WATER RIGHTS LAWS
IN THE
NINETEEN WESTERN STATES

By

Wells A. Hutchins, J.D.

Completed by

Harold H. Ellis, B.S., M.S., J.D.

and

J. Peter DeBraal, B.A., LL.B., M.S.

Volume I

Miscellaneous Publication No. 1206
Natural Resource Economics Division
Economic Research Service
United States Department of Agriculture

Washington, D.C.: 1971

Library of Congress Catalogue Card Number: 76-611995

IN MEMORIAM

This multivolume work on water rights laws in the Western States is the culmination and capstone of the long, dedicated, and distinguished career of Wells A. Hutchins. A nationally recognized authority on the subject, his extensive and far-ranging studies of Western water laws have been widely acclaimed and have made an invaluable contribution to this field of knowledge. His much sought-after advice by the many States that he assisted in formulating improved water laws bears testimony to the rich legacy of outstanding service our esteemed colleague has left to the Nation.

Harold H. Ellis

J. Peter DeBraal

FOREWORD

Wells A. Hutchins was nearing completion of this three-volume report on water rights in the 19 Western States at the time of his death on September 19, 1970. This work culminates more than 62 years of public service and of dedication to the subject matter contained herein. These volumes are, therefore, a monument to Wells A. Hutchins. They are also a monument to the role of water in the development and prosperity of the West.

One hallmark of economic development, and indeed of civilization itself, may be found in the rules men devise to order their access to resources. When ambitious men began to develop the West, they found English common law deficient in many respects. It failed to provide workable rules among men as they struggled to get, develop, and use water where water was relatively scarce and often vital to life itself. So new laws and new institutions had to be developed. They are still developing. The crucial role of these laws and institutions led Wells A. Hutchins to devote his professional life to their study and articulation.

Mr. Hutchins was born February 20, 1888, in Beatrice, Nebraska. He graduated in 1906 from Lawrenceville Academy in New Jersey and in 1909 he received a law degree, with highest honors, from George Washington University, Washington, D.C. Mr. Hutchins began his government career in 1908. Although in his long career he served under a number of different bureaus in the Department of Agriculture, his interests and field of work remained steadfastly on water laws. Except for military service as a 1st Lieutenant in the Infantry in World War I, he spent most of his long government career in Berkeley, California.

As a leading authority on water rights laws in the Western States, Mr. Hutchins wrote numerous books, reports, articles, and papers on the subject. He also assisted many States in formulating improved water laws. From 1942 to 1946, he served as chairman of a committee of the National Reclamation Association (now the National Water Resources Association) to formulate desirable water law principles for the West. He also lectured on water law and institutions at the University of California at Davis and Berkeley. Mr. Hutchins received the Superior Service Award from the Department of Agriculture, was made a life member of the National Reclamation Association in 1958 for outstanding services to the West, and received a number of other honors for his knowledge and accomplishments.

Mr. Hutchins' important and widely used book entitled "Selected Problems in the Law of Water Rights in the West" was published in 1942. In the 1950's, he initiated the research for this voluminous sequel to that book. Since his death, Harold H. Ellis and J. Peter DeBraal of the Economic Research Service have completed this publication.

The findings of this study are a significant and valuable contribution to our knowledge of the legal aspects of the use of water resources. These findings will be of lasting value and utility to the wide variety of people who are concerned with the laws relating to water. We all stand deeply in debt to Wells A. Hutchins for his mastery of the subject and for his contributions to our literature on it.

Washington, D. C.   *M. L. UPCHURCH*
November 1971   *Administrator*
                                                          Economic Research Service

PREFACE

This three-volume work on the water rights laws in the 19 Western States is a comprehensive sequel to the 1942 single-volume publication authored by Wells A. Hutchins entitled "Selected Problems in the Law of Water Rights in the West." That book was extensively used and the supply was soon exhausted. In the 1950's, he initiated the research needed to prepare the manuscript for this multivolume work. Since the appearance of the 1942 book, there has been a great amount of additional legislation and court decisions and two new Western States had to be considered. Moreover, the present, much more extensive, work treats more facets of the subject and discusses a number of items in greater detail.

Rights to the use of water from various surface and underground sources often are of crucial importance in the Western States. The 19 States to which this study relates include the 17 contiguous Western States plus Alaska and Hawaii. The 17 contiguous States comprise the six extending from North Dakota to Texas, the three bordering the Pacific Ocean, and the intervening eight States.

This work is a comparative analysis of the development and status of the constitutional provisions, statutes, reported court decisions, and some administrative regulations, practices, and policies regarding water rights laws in the Western States. The analysis includes the nature of such water rights and their acquisition, control, exercise, transfer, protection, and loss. In addition to the relevant State laws, Federal, interstate, and international matters are also discussed. An extensive appendix includes summaries of selected components of the water rights systems of each State. Although critical or laudatory comments are occasionally included, Mr. Hutchins' general purpose was to objectively portray the development and status of the laws rather than to propound his views on what the laws should be.

The general coverage and arrangement of the work is set forth in the summary of contents. The more detailed aspects of the subject are reflected in the extensive table of contents for each volume which should help to guide the reader through the numerous topics and subtopics. Volume three will include indexes to the entire publication to further assist the reader. To facilitate the use of this work as a source book on Western water rights laws, different ramifications of particular statutes, cases, or other items are treated in two or more places.

This study should be useful to the wide variety of private persons, organizations, institutions, and Federal, State, and local government officials concerned with the laws regarding the use of water resources. These may include lawyers, judges, legislators, administrators, economists, engineers, other social, political, and physical scientists and research workers, educators, agricultural and other water users, as well as organizations and agencies concerned with water supply, allocation, distribution, development, conservation, planning, and affiliated functions.

The intricate mosaic of constitutional, legislative, judicial, administrative, contractual, and other provisions that may make up the involved structure and operation of the water rights laws in the Western States is so extensive that, even in a work of this size, not all of its myriad facets could possibly be examined. Moreover, various related laws are not dealt with or are only briefly discussed, such as those dealing with the organization of irrigation, drainage, and other districts, river control in aid of navigation, flood prevention, and water quality regulatory programs. In view of such considerations, as well as the fact that the laws may change and their application may depend upon the particular circumstances, the discussion should not be regarded as a substitute for competent legal advice on specific problems.

While the research was underway, several requests were made urging Mr. Hutchins to prepare reports on the water rights laws of particular Western States, as he had done previously for the Territory of Hawaii. In response, separate reports were written for nine of the 19 Western States, including California, Idaho, Kansas, Montana, New Mexico, Nevada, Oklahoma, Texas, and Utah. Citations of these and the other numerous publications of Mr. Hutchins are included at the end of volume three.

Mr. Hutchins was completing the manuscript for this publication at the time of his death on September 19, 1970. Since that time, the undersigned colleagues of Mr. Hutchins, Harold H. Ellis and J. Peter DeBraal, have conducted the work considered necessary to complete the publication. Mr. Ellis provided leadership for this and other water law studies in recent years. He and Mr. DeBraal have made final updating and a variety of other revisions and additions in the manuscript. It has been updated so as to incorporate discussions of significant recent legislative changes and reported court decisions to January 1, 1970.

In view of the magnitude of the undertaking, at Mr. Hutchins' request a few chapters in volumes two and three are authored by different persons. These chapters and their authors will be identified in those volumes.

Grateful acknowledgement is made of the assistance of law student assistants Bonnie Lea, John Fruth, Michael Hughes, and R. Kent Gardner as well as the editorial work of Daniel W. Michaels and the typing and secretarial services of Gertrude Lane, Mildred Naughton, and Brenda Adams.

Special thanks is due Mrs. Wells A. Hutchins for her untiring and invaluable interest, encouragement, and assistance.

Harold H. Ellis

J. Peter DeBraal

SUMMARY OF CONTENTS

VOLUME I

TABLE OF CONTENTS

WATER RIGHTS LAWS

IN THE

NINETEEN WESTERN STATES

VOLUME I

Chapter 1

STATE WATER POLICIES

ATTAINMENT OF STATEHOOD IN THE WEST

The governmental histories of the 19 Western States (17 contiguous plus Alaska and Hawaii) have importantly affected the development of the water rights laws in the respective States. One facet of State governmental history, which will be referred to throughout this work, concerns the attainment of statehood. The dates on which the Western States were admitted to the Union cover more than a century—1845 to 1959 (table 1).

On December 29, 1845, Texas became the first to be admitted, after having first been under Spanish and Mexican rule and then existing as an independent republic. With the outbreak of the Civil War in 1861, Texas seceded from the Union. Statehood was reestablished in 1870.[1]

California was admitted to the Union in 1850, without having had Territorial status (table 2). Over the next quarter century, five Western States were created out of Territories—Oregon in 1859, Kansas in 1861, Nevada in 1864, Nebraska in 1867, and Colorado in 1876.[2]

Toward the close of the 19th century, seven more States of the West came into the Union—in 1889, within a few days of each other, North Dakota, South Dakota, Montana, and Washington; in 1890, Idaho and Wyoming; and in 1896, Utah.[3]

In the early 1900's, the remaining three of the western block of 17 contiguous States were admitted—Oklahoma in 1907, and New Mexico and Arizona in 1912.[4] Finally, in 1959, the two outlying States—Alaska and Hawaii—were admitted.[5]

ARIDITY AND WATER RIGHTS SYSTEMS

The 17 contiguous Western States comprise a solid block extending from east of the 100th meridian to the Pacific Coast. As a result of features noted

---

[1] Admission December 29, 1845: 9 Stat. 108. Secession effective March 2, 1861: 3 Tex. Const. Ann. 597 (Vernon, 1955). Readmission March 30, 1870: 16 Stat. 80.

[2] California, September 9, 1850: 9 Stat. 452. Oregon, February 14, 1859: 11 Stat. 383. Kansas, January 29, 1861: 12 Stat. 126. Nevada, October 31, 1864: 13 Stat. 749. Nebraska, March 1, 1867: 14 Stat. 820. Colorado, August 1, 1876: 19 Stat. 665.

[3] North Dakota, November 2, 1889: 26 Stat. 1548. South Dakota, November 2, 1889: 26 Stat. 1549. Montana, November 8, 1889: 26 Stat. 1551. Washington, November 11, 1889: 26 Stat. 1552. Idaho, July 3, 1890: 26 Stat. 215. Wyoming, July 10, 1890: 26 Stat. 222. Utah, January 4, 1896: 29 Stat. 876.

[4] Oklahoma, November 16, 1907: 35 Stat. 2160. New Mexico, January 6, 1912: 37 Stat. 1723. Arizona, February 14, 1912: 37 Stat. 1728.

[5] Alaska, January 3, 1959: 73 Stat. c16. Hawaii, August 21, 1959: 73 Stat. c74.

(1)

Table 1. Admission to Statehood in the West
(States arranged by date of admission)

Texas	Admitted	December 29, 1845	9 Stat. 108
	Seceded	March 2, 1861	3 Tex. Const. Ann. 597
	Readmitted	March 30, 1870	16 Stat. 80
California	Admitted	September 9, 1850	9 Stat. 452
Oregon	Admitted	February 14, 1859	11 Stat. 383
Kansas	Admitted	January 29, 1861	12 Stat. 126
Nevada	Admitted	October 31, 1864	13 Stat. 749
Nebraska	Admitted	March 1, 1867	14 Stat. 820
Colorado	Admitted	August 1, 1876	19 Stat. 665
North Dakota	Admitted	November 2, 1889	26 Stat. 1548
South Dakota	Admitted	November 2, 1889	26 Stat. 1549
Montana	Admitted	November 8, 1889	26 Stat. 1551
Washington	Admitted	November 11, 1889	26 Stat. 1552
Idaho	Admitted	July 3, 1890	26 Stat. 215
Wyoming	Admitted	July 10, 1890	26 Stat. 222
Utah	Admitted	January 4, 1896	29 Stat. 876
Oklahoma	Admitted	November 16, 1907	35 Stat. 2160
New Mexico	Admitted	January 6, 1912	37 Stat. 1723
Arizona	Admitted	February 14, 1912	37 Stat. 1728
Alaska	Admitted	January 3, 1959	73 Stat. c16
Hawaii	Admitted	August 21, 1959	73 Stat. c74

below, these States fall into three broad groups: (1) the easternmost six States extending from North Dakota to Texas, (2) the three States bordering the Pacific Ocean, and (3) the eight intermediate States traversed by the Continental Divide and containing most of the Great Basin and the Southwest Desert. It is to these 17 States in this compact group that the instant subtopic relates.

In the overall view, both the eastern and western tiers of States include both humid and semiarid areas and hence, on the whole, are "generally less arid," and the eight intermediate States are "generally more arid." Again in general, the more humid parts of the eastern tier lie east of the 100th meridian, where their climatic characteristics grade into those of the adjoining Mississippi Valley States; whereas in the Far West it is the extreme westernmost areas between the mountain ranges and the ocean that receive the greater rainfall. Thus, the drier or semiarid parts of the nine "generally less arid" States adjoin and climatically blend into those of the eight interior "generally more arid" States.

This broad separation into "generally more arid" and "generally less arid" regions—which is made for purposes of comparison—corresponds in some measure to the classification of basic water rights principles that prevails in the component States. That is, the eight interior States with the lesser rainfall adhere to what is termed the arid region doctrine of prior appropriation of water, generally to the exclusion of the humid region riparian doctrine; whereas in the other nine States, both of these conflicting principles are recognized concurrently in legal theory, although the measure of practical importance of

Table 2. Establishment of Territorial Status in the West
(States alphabetically arranged)

Alaska	August 24, 1912	37 Stat. 512
Arizona	February 24, 1863	12 Stat. 664
California	None	
Colorado	February 28, 1861	12 Stat. 172
Hawaii	June 14, 1900	31 Stat. 141
Idaho	March 3, 1863	12 Stat. 808
Kansas	May 30, 1854	10 Stat. 277
Montana	May 26, 1864	13 Stat. 85
Nebraska	May 30, 1854	10 Stat. 277
Nevada	March 2, 1861	12 Stat. 209
New Mexico	September 9, 1850	9 Stat. 446
North Dakota	March 2, 1861	12 Stat. 239
Oklahoma	May 2, 1890	26 Stat. 81
Oregon	August 14, 1848	9 Stat. 323
South Dakota	March 2, 1861	12 Stat. 239
Texas	None	
Utah	September 9, 1850	9 Stat. 453
Washington	March 2, 1853	10 Stat. 172
Wyoming	July 25, 1868	15 Stat. 178

the riparian doctrine varies from "underlying and fundamental" in some jurisdictions to quite limited in others.

This is not to imply that in a dual-system State one water rights doctrine applies in the more arid portions and a different doctrine where the precipitation is greater. Whatever water rights laws prevail in a State, these laws operate uniformly within its boundaries.[6]

DECLARATIONS OF POLICY

The Place of Water in the State's Economy

Constitutional Declarations

Declarations with respect to the essential part played by the utilization of water in the State's economy are found in several of the fundamental laws of the West.

Thus, the constitution of Wyoming, which was formed by the people before admission to the Union, established for the State a system of centralized control over the appropriation and distribution of water and adjudication of water rights. The foundation for this was laid in the Declaration of Rights, wherein it is declared that because water is essential to industrial prosperity, its control must be in the State, the duty of which is to guard all the interests involved.[7]

---

[6] The earlier water appropriation statutes of Texas were by their terms applicable only in the parts of the State where rainfall was inadequate for agricultural purposes—the boundaries of such regions not being defined by statute—but the 1913 and succeeding statutes were made effective throughout the entire State. Tex. Gen. Laws 1889, ch. 88, § 1; Laws 1895, ch. 21, § 1; Laws 1913, ch. 171, § 1.

[7] Wyo. Const., art. I, § 31.

The foundation of State control in Nebraska is the declaration that the necessity of water for domestic and irrigation uses in the State is a natural want.[8]

In Texas, the basis of important water control measures is a constitutional amendment declaring that the conservation and development of all the natural resources of the State, including (but not limited to) the control, storing, preservation, and distribution of its waters for useful purposes and the irrigation and drainage of lands, are public rights and duties, with a mandate to the legislature to pass all laws appropriate thereto.[9]

An amendment to the constitution of California (1) declares that because of the conditions prevailing in the State, the general welfare requires that its water resources be put to beneficial use to the fullest extent of which they are capable, (2) forbids waste, unreasonable use, and unreasonable methods of use of water, and (3) commands that the conservation of waters be exercised with a view to their reasonable beneficial use in the interest of the people and for the public welfare.[10]

Some Legislative Statements

Declarations of the importance to the public of the use of water are found in some statutes. For example, the Water Code of California repeats the declarations in the constitution noted immediately above, and the South Dakota legislature included them in substantially identical language in the 1955 revision and reenactment of the water law of that State.[11] The legislature of Texas enacted the substance of the constitutional amendment referred to above, except as to the mandate to itself to enact appropriate laws.[12]

Some Judicial Observations

Courts have taken notice of constitutional and statutory declarations and have added some of their own. To cite a few examples:

—"That domestic use is the most beneficial use for water and that irrigation is the next most beneficial use in the arid western states is a self-evident and well recognized fact regardless of any statute."[13]

—"We historically know that the lands in the western portion of the state are comparatively in some seasons useless for agricultural purposes unless they are irrigated."[14]

---

[8] Nebr. Const., art. XV, § 4.

[9] Tex. Const., art. XVI, § 59a.

[10] Cal. Const., art. XIV, § 3.

[11] Cal. Water Code § 100 (West 1956); S. Dak. Code § 61.0101 (1939), as reenacted by Laws 1955, ch. 430, now Comp. Laws Ann. § 46-1-4 (1967). The South Dakota statute does not repeat the declarations in the California constitution and California Water Code with respect to riparian rights.

[12] Tex. Rev. Civ. Stat. Ann. art. 7466 (1954). See also *id.* art. 7472d.

[13] *Tanner* v. *Bacon,* 103 Utah 494, 508, 136 Pac. (2d) 957 (1943).

[14] *Tolle* v. *Correth,* 31 Tex. 362, 365, 98 Am. Dec. 540 (1868).

—"The court knows judicially that water in many sections of this great Western country is its very lifeblood."[15]

The State policy of Arizona has ever been "to make the largest possible use of the comparatively limited quantity of water within its boundaries."[16] In California, with the passing of the years and the growth of industries, it has become "an obvious proposition that the development of the state's resources—its agricultural, horticultural, stock-raising, power, and other like industries—depends largely upon the fullest use of the water supply of the state."[17] It is the policy not only in Montana, said the supreme court of that State, but of all Western States, to require the highest and greatest possible duty from the waters of the State in the interest of agriculture and other useful and beneficial purposes.[18]

The rule is well settled that courts may take judicial notice, as a matter of common knowledge, of the natural features of the State, including the general location of its mountains, the courses of its rivers, and their general history.[19]

Ownership of Water Supplies

In various Western States there are constitutional and statutory declarations and judicial acknowledgments that waters within their respective State boundaries belong to the public or to the State. "The modern expression is that such waters are owned by the state in trust for the people."[20] The declaration of ownership sometimes applies specifically to unappropriated waters, or it is made subject to the right of appropriation for beneficial use or subject to existing rights of use.

Property of the Public

Thus, in the Colorado and New Mexico constitutions, the declaration of public ownership of water applies to every natural stream.[21] Declarations of public ownership of water of all sources, or of sources specifically named, appear in the statutes of some Western States.[22]

---

[15] *Pacific Live Stock Co.* v. *Read*, 5 Fed. (2d) 466, 468 (9th Cir. 1925).

[16] *Pima Farms Co.* v. *Proctor*, 30 Ariz. 96, 102, 112-113, 245 Pac. 369 (1926).

[17] *Waterford Irr. Dist.* v. *Turlock Irr. Dist.*, 50 Cal. App. 213, 220, 194 Pac. 757 (1920).

[18] *Worden* v. *Alexander*, 108 Mont. 208, 90 Pac. (2d) 160 (1939).

[19] *State of Texas* v. *Bradford*, 121 Tex. 515, 527, 50 S. W. (2d) 1065 (1932).

[20] *Murphy* v. *Kerr*, 296 Fed. 536, 540 (D. N. Mex. 1923), affirmed, 5 Fed. (2d) 908 (8th Cir. 1925).

[21] Colo. Const., art. XVI, § 5; N. Mex. Const., art. XVI, § 2.

[22] See Ariz. Rev. Stat. Ann. § 45-101 (1956); Colo. Rev. Stat. Ann. § § 148-2-1 and 148-21-2 (Supp. 1969); Nev. Rev. Stat. § 533.025 (Supp. 1969); *Bergman* v. *Kearney*, 241 Fed. 884, 893 (D. Nev. 1917); N. Mex. Stat. Ann. § 75-1-1 (1968); N. Dak. Cent. Code Ann. § 61-01-01 (1960); Oreg. Rev. Stat. § 537.110 (Supp. 1969); Utah Code Ann., § 73-1-1 (1968); Wash. Rev. Code § 90.03.010 (Supp. 1961). With respect to Montana, see *Mettler* v. *Ames Realty Co.*, 61 Mont. 152, 161-162, 201 Pac. 702 (1921).

Property of the State or of the People

Under the North Dakota constitution, all flowing streams and natural watercourses are to remain forever the property of the State for mining, irrigating, and manufacturing purposes.[23] The Wyoming declaration of State ownership relates to the water of all natural streams, springs, lakes, or other collections of still water within the State boundaries.[24] The constitutions of Colorado and Nebraska dedicate the use of the water of all natural streams to the people of the State.[25]

Statutes of several other States contain similar declarations.[26]

The Idaho Supreme Court considered it clear that title to the public waters of the State is vested in the State for the use and benefit of all citizens under such rules and regulations as may be prescribed from time to time by the legislature.[27] This is not an interest or title in the proprietary sense, but rather in a sovereign capacity as representative of all the people for the purpose of guaranteeing that the common rights of all shall be equally protected.

In 1900 the Montana Supreme Court observed that "the state of Montana has by necessary implication assumed to itself the ownership, *sub modo,* of the rivers and streams of this state, and, by section 1880 *et seq.* of the Civil Code, has expressly granted the right to appropriate the waters of such streams, * * * ."[28] When, two decades later, this court repudiated the riparian doctrine *in toto* and held that the comment upon riparian rights in each of its previous decisions was purely *obiter dictum,* it held that the *corpus* of running water in natural streams in the State was *publici juris*—the property of the public.[29]

Public Supervision over Waters

Basis of State Control

The Wyoming constitution declares that the control of waters must be in the State, which in providing for its use shall equally guard all the various interests involved.[30] An Idaho statute makes a similar declaration.[31]

Still other statutes assert the public interest in this public function. For example, laws of both California and South Dakota say that the protection of

---

[23] N. Dak. Const., art. XVII, § 210.
[24] Wyo. Const., art. VIII, § 1.
[25] Colo. Const., art. XVI, § 5; Nebr. Const., art. XV, § 5.
[26] Cal. Water Code § 102 (West 1956); Idaho Code § 42-101 (1948); Kans. Stat. Ann. § 82a-702 (1969); S. Dak. Comp. Laws Ann. § 46-1-3 (1967); Tex. Rev. Civ. Stat. Ann. art. 7467 (1970).
[27] *Walbridge* v. *Robinson,* 22 Idaho 236, 241-242, 125 Pac. 812 (1912). See *Coulson* v. *Aberdeen-Springfield Canal Co.,* 39 Idaho 320, 323-324, 227 Pac. 29 (1924).
[28] *Smith* v. *Deniff,* 24 Mont. 20, 21-22, 60 Pac. 398 (1900).
[29] *Mettler* v. *Ames Realty Co.,* 61 Mont. 152, 161-162, 201 Pac. 702 (1921).
[30] Wyo. Const., art. I, § 31.
[31] Idaho Code § 42-101 (1948).

the public interest in the development of the water resources of the State is of vital concern to the people thereof, and that the State shall determine what surface and ground water can be controlled and developed for the greatest public benefit and in what way it should be done.[32]

The public interest in State control of waters and water rights in the arid land States, say the courts, is "definite and substantial," and they have the power to legislate with respect thereto as they deem wise.[33] "It has *long been the settled law* in the arid and semiarid states that a state, *in the exercise of its police power,* may regulate the manner of appropriation and distribution of water from natural streams for purposes of irrigation."[34] [Emphasis supplied.] A Federal court remarked with respect to the Nevada law that:[35]

The idea that the individual has a vested right to enjoy the use of running water without public regulation or control is subversive of the sovereignty of the State. The state cannot divest itself of, or surrender, grant, or bargain away this authority.* * *

Supervisory Functions

Most of the Western States provide by statute for State control over the acquisition of appropriative rights to the use of public waters and over the distribution of water to those entitled to receive it, and vest these duties in a centralized group of water administrative officials. Many States also provide special procedures for the adjudication of water rights; in most of these States, State officials play an active part. Provisions for these administrative and judicial functions comprise a major part of the State statutory water law.

In Wyoming, which pioneered in setting up a completely integrated centralized administrative procedure, these are constitutional as well as statutory functions. The original constitution of the new State directed the legislature to divide the State into four water divisions, each to have a superintendent; provided for a State Engineer as the chief water administrative officer; and provided also that the State Engineer and the four division superintendents

---

[32] Cal. Water Code § § 104 and 105 (West 1956); S. Dak. Comp. Laws Ann. § 46-1-2 (1967).

[33] *California Oregon Power Co.* v. *Beaver Portland Cement Co.,* 295 U.S. 142, 163-165 (1935).

[34] *Humboldt Lovelock Irr. Light & Power Co.* v. *Smith,* 25 Fed. Supp. 571, 573 (D. Nev. 1938). See *In re Willow Creek,* 74 Oreg. 592, 617, 144 Pac. 505 (1914), 146 Pac. 475 (1915). To accomplish its purposes, the State has a right to exercise a superintending control over entire stream systems: *Ormsby County* v. *Kearney,* 37 Nev. 314, 336-338, 142 Pac. 803 (1914).

[35] *Bergman* v. *Kearney,* 241 Fed. 884, 893 (D. Nev. 1917). With respect to the New Mexico constitutional declaration that beneficial use shall be the basis, the measure, and the limit of the right to the use of water, the supreme court of that State has held that the provision "merely declares the basis of the right to the use of water, and in no manner prohibits the regulation of the enjoyment of that right." *Harkey* v. *Smith,* 31 N. Mex. 521, 526-527, 247 Pac. 550 (1926).

should constitute a Board of Control with supervision over the waters of the State.[36]

Use of Water

Use of Water a Public Use

A foundation for such public functions as control of the use of water, regulation of water rates, and exercise of the power of eminent domain is laid in provisions of various Western State constitutions.

Public use in general.—Some features of public use of water are discussed above under "Public Supervision over Waters."

The constitution of Washington declares that the use of water for irrigation, mining, and manufacturing purposes shall be deemed a public use.[37] In South Dakota, the irrigation of public lands is a public purpose, and legislation for the organization of irrigation districts is authorized.[38] Nebraska declares that the necessity of water for domestic use and irrigation is a natural want.[39] The control and management of waters for useful purposes are declared by the Texas amendment to be public rights and duties, concerning which the legislature is commanded to pass appropriate laws.[40]

Sale and rental of water.—The constitutions of California, Idaho, and Montana declare that the use of water appropriated for sale, rental, or distribution is a public use.[41] Idaho provides further for the exclusive dedication of such waters to agricultural and domestic purposes when used therefor, upon proper payment, and for priority in water service.[42]

Condemnation by individuals.—Statutes of many Western States grant the power of condemnation for rights of way to individuals for their own private irrigation purposes on the theory that the use of water for irrigation is a public use even when made by individuals for personal use on their own private lands, and the validity of the principle has judicial sanction. For example, the Supreme Court of Utah upheld the constitutionality of a statute of that State authorizing individuals to condemn rights of way across lands owned by others by enlargement of existing ditches thereon, in order to bring water to irrigate their own land.[43] In affirming the judgment of the State court, the United States Supreme Court took note that the water rights principles and laws of many Western States differed markedly from those in the East, and felt constrained to recognize the physical differences that rendered necessary the

---

[36] Wyo. Const., art. VIII, § § 2, 4, and 5.
[37] Wash. Const., art. XXI, § 1.
[38] S. Dak. Const., art. XXI, § 7.
[39] Nebr. Const., art. XV, § 4. See *State v. Birdwood Irr. Dist.,* 154 Nebr. 52, 55, 46 N. W. (2d) 884 (1951).
[40] Tex. Const., art. XVI, § 59a.
[41] Cal. Const., art. XIV, § 1; Idaho Const., art. XV, § 1; Mont. Const., art. III, § 15.
[42] Idaho Const., art. XV, § § 4 and 5.
[43] *Nash v. Clark,* 27 Utah 158, 162-168, 75 Pac. 371 (1904).

enactment of these different Western laws for the purpose of furthering the growth and prosperity of these States by means of irrigation.[44]

Declaring the beneficial use of water to be a public use, a Washington statute authorizes any person to condemn property or rights necessary to effectuate such beneficial use, including the right to condemn an inferior use of water for a superior one.[45]

Beneficial Use of Water

Need of a useful or beneficial purpose.—The concept that to accord with the public policy of the State, use of the public water must be made for a useful or beneficial purpose, is fundamental in the water law philosophy of the West. This holds true regardless of classification of the particular State as arid or semiarid.

The concept is declared in specific terms in the majority of Western State constitutions. Positive statements and necessary implications appear in all western "water codes." The principle runs through the leading water rights decisions of the courts. Exceptions and deviations from a strict application of the long-established principle exist and in some situations have caused serious difficulties. Nevertheless, the declaration that "Beneficial use shall be the basis, the measure, and the limit of the right to the use of water" has been controlling in the acquisition and exercise of appropriative rights throughout the history of the West and it has come more and more to pervade riparian philosophy as well.

(1) *Constitutional declarations.*—Thus, in Arizona, New Mexico, and Utah, existing rights to the use of water for "useful or beneficial" purposes are recognized and confirmed (see "Rights to the Use of Water," below).[46] The constitutions of Colorado, Idaho, Nebraska, New Mexico, and Wyoming link the right of appropriation of water with its beneficial use.[47] New Mexico adds the time-honored rule that "Beneficial use shall be the basis, the measure and the limit of the right to the use of water."[48] Montana holds the use of water appropriated, not only for sale, rental, or distribution, but also for "other beneficial use" to be a public use.[49] The Texas constitutional amendment includes within public rights and duties the control, storing, preservation, and distribution of waters for all useful purposes.[50] The California amendment declares that the water right is limited to the quantity of water reasonably required for the beneficial use to be served, and does not extend to the "waste or unreasonable use or unreasonable method of use or unreasonable method of diversion of water."[51]

---

[44]*Clark* v. *Nash,* 198 U.S. 361, 370 (1905).
[45] Wash. Rev. Code § 90.03.040 (Supp. 1961). See *State ex rel. Andersen* v. *Superior Court,* 119 Wash. 406, 411, 205 Pac. 1051 (1922).
[46] Ariz. Const., art. XVII, § 2; N. Mex. Const., art. XVI, § 1; Utah Const., art. XVII, § 1.
[47] Colo. Const., art. XVI, § 6; Idaho Const., art. XV, § 3; Nebr. Const., art. XV, § § 5 and 6; N. Mex. Const., art. XVI, § 2; Wyo. Const., art. VIII, § 3.
[48] N. Mex. Const., art. XVI, § 3.
[49] Mont. Const., art. III, § 15.
[50] Tex. Const., art. XVI, § 59a.
[51] Cal. Const., art. XIV, § 3.

(2) Some typical legislative and judicial statements.—The handling of this concept of beneficial use of water in the many relevant statutes and court decisions is general and without significant dissent, irrespective of geographical location. Some typical examples follow.

Consider first the generally more arid States: Statutes of Nevada not only declare that beneficial use shall be the basis, the measure, and the limit of the right to the use of water, but restrict such rights to such quantity of water as may be necessary, when reasonably and economically used for beneficial purposes, irrespective of the carrying capacity of the ditch.[52] In an early decision in a controversy arising in Nevada, a Federal court stated that an excessive diversion of water for any purpose cannot be regarded as a diversion to a beneficial use, inasmuch as water in this State "is too scarce, needful, and precious for irrigation and other purposes, to admit of waste."[53]

The Supreme Court of Colorado held in two of its earliest water rights decisions that the first appropriator of water from a natural stream for a beneficial purpose has the prior right thereto, and that the true test of an appropriation of water "is the successful application thereof to the beneficial use designed."[54]

The Montana Supreme Court called attention to the fact that in the early days of irrigation in the Territory and State, extravagant quantities of water were awarded to the litigants by the courts, which were not always to blame; but that the position was eventually taken that "If comparison between the principles regulating the appropriation and use of water is permissible it may be said that the principle of beneficial use is the one of paramount importance."[55]

Next, consider the six States lying on the 100th meridian (on the eastern border of the compact group of 17 contiguous States), the western parts of which in general are drier than the eastern parts and adjoin the interior block of generally more arid States: The Nebraska Supreme Court, after citing the constitutional declaration that the necessity of water for domestic and irrigation purposes in the State is a natural want,[56] observed that the statutory and judicial laws of Nebraska on the subject of irrigation show a clear intention to enforce and maintain a rigid economy in the use of the public waters.[57] Further, said the court, it is the policy of the law in all the arid States to compel an economical use of the waters of natural streams.

A statute of Kansas provides that all appropriations of water must be for some beneficial purpose, and that an appropriation in excess of the reasonable needs of the appropriators shall not be allowed.[58]

---

[52] Nev. Rev. Stat. § § 533.035 (Supp. 1969) and 533.060 (Supp. 1967).

[53] *Union Mill & Min. Co.* v. *Dangberg,* 81 Fed. 73, 97 (D. Nev. 1897).

[54] *Coffin* v. *Left Hand Ditch Co.,* 6 Colo. 443, 447 (1882); *Thomas* v. *Guirard,* 6 Colo. 530, 533 (1883).

[55] *Allen* v. *Petrick,* 69 Mont. 373, 377-378, 222 Pac. 451 (1924).

[56] Nebr. Const., art. XV, § 4.

[57] *State* v. *Birdwood Irr. Dist.,* 154 Nebr. 52, 55, 46 N. W. (2d) 884 (1951).

[58] Kans. Stat. Ann. § § 82a-707 and 82a-718 (1969).

Texas declares by statute that the use of water under an appropriative right shall not exceed in any case "the limit of volume to which the user is entitled and the volume which is necessarily required and can be beneficially used for irrigation or other authorized uses;" and it spells out the definition of beneficial use as "the use of such a quantity of water, when reasonable intelligence and reasonable diligence are exercised in its application for a lawful purpose, as is economically necessary for that purpose."[59]

The Supreme Court of Oklahoma in an early case held it necessary to the completion of an appropriation that the water shall have been actually applied to beneficial uses.[60]

Finally, on the Pacific Coast: The earliest water rights statute of California, enacted in 1872, declared that the appropriation of water must be for some useful or beneficial purpose, and that when the appropriator or his successor in interest ceases to use the water for such purpose, the right ceases.[61] Twelve years earlier, the California Supreme Court had stated that a claim of appropriative right to be valid must be for some useful or beneficial purpose, or in contemplation of a future appropriation therefor.[62] To the essential requirement of beneficial use have been added the qualifications of "economical use" and "reasonable use";[63] and eventually the qualifying phrase became "reasonable beneficial use" as commanded in 1928 by the State constitution.[64] This mandate applied not only to appropriative rights, but expressly to riparian rights as well. By necessary implication it applied also to ground water rights and "to the use of all water, under whatever right the use may be enjoyed."[65]

This represented a marked change in the attitude of the California judiciary toward the riparian right. Previously, as against the owners of lands contiguous to the same stream, the riparian owner was held to reasonable use of the water for a useful or beneficial purpose, but—by contrast to the courts of the Pacific Coast neighbors Oregon and Washington,[66]—as against an appropriator he was "not limited by any measure of reasonableness."[67]

---

[59] Tex. Rev. Civ. Stat. Ann. arts. 7542 and 7476 (1954).
[60] *Gates* v. *Settlers' Mill., Canal & Res. Co.*, 19 Okla. 83, 89, 91, 91 Pac. 856 (1907).
[61] Cal. Civ. Code § 1411 (1872). This was repealed by Laws 1943, ch. 368, pt. 12, p. 1895, Water Code § 150001 (West 1966), and replaced without change in language by Laws 1943, ch. 368, pt. 2, ch. 1, art. 4, § 1240, p. 1615, Water Code § 100 (West 1956).
[62] *Weaver* v. *Eureka Lake Co.*, 15 Cal. 271, 275 (1860). Compare *Ketchikan Co.* v. *Citizens' Co.*, 2 Alaska 120, 124 (1903).
[63] *Hufford* v. *Dye*, 162 Cal. 147, 159, 121 Pac. 400 (1912); *California Pastoral & Agricultural Co.* v. *Madera Canal & Irr. Co.*, 167 Cal. 78, 84-86, 138 Pac. 718 (1914).
[64] Cal. Const., art. XIV, § 3.
[65] *Peabody* v. *Vallejo*, 2 Cal. (2d) 351, 367-369, 383, 40 Pac. (2d) 486 (1935); *Joslin* v. *Marin Mun. Water Dist.*, 67 Cal. (2d) 132, 134-140, 429 Pac. (2d) 889, 60 Cal. Rptr. 377 (1967).
[66] *In re Hood River*, 114 Oreg. 112, 116, 191, 207, 211-212, 227 Pac. 1065 (1924); *Brown* v. *Chase*, 125 Wash. 542, 553, 217 Pac. 23 (1923).
[67] *Miller & Lux* v. *Madera Canal & Irr. Co.*, 155 Cal. 59, 64, 99 Pac. 502 (1907, 1909). See *Pabst* v. *Finmand*, 190 Cal. 124, 132, 211 Pac. 11 (1922); *Herminghaus* v. *Southern California Edison Co.*, 200 Cal. 81, 100-101, 252 Pac. 607 (1926).

The question of waste of water.—Unnecessary waste of water generally has no rightful place in the water use economy of the West. Said a Federal court: "As a general principle, equity abhors waste, and delights to restrain it in a proper case."[68] To waste water is to injure the public welfare; hence, it is the undoubted policy of the law to prevent its waste.[69] "Let it be remembered that no one can acquire a vested right to waste water in any form."[70] These and other declarations of the Utah courts as to the State policy of encouraging development of precious waters and preventing wastage thereof[71] undoubtedly reflect the public policy of that State. This is in accordance with the water policies of the other arid States, despite what the author believes to have been an inadvertent generalization in a *dictum* that appears in two other opinions of the Utah Supreme Court.[72]

The strictures apply essentially to unnecessary waste.—In the operation of diversion and distribution systems, it is impracticable to save every acre-foot of water. Some so-called waste is inevitable, depending quantitatively on the surrounding circumstances. Because of practical considerations, therefore, the inhibition against waste of water means *unnecessary* waste, which is not tolerated in the State policies relating to beneficial use of water.

The constitution of California absolutely forbids waste of water, and declares that it is not included in a right of use.[73] However, the supreme court of that State says that as denounced by the constitutional amendment the term is necessarily relative,[74] and that the question as to what is waste of water depends upon the circumstances of each case and the time when the waste is required to be prevented.[75]

---

[68] *Finney County Water Users' Assn.* v. *Graham Ditch Co.,* 1 Fed. (2d) 650, 652 (D. Colo. 1924).

[69] *Brian* v. *Fremont Irr. Co.,* 112 Utah 220, 224-225, 186 Pac. (2d) 588 (1947); *Little Cottonwood Water Co.* v. *Kimball,* 76 Utah 243, 247, 289 Pac. 116 (1920).

[70] *Eden Irr. Co.* v. *District Court,* 61 Utah 103, 113, 211 Pac. 957 (1922).

[71] See also *Yates* v. *Newton,* 59 Utah 105, 110, 202 Pac. 208 (1921); *Big Cottonwood Tanner Ditch Co.* v. *Moyle,* 109 Utah 197, 203, 220-221, 159 Pac. (2d) 596 (1945), 174 Pac. (2d) 148 (1946).

[72] The opinion in *Adams* v. *Portage Irr., Res. & Power Co.,* 95 Utah 1, 11, 72 Pac. (2d) 648 (1937), says in effect that in Utah private waters (as distinguished from public waters) are not only subject to exclusive control and ownership, but may be used, sold, or *wasted.* A dissenting opinion in *In re Bear River Drainage Area,* 2 Utah (2d) 208, 216, 271 Pac. (2d) 846 (1954), included this passage in an extensive quotation from the *Adams* opinion. Obviously, an acknowledgment that water may be wasted is squarely in conflict with the many declarations in Utah concerning conservation of water and the public necessity of preventing waste. It is not a correct statement of the Utah law of water rights. Undoubtedly, it was made inadvertently. As a matter of fact, the writer of the dissenting opinion in *Bear River* declared, before making this quotation, that water is the life of an arid State such as Utah and that the right to its use must be carefully guarded and perpetually regulated to achieve the greatest good therefrom.

[73] Cal. Const., art. XIV, § 3.

[74] *Meridian* v. *San Francisco,* 13 Cal. (2d) 424, 447, 90 Pac. (2d) 537 (1939).

[75] *Peabody* v. *Vallejo,* 2 Cal. (2d) 351, 368, 40 Pac. (2d) 486 (1935).

A Kansas statute provides that an appropriation of water is effectual only as to so much water as is applied to beneficial use, together with a reasonable allowance for waste, seepage, and evaporation.[76]

The water appropriation statute of Nevada requires that in determining the quantity of water to be allowed in a permit, there be taken into consideration various factors including reasonable transportation losses between the places of diversion and use, and reservoir evaporation losses in case of storage of water.[77]

Courts recognize that absolute efficiency in the diversion, conveyance, and appropriation of water is not practicable, and that at times some so-called "waste" is inevitable.[78] A water user thus is entitled to a reasonable allowance—but only that—in conducting his water from the point of diversion to the place of use.[79] The limitation of economy of use of water is to be applied within reasonable limits; it is to be emphasized, but not "to such an extent as to imperil success."[80] In the last analysis, it precludes any waste of water that can be reasonably avoided.[81]

Rights to the Use of Water

Constitutional confirmation of existing water rights.—In the constitutions of Arizona, New Mexico, and Utah, all rights to the use of water in the State for useful or beneficial purposes, existing at the time of adoption of the constitutional declaration, are recognized and confirmed.[82]

Appropriation of water: Recognition and safeguarding of the right.—The constitutions of Colorado and New Mexico declare that waters of natural streams are subject to appropriation under the laws of the State.[83] The Colorado constitution contains a further provision that the right to divert the unappropriated waters of any natural stream to beneficial uses shall never be denied.[84] In three other States, there is a safeguard similar to that of Colorado but with important qualifications—there shall be no denial of the right to appropriate water except (1) in Nebraska and Wyoming, when the denial is demanded by the public interest, and (2) in Idaho, where the State may regulate and limit the use of water for power purposes.[85]

Each of the 17 contiguous Western States and Alaska has a statute that authorizes the appropriation of water in natural watercourses, and each provides statutory procedure under which such rights may be acquired. (The

---

[76] Kans. Stat. Ann. § 42-302 (1964).

[77] Nev. Rev. Stat. § 533.070 (Supp. 1967).

[78] *Bidleman* v. *Short,* 38 Nev. 467, 470-471, 150 Pac. 834 (1915).

[79] *Basinger* v. *Taylor,* 36 Idaho 591, 597, 211 Pac. 1085 (1922).

[80] *Allen* v. *Petrick,* 69 Mont. 373, 376, 380, 222 Pac. 451 (1924).

[81] *Vineyard Land & Stock Co.* v. *Twin Falls Oakley Land & Water Co.,* 245 Fed. 30, 33-34, 35 (9th Cir. 1917).

[82] Ariz. Const., art. XVII, § 2; N. Mex. Const., art. XVI, § 1; Utah Const., art. XVII, § 1.

[83] Colo. Const., art. XVI, § 5; N. Mex. Const., art. XVI, § 2.

[84] Colo. Const., art. XVI, § 6.

[85] Nebr. Const., art. XV, § 6; Wyo. Const., art. VIII, § 3; Idaho Const., art. XV, § 3.

extent to which the appropriation doctrine also may apply to other sources of water is considered later. See chapter 7.) Most of these statutes, as noted above (see "Public Supervision over Waters—Supervisory Functions"), vest centralized administration of this function in State agencies. In each of these Western States there are also high court decisions that recognize the right of appropriation. The aggregate of these decisions comprises a large body of case law.

Appropriation of water: Priority of the right.—By the constitutions of New Mexico and Wyoming, priority of appropriation, without qualification, is declared to give the better right.[86] The principle of priority is declared in Colorado and Idaho likewise, but with certain exceptions in times of water shortage. (See "Preferences in Use of Water," below.)[87]

Aside from certain deviations made applicable in some of the water appropriation statutes under exceptional circumstances, the principle of "First in time, first in right" prevails throughout the statutory and case law of the West.

Riparian doctrine: Repudiated.—The constitution of Arizona declares that the common law doctrine of riparian water rights shall not obtain or be of any force or effect in the State.[88] In 1887—a quarter century prior to statehood—the Territorial legislature of Arizona had repudiated the riparian doctrine,[89] and the declaration in the State constitution restated the provision in substantially identical language.

The courts of the compact group of eight "generally more arid" States have generally repudiated the riparian water-rights doctrine as unsuited to the conditions within these jurisdictions.[90] (See chapters 6 and 10).

Riparian doctrine: Recognized and limited.—The courts were chiefly responsible for creating the riparian water law of the West. While generally repudiating this doctrine in the eight "generally more arid" States as noted above, they have recognized its existence in the other 11 States—although within limitations, the nature and extent of which have varied considerably from one jurisdiction to another. These limitations often have resulted from or have been influenced by State legislative or constitutional provisions. A brief discussion of such provisions is included below. In a number of States, various questions regarding the effect or validity of these limitations have not been resolved by the courts. This is explained more fully later. (See chapter 6.)

---

[86] N. Mex. Const., art. XVI, § 2; Wyo. Const., art. VIII, § 3.

[87] Colo. Const., art. XVI, § 6; Idaho Const., art. XV, § 3.

[88] Ariz. Const., art. XVII, § 1.

[89] Terr. Ariz. Rev. Stat. § 3198 (1887).

[90] Arizona: *Clough* v. *Wing,* 2 Ariz. 371, 380-381, 17 Pac. 453 (1888); Colorado: *Coffin* v. *Left Hand Ditch Co.,* 6 Colo. 443, 446-447 (1882); Idaho: *Hutchinson* v. *Watson Slough Ditch Co.,* 16 Idaho 484, 490-495, 101 Pac. 1059 (1909); Montana: *Mettler* v. *Ames Realty Co.,* 61 Mont. 152, 157-158, 165, 166, 201 Pac. 702 (1921); Nevada: *Jones* v. *Adams,* 19 Nev. 78, 84-88, 6 Pac. 442 (1885); New Mexico: *Trambley* v. *Luterman,* 6 N. Mex. 15, 25, 27 Pac. 312 (1891); Utah: *Stowell* v. *Johnson,* 7 Utah 215, 225-226, 26 Pac. 290 (1891); Wyoming: *Moyer* v. *Preston,* 6 Wyo. 308, 318-319, 44 Pac. 845 (1896).

Despite California's judicial recognition of the doctrine of riparian rights throughout almost the entire history of the State, it was not until 1928 that the State constitution for the first time specifically named this doctrine in an amendment which, however, placed an important limitation on the extent of the right.[91] The amendment declares that riparian rights in the water of a stream "attach to, but to no more than" the quantity of water required or used reasonably and beneficially for the purposes for which the riparian lands are or may be made adaptable.

In the early years of statehood, the California Supreme Court recognized the riparian doctrine as a fundamental part of the State water law, and in its many subsequent water rights decisions it has never deviated from a policy of according to that doctrine outstanding importance. However, notwithstanding its long line of proriparian decisions, the supreme court accepted the constitutional amendment of 1928 as being the supreme law of the State, having superseded all State laws inconsistent therewith,[92] and acknowledged that its duty was "to cause the law to conform to the state policy now commanded by our fundamental law."[93]

Early statutes of the Dakotas and of Oklahoma declared that the landowner might use water running in a definite stream over or under the surface of his land, but might not prevent its natural flow nor pursue nor pollute it.[94] This, according to the South Dakota Supreme Court, was a concise statement of the common law riparian doctrine.[95] As such, these statutes are unique in riparian legislation in the West which, aside from disclaiming interference with vested riparian rights,[96] has been directed chiefly toward restricting the operation of the riparian doctrine.

Important legislative limitations upon riparian rights include those of Oregon, South Dakota, and Kansas, which appear to have generally restricted the exercise of such rights, as vested riparian rights, to the extent of actual application of water to beneficial use made at the time of the enactment of water appropriation statutes or, in certain cases, shortly thereafter.[97]

---

[91] Cal. Const., art. XIV, § 3. This provision is repeated in Cal. Water Code § § 100 and 101 (West 1956).

[92] *Gin S. Chow* v. *Santa Barbara,* 217 Cal. 673, 700, 22 Pac. (2d) 5 (1933).

[93] *Peabody* v. *Vallejo,* 2 Cal. (2d) 351, 365, 40 Pac. (2d) 486 (1935).

[94] Terr. Dak. Laws 1865-1866, ch. 1, § 256, Civ. Code § 255 (1877), N. Dak. Cent. Code Ann. § 47-01-13, repealed, Laws 1963, ch. 419, § 7; S. Dak. Code § 61.0101 (1939), repealed, Laws 1955, ch. 430, § 1; Terr. Okla. Stat. § 4162 (1890), Stat. Ann. tit. 60, § 60 (Supp. 1961), amended, Laws 1963, ch. 419, § 7, Stat. Ann. tit. 60, § 60 (Supp. 1970).

[95] *Lone Tree Ditch Co.* v. *Cyclone Ditch Co.,* 15 S. Dak. 519, 525-526, 91 N. W. 352 (1902).

[96] See, e.g., Tex. Rev. Civ. Stat. Ann. art. 7507 (1954).

[97] Oreg. Rev. Stat. § 539.010 (Supp. 1955); S. Dak. Comp. Laws Ann. § 46-1-9 (1967); Kans. Stat. Ann. § 82a-701 (1969).

Courts have sustained the validity of Oregon and Kansas statutes on several points presented for determination. *In re Willow Creek,* 74 Oreg. 592, 610-620, 625-628, 144

The Texas water appropriation statute provides that nothing in it is to be construed as a recognition of any riparian right in any land the title to which passed out of the State after July 1, 1895.[98] Texas legislation in 1967 added a provision similar to the Oregon, South Dakota, and Kansas legislative limitations on riparian rights discussed above.[99]

Without prior legislative direction, the high courts of Washington and Nebraska have restricted the operation of the riparian doctrine. The Washington court has said that water in excess of the amount a riparian owner can beneficially use, either directly or within a reasonable time, is subject to appropriation.[100] Washington legislation enacted in 1967 has specified some different requirements in this regard.[101]

A 1903 Nebraska decision ruled that if the riparian owner did not make actual use of the water before conflicting appropriative rights vested, he had no recourse other than to recover such damages for the impairment of his riparian rights as he could prove.[102] However, the Nebraska Supreme Court in a 1966 decision has relaxed, to some extent, the restrictions placed upon the remedies available to riparian owners and has given them, in appropriate cases, the

---

Pac. 505 (1914), 146 Pac. 475 (1915); *In re Hood River,* 114 Oreg. 112, 173-182, 227 Pac. 1065 (1924); *California-Oregon Power Co.* v. *Beaver Portland Cement Co.,* 73 Fed. (2d) 555, 562, 564, 567-569 (9th Cir. 1934), affirmed, but without deciding the validity of the Oregon statute, in 295 U.S. 142, 153-165 (1935); *State ex rel. Emery* v. *Knapp,* 167 Kans. 546, 555-556, 207 Pac. (2d) 440 (1949); *Baumann* v. *Smrha,* 145 Fed. Supp. 617 (D. Kans. 1956), affirmed per curiam, 352 U.S. 863 (1956); *Williams* v. *City of Wichita,* 190 Kans. 317, 374 Pac. (2d) 578 (1962), appealed dismissed, 375 U.S. 7 (1963).

See also *Belle Fourche Irr. Dist.* v. *Smiley,* ___ S. Dak. ___, 176 N.W. (2d) 239, 245 (1970), regarding the South Dakota legislation; and *Baeth* v. *Hoisveen,* 157 N. W. (2d) 728 (N. Dak. 1968), construing North Dakota legislation. These cases are discussed in chapter 6.

[98] Tex. Rev. Civ. Stat. Ann. art. 7619 (1954). See also *Motl* v. *Boyd,* 116 Tex. 82, 108, 286 S. W. 458 (1926), regarding the limitation of riparian rights to the ordinary streamflow.

[99] Tex. Rev. Civ. Stat. Ann. art. 7542a, § 4 (Supp. 1970). This limitation does not apply to the use of water for domestic or livestock purposes.

Oklahoma legislation provides that a riparian owner has a right to use a stream for domestic purposes as defined in the legislation. Okla. Stat. Ann. tit. 60, § 60 (Supp. 1970) and tit. 82, § 1-A (1970).

[100] *In re Sinlahekin Creek,* 162 Wash. 635, 640-641, 299 Pac. 649 (1931); *State* v. *American Fruit Growers,* 135 Wash. 156, 161, 237 Pac. 498 (1925).

[101] See Wash. Rev. Code § § 90.14.170 and 90.14.020(3) (Supp. 1970) and Laws 1967, ch. 233, § 12, creating Rev. Code § 90.14.120, repealed, Laws 1969, ch. 284, § 23. This legislation is discussed in chapter 6.

[102] *McCook Irr. & Water Power Co.* v. *Crews,* 70 Nebr. 109, 121-127, 96 N.W. 996 (1903), 102 N.W. 249 (1905). See also *Cline* v. *Stock,* 71 Nebr. 70, 80-83, 98 N.W. 454 (1904), 102 N.W. 265 (1905).

possibility of obtaining injunctive relief against conflicting appropriative rights.[103]

In Hawaii, riparian rights have been recognized in a limited degree, but the appropriation system of surface water rights has never been in effect.[104] Alaska courts early recognized the appropriation doctrine. They have declared that a Territorial mining statute of 1917 enacted the law of riparian rights to a limited extent.[105] However, the Alaska Water Use Act of 1966 apparently purports to phase out such riparian rights.[106]

Purpose of Use of Water

In general, the State water policies contemplate that appropriative water rights may relate to any specific purpose of use of water that is beneficial to the user and that does not conflict with the public welfare.

In the constitutions of Western States in which purposes of use of water are mentioned, irrigation (or agriculture) occurs most frequently, followed by manufacturing, power, domestic, and mining.

Thus, certain preferences as among domestic, agriculture, and manufacturing purposes are accorded in the Colorado, Nebraska, and Idaho constitutions, with the addition of mining in the last named.[107] (See "Preferences in Use of Water," below.) Use of water for irrigation, mining, and manufacturing purposes is a public use in Washington; and for these purposes, stream waters in North Dakota remain the property of the State.[108] In Texas and South Dakota, irrigation of arid lands is a public purpose; and in the former, the control of water for irrigation, power, and other useful purposes is a public right and duty.[109] The constitutions of Oklahoma, South Dakota, and Texas

---

[103] *Wasserburger* v. *Coffee,* 180 Nebr. 147, 161-164, 141 N.W. (2d) 738 (1966), modified, 180 Nebr. 569, 144 N.W. (2d) 209 (1966).

[104] *Carter* v. *Territory of Hawaii,* 24 Haw. 47, 57-71 (1917); *Territory of Hawaii* v. *Gay,* 31 Haw. 376, 394-417 (1930), affirmed, 52 Fed. (2d) 356 (9th Cir. 1931), certiorari denied, 284 U.S. 677 (1931).

[105] *Noland* v. *Coon,* 1 Alaska 36, 37-38 (1890); *Balabanoff* v. *Kellogg,* 10 Alaska 11, 118 Fed. (2d) 597, 599 (9th Cir. 1940), certiorari denied, 314 U.S. 635 (1941).

[106] The 1966 act repealed this mining statute (Alaska Laws 1966, ch. 50, § 2) and provides *inter alia* that waters occurring in a natural state are reserved to the people for common use, subject to appropriation and beneficial use. Alaska Stat. § 46.15.030 (1966). Without mentioning the term "riparian," the act also provides that a water right lawfully acquired before the effective date of the act, or a beneficial use on the effective date thereof, or made within 5 years prior thereto, or in conjunction with works then under construction under a common-law or customary appropriation or use, is a lawful appropriation under the act and is subject to its applicable provisions. *Id.* § 46.15.060. This and related provisions of the act are discussed in chapter 6.

[107] Colo. Const., art. XVI, § 3; Nebr. Const., art. XV, § 6; Idaho Const., art. XV, § 3.

[108] Wash. Const., art. XXI, § 1; N. Dak. Const., art. XVII, § 210.

[109] Tex. Const., art. XVI, § 59a; S. Dak. Const., art. XXI, § 7.

authorize the respective legislatures to provide for irrigation improvements to be paid for by taxation of the benefited lands.[110] Waters appropriated and used for agricultural and domestic purposes under sale or rental in Idaho are exclusively dedicated to such use.[111] The necessity of water for domestic and irrigation purposes in Nebraska is a natural want.[112]

The Idaho constitution provides that the State may control and promote the development of the unused water power within its boundaries; and it reserves to the State the right to regulate and limit the use of water for power purposes.[113] That of Oregon declares that the right to all water for the development of water power and to water power sites owned by the State shall be held by it in perpetuity; and it clothes the State with broad powers to control and develop water power and to distribute electric energy either alone or in cooperation with the United States, other States, and political subdivisions.[114] In Nebraska, the use of water for power purposes is deemed to be a public use; and it must never be alienated, but may be leased or otherwise developed as prescribed by law.[115]

Some statutes particularize purposes for which water may be appropriated.[116] Others authorize appropriations of water for beneficial use, and contain provisions respecting certain purposes but without placing any limitation upon the purpose of use if it is beneficial.[117]

Courts have indicated in some instances their approval of the appropriability of water for certain purposes not stated in the statutes,[118] and in other instances they have voiced their disapproval because of the circumstances of the particular case.[119]

Formerly, in Alaska, use of water for mining was preeminent. Most of the litigated controversies have been in this field. However, water appropriation has always been possible not only for mining but for other useful purposes as

---

[110] Okla. Const., art. XVI, § 3; S. Dak. Const., art. XXI, § 7; Tex. Const., art. III, § 52, and art. XVI, § 59c.

[111] Idaho Const., art. XV, § § 4 and 5.

[112] Nebr. Const., art. XV, § 4.

[113] Idaho Const., art. VIII, § 2 and art. XV, § 3.

[114] Oreg. Const., art. XI-D.

[115] Nebr. Const., art. XV, § 7.

[116] The Texas statute contains a long list of purposes: Tex. Rev. Civ. Stat. Ann. arts. 7470 and 7471 (Supp. 1970).

[117] See Okla. Stat. Ann. tit. 82, § § 1-A and 33 (1970).

[118] Swimming pool or fishpond: *Osnes Livestock Co.* v. *Warren,* 103 Mont. 284, 300-302, 62 Pac. (2d) 206 (1936); propagation of fish: *Faden* v. *Hubbell,* 93 Colo. 358, 368, 28 Pac. (2d) 247 (1933).

[119] Extermination of pests: *Tulare Irr. Dist.* v. *Lindsay-Stratnmore Irr. Dist.,* 3 Cal. (2d) 489, 567-568, 45 Pac. (2d) 972 (1935); formation of icecap to promote retention of moisture: *Blaine County Investment Co.* v. *Mays,* Idaho 766, 773, 291 Pac. 1055 (1930); disposal of debris: *In re Deschutes River and Tributaries,* 134 Oreg. 623, 665, 286 Pac. 563, 294 Pac. 1049 (1930).

well.[120] Until 1966, a mining claim that included within its boundaries both banks of a stream was vested by statute with certain riparian rights.[121]

Preferences in Use of Water

Although, in the consitution of Colorado, the principle of priority in time of appropriating water is declared, this principle is made applicable as between persons who use the water for the same purpose, with a further proviso that when the waters of a stream are not adequate for all desired uses, domestic purposes have the preference over all others and agriculture is preferred to manufacturing.[122] Despite the failure of this section to provide for compensation to the holder of the inferior right, the Colorado Supreme Court held that the section does not authorize one desiring to use water for domestic purposes to take it from another who has previously appropriated it for some other purpose, without just compensation.[123]

The Idaho constitution contains a preference provision similar to that of Colorado, but with these important differences: (1) The preference accorded domestic uses is subject to such limitations as may be prescribed by law. (2) In any organized mining district, uses of water for mining purposes, or for milling purposes associated with mining, have preference over manufacturing or agricultural purposes. (3) Usage by subsequent appropriators is subject to the laws regulating the condemnation of property for public or private use.[124] According to the Idaho Supreme Court, the constitutional preference in favor of uses of water for domestic purposes is subject to other constitutional provisions regulating the taking of private property for public use.[125]

To the constitution of Nebraska there was added in 1920 a preference provision applicable in the event of insufficiency of the water supply, similar to that of Colorado, but with the important qualification that no inferior right to the use of water shall be acquired by a superior right without payment of just compensation.[126] An earlier statutory provision, still in the law, granted this preference but without a proviso for compensation.[127] Concerning this, the Nebraska Supreme Court observed in 1914 that "it must follow that vested

---

[120] See Alaska Comp. Laws Ann. § 47-3-7 (1949), deleted from Alaska Stat., Tables (Supp. 1965); *Kernan* v. *Andrus,* 6 Alaska 54, 59 (1918).

[121] Alaska Stat. § § 27.10.080 and 38.05.260 (Supp. 1962), repealed, Laws 1966, ch. 50, § 2. *Balabanoff* v. *Kellogg,* 10 Alaska 11, 118 Fed. (2d) 597, 599 (9th Cir. 1940), certiorari denied, 314 U.S. 635 (1941). See note 106 *supra,* regarding the Alaska Water Use Act of 1966 which is an appropriation doctrine act and apparently purports to phase out such riparian rights.

[122] Colo. Const., art. XVI, § 6.

[123] *Sterling* v. *Pawnee Ditch Extension Co.,* 42 Colo. 421, 426, 94 Pac. 339 (1908).

[124] Idaho Const., art. XV, § 3.

[125] *Basinger* v. *Taylor,* 30 Idaho 289, 294-295, 164 Pac. 522 (1917). See also *Montpelier Mill. Co.* v. *Montpelier,* 19 Idaho 212, 219-220, 113 Pac. 741 (1911).

[126] Nebr. Const., art. XV, § 6.

[127] Nebr. Rev. Stat. § 46-204 (1968).

rights of completed appropriations cannot be destroyed without compensation."[128]

Statutes of Oregon and Utah purport to give preference to the use of water for certain purposes in time of water shortage.[129] Neither statute specifically requires the payment of compensation to appropriators whose rights would be thus impaired or destroyed. But so far as has been ascertained, neither statute has been construed on this point in any reported court decision.

Still other statutory preferences apply to the acquisition of appropriative rights, rather than as between uses of water for which rights have been obtained. For example, Arizona legislation provides that when pending applications conflict, first preference goes to domestic (including small garden) and municipal uses, second to irrigation and stockwatering, third to power and mining, and last to recreation and wildlife, including fish.[130] These statutory preferences are discussed in chapter 7.

---

[128] *Kearney Water & Electric Powers Co.* v. *Alfalfa Irr. Dist.,* 97 Nebr. 139, 146, 149 N. W. 363 (1914).

[129] Oreg. Rev. Stat. § 540.140 (Supp. 1969); Utah Code Ann. § 73-3-21 (1968). See also Oreg. Rev. Stat. § 536.310(12) (Supp. 1969); Kans. Stat. Ann. § 82a-707 (1969); N. Dak. Cent. Code Ann. § 61-01-01.1 (Supp. 1969). These statutes are discussed in chapter 7.

[130] Arizona Rev. Stat. Ann. § § 45-141(c) (1956) and 45-147 (Supp. 1970).

Chapter 2

CLASSIFICATION, DEFINITION, AND DESCRIPTION OF AVAILABLE WATER SUPPLIES

A *water supply*, as the term is used in this study of water rights laws, is a natural body of water, either on or under the surface of the ground, available for diversion of the water therefrom and for its application to beneficial use. The water may be in motion, such as in the channel of a watercourse or in a stratum of rock or soil; or may be substantially at rest, such as in a lake or pond in a closed ground water reservoir.[1]

A *common water supply*, as the term is used herein, is a combination of water supplies, on or under the surface of the ground, or both, which are so interconne ted that diversions from one component water supply result in reducing the quantities of water which otherwise would be available in other component water supplies.

Supplies of water required for useful purposes, therefore, are available on or below the surface of the earth. The science of weather modification, chiefly "rainmaking," though now in its infancy, has progressed far enough to indicate a "great economic potential," accompanied by new legal doctrines of rights and liabilities.[2] At present, however, waters in the atmosphere, though highly important physically, generally do not constitute an "available water supply" to which separate rights of use attach.

For the purpose of discussing laws of water rights, there is adopted the following classification of available water supplies occurring in natural geological formations or on their surface:

(1) Watercourses. This group comprises, without subclassification, waters flowing in well-defined channels, and waters in lakes and ponds whether or not connected with stream systems.

(2) Diffused surface water.

(3) Other waters at the surface:

    (a) Salvaged and developed waters.

    (b) Waste, seepage, drainage, and return waters.

    (c) Spring water.

(4) Ground waters:

---

[1] The definitions of terms in this chapter are based largely on National Reclamation Association, "Desirable Principles of State Water Legislation," pp. 1-2 (1946), which was prepared by a committee of the National Reclamation Association, Wells A. Hutchins, chairman.

[2] Stark, Donald D., "Weather Modification:Water—Three Cents per Acre-Foot?" 45 Cal. Law Rev. 698 (1957). See also Davis, R. J., "The Legal Implications of Atmospheric Water Resources Development and Management," (Ariz. Univ., Coll. of Law, 1968).

(21)

(a) Definite underground streams.
(b) Underflow of surface streams.
(c) Percolating water.
(d) Artesian water.

These terms may be defined as follows:

Watercourse is a definite stream of water in a definite natural channel, originating from a definite source or sources of supply. It includes the underflow. The stream may flow intermittently or at irregular intervals, if that is a characteristic result of the sources of water supply in the area.

Lake or *pond* is a compact body of water with defined boundaries, substantially at rest. The difference between a lake and a pond is in size. A pond is a small lake.

Diffused surface water is water that occurs, in its natural state, in places on the surface of the ground other than in a watercourse or lake or pond.

Salvaged and developed waters are made available for use by the labor of man.

Salvaged water is that portion of water in a water supply which under natural conditions is lost, but which by means of artificial devices is recovered and made available for beneficial use.

Developed water is water which in its natural state does not augment a water supply, but which by means of artificial works is added to a water supply or is otherwise made available for beneficial use.

Waste, seepage, drainage, and return waters are closely associated and their classifications overlap.

Waste water, which may be flowing on the surface or seeping under it, includes water purposely turned back into streams from which diverted, because of operation conditions and requirements affecting the diversion systems; water leaking from ditches and structures; and water flowing from irrigated lands as a result of excessive applications to the soil.

Seepage or seepage water is water seeping through the soil, from natural or artificial sources, and entering stream channels or appearing elsewhere on the surface.

Drainage water is water flowing in an artificial drain, originating from either natural or artificial sources.

Return water consists of portions of water diverted for irrigation or other uses that return to the stream from which diverted, or to some other stream, or that would do so if not intercepted by some obstacle, and may thus include waste water, seepage, and drainage water.

Spring water is water that breaks out upon the surface of the earth through natural openings in the ground.

Ground water is water under the surface of the ground, whatever may be the geologic structure in which it is standing or moving.

Definite underground stream is a watercourse buried in the ground.

Underflow of surface stream is the subsurface portion of a watercourse the whole of which comprises waters flowing in close association both on and beneath the surface.

Percolating water is water moving through the ground but not constituting part of a definite underground stream.

Artesian water is ground water under sufficient hydrostatic pressure to rise above the saturated zone.

An available supply of water differs from that of certain other natural resources—such, for example, as deposits of iron ore or precious metals, or even oil—in that it is in a state of continuous or intermittent replenishment from other sources of water supply, through the cyclical operation of physical laws. Thus, in the western United States, watercourses and diffused surface waters are supplied chiefly by precipitation in storms originating over the Pacific Ocean and the Gulf of Mexico; diffused surface waters sink into the ground or become concentrated in stream channels, thereby augmenting the supply of ground water or of surface streams; surface streams feed subterranean supplies at some places and are fed from subterranean sources at others, and disappear into the ground or flow into the sea or into lakes either with or without known surface outlets; and water evaporates from all surface supplies and from subterranean supplies close to the surface and is deposited in the form of precipitation elsewhere.

A water supply, therefore, is almost never in truly static condition, awaiting exploitation by man. Its particles are generally in motion—they have come from some other water supply or supplies, and are en route to still others. Therefore, diversion of water from a particular source of supply interrupts the natural replenishment of some other available source of supply. Recognition of this fundamental relationship is necessary to an orderly discussion of water rights.

The point at which water is physically appropriated for use—that is, diverted from its natural state and brought under control by artificial devices— determines the initial legal classification of such water for such use. Thus, waters taken from a stream into a canal, through a headgate installed on the bank of the stream, are classified at the point of diversion as waters of a watercourse. Waters diffused over the ground and which if not intercepted would flow over a bank into a stream, but which before doing so are captured by means of an artificial dike and thereby simply detained or directed into a canal, are classified at the point of interception as diffused surface waters. Waters moving through the soil, which if not intercepted would seep into a surface watercourse through the banks or bottom of the channel, but which are captured and brought to the surface by means of a pumping plant installed some distance away from the stream and its subterranean channel, are classified at the point of interception as percolating waters or as waters of definite underground streams, depending upon the geological structure through which they are moving. However, a watercourse flow, or a ground water reservoir, may contain undivided segments of commingled waters to which different rights of use may attach.

The point of diversion of water from a natural water supply is an element of the right to make such diversion. The exercise of this right at this place depends upon rules that pertain to the particular source of supply—for example, a watercourse—which in a given jurisdiction may be different from those that pertain to another source such as a supply of percolating ground water. In many instances, these rules have been formulated without due consideration for the physical interrelationships of the several components of common water supplies. This has come about in certain situations, for example, because rival claimants of rights in a ground water supply have litigated their rights as between themselves, without intervention by claimants of rights to waters of a surface stream to which the ground waters involved in the litigation were physically tributary; and the result of such decisions has been to establish a rule of property, repeated and reemphasized in subsequent decisions, and therefore difficult to overturn in later years when these physical relationships had become more clearly recognized. In some States there has been a measure of correlation between rights to the use of waters of various interconnected sources of supply—or common water supplies, while in others there has been little or none. Furthermore, in some jurisdictions, rights to some of these available sources of supply have not yet been adequately defined.

Most water to which rights of use attach comprises (1) water of watercourses and (2) percolating ground water. Of these, by far the larger amount of statutory and case law relates to watercourses, although in the last few decades, with the marked development of pumped water supplies that has occurred in various jurisdictions, the ground water share of the total has materially increased.

Principles governing rights to the use of water of surface streams were formulated, applied, and in greater or less degree established, and substantial experience in their administration was acquired, before the ever-increasing use of ground water was well underway. In the Western States, most of the legislation dealing with water rights in streams governs appropriative rights; and in some of them, much of the litigation over stream water rights has been concerned with conflicts between the appropriation and riparian philosophies. Likewise with respect to ground water rights in the West, there has been a somewhat comparable experience—much of the legislation and litigation has been concerned with efforts to apply to percolating ground water, often in the face of conflicting rules previously applied or claimed to have been applied thereto, the law of appropriation as developed with respect to surface watercourses in the particular jurisdiction, with only such variations as were required by differences in the physical occurrence and behavior of these surface and subterranean water supplies.

In this study of Western State laws, water rights principles pertaining to watercourses, diffused surface water, etc., will be presented in the order of classification of available water supplies given above in this chapter. The quantity of materials applicable to watercourses is so large, by contrast with other water supplies, as to require presentation in several separate chapters.

First, attention is given to the considerable number of topics relating to characteristics of a watercourse and to the property nature of water and water rights therein. The succeeding chapters will concentrate on rights to the use of water.

Chapter 3

CHARACTERISTICS OF WATERCOURSE

"The stream or body of water, although its particles are transient and ever changing, is deemed, for purposes of legal definition, a fixed object so long as it can thus be identified.* * *."[1]

DEFINITION AND GENERAL DESCRIPTION

"A river is more than an amenity, it is a treasure. It offers a necessity of life that must be rationed among those who have power over it."[2] This discerning statement by Justice Holmes, made in an interstate case involving the Delaware River and its tributaries, was directed at the major type of watercourse universally known as a river. But its truth applies just as surely to much smaller streamflows called rivers in the arid part of the nation, where great rivers are few and far between, and likewise to even smaller ones with channels that become dry and are expected to remain dry during a part of every year.

The purpose of the brief discussion that follows is to present a broad summary of the major characteristics of the vitally important natural feature known legally as a watercourse. In later parts of this chapter, the physical characteristics of a watercourse and their legal implications are discussed, in some detail, with supporting authorities.

The Legal Composition of a Watercourse

Surface waters in watercourses are waters flowing continuously or intermittently in natural surface channels from definite sources of supply, and waters flowing through lakes, ponds, and marshes which are integral parts of a stream system.

The term "watercourse" is in common use. It means a definite stream in a definite channel with a definite source or sources of supply, and it includes the underflow. The term "stream" is often used alone, in which case it is practically synonymous with "watercourse." For example, the term "natural stream" as used in the Colorado constitution[3] has been construed by the State Supreme Court as including all "watercourses" and their tributaries.[4] The South Dakota Supreme Court made a distinction between "definite stream" as used in a special statute of the State and "watercourse."[5] The court

---

[1] *Utah Metal & Tunnel Co.* v. *Groesbeck*, 62 Utah 251, 256, 219 Pac. 248 (1923).
[2] *New Jersey* v. *New York*, 283 U.S. 336, 342 (1931).
[3] Colo. Const., art. XVI, § § 5 and 6. See "State Water Policies—Declarations of Policy," in chapter 1.
[4] *In re German Ditch & Res. Co.*, 56 Colo. 252, 271, 139 Pac. 2 (1913).
[5] *Benson* v. *Cook*, 47 S. Dak. 611, 616, 201 N. W. 526 (1924). The special statute, S. Dak. Rev. Code § 348 (1919), Code § 61.0101 (1939), was repealed by Laws 1955, ch. 430.

commented on the looseness and inaccuracy of using the terms as though they were synonymous, for they do not have the same meaning. While there cannot be a running stream without a watercourse, said the court, nothing is more common than a watercourse without a stream.

It is true that in strict legal parlance a stream of water is not a watercourse—it is assuredly one of the essential elements of an overall natural system called a watercourse, but only one of them. When exact terminology is required in this book, the term watercourse is used to designate this overall system of which the stream is only a part. Otherwise, to avoid montonous repetition, such terms as stream, creek, river, tributary, etc., may be used when appropriate.

The Surface Stream System

The concept of a surface stream system has long been recognized in discussions of the right to make use of the water of surface watercourses. The stream system consists of the main channel and of all tributary channels through which water naturally flows by gravity into the main channel. It comprises a main watercourse and a number of tributary watercourses of varying size. This concept is particularly important in the determination of rights to the use of water in the arid and semiarid West—not only rights of prior appropriation and beneficial use, but riparian rights as well. The use of water under the appropriation doctrine is not confined to lands contiguous to the stream channels, for the doctrine—subject to priorities of right—sanctions the diversion of waters from main streams and from their tributaries, flowing through either agricultural or nonagricultural country, and conveyance of the diverted water to areas from which there will be no natural return to the main channel. The prior appropriator is protected by law against diversions from upstream tributaries under junior rights which would materially interfere with the exercise of his own prior rights. Likewise, in the jurisdictions in which the riparian doctrine is substantially recognized, upstream diversions either from the main stream or from tributaries may be restricted—or, indeed, completely stopped—to the extent that they interfere with the rights of downstream riparian owners.

Gains and Losses of Water

Surface watercourses are fed by the flow in tributary channels, by diffused surface water flowing over the banks of the stream, by waste water discharged into the channel, and by ground water seeping into the channel through its banks and bed. The tributary sources of supply may be natural sources altogether, such as rains and melting snows, or they may, and in the irrigated areas usually do, include waste and seepage waters or return flow from irrigated lands.

The sides and bottom of the channel may be impervious in some places and not in others; where not impervious, the soil across and through which the channel is formed necessarily contains water in greater or less degree, and this water-bearing zone may be very limited in extent or may extend to considerable depths and for considerable distances on each side. The water-bearing zone adjacent to a previous surface channel is called in the court decisions the "underflow" or "subflow" of the surface watercourse. It may be in contact with the ground water table in the region through which the stream flows, or may be separated from it. A surface stream throughout part of its course may be discharging water into the ground; elsewhere, it may be taking water from the ground; and in other places, there may be neither an underground inflow nor outflow, but only a surface flow supported by the water in the subterranean channel or reservoir—a physical balance. At a given point on a stream channel, there may be an inflow from the ground at one time and an outflow into the ground at another time. Some of the water that passes from the surface stream channel into the ground becomes permanently separated from the subflow and enters the classification of percolating water. Other surface stream water that seeps into the subflow remains therein and moves downstream as a part of that subterranean body of water.

Therefore, the flow in a watercourse does not mean solely the visible surface stream, but includes likewise the underflow, where there is one. The underflow is as much a part of the watercourse and as important from the standpoint of rights in the watercourse as is the surface flow; for if the waters within this subterranean area are withdrawn, the surface waters tend to sink into the voids to take their place. The legal implications of this are widely recognized in court decisions. Although definitions of a surface watercourse seldom refer to associated waters in the ground, nevertheless the underflow is a physical part of the whole and the courts have held it to be a component part.

The association between surface watercourses and diffused surface waters and ground waters is therefore very marked. The legal significance of this association is highly important, although it has not been established in all instances.

ELEMENTS OF WATERCOURSE

Typical Definitions

Judicial

Definitions of "watercourse" and of its component parts appear in high court decisions rendered throughout the West. The accompanying footnote brings together citations of cases in which some typical definitions have been given by western courts over the 90-year period from 1875 to 1965, arranged chronologically.[6]

---

[6]*Barnes* v. *Sabron*, 10 Nev. 217, 236-239 (1875); *Geddis* v. *Parrish*, 1 Wash. 587, 589, 21 Pac. 314 (1889); *Simmons* v. *Winters*, 21 Oreg. 35, 41-42, 27 Pac. 7 (1891); *Rait* v. *Furrow*, 74 Kans. 101, 105, 107, 85 Pac. 934 (1906); *Jaquez Ditch Co.* v. *Garcia*, 17 N. Mex. 160, 161, 124 Pac. 891 (1912); *In re German Ditch & Res. Co.*, 56 Colo. 252,

Substantial agreement as to basic elements. –On the whole, despite some variations, little change has apparently occurred in prevailing judicial concepts of what is basically necessary to constitute a watercourse. There is substantial agreement among the high courts as to the essential elements of a watercourse. (See "The Three Essential Elements," below.) The variations occur chiefly in interpretations of these requirements, arising out of their applicability to widely varying sets of circumstances. To illustrate this point, brief mention may be made of significant variations in this field in the jurisprudence of South Dakota, which are discussed elsewhere in this chapter in connection with the features to which they pertain.

Variations in interpretations. –In 1917, the South Dakota Supreme Court observed that the term "watercourse" had come to have two distinct meanings–one as a watercourse to which riparian rights attach, and the other a watercourse through which an upper landowner may discharge drainage water from his land.[7] With respect to the latter, the court adopted a definition and description that included a uniform flow over a given course having reasonable limits as to width; and this feature was adhered to in 1946.[8] However, in the 1946 opinion, no mention was made of other features adopted in 1917, particularly a rejection of the requirement that the given course be a channel with definite sides or banks carved by the action of the flowing water. In the meantime, the court decided two cases involving water rights, in which there were definite channels classified as "draws," the waters of which were held to be "mere surface water" because they were only temporary streamflows from impermanent sources of melting snow and summer rain.[9] This series of cases contains several variations from generally prevailing interpretations of watercourse characteristics–definite bed and banks to the channel, noncontinuity of flow of stream, and permanence of source consisting of melting snow and rain.

Legislative

Some legislatures have defined watercourse in connection with specific statutory authorizations. For example:

271, 139 Pac. 2 (1913); *Hoefs* v. *Short,* 114 Tex. 501, 505-511, 273 S. W. 785 (1925); *Maricopa County M.W.C. Dist.* v. *Southwest Cotton Co.,* 39 Ariz. 65, 85-86, 4 Pac. (2d) 369 (1931); *Wyoming* v. *Hiber,* 48 Wyo. 172, 183-185, 44 Pac. (2d) 1005 (1935); *Garrett* v. *Haworth,* 183 Okla. 569, 570-571, 83 Pac. (2d) 822 (1938); *Scott* v. *Watkins,* 63 Idaho 506, 517-518, 122 Pac. (2d) 220 (1942); *Johnson* v. *Metropolitan Life Ins. Co.,* 71 S. Dak. 155, 161, 22 N.W. (2d) 737 (1946); *Costello* v. *Bowen,* 80 Cal. App. (2d) 621, 627, 182 Pac. (2d) 615 (1947); *State* v. *Brace,* 76 N. Dak. 314, 322, 36 N. W. (2d) 330 (1949); *Jack* v. *Teegarden,* 151 Nebr. 309, 315, 37 N.W. (2d) 387 (1949); *Doney* v. *Beatty,* 124 Mont. 41, 45, 51, 220 Pac. (2d) 77 (1950); *South Santa Clara Valley Water Cons. Dist.* v. *Johnson,* 231 Cal. App. (2d) 388, 393-395, 41 Cal. Rptr. 846 (1964).

[7] *Thompson* v. *Andrews,* 39 S. Dak. 477, 483-484, 165 N. W. 9 (1917).

[8] *Johnson* v. *Metropolitan Life Ins. Co.,* 71 S. Dak. 155, 161, 22 N. W. (2d) 737 (1946).

[9] *Benson* v. *Cook,* 47 S. Dak. 611, 616-617, 201 N. W. 526 (1924); *Terry* v. *Heppner,* 59 S. Dak. 317, 319-320, 239 N. W. 759 (1931).

The "General Provisions" chapter of the North Dakota water statute contains the following definition of a watercourse:[10]

A watercourse entitled to the protection in the law is constituted if there is a sufficient natural and accustomed flow of water to form and maintain a distinct and a defined channel. It is not essential that the supply of water should be continuous or from a perennial living source. It is enough if the flow arises periodically from natural causes and reaches a plainly defined channel of a permanent character.

The New Mexico statute providing for the appropriation of natural waters flowing in "streams and watercourses" contains the following definition:[11]

A watercourse is hereby defined to be any river, creek, arroyo, canyon, draw, or wash, or any other channel having definite banks and bed with visible evidence of the occasional flow of water.

The Nebraska law authorizing individual landowners to drain their lands "into any natural watercourse or into any natural depression or draw" contains the following provision:[12]

Any depression or draw two feet below the surrounding lands and having a continuous outlet to a stream of water, or river or brook shall be deemed a watercourse.

The Three Essential Elements

As noted in chapter 2, "Classification, Definition, and Description of Available Water Supplies," a watercourse comprises three essential elements: (1) a definite *stream of water*, (2) flowing in a definite natural *channel*, and (3) originating from a definite *source or sources* of supply. However, the several elements and their associated characteristics are all subject to judicial constructions that are not always harmonious and cannot be expected to be, because their applications to particular sets of physical conditions depend upon the facts of each case. As the Wyoming Supreme Court well said, too much stress ought not, perhaps, to be placed upon any one element, and all should be given due consideration.[13] The ensuing discussion of these matters contains a selection of examples intended to illustrate some of the varying circumstances under which western courts have decided that watercourses exist.

Stream

Moving Body of Water

The stream throughout most of its course is a moving body of water,[14] with a continuous or intermittent flow in one direction.[15] The streamflow is

---

[10] N. Dak. Cent. Code Ann. § 61-01-06 (1960).

[11] N. Mex. Stat. Ann. § 75-1-1 (1968).

[12] Nebr. Rev. Stat. § 31-202 (1968).

[13] *Wyoming* v. *Hiber,* 48 Wyo. 172, 183, 44 Pac. (2d) 1005 (1935).

[14] *Hutchinson* v. *Watson Slough Ditch Co.,* 16 Idaho 484, 488, 101 Pac. 1059 (1909); *Doney* v. *Beatty,* 124 Mont. 41, 51, 220 Pac. (2d) 77 (1950).

[15] *St. Paul Fire & Marine Ins. Co.* v. *Carroll,* 106 S. W. (2d) 757, 758 (Tex. Civ. App. 1937, error dismissed).

sometimes spoken of as a current.[16] The streamflow is also referred to as a living stream,[17] and as a running stream.[18] Necessarily, the current is running water, though it need not run continuously.[19]

Definite and Substantial Existence

Definite stream.—There must be a *definite stream,*[20] the *existence* of which must be well defined.[21] In a leading case, the South Dakota Supreme Court held that water that ran at intervals down a coulee did not have the characteristics of a definite running stream, which means the presence or existence of running water, running down a fixed channel, with some permanent source of supply.[22] The court admitted that a river might run dry in a dry season without losing its character as a river, but insisted that it must be something more than just a wash or runoff caused by melting snow or a heavy rain. (The treatment of source of supply in this case is discussed below under "Source of Supply.")

Indications of existence.—To meet the requirement that the stream shall have a substantial existence,[23] there must be substantial indications of that fact.[24] The Kansas Supreme Court held that prior to the occurrence of a particular flood there was water in a depression only in wet weather, leaving no impress of permanent running water; but that since the flood there had been a regular channel with a flow of water so steady and persistent as to show that the stream then had a well-defined and substantial existence.[25] Under such circumstances, the short life of the watercourse was no bar to its classification as such.

Therefore, visible evidence of the flow of water, either regular or at least occasional, is required.[26] In a Wyoming case, seepage from irrigated land that

[16] *Hoefs* v. *Short,* 114 Tex. 501, 507, 273 S. W. 785 (1925). Current, or flow, one of the essential elements of a watercourse, is stressed in many court decisions: *De Ruwe* v. *Morrison,* 28 Wash. (2d) 797, 810, 184 Pac. (2d) 273 (1947).

[17] *Meine* v. *Ferris,* 126 Mont. 210, 212, 247 Pac. (2d) 195 (1952).

[18] *Costello* v. *Bowen,* 80 Cal. App. (2d) 621, 627, 182 Pac. (2d) 615 (1947); *Denver, Texas & Fort Worth R.R.* v. *Dotson,* 20 Colo. 304, 305-306, 38 Pac. 322 (1894); *Benson* v. *Cook,* 47 S. Dak. 611, 616, 201 N. W. 526 (1924).

[19] *Maricopa County M.W.C. Dist.* v. *Southwest Cotton Co.,* 39 Ariz. 65, 85-86, 4 Pac. (2d) 369 (1931).

[20] *Terry* v. *Heppner,* 59 S. Dak. 317, 319-320, 239 N. W. 759 (1931).

[21] *Cooper* v. *Sanitary Dist. No. 1 of Lancaster County,* 146 Nebr. 412, 419, 19 N. W. (2d) 619 (1945); *Allison* v. *Linn,* 139 Wash. 474, 477-478, 247 Pac. 731 (1926).

[22] *Benson* v. *Cook,* 47 S. Dak. 611, 615-616, 201 N. W. 526 (1924).

[23] *Barnes* v. *Sabron,* 10 Nev. 217, 237 (1875); *Shively* v. *Hume,* 10 Oreg. 76, 77 (1881); *Sierra County* v. *Nevada County,* 155 Cal. 1, 8, 99 Pac. 371 (1908); *Tierney* v. *Yakima County,* 136 Wash. 481, 484, 239 Pac. 248 (1925); *St. Paul Fire & Marine Ins. Co.* v. *Carroll,* 106 S. W. (2d) 757, 758 (Tex. Civ. App. 1937, error dismissed); *Mader* v. *Mettenbrink,* 159 Nebr. 118, 127, 65 N. W. (2d) 334 (1954).

[24] *Hutchinson* v. *Watson Slough Ditch Co.,* 16 Idaho 484, 488, 101 Pac. 1059 (1909); *Doney* v. *Beatty,* 124 Mont. 41, 51, 220 Pac. (2d) 77 (1950).

[25] *Rait* v. *Furrow,* 74 Kans. 101, 105-106, 85 Pac. 934 (1906).

[26] N. Mex. Stat. Ann. § 75-1-1 (1968).

collected in a gulch finally developed, over a period of 30 years, a visible stream of running water which was held to have met, by that time, the requirements of a definite stream.[27]

Size or Velocity Immaterial

The volume of water flowing in the stream does not alone determine the character of the stream as an element of a watercourse. The flow in many cases may be very small;[28] but if the other requirements of a stream are met and the other elements of a watercourse are present, the qualifications or classification as a watercourse may be satisfied whether the streamflow is that of a small brook or a great river. The size or velocity of the stream is not material; the flow may be small in volume, but "it must, however, be a stream in fact as distinguished from mere temporary surface drainage occasioned by freshets or other extraordinary causes."[29]

Continuity of Flow Generally not Required

The general rule. – It is the general rule—with some exceptions exemplified by cases mentioned immediately below—that to constitute a watercourse, the stream need not flow continually throughout the year nor throughout its accustomed course. Important variations enter into the interpretation of this principle.

The inference in a Kansas case decided in 1906—*Rait* v. *Furrow*—is that a wet-weather flow is only a temporary stream, therefore lacks the element of permanence, and consequently does not satisfy the requirements for a watercourse.[30] The decisions in two South Dakota cases of later date were along the same line, although here the emphasis was laid upon the impermanence of melting snow and summer rains as sources of supply in that they yielded only temporary streamflows.[31] (See "Source of Supply," below.)

The great weight of authority, however, is to the effect that the flow need not be continuous, with respect either to time[32] or to distance throughout its

---

[27] *Binning* v. *Miller*, 55 Wyo. 451, 474-476, 102 Pac. (2d) 54 (1940).

[28] *Jaquez Ditch Co.* v. *Garcia*, 17 N. Mex. 160, 161, 124 Pac. 891 (1912); *Holman* v. *Christensen*, 73 Utah 389, 397, 274 Pac. 457 (1929); *Popham* v. *Holloron*, 84 Mont. 442, 447-451, 275 Pac. 1099 (1929); *Heard* v. *Refugio*, 129 Tex. 349, 352-353, 103 S. W. (2d) 728 (1937); *Alexander* v. *Muenscher*, 7 Wash. (2d) 557, 559-560, 110 Pac. (2d) 625 (1941); *Scott* v. *Watkins*, 63 Idaho 506, 517, 122 Pac. (2d) 220 (1942); *Snyder* v. *Platte Valley Public Power & Irr. Dist.*, 144 Nebr. 308, 313-314, 13 N. W. (2d) 160 (1944).

[29] *Miksch* v. *Tassler*, 108 Nebr. 208, 213, 187 N. W. 796 (1922).

[30] *Rait* v. *Furrow*, 74 Kans. 101, 105-107, 85 Pac. 934 (1906).

[31] *Benson* v. *Cook*, 47 S. Dak. 611, 615-616, 201 N. W. 526 (1924); *Terry* v. *Heppner*, 59 S. Dak. 317, 319-320, 239 N. W. 759 (1931).

[32] *Maricopa County M.W.C. Dist.* v. *Southwest Cotton Co.*, 39 Ariz. 65, 86, 4 Pac. (2d) 369 (1931); *Hutchinson* v. *Watson Slough Ditch Co.*, 16 Idaho 484, 488, 101 Pac. 1059 (1909); *Le Munyon* v. *Gallatin Valley Ry.*, 60 Mont. 517, 523, 199 Pac. 915 (1921); *Reed* v. *Jacobson*, 160 Nebr. 245, 248, 69 N. W. (2d) 881 (1955); *Jaquez Ditch Co.* v. *Garcia*, 17 N. Mex. 160, 161, 124 Pac. 891 (1912); *Wyoming* v. *Hiber*, 48 Wyo. 172, 184, 44 Pac. (2d) 1005 (1935).

course.[33] Many courts have recognized that a stream channel may be dry at times.[34] In fact, less than two decades after rendering the decision in *Rait* v. *Furrow*, discussed above, the Kansas Supreme Court stated that to give the requisite degree of permanence, it is not necessary that the water shall flow continuously in the channel; the fact that the stream may be intermittent in its flow, or that there may be no flow in droughty periods, will not deprive it of its character as a watercourse.[35] Nor is the principle changed by the fact that the channel may be dry during a large part of the year.[36] The implications of two cases from New Mexico are that the principle would be equally applicable to channels flush with water from heavy rains in hilly or mountainous regions but dry throughout the entire year in periods of extreme drought.[37] Water remaining in long, deep pools or holes in the channel of a Texas river after the stream had ceased to flow were held to be part of the normal flow of the stream.[38]

Some expressions of the principle.—Within the widely recognized principle that the streamflow need not be continuous either in time or distance, but may be recurrent without sacrificing the classification of the system as a watercourse, courts have used various expressions as to how, to support the classification, the recurrence is manifested. Examples of this are: a frequent flow of water;[39] uniform or habitual flows;[40] usual or periodical flow;[41] regular discharge through the channel.[42]

The streamflow need not be continual, but must be at least periodical, such as may be expected during a portion of each year.[43] The supreme courts of Oregon and Utah have approved the classification where the streamflow was "fairly regular,"[44] and where it occurred with "some degree of regularity."[45] In California, the supreme court gave its approval with respect to a stream in which the flow in ordinary seasons began in November or December and ceased

---

[33] *St. Paul Fire & Marine Ins. Co.* v. *Carroll,* 106 S. W. (2d) 757, 758 (Tex. Civ. App. 1937, error dismissed). See "Channel—Continuity of Channel," below.

[34] *Costello* v. *Bowen,* 80 Cal. App. (2d) 621, 627, 182 Pac. (2d) 615 (1947); *In re German Ditch & Res. Co.,* 56 Colo. 252, 271, 139 Pac. 2 (1913); *Barnes* v. *Sabron,* 10 Nev. 217, 237 (1875); *Shively* v. *Hume,* 10 Oreg. 76, 77 (1881); *Heard* v. *Refugio,* 129 Tex. 349, 352-353, 103 S. W. (2d) 728 (1937); *In re Johnson Creek,* 159 Wash. 629, 630, 294 Pac. 566 (1930).

[35] *Hornor* v. *Baxter Springs,* 116 Kans. 288, 289-290, 226 Pac. 779 (1924).

[36] *Popham* v. *Holloron,* 84 Mont. 442, 450-451, 275 Pac. 1099 (1929).

[37] *Jaquez Ditch Co.* v. *Garcia,* 17 N. Mex. 160, 162-164, 124 Pac. 891 (1912); *Martinez* v. *Cook,* 56 N. Mex. 343, 348-351, 244 Pac. (2d) 134 (1952).

[38] *Humphreys-Mexia Co.* v. *Arseneaux,* 116 Tex. 603, 609-611, 297 S. W. 225 (1927).

[39] *Town* v. *Missouri Pacific Ry.,* 50 Nebr. 768, 773-774, 70 N. W. 402 (1897).

[40] *Johnson* v. *Metropolitan Life Ins. Co.,* 71 S. Dak. 155, 161, 22 N. W. (2d) 737 (1946).

[41] *Costello* v. *Bowen,* 80 Cal. App. (2d) 621, 627, 182 Pac. (2d) 615 (1947).

[42] *Garrett* v. *Haworth,* 183 Okla. 569, 570-571, 83 Pac. (2d) 822 (1938).

[43] *Lux* v. *Haggin,* 69 Cal. 255, 417, 4 Pac. 919 (1884), 10 Pac. 674 (1886).

[44] *Hansen* v. *Crouch,* 98 Oreg. 141, 146, 193 Pac. 454 (1920).

[45] *Holman* v. *Christensen,* 73 Utah 389, 397, 274 Pac. 457 (1929).

about June—a stream, said the court, of the character familiar in the State and in other semiarid regions;[46] and a district court of appeal said that the requirement means a stream in the real sense, which flows at those times when the streams of the region habitually flow.[47] In Arizona, under conditions of irregularity of precipitation, both as to time and location, the supreme court found no difficulty in holding that a watercourse exists where the precipitation runs off the hills in a well-defined channel at irregular intervals.[48]

Some variations in interpreting the principle.—It is evident that interpretations vary considerably regarding the requirement that while the streamflow must be definite and substantial, it need not be continuous. Doubtless, this is owing in large measure to the wide range in meteorological conditions throughout the West. To hold that a stream is not a watercourse because the channel is dry half or more of the year would eliminate from this category important sources of supply of many irrigated areas, for in the arid regions cessation of flow of streams during certain seasons of the year is a common phenomenon. For example, in New Mexico—which with respect to topographic and hydrological conditions is typical of the arid Southwest—the supreme court stressed the "enormous number of arroyos" which serve the purpose of drainageways during the rainy seasons but are dry at other times, and the unsuitability to southwestern conditions of a rule that to constitute a watercourse, water must be carried in the channel throughout the entire year or a majority of the time.[49] During extremely dry cycles, some streams in the West, particularly the Southwest, carry little or no water for two or more consecutive seasons.

A reasonable and practicable measure of recurrence of flow necessary to constitute the stream a watercourse is the condition prevalent in the general area in which the stream is found—that the water passes down the channel "in those seasons of the year and at those times when the streams in the region are accustomed to flow."[50] On that premise, a permanent stream may be one that not only flows intermittently, but infrequently and at irregular intervals, if that kind of flow is characteristic of the area in question.

Had the foregoing measure been applied by the South Dakota Supreme Court in the cases cited above under "The general rule,"[51] the waters of the two draws in litigation would have been classed as those of natural streams or watercourses, to which the dry draw appropriation statute would have applied.

---

[46] *Lindblom* v. *Round Valley Water Col.*, 178 Cal. 450, 452-453, 173 Pac. 994 (1918).

[47] *McManus* v. *Otis*, 61 Cal. App. (2d) 432, 440, 143 Pac. (2d) 380 (1943).

[48] *Globe* v. *Shute*, 22 Ariz. 280, 289, 196 Pac. 1024 (1921).

[49] *Martinez* v. *Cook*, 56 N. Mex. 343, 349-350, 244 Pac. (2d) 134 (1952).

[50] *San Gabriel Valley Country Club* v. *County of Los Angeles*, 182 Cal. 392, 397, 188 Pac. 554 (1920). See *McManus* v. *Otis*, 61 Cal. App. (2d) 432, 440, 143 Pac. (2d) 380 (1943).

[51] *Benson* v. *Cook*, 47 S. Dak. 611, 615-617, 201 N. W. 526 (1924); *Terry* v. *Heppner*, 59 S. Dak. 317, 319-320, 239 N. W. 759 (1931).

The flows were characteristic of those of many draws in western South Dakota.[52] However, the court chose to rest its rejection of the concept of a definite stream chiefly on its interpretation of the water sources as impermanent. (See "Source of Supply," below.)

Channel

The channel is a definite element of a watercourse—an indispensable one. Although some divergence appears in the holdings with respect to character of the channel, western courts are in substantial agreement that a channel must exist.

General Features

The channel must be definite—usually, but not in all cases necessarily, with well-defined bed and banks or sides. Any groove in the earth's surface through which water flows is, of course, from a physical standpoint, a channel for passage of the water; but the requirements of a watercourse made by many—but not all—courts are that the channel bear the unmistakable impress of the action of running water, that it be more than just a grassy swale or wide depression. This means, in effect, that the channel must have been created by the flow of the water itself, or enlarged by it, or otherwise so altered by the action of the water as to make it appear to an observer that water has been accustomed to run there with some frequency. The erosive action of water flowing along a depression naturally leaves a bed and banks; hence the frequent criterion that the channel of a watercourse have a bed and banks. These matters are discussed in some detail under subsequent topics.

The appearance of the channel is important,[53] as well as its local reputation as a named "creek," or other watercourse.[54]

Length of the channel may be of some importance in borderline cases, but more as an aid in reaching a conclusion than as an independent criterion. It is not of itself a determining factor if the requirements of a watercourse are otherwise satisfied, for a watercourse may attain all its necessary elements at a particular point and then flow for a very short distance to its termination.[55] In any event, the channel need not continue indefinitely, for the water must have an outlet somewhere. (See "Other Factors—Termination of the Watercourse," below.) In a case decided by the Oregon Supreme Court in 1959, the evidence clearly established the fact that water flowed from two springs throughout the

---

[52] In *Benson* v. *Cook,* 47 S. Dak. 611, 616, 201 N. W. 526 (1924), the court remarked that the presence of a meandering depression in the channel of Ash Coulee, worn by the action of running water, with bed and banks down which the water ran when there was water to run, was true of practically every other coulee or dry draw in the land.

[53] *Gibbs* v. *Williams,* 25 Kans. 214, 220-221 (1881).

[54] *Geddis* v. *Parrish,* 1 Wash. 587, 588-589, 21 Pac. 314 (1889).

[55] The watercourse that was held to exist in the much cited case of *Rait* v. *Furrow,* 74 Kans. 101, 109, 85 Pac. 934 (1906), was apparently of very short length. This did not influence the decision.

year in a definite channel having well-defined banks through most of its course.[56] Although the stream ran only a short distance from the springs to its outlet in Rogue River, and in so doing never completely left a single holding of land—but did touch neighboring land for a short distance before reaching the river—the supreme court was satisfied from the testimony that the water flowed in a watercourse.

Some judicial expressions.—In quoting a definition of a watercourse, the Nebraska Supreme Court stated, among other things, that it must appear that the water usually flows in a particular direction and by a regular channel having a bed with banks and sides.[57] This is the usual approach in the West.

Holdings of the Supreme Court of South Dakota have departed from the norm; but it is important to bear in mind that these deliberate departures have been made in cases involving the right to drain water from one's land into a watercourse—not the right to divert water from a watercourse in the exercise of a right of use. In 1946, this court held that: "A natural watercourse is defined as: 'If the surface water in fact uniformly or habitually flows off over a given course, having reasonable limits as to width, the line of its flow is *within the meaning of the law applicable to the discharge of surface water,* a watercourse.' "[58] [Emphasis supplied.] This was based upon a decision rendered some three decades earlier in which the South Dakota court observed that the term "watercourse" had come to have two distinct meanings—one referring to a watercourse to which riparian rights attach, and the other to a watercourse through which an upper landowner has the statutory right to discharge waters from his land.[59] With respect to the drainage situation, the court adhered in this earlier case to a definition that it had previously adopted, the last paragraph of which is quoted in the 1946 opinion. Included in the description preceding this last paragraph was a statement denying the importance of a requirement that the force of the water be sufficient to cut a channel with definite and well-marked sides or banks. The wording of the 1946 definition, which is quoted in full above in this paragraph, simply ignores the question of a waterworn channel, or channel with bed and banks or sides; but it does not dispense with the necessity of a particular course "uniformly or habitually" used by the water. (See further discussion of these cases under "Definiteness of Channel" and "Bed and Banks or Sides," below.)

Some legislative requirements.—The New Mexico legislature, in defining watercourses, refers to a "channel having definite banks and bed."[60] The Nebraska statutory definition says, on this feature, "Any depression or draw two feet below the surrounding lands."[61] The North Dakota statutory

---

[56] *Fitzstephens* v. *Watson,* 218 Oreg. 185, 193-194, 344 Pac. (2d) 221 (1959).
[57] *Mader* v. *Mettenbrink,* 159 Nebr. 118, 127, 65 N. W. (2d) 334 (1954).
[58] *Johnson* v. *Metropolitan Life Ins. Co.,* 71 S. Dak. 155, 161, 22 N. W. (2d) 737 (1946).
[59] *Thompson* v. *Andrews,* 39 S. Dak. 477, 483-484, 165 N. W. 9 (1917).
[60] N. Mex. Stat. Ann. § 75-1-1 (1968).
[61] Nebr. Rev. Stat. § 31-202 (1968).

definition refers to "a distinct and a defined channel" and "a plainly defined channel of a permanent character,"[62] and the designation of public,
appropriable waters include those "flowing in well defined channels or
flowing through lakes, ponds, or marshes which constitute integral parts of a
stream system."[63]

The special water rights laws of South Dakota that apply only to streams of
minor flows relate to "dry draw," "ravine or watercourse" (See "Some Local
Situations—Draws and Coulees," below).[64]

Terms designating channels.—The terms "river," "creek," and "brook" all
refer to channels through which water flows either continuously or with a
considerable degree of regularity, depending on the climate of the area and the
particular season. Their chief differences are in size of channel and volume of
streamflow.

It is of course true that some channels named or locally known as creeks or
brooks would not meet the accepted legal requirements of a watercourse. For
example, the waters of a natural drainway known as Plum Creek, in
southwestern South Dakota, were held to be "mere surface waters," not
subject to appropriation under the "dry draw law"—although the court felt
bound by an analogous precedent of 7 years' standing and admitted that the
question was "a close one."[65] However, in many and probably most instances,
what are locally called creeks or brooks would be expected to meet
watercourse requirements, for mere size is not of itself a controlling factor.

Other terms designate channels which may or may not meet the watercourse
requirements under particular sets of existing circumstances. These include
"arroyo," "coulee," "canyon," "ravine," "gulch," "gulley," "draw," "wash."
Whether or not created by the action of flowing water as many of them were,
the classifications of these physical features as watercourse depend upon the
present situation with respect to condition of the channel, source of water, and
streamflow.

Natural Channel

To meet the requirements of a watercourse, the channel must be
natural[66] —of natural origin.[67]

Exceptional circumstances under which a watercourse of artificial origin
may be accepted in the category of a natural watercourse are noted below (see

---

[62] N. Dak. Cent. Code Ann. § 61-01-06 (1960).

[63] *Id.* § 61-01-01(1).

[64] S. Dak. Comp. Laws Ann. § 46-1-6(3) (1967).

[65] *Terry* v. *Heppner*, 59 S. Dak. 317, 319-320, 239 N. W. 759 (1931), following *Benson* v.
Cook, 47 S. Dak. 611, 615-617, 201 N. W. 526 (1924). The holding in the *Benson* case
with respect to requisite source of supply was an extreme one. See "Source of
Supply," below.

[66] *Jaquez Ditch Co.* v. *Garcia*, 17 N. Mex. 160, 161, 124 Pac. 891 (1912); *Allison* v. *Linn*,
139 Wash. 474, 477-478, 247 Pac. 731 (1926).

[67] *State* v. *Brace*, 76 N. Dak. 314, 322, 36 N. W. (2d) 330 (1949).

"Collateral Questions Respecting Watercourses—Watercourse Originally Made Artificially").

Definiteness of Channel

Definite channel.—Western courts long ago declared that the channel of a watercourse must be definite.[68] That the channel may be "reasonably" definite or well defined has been acknowledged by courts in some later cases.[69]

Other statements have been to the effect that the channel is well defined,[70] created by the eroding force of the running water itself,[71] and through which the water is accustomed to flow.[72] However, it is held in South Dakota that to constitute a watercourse with respect to the statutory right to drain one's land into a natural watercourse or depression, it is sufficient that the conformation of the land be such as to give the diffused surface water flowing from one tract to another a fixed and determinate course so as to discharge it uniformly upon the servient tract at a fixed and definite point; and that it is not necessary that the force of the water be sufficient to wear out a channel having definite and well-marked sides or banks—this depending on the nature of the soil and force and rapidity of the flow.[73] (See "General Features," above, and "Bed and Banks or Sides," below).

The description in another case was that of a natural and "regular" watercourse, rather than that of a mere casual overflow.[74]

Visual indications of definiteness.—In close contests over the existence of a definite natural channel, the readiness with which an observer can discern such existence, particularly when the ground is dry, is important in establishing the watercourse as such.

Hence, we find such expressions as these: the channel is easily distinguished;[75] it is rendered perceptible by a difference of vegetation;[76] any person

[68] *Pyle* v. *Richards,* 17 Nebr. 180, 182, 22 N. W. 370 (1885); *Rigney* v. *Tacoma Light & Water Co.,* 9 Wash. 576, 579, 38 Pac. 147 (1894); *Jaquez Ditch Co.* v. *Garcia,* 17 N. Mex. 160, 161, 124 Pac. 891 (1912); *Hutchinson* v. *Watson Slough Ditch Co.,* 16 Idaho 484, 488, 101 Pac. 1059 (1909).

[69] *Alexander* v. *Muenscher.* 7 Wash. (2d) 557, 559-560, 110 Pac. (2d) 625 (1941); *Scott* v. *Watkins,* 63 Idaho 506, 517, 122 Pac. (2d) 220 (1942); *State* v. *Brace,* 76 N. Dak. 314, 322, 36 N. W. (2d) 330 (1949).

[70] *Watkins Land Co.* v. *Clements,* 98 Tex. 578, 582-583, 86 S. W. 733 (1905); *Holman* v. *Christensen,* 73 Utah 389, 397, 274 Pac. 457 (1929); *Popham* v. *Holloron,* 84 Mont. 442, 450-453, 275 Pac. 1099 (1929); *Maricopa County M.W.C. Dist.* v. *Southwest Cotton Co.,* 39 Ariz. 65, 85-86, 4 Pac. (2d) 369 (1931).

[71] *Palmer* v. *Waddell,* 22 Kans. 352, 355-356 (1879); *Miller* v. *Marriott,* 48 Okla. 179, 183-186, 149 Pac. 1164 (1915); *Doney* v. *Beatty,* 124 Mont. 41, 45, 220 Pac. (2d) 77 (1950).

[72] *San Gabriel Valley Country Club* v. *County of Los Angeles,* 182 Cal. 392, 397, 188 Pac. 554 (1920); *Hansen* v. *Crouch,* 98 Oreg. 141, 146, 193 Pac. 454 (1920).

[73] *Thompson* v. *Andrews,* 39 S. Dak. 477, 483-484, 165 N. W. 9 (1917). See *Johnson* v. *Metropolitan Life Ins. Co.,* 71 S. Dak. 155, 161, 22 N. W. (2d) 737 (1946).

[74] *Dahlgren* v. *Chicago, M. & P.S. Ry.,* 85 Wash. 395, 405, 148 Pac. 567 (1915).

[75] *Rigney* v. *Tacoma Light & Water Co.,* 9 Wash. 576, 579, 38 Pac. 147 (1894).

[76] *Lux* v. *Haggin,* 69 Cal. 255, 419, 4 Pac. 919 (1884), 10 Pac. 674 (1886).

examining the premises can see by the growth of willows where the natural channel runs;[77] to the casual glance, the channel bears the unmistakable impress of the frequent action of running water;[78] an observer should be able to perceive that a watercourse exists,[79] and to determine where the water would flow in the case of rain or melting snow.[80]

The New Mexico legislature includes in its definition of watercourse "visible evidence of the occasional flow of water."[81]

Bed and Banks or Sides

Necessary in most cases to classification of channel.—The requirement that the channel of a watercourse have a bed with banks or sides has been expressed by many courts and included in many definitions of a watercourse.[82] It is the usual requirement in the West.

The California Supreme Court held Rubio Canyon Wash near Pasadena to be a watercourse in the legal sense, saying that: "It is a channel with defined beds and banks made and habitually used by water passing down as a collected body or stream in those seasons of the year and at those times when the streams in the region are accustomed to flow."[83] This definition expresses the view of a large majority of the courts.

Exception in South Dakota.—The requirement that the channel have a bed and banks or sides cut by the flowing water has been downgraded in South Dakota, at least insofar as it pertains to watercourses of the character contemplated by the statute[84] authorizing proprietors to drain their lands in the general course of natural drainage into any natural watercourse, or into any natural depression whereby the water will be carried into some natural watercourse.[85] This has been mentioned before under the topics "General Features" and "Definiteness of Channel."

According to the definition and description of a "drainage" watercourse given in 1917, a fixed and determinate course uniformly followed by surface

---

[77] *Wright v. Phillips*, 127 Oreg. 420, 426, 272 Pac. 554 (1928).
[78] *Simmons v. Winters*, 21 Oreg. 35, 41-42, 27 Pac. 7 (1891); *International & G.N.R.R. v. Reagan*, 121 Tex. 233, 241-242, 49 S. W. (2d) 414 (1932); *Doney v. Beatty*, 124 Mont. 41, 45, 220 Pac. (2d) 77 (1950).
[79] *Wyoming v. Hiber*, 48 Wyo 172, 187-188, 44 Pac. (2d) 1005 (1935).
[80] *Muhleisen v. Krueger*, 120 Nebr. 380, 381-382, 232 N. W. 735 (1930).
[81] N. Mex. Stat. Ann. § 75-1-1 (1968).
[82] See *Maricopa County M.W.C. Dist. v. Southwest Cotton Co.*, 39 Ariz. 65, 85-86, 4 Pac. (2d) 369 (1931); *Hutchinson v. Watson Slough Ditch Co.*, 16 Idaho 484, 488, 101 Pac. 1059 (1909); *Mader v. Mettenbrink*, 159 Nebr. 118, 127, 65 N. W. (2d) 334 (1954); *Froemke v. Parker*, 41 N. Dak. 408, 416, 171 N. W. 284 (1919); *Hansen v. Crouch*, 98 Oreg. 141, 146, 193 Pac. 454 (1920); *Alexander v. Muenscher*, 7 Wash. (2d) 557, 559-560, 110 Pac. (2d) 625 (1941); *Binning v. Miller*, 55 Wyo. 451, 463, 474-475, 102 Pac. (2d) 54 (1940); N. Mex. Stat. Ann. § 75-1-1 (1968).
[83] *San Gabriel Valley Country Club v. County of Los Angeles*, 182 Cal. 392, 397, 188 Pac. 554 (1920).
[84] S. Dak. Comp. Laws Ann. § 46-20-31 (1967).
[85] *Thompson v. Andrews*, 39 S. Dak. 477, 483-484, 165 N. W. 9 (1917). See *Johnson v. Metropolitan Life Ins. Co.*, 71 S. Dak. 155, 161, 22 N. W. (2d) 737 (1946).

water discharged at a fixed and definite point on the servient tract is a watercourse within the meaning of the rule applicable to such drainage. Conceding that to accomplish this purpose, such course must follow a ravine, swale, or depression of some depth, the fact that the force of the flowing water is not sufficient to carve out a channel with definite and well-marked sides or banks seemed unimportant to the court; that result would depend on the nature of the soil and velocity of the water.[86] The concluding sentence of the definition, which was adopted in 1946 as the court's accepted definition of a natural drainage watercourse,[87] was simply that: if the diffused surface water " 'in fact uniformly or habitually flows off over a given course, having reasonable limits as to width, the line of its flow is, within the meaning of the law applicable to the discharge of such water, a watercourse.' "[88]

In the 1917 case, before embarking upon this description and definition, the South Dakota Supreme Court observed that the term "watercourse" had come to have two distinct meanings—one as a watercourse to which riparian rights may attach, and the other to a watercourse through which an upper landowner has the statutory right to discharge drainage waters from his land.[89]

What constitutes bed and banks.—The bottom and sides of a characteristic watercourse, formed as such by water erosion, distinguish the channel from a normally smooth or rounded depression in the earth's surface.

In borderline contests over the classification of flows of water as watercourses or as diffused surface waters, testimony as to the angle of inclination of the sides, condition of the bottom, and character of vegetation on the bed has been important. For example, there was evidence that where a certain California slough crossed the lands of the parties it had a well-defined channel and distinct banks of sufficient depth and declivity to preclude the crossing of vehicles at most places.[90] Because of this and of other necessary elements, it was held that a watercourse existed along that section.

The denuded condition of a Texas channel, absence of soil and vegetation, and presence of boulders and gravel showed without question the long persistence of a current; the channel was of such substantial, stable, and permanent character that its existence was easily recognized.[91] In connection with evidence as to the stream of water and its source, a watercourse was held to exist.

On the other hand, in the following situations the courts held that the features of the several depressions in litigation did not satisfy the requirements of a watercourse channel: (1) A depression 3 to 5 feet deep, 30 to 40 feet wide, no sharp and distinct banks; grass throughout most of its length, and

---

[86] *Thompson* v. *Andrews,* 39 S. Dak. 477, 484, 165 N. W. 9 (1917).
[87] *Johnson* v. *Metropolitan Life Ins. Co.,* 71 S. Dak. 155, 161, 22 N. W. (2d) 737 (1946).
[88] *Thompson* v. *Andrews,* 39 S. Dak. 477, 484, 165 N. W. 9 (1917).
[89] *Id.* at 484.
[90] *Haun* v. *De Vaurs,* 97 Cal. App. (2d) 841, 842-843, 218 Pac. (2d) 996 (1950).
[91] *Hoefs* v. *Short,* 114 Tex. 501, 505-507, 273 S. W. 785 (1925).

mowing machines run in it; no general cut in the soil by the frequent flow of water.[92] (2) A depression several miles long, some 80 feet wide, a few inches deep; gently sloping sides; cultivated to grain when dry and part planted to vines.[93] (3) A draw covered with grass; no banks; no waterworn channel; easily crossed by a vehicle almost everywhere.[94] (4) The evidence silent as to whether Garrison Draw—one-fourth to one-half mile wide and several miles long—has a channel with well-defined bed and banks; held to be a wide valley, a typical West Texas draw.[95]

According to the California Supreme Court, in a decision rendered in 1902, cited and quoted with approval in 1959 by a district court of appeal, the most approved definitions are to the effect that banks of watercourses are those boundaries which contain the waters at their highest flow—that is, the fast land which confines the water in its channel or bed in its whole width as determined by its highest flow.[96] The bed of a river is thus bounded by the permanent or fast banks by which its waters are confined, even though during most of the year the actual flow follows a winding channel in the overall channel, parts of the bed being cultivated when the streamflow permits.

The Supreme Court of Arizona thus defined these characteristics of a channel:[97] The bed is that portion of the channel which carries the waters at their ordinary stage. The banks are the elevations of land which confine the waters to their natural channel when they rise to the highest point at which they are confined to a definite course and channel.

Questions relating to streambed and banks have been considered in a number of Texas cases where, in considerable degree, their importance has grown out of the statutory definition of navigable streams and its relation to land titles.[98] After a series of court decisions on this matter, the Texas Supreme Court adopted, as a definition of a streambed, that portion of its soil that is covered by the water, not at either its high stage or its low watermark, but at its height under normal conditions and seasons.[99]

---

[92] *Gibbs* v. *Williams,* 25 Kans. 214, 215-216, 221 (1881).

[93] *Sanguinetti* v. *Pock,* 136 Cal. 466, 470-471, 69 Pac. 98 (1902).

[94] *Wyoming* v. *Hiber,* 48 Wyo. 172, 187-188, 44 Pac. (2d) 1005 (1935).

[95] *Turner* v. *Big Lake Oil Co.,* 62 S. W. (2d) 491, 493 (Tex. Civ. App. 1933), affirmed, 128 Tex. 155, 96 S. W. (2d) 221 (1936).

[96] *Ventura Land & Power Co.* v. *Meiners,* 136 Cal. 284, 290, 68 Pac. 818 (1902), cited approvingly in *Bishel* v. *Faria,* 342 Pac. (2d) 278, 280-281 (Cal. 1959). See *Bishel* v. *Faria,* 53 Cal. (2d) 254, 258-261, 347 Pac. (2d) 289, 1 Cal. Rptr. 153 (1959).

[97] *Maricopa County M.W.C. Dist.* v. *Southwest Cotton Co.,* 39 Ariz. 65, 85-86, 4 Pac. (2d) 369 (1931).

[98] Tex. Rev. Civ. Stat. Ann. art. 5302 (1962). The rule prescribed by the statute for determining the navigability of streams was made for the purpose of the statute, which related to the surveying for individuals of lands lying on navigable watercourses.

[99] *Motl* v. *Boyd,* 116 Tex. 82, 108-109, 286 S. W. 458 (1926). The more detailed rule on which this conclusion was based has been stated in *Alabama* v. *Georgia,* 64 U. S. 505, 515 (1859).

The Texas Supreme Court also adopted a definition of the United States Supreme Court defining the interstate boundary line between Texas and Oklahoma[100] as consistent with the Spanish or Mexican law on the subject.[101] This is to the effect that the banks of a stream are the water-washed and relatively prominent elevations of activities, commonly called "cut banks," at the outer lines of the streambed which separate the bed from the adjacent land, whether valley or hill, and which usually serve to confine the waters within the bed and to preserve the course of the river. The boundary between the States—or between public and private ownership along the banks of a navigable stream—is the mean level attained by the waters when they reach and wash the bank without overflowing it or, expressed differently, when they rise to the highest point at which they are still confined to a definite channel.[102]

The Flood Plain

The flood plain of an ordinary stream is a part of the watercourse.—The flood channel or flood plain of a live stream is the land adjacent to the ordinary channel that is overflowed in times of high water, from which the floodwaters return to the channel of the stream at lower points.[103] In an ordinary situation, this is as much a part of the overall watercourse system as are its bed, banks, and ordinary channel.

The Texas and Nebraska cases cited in the immediately preceding paragraph were concerned with obstructions of the flow of floodwaters within the flood plains of the streams, not with rights to the use of the water.

On the other hand, in the California Supreme Court case cited above under "Bed and Banks or Sides—What constitutes bed and banks"—in which it was held that the bed of a river is bounded by its permanent and fast banks—the question was whether certain lands lying between some lower banks and the high banks of Ventura River were riparian to the river; and the court held that they were.[104] The opinion in this case was written by a commissioner and concurred in by the justices of the California Supreme Court. The justices stated that "this case differs materially from the ordinary case where a stream

---

[100] *Oklahoma* v. *Texas,* 260 U.S. 606, 631-632 (1923); *Oklahoma* v. *Texas,* 261 U.S. 340, 341-342 (1923); *Oklahoma* v. *Texas,* 265 U.S. 500, 501 (1924).

[101] *Motl* v. *Boyd,* 116 Tex. 82, 109, 286 S. W. 458 (1926).

[102] In *Maufrais* v. *State of Texas,* 142 Tex. 559, 565-566, 180 S. W. (2d) 144 (1944), the Texas Supreme Court again reviewed with approval the rules as to bed and banks that had been expressed in the previous decisions of the United States Supreme Court and that were followed in *Motl* v. *Boyd,* 116 Tex. 82, 109, 286 S. W. 458 (1926), and in *Diversion Lake Co.* v. *Heath,* 126 Tex. 129, 140-141, 86 S. W. (2d) 441 (1935). See also *Heard* v. *Refugio,* 129 Tex. 349, 352-353, 103 S. W. (2d) 728 (1937); and *Brown* v. *Linkenhoger,* 175 S. W. (2d) 975, 976 (Tex. Civ. App. 1943, error refused want merit).

[103] *Bass* v. *Taylor,* 126 Tex. 522, 529-530, 90 S. W. (2d) 811 (1936); *Bahm* v. *Raikes,* 160 Nebr. 503, 514-515, 70 N. W. (2d) 507 (1955).

[104] *Ventura Land & Power Co.* v. *Meiners,* 136 Cal. 284, 290-291, 68 Pac. 818 (1902).

runs through a valley between rather low banks which usually, but not always, contain its waters, and where the land adjacent to the banks differs in character from the bed of the stream, and is composed of arable and fertile land." In the instant case, a large part of the land between the low and high banks was composed characteristically of boulders, sand, and gravel, although some parts were susceptible of cultivation and some actually had been cultivated. Five years later the supreme court cautioned that the discussion in the *Ventura Land & Power Company* case—as to the character of the ground lying between the edge of the stream at its ordinary flow and the line of high water when in flood—had no reference to the right of the owner of the intervening land, as a riparian owner, to use the stream water for any useful purpose which his position on the stream enabled him to make of it.[105]

The principle does not govern great rivers.—The principle above stated with respect to ordinary watercourses does not govern the major streamways of the nation. To apply it to a great valley through which a major river system flows would be an unwarranted and impracticable extension of the principle.

Hence, the whole floor of such a great valley is not to be considered the high water channel of the river simply because in times of flood extensive areas are overflowed. In a Mississippi River case, the United States Supreme Court[106] emphasized not only the unsoundness, but also the absurdity of the theory that:

> the valley through which the river travels, in all its length and vast expanse, with its great population, its farms, its villages, its towns, its cities, its schools, its colleges, its universities, its manufactories, its network of railroads—some of them transcontinental, are virtually to be considered from a legal point of view as constituting merely the high water bed of the river and therefore subject, without any power to protect, to be submitted to the destruction resulting from the overflow by the river of its natural banks.[107]

Nor, it has been held, is a great catchment area (Sutter Basin, California)—a very wide and very shallow basin that exists principally for the reception of the floodwaters of a long river (Sacramento River) that normally carries heavy winter and spring flows—a watercourse.[108] "The whole space between the foothills and a river is not to be called the channel because it sometimes overflows."

---

[105] *Anaheim Union Water Co.* v. *Fuller,* 150 Cal. 327, 328-329, 88 Pac. 978 (1907). With respect to the right of the landowner to make reasonable use of the water, the court was of the opinion that bottom lands riparian to a stream, even though lying between high bluffs on each side, are not to be distinguished from other land abutting on the stream.

[106] Speaking through Chief Justice White, himself a native of the Mississippi Valley.

[107] *Cubbins* v. *Mississippi River Comm'n.,* 241 U.S. 351, 368 (1916).

[108] *Gray* v. *Reclamation Dist. No. 1500,* 174 Cal. 622, 647-648, 163 Pac. 1024 (1917).

Continuity of Channel

An apparently well-established principle states that continuity of a watercourse is not broken by interruptions in continuity of the channel—that is, changes in character of the channel which depart from the normal requirements in greater or less degree but do not permanently interrupt the flow of water. This is important to a water user on the lower part of such a watercourse, for it protects him against injury occasioned by diversions from the upper part by junior appropriators or others who seek to show that there are really two or more independent watercourses.

Thus, while the rule is ordinarily expressed that a watercourse must have a well-defined channel, bed, and banks, instances have been noted in which these features were recognized as slight, imperceptible, or even absent at points along an otherwise undoubted watercourse, without destroying its classification as such.[109] Again, segregated swamps and marshes would scarcely be classified as watercourses under ordinary circumstances,[110] yet "There may be a continuous watercourse through a body of swamplands."[111] As stated by several courts, the fact that a stream flows through a swamp along part of its course does not deprive it of the character of a watercourse.[112]

It is not essential to a watercourse, said the California Supreme Court in an early leading riparian water rights case, that the banks shall be unchangeable throughout its course, or that there shall be everywhere a visible change in the angle of ascent, making the line between bed and banks.[113] It may spread out over a wide, shallow place,[114] even without enclosure by apparent banks,[115] without thereby losing its classification as a watercourse and turning into diffused surface water.[116] Although the rule that there must be well-defined banks is relaxed under these circumstances, it is still necessary that the current and course of the water must be clearly perceptible[117] —unless the connection between the upper and lower courses of the main channel be established by other means, as noted below.

Ways in which this has been handled may be shown by a few examples. Thus, where the bed of the stream is such that, except during high water flows, the water disappears at various points and comes to the surface lower down,

---

[109] *Hoefs* v. *Short*, 114 Tex. 501, 507, 273 S. W. 785 (1925).
[110] *Id.* at 508.
[111] *Lux* v. *Haggin*, 69 Cal. 255, 413, 4 Pac. 919 (1884), 10 Pac. 674 (1886).
[112] *Tonkin* v. *Winzell*, 27 Nev. 88, 99, 73 Pac. 593 (1903); *Wright* v. *Phillips*, 127 Oreg. 420, 426, 272 Pac. 554 (1928); *Alexander* v. *Muenscher*, 7 Wash. (2d) 557, 560, 110 Pac. (2d) 625 (1941).
[113] *Lux* v. *Haggin*, 69 Cal. 255, 418, 4 Pac. 919 (1884), 10 Pac. 674 (1886).
[114] *Cederburg* v. *Dutra*, 3 Cal. App. 572, 574-575, 86 Pac. 838 (1906).
[115] *West* v. *Taylor*, 16 Oreg. 165, 170-171, 13 Pac. 665 (1887); *Hofeldt* v. *Elkhorn Valley Drainage Dist.*, 115 Nebr. 539, 544, 213 N. W. 832 (1927).
[116] *Harrington* v. *Demaris*, 46 Oreg. 111, 117-118, 77 Pac. 603, 82 Pac. 14 (1904).
[117] *Hough* v. *Porter*, 51 Oreg. 318, 415-416, 95 Pac. 732 (1908), 98 Pac. 1083 (1909), 102 Pac. 728 (1909).

but the testimony shows that there is a connected stream, it is held that there is one watercourse.[118] In this case, the referee had found that Johnson Creek was a natural watercourse, and that the bed of the stream was of such character that the water rose and sank along its course, coming to the surface with the bedrock, and sinking in other sections where the soils were porous. In the spring during the snow runoff, water ran on the surface the entire length of the stream. If that finding was correct, said the court, "then Johnson Creek is a stream, even though it does not flow continuously and at times is dry in places." A prior appropriator will be protected against material interference with his rights to such flow under these or comparable circumstances.[119]

Continuity of a watercourse is not broken because a stream enters a meadow in one channel and leaves it in another, there being no definite channel across the meadow—simply low depressions and partial channels in which water flows—but the evidence being uncontradicted that the inlet channel is the source of supply of the outlet channel.[120] An appropriator on the outlet will be protected against the effects of a junior diversion of the inlet.

Nor is continuity broken where the flow from springs leaves its channel and proceeds under the surface of the ground for one-half mile to the surface stream to which it is tributary.[121]

In these several cases, the essential feature is continuity of the flow of water—either on the surface or partly on and partly under the surface—not of character of the channel.

Some Local Situations

Southwestern arroyos.—The term "arroyo" is applied in the Southwest to a channel, worn by the erosive action of running water—often torrential—but dry much or most of the time. Where such an arroyo emerges from the hills, it may have a wide bed cut some feet or yards below the surrounding lands. The usually "dry arroyo" may suddenly become bank full with the runoff from a torrential rain or cloudburst; it may run swiftly thus for a short time; and after the passage of the flood it may dry gradually and again remain quiescent for days or weeks or even for many months. In fact, there are comparatively few streams in the smaller valleys of the southwestern region that flow much of the time.

The significance of these spasmodic occurrences is discussed below under "Source of Supply."[122] It may be noted here that in view of the topographic and meteorological conditions of the region, the courts of New Mexico and Arizona accept the typical arroyo emerging upon the plains from high ground as the channel of a watercourse.

---

[118] *In re Johnson Creek,* 159 Wash. 629, 630, 294 Pac. 566 (1930).

[119] See *Barnes* v. *Sabron,* 10 Nev. 217, 236-239 (1875).

[120] *Anderson Land & Stock Co.* v. *McConnell,* 188 Fed. 818, 829-831 (C.C.D. Nev. 1910).

[121] *Strait* v. *Brown,* 16 Nev. 317, 323-324 (1881).

[122] Under "Source of Supply—Definiteness and Permanence," the article cited in "Agricultural Research" for August 1959 well illustrates this general situation.

The opinion in a case that was appealed to the United States Supreme Court from the Territorial Supreme Court of New Mexico[123] was written by Justice Brewer, who formerly had been on the bench of the Kansas Supreme Court. In writing the New Mexico opinion, the justice was doubtless influenced by his previous Kansas experience with watercourse and diffused surface water classifications.[124] In any event, he ignored the significance of the essential differences in nature's handling of the runoff from rainfall on Kansas prairies and that from cloudbursts in the mountains of New Mexico. In each of the above-cited cases, despite the physical contrasts, he held the channel to be simply a passageway for diffused surface water. From two subsequent decisions of the New Mexico Supreme Court, it may be gathered that the court has never approved of the high Court's classification of the arroyos in the *Walker* case. In 1912, the New Mexico court "adroitly distinguished" the highest Court's decision; in 1952, it rejected the decision completely as authority in the jurisdiction of this important matter, declaring that it was ill suited to conditions in the State and would no longer be followed.[125] The legislature of New Mexico is in accord.[126]

The Arizona Supreme Court, in an opinion that contained no description of the channel in litigation, indicated its approval of the concept that a ravine or wash is a natural stream or watercourse where precipitation on adjacent hills flows down through the ravine in a well-defined channel at irregular intervals.[127]

Draws and coulees.—The term "draw" is used in various parts of the West to indicate a depression through which water drains. As contrasted with a canyon or ravine, a draw in many instances is characteristically wide and shallow, without steeply sloping sides. "Coulee" has been defined as a deep gulch or ravine formed by rainstorms or melting snow, often dry in summer.[128]

---

[123] *Walker* v. *New Mexico & S.P.R.R.,* 165 U.S. 593, 599-602 (1897).

[124] See *Gibbs* v. *Williams,* 25 Kans. 214, 215-216, 221 (1881).

[125] *Jaquez Ditch Co.* v. *Garcia,* 17 N. Mex. 160, 162-164, 124 Pac. 891 (1912); *Martinez* v. *Cook,* 56 N. Mex. 343, 348-351, 244 Pac. (2d) 134 (1952). In the latter case, at 349-350, the court emphasized that New Mexico is a State with an enormous number of arroyos that serve as drainageways in rainy seasons but are dry at other times; and that a rule that to constitute a watercourse, water must be carried in the channel throughout the year or most of the time is not suited to local conditions. The court added that "Likewise, the holding in the *Walker* case that because a deep arroyo terminated in the flat country although the water thereafter traveled to a river through defined channels, that dams may be thrown across such channels and the water cast back on higher lands, is ill suited to conditions in this State and the case will not longer be followed."

[126] A watercourse is defined by statute as any channel—including arroyo—having definite banks and bed with visible evidence of the *occasional* flow of water: N. Mex. Stat. Ann. § 75-1-1 (1968).

[127] *Globe* v. *Shute,* 22 Ariz. 280, 289, 196 Pac. 1024 (1921).

[128] "The American Heritage Dictionary of the English Language," Houghton Mifflin Co., 1969.

However, the South Dakota Supreme Court stated with respect to a depression in Harding County, in the northwestern corner of the State, that: "Ash coulee, as the name implies, is a long shallow draw."[129] A few examples follow. (See also "Bed and Banks or Sides—What constitutes bed and banks," above.)

A depression in Reagan County, Texas, one-fourth to one-half mile wide and several miles long, draining a considerable area, but in which water flowed only after "a good rain," was held to lack under the testimony any of the essential characteristics of a watercourse. According to the court, "it would seem that Garrison Draw is just a wide valley; a typical West Texas draw."[130]

Adamson Draw in Johnson County, Wyoming, was said to be "just a swale," a "small water drainage" for local precipitation, and was held to be not a watercourse. The bottom was "well grassed," there was no evidence of well-defined banks or creek channel; and it was easily crossed by a vehicle almost anywhere.[131]

This is not to imply that a draw is to be completely dissociated from the category of watercourses. In the two examples just noted, the physical features of the draws in question did not meet the specifications of a watercourse channel. Had they done so, with the requisite elements of source and streamflow—or had there been an accepted channel running along their beds, no matter how wide the draws—classification as watercourses might well have resulted. It is true that the South Dakota Supreme Court in *Benson* v. *Cook* stated that extending throughout the length of Ash Coulee, in Harding County in the northwestern part of the State, is a meandering depression that had been worn by the action of running water, with a bed and banks forming a continuous channel down which water ran when there was water to run—"the same" being "true of practically every other coulee or dry draw in the land." But the court stated that the water flowing down the coulee had never lost its character as "mere surface water."[132] In dealing with the question of source of supply, the holding in this case is an extreme one. In the author's opinion, the streamflows in this case and in *Terry* v. *Heppner* decided 7 years later[133] could better have been classed as appropriable waters of watercourses. (See "Source of Supply," below.)

The statutes of South Dakota make provision for obtaining rights to the use of water of minor streamflows under special procedure.[134] It applies to any dry draw not exceeding 160 acres in drainage area for any purpose, or to any dry draw or watercourse for livestock purposes; "dry draw" being any ravine or watercourse not having an average daily flow of at least 0.4 cubic foot per

---

[129] *Benson* v. *Cook*, 47 S. Dak. 611, 613, 201 N. W. 526 (1924).
[130] *Turner* v. *Big Lake Oil Co.*, 62 S. W. (2d) 491, 493 (Tex. Civ. App. 1933), affirmed, 128 Tex. 155, 96 S. W. (2d) 221 (1936).
[131] *Wyoming* v. *Hiber*, 48 Wyo. 172, 178-179, 187-188, 44 Pac. (2d) 1005 (1935).
[132] *Benson* v. *Cook*, 47 S. Dak. 611, 613, 616-617, 201 N. W. 526 (1924).
[133] *Terry* v. *Heppner*, 59 S. Dak. 317, 319-320, 239 N. W. 759 (1931).
[134] S. Dak. Comp. Laws Ann. § § 46-1-6(3) and 46-4-1 to 46-4-8 (1968).

second during the period May 1 to September 30, inclusive. In *Benson* v. *Cook* and *Terry* v. *Heppner*, it was held that the waters flowing in the draws or coulees in litigation were diffused surface waters not subject to appropriation under the "dry draw law."

Slough connected with watercourse.—It has long been recognized that a slough connected with a watercourse and supplied with water therefrom is a part of the watercourse. In California, where the doctrine of riparian rights is recognized and applied, lands contiguous to the slough have riparian rights in the waters of the river with which it is connected during such times as the water of that stream is present in the slough.[135] It is not necessary that the water in a slough be flowing; riparian rights "exist in any body of water, whether flowing or not."[136]

In *Herminghaus* v. *Southern California Edison Company*, so important in the riparian water law of California, a tract of about 18,000 acres of land extending along the San Joaquin River was intersected by 22 sloughs through which the river waters flowed out into the tract, the residue thereof eventually reaching the river.[137] These sloughs had definite beginnings, definite channels with banks and bottoms, and a definite ending in Fresno Slough; and they regularly took water during certain seasons of the year from San Joaquin River. It was held that they were watercourses, and that the lands bordering them were riparian lands with rights to the use of the water of the river correlated with those of upper riparian owners on the main river.

An early map showed the upper reaches of Warm Springs Creek in Idaho as a flat, boggy area and referred to it as Warm Springs Slough.[138] The fact that these waters flowed through sloughs, said the supreme court, would not necessarily change the character of the watercourse nor render the waters not subject to appropriation.

In another Idaho case, one point was whether Watson Slough was a natural watercourse, or merely a high-water channel for overflow waters of Snake River.[139] It was a channel that left the main stream and returned to it about 8 miles below; and it was held to be a watercourse within accepted definitions thereof, even though the evidence conflicted as to whether only high water

---

[135] *Turner* v. *James Canal Co.*, 155 Cal. 82, 91, 99 Pac. 520 (1909). While the water is running into Fresno Slough from Kings River, the slough is a part of the river and the riparian needs of lands riparian to the slough are fixed by reference to the similar needs of other lands riparian to the river. Fresno Slough is also connected with San Joaquin River, and the same relationships between lands riparian to the slough and those riparian to San Joaquin River apply except when the waters of Kings River are flowing in the slough: *Miller & Lux* v. *Enterprise Canal & Land Co.*, 169 Cal. 415, 420-421, 147 Pac. 567 (1915).

[136] *Turner* v. *James Canal Co.*, 155 Cal. 82, 87-88, 99 Pac. 520 (1909).

[137] *Herminghaus* v. *Southern California Edison Co.*, 200 Cal. 81, 92, 252 Pac. 607 (1926).

[138] *Bachman* v. *Reynolds Irr. Dist.*, 56 Idaho 507, 512, 55 Pac. (2d) 1314 (1936).

[139] *Hutchinson* v. *Watson Slough Ditch Co.*, 16 Idaho 484, 488-489, 101 Pac. 1059 (1909).

passed through it. However, a slough that led from Sacramento River, California, and did not return, but which served simply as a conduit by which some of the floodwaters of the river occasionally escaped into lower lands adjoining, as they did at other low places along the banks, was held not to be a watercourse.[140]

A certain California slough was originally a branch of Mariposa Creek, from which it received a portion of the streamflow thereof.[141] The flow from the creek was later cut off by filling in the upper part of the slough, but water continued to flow into the lower part from rainfall on adjoining lands and from drains of an irrigation district. Evidence as to the character of the slough channel where it crossed the lands of the parties was favorable and conclusive. The court held that the artificial separation of the slough from Mariposa Creek and the cutting off of the creek waters did not destroy the character of the slough as a natural channel or watercourse.

Source of Supply

Particularity of the source of supply is not material to the classification of a watercourse, provided the source is determinable. A single stream of water may have one or more of a large number of possible sources of supply. The Idaho Supreme Court quoted from *Corpus Juris* to the effect that:[142]

"The particular source is immaterial. Thus, the supply of a natural watercourse may come from springs, swamp, surface water, artificially controlled water over which the creator has lost control, artesian wells, lake, or a pond formed by surface water, the overflow of a lake because of rainfall, or from a glacier."

The Ultimate Source

It is pertinent to quote here the observations of high courts of two arid Western States as to the ultimate sources of supply of flowing streams and their relation to the water sheds they drain.

The Colorado Supreme Court stated:[143]

The volume of these streams is made up of rains and snowfall on the surface, the springs which issue from the earth, and the water percolating under the surface, which finds its way to the streams running through the watersheds in which it is found. It is likewise proper to take judicial notice of the fact that upon account of the elevation of the state and other

---

[140] *Lamb* v. *Reclamation Dist. No. 108,* 73 Cal. 125, 134-135, 14 Pac. 625 (1887).

[141] *Haun* v. *De Vaurs,* 97 Cal. App. (2d) 841, 842-843, 218 Pac. (2d) 996 (1950).

[142] *Scott* v. *Watkins,* 63 Idaho 506, 517-518, 122 Pac. (2d) 220 (1942), quoting from 67 C.J. *Waters* § 5 (1954). See also *Hildebrandt* v. *Montgomery,* 113 Oreg. 687, 691, 234 Pac. 267 (1925).

[143] *In re German Ditch & Res. Co.,* 56 Colo. 252, 271, 139 Pac. 2 (1913).

reasons, the precipitation is quite small, and that a large number of streams in the state are, and always have been, dry during a portion of each year. When these facts are taken into consideration it is evident that the words "natural stream" as used in the constitution were intended to be used in their broadest scope and include within their definition all the streams of the state supplied in the manners above referred to, including tributaries and the streams draining into other streams.

The Utah Supreme Court declared:[144]

We must know judicially that the water in a river between any two points is not accumulated there solely from the contributions thereto from marginal sources, but that the major portion thereof comes by natural flow from upstream sources which have fed the channel itself, step by step, clear back to its ultimate source or sources. The entire watershed to its uttermost confines, covering thousands of square miles, out to the crest of the divides which separate it from adjacent watersheds, is the generating source from which the water of a river comes or accumulates in its channel. Rains and snows falling on this entire vast area sink into the soil and find their way by surface or underground flow or percolation through the sloping strata down to the central channel. This entire sheet of water, or water table, constitutes the river and it never ceases to be such in its centripetal motion towards the channel. Any appropriator of water from the central channel is entitled to rely and depend upon all the sources which feed the main stream above his own diversion point, clear back to the farthest limits of the watershed. * * *

Definiteness and Permanence

It is the consensus of western courts that there must be a definite and permanent source of supply, though not necessarily unfailing at all times. However, under the widely varying topographic and meteorological conditions that are found in the West, there is no uniform concept of either definiteness or permanence of source. Some treatment of this variability appears in the discussion under "Stream," above. Inasmuch as a stream of water can flow only if it has a source or sources of supply, definiteness and permanence of the stream are bound up inextricably with these attributes of its source of supply.[145] The discussions unavoidably overlap.

An appropriate quotation to insert at this point is taken from a decision of the Supreme Court of Texas, which said:[146]

---

[144] *Richlands Irr. Co.* v. *Westview Irr. Co.,* 96 Utah 403, 418, 80 Pac. (2d) 458 (1938).

[145] In 1906, the Kansas Supreme Court found that a new stream exhibited the element of permanence, and stated that in that event the particular source was immaterial. *Rait* v. *Furrow,* 74 Kans. 101, 106-107, 85 Pac. 934 (1906). It was enough that there was "a living source—a steady supply." Apparently permanence of the source was deduced from the finding that there was a permanent stream.

[146] *Hoef* v. *Short,* 114 Tex. 501, 506, 273 S. W. 785 (1925).

With reference to the phrase "definite and permanent source of supply of water," frequently used by the courts as describing a necessary requisite of an irrigable stream, all that is meant is that there must be sufficient water carried by the stream at such intervals as may make it practicable to irrigate from or use the stream.

A few other examples of judicial observations follow:

Definite source.—The current (stream) consists of water from a definite source of supply.[147]

When water has a definite source, such as a spring, and takes a definite channel, it is a watercourse.[148] Here a spring is singled out as a definite source. A spring that yields a stream flowing in a channel is an excellent and obvious example.

Permanent source.—Water that appears on the surface in a diffused state with no permanent source of supply or regular course is valuable to no one and is not classified as a watercourse.[149]

Certain sloughs that had definite beginnings, definite channels with banks and bottoms and a definite ending in the main Fresno Slough, and a "permanent source" (San Joaquin River) from which they took water during certain seasons of the year, were held to be watercourses both in fact and in law.[150] As a result, the contiguous lands were held to have riparian rights in the waters of the slough.

The Montana Supreme Court has said a stream must be "fed from other and more permanent sources than mere surface water."[151] The implication of this observation is that flows of diffused surface water are too short lived and unstable to themselves constitute watercourses, even when flowing briefly in natural depressions and in large quantity therein—which thus far is true—and therefore cannot be considered permanent sources of watercourses. However, as noted below (see "Diffused Surface Water"), this broad exclusion of diffused surface water from classification as a source of a watercourse is not justified, because part of the precipitation that falls on the slopes of a watershed—the ultimate source of its water supply—will reach the draining watercourses in the form of diffused surface water.

Some interpretations of definiteness and permanence.—An extreme view of this requirement of a watercourse is that the supply must be permanent to the exclusion of rain and snow and diffused surface water generally; and perhaps the best known exponent of this view in the West is the decision of the South

---

[147] *Maricopa County M.W.C. Dist.* v. *Southwest Cotton Co.,* 39 Ariz. 65, 86, 4 Pac. (2d) 369 (1931). No criteria of definiteness are stated.

[148] *Snyder* v. *Platte Valley Public Power & Irr. Dist.,* 144 Nebr. 308, 314, 13 N. W. 160 (1944).

[149] *Cooper* v. *Sanitary Dist. No. 1 of Lancaster County,* 146 Nebr. 412, 419, 19 N. W. (2d) 619 (1945).

[150] *Herminghaus* v. *Southern California Edison Co.,* 200 Cal. 81, 92, 252 Pac. 607 (1926).

[151] *Le Munyon* v. *Gallatin Valley Ry.,* 60 Mont. 517, 523, 199 Pac. 915 (1921).

Dakota Supreme Court in *Benson* v. *Cook*,[152] which has been given some attention in the discussion of "Stream," above. The controversy arose over the right to use water flowing down Ash Coulee for irrigation purposes, and the controlling question was whether Ash Coulee was a "definite stream" within the meaning of a statute relating to "dry draws."[153] In holding that this channel did not contain a "definite stream," the supreme court found that the channel had no permanent source of supply. It contained some water while snow was melting in the spring, varying generally from a few days to a few weeks; and after heavy summer rains, from a few hours to a day or two. Although there were some springs at intervals along the coulee, their flow failed to form streams for more than very short distances.

Seven years later, in a comparable situation, the South Dakota court had an opportunity to review this interpretation of "permanent source," the question being "admittedly a close one."[154] However, as the principle established in *Benson* v. *Cook* had been the law of the State for some 7 years, the court felt constrained to follow it, believing that an attempt now to establish a different rule would be neither salutary nor advisable. One may infer that if this had been a matter of first impression in the State, the supreme court might then have been less extreme in its imputation of impermanence of melting snow and rainfall supplies.

In any event, to adopt generally and literally the view taken in *Benson* v. *Cook* would result in excluding many definite and substantial streams from the category of watercourses. Consequently, sources of this character that yield large quantities of water over considerable periods of time in regular seasons have been held in various jurisdictions to be definite sources.

For example, the existence of a watercourse was in controversy with respect to a California stream which the supreme court found to be "of the character familiar in this state, and in other semiarid regions."[155] It carried a substantial current during the rainy season and thereafter while snows in the surrounding mountains were melting, but the flow ceased entirely as the dry summer advanced. The evidence was clear to the effect that the flow in the well-defined stream channel consisted of the runoff of the usual and annually recurring fall of rain and snow. This the supreme court held to be a watercourse to which riparian rights attached.

Another good example appears in a Texas case in which the primary question was whether a certain creek was a stream to which irrigation rights attached.[156] The creek occupied a channel with well-defined bed and banks, its stream being fed by the rainfall on its watershed of approximately 225,000

---

[152] *Benson* v. *Cook*, 47 S. Dak. 611, 615-617, 201 N. W. 526 (1924).
[153] The present "dry draw law" is found in S. Dak. Comp. Laws Ann. § § 46-1-6 and 46-4-1 to 46-4-8 (1967).
[154] *Terry* v. *Heppner*, 59 S. Dak. 317, 319-320, 239 N. W. 759 (1931).
[155] *Lindblom* v. *Round Valley Water Co.*, 178 Cal. 450, 452-453, 173 Pac. 994 (1918).
[156] *Hoefs* v. *Short*, 114 Tex. 501, 503-504, 506, 510, 273 S. W. 785 (1925).

acres. The stream flowed after rainfall, from 1 to 22 times a year, from "a day or two" to "a good while," at more or less regular seasons. The evidence was uncontradicted that the flow occurred with sufficient regularity, one year after another, to make it valuable and useful for agricultural purposes. This, said the Texas Supreme Court, satisfied every legal requirement as to permanence of source of water supply. It showed the waters of the creek to be not mere diffused surface waters, but those of a natural watercourse to which water rights, whether riparian or by appropriation, attached.

The viewpoint that snow and rainfall sources that yield large quantities of water in regular seasons are sufficiently definite and permanent to serve as elements of a watercourse is often a rational one under typical southwestern conditions, in an area distant from sources of supply in high mountains. The situation that prevails in parts of the Southwest is well portrayed in a periodical of the Agricultural Research Service, United States Department of Agriculture, issued in the summer of 1959.[157] Under the caption "Saving Floodwaters," the article stated that much of the limited rainfall—almost totally lost through runoff—that occurs in the Southwest might be held in the area in which it falls. Specifically, the annual precipitation of 7 to 15 inches in the Tucson, Arizona, area falls largely in the summer and winter, much of it in small, local but intense thunderstorms. About 95 percent of the water from intense storms promptly runs off. Steep slopes and straight stream channels develop high water velocities and heavy sediment. The water runs into the river channels in abrupt wave movements, causing flash floods. "In Walnut Gulch watershed near Tombstone, Arizona, a dry streambed became a raging torrent in 17 minutes of rainfall, with 20,000 cubic feet of water racing by per second." Ways of making beneficial savings of the runoff are suggested.

Precipitation

Runoffs from rainfall and melting snow have been recognized in many jurisdictions as definite and permanent sources of water supply of watercourses. Although the decisions are not harmonious, this is apparently the majority viewpoint when runoffs from substantial areas are in litigation.

Majority viewpoint respecting watershed runoff.—Thus, the courts speak of "rains and snowfall" in the watersheds of streams;[158] and "run-off from the usual, and annually recurring fall of rain and snow."[159]

Volume of runoff is sometimes a factor. For example, the Nevada Supreme Court agreed that a watercourse could be supplied at certain seasons from snows on the watershed mountains, as distinguished from occasional bursts of

---

[157] U.S. Dept. Agr., "Agricultural Research," August 1959, p. 16; findings of R. V. Keppel and J. E. Fletcher.
[158] *In re German Ditch & Res. Co.*, 56 Colo. 252, 271, 139 Pac. 2 (1913).
[159] *Lindblom* v. *Round Valley Water Co.*, 178 Cal. 450, 453, 173 Pac. 994 (1918).

water in gulches or ravines in times of freshets or melting of ice and snow.[160] And the Oklahoma court speaks of a large quantity of water, "after heavy rain or after the melting of large bodies of snow."[161] On the other hand, a natural watercourse was held to have been formed in Montana by waters flowing in a gulch with regularity from year to year in times of storms and melting snow, even though inconsiderable in quantity.[162]

In cases arising in several States of the Northwest, where winter snows accumulate in large quantities in the mountains, recognized sources of supply have been designated variously as spring rains and melting snows;[163] rains and snows falling on the watersheds;[164] and snow runoff in the spring.[165]

Of course, snow falls on mountains of the Southwest as well, but in large areas there in most years the precipitation is chiefly in the form of rain. As already noted, there are areas in which heavy rainstorms, followed by torrential runoff or flash floods, are not uncommon. In other regions, the rainstorms, although productive of considerable runoff, are normally less violent. Whatever the nature of the particular occurrence, high courts of the Southwest are liberal in their acceptance of these precipitation phenomena as definite and permanent supplies of water for watercourses. Thus, in Arizona, we have rains or snows falling on adjacent hills, whence their runoff flows down ravines or washes at irregular intervals;[166] in New Mexico, surface water in a hilly region, seeking an outlet through a gorge or ravine during the rainy season, where the size of the stream is immaterial;[167] arroyos that serve the purpose of drainageways during the rainy season, but are dry at other times.[168]

The Texas Supreme Court, in its decision in *Hoefs* v. *Short*, the *locus* of which was in an arid or semiarid region (Reeves County), handles the question of rainfall as a source of water supply with lucidity and good reasoning.[169] Rain falling on the watershed of Barilla Creek from 1 to 22 times each year, in sufficient quantity to permit irrigation from the stream, was held to be a permanent source of water supply. The court went on to say that the watershed is permanent, the meteorological laws that cause the rain to fall there are permanent, and the streambed by which the waters reach the locality in controversy was to all intents and purposes permanent. But, said the court, still more convincing than these is the admitted fact that the rain does fall and

---

[160] *Barnes* v. *Sabron*, 10 Nev. 217, 236-237 (1875).

[161] *Chicago, R.I. & P.Ry.* v. *Groves*, 20 Okla. 101, 117-118, 93 Pac. 755 (1908).

[162] *Popham* v. *Holloron*, 84 Mont. 442, 447, 450-451, 275 Pac. 1099 (1929).

[163] *West* v. *Taylor*, 16 Oreg. 165, 172, 13 Pac. 665 (1887); *Wright* v. *Phillips*, 127 Oreg. 420, 426, 272 Pac. 554 (1928).

[164] *Richlands Irr. Co.* v. *Westview Irr. Co.*, 96 Utah 403, 418, 80 Pac. (2d) 458 (1938).

[165] *In re Johnson Creek*, 159 Wash. 629, 630, 294 Pac. 566 (1930).

[166] *Globe* v. *Shute*, 22 Ariz. 280, 289, 196 Pac. 1024 (1921).

[167] *Jaquez Ditch Co.* v. *Garcia*, 17 N. Mex. 160, 161-164, 124 Pac. 891 (1912).

[168] *Martinez* v. *Cook*, 56 N. Mex. 343, 349-350, 244 Pac. (2d) 134 (1952). Note the handling in this case of the United States Supreme Court decision rendered much earlier in *Walker* v. *New Mexico & S.P.R.R.*, 165 U.S. 593, 600-605 (1897).

[169] *Hoefs* v. *Short*, 114 Tex. 501, 506-507, 273 S. W. 785 (1925).

run down the creek in sufficient quantity and with such regularity and frequency as to be valuable for irrigation, and that people for years have been and now are successfully irrigating from it. The facts as to bed, banks, and permanency of source or water supply are mere evidentiary facts that a stream can be used for irrigation or water right purposes. When the fact of utility is conceded or established, as it is here, said the court, the stream is one to which water rights attach, regardless of variations from the ideal stream of physiographers and meteorologists.

The minority viewpoint.—The South Dakota cases that rejected the water sources of Ash Coulee as impermanent represent the extreme point of view with respect to melting snow and rainfall as sources of supply of watercourses.[170] (See "Source of Supply," above.) Admittedly, the water supplies in question were neither large nor did they last long into the summer, but this is a phenomenon not at all uncommon in the West. The two cases contain borderline decisions which might easily have gone the other way.

Localized precipitation and runoff.—As the field narrows from overall concepts of watersheds and their drainage stream systems to more localized situations, standards of definiteness and permanence tend to become more exacting. The South Dakota borderline cases noted immediately above are on the physical borderline also.

Thus, there is the early observation of the Nevada Supreme Court distinguishing occasional bursts of water in localized areas from snows on the mountain watersheds, and there is also the emphasis placed in Oklahoma upon *heavy* rain and *large* bodies of snow,[171] both noted above in discussing the majority viewpoint.

The concept as to localized sources is embodied in two decisions of the Nebraska Supreme Court rendered in the 1890's.[172] Both involved interception of water by railroad embankments. In each, an essential question of law was whether the law of watercourses or that of diffused surface waters should be applied.

In the *Morrissey* case, existence of the water in litigation was traceable directly to falling rains, when there were extraordinary freshets. It was not shown that in its undiverted course, the water originated from or returned to Yankee Creek. Its course was along the valley, but not as a part of the stream or in any defined watercourse of its own. The supreme court agreed with the trial court that this was diffused surface water.

The jury in the *Town* case believed that there was a well-defined channel for the drainage of rainfall, melting snow, or diffused surface water only, although

---

[170] *Benson* v. *Cook*, 47 S. Dak. 611, 613-617, 201 N. W. 526 (1924); *Terry* v. *Heppner*, 59 S. Dak. 317, 319-320, 239 N. W. 759 (1931).

[171] *Barnes* v. *Sabron*, 10 Nev. 217, 236-237 (1875); *Chicago, R.I. & P.Ry.* v. *Groves*, 20 Okla. 101, 117-118, 93 Pac. 755 (1908).

[172] *Morrissey* v. *Chicago, B. & Q.R.R.*, 38 Nebr. 406, 430-431, 56 N. W. 946 (1893); *Town* v. *Missouri Pac. Ry.*, 50 Nebr. 768, 772-774, 70 N. W. 402 (1897).

there was evidence that there was vegetation on the entire ground surface at the place where the embankment was built, and that the land was cultivated, with less of the appearance of a channel than of a mere depression in the prairie. According to a finding of the jury, said the supreme court, the outlet for the water had some of the essential, distinctive attributes of a watercourse, but lacked others—among them, a frequent flow of water, or a flow which had any definite and other than an occasional source. The water in question was held to be diffused surface water.

In both these Nebraska cases the supreme court was dealing with localized sources of water supply. The court failed to find enough, in the overall circumstances of either case, to satisfy what it believed to be the requisite elements of a watercourse.

Diffused Surface Water

"Streams are usually formed by surface waters gathering together in one channel and flowing therein. The waters then lose their character as surface waters and become stream waters."[173]

Under "Definiteness and Permanence," above, attention is called to a case in which the Montana Supreme Court adopted with approval a definition of watercourse which excluded sources as impermanent as diffused surface water.[174] The question at issue was not whether a legally constituted watercourse might be supplied wholly by diffused surface water; it was whether the water in litigation was that of a watercourse or was diffused surface water. It was held that the evidence disclosed none of the elements required to constitute a watercourse. Therefore, this case is not good authority for the proposition—which is controverted by the great weight of authority in the West—that a stream fed solely by diffused surface water is not a watercourse.

A number of western courts have recognized diffused surface water as a valid source of a watercourse both in fact and in law.[175]

An opinion of the Texas Supreme Court contains several quotations of authorities squarely in point.[176] One in particular is to the effect that although

---

[173] *Mogle* v. *Moore,* 16 Cal. (2d) 1, 9, 104 Pac. (2d) 785 (1940).

[174] *Le Munyon* v. *Gallatin Valley Ry.,* 60 Mont. 517, 523, 199 Pac. 915 (1921).

[175] Streams may be composed wholly of diffused surface water: *Rait* v. *Furrow,* 74 Kans. 101, 106-107, 85 Pac. 934 (1906). Where diffused surface waters flow into and become physically part of a stream, their classification changes and they become legally part of the stream: *Jack* v. *Teegarden,* 151 Nebr. 309, 314, 37 N. W. (2d) 387 (1949). See also *Jaquez Ditch Co.* v. *Garcia,* 17 N. Mex. 160, 161, 124 Pac. 891 (1912); *Borman* v. *Blackmon,* 60 Oreg. 304, 309-310, 118 Pac. 848 (1911); *Johnson* v. *Metropolitan Life Ins. Co.,* 71 S. Dak. 155, 161, 22 N. W. (2d) 737 (1946); *Richlands Irr. Co.* v. *Westview Irr. Co.,* 96 Utah 403, 418, 80 Pac. (2d) 458 (1938); *Alexander* v. *Muenscher,* 7 Wash. (2d) 557, 559-560, 110 Pac. (2d) 625 (1941).

[176] *International & G.N.R.R.* v. *Reagan,* 121 Tex. 233, 241-242, 49 S. W. (2d) 414 (1932). The one paraphrased here is from 27 Ruling Case Law, p. 1066, §6.

there is apparently some authority for the proposition that the supply of a legally constituted watercourse must be more permanent than mere diffused surface water, it is not satisfactory to conclude that no watercourse exists merely because that is the source, for a stream may be composed wholly of such water. In addition, even diffused surface water becomes a watercourse at the point where it begins to form a legally acceptable channel and stream of water.

The foregoing conclusion is inevitable. A Colorado decision states that the flow of natural streams "is made up of rains and snowfall on the surface," as well as springs and percolating ground water.[177] Part of the water from the rain and snowfall sinks into the ground and joins streams in the watershed by that route, and part reaches the streams by another route—diffused flows over the surface. Decisions to the effect that these diffused flows are acceptable as sources of watercourses are in the large majority in the West, and they are supported by the better reasoning.

Spring Water

"We have also held that where springs form the fountain head of living watercourses they are a part and parcel of the stream."[178]

The physical characteristics of springs, and rights to the use of spring waters, are treated later, in chapter 18. At this point it is sufficient to note that (1) in some instances, the flow from a spring simply forms a marshy area in the immediate vicinity, where it sinks into the ground or evaporates without moving away on the surface, and hence fails to satisfy the legal requirements of a watercourse; whereas (2) in other cases, spring water collects in a channel and becomes a watercourse, or it spills over the bank of a flowing stream and thus is physically tributary to the watercourse to the same extent as other sources of supply.[179]

Spring water is defined in chapter 2 as water that breaks out upon the surface of the earth through natural openings in the ground. There is little question about classifying as a definite source a spring the discharge from which augments the flow of a watercourse year after year.[180] Questions have

---

[177] *In re German Ditch & Res. Co.,* 56 Colo. 252, 271, 139 Pac. 2 (1913).

[178] *In re Ahtanum Creek,* 139 Wash. 84, 100, 245 Pac. 758 (1926).

[179] But see *Texas Co.* v. *Burkett,* 117 Tex. 16, 28-29, 296 S. W. 273 (1927), in which the Texas Supreme Court was unable to say on the evidence whether the flow from springs along the banks of a stream was of sufficient volume to be of any value to riparian proprietors, or added perceptibly to the general volume of water in the bed of a stream, and hence held that they belonged to the owner of the land on which the springs arose. In *Barnes* v. *Sabron,* 10 Nev. 217, 237-239 (1875), the evidence showed that water from springs along the banks and bed of a stream disappeared in the earth in certain seasons; but it also showed that in most instances this disappearance coincided with heavy upstream diversions of creek waters, or else the water reappeared shortly in the streambed.

[180] A definite source, as a spring: *Pyle* v. *Richards,* 17 Nebr. 180, 182, 22 N. W. 370 (1885).

arisen, however, about the nature of the channel that carries the water away from the spring. For example, in an early Nevada case, waters from springs that where tributary to a creek passed part way through the ground either as percolation's or by unknown subterranean channels.[181] As there was no uncertainty that these creek waters actually came from these springs, their partly uncertain course through the ground was held immaterial. Again, a stream that flows from a spring with regularity in a well-defined channel is held to be a watercourse,[182] even though it enters the channel through an outlet in a marsh or swamp fed by living springs.[183]

In a Washington case, there was a curious conflict in the testimony as to the circumstances concerning the flow of water from a spring.[184] Two-thirds of the witnesses testified that the spring waters flowed in a natural channel to, upon, and across a part of plaintiff's lands throughout the year; the other third thought there was no stream. However, plaintiff and his predecessors in interest had found sufficient water in the stream to divert it and thereby supply their domestic and other purposes. Furthermore, the trial judge found on visiting the premises that there was a well-defined stream for about 200 feet on plaintiff's lands. Even if water then disappeared into the ground, or if there was no mouth to the stream, the supreme court was of the opinion that a holding was required that a well-defined stream ran upon and over at least a part of plaintiff's lands.

Some other typical cases recognizing the acceptability of springs as sources of a watercourse are given in the accompanying footnote.[185]

Waste and Seepage Waters

The fact that waste and seepage waters contribute to and therefore are sources of supply of watercourses is not to be confused with questions of rights to the use of waste and seepage waters before they actually enter the stream channel, and with rights of use, recapture, and reuse after they have mingled with the waters already flowing there. Holdings of the courts on these claims of right are not uniform, as noted later in chapter 18.

Disregarding for the present purpose, rights of ownership, use, recapture, and reuse, it has been noted in various decisions of western courts that with the establishment and expansion of irrigated areas, seepage into stream channels over a period of years develops substantial streams of water therein. Such

---

[181] *Strait* v. *Brown,* 16 Nev. 317, 323-324 (1881).

[182] *Holman* v. *Christensen,* 73 Utah 389, 397, 274 Pac. 457 (1929).

[183] *Pays* v. *Roseburg,* 123 Wash. 82, 84-85, 211 Pac. 750 (1923). See *Alexander* v. *Muenscher,* 7 Wash. (2d) 557, 560, 110 Pac. (2d) 625 (1941).

[184] *Allison* v. *Linn,* 139 Wash. 474, 477-478, 247 Pac. 731 (1926).

[185] *In re German Ditch & Res. Co.,* 56 Colo. 252, 271, 139 Pac. 2 (1913); *Rait* v. *Furrow,* 74 Kans. 101, 106-107, 85 Pac. 934 (1906); *Wright* v. *Phillips,* 127 Oreg. 420, 426, 272 Pac. 554 (1928); *Pecos County W.C. & I. Dist. No. 1* v. *Williams,* 271 S. W. (2d) 503, 504 (Tex. Civ. App. 1954, error refused n.r.e.); *Hollett* v. *Davis,* 54 Wash. 326, 329, 103 Pac. 423 (1909).

accumulations may create watercourses where none previously existed, by raising the flows in the channels to the status of definite streams.[186] In the process of this buildup, these "vagrant, fugitive" waste, seepage, return, and percolating waters lose their character as such and become part of the watercourse stream which they create or augment.[187]

Percolating Ground Water

It has been said by eminent ground water hydrologists that practically all ground water "is moving toward some stream, perhaps at a considerable distance, the flow of which it is helping to maintain."[188]

The contributions made by ground water to the flow of surface streams, and the reverse process by which the surface stream discharges water into the ground, are well-known phenomena. The implications with respect to water rights in these physically interconnected sources of supply are discussed later, in chapter 19.

The supreme courts of both Colorado and Utah have made sweeping comments on watershed relationships between streamflow and sources of supply, including intermediate percolating water.[189] Percolating water loses its character as such when it reaches a natural surface channel and mingles with the water flowing there. It then constitutes a part of the watercourse.[190]

Underflow

The underflow of a surface stream is the subsurface portion of a watercourse the whole of which comprises waters flowing in close association both on and beneath the surface.

---

[186] *Binning* v. *Miller,* 55 Wyo. 451, 462, 475-476, 102 Pac. (2d) 54 (1940). See *Hansen* v. *Crouch,* 98 Oreg. 141, 146, 193 Pac. 454 (1920). See also Hutchins, Wells, A., U.S. Dept. Agr., Tech. Bul. 439, "Policies Governing the Ownership of Return Waters from Irrigation" (1934).

[187] *Popham* v. *Holloron,* 84 Mont. 442, 452-453, 275 Pac. 1099 (1929); *Rock Creek Ditch & Flume Co.* v. *Miller,* 93 Mont. 248, 260, 17 Pac. (2d) 1074 (1933). See *In re German Ditch & Res. Co.,* 56 Colo. 252, 267-271, 139 Pac. 2 (1913). The fact that tributary waters flowed through sloughs in flat, boggy areas would not necessarily change the character of the watercourse of which they become a part: *Bachman* v. *Reynolds Irr. Dist.,* 56 Idaho 507, 512, 55 Pac. (2d) 1314 (1936).

[188] Thompson, David G., and Fiedler, Albert G., "Some Problems Relating to Legal Control of Use of Ground Waters," 30 Jour. Amer. Water Works Assn., 1049-1091 at p. 1060 (July, 1938).

[189] Streamflow is made up of rains and snowfall on the surface, springs, and water percolating under the surface, which finds its way to the streams running through the watersheds in which it occurs: *In re German Ditch & Res. Co.,* 56 Colo. 252, 271, 139 Pac. 2 (1913). Rains and snows falling on the vast watershed area sink into the soil and find their way through the sloping strata to the center channel; the entire sheet of water, or water table, constitutes the river: *Richlands Irr. Co.* v. *Westview Irr. Co.,* 96 Utah 403, 418, 80 Pac. (2d) 458 (1938).

[190] *Rock Creek Ditch & Flume Co.* v. *Miller,* 93 Mont. 248, 260, 17 Pac. (2d) 1074 (1933).

The sides and bottom of the stream channel may be impervious in some places and not in others; where not impervious the soil across and through which the channel is formed necessarily contains water in greater or less degree, and this water-bearing zone may be very limited in extent or may extend to considerable depths and for considerable distances on each side. The water-bearing zone adjacent to a previous surface channel is called in the court decisions the "underflow", "subflow," or "supporting flow" of the surface stream. Where this underflow or subflow exists—as it does frequently though not invariably—it is a component part of the watercourse part of which lies above and part below the ground surface.

Essential Features

The underflow or subflow of a surface stream consists of water slowly finding its way through the soil, sand, and gravel constituting the bed of the open stream,[191] or through the lands under the bed or immediately adjacent at the sides of the stream,[192] which supports the surface stream in its natural state or feeds it directly.[193]

To constitute underflow, it is essential that the surface and subsurface flows be in contact and that the subsurface flow shall have a definite direction corresponding to the surface flow. In a leading decision rendered in 1899, the California Supreme Court said that:[194]

It is agreed that all the waters of the San Fernando valley, except what is lost by evaporation or consumed in plant life, flow out through the narrow pass between the eastern extremity of the Cahuenga range and the Verdugo hills, either on or beneath the surface, and there is abundant testimony to warrant the conclusion that at ordinary stages of the river the water flowing on the surface and that which is beneath the surface are in intimate contact and moving in the same direction.* * *

Subterranean Side Flow

The underflow may and often does include water moving not only in the loose, porous material that constitutes and underlies the bed of the surface stream, but also the lateral extensions of the water-bearing material on each side of the surface channel.[195] It moves along the course of the stream and on each side, tending to reach farther laterally with increases in volume.[196] But it

---

[191] *Verdugo Canyon Water Co.* v. *Verdugo,* 152 Cal. 655, 663, 93 Pac. 1021 (1908); *Texas Co.* v. *Burkett,* 117 Tex. 16, 28, 296 S. W. 273 (1927); *In re Johnson Creek,* 159 Wash. 629, 630-631, 294 Pac. 566 (1930).

[192] *Maricopa County M.W.C. Dist.* v. *Southwest Cotton Co.,* 39 Ariz. 65, 96, 4 Pac. (2d) 369 (1931); *Larsen* v. *Apollonio,* 5 Cal. (2d) 440, 444, 55 Pac. (2d) 196 (1936).

[193] *Huffner* v. *Sawday,* 153 Cal. 86, 92-93, 94 Pac. 424 (1908); *San Bernardino* v. *Riverside,* 186 Cal. 7, 14, 198 Pac. 784 (1921).

[194] *Los Angeles* v. *Pomeroy,* 124 Cal. 597, 617, 57 Pac. 585 (1899).

[195] *Larsen* v. *Apollonio,* 5 Cal. (2d) 440, 444, 55 Pac. (2d) 196 (1936).

[196] *Kansas* v. *Colorado,* 206 U.S. 46, 114-115 (1907).

must be moving in a course and confined within a space reasonably well defined, so that the existence and general direction of the body of water moving through the ground may be determined with reasonable accuracy.[197]

There was evidence in one California case that, because of the geological formation in a valley, the creek traversing it was not only a surface but a subsurface stream as well.[198] The subsurface stream extended a considerable distance on either side of the trough through which the surface stream flowed.

When rights to the use of the underflow are in issue, it becomes necessary to establish the lateral limits of this water by competent evidence—often a difficult task. As stated by the California Supreme Court, there may be a point of distance from the stream at which a diversion of such ground water will have so little effect on the stream that it will not be actionable; it is ordinarily a question for the trial court to determine whether or not this is true in the particular case before it.[199]

The Underflow is a Part of the Watercourse

Affinity of surface and subsurface flows.—The portion of the water of a stream that goes along through the ground in association with the surface flow, under the conditions above noted, is as much a part of the watercourse as is the part that flows on the surface.[200] Water "passing through the voids of any loose permeable material filling or partially obstructing the channel of a stream is still water of the stream."

In an interstate suit over the waters of Arkansas River, the United States Supreme Court disagreed with what "seems to be the contention" of Kansas that beneath the surface of the river there was a second river, with the same course as that on the surface, but with a distinct and continuous flow as of a separate stream.[201] The Court was of opinion that the testimony did not warrant the finding of "such second and subterranean stream," and that it was not properly so denominated. Rather, it was to be regarded as merely the accumulation of water in the porous bed of the stream, percolating along either side of the stream as well as in the course of the stream itself.

The California Supreme Court has said, "With reference to a stream of the sort that Mill Creek is shown by the evidence to be—that is, a mountain creek flowing in a rocky and precipitous canyon partially blocked by detritus and having many 'narrows'—it is not possible logically to consider the flow and the underflow as separate and distinct sources of water supply."[202] It is "well established that the underground and surface portions of the stream constitute one common supply."[203]

---

[197] *Los Angeles* v. *Pomeroy*, 124 Cal. 597, 623-624, 57 Pac. 585 (1899).

[198] *Peabody* v. *Vallejo*, 2 Cal. (2d) 351, 375, 40 Pac. (2d) 486 (1935).

[199] *San Bernardino* v. *Riverside*, 186 Cal. 7, 14, 198 Pac. 784 (1921).

[200] *Los Angeles* v. *Pomeroy*, 124 Cal. 597, 623-624, 631, 57 Pac. 585 (1899).

[201] *Kansas* v. *Colorado*, 206 U.S. 46, 114-115 (1907).

[202] *Barton Land & Water Co.* v. *Crafton Water Co.*, 171 Cal. 89, 95, 152 Pac. 48 (1915).

[203] *Rancho Santa Margarita* v. *Vail*, 11 Cal. (2d) 501, 555, 81 Pac. (2d) 533 (1938).

The high courts of a number of Western States have declared or voiced approval of this principle.[204]

Effect of withdrawal of subsurface waters.—If drawing off the subsurface water tends to diminish appreciably and directly the flow of a surface stream, said the Arizona Supreme Court, it is subflow and is subject to the same rules that apply to the surface stream itself.[205] In that event, the withdrawal of water from the subflow is a taking of a part of the whole streamflow, and as much a depletion of the natural watercourse as though diverted from the surface.[206]

Burden of proof.—Several courts have held that one who diverts part of the underflow of a stream has the burden of proving that such action does not result in depleting the streamflow at points farther down.

In 1898, the Colorado Supreme Court held that when water flowing in a natural channel reaches the banks of a stream and there disappears in the sands of the streambed, the presumption will be that it augments the flow in the main stream by percolation, until the contrary is shown; and the burden of proof is on the party who diverts such water to establish that it does not mingle with the main flow of the stream.[207]

Subsequently, in a California case, there was testimony to the effect that no surface flow would show in the porous bed of a certain creek until the gravel was full of water from the bedrock to the surface.[208] With such a porous creek bed, said the court, no evidence was necessary to establish the fact that the taking of a substantial part of the underflow from the channel at any point on the stream would cause a corresponding diminution in the surface water flow—the law of gravitation would raise a presumption to that effect. Hence, one who would establish the contrary has the burden of proving conditions which would prevent this result.

The Idaho Supreme Court held that where there is evidence of subflow in a stream, the burden of proving that the water will not reach a lower prior appropriator is upon a later upper appropriator who asserts that such is the case.[209]

---

[204] See *Maricopa County M.W.C. Dist.* v. *Southwest Cotton Co.*, 39 Ariz. 65, 96, 4 Pac. (2d) 369 (1931); *Huerfano Valley Ditch & Res. Co.* v. *Huerfano Valley Investment Co.*, 73 Colo. 300, 302, 215 Pac. 132 (1923); *Smith* v. *Duff*, 39 Mont. 382, 390, 102 Pac. 984 (1909); *Texas Co.* v. *Burkett*, 117 Tex. 16, 28, 296 S. W. 273 (1927): *In re Johnson Creek*, 159 Wash. 629, 630-631, 294 Pac. 566 (1930).

[205] *Maricopa County M.W.C. Dist.* v. *Southwest Cotton Co.*, 39 Ariz. 65, 96, 4 Pac. (2d) 369 (1931).

[206] *Montecito Valley Water Co.* v. *Santa Barbara*, 144 Cal. 578, 585-586, 588, 77 Pac. 1113 (1904); *Verdugo Canyon Water Co.* v. *Verdugo*, 152 Cal. 655, 663, 93 Pac. 1021 (1908); *Buckers Irr., Mill. & Improvement Co.* v. *Farmers' Independent Ditch Co.*, 31 Colo. 62, 70-71, 72 Pac. 49 (1903); *Emporia* v. *Soden*, 25 Kans. 588, 608-609, 37 Am. Rep. 265 (1881).

[207] *Platte Valley Irr. Co.* v. *Buckers Irr., Mill & Improvement Co.*, 25 Colo. 77, 82, 53 Pac. 334 (1898).

[208] *Perry* v. *Calkins*, 159 Cal. 175, 180, 113 Pac. 136 (1911).

[209] *Jackson* v. *Cowan*, 33 Idaho 525, 527-528, 196 Pac. 216 (1921).

Negating Circumstances

To facilitate comparison, some of the controlling circumstances or combinations of circumstances that have led the courts to decide against the existence of watercourses are brought together below.

Topography

—The water was not confined by any well-defined bed and banks.[210]

—In the general level of the country, there was only a slight natural depression with a gentle slope.[211]

—There was no semblance of a definite channel. The depression or swale in which it was attempted to carry off waste water was planted to crops and was cultivated year after year.[212]

—Sutter Basin was not a watercourse, but was a great catchment area which served principally for reception of the floodwaters of Sacramento River.[213]

Water

Flows of water.
—There was not a perennial stream.[214]

—There was no converging of the water into a single stream; it was not obvious where the runoff would flow.[215]

—The term "stream" was said not to mean water deposited during times of storm which immediately runs off and leaves in its course a mere stretch of sand and rock.[216]

—From the case record, it was not sufficiently clear whether or not the waters comprised a mere collection of floodwaters from rains and melting snow that ran off in the winter and spring, and did not actually comprise or enter any natural stream or other body of water.[217]

Source of water supply.—As noted under "Source of Supply," above, in two borderline cases where the resulting streamflows were not large and did not last long, the South Dakota Supreme Court rejected melting snow and rainfall as acceptable sources of supply.[218] Elsewhere in much of the West, in comparable situations, the majority viewpoint would probably accept these water supplies as sources of watercourses.

---

[210] *Eastern Oregon Live Stock Co.* v. *Keller,* 108 Oreg. 256, 257-258, 216 Pac. 556 (1923).

[211] *Dyer* v. *Stahlhut,* 147 Kans. 767, 770, 78 Pac. (2d) 900 (1938).

[212] *Loosli* v. *Heseman,* 66 Idaho 469, 481, 162 Pac. (2d) 393 (1945).

[213] *Gray* v. *Reclamation Dist. No. 1500,* 174 Cal. 622, 648, 163 Pac. 1024 (1917).

[214] *Eastern Oregon Live Stock Co.* v. *Keller,* 108 Oreg. 256, 257-258, 216 Pac. 556 (1923).

[215] *Muhleisen* v. *Krueger,* 120 Nebr. 380, 381-382, 232 N. W. 735 (1930).

[216] *San Pedro, L.A. & S.L.R.R.* v. *Simons Brick Co.,* 45 Cal. App. 57, 61-62, 187 Pac. 62 (1919).

[217] *Washington County Irr. Dist.* v. *Talboy,* 55 Idaho 382, 389, 43 Pac. (2d) 943 (1935).

[218] *Benson* v. *Cook,* 47 S. Dak. 611, 613-617, 201 N. W. 526 (1924); *Terry* v. *Heppner,* 59 S. Dak. 317, 319-320, 239 N. W. 759 (1931).

The Overall Situation: Water and Topography

In the numerous factual situations that have been judicially considered and appraised with respect to existence of watercourses, it is evident that the courts often study not only the individual criteria separately, but also the whole combination of circumstances to which they belong. For example, in a Nebraska situation in which water directly traceable to falling rains appeared only when there were extraordinary freshets, and moved along a valley in which there was an undisputed watercourse—of which the water in litigation did not form a part and from which it did not originate nor return to—the contrast of this water situation was so great in every respect from that of an undisputed watercourse in the neighborhood that the court had no hesitancy in classifying it as diffused surface water.[219] Another Nebraska situation litigated in the same general period involved water actually draining from rain, melting snow, and diffused surface water—the flow of which had no permanence or regularity as to time and was "dependent upon transient causes alone." The water was obstructed by an embankment at a place which the jury believed to be a well-defined channel, but was shown by evidence to be covered with vegetation and cultivated, having the appearance of a mere depression in the prairie.[220] Here again, in the face of jury findings that (1) there was a clearly defined watercourse, which however, (2) was carrying diffused surface water, the court undoubtedly considered the overall situation in conceding that the outlet for the water had some of the essential, distinctive, attributes of watercourses but lacked others—among them, a frequent flow of water or a flow with a definite and more than occasional source.

Some other combinations of water and topography follow:

—Runoff that is broadly diffused over the ground is not stream water.[221]

—A watercourse comprises more than mere surface drainage over land occasioned by unusual freshets or other extraordinary causes.[222]

—Insufficient for the classification of a watercourse is water from precipitation that at times collects or stands in low places, depressions, potholes, or shallow basins;[223] or the existence of holes, gullies, or ravines in which diffused surface water from rain or melting snow is discharged at

---

[219] *Morrissey* v. *Chicago, B. & Q.R.R.*, 38 Nebr. 406, 430-431, 56 N. W. 946 (1893).

[220] *Town* v. *Missouri Pacific Ry.*, 50 Nebr. 768, 772-775, 70 N. W. 402 (1897).

[221] *Sun Underwriters Ins. Co. of New York* v. *Bunkley*, 233 S. W. (2d) 153, 155 (Tex. Civ. App. 1950, error refused).

[222] *Sanguinetti* v. *Pock*, 136 Cal. 466, 471-472, 69 Pac. 98 (1902); *Hutchinson* v. *Watson Slough Ditch Co.*, 16 Idaho 484, 488, 101 Pac. 1059 (1909); *Miksch* v. *Tassler*, 108 Nebr. 208, 213, 187 N. W. 796 (1922); *Hoefs* v. *Short*, 114 Tex. 501, 508, 273 S. W. 785 (1925); *Maricopa County M.W.C. Dist.* v. *Southwest Cotton Co.*, 39 Ariz. 65, 85-86, 4 Pac. (2d) 369 (1931).

[223] *Doney* v. *Beatty*, 124 Mont. 41, 50, 220 Pac. (2d) 77 (1950).

irregular intervals from a higher to a lower level;[224] or temporary flows in shallow depressions that were only slightly lower than the surrounding land.[225]

—Exempted from classification as watercourses are west Texas draws that ordinarily are dry.[226]

—Nor was a slough connected with Sacramento River to be classed as a watercourse simply because it was a connecting slough, when the only water it carried consisted of insignificant quantities in times of flood—a role performed by every other low place along the bank.[227]

Other Factors

Beginning of the Watercourse

The channel of the watercourse necessarily has a definite beginning somewhere.[228]

In general, the watercourse begins at the place at which it first evidences all the characteristics necessary to its classification as such. This matter is closely associated with the source of the watercourse (see "Source of Supply," above). If it originates in the discharge of a spring, the watercourse begins at the place at which the water flows away from the spring in a well-defined channel. Likewise, if its source is a lake, it begins at the outlet of the lake. "Whether the water comes from a spring, subterranean vein, or surface-water, it becomes a watercourse from the point where it comes to or collects on the surface and flows in a well-defined channel or bed, with such banks as will ordinarily confine the water and cause it to run in a definite and certain direction."[229]

Determination of the point of beginning of a watercourse the upper part of which is fed mainly by diffused surface water involves not only selection of criteria for distinguishing watercourses from diffused surface waters, but also application of the selected criteria to the factual situation, which may be complicated. As to criteria, the South Dakota Supreme Court observed that: "At what time water, originating as surface water, by reaching and flowing in a definite channel or natural drainway, ceases to become mere surface water, and

---

[224] *Sanguinetti* v. *Pock,* 136 Cal. 466, 471-472, 69 Pac. 98 (1902); *Doney* v. *Beatty,* 124 Mont. 41, 51, 220 Pac. (2d) 77 (1950); *Wyoming* v. *Hiber,* 48 Wyo. 172, 184-185, 44 Pac. (2d) 1005 (1935).

[225] *Sun Underwriters Ins. Co. of New York* v. *Bunkley,* 233 S. W. (2d) 153, 156 (Tex. Civ. App. 1950, error refused).

[226] *Turner* v. *Big Lake Oil Co.,* 62 S. W. (2d) 491, 493 (Tex. Civ. App. 1933), affirmed, 128 Tex. 155, 96 S. W. (2d) 221 (1936). See *St. Paul Fire & Marine Ins. Co.* v. *Carroll,* 106 S. W. (2d) 757, 759 (Tex. Civ. App. 1937, error dismissed), which did not involve the classification of these dry draws as watercourses, but in which the court refused to hold them to be, as a matter of law, statutory navigable streams.

[227] *Lamb* v. *Reclamation Dist. No. 108,* 73 Cal. 125, 134-135, 14 Pac. 625 (1887).

[228] See *Herminghaus* v. *Southern California Edison Co.,* 200 Cal 81, 92, 252 Pac. 607 (1926).

[229] *Rait* v. *Furrow,* 74 Kans. 101, 107, 85 Pac. 934 (1906).

takes on the characteristics of a definite stream, is a nice question upon which the authorities are not in harmony."[230] As indicated under "Source of Supply—Definiteness and Permanence," above, the expressed views of the South Dakota court on this matter are not in harmony with those generally accepted in the West.

"Nevertheless surface waters may, without artificial aid, converge so as to form a defined channel and if they would naturally flow therein it would be construed to be a natural watercourse from the point at which the channel begins to take form."[231] A statement of principle that has found considerable favor is to the effect that diffused surface water becomes a natural watercourse at the point where it begins to form a reasonably well-defined channel, with bed and banks, or sides and current, although the stream itself may be very small and the water may not flow continuously.[232] Even when further complicated by the building of an insignificant flow up to a point at which it becomes legally acceptable as the stream component of a watercourse, the same principles apply.[233]

The precise point at which the flow of diffused surface water ceases to be such and becomes that of a watercourse is often difficult to determine as a matter of fact, because the transition may be a gradual one. The question is often one of fact, to be determined by a jury or by the court.[234] But from the point of beginning, wherever fixed, the law of watercourses applies. "While this dividing point may be difficult to determine physically, its meaning in law is definite."[235]

Termination of the Watercourse

Not only does a watercourse necessarily have a definite beginning somewhere—it likewise necessarily terminates somewhere. However, the character or place of discharge of the water does not determine the classification of a watercourse and therefore is not properly one of its elements.

In general.—Some definitions of a watercourse state that it usually discharges water into some other stream or body of water (see "Some particulars," below). That is generally true. Most of the larger western streams belong to systems which eventually discharge into the Gulf of Mexico, the Pacific Ocean, or bays or gulfs opening to the Pacific Ocean. However, the

---

[230] *Terry* v. *Heppner*, 59 S. Dak. 317, 319, 239 N. W. 759 (1931).

[231] *Weck* v. *Los Angeles County Flood Control Dist.*, 80 Cal. App. (2d) 182, 196, 181 Pac. (2d) 935 (1947).

[232] *International & G. N. R.R.* v. *Reagan*, 121 Tex. 233, 242, 49 S. W. (2d) 414 (1932), quoting from 27 Ruling Case Law 1066, §6; *Alexander* v. *Muenscher*, 7 Wash. (2d) 557, 560, 110 Pac. (2d) 625 (1941); *Mogle* v. *Moore*, 16 Cal. (2d) 1, 9, 104 Pac. (2d) 785 (1940).

[233] *Popham* v. *Holloron*, 84 Mont. 442, 447-453, 275 Pac. 1099 (1929); *Binning* v. *Miller*, 55 Wyo. 451, 465, 474-476, 102 Pac. (2d) 54 (1940).

[234] *Costello* v. *Bowen*, 80 Cal. App. (2d) 621, 627, 182 Pac. (2d) 615 (1947).

[235] Harding, S. T., "Water Rights for Irrigation," p. 9 (1936).

streams in the Great Basin, and some small streams elsewhere, flow into sumps or lakes with no surface outlets, or disappear into the ground. A stream that has the three elements of a watercourse generally held to be essential—definite channel, substantial stream, and definite source of supply—is not barred from that classification simply because the water eventually disappears into the ground or is discharged into a marsh or lake from which there is no perceptible surface outlet.

Some particulars.—Classification of the watercourse depends upon circumstances that prevail from its beginning to its end, and is not determined by the manner of its ending nor by the character of discharge of the water at the point at which the legal classification ceases. The fact that a stream of water loses its identity or vanishes from sight in one way or another "does not deprive the part which flows regularly through a channel of its character as a watercourse."[236] In a Washington case, the supreme court held that the trial judge "was guided too much by what he saw at the dry season of the year, and was temporarily misled by the idea that, in order for there to be a stream in a legal sense, 'it must flow on down to a certain place and have a mouth somewhere.' "[237] Disappearance of the water into the ground, or absence of a mouth to the stream, as the trial court suggested, should make no difference in classifying the upper portion as a watercourse.

"Streams usually empty into other streams, lakes, or the ocean, but a stream does not lose its character as a watercourse even though it may break up and disappear."[238] According to the Kansas Supreme Court, "The fact that the channel of the stream in question grew less distinct and that it practically passed out of sight before the waters reached Dry Creek does not argue that the stream lacks the characteristics of a watercourse."[239]

Thus, the watercourse may terminate with the discharge of the water into another stream,[240] or into a lake,[241] or the sea;[242] or it may have a definite ending in a slough connected with a watercourse.[243] It may discharge into a swamp or sandy basin.[244] Or the stream "may spread out over the land."[245]

In the usual situation—although, as above stated, not the only controlling one—the watercourse discharges its flow into some other stream or body of

---

[236] *Rait* v. *Furrow*, 74 Kans. 101, 109, 85 Pac. 934 (1906).
[237] *Allison* v. *Linn*, 139 Wash. 474, 477-478, 247 Pac. 731 (1926).
[238] *Mogle* v. *Moore*, 16 Cal. (2d) 1, 9, 104 Pac. (2d) 785 (1940).
[239] *Brown* v. *Schneider*, 81 Kans. 486, 488, 106 Pac. 41 (1910).
[240] *Sanguinetti* v. *Pock*, 136 Cal. 466, 472, 69 Pac. 98 (1902).
[241] *Duckworth* v. *Watsonville Water & Light Co.*, 150 Cal. 520, 529, 89 Pac. 338 (1907); *Costello* v. *Bowen*, 80 Cal. App. (2d) 621, 627, 182 Pac. (2d) 615 (1947).
[242] *Costello* v. *Bowen*, 80 Cal. App. (2d) 621, 627, 182 Pac. (2d) 615 (1947).
[243] *Herminghaus* v. *Southern California Edison Co.*, 200 Cal. 81, 92, 252 Pac. 607 (1926).
[244] *Duckworth* v. *Watsonville Water & Light Co.*, 150 Cal. 520, 528-529, 89 Pac. 338 (1907); *Costello* v. *Bowen*, 80 Cal. App. (2d) 621, 627, 182 Pac. (2d) 615 (1947).
[245] *Rait* v. *Furrow*, 74 Kans. 101, 109, 85 Pac. 934 (1906).

water.[246] Under certain circumstances, the flow may disappear into the ground and thus join the ground water of the area.[247] In the above discussions of "Stream" and "Channel," it was brought out that the disappearance of stream water in the bed of a channel, followed by its reappearance downstream and establishment as the same flow of water, does not break the continuity of stream and channel and hence does not preclude classification of the entire structure as a watercourse.[248] Where the course of the water is not traced beyond the place at which it disappears in the stream channel, the watercourse ends at that place.

Permanence of Existence

The age of a watercourse is not determinative of its classification as such, provided that it has existed long enough to exhibit the elements of permanence and that it meets the other requirements of a watercourse.

Long existence persuasive in determining permanence.—Although the element of permanence is necessary, great age is not essential.[249] But a long existence undoubtedly lends weight to the requirements of definiteness, stability, and permanence, and its value in that regard has been recognized by many courts. Expressions in support of this that appear in reported decisions include statements or findings such as the following: the stream flows and has ever flowed;[250] many years of recurring flow;[251] a stream flowing intermittently for many years in a channel that is not ephemeral in character;[252] the stream has flowed in its present course more than 20 years;[253] the established condition has existed for more than 60 years;[254] the present situation has been the case so far as the memory of man runs;[255] the watercourse has existed from time immemorial.[256]

---

[246] *Sierra County* v. *Nevada County*, 155 Cal. 1, 8 99 Pac. 371 (1908); *Hutchinson* v. *Watson Slough Ditch Co.*, 16 Idaho 484, 488, 101 Pac. 1059 (1909); *Rait* v. *Furrow*, 74 Kans. 101, 109, 85 Pac. 934 (1906); *Mader* v. *Mettenbrink*, 159 Nebr. 118, 127, 65 N. W. (2d) 334 (1954).

[247] The stream may "percolate into the soil, or lose itself in some subterranean channel:" *Rait* v. *Furrow*, 74 Kans. 101, 109, 85 Pac. 934 (1906). Classification of a watercourse should not be affected by the eventual disappearance of the water into the ground: *Allison* v. *Linn*, 139 Wash. 474, 477-478, 247 Pac. 731 (1926).

[248] See *Strait* v. *Brown*, 16 Nev. 317, 323-324 (1881); *In re Johnson Creek*, 159 Wash. 629, 630, 294 Pac. 566 (1930). See *St. Paul Fire & Marine Ins. Co.* v. *Carroll*, 106 S. W. (2d) 757, 758 (Tex. Civ. App. 1937, error dismissed).

[249] *Scott* v. *Watkins*, 63 Idaho 506, 517, 122 Pac. (2d) 220 (1942).

[250] *Chicago, R.I. & P.Ry.* v. *Groves*, 20 Okla. 101, 118, 93 Pac. 755 (1908).

[251] *Hellman Commercial Trust & Savings Bank* v. *Southern Pacific Co.*, 190 Cal. 626, 634, 214 Pac. 46 (1923).

[252] *Hoefs* v. *Short*, 114 Tex. 501, 505, 510, 273 S. W. 785 (1925).

[253] *Popham* v. *Holloron*, 84 Mont. 442, 452-453, 275 Pac. 1099 (1929).

[254] *In re Bassett Creek and Its Tributaries*, 62 Nev. 461, 466-467, 155 Pac. (2d) 324 (1945).

[255] *Palmer* v. *Waddell*, 22 Kans. 352, 355-356 (1879); *Jaquez Ditch Co.* v. *Garcia*, 17 N. Mex. 160, 161, 124 Pac. 891 (1912).

[256] *Hansen* v. *Crouch*, 98 Oreg. 141, 146, 193 Pac. 454 (1920); *International & G. N. R. R.* v. *Reagan*, 121 Tex. 233, 242, 49 S. W. (2d) 414 (1932); *Doney* v. *Beatty*, 124 Mont. 41, 45, 220 Pac. (2d) 77 (1950).

But short existence alone does not bar permanence.—In 1906, the Kansas Supreme Court held in *Rait* v. *Furrow* that to give a stream the necessary degree of permanence in classifying it as a watercourse, it is not necessary that the stream shall have flowed in its present course for any particular length of time, provided that it now exhibits the attributes of permanence in its present course, this being a question of fact for the trial court to decide.[257] In this case, the watercourse had originated in a flood, prior to which time there had been no definite or visible channel or course formed by water flowing occasionally down a depression. The flood, however, did cut a channel, well defined with banks, down through the depression in which water flowed steadily. Counsel "plausibly contended" that the water had not flowed in the stream for such length of time as to indicate permanence; that as it had not flowed from time immemorial, it could not be regarded as an ancient watercourse. The matter of permanence, however, said the supreme court, is a question of fact for the trial court; and although the existence of the watercourse in litigation originated in a flood, and only a year or two earlier, the facts stated appeared to be sufficient to support the court's finding.

It is true that this decision in *Rait* v. *Furrow* implies that practically continuous flow of water is a prerequisite. On that point, it does not conform to the weight of authority as discussed above under "Stream—Continuity of Flow Generally not Required." The importance of the decision lies in its stressing of the element of permanence of supply, the determination of which is governed by present conditions and indications—not solely by long history, which is persuasive but not necessarily controlling. In this case, all the elements of a watercourse appeared to be permanent, even though of recent origin.

The precedent set by the Kansas court on this point was followed by the Supreme Court of Texas.[258] It was contended in this Texas case that a creek had not existed in 1874. The evidence showed that as early as 1884 or 1885 there was a channel, which at the time of the trial was well defined and in which water had been flowing for many years. Hence, the supreme court rejected the contention as to the effect of the absence of the stream in 1874. But besides, said the court, citing *Rait* v. *Furrow,* it is not necessary for the attachment of water rights to a stream that it should have crossed a particular tract of land for any particular length of time, if the stream now has a substantial existence and is of value as an irrigation stream.

Utility of the Watercourse

Value to adjacent lands.—An important but not essential characteristic of a watercourse is that it shall have flowed for such length of time and shall have attained a sufficient volume of water to furnish the advantages usually

[257] *Rait* v. *Furrow,* 74 Kans. 101, 102-104, 108-109, 85 Pac. 934 (1906).
[258] *Hoefs* v. *Short,* 114 Tex. 501, 510-511, 273 S. W. 785 (1925).

attendant upon streams. Thus, the stature of a watercourse may be attained where the channel carries a stream of water of such well-defined existence and size as to make its flow valuable to the owners of land along its course.[259]

This feature is not to be confused with the fact that there are times when the flow of a stream can be a detriment to the adjacent lands—a common phenomenon. That is, generally speaking, the stream is something of value to these lands, but when augmented with storm or floodwaters it is quite the reverse, unless provision is made for protection of the threatened lands[260] or for storage of the floodwaters.[261] The watercourse classification of a stream that is useful to the valley through which it flows is not affected by its behavior when overladen with storm waters.

Water rights.—The fact that a watercourse furnishes the advantages usually attendant upon streams of water may include its uses by appropriators of the water as well as by riparian landowners. If it is of this character, it may be held as it was in *Hoefs* v. *Short,* to meet the requirements of a natural watercourse to which water rights, whether riparian or by appropriation, attach.[262]

In *Hoefs* v. *Short,* the Texas Supreme Court was impressed by the facts that rainwater ran down Barilla Creek in sufficient quantity and with such regularity and frequency as to be valuable for irrigation, that for years people had been irrigating successfully from the creek, and that they were still doing so. Hence, the court reasoned that the facts as to bed, banks, and permanency of source of water supply were merely evidentiary that the stream could be used for exercising irrigation water rights. When the fact of utility is conceded or established, as here, said the court, the stream necessarily is one to which water rights attach, regardless of variations from the ideal stream of physiographers and meteorologists—conclusions supported not only by common sense and reason but by authority as well. Two years later, the same court applied the same principle to another Texas stream, in the section involved in litigation, "whether in flood stage, normal flow stage, or standing in pools."[263]

In holding that the flow from a certain spring constituted a watercourse, the Washington Supreme Court stated that: "Another thing should be taken into consideration. For many years appellant and his predecessors in interest had

---

[259] *Weck* v. *Los Angeles County Flood Control Dist.,* 104 Cal. App. (2d) 599, 609, 232 Pac. (2d) 293 (1951); *Jack* v. *Teegarden,* 151 Nebr. 309, 314, 37 N. W. (2d) 387 (1949); *Sun Underwriters Ins. Co. of New York* v. *Bunkley,* 233 S. W. (2d) 153, 156 (Tex. Civ. App. 1950, error refused).

[260] *Weck* v. *Los Angeles County Flood Control Dist.,* 104 Cal. App. (2d) 599, 609, 232 Pac. (2d) 293 (1951).

[261] *Motl* v. *Boyd,* 116 Tex. 82, 115-116, 286 S. W. 458 (1926).

[262] *Hoefs* v. *Short,* 114 Tex. 501, 506-507, 510, 273 S. W. 785 (1925).

[263] *Humphreys-Mexia Co.* v. *Arseneaux,* 116 Tex. 603, 610, 297 S. W. 225 (1927).

found sufficient water in the stream to divert it and thus supply their domestic and other purposes."[264]

The value of a stream in serving irrigation water rights—or water rights for other purposes—great as it is in western economy, is not essential to the classification of a watercourse. It is useful in reaching a decision, but other values will do. This point had the attention of the Texas Supreme Court in the case noted below under "Drainageway" in which it was held that the waters of Mineral Creek were those of a stream, not diffused surface waters.[265] In reaching this conclusion, the court made it clear that it was not saying that the creek was a stream to which riparian or statutory water rights may attach. That question was not before the court. It depended upon other factors not involved in the instant case, and its answer had no bearing on the immediate decision or on the classification of Mineral Creek therein.

Drainageway.—A watercourse has been held to exist even though it serves as a "mere channel" by means of which a particular watershed is drained.[266] It may also serve a useful purpose in carrying away water that otherwise would accumulate locally.[267]

However, not all channels are classed as watercourses simply because they serve as drainageways. Any local depression that slopes enough to carry water from the higher to the lower part of a small land area may serve this function, even though the only water that it carries at any time is short-lived runoff from rainfall on the immediate terrain. Undoubtedly, in most extreme cases of this character, the runoff would be classed as diffused surface water. In most parts of the country, more than the performance of this local drainage service would be needed to satisfy the requirements of a watercourse.

The importance of this feature of watercourse utility when it rises above small local service and actually benefits an entire community—as contrasted with the flow of diffused surface water—was emphasized by the Texas Supreme Court in a case involving a claim for flood damage.[268] Mineral Creek, the overflow from which was in litigation, was a substantial stream. It had tributaries and a substantial watershed. It carried water at least seasonally, and a great deal of water during periods of rainfall, in a well-defined channel. On the whole, said the court, the watercourse performed a necessary and

---

[264] *Allison* v. *Linn,* 139 Wash. 474, 477-478, 247 Pac. 731 (1926). A "never failing supply of water for the development of valuable grain lands:" *Popham* v. *Holloron,* 84 Mont. 442, 453, 275 Pac. 1099 (1929).

[265] *International & G. N. R. R.* v. *Reagan,* 121 Tex. 233, 240, 49 S. W. (2d) 414 (1932).

[266] *Costello* v. *Bowen,* 80 Cal. App. (2d) 621, 627, 182 Pac. (2d) 615 (1947).

[267] *Hansen* v. *Crouch,* 98 Oreg. 141, 146, 193 Pac. 454 (1920).

[268] *International & G. N. R. R.* v. *Reagan,* 121 Tex. 233, 238-240, 49 S. W. (2d) 414 (1932).

substantial service for a large territory, making its watershed tillable and habitable. It was not a mere rivulet into which surface water gathered from a diffused state before entering some streamway on its journey to the sea. What the court held and specifically intended to hold was that the waters in this creek were those of a substantial natural drainageway, to be governed by the law applicable to streams, as distinguished from the law that governs diffused surface waters.

Navigation.—The constitution of Texas, in declaring that the preservation and conservation of the natural resources of the State are public rights and duties, includes "the navigation of its inland and coastal waters."[269] And the State Supreme Court has said that title to the waters of the public navigable streams of Texas is in the State, in trust for the public, and that the use of the waters for navigation purposes concerns all the people and is ordinarily regarded as a superior right.[270]

Navigability has not—to the knowledge of the author—been included in the list of essential characteristics of a watercourse, in Texas or elsewhere. If it were, some very small streams of water flowing from springs that otherwise would qualify as watercourses would be ruled out. Small streams have been classified as watercourses without consideration of their potential in this regard, even under broad interpretations of a navigable stream. On the other hand, without the recognized attributes of a watercourse, the utility of flowing water for navigation purposes would be small or nonexistent. And so a stream of flowing water that is navigable in fact would almost certainly be possessed of these attributes.

Relation of Watercourse to Connected Sources of Water Supply

The term "watercourse" comprehends not only a stream of water and the reasonably definite channel in which it flows, but also " 'springs, lakes or marshes in which such a stream originates or through which it flows.' "[271]

Lakes and ponds.—As noted elsewhere (see chapter 2, above, and "Lakes and Ponds," below), a lake or pond is a compact body of water with defined boundaries, substantially at rest, and a pond is essentially a small lake.

Most western lakes are clearly connected with surface stream channels. The lake may constitute the source of a watercourse, or it may be the terminus of one or more, or it may be so situated that one stream flows into it and another flows out of it. A number of high-level lakes have several or even many small inlets and only one outlet. In such cases, the waters in the inlet and outlet

---

[269] Tex. Const., art. XVI, § 59(a).
[270] *Motl* v. *Boyd,* 116 Tex. 81, 111, 286 S. W. 458 (1926).
[271] *State* v. *Brace,* 76 N. Dak. 314, 322, 36 N. W. (2d) 330 (1949), quoting from Restatement of Torts § 841 (1939).

channels and in the lake itself are directly connected and constitute one source of water supply, for diversions from the inlet channel or channels reduce the quantity of water otherwise available in the lake and its outlet channel, and diversions from the lake itself reduce the available supply flowing in the outlet. From the standpoint of rights to the use of the common water supply, there is no fundamental distinction between such a lake and any wide portion of the main stream channel, where the question of maintenance of the natural water level is not the determining factor; each is an integral portion of the stream system, and in the absence of the question of maintenance of the water level, rights to the use of the water apparently are not affected by the precise characterization of the particular body of water as a lake or as a watercourse.

Lake: Integration of connected sources.—According to the California Supreme Court, a lake physically connected with a watercourse is legally a part of it. The fact that a flowing stream ends in a lake "will not defeat the right to make the statutory appropriation therefrom, and we can see no reason why the appropriation in such a case may not be made from the lake in which the stream terminates, and which therefore constitutes a part of it, as well as from any other part of the watercourse."[272]

In a Kansas case, the parties agreed, and the court so found, that Silver Lake, with the draw or ravine entering it from the west and with its outlet through the east end of the lake to the river, constituted a natural watercourse.[273] The relative water rights of owners of land along the lake were held to be those of riparian proprietors.

Lake: Reciprocal importance of lake level and outflow.—Lake levels are important to the use of littoral lands in several respects: (1) material lowering of the water moves the shoreline out and down and thus bares previously covered land, which may result in exposure of mudflats, stagnant waters, and impairment of recreational values of the littoral land; (2) material raising of the level causes flooding of previously uncovered land, which may result in flood damage and impairment of usefulness of the land; (3) excessive changes in level may complicate pumping diversions of water from the lake itself. Lake levels are important also to those who depend upon the outflow, which may be materially affected by artificial regulation of the level and by legal and contractual restrictions thereon.

Importance of relationships between water levels of a lake and outflow of water in the outlet channel may be illustrated by two examples in the Far West.

Lake Tahoe lies across the California-Nevada stateline. It has many definite inlets in the form of small streams, and but one outlet—Truckee River, which

---

[272] *Duckworth* v. *Watsonville Water & Light Co.,* 150 Cal. 520, 528-529, 89 Pac. 338 (1907).
[273] *Dougan* v. *Board of County Comm'rs.,* 141 Kans. 554, 562, 43 Pac. (2d) 223 (1935).

flows from the California side of the lake into Nevada. There the Truckee terminates in another lake—Pyramid Lake—which has no surface outlet. In the many-sided controversy over the waters of Lake Tahoe—which has persisted in one form or another for decades—have been questions of use of water of Truckee River, use of the lake for temporary storage of the inflow, damage from maintenance of high lake levels, maintenance of the natural rim at the outlet, water requirements within the Tahoe basin, protection against contamination of the marginal lake water by return flow in the form of sewage, and water requirements of the Pyramid Lake Indians. Negotiations are underway in an effort to consummate an interstate compact to provide an equitable solution for major water problems in the Tahoe basin and Truckee River watershed.[274]

The intrastate Clear Lake in California has a number of tributaries and one outlet—Cache Creek, which flows from the mountainous Clear Lake basin out upon the valley floor of Sacramento Valley and into Sacramento River. Early litigation involved conflicting claims, riparian and appropriative, to the use of waters of Cache Creek in the foothill and valley agricultural lands. What was apparently the first attempt to control the outlet of the lake by a milldam ended in 1868.[275] Forty-five years later, the owners of the irrigation company which had acquired the water rights on Cache Creek built a dam at the lake outlet to control the flow into Cache Creek. In 1920, during an extremely dry period, the company was contemplating a deepening of the outlet channel to increase the outflow into Cache Creek when a proceeding was commenced

---

[274] Much pertinent information and analysis of Tahoe water problems are brought together by King, Keith C., and Warren, Earl, Jr., "The Tahoe Controversy—Compact or Litigation?" (December 16, 1959), published by California-Nevada Interstate Compact Commission of California, Sacramento, California.

[275] The dam was so operated as to cause flooding of littoral land and, after ineffective recourse to the courts, it was destroyed by a mob: U.S. Dept. Agr. Bull. 100, "Report of Irrigation Investigations in California": Wilson, J. M. "Irrigation Investigations on Cache Creek," pp. 182-183 (1901). This article states that "tradition reports that the presiding judge, whose sympathies were evidently with the sufferers," decided that his court could furnish no legal remedy but "intimated that there was a law 'higher than statute or procedure of court,' which when the necessity arose might be invoked. A few days later a force of citizens of Lake County appeared at the mill, and, after carefully removing everything that was movable, destroyed the works. This was in 1868. The milldam and mill were never replaced, but Lake County is still paying interest on bonds issued to liquidate the damages incurred through this appeal to 'higher law.' "

Harding, S. T., "Water in California," p. 36 (1960), cites this Clear Lake-Cache Creek incident as an example of well-organized "extralegal" action in solving water rights problems. After describing the circumstances in detail, he refers to reports of the group action as including accounts of its organization, placing of pickets to prevent seeking of outside relief, and its general military type, and concludes by stating that while it was sometimes referred to as "riot action," nevertheless it was not the usual impulsive type of action but a deliberate and planned undertaking.

which resulted in the stipulated "Gopcevic decree." This decree permanently enjoined the company from deepening the outlet excessively, fixed maximum and minimum lake levels, and placed restrictions on the rapidity with which the level might be reduced. All this was for the purpose of allowing the company to impound floodwaters and to withdraw them for irrigation downstream, while at the same time affording the protection of a fixed water level to Lakeport, the county seat, and to the owners of homes, farms, and resorts on the lake borders.[276] The Gopcevic decree thus placed an effective legal limit upon the extent to which Clear Lake could be used as a storage reservoir for the service of downstream lands.[277]

Other surface sources.—The oft repeated statement that a watercourse usually discharges its flow into some other watercourse[278] takes on special significance when one considers the structure of a surface stream system (see "Definition and General Description—The Surface Stream System," above), which comprises a main watercourse and its branches or tributaries of varying size, many of which are themselves classifiable as watercourses.

Interconnection of watercourses and sloughs, and the legal implications thereof, have also been noted in various cases.[279] The same comment applies to interconnection of a swamp or marsh with a river.[280]

Some springs contribute to the supply of watercourses, and others do not. The association between headsprings and watercourses has been noted above under "Source of Supply—Spring water."

Ground waters.—A phenomenon of vital importance in the hydrology and water-rights jurisprudence of the West is the association of surface streams and ground waters, which together comprise most of the water to which rights of use attach. The physical interconnections are referred to in chapter 2 and under "Source of Supply—Percolating ground water," above. The legal implications are discussed later, in chapter 19.

---

[276] The Gopcevic decree provided that a specified higher rise in level for specified time periods by reason of storm or flood conditions beyond control of the company should not be deemed a violation of the decree. A judgment against the company for contempt of court in allowing the lake level to remain above the maximum for a period longer than authorized by the decree was affirmed by the California District Court of Appeal; *Clear Lake Water Co.* v. *Superior Court of Mendocino County,* 33 Cal. App. (2d) 710, 92 Pac. (2d) 921 (1939).

[277] An authoritative statement of the Clear Lake-Cache Creek relationship, based upon exhaustive research, is presented by More, Rosemary Macdonald, "The Influence of Water-rights Litigation upon Irrigation Farming in Yolo County, California," thesis submitted for the degree of Master of Arts in Geography, University of California (1960).

[278] For example, *Sierra County* v. *Nevada County,* 155 Cal. 1, 8, 99 Pac. 371 (1908); *Hutchinson* v. *Watson Slough Ditch Co.,* 16 Idaho 484, 488, 101 Pac. 1059 (1909).

[279] See *Turner* v. *James Canal Co.,* 155 Cal. 82, 87-88, 91-92, 99 Pac. 520 (1909); *Herminghaus* v. *Southern California Edison Co.,* 200 Cal. 81, 92, 252 Pac. 607 (1926); *Bachman* v. *Reynolds Irr. Dist.,* 56 Idaho 507, 512, 55 Pac. (2d) 1314 (1936).

[280] *Hall* v. *Webb,* 66 Cal. App. 416, 420, 226 Pac. 403 (1924).

FLOODFLOWS
Classification
Use of Terms

In ordinary parlance, a flood may be a high moving body of water whether (1) confined within the banks of a stream channel or (2) overflowing the banks. As the swelling waters of a stream rise toward the tops of the banks, the stream is "in flood," whether or not the water actually spills over the top and inundates the adjacent land.

There is no uniform concept of "flood" in the water rights decisions of the West. In many of them, the term is used without particular attention to the confined or unconfined state of the high waters. Thus, the Texas Supreme Court defines "floodwaters" as those waters that rise above the line of highest ordinary flow of a stream;[281] and the Texas Court of Civil Appeals has added to this the concept that "generally speaking, [they] have overflowed a river, stream or natural watercourse and have formed a continuous body with the water flowing in the ordinary channel."[282] In the last cited case the court, in construing the language of a policy that insured against loss or damage caused by a "Flood (meaning the rising of natural bodies of water)," held that water that ran into certain chickenhouses was not backed up from a river, creek, or other natural watercourse and must be regarded as diffused surface water, not as a flood within the meaning of the insurance policy.

The Nebraska and Washington supreme courts apply the term "floodwater" to the water flowing within the flood channel or flood plain of a stream.[283]

In California and Arizona, waters that have escaped from a stream in great volume and are "flowing wild" over the country are characterized as "floodwaters."[284] The purpose of this classification is to distinguish these flows from diffused surface waters, which also flow vagrantly over the country but are not, in these jurisdictions, waters that have escaped from a watercourse. In California, however, high waters within stream channels, and those that

---

[281] *Motl* v. *Boyd,* 116 Tex. 82, 111, 286 S. W. 458 (1926); *Texas Co.* v. *Burkett,* 117 Tex. 16, 28, 296 S. W. 273 (1927).

[282] *Sun Underwriters Ins. Co. of New York* v. *Bunkley,* 233 S. W. (2d) 153, 155 (Tex. Civ. App. 1950, error refused).

[283] *Courter* v. *Maloley,* 152 Nebr. 476, 486, 41 N. W. (2d) 732 (1950); *Bahm* v. *Ralkes,* 160 Nebr. 503, 514-515, 70 N. W. (2d) 507 (1955); *Sund* v. *Keating,* 43 Wash. (2d) 36, 41-45, 259 Pac. (2d) 1113 (1953).

[284] *Mogle* v. *Moore,* 16 Cal. (2d) 1, 9, 104 Pac. (2d) 785 (1940); *Everett* v. *Davis,* 18 Cal. (2d) 389, 393, 115 Pac. (2d) 821 (1941); *Southern Pacific Co.* v. *Proebstel,* 61 Ariz. 412, 416-420, 150 Pac. (2d) 81 (1944).

overflow in periodically inundating adjacent lands but that eventually recede into the channel, are also spoken of as floodwaters.[285]

The term "overflow" as used in these high stream water cases refers to the water that overtops the banks of a main stream channel, or that escapes from the flood plain of the watercourse. A flood overflow at a particular time may be classified as part of the watercourse, or as escaped floodwater, or as diffused surface water, depending upon the physical factual situation at such time and on the particular jurisdiction in which it occurs.

Purpose of Classification

Principles governing the classification of floodwaters are developed in connection with actions based upon the physical damage to property caused by obstruction or deflection of flow of the water, and have been chiefly of importance in determining the liability for such damage. Often these obstructions were caused by railway embankments, or by levees built to protect riparian lands from floods. Liability for damage, then, usually depended upon the classification of the flood as ordinary or extraordinary, or the classification of the overflow as part of the stream or as diffused surface water.

In other cases, the classification of floodwaters has been important in connection with water rights controversies. This has occurred in some cases in which riparian owners have claimed that the natural overflows benefited their lands, as distinguished from cases in which they complained of injury caused from obstruction or deflection of the water by others; and in other cases where rights to the use of water have been involved in distinctions between ordinary flows and floodflows in the stream.

Questions of rights and liabilities are considered below under "Collateral Questions Respecting Watercourses." First, the physical features will be discussed.

Ordinary and Extraordinary Floods

The distinction between floods which are "usual and ordinary" and those that are "unprecedented and extraordinary" is an old one. In a Mississippi River case, Chief Justice Brewer pointed out the ancient recognition of the duty not to unduly change the flow of a river by works constructed for individual benefit, as qualified by the limitation that individuals could protect their property from the consequences of "accidental or extraordinary" floods.[286] He added that the limitation is recognized in this country as well,

---

[285] See *Miller & Lux* v. *Madera Canal & Irr. Co.*, 155 Cal. 59, 76-80, 99 Pac. 502 (1907); *Collier* v. *Merced Irr. Dist.*, 213 Cal. 554, 558, 2 Pac. (2d) 790 (1931); *Chowchilla Farms* v. *Martin*, 219 Cal. 1, 36-38, 25 Pac. (2d) 435 (1933); *Peabody* v. *Vallejo*, 2 Cal. (2d) 351, 368, 40 Pac. (2d) 486 (1935).

[286] *Cubbins* v. *Mississippi River Comm'n.*, 241 U.S. 351, 366-367 (1916).

"although it is true to say that much contrariety and confusion exist in the adjudged cases as to when it is applicable, some cases extending the rule so far as to virtually render the limitation inoperative, others extending the limitation to such a degree as really to cause it to abrogate the rule itself."

The distinction, rather widely recognized at one time, has become of less importance—perhaps because of the difficulty in making the distinction, and the growing tendency to call a high proportion of all floods "usual and ordinary."[287] In various jurisdictions, however, it still prevails.

Distinctions

Ordinary floods.—Floods or freshets that occur annually with practical regularity cannot be said to be unprecedented or extraordinary.[288] In a Nebraska case, the evidence disclosed that floods, like the one in instant litigation, were likely to occur annually, hence did not conform to the concept of a flood that is not only extraordinary but unprecedented and not reasonably to be foreseen.[289] If floods regarded as unusual have actually occurred again and again even at irregular intervals, it is only reasonable to anticipate that they will recur in the future.[290]

Decisions of the California Supreme Court with respect to major streams rising in the Sierra Nevada and flowing down into the San Joaquin Valley have been uniformly to the effect that the high waters thereof were flows that were expected annually and hence not unusual, extraordinary, or unexpected.[291] In an early case, the Supreme Court of California observed that "Nor can that flow be said to be an extraordinary flood which can be counted on as certain to occur annually, and to continue for months."[292]

In an early Texas case, it was held that a defense that floods not provided for have occurred only at long intervals will not avail a party who knows that an unprecedented inundation has occurred more than once and for that reason may occur again.[293]

On the Pacific Coast, when discussing a heavy rainfall of flood proportions in recent years, the Oregon Supreme Court said that:[294]

---

[287]See discussions of the distinction in Annots., 16 A.L.R. 629, 634 (1922), 23 A. L. R. (2d) 750, 757 (1952).

[288]*Longmire* v. *Yakima Highlands Irr. & Land Co.*, 95 Wash. 302, 305-306, 163 Pac. 782 (1917). See *Still* v. *Palouse Irr. & Power Co.*, 64 Wash. 606, 609-610, 117 Pac. 466 (1911).

[289]*Clark* v. *Cedar County*, 118 Nebr. 465, 468-470, 225 N. W. 235 (1929).

[290]*Kansas City* v. *King*, 65 Kans. 64, 66-67, 68 Pac. 1093 (1902). Repetition even at uncertain intervals does not take the flood out of the classification as "ordinary": *Jefferson* v. *Hicks*, 23 Okla. 684, 686-687, 102 Pac. 79 (1909).

[291] Hutchins, Wells A., "The California Law of Water Rights," p. 26 (1956).

[292] *Heilbron* v. *Fowler Switch Canal Co.*, 75 Cal. 426, 432, 17 Pac. 535 (1888).

[293] *Gulf, C. & S. F. Ry.* v. *Pomeroy*, 67 Tex. 498, 502, 3 S. W. 722 (1887).

[294]*Schweiger* v. *Solbeck*, 191 Oreg. 454, 464, 230 Pac. (2d) 195 (1951), quoted with approval in *Wellman* v. *Kelley*, 197 Oreg. 553, 561, 252 Pac. (2d) 816 (1953).

Taking into consideration the heavy rainfall which is normal in the area involved in this case, it is impossible to conclude from the evidence that that which immediately preceded the disaster was at all extraordinary. It was a heavy rain, but not of unprecedented proportions. In its occurrence and magnitude, it might have been anticipated by a person of reasonable prudence. * * *

Extraordinary floods.—In this category, the Texas Supreme Court has placed "an extraordinary and unprecedented flood * * * of such a size as had not been known or heard of before, and which a person of ordinary care and prudence, under the circumstances, could not have foreseen or anticipated, * * *."[295] To the same effect, in an Oregon case, it is said that "An extraordinary flood is one 'whose comings are not foreshadowed by the usual course of nature, and whose magnitude and destructiveness could not have been anticipated or provided against by the exercise of ordinary foresight.' "[296]

In accord with the foregoing is an early Kansas statement that in constructing railway lines across watercourses, railroads were not bound to anticipate extraordinary changes of seasons, nor unusual freshets or rainfalls, that could not be detected by a skillful and careful appraisal of the local situation, "nor to guard against every possible contingency."[297]

Criteria

In a North Dakota case decided in 1950, the undisputed testimony was that the waters of the flood in litigation were greater in volume and rose higher than had ever before occurred within the recollection or knowledge of any of the witnesses, some of whom had been living in the vicinity for 40 or more years.[298] A United States Weather Bureau published report received in evidence tended to corroborate this testimony; but it also showed that floods on this and other tributaries of the Missouri River in this area were not unusual, particularly at the time of the spring runoff, and that ice jams or gorges were often formed. Also, one witness testified that a few years prior to the instant flood there was another almost as great as this one. The court said that:

In passing upon the question of whether a flood is extraordinary and unprecedented it is proper and necessary to consider the topography of the area traversed and drained by the flooded stream; the climatic conditions ordinarily prevailing there; whether the stream is subject to ice jams during the spring run-off; the character of tributary streams as to their volume and velocity; the laws of hydraulics known to the ordinary man; the extent of

---

[295] *Fort Worth & D. C. Ry.* v. *Kiel,* 143 Tex. 601, 605-606, 187 S. W. (2d) 371 (1945).
[296] *Schweiger* v. *Solbeck,* 191 Oreg. 454, 464, 230 Pac. (2d) 195 (1951), quoting from 56 Am. Jur. *Waters* § 91 (1945).
[297] *Union Trust Co.* v. *Cuppy,* 26 Kans. 754, 762-763 (1882).
[298] *Ferderer* v. *Northern Pac. Ry.,* 77 N. Dak. 169, 181-182, 42 N. W. (2d) 216 (1950).

the drainage area; the existence or non-existence of conditions tending to retard the flow of the water therein; and whether there have been other floods and the frequency and magnitude thereof. If all the attendant conditions and circumstances are such that men of ordinary experience and prudence reasonably could have foreseen that such a flood as did occur might occur, it would not be extraordinary and unprecedented within the meaning of those terms as they were defined in the instructions to the jury. The question is one of fact, to be determined as any other question of fact. In the instant case the evidence is such that reasonable men might differ as to the answer to be made to the special interrogatory. Therefore, we cannot say that the jury's determination was not warranted by the evidence.

The jury found the flood in question to be not extraordinary and unprecedented.

Flood Overflows

Much water which, in times of flood, overflows the banks of a stream and inundates adjacent lands, drains back into the stream channel as the flood subsides. Part of the overflow, however, may become completely and permanently separated from the stream; and of this, part may join another stream, and part may spread out over marshy land and there evaporate or seep into the soil.

In a 1953 case the Washington Supreme Court spoke of the "almost incredible conflict of authorities" as to when and under what circumstances floodwaters of a stream become diffused surface waters, so as to be governed by the rules relating to the latter rather than by the rules applicable to water of watercourses.[299]

The principle that diffused surface water, on joining the flowing stream of a watercourse and becoming subject to its current, ceases to possess the characteristics of vagrant diffused surface water and becomes part of the stream both physically and legally, is supported in the West by the great weight of authority. (See "Elements of Watercourse–Source of Supply–Diffused Surface Water," above.) It is the classification of stream waters–whatever their origin–on overflowing the stream banks in times of flood that has involved both real and apparent conflicts.

Overflows not Separated from the Stream

The general rule.–The more generally accepted rule is that floodwater overflowing the banks of a stream channel, not becoming permanently separated from the stream but receding into the main channel as the flood subsides, is classified as a part of the stream, not as diffused surface water.

"It is well determined by the authorities," said the California Supreme Court a half century ago, "that waters flowing under circumstances such as

---

[299] *Sund* v. *Keating,* 43 Wash. (2d) 36, 42, 259 Pac. (2d) 1113 (1953).

these, notwithstanding they may consist of a large expanse of water on either side of the main channel, constitute but a single watercourse and that riparian rights pertain to the whole of it."[300] The Oregon Supreme Court has reaffirmed the principle that so long as overflow waters form one continuous body, flowing in the ordinary course of the stream and returning to the natural channel as they recede, they are waters of a watercourse, although not confined within the banks of the stream.[301] And there have been decisions in some other States to the same effect.[302]

Some of the decisions—chiefly but not wholly the more recent ones—specifically adopt the "flood plain" or "flood channel" concept of a watercourse in time of high floods. As above noted (see "Elements of Watercourse—Channel—Flood plain"), the flood channel or flood plain of a live ordinary stream has been defined as the land adjacent to the ordinary channel which is overflowed in times of high water, from which the floodwater returns to the main channel at lower points as the flood subsides.

Thus, in 1953, the Washington Supreme Court, discussing the authorities, held that (1) a stream must be viewed as consisting of its normal banks and what is termed its "flood channel"; (2) that so long as overflow waters remain within this flood channel, these overflow floodwaters are properly classified as riparian waters rather than diffused surface waters; and (3) that being riparian waters, the rules relating to watercourses would apply.[303] (Previous holdings of the Washington court are noted below.)

The Nebraska Supreme Court, declaring in a series of decisions its adherence to this rule, designated the water flowing in the flood channel or flood plain as "floodwater."[304]

The situation in Washington.—In 1896, the Washington Supreme Court held that water escaping from a river in time of flood was diffused surface water—an outlaw and a common enemy.[305] The overflow water in litigation in this case gathered in a low part of plaintiff's land, where it "passes off through the soil, or sinks beneath the surface." Such water of course had permanently escaped from the stream channel. This holding has been reaffirmed in decisions in which the significance of the return, or failure to return, of the escaped waters to the original stream was not dwelt upon. In one of them, in which the rim of

---

[300] *Miller & Lux* v. *Madera Canal & Irr. Co.,* 155 Cal. 59, 77, 99 Pac. 502 (1907).

[301] *Wellman* v. *Kelley,* 197 Oreg. 553, 565, 252 Pac. (2d) 816 (1953).

[302] See *Broadway Mfg. Co.* v. *Leavenworth Terminal Ry. & Bridge Co.,* 81 Kans. 616, 621-622, 106 Pac. 1034 (1910), supplanting the opposite principle declared in *Missouri Pacific Ry.* v. *Keys,* 55 Kans. 205, 216-218, 40 Pac. 275 (1895); *Wine* v. *Northern Pacific Ry.,* 48 Mont. 200, 208, 136 Pac. 387 (1913); *Buchanan* v. *Seim,* 104 Nebr. 444, 446, 177 N. W. 751 (1920); *Franks* v. *Rouse,* 192 Okla. 520, 137 Pac. (2d) 899 (1943); *Bass* v. *Taylor,* 126 Tex. 522, 529, 90 S. W. (2d) 811 (1936).

[303] *Sund* v. *Keating,* 43 Wash. (2d) 36, 42-45, 259 Pac. (2d) 1113 (1953). See also *Bass* v. *Taylor,* 126 Tex. 522, 529-530, 90 S. W. (2d) 811 (1936).

[304] See *Bahm* v. *Raikes,* 160 Nebr. 503, 514-515, 70 N. W. (2d) 507 (1955).

[305] *Cass* v. *Dicks,* 14 Wash. 75, 77, 44 Pac. 113 (1896).

the channel was higher than adjoining bottom land except at certain points where it was "broken by natural watercourses running into said river," high waters overflowing the banks in time of flood continued to flow in the same general direction as the channel, "and such portions thereof as do not flow over the rim, are discharged into the channel of the river when the flood subsides, through numerous natural water courses and channels, carrying and draining themselves into the river."[306] In another one, the overflow waters returned to the stream "by way of Lincoln Creek," a tributary located apparently at the west end of the flooded area.[307] A third case involved the navigability of a "slough" for transporting logs, and the right to protect land against floodwaters that escaped into the "alleged sloughs" from the banks of a river during freshets.[308] According to the findings of the trial judge, there were certain "depressions or sloughs, more or less well defined, * * * with an outlet towards the southwest over the adjoining land to the Snoqualmie River; * * *." The opinion of the supreme court contained no statement as to the possibility, or otherwise, of these overflow waters draining back into the river as the floods subsided.

In all these cases, the overflow waters were held to be diffused surface water, an outlaw and common enemy, without reference to the question of their eventually returning or not returning to the river. Nor was the question raised in the opinion of the supreme court in *Sund* v. *Keating,* decided in 1953, in which several of the previous decisions were reviewed.[309]

The case of *Sund* v. *Keating* is important not only in reaffirming the diffused surface water principle, but in explaining its development, in substance as follows: In *Cass* v. *Dicks,* because the floodwaters were not confined within the channel of a natural watercourse, it was assumed without discussion that the case was governed by the law of diffused surface waters. In the *Harvey* case, noting that the floodwaters had already escaped over the banks of the stream, they were treated as diffused surface water on the authority of *Cass* v. *Dicks.* And in *Morton* v. *Hines,* the rule was accepted that waters *escaping* from the banks of a stream become diffused surface water, subject to the laws applicable thereto.[310] As above stated, the opinion in *Sund* v. *Keating* took no notice of the question of complete separation or eventual return of the escaped waters to the stream. Actually, this question was not involved in the case's factual situation. The controversy arose over the artificial

---

[306] *Harvey* v. *Northern Pacific Ry.,* 63 Wash. 669, 671, 673, 674-677, 116 Pac. 464 (1911). This factual statement was taken from the amended complaint, the sufficiency of which was said by the supreme court to be the "only question before us."

[307] *Morton* v. *Hines,* 112 Wash. 612, 617-619, 192 Pac. 1016 (1920).

[308] *Healy* v. *Everett & Cherry Valley Traction Co.,* 78 Wash. 628, 631, 634-635, 139 Pac. 609 (1914).

[309] *Sund* v. *Keating,* 43 Wash. (2d) 36, 41-42, 259 Pac. (2d) 1113 (1953).

[310] Also cited was *De Ruwe* v. *Morrison,* 28 Wash. (2d) 797, 184 Pac. (2d) 273 (1947), but not *Healy* v. *Everett & Cherry Valley Traction Co.,* 78 Wash. 628, 139 Pac. 609 (1914).

cutting of a streambank through which damaging floodwaters were allowed to escape—interference, that is, not with escaped floodwaters, but with the natural flow of floodwaters within the stream channel. Continuing, the supreme court stated that in none of the cited cases had it been decided whether floodwaters, *still remaining* within the confines of the flood channel of a stream, are an integral part of the watercourse or whether they have become diffused surface water. The court then held in *Sund* v. *Keating,* as noted above under "The general rule," that the floodwaters remained a part of the watercourse—that unless floodwaters top the banks of the flood channel or escape from some *natural* outlet, they are riparian in character, interference with which (except in the exercise of a lawful riparian right) to the damage of others is actionable.[311]

As a result of the foregoing decisions, the rule in Washington appears to be that floodwaters remain part of the watercourse while they remain within the flood plain of the stream, but on escaping therefrom they become diffused surface waters—the significance of their eventually returning to the stream, over the banks or by way of tributary channels, having not been specifically passed upon by the supreme court.

Overflows Permanently Escaped from the Stream

No contact with any watercourse.—Overflows that escape from a stream and that fail to rejoin the original stream or to flow into any other one are no longer waters of a watercourse, and the rules governing watercourses are no longer applicable.[312] There is no serious conflict of authority on this. The courts are not agreed, however, as to how these escaped waters should be classified.

Classification: Diffused surface water.—In most western jurisdictions in which litigation on this matter has reached the high courts, "Overflow water that escapes from the banks of a running stream, and that does not return to its banks, nor find its way to another stream or watercourse," is classified as diffused surface water.[313]

Overflow water that "has ceased to be a part of a general current following the channel," and that "spreads out over the open country and settles in stagnant pools or finds some other outlet," loses its character as part of the watercourse and becomes diffused surface water.[314]

---

[311] The court reached a similar conclusion in a 1967 case. *Marshland Flood Control District of Snohomish County* v. *Great Northern Railway Co.,* 71 Wash. (2d) 365, 428 Pac. (2d) 531 (1968). In this case, the court relied heavily upon *Conger* v. *Pierce County,* 116 Wash. 27, 198 Pac. 377 (1921).

[312] *Brinegar* v. *Copass,* 77 Nebr. 241, 243-244, 109 N. W. 173 (1906).

[313] *Hengelfelt* v. *Ehrmann,* 141 Nebr. 322, 327, 3 N. W. (2d) 576 (1942). This is the case with respect to overflow waters separated from the main body and spread out over the adjoining country without following any definite watercourse or channel: *Wellman* v. *Kelley,* 197 Oreg. 553, 565, 252 Pac. (2d) 816 (1953). Likewise with respect to overflow waters that escape from the flood plain of the stream: *Sund* v. *Keating,* 43 Wash. (2d) 36, 41-44, 259 Pac. (2d) 1113 (1953).

[314] *Broadway Mfg. Co.* v. *Leavenworth Terminal Ry. & Bridge Co.,* 81 Kans. 616, 622, 106 Pac. 1034 (1910). This is so if the floodwater leaves the main current "never to return." *Fordham* v. *Northern Pacific Ry.,* 30 Mont. 421, 431, 76 Pac. 1040 (1904).

Classification: Floodwater. —Waters that were once part of a stream or other body of water and that have escaped therefrom and overflow the adjacent territory are defined in the judicial nomenclature of California as "flood waters."[315] Implicit in their definition is the element of abnormality, in that they escape from the usual channels under conditions which do not ordinarily occur. Therefore, they can never be the flow of a stream at the end of its channel.[316]

Floodwaters are extraordinary vagrant waters which will not return to the stream when the high water therein recedes.[317] They retain their character as such while "flowing wild" over the country.[318] The essential distinction between floodwaters and diffused surface waters—both of which may be "flowing wild" over the country—is that floodwaters have broken away from a watercourse, whereas diffused surface waters have not yet become part of a watercourse.[319]

The fact that floodwaters happen to follow some natural channel, gully, or depression after breaking away from the stream does not affect their character as floodwaters or give to the course which they follow the character of a natural watercourse.[320]

The Arizona Supreme Court has adopted the classification of escaping overflow waters as floodwaters, and the distinction between floodwaters and diffused surface waters, as developed in the courts of California.[321]

Rejoinder with Original Watercourse

A conflict in the authorities exists with respect to overflows that escape from the original stream but eventually rejoin it. The Nebraska Supreme Court held that overflow waters do not cease to be a part of the stream unless or until separated therefrom so as to prevent their return to its channel.[322] In Washington, on the other hand, overflow waters that escaped from streams but returned at lower points by way of tributary channels were classified as outlaw

---

[315] *Everett* v. *Davis,* 18 Cal. (2d) 389, 393, 395, 115 Pac. (2d) 821 (1941).

[316] In *Everett* v. *Davis,* 18 Cal. (2d) 389, 394-395, 115 Pac. (2d) 821 (1941), the court corrected a statement that it had made during the preceding year, in *Mogle* v. *Moore,* 16 Cal. (2d) 1, 12, 104 Pac. (2d) 785 (1940), to the effect that flood waters constituted overflow waters whether they escaped over the stream banks "or at the end of the channel."

[317] *Costello* v. *Bowen,* 80 Cal. App. (2d) 621, 629, 182 Pac. (2d) 615 (1947).

[318] *Mogle* v. *Moore,* 16 Cal. (2d) 1, 9, 104 Pac. (2d) 785 (1940).

[319] *McManus* v. *Otis,* 61 Cal. App. (2d) 432, 440, 143 Pac. (2d) 380 (1943).

[320] *Id.*

[321] *Southern Pacific Co.* v. *Proebstel,* 61 Ariz. 412, 416-420, 150 Pac. (2d) 81 (1944); *Maricopa County M.W.C. Dist.* v. *Warford,* 69 Ariz. 1, 12, 206 Pac. (2d) 1168 (1949); *Diedrich* v. *Farnsworth,* 100 Ariz. 269, 413 Pac. (2d) 774 (1966).

[322] *Brineger* v. *Copass,* 77 Nebr. 241, 243-244, 109 N. W. 173 (1906). The question has been settled in this State: *Murphy* v. *Chicago B. & Q. R.R.,* 101 Nebr. 73, 77, 161 N. W. 1048 (1917).

or diffused surface waters.[323] (See "Overflows not Separated from the Stream—The situation in Washington," above.) Had they never left the flood plain of the original stream, these waters would have remained part of the watercourse.[324]

Joinder with Another Watercourse

Some authority exists for classification of overflow floodwater in the unusual situation in which it separates completely from the original stream and joins another one. The Oklahoma Supreme Court held that waters that overflowed the banks of a stream and pursued "a general course back into the same water course, or into another watercourse, although they do not follow a channel with well-defined banks," did not become diffused surface water but continued to be floodwaters of the watercourse.[325] The same rule was applied by the Nebraska Supreme Court to overflow waters that separated completely from Omaha Creek and followed a slight natural depression, in a definite and well-defined course, to an outlet in a lake or lakebed about 2 miles away.[326]

COLLATERAL QUESTIONS RESPECTING WATERCOURSES

Overflows: Rights of Landowners

Rights of landowners with respect to flood overflows are in two categories: (1) The right to protect their lands from inundation; and (2) the right to have the overflows occur naturally for beneficial use. The first case thus involves avoidance and riddance of the floodwaters; the second, their unobstructed overflow for natural irrigation of the contiguous land.

Protection of Lands Against Inundation

The rules with respect to the right of a landowner to embank against flood overflows for the protection of his land vary from one western jurisdiction to another. Variations relate to distinctions between so-called ordinary and extraordinary floods; to floodwaters in the streamway and floodwaters escaped from it; and to the right to protect lands and the limitations upon this right. The general western situation can best be described by noting briefly the rules in several of the States which, in the aggregate, include probably most of the important points that have been litigated in the high courts.

---

[323] *Harvey* v. *Northern Pacific Ry.*, 63 Wash. 669, 674-677, 116 Pac. 464 (1911); *Morton* v. *Hines*, 112 Wash. 612, 617, 192 Pac. 1016 (1920).

[324] See *Sund* v. *Keating*, 43 Wash. (2d) 36, 41-42, 259 Pac. (2d) 1113 (1953).

[325] *Jefferson* v. *Hicks*, 23 Okla. 684, 692-693, 102 Pac. 79 (1909), restated in the syllabus by the court in *Franks* v. *Rouse*, 192 Okla. 520, 137 Pac. (2d) 899 (1943).

[326] *Murphy* v. *Chicago, B. & Q. R.R.*, 101 Nebr. 73, 77-80, 161 N. W. 1048 (1917). Twenty-five years later, in *Hengelfelt* v. *Ehrmann*, 141 Nebr. 322, 327, 3 N. W. (2d) 576 (1942), this court quoted from one of its previous decisions to the effect that overflow water that escapes from the banks of a running stream, "and that does not return to its banks, nor find its way to another stream or watercourse," is diffused surface water.

California.—Flood overflows of rivers are a common enemy which may be guarded against or warded off by one whose property is invaded or threatened, by structures that are merely defensive in nature and not calculated to interfere with the current of the water in its natural channel.[327] A landowner who takes these measures to protect his lands is not liable for damage to lower and adjoining lands by exclusion of floodwaters from his own property, even though the damage to the other lands is increased thereby. Owners of these other lands have not only the same right, but also the duty of self-protection.[328] These rights and responsibilities of landowners apply to streamflows without regard to their so-called ordinary or extraordinary character.

The same principles apply both to the right of a landowner to build works that will confine these high waters in the stream channel, and to his right to protect his land against floodwaters that have escaped from the stream and are "flowing wild" over the country. For that purpose, he may obstruct the flow of these floodwaters onto his land, even though such obstruction causes the water to flow onto the land of another.[329]

Idaho.—Owners of lands abutting upon a stream have the right to place such barriers as will prevent their lands from being overflowed or damaged by the stream and for the purpose of keeping it within its natural channel.[330] This is particularly true with respect to streams that have well-defined banks and a permanent channel or bed. With respect to other streams, the courts must take into consideration the facts and conditions concerning the stream in litigation.[331]

Kansas—Distinctions between ordinary and extraordinary floods have been recognized, chiefly in the settlement of controversies over railroad structures across and along watercourses. The requirement was that provision be made for ordinary floods.[332]

Overflows that subsequently rejoin a stream remain a part of it; but overflow water permanently separated from a watercourse loses its character as stream water and becomes diffused surface water.[333] The flow of the latter may not be obstructed to the damage of an upper owner.[334]

---

[327] *Weinberg Co.* v. *Bixby*, 185 Cal. 87, 95, 96, 101, 196 Pac. 25 (1921).

[328] *Clement* v. *State Reclamation Bd.*, 35 Cal. (2d) 628, 635-636, 642-643, 220 Pac. (2d) 897 (1950).

[329] *Mogle* v. *Moore*, 16 Cal. (2d) 1, 10, 12, 104 Pac. (2d) 785 (1940); *Horton* v. *Goodenough*, 184 Cal. 451, 452-453, 194 Pac. 34 (1920).

[330] *Fischer* v. *Davis*, 19 Idaho 493, 498-499, 116 Pac. 412 (1911); *Boise Development Co.* v. *Idaho Trust & Savings Bank*, 24 Idaho 36, 51-53, 133 Pac. 916 (1913).

[331] *Fischer* v. *Davis*, 24 Idaho 216, 229-230, 133 Pac. 910 (1913).

[332] See *Clement* v. *Phoenix Utility Co.*, 119 Kans. 190, 195-197, 237 Pac. 1062 (1925).

[333] *Broadway Mfg. Co.* v. *Leavenworth Terminal Ry. & Bridge Co.*, 81 Kans. 616, 622, 106 Pac. 1034 (1910). Previously, the court had classified as diffused surface water, overflows from a stream in time of flood that later rejoined it: *Missouri Pacific Ry.* v. *Keys*, 55 Kans. 205, 216-218, 40 Pac. 275 (1895).

[334] *Dyer* v. *Stahlhut*, 147 Kans. 767, 770, 78 Pac. (2d) 900 (1938).

A Kansas statute authorizes a landowner (1) to build a levee along a natural watercourse to repel floodwater if his plans have the approval of the Chief Engineer of the State Division of Water Resources, and (2) with the approval of that official, to build a levee on his own land to repel overflows (which the statute terms "surface water") on upper lands in the event that the upper landowners have not themselves diked against the overflows.[335] In situations to which the statute applies, overflow from a watercourse is thus classified by the statute as diffused surface water regardless of its subsequent connection with or separation from the stream. However, as the statute covers these situations whatever the waters are called, the statutory classification of such water is of no practical importance.

Nebraska.—"We think our decisions have committed us to the doctrine that a riparian owner may not embank against the overflow of running streams when the effect is to cause an increased volume of water on the land of another riparian owner to his injury, and if he does so he is answerable in damages."[336] The same rule applies to diking against floodwaters within the flood channel or flood plain of a running stream.[337] This applies also to overflows that return to the stream after separation therefrom, or that find their way to another stream or watercourse; but other overflows that permanently escape contact with watercourses are diffused surface waters, a common enemy.[338]

Oklahoma.—The right of a riparian owner to protect his land against overflow resulting from any change in the natural state of a stream, and to prevent the old course of a stream from being altered, was declared by a Federal court in 1900, while Oklahoma was a Territory.[339]

The State court decisions in Oklahoma with respect to repulsion of stream water distinguish between ordinary and extraordinary floods of a watercourse, and hold that the owner of abutting land has no right to erect a barrier which in time of ordinary flood will throw the water in larger volume on the lands of another so as to overflow and injure them; and that if he does so, the injured party has the right to repel the water.[340] The limits of the protective right of the landowner are the same, whether the floodwater comes down the main channel, or whether the overflow spreads out over adjacent lowlands and

---

[335] Kans. Stat. Ann. § 24-105 (1964).

[336] *Hofeldt* v. *Elkhorn Valley Drainage Dist.,* 115 Nebr. 539, 546, 213 N. W. 832 (1927).

[337] *Bahm* v. *Raikes,* 160 Nebr. 503, 514-515, 70 N. W. (2d) 507 (1955).

[338] *Hengelfelt* v. *Ehrmann,* 141 Nebr. 322, 327, 3 N. W. (2d) 576 (1942).

[339] *Gulf, C. & S. F. Ry.* v. *Clark,* 101 Fed. 678, 680-681 (8th Cir. 1900). The declaration was that: "A riparian owner may construct the necessary embankments, dikes, or other structures to maintain his bank of the stream in its original condition, or to restore it to that condition, and to bring the stream back to its natural course; and, if he does no more, riparian owners upon the opposite or upon the same side of the stream can recover no damages for the injury his actions causes them."

[340] *Jefferson* v. *Hicks,* 23 Okla. 684, 689, 102 Pac. 79 (1909); *George* v. *Greer,* 207 Okla. 494, 495, 250 Pac. (2d) 858 (1952); *Dowlen* v. *Crowley,* 170 Okla. 59, 62, 37 Pac. (2d) 933 (1934).

eventually returns to the stream from which it came or joins another watercourse.[341]

Oregon.—A riparian landowner may protect his premises against overflow of the stream and may protect the banks,[342] which he has a right to maintain at their usual or natural height.[343]

A distinction is made between overflows from ordinary floods and those from extraordinary floods. Unanticipated appearances of water in volume in the form of extraordinary floods constitute a "common enemy" and may be repelled by the owner of lands over which the water flows. But floodwaters that are seasonal and expected and that have been recurring at substantially the same periods of the year and in approximately the same volume are ordinary floodwaters.[344]

So long as ordinary floodwaters form one continuous body, flowing in the ordinary course of the stream and returning to the natural channel as they recede, they are waters of a watercourse, although not confined to the banks of a stream, in which case the lower landowner is inhibited from obstructing the runoff when following its natural course over his land.[345]

Stream waters which in times of flood become separated from the main body and spread out over the adjoining country without following any definite watercourse or channel cease to be a part of the stream and are regarded as diffused surface water. The rule with regard to their obstruction by the lower owner is the same as in case of ordinary floodwaters temporarily cut off from the main stream.[346]

Texas.—Subject to the limitations noted below, a riparian owner may lawfully erect a levee on his own land for the purpose of controlling overflows and freshets in streams along the land.[347] This conforms to the principle that the reclamation of land and its protection from overflow are private rights as well as being in the interest of the public welfare.

Under the limitation of the law, the landowner cannot exercise this right, even for his own benefit, for the purpose of constructing a levee on his side of the channel if the effect will be to cause the water, in times of ordinary overflow, to flow unnaturally over the ground of the opposite owner to his

---

[341] *Jefferson* v. *Hicks,* 23 Okla. 684, 692-694, 102 Pac. 79 (1909); *Franks* v. *Rouse,* 192 Okla. 520, 525, 137 Pac. (2d) 899 (1943).

[342] *Cox* v. *Bernard,* 39 Oreg. 53, 61, 64 Pac. 860 (1901).

[343] *Mace* v. *Mace,* 40 Oreg. 586, 589-590, 67 Pac. 660, 68 Pac. 737 (1902).

[344] *Wellman* v. *Kelley,* 197 Oreg. 553, 560-562, 252 Pac. (2d) 816 (1953).

[345] *Wellman* v. *Kelley,* 197 Oreg. 553, 561-563, 252 Pac. (2d) 816 (1953). See also *Price* v. *Oregon Ry.,* 47 Oreg. 350, 359, 83 Pac. 843 (1906).

[346] *Wellman* v. *Kelley,* 197 Oreg. 553, 566-567, 252 Pac. (2d) 816 (1953); *Price* v. *Oregon Ry.,* 47 Oreg. 350, 359, 83 Pac. 843 (1906).

[347] *Knight* v. *Durham,* 136 S. W. 591, 594 (Tex. Civ. App. 1911); *Jackson* v. *Knight,* 268 S. W. 773, 775 (Tex. Civ. App. 1925, error dismissed). See *Fort Worth Impr. Dist. No. 1* v. *Fort Worth,* 106 Tex. 148, 154-160, 158 S. W. 164 (1913).

injury.[348] This limitation has been recognized, as a principle of equity, without reference to any statutory limitation;[349] but it applies only with respect to a *material* injury.[350]

Rights of Use

Under certain circumstances, riparian proprietors in States having dual systems of water rights (riparian and appropriative) have claimed and have obtained sanction of rights to the use of high flood overflows for the purpose of natural irrigation of their riparian lands, where the overflows substantially benefited the land.

In the case arising in Oregon, a Federal court held that a riparian owner was entitled to the ordinary and usual flow of the stream of any beneficial use to him including, under certain circumstances, flood or overflow waters reasonably to be anticipated in ordinary seasons.[351] Here about 300 acres of low-lying land adjacent to a creek was rendered productive of wild grass and other hay crops by the natural overflow of the creek, thus adding measurably to the value of the land. The owner was entitled to have this right protected against a proposed diversion that would cause substantial injury.

The Washington Supreme Court held that the riparian proprietor is entitled to the use of the natural flow of stream waters in their natural and accustomed channels, including floods or freshets that occur annually with practical regularity, where the riparian owner is accustomed to spreading of the water over his land to its enrichment and would be substantially injured by deprivation of the overflows by reason of upstream storage.[352] In the *Longmire* case, the court acknowledged that it "may be" that the rule would not apply if the floodwaters were unprecedented and extraordinary. That question, however, was moot in the *Still* case, where the high waters were of practically regular annual occurrence.

Although the California courts have not distinguished between ordinary and extraordinary floodflows in streams with respect to rights of landowners to embank against them, they formerly did make some distinction insofar as rights of riparian owners to use the overflows were involved. Thus, in several cases, it was held that riparian landowners were not entitled to enjoin hostile diversions of flood or freshet flows that did not injure their lands or impair

---

[348] *Jackson* v. *Knight,* 268 S. W. (2d) 773, 775 (Tex. Civ. App. 1925, error dismissed).

[349] *Bass* v. *Taylor,* 126 Tex. 522, 527-528, 90 S. W. (2d) 811 (1936).

[350] *Knight* v. *Durham,* 136 S. W. 591, 593-594 (Tex. Civ. App. 1911).

[351] *Eastern Oregon Land Co.* v. *Willow River Land & Irr. Co.,* 201 Fed. 203, 213-214 (9th Cir. 1912).

[352] *Still* v. *Palouse Irr. & Power Co.,* 64 Wash. 606, 608-610, 117 Pac. 466 (1911); *Longmire* v. *Yakima Highlands Irr. & Land Co.,* 95 Wash. 302, 305-307, 163 Pac. 782 (1917).

their water rights.[353] On the other hand, decisions with respect to streams flowing from the Sierra Nevada into San Joaquin Valley were uniformly to the effect that the high waters thereof were flows that were expected annually and hence were not unusual, extraordinary, or unexpected, and that they constituted waters to which riparian rights attached.[354] In construing the constitutional amendment of 1928, which limited riparian rights to reasonable beneficial use under reasonable methods of diversion and use, the California Supreme Court stated that "distinctions heretofore made between the unusual or extraordinary and the usual or ordinary flood and freshet waters of a stream are no longer applicable."[355]

Change of Channel

Effect on Property Boundaries

Gradual change of channel.—Stream channels may shift slowly and imperceptibly from one location to another over considerable distances. This may result from the gradual addition of alluvium to one bank along the waterline, called *accretion,* or the gradual withdrawal of the water from the land on that side, called *reliction,* and from the gradual erosion of land from the opposite bank.[356]

Where such change comes about gradually, a boundary line consisting of the thread of a stream will ordinarily shift with the accretion and decrement caused by the water.[357] Thus, the one riparian owner, by accretion or reliction, acquires land not previously owned by him, and the other whose land is carried away by erosion loses title to the eroded area.[358] Furthermore, it has been held that the lost title to an eroded area is not regained if the submerged land reappears as the result of another recession of the river; the new land becomes

---

[353] *Edgar* v. *Stevenson,* 70 Cal. 286, 289-291, 11 Pac. 704 (1886); *Modoc Land & Live Stock Co.,* v. *Booth,* 102 Cal. 151, 156-158, 36 Pac. 431 (1894); *Fifield* v. *Spring Valley Water Works,* 130 Cal. 552, 553-555, 62 Pac. 1054 (1900); *Gallatin* v. *Corning Irr. Co.,* 163 Cal. 405, 413, 126 Pac. 864 (1912); *Gin S. Chow* v. *Santa Barbara,* 217 Cal. 673, 683, 686, 22 Pac. (2d) 5 (1933).

[354] *Miller & Lux* v. *Madera Canal & Irr. Co.,* 155 Cal. 59, 76, 99 Pac. 502 (1907); *Herminghaus* v. *Southern California Edison Co.,* 200 Cal. 81, 88, 103, 252 Pac. 607 (1926); *Collier* v. *Merced Irr. Dist.,* 213 Cal. 554, 558, 2 Pac. (2d) 790 (1931); *Chowchilla Farms* v. *Martin,* 219 Cal. 1, 26-33, 39, 25 Pac. (2d) 435 (1933).

[355] *Peabody* v. *Vallejo,* 2 Cal. (2d) 351, 368, 40 Pac. (2d) 486 (1935).

[356] Wiel, S. C., "Water Rights in the Western States," 3rd ed., vol. 1, § 901 (1911). Kinney, C. S., "A Treatise on the Law of Irrigation and Water Rights," 2d ed., vol. 1, § 927 (1912).

[357] *Campbell* v. *Weisbrod,* 73 Idaho 82, 88, 245 Pac. (2d) 1052 (1952); *State* v. *Ecklund,* 147 Nebr. 508, 521, 23 N. W. (2d) 782 (1946). The boundary of land bordering the stream changes with the changing course of the stream: *Hirt* v. *Entus,* 37 Wash. (2d) 418, 423, 224 Pac. (2d) 620 (1950).

[358] *Manry* v. *Robison,* 122 Tex. 213, 225, 56 S. W. (2d) 438 (1932). See *Hogue* v. *Bourgois,* 71 N. W. (2d) 47 (N. Dak. 1955).

an accretion to other lands.[359] Regardless of the rapidity of changes in the channel, so long as the change is not of the character known as avulsion, discussed immediately below, the rules with respect to erosions and accretions apply.[360]

Abrupt change of channel.—A sudden and violent change of channel is known as *avulsion*.[361] When a stream suddenly abandons its old channel and creates a new one, or suddenly washes from one of its banks a considerable body of land and deposits it on the other side, the boundary does not change with the changed course of the stream but remains as it was before.[362]

If a stream suddenly leaves its accustomed channel and takes a new course distinct from the old, the law of avulsion definitely applies. In some cases in which the stream cuts land from one side of its channel and deposits the soil on the opposite side, classification of the change may be less obvious. The distinction appears to be that to constitute avulsion, the change must be on a considerable scale, violent, and so sudden and abrupt as to be completed within a very short time—in some circumstances, but not necessarily, practically overnight; to be classed as accretion and erosion, there is good authority that changes may be rapid, but in the overall view the shifting of channel is gradual and, over a long time, perhaps continuous.

An example of avulsive action that affected private interests only was the effect of a change of stream channel on the ownership of a gravel bed in southern Oregon.[363] When the lands owned by plaintiffs and defendant were surveyed in 1859, their common boundary was the center of the channel of Rogue River, the gravel bed being north of the river on plaintiffs' land. The instant dispute arose over the ownership of receipts from defendant's sale of gravel taken from the bed, which plaintiffs claimed belonged to them. By accretion, the river shifted gradually until in 1877 it was north of the gravel bed. Between 1891 and 1900, there was a sudden and violent change by which the channel was moved more than one-fourth mile south of the gravel bed. The court held that plaintiffs' south boundary followed the thread of the stream northward to its location in 1877, and remained there unaltered despite the avulsion of the 1890's. Consequently, as a legal question the gravel bed did not

---

[359] *Hancock* v. *Moore,* 135 Tex. 619, 623, 146 S. W. (2d) 369 (1941).

[360] *Nebraska* v. *Iowa,* 143 U.S. 359, 369-370 (1892); *Hancock* v. *Moore,* 135 Tex. 619, 623, 146 S. W. (2d) 369 (1941).

[361] Wiel, *supra* note 356, § 862.

[362] *Hirt* v. *Entus,* 37 Wash. (2d) 418, 423, 224 Pac. (2d) 620 (1950); *Ross* v. *Green,* 135 Tex. 103, 107, 139 S. W. (2d) 565 (1940); *Tomasek* v. *State,* 196 Oreg. 120, 138-139, 248 Pac. (2d) 703 (1952). The great weight of authority, as shown by decisions in many cases, is to the effect that when avulsion occurs the line dividing the property of riparians remains according to the former boundary, not according to the boundaries created by the avulsion: *Maufrais* v. *State of Texas,* 142 Tex. 559, 568, 180 S. W. (2d) 144 (1944).

[363] *Wyckoff* v. *Mayfield,* 130 Oreg. 687, 689-692, 280 Pac. 340 (1929).

belong to the plaintiffs, either immediately before the avulsion, or afterward to the time the gravel was sold.

Many "oxbows" or crescent shaped bends may be located along the courses of winding rivers, of which the Mississippi is a conspicuous example. In periods of high floodflow, the swollen stream may cut across the neck or open end of the bend and may make the cutoff the permanent new channel, leaving the abandoned channel around the curve of the bend to contain only such overflow as may spill over at the peak of high floods. These channel changes are clear examples of avulsion.

Effect on Political Boundaries

The United States Supreme Court has held that the laws of accretion and avulsion apply to State boundary lines as well as to those of individual property holdings. In 1892 the Court held that:[364]

> Our conclusions are that, notwithstanding the rapidity of the changes in the course of the channel, and the washing from the one side and on to the other, the law of accretion controls on the Missouri River, as elsewhere; and that not only in respect to the rights of individual land owners, but also in respect to the boundary lines between States. The boundary, therefore, between Iowa and Nebraska is a varying line, so far as affected by these changes of diminution and accretion in the mere washing of the waters of the stream.
>
> It appears, however, from the testimony, that in 1877 the river above Omaha, which has pursued a course in the nature of an ox-bow, suddenly cut through the neck of the bow and made for itself a new channel. This does not come within the law of accretion, but of that of avulsion. By this selection of a new channel the boundary was not changed, and it remained as it was prior to the avulsion, the centre line of the old channel; and that, unless the waters of the river returned to their former bed, became a fixed and unvarying boundary, no matter what might be the changes of the river in its new channel.

Another example of change of the Missouri River channel by avulsive action at the neck of an oxbow, which also involved a question of interstate boundary, appeared in *Missouri* v. *Nebraska*[365] and is noted here in detail because of pertinence of the factual circumstances. The middle of the channel of the Missouri River had been fixed by Congress as the interstate boundary between these two States. On July 5, 1867 (after Nebraska had been admitted to the Union), within a period of 24 hours and in a time of very high water, the

---

[364] *Nebraska* v. *Iowa,* 143 U.S. 359, 369-370 (1892). In *Oklahoma* v. *Texas,* 260 U.S. 606, 636-638 (1923), applicability of the doctrine of erosion and accretion to the Red River, particularly in western Oklahoma, was questioned by litigants because of the rapidity and material changes effected during rises in the river. "But we think the habit of this river is so like that of the Missouri in this regard that the rule relating to the latter in *Nebraska* v. *Iowa,* 143, U.S. 359, 368, is controlling."

[365] *Missouri* v. *Nebraska,* 196 U.S. 23, 34-37 (1904).

river cut a new channel across the neck of an oxbow and through what was admittedly at that time territory of Nebraska. This change of channel was not only sudden, but was permanent. The result was that land within the oxbow which previously had been west of the river was now east of it. The Supreme Court held that the midchannel of the river according to its course prior to the avulsion—around the oxbow—remained the true interstate boundary. The Court cited its decision in *Nebraska* v. *Iowa* as authority for holding that a cutting of this river across the neck of an oxbow came within the law of avulsion, not that of accretion, and quoted therefrom: " 'Accretion, no matter to which side it adds ground, leaves the boundary still the centre of the channel. Avulsion has no effect on boundary, but leaves it in the centre of the old channel.' "[366]

Protection of Land Against Change of Channel

In a very early California case, it was held that a riparian owner has the right to protect his land against a threatened change of the original channel—which if not prevented would probably cut across his land—by building a bulkhead as high as was the original bank before it was washed away.[367]

A prompt reconstruction of the bank to its original height would not violate the principle that a riparian owner is entitled to have the stream flow as it was wont to flow. Hence, this does not conflict with the principle that a riparian owner may make changes in the stream channel that benefit him, provided the changes do not work a material injury upon other riparians. (See "Obstruction, Alteration, Diversion of Flow—The limitation to noninjurious changes," below.) This is recognized in a Nebraska decision in observing, in effect, that the riparian owner would be entitled to keep the stream in its original channel, provided the work is done in a reasonable time and without violating the principle that all riparian owners are entitled to have the stream run as it is wont to run according to natural drainage.[368]

Restoration of Original Channel

A riparian owner may restore to its former channel a stream which erosion has caused to flow in a new channel upon his land, provided he does so within a reasonable time after the new channel formed and before the interests of lower riparian proprietors along the course of the old channel would be injuriously affected by such action on his part.[369]

A California district court of appeal has stated this rule and applied it to the facts of the case under consideration as follows:[370]

> Without doubt a riparian owner, having lost his rights as such by avulsion, may ditch the water back to its original channel if he does not

---

[366] *Id.* at 35.
[367] *Barnes* v. *Marshall*, 68 Cal. 569, 570-571, 10 Pac. 115 (1886).
[368] *Stolting* v. *Everett*, 155 Nebr. 292, 301, 51 N. W. (2d) 603 (1952).
[369] *Ballmer* v. *Smith*, 158 Nebr. 495, 499, 63 N. W. (2d) 862 (1954).
[370] *McKissick Cattle Co.* v. *Alsaga*, 41 Cal. App. 380, 388-389, 182 Pac. 793 (1919).

delay doing so beyond a reasonable time. * * * But in restoring the water to its original channel, he will not be permitted to disturb the rights of appropriators, nor has he the right to go upon the lands of others, without their consent or acquiescence, and build thereon dams and ditches, or either, whereby he may restore the lost waters to their original bed. The defendant in this case entered upon the lands of the plaintiff and constructed the ditch complained of without the consent of the latter, and, as in no other way can he bring back to the portion of the channel of Secret Creek passing over and across a corner of his lands the waters which had theretofore flowed therein, he stands as one who has lost his riparian rights with respect to the creek in question.

Obstruction, Alteration, Diversion of Flow

The general rule.—It is the general rule that no one has the right to obstruct the flow of a natural watercourse, or to divert the water from its natural channel into another channel, if the result of the change is to cause an overflow upon the land of another that would not have reached such land had the artificial change not been made.[371] Stated differently, water flowing in a well-defined watercourse cannot be lawfully diverted and cast upon the lands of another to his damage where it was not wont to run in the course of natural drainage.[372] Any damage caused by such obstruction or diversion is actionable.[373]

The same inhibition applies to waters within the flood channels or flood plains of watercourses.[374]

Whether, in these cases of obstructing or changing natural streamflows, the damaging inundation is directly caused by a dam across the stream, or by a structure extending out into the stream, or by a dike or embankment along its sides, or by any other artificial means, the same rule as to liability applies.[375]

---

[371] See Clement v. State Reclamation Bd., 35 Cal. (2d) 628, 636, 642-643, 220 Pac. (2d) 897 (1950); Scott v. Watkins, 63 Idaho 506, 522, 122 Pac. (2d) 220, 226-227 (1942); Martinez v. Cook, 56 N. Mex. 343, 347-348, 224 Pac. (2d) 134 (1952); Schweiger v. Solbeck, 191 Oreg. 454, 464-467, 230 Pac. (2d) 195 (1951); Wilson v. Hagins, 50 S. W. (2d) 797, 798-799 (Tex. Com. App. 1932). Compare Jordan v. Mt. Pleasant, 15 Utah 449, 451-452, 49 Pac. 746 (1897).

[372] Pint v. Hahn, 152 Nebr. 127, 130-131, 40 N. W. (2d) 328 (1949).

[373] Archer v. Los Angeles, 19 Cal. (2d) 19, 26, 28, 119 Pac. (2d) 1 (1941). According to the Court of Civil Appeals of Texas, materiality of such an injury is an important consideration, because an injury that is not material is not actionable: Knight v. Durham, 136 S. W. 591, 594 (Tex. Civ. App. 1911).

[374] "The settled doctrine in this state is that no man has the right, without the consent of other riparian proprietors, to interfere with these flood-channels in such a way as to increase or diminish the water coming to other proprietors, to their injury and without their consent, * * * ." Krueger v. Crystal Lake Co., 111 Nebr. 724, 729, 197 N. W. 675 (1924). See Bahm v. Raikes, 160 Nebr. 503, 515, 70 N. W. (2d) 507 (1955).

[375] Chandler v. Drainage Dist. No. 2, 68 Idaho 42, 46, 187 Pac. (2d) 971 (1947); Reed v. Jacobson, 160 Nebr. 245, 249-250, 69 N. W. (2d) 881 (1955).

The limitation to noninjurious changes.—It has been held that an artificial change in the stream is not, of itself alone, objectionable if done for a proper purpose; that the gravamen of the action is resulting injury to others. Thus, the Colorado Supreme Court observed that the defendant, in cutting an artificial channel on his own land to prevent further erosion and damage from a stream, was within his right to do on his own property such things as were thought to be for its protection, but that in the enjoyment of this right he could not adopt a method that would damage or create a new injury to others.[376]

In North Dakota, also, it was held that the defendant railroad had the right to dam and divert the Cannonball River—a nonnavigable stream—but that in doing so it was bound to see that no injury should result therefrom and to make provisions to take care of not only the normal flow but also any flood that men of ordinary experience and prudence could have foreseen; this duty being a continuing one.[377]

The State Highway Commission of Oregon, presumably acting properly and in accordance with the necessities of the occasion as determined by it, closed approximately 70 percent of the flood plain of a stream and thus changed the velocity and course of the flow, the result of which was a partial destruction of plaintiff's land.[378] The supreme court held that this constituted a taking for a public purpose by the State within the meaning of the constitutional limitation upon the power of eminent domain.

A Texas statute makes it unlawful to divert or impound the natural flow of surface streams in such manner as to damage the property of another; flood control improvements and canals for conveying water for irrigation and other purposes not being affected by the statute.[379] "It is an elemental rule of law that, while a riparian, or another with proper authority, may construct dams in streams for the purpose of making reservoirs, still in doing so, they are not permitted to flood the lands of other riparians, or to back the water past the line of other owners of the streamway."[380]

---

[376] *Wyman* v. *Jones,* 123 Colo. 234, 243-245, 228 Pac. (2d) 158 (1951). The underlying purpose of plaintiff in bringing this action was to prevent formation of a new river channel through his premises. In an early Colorado case, *Crisman* v. *Heiderer,* 5 Colo. 589, 596 (1881), the court acknowledged the right of an appropriator to enter the bed of the stream above his ditch and to remove obstructions that were deflecting the current from his ditch, this being implied by his appropriation, but that the most reasonable mode of effectuating this must be adopted and executed in such manner as to occasion the least possible damage to neighbors.

[377] *Ferderer* v. *Northern Pacific Ry.,* 77 N. Dak. 169, 180, 42 N. W. (2d) 216 (1950).

[378] *Tomasek* v. *State,* 196 Oreg. 120, 138, 151, 248 Pac. (2d) 703 (1952).

[379] Tex. Rev. Civ. Stat. Ann. art. 7589a (1954).

[380] *Humphreys-Mexia Co.* v. *Arseneaux,* 116 Tex. 603, 612-614, 297 S. W. 225 (1927). The statutory right to appropriate and impound floodwaters does not authorize an appropriator or even a lower riparian owner to violate this principle. See Tex. Rev. Civ. Stat. Ann. arts. 7468 (Supp. 1970) and 7469 (1954).

Watercourse Originally Made Artificially

May Become in Effect a Natural Watercourse

The fact that a waterway was originally created artificially, in whole or in part, does not deprive it of the attributes of a watercourse if it performs the functions of a natural watercourse and has been treated as such by the interested parties for a long period of time.[381]

A channel connecting Kings and San Joaquin rivers in California, which had been made as a result of artificial work, was held by the supreme court to have become, in legal contemplation, a natural watercourse.[382] In view of the authorities the court felt warranted in holding "that a watercourse, although originally constructed artificially, may from the circumstances under which it originated and by long-continued use and acquiescence by persons interested therein become and be held to be a natural watercourse, and that riparian owners thereon and those affected thereby may have all the rights to the waters therein as they would have in a natural stream or watercourse."

Thus, a channel may have existed for such a length of time and may have been used under such circumstances that the manner of its creation is not material.[383] In the cited case, Rubio Canyon Wash was created as a result of settlement of the region and became the natural drainageway for the tributary watershed; its existence and function were accepted by those who settled in the area.

Important Factors

Characteristics of watercourse.—In order that an artificial channel may come to be considered a natural watercourse, it must have all the essential elements of such a watercourse.[384] This requirement has not been noted in many court decisions, but it is a logical factor. In the *Auchmuty* case, just cited, the Wyoming Supreme Court rejected a contention that the artificial ditch in litigation had become a natural watercourse by reason of long usage, saying that: "In the case at bar we have not been informed as to the width or the depth of the drainage ditch in question and whether it has banks such as are required in order to constitute a watercourse."

Indications of permanence.—As with the wholly natural creation of a watercourse (see "Elements of Watercourse—Other Factors—Permanence of Existence," above), an important element of a watercourse created artificially is the indication that it is designed to be permanent.[385] With passage of time, the implication of permanence becomes increasingly important.[386]

---

[381] *Missouri Pacific Ry.* v. *Keys,* 55 Kans. 205, 215, 40 Pac. 275 (1895); *Hornor* v. *Baxter Springs,* 116 Kans. 288, 290, 226 Pac. 779 (1924). In the latter case, it is said that: "The straightening of a crooked watercourse in order to facilitate the flow and avoid the flooding of bordering lands is not uncommon." See *Auchmuty* v. *Chicago, Burlington & Quincy R.R.,* 349 Pac. (2d) 193, 196 (Wyo. 1960).

[382] *Chowchilla Farms* v. *Martin,* 219 Cal. 1, 18-20, 25 Pac. (2d) 435 (1933).

[383] *San Gabriel Valley Country Club* v. *County of Los Angeles,* 182 Cal. 392, 397, 188 Pac. 554 (1920).

[384] *Auchmuty* v. *Chicago, Burlington & Quincy R.R.,* 349 Pac. (2d) 193, 196 (Wyo. 1960).

[385] *Jack* v. *Teegarden,* 151 Nebr. 309, 315-316, 37 N. W. (2d) 387 (1949).

[386] *Hollett* v. *Davis,* 54 Wash. 326, 332-333, 103 Pac. 423 (1909); *Gardner* v. *Dollina,* 206

The time element.—The time element is less important in itself than in the opportunity it affords for creation of new conditions the impairment or destruction of which would be inequitable, if the old ones were restored. The periods in which new conditions have been held to be sufficiently permanent to justify their retention vary considerably. Thus, in one case, a failure to restore the old conditions within slightly more than 3 years, within which time other rights had intervened, was held to have forfeited the right to make the restoration.[387] In another case, the elapsed time was 30 years,[388] and in still another, it was most of a period of 90 years.[389] The opinion in an early Oklahoma case says that where water has flowed in its accustomed, originally artificial channel from time immemorial, there is an ancient natural watercourse.[390]

The question of prescription.—Prescription is mentioned in some of the cases in connection with the basis of the right to retain the new channel in preference to the old. Accrual of an easement by prescription may arise against persons *unfavorably* affected by the change from a natural to an artificial channel by adverse user for the period prescribed by the statute of limitations, but not against persons *favorably* affected.[391] A contention in an Oklahoma case that a canal had become a watercourse by prescription was rejected by the supreme court because there was no adverse possession or continuous invasion of the other's rights as would be necessary to establishment of a prescriptive easement.[392]

The length of the prescriptive period appears to have suggested itself to the courts in some cases as an appropriate time within which, under the circumstances of the instant controversy, the right to restore the original channel conditions should have been exercised—for reasons other than adverse use, but for periods analogous to the statute of limitations. Thus, the Oregon Supreme Court held that as an opening of certain artificial channels had been acquiesced in by all parties on the stream for a period longer than that prescribed by the statute of limitations, the channel had become fixed.[393] Shortly afterward, the Washington Supreme Court approved the principle that one who diverts a stream into an artificial channel and suffers it to remain there for a period exceeding the statute of limitations, is estopped, as against a person making beneficial use of the water, from returning it to the original stream to this person's injury.[394] The court went on to say that the user does

---

Oreg. 1, 42-43, 288 Pac. (2d) 796 (1955).

[387] *Johnk* v. *Union Pacific R.R.,* 99 Nebr. 763, 766-769, 157 N. W. 918 (1916).

[388] *Matheson* v. *Ward,* 24 Wash. 407, 410-411, 64 Pac. 520 (1901).

[389] *Gardner* v. *Dollina,* 206 Oreg. 1, 42-43, 288 Pac. (2d) 796 (1955).

[390] *Chicago, R. I. & P. Ry.* v. *Groves,* 20 Okla. 101, 115-116, 93 Pac. 755 (1908).

[391] *Johnk* v. *Union Pacific R.R.,* 99 Nebr. 763, 767-768, 157 N. W. 918 (1916).

[392] *Branch* v. *Altus,* 195 Okla. 625, 627, 159 Pac. (2d) 1021 (1945).

[393] *Hough* v. *Porter,* 51 Oreg. 318, 415, 95 Pac. 732 (1908), 98 Pac. 1083 (1909), 102 Pac. 728 (1909).

[394] *Hollett* v. *Davis,* 54 Wash. 326, 332-333, 103 Pac. 423 (1909).

not have to show a prescriptive right in himself, or a use by himself for the period of the statute of limitations in order to prevent the return of the water to the original channel; "all he needs to show is that the person diverting it has suffered it to remain in its changed state *for that period* [emphasis supplied] and that he has made a beneficial use of the water relying upon the permanency of the change."

Long acquiescence of parties affected.—Generally speaking, an important element in converting a new artificial channel into a natural one is acquiescence of the landowners or water users affected by the change for an unreasonable period of time.[395] The actual length of time in any particular case depends upon the circumstances thereof.

Estoppel.—It is also held that one who makes such a change by agreement with other interested parties, who expend funds and labor in the course of acceptance of the new conditions, is estopped from restoring the water to its former channel.[396] The California Supreme Court held that one who makes substantial expenditures in reliance on long-continued diversion of water by another has the right to have the diversion continued if his investment would otherwise be destroyed.[397]

Dedication.—Even implied dedication has been suggested as a base. The opinion in a Nebraska decision referred to certain cases holding that where a change appeared to be permanent and was accepted by others who would be injured by restoration of the old conditions, the one responsible for the change could not, after a material time less than the prescriptive period, make the restoration without their consent.[398] In these cases, said the supreme court, the question was considered to be somewhat of the nature of one pertaining to the dedication of a highway.

Effect upon Riparian Rights

Questions of riparian water rights have been involved in cases in which new stream channels have been substituted for original ones, or have been created in addition thereto. Thus, when a new channel becomes, in legal contemplation, a natural watercourse, "lands bordering thereon are riparian thereto in the same manner and to the same extent as are lands bordering on streams natural in their origin."[399] In the case of a change made by mutual action of riparian owners, their rights and duties respecting the artificial channel will be the same as if it were the natural one.[400]

---

[395] *Matheson* v. *Ward,* 24 Wash. 407, 410-411, 64 Pac. 520 (1901).

[396] *Whipple* v. *Nelson,* 143 Nebr. 286, 291-292, 9 N. W. (2d) 288 (1943).

[397] *Natural Soda Products Co.* v. *Los Angeles,* 23 Cal. (2d) 193, 197, 143 Pac. (2d) 12 (1943); *People* v. *Los Angeles,* 34 Cal. (2d) 695, 697-699, 214 Pac. (2d) 1 (1950).

[398] *Johnk* v. *Union Pacific R.R.,* 99 Nebr. 763, 766-767, 157 N. W. 918 (1916).

[399] *Chowchilla Farms* v. *Martin,* 219 Cal. 1, 19-20, 25 Pac. (2d) 435 (1933).

[400] *Jack* v. *Teegarden,* 151 Nebr. 309, 315-316, 37 N. W. (2d) 387 (1949); *Harrington* v. *Demaris,* 46 Oreg. 111, 118-119, 77 Pac. 603, 82 Pac. 14 (1904). In another case, the Oregon Supreme Court observed that: "It seems to be a rule of law that, where owners

LAKES AND PONDS

Physical Characteristics

Lakes and ponds are compact bodies of water, with defined boundaries. Perceptible currents may or may not be flowing through these bodies of water, but in contrast to streams, they are substantially at rest. A necessary characteristic of a lake is a reasonably permanent existence, even though it may dry up in periods of drought.[401]

Usually, currents of water flowing through a lake are not perceptible, even where the lake is connected with a stream system, except of course in the inlet and outlet regions. That a current or flow of water is one of the essential elements of a watercourse has been stated heretofore (see "Elements of Watercourse—Stream").[402] The Arizona Supreme Court has said, in this connection, that:[403]

> This element of a current is one of the controlling distinctions between a river or stream, and a pond or lake. In the former case the water has a natural motion or current, while in the latter the water is in its ordinary state substantially at rest, with its surface perpendicular to a radius of the earth. The *exit* of a lake is a river or stream, having a current, but the lake itself has substantially none. * * *

Although the weight of authority appears to be that the controlling distinction between a lake and a watercourse is that in the former the water is substantially at rest whereas in the latter it is in perceptible motion,[404] nevertheless the existence or nonexistence of a current does not necessarily determine the classification of the body of water in question.[405]

---

of different parcels of land conduct water across the same in an artificial channel, and do not define their respective interests in the water, their reciprocal rights thereto are to be measured and determined as if they were riparian owners upon a natural stream * * * ." *Cottel* v. *Berry,* 42 Oreg. 593, 596, 72 Pac. 584 (1903). This comment was *dictum* in view of the fact that the rights of the parties in this case were not determined by rules governing riparian owners on a natural stream, but by an agreement they had made regarding disposition of water developed by a certain ditch. The Kansas Supreme Court says that: "The diversion of a stream by substituting an artificial channel for part of a natural one, by common consent, running in the same general direction, which has existed for a considerable time, may have the characteristics of a watercourse, to which riparian rights would attach." *Hornor* v. *Baxter Springs,* 116 Kans. 288, 290, 226 Pac. 779 (1924).

[401] *Block* v. *Franzen,* 163 Nebr. 270, 277, 79 N. W. (2d) 446 (1956). See *Froemke* v. *Parker,* 41 N. Dak. 408, 415, 171 N. W. 284 (1919).

[402] See *De Ruwe* v. *Morrison,* 28 Wash. (2d) 797, 810, 184 Pac. (2d) 273 (1947).

[403] *Maricopa County M.W.C. Dist.* v. *Southwest Cotton Co.,* 39 Ariz. 65, 86, 4 Pac. (2d) 369 (1931).

[404] *Froemke* v. *Parker,* 41 N. Dak. 408, 415, 171 N. W. 284 (1919); *Block* v. *Franzen,* 163 Nebr. 270, 277, 79 N. W. (2d) 446 (1956).

[405] See Kinney, C. S., "A Treatise on the Law of Irrigation and Water Rights," 2d ed., vol. 1, § 294 (1912). Compare Wiel, S. C., "Water Rights in the Western States," 3d ed., vol. 1, § 346 (1911).

A natural pond is really a small lake. The Nebraska Supreme Court quotes with approval a statement that although a distinction is sometimes made between lakes and ponds—the term "lake" connoting a large body of water, and "pond" connoting a small one ordinarily containing considerable aquatic growth—nevertheless this distinction is based chiefly on the size of the body of water and is not essential for legal purposes.[406] These natural bodies of water, with defined boundaries, belong in the same legal classification.

Lakes and ponds are distinguished from marshes in being definite bodies of standing water, rather than areas of soft, low-lying, water-logged land which may or may not have water standing in places on the surface.[407] The distinction obviously may be close under some circumstances.

As noted above (see "Elements of Watercourse—Other Factors—Relation of Watercourse to Connected Sources of Water Supply"), most western lakes are clearly connected with surface stream channels. On the other hand, there are lakes and ponds with no visible tributary channels or outlet channels. They may be fed from precipitation upon the water surface, from diffused surface waters, and from underground sources; and they discharge water into the atmosphere and in many cases into the ground. They may constitute definite sources of water supply to which rights exist or may be acquired independently of rights to other sources of supply.

A Washington case, *De Ruwe* v. *Morrison,* began as an action to compel neighbors to remove a dam, erected on their own property, which plaintiffs contended obstructed a natural watercourse and flooded their land at certain seasons.[408] In a decision rendered by a divided court, it was held that the lake basin in litigation was not a natural watercourse; that the overflow outlet was not a true outlet in the typical situation in which water enters a lake at one point and flows out at another, thus preserving the continuity of a watercourse. Here the inflow came to rest in the lake and escaped as outflow only at certain seasons of the year and even then shortly disappeared into a sink hole. The waters that periodically inundated the basin were classed as "flood and surface waters."

Standing alone, the decision on this point in *De Ruwe* v. *Morrison* is an extreme one insofar as it purports to hold that a closed lake outlet determines the classification of waters that come to rest in a lakebed. Compare the North Dakota case of *Froemke* v. *Parker,* in which the court held that when diffused

---

[406] *Block* v. *Franzen,* 163 Nebr. 270, 276-277, 79 N. W. (2d) 446 (1956), quoting from Restatement of Torts § 842 p. 324 (1939).

[407] Kinney, C. S., *supra* note 405, § 317.

[408] *De Ruwe* v. *Morrison,* 28 Wash. (2d) 797, 805, 810, 184 Pac. (2d) 273 (1947). Judgment of dismissal appealed and affirmed. Plaintiffs invoked the rule relative to natural watercourses and relied on their riparian rights thereunder. Under the facts, the supreme court held that appellants had no cause of action on this theory. The supreme court held also with the trial court that the lake was not a natural watercourse. The waters in the basin were held to be "flood and surface waters," against which the defendants had the right to protect their property.

surface waters collected in a slough and there remained—except for occasional overflow—for purposes of evaporation or seepage into the soil, they lost their characteristics as diffused surface waters and became waters of a pond, the principles of law applicable thereto being similar to those applicable to watercourses.[409] However, the overall decision in *De Ruwe* v. *Morrison* was actually based on a complicated factual situation which included, among other things, the construction of drainage ditches by the defendants' predecessors for the purpose of draining and reclaiming the lakebed for valuable farming land, in which the plaintiffs and their predecessors had acquiesced for many years.[410]

Governing Principles of Law

The principles of law applicable to lakes and ponds are similar to those governing watercourses.[411] This is subject to qualification where physical differences are important, such as elevation of the lake level. (See "Lake: Reciprocal importance of lake level and outflow" under "Elements of Watercourse—Other Factors—Relation of Watercourse to Connected Sources of Water Supply," above.)

---

[409] *Froemke* v. *Parker,* 41 N. Dak. 408, 415, 171 N. W. 284 (1919).

[410] Each year a large part of the lakebed was subject to overflow in the high-water season, but because of the greatly deepened outlet and the extensive drainage system, the waters were drained off and the lands made available for pasture and crops through the summer and fall.

[411] *Froemke* v. *Parker,* 41 N. Dak. 408, 415, 171 N. W. 284 (1919); *Block* v. *Franzen,* 163 Nebr. 270, 279, 79 N. W. (2d) 446 (1956). In *Roberts* v. *Taylor,* 47 N. Dak. 146, 153, 181 N. W. 622 (1921), both parties were seeking to exclude any public use or public right in the open waters or bed of a lake and to fix the status as wholly private. In this regard in North Dakota, a lake is differentiated from a watercourse only in that it is simply an enlarged watercourse wherein the waters may flow, or a basin wherein the waters are quiescent.

Chapter 4

NAVIGABLE WATERS

The general subject of navigation and navigable waters is one of considerable proportions, including important subtopics not germane to the theme of rights to the use of water in the West. However, other subtopics that are directly or indirectly related must be considered herein.

For a compact, well-considered statement of important facets of the overall topic of navigation, reference is made to the President's 1950 Water Resources Policy report dealing with water resources law.[1] The report shows that the constitutional power of Congress to regulate navigation under the commerce clause comprehends control of navigable waters of the United States and, if necessary, nonnavigable waters connected with them and essential to their navigable capacity, and control over the removal of obstructions to their navigation. It is also shown that subject to the powers conferred upon the Federal Government, the States have proprietary control over navigable waters and their beds within the boundaries of the respective States. Of particular importance with respect to the acquisition and exercise of water rights, the report notes that the protective power of Congress over navigable waters extends to control over the installation of structures across and in such waters and their connecting waters as well—bridges, dams, dikes, causeways, wharves, piers, and other obstructions to their navigable capacity—and to prohibition of any diversion of water that tends to impair or destroy such capacity.

CONTROL OVER NAVIGATION AND NAVIGABILITY

Paramount authority over navigation and the navigability of waterways useful to interstate and foreign commerce is vested in the United States, acting through the Congress and through Federal administrative agencies pursuant to congressional direction. Subject to this Federal control, or in the absence of it, the States have concurrent jurisdiction within their boundaries.

Exercise of Sovereign Power

Whether exercised by the United States or by a State, "This power over navigable waters and over navigation is essentially an attribute of sovereignty, and some of its forms find expression in the exercise of the police power."[2]

---

[1] "The Report of the President's Water Resources Policy Commission," vol. 3, "Water Resources Law," pp. 8-17, 73-125 (1950).

[2] *Gray* v. *Reclamation Dist. No. 1500,* 174 Cal. 622, 637, 163 Pac. 1024 (1917).

In 1904, the California Supreme Court held that the effect of diversions by appropriators of water of a navigable stream upon the navigability of that stream is the concern of the Federal or State governments, and it is not a proper subject of litigation in a suit over conflicting water rights involving only private claimants who are unaffected by the effect on navigability.[3]

United States: Paramount Authority[4]

The framers of the United States Constitution expressly delegated to Congress the power to regulate commerce with foreign nations and among the several States, as well as with the Indian tribes.[5] Out of this developed the considerable body of Federal law relating to interstate commerce. As commerce includes navigation—which, in the early years of the Republic, was of outstanding importance—regulation of transportation over the inland waterways and control of navigable waters for such purpose became established congressional prerogatives.[6] And the later development of this field has included extension of Federal regulation of navigable waters to uses other than navigation, as well as broadening of the classification of waters subject to this regulation.

The paramount authority of the United States, acting through the Congress, to control navigable waters of the United States—and other waters to the extent that their control is required in exercising this paramount function—has been repeatedly asserted by Congress and has been, in many decisions, consistently sustained by the United States Supreme Court. To cite a few examples:

"* * * the great and absolute power of Congress over the improvement of navigable rivers * * * comes from the power to regulate commerce between the States with foreign nations. It includes navigation and subjects every navigable river to the control of Congress."[7]

"Commerce includes navigation. * * * The power to regulate interstate commerce embraces the power to keep the navigable rivers of the United States free from obstructions to navigation and to remove such obstructions when they exist."[8]

In the so-called *New River* decision, rendered in 1940,[9] it is said that "there is no doubt that the United States possesses the power to control the erection

---

[3] *Miller & Lux* v. *Enterprise Canal & Land Co.,* 142 Cal. 208, 213-214, 75 Pac. 770 (1904).

[4] See also the later discussion of this and related subjects in chapter 21.

[5] U.S. Const., art. I, § 8, cl. 3.

[6] "It was held early in our history that the power to regulate commerce necessarily included power over navigation." *United States* v. *Appalachian Electric Power Co.,* 311 U.S. 377, 404 (1940). See *United States* v. *Chicago, M., St. P. & P. R. R.,* 312 U.S. 592, 595-596 (1941).

[7] *United States* v. *Chandler-Dunbar Water Power Co.,* 229 U.S. 53, 62 (1913).

[8] *Ashwander* v. *Tennessee Valley Authority,* 297 U.S. 288, 328 (1936).

[9] *United States* v. *Appalachian Electric Power Co.,* 311 U.S. 377 (1940). See *United States* v. *Chandler-Dunbar Water Power Co.,* 229 U.S. 53, 64 (1913).

of structures in navigable waters."[10] "This power of Congress to regulate commerce is so unfettered that its judgment as to whether a structure is or is not a hindrance is conclusive. Its determination is legislative in character."[11]

The power of Congress extends not only to keeping clear the channels of interstate navigation by prohibiting or removing actual obstructions, but includes improvement and enlargement of their navigability and determination of the necessity therefor.[12] Whether, under local law, the State retains title to the streambed or the riparian owner holds to the thread of the stream or to low watermark, the title-holder's rights are subordinate to the dominant power of the United States in respect of navigation. This dominant power extends to the entire bed of the stream, which includes lands below ordinary high watermark.

The power of Congress to create the Mississippi River Commission and to appropriate millions of dollars to build levees and improve the river and its navigable capacity derives from its paramount vested authority to improve the navigability of the river.[13]

In the course of the long-continuing interstate controversy over waters of the Colorado River, the Court observed that: "The Colorado River is a navigable stream of the United States. The privilege of the states through which it flows and their inhabitants to appropriate and use the water is subject to the paramount power of the United States to control it for the purpose of improving navigation."[14] Again, the United States has the power to create an obstruction in a navigable river, such as the Colorado, by the building of a dam for the purpose of improving navigation; and it may perform its functions without conforming to the police regulations of a State.[15]

Exercise of paramount authority under the commerce clause does not stop at the geographical boundaries of waters that are within the definition of "navigable waters of the United States." It extends to nonnavigable parts of stream systems insofar as such waters are needed to protect the navigable capacity of other parts. "As repeatedly recognized" in the Supreme Court decisions, "the exercise of the granted power of Congress to regulate interstate commerce may be aided by appropriate and needful control of activities and agencies which, though intrastate, affect that commerce."[16] This matter is discussed further below (see "Classification of Navigable Waters").

State: Concurrent and Subordinate Power

The vesting of paramount control over navigation so far as foreign and interstate commerce is concerned does not destroy the concurrent and

---

[10] 311 U.S. 377, 405 (1940).
[11] *Id.* at 424.
[12] *United States* v. *Chicago, M., St. P. & P. R. R.,* 312 U.S. 592, 596 (1941).
[13] *Cubbins* v. *Mississippi River Commission,* 241 U.S. 351, 369 (1916).
[14] *Arizona* v. *California,* 298 U.S. 558, 569 (1936).
[15] *Arizona* v. *California,* 283 U.S. 423, 451-452 (1931).
[16] *Oklahoma* v. *Guy F. Atkinson Co.,* 313 U.S. 508, 526 (1941).

subordinate power of the State, which may act in the absence of action by the Federal Government. In the words of the United States Supreme Court:[17]

> The power of Congress to regulate commerce among the States involves the control of the navigable waters of the United States over which such commerce is conducted is undeniable; but it is equally well settled that the control of the State over its internal commerce involves the right to control and regulate navigable streams within the State until Congress acts on the subject. * * *

A decade earlier, the Court observed that the jurisdiction of the general government over interstate commerce and its natural highways vests in that government the right to take all needed measures to preserve the navigability of the navigable watercourses of the country "even against any state action."[18] It was acknowledged that frequent decisions had recognized the power of the State, in the absence of congressional legislation, to assume control of even navigable waters within its limits to the extent of creating obstructions to navigability. Until, in some way, Congress asserts its superior power, the power of the State to thus legislate for the interests of its own citizens is conceded. "All this proceeds upon the thought that the non-action of Congress carries with it an implied assent to the action taken by the State."

The privilege of the States through which a navigable stream flows, and of their inhabitants, to appropriate and use the water is subject to the paramount power of the United States to control it for the purpose of improving navigation.[19] The same limitation applies to appropriations of water of nonnavigable portions or tributaries of a navigable stream.[20]

With respect to the power of the Federal and State Governments to regulate and control the navigable streams and their navigable streams and their navigable and nonnavigable tributaries, the California Supreme Court has said that:[21]

> This general power, so far as the national government is concerned, is found in the constitutional grant to the United States of the right to regulate commerce with foreign nations and among the states, and the state's power in this regard is limited only by the supervisory control which the paramount authority may exercise over it. This power over navigable waters and over navigation is essentially an attribute of sovereignty, and some of its forms find expression in the exercise of the police power.

---

[17] *Coyle* v. *Oklahoma*, 221 U.S. 559, 573 (1911).
[18] *United States* v. *Rio Grande Dam & Irr. Co.*, 174 U.S. 690, 703-704 (1899).
[19] *Arizona* v. *California*, 298 U.S. 558, 569 (1936).
[20] *United States* v. *Rio Grande Dam & Irr. Co.*, 174 U.S. 690, 706-707 (1899).
[21] *Gray* v. *Reclamation Dist. No. 1500*, 174 Cal. 622, 637, 163 Pac. 1024 (1917).

The "contrariety of interests" created by this dual power of sovereignty over navigable waters was thus commented upon by the United States Supreme Court in the *New River* decision:[22]

The states possess control of the waters within their borders, "subject to the acknowledged jurisdiction of the United States under the constitution in regard to commerce and the navigation of the waters of rivers." It is this subordinate local control that, even as to navigable rivers, creates between the respective governments a contrariety of interests relating to the regulation and protection of waters through licenses, the operation of structures and the acquisition of projects at the end of the license term. But there is no doubt that the United States possesses the power to control the erection of structures in navigable waters.

CLASSIFICATION OF NAVIGABLE WATERS

Navigable Waters of the United States

Navigable waters of the United States are those usable as such in interstate or foreign commerce[23] "when they form in their ordinary condition by themselves, or by uniting with other waters, a continued highway over which commerce is or may be carried on with other States or foreign countries in the customary modes in which such commerce is conducted by water."[24]

Navigable Waters of a State

Navigable waters of a stream within a State, which do not conform to the definition of navigable waters of the United States, are navigable waters of that State.

In a decision involving title to the ownership of beds of portions of several rivers lying within Utah, the Supreme Court held it to be "undisputed that none of the portions of the rivers under consideration constitute navigable waters of the United States, that is, they are not navigable in interstate or foreign commerce, and the question is whether they are navigable waters of the State of Utah."[25] The importance of determining the question of navigability lay in the fact—as will be discussed below under "Lands Underlying Navigable Waters"—that title to the beds of rivers then navigable passed to the State of Utah when it was admitted to the Union, and title to those of nonnavigable rivers remained in the United States. This is a Federal question, and "State laws

---

[22] *United States* v. *Appalachian Electric Power Co.*, 311 U.S. 377, 405 (1940).
[23] *United States* v. *Utah*, 283 U.S. 64, 75 (1931).
[24] *The Daniel Ball*, 77 U.S. (10 Wall.) 557, 563 (1871).
[25] *United States* v. *Utah*, 283 U.S. 64, 75 (1931).

cannot affect titles vested in the United States." In a marginal note, the Court referred to the fact that in 1927 the Utah Legislature passed an act declaring "The Colorado River in Utah and the Green River in Utah" to be navigable streams.[26]

Notwithstanding the recognition of the Supreme Court in *United States* v. *Utah* that none of the river sections in litigation constituted navigable waters of the United States, but that certain sections were found to be navigable and their beds therefore the property of the State of Utah, the master recommended insertion of a proviso in the decree that the United States "shall in no wise be prevented from taking any such action in relation to said rivers or any of them as may be necessary to protect and preserve the navigability of any navigable waters of the United States."[27] Utah excepted to this recommendation. The Court stated that while a statement to that effect was not necessary, as the United States would have that authority in any event, nevertheless the provision was not inappropriate in a decree determining the right, title, or interest of the United States and of Utah, respectively, in relation to the beds of the rivers in question.[28] Protection of navigability of the downstream course of the Colorado River was not involved in the instant case; but the Colorado certainly was[29] and is a navigable stream of the United States. Undoubtedly, the right of protective action on the part of the United States acknowledged by the Court and approved in the decree would apply equally to all the upstream channels involved in the litigation, regardless of classification of the several sections as navigable or nonnavigable.

As ordered by the decree entered in *United States* v. *Utah,* title to the beds of the navigable portions of these rivers within the borders of Utah was vested in the State of Utah, and title to the nonnavigable portions was vested in the United States.

Other Waters Related to Navigability

Nonnavigable Stretches of a Stream

It is well recognized that navigability, in behalf of which the commerce clause may be invoked, "may be of a substantial part only of the waterway in question."[30]

A Supreme Court decision was rendered in 1931 in an original suit brought by the United States against the State of Utah to quiet title to portions of

---

[26] Citing Utah Laws 1927, ch. 9, p. 8.

[27] *United States* v. *Utah,* 283 U. S. 64, 90 (1931).

[28] The statement was inserted in the decree: *United States* v. *Utah,* 283 U.S. 801, 804 (1931).

[29] In *Arizona* v. *California,* 283 U.S. 423, 452-456 (1931), the Supreme Court declared the Colorado to be a navigable river of the United States.

[30] *United States* v. *Appalachian Electric Power Co.,* 311 U. S. 377, 410 (1940).

riverbeds within the State—Colorado River, and its tributary Green and San Juan Rivers.[31] Certain portions of these rivers were found to be navigable— navigable waters of the State of Utah, not of the United States because they were not navigable in interstate or foreign commerce. As stated above under "Navigable Waters of a State", the Court held that a recommendation of the master that the decree contain a proviso authorizing the United States to protect the navigability of any navigable waters of the United States was not necessary, but that under the circumstances the provision was not inappropriate.

In a controversy decided in 1922 over the ownership of underlying lands, the Supreme Court held that no part of the Red River within Oklahoma was navigable.[32] At issue in a decision rendered with respect to the same stream in 1941 was an entirely different question—constitutionality of an Act of Congress[33] insofar as it authorized the construction of a reservoir on the Red River in Texas and Oklahoma.[34] Here, the Court, without disturbing its previous declaration as to navigability within Oklahoma, noted that navigation of the Red River had been practiced in past years almost as high upstream as the Oklahoma boundary, and currently to a point within Louisiana 122 miles above the river mouth. Among other things, the Court held (1) that the fact that portions of the river are no longer used for commerce does not dilute the power of Congress over them; (2) that clearly, Congress may exercise its control over the nonnavigable stretches of a river in order to preserve or promote commerce on the navigable portions; and (3) that the power of flood control extends to the tributaries of navigable streams.

Nonnavigable Tributaries

The relation of nonnavigable tributaries to the navigable parts of a stream system was considered in 1899 in a water rights controversy arising in New Mexico.[35] The bill was brought by the United States to restrain construction of a dam across the Rio Grande and appropriation of the stream waters for purposes of irrigation, the result of which would seriously obstruct the navigability of the entire river below the dam. The United States Supreme Court reversed the judgment of the Territorial Supreme Court, which had held that the river was not navigable within the limits of the Territory of New Mexico and that the United States therefore had no jurisdiction over the stream.

In the *Rio Grande Dam* case, the high Court held that in the absence of specific authority from Congress, (1) a State cannot by legislation destroy the

---

[31] *United States* v. *Utah,* 283 U.S. 64, 75, 90 (1931).
[32] *Oklahoma* v. *Texas,* 258 U.S. 574, 591 (1922).
[33] 52 Stat. 1215 (Act of June 28, 1938).
[34] *Oklahoma* v. *Guy F. Atkinson Co.,* 313 U.S. 508, 510, 523, 525 (1941).
[35] *United States* v. *Rio Grande Dam & Irr. Co.,* 174 U.S. 690, 703, 704-708 (1899).

right of the United States to the continued flow of the stream waters necessary for the use of contiguous government property, and (2) it is limited by the superior power of the United States to secure the uninterrupted navigability of all navigable streams within the nation. The Court referred to the series of enactments beginning in 1866[36] by which "Congress recognized and assented to the appropriation of water," so far as the public lands were concerned, under local customs, laws, and decisions of courts, "in contravention of the common law rule as to continuous flow." But it is not to be inferred therefrom that Congress intended to release its control over the navigable streams of the country and to suffer impairment of their navigability for the benefit of western mining and land reclamation. On this important matter the Court said that:[37]

> To hold that Congress, by these acts, meant to confer upon any State the right to appropriate all the waters of the tributary streams which unite into a navigable watercourse, and so destroy the navigability of that watercourse, in derogation of the interests of all the people of the United States, is a construction which cannot be tolerated. It ignores the spirit of the legislation and carries the statute to the verge of the letter and far beyond what under the statute to the verge of the letter and far beyond what under the circumstances of the case must be held to have been the intent of Congress.

The Court referred to a congressional declaration in 1890 prohibiting the creation of any obstruction, not affirmatively authorized by law, to the navigable capacity of any waters in respect to which the United States has jurisdiction.[38] This, said the Court:[39]

> * * * did not, of course, disturb any of the provisions of prior statutes in respect to the mere appropriation of water of non-navigable streams in disregard of the old common law rule of continuous flow, and its only purpose, as is obvious, was to affirm that as to navigable waters nothing should be done to obstruct their navigability without the assent of the National Government. It was an exercise by Congress of the power, oftentimes declared by this court to belong to it, of national control over navigable streams; * * * .

Thus, Congress, while subjecting surplus waters of nonnavigable sources on the public domain to appropriation by the public,[40] has reserved its control over the maintenance of navigability of navigable watercourses.[41]

---

[36] 14 Stat. 253, § 9 (1866); 16 Stat. 218 (1870); 19 Stat. 377 (1877), 43 U.S.C. § 321 (1964); 26 Stat. 1101, § 18 (1891), 43 U.S.C. § 946 (1964).

[37] 174 U.S. 690, 706-707 (1889).

[38] 26 Stat. 426, 454, § 10.

[39] 174 U.S. 690, 708 (1899).

[40] 19 Stat. 377, 43 U.S.C. § 321 (1964).

[41] 26 Stat. 426, 454, § 10.

In the *Rio Grande Dam* case, the Supreme Court pointed out that pursuant to the statute of 1890, the creation of any such obstruction may be enjoined by proper proceedings in equity under the direction of the Attorney General of the United States. It then "becomes a question of fact whether the act sought to be enjoined is one which fairly and directly tends to obstruct (that is, interfere with or diminish) the navigable capacity of a stream." In the instant case, the question was whether the appropriation of the upper waters of a navigable river "substantially interferes with the navigable capacity within the limits where navigation is a recognized fact."[42]

Texas Statutory Navigable Streams

A statute originally enacted by the Republic of Texas—and still extant—which relates to the surveying for individuals of lands lying on navigable watercourses, provides that *for the purpose of the statute* all streams shall be considered navigable as far up from their mouths as they retain an average width of 30 feet, and that no such stream shall be crossed by the lines of a survey.[43] The apparent object of this early act *was not to regulate navigation,* but to prevent persons locating on the public domain from monopolizing the waters of the State.[44] However, the inevitable result of the statute is that streams of the stated width were made public and title to their beds was reserved to the Republic and to the succeeding State, so that in these respects such streams, whether or not navigable in fact, have the same legal quality and character as streams actually navigable.[45]

Unquestionably, when the evidence brings a stream within the statute, the statute is controlling.[46] However, some interpretations of the applicability of the statute have been made by the courts.[47]

---

[42] 174 U.S. 690, 709 (1899).

[43] Tex. Rev. Civ. Stat. Ann. art. 5302 (1962), first enacted, Tex. Acts 1837, p. 63; 1 Sayles' Tex. Early Laws, pp. 266, 271. In the "Small Bill," enacted in 1929, the State's title to beds or abandoned beds of watercourses of navigable streams was relinquished to certain grantees whose grants actually crossed them: Tex. Rev. Civ. Stat. Ann. art. 5414a (1962).

[44] *Austin* v. *Hall,* 93 Tex. 591, 596-598, 57 S. W. 563 (1900).

[45] *Diversion Lake Club* v. *Heath,* 126 Tex. 129, 137-140, 86 S. W. (2d) 441 (1935).

[46] *Burr's Ferry, B. & C. Ry.* v. *Allen,* 164 S. W. 878, 880 (Tex. Civ. App. 1914, error refused).

[47] It is common knowledge that most streams in the State only 30 feet wide—and all of such streams in the arid sections—are not navigable streams in the sense of the common law; the statutory designation of navigable streams does not mean streams so designated at common law: *Barrett* v. *Metcalfe,* 12 Tex. Civ. App. 247, 255, 33 S. W. 758 (1896, error refused). A Federal court indicated its disbelief that the statute was intended to apply to surveys of lands located on tidewaters which, while navigable waters, are not streams at all in the usual meaning of the term: *Texas* v. *Chuoke,* 154 Fed. (2d) 1, 3 (5th Cir. 1946). The statute applies to streams only, not to lakes: *Taylor Fishing Club* v. *Hammett,* 88 S. W. (2d) 127, 129 (Tex. Civ. App. 1935, error dismissed). The statute is not applicable to ordinarily dry gullies, draws, and branches

Most of the public lands in Texas, owned by the Republic of Texas, were retained for disposition by the State upon its admission to statehood.[48] Those cases cited and discussed above in which the statute was held to be applicable appear to have dealt with the statute's effect upon the disposition of such lands.

DETERMINATION OF NAVIGABILITY FOR COMMERCE POWER AND BED TITLE PURPOSES

A Federal Question

The question of whether particular waters are navigable waters of the United States that are subject to the paramount Federal power over interstate and foreign commerce is a Federal question, not a local one. It is to be determined according to the law and usages recognized and applied in the Federal courts. Also a Federal question is that of whether particular waters are navigable waters, title to the beds of which passed from the Federal Government to the State upon statehood, discussed later.[49] This is so, even though no portions of the bodies of water under consideration are navigable in interstate or foreign commerce, so that these particular bodies of water are not navigable waters of the United States.[50]

Determining Agencies

Courts

Many determinations as to the navigability or nonnavigability of watercourses have been made by the courts, based upon the facts before them. But in one of the Colorado River decisions, the United States Supreme Court stated that while it is true that whether a stream is navigable in law depends upon whether it is navigable in fact, nevertheless "a court may take judicial notice that a river within its jurisdiction is navigable."[51] In this instance, the Court knew judicially, from the evidence of history, that a large part of the lower river was formerly navigable, and that corrections of the changed geographical conditions would, in the opinion of government engineers, restore the feasibility of navigation. In a case decided previously but in the same year, the Court said that:[52]

in the semiarid part of the State: *St. Paul Fire & Marine Ins. Co.* v. *Carroll,* 106 S. W. (2d) 757, 758-759 (Tex. Civ. App. 1937, error dismissed).

[48] See *Austin* v. *Hall, supra* note 44; Hutchins, W. A., "The Texas Law of Water Rights," pp. 49-50 (1961); Gates, P. W., "History of Public Land Law Development," pp. 82-83 (Nov. 1968).

[49] *United States* v. *Oregon,* 295 U.S. 1, 14 (1935). See *Ozark-Mahoning Co.* v. *State,* 76 N. Dak. 464, 467-468, 37 N. W. (2d) 488 (1949); *Lynch* v. *Clements,* 263 Pac. (2d) 153, 155 (Okla. 1953).

[50] *United States* v. *Utah,* 283 U.S. 64, 75, 82-83 (1931). The navigable portions of the streams in litigation were held to be navigable waters of the State of Utah.

[51] *Arizona* v. *California,* 283 U. S. 423, 452-454 (1931).

[52] *United States* v. *Utah,* 283 U.S. 64, 77 (1931).

Even where the navigability of a river, speaking generally, is a matter of common knowledge, and hence one of which judicial notice may be taken, it may yet be a question, to be determined upon evidence, how far navigability extends.

The syllabus by the Oklahoma Supreme Court in a case relating to the Arkansas River contains the following:[53]

. . . Where the United States Supreme Court has judicially determined that an Oklahoma river is navigable below a certain point, although such decision and its findings may not be binding upon the parties to subsequent actions in the federal courts, this court will take judicial notice that such stream is navigable below that point, and that title to the river bed where navigable, and also previously conveyed by federal grant, vested in the State of Oklahoma upon its admission as a state.

The decision of a State supreme court that a river is navigable, in a litigation to which the United States is not a party, does not bind the United States.[54] Nor is a judgment of a State court as to the navigability of a river within the limits of the State binding on the Federal courts in determining whether or not title to the riverbed passed with a Federal grant made prior to the admission of the State to the Union[55] or thereafter[56].

Congress

The power of Congress over navigable streams includes improvement and enlargement of their navigability.[57] "And the determination of the necessity for a given improvement of navigable capacity, and the character and extent of it, is for Congress alone."

Determinations of navigability are made by Congress in specific terms, or clearly implied, in legislating for the control and improvement of waterways. For example, in the Boulder Canyon Project Act, one of the purposes listed by Congress for the authorized construction was "improving navigation and regulating the flow of the Colorado River."[58] At that time, there was no navigation on the section of the river where the proposed dam was to be located. The Supreme Court, however, took judicial notice of its former navigability and expressly recognized that "the river is navigable." The Court held that the means provided in the act for regulating the streamflow were not unrelated to the control of navigation. It refused to inquire into the motives

---

[53]*Lynch* v. *Clements*, 263 Pac. (2d) 153 (Okla. 1953).

[54]*Oklahoma* v. *Texas*, 258 U.S. 574, 591 (1922).

[55]*Aladdin Petroleum Corp.* v. *State ex rel. Commissioners of Land Office*, 200 Okla. 134, 138-139, 191 Pac. (2d) 224 (1948).

[56]*United States* v. *Holt State Bank*, 270 U.S. 49, 52, 55-56 (1925).

[57]*United States* v. *Chicago, M., St. P. & P. R. R.*, 312 U. S. 592, 596 (1941).

[58]45 Stat. 1057, 43 U.S.C. § 617 (1964).

that influenced members of Congress to enact the measure, or into the adequacy or reasonableness of the authorized structures, these being matters of legislative policy only.[59]

In the important case of *United States* v. *Chandler-Dunbar,*[60] the Supreme Court held that the control of Congress over navigable streams of the country is so unfettered that its judgment as to whether a construction in or over such a river is or is not a hindrance to navigation is conclusive; that such questions are legislative in character; and that when Congress determines that a whole river throughout its entire length is "necessary for the purposes of navigation of said waters and the waters connected therewith," that determination is conclusive.

An avenue for congressional determinations of navigability not originally contemplated has been made available as a result of broadening the early definitions of "waters navigable in fact." A much cited definition of such waters by the Supreme Court includes "when they are used, or are susceptible of being used, *in their ordinary condition,* as highways for commerce, * * * ." [Emphasis supplied.][61] In the Federal Power Act of 1920, Congress defines "navigable waters" as those "which either in *their natural or improved condition* * * * are used or suitable for use" in interstate or foreign commerce, "together with such other parts of streams as shall have been authorized by Congress for improvement by the United States or shall have been recommended to Congress for such improvement after investigation under its authority."[62] [Emphasis supplied.]

This recognition by Congress that artificial aids may be needed to make a waterway suitable for commercial navigation was noted and approved by the Supreme Court in the *New River* decision.[63] There, the Court held that to appraise the evidence of navigability solely on natural conditions is erroneous; that *availability* for navigation must also be considered. Hence, determinations of navigability may rest upon a consideration of improvements needed to make the waterway suitable for commerce, even though the improvements are not actually completed or even authorized. A recent commentator says of this holding that "It would appear from this that if any portion of a river system can be made navigable by reasonable improvements, federal jurisdiction attaches to that portion and also to upper stretches and tributaries, under the *Rio Grande* doctrine, even though they cannot be made navigable."[64]

Thus, in authorizing improvements needed to make a stream navigable in fact, Congress determines its navigability and so asserts the paramount

---

[59] *Arizona* v. *California,* 283 U. S. 423, 452-456 (1931).

[60] *United States* v. *Chandler-Dunbar Water Power Co.,* 229 U. S. 53, 64-65 (1913).

[61] *The Daniel Ball,* 77 U. S. (10 Wall.) 557, 563 (1871).

[62] 41 Stat. 1063, § 3, 16 U.S.C. § 796(8) (1964).

[63] *United States* v. *Appalachian Electric Power Co.,* 311 U. S. 377, 407-408 (1940).

[64] Sato, Sho, "Water Resources—Comments upon the Federal-State Relationship," 48 Cal. L. Rev. 43 (1960), referring to *United States* v. *Rio Grande Dam & Irr. Co.,* 174 U. S. 690 (1899).

authority of the United States under the commerce clause. The broad scope of this authority includes, for example, (1) improvement of the present navigability of a river, such as the Mississippi, 'the historical and present navigability of which was unquestioned;[65] (2) restoration of the historical navigability of a river, such as the Colorado, which had become nonnavigable;[66] and (3) on a river such as New River, which had been held not navigable by both the United States District Court and the Court of Appeals, 4th Circuit,[67] improvements needed to make it usable for commercial navigation— that is, navigable in fact.

Criteria

"Behind all definitions of navigable waters lies the idea of public utility."[68]

Earlier Tests of Navigability

Reference has been made (see "Determining Agencies–Congress," above) to *The Daniel Ball* case, in which, a century ago, the United States Supreme Court held that:[69]

> Those rivers must be regarded as public navigable rivers in law which are navigable in fact. And they are navigable in fact when they are used, or are susceptible of being used, in their ordinary condition, as highways for commerce, over which trade and travel are or may be conducted in the customary modes of trade and travel on water. * * *

For a long time, the foregoing statement continued to be the settled rule in this country.[70] In an original suit by the United States against the State of Oregon, decided in 1935, the special master based his conclusion that the waters in litigation were not navigable in fact when Oregon was admitted to the Union, or afterward, on his finding of fact that:[71]

> " * * * neither trade nor travel did then or at any time since has or could or can move over said Divisions, or any of them, in their natural or ordinary conditions according to the customary modes of trade or travel over water; nor was any of them on February 14, 1859, nor has any of them since been used or susceptible of being used in the natural or ordinary condition of any of them as permanent or other highways or channels for useful or other commerce."

---

[65] *Cubbins* v. *Mississippi River Commission,* 241 U. S. 351, 369 (1916).

[66] *Arizona* v. *California,* 283 U. S. 423, 452-454 (1931).

[67] See *United States* v. *Appalachian Electric Power Co.,* 311 U. S. 377, 398 (1940).

[68] *Welder* v. *State,* 196 S. W. 868, 873 (Tex. Civ. App. 1917, error refused).

[69] *The Daniel Ball,* 77 U. S. (10 Wall.) 557, 563 (1871).

[70] *Oklahoma* v. *Texas,* 258 U. S. 574, 586 (1922). See *Arizona* v. *California,* 283 U. S. 423, 452 (1931); *Clark* v. *Cambridge & Arapahoe Irr. & Improvement Co.,* 45 Nebr. 798, 804-805, 64 N. W. 239 (1895); *Taylor Fishing Club* v. *Hammett,* 88 S. W. (2d) 127, 129 (Tex. Civ. App. 1935, error dismissed); *State* v. *Rolio,* 71 Utah 91, 103, 262 Pac. 987 (1927).

[71] *United States* v. *Oregon,* 295 U. S. 1, 15 (1935).

After quoting this finding by the special master, the Supreme Court stated that: "It is not denied that this finding embodies the appropriate tests of navigability as laid down by the decisions of this Court." This case dealt with the question of navigability for determining whether or not title to the bed of the waters involved passed to the State on admission to statehood. The court said that this question is "to be determined according to the law and usages recognized and applied in the federal courts, even though, as in the present case, the waters are not capable of use for navigation in interstate or foreign commerce."[72]

In a case decided in 1894, the Texas Court of Civil Appeals held that the issue of navigability of a body of water should be determined by the jury as one of fact; that evidence of navigability should not be confined to present or past uses of the water as a highway of commerce; and that capacity for such uses should be considered in connection with the future development of the country.[73]

With respect to the navigability of certain river sections within Utah at the time of admission to the Union, the United States Supreme Court declared that the *extent* of existing commerce was not the test; that *susceptibility* rather than mere manner or extent of actual use was the crucial question.[74] That is, although evidence of actual use, especially where extensive and continued, was persuasive, yet even in its absence owing to conditions of exploration and settlement, susceptibility to use as a highway of commerce and capacity to meet the needs of expanding population and economic development could still be satisfactorily proved.

Later Tests of Navigability

The landmark case in developing currently recognized criteria of navigability for determining waters subject to the paramount authority of the United States under the commerce power is the *New River* decision rendered by the Supreme Court in 1940.[75] "The navigability of the New River is, of course," said the Court, "a factual question but to call it a fact cannot obscure the diverse elements that enter into the application of the legal tests as to navigability."[76]

Note has been made of statements in the *New River* opinion that availability of a stream for navigation must be considered in addition to evidence of navigability under natural conditions; but consideration of improvements needed to make a stream suitable for commerce, even though not completed or even authorized, may control determinations of navigability (see "Determining Agencies—Congress," above). In addition, said the Court, a waterway is not

---

[72] *Id.* at 14.
[73] *Jones* v. *Johnson*, 6 Tex. Civ. App. 262, 265-266, 25 S. W. 650 (1894, error refused).
[74] *United States* v. *Utah*, 283 U. S. 64, 76-87 (1931).
[75] *United States* v. *Appalachian Electric Power Co.*, 311 U. S. 377, 405-410, (1940).
[76] *Id.* at 405.

barred from classification as navigable merely because artificial aids are needed before commercial navigation may be undertaken—which Congress recognized in the Federal Power Act of 1920.[77] Limits to such improvements are a matter of degree; a balance between cost and need when the improvement would be useful. "The power of Congress over commerce is not to be hampered because of the necessity for reasonable improvements to make an interstate waterway available for traffic."[78]

The court said that "Although navigability to fix ownership of the river bed or riparian rights is determined ... as of ... the admission to statehood ... navigability, for the purpose of the regulation of commerce, may later arise."[79]

Some other points made in the *New River* decision are: it is not necessary for navigability that the use should be continuous. Even nonuse over long periods of years because of changed conditions, competition from railroads or improved highways, or other developments, does not affect the navigability of rivers in the constitutional sense. "When once found to be navigable, a waterway remains so."[80] And it is well recognized that the navigability of a waterway may be only of a substantial part of its course.

It should be noted that for various purposes some Western States have applied somewhat different tests of navigability. For example, unlike Federal criteria which have emphasized capacity for commercial navigation, some State courts have indicated that navigable waters may include waters that are only navigable for pleasure purposes. This is discussed below under "Uses of Navigable Water—Other Uses—Non-Federal."

USES OF NAVIGABLE WATER

Navigation

Water rights, titles, and related interests are subject to the dominant power of the Federal Government to control the navigability of a navigable stream of the United States.

In leading up to a discussion of tests of navigability in the *New River* case, the United States Supreme Court said that:[81]

> We are dealing here with the sovereign powers of the Union, the Nation's right that its waterways be utilized for the interests of the commerce of the whole country. It is obvious that the uses to which the streams may be put vary from the carriage of ocean liners to the floating out of logs; that the

---

[77] 41 Stat. 1063, § 3, 16 U.S.C. § 796(8) (1964).
[78] 311 U. S. 377, 408 (1940).
[79] *Id.* at 408.
[80] *Id.*
[81] *Id.* at 405-406.

density of traffic varies equally widely from the busy harbors of the seacoast to the sparsely settled regions of the Western mountains. The tests as to navigability must take these variations into consideration.

Other Uses

The use of navigable streams is not confined to navigation. Their waters may be put to other uses, subject to the dominant public easement for navigation. And the Federal Government has improved navigable streams for uses other than navigation.

Federal[82]

In 1950, the United States Supreme Court observed that the custom of invoking the navigation power in authorizing improvements appears to have had its origin when the power of the Federal Government to make internal improvements was contested and in doubt.[83]

Thus, two decades earlier, in answering Arizona's allegation that the recital in the Boulder Canyon Project Act concerning improvement of navigation on the Colorado River (as well as flood control, river regulation, storage and delivery of water for reclamation of public lands and other uses, and generation of electrical energy)[84] was a mere subterfuge, the Court held that as the river was navigable "and the means which the Act provides are not unrelated to the control of navigation," construction and maintenance of the dam and reservoir were clearly within the powers of Congress.[85] The fact that purposes other than navigation would also be served could not invalidate this authority, "even if those other purposes would not alone have justified an exercise of Congressional power." That being so, the Court found no occasion to decide whether authority to construct the dam and reservoir might not also have been constitutionally conferred for the other purposes—irrigation of public lands, regulating streamflow and preventing floods, conserving and apportioning waters among the States equitably entitled thereto, or performing international obligations.

In the *New River* decision, however, the United States Supreme Court went far beyond its earlier decisions and, in making positive declarations, effectively discarded previous implications as to the relation of commerce regulation to purposes other than navigation.[86] It was held flatly that the constitutional

---

[82] See also the later discussion of this and related subjects in chapter 21.

[83] *United States* v. *Gerlach Live Stock Co.,* 339 U. S. 725, 738, (1950).

[84] 45 Stat. 1057, 43 U.S.C. § 617 (1964).

[85] *Arizona* v. *California,* 283 U. S. 423, 455-458 (1931). With respect to means "not unrelated to the control of navigation," the Court cited *United States* v. *River Rouge Improvement Co.,* 269 U. S. 411, 419 (1926), wherein it was said that while the right of the United States in navigable waters within the several States was limited to the control thereof for purposes of navigation, Congress in the exercise of this power might adopt any means having some real, substantial, positive relation to the control of navigation.

[86] *United States* v. *Appalachian Electric Power Co.,* 311 U. S. 377, 424-427 (1940).

power of the United States over its water is *not* limited to control for navigation in the sense that navigation means no more than operation of boats and improvement of the waterway itself. The authority of the United States is the regulation of commerce on its waters—prescribing the rule by which commerce is to be governed—in which sense technical navigability is but a part of this whole. "Flood protection, watershed development, recovery of the cost of improvements through utilization of power are likewise parts of commerce control." The authority of the Federal Government over a navigable stream is as broad as the needs of commerce; and in the broad regulation of commerce, navigable waters are subject to national planning and control. And so, possessing this plenary power over structures in the flowage of navigable waters, "the United States may make the erection or maintenance of a structure in a navigable stream dependent upon a license."

In the following year, referring to the holding in the *New River* decision that flood control is a part of commerce control,[87] the Court said that:[88]

> And we now add that the power of flood control extends to the tributaries of navigable streams. For, just as control over the non-navigable parts of a river may be essential or desirable in the interests of the navigable portions, so may the key to flood control on a navigable stream be found in whole or in part in flood control on its tributaries. As repeatedly recognized by this Court * * *, the exercise of the granted power of Congress to regulate interstate commerce may be aided by appropriate and needful control of activities and agencies which, though intrastate, affect that commerce.

The court further indicated that one phase of a project, such as power, may carry some of the cost of another phase, such as flood control, and that the several phases need not be of equal importance.[89]

In the *Gerlach Live Stock Company* case, noted briefly at the beginning of this subtopic, the Supreme Court expressed itself as without doubt that the totality of a plan so comprehensive as the Central Valley Project of California has some legitimate relation to control of inland navigation, or that particular components might be described without pretense as navigation and flood control projects.[90] This made it appropriate that Congress should justify this undertaking by general reference to its control over commerce and navigation; and the general direction of the purpose of Congress in this legislation, the Court believed, was intended to help meet any objection to its constitutional authority to undertake this array of big projects. Noting that the custom of invoking the commerce clause in authorizing improvements arose when the power to make internal improvements was still in doubt, the Court now agreed

---

[87] *Oklahoma* v. *Guy F. Atkinson Co.,* 313 U. S. 508, 525-530 (1941).
[88] *Id.* at 525-526.
[89] *Id.* at 530-534.
[90] *United States* v. *Gerlach Live Stock Co.,* 339 U. S. 725, 736-739 (1950).

that Congress has a substantive power to tax and appropriate for the general welfare, limited only by the requirement that it shall be exercised for the common benefit as distinguished from some mere local purpose. Continuing, the Court said that:[91]

> Thus the power of Congress to promote the general welfare through large-scale projects for reclamation, irrigation, or other internal improvement, is now as clear and ample as its power to accomplish the same results indirectly through resort to strained interpretation of the power over navigation. But in view of this background we think that reference to the navigation power was in justification of federal action on the whole, not for effect on private rights at every location along each component project.
>
> Even if we assume, with the Government, that Friant Dam in fact bears some relation to control of navigation, we think nevertheless that Congress realistically elected to treat it as a reclamation project. It was so conceived and authorized by the President and it was so represented to Congress. Whether Congress could have chosen to take claimants' rights by the exercise of its dominant navigation servitude is immaterial. * * *

The court held that Congress elected to take any State—created rights on the San Joaquin River—navigable on the lower portion of its course—under its power of eminent domain for reclamation purposes.[92]

The foregoing paragraphs summarize the transition in the thinking of the United States Supreme Court on the scope of congressional authority under the commerce clause. It is no longer constitutionally necessary to invoke the navigation power in authorizing construction of a dam on a navigable stream for the sole purpose of storing water for irrigation purposes in furtherance of the general welfare. But when the constitutional general welfare power is relied upon rather than its dominant commerce power, the Federal Government may more likely be required to provide compensation for injury to private water rights and property. Such matters are discussed later in chapter 21. The Supreme Court has indicated that no such compensation to property interests along navigable waters of the Unites States is generally required under a valid exercise of the commerce power unless property above the ordinary high watermark of the navigable stream is flooded or directly injured.[93]

---

[91] *Id.* at 738-739.

[92] *Id.* at 739, 754-755 (1950).

[93] See *United States* v. *Virginia Elec. & Power Co.,* 365 U. S. 624 (1961); *United States* v. *Rands,* 389 U. S. 121 (1967); and other cases cited in these cases. See also *Colberg, Inc.* v. *State,* 67 Cal. (2d) 408, 432 Pac. (2d) 3, 11, 62 Cal. Rptr. 401, 409 (1967).

The extent to or circumstances in which compensation may or may not be required when rights to use, or property along, nonnavigable tributaries of such navigable waters are impaired by the exercise of the commerce power appears to be rather unsettled. See Bartke, R. W., "The Navigation Servitude and Just Compensation—Struggle for a Doctrine," 48 Ore. L. Rev. 1 (1968); Hanks, E. H., "The Commerce Clause and The Navigation Power" in 2 "Waters and Water Rights" § 101 (R. E. Clark ed. 1967).

Non-Federal

The relationship under the immediately preceding topic is between actual navigation and other uses of navigable waters under the control of Congress in the exercise of its constitutional power to regulate commerce. In the discussion immediately below, the relationship is between navigation under the dominant power of Congress, and other uses of navigable waters by States or other non-Federal entities, organizations, or individuals.

Subject to the dominant power of Congress to regulate navigation, utilization of navigable waters for other beneficial purposes is permissible. Thus, in one of the Colorado River cases, the Supreme Court said that the river is a navigable stream of the United States, and that the privilege of the States through which it flows and their inhabitants to appropriate and use the water is subject to the paramount power of the United States to control it for the purpose of improving navigation.[94] In the *River Rouge* case, the Court held it to be well settled that in the absence of a controlling local law, the owner of land contiguous to a navigable stream has the rights of a riparian owner, subject to the exercise of the absolute power of Congress over the improvement of navigable rivers.[95] The Texas Supreme Court, upon concluding that the watercourse in litigation was a public navigable stream, stated that its waters were held in the State in trust for the public for uses and benefits of which the first and superior right is navigation.[96] (See "Water Rights in Navigable Waterways," below.)

S. T. Harding, writing in 1936, noted that diversions for irrigation purposes had at times restricted navigation in the summer months on portions of the Sacramento River, California, and that the War Department, acting for Congress, had sometimes served notice that it might be necessary to restrict such diversions in the interest of navigation but had not yet actually required the closing of headgates.[97] He went on to say that:

> While the legal right of navigation to take precedence over other uses is well established, its exercise has been based on questions of public policy, and it is not to be expected that the legal preference of navigation will be enforced to prevent other uses except where navigation represents a greater public interest than such other purposes. Other methods of transportation are generally available, while alternate sources of water supply for irrigation are seldom obtainable. It is not to be expected that the rights of navigation will be asserted in the future to an extent that will restrict irrigation or other developments affecting navigable streams.

As noted earlier, it is a Federal, not a local, question, as to whether particular waters are navigable for the purpose of determining the applicability

---

[94] *Arizona* v. *California,* 298 U. S. 558, 569 (1936).

[95] *United States* v. *River Rouge Improvement Co.,* 269 U. S. 411, 418-419 (1926).

[96] *Motl* v. *Boyd,* 116 Tex. 82, 111, 286 S. W. 458 (1926).

[97] Harding, S. T., "Water Rights for Irrigation," p. 14 (1936).

of the paramount Federal commerce power or whether title to the beds underlying particular waters passed from the Federal Government to the State upon statehood. If any State criteria of navigability differ from Federal criteria for such purposes the State criteria may be held to be invalid to this extent. But it appears that different State criteria may be validly employed for certain other purposes. For example, unlike Federal criteria, which emphasize *commercial* navigability, the Oregon Supreme Court has indicated that public rights of boating may exist on waters that are only navigable for pleasure boating purposes.[98] The Oklahoma Supreme Court appears to have similarly indicated that such streams may be used for public fishing and other recreational purposes. The court said, "Our precise holding is that Kiamichi River is an open stream, navigable in fact and can be fished on from boats if the fisherman gets on the stream without trespass against the will of the abutting owner, but the fisherman cannot fix or station trot lines on the bottom of that part of the stream owned by the abutting land owner without permission of such owner."[99]

---

[98] *Luscher* v. *Reynolds,* 153 Oreg. 625, 56 Pac. (2d) 1158 (1936). The court said, among other things, that "There are hundreds of similar beautiful, small inland lakes in this state well adapted for recreational purposes, but which will never be used as highways of commerce in the ordinary acceptation of such terms. . . .Regardless of the ownership of the bed, the public has the paramount right to the use of the waters of the lake for the purpose of transportation and commerce." 56 Pac. (2d) at 1162.

See also the *dicta* in *Day* v. *Armstrong,* 362 Pac. (2d) 137, 143 (Wyo. 1961), to the effect that to satisfy Federal criteria of navigability for commerce power purposes waters must be capable of use in interstate or international commerce but that the State may employ different criteria for other purposes. The court held, however, that it was unnecessary to determine the navigability of the water in dispute "because by our Constitution and its Congressional approval, the title of *all* waters of the State is placed in public ownership." (Emphasis supplied). *Id.* at 144, referring to Wyo. Const., art. VIII, § 1, which declares that all natural streams, springs, lakes, or other collections of still water are the property of the State. The court concluded that: "Irrespective of the ownership of the bed or channel of waters, and irrespective of their navigability, the public has the right to use public waters of this State for floating usable craft and that use may not be interfered with or curtailed by any landowner. It is also the right of the public while so lawfully floating in the State's waters to lawfully hunt or fish or do any and all other things which are not otherwise made unlawful." *Id.* at 147. For a similar interpretation of a similar type of constitutional provision in New Mexico, see *State ex rel. State Game Comm'n.* v. *Red River Valley Co.,* 51 N. Mex. 207, 182 Pac. (2d) 421, 430-432, 464 (1945). But the Colorado Supreme Court rejected such an interpretation of a similar constitutional provision in that State. *Hartman* v. *Tresise,* 36 Colo. 146, 84 Pac. 685, 686-687 (1905).

[99] *Curry* v. *Hill,* 460 Pac. (2d) 933, 936 (Okla. 1969). The court also said that "The question of whether such streams similar to the Kiamichi River were navigable in fact at least so far as fishing and use for pleasure purposes is concerned has been troublesome to the courts in various jurisdictions for many years." *Id.* at 935. The court indicated the river had been extensively used for boating, fishing, recreation, and

The South Dakota Supreme Court has broadened definitions of navigable waters to include "waters not navigable in the ordinary sense."[100] Rather, navigability is made to depend upon the natural availability of waters for public purposes—including rowing, fishing, fowling, bathing, and the like[101] — taking into consideration their natural character and surroundings. Under this view, to say that stream or lake waters are public is equivalent to saying that they are navigable.[102] In each of the three cited cases in which this definition was employed, the court held that the lake involved was navigable and that its bed was owned by the State rather than the riparian landowners. However, to the extent that this definition may have been applied for the purpose of determining whether title to the bed underlying particular waters passed from the Federal Government to the State upon statehood, it may have been erroneous, as it is a broader definition than the controlling Federal criteria of navigability for such purposes discussed above.[103] Nevertheless, it apparently could generally be effective to preclude owners of riparian lands along such waters that are nonnavigable by Federal criteria from acquiring ownership of the bed if they hold title under Federal patents issued after statehood.[104] But

---

pleasure. At one point, the court mentioned that the river at one time had been used for commercial log floatage. *Id.* at 935. But since such commercial use was not alluded to in the quoted "question" posed by tne court, or otherwise referred to, it may be doubted whether the court made it an element of its test of navigability for public fishing purposes.

See also *Bohn* v. *Albertson,* 107 Cal. App. (2d) 738, 238 Pac. (2d) 128, 132-135, 139-140 (1951). A recent Washington case held that the public had rights of "fishing, boating, swimming, water skiing, and other related recreational purposes generally regarded as corollary to the right of navigation and the use of public waters" over privately owned portions of the bed of a navigable lake during the times they are submerged. The navigability of the lake involved was conceded and not in issue. *Wilbour* v. *Gallager,* ____ Wash. (2d) ____, 462 Pac. (2d) 232, 233, 239 (1969).

[100] *Hildebrand* v. *Knapp,* 65 S. Dak. 414, 417, 274 N. W. 821 (1937).

[101] In this regard, see also *Anderson* v. *Ray,* 37 S. Dak. 17, 21, 156 N. W. 591 (1916).

[102] In this regard, see also *Flisrand* v. *Madson,* 35 S. Dak. 457, 469, 152 N. W. 796 (1915).

[103] See Johnson, R. W., and Austin, R. A., Jr., "Recreational Rights and Titles to Beds in Western Lakes and Streams," 7 Nat. Res. J. 1, 32 (1967). See also *United States* v. *Oregon,* 295 U.S. 1, 14, 26-29 (1935), *supra* note 71, which dealt with an Oregon statute.

[104] In *United States* v. *Oregon,* 295 U. S. 1, 27-28 (1935), which dealt with Federal grants after statehood of lands adjoining a non-navigable watercourse by Federal criteria, the United States Supreme Court said that while Federal, not State, laws control the disposition of titles to Federal lands, the construction of Federal grants may involve consideration of State law "insofar as it may be determined as a matter of federal law that the United States has impliedly adopted and assented to a state rule of construction as applicable to its conveyances." It added that "if its intention be not otherwise shown it will be taken to have assented that its conveyance should be construed and given effect in this particular according to the law of the state in which the land lies."

since the State did not acquire title to their beds upon statehood, the Federal, not the State, Government ordinarily may still own such beds.[105]

As suggested by some of the cases discussed above, in a number of States the public may have rights to use the surface of navigable waters for various purposes in addition to navigation, such as fishing, hunting, and swimming. A number of questions regarding the correlation of such uses with riparian or appropriative rights do not appear to have been settled in several States. Such matters are alluded to in chapters 7 to 10.

Irrigation and other consumptive uses of navigable water have been involved in determinations of water rights questions (see the immediately succeeding topic).

WATER RIGHTS IN NAVIGABLE WATERWAYS

Appropriative Rights

Subject to the paramount authority of the Federal Government to control navigation and to protect the navigability of navigable streams, the right to appropriate such waters is generally recognized throughout the West. Many diversions under appropriative rights are made from navigable streams. The effect of acquisition of an appropriative right on a navigable stream is to establish the appropriator's right to make his diversion during the periods in which it does not impair the navigable capacity of the stream.

Federal Law

By the Acts of 1866 and 1870, Congress recognized and confirmed the acquisition of appropriative rights on the public domain pursuant to local customs, laws, and court decisions.[106] By the Desert Land Act of 1877, it was provided that the surplus unappropriated water of nonnavigable sources on the public domain should be available for appropriation by the public for irrigation, mining, and manufacturing purposes.[107] In 1890, Congress prohibited creation of obstructions to the navigable capacity of waters over which the United States has jurisdiction.[108] As noted earlier (see "Classification of Navigable Waters—Other Waters Related to Navigability"), Congress thereby subjected surplus waters of nonnavigable sources on the public domain to appropriation, but reserved its control over the maintenance of navigability of navigable watercourses; and it did not confer upon any State the right to

---

[105] Unless they were acquired by the State under Federal land grants to the State. But this seems rather unlikely.

For a detailed discussion of this complicated subject, see Mann, F. L., Ellis, H. H., and Krausz, N. G. P., "Water-Use Law in Illinois," pp. 82-108 (1964).

[106] 14 Stat. 253, § 9; 16 Stat. 218.

[107] 19 Stat. 377, 43 U.S.C. § 321 (1964).

[108] 26 Stat. 454, § 10.

· appropriate all waters of tributary streams that unite into a navigable watercourse and so destroy its navigability.[109] On this latter point, referring to the *Rio Grande Dam* case, the Oregon Supreme Court observed that the Desert Land Act was not intended to permit appropriators to deplete the flow of nonnavigable water sources to such an extent as to impair materially navigation of the rivers to which such streams directly or indirectly may be tributary, and that:[110]

> The reason for this is plain: To permit an interference with navigation would be to deprive the entire public of a valuable right, which at all times has been recognized as paramount to that of the individual desiring such interference; while to permit an appropriation of water depriving the owner of the land through which it may flow of its use for irrigation, affects such person only. * * *

That waters of navigable streams of the United States may be appropriated, subject to the dominant Federal easement, has been specifically recognized by the United States Supreme Court. In *Arizona* v. *California,* the Court, declaring the Colorado River to be a navigable stream of the United States, recognized the privilege of the States and individuals therein to appropriate and use the water by holding that this privilege is subject to the paramount navigation authority.[111] In *United States* v. *Gerlach Live Stock Company,* the Court sustained the power of Congress to build the Friant Dam on the San Joaquin River—the lower sections of which are not only navigable in fact but are navigated—and approved the "realistic" election of Congress to treat it as a reclamation project.[112] Two large canals emanating from the ends of the dam carry away from the San Joaquin River large quantities of stored water appropriated for irrigation and other purposes. In the plan of the overall Central Valley Project, of which Friant Dam is a part, the paramount authority of the United States is asserted by naming navigation of the Sacramento and San Joaquin Rivers as one of the purposes.

State Law

According to the Washington Supreme Court, "no reason is apparent why the [respective] rights of appropriators should depend upon the navigability or nonnavigability of the water appropriated."[113]

A California district court of appeal has said:

---

[109] *United States* v. *Rio Grande Dam & Irr. Co.,* 174 U. S. 690, 703, 704-708 (1899).

[110] *Hough* v. *Porter,* 51 Oreg. 318, 405, 95 Pac. 732 (1908), 98 Pac. 1083 (1909), 102 Pac. 728 (1909).

[111] *Arizona* v. *California,* 298 U. S. 558, 569 (1936).

[112] *United States* v. *Gerlach Live Stock Co.,* 339 U. S. 725, 738-739, 742 (1950). See *Blake* v. *United States,* 295 Fed. (2d) 91, 96 (4th Cir. 1961), distinguishing the power of eminent domain from the power to control navigation.

[113] *In re Crab Creek and Moses Lake,* 134 Wash. 7, 14, 235 Pac. 37 (1925).

It may further be added that the policy of the state with respect to the waters flowing in non-navigable streams, or even in navigable streams where the use of the waters thereof for purposes other than navigation may be had without material interference with the navigability of such streams, is that such waters shall be so utilized as to produce the greatest amount of good to the industries of the state that they are capable of.[114]

The court in its *dicta* regarding navigable streams did not expressly specify whether its words "without material interference with the navigability of such streams" had reference to applicable Federal or State laws, or both.[115]

The California Supreme Court has said the effect of an appropriative diversion from a navigable stream upon its navigability is the concern of the Federal or State governments.[116] In the absence of governmental action, the matter is not subject to litigation in a private suit between claimants of water rights who are unaffected by the effect on navigability.

Provisions of the water appropriation statutes of North Dakota and South Dakota exempting navigable waters from appropriation were deleted in 1939 and 1955, respectively.[117] None of the current water appropriation statutes in the West include this exemption.

Riparian Rights

In a discussion of riparian rights in the water of navigable streams, it is necessary to distinguish (1) rights in the flow of the stream itself from (2) rights in the bed of the stream and (3) rights in the fast land contiguous to the channel.[118] It is to the first-named category—commonly termed water rights—that this discussion relates.

---

[114] *Waterford Irr. Dist.* v. *Turlock Irr. Dist.*, 50 Cal. App. 213, 220, 194 Pac. 757 (1920).

[115] The court's *dicta* appears to have been intended to apply to appropriative rights because the case dealt with such rights.

[116] *Miller & Lux* v. *Enterprise Canal & Land Co.*, 142 Cal. 208, 213-214, 75 Pac. 770 (1904). The court indicated some skepticism as to the practical value of navigation on the San Joaquin River. In commenting upon the fact that the State had allowed the maintenance of the dam in litigation for a long period of time, the court said that the State "may never conclude to interfere to inquire into its lawfulness in the interest of a mere potential navigability which is apparently of little consequence, when such interference might destroy what, in this instance at least, seems to be a much more valuable public use of the water of the stream for irrigation." In any event, the decision in the instant case was to be made in accordance with the rights of the individual parties as against each other, "leaving the state or the federal government to determine whether or not it will initiate proper proceedings" to inquire into what was alleged to be a public nuisance.

[117] N. Dak. Comp. Laws § 8235 (1913), amended by Laws 1939, ch. 255; S. Dak. Code § 61.0101 (1939), repealed by Laws 1955, § 1.

[118] See, for example, *Curry* v. *Hill*, 460 Pac. (2d) 933, 936 (Okla. 1969), discussed at note 99 *supra*.

Federal Law

"Ownership of a private stream wholly upon the lands of an individual is conceivable; but that the running water in a great navigable stream is capable of private ownership is inconceivable."[119]

In the absence of controlling local laws limiting the rights of a riparian owner upon a navigable stream, he has private property rights such as those of access and wharfage.[120] Such rights, however, are subordinate to the public right of navigation and are of no avail against the absolute power of Congress over the improvement of navigable rivers.[121] From the beginning, said the Supreme Court, it has been recognized that all riparian interests in navigable streams are subject to a dominant public interest in navigation.[122] Further:[123]

> Whatever rights may be as between equals such as riparian owners, they are not the measure of riparian rights on a navigable stream relative to the function of the Government in improving navigation. Where these interests conflict they are not to be reconciled as between equals, but the private interest must give way to a superior right, or perhaps it would be more accurate to say that as against the Government such private interest is not a right at all.

In the *New River* case, the Supreme Court observed that the power company litigant was a riparian owner with a valid State license to develop the water-power resource, and that consequently it had as complete a right to the use of the riparian lands, the water, and the riverbed as could be obtained under State law.[124] But the State and the power company alike hold the water and the lands under them subject to the power of Congress to control the waters under the commerce clause. As the flow of a navigable stream is in no sense private property, "Exclusion of riparian owners from its benefits without compensation is entirely within the Government's discretion."[125] Furthermore, the United States may make the erection or maintenance of a structure in a navigable stream dependent upon a license.

Thus, when the commerce power of the Federal Government is invoked, riparian water rights of contiguous landowners may be taken for the superior

---

[119] *United States* v. *Chandler-Dunbar Water Power Co.*, 229 U. S. 53, 69 (1913).

[120] *United States* v. *River Rouge Improvement Co.*, 269 U. S. 411, 418-419 (1926).

[121] *United States* v. *Chandler-Dunbar Water Power Co.*, 229 U. S. 53, 62 (1913).

[122] *United States* v. *Willow River Power Co.*, 324 U. S. 499, 507 (1945).

[123] *Id.* at 510.

[124] *Unites States* v. *Appalachian Electric Power Co.*, 311 U. S. 377, 423-424 (1940).

[125] *Id.* at 424. Compare the Court's language in *Unites States* v. *Chandler-Dunbar Water Power Co.*, 229 U. S. 53, 66 (1913): "But the flow of the stream was in no sense private property, and there is no room for a judicial review of the judgment of Congress that the flow of the river is not in excess of any possible need of navigation, or for a determination that if in excess, the riparian owners had any private property right in such excess which must be paid for if they have been excluded from the use of the same."

navigation use without compensation. It is otherwise, however, when Congress "realistically" elects to treat an internal improvement (Friant Dam, California) as a reclamation project and provides that construction funds shall be reimbursable in accordance with the reclamation laws.[126] Such direction, said the Supreme Court, cannot be twisted into an election on the part of Congress under its navigation power to take such water rights without compensation. Whether Congress could have done so is immaterial; what it did was to elect to recognize any State-created rights and to take them under its power of eminent domain.

State Law

Decisions in the Western States which recognize the riparian doctrine so far as nonnavigable waters are concerned are not uniform in extending that doctrine to the waters of navigable streams. This is discussed in more detail later in chapter 10.

The California courts hold that the riparian doctrine attaches to navigable waters to the extent that their navigability is not interfered with. According to the supreme court, "The riparian owner on a non-tidal, navigable stream has all the rights of a riparian owner not inconsistent with the public easement."[127] A district court of appeal expressed the belief that a lake is not excluded from the application of the water rights constitutional amendment of 1928 merely because it is navigable.[128]

Under "Riparian Rights—Federal Law," above, it is noted that in the case involving Friant Dam, California, the United States Supreme Court held that Congress elected to take any State-created rights on the San Joaquin River—navigable on the lower portion of its course—under its power of eminent domain for reclamation purposes.[129] Whether Congress could have taken them under its dominant commerce power was therefore immaterial. Riparian lands that had previously benefited from the annual inundations of San Joaquin River, which ceased with construction of Friant Dam behind which the high floodflows were impounded, were held to have valid riparian water rights under California law for the deprivation of which compensation must be paid.

---

[126] *United States* v. *Gerlach Live Stock Co.*, 339 U. S. 725, 739 (1950). Also see *Blake* v. *United States*, 295 Fed. (2d) 91, 96 (4th Cir. 1961).

[127] *Heilbron* v. *Fowler Switch Canal Co.*, 75 Cal. 426, 432-433, 17 Pac. 535 (1888). The fact that San Joaquin River between two indicated points is navigable "does not affect riparian rights." *Miller & Lux* v. *San Joaquin Light & Power Corp.*, 120 Cal. App. 589, 612, 8 Pac. (2d) 560 (1932). In *Antioch* v. *Williams Irr. Dist.*, 188 Cal. 451, 456, 205 Pac. 688 (1922), the claims of riparian rights of the City of Antioch in San Joaquin River, which is actually navigable in this locality, were passed upon by the supreme court without regard to the question of navigability.

[128] *Los Angeles* v. *Aitken*, 10 Cal. App. (2d) 460, 474, 52 Pac. (2d) 585 (1935, hearing denied by supreme court, 1936). The constitutional amendment is Cal. Const., art. XIV, § 3.

[129] *United States* v. *Gerlach Live Stock Co.*, 339 U. S. 725, 739, 754-755 (1950).

The Texas courts have held consistently that in the case of attachment of water rights to a watercourse the navigability or nonnavigability of its waters is not material. In 1896, the old court of civil appeals rejected a claim by one of the parties that there could be no right for purposes of irrigation as an incident to the ownership of land on a navigable stream.[130] That riparian rights may attach to navigable waters has been held or recognized in a number of subsequent cases.[131] One of the conclusions expressed by the supreme court, although *dictum,* in *Motl* v. *Boyd* was that the creek in litigation was a public navigable stream under the State statute, and that title to its waters was in the State in trust for the public for certain purposes of which navigation was first and use by the riparian owners second.[132]

On the other hand, the Washington Supreme Court has held that owners of uplands bordering upon navigable waters cannot assert riparian rights for irrigation as against the claims of appropriators.[133]

LANDS UNDERLYING NAVIGABLE WATERS

Original Title Vests in the Sovereign

"Dominion over navigable waters and property in the soil under them are so identified with the sovereign power of government that a presumption against their separation from sovereignty must be indulged, in construing either grants by the sovereign of the lands to be held in private ownership or transfer of sovereignty itself."[134]

Title to lands under navigable waters in the West vested in the United States on the transfer thereto of sovereignty over the several western additions, exclusive of lands previously granted by the previous governments and of lands owned by the Republic of Texas. Texas, which was annexed to the United States as a full-fledged State, retained for the State the lands previously

---

[130] *Barrett* v. *Metcalfe,* 12 Tex Civ. App. 247, 254, 33 S. W. 758 (1896, error refused).

[131] See, for example, *Bigham Bros.* v. *Port Arthur Channel & Dock Co.,* 100 Tex. 192, 97 S. W. 686 (1906); *King* v. *Schaff,* S. W. 1039, 1042 (Tex. Civ. App. 1918); *Heard* v. *State of Texas,* 146 Tex. 139, 146, 148, 204 S. W. (2d) 344 (1947).

[132] *Motl* v. *Boyd,* 116 Tex. 82, 111, 286 S. W. 458 (1926).

[133] *State ex rel. Ham, Yearsley & Ryrie* v. *Superior Court,* 70 Wash. 442, 453, 126 Pac. 945 (1912). In the language of the court: "We are of the opinion that common law riparian rights in navigable waters, if it can be said that the common law recognized such rights, have not existed or been recognized in this state since the adoption of our constitution; at least so far as the upland owner having any right to occupy in any way the beds or shore lands of such waters or to take from such waters water for irrigation as against the state, its grantees, or those who have appropriated such water for purposes of irrigation in compliance with the laws of the state." See also Johnson, R. W.,"Riparian and Public Rights to Lakes and Streams," 35 Wash. L. Rev. 580, 601-605 (1960).

[134] *United States* v. *Oregon,* 295 U. S. 1, 14 (1935).

owned by the Republic.[135] Title to lands under navigable waters acquired by the United States elsewhere in the West remained in the Federal Government prior to admission of the States in which such lands were located.

Most of the cases examined in connection with this subtopic relate to watercourses. However, the principles apply equally to lakes and tidewaters.

Title Passes to State on Creation

In *United States* v. *Oregon,* the Supreme Court reiterated a long-established principle of fundamental importance—that on admission of a State to the Union, title to lands underlying waters within its boundaries, navigable in fact at such time, passes from the Federal Government to the State as incident to the transfer thereto of local sovereignty.[136] This accords with the constitutional principle of equality among the States whereby each new State becomes, as was each of the original States, the owner of the soil underlying the navigable waters within its borders.[137] When a new State is admitted to the Union, it is so admitted with all the powers of sovereignty and jurisdiction that pertain to the original States, which powers may not be constitutionally diminished, impaired, or shorn away by any conditions, compacts, or stipulations embraced in the enabling act which would not be valid and effectual if they were the subject of Congressional legislation after establishment of statehood.[138]

Thus, becoming endowed with the same rights and powers in this regard as the original States,[139] the new ones may use and dispose of the lands underlying navigable waters as they may respectively direct—subject always to the rights of the public in such waters, and to the paramount authority of Congress to control their navigation so far as may be necessary for the regulation of commerce among the States and with foreign nations.[140]

As the effect upon title to lands underlying bodies of water is the result of Federal action in admitting a State into the Union, the question whether the

---

[135] 5 Stat. 797 (1845); 9 Stat. 108 (1845).

[136] *United States* v. *Oregon,* 295 U. S. 1, 14 (1935).

[137] *Oklahoma,* v. *Texas,* 258 U. S. 574, 583 (1922); *United States* v. *Utah,* 283 U. S. 64, 75 (1931).

[138] *Coyle* v. *Oklahoma,* 221 U. S. 559, 568, 570, 573 (1911). This case did not involve navigable waters. It related to a provision in the Enabling Act of 1906 prescribing the location of the State capital and forbidding its removal therefrom prior to 1913, whereas Oklahoma became a State in 1907. The Supreme Court held this provision to be not a valid limitation upon the power of the State to change the location of the capital after its admission.

[139] *Scott* v. *Lattig,* 227 U. S. 229, 242-243 (1913).

[140] See *Hardin* v. *Jordan,* 140 U.S. 371, 381-382 (1891). See also *Callahan* v. *Price,* 26 Idaho 745, 754-755, 146 Pac. 732 (1915); *State* v. *Brace,* 76 N. Dak. 314, 317, 320-321, 36 N. W. (2d) 330 (1949); *Lynch* v. *Clements,* 263 Pac. (2d) 153, 155 (Okla. 1953); *State* v. *Rolio,* 71 Utah 91, 97, 262 Pac. 987 (1927).

waters within the State under which the lands lie are navigable or nonnavigable is a Federal question, not a local one, and is to be determined according to the law and usages applied in the Federal courts.[141]

Technical Title a Question of Local Law

It is for the State to decide what shall be done with respect to its acquired title to the lands underlying navigable waters—whether to retain title, or to confer it upon the owners of riparian lands. As to this the Supreme Court has said that:[142]

> The technical title to the beds of the navigable rivers of the United States is either in the States in which the rivers are situated, or in the owners of the land bordering upon such rivers. Whether in one or the other is a question of local law. * * *[143]

Retention of Title Elected by State

Many of the States have elected to retain title to the beds of navigable waters. For example, the State of California is declared by its legislature to be the owner of all land in the State below tidewater, below ordinary high watermark bordering upon tidewater, and below the water of a navigable lake

---

[141] *United States* v. *Oregon*, 295 U. S. 1, 14 (1935); *United States* v. *Utah*, 283 U. S. 64, 75 (1931); *Ozark-Mahoning Co.* v. *State*, 76 N. Dak. 464, 467-468, 37 N. W. (2d) 488 (1949); *Lynch* v. *Clements*, 263 Pac. (2d) 153, 155 (Okla. 1953).

[142] *United States* v. *Chandler-Dunbar Water Power Co.*, 229 U. S. 53, 60 (1913). In *Donnelly* v. *United States*, 228 U. S. 243, 262 (1913), the Court stated: "But it results from the principles already referred to that what shall be deemed a navigable water within the meaning of the local rules of property is for the determination of the several States. Thus, the State of California, if she sees fit, may confer upon the riparian owners the title to the bed of any navigable stream within her borders."

[143] In one line of cases, including *Illinois Cent. R.R.* v. *Illinois*, 146 U. S. 387 (1892), the Supreme Court has expressed the view that the title to such beds is to be held in trust for the use of the people of the State for navigation and other public purposes and that this trust shall not be relinquished by transferring the title to private persons or others except to be used for the improvement of such public use or so as not to substantially impair it. This doctrine appears to have been particularly applied to the Great Lakes and the seacoast harbors and other tidal waters. However, there have been a number of other Federal cases approving of such transfer of beds under inland streams or small lakes subject only to the paramount Federal commerce power. Hence, the public trust doctrine apparently has presented little or no barrier in this regard. See, for example, *St. Louis* v. *Rutz*, 138 U.S. 226, 242 (1891), where the court applied the Illinois rule that riparian landowners acquired ownership of the bed of navigable streams and made no reference to the public trust doctrine mentioned in *Illinois Cent. R. R.* v. *Illinois, supra.* For a fuller discussion of this matter, see Mann, F. L., Ellis, H. H., and Krausz, N. G. P., "Water-Use Law in Illinois," pp. 85-87 note 10 (1964).

or stream. The State of Montana is declared by its legislature to be the owner of all land below the water of a navigable lake or stream.[144] By its constitution, the State of Washington asserts ownership of the beds and shores of all navigable waters in the State up to and including the line of ordinary high tide in waters where the tide ebbs and flows, and up to and including the line of ordinary high water within the banks of all navigable rivers and lakes.[145]

Some points involved in litigation in a few of the Western States that follow this rule may be noted, thus:

In Kansas, the owner of land riparian to a navigable watercourse owns only to the bank of the stream, and ice formed on the stream opposite his land is not his property but may be appropriated by the first person who takes possession of it.[146] The sand on the streambed is the property of the State.[147] But the accumulation of water above a dam built by a riparian owner in a navigable stream is, in a sense, a reducing of personal property to possession.[148] Therefore, it was held in this case that the grant of a right to use water thereby created need not be made by deed, but may be made by parol.

In North Dakota, title to the lands below low watermark of a navigable stream is coextensive with the streambed as it may exist from time to time—a necessary corollary to the rule that the owner of lands riparian to a navigable stream owns title to the low watermark.[149] The legislature may not adopt a retroactive definition of navigability that would destroy a private title already vested under a Federal grant; and the State may not now successfully assert title, on the ground of navigability, to lands beneath navigable waters of streams or lakes unless they were in fact navigable at the time of statehood, absent subsequent conveyances to the State.[150]

If the bed of a nonnavigable river has passed to private ownership by Federal grant at the time a State is admitted to the Union, the State cannot

---

[144] Cal. Civ. Code § 670 (West 1954); Mont. Rev. Codes Ann. § 67-302 (1970). See also Cal. Civ. Code § 830 (West 1954) which specifies the low watermark of nontidal navigable lakes and streams. In *United States* v. *Gossett*, 277 Fed. Supp. 11, 13 (C. D. Cal. 1967), the Federal District Court said "Since the enactment of California Civil Code § 830, it has been the law in California that the state's title to the lands under navigable streams extends only to low watermark ...." citing *Crews* v. *Johnson*, 202 Cal. App. (2d) 256, 21 Cal. Rptr. 37 (1962); *City of Los Angeles* v. *Aitken*, 10 Cal. App. (2d) 460, 52 Pac. (2d) 585 (1935), which dealt with a lake. The court added that "California is not the only state to limit its title to low-water mark. *United States* v. *Eldredge* (D. C. Montana), 33 F. Supp. 337 (1940)."

[145] Wash. Const., art. XVII, § 1. See *Narrows Realty Co.* v. *State*, 52 Wash. (2d) 843, 846-847, 329 Pac. (2d) 836 (1958).

[146] *Wood* v. *Fowler*, 26 Kans. 682, 689-690 (1882).

[147] *Dreyer* v. *Siler*, 180 Kans. 765, 308 Pac. (2d) 127 (1957).

[148] *Johnston* v. *Bowersock*, 62 Kans. 148, 161-162, 61 Pac. 740 (1900).

[149] *Hogue* v. *Bourgois*, 71 N. W. (2d) 47, 52 (N. Dak. 1955).

[150] *State* v. *Brace*, 76 N. Dak. 314, 317-318, 36 N. W. (2d) 330 (1949).

divest this private title by declaring through the courts or the legislature that the river is navigable.[151]

Title to an island that arose on the bed of the Missouri River, a navigable stream in North Dakota, which had not become fast dry land at the time the State was admitted to the Union, vested in the State by reason of its then acquired ownership of the streambed.[152] But islands in the Idaho portion of Snake River, also a navigable stream, which were already in existence when Idaho became a State, were not part of the bed of the stream or land under water, hence their ownership did not pass to the State or come within the disposing influence of its laws but remained public land as before.[153]

With respect to Willamette River, a navigable stream, the Oregon Supreme Court stated that from and after February 14, 1859, when Oregon was admitted to statehood, the State became the owner of the riverbed *and all islands situated therein,* lying between the high watermarks of the riverbanks.[154] To be in harmony with *Scott* v. *Lattig* and *Moss* v. *Ramey,* this statement would be correct with respect to the riverbed lying between the high watermarks of the banks, but it would have to be modified to relate only to islands lying *below* the high watermark at the time of admission to the Union. The only pertinent evidence showed that Meldrum Bar was an island on June 30, 1852, and was an "island overflowed at high water" in 1851. In the absence of evidence to overcome or rebut the statutory presumption that the status of an island overflowed at high water continued until statehood was acquired, it would seem to follow as a legal conclusion that the island was not "fast dry land" at that time and so it would then have been part of the streambed and hence would have become the property of the State of Oregon. The author's impression of this case is that the status of Meldrum Bar as an "island overflowed at high water" in 1851-52, and hence by unrebutted presumption in 1859, *ipso facto* disposed of any question of its ownership by the State as against the United States; and that in the absence of any controversy over it, the court was led to word its statement as to ownership of "all islands" so broadly.

As Snake River forms part of the western boundary of Idaho, the thread of the stream being the true boundary, ownership of the bed on the Idaho side

---

[151] *Aladdin Petroleum Corp.* v. *State ex rel. Commissioners of Land Office,* 200 Okla. 134, 139, 191 Pac. (2d) 224 (1948).

[152] *Hogue* v. *Bourgois,* 71 N. W. (2d) 47, 53 (N. Dak. 155).

[153] *Scott* v. *Lattig,* 227 U. S. 229, 244 (1913), reaffirmed in *Moss* v. *Ramey,* 239 U. S. 538, 545-546 (1916), wherein the Court said, with respect to another island in Snake River which was in its present condition when Idaho became a State: "It was fast dry land, and neither a part of the bed or the river nor land under water, and therefore did not pass to the State of Idaho on her admission into the Union but remained public land as before."

[154] *Freytag* v. *Vitas,* 213 Oreg. 462, 465-467, 326 Pac. (2d) 110 (1958).

passed from the Unites States to the State upon admission to the Union; and the subsequent disposal of fractional subdivisions on the eastern bank (Idaho side) carried with it no right to the bed of the river, "save as the law of Idaho may have attached such a right to private riparian ownership."[155] The original and the altered positions of the Idaho Supreme Court on this question are noted under the immediately succeeding topic.

Title Conferred by State upon Riparian Landowners

Some States have not elected to retain title to lands under the navigable waters within their boundaries.[156]

"The state does not hold title to the river beds in Nebraska. * * * Such river beds are as effectually the subject of private ownership as other property, except that, in the case of navigable streams, there is an easement for public navigation."[157] Title in the case of navigable streams is in the riparian proprietor to the thread of the stream, subject to the navigation easement.[158]

The earlier decisions of the Idaho Supreme Court specifically recognized the principle previously announced in Nebraska. A case decided in 1908 includes the following in the syllabus by the court:[159]

> . . . In this state the doctrine is announced and adopted, that a riparian owner upon the streams of this state, both navigable and non-navigable, takes to the thread of the stream, subject, however, to an easement for the use of the public.

A subsequent decision reaffirmed the rule, holding that patentees of land on the east bank of Snake River took title to the middle thread of its navigable channel, including an island between the thread and the meander line.[160] This decision was reversed by the United States Supreme Court in *Scott v. Lattig,* discussed above under "Retention of Title Elected by State."[161] The High Court held that title to the streambed on the Idaho side had passed to the State, but that the island was fast land at the time Idaho was admitted to the Union and hence, although surrounded by river waters, it remained the

---

[155] *Scott* v. *Lattig,* 227 U. S. 229, 243 (1913).

[156] "Upon the admission of the State of Michigan into the Union the bed of the St. Marys River passed to the State, and under the law of that State the conveyance of a tract of land upon a navigable river carries the title to the middle thread." *United States* v. *Chandler-Dunbar Water Power Co.,* 229 U. S. 53, 60-61 (1913).

[157] *Thies* v. *Platt Valley Public Power & Irr. Dist.,* 137 Nebr. 344, 346, 289 N. W. 386 (1939).

[158] *Kinkead* v. *Turgeon,* 74 Nebr. 573, 580, 583-591, 104 N. W. 1061 (1905), 109 N. W. 744, 745-748 (1906).

[159] *Johnson* v. *Johnson,* 14 Idaho 561, 562, 95 Pac. 499 (1908).

[160] *Lattig* v. *Scott,* 17 Idaho 506, 518, 532-533, 107 Pac. 47 (1910).

[161] *Scott* v. *Lattig,* 227 U. S. 229, 243-244 (1913).

property of the United States and subject to disposal under Federal law only.[162] The Court also stated that as the riverbed itself became the property of the State, subsequent disposal by the United States of riparian tracts on the Idaho side carried with it no right to the bed of the river, "save as the law of Idaho may have attached such a right to private riparian ownership."

The error of the Idaho court in holding that riparian patentees took title to the island, which was Government property, was thus corrected. But the previously announced principle that the riparian proprietor takes title to the thread of a navigable stream was not held by the United States Supreme Court to be in error. What the Supreme Court held was that the east bank patentees obtained with their grants no right to the riverbed *unless* the State law has conferred it—which is what the Idaho court previously had purported to do. However, within a few years thereafter, the Idaho Supreme Court overruled its previous decisions and held the settled law in the jurisdiction to be that the State holds title to the beds of navigable lakes and streams below the natural high watermark for the use and benefit of the whole people, and that the title of upland proprietors to such shores is determined by State law, subject only to rights vested by the constitution of the United States.[163] This holding has been reaffirmed in several cases.[164]

LANDS UNDERLYING NONNAVIGABLE WATERS

Title Remains in the United States

Where waters are not navigable in fact at the time of establishment of a new State, title of the United States to land underlying them remains unaffected by the change to statehood.[165]

The provision of the North Dakota Constitution that all flowing streams and natural watercourses shall forever remain the property of the State for mining, irrigating and manufacturing purposes[166] does not apply to lands underlying nonnavigable streams and watercourses, nor to lands underlying nonnavigable

---

[162] Reaffirmed in *Moss* v. *Ramey,* 239 U. S. 538, 545-546 (1916).

[163] *Callahan* v. *Price,* 26 Idaho 745, 754-755, 146 Pac. 732 (1915).

[164] See particularly *Gasman* v. *Wilcox,* 54 Idaho 700, 703, 35 Pac. (2d) 265 (1934), followed in *Driesbach* v. *Lynch,* 71 Idaho 501, 505-506 234 Pac. (2d) 446 (1951). See also *Smith* v. *Long,* 76 Idaho 265, 271-272, 281 Pac. (2d) 483 (1955).

[165] *United States* v. *Oregon,* 295 U. S. 1, 14 (1935); *United States* v. *Utah,* 283 U. S. 64, 75 (1931). In *Oklahoma* v. *Texas,* 258 U. S. 574, 591-592 (1922), it was held that as no part of the Red River within Oklahoma was navigable, the State acquired no title to the bed, and any lawful claim to any part thereof was only such as might be incidental to its ownership of riparian lands on the north bank; and so as to its grantees and licenses. See *State* v. *Brace,* 76 N. Dak. 314, 317, 320-321, 36 N. W. (2d) 330 (1949).

[166] N. Dak. Const., art. XVII, § 210.

lakes.[167] If construed as attempting to destroy vested rights of property in the beds of such water sources, derived from grants of land by the United States without reservation and conferred by the State law, this State constitutional provision would itself be unconstitutional.[168]

Disposal of Upland and Riverbed

In no case has the United States Supreme Court held that a State can deprive the United States of its title to lands underlying nonnavigable waters without its consent, or that a grant of uplands to private individuals, which does not in terms or by implication include the adjacent land under water, nevertheless operates to pass it to the State. On the contrary, the Court has said:[169]

> The laws of the United States alone control the disposition of title to its lands. The States are powerless to place any limitation or restriction on that control. * * * The construction of grants by the United States is a federal not a state question, * * * and involves the consideration of state questions only insofar as it may be determined as a matter of federal law that the United States has impliedly adopted and assented to a state rule of construction as applicable to its conveyances. * * * In construing a conveyance by the United States of land within a State, the settled and reasonable rule of construction of the State affords an obvious guide in determining what impliedly passes to the grantee as an incident to land expressly granted. * * *

Where the United States owns the bed of a nonnavigable stream and the upland on one or both sides, it is free when disposing of the upland to retain all or any part of the riverbed.[170] Whether in any particular instance the Government has done so is essentially a question of what the Government intended. Its intention, if not otherwise shown, will be that the conveyance be construed and given effect in this particular *according to the law of the State in which the land lies.* If there is no attempt or intent to dispose of a riverbed separately from the upland, the common law rule would be that conveyances of riparian tracts extend not merely to the waterline, but to the middle of the stream. The Court rejected a contention that the common law rule to this effect adopted in Oklahoma had been impliedly abrogated by the legislature.

Late in 1959, the California Supreme Court made its first definite determination of what, in the settlement of a boundary line, is the center of a

---

[167] *Ozark-Mahoning Co.* v. *State,* 76 N. Dak. 464, 472-473, 37 N. W. (2d) 488 (1949). See *State* v. *Brace,* 76 N. Dak. 314, 322-323, 36 N. W. (2d) 330 (1949).

[168] *Bigelow* v. *Draper,* 6 N. Dak. 152, 163, 69 N. W. 570 (1896).

[169] *United States* v. *Oregon,* 295 U. S. 1, 27-28 (1935).

[170] *Oklahoma* v. *Texas,* 258 U. S. 574, 591-592, 594-596 (1922). See *Ozark-Mahoning Co.* v. *State,* 76 N. Dak. 464, 469-470, 37 N. W. (2d) 488 (1949).

nonnavigable stream—the determination of which is held to be a local matter.[171] Under the rule in this State and at common law, said the court, abutting owners on a nonnavigable, nontidal stream are deemed to be the owners "to the middle of the stream," "to the thread of the stream," or "to the filium acquae," as it is variously expressed. While the high banks are the true boundaries of a river for certain purposes, this is not necessarily true in determining where the main channel lies. Noting a conflict of authority in the matter, the California court approved and adopted an apparently logical rule for determining the imaginary line known as the thread of a nonnavigable river or the middle of the main channel thereof—the rule that the thread of such a river is to be ascertained from measurement of the water *at its lowest stage*. In doing so, the supreme court vacated an opinion to the contrary by a district court of appeal.[172]

---

[171] *Bishel* v. *Faria*, 53 Cal. (2d) 254, 258-261, 347 Pac. (2d) 289, 1 Cal. Rptr. 153 (1959).

[172] *Bishel* v. *Faria*, 342 Pac. (2d) 278 (Cal. App. 1959). The court of appeal had held that "middle of the river," as this term was used in describing the boundary of Fresno County, meant the point midway between the permanent banks of San Joaquin River which confine the waters to its channel throughout the entire width when the stream is carrying its maximum, usual, and normal quantity of water.

Chapter 5

PROPERTY NATURE OF WATER AND WATER
RIGHTS PERTAINING TO WATERCOURSES

WATER FLOWING IN NATURAL STREAM
Rights of Ownership of the Water

No Private Ownership: The General Rule

Water flowing in a natural stream is not the subject of private ownership. Private rights that attach thereto—whether appropriative or riparian—are strictly usufructuary rights to take the water from the stream into physical possession for the purpose of putting it to beneficial use. This, in western water law—despite the existence of some real or apparent exceptions, noted below—is a very old and well-established principle.

In its earliest decision as between conflicting claims of rights to the use of water, the California Supreme Court observed that the right of property in water flowing in a stream is not in the *corpus* of the water, but is usufructuary and continues only with its possession.[1]

It has been noted in chapter 1, "State Water Policies," under "Declarations of Policy—Ownership of Water Supplies", that in various Western States there are constitutional and statutory declarations and judicial acknowledgments that waters within their boundaries belong to the public or to the State.

Whether, in a given jurisdiction, natural stream waters are regarded as the property of the sovereign or of the public, or whether there has been no authoritative pronouncement therein as to who "owns" the flowing waters or whether they belong to no one, it is a widely recognized principle—and an elementary one[2]—that private rights of ownership do not attach to the *corpus* of the water so long as it remains in the stream in its natural state.[3] "The true

---

[1] *Eddy* v. *Simpson*, 3 Cal. 249, 252, 58 Am. Dec. 408, 15 Morr. Min. Rep. 175 (1853).

[2] *Custer* v. *Missoula Public Service Co.*, 91 Mont. 136, 142, 6 Pac. (2d) 131 (1931).

[3] *Maricopa County M.W.C. Dist.* v. *Southwest Cotton Co.*, 39 Ariz. 65, 73, 4 Pac. (2d) 369 (1931); *Albrethsen* v. *Wood River Land Co.*, 40 Idaho 49, 59-60, 231 Pac. 418 (1924); *Wallace* v. *Winfield*, 98 Kans. 651, 653-654, 159 Pac. 11 (1916); *Meng* v. *Coffee*, 67 Nebr. 500, 504, 93 N. W. 713 (1903); *Application of Filippini*, 66 Nev. 17, 21-22, 202 Pac. (2d) 535 (1949); *Albuquerque Land & Irr. Co.* v. *Gutierrez*, 10 N. Mex. 177, 236-237, 61 Pac. 357 (1900); *Nevada Ditch Co.* v. *Bennett*, 30 Oreg. 59, 89, 45 Pac. 472 (1896); *Haas* v. *Choussard*, 17 Tex. 588, 589 (1856); *Adams* v. *Portage Irr., Res. & Power Co.*, 95 Utah 1, 12, 72 Pac. (2d) 648 (1937); *Johnston* v. *Little Horse Creek Irrigating Co.*, 13 Wyo. 208, 227-228, 79 Pac. 22 (1904). In *Pulaski Irrigating Ditch Co.* v. *Trinidad*, 70 Colo. 565, 568-570, 203 Pac. 681 (1922), and *Wyoming Hereford Ranch* v. *Hammond Packing Co.*, 33 Wyo. 14, 42-44, 236 Pac. 764 (1925), the principle was applied to sewage discharged into the stream from which the

reason for the rule that there can be no property in the *corpus* of the water running in a stream is not that it is dedicated to the public, but because of the fact that so long as it continues to run there cannot be that possession of it which is essential to ownership."[4]

The principle has been declared as a part of legislative policy as well.[5]

The courts have held that this principle applies not only to appropriators, who merely acquire rights to divert and use the water for the purpose of their appropriations,[6] but to riparian owners as well.[7] "Under either doctrine," said the Montana Supreme Court, "the *corpus* of running water in a natural stream is not the subject of private ownership, though this elementary principle is apparently overlooked in some of the decided cases."[8]

---

municipal water had been diverted. The South Dakota Supreme Court acknowledged that "In a certain limited sense water flowing in a natural stream belongs to the public," subject to private rights of use by riparians and appropriators: *St. Germain Irrigating Ditch Co.* v. *Hawthorne Ditch Co.,* 32 S. Dak. 260, 268, 143 N. W. 124 (1913).

Compare the statement in *Dougan* v. *Board of County Commissioners,* 141 Kans. 554, 562, 43 Pac. (2d) 223 (1935), that the riparian landowner owned the water in the stream just as much as he owned the bed or banks thereof. The ownership that the court was talking about probably pertained to rights of use rather than particles of water. The same question may be raised about statements in *Dunsmuir* v. *Port Angeles Gas, Water, Electric Light & Power Co.,* 24 Wash. 104, 114, 63 Pac. 1095 (1901), and *Colburn* v. *Winchell,* 97 Wash. 27, 29, 165 Pac. 1078 (1917), to the effect that waters of a nonnavigable stream are deemed to be a part of the soil over which they flow, particularly in view of statements in other opinions (*Crook* v. *Hewitt,* 4 Wash. 749, 31 Pac. 28 (1892), and *Rigney* v. *Tacoma Light & Water Co.,* 9 Wash. 576, 583, 38 Pac. 147 (1894)) to the effect that the riparian proprietor has no property in the water itself, but a simple usufruct while it passes along.

[4] *Palmer* v. *Railroad Commission,* 167 Cal. 163, 168, 138 Pac. 997 (1914).

[5] The California Water Code § 1001 (West 1956), provides that nothing in the division relating to appropriative water rights shall be construed as giving or confirming any right in the *corpus* of any water. The Kansas appropriation statute provides that an appropriation of surface or ground water shall not constitute ownership of such water: Kans. Stat. Ann. § 82a-707 (1969).

[6] *Bader Gold Min. Co.* v. *Oro Electric Corp.,* 245 Fed. 449, 451-452 (9th Cir. 1917); *South Texas Water Co.* v. *Bieri,* 247 S. W. (2d) 268, 272 (Tex. Civ. App. 1952, error refused n.r.e.).

[7] *Rancho Santa Margarita* v. *Vail,* 11 Cal. (2d) 501, 554-555, 81 Pac. (2d) 533 (1938); *Crawford Co.* v. *Hathaway,* 67 Nebr. 325, 352, 93 N. W. 781 (1903), overruled on different matters by *Wasserburger* v. *Coffee,* 180 Nebr. 147, 141 N. W. (2d) 738 (1966); *In re Hood River,* 114 Oreg. 112, 181, 213, 227 Pac. 1065 (1924); *Redwater Land & Canal Co.* v. *Reed,* 26 S. Dak. 466, 474-476, 128 N. W. 702 (1910); *Texas Co.* v. *Burkett,* 117 Tex. 16, 25, 296 S. W. 273 (1927); *Rigney* v. *Tacoma Light & Water Co.,* 9 Wash. 576, 583, 38 Pac. 147 (1894).

[8] *Mettler* v. *Ames Realty Co.,* 61 Mont. 152, 161-162, 201 Pac. 702 (1921). With respect to streamflow, the rights of the appropriator, "like those of a riparian owner, are strictly usufructuary." *Kidd* v. *Laird,* 15 Cal. 161, 179-180, 76 Am. Dec. 472, 4 Morr. Min. Rep. 571 (1860). "Neither at common law, nor under the law of appropriation, does the proprietor or appropriator own the water in the stream." *Salt Lake City* v. *Salt Lake City Water & Electrical Power Co.,* 25 Utah 456, 465, 71 Pac. 1069 (1903).

No Private Ownership: Some Real or Apparent Contradictions

It is true, as the Montana Supreme Court observed above,[9] that some courts have stated real or apparent exceptions to the general rule that the *corpus* of running water in a natural stream is not the subject of private ownership.

The Kansas Supreme Court said in 1935 that certain landowners owned the water in the navigable water course to which their lands were riparian "just as much and under the same rights as they own the bed of the stream, or the banks, or the trees thereon."[10] However, a reading of the entire passage from which this was taken suggests that the statement was directed to ownership of the right to use the water, rather than title to the particles of the water themselves.

The same comment may be offered about two opinions of the Washington Supreme Court to the effect that waters of a nonnavigable stream are deemed to be a part of the soil over which they flow.[11] This is particularly so in view of the statements in other opinions of this court to the effect that the riparian proprietor has no property in the water itself, but a simple usufruct while it passes along.[12]

Even in California, where the general rule of nonprivate ownership of particles of running water has been so long and apparently so well established, two examples of apparent nonconformity may be noted. In one case, the supreme court held that the plaintiff had stated facts constituting a good cause of action to quiet title to the stream water "as part of his real estate," such flowing water being "parcel of the riparian land, inseparably annexed to it."[13] As noted below under "Water Reduced to Physical Possession by Means of Artificial Structures—Property Classification of the Water," the same result could have been reached by allowing the injunction for injury to the plaintiff's riparian *water right*, rather than to his title to the *water* as part of his riparian land.

In the other California case, the principal question was whether an artificial addition to the flow of a natural stream—"foreign water" originating in another watershed—inured to the benefit of owners of land riparian thereto, or was merely "in the nature of abandoned personalty" which might be appropriated by the first person who could take it from the stream.[14] The supreme court

---

[9] In *Mettler* v. *Ames Realty Co.,* 61 Mont. 152, 161-162, 201 Pac. 702 (1921).

[10] *Dougan* v. *Board of County Commissioners,* 141 Kans. 554, 562, 43 Pac. (2d) 223 (1935).

[11] *Dunsmuir* v. *Port Angeles Gas, Water, Electric Light & Power Co.,* 24 Wash. 104, 114, 63 Pac. 1095 (1901); *Colburn* v. *Winchell,* 97 Wash. 27, 29, 165 Pac. 1078 (1917).

[12] *Crook* v. *Hewitt,* 4 Wash. 749, 31 Pac. 28 (1892); *Rigney* v. *Tacoma Light & Water Co.,* 9 Wash. 576, 583, 38 Pac. 147 (1894).

[13] *Shurtleff* v. *Bracken,* 163 Cal. 24, 26, 124 Pac. 724 (1912).

[14] *E. Clemens Horst Co.* v. *New Blue Point Min. Co.,* 177 Cal. 631, 637-640, 171 Pac. 417 (1918).

denied the riparian claim and sustained that of the first taker, saying that although a riparian owner has a right to the usufruct of the natural flow in the stream, "an appropriator of the waters artificially added is a taker of the *corpus* of that which exists in the stream only by virtue of its abandonment." However, the essential difference here is that the only water the ownership of which was in question was the artificial increment consisting of foreign water that had been once reduced to private possession and thereafter abandoned into the stream. The court did not reject the general rule that the *corpus* of water naturally flowing in a stream is not the subject of private ownership. It held only that the *corpus* of water (which had come into private possession by reason of exercise of the original diverter's usufructuary right in the watershed of the Yuba River, and which after such diversion and use had been abandoned into the foreign Wolf Creek watershed) did not by reason of commingling with the waters of Wolf Creek become a part of the natural flow thereof.

Ownership by the Public, State, or No One, Subject to Private Rights of Capture, Possession, and Use

Natural streamflow belongs to the public, State, or no one.—One of the "first principles" of the law of watercourses, as deduced by Wiel, is that the running water of a natural streams is, as a *corpus*, the property of no one—variously expressed as being in the "negative community," "common," *"publici juris,"* "the property of the public," or "the property of the State in trust for the people."[15]

The doctrine of public (or State) ownership of available water supplies has been declared in many of the Western States[16] as shown in chapter 1 (see "Declarations of Policy—Ownership of Water Supplies"). Constitutional or statutory declarations of "ownership by no one" have not been found.[17] This

---

[15] Wiel, S. C., "Water Rights in the Western States," 3d ed., vol. 1, § 63 (1911).

[16] This, of course, would be subject to the paramount Federal authority regarding navigable waters of the United States discussed in chapter 4.

[17] After the Utah legislature had declared that all waters in the State, whether above or in the ground, were the property of the public, subject to all existing rights of use, the Utah Supreme Court decided a case involving the taking of water from streams for camp purposes and for the watering of animals therein without the formality of making a statutory appropriation of the water: *Adams* v. *Portage Irr., Res. & Power Co.*, 95 Utah 1, 72 Pac. (2d) 648 (1937). In holding that the taking was lawful, subject to existing preferential rights of prior appropriation, the court observed that the title to such running water is in the public, all members being equal owners or having equal rights therein; that while flowing naturally in the stream the water must of necessity continue common by the law of nature, "and therefore is *nobody's property,* [emphasis supplied] or property common to everybody;" and that being common property, all members of the public may exercise the same privileges in respect thereto, subject not only to the same rights in others but to special rights of diversion and use that have theretofore vested under the doctrine of prior appropriation. *Id.* at 11-12. As to whether this was a purposeful attempt to rationalize the terms "public property," "common property," and "nobody's property," the author is not advised.

is readily understandable, for the purpose of a constitutional or statutory declaration of public or State ownership is to lay the foundation for State control over the management and use of stream waters, and the principle of public or State ownership is more compatible with State control than would be that of ownership by no one. Wiel, writing in 1911, commented further on the confusion in the early authorities over terms used to designate the status of flowing waters, and stated that whether called *"publici juris"* or *"res communes,"* "it is now settled that either form of expression means only that the *corpus* of naturally flowing water is not the subject of private ownership, and is not property in any sense of the word."[18] Certainly in the Western States, any distinctions that may exist in concepts of public ownership, State ownership, and ownership by no one, in the waters flowing in natural streams have not been reflected in the laws of these States that govern rights to the use of water, nor in their administration. With full realization that the currently expanding water economy of the West is accompanied by searching reappraisals of water rights doctrines and proposals for changes, it is correct to say that such distinctions have not had practical importance in this area. So far as State control and actual use of these flowing waters is concerned, the significant and essential principle is that *private* ownership in the *corpus* of the water does not exist.

This positive or negative ownership is subject to private water rights. —The foregoing principle, so well settled in the arid and semiarid regions of the country recognizes, of course, that denial of private ownership in the *corpus* of flowing stream water does not preclude but, on the contrary, is expressly subject to the existence and protection of valid private rights to capture, possess, and beneficially use the public waters.[19] Water in Wyoming, although owned by the State, is held in trust for the use of its people—not indiscriminately, but under public control exercised in the public interest.[20] In

---

[18] Wiel, *supra,* note 15, § 699.

[19] *Oldroyd* v. *McCrea,* 65 Utah 142, 151, 235 Pac. 580 (1925). "In a certain limited sense" natural streamflow belongs to the public, but the right to the use thereof is the subject of private property and ownership by riparian owners and appropriators, subject to public and judicial regulation: *St. Germain Irrigating Ditch Co.* v. *Hawthorne Ditch Co., 32* S. Dak. 260, 268, 143 N. W. 124 (1913).

[20] *Lake DeSmet Res. Co.* v. *Kaufmann,* 75 Wyo. 87, 99, 292 Pac. (2d) 482 (1956); *Hunziker* v. *Knowlton,* 78 Wyo. 241, 252, 322 Pac. (2d) 141, (1958). Compare the declaration of the Colorado Supreme Court in 1912: "The state has never relinquished its right of ownership and claim to the waters of our natural streams, though it has granted to its citizens, upon prescribed conditions, the right to the use of such waters for beneficial purposes and within its own boundaries." *Stockman* v. *Leddy,* 55 Colo. 24, 27-28, 129 Pac. 220 (1912). And in that same year, the Supreme Court of Nebraska held that as running water in this jurisdiction is *publici juris,* its use being owned by the public and controlled by the State in its sovereign capacity, "This state then has such a proprietary interest in the running water of its streams and in the beneficial use thereof that it may transfer a qualified ownership or right of use thereof. When it grants such ownership or right of use it may impose such limitations and

Texas, title to the waters of public streams is in the State in trust for the public: First, for navigation purposes; second, for the use of riparian owners; third, for users of nonriparian waters; and fourth, for other uses and benefits.[21] These rights of capture and use are "water rights." Systems of administering them, whether in the executive or judicial branches of the government, take cognizance of the principle of public ownership of the flowing waters to which the rights of use attach.

The right to take water from a public stream into private possession under either the doctrine of appropriation or the riparian doctrine is a strictly usufructuary right.[22] Said the California Supreme Court in the landmark riparian rights case of *Lux* v. *Haggin*: "As to the *nature* of the right of the riparian owner in the water, by all the modern as well as ancient authorities the right in the water is *usufructuary,* and consists not so much in the fluid itself as in its uses, including the benefits derived from its momentum or impetus."[23] From the earliest times, this usufructuary right, whether riparian or appropriative, has been consistently regarded and protected as property.[24]

Property Classification of the Water

Wiel, writing in 1911, commented with disapproval on the tendency in some cases to state that flowing water in its natural state is not personal but real property—as much a part of the land over which it flows as are the soil and rocks

---

conditions as its public policy demands. Under such circumstances, the state may reserve such a right of ownership and control of the beneficial use of the running waters of the streams as will enable it to prohibit the transmission or use thereof beyond the confines of the state." *Kirk* v. *State Board of Irrigation,* 90 Nebr. 627, 631, 134 N. W. 167 (1912).

The power of the State to impose reasonable limitations upon the acquisition and exercise of private water rights is generally recognized in the West.

Note the handling of a "trust theory" propounded by the California Supreme Court with respect to the relation of California law to Federal reclamation law, particularly the excess land limitation provision (160 acres) in *Ivanhoe Irr. Dist.* v. *All Parties,* 47 Cal. (2d) 597, 306 Pac. (2d) 824 (1957); *Ivanhoe Irr. Dist.* v. *McCracken,* 357 U. S. 275 (1958); *Ivanhoe Irr. Dist.* v. *All Parties and Persons,* 53 Cal. (2d) 692, 350 Pac. (2d) 69, 3 Cal. Rptr. 317 (1960).

[21] *Motl* v. *Boyd,* 116 Tex. 82, 111, 286 S. W. 458 (1926).

[22] *Sauve* v. *Abbott,* 19 Fed. (2d) 619, 620 (D. Idaho 1927); *Brennan* v. *Jones,* 101 Mont. 550, 567, 55 Pac. (2d) 697 (1936); *Crawford Co.* v. *Hathaway,* 67 Nebr. 325, 93 N.W. 781 (1903), overruled on different matters by *Wasserburger* v. *Coffee,* 180 Nebr. 147, 141 N.W. (2d) 738 (1966); *In re Manse Spring and Its Tributaries,* 60 Nev. 280, 286, 108 Pac. (2d) 311 (1940); *Snow* v. *Abalos,* 18 N. Mex. 681, 693, 694-695, 140 Pac. 1044 (1914); *In re Hood River,* 114 Oreg. 112, 181, 227 Pac. 1065 (1924); *California-Oregon Power Co.* v. *Beaver Portland Cement Co.,* 73 Fed. (2d) 555, 567 (9th Cir. 1934); *Salt Lake City* v. *Salt Lake City Water & Electrical Power Co.,* 24 Utah 249, 266, 67 Pac. 672 (1902), 25 Utah 456, 465, 71 Pac. 1069 (1903); *Rigney* v. *Tacoma Light & Water Co.,* 9 Wash. 576, 583, 38 Pac. 147 (1894).

[23] *Lux* v. *Haggin,* 69 Cal. 255, 390, 4 Pac. 919 (1884), 10 Pac. 674 (1886).

[24] *Kidd* v. *Laird,* 15 Cal. 161, 179-180 (1860); *Fleming* v. *Davis,* 37 Tex. 173, 201 (1872,

and trees—saying that the error is in assuming that it *must* be real *or* personal, when the law says it is *neither* and not property in any sense of the word.[25]

However, in a series of cases, the California courts have held uniformly that water flowing in a natural channel is real property, a part of the land.[26] "That water in its natural situation upon the surface of the earth, whether as a flowing stream, as a lake or pond, or as percolations in the soil, is real property, will not be disputed."[27]

The concept that water of a nonnavigable stream is a part of the land over which it flows, but that it is not owned by the riparian proprietor while so flowing, can lead to confusion. In a case decided by the California Supreme Court in 1912, after stating that water flowing in a stream is real property, parcel of the riparian land and inseparably annexed to it, the court held that diversion of the water was an injury to the freehold of the riparian owner and enjoinable.[28] The same result could have been reached by holding clearly that the diversion was an injury to the *water right* of the riparian owner and that an action would lie to quiet the landowner's title to the *riparian water right* as part of his real estate. Title to the riparian water right, of course, is as much entitled to protection as is title to the riparian land itself. The landowner's remedy for infringement is not strengthened by holding that the injurious diversion of the water affects the title to the water as such.

The view taken by the California Supreme Court as to the real property nature of flowing water harmonizes with its holding that water diverted from streams into ditches or other conduits and delivered therefrom upon land for the irrigation thereof never loses its character as real property. This is discussed under the immediately succeeding topic.

WATER REDUCED TO PHYSICAL POSSESSION BY MEANS OF ARTIFICIAL STRUCTURES

Rights of Ownership of the Water

Necessity of Obtaining Physical Possession of the Water

As the water of a public stream while flowing in its natural channel is the property of the public (or the State, or no one), one who has a right of use

---

military court); *Dalton* v. *Bowker,* 8 Nev. 190, 201(1873); *Fairbury* v. *Fairbury Mill & Elevator Co.,* 123 Nebr. 588, 592, 243 N. W. 774 (1932); *Atchison, Topeka & Santa Fe Ry.* v. *Hadley,* 168 Okla. 588, 591, 35 Pac. (2d) 463 (1934); *St. Germain Irrigating Ditch Co.* v. *Hawthorne Ditch Co.,* 32 S. Dak. 260, 267. 143 N. W. 124 (1913).

[25] Wiel, *supra* note 15 § 696 and n. 7, p. 766.

[26] Undoubtedly real property: *Fudickar* v. *East Riverside Irr. Dist.,* 109 Cal. 29, 36, 41 Pac. 1024 (1895).

[27] *Stanislaus Water Co.* v. *Bachman,* 152 Cal. 716, 725, 93 Pac. 858 (1908). See *Copeland* v. *Fairview Land & Water Co.,* 165 Cal. 148, 154, 131 Pac. 119 (1913).

[28] *Shurtleff* v. *Bracken,* 163 Cal. 24, 26, 124 Pac. 724 (1912). "The facts stated constitute a good cause of action to quiet the plaintiff's title to the water, as a part of his real estate, and to enjoin the threatened diversion."

therein does not become the owner of the body of the water to which his right attaches until he has acquired control of it in conduits or reservoirs constructed by artificial means.[29] As said by the Utah Supreme Court in 1902:[30]

> Nor has the city, by virtue of its appropriation, acquired a right to the corpus of the water in the lake or river. Not until the water is conducted into its canal does the corpus belong to the city. * * *

To obtain a usufructuary interest in the streamflow to which his claimed water right attaches, the claimant must actually lay hold of whatever quantity of water is required for his proposed use.[31] This involves a diversion of the water whereby the claimant is enabled thereafter to assert absolute control over it, and an actual application of the water to some beneficial purpose.

The Kansas Supreme Court held that one who had acquired by prescription water power rights in a river—but who had not withdrawn the water from the river and reduced it to possession, nor taken any steps that had changed the character of the water and given him a property right in it—had no title to the water in the river, no right to sell the water, and no right to recover the sale price of water taken from the river.[32]

To meet the need of obtaining physical possession of the water, valid rights of use, or water rights, are essential. The subject thus merges into that of requirements that pertain to water rights, discussed below.

Private Rights of Ownership of the Water

Upon severance from the streamflow, water generally becomes private property.—The general rule is that one who diverts water from a natural stream pursuant to a valid right of diversion and use becomes the owner of the particles of water.

The general rule has been stated affirmatively by some courts, as noted below under "Property Classification of the Water." Some other courts have handled the proposition in a negative way,[33] or with caution.[34] Still others

---

[29] *Parks Canal & Min. Co.* v. *Hoyt,* 57 Cal. 44, 46 (1880), cited with approval in *Riverside Water Co.* v. *Gage,* 89 Cal. 410, 418, 26 Pac. 889 (1891); *Bader Gold Min. Co.* v. *Oro Electric Corp.,* 245 Fed. 449, 451-452 (9th Cir. 1917).

[30] *Salt Lake City* v. *Salt Lake City Water & Electric Power Co.,* 24 Utah 249, 266, 67 Pac. 672 (1902).

[31] *Nevada Ditch Co.* v. *Bennett,* 30 Oreg. 59, 89, 45 Pac. 472 (1896). "Granting that plaintiff does not own the corpus of the water *until it shall enter its ditch*, yet the right to have it flow into the ditch appertains to the ditch." [Emphasis supplied.] *Lakeside Irr. Co.* v. *Markham Irr. Co.,* 116 Tex. 65, 76-77, 285 S. W. 593 (1926).

[32] *Wallace* v. *Winfield,* 98 Kans. 651, 653-654, 159 Pac. 11 (1916). Having acquired no ownership in the water, the extent of the recovery, by the holder of prescriptive rights, for deprivation of use of the water was reasonable damages for the injury thus sustained.

[33] For example, appropriated water never becomes the property of any appropriator until reduced to possession in his own ditch: *Bader Gold Min. Co.* v. *Oro Electric Corp.,* 245 Fed. 449, 452 (9th Cir. 1917).

[34] For the purpose of the decision, "it may be admitted" that the water "becomes, after it has passed into the ditch, the personal property of the appropriator." *Parks Canal &*

have noted qualifications or exceptions (See "Some exceptions to the general rule," below).

The old community acequias of New Mexico are usually owned by the builders as tenants in common, although the appropriated water rights of the owners are held by them in severalty. According to the New Mexico Supreme Court, "After the water, the right to divert which, as stated, is vested in the several parties, has been actually diverted under such several rights, into the ditch, and reduced to possession, and by such diversion becomes intermingled, such waters are probably owned by the parties as tenants in common."[35]

In some of the decisions, it is pointed out that the ownership of water which the diverter from the public stream acquires is not unqualified. Although one who lawfully diverts water from a public water supply into his own works becomes the owner of the *corpus* of the water, said the Idaho Supreme Court, his ownership is subject to the necessity of making beneficial use of the water.[36] This private property right is impressed with a public trust to apply the water to a beneficial use.[37] It is only after water has been diverted from the public source into private conduits by permission of the State, said the Utah Supreme Court, that the party who makes the diversion acquires a *qualified* ownership in the water.[38]

Some exceptions to the general rule.—Some State supreme court decisions have been to the effect that the one who makes a lawful diversion of water from a public stream does not thereupon become the owner of the *corpus*. He becomes the lawful custodian of the diverted water, with the rights and responsibilities that pertain thereto. As indicated by the following examples, the duration of this custodianship depends on the judicial view in the particular jurisdiction in which it is exercised.

Min. Co. v. *Hoyt,* 57 Cal. 44, 46 (1880). Defendant could not acquire "an ownership in the corpus of the water, except, perhaps, so much thereof as it has actually reduced to possession in its reservoir." *Lindblom* v. *Round Valley Water Co.,* 178 Cal. 450, 456, 173 Pac. 994 (1918).

[35] *Snow* v. *Abalos,* 18 N. Mex. 681, 695, 140 Pac. 1044 (1914).

[36] *Glavin* v. *Salmon River Canal Co.,* 44 Idaho 583, 588-589, 258 Pac. 532 (1927). The right of usufruct in the water is "subject to a reasonable use and consumption for domestic and other purposes." *Big Rock Mutual Water Co.* v. *Valyermo Ranch Co.,* 78 Cal. App. 266, 274, 248 Pac. 264 (1926), hearing denied by supreme court (1926).

[37] *Washington County Irr. Dist.* v. *Talboy,* 55 Idaho 382, 389, 43 Pac. (2d) 943 (1935).

[38] *Spanish Fork Westfield Irr. Co.* v. *District Court,* 99 Utah 527, 536, 104 Pac. (2d) 353 (1940). Compare the *dictum* in *Adams* v. *Portage Irr., Res. & Power Co.,* 95 Utah 1, 11, 72 Pac. (2d) 648 (1937) – repeated by quotation in a dissenting opinion in *In re Bear River Drainage Area,* 2 Utah (2d) 208, 216, 271 Pac. (2d) 846 (1954) -- to the effect that in Utah, private waters (as distinguished from public waters) are not only subject to exclusive control and ownership, but may be used, sold, or *wasted.* This unqualified judicial acknowledgement that water may be wasted is in direct conflict with State policies as declared in Utah and elsewhere in the West (see "State Water Policies–Declarations of Policy–Use of Water–Beneficial use of water," above). Undoubtedly, it was an inadvertent generalization.

According to the Supreme Court of Arizona:[39]

Water, being public property in a running stream, continues to be public property even when diverted for beneficial uses, and remains such until actually applied to such uses. Our statutes do not recognize the right of ownership of water, as distinct from its use or application.

In determining a question of ownership of water for rate-making purposes, the Colorado Supreme Court held that:[40]

Neither the carrier nor the landowner owns the water diverted from the natural stream. They have only the use thereof under regulations prescribed by the state. Ownership of the water of natural streams still remains with the state. Its use by the carrier and landowner under the ditch is by permission of the state. * * *

Although the New Mexico Supreme Court has held to the general rule that water that is reduced to possession by artificial means becomes personal property,[41] the private property of those entitled to its use,[42] an exceptional situation was the subject of a decision rendered in 1945.[43] The question involved in this case was whether the public, when properly authorized by the State Game Commission, could participate in fishing and other recreational activities with respect to waters impounded by a dam across the channel of a public stream, access to the waters of which could be had without trespassing upon private property. The capacity of the reservoir was some 600,000 acre-feet of water, of which part was designed for downstream irrigation, about 100,000 acre-feet was classified as dead storage, and some was impounded for flood control, to be released as waste water as the occasion should demand. The supreme court held that the entire quantity in storage was public water until beneficially applied to the purposes for which its presence afforded a potential use; and as to some of the storage, it was not contemplated that application to beneficial use in New Mexico would be made at all. To constitute an appropriation, said the court, there must be a diversion and application to beneficial use, consequently these artificially impounded waters were not appropriated in advance of their application to use. Accordingly, not only before being stored but also while impounded by the dam, these were public waters, and the organization that impounded them had no exclusive

---

[39] *Slosser* v. *Salt River Valley Canal Co.,* 7 Ariz. 376, 390, 65 Pac. 332 (1901). See also *Gould* v. *Maricopa Canal Co.,* 8 Ariz. 429, 446-447, 76 Pac. 598 (1904).

[40] *Northern Colorado Irr. Co.* v. *Board of Commissioners of Arapahoe County,* 95 Colo. 555, 567, 38 Pac. (2d) 889 (1934). See also the much earlier case of *Wright* v. *Platte Valley Irr. Co.,* 27 Colo. 322, 329, 61 Pac. 603 (1900).

[41] *Hagerman Irr. Co.* v. *McMurry,* 16 N. Mex. 172, 180, 113 Pac. 823 (1911).

[42] See *Snow* v. *Abalos,* 18 N. Mex. 681, 695, 140 Pac. 1044 (1914).

[43] *State ex rel. State Game Commission* v. *Red River Valley Co.,* 51 N. Mex. 207, 223-229, 182 Pac. (2d) 421 (1945).

privilege in their use while they remained public and no right of recreation or fishery distinct from the right of the general public therein.

Property Classification of the Water

Granting that water lawfully diverted from a public stream pursuant to a valid right of diversion and use becomes *private* property, how is it classified from standpoints of sale, theft, or taxation?

The General Rule

The high courts of most Western States hold that water lawfully diverted from its natural course and reduced to possession by means of artificial devices becomes the *personal* property of the appropriator or riparian owner who takes this action. "As a general principle of law," said the Washington Supreme Court, "water, after it has been diverted from a natural stream and taken into a reservoir and distributing pipes, takes the character of personal property, the ownership of which rests in the appropriator, although some authorities make exceptions."[44]

Some examples of the circumstances under which this conclusion has been reached are as follows:

In a Kansas case decided in 1900, it was held that as the water flowing in a navigable stream was not a part of the riparian owner's estate, his possessory right to the water accumulated by a dam built to impound the water was in a sense a reducing of personal property to possession, much like the collection of a crop of ice.[45] Hence, transfer of the water or ice so accumulated was not required to be made by deed.

The New Mexico Supreme Court held in 1911 that water impounded and reduced to possession and control becomes personal property.[46] As such, it may be made the subject of purchase and sale, or of larceny. It makes no difference in that respect, said the court, whether the captured fluid is held in a skin or cask, by an itinerant water vendor, or in the pipes of a modern aqueduct company. Much more recently, however, as noted above (under "Rights of Ownership of the Water—Private Rights of Ownership of the Water—Some exceptions to the general rule"), the same court has held that there must be a diversion and application of water to a beneficial use to constitute an appropriation; that the water of a perennial stream remained public water after the construction of a dam across the channel of the stream by means of which a large volume of water had been artificially impounded for irrigation purposes and for flood control, part being classified as dead storage;

---

[44] *Madison* v. *McNeal*, 171 Wash. 669, 674, 19 Pac. (2d) 97 (1933).

[45] *Johnston* v. *Bowersock*, 62 Kans. 148, 161-162, 61 Pac. 740 (1900). It had been held in *Wood* v. *Fowler*, 26 Kans. 682, 689-690, 40 Am. Rep. 330 (1882), that the waters of a navigable stream belong to the public, not to the owner of the adjacent riparian land. The riparian has no more ownership in the ice formed on the surface of the river than he would have to the fish that swim in the stream.

[46] *Hagerman Irr. Co.* v. *McMurry*, 16 N. Mex. 172, 180, 113 Pac. 823 (1911).

and that the owner of the dam had no right of recreation or fishery distinct from the right of the general public thereto.[47]

In determining questions of abandonment and appropriation of waste water, the Supreme Court of Oregon held that water appropriated and diverted from a natural stream and taken into possession and confinement in ditches or other artificial works becomes personal property.[48] On the theory that such water is personal property, it belongs to the appropriator from the natural stream and it cannot be appropriated from the artificial works. Only specific quantities of the water may be abandoned.

The South Dakota Supreme Court had occasion to construe a statutory grant of power to a municipality "to acquire a suitable supply of water" for the use of the city.[49] In disagreeing with the contention that under the contract the city did not "acquire" any supply of water, the court held that water when impounded and reduced to possession is personal property; that when separated from its source it may be bought and sold like other commodities. The very apparent legislative intent, said the court, was to grant to municipal corporations the power to obtain water.

For purposes of taxation, the Utah Supreme Court differentiated between (1) water flowing in a natural stream or in a ditch and (2) water in the pipes of a distributing system.[50] The former, said the court, is not subject to ownership so far as the *corpus* of the water is concerned, the right to use it being a hereditament appurtenant to land and exempt from taxation when the land itself is subject to taxation. On the other hand, water in the pipes of a distributing system is personal property, the ownership being in the water itself. At common law such water was the subject of larceny. Not being appurtenant to any land, it was not within the Utah statutory exemption from taxation. In another case—an action for damages for injury to fish and fishponds in which the owners of the fishponds were not the owners of the real estate on which they were located—the Supreme Court of Utah held that the action was one for injury to "personal property pure and simple."[51] Still another Utah action involved the right of a shareholder of a mutual irrigation corporation to have water to which she was entitled delivered into her own private pipeline, to be taken and used for culinary purposes outside the territory irrigated by the company's own canal system.[52] In sustaining the right

---

[47] *State ex rel. State Game Commission* v. *Red River Valley Co.*, 51 N. Mex. 207, 223-229, 182 Pac. (2d) 421 (1945).

[48] *Vaughn* v. *Kolb*, 130 Oreg. 506, 511-512, 280 Pac. 518 (1929). See also *Barker* v. *Sonner*, 135 Oreg. 75, 85, 294 Pac. 1053 (1931).

[49] *Robbins* v. *Rapid City*, 71 S. Dak. 171, 177-179, 23 N. W. (2d) 144 (1946).

[50] *Bear Lake & River Waterworks & Irr. Co.* v. *Ogden*, 8 Utah 494, 496, 33 Pac. 135 (1893). See also *Utah Metal & Tunnel Co.* v. *Groesbeck*, 62 Utah 251, 256, 219 Pac. 248 (1923).

[51] *Reese* v. *Qualtrough*, 48 Utah 23, 30, 156 Pac. 955 (1916).

[52] *Baird* v. *Upper Canal Irr. Co.*, 70 Utah 57, 69, 257 Pac. 1060 (1927). Plaintiff installed her private pipeline at her own expense with the acquiescence of the company manage-

of the shareholder to take her share of the water in this way, the court held that when she had the water to which she was entitled delivered into her private pipeline, it became her personal property, subject to her own use and disposal in any way desired so long as the rights of others were not interfered with.

In a case involving foreclosure of a mortgage on a system of waterworks, the Supreme Court of Washington observed that while water in a stream is deemed in law a part of the land over which it flows, nevertheless after being diverted from the original channel and conveyed elsewhere in pipes for distribution or sale, it loses its original character and becomes personal property.[53] The same court held in a later case that water in an artificial ditch is private and personal property and, as such, it is subject to an agreement for its sale or use and may be made a consideration for exchange of a right of way for a ditch.[54] The water so agreed upon is as much the property of the person to whom it is given as would be money paid for the right of way if purchased for a cash consideration.

The California Rule

The rule in California is that water in canals and other artificial conduits or reservoirs does not become personalty as soon as it is diverted from its natural channel or situation, but usually retains its character as realty until severance from the artificial conduits is completed by delivery therefrom to the consumer; and that water in use in irrigation is not personal property.

Water flowing in conduits or stored in reservoirs. —Water while flowing by right in a canal or pipe, which is real property, is likewise real property.[55]

In *Stanislaus Water Company* v. *Bachman*, the California Supreme Court stated that where the right to water in pipes and the pipes themselves constitute an appurtenance to real property, which is usually the case, the water usually retains its character as realty until severance is completed by its delivery from the pipes to the consumer.[56] The court distinguished the decision in a very early case, which was believed to have given rise to the mistaken notion that when water is confined in artificial channels it thereupon

---

ment and applied for its connection with the main company line within the irrigated territory. However, new officers were elected and the shareholders directed the board not to make connections that would divert any culinary water outside the territory covered by the company's canal system. Plaintiff's pipeline would do this. Plaintiff sued to compel connection. The supreme court held that the board owed the legal duty to distribute to the stockholding plaintiff her proper proportion of the available water, and that a regulation limiting the use of culinary water to homes and premises within the irrigated area was an unwarranted interference with the rights of nonconsenting shareholders.

[53] *Dunsmuir* v. *Port Angeles Gas, Water, Elec. Light & Power Co.,* 24 Wash. 104, 114, 63 Pac. 1095 (1901).
[54] *Methow Cattle Co.* v. *Williams,* 64 Wash. 457, 460, 117 Pac. 239 (1911).
[55] *Fudickar* v. *East Riverside Irr. Dist.,* 109 Cal. 29, 36-37, 41 Pac. 1024 (1895).
[56] *Stanislaus Water Co.* v. *Bachman,* 152 Cal. 716, 725-726, 93 Pac. 858 (1908).

becomes personal property.[57] The language used in that early case, said the court, "is apt for the disposition of the question to which it was addressed, but it is by no means tantamount to a decision that water becomes personalty as soon as it is diverted from its natural channel or situation. No such question was involved in that case."[58]

The handling of this matter in *Stanislaus Water Company* v. *Bachman* was approved in a later decision, in which it was held that water stored in a reservoir is "real property, the right to the use of which may become appurtenant to land."[59]

Water diverted for irrigation or in use therefor.—Water diverted from a natural source of supply into artificial conduits for the purpose of conducting it to land for irrigation has been uniformly classed in California as real property, and it does not change its character from realty to personalty upon being delivered upon the land for the irrigation thereof.[60]

The reason for this rule is that in the case of water delivered in ditches or pipes for irrigation purposes, severance from the realty does not take place at all.[61] Such water "remains real property throughout the process and until it serves its purpose by being absorbed into the land which it moistens."[62]

Water severed from the realty.—In *Stanislaus Water Company* v. *Bachman,* the supreme court considered it evident that water may become personalty by being severed from the land and confined in portable receptacles.[63]

Water separated from the source or body of which it constitutes a part may be bought and sold like other commodities in the character of personal property, such as when it is supplied through artificial conduits for domestic use. The same reasoning applies to water supplied for industrial use.[64] Hence, water delivered to an oil company for use in its drilling operations no more partakes of the characteristics of realty than does domestic water delivered by a municipality to its inhabitants for use within their homes or to an industrial plant for use within its factory. In this case, such water was held to have become severed from the real property on which it was produced, and to have become personalty.

---

[57] *People ex rel. Heyneman* v. *Blake,* 19 Cal. 579, 594 (1862).

[58] *Stanislaus Water Co.* v. *Bachman,* 152 Cal. 716, 93 Pac. 858 (1908).

[59] *Copeland* v. *Fairview Land & Water Co.,* 165 Cal. 148, 153-154, 131 Pac. 119 (1913).

[60] *Stanislaus Water Co.* v. *Bachman,* 152 Cal. 716, 726, 728, 93 Pac. 858 (1908). See also *Fawkes* v. *Reynolds,* 190 Cal. 204, 211, 211 Pac. 449 (1922); *Relovich* v. *Stuart,* 211 Cal. 422, 428, 295 Pac. 819 (1931); *Schimmel* v. *Martin,* 190 Cal. 429, 432, 213 Pac. 33 (1923); *Chrisman* v. *Southern California Edison Co.,* 83 Cal. App. 249, 258, 256 Pac. 618 (1927), hearing denied by supreme court (1927); *Northern California Power Co., Consolidated* v. *Flood,* 186 Cal. 301, 305, 199 Pac. 315 (1921).

[61] *Copeland* v. *Fairview Land & Water Co.,* 165 Cal. 148, 154, 131 Pac. 119 (1913).

[62] *Stanislaus Water Co.* v. *Bachman,* 152 Cal. 716, 728, 93 Pac. 858 (1908).

[63] *Id.* at 725.

[64] *Lewis* v. *Scazighini,* 130 Cal. App. 722, 724, 20 Pac. (2d) 359 (1933), hearing denied by supreme court (1933).

Approval of the California rule by a Texas court.—In deciding questions relating to the property nature of a right to use water from an irrigation canal, the San Antonio Court of Civil Appeals quoted with approval from *Stanislaus Water Company* v. *Bachman*[65] to the effect that *water* while in canals for irrigation purposes is real property.[66] Some further points included in the quotation are that the *right* in such water is real property, and that the right of a landowner to use part of such water is a servitude on the canal and is real property.

WATER RIGHTS
Usufructuary Right

A water right is a right to the use of water, accorded by law.[67]

Whether appropriative or riparian, the right that attaches to the flow of a natural watercourse is not an ownership of the *corpus* of the flowing water. (See "Water Flowing in Natural Stream—Rights of Ownership of the Water," above.) As the above definition states, it is a right to the *use* of the water—a usufructuary right.

The property nature of appropriative and riparian rights is discussed further in chapters 8 and 10.

Appropriative Right

Right of Private Property

The appropriative right is a species of property.—At the beginning of the development of water law in California—in the earliest years of statehood—it was established that the right which an appropriator gains is a private property right, subject to ownership and disposition by him as in the case of other kinds of private property.[68]

This view of the property nature of the appropriative right has been consistently taken by the western courts that have had occasion to pass upon or to discuss it.[69]

---

[65] *Stanislaus Water Co.* v. *Bachman,* 152 Cal. 716, 93 Pac. 858 (1908).

[66] *Mudge* v. *Hughes,* 212 S. W. 819, 823-824 (Tex. Civ. App. 1919).

[67] National Reclamation Association, "Desirable Principles of State Water Legislation," p. 2 (1946).

[68] *Thayer* v. *California Development Co.,* 164 Cal. 117, 125, 128 Pac. 21 (1912). See *Tartar* v. *Spring Creek Water & Min. Co.,* 5 Cal. 395, 399 (1855); *Hoffman* v. *Stone,* 7 Cal. 46, 49 (1857).

[69] See, for example, *Denver* v. *Sheriff,* 105 Colo. 193, 199, 96 Pac. (2d) 836 (1939); *Payette Lakes Protective Assn.* v. *Lake Res. Co.,* 68 Idaho 111, 122, 189 Pac. (2d) 1009 (1948); *Lindsay* v. *McClure,* 136 Fed. (2d) 65, 70 (10th Cir. 1943); *Osnes Livestock Co.* v. *Warren,* 103 Mont. 284, 294, 62 Pac. (2d) 206 (1936); *Crawford Co.* v. *Hathaway,* 67 Nebr. 325, 356, 93 N. W. 781 (1903), overruled on different matters by *Wasserburger* v. *Coffee,* 180 Nebr. 147, 141 N. W. (2d) 738 (1966); *Application of Filippini,* 66 Nev. 17, 22, 202 Pac. (2d) 535 (1949); *New Mexico Products Co.* v. *New*

Valuable property.—Not only is the appropriative right property—it is valuable property.[70] In an early case, it was termed "a substantive and valuable property."[71] In a recent one, "a property right of high order."[72]

Real Property: The General Rule

The appropriative right is real property.—In 1894, the Wyoming Supreme Court said:

> Thus it seems that the doctrine is very general in the states of the arid region that a water right becomes appurtenant to the land upon which the water is used, and the ditch, water-pipe, or other conduit for the water, becomes attached to the land either as appurtenant, or incident to the land and necessary to its beneficial enjoyment, and therefore becomes part and parcel of the realty.[73]

In one of its earliest water rights decisions, the California Supreme Court held that the right of prior appropriation and use of water "has none of the characteristics of mere personalty."[74] The rule that the appropriative right is an interest in real property is recognized generally throughout the West.[75] (The Montana rule is noted below.)

Mexico Power Co., 42 N. Mex. 311, 321, 77 Pac. (2d) 634 (1937); *In re Scholl-meyer,* 69 Oreg. 210, 215, 138 Pac. 211 (1914); *Clark* v. *Briscoe Irr. Co.,* 200 S. W. (2d) 674, 679 (Tex. Civ. App., 1947); *In re Bear River Drainage Area,* 2 Utah (2d) 208, 211, 271 Pac. (2d) 846 (1954). *Merrill* v. *Bishop,* 74 Wyo. 298, 312-313, 287 Pac. (2d) 620 (1955).

[70] *Reno* v. *Richards,* 32 Idaho 1, 15, 178 Pac. 81 (1918); *In re Barber Creek and Its Tributaries (Scossa* v. *Church),* 46 Nev. 254, 262, 205 Pac. 518, 210 Pac. 563 (1922); *In re Willow Creek,* 74 Oreg. 592, 616-617, 144 Pac. 505 (1914), 146 Pac. 475 (1915); *Hammond* v. *Johnson,* 94 Utah 20, 27-28, 66 Pac. (2d) 894 (1937).

[71] *McDonald* v. *Bear River & Auburn Water & Min. Co.,* 13 Cal. 220, 232 (1859)

[72] *Posey* v. *Dove,* 57 N. Mex. 200, 210, 257 Pac. (2d) 541 (1953). In Arizona, "It is common knowledge that the value of land requiring irrigation consists principally in the water supply." *Ramirez* v. *Electrical Dist. No. 4,* 37 Ariz. 360, 363, 294 Pac. 614 (1930). In Montana, the value of a water right was held to be a proper item of value to be considered in fixing the rates of a public utility for the sale of power, inasmuch as it was a part of the production system of the utility company: *Tobacco River Power Co.* v. *Public Service Commission,* 109 Mont. 521, 532, 98 Pac. (2d) 886 (1940).

[73] *Frank* v. *Hicks,* 4 Wyo. 502, 531, 35 Pac. 475 (1894).

[74] *Hill* v. *Newman,* 5 Cal. 445, 446 (1855). More recently: "An appropriative right constitutes an interest in realty." *Wright* v. *Best,* 19 Cal. (2d) 368, 382, 121 Pac. (2d) 702 (1942).

[75] *Comstock* v. *Olney Springs Drainage Dist.,* 97 Colo. 416, 419, 50 Pac. (2d) 531 (1935); *In re Robinson,* 61 Idaho 462, 469, 103 Pac. (2d) 693 (1940); *Nenzel* v. *Rochester Silver Corp.,* 50 Nev. 352, 357, 259 Pac. 632 (1927); *Posey* v. *Dove,* 57 N. Mex. 200, 210, 257 Pac. (2d) 541 (1953); *Oviatt* v. *Big Four Min. Co.,* 39 Oreg. 118, 122, 65 Pac. 811 (1901); *Goodwin* v. *Hidalgo County W. C. & I. D. No. 1,* 58 S. W. (2d) 1092, 1094 (Tex. Civ. App. 1933, error dismissed); *In re Bear River Drainage Dist.,* 2 Utah (2d) 208, 211, 271 Pac. (2d) 846 (1954); *Madison* v. *McNeal,* 171 Wash. 669, 675, 19 Pac. (2d) 97 (1933). An appropriative right appurtenant to the realty in connection with which the use of the water is applied "savors of, and is a part of, the realty itself."

Quiet title actions.—As a corollary, an action to quiet title to an appropriative right and to establish the right to divert and use the water is in the nature of an action to quiet title to real estate.[76] Hence, said the Texas Supreme Court, the quiet title suit must be brought in the jurisdiction in which the land is located.[77] And in such an action, according to the Supreme Court of Idaho, one must rely upon the strength of his own title to establish his claimed right, not upon the weakness of that of his adversary.[78] Furthermore, according to the Idaho Supreme Court, questions of ownership of water rights cannot be litigated in a mandamus proceeding.[79] The Montana Supreme Court has held at least twice with respect to water rights adjudications, title to a substantive property right of this kind cannot be adjudicated through the medium of a contempt proceeding.[80] The Nevada Supreme Court held to the same effect: "Such a right cannot be adjudicated incidentally to a proceeding in which the adjudication of such right is not the main question involved; and specifically, it cannot be adjudicated in a contempt proceeding."[81]

Real Property: The Montana Rule

Applicability of the general rule in Montana.—The Montana Supreme Court follows the general rule to this extent: (1) It acknowledges that the appropriative right, although "not land in any sense,"[82] partakes of the nature of real estate insofar as a conveyance of the usufruct is concerned.[83] (2) An action to ascertain, determine, and decree the extent and priority of the usufructuary right partakes of the nature of an action to quiet title to real estate.[84]

The Montana rule with respect to taxation.—In 1908, the Supreme Court of Montana held that for purposes of taxation, an appropriative right under which

---

Rickey Land & Cattle Co. v. *Miller & Lux,* 152 Fed. 11, 15 (9th Cir. 1907). A water right perfected by appropriation and beneficial use of water "constitutes realty in the nature of a possessory right." *Knapp* v. *Colorado River Water Conservation Dist.,* 131 Colo. 42, 52-53, 279 Pac. (2d) 420 (1955). See Kans. Stat. Ann. § 82a-701 (g) (1969).

[76] *Rickey Land & Cattle Co.* v. *Miller & Lux,* 152 Fed. 11, 14, 15 (9th Cir. 1907); *Pecos Valley Artesian Conservancy Dist.* v. *Peters,* 52 N. Mex. 148, 154, 193 Pac. (2d) 418 (1948); *Hammond* v. *Johnson,* 94 Utah 20, 27-28, 66 Pac. (2d) 894 (1937); *Hunziker* v. *Knowlton,* 78 Wyo. 254, 255-256, 324 Pac. (2d) 266 (1958).

[77] *Lakeside Irr. Co.* v. *Markham Irr. Co.,* 116 Tex. 65, 74-75, 285 S. W. 593 (1926).

[78] *Harris* v. *Chapman,* 51 Idaho 283, 293, 5 Pac. (2d) 733 (1931).

[79] *Nampa & Meridian Irr. Dist.* v. *Welsh,* 52 Idaho 279, 283-285, 15 Pac. (2d) 617 (1932).

[80] *State ex rel. Zosel* v. *District Court,* 56 Mont. 578, 581, 185 Pac. 1112 (1919); *State ex rel. Reeder* v. *District Court,* 100 Mont. 376, 380, 47 Pac. (2d) 653 (1935).

[81] *In re Barber Creek and Its Tributaries (Scossa* v. *Church),* 46 Nev. 254, 260, 262, 205 Pac. 518, 210 Pac. 563 (1922).

[82] *Verwolf* v. *Low Line Irr. Co.,* 70 Mont. 570, 578, 227 Pac. 68 (1924).

[83] *Middle Creek Ditch Co.* v. *Henry,* 15 Mont. 558, 572, 39 Pac. 1054 (1895).

[84] *Whitcomb* v. *Murphy,* 94 Mont. 562, 566, 23 Pac. (2d) 980 (1933).

water was being distributed to the City of Helena and its inhabitants for their consumptive use must be considered personal property.[85]

A year later, the court attempted to explain this by saying (1) that when viewed as independent property rights, ditches and the right to use the water conveyed by them are property subject to taxation; but (2) a different situation arises when the water rights are made appurtenant to land, for they then have no independent use.[86] Such an appurtenant water right is not taxable separately. Its value enters as an element into the value of the principal estate to which it is appurtenant. Hence, it bears a proportionate burden of taxation by the added taxable value which it gives to the land.[87]

The Montana Supreme Court has thus summed up the situation:[88]

The water right—a right to the use of water—while it partakes of the nature of real estate * * *, is not land in any sense, and, when considered alone and for the purpose of taxation, is personal property. * * * When considered otherwise, it is not subject to taxation independently of the land to which it is appurtenant, * * *.

Riparian Right

It will be noted in chapter 6, in discussing the status of the riparian doctrine in the several Western States, that with the passing of the years the practical and legal importance of this doctrine has undergone some marked changes. In some of the dual-system States, the relative importance of riparianism has progressively declined. This fact, however, does not affect the correctness of statements concerning the property nature of the riparian right that were made by the courts of such States during the time they accepted the riparian doctrine as of greater significance in their jurisdictions. Therefore, the citations in the ensuing discussion of the property nature of the riparian right are submitted as valid in the overall view of this topic, regardless of the current force or lack of force of the doctrine in the jurisdictions from which they are taken.

Right of Private Property

The riparian right is a right of property.—An incident to the ownership of land abutting upon a stream,[89] the riparian right is property within the meaning of that word.[90] "It is property within the constitutional

---

[85] *Helena Water Works Co.* v. *Settles,* 37 Mont. 237, 239-240, 95 Pac. 838 (1908).

[86] *Hale* v. *County of Jefferson,* 39 Mont. 137, 142, 101 Pac. 973 (1909).

[87] *State ex rel. Schoonover* v. *Stewart,* 89 Mont. 257, 273, 297 Pac. 476 (1931).

[88] *Verwolf* v. *Low Line Irr. Co.,* 70 Mont. 570, 578, 227 Pac. 68 (1924); *Brady Irr. Co.* v. *Teton County,* 107 Mont. 330, 333-334, 85 Pac. (2d) 350 (1938).

[89] *Benton* v. *Johncox,* 17 Wash. 277, 281, 283, 49 Pac. 495 (1897).

[90] *Crawford Co.* v. *Hathaway,* 67 Nebr. 325, 346-347, 93 N. W. 781 (1903), overruled on different matters by *Wasserburger* v. *Coffee,* 180 Nebr. 147, 141 N. W. (2d) 738

guaranties."[91] It is often said to be a vested property right.[92] Although they are qualified and not absolute rights of property,[93] "riparian rights are substantial property rights which may not be arbitrarily destroyed."[94] That a riparian right is a property right, said the Kansas Supreme Court in an early decision, "is unquestioned and familiar law."[95]

Private property. —The riparian right is a right of private property,[96] vested exclusively in the owner of the abutting land for use only on that land; and it is not of a political nature.[97]

Real Property

That the riparian right is real estate has been acknowledged uniformly by the courts of the West that have had occasion to pass upon or to discuss the property nature of the right. This has been done in various ways. Some examples follow:

The water right that attaches to riparian land by virtue of its location is real estate: It is identified with the realty,[98] and is a part thereof.[99] It is a part of the riparian owner's estate.[100] The riparian right is incident to the ownership of upland and it enters materially into the actual value thereof.[101] This property right, like any other part of the realty, is subject to taking for public use under the power of eminent domain and to loss in other ways provided by law.[102] A contract for the sale of riparian waters was held by the Supreme Court of Texas to be one affecting real estate to such an extent as to be within the

---

(1966). The right to the continued existence of the stream conditions at the landowner's land is property: *Atchison, Topeka & Santa Fe Ry.* v. *Hadley,* 168 Okla. 588, 591, 35 Pac. (2d) 463 (1934).

[91] *Parker* v. *El Paso County W. I. Dist. No. 1,* 116 Tex. 631, 643, 297 S. W. 737 (1927).

[92] *St. Germain Irrigating Ditch Co.* v. *Hawthorne Ditch Co.,* 32 S. Dak. 260, 267, 143 N. W. 124 (1913). "We, therefore, here, reassert the riparian right to be a vested property right inhering in and a part and parcel of the abutting lands* * *." *Fall River Valley Irr. Dist.* v. *Mt. Shasta Power Corp.,* 202 Cal. 56, 65, 259 Pac. 444 (1927).

[93] *Martin* v. *British American Oil Producing Co.,* 187 Okla. 193, 195, 102 Pac. (2d) 124 (1940).

[94] *California-Oregon Power Co.* v. *Beaver Portland Cement Co.,* 73 Fed. (2d) 555, 562 (9th Cir. 1934). "Such rights are not unlimited, but they are substantial." *Greenman* v. *Fort Worth,* 308 S. W. (2d) 553, 555 (Tex. Civ. App. 1957, error refused n.r.e.).

[95] *Emporia* v. *Soden,* 25 Kans. 588, 604, 37 Am. Rep. 265 (1881).

[96] *San Bernardino* v. *Riverside,* 186 Cal. 7, 13, 198 Pac. 784 (1921).

[97] *Antioch* v. *Williams Irr. Dist.,* 188 Cal. 451, 456, 205 Pac. 688 (1922).

[98] *Lux* v. *Haggin,* 69 Cal. 255, 391, 4 Pac. 919 (1884), 10 Pac. 674 (1886).

[99] *Palmer* v. *Railroad Commission,* 167 Cal. 163, 173, 138 Pac. 997 (1914); *Frizell* v. *Bindley,* 144 Kans. 84, 91, 58 Pac. (2d) 95 (1936).

[100] *Bernot* v. *Morrison,* 81 Wash. 538, 544, 143 Pac. 104 (1914).

[101] *Parsons* v. *Sioux Falls,* 65 S. Dak. 145, 151, 272 N. W. 288 (1937).

[102] *Crawford Co.* v. *Hathaway,* 67 Nebr. 325, 346-347, 93 N. W. 781 (1903), overruled on different matters by *Wasserburger* v. *Coffee,* 180 Nebr. 147, 141 N. W. (2d) 738 (1966).

statute of frauds.[103] An argument of counsel that riparian rights are real property rights attached to the land does not put them beyond reach of the police power.[104]

There is eminent authority, said the North Dakota Supreme Court in 1896, for the doctrine that a riparian right is real estate; and that it might be condemned without also taking the fee of the land does not admit of doubt.[105]

Real Property: Part and Parcel of the Soil

The right of a proprietor of riparian land in a riparian rights jurisdiction to have the water flow to his land to meet the requirements of his water right as recognized in the jurisdiction is annexed to the soil, not as a mere easement or appurtenance, but as part and parcel of the land itself.

The essence of the statement that the riparian right is part and parcel of the soil—as a rule of the common law—has been included in the opinions of courts of a number of the Western States in which the common law riparian doctrine has been recognized.[106] It has been repeated through the years in one form or another in many decisions of the California courts.[107] The California Supreme Court made the statement at least as early as 1882.[108] In 1927, this court reexamined the riparian right in the light of the facts of the case then before it, considered itself entirely satisfied with previous pronouncements thereupon, and specifically reasserted the right to be a vested property right inhering in the riparian land.[109]

---

[103] *Texas Co.* v. *Burkett,* 117 Tex. 16, 29-30, 296 S. W. 273 (1927).

[104] *California-Oregon Power Co.* v. *Beaver Portland Cement Co.,* 73 Fed. (2d) 555, 567 (9th Cir. 1934).

[105] *Bigelow* v. *Draper,* 6 N. Dak. 152, 161-162, 69 N. W. 570 (1896).

[106] See *Smith* v. *Miller,* 147 Kans. 40, 42, 75 Pac. (2d) 273 (1938); *Crawford Co.* v. *Hathaway,* 67 Nebr. 325, 343, 93 N. W. 781 (1903), overruled on different matters by *Wasserburger* v. *Coffee,* 180 Nebr. 147, 141 N. W. (2d) 738 (1966); *St. Germain Irrigating Ditch Co.* v. *Hawthorne Ditch Co.,* 32 S. Dak. 260, 266-267, 143 N. W. 124 (1913); *Parker* v. *El Paso County W. I. Dist. No. 1,* 116 Tex. 631, 642-643, 297 S. W. 737 (1927); *Rigney* v. *Tacoma Light & Water Co.,* 9 Wash. 576, 583, 38 Pac. 147 (1894).

[107] It has been noted in more than 30 cases in the supreme court and district courts of appeal of this State.

[108] *St. Helena Water Co.* v. *Forbes,* 62 Cal. 182, 184 (1882).

[109] *Fall River Valley Irr. Dist.* v. *Mt. Shasta Power Corp.,* 202 Cal. 56, 65, 259 Pac. 444 (1927).

Chapter 6

WATER RIGHTS SYSTEMS PERTAINING

TO WATERCOURSES

THE DUAL SYSTEMS OF WATER RIGHTS

Two basic doctrines govern rights to the use of water of western watercourses. They are (1) the doctrine of prior appropriation, and (2) the riparian doctrine. The appropriation doctrine is established in each of the 17 contiguous Western States and Alaska. In 10 of these States, the riparian doctrine is recognized in some degree concurrently with the doctrine of appropriation, and in Hawaii, without such concurrence. This degree of riparian recognition varies widely from one jurisdiction to another: in some States, riparianism, both in law and in fact, is an important part of the State water jurisprudence; in others, very little vestige of the doctrine is left. Eight Western States have generally repudiated the riparian doctrine of water rights. Where the two doctrines exist simultaneously, they are often in conflict. The conflicts between the doctrines and their adjustment have occupied a large part of the attention of western courts throughout the last century.[1] A major conflict was heard in the appellate courts of Texas in 1959-62.[2]

The *appropriation doctrine* contemplates the acquisition of rights to the use of water by diverting water and applying it to reasonable beneficial use for a beneficial purpose, in accordance with procedures and under limitations specified by constitutional and statutory law or acknowledged by the courts. The water may be used on or in connection with lands away from streams, as well as lands contiguous to streams. A distinctive feature of the doctrine as it was developed in the West is the principle of "first in time, first in right"—the prior exclusive right of the earliest appropriator of water from a particular watercourse to the use of the water to the extent of his appropriation, without material diminution in quantity or deterioration in quality, whenever the water is available; each later appropriator has a like priority with respect to all

---

[1] See Hutchins, Wells A., "History of the Conflict between Riparian and Appropriative Rights in the Western States," Proc., Water Law Conferences, Univ. of Texas, pp. 106-137 (1952, 1954).

[2] *State* v. *Valmont Plantations,* No. B-20791, Dist. Ct. Hidalgo County, Texas (1959). Appealed to San Antonio Court of Civil Appeals, 346 S. W. (2d) 853 (1961), and appealed to the Texas Supreme Court, *Valmont Plantations* v. *State of Texas,* 163 Tex. 381, 355 S. W. (2d) 502 (1962). See also *State* v. *Hidalgo County Water Control & Improvement Dist. No. 18,* 443 S. W. (2d) 728 (Tex. Civ. App. 1969), citing other connected cases.

(157)

those who are later in time than himself. In the absence of constitutional or statutory modifications, the principle of "first in time, first in right" is still valid. However, certain States have authorized preferences and imposed restrictions upon appropriations made under prescribed statutory procedures, the effects of which under some circumstances is at variance from the right of the first applicant to be accorded the first priority. The appropriative right relates to a specific quantity of water, and is good as long as the right continues to be properly exercised. The right may be acquired for any use of water that is beneficial and reasonable.

The *riparian doctrine,* where given full recognition in the West, accords to the owner of land contiguous to a watercourse a right to the use of water on such land for various beneficial purposes. Generally, the use of water for domestic purposes is the highest use, and subject thereto, use of the water for irrigation and industrial purposes must be reasonable in relation to the reasonable requirements of all other owners of lands riparian to the same source of supply. The riparian right is a part of the land; it is not based upon use, and in the absence of prescription it is not lost by disuse. No riparian owner acquires priority over other riparian owners by reason of the time of beginning use of the water. The riparian right is proportionate, not exclusive. It is not measured by a specific quantity of water except when apportioned by a court decree adjudicating the rights of the riparian owners among themselves, or except in an adjudication of rights as against appropriators.

IRRIGATION AGRICULTURE

To say that irrigation is essential to agriculture in the arid portions of the Western States is axiomatic.

The quantity of water available in this vast region is far short of the quantity that would be required for the farming of all agricultural lands. The degree of the necessity for irrigating varies widely, the chief consideration in a given area being the deficiency of precipitation during the growing season with regard to the quantity of water required for crop growth. In some portions of the West, then, irrigation is seldom required; in other areas, it contributes to a wider range of crop production and to greater production than would be possible with the use solely of precipitation on the cropped land; and in still others, it is necessary to practically every form of dependable agricultural development.

The sources of water are snow and rain on the mountain ranges and other higher lands, which in seeking lower levels flow over and under the surface in streams and in diffused flows. As water is much less abundant than good land in the West, the problem is to distribute these water supplies where they can be most beneficially and economically utilized. The physical, economic, and legal problems involved go far beyond those concerned with the simple operation of diverting a little water from a stream for domestic use and incidental irrigation in an area in which the rainfall in most seasons is adequate for farming purposes.

The common law riparian doctrine was found to be unsuited to water development in the more arid areas. Had the riparian doctrine remained the only accepted rule, the lands contiguous to surface streams would have had the prior claim to the flowing waters, solely by reason of location, and diversions for use on nonriparian lands would have been made at the sufferance of the riparian owners. This would have been the case, regardless of the relative productive capacities of riparian and nonriparian lands. It was natural that some other rule, laying greater emphasis upon beneficial use, and affording protection to enterprises based upon feasibility of diversion of water and application to lands whether or not contiguous to watercourses, should have developed from the necessities of the environment. The alternative doctrine of prior appropriation appeared adequate for this purpose. While by no means a perfect system, it has proved more generally satisfactory for conditions in most of the West than has the common law riparian doctrine.

It is implicit in the foregoing statement that, in general, efficient utilization of a limited water supply can contribute as much to the public welfare under a riparian right as under an appropriative right. The difficulty has been that when the unmodified riparian right entitled the holder to use the water inefficiently and wastefully at his own discretion, or to keep the right intact indefinitely while making no use of the water, then the successful assertion of this right could become an impediment to water development. In several States, modifications of riparian principles in the public interest, as the result of conflicts, have consisted of lessening or removing the obstructive aspects of the early common law principles but without repudiating the doctrine completely.

Problems involved in the interrelationship of the appropriation and riparian doctrines in the States in which both doctrines are recognized will be referred to later in this chapter as well as in other chapters.

ESTABLISHMENT OF THE APPROPRIATION DOCTRINE IN THE WEST

Origins of the Appropriation Doctrine

The prevailing Western doctrine of prior appropriation, as it is now recognized and applied throughout the 17 contiguous Western States and Alaska, is traceable chiefly to local customs and regulations developed spontaneously on public lands. The basic principles resulted from experience under varying conditions which, however, had an outstanding feature in common—inadequacy of water to supply completely the rapidly growing demands of industry and agriculture with use of the water control facilities then available. With considerable uniformity, these simple but effective principles became formalized into legal doctrine by decisions of courts and enactments of legislatures. Upon this foundation have been built the current complicated and voluminous water codes and case laws of the West.

As of the middle of the 19th century, the seeds of the appropriation doctrine are discernible in the status of three general movements of great historical and economic importance, which for the most part were probably unrelated—(1) Spanish settlements in parts of the Southwest, (2) the Mormon colonization of Utah, and (3) the California Gold Rush. Irrigation, although on the whole in its infancy, was being practiced in parts of the Southwest, chiefly under the Spanish-American community acequias[3] and to a moderate extent by individuals in other scattered western areas. The Mormon irrigation agriculture development in Utah was getting under way. In California, the Gold Rush had started and mining ditches were being dug.

The early Utah and California water law situations have been the subject of much legal and historical literature, which facilitates appraisals of prevailing doctrine. In the southwestern areas, however, the situation with respect to appropriation of water is less clear and opinions concerning it differ.

Spanish Settlements in Parts of the Southwest

Irrigation in Arizona and New Mexico in aid of crop production is of prehistoric origin.[4]

According to the Arizona Supreme Court, recognition of the right to appropriate and use water for irrigation antedates history and even tradition.[5] However, the supreme court has also stated that in the Mexican State of Sonora, of which Arizona formed a part before the cession from Mexico, rights of prior appropriators arose under Mexican law only as a result of grants from the government, but that appropriations were permitted to some extent by local custom.[6] In a later case, the court stated that the declarations by the first Territorial legislature in the Howell Code[7] established, with respect to watercourses, "the law of prior appropriation as it had existed for centuries in Mexico as best suited to our conditions."[8]

---

[3] Hutchins, Wells A., "The Community Acequia: Its Origin and Development," 31 Southwestern Historical Quarterly 261 (1928). See also Hutchins, Wells A.,"Community Acequias or Ditches in New Mexico," State Eng., N. Mex., 8th Bien. Rept. 1926-1928, 227-237 (1928); *Biggs* v. *Utah Irrigating Ditch Co.,* 7 Ariz. 331, 348-349, 64 Pac. 494 (1901); *Snow* v. *Abalos,* 18 N. Mex. 681, 691, 692-693, 140 Pac. 1044 (1914).

[4] Hutchins, "The Community Acequia: Its Origin and Development," *supra* note 3, pp. 261-262.

[5] *Clough* v. *Wing,* 2 Ariz. 371, 380, 17 Pac. 453 (1888). Early irrigation practices and water rights in what is now Arizona, and elsewhere, are also referred to in *Biggs* v. *Utah Irrigating Ditch Co.,* 7 Ariz. 331, 348-349, 64 Pac. 494 (1901); *Slosser* v. *Salt River Valley Canal Co.,* 7 Ariz. 376, 385-386, 65 Pac. 332 (1901); *Boquillas Land & Cattle Co.* v. *St. David Cooperative Commerical & Development Assn.,* 11 Ariz. 128, 135-139, 89 Pac. 504 (1907); *Maricopa County M. W. C. Dist.* v. *Southwest Cotton Co.,* 39 Ariz. 65, 73-75, 4 Pac. (2d) 369 (1931).

[6] *Maricopa County M. W. C. Dist.* v. *Southwest Cotton Co.,* 39 Ariz. 65, 74-75, 4 Pac. (2d) 369 (1931). See also *Boquillas Land & Cattle Co.* v. *St. David Cooperative Commercial & Development Assn.,* 11 Ariz. 128, 129, 89 Pac. 504 (1907).

[7] Terr. Ariz. Howell Code, Bill of Rights, art. 22; ch. LV (October 4, 1864).

[8] *Tattersfield* v. *Putnam,* 45 Ariz. 156, 165, 41 Pac. (2d) 228 (1935).

In 1898, the Territorial Supreme Court of New Mexico said that:[9]

The law of prior appropriation existed under the Mexican republic at the time of the acquisition of New Mexico, and one of the first acts of this government was to declare that "the laws heretofore in force concerning water courses * * * shall continue in force." Code proclaimed by Brigadier General Kearney, September 22, 1846. * * * The doctrine of prior appropriation has been the settled law of this territory by legislation, custom and judicial decision. Indeed, it is no figure of speech to say that agriculture and mining life of the whole country depends upon the use of the waters for irrigation, and, if rights can be acquired in waters not navigable, none can have greater antiquity and equity in their favor than those which have been acquired in the Rio Grande valley in New Mexico.

A half-century later, the State supreme court observed that the constitutional provision, that the doctrine of prior appropriation applies to unappropriated waters of all natural streams,[10] is only declaratory of prior existing law and always has been the rule and practice under Spanish and Mexican dominion; that this doctrine, based on the theory that all waters subject to appropriation are public, obtained under Mexican sovereignty and continued after the American acquisition.[11]

In 1901, the Arizona Supreme Court stressed the common ancestry of water laws of Arizona and New Mexico, and asserted that Arizona legislation on the right to appropriate water for beneficial use differed fundamentally from that of other States and Territories with the single exception of New Mexico.[12] Continuing, the court said that:

Whatever, therefore, may be the law as declared by the supreme court or court of appeals of Colorado, or the courts of last resort of other states and territories having a dissimilar history, or whose water laws have grown out of the local customs of miners, as in California and Nevada, these are not controlling, and are not even authoritative in the decision of questions which arise, as in this instance, wholly and entirely under our own peculiar statutes. * * *

Thus have the Arizona and New Mexico courts expressed their convictions that the doctrine of appropriation existed in these jurisdictions prior to American sovereignty—that the now existing appropriation philosophy was derived from principles and practices of the Spanish-Mexican occupations of

---

[9] *United States* v. *Rio Grande Dam & Irr. Co.*, 9 N. Mex. 292, 306-307, 51 Pac. 674 (1898), reversed, but not on the point discussed here, 174 U. S. 690 (1899).

[10] N. Mex. Const., art. XVI, § 2.

[11] *State ex rel. State Game Commission* v. *Red River Valley Co.*, 51 N. Mex. 207, 217, 182 Pac. (2d) 421 (1945). See also *Hagerman Irr. Co.* v. *McMurry*, 16 N. Mex. 172, 181-182, 113 Pac. 823 (1911).

[12] *Slosser* v. *Salt River Valley Canal Co.*, 7 Ariz. 376, 385-386, 65 Pac. 332 (1901).

these regions, not from those of lesser antiquity development in other parts of the West. On the other hand, it is noteworthy that the Spaniards made settlements in California and Texas as well; yet that there is nothing in the water laws of either of these States to suggest that a principle of prior appropriation of water prevailed under Spanish or Mexican sovereignty.[13]

Opinions differ as to just how the appropriation doctrine came to the southwestern areas that had been occupied by the Spaniards and Mexicans. According to one school of thought, the Spanish settlers brought this doctrine from Europe with their civil law, which had been derived from the civil law of Rome. Thus, with respect to the Spanish, French, and Mexican penetration of what is now the American Southwest, it is said that:[14]

> The extent to which this early western development has spread over and influenced the customs and laws of the subsequently created states may be debatable. But that such an influence existed, having as its background the old Roman water law, cannot be denied. How remarkably alike, in many vital respects, are the Roman laws concerning water and water rights and the doctrine of appropriation as interpreted and applied, for example, in Colorado. * * *

Another view is that exclusive rights in the Spanish and Mexican settlements arose only by way of grants from the sovereign, or as the result of local custom—as noted by the Arizona Supreme Court, above[15]—which would be prescription.[16]

Apparently, exclusive rights to the use of water on nonriparian lands in the New World of Spain were obtainable and, in various instances, they doubtless were obtained from the sovereign. Perhaps some form of "appropriation" of water can be found in some of the local customs. But in view of the paucity of historical examples, establishment of the well-known principle of *priority of appropriation* under the Spanish-Mexican regime, in the form in which it is so widely applied in the West today, is lacking in satisfactory proof and therefore, to say the least, is questionable.

Mormon Colonization of Utah

The colonization of Utah began in 1847 when the Mormons, under the personal leadership of Brigham Young, entered the Great Salt Lake Valley. This desert, unoccupied except by some Indians, then belonged to Mexico.

---

[13] Compare Hutchins, Wells A.: "The California Law of Water Rights," pp. 41-51 (1956), and "The Texas Law of Water Rights," pp. 102-106 (1961).

[14] Report and Recommendations of Committee of National Reclamation Association, "Preservation of Integrity of State Water Laws," 165-168 (1943).

[15] *Maricopa County M. W. C. Dist.* v. *Southwest Cotton Co.,* 39 Ariz. 65, 74-75, 4 Pac. (2d) 369 (1931).

[16] Mann, G. C., "Riparian Irrigation Rights as Declared and Enforced by the Courts, and Protected by the Statutes, of Texas," Proceedings, Water Law Conferences, Univ. of Texas, pp. 169, 172 (1952, 1954).

Apparently, there had been in this area certain large and to some degree indefinite land grants, but as a practical matter Mexican land and water law had not been extended into the area and had no effect upon the systems of property rights that were destined to become effective there.[17]

In the year following the arrival of the first pioneers, this region was ceded to the United States by the Treaty of Guadalupe Hidalgo, which was proclaimed July 4, 1848.[18] Without direction or interference from the United States Government, the Mormons improvised a temporary system of land titles, pending the acquisition of definitive Federal grants, and the roots of a permanent system of water titles. This was done, and probably could only have been done under the circumstances, under a strong and effective church leadership, which altogether sponsored the material as well as the spiritual welfare of the members.[19]

The Mormon Church took possession of the country, laid out townsites and farm sites, and allotted parcels to members of the church. These early possessory titles were recognized successively by the State of Deseret and the Territory of Utah. Owing to the small size of the Mormon holdings, when Federal land laws became available many separately occupied parcels were actually located within a single minimum government entry. To meet this situation, an entryman chosen by the settlers obtained the patent and deeded the several parcels to their respective occupants.[20]

Establishment of a system of water titles likewise was a product of the environment. During the earliest years, in the absence of political law, the Mormon Church approved the custom of diverting water by group effort and applying it to beneficial use, and supervised these operations. Early legislation made grants of water privileges, authorized the making of grants, and vested in the county courts control over appropriations of water.[21] A statute passed in 1880 recognized accrued rights to water acquired by appropriation or adverse use, but did not contain a specific authorization to appropriate water.[22] The principle of priority in time appears to have been recognized by custom before there was any general law on the subject.

---

[17] Hutchins, Wells A., "Mutual Irrigation Comapnies in Utah," Utah Agr. Expt. Sta. Bull. 199, p. 13 (1927).

[18] 9 Stat. 928 (1848).

[19] The Mormon Church was the only authority, and at no time was this authority relaxed. See Geddes, Joseph A., "The United Order among the Mormons," p. 94 (1924).

[20] Thomas, George, "The Development of Institutions under Irrigation," ch. III, "Land Systems" (1920); Brough, Charles H., "Irrigation in Utah," pp. 12-34 (1898); Hutchins, *supra* note 17, pp. 13-16.

[21] Laws and Ordinances of the State of Deseret (Utah), Compilation 1851 (Salt Lake City, Utah, 1919). Thomas, *supra* note 20, ch. IV, "Water Legislation 1849-1880," and ch. V, "County Courts and the Control of Irrigation Water."

[22] Utah Laws 1880, ch. XX.

California Gold Rush

Gold was discovered in the foothills of the Sierra Nevada, California, in January 1848. This development and the resulting mining industry had a profound influence upon the political and economic growth of California and on the development of water law throughout the West. As water was required in much of the gold mining processes, rights to the use of water were of fundamental importance. This mineral area was Mexican territory when gold was discovered but was ceded to the United States less than 6 months later by the Treaty of Guadalupe Hidalgo. There was no organized government there in the early years, nor much law except that made by the miners who helped themselves to the land, gold, and water under rules and regulations of their own making as they went along. In the words of the United States Supreme Court, speaking through Justice Field who had been Chief Justice of California, the miners "were emphatically the law-makers, as respects mining, upon the public lands in the State."[23]

The rules and regulations of the miners were made by and for the individual camps and hence varied from one locality to another, but essentially the principles that they embodied were of marked uniformity. These principles related to the acquisition, holding, and forfeiture of individual mining claims, based upon priority of discovery and diligence in working them. And to the acquisition and exercise of rights to the needed water were applied comparable principles—posting and recording notice of intention to divert a specific quantity of water, actual diversion and application of water to beneficial use with reasonable diligence, continued exercise of the right, priority in time of initiating the appropriation, and forfeiture of priority for noncompliance with the rules—in other words, the doctrine of prior appropriation of water for beneficial use. These property rights in land and water were thus had, held, and enjoyed under local rules and were enforced by community action.

The California legislature took note of the miners' practices,[24] but did not authorize appropriation of water until 1872.[25] This was done in a short statute which essentially codified principles and practices that had been developed in the mining camps of the Sierra. In the meantime, these customs had been copied in mining areas of other States and Territories. Many water cases decided in the early years in several Western States involved relative rights to the use of water for mining purposes or for milling connected with mining.[26]

---

[23] *Jennison* v. *Kirk,* 98 U. S. 453, 457 (1879).

[24] For example, the California practice act (Cal. Stat. 1851, ch. 5, § 621) provided that: "In actions respecting 'Mining Claims,' proof shall be admitted of the customs, usages, or regulations established and in force at the bar, or diggings, embracing such claim; and such customs, usages, or regulations, when not in conflict with the Constitution and Laws of this State, shall govern the decision of the action."

[25] Cal. Civ. Code, § § 1410-1422 (1872).

[26] See, for example, Hutchins, Wells A., "The California Law of Water Rights," p. 146 (1956), and "The Montana Law of Water Rights," pp. 6-7 (1958).

The miner's inch unit for measuring water in the mining camps is still used in some Western States, although its quantitative value varies from one area to another.[27] The spreading influence of these mining customs is attested to by the considerable number of western jurisdictions in which early statutes authorizing appropriation of water contained the requirements of posting notice of appropriation, filing it for record, and diverting the water and putting it to beneficial use which were featured in the California statute of 1872.[28] The present long, detailed "water codes," with their centralized administrative procedures, developed inevitably from these early brief declarations of a few basic principles.

There is no doubt that the major contribution to the arid region doctrine of appropriation as it is now recognized and applied throughout the West was made by these gold miners. But as to whether the mining water rights doctrine was actually made up out of whole cloth in the Gold Rush days, substantial doubt has been expressed. A writer who studied the scene on the ground a few decades after its height,[29] and another whose research was published in 1935,[30] concluded that the rules and regulations then established were strikingly characteristic of much earlier mining enterprises in the Old World. The earlier writer compared the principle of "mining freedom" of the Germanic and Cornwall miners with that of the modern mining camps in California and other western jurisdictions. A half-century later, Professor Colby's well-documented article discussed the right of free mining and free use of flowing water for mining purposes as a part of the customs of Germanic miners in the Middle Ages, and the similarity of conditions under which the California and Germanic miners developed their rules, usages, and customs related to mining practices and uses of water for mining purposes. This principle of "free mining," with free use of water therefor, spread from the Germanic lands to various European countries and their colonies. In fact, Professor Colby's main thesis, with numerous examples, is the widespread existence of the doctrine of prior appropriation of water in the important mining regions of the world. Certain it is that the "Forty-niners" came to California from many countries. They may well have brought with them some knowledge of the old Germanic customs and applied this knowledge in their new environment.

---

[27] With respect to mining water rights in general, see Hutchins, Wells A., "Water Laws Relating to Mining," Mining Engineering, February 1960, pp. 153-158.

[28] Ariz. Laws 1893, No. 86, p. 135; Terr. Dak. Laws 1881, ch. 142; Idaho Laws 1881, p. 267; Kans. Laws 1886, ch. 115; Mont. Laws 1885, p. 130; Nebr. Laws 1889, ch. 68; Oreg. Laws 1891, p. 52; Oreg. Laws 1899, pp. 172-180; Oreg. Laws 1905, ch. 228; Utah Laws 1897, ch. 52; Wash. Gen. Stat. 1891, ch. 142. The influence is also apparent in N. Mex. Laws 1891, ch. 71; Tex. Laws 1889, ch. 88.

[29] Shinn, C. H., "Mining Camps, A Study in American Frontier Government," pp. 11-35 (1948, originally published in 1885).

[30] Colby, William E., "The Freedom of the Miner and Its Influence on Water Law," published in "Legal Essays, in Tribute to Orrin Kipp McMurray," pp. 67-84 (1935).

Development of the Appropriation Doctrine

State and Local Laws and Customs

Possessory rights on the public domain.—The appropriation doctrine developed chiefly on the public domain. For years the owner of these lands—the Federal Government—made no move either to assert or to grant away its water rights. The miners were trespassers, and so their claims to the use of water were not good as against the Government. However, in the absence of specific State or Federal legislation authorizing the appropriation of water, the customs established in the mining camps of recognizing rights to the use of water by appropriation—"first in time, first in right"—eventually became valid local law. This came about because of the policy of the courts to recognize miners' claims as possessory rights that were good among themselves and as against any other claimant but the Government.

An enlightening account of the events leading up to the establishment of the appropriative doctrine in California is contained in an opinion of the United States Supreme Court written in 1879 by Justice Field, who had been Chief Justice of the California Supreme Court during a part of this dynamic period.[31] Justice Field said that the discovery of gold was followed by an immense immigration into the State; that the gold-bearing lands, which belonged to the United States, were unsurveyed and not open to settlement; that the immigrants in vast numbers entered the Sierra Nevada with a love of order, system, and fair dealing. He continued:

> In every district which they occupied they framed certain rules for their government, by which the extent of ground they could severally hold for mining was designated, their possessory right to such ground secured and enforced, and contests between them either avoided or determined. These rules bore a marked similarity, varying in the several districts only according to the extent and character of the mines; distinct provisions being made for different kinds of mining, such as placer mining, quartz mining, and mining in drifts or tunnels. They all recognized discovery, followed by appropriation, as the foundation of the possessor's title, and development by working as the condition of its retention. And they were so framed as to secure to all comers, within practicable limits, absolute equality of right and privilege in working the mines. Nothing but such equality would have been tolerated by the miners, who were emphatically the law-makers, as respects mining, upon the public lands in the State. The first appropriator was everywhere held to have, within certain well-defined limits, a better right than others to the claims taken up; and in all controversies, except as against the government, he was regarded as the original owner, from whom title was to be traced. But the mines could not be worked without water. Without water the gold

---

[31] *Jennison* v. *Kirk,* 98 U. S. 453, 457-458 (1879).

would remain forever buried in the earth or rock. To carry water to mining localities, when they were not on the banks of a stream or lake, became, therefore, an important and necessary business in carrying on mining. Here, also, the first appropriator of water to be conveyed to such localities for mining or other beneficial purposes, was recognized as having, to the extent of actual use, the better right. The doctrines of the common law respecting the rights of riparian owners were not considered as applicable, or only in a very limited degree, to the condition of miners in the mountains. The waters of rivers and lakes were consequently carried great distances in ditches and flumes, constructed with vast labor and enormous expenditures of money, along the sides of mountains and through cañons and ravines, to supply communities engaged in mining, as well as for agriculturists and ordinary consumption. Numerous regulations were adopted, or assumed to exist, from their obvious justness, for the security of these ditches and flumes, and the protection of rights to water, not only between different appropriators, but between them and the holders of mining claims. These regulations and customs were appealed to in controversies in the State courts, and received their sanction; and properties to the values of many millions rested upon them. * * * Until 1866, no legislation was had looking to a sale of the mineral lands. * * *

Resort to common law principles.—An ever-recurring consciousness of the importance of mining and associated water rights is evident in the early decisions of the California Supreme Court.[32] In 1857, the court observed that the California judiciary had incurred responsibilities not faced by other American courts with respect to a large class of cases involving a great mining interest dependent upon the use of water; that without direct precedent or specific legislation, it was necessary to resort to analogies of the common law.[33] One such analogy related to controversies over possession of land between persons without title in which the real owner was absent,[34] the matter being decided according to the rules of law regarding priority of possession of land. "The diversion of water was declared to be the equivalent of possession and the doctrine was laid down that he who was first in time was first in right."

Another indulgence in common law principles related to the doctrine of presumption, under which it was presumed from the general legislative situation that everyone who wished to appropriate water or to dig gold on the public domain within California had a license from the State to do so, provided that the prior rights of others were not thereby infringed.[35] These two

---

[32] See, for example, *Hoffman* v. *Stone,* 7 Cal. 46, 49 (1857); *Crandall* v. *Woods,* 8 Cal. 136, 141 (1857).

[33] *Bear River & Auburn Water & Min. Co.* v. *New York Min. Co.,* 8 Cal. 327, 332-333 (1857).

[34] *Palmer* v. *Railroad Commission,* 167 Cal. 163, 170-171, 138 Pac. 997 (1914).

[35] *Conger* v. *Weaver,* 6 Cal. 548, 556-558 (1856); *Hill* v. *King,* 8 Cal. 336, 338 (1857).

privileges—mining and diverting water—were equally conferred and stood on an equal footing.[36] On the public domain, therefore, the right to the use of running water existed without private ownership of the soil, on the basis either of prior location on the land or of prior appropriation and use of the water,[37] conflicts between land claimants and water claimants being decided by the fact of priority in time of either land location or water diversion.[38]

Relative rights of appropriators.—The first appropriator of water for mining or other beneficial purposes was recognized in the local communities as having, to the extent of actual use, the better right. And priority of appropriation—a fundamental feature of the appropriation doctrine—was repeatedly recognized in specific terms by the courts in the early California water cases.[39]

The priority principle was applied in the first California cases as between appropriators of water for mining purposes,[40] and was soon extended to other purposes as well. This extension required the authority of the courts, for in the mining areas it was argued that a prior appropriation could be made solely for the purpose of mining and there was as yet no Federal or State legislation on the subject. Thus, in one controversy, the right to use the water of a stream was claimed by a prior appropriator for operating a sawmill and by a subsequent appropriator for working mines.[41] The upstream mining diversions from a water supply insufficient for both claimants prevented operation of the mill for 5 months of the year. The California Supreme Court resolved the vital issue by affirming the judgment of the trial court in issuing an injunction against the miners. The ground for this decision was that under the State policy the prior appropriation of either land or water on the public domain entitled the holder to protection in its quiet enjoyment.

In a later California case, the plaintiff, a prior appropriator of water, had constructed a reservoir for impounding the waters of a ravine for the purpose of irrigating a garden and fruit trees on the public domain.[42] Defendants entered the enclosed premises, proceeded to dig and sluice the same for mining purposes, and threatened to divert the water from plaintiff's reservoir. The supreme court decided that regardless of the rights of defendants to enter public lands for mining purposes,[43] the threatened diversion of water from the

---

[36] *Irwin* v. *Phillips*, 5 Cal. 140, 147 (1855).

[37] *Hill* v. *Newman*, 5 Cal. 445, 446 (1855).

[38] *Irwin* v. *Phillips*, 5 Cal. 140, 147 (1855); *Crandall* v. *Woods*, 8 Cal. 136, 144 (1857).

[39] See *Stiles* v. *Laird*, 5 Cal. 120, 122 (1855); *Hill* v. *Newman*, 5 Cal. 445, 446 (1855); *Hill* v. *King*, 8 Cal. 336, 337, 338 (1857). See also *Jennison* v. *Kirk*, 98 U. S. 453, 458 (1879).

[40] *Eddy* v. *Simpson*, 3 Cal. 249, 252 (1853).

[41] *Tartar* v. *Spring Creek Water & Min. Co.*, 5 Cal. 395, 397-399 (1855).

[42] *Rupley* v. *Welch*, 23 Cal. 452, 455-457 (1863).

[43] An exception from the right of the prior appropriator of water to be protected against all the world but the true owner was expressed in early California State legislation requiring the agriculturist to yield to the miner under certain circumstances: Cal. Stat. ch. 82 (1852); Stat. ch. 119 (1855).

reservoir of plaintiff was a clear violation of a vested right of property, acquired by virtue of a prior appropriation, of which he could not be divested for any private purposes or for the benefit of a few individuals.

While the elemental principles of prior appropriation of water for various beneficial purposes were being developed more than a century ago in repeated decisions of the California Supreme Court, mining and water customs were coming to the fore in other western jurisdictions as well. An example is found in Montana, where the appropriation doctrine was first established primarily in mining regions pursuant to customs and rules of mining camps introduced from similar developments in California.[44] Another example is Nevada, where in its first reported decision on water rights law the supreme court followed the "doctrine * * * well settled in California" that as between persons claiming rights to the use of water by appropriation alone, the one "has the best right who is the first in time."[45] Likewise in Idaho, the supreme court in its first reported decision relating to rights to the use of water stated the law of the jurisdiction to be that the first appropriation of water for a useful or beneficial purpose gives the better right thereto;[46] and in another early one, it severely criticized the trial court for rendering a judgment that not only failed to take account of plaintiff's prior appropriation, but purported to award priorities in an aggregate amount much greater than the maximum quantity of water flowing in the stream at its highest stage.[47] On the other hand, the Kansas Supreme Court held that prior to the enactment of the water appropriation statute of 1886,[48] there had been in the State no legislative or judicial recognition of rights to the use of water by priority of possession; that local customs to that effect were invalid.[49]

---

[44] Stearns, v. Benedick, 126 Mont. 272, 274-275, 247 Pac. (2d) 656 (1952); Bailey v. Tintinger, 45 Mont. 154, 166, 122 Pac. 575 (1912); Maynard v. Watkins, 55 Mont. 54, 55, 173 Pac. 551 (1918).

[45] Lobdell v. Simpson, 2 Nev. 274, 277, 278 (1866). See Ophir Silver Min. Co. v. Carpenter, 4 Nev. 534, 543 (1869); Barnes v. Sabron, 10 Nev. 217, 233 (1875).

[46] Malad Valley Irr. Co. v. Campbell, 2 Idaho 411, 414, 18 Pac. 52 (1888).

[47] Hillman v. Hardwick, 3 Idaho 255, 259-262, 28 Pac. 438 (1891). Among other things, the supreme court said that: "In fact, the decision of the learned district judge in this case stands alone. We have been unable, by the most diligent search, to find a precedent or parallel for it. Heroically setting aside the statute, the decisions and the evidence in the case, he assumes the role of Jupiter Pluvius, and distributes the water of Gooseberry Creek with a beneficent recklessness, which makes the most successful efforts of all the rain wizards shrink into insignificance, and which would make the hearts of the ranchers on Gooseberry dance with joy, if only the judicial decree could be supplemented with a little more moisture. The individual who causes two blades of grass to grow where but one grew before is held in highest emulation as a benefactor of his race. How, then, shall we rank him who, by judicial fiat alone, can cause four hundred inches of water to run where nature only put one hundred inches? (We veil our faces, we bow our heads, before this assumption of judicial power and authority.)" Id. at 260.

[48] Kans. Laws 1886, ch. 115.

[49] Clark v. Allaman, 71 Kans. 206, 240-241, 80 Pac. 571 (1905).

Two cases decided by the Montana Supreme Court in 1872, recognizing the appropriation doctrine, were affirmed by the United States Supreme Court in landmark decisions that fully supported the principles that had been developed in California.[50]

In *Atchison* v. *Peterson,* which involved the respective water rights of miners on the public domain, the United States Supreme Court stated that the doctrines of the common law declaratory of the rights of riparian owners had been found inapplicable or applicable only in a very limited extent to the necessities of miners and inadequate for their protection, and that as the Government was the sole proprietor of the public lands there was no occasion to apply such doctrine in the mining regions.[51] Hence, the doctrine of appropriation had grown up, at first with the silent acquiescence of the Government, and then with congressional recognition; and in the meantime, it had been recognized by legislation and enforced by the courts in the Pacific States and Territories. Under this doctrine, priority gives the better right.

In the other decision, *Basey* v. *Gallagher,* water on the public lands had been appropriated for irrigation purposes, neither party having any title from the United States. Referring to *Atchison* v. *Peterson,* then recently decided, the Supreme Court stated that the views and rulings therein contained were equally applicable to the use of water on the public lands for purposes of irrigation. It was further stated that no distinction was made in the Western States and Territories by the customs of miners or settlers, or by the courts, in the rights of the first appropriator from the use made of the water, provided the use is a beneficial one.

General Recognition of the Appropriation Doctrine

During the first 25-year period following the Gold Rush[52] —approximately 1850 to 1875—the appropriation doctrine was adopted by State or Territorial statute, or was recognized by high court decision, or both, in Arizona, California, Colorado, Montana, Nevada, New Mexico, and Wyoming.[53] It was

---

[50] *Gallagher* v. *Basey,* 1 Mont. 457, 460-462 (1872), affirmed, 87 U. S 670, 681-682, 685-686 (1875); *Atchison* v. *Peterson,* 1 Mont. 561, 569 (1872), affirmed, 87 U. S. 507, 510-516 (1874).

[51] Compare the discussion of establishment of the riparian doctrine in California, below (see "Establishment of the Riparian Doctrine in the West"), and the treatment by the California Supreme Court of water rights on the public domain *analogous* to riparian rights.

[52] See Hutchins, Wells A., "History of the Conflict between Riparian and Appropriative Rights in the Western States," Proceedings, Water Law Conferences, Univ. of Texas, p. 106 (1952, 1954).

[53] Arizona: Terr. Ariz., Howell Code, Ch. LV (1864); *Campbell* v. *Shivers,* 1 Ariz. 161, 174, 25 Pac. 540 (1874). California: Cal. Civ. Code, § § 1410-1422 (1872); *Eddy* v. *Simpson,* 3 Cal. 249, 252 (1853). Colorado: Colo. Laws 1861, p. 67; *Yunker* v. *Nichols,* 1 Colo. 551, 555, 570 (1872). Montana: Bannack Stat., p. 367 (1865); *Thorp* v. *Woolman,* 1 Mont. 168, 172 (1870). Nevada: *Lobdell* v. *Simpson,* 2 Nev. 274, 278-279, 90 Am. Dec. 537 (1866). New Mexico: N. Mex. Laws 1851; see *State ex rel.*

widely practiced in the settled parts of Utah without general authority from the legislature and without specific recognition by the supreme court. In various other parts of the West, also, in both mining and agricultural areas, appropriations of water were being made without general authority or judicial recognition by the States and Territories concerned but pursuant to local customs.

The second period—about 1875 to 1900—witnessed the local statutory recognition of the appropriation doctrine in all of the contiguous Western States and Territories in which this had not occurred previously. During this period, the intent of the legislature to authorize the prior appropriation of water for beneficial purposes generally was expressed in each of the present jurisdictions of Idaho, Kansas, Nebraska, North Dakota, Oklahoma, Oregon, South Dakota, Texas, Utah, and Washington.[54] But in many areas in these jurisdictions, water was used for mining and agricultural purposes long before the local appropriation customs were thus legalized. In Alaska, recognition of the doctrine of prior appropriation was, until 1966, chiefly judicial. The United States District Court at Sitka recognized and applied the principle as early as 1890, holding that prior appropriations were entitled to protection under the Act of Congress of 1866.[55] This Act of 1866 and the amendment thereof in 1870[56] were reproduced in the first Territorial compilation, issued in 1913.[57] In 1966, a century after the Act of 1866, the legislature of the State of Alaska enacted a Water Use Act.[58] This act provides a system for the appropriation and use of water under authority of the Department of Natural Resources and establishes a Water Resources Board, the chief duty of which is to inform and advise the Governor on all matters relating to the use and appropriation of all water in the State.

The appropriation doctrine has never been recognized in Hawaii.[59]

Congressional Legislation

As noted earlier, the United States was the owner of the lands upon which the American customs of appropriating water for mining purposes originated,

---

State Game Commission v. *Red River Valley Co.,* 51 N. Mex. 207, 217, 182 Pac. (2d) 421 (1945). Wyoming: Terr. Wyo. Comp. Laws 1876, ch. 65.

[54] Idaho: Idaho Laws 1881, p. 267. Kansas: Kans. Laws 1886, ch. 115. Nebraska: Nebr. Laws 1889, ch. 68; see Laws 1877, p. 168. North Dakota: Terr. Dak. Laws 1881, ch. 142, repealed N. Dak. Rev. Codes 1895, p. 1518, new enactment, Laws 1899, ch. 173. Oklahoma: Terr. Okla. Laws 1897, ch. XIX. Oregon: Oreg. Laws 1891, p. 52. South Dakota: Terr. Dak. Laws 1881, ch. 142. Texas: Tex. Gen. Laws 1889, ch. 88. Utah: Utah Laws 1880, ch. XX; Laws 1897, p. 219. Washington: Wash. Sess. Laws 1889-1890, p. 706; Sess. Laws 1891, ch. CXLII.

[55] *Noland* v. *Coon,* 1 Alaska 36, 37-38 (1890).

[56] 14 Stat. 153, § 9 (1866); 16 Stat. 218 (1870).

[57] Terr. Alaska Comp. Laws § § 151 and 152 (1913).

[58] Alaska Laws 1966, ch. 50, Stat. § 46.05.010 *et seq.* (Supp. 1966).

[59] *Carter* v. *Territory of Hawaii,* 24 Haw. 47, 57 (1917).

and on which lands these customs were practiced in the early development of the appropriation doctrine. The significance of this fact in its impact upon the establishment of the doctrine in the West calls for strong emphasis.

Period of silent acquiescence.—After the discovery of gold, diversions of water on the public domain for mining and other purposes were made for years before Congress took direct notice. Possessory titles to land and water representing in the aggregate great wealth were acquired and conveyed from one holder to another, with the sanction of the courts, on the assumption that the silence of Congress indicated tacit consent.[60]

Shortly after the close of the Civil War in 1865, proposals were made in Congress that the Government withdraw the mines on the public domain from the miners, and operate and sell them in order to obtain revenue to help pay the war debt. Western Senators and Representatives thereupon made a forceful and successful campaign to halt this movement, the culmination of which was the enactment on July 26, 1866, of an act expressly confirming the rights of miners and appropriators that had been recognized only tacitly theretofore.[61]

Act of 1866.—The Act of 1866 was primarily a mining law, which declared that the mineral lands of the public domain, both surveyed and unsurveyed, were free and open to exploration and occupation by citizens of the United States and those who had declared their intention to become citizens.[62] However, section 9 contained these provisions: Whenever, by priority of possession, rights to the use of water for mining, agriculture, manufacturing, or other purposes had vested and accrued and were recognized and acknowledged by local customs, laws, and court decisions, their possessors should be protected in the same. Rights of way for the construction of ditches and canals for such purposes were acknowledged and confirmed. Any party who in the course of construction of a conduit damaged the possession of any settler on the public domain should be held liable to the injured party.

The Act of 1866 thus gave formal sanction of the Government to appropriations of water on public lands of the United States, whether made before or after passage of the act, and rights of way in connection therewith, provided that the appropriations conformed to principles established by customs of local communities, State or Territorial laws, and decisions of courts. The act contained no procedure by which such rights could be acquired from the United States while the lands remained part of the public domain. What it did was to take cognizance of the customs and usages that had grown up on the public lands under State and Territorial sanction and to make compliance therewith essential to enjoyment of the Federal grant.

According to the United States Supreme Court, this Congressional act was more than the establishment of a rule for the future.[63] It also constituted

---

[60] See *Forbes* v. *Gracey,* 94 U. S. 762, 766-767 (1877).

[61] Wiel, S. C., "Water Rights in the Western States," 3d ed., vol. 1, § 93 (1911).

[62] 14 Stat. 253 (1866).

[63] *Broder* v. *Water Co.,* 101 U. S. 274, 276 (1879).

recognition of a preexisting right, which reached back to the time of formation of the State of California. The established doctrine of the Supreme Court was said to be that the rights of miners and appropriators of water for mining and agricultural purposes in regions in which such use of the water was an absolute necessity were rights which "the government had, by its conduct, recognized and encouraged and was bound to protect, before the passage of the act of 1866." The section of the Act of 1866 confirming such rights was, in the Court's opinion, "rather a voluntary *recognition of a pre-existing right of possession,* constituting a valid claim to its continued use, than the establishment of a new one."[64] The act merely recognized the obligation of the Government to respect private rights which had grown up under its tacit consent and approval.[65] It proposed no new system, but sanctioned, regulated, and confirmed the system already established, to which the people were attached.

Act of 1870.—An amendment of the Act of 1866, enacted July 9, 1870, provided that all patents granted, or preemption or homestead rights allowed, should be subject to any vested water rights, or rights to ditches and reservoirs used in connection therewith, as may have been acquired under or recognized by section 9 of the Act of 1866.[66]

The Act of 1866 had recognized water rights and rights of way on public lands as against the Government. The amendment of 1870 clarified the intent of Congress that the water rights and rights of way to which the 1866 legislation related were effective not only as against the United States, but also against its grantees—that anyone who acquired title to public lands took such title burdened with any easements for water rights or rights of way that had been previously acquired, with the Government's consent, against such lands while they were in public ownership. The Oregon Supreme Court characterized the amendment as a precautionary measure to remove doubts as to the legal effect of such patents.[67]

Desert Land Act of 1877.—This act provided that water rights on tracts of desert land should depend upon bona fide prior appropriation; and that all surplus water over and above actual appropriation and necessary use, together with the water of all lakes, rivers, and other sources of water upon the public lands and not navigable, should be held free for appropriation by the public for irrigation, mining, and manufacturing purposes, subject to existing rights.[68] This act applied specifically to Arizona, California, Idaho, Montana, Nevada, New Mexico, North Dakota, Oregon, South Dakota, Utah, Washington, and Wyoming. An amendment in 1891 extended the provisions to Colorado.[69]

---

[64] *Id.*

[65] *Jennison* v. *Kirk,* 98 U. S. 453, 459 (1879).

[66] 16 Stat. 217 (1870).

[67] *Hough* v. *Porter,* Oreg. 318, 383-386, 95 Pac. 732 (1908), 98 Pac. 1083 (1909), 102 Pac. 728 (1909).

[68] 19 Stat. 377 (1877), 43 U. S. C. § 321 *et seq.* (1964).

[69] 26 Stat. 1096, 1097 (1891), 43 U. S. C. § 321 *et seq.* (1964).

The question whether the desert land legislation was limited to desert lands was not decided by the United States Supreme Court until 1935, after the high courts of four States had divided equally on the matter. In 1909, in *Hough* v. *Porter,* the Oregon Supreme Court expressed the opinion that *all* public lands settled upon after the enactment of that legislation were accepted with the implied understanding that, except for domestic use, the first appropriator should have the superior right.[70] The Washington court, in a decision rendered in 1911, refused to follow the lead of Oregon, and held that the Desert Land Act related to the reclamation of desert lands only; and it reaffirmed the principle in 1914.[71] In 1921, the South Dakota Supreme Court expressly adopted the principle as stated in *Hough* v. *Porter,* stating that the reasoning in the opinion in that case was so lucid and convincing that it felt justified in resting its ruling thereon.[72] But in the following year, the California court declined to adopt the Oregon construction and held that the Desert Land Act did not affect other than desert lands.[73]

The question was settled by the United States Supreme Court in 1935 in the *California Oregon Power Company* case, wherein it was held that the Desert Land Act applied to all the public domain in the States and Territories named, and that it severed the water from the public lands and left the unappropriated waters of nonnavigable sources open to appropriation by the public under the laws of the several States and Territories.[74] This case, arising in Oregon, concerned the right of an owner of riparian lands—which had been acquired in 1885 by a predecessor in interest by patent under the Homestead Act of 1862—who had never diverted water for beneficial use nor sought to make an appropriation thereof, to enjoin an appropriator the water rights claims of which were based upon adjudicated rights and permits from the State. The Supreme Court referred to the decisions from the four States noted above, and said that the decision of the Oregon court in *Hough* v. *Porter* was well reasoned and reached the right conclusion, whereas to accept the view of the Washington and California courts would be, in large measure, to subvert the policy Congress had in mind to further the disposition and settlement of the public domain. The language in the Desert Land Act, the court said, applied not only to desert land entries but to entries under other land laws as well.

The expressions of the Supreme Court as to the impact of the Desert Land Act upon the doctrine of riparian water rights are considered in Chapter 10.

---

[70] *Hough* v. *Porter,* 51 Oreg. 318, 383-399, 404-406, 95 Pac. 732 (1908), 98 Pac. 1083 (1909), 102 Pac. 728 (1909).

[71] *Still* v. *Palouse Irr. & Power Co.,* 64 Wash. 606, 612, 117 Pac. 466 (1911); *Bernot* v. *Morrison,* 81 Wash. 538, 559-560, 143 Pac. 104 (1914).

[72] *Cook* v. *Evans,* 45 S. Dak. 31, 38-39, 185 N. W. 262 (1921).

[73] *San Joaquin & Kings River Canal & Irr. Co.* v. *Worswick,* 187 Cal. 674, 690, 203 Pac. 999 (1922). "We think the conclusion of the Washington Supreme Court was correct."

[74] *California Oregon Power Co.* v. *Beaver Portland Cement Co.,* 295 U. S. 142, 160-163 (1935).

Limitations on Congressional recognition.—There were two important limitations upon the recognition by Congress of the doctrine of appropriation in the Act of 1866 and subsequent legislation: (1) It was restricted to the public lands of the United States, and thus had no effect upon the water rights of private lands. (2) It applied only to appropriative rights that accrued under State laws.

However, in view of the fact that so much land in the West was in public ownership during the period under consideration, the Congressional legislation was a powerful factor in the spread of the appropriative principle throughout the West.

Appropriations under State procedures.—This discussion of the important relation of early Congressional legislation to the development of the appropriation doctrine in the West may have little bearing on the current Federal-State conflict over the ownership of water on the public domain and paramount rights of the United States therein. But it emphasizes the fact that in this series of statutes Congress recognized State customs and laws as applied to the appropriation of nonnavigable waters on the public domain, and neither set up nor authorized a general procedure under which an individual must initiate or perfect a right to appropriate such water. Whether initiated on the public domain or on private land, the individual made his application under the then existing State procedure.

State Water Rights Administration

Early appropriation procedures.—As noted earlier, all of the 17 contiguous Western States and Alaska have statutes providing for the appropriation of water. The earlier enactments were generally short; many of them provided for posting of a notice at the point of diversion and for filing a copy of the notice in the county records. They usually specified, also, a certain time within which construction must be commenced.

In various States, the earliest statutes were enacted long after irrigation development had begun. In California, for example, the first legislative authorization to appropriate water was in 1872, whereas decisions of the California Supreme Court in controversies over water rights for mining, milling, and agriculture had been rendered at various times during the two preceding decades.[75] Irrigation in Nevada began about 1849, as an incident to the early development of mining; yet there was no general legislation on the subject of irrigation water rights until 1866.[76] The Nevada Supreme Court stated in 1914 that the greater portion of water rights in Nevada had been acquired before the passage of any statute prescribing a method of appropriation, and that such rights had been recognized uniformly by the courts as being vested under the

---

[75] Hutchins, Wells A., "The California Law of Water Rights," pp. 41-51 (1956).
[76] Hutchins, Wells A., "The Nevada Law of Water Rights," pp. 3-5 (1955).

common law of the State.[77] Irrigation in Utah began when the Mormon pioneers entered Great Salt Lake Basin in 1847. The earliest legislation made grants of water privileges and authorized public officials to make grants; and a statute passed in 1880 recognized accrued rights to water acquired by appropriation or adverse use, but did not contain a specific authorization to appropriate. (See "Origins of the Appropriation Doctrine—Mormon Colonization of Utah," above.) It was not until 1897 that Utah, a State in which agriculture is so important and so largely dependent upon irrigation, provided by statute for the future appropriation of water by individuals.[78] In the meantime, the Utah courts had recognized the appropriative right,[79] and had repudiated the riparian doctrine.[80] Irrigation was being practiced in various portions of the Southwest at the time of its accession to the United States, and the beginnings of the practice in some of these areas are lost in antiquity.

What statutes in various States did was to give legislative sanction to methods of appropriation already developed by custom. In the States in which there had been little development prior to legislation on irrigation, the legislatures generally adopted the statutes then in effect in other States, so that the initiation of an appropriative right by posting and filing a notice became the general method throughout much of the West. The right became vested by reason of application of the water to beneficial use; and if the appropriator was diligent, his priority related back to the time of taking the first statutory step.

Current administrative procedures.—Administrative procedure governing the acquisition, determination, and administration of water rights, in contrast with its early stages, has become highly developed throughout the West. Some indication as to the contrast between these initial statutes and the present "water codes" may be had by reference to California. There the first statute, a part of the Civil Code of 1872, comprised 13 sections which could be reproduced on one printed page. In the present California Water Code, the functions relating to the procedure for appropriating water—corresponding to the 1872 Civil Code—and those for determining or adjudicating water rights and for the distribution of water in watermaster service areas comprise several hundred sections covering many printed pages. Added to all these provisions are others dealing with State policies, State administration generally (even down to regulation of weather modification), witnesses and production of evidence, liability within a watershed, joint use and development, recordation of water extractions and diversions, and supervision of dams, wells, pumping plants, conduits, and streams.

Present administrative procedures are based largely upon those which originated in Colorado and Wyoming. The State's supervision and control are usually exercised through the State Engineer or other corresponding official,

---

[77] *Ormsby County* v. *Kearney*, 37 Nev. 314, 352, 142 Pac. 803 (1914).

[78] Utah Laws 1897, p. 219 *et seq.*

[79] *Crane* v. *Winsor*, 2 Utah 248 (1878).

[80] *Stowell* v. *Johnson*, 7 Utah 215, 26 Pac. 290 (1891).

and the courts. In some States a board or department of the State government exercises control.

In Wyoming, all these functions are vested primarily in State administrative officers. The exclusive procedure for initiating the acquisition of a water right in Wyoming is to apply to the State Engineer for a permit to make the appropriation.[81] Adjudications or determinations of existing rights are made by the Board of Control.[82] composed of the State Engineer and the water division superintendents,[83] all of whom are constitutional officers, from which appeals lie to the courts.[84] The distribution of water according to priorities of right is under the control of the organization of division superintendents and district commissioners, headed by the State Engineer.[85]

The Colorado system provides for judicial or judicially supervised determinations of water rights and priorities.[86] Responsibility for the administration, distribution, and regulation of waters, subject to such determinations, is placed upon the division engineers, under the general supervision of the State Engineer.[87] However, permits to appropriate water are not required.[88] If an appropriator desires a determination of his water right and the amount and priority thereof, he shall file an application for such determination with the water clerk.[89] Jurisdiction to hear and adjudicate such questions is vested exclusively in the water judges and their designated referees.[90]

In many of the States, the statutory procedure to appropriate water is held or conceded to be the exclusive method by which an appropriative right may

---

[81] Wyo. Stat. Ann. § 41-201 (1957).

[82] Id. § 41-165.

[83] Id. § 41-154.

[84] Id. §§ 41-193 and 41-126.

[85] Id. § 41-57; Wyo. Stat. Ann. § 41-64 (Supp. 1964).

[86] Colo. Rev. Stat. Ann. §§ 148-21-10 to -23 (Supp. 1969).

[87] Id. §§ 148-21-17 and -34.

[88] Prior to 1969, the intending appropriator began his work and then filed a claim with the State Engineer. Colo. Rev. Stat. Ann. § 148-4-1 to -7 (1963). This requirement was important in providing orderly records of water appropriations and was of evidentiary value in establishing a claimant's right, but it was not essential to the validity of the appropriative right. De Hass v. Benesch, 116 Colo. 344, 351-352, 181 Pac. (2d) 453 (1947); Archuleta v. Boulder & Weld County Ditch Co., 118 Colo. 43, 53, 192 Pac. (2d) 891 (1948). In 1969, this claim-filing requirement was repealed. Colo. Laws 1969, ch. 373, § 20.

It may be noted that the Colorado constitution provides that "The right to divert the unappropriated waters of any natural stream to beneficial uses shall never be denied." Colo. Const., art. XVI, § 6.

[89] Colo. Rev. Stat. Ann. § 148-21-18(1) (Supp. 1969).

[90] Id. §§ 148-21-10(1) and (2). This is subject to rights of appeal to higher courts. Id. § 148-21-20(9). The 1969 legislation provided for these special water clerks, water judges, and their designated referees. Such matters were previously handled by regular courts and judicial officers. For further discussions of these and other provisions of the 1969 Colorado "Water Right Determination and Administration Act," see chapters 7, 8, and 15, and the summary for Colorado in the State summaries in the appendix.

be acquired. Idaho is a definite exception; there, at his option, an intending appropriator may acquire an equally valid right by following either the "constitutional" procedure of diverting water and applying it to beneficial use, or the formal statutory procedure.[91] The latter, while thus not exclusive, may be advantageous to an appropriator in the matter of establishing the date of priority. In Montana, the statutory procedure is exclusive as to appropriations of water from adjudicated streams made after the date of the amended statute.[92] However, there is no control over the appropriation of water centered by statute in the State administrative organization.

Whatever the method of determining water rights—a form of property— jurisdiction in the last analysis is necessarily vested in the courts. For example, although the powers of the Wyoming Board of Control are quasi-judicial,[93] it is true that appeal from the Board's determinations may be taken to the courts.[94] In no event are individuals precluded from recourse to the courts for protection of their water rights. These matters are discussed in more detail in chapter 7 and the respective State summaries in the appendix.

Modification of the Strict Priority Rule

An essential feature of the appropriation doctrine as originally practiced in the West was the rule that he who is first in time is first in right. However, in the economic and legal development of the doctrine there have been engrafted upon the procedure for acquiring new appropriative rights so many important and controlling provisions that the simple formula "first in time, first in right" has tended to become a qualified rather than an absolute rule. To preclude possible misapprehension as to the inelasticity of the rule, which amounted to dogma in the earlier historical phases but has since yielded to development pressures, several matters must be emphasized.

Priorities in time of acquiring water rights.—The principle of priority in time of appropriating water still prevails in general in the acquisition of new water rights, but with certain important statutory exceptions in various States. Among these are: (1) Authority vested in the administrator to reject an application to appropriate water that is deemed to be a menace to the safety or against the interests and welfare of the public. (2) Preferences accorded to certain uses of water as among pending applications to appropriate water, regardless of relative dates of filing, and preferences even in favor of prospective applications as against those already filed. (3) Preferences and reservations in favor of municipal uses. (4) Withdrawal of waters from general

---

[91] Idaho Const., art. XV, § 3; Code Ann. § 42-101 *et seq.* (1948). *Nielson* v. *Parker,* 19 Idaho 727, 730-731, 733, 115 Pac. 488 (1911).

[92] Mont. Laws 1921, ch. 228, Rev. Codes Ann. §§ 89-829 to -844 (1964), construed in *Anaconda Nat'l Bank* v. *Johnson,* 75 Mont. 401, 411, 244 Pac. 141 (1926), followed and applied in *Donich* v. *Johnson,* 77 Mont. 229, 246, 250 Pac. 963 (1926).

[93] Wyo. Stat. Ann. § 41-165 (1957).

[94] *Id.* §§ 41-193 and 41-216.

appropriation in favor of existing or proposed public projects. For example, the California Water Code directs the State Board of Water Rights, among other things, (a) to reject an application when in its judgment the proposed appropriation would not best conserve the public interest; (b) in acting upon an application, to consider the relative benefit to be derived from all uses of the water concerned; and (c) to consider an application by a municipality for domestic purposes first in right, "irrespective of whether it is first in time."

Priorities in periods of water shortage.—The value to an early appropriator of his priority over later comers is that when the water supply is not enough for all who have rights of use in the common supply, the earliest priority must be fully satisfied before any water may be taken by junior claimants. Yet the constitutions and statutes of certain States provide that when the waters in a particular source of supply are not sufficient to satisfy the wants of all who have rights of use, domestic purposes shall have first preference and agriculture second, regardless of priority in time. Whether or not it is therein declared that compensation must be paid to one whose prior right is thus subordinated, courts that have passed on the question have held that it must be done.

Condemnation of inferior uses of water.—In certain States, holders of junior rights for uses of water declared by statute to be superior may condemn appropriative rights already acquired by others senior in time but for inferior uses.

Priorities in large developments.—In a few States, the consumers served by large irrigation enterprises are the appropriators with priorities as among themselves; elsewhere, priorities throughout the service area of an enterprise, or throughout a given subdivision, are the same provided that the appropriation made by the organization covers the area in question. Needless to say, enforcement of individual priorities in a large project, if based strictly upon times of beginning use of water by the several consumers, would be indeed a complicated procedure and would not necessarily result in the most efficient use of the available water supply.

The trend in water development is toward large projects. One reason is the increasing unavailability of small sources of surface water supply, owing to the steady increase in water uses and in competition for them beginning about the middle of the 19th century. Another of course is increasing cost, resulting not only from the size of undertakings now necessary to develop less accessible supplies, but also from higher and higher costs of labor and materials. In the face of diminishing supplies of unappropriated water and of mounting costs of development and operation—aside from increasingly exceptional instances in which the individual appropriates and diverts from a stream his own independent water supply—some sort of group organization is necessary. In the overall view, appropriations of water are being made, and doubtless will continue to be made, chiefly by high level entities or organizations on behalf of the ultimate consumers. From this it should follow that as time goes on there will be more and more individual rights to the service of water based on relations between consumers and distributing agencies—such as contracts with companies or districts, holding of shares of stock in corporations, and ownership of land within public districts—and fewer and fewer appropriations of water by individuals.

ESTABLISHMENT OF THE RIPARIAN DOCTRINE IN THE WEST

Origins and Asserted Origins of the Riparian Doctrine

The riparian doctrine is not an arid region doctrine of water law. There is nothing in it as stated in early court decisions in the East or abroad to suggest that a comparable philosophy of water rights law could have been indigenous a century ago to the undeveloped West, where the water potential fell far short of meeting the needs of large areas of arable land. The history of western agriculture and water law refutes such a possibility. As a practical matter, the riparian doctrine was found to be unsuited to water development in the more arid areas, and as a legal matter it was repudiated in the predominantly arid jurisdictions. Had the riparian doctrine been recognized and applied in Utah, said the supreme court of that State, "It would still be a desert."[95]

It is clear that the so-called riparian doctrine in its simplest form—although molded and developed by some westerners to meet the demands of expanding economies, and by others rejected completely—was not a native of the West. It came to the West as a part of the common law of England. But questions as to when it was introduced into the English common law before the latter came west have been and still are being raised. Furthermore, assertion of Spanish origin was urged and rejected in the *Valmont Plantations* case.[96]

Common Law of England

Adoption of riparian doctrine in Western States.—Certain Western States that adopted the common law of England also adopted by virtue thereof the riparian doctrine of rights in water of watercourses. In others, notwithstanding adoption of the common law, constitutional or statutory provisions repudiated the riparian doctrine, or court decisions held that it had not become a part of the State law because unsuited to the local natural environment.

Association of the riparian doctrine, in its earliest and most simplified aspects, with English common law has been practically uniform in western judicial writings. The "common law riparian doctrine" is a familiar phrase. Sometimes the statement is merely "the common law doctrine," or "common

---

[95] *Stowell* v. *Johnson,* 7 Utah 215, 225-226, 26 Pac. 290 (1891).

[96] *State* v. *Valmont Plantations,* 346 S. W. (2d) 853 (Tex. Civ. App. 1961), affirmed, 163 Tex. 381, 355 S. W. (2d) 502 (1962).

law water rights," although the latter may comprehend a certain class of ground water rights as well.[97]

The courts of California base their judicially sponsored riparian principles on the common law of England, which was adopted by the legislature in the year of admission to the Union.[98] In the comprehensive, detailed examination of the subject in *Lux* v. *Haggin* (the opinion is 200 pages in length), the California Supreme Court declared unequivocally that the legislature had adopted the common law of England—not the civil law, nor the Roman "law of nature", nor the Mexican law, nor any hybrid system.[99] In Texas, which while a Republic adopted the common law a decade earlier than did California,[100] the judicial law of riparian water rights grew up in a predominantly common law atmosphere. However, the civil law and Spanish-Mexican law were cited by the Texas Supreme Court in certain cases, and the situation was further complicated by the long opinion in *Motl* v. *Boyd*[101] which contained references to the Mexican origin of the doctrine which, although *dicta,* were cited with approval in subsequent decisions. The courts of other Western States that adopted the riparian doctrine (Hawaii, Kansas, Nebraska, Nevada, North Dakota, Oklahoma, Oregon, South Dakota, and Washington) likewise invoked the common law.[102]

Disagreement as to earlier history.—Researchers differ, not as to the fact that the riparian doctrine became a part of the common law of England, but as to when it occurred. As the disputed period antedates adoption of the riparian doctrine in the Western States, the matter there is probably *stare decisis.* In other areas, it is considered to be of practical as well as historical significance. This is the subject of the immediately succeeding discussion.

French Civil Law

Wiel's thesis.—Probably the chief controversy centers upon the thesis of Samuel C. Wiel, best known for his scholarly works of more than a half-century ago on western water law.[103] The thesis in question was advanced in law review articles published in 1918 and 1919.[104]

---

[97] The present water appropriation statutes of Kansas and Alaska make provision for "common law" claims of vested rights in surface or ground waters, without using the term "riparian": Kans. Stat. Ann. § 82a-701 *et seq.* (1969); Alaska Stat. § 46.15.060 (Supp. 1966).

[98] Cal. Stat. 1850, p. 219.

[99] *Lux* v. *Haggin,* 69 Cal. 255, 384, 4 Pac. 919 (1884), 10 Pac. 674 (1886).

[100] Tex. Act of January 20, 1840, p. 3.

[101] *Motl* v. *Boyd,* 116 Tex. 82, 99-108, 286 S. W. 458 (1926).

[102] Decisions are cited under "Interrelationships of the Dual Water Rights Systems," below.

[103] His major text is "Water Rights in the Western States" (3d ed. 1911).

[104] Wiel, Samuel C., "Origin and Comparative Development of the Law of Watercourses in the Common Law and in the Civil Law," 6 Cal. Law Rev. 245, 342 (1918); "Waters: American Law and French Authority," 33 Harvard Law Rev. 133, 147 (1919).

Mr. Wiel's thesis asserts that the common law of watercourses is not the ancient result of English law, but is a modern French doctrine received into English law only through the influence of two eminent American jurists; that Blackstone's rule of prior appropriation was accepted by the English courts at the beginning of the 19th century and as late as 1831; that toward the close of this period, and at about the same time, the American jurists Story and Kent had expounded the civil law doctrine of "riparian" proprietorship, with Kent citing the French sources; that subsequently, in 1833, the modern doctrine was first laid down by the English courts in *Mason* v. *Hill*,[105] but without using the term "riparian" or citing either of these American jurists; and that the English law wavered from then on until the decision in 1849 in *Wood* v. *Waud*,[106] in which the term "riparian" was apparently first used by the English authorities, main reliance being placed upon Kent and Story, contention thereby being set at rest. This he believed to have marked the definite adoption of the riparian doctrine as a part of the common law of England.

Dissents.—For several decades Wiel's exposition was cited by many writers (including the present one) without contradiction.

The first disagreement that came to the author's attention was in an address by Associate Justice Wilson of the Texas Supreme Court, in collaboration with one given by Dean White of the School of Law, University of Houston.[107] Judge Wilson stated that Texas had received the riparian system from the common law of England, and that he and Dean White questioned the conclusions of Mr. Wiel upon the history of the riparian doctrine contained in his Harvard Law Review article. Further:

Although we have had neither the time nor access to the sources needed to make an exhaustive study of this, we are of the opinion now that the English did not get this doctrine from the writings of Kent and Story as suggested by Mr. Weil [Wiel], but rather the converse is true. Story's citations are all common law. The riparian is an old common law doctrine whose roots can be traced to the year books. It may well be that it is parallel to the French water law in that both the English common law and land title system and much of the French law and land title system had a common origin in Norman feudalism, but only in this sense is the English riparian doctrine of French origin.

An article by Maass and Zobel published in 1960 takes issue with Wiel's entire thesis.[108] Having found no detailed study of Wiel's 1919 article by

---

[105] *Mason* v. *Hill*, 5 Barn. & Adol. 1, 110 Eng. Reprint 692 (1833).

[106] *Wood* v. *Waud*, 3 Exch. 748, 154 Eng. Reprint 1047 (1849).

[107] Wilson, Will, "Reappraisal of Molt v. Boyd," and White, A.A., "The Flow and Underflow of Motl v. Boyd," Proceedings, Water Law Conferences, Univ. of Texas, pp. 38, 44 (1955).

[108] Maass, Arthur and Zobel, Hiller B., "Anglo-American Water Law: Who Appropriated the Riparian Doctrine?" Graduate School of Public Administration, Harvard, 10 Public Policy 109-156 (1960).

anyone who had cited it as authority, the authors embarked upon the considerable undertaking of making a comprehensive study of the article and the original sources. This they believed to be of great importance, apparently because constantly increasing demands upon available water supplies in Eastern States have stimulated proposals to revise the common law riparian system in an effort to cope with the situation. The authors' study convinced them that Wiel was wrong in the essential facets of his thesis—that his errors resulted largely from errors in interpretation of the sources on which he relied. Their article is devoted to dissecting Wiel's thesis and to proving their own points.

If the conclusions of these authors are correct, the riparian doctrine was not introduced into English law from the Code Napoleon by Story and Kent. On the contrary, say these researchers, the common law has been riparian in character from early times, and American common law, even before Story and Kent, was riparian.

Spanish-Mexican Law

What is now the southwestern part of the United States was occupied by Spanish and Mexican settlers and contained land grants of various sizes made by or under the authority of the governments of Spain and Mexico. Parts of this erstwhile Hispanic domain are principally included in what is now California, Arizona, New Mexico, Texas, Colorado, Utah, and Nevada. Of these States, only California and Texas have generally recognized the riparian water-rights doctrine.

California.—The question whether Spanish or Mexican land grants in California carried with them as appurtenances riparian rights to the use of water for irrigation of lands contiguous to streams has apparently never been a major issue. Such lands bordering on streams have been recognized as having riparian rights, but neither greater nor less than lands acquired from the United States Government. That is, recognition of the common law riparian doctrine served to clothe the proprietors of riparian lands granted prior to statehood with the same water privileges that it accorded to early possessors of lands contiguous to streams on the public domain of the United States and to subsequent grantees of such lands. Controversies over riparian rights arising on lands originally granted by Spain or Mexico which reached the California Supreme Court have been settled according to riparian principles applicable to privately owned lands in general, regardless of the source of private title.[109]

On the whole, Spanish-Mexican water law made little impression on the water law of California other than with respect to water rights of American cities that succeeded Spanish and Mexican pueblos.[110]

---

[109] Some cases in which lands in Spanish and Mexican grants contiguous to streams were recognized as having riparian rights are cited in Hutchins, *supra* note 75, p. 179.

[110] See Hutchins, Wells A., "Pueblo Water Rights in the West," 38 Tex. Law Rev. 748-762 (1960).

Texas.—In Texas, on the contrary, the relation of Spanish-Mexican law to present day riparian rights chiefly for irrigation use has been a major issue.[111]

During the long period extending from the date of the first riparian case to 1926, when *Motl* v. *Boyd*[112] was decided, the Texas courts in discussing riparian questions were concerned chiefly with the common law and, except in one early case, had little to say about the civil law or about Spanish-Mexican colonization laws.[113] In *Motl* v. *Boyd,* however, speaking through Chief Justice Cureton, the Texas Supreme Court by *dictum* broke away from this long trend and dealt at length with Mexican colonization laws and with laws and policies of the succeeding Republic and State governments—including adoption of the common law—as sources of riparian water rights. The court was of the opinion that the policy of the Mexican Government—as well as its successors—in granting lands was to recognize the right of the riparian owner to use water not only for domestic and household purposes, but for irrigation as well. It is important to emphasize the fact that this statement was *dictum.*

Until 1962, the supreme court had not questioned the soundness of the holdings in *Motl* v. *Boyd;* although, their accuracy and legal soundness as precedents had been seriously questioned by some writers and speakers while stoutly defended by others.[114] In 1962, the supreme court in *Valmont Plantations* v. *State of Texas,* affirmed the decision of a lower appellate court holding that the dictum in *Motl* v. *Boyd* was erroneous and that no Texas court until that time had been called upon to decide whether Spanish and Mexican land grants have appurtenant irrigation rights similar to the common law riparian right.[115] A brief discussion of the events leading to this decision follows.

---

[111] *State* v. *Valmont Plantations,* 346 S. W. (2d) 853 (Tex. Civ. App. 1961), affirmed, 163 Tex. 381, 355 S. W. (2d) 502 (1962).

[112] *Motl* v. *Boyd,* 116 Tex. 82, 286 S. W. 458 (1926).

[113] See Hutchins, Wells A., "The Texas Law of Water Rights," pp. 3-6, 131-151 (1960).

[114] For diverse viewpoints, see Proceedings, Water Law Conferences, Univ. of Texas: Mann, G. C., "Riparian Irrigation Rights as Declared and Enforced by the Courts, and Protected by the Statutes, of Texas," pp. 167-187 (1952, 1954); Davenport, Harbert, "Riparian vs. Appropriative Rights: The Texas Experience," pp. 138-168 (1952, 1954); King, Neal, "Some Irrigation Law Problems Peculiar to the Lower Rio Grande," pp. 294-307 (1952, 1954); Wilson, Will, "Reappraisal of Motl v. Boyd," pp. 38-43 (1955); White, A. A., "The Flow and Underflow of Motl v. Boyd," pp. 44-60 (1955). See also Davenport, Harbert and Canales, J. T., "The Texas Law of Flowing Waters, with Special Reference to Irrigation from the Lower Rio Grande," p. 82 (1949), republished in 9 Baylor Law Rev. 138, 283 (1956); Davenport, "Development of the Texas Laws of Waters," 21 Tex. Rev. Civ. Stat. Ann. pp. XIII to XXXIX (1953); White and Wilson, "The Flow and Underflow of Motl v. Boyd," 9 Southwestern Law Journal 1, 377 (1955). See also, in this connection, Dobkins, Betty Eakle, "The Spanish Element in Texas Water Law," particularly ch. V, "Spanish Water Law in Texas, 1821-1958," and ch. VI, "Rulings on Spanish Grants in Texas v. Valmont Plantations" (1959).

[115] *Valmont Plantations* v. *State of Texas,* 163 Tex. 381, 355 S. W. (2d) 502 (1962), affirming, 346 S. W. (2d) 853 (Tex. Civ. App. 1961).

In 1956, a suit was brought to determine the relative rights of all diverters of water from the Rio Grande below Falcon Dam, in which an essential issue of law was the extent of the vested riparian right as it relates to the use of water for irrigation.[116] As a result of a cross-petition filed by the Texas Attorney General and certain litigant districts late in 1957, the cause of action stated therein was severed from the main suit in order to determine the fundamental riparian irrigation issue.[117] Severance was ordered because of the court's finding that claims other than riparian could not be adjudicated in this cause without joining hundreds of additional parties and unwarranted delay.

At the trial in the *Valmont* case, which was held by the district court without a jury, the real issue was whether a grant of land abutting on the Rio Grande, when made by the proper officers of the King of Spain, carried with it the right of irrigation as an appurtenance to the land, or whether it was necessary to get also a grant of water for such purpose. Much expert testimony was presented and arguments heard on both sides of the controversy. In reaching its conclusions the court took notice of the contents of memoranda that were presented on Spanish and Mexican law relating to waters in Spanish America, in several of which the original Spanish materials and corresponding English translations were printed on facing pages.

The trial court in the *Valmont* case was of the opinion that when the Government of Spain made the original grants of land in question, "such grants did not, as an appurtenance thereto, carry with them a right of irrigation upon the lands involved." However, under the doctrine of *stare decisis*, the trial court was constrained to follow the consistent holdings of the supreme court, on various grounds, that lands abutting upon a stream such as the Rio Grande do have a riparian right of irrigation. Judgment was rendered accordingly in September 1959, and appeal was taken to the San Antonio Court of Civil Appeals.

The San Antonio Court of Civil Appeals held that despite an erroneous *dicta* in *Motl* v. *Boyd,* no Texas court had until now been called upon to decide whether Spanish and Mexican land grants have appurtenant irrigation rights similar to the common law riparian right, and that there was no *stare decisis* on the subject. The court held that the Spanish and Mexican grants of land adjacent to the Rio Grande did not carry with them an implied grant of riparian waters for irrigation, and reversed the trial court's determination of the conflict.[118] The Texas Supreme Court affirmed the decision of the San Antonio Court of Civil Appeals holding that lands riparian to the lower Rio Grande, held under Spanish and Mexican grants, have no appurtenant right to irrigate with river waters.[119]

---

[116] *State of Texas v. Hidalgo County W. C. & I. Dist. No. 18,* No. B-20576, 93rd Dist. Court, Hidalgo County, Texas.

[117] *State of Texas* v. *Valmont Plantations,* No. B-20791, 93rd Dist. Court, Hidalgo County, Texas.

[118] *State* v. *Valmont Plantations,* 346 S. W. (2d) 853 (Tex. Civ. App. 1961).

[119] *Valmont Plantations* v. *State of Texas,* 163 Tex. 381, 355 S. W. (2d) 502 (1962). See also *Duke* v. *Reily,* 431 S. W. (2d) 769, 771 (Tex. Civ. App. 1968).

Early Development of the Riparian Doctrine in
Specified Jurisdictions

Transplantation of the common law riparian doctrine in the undeveloped West was favored by environment in some of the States, notably those lying on the 100th meridian and on the Pacific Coast in large parts of which humid conditions prevailed. In several of the more arid ones, on the contrary, the environment was so hostile that the court decision reports reflect no encouragement; in others, deviations or uncertainty appeared at times, to be cleared up later; and in one, the riparian doctrine was definitely recognized for some 13 years and then, after considerable criticism and turmoil, was abrogated. These matters are noted later under "Interrelationships of the Dual Water Rights Systems."

Diverse ways in which the riparian doctrine was implanted and developed in the West may be illustrated by early experiences in California, Texas, the Dakota Territory, and Oklahoma. More recent developments in these and other areas in the Western States are discussed later in this chapter.

California

California's experience begins, of course, with the momentous Gold Rush, when demands for water for use in extracting gold from the ground led to adoption of two different systems of rights of use. The interplay of forces in the ensuing century of conflict between these systems is left for later discussion. Here we are concerned only with riparian rights.

Easterners who came to California after the discovery of gold included many lawyers, who worked as miners pending the time when their professional services would be needed.[120] They were versed in the common law and in the eastern court decisions in which the riparian doctrine had been held to be included therein. They were on the ground when controversies over mining claims and uses of water reached the regularly established courts, the disputants being trespassers on the public domain, the owner of the land (the Government) not being in court, the mining industry rapidly becoming or having become predominant in the economy of the new State, and questions being posed for which no direct precedent could be found. Under these circumstances, we find the California Supreme Court resorting for solution of these questions to analogies of the common law. (See "Establishment of the Appropriation Doctrine in the West—Development of the Appropriation Doctrine," above.)

Thus, there was established in the mining litigation the rule that as between persons without title to land when the real owner is absent, priority of possession of the land gives the better right, diversion of water being regarded as equivalent to possession. Having gone that far, it is not surprising to find the

---

[120] Shinn, C. H., "Mining Camps, A Study in American Frontier Government," pp. 114-115 (1948, originally published in 1885).

court regarding a contiguous mining claim as a tract of riparian land, despite the true landowner's absence from the litigation, rights of use of the water to be decided according to principles of the common law riparian doctrine. These water rights served their purpose for the time being during that formative period; but they were not permanent riparian rights in the full sense of that term, for they could not survive the "working out" of the claims and their abandonment by the trespassing miners. A better designation of them is "rights analogous to riparian rights."

Regardless of the value of expediency in creating a class of analogous water rights, the pattern of a riparian system was thus set in the mining area by the common-law-conscious court.[121] Fifteen years after the attainment of statehood, the supreme court decided in an agricultural area what appears to have been its first case in which rights of riparian proprietors only were involved, with no question of use of water on nonriparian land.[122] Plaintiff used the water of a creek for irrigating a commercial vegetable garden. Some 7 or 8 years after this project was begun, defendant diverted the entire flow upstream for watering stock. Although the supreme court decision purported to be based on the common law rights of riparian proprietors as against each other, it recognized that irrigation in Solano County was a proper riparian use of the water. The court held that each proprietor had a right to the use of water for domestic, stockwatering, and reasonable irrigation, and that neither one had the right to so obstruct the stream as to prevent running of the water substantially as in a state of nature it was accustomed to run; that the maxim each one was bound to respect, while availing himself of his right, is *sic utere tuo ut alienum non laedas* (use your property so as not to injure that of others). Thus, the court applies a modification of the strict original common law rule in holding that plaintiff "had the right to the water of the creek in the natural flow, subject only to the use thereof by the defendant in a reasonable manner, *without unnecessary obstruction or diminution.*" [Emphasis supplied.]

During the ensuing two decades the California Supreme Court rendered several decisions in which the rights of riparian proprietors were recognized and matters respecting them were actually litigated.[123] Then came the landmark case of *Lux* v. *Haggin,* in which the supreme court unequivocally established the principle that the riparian owner in California is entitled to a reasonable use of water for irrigation in relation to the reasonable needs of all other riparian proprietors on the same stream.[124] The principle has been restated in numerous court decisions.[125]

[121] See *Irwin* v. *Phillips,* 5 Cal. 140, 145-146 (1855); *Hill* v. *Newman,* 5 Cal. 445, 446 (1855); *Kelly* v. *Natoma Water Co.,* 6 Cal. 105, 108 (1856); *Hill* v. *King,* 8 Cal. 336, 338 (1857); *Kidd* v. *Laird,* 15 Cal. 161, 180 (1860).

[122] *Ferrea* v. *Knipe,* 28 Cal. 340, 343-345 (1865).

[123] The cases are cited by Hutchins, *supra* note 75, p. 53, n. 7.

[124] *Lux* v. *Haggin,* 69 Cal. 255, 408-409, 4 Pac. 919 (1884), 10 Pac. 674 (1886).

[125] For some examples see Hutchins, *supra* note 75, p. 241, n. 46.

The riparian doctrine has considerable significance in California. In no other Western State has the riparian owner been accorded greater privileges in respect to his water right than in California. It is a far cry from his position to that of the owner "of an estate on the Thames."[126] But exercise of the right is subjected by constitutional amendment to reasonable beneficial use under reasonable methods of diversion and use.[127]

Texas

Unlike the situation in California, the riparian doctrine in Texas got underway gradually without the impetus of an overriding economic development in the fashioning of two competing systems of water rights and in sending them on into history. As in California, however, the decisions began to be rendered in the 1850's, and they were based predominantly on the common law.

The first riparian case in the Texas Supreme Court was a suit by one riparian landowner against another for backing water upon his land, not a controversy over rights to the use of water.[128] However, the decision was given a strong common law flavor by the court's observation that plaintiff has a right to the use of the water on his adjacent land as it flowed in its natural channel, and by the support of quotations from Kent's *Commentaries on American Law.* These were to the effect, *inter alia,* that all proprietors of lands on the banks of a stream have equal rights to the use of the water as it was wont to run, without diminution or alteration; that each proprietor may use the water while it runs over his land; that he cannot unreasonably detain it and must return it to its ordinary channel when it leaves his estate; and that without a grant, express or implied, he cannot divert or diminish the quantity of water which would otherwise descend to the proprietors below, nor throw the waters back upon those above. Another case that did not involve the right to use water in any form contains *dicta* concerning both the common law and the civil law.[129]

The decision of *Tolle* v. *Correth,* rendered by the supreme court in 1868, is historically important, but it has no value as a precedent because it was rendered by the military court during the reconstruction era.[130] It invoked the Mexican colonization laws as sources of water rights and refused to be guided by common law inhibitions.

In *Tolle* v. *Correth* the court rejected the maxims "The water runs and let it run" and "Every one has a right to have the advantage of a flow of water in his

---

[126] The United States Supreme Court, in affirming a decision of the supreme court of the Territory of Arizona, commented that adoption of the common law by the Territorial legislature "is far from meaning that patentees of a ranch on the San Pedro are to have the same rights as owners of an estate on the Thames." *Boquillas Land & Cattle Co.* v. *Curtis,* 213 U. S. 339, 345 (1909).

[127] Cal. Const., art. XIV, § 3.

[128] *Haas* v. *Choussard,* 17 Tex. 588, 589-590 (1856).

[129] *Rhodes* v. *Whitehead,* 27 Tex. 304, 309-310, 315, 84 Am. Dec. 631 (1863).

[130] *Tolle* v. *Correth,* 31 Tex. 362, 365-366, 98 Am. Dec. 540 (1868).

land without diminution or alteration," which guided the courts of Eastern States and England. This was done by (1) acknowledging their applicability in regions in which the flow serves mechanical or manufacturing purposes, and (2) denying it where water is useful for agriculture and where the sovereign power grants, for a nominal consideration, water for irrigation purposes. Where the latter conditions obtain, in place of these inapplicable maxims "we must substitute, 'water irrigates, and let it irrigate.' " The court specifically disclaimed any intent to decide *to what extent* a stream could be used for irrigation, inasmuch as the relative rights or exclusive rights of proprietors were not in issue. The holding was that the upper riparian proprietor could divert and use water for irrigation of his land, even though the streamflow was thereby lessened before reaching the lower riparian land.

Although the decision in *Tolle* v. *Correth* was severely criticized 4 years later by the "semicolon court"[131] as setting forth an impossible physical situation and as furnishing no rule of decision,[132] a later postreconstruction court indicated its belief that the departure in *Tolle* v. *Correth* from the strict common law maxims in favor of irrigation was correct as applied to the instant case.[133]

Texas case law contains a number of decisions in which the right of riparian owners to irrigate their riparian land has been recognized. Some of them are *dicta,* such as the famous pronouncement of Chief Justice Cureton in *Motl* v. *Boyd* to the effect that lands granted from the time of the Mexican decree of 1823 down to the passage of the appropriation act in 1889 carried with them the right of the riparian owner to use water, not only for his domestic and household uses, but for irrigation as well.[134] However, the most famous and controlling case in the *Valmont Plantations* case[135] in which the supreme court affirmed the holding that lands riparian to the lower Rio Grande, held under Spanish and Mexican grants, have no appurtenant right to irrigate with the river water. This did not affect anything previously said regarding such common law rights.

The Texas Legislature, on its part, has disclaimed any intent to impair vested riparian rights or rights of property, but has recognized no riparian right in the owner of any land that passed out of State ownership after enactment of the appropriation act of 1895.[136] In none of the complete water appropriation

---

[131] For historical background of the three reconstruction courts of Texas and a study of the last one, the "semicolon court," see Norvell, James R., "Oran M. Roberts and the Semicolon Court," 37 Tex. Law Rev. 279 (1959).

[132] *Fleming* v. *Davis* 37 Tex. 173, 194 (1872).

[133] *Mud Creek Irr., Agric. & Mfg. Co.* v. *Vivian,* 74 Tex. 170, 173-174, 11 S. W. 1078 (1889). See also *Watkins Land Co.* v. *Clements,* 98 Tex. 578, 586, 587-588, 86 S. W. 733, 107 Am. St. Rep. 653, 70 LRA 964 (1905).

[134] *Motl* v. *Boyd,* 116 Tex. 82, 107-108, 286 S. W. 458 (1926).

[135] *Valmont Plantations* v. *State of Texas,* 163 Tex. 381, 355 S. W. (2d) 502 (1962).

[136] Tex. Rev. Civ. Stat. Ann. arts. 7507, 7619, and 7620 (1954).

statutes[137] has the legislature specifically declared or recognized irrigation as a lawful riparian use of water.

Territory of Dakota

A Territorial statute enacted in 1866 read as follows:[138]

The owner of the land owns water standing thereon, or flowing over or under its surface, but not forming a definite stream. Water running in a definite stream, formed by nature over or under the surface, may be used by him as long as it remains there; but he may not prevent the natural flow of the stream, or of the natural spring from which it commences its definite course, nor pursue, nor pollute the same.

Toward the end of the Territorial regime, the supreme court held that on the filing of a homestead entry for which a patent was subsequently issued, rights in the stream flowing over the land vested in the entryman.[139] In affirming this judgment, the United States Supreme Court approved the principle that a proprietor of land bordering upon a running stream is entitled to the benefit to be derived from the flow of its waters as a natural incident to his estate; that when the Government ceases to be the sole proprietor, the right of the riparian owner attaches and cannot be subsequently invaded.[140] "As the riparian owner has the right to have the water flow *ut currere solebat,* undiminished except by reasonable consumption of upper proprietors, and no subsequent attempt to take the water only can override the prior appropriation of both land and water, it would seem reasonable that lawful riparian occupancy with intent to appropriate the land should have the same effect." The Court quoted with approval the Dakota Civil Code section 255 cited immediately above.

North Dakota and South Dakota. – The Territorial Civil Code section 255 was carried over into the laws of both North Dakota and South Dakota on their creation in 1889.[141] It was cited as current authority by the supreme courts of both States in decisions in which riparian rights were involved or considered.[142]

---

[137] Tex. Laws 1889, ch. 88; Laws 1895, ch. 21; Laws 1913, ch. 171; Laws 1917, ch. 88.

[138] Terr. Dak. Laws 1865-1866, ch. 1, § 256, Civ. Code § 255 (1877).

[139] *Sturr v. Beck,* 6 Dak. 71, 50 N. W. 486 (1888).

[140] *Sturr v. Beck,* 133 U. S. 541, 547, 551 (1890).

[141] The Enabling Act provided that all Territorial laws in force at the time of admission of the States to the Union "shall be in force in said States, except as modified or changed by this act or by the constitutions of the States, respectively." 25 Stat. 676, § 24. See also N. Dak. Const., Schedule, § 2. For subsequent history in the two States, see: (1) North Dakota: N. Dak. Rev. Codes § 3362 (1895); Rev. Code § 4798 (1905); Comp. Laws § 5341 (1913); Rev. Code § 47-0113 (1943); Cent. Code Ann. § 47-01-13 (1960), repealed, Laws 1963, ch. 419, § 7. (2) South Dakota: S. Dak. Rev. Codes, C. C. § 278 (1903); Rev. Code § 348 (1919); Comp. Laws § 348 (1929); Code § 61.0101 (1939), repealed, Laws 1955, ch. 430, § 1.

[142] See *McDonough v. Russell-Miller Mill. Co.,* 38 N. Dak. 465, 471-472, 165 N. W. 504 (1917); *Johnson v. Armour & Co.,* 69 N. Dak. 769, 776-777, 291 N. W. 113 (1940); *Lone Tree Ditch Co. v. Cyclone Ditch Co.,* 15 S. Dak. 519, 525-527, 91 N. W. 352 (1902); *Redwater Land & Canal Co. v. Reed,* 26 S. Dak. 466, 474, 128 N. W. 702 (1910).

The ancestry of section 255 of the Territorial Civil Code was noted in both of the South Dakota decisions. In *Lone Tree Ditch Company* v. *Cyclone Ditch Company,* the court declared the section to be a concise statement of the common law doctrine applicable to the rights of riparian owners. This was said to be apparent from the fact that the section was a literal copy of section 256 of the proposed civil code for the State of New York and that the code commissioners of that State, in a note to that section, cited a large number of English and American decisions in which the doctrine of the common law as applied to riparian owners was discussed. The common law, said the South Dakota court, "seems to have recognized" the right of the riparian owner to use a reasonable amount of water for irrigating purposes. In *Redwater Land & Canal Company* v. *Reed,* the supreme court repeated its statement that section 278 of the Revised Civil Code of South Dakota (which was taken from section 255 of the Territorial Civil Code) was the same as the New York section as proposed by the commissioners, and concluded on this point that:[143]

> There is no suggestion in the report of the commissioners of an intention to change the common law respecting riparian rights. Therefore section 278 of our Civil Code should be regarded as merely declaratory of the common law as understood by the commissioners when their report was prepared.

The South Dakota provision, after several amendments, was repealed in 1955.[144] The North Dakota section was repealed in 1963.[145]

Oklahoma

The Dakota Civil Code section 255[146] was copied literally by the First Territorial Legislative Assembly of Oklahoma.[147] It was continued in the State statutes and remained in force until amended in 1963.[148]

The Territorial statute of 1890 has been quoted or cited by the Oklahoma Supreme Court in several cases concerning rights of landowners to use water of natural streams flowing over their land.[149] In two of them, interpretation of the statute was an important part of the court's decision. Undoubtedly, this early statute was important in such development of the riparian doctrine as has taken place in Oklahoma with respect to rights of use of riparian waters. However, in both early and late decisions, without referring to the statute of

---

[143] *Redwater Land & Canal Co.* v. *Reed,* 26 S. Dak. 466, 474, 128 N. W. 702 (1910).

[144] S. Dak. Code § 61.0101 (1939), repealed by Laws 1955, ch. 430, § 1.

[145] N. Dak. Cent. Code Ann. § 47-01-13 (1960), repealed by Laws 1963, ch. 419, § 7.

[146] Then Terr. Dak. Comp. Laws § 2771 (1887).

[147] Terr. Okla. Stat. § 4162 (1890).

[148] Okla. Stat. Ann. tit. 60, § 60 (Supp. 1961), amended by Laws 1963, ch. 205 § 1, Stat. Ann. tit. 60, § 60 (Supp. 1970).

[149] *Broady* v. *Furray,* 163 Okla. 204, 205, 21 Pac. (2d) 770 (1933); *Grand-Hydro* v. *Grand River Dam Authority,* 192 Okla. 693, 695, 139 Pac. (2d) 798 (1943); *Smith* v. *Stanolind Oil & Gas Co.,* 197 Okla. 499, 501, 172 Pac. (2d) 1002 (1946).

1890, the supreme court recognized the existence in this jurisdiction of the common law doctrine of rights and liabilities of riparian owners with respect to watercourses.[150] Most of these cases involved injuries to riparian uses of other proprietors—nuisance cases rather than controversies between riparian owners who were claiming coequal rights of use of water. Only one case involved relative rights of riparians to divert water from a common stream for beneficial use.[151]

Status of the Riparian Doctrine in the West

Nonrecognition

The riparian water-rights doctrine is not usually recognized in the eight, generally arid, interior States—Idaho, Montana, Wyoming, Nevada, Utah, Colorado, Arizona, and New Mexico. In these jurisdictions, rights to the use of water of watercourses usually do not accrue, by operation of general law, to the owners of lands bordering on or crossed by such watercourses solely because of the natural juxtaposition of land and water. See chapter 10.

However, there are cases in some of these jurisdictions (as well as in other Western States[152]) which have declared or implied that a riparian owner may apply the water to beneficial use by virtue of his riparian status, so long as he does not interfere with the recognized operation of the appropriation doctrine.[153] In addition, the definition of riparian rights encompasses more than just the right to use water, some features of which have been recognized by various courts in certain of these jurisdictions. For example, the common

---

[150] See *Markwardt* v. *Guthrie*, 18 Okla. 32, 34-36, 55, 90 Pac. 26 (1907); *Chicago, R. I. & P. Ry.* v. *Groves*, 20 Okla. 101, 111, 93 Pac. 755 (1908); *Zalaback* v. *Kingfisher*, 59 Okla. 222, 223-224, 158 Pac. 926 (1916); *Kingfisher* v. *Zalaback*, 77 Okla. 108, 109-110, 186 Pac. 936 (1920); *Enid* v. *Brooks*, 132 Okla. 60, 61-63, 269 Pac. 241 (1928); *Martin* v. *British American Oil Producing Co.*, 187 Okla. 193, 194-195, 102 Pac. (2d) 124 (1940).

[151] *Smith* v. *Stanolind Oil & Gas Co.*, 197 Okla. 499, 500-503, 172 Pac. (2d) 1002 (1946).

[152] See, for example, *Fitzstephens* v. *Watson*, 218 Oreg. 185, 344 Pac. (2d) 221 (1959).

[153] See *Hutchinson* v. *Watson Slough Co.*, 16 Idaho 484, 490-496, 101 Pac. 1059 (1909); *Weeks* v. *McKay*, 85 Idaho 617, 624, 382 Pac. (2d) 788 (1963); *United States Freehold Land & Emmigration Co.* v. *Galleges*, 89 Fed. 769, 772-773 (8th Cir. 1898), discussed in *Sternberger* v. *Seaton Min. Co.* 45 Colo. 401, 405, 102 Pac. 168 (1909).

For a somewhat confused discussion of ordinary domestic use, perhaps being treated as a recognized riparian right protected against appropriative rights in Colorado, see *Montrose Canal Co.* v. *Loutsenhizer Ditch Co.*, 23 Colo. 233, 237, 48 Pac. 532 (1896); *Broadmoor Dairy & Livestock Co.* v. *Brookside Water & Improvement Co.*, 24 Colo. 541, 545-546, 550, 52 Pac. 792 (1898). But the court's language in these two cases appears to have been *dicta*. These and related Colorado cases are discussed in the State summary for Colorado in the appendix.

law riparian rights regarding accretions have been recognized and applied in Arizona.[154] Likewise, the common law right of fishery has been applied in Colorado and Montana.[155] Other features of the riparian doctrine which have been recognized in some of these jurisdictions include, for example, bed ownership, the right to unpolluted water, the right to protect streambanks against erosion, and the right to have access to the adjoining watercourse.[156]

Recognition in Varying Degree

In the other generally less arid Western States—North Dakota, South Dakota, Nebraska, Kansas, Oklahoma, and Texas on the 100th meridian, Washington, Oregon, and California on the Pacific Coast, and Alaska and Hawaii—the riparian doctrine of water rights has been recognized, but the degree of its importance and the way in which it has been recognized or curtailed varies markedly from one jurisdiction to another. The following discussion highlights some of the major approaches and developments in these States throughout the years. The order in which the States are presented is not necessarily intended to signify the relative importance of the doctrine in the different States. (See chapter 4 for additional considerations regarding navigable waters and their tributaries.)

California.—The riparian doctrine has been of major importance in this State. From the time of the earliest court decisions more than a century ago, integrity of the California riparian right has withstood repeated attacks. The right is an important property right and it may have substantial utility and value. Exercise of the right has been subjected to regulation under the police power by the State constitution, which commands reasonable beneficial diversion and utilization of water and forbids waste.[157] The right is perpetual, whether exercised or not, but it may be lost by prescription. For any substantial deprivation of his riparian right, the owner is entitled to compensation, or to a physical solution.

Texas.—In this State, the riparian doctrine has been of major importance for many years but with the passage of legislation in 1967 its significance has been limited.[158] In many decisions rendered over a period of more than 100 years,

---

[154] *State* v. *Jacobs,* 93 Ariz. 336, 339, 380 Pac. (2d) 998 (1963); *State* v. *Gunther & Shirley Co.,* 5 Ariz. App. 77, 423 Pac. (2d) 352, 357 (1967); *State* v. *Bonelli Cattle Co.,* 11 Ariz. App. 412, 464 Pac. (2d) 999, 1005, 1006 (1970).

[155] *Hartman* v. *Tresise,* 36 Colo. 146, 150-151, 84 Pac. 685 (1905); *Herrin* v. *Sutherland,* 74 Mont. 587, 595-596, 241 Pac. 328 (1925). Compare *State ex rel. State Game Comm'n* v. *Red River Valley Co.,* 51 N. Mex. 207, 215, 182 Pac. (2d) 421 (1945). See also the dissents in this case, 51 N. Mex. at 229 *et seq.*

[156] For a brief discussion of the protection provided these and related riparian rights by some of the courts in these jurisdictions (as well as in other Western States), see Note, "Riparian Rights in Appropriation States," 9 Wyo. L. J. 130 (1954). See also the disccussion of some of these matters in *Fitzstephens* v. *Watson,* 218 Oreg. 185, 344 Pac. (2d) 221 (1959).

[157] Cal. Const., art. XIV, § 3.

[158] Tex. Rev. Civ. Stat. Ann. art. 7542 *et seq.* (Supp. 1970).

the courts have recognized that the riparian doctrine is a part of the State water law, and at various times the legislature has referred on one occasion or another to riparian rights.[159] Use of water for domestic purposes on riparian land has been involved in litigation; it has come to be accepted not only as a legitimate purpose but as a natural use superior to irrigation, an artificial use.[160] The riparian right has been limited to use of the normal streamflow.[161]

The proposition that irrigation is a proper riparian purpose has aroused much contention in Texas. So far as opinions expressed in decisions of the high courts are concerned, there is no doubt that, until 1962, it had been regarded favorably, whether by *dictum* or by actual decision. However, unrelenting opposition finally resulted in forcing the riparian irrigation question as an essential issue of law in an important areawide adjudication in lower Rio Grande Valley. In the resulting *Valmont Plantations* case, the Texas Supreme Court ruled that lands riparian to the Lower Rio Grande, held under Spanish and Mexican grants, have no appurtenant right to irrigate with the river water.[162] But this did not affect anything previously said with respect to such common law rights.

Texas legislation has disclaimed any intent to impair vested riparian rights or rights of property but has recognized no riparian right in the owner of any land that passed out of State ownership after July 1, 1895.[163] A 1967 statute has limited riparian rights, except for domestic or livestock purposes, to the extent of maximum actual application of water to beneficial use made during any calender year from 1963 to 1967.[164] This legislation is similar to the general approach taken by the Oregon legislation limiting riparian rights, discussed below.

Oregon.—Although the riparian doctrine is historically an important part of the water law of Oregon, State legislation, favorably construed by the courts, has effectively limited the extent and operation of the doctrine.[165]

Progressive modification of the common law doctrine by the courts was influenced by such factors as incompatibility of appropriative and riparian

---

[159] See the earlier discussion under "Establishment of the Riparian Doctrine in the West—Early Development of the Riparian Doctrine in Specified Jurisdictions—Texas."

[160] *Watkins Land Co.* v. *Clements,* 98 Tex 578, 585-590, 86 S. W. 733 (1905).

[161] *Motl* v. *Boyd,* 116 Tex. 82, 111, 121-126, 286 S. W. 458 (1926).

[162] *Valmont Plantations* v. *State of Texas,* 163 Tex. 381, 355 S. W. (2d) 502 (1962).

[163] Tex. Rev. Civ. Stat. Ann. arts. 7507, 7619, and 7620 (1954).

The Texas Supreme Court has said grantees of public lands from 1840, when the common law was adopted in Texas, to the passage of the first water appropriation act in 1889 became vested with riparian rights in the waters of contiguous streams. *Motl* v. *Boyd,* 116 Tex. 82, 107-108, 286 S. W. 458 (1926).

[164] Or until the end of 1970 if works were under construction before the act's effective date. Tex. Rev. Civ. Stat. Ann. art. 7542a, § 4 (Supp. 1970).

[165] See Hutchins, Wells A., "The Common-Law Riparian Doctrine in Oregon: Legislative and Judicial Modification," 36 Oreg. Law Rev. 193 (1957).

rights, difficulty of apportionment of water among riparians, disapproval of simultaneous claiming of both appropriative and riparian rights by a riparian landowner, and interpretation of the Congressional Desert Land Act of 1877[166] as abrogating the common law rule in respect to riparian rights for irrigation and other artificial purposes on all public lands entered thereafter.[167] The State water code of 1909 limited vested riparian rights to the extent of actual application of water to beneficial use prior to its enactment, or within a reasonable time thereafter by means of works then under construction, all such rights to be adjudicated under the statutory procedure provided therein.[168] This legislation was sustained by both the Oregon Supreme Court and the United States Court of Appeals, 9th Circuit.[169]

The result of this harmonized legislative and judicial modification of the common law riparian doctrine in Oregon has been to substantially reduce that doctrine. So far as rights to the use of water for beneficial purposes are concerned, and except for certain vested rights chiefly for domestic and stockwatering purposes,[170] very little vestige of the doctrine remains as against appropriative rights under the water code, although it may apply in situations not controlled by the water code.[171]

South Dakota.—Riparian rights have been recognized in a number of South Dakota court decisions. They are held to be incident to and part of the riparian land itself, and unaffected by a statutory dedication to the public of all water within the State.

However, the South Dakota water appropriation act was completely rewritten in 1955, one of the chief purposes being to eliminate so far as possible the obstructive aspects of the common law riparian doctrine. To that end, the precedent set by the Oregon Legislature was followed in including under the definition of "Vested Rights" the right of a riparian owner to continue the use of water actually applied to any beneficial purpose at the time of the enactment, or within the immediately preceding 3 years, or with the use of works under construction at the time of the enactment provided the works are completed and water actually applied to beneficial use within a reasonable time thereafter. But use of water for domestic purposes is unqualifiedly declared a vested right.[172]

---

[166] 19 Stat. 377, 43 U. S. C. § 321 (1964).

[167] *Hough* v. *Porter,* 51 Oreg. 318, 383-399, 404-406, 95 Pac. 732 (1908), 98 Pac. 1083 (1909), 102 Pac. 728 (1909).

[168] Oreg. Laws 1909, ch. 216, Rev. Stat. § 539.010 (Supp. 1955).

[169] *In re Willow Creek,* 74 Oreg. 592, 610-620, 625-628, 144 Pac. 505 (1914), 146 Pac. 475 (1915); *California-Oregon Power Co.* v. *Beaver Portland Cement Co.,* 73 Fed. (2d) 555, 562-569 (9th Cir. 1934).

[170] Hutchins, Wells A., *supra* note 165, at 218-219, which includes a discussion of questions regarding these domestic and stockwatering purposes.

[171] *Fitzstephens* v. *Watson,* 218 Oreg. 185, 344 Pac. (2d) 221 (1959).

[172] S. Dak. Laws 1955, Ch. 430, Comp. Laws Ann. § 46-1-9 (1967).

The constitutionality of this 1955 legislation has been upheld by the South Dakota Supreme Court.[173]

Kansas.—The common law doctrine of riparian rights was declared by the Kansas Supreme Court to be fundamental in the jurisprudence of the State. It included the reasonable use of water for irrigation purposes after the primary uses for domestic purposes had been subserved. Prior to 1945, statutes designed to encourage irrigation were ineffective in modifying the riparian doctrine.[174] In that year, however, the legislature passed an act that accomplished its purpose of modifying the common law doctrine sufficiently to effectuate rights of prior appropriation. A number of amendments were made in 1957.[175]

The new legislation followed the lead of the Oregon water code in declaring vested rights to be rights to continue the use of water actually applied to any beneficial use at the time of the passage of the act, as well as rights to begin use with works then under construction provided they are completed and water applied to a beneficial use within a reasonable time thereafter.[176] And the Nebraska judicial precedent, discussed below, was followed by providing in the act that common law claimants are entitled to compensation in an action at law for proved damages for property taken by an appropriator in connection with an appropriation, and that appropriators shall have injunctive relief against subsequent diversions by common law claimants with no vested rights without first being required to condemn the latters' rights.[177]

The validity of the Kansas statute has been sustained by both State and Federal courts on the several points presented for determination.[178]

Nebraska.—Existence of the riparian doctrine in Nebraska was recognized in early court decisions as applicable throughout the State. However, other decisions rendered early in the present century had the effect of putting a riparian owner who does not make actual use of water before the time of vesting of appropriative rights in a position in which he has no recourse other

---

[173]*Belle Fourche Irr. Dist.* v. *Smiley,* 176 N. W. (2d) 239 (S. Dak. 1970); *Knight* v. *Grimes,* 80 S. Dak. 517, 127 N. W. (2d) 708 (1964). In the *Belle Fourche* case the court said that the "Decision in the Knight case concerned with underground waters is equally applicable to surface waters." 176 N. W. (2d) at 245.

[174]*State ex rel. Peterson* v. *State Bd. of Agriculture,* 158 Kans. 603, 605-614, 148 Pac. (2d) 604 (1944).

[175]Kans. Laws 1945, ch. 390, Laws 1957, ch. 539, Stat. Ann. § 82a-701 *et seq.* (1969).

[176]Kans. Stat. Ann. § 82a-701(d) (1969).

[177]*Id.* §§ 82a-716 and -717a.

[178]*State ex rel. Emery* v. *Knapp,* 167 Kans. 546, 555-556, 207 Pac. (2d) 440 (1949); *Baumann* v. *Smrha,* 145 Fed. Supp. 617 (D. Kans. 1956), affirmed per curiam, 352 U. S. 863 (1956); *Williams* v. *Wichita,* 190 Kans. 317, 374 Pac. (2d) 578 (1962), appeal dismissed "for want of a substantial Federal question," 375 U. S. 7 (1963), rehearing denied, 375 U. S. 936 (1963); *Hesston & Sedgwick* v. *Smrha,* 192 Kans. 647, 391 Pac. (2d) 93 (1964). For a discussion of these cases, see note 245, *infra.*

than to recover such damages as he can actually prove.[179] But in 1966, the court said that:[180]

> We think [these] cases have been misread. The appropriative rights [in these cases] seem to have been asserted by irrigation companies offering a public service. The court attached significance to the public benefit, to the appropriation project completed in good faith and at great cost, and to the tardy initiation of the riparian use. If the court went too far, the limitations themselves have remained. We reject the startling proposition [urged by the defendant appropriators] that equity sends every riparian proprietor packing. Defendants are private appropriators—not champions of the public interest. . . .The remedy rests on other considerations.

The court concluded that the defendant appropriators should be enjoined for injury to a recognized riparian right where the harmful use was unreasonable with respect to the riparian proprietor. The court set forth criteria for determining such reasonableness as well as criteria for determining the appropriativeness of the injunction.[181]

Washington.—The riparian doctrine has been recognized repeatedly in the court decisions of Washington. The supreme court held that riparian rights existed in the arid as well as the humid parts of the State.[182] However, the common law doctrine has been modified by limiting the riparian claimant's right as against appropriators to the quantity of water that can be used beneficially, either directly or prospectively, within a reasonable time on or in connection with riparian land.[183] The supreme court's own appraisal of its decisions has been that the common law rule of riparian rights has been "stripped of some of its rigors,"[184] and that the trend has been to restrict and narrow this doctrine. As a result, the advantage of position of riparian lands with reference to water rights has been materially reduced.

Legislation enacted in 1967 provides that a riparian landowner who abandons or voluntarily fails, without sufficient cause, to divert or withdraw water to which he is entitled for 5 successive years shall relinquish the right to do so.[185]

---

[179] *McCook Irr. Water Power Co.* v. *Crews,* 70 Nebr. 109, 96 N. W. 996 (1903), 102 N. W. 249 (1905); *Cline* v. *Stock,* 71 Nebr. 70, 98 N. W. 454 (1904), 102 N. W. 265 (1905).

[180] *Wasserburger* v. *Coffee,* 180 Nebr. 147, 141 N. W. (2d) 738, 747 (1966).

[181] *Id.* at 746-748. For a critical discussion of this case, see Comment, "The Dual-System of Water Rights in Nebraska," 48 Nebr. L. Rev. 488, 497-498 (1969).

[182] *Benton* v. *Johncox,* 9 Wash. 576, 38 Pac. 147 (1894).

[183] *Brown* v. *Chase,* 125 Wash. 542, 549, 553, 217 Pac. 23 (1923); *In re Alpowa Creek,* 129 Wash. 9, 13, 224 Pac. 29 (1924); *Proctor* v. *Sim,* 134 Wash. 606, 616-619, 236 Pac. 114 (1925); *In re Sinlahekin Creek,* 162 Wash. 635, 640-641, 229 Pac. 649 (1931). For a greater restriction regarding navigable waters, see chapter 4 at note 133.

[184] *In re Alpowa Creek,* 129 Wash. 9, 13, 224 Pac. 29 (1924).

[185] Wash. Laws 1967, ch. 233, Rev. Code § 90.14.170 (Supp. 1970).

North Dakota.—In the very few cases in the early Territorial and State supreme courts in which riparian water rights were considered, the courts adhered to the riparian doctrine.

A territorial statute provided that water running in a definite natural stream might be used by the landowner as long as it remains there, but that he might not prevent the natural flow of the stream nor pursue nor pollute it.[186] The North Dakota Legislature declared in 1955 that the several and reciprocal rights of a riparian owner, other than a municipal corporation, in the waters of the State comprise the ordinary or natural use of water for domestic and stockwatering purposes.[187] Both provisions were eliminated in 1963 and different ones enacted which relate to priority of water rights and preferences in the use of water.[188]

As amended by the 1955 legislation, the statute declares, among other things, that waters flowing in watercourses belong to the public and are subject to appropriation.[189] In a recent case, the North Dakota Supreme Court appears to have concluded that unused riparian rights to irrigate from an underground stream could be validly abrogated by this and related legislation, at least as against appropriative rights acquired thereafter, and that the riparian owner could be validly required to apply for and be governed by an appropriative-right permit. But the court qualified this by stating that it did not approve of the State Water Commission's granting to one of two adjacent landowners who had applied "at approximately the same time . . . so much water that the other was in effect denied use of any water."[190] This case did not involve any consideration of the 1963 legislation.

Oklahoma.—An Oklahoma territorial statute provided that water running in a definite natural stream might be used by the landowner as long as it remains there, but that he might not prevent the natural flow of the stream nor pursue nor pollute it.[191] The Oklahoma territorial and State legislatures subsequently enacted various water appropriation statutes.

The tenor of Oklahoma court decisions is that the riparian doctrine is established as a facet of the State water law but its extent and its correlation with appropriative water rights is rather unclear. Most of the decisions involved other matters than rights to the use of stream water on riparian land, important among which is pollution of water. In 1963, the Oklahoma legislature attempted to clarify the matter by, among other things, recognizing a riparian right to domestic use of water but by otherwise restricting unused riparian

---

[186] Terr. Dak. Laws 1865-1866, ch. 1, § 256, Civ. Code § 255 (1877); N. Dak. Cent. Code Ann. § 47-01-13 (1960).

[187] N. Dak. Laws 1955, ch. 345, § 2. Cent. Code Ann. § 61-01-01.1 (1960).

[188] N. Dak. Laws 1963, ch. 419, Cent. Code Ann. § 61-01-01.1 (Supp. 1969).

[189] N. Dak. Cent. Code Ann. § 61-01-01 (1960), created by Laws 1905, ch. 34, § 1.

[190] *Baeth* v. *Hoisveen*, 157 N. W. (2d) 728, 733-734 (N. Dak. 1968).

[191] Terr. Okla. Stat. § 4162 (1890), Stat. Ann. tit. 60, § 60 (Supp. 1961).

rights.[192] As the courts construe this legislation, the importance of riparianism and its correlation with appropriative water rights in Oklahoma may become more settled.[193]

Alaska.—A territorial statute enacted in 1917 applied riparian principles to mining claims that included within their boundaries both banks of a stream, in the absence of prior appropriation of water.[194] The United States Court of Appeals, 9th Circuit, stated (probably as *dictum*) that this statute enacted the law of riparian rights to a limited extent.[195] But in 1966, the State legislature enacted the Water Use Act,[196] which is fundamentally an appropriation doctrine statute. Without mentioning the term "riparian," it apparently purports to phase out that water-rights doctrine. It repealed the earlier mining legislation[197] and, among other things, declared that a water right acquired by law before the effective date of the act, or a beneficial use of water on such date, or such a use made within 5 years before it or in conjunction with works under construction, "under a lawful common law or customary appropriation or use, is a lawful appropriation under this chapter . . . subject to applicable provisions of this chapter. . . ."[198] This and related provisions of the 1966 act are discussed in more detail later.[199]

Hawaii.—The riparian doctrine has been recognized by the Hawaii Supreme Court in a few decisions, only two of which specifically adjudicated riparian water rights.[200] The result was to apply the riparian doctrine, as between "konohiki" or landlord units, to the surplus freshet waters of streams but not to the normal flow. Owing to the physiography and hydrology of the islands, the question of riparian rights is probably not of great practical importance in their economy. Moreover, unlike the other States previously discussed in this subsection, there is no appropriation system of surface water rights.

---

[192] Okla. Laws 1963, ch. 205, Stat. Ann. tit. 60, § 60 (Supp. 1970) and tit. 82, § 1-A (1970).

[193] A recent case, *Oklahoma Water Resources Bd.* v. *Central Oklahoma Master Conservancy Dist.*, 464 Pac. (2d) 748 (Okla. 1968), is discussed later under "Interrelationships of the Dual Water Rights Systems—The Status in Summary: By States—Oklahoma."

[194] Alaska Laws 1917, ch. 57, Comp. Laws Ann. § 47-3-35 (1949), Stat. § § 27.10.080 (Supp. 1962) and 38.05.260 (Supp. 1965).

[195] *Balabanoff* v. *Kellog*, 10 Alaska 11, 16-17, 118 Fed. (2d) 597, 599 (9th Cir. 1940), certiorari denied, 314 U. S. 635 (1941).

[196] Alaska Laws 1966, ch. 50, Stat. § 46.15.010 *et seq.* (Supp. 1966).

[197] Alaska Laws 1966, ch. 50, § 2.

[198] Alaska Stat. § 46.15.060 (Supp. 1966).

[199] See "Interrelationships of the Dual Water Rights Systems—The Status in Summary: By States—Alaska."

[200] *Carter* v. *Territory of Hawaii*, 24 Haw. 47 (1917); *Territory of Hawaii* v. *Gay*, 31 Haw. 376 (1930), affirmed, 52 Fed. (2d) 356 (9th Cir. 1931), certiroari denied, 284 U. S. 677 (1931).

INTERRELATIONSHIPS OF THE DUAL WATER RIGHTS SYSTEMS

A Century of Conflict and Adjustment

Several years ago the author prepared a paper in which the conflict between riparian and appropriative rights in the West was discussed from an historical standpoint.[201] For convenience in tracing the threads of the farflung conflict and the trends, the approximate century was divided into four periods of about 25 years each, followed by general observations. Some general matters included in this present discussion were first written in that paper, and the subtopic "Some Features of the Conflict," below, reproduces the conclusions with but few changes.

Reasons for the Conflict

The riparian right to the use of water of watercourses inheres in the ownership of riparian land solely by reason of its contiguity to the source of water supply; hence, one who acquires title to the land acquires ownership of the water right as well. In its early common law form, the riparian doctrine accorded to the riparian landowner the right to the flow of water in the channel as it had been accustomed to flow, undiminished in quantity and unpolluted in quality. Although that rule was adequate for propulsion of mill machinery, for floating logs, or for recreational purposes, it obviously was not adapted to consumptive uses of the water on a substantial scale. Increasing demands upon water supplies for utilitarian purposes resulted in so modifying the doctrine in various jurisdictions as to allow consumption of water not only for domestic uses, but also for irrigation of agricultural land and for industrial needs.

At this stage there arises a potential conflict, not only between riparian landowners who seek use of the same source of water for increasing their crop production, but also between, on the one hand, riparian proprietors and, on the other hand, possessors of noncontiguous lands with agricultural possibilities. This is the general situation that developed in the middle of the 19th century, in the early stages of the formidable westward migration and settlement of arable farmlands both along and distant from stream channels. So there began during this western expansion, and there has continued to the present time, a century (and more) of conflict between the now familiar riparian and appropriation doctrines. In some of the States, as already noted, the conflict never progressed far, or was speedily or gradually terminated by

---

[201] Hutchins, Wells A., "History of the Conflict Between Riparian and Appropriative Rights in the Western States," Proceedings, Water Law Conferences, Univ. of Texas, pp. 106 (1952, 1954).

the expedient of ignoring or specifically repudiating the riparian doctrine in favor of one founded on the rock of priority in time of diverting water and putting it to beneficial use on land, regardless of contiguity of the land to the source of water supply—the appropriation doctrine. This was accomplished more readily in the generally more arid States than in those that contained considerable areas in which crops grew well with the use of precipitation alone. These latter States recognized both doctrines of water law.

In the dual-system States, the water rights of lands that bordered streams were superior to those of noncontiguous lands solely because of their location. Under the riparian doctrine this location gave them prior claims to the water. With development of the country and growing competition for water for irrigation purposes, it was inevitable that controversies should arise between these antagonistic groups—owners of lands riparian to a stream, and persons who wished to extend use of the waters to areas perhaps far from the channel and thereby to increase the irrigated area and the usefulness of the water supply.

The appropriation doctrine proved to be better suited to the needs of a pioneer arid region than did the riparian doctrine. There is no doubt that it contributed far more to the building up of the West than its rival could account for.

On the other hand, it is equally without doubt that no particular magic is inherent in the term "appropriative right"—that "appropriation" is not necessarily synonymous with best possible use of water, and "riparian" with waste. As a matter of fact, although waste of water never has been compatible with the appropriative principle of beneficial use, trouble in certain exclusive appropriation doctrine areas has been experienced with early court decrees that awarded excessive quantities of water to early priorities.

In general, efficient utilization of a limited water supply can be attained under either the riparian or the appropriation doctrine, provided the governing principles are adequately defined and applied and the serious problem of the unused riparian right adequately dealt with. Under these circumstances, efficient utilization should be able to contribute as much to the public welfare under one doctrine as under the other. The difficulty has been with those concepts of the riparian right that sanctioned inefficient and wasteful use of water, or indefinite holding of the right without putting the water to use even though some appropriator might be willing and able to use the water beneficially according to accepted standards. As said by the United States Supreme Court when discussing the former California situation: "Riparianism, pressed to the limits of its logic, enabled one to play dog-in-the-manger."[202]

---

[202] *United States* v. *Gerlach Live Stock Co.,* 339 U. S. 725, 751 (1950).

Various modifications through the years in various States, as the result of statutes and court decisions, have been directed toward removal of obstructive aspects of the riparian doctrine. They have accomplished a large measure of reduction in excessive riparian demands upon water supplies and in so releasing, for utilization on nonriparian lands, waters theretofore legally unavailable. This has been done in recognition of rights of reasonable use that had actually vested, and of the fact that new rights in a particular source of supply must necessarily be subject to those validly existing.

Some Features of the Conflict

Purpose of use of water. —The century-long conflict has not been essentially a struggle between users of water for different purposes. It began with the disputes over mining water rights and extended to industrial and irrigation uses as well. But the miners as a class were not arrayed in reliance upon one water law doctrine as against another, nor were the industrialists or irrigationists later. Despite those individual conflicts between riparian and appropriative claimants of water for different purposes—some of major importance—most of the controversies have been fought out in the agricultural areas between users or prospective users of water for irrigation.

Sources of conflict. —As noted above (see "Reasons for the Conflict"), controversies between claimants who invoked different doctrines stemmed from the superiority which the riparian owner enjoyed by reason of the situation of his land on the banks of the stream, which entitled him to have the stream flow to his land. Even though the common law doctrine has been so modified as to allow a reasonable consumption of the water for irrigation, so that the riparian proprietor was required to suffer some diminution of the flow as the result of diversions by other riparian owners, his right to the uninterrupted flow was still good as against diversions to nonriparian lands. When appropriators attempted to make upstream diversions of water that from time immemorial had been flowing to riparian lands, conflicts with the riparian owners ensued, naturally. Bitter conflicts in some areas were precipitated by riparian claims of right to use water wastefully, or to withhold use without sacrificing the right, as against nonriparian diversions for useful purposes. But other conflicts resulted simply from competition between early and latecomers for the use of water supplies of valleys, just as many contests arose in that way between senior and junior claimants of appropriative rights only.

Results in the arid States. —The riparian water rights doctrine was generally eliminated in the arid jurisdictions on the ground that it was unsuited to the conditions that obtained there. In several of the States this action was taken promptly, before there had been much litigation over water. It was not taken in Montana until quite late, after more than 90 decisions in water rights controversies had been rendered by the State supreme court.[203] And in

---

[203] *Mettler* v. *Ames Realty Co.*, 61 Mont. 152, 170-171, 201 Pac. 702 (1921).

Nevada the supreme court made its final decision to abandon the riparian doctrine after having accepted that doctrine for 13 years.[204]

Results in the other States.—All of the contiguous States on the 100th meridian and those on the Pacific Coast, portions of which are generally humid and other portions generally arid or semiarid, originally accepted both the riparian doctrine and the doctrine of prior appropriation. These two theories proved so conflicting when applied to the assertion of both kinds of rights on the same stream that adjustments in most jurisdictions resulted in modification of riparian principles. But this was not done uniformly. Hence, the extent of modification of the riparian doctrine and the accompanying degree of effectiveness of the appropriative principle vary considerably throughout these nine dual system States.

Alaska, since the latter part of the 19th century, has recognized the appropriation doctrine, and by statute in 1917 applied riparian principles to a limited extent to certain mining claims.[205] However, as noted in more detail later under "The Status in Summary: By States—Alaska," the Alaska Water Use Act of 1966 apparently purports to phase out the riparian doctrine as such by, among other things, recognizing existing beneficial uses of water under the common law or customary appropriation or use and declaring them to be lawful appropriations under the Water Use Act.[206] In Hawaii, on the other hand, riparian rights have been recognized in some degree but appropriations of water not at all.[207]

Recourse of the appropriator where riparian rights attached to all the water.—To hold that the rights of owners of riparian lands along a stream attached to all the water of the source necessarily left no water open to appropriation. In such case, an appropriation could become effective only upon the nullification of impeding riparian rights by some process sanctioned by law, such as grant, condemnation, or prescription.

The right of eminent domain may be exercised for irrigation purposes by public entities and public service companies generally, and in some jurisdictions in greater or less degree by other enterprises, even including individuals. Riparian claims have been satisfied in various cases by contract or condemnation, but this necessitated finanical resources beyond the ability of small groups even where they had the power to condemn. Prescription, however, has been a potent factor in establishing appropriative rights despite the existence of downstream riparian lands for which riparian rights could have been adjudicated had their owners chosen to assert them.

[204] *Jones* v. *Adams,* 19 Nev. 78, 84-88, 6 Pac. 442 (1885).

In these regards, see chapter 10 and the earlier discussion at notes 152 to 156.
[205] Alaska Laws 1917, ch. 57, Comp. Laws Ann. § 47-3-35 (1949).
[206] Alaska Stat. § 46.15.060 (Supp. 1966).
[207] *Carter* v. *Territory of Hawaii,* 24 Haw. 47, 57-71 (1917); *Territory of Hawaii* v. *Gay,* 31 Haw. 376, 394-417 (1930), affirmed, 52 Fed. (2d) 356 (9th Cir. 1931), certiorari denied, 284 U. S. 677 (1931).

Modification of riparian principles.—Where the riparian right entitled the holder to use water inefficiently and wastefully, or to keep the right intact indefinitely while making no use of the water, then the successful assertion of that right could become or could threaten to become an impediment to water development. As above noted (see "Reasons for the Conflict"), modifications of riparian principles in the public interest in various States, as a result of conflicts, have consisted of lessening or removing the obstructive aspects of the early common law principles.

Measures to solve the problem of the unused riparian right were undertaken early in the 20th century. These developments have continued. Following are brief descriptions of some of the approaches that have been taken:

Important legislative limitations upon riparian rights include those of Oregon, South Dakota, and Kansas, which appear to have generally restricted the exercise of such rights, as vested riparian rights, to the extent of actual application of water to beneficial use made at the time of the enactment of water appropriation statutes or, in certain cases, shortly thereafter.[208] In Kansas, common law claimants may recover provable damages for property taken by an appropriator, but an appropriator may enjoin diversions begun subsequently by riparian claimants.[209] The Alaska Water Use Act of 1966 apparently purports to phase out the riparian doctrine by, among other things, recognizing existing beneficial uses of water under the common law and declaring them to be lawful appropriations under the act.[210] The riparian right has been of major importance in California, although a 1928 constitutional amendment has limited the exercise of water rights to "reasonable beneficial use."[211] These and other approaches that have been taken in the different States are discussed in more detail elsewhere in this chapter.

The question of abrogating riparian rights.—The courts of the more arid States, which have generally repudiated the riparian water rights doctrine, usually took the view that in those jurisdictions the doctrine had never existed. Riparian rights, that is, never had vested. But in a Federal case arising in Nevada,[212] the Federal court said riparian rights of contesting riparians that were adjudicated in conformance with an early decision of the Nevada Supreme Court recognizing such rights[213] were not affected by the overruling of that decision and negation of the riparian doctrine 13 years later.[214]

---

[208] Oreg. Rev. Stat. § 539.010 (Supp. 1955); S. Dak. Comp. Laws Ann. § 46-1-9 (1967); Kans. Stat. Ann. § 82a-701 (1969).

[209] Kans. Stat. Ann. §§ 82a-716 and -717a (1969).

[210] Alaska Stat. § 46.15.060 (Supp. 1966).

[211] Cal. Const., art. XIV, § 3.

[212] *Union Mill & Min. Co.* v. *Dangberg,* 81 Fed. 73, 85, 92, 115-116 (C.C.D. Nev. 1897).

[213] *Vansickle* v. *Haines,* 7 Nev. 249 (1872).

[214] In *Jones* v. *Adams,* 19 Nev. 78, 6 Pac. 442 (1885).

In some States in which both the riparian and the appropriation doctrines are recognized, the riparian right has been shorn of unreasonable advantages and the riparian proprietor held to the same standard of reasonable beneficial use as the appropriator. The measures taken to curb the unreasonable assertion of riparian claims have not attempted to abrogate riparian rights actually in use, nor to interfere with uses of water that conformed to reasonable standards. They have purported to invoke the police power of the State in regulating uses of water in the public interest.

The question of possible confiscation of a right in actual use was touched upon by the United States Supreme Court in discussing the California constitutional amendment of 1928.[215] The case arose upon claims for compensation by riparian owners for deprivation of the natural overflow of the San Joaquin River by reason of operation of Friant Dam. The Court acknowledged that in framing the amendment there had been a studied purpose to preserve existing values, but said: "We must conclude that by the Amendment California unintentionally destroyed and confiscated a recognized and adjudicated private property right, or that it remains compensable although no longer enforcible by injunction. The right of claimants at least to compensation prior to the Amendment was entirely clear." The implication is that if the effect of the amendment has been to deny compensation as well as injunctive relief to a riparian owner who had been accepting the benefits of natural overflow and deriving value from them, the amendment would have been unconstitutional.

Control measures put into operation in several States went considerably farther than the regulation of rights actually in use. Their effect was to subject unused riparian rights to loss, in some cases with and in other cases without compensation. These measures met the approval of the courts of those particular States. On the other hand, limiting statutes passed by the legislatures of two States—California and Texas—were held inoperative as against the water rights of riparian landowners.[216]

It has been insisted at various times that to subject the unused riparian right to loss, in a State in which the riparian owner's right to the flow of the water has been previously recognized, amounts to a denial of due process. However, the United States Court of Appeals, 9th Circuit,[217] agreed with the Oregon Supreme Court[218] that the Oregon statute[219] was valid. The United States Supreme Court, in affirming the judgment, passed over that particular question as not

---

[215] *United States* v. *Gerlach Live Stock Co.*, 339 U. S. 725, 751-755 (1950).

[216] *Tulare Irr. Dist.* v. *Lindsay-Strathmore Irr. Dist.*, 3 Cal. (2d) 489, 530-531, 45 Pac. (2d) 472 (1935); *Freeland* v. *Peltier*, 44 S. W. (2d) 404, 408 (Tex. Civ. App. 1931).

[217] *California-Oregon Power Co.* v. *Beaver Portland Cement Co.*, 73 Fed. (2d) 555, 568-569 (9th Cir. 1934).

[218] *In re Hood River*, 114 Oreg. 112, 173-182, 227 Pac. 1065 (1924).

[219] Oreg. Laws 1909, ch. 216, § 70, Rev. Stat. § 539.010 (Supp. 1955).

necessary to the decision.[220] The Oregon statute has been in effect now since the first decade of the 20th century.

The water law philosophy of some States, therefore, denies to the riparian proprietor a vested right of nonuse of water, and holds that deprivation of any such claimed privilege is not abrogation of a right. That of other States accords him a right of future use of the same validity as his right of present use. Whether the courts have considered the matter *stare decisis* has necessarily had great weight in determining the constitutional question.

The Status in Summary: By States

The overall riparian status in the West has been discussed heretofore under "Establishment of the Riparian Doctrine—Status of the Riparian Doctrine in the West," but without necessarily emphasizing the riparian-appropriation relationship.

Briefly, after the century of conflict the riparian doctrine is found to be recognized in theory or in practice or both, in 11 States, but with wide ranges in the degree of recognition and in the way it has been applied or curtailed. Such matters are discussed in the following summaries of the status of the interrelationships of the riparian and appropriation doctrines in the respective States.

States in Which There Generally Are No Interrelationships

Arizona, Colorado, Idaho, Montana, Nevada, New Mexico, Utah, and Wyoming recognize appropriative water rights but generally not riparian water rights.[221] Hence, in these States, there generally are no doctrinal interrelationships. Moreover, while Hawaii recognizes riparian rights, it does not have an appropriation system of surface water rights.

Alaska

A statute enacted in 1917 declared that owners of mining claims that embraced both banks of a stream were entitled to use all water necessary for working their claims, subject to appropriative rights already vested but superior to those of subsequent date. Later appropriators were entitled to the use of the water during such times as it was not needed by the riparian claimants.[222] The United States Court of Appeals, 9th Circuit, stated (probably as *dictum*) that

---

[220] *California Oregon Power Co.* v. *Beaver Portland Cement Co.*, 295 U. S. 142, 154-165 (1935).

[221] See "Establishment of the Riparian Doctrine in the West—Status of the Riparian Doctrine in the West—Nonrecognition," earlier. See also chapter 10.

[222] Alaska Laws 1917, ch. 17, Comp. Laws Ann. § 47-3-35 (1949), Stat. § § 27.10.080 (Supp. 1962) and 38.05.260 (Supp. 1965).

A more detailed discussion of the historical development of early mining court decisions and this legislation is included in the State summary for Alaska in the appendix.

this statute enacted the law of riparian rights to a limited extent.[223] However, in 1966 the State legislature enacted the Water Use Act,[224] which is fundamentally an appropriation doctrine statute.[225] Without mentioning the term "riparian" it apparently purports to phase out that water rights doctrine. The 1966 act repealed the earlier mining legislation[226] and provides that:

> *A water right acquired by law before the effective date of this chapter* or a beneficial use of water on the effective date of this chapter, or made within five years before the effective date, or made in conjunction with works under construction on the effective date, *under a lawful common law or customary appropriation or use, is a lawful appropriation* under this chapter. The appropriation is *subject to applicable provisions of this chapter* and rules and regulations adopted under this chapter. [Emphasis supplied.] [227]

This apparently purports to convert any riparian rights to appropriative rights. While this language appears to be broad enough to recognize both used and unused riparian rights, the act does not appear to include any procedure for establishing evidence of and preserving *unused* rights.[228] At any rate, the act apparently contemplates that any such rights may be declared forfeited if they have not been beneficially used, without sufficient cause, within 5 years after the act's effective date.[229]

California

Appropriations made on *private* lands are *inferior* to the riparian rights that attach to tracts of land *above* the appropriator's point of diversion even though the upstream tracts were part of the Federal public domain at the time the

---

[223] *Balabanoff* v. *Kellog,* 10 Alaska 11, 16-17, 118 Fed. (2d) 597, 599 (9th Cir. 1940), certiorari denied, 314 U. S. 635 (1941).

[224] Alaska Laws 1966, ch. 50 Stat. § 46.15.010 *et seq.* (Supp. 1966).

[225] The act provides *inter alia* that "Wherever occurring in a natural state, the waters are reserved to the people for common use and are subject to appropriation and beneficial use as provided in this chapter." Alaska Stat. § 46.15.030 (Supp. 1966).

[226] Alaska Laws 1966, ch. 50, § 2.

[227] Alaska Stat. § 46.15.060 (Supp. 1966). See also § § 46.15.260 (2) and 46.15.030. The act's effective date was July 1, 1966. Alaska Laws 1966, ch. 50, § 3.

[228] Except where works were under construction on the act's effective date.
    See Alaska Stat. § 46.15.135(a) (Supp. 1966) and Alaska Reg. 801.01, discussed in Trelease, F. J., "Alaska's New Water Use Act," 2 Land & Water L. Rev. 1, 31-32 (1967).

[229] Alaska Stat. § 46.15.140(b) (Supp. 1966) provides that "The commissioner [of natural resources] may declare an appropriation to be wholly or partially forfeited and shall revoke the certificate of appropriation if an appropriator voluntarily fails or neglects, without sufficient cause, to make use of all or a part of his appropriated water for a period of five successive years." The act apparently purports to convert any unused riparian rights to appropriative rights, as discussed above.

appropriation accrued and *subsequently* passed into private ownership.[230] The status of such appropriations with respect to riparian rights attached to such tracts of land *below* the appropriator's point of diversion apparently has not been specifically decided by the California appellate courts. Appropriations made on *Federal public domain* and *State* lands *after* riparian lands on the same stream passed into private ownerhip are *inferior* to the riparian rights attached to such lands.[231] However, appropriations made on such lands *before* riparian lands on the same stream passed into private ownership are *superior* to the riparian rights attached to such lands,[232] provided that, at least in the case of an appropriation on Federal public domain lands, the appropriation was made *before* the riparian's *settlement* on the land. If the appropriation was made *before* the time title to the riparian land *passed into* private ownership, but *after* the riparian's *settlement* occurred, the appropriation (by anyone other than the United States) is *inferior* to the riparian right. For the California Supreme Court has said that:[233]

> While it is true that as against the United States the inception of the right of a [riparian] settler relates only to the date of filing application, actual settlement gives to such settler a preference as to such filing, so that, as to subsequent parties other than the United States, the inception of the right is the date of settlement. In view of the fact that the rights of both the appropriator and the settler are based upon priority in time of taking the initial step, actual settlement upon the land with the intention of subsequently acquiring a completed title by patent is sufficient, we think, to create an equitable right in the land so settled upon by a bona fide settler as to cut off all intervening rights, including those of a subsequent appropriator. The right acquired by a prior appropriator relates back to the first step taken, and we are of the opinion that the right of a settler should likewise date back to the first step taken, which in this case was actual settlement, rather than to the intermediate step of filing a formal application in the land office.

---

[230] *Cave* v. *Tyler*, 133 Cal. 556, 570, 65 Pac. 1089 (1901); *Holmes* v. *Noy*, 186 Cal. 231, 234-235, 199 Pac. 325 (1921); *San Joaquin & Kings River Canal & Irr. Co.* v. *Worswick*, 187 Cal. 674, 683-685, 203 Pac. 999 (1922).

[231] Federal public domain: *Barrows* v. *Fox*, 98 Cal. 63, 64-67, 32 Pac. 811 (1893); *Witherill* v. *Brehm*, 74 Cal. App. 286, 298-299, 240 Pac. 529 (1925). See *Alhambra Addition Water Co.* v. *Mayberry*, 88 Cal. 68, 74-75, 25 Pac.1101 (1891). See also *Wood* v. *Etiwanda Water Co.*, 122 Cal. 152, 158-159, 54 Pac. 726 (1898). State lands: *Lux* v. *Haggin*, 69 Cal. 255, 368, 374, 4 Pac. 919 (1884). See also *Shenandoah Min. & Mill. Co.* v. *Morgan*, 106 Cal. 409, 416, 39 Pac. 802 (1895).

[232] Federal public domain: *Cave* v. *Crafts*, 53 Cal. 135, 138 (1878); *Osgood* v. *El Dorado Water & Deep Gravel Min. Co.*, 56 Cal. 571, 578-581 (1880); *Haight* v. *Costanich*, 184 Cal. 426, 430, 194 Pac. 26 (1920). See *Farley* v. *Spring Valley Min. & Irr. Co.*, 58 Cal. 142, 143-144 (1881). State lands: *Lux* v. *Haggin*, 69 Cal. 255, 373-374, 4 Pac. 919 (1884).

[233] *Pabst* v. *Finmand*, 190 Cal. 124, 131, 211 Pac. 11 (1922).

Most California law with respect to conflicting riparian-appropriation interrelationships was made in controversies in which the riparian right was adjudged superior. The riparian doctrine was firmly established in 1886 in *Lux* v. *Haggin*.[234] Forty years later in *Herminghaus* v. *Southern California Edison Company,* prevailing riparian principles were so interpreted and applied by the supreme court as to result in segregating a large quantity of water from appropriative use to accomplish a comparatively small riparian benefit.[235] Among other things, the supreme court repeated an observation that it had made twice before to the effect that as against an appropriator, a riparian owner "is not limited by any measure of reasonableness."[236]

The cumulative effect of this 40-year period of litigation, culminating in the *Herminghaus* case, was that the position of the riparian owner in California in relation to that of an appropriator, whether or not the riparian had made any use of the water, became so fortified in judicial law—and so unbearable to advocates of resource development—that the voters of the State were constrained to write into their constitution a mandate that beneficial utilization of the State's water resources be made "to the fullest extent of which they are capable."[237] The amendment forbids waste or unreasonable use or unreasonable method of use or unreasonable method of diversion of water. It declares that riparian rights in a stream attach to only so much of the flow as may be required or used for reasonable and beneficial purposes.

The constitutional amendment has been construed, accepted as commanding a new State water policy, and applied by the courts in a number of key cases.[238]

The present situation in California is that the riparian owner as well as the appropriator is now limited to reasonable beneficial use of water under reasonable methods of diversion and use. The riparian owner can no longer insist that an upstream appropriator refrain from diverting water the taking of which will prevent the riparian owner from using the full natural flow of the stream for the sole purpose of lifting a comparatively small quantity of water over the banks for natural flooding and irrigation of the riparian land by natural processes. But the amendment did not destroy the riparian right. It merely restricted the unreasonable exercise of the right. The riparian owner is

---

[234] *Lux* v. *Haggin,* 69 Cal. 255, 4 Pac. 919 (1884), 10 Pac. 674 (1886).

[235] *Herminghaus* v. *Southern California Edison Co.,* 200 Cal. 81, 252 Pac. 607 (1926).

[236] *Id* at 100-101, quoting, *Miller & Lux* v. *Madera Canal & Irr. Co.,* 155 Cal. 59, 64, 99 Pac. 502 (1907). See also *Pabst* v. *Finmand,* 190 Cal. 124, 132, 211 Pac. 11 (1922).

[237] Cal. Const., art. XIV, § 3, adopted November 26, 1928.

[238] In particular, *Peabody* v. *Vallejo,* 2 Cal. (2d) 351, 365-375, 40 Pac. (2d) 486 (1935); *Tulare Irr. Dist.* v. *Lindsay-Strathmore Irr. Dist.,* 3 Cal. (2d) 489, 524-530, 45 Pac. (2d) 972 (1935); *Meridian* v. *San Francisco,* 13 Cal. (2d) 424, 445-450, 90 Pac. (2d) 537 (1939); *Pasadena* v. *Alhambra,* 33 Cal. (2d) 908, 934-935, 207 Pac. (2d) 17 (1949); *United States* v. *Gerlach Live Stock Co.,* 339 U. S. 725, 752-755 (1950).

still entitled to compensation for any substantial deprivation of his riparian right, or to a physical solution—a valid exercise of the State's police power.[239]

Kansas

The doctrine of riparian rights was recognized and applied in early decisions of the Kansas Supreme Court, which agreed that it might exist in the same State with the doctrine of prior appropriation. The appropriation doctrine, however, could not operate to the destruction of previously vested common law rights.[240]

Following a period of uncertainty resulting from a supreme court decision,[241] and attempted corrective legislation,[242] another supreme court decision resulted in rendering the legislation completely ineffective.[243]

---

[239] In *Joslin* v. *Marin Mun. Water Dist.,* 67 Cal. (2d) 132, 142-143, 429 Pac. (2d) 889, 60 Cal. Rptr. 377 (1967), the California Supreme Court said " . . . since there was and is no property right in an unreasonable use, there has been no taking or damaging of property by the deprivation of such use and, accordingly, the deprivation is not compensable." The court said that in view of the State's constitutional amendment limiting the use of water only to beneficial uses "to the fullest extent of which they are capable," and providing that "waste or unreasonable use" shall be prevented and that conservation shall be exercised "in the interest of the people and for the public welfare," "in the instant case the use of such waters as an agent to expose or to carry and deposit sand, gravel and rocks, is as a matter of law unreasonable within the meaning of the constitutional amendment. (See Peabody v. City of Vallejo, supra, 2 Cal. 2d 351, 369, 40 P. 2d 486.)" 67 Cal. (2d) at 141. The court held that a riparian landowner could not require that an upstream appropriator pass along the streamflow to serve "the amassing of mere sand and gravel which for aught that appears subserves *no* public policy . . . ." *Id.* The court said that "unlike the unanimous policy pronouncements relative to the use and conservation of natural waters, we are aware of none relative to the supply and availability of sand, gravel and rocks in commercial quantities." 67 Cal. (2d) at 140-141. The court noted that in *Peabody* v. *Vallejo* a lower riparian had asserted a right as against an upstream appropriator to have all the waters flow without interruption since by normally overflowing his land they not only deposited silt thereon but also washed out salt deposits on portions of his land. 67 Cal. (2d) at 139. In that case the court said: "So far as we are advised, this asserted right does not inhere in the riparian right at common law, and as a natural right cannot be asserted as against the police powers of the State in the conservation of its waters. This asserted right involves an unreasonable use—as contemplated by the Constitution." 2 Cal. (2d) at 369, quoted in 67 Cal. (2d) at 139. In the instant case, at 429 Pac. (2d) 898, the court distinguished *United States* v. *Gerlach Live Stock Co.,* 339 U. S. 725 (1950), discussed at note 215 *supra,* as a case involving the use of the natural overflow for irrigation, a recognized reasonable use.

[240] *Clark* v. *Allaman,* 71 Kans. 206, 237-239, 241, 80 Pac. 571 (1905).

[241] *Frizell* v. *Bindley,* 144 Kans. 84, 91-93, 58 Pac. (2d) 95 (1936).

[242] Kans. Laws 1941, ch. 261.

[243] *State ex rel. Peterson* v. *State Board of Agriculture,* 158 Kans. 603, 605-614, 149 Pac. (2d) 604 (1944).

In the next year, 1945, the legislature passed a new act, which was extensively amended in 1957.[244] This legislation followed the much earlier Oregon example of limiting vested rights of common law claimants to use of water actually applied to beneficial use at the time of the 1945 enactment or within a reasonable time thereafter with use of works then under construction. Common law claimants without vested rights could be enjoined by appropriators from making subsequent diversions, although compensation could be had in an action at law for damages proved for any property taken from a common law claimant by an appropriator. The validity of the Kansas statute has been sustained by both State and Federal courts on the several points presented for determination.[245]

Nebraska

After decisions had been rendered late in the last century recognizing the common law riparian doctrine, the Nebraska Supreme Court in 1903 discussed at considerable length principles underlying the relative rights of riparian landowners and appropriators on the same stream. Concurrence of the two doctrines was recognized, preference between conflicting claimants to be determined by the time when either right accrued.[246] This decision, in *Crawford Company* v. *Hathaway,* has been superseded in certain respects by the more recent 1966 decision in *Wasserburger* v. *Coffee.*[247] The court indicated that a riparian right to the use of a watercourse "may be superior" to a competitive appropriative right if the riparian land passed into private ownership from the public domain prior to April 4, 1895, the effective date of the irrigation act of 1895, and provided the riparian land has not subsequently

---

[244] Kans Laws 1945, ch. 390, Laws 1957, ch. 539, Stat. Ann. § 82a-701 *et seq.* (1969).

[245] *State ex rel. Emery* v. *Knapp,* 167 Kans. 546, 555-556, 207 Pac. (2d) 440 (1949); *Baumann* v. *Smrha,* 145 Fed. Supp. 617 (D. Kans. 1956), affirmed per curiam, 352 U. S. 863 (1956); *Williams* v. *Wichita,* 190 Kans. 317, 374 Pac. (2d) 578 (1962), appeal dismissed "for want of a substantial Federal question," 375 U. S. 7 (1963), rehearing denied, 375 U. S. 936 (1963); *Hesston & Sedgwick* v. *Smrha,* 192 Kans. 647, 391 Pac. (2d) 93 (1964).

The *Emery* case, *supra,* involved a surface watercourse. The other cases involved percolating groundwaters. The opinion in the *Hesston* case, *supra,* does not disclose the source of water it involved but a former opinion in the case indicates it dealt with rights to use waters of the Equus Beds. 184 Kan. 233, 336 Pac. (2d) 428 (1959). In this regard, it may be noted that in a recent decision upholding the validity of 1955 South Dakota legislation, the court said that a previous decision upholding its validity in a case involving underground waters was equally applicable to surface watercourses. *Belle Fourche Irr. Dist.* v. *Smiley,* 176 N. W. (2d) 239, 245 (S. Dak. 1970). See also *Baeth* v. *Hoisveen,* 157 N. W. (2d) 728 (N. Dak. 1968).

[246] *Crawford Co.* v. *Hathaway,* 67 Nebr. 325, 93 N. W. 781 (1903). As against appropriators, riparian rights extend only to the ordinary flow, not to floodwaters. *Id.*

[247] *Wasserburger* v. *Coffee,* 180 Nebr. 147, 141 N. W. (2d) 738 (1966), modified at 180 Nebr. 569, 144 N. W. (2d) 209 (1966).

lost its riparian status by severance.[248] But the court concluded that an appropriator may be liable for injury to a recognized riparian right "if, but only if, the harmful appropriation is unreasonable in respect to the [riparian] proprietor."[249] The court indicated that if riparian lands passed into private ownership *after* April 4, 1895 a competing appropriative right "outranks the riparian right under the facts of the present case."[250] A 1969 case appears to have added some uncertainty regarding the status of domestic use of water.[251]

Shortly after the 1903 decision in *Crawford Company* v. *Hathaway,* two cases were decided which dealt with the remedial rights of riparian claimants rather than with substantive rights or interests in property. In one of these cases, it was held that an appropriator might restrain upstream riparians—who had made no diversion of water until after plaintiff's rights had accrued—from now diverting an injurious quantity from the stream; leaving the defendant riparians to an action to recover damages if any had been sustained.[252] In the other case, decided on general demurrer, the court stated that a lower riparian owner could not enjoin continued use of water by an upstream appropriator who had lawfully acquired an appropriative right, constructed works, and put the water to beneficial use, but must rely upon his action to recover such damages, if any, as he might sustain thereby.[253] However, in *Wasserburger* v.

---

[248] *Id.* at 742, 743, 745. The court referred to patents that "had been initiated by entries filed." In *Osterman* v. *Central Nebr. Pub. Power & Irr. Dist.,* 131 Nebr. 356, 268 N. W. 334, 337 (1936), the court said riparians' titles were "initiated by settlement." Also see above at note 233.

[249] *Id.* at 745. The court set forth criteria for determining such reasonableness as well as criteria for determining the appropriateness of an injunction. See Nebraska State summary in the appendix. For a critical discussion of the case, see Comment, "The Dual-System of Water Rights in Nebraska," 48 Nebr. Law Rev. 488, 497-498 (1969).

Some of the permits of the defendant appropriators bore adjudicated dates prior to the time any of the plaintiff riparians' lands had passed into private ownership from the public domain. This apparently raised the question of the relative status of appropriative and riparian rights where both were initiated prior to the effective date of the 1895 statute and where the appropriative right was earlier in time. In this regard, the court said that "Under the 1895 statute the board of irrigation fixed the priority dates of appropriators who had acquired rights earlier than the effective date of the statute. The board determined appropriative priorities but not riparian rights. . . . The adjudication established the time when the appropriations had been initiated, but time is only one of the elements to be considered in the adjustment of the competing rights.

"On the facts of this case the riparian right is superior. Plaintiffs' need for livestock water is greater than defendants' need for irrigation, and the difference is not neutralized by time priorities." 141 N. W. (2d) at 747.

[250] 141 N. W. (2d) at 742.

[251] *Brummund* v. *Vogel,* 184 Nebr. 415, 168 N. W. (2d) 24 (1969). This is discussed in the State summary for Nebraska in the appendix. 19 Nebr. State Bar J. 63, 64-69 (1970) includes a report of the Special Committee on Water Resources regarding the alleged uncertainty created by this case and some suggested alternative interpretations of it. The report includes a dissenting view of one of the committee members.

[252] *McCook Irr. Water Power Co.* v. *Crews,* 70 Nebr. 109, 96 N. W. 996 (1903), 102 N. W. 249 (1905).

[253] *Cline* v. *Stock,* 71 Nebr. 70, 98 N. W. 454 (1904), 102 N. W. 265 (1905).

offee the court said that:[254]

We think [these] cases have been misread. The appropriative rights [in these cases] seem to have been asserted by irrigation companies offering a public service. The court attached significance to the public benefit, to the appropriation project completed in good faith and at great cost, and to the tardy initiation of the riparian use. If the court went too far, the limitations themselves have remained. We reject the startling proposition [urged by the defendant appropriators] that equity sends every riparian proprietor packing. Defendants are private appropriators—not champions of the public interest. . . . The remedy rests on other considerations.

The court set forth tests to determine the appropriateness of an injunction against an intentional tort in a given case, thereby establishing that in an appropriate case an injunction will lie.

North Dakota

Both riparian and appropriation doctrines have been recognized in North Dakota since early in the history of the Dakota Territory, but interrelationships between claimants of the opposing systems have been relatively meager.[255]

A statute of the Territory of Dakota provided, among other things, that water running in a definite natural stream might be used by the landowner as long as it remains there, but that he might not prevent the natural flow of the stream nor pursue nor pollute it.[256] In 1955, the State legislature declared that the several and reciprocal rights of a riparian owner, other than a municipal corporation, in the waters of the State comprise the ordinary or natural use of water for domestic and stockwatering purposes.[257] Both provisions were eliminated in 1963.[258] Different provisions were enacted which relate to priority of water rights and preferences in the use of water. Among other things, this 1963 legislation provides (in section 61-01-01.1) that in all cases

---

[254] *Wasserburger* v. *Coffee,* 180 Nebr. 147, 141 N. W. (2d) 738, 747 (1966).

[255] *Sturr* v. *Beck,* 6 Dak. 71, 50 N. W. 486 (1888), affirmed, 133 U. S. 541 (1890); *Bigelow* v. *Draper,* 6 N. Dak. 152, 69 N. W. 570 (1896); *Brignall* v. *Hannah,* 34 N. Dak. 174, 157 N. W. 1042 (1916); *Ozark-Mahoning Co.* v. *State,* 76 N. Dak. 464, 37 N. W. (2d) 488 (1949).

The early case of *Sturr* v. *Beck, supra,* generally cited as definitely recognizing both the riparian and appropriation doctrines, held that an earlier homesteader had made a prior appropriation of both land and water even without making use of the water, as against a later downstream entryman who trespassed upon the upper land in order to locate a water right thereon. This is suggestive of an offbeat example of interdoctrinal conflict, but it is not a satisfactory one.

A recent and more important case in regard to interdoctrinal conflicts is *Baeth* v. *Hoisveen,* 157 N. W. (2d) 728 (N. Dak. 1968). This case is discussed below.

[256] Terr. Dak. Laws 1865-1866, ch. 1, § 256, Civil Code § 255 (1877).

[257] N. Dak. Laws 1955, ch. 345, § 2.

[258] N. Dak. Laws 1963, ch. 419. Deletion of the substance of the 1955 riparian section, N. Dak. Cent. Code Ann. § 61-01-01.1 (1960), was accomplished, not by literally

where the use of water for different purposes conflicts, such uses shall conform to a specified order of priority. Domestic use, as defined, has first priority. As between appropriations for the same type of use, priority in time shall give the better right. No permit shall be required for domestic and livestock uses.[259]

Section 61-01-01 of the North Dakota statutes, as amended by the 1955 legislation referred to above, declares, among other things, that waters flowing in surface or underground watercourses and percolating ground waters belong to the public and are subject to appropriation for beneficial use. In a 1968 case, the North Dakota Supreme Court appears to have concluded that inasmuch as the right of a riparian landowner to use an underground stream for irrigation purposes had not been exercised before the 1955 legislation, the unused right could be validly abrogated without compensation by the legislation, at least as against appropriative rights acquired thereafter, and that the riparian owner could validly be required by the legislation to apply for and be governed by an appropriative-right permit.[260] However, the court qualified this as follows:

> In upholding the constitutionality of Section 61-01-01, N.D.C.C., we do not approve the procedure followed by the State Water Commission in the instant case, which resulted in granting to one of two landowners, who owned adjacent land and who made application at approximately the same time for beneficial use of water, the use of so much water that the other was in effect denied use of any water. The failure on the part of the State Water Commission to determine the actual amount of water available before granting the first neighbor's application resulted in a very disproportionate granting of water rights. Such a procedure, if followed in the future, might

repealing it, but by amending the section so as to delete the entire original wording and to substitute therefor entirely different provisions relating to priority of water rights and preferences in the use of conflicting purposes.

[259] Regardless of the proposed use, however, all water users shall secure a permit before constructing an impoundment capable of retaining more than 12½ acre feet of water. This proviso was added by Laws 1965, ch. 447.

[260] *Baeth* v. *Hoisveen*, 157 N. W. (2d) 728 (N. Dak. 1968). The court decided that unused riparian rights to use water for irrigation did not constitute "vested rights." In doing so, it construed the above-mentioned statutory declarations regarding riparian rights and the declaration regarding waters being owned by the public and subject to appropriation for beneficial use, and it indicated that these should be construed in association with the statement in N. Dak. Cent. Code Ann. § 61-01-02 that "Beneficial use shall be the basis, the measure, and the limit of the right to use water." The court added at 157 N. W. (2d) 733 that:

"Notwithstanding what this court said in Bigelow v. Draper, 6 N. D. 152, 69 N. W. 570 [1896] and in subsequent supporting decisions which may be construed to the contrary to what is said in the instant case, we hold that there is no deprivation of a constitutional right or rights, and that the action taken by the legislature in enacting Section 61-01-01, N.D.C.C., is within the police power of the State, as a reasonable regulation for the public good."

well justify legislative action directed toward preventing the reoccurrence of such inequitable results.[261]
One concurring justice said, among other things, that:

> ... a provision not objectionable on its face may be adjudged unconstitutional because of its effect in operation upon a showing of a fixed and continuous policy of unjust and discriminatory application by the officials in charge of its administration.[262]

Another concurring justice said:

> ... the action taken by the Water Commission may not be within a valid exercise of the police power, and thus constitutes an unconstitutional application of the law.[263]

This case did not involve any consideration of the 1963 legislation. Applications for the water uses in controversy were initiated before it was enacted.

Oklahoma

A statute passed by the first Oklahoma Territorial legislative Assembly provided, among other things, that water running in a definite natural stream might be used by the landowner as long as it remains there, but that he might not prevent the natural flow of the stream nor pursue nor pollute it.[264] This was copied from the early statute of the Territory of Dakota cited under "North Dakota," above. This statute was quoted or cited in several decisions of the Oklahoma Supreme Court,[265] which in numerous cases decided questions relating to various aspects of the riparian right, and of the appropriative right, but none involving conflicts between riparian claimants on the one hand and appropriators on the other.[266] The Oklahoma territorial and State legislatures had enacted various water appropriation statutes.[267]

The 1963 Oklahoma legislature made the first move in the field of interdoctrinal relationships. The early 1890 statute, unchanged since enactment, was amended in several vital respects.[268] Pursuant to the amendment, water running in a definite natural stream may be used by the landowner *for domestic purposes* as long as it remains there, but he may not prevent the

---

[261] 157 N. W. (2d) at 733-734. This is discussed in Bard, D. F., & Beck, R. E., "An Institutional Overview of the North Dakota State Water Conservation Commission: Its Operation and Setting," 46 N. Dak. Law Rev. 31, 42 (1969); Case Note, 4 Land & Water Law Rev. 185 (1969).

[262] 157 N. W. (2d) at 734.

[263] *Id.*

[264] Terr. Okla. Stat. 1890, § 4162, Stat. Ann. tit. 60, § 60 (Supp. 1961).

[265] *Broady* v. *Furray,* 163 Okla. 204, 205, 21 Pac. (2d) 770 (1933); *Grand-Hydro* v. *Grand River Dam Authority,* 192 Okla. 693, 695, 139 Pac. (2d) 798 (1943); *Smith* v. *Stanolind Oil & Gas Co.,* 197 Okla. 499, 501, 172 Pac. (2d) 1002 (1946).

[266] Hutchins, Wells A., "The Oklahoma Law of Water Rights," pp. 13-22 (1955).

[267] See Terr. Okla. Laws 1897, ch. XIX; Okla. Stat. Ann. tit. 82 (1970).

[268] Okla. Sess. Laws 1963, ch. 205, § 1.

natural flow of the stream nor pursue nor pollute it, *as such water then becomes public water and is subject to appropriation for the benefit and welfare of the people of the State as provided by law.*[269] Section 2 of this 1963 statute (which became Section 1-A of Title 82, Okla. Stat. (1970)) relates to rights to use water, domestic use, and priorities. Water taken for domestic use is not subject to the provisions of the appropriation law. "Any natural person has the right to take water for domestic use from a stream to which he is riparian or to take stream water for domestic use from wells on his premises," as provided in section 1. Domestic use is defined to include the use of water "for household purposes, for farm and domestic animals up to the normal grazing capacity of the land, and for the irrigation of land not exceeding a total of three (3) acres in area for the growing of gardens, orchards and lawns. . . ."[270]

By the 1963 amendment, the legislature has undertaken to respect existing claims of water rights based upon beneficial use, but to restrict the exercise of unused riparian rights to water for domestic purposes only, as defined in the act. Provision has been made for obtaining priorities based on present beneficial riparian use initiated before the effective date of the act, dating from initiation of the beneficial use. But no such priority right for a beneficial use initiated after statehood shall take precedence over those for a beneficial use with a priority date earlier than the effective date of the 1963 amendment arising by compliance with the appropriation statutes.[271] Provision is made for

---

[269] The italicized words have been added by the amendment in Okla. Stat. Ann. tit. 60, § 60 (Supp. 1970). Tit. 60, § 60, in its first sentence, had provided and still provides that the owner of the land owns water standing thereon or flowing over its surface but not forming a definite stream. As amended, following this and the provision regarding domestic use described above, the following wording has been added in tit. 60, § 60:

> Provided however, that nothing contained herein shall prevent the owner of land from damming up or otherwise using the bed of a stream on his land for the collection or storage of waters in an amount not to exceed that which he owns, by virtue of the first sentence of this Section so long as he provides for the continued natural flow of the stream in an amount equal to that which entered his land less the uses allowed in this Act; provided further, that nothing contained herein shall be construed to limit the powers of the Oklahoma Water Resources Board to grant permission to build or alter structures on a stream pursuant to Title 82 to provide for the storage of additional water the use of which the land owner has or acquires by virtue of this Act.

It also may be noted that Okla. Stat. Ann. tit. 82, § 1-A(a) (1970) provides that "this Act shall not apply to farm ponds or gully plugs which have been constructed under the supervision and specifications of the Soil and Water Conservation Districts prior to the effective date of this Act."

[270] Water for such purposes may be stored in an amount not to exceed 2-years' supply.

[271] Moreover, such a priority might have been lost in whole or in part because of nonuse. Okla. Stat. Ann. tit. 82, § 1-A(b)6 (1970), referring to § 32. By virtue of Laws 1965, ch. 336, §§ 32A and 32B of tit. 82 provide that vested rights of use may be declared lost in whole or in part due to 7-years' nonuse. See Rarick, J. F., "Oklahoma Water

protection of priorities based on beneficial use theretofore made under various combinations of circumstances.

In a recent case, the Oklahoma Supreme Court held that this 1963 legislation did not apply to situations in which it concluded that the rights of the litigants had vested under the laws in existence prior to this amendment, although it was held to have retroactively eliminated certain procedural requirements in previous appropriation statutes.[272] The court's opinion includes some discussion of the question of the correlation of riparian and appropriative rights under the pre-1963 Oklahoma laws.[273]

Law, Stream and Surface Under the 1963 Amendments" 23 Okla. Law Rev. 19, 42, 44 (1970).

Certain existing riparian rights conceivably might be affected and protected by the following provisions of the 1963 legislation: (1) Okla. Stat. Ann. tit. 82, § 1-A(b) (1970) pertains to beneficial uses initiated before statehood. (2) Section 1-A(b)2 specifies that priorities established in adjudications under prior legislation will be accorded priority as assigned in the adjudication decrees if they have not been lost in whole or in part because of nonuse as provided in § 32 of tit. 82. See Rarick, *supra* at 42; Rarick, J. F., "Oklahoma Water Law, Stream and Surface in the Pre-1963 Period," 22 Okla. Law Rev. 1, 38 (1969).

[272] *Oklahoma Water Resources Bd.* v. *Central Oklahoma Master Conservancy Dist.*, 464 Pac. (2d) 748 (Okla. 1968). The Court in its 1968 opinion held that the 1963 legislation had no application to the case because "This act was passed both *after* the initiation of the appropriation by the District and *after* the commencement of the Draper Dam project [by Oklahoma City, the coplaintiff on appeal]. The rights of the District and of the City vested under the law in existence before the cited amendment was enacted." *Id.* at 755. Nevertheless, in its 1969 supplemental opinion on rehearing, the court held the 1963 legislation had eliminated "pre-1963 statutory conditions precedent for the perfection of a water right, i.e., hydrographic survey and adjudication proceedings . . ." with which the District had not complied. *Id.* at 756. The court held these to be procedural requirements and that "no one has a vested right in any particular mode of procedure for the enforcement or defense of his rights. Hence, the general rule that statutes will be construed to be prospective only does not apply to statutes affecting procedure; but such statutes, unless the contrary intention is clearly expressed or implied, apply to all actions falling within their terms, whether the right of action existed before or accrued after the enactment. . . ." *Id.* This case is critically reviewed in Rarick, *supra* note 271, 23 Okla. Law Rev. at 52-70.

[273] This case involved the relative rights of Oklahoma City which had constructed a dam in a nonnavigable stream and the conservancy district which had acquired a prior appropriative right at a downstream location. The court said: "Since pre-statehood days the system of prior appropriation has coexisted in Oklahoma with that of recognized riparian and proprietary rights in water. Gates v. Settlers' Milling, Canal & Reservoir Co., 19 Okl. 83, 91 P. 856 (1907). This court has not been called upon before to correlate these two separate doctrines of property which are to a substantial degree incompatible." 464 Pac. (2d) 748, 752 (1968).

The court further said: "In Jan. 1961, when the City was granted a license to construct Stanley Draper Dam and to interrupt the flow of East Elm Creek, its rights to the creek were governed by 60 O. S. 1951, § 60, the statute then in force. Under the terms of that statute the City had no right to store surface water in the bed of a definite stream and continue to claim them as its property. Nor could it obstruct the course of a definite stream [citing previous Oklahoma cases]. Its rights in that stream, which were not proprietary but merely riparian, could not be increased by the

Oregon

The interdoctrinal situation in this State is briefly referred to earlier under "Establishment of the Riparian Doctrine in the West—Status of the Riparian Doctrine in the West—Recognition in Varying Degree—Oregon."

Judicial modification of the common law riparian doctrine in Oregon began in the last century and reached an important peak in the landmark case of *Hough* v. *Porter* in 1909—the year in which the legislative modification in the water code took place.[274] The Oregon Supreme Court construed the Congressional Acts of 1866, 1870, and 1877[275] as dedicating to the public all rights of the Government with respect to the waters and purposes named, and as abrogating the modified common law rules, except with respect to domestic purposes, so far as applicable to all public lands—not only desert lands—entered after March 3, 1877.[276] The United States Supreme Court agreed.[277]

The water code of 1909 undertook to recognize and to limit the vested right of a riparian claimant who had actually applied water to beneficial use prior to the enactment, to the extent that it had not been abandoned for a continuous period of 2 years; to recognize a similar right with respect to uncompleted works if completed and the water devoted to beneficial use within a reasonable time thereafter; and to bring adjudication of such rights within the procedures newly set up in the statute. Validity of the water code with its provisions relating to riparian rights was sustained in both State and

---

construction of the dam. The City does not contend here that its riparian rights are adversely affected by the District's prior appropriation. Its claim to the water in question is predicated solely on its asserted [but disallowed] ownership of the surface water originating in the watershed." *Id.* at 754.

In its supplemental opinion on rehearing, the court said: "The City urges on rehearing that the law in effect before the 1963 amendment to our statutes [discussed above] invested it with a riparian right to the reasonable use of the stream waters in question." *Id.* at 755. But the court held that under the riparian doctrine the city's riparian status did not entitle it to abstract water for distribution to its inhabitants for domestic purposes. Hence, it appears that relatively little was expressly and clearly decided about the correlation of riparian and appropriative rights.

There being no errors in law, the court affirmed the district court's judgment in which "The City was directed 'to forthwith release [from its Draper Lake reservoir] the average annual run-off of surface waters occurring north of * * * [the dam] within the watershed of East Elm Creek * * * impounded [there] as of October 1, 1966.' " *Id.* at 751. The district court's specific provisions regarding release of the water were not otherwise discussed by the Supreme Court. These provisions are discussed in Rarick, *supra* note 271, 23 Okla. Law Rev. at 69-70.

[274] *Hough* v. *Porter*, 51 Oreg. 318, 95 Pac. 732 (1908), 98 Pac. 1083 (1909), 102 Pac. 728 (1909). Oreg. Laws 1909, ch. 216, Rev. Stat. ch. 539 (Supp. 1955).

[275] 14 Stat. 353, § 9; 16 Stat. 218; 19 Stat. 377, 43 U.S.C. § 321 (1964).

[276] *Hough* v. *Porter*, 51 Oreg. 318, 383-407, 95 Pac. 732 (1908), 98 Pac. 1083 (1909), 102 Pac. 728 (1909).

[277] *California Oregon Power Co.* v. *Beaver Portland Cement Co.*, 295 U. S. 142, 160-163 (1935).

Federal courts.[278] The act was construed as having validly abrogated the common law riparian rule as to "continuous flow" of a stream except where the water had been actually applied to beneficial use.[279]

The United States Supreme Court held that after enactment of the Desert Land Act of 1877, a patent issued for land in any desert land State or Territory carried with it *of its own force,* no common law right to water flowing through or by the land conveyed; and that following that enactment, if not before, the States to which the act applied had the right to determine for themselves to what extent the appropriation or riparian rule should obtain within their boundaries. However, the Court expressed no opinion as to whether the common law right in controversy in Oregon had been validly modified by the State legislation as construed by the State supreme court.[280]

The measure of a vested riparian right in Oregon as against an appropriator is actual application of water to beneficial use prior to passage of the "water code" or shortly thereafter.[281] One who asks for an adjudication of a claimed riparian right, but for a specific quantity of water and a fixed date of beginning use, assumes the character of an appropriator and waives his riparian claims for the purpose of such adjudication. As a matter of fact, water rights determined and decreed in the Oregon statutory adjudication proceedings have been based almost entirely—but not quite—on actual appropriation and use.

Although the riparian doctrine in Oregon is sometimes said to be now little more than a legal fiction, a 1959 decision of the supreme court discloses that the doctrine still has some substance. Although admittedly very little vestige of the doctrine remains in this State insofar as it may be asserted against those who base their claims to use of water on priority of appropriation under the "water code," occasionally riparian rights are still recognized in statutory adjudication proceedings. It is not correct to say, according to the supreme court, that the statutory system of appropriation abrogates the riparian doctrine in Oregon. Rather, the statute is a *modification* only of the law of riparian proprietorship. Unless under the circumstances of the particular case the "water code" is controlling, such a riparian right is a right of private property which will be protected under well-recognized principles of real property law.[282]

---

[278] *In re Willow Creek,* 74 Oreg. 592, 610-620, 625-628, 144 Pac. 505 (1914), 146 Pac. 475 (1915).

[279] *In re Hood River,* 114 Oreg. 112, 173-182, 227 Pac. 1065 (1924), vote of 4 to 3; *California-Oregon Power Co.* v. *Beaver Portland Cement Co.,* 73 Fed. (2d) 555, 562-569 (9th Cir. 1934), vote of 2 to 1.

[280] *California Oregon Power Co.* v. *Beaver Portland Cement Co.,* 295 U. S. 142, 155-165 (1935).

[81] For a discussion of questions regarding riparian rights for domestic and stockwatering purposes, see Hutchins, Wells A., "The Common-Law Riparian Doctrine in Oregon: Legislative and Judicial Modification," 36 Oreg. L. Rev. 193, 218-219 (1957). See above at note 170.

[282] *Fitzstephens* v. *Watson,* 218 Oreg. 185, 344 Pac. (2d) 221 (1959).

The rule invoked by the Oregon Supreme Court, therefore, is quite the opposite of a "legal fiction." Pragmatically speaking, however, in the present considerable irrigation economy of Oregon, the water law aspects of which are predicated predominantly upon the appropriation doctrine, the sum total of these remnants of riparianism is small.

South Dakota

The Dakota Territorial statute of 1865-66 provided, *inter alia,* that water running in a definite natural stream over or under the surface might be used by the landowner as long as it remains there, but that he might not prevent the natural flow of the stream nor pursue nor pollute it. This was carried over into the laws of South Dakota as well as North Dakota.[283] After being reenacted with some modifications, the section was repealed in 1955 in connection with the complete revision and the reenactment of the water appropriation law.[284]

The first judicial recognition of the riparian doctrine in the Dakotas was in 1890 in *Sturr* v. *Beck,* by both the Territorial supreme court and the United States Supreme Court.[285] In 1910, the State supreme court referred to the Territorial act of 1866 as a literal copy of one section of the proposed Civil Code for the State of New York, and that the South Dakota copy should be regarded as merely declaratory of the common law riparian doctrine as understood by the New York code commissioners when their report was prepared.[286]

In the *Lone Tree Ditch* case, the South Dakota Supreme Court held that two water rights systems prevailed: One for acquiring the right to use water for irrigation purposes by appropriation; the other, the common law right to the use of water, not so appropriated for irrigation purposes, by the riparian owner.[287]

The appropriative right accrues as of the date of priority of the right. The riparian right accrues at the time the riparian owner or his predecessor settled on the riparian tract of public land with the intention of perfecting the title which he finally acquired from the Govermment.[288] The results, according to

---

[283] Terr. Dak. Laws 1865-1866, ch. 1, § 256, Civil Code § 255 (1877), S. Dak. Laws 1890, ch. 105.

[284] S. Dak. Laws 1955, ch. 430, § 1, repealing, Code § 61.0101 *et seq.* (1939). Section 61.0101 of 1939, which contained the riparian declarations, was replaced in 1955 by § 61.0137, now S. Dak. Comp. Laws Ann. § § 46-5-1 to -3 (1967), which recognizes no riparian rights of landowners in streamflow crossing their lands.

[285] *Sturr* v. *Beck,* 6 Dak. 71, 50 N. W. 486 (1888), affirmed, 133 U. S. 541 (1890).

[286] *Lone Tree Ditch Co.* v. *Cyclone Ditch Co.,* 15 S. Dak. 519, 525-527, 91 N. W. 352 (1902); *Redwater Land & Canal Co.* v. *Reed,* 26 S. Dak. 466, 474, 128 N. W. 702 (1910).

[287] *Lone Tree Ditch Co.* v. *Cyclone Ditch Co.,* 15 S. Dak. 519, 527-530, 91 N. W. 352 (1902).

[288] *Id.* at 521-522; *Stenger* v. *Tharp,* 17 S. Dak. 13, 20, 94 N. W. 402 (1903); *Redwater Land & Canal Co.* v. *Jones,* 27 S. Dak. 194, 203-204, 130 N. W. 85 (1911).

the decisions, is that on a stream, the waters of which are claimed by both appropriators and riparians, the superiority of rights of any appropriator as against any riparian proprietor, or vice versa, depends upon their respective times of accrual. And it is the surplus flow of a stream over what might be legally used by riparians and prior appropriators that is subject to appropriation.[289]

In 1955, the South Dakota Legislature repealed the water appropriation legislation in its entirety and in place thereof substituted two acts—one relating to surface waters and the other to ground waters and wells.[290] In enacting the current law relating to appropriation of water of watercourses, the legislature undertook to define and to protect vested rights to the use of water so far as they pertain to beneficial use. Use of water for defined domestic purposes is unqualifiedly declared to be a vested right. The right of a riparian owner, at the time the act was passed, to continue to use water then being used for irrigation or other "artificial" purposes, or recently so used or in preparation therefor, was a vested right.[291] But failing such use or immediately prospective use, the riparian right to use water for irrigation or other "artificial" purposes is not recognized. On the contrary, "Subject to vested rights and prior appropriations, all waters flowing in definite streams of the State may be appropriated as herein provided."[292]

The constitutionality of this 1955 water rights legislation has been sustained by the South Dakota Supreme Court.[293]

Texas

During the 70 years that elapsed from the decision in the first riparian case of *Haas* v. *Choussard* in 1856 to that rendered in *Motl* v. *Boyd* in 1926, the Texas courts in discussing riparian rights questions were concerned chiefly with the common law and had little to say about the civil law or Spanish-American colonization law.[294]

In *Motl* v. *Boyd* the supreme court broke away from this long trend and dealt at length by *dictum* with Mexican colonization laws and with laws and

---

[289] *St. Germain Irrigating Ditch Co.* v. *Hawthorne Ditch Co.,* 32 S. Dak. 260, 268, 143 N. W. 124 (1913).

[290] S. Dak. Laws 1955, chs. 430 and 431, respectively, Comp. Laws Ann. chs. 46-1 to -8 (1967).

[291] S. Dak. Comp. Laws Ann. § 46-1-9 (1967).

[292] *Id.* § 46-5-5.

[293] *Belle Fourche Irr. Dist.* v. *Smiley,* 176 N. W. (2d) 239 (S. Dak. 1970); *Knight* v. *Grimes,* 80 S. Dak. 517, 127 N. W. (2d) 708 (1964). In the *Belle Fourche* case, the court said that the "Decision in the Knight case concerned with underground waters is equally applicable to surface waters." 176 N. W. (2d) at 245.

[294] *Haas* v. *Choussard,* 17 Tex. 588 (1856); *Motl* v. *Boyd,* 116 Tex. 82, 286 S. W. 458 (1926). An early exception was *Tolle* v. *Correth,* 31 Tex. 362, 98 Am. Dec. 540 (military court 1898).

policies by the succeeding Republic and State governments as sources of riparian water rights. But several decades later, in 1962, the Texas Supreme Court in *Valmont Plantations* v. *State of Texas* affirmed a decision of the San Antonio court of civil appeals to the effect that despite the erroneous *dicta* in *Motl* v. *Boyd*, no Texas court had until now been called upon to decide whether Spanish and Mexican land grants have appurtenant irrigation rights similar to the common law riparian right, and that there was no *stare decisis* on the subject. The court decided that lands riparian to the lower Rio Grande held under Spanish and Mexican grants have no appurtenant right to irrigate with the river waters.[295]

There was no issue of common law riparian rights in the *Valmont Plantations* case. Nothing said in either of the majority opinions in the case affected anything that had been said previously with respect to such common law rights. Certain statements in *Motl* v. *Boyd* that were not affected by the *Valmont Plantations* decision were that from 1840—when the common law was adopted by the Republic of Texas—down to the passage of the first water appropriation act in 1889, all grantees of public lands of the Republic and State became vested thereby with riparian rights in the waters of contiguous streams, for irrigation as well as for domestic use.[296] The legislature's own declaration in the water appropriation statutes is that nothing contained therein is to be construed as a recognition of any riparian right in the owner of any lands the title to which passed out of the State after July 1, 1895.[297]

During most of the history of the riparian doctrine in Texas, the courts took the position that the riparian doctrine is underlying and fundamental, formerly without regard to segments of streamflow,[298] but limited in *Motl* v. *Boyd* to the normal flow and underflow of the stream. Waters rising above the "line of highest ordinary flow" are to be regarded as floodwaters to which riparian rights do not attach, but are subject to appropriation under the statute.[299] The supreme court concluded in *Motl* v. *Boyd* that the appropriation statutes of 1889 down to 1917, inclusive, were valid and constitutional insofar as they authorized the appropriation of storm and floodwaters, and other waters without violation of riparian rights.[300]

---

[295] *Valmont Plantations* v. *State of Texas*, 163 Tex. 381, 355 S. W. (2d) 502 (1962), affirming, 346 S. W. (2d) 853 (Tex. Civ. App. 1961). Nevertheless, see chapter 7 at notes 656-659 regarding "equitable" rights recognized in a 1969 Texas Court of Civil Appeals case.

[296] *Motl* v. *Boyd*, 116 Tex. 82, 107-108, 286 S. W. 458 (1926).

[297] Tex. Rev. Civ. Stat. Ann. art. 7619 (1954). These matters are discussed in more detail in the State summary for Texas in the appendix.

[298] *Biggs* v. *Miller*, 147 S. W. 632, 636-637 (Tex. Civ. App. 1912); *Matagorda Canal Co.* v. *Markham Irr. Co.*, 154 S. W. 1176, 1180-1181 (Tex. Civ. App. 1913); *Zavala County W. I. Dist. No. 3* v. *Rogers*, 145 S. W. (2d) 919, 923 (Tex. Civ. App. 1940).

[299] *Motl* v. *Boyd*, 116 Tex. 82, 111, 121-122, 286 S. W. 458 (1962). The underflow of a stream is included in riparian waters: *Texas Co.* v. *Burkett*, 117 Tex. 16, 28, 296 S. W. 273 (1927).

[300] *Motl* v. *Boyd*, 116 Tex. 82, 124, 286 S. W. 458 (1926).

An important limitation to reasonable and necessary use of water by a riparian as against an appropriator was made in 1912. Riparian owners were entitled to quantities of water reasonably sufficient for irrigation, stockraising, and domestic purposes, waters in excess thereof being subject to statutory appropriation.[301]

A method of distributing waters of Pecos River to both riparian and nonriparian lands according to a schedule of rotation of the entire flow, rather than by simultaneous diversions of segments thereof, received judicial approval.[302]

A 1967 Texas statute has restricted the exercise of riparian rights to the extent of the maximum actual application of water to beneficial use without waste made during any calender year from 1963 to 1967, inclusive (or until the end of 1970 if works were under construction before the act's effective date).[303] But this does not apply to the use of water for domestic or livestock purposes.

Washington

From the earliest times in Washington, the dual systems of water rights—appropriation and riparian—were recognized and applied in actual controversies. This was and is a continuing process.

The earlier holdings were to the effect that appropriations made on the public domain of the United States took precedence over riparian rights of lands that subsequently passed to private ownership.[304] A principle complementary to the foregoing—of equally vital importance—was early announced to the effect that an entryman who settled upon public land and acquired title thereto by complying with the laws of the United States was entitled to the common law rights of a riparian proprietor, as against subsequent appropriators of the water, from the date of his occupancy with intent to acquire title thereto from the Government.[305] These complementary principles were summarized in a decision rendered in 1923.[306]

---

[301] *Biggs* v. *Lee*, 147 S. W. 709, 710-711 (Tex. Civ. App. 1912, error dismissed).

[302] *Ward County W. I. Dist. No. 3* v. *Ward County Irr. Dist. No. 1*, 237 S. W. 584 588 (Tex. Civ. App. 1921), reformed and affirmed, 117 Tex. 10, 14-16, 295 S. W. 917 (1927).

[303] If valid under existing law, claims for such rights as required shall be filed with the Texas Water Rights Commission to prevent their being extinguished. Tex. Rev. Civ. Stat. Ann. art. 7542a, § 4 (Supp. 1970).

Previously existing legislation has disclaimed any intent to impair vested rights or rights of property. Tex. Rev. Civ. Stat. Ann. arts. 7507 and 7620 (1954). Relevant provisions in the 1967 statute include Tex. Rev. Civ. Stat. Ann. art. 7542a, § § 12 and 14 (Supp. 1970).

[304] *Geddis* v. *Parrish*, 1 Wash. 587, 589-592, 21 Pac. 314 (1889). Reiterated in the opinions in many cases, for example: *In re Sinlahekin Creek*, 162 Wash. 635, 642-643, 299 Pac. 649 (1931).

[305] *Benton* v. *Johncox*, 17 Wash. 277, 279-290, 49 Pac. 495 (1897). This likewise became an established principle: *Bernot* v. *Morrison*, 81 Wash. 538, 544, 143 Pac. 104 (1914). "Riparian rights date from the first step taken to secure title from the government." *In re Alpowa Creek*, 129 Wash. 9, 13, 224 Pac. 29 (1924).

[306] *In re Doan Creek*, 125 Wash. 14, 20, 215 Pac. 343 (1923).

Originally, there was derived the broad rule that "the doctrine of appropriation applies only to public lands, and when such lands cease to be public and become private property, it is no longer applicable."[307] This was reiterated in one form or another in many decisions and was actually applied on the pleadings in *Wallace* v. *Weitman,* decided in 1958.[308] In other cases decided in the meantime, however, the Washington Supreme Court rejected arguments that "a valid appropriation can be made only upon government lands."[309] Finally in 1959, some 9 months after the date of the decision in *Wallace* v. *Weitman* and without reference to the opinion in that case, the Washington Supreme Court said that: "Defendants' contention that the doctrine of appropriation of water applies only to public lands has been rejected by this court."[310]

Notwithstanding these contradictions, it was established in a series of decisions rendered in the 1920's that the riparian owner's right of use as against an appropriator in Washington is now limited to such quantity of water as he can *beneficially use* on his riparian lands, either *directly* or *prospectively within a reasonable time.* All water in excess thereof may be appropriated.[311] The court's thesis was that while it had recognized the common law doctrine of riparian rights, it had also modified and enlarged upon that doctrine by engrafting upon it the necessity of beneficial use by the riparian owner, the question of relief to such owner depending upon whether he was substantially damaged either presently or prospectively within a reasonable time. The common law rule of riparian rights "has been stripped of some of its rigors."[312]

As a result, before the riparian owner in Washington now has any rights to protect as against an appropriator he must show with reasonable certainty that either at present or within the near future, he will make use of the water for beneficial purposes.[313]

---

[307] *Benton* v. *Johncox,* 17 Wash. 277, 289, 49 Pac. 495 (1897).

[308] *Wallace* v. *Weitman,* 52 Wash. (2d) 585, 586-587, 328 Pac. (2d) 157 (1958).

[309] *Weitensteiner* v. *Engdahl,* 125 Wash. 106, 113, 215 Pac. 378 (1923); *Hunter Land Co.* v. *Laugenour,* 140 Wash. 558, 570, 250 Pac. 41 (1926).

[310] *Drake* v. *Smith,* 54 Wash. (2d) 57, 61, 337 Pac. (2d) 1059 (1959).

[311] *Brown* v. *Chase,* 125 Wash. 542, 549, 553, 217 Pac. 23 (1923); *In re Alpowa Creek,* 129 Wash. 9, 13, 224 Pac. 29 (1924); *Proctor* v. *Sim,* 134 Wash. 606, 616-619, 236 Pac. 114 (1925); *In re Sinlahekin Creek,* 162 Wash. 635, 640-641, 299 Pac. 649 (1931); foreshadowed in *State ex rel. Liberty Lake Irr. Co.* v. *Superior Court,* 47 Wash. 310, 313-314, 91 Pac. 968 (1907). See also *United States* v. *Ahtanum Irr. Dist.,* 330 Fed. (2d) 897, 904-905 (9th Cir. 1964), rehearing denied, 338 Fed. (2d) 307, certiorari denied, 381, U. S. 924 (1965).

A number of conjectured alternative meanings of this limitation on riparian rights are discussed in Corker, C. E., & Roe, C. B., Jr., "Washington's New Water Rights Law—Improvements Needed," 44 Wash. Law Rev. 85, 113-128 (1968).

[312] *In re Alpowa Creek,* 129 Wash. 9, 13, 224 Pac. 29 (1924).

[313] *State* v. *American Fruit Growers, Inc.,* 135 Wash. 156, 161, 237 Pac. 498 (1925).

For a greater restriction regarding navigable waters, see chapter 4 at note 133.

An act enacted in 1967 provides that anyone entitled to divert or withdraw water by virtue of his ownership of land abutting a stream, lake or watercourse who abandons the same, or voluntarily fails, without sufficient cause," to beneficially use all or any part of such a right for any period of 5 successive years after the act's effective date shall relinquish such right or portion thereof which shall revert to the State and the affected waters become available for appropriation).[314] This legislation has not yet been construed by the Washington Supreme Court.

---

[314]Laws 1967, ch. 233, Rev. Code § 90.14.170 (Supp. 1970). See also § 90.14.020 (3). The act's effective date was July 1, 1967. *Id.* § 90.14.900 (Supp. 1970). A rather elaborate definition of "sufficient cause" and certain exceptions are included in § 90.14.140. Procedures for holding hearings and issuing orders determining any such relinquishment for nonuse are included in § 90.14.130.

The 1967 legislation, as revised in 1969, also requires that anyone claiming water rights other than under permit or certificate from the Department of Ecology shall file a claim with the department by June 30, 1974. Failure to do so shall be "conclusively deemed to have waived and relinquished" such rights. Laws 1967, ch. 233, Laws 1969, ch. 284, Rev. Code § § 90.14.010 to -.121 (Supp. 1970). This legislation may present a question somewhat similar to that discussed above regarding a 1966 Alaska statute concerning the question of the application of the claim registration provisions to unused riparian rights. But in any event, a number of such unused rights might be extinguished for 5-years' nonuse since July 1, 1967, under the statutory provision discussed above, prior to the final June 30, 1974, date for filing water rights claims.

The 1967 legislation also stated that "The legislature hereby affirms the rule that no right to withdraw or divert any water shall accrue to any riparian unless said riparian shall have complied with the provisions of law applicable to the appropriation of water." But this provision (critically discussed in Corker and Roe, *supra* note 311, at 106 *et seq.*) was repealed in 1969. Laws 1967, ch. 233, § 12, creating Rev. Code § 90.14.120 (Supp. 1970), repealed, Laws 1969, ch. 284, § 23.

Chapter 7

APPROPRIATION OF WATER

With one exception, all of the 19 Western States to which this study relates recognize the appropriation doctrine. The one exception is Hawaii. "The law of priority of appropriation which prevails in the arid sections of the mainland of the United States has never been recognized in this jurisdiction."[1]

DEFINITIONS

Following are definitions of terms frequently used in this chapter:

Water right is a right to the use of water, accorded by law.[2]

Appropriative right is an exclusive right, acquired under the procedure provided by law, to divert from a public water supply a specific quantity of water—provided it is available there in excess of the requirements of all existing vested rights—and to apply such water to a specific beneficial use or uses in preference to all appropriative rights of later priority.

Inchoate appropriative right is an incomplete appropriative right in good standing. It comes into being as the first step provided by law for acquiring an appropriative right is taken. It remains in good standing so long as the requirements of law are being fulfilled. And it matures into an appropriative right on completion of the last step provided by law.

Appropriation is the process or series of operations by which an appropriative right is acquired. A complete appropriation thus results in an appropriative right.

To appropriate water, or *to make an appropriation,* is to take the steps required by law for the acquisition of an appropriative right.

Appropriated water is the water to which a completed appropriation in good standing relates.

Priority of an appropriative right is the superiority of the right over all rights of later priority when the available water supply is not enough for all. The priority relates to a specific date, and in some cases to a specific hour of such date.

---

[1] *Carter* v. *Territory of Hawaii,* 24 Haw. 47, 57 (1917). Nevertheless, see chapter 20 regarding Hawaiian ground water regulatory legislation which includes some features that appear to be modifications of the appropriation doctrine. Haw. Rev. Stat. § § 177-1 to -35 (1968).

[2] Definitions of terms in this section are based largely on National Reclamation Association, "Desirable Principles of State Water Legislation," pp. 1-5 (1946), which was prepared by a committee of the National Reclamation Association, Wells A. Hutchins, chairman, and on Texas State Board of Water Engineers, "Rules, Regulations and Modes of Procedure," rule 115.1 (1955).

WATERS SUBJECT TO APPROPRIATION

In the development of the appropriation doctrine in the Western States, diversions of water for mining, domestic, and irrigation purposes were commonly made from "streams"—watercourses and their tributary creeks and springs. Western water law developed chiefly with respect to these sources. For example, the California Civil Code of 1872, which was the inspiration for many other early western water statutes, authorized acquisition by appropriation of the right to use water flowing in a river or stream or down a canyon or ravine.[3]

"The secret, changeable, and uncontrollable character of underground water" which, according to a Vermont court more than a century ago, "sometimes rises to a great height, and sometimes moves in collateral directions, by some secret influences, beyond our comprehension,"[4] kept the law of rights to the use of percolating ground water within the domain of landownership, well away from prior appropriation, throughout decades in which a large volume of statutory and case law was being developed respecting the appropriation doctrine. Then, as the appropriative principle was eventually applied to percolating ground water in one western jurisdiction after another, statutory authorizations were either added to existing laws by amendment and enlargement, or were granted in separate enactments.

As a result of these several developments, statutory declarations of appropriable waters (1) came to relate simply to all waters in the jurisdiction, or (2) were made in the form of classifications, or (3) in other instances were applied separately to surface waters and to ground waters.

Classifications made in the current statutes with respect to appropriable waters are noted below. Some statutes specifically carry the provison that they are subject to vested rights, or its equivalent. Others omit such a limitation which, in view of well-known constitutional requirements, would apply whether or not the legislature mentions it.

Statutory Declarations

Nearly all the water appropriation statutes of the Western States specify either all waters, or classes of waters, that are subject to appropriation in accordance with the express legislative provisions.

All Waters

In Oregon, all waters within the State are subject to appropriation for beneficial use, although certain waters are specifically withdrawn from appropriation for scenic and other public welfare purposes by the legislature.[5]

---

[3] Cal. Civ. Code § 1410 (1872).

[4] *Chatfield* v. *Wilson*, 28 Vt. 49, 54 (1855).

[5] Oreg. Rev. Stat. § 537.120 (Supp. 1969) and ch. 538 (Supp. 1967).

In Kansas, all waters may be appropriated subject of course to vested rights.[6] Also in Kansas, as well as in Nevada and Utah, declarations relate to all waters whether on the surface or in the ground.[7]

Although a Washington statute declares public ownership of "all waters" within the State and generally relates rights of acquisition to appropriation there is also a later ground water law which specified what ground waters ar public and appropriable, the effect of which is to exclude broadly diffused percolating water.[8]

A general Oklahoma statute likewise does not specify any class of appropriable water. It provides the procedure by which one who intends to acquire the right to the beneficial use of "any water" shall go about acquiring such rights and uses general terms in other sections.[9] However, one section provides procedure relating to "each stream system and source of water supply"[10] and a later statute provides specific procedures for appropriating ground water.[11]

In 1966, the State of Alaska enacted a statute providing a system for the appropriation and use of all water and establishing a water resources board.[12]

Stream Waters

The Colorado constitution declares the water of every natural stream to be the property of the public, subject to appropriation.[13] The South Dakota surface water appropriation statute applies to "all waters flowing in definite streams of the State."[14] As noted below, South Dakota has a separate ground water statute. In New Mexico, the constitution subjects to appropriation all natural waters flowing in streams and watercourses, whether perennial or torrential. A statute further defines a watercourse as "any river, creek, arroyo canyon, draw, or wash, or any other channel having defined banks and bed with visible evidence of the occasional flow of water."[15]

Natural Streams

The qualifying word "natural" is used in several water rights statutes—water of a "natural stream" or water flowing in a "natural channel."

The Arizona Supreme Court held that this usage in the statute limits the sources of water appropriable thereunder and excludes sources of artificia

---

[6] Kans. Stat. Ann. § 82a-703 (1969).

[7] Id. §§ 82a-703 and 82a-707; Nev. Rev. Stat. §§ 533.025 and 533.030 (Supp. 1969); Utah Code Ann. §§ 73-1-1 and 73-3-1 (1968).

[8] Wash. Rev. Code §§ 90.03.010, 90.44.020, 90.44.035 (Supp. 1961).

[9] Okla. Stat. Ann. tit. 82, §§ 21, 1-A(a), 2, 12-14, and 27 (1970).

[10] Id. § 11.

[11] Id. § 1001 et seq.

[12] Alaska Stat. § 46.15.010 et seq. (Supp. 1966).

[13] Colo. Const., art. XVI, §§ 5 and 6.

[14] S. Dak. Comp. Laws Ann. § 46-5-5 (1967).

[15] N. Mex. Const., art. XVI, § 2; Stat. Ann. § 75-1-1 (1968).

rigin.[16] In Nebraska, it is held to exclude strictly artificial conditions such as drainage ditches.[17] And in New Mexico, waters flowing in a drainage ditch are not appropriable under the constitution or the statute, nor in the absence of statute.[18]

Multiple Classifications of Watercourses

The most extensive classifications of appropriable watercourses are in the statutes of Arizona and Texas. The Arizona classification includes waters of all sources, flowing in streams, canyons, ravines, or other natural channels, or in definite underground channels, whether perennial or intermittent, flood, waste, or surplus water, and waters of lakes, ponds, and springs on the surface. The Texas classification includes waters of the ordinary flow and underflow and tides of every flowing river or natural stream; of all lakes, bays, or arms of the Gulf of Mexico; and the storm, flood, or rainwaters of every river or natural stream, canyon, ravine, depression, or watershed in the State.[19]

Other authorizations with multiple classifications, emphasizing watercourses and elaborating upon or adding to them, are those of California, Idaho, Montana, Nebraska, North Dakota, and Wyoming.[20]

Navigable Waters

In chapter 4, it is noted that provisions formerly contained in the water administration statutes of North Dakota and South Dakota exempted navigable waters from appropriation. These exemptions were deleted from these statutes in 1939 and 1955, respectively.[21]

No current water appropriation statute in the West exempts navigable waters from the statute.

---

[16] *Fourzan* v. *Curtis,* 43 Ariz. 140, 143, 29 Pac. (2d) 722 (1934). "* * * the test of the right of appropriation, both in quantity and quality, depends on their natural condition, and not on what may occur after that condition is artifically changed."

[17] *Drainage Dist. No. 1 of Lincoln County* v. *Suburban Irr. Dist.,* 139 Nebr. 460, 468-471, 298 N. W. 131 (1941).

[18] *Hagerman Irr. Co.* v. *East Grand Plains Drainage Dist.,* 25 N. Mex. 649, 656-658, 187 Pac. 555 (1920).

See also *Pikes Peak Golf Club, Inc.* v. *Kuiper,* __Colo.__, 455 Pac. (2d) 882 (1969), regarding increased drainage waters resulting from the reclamation of swampland.

[19] Ariz. Rev. Stat. Ann. § 45-101 (1956); Tex. Rev. Civ. Stat. Ann. art 7467 (Supp. 1970).

[20] Cal. Water Code § § 1200 and 1201 (West 1956); Idaho Code Ann. § § 42-101, 42-103, and 42-107 (1948); Mont. Rev. Codes Ann. § § 89-810 and 89-829 (1964); Nebr. Rev. Stat. § § 46-202, 46-233, 46-240, and 46-259 (1968); N. Dak. Cent. Code Ann. § 61-01-01 (1960); Wyo. Const., art. VIII, § 1.

[21] N. Dak. Comp. Laws § 8235 (1913), amended, Laws 1939, ch. 255; S. Dak. Code § 61.0101 (1939), repealed, Laws 1955, ch. 430, § 1.

Ground Waters

Historically, as noted in chapter 2, distinctions were made between water of a *definite underground stream* and *percolating water*. A definite underground stream is a watercourse, moving in a definite subterranean channel. Percolating water moves through the ground but without constituting part of a definite underground stream. Based upon legal recognition of such a physical distinction, different principles were applied to waters of the two classes in determining rights of use (see chapter 19). This influenced the wording of declarations of western legislatures that applied the appropriative principle to various or all kinds of ground waters.

All ground waters.—That the water appropriation statutes of certain Western States purport to subject all waters of the State to appropriation, subject necessarily to vested rights, is noted above under "All Waters." However, in some of these States there are provisions of the general appropriation statute, or separate statutes entirely, which in express terms relate to ground water. In the immediately following paragraphs, the ground water situation is treated independently of declarations in the general appropriation statutes.

In a number of Western States, all ground waters, without restriction, are expressly subjected to appropriation. Thus, in Kansas the designation is simply ground water and in Nevada, all underground water or ground water.[22] Idaho, South Dakota, Oklahoma, and North Dakota agree in designating all water under the surface of the ground. The first three, however, reinforce their declarations by making them applicable whatever may be the geology of the water-bearing formation. North Dakota does so by adding that all such water is included whether flowing in defined subterranean channels or percolating in the ground.[23] Wyoming's designation is any water under the surface of the land or the bed of any stream, lake, reservoir, or other body of surface water.[24] Utah's all-inclusive declaration is all waters, whether above or under the ground.[25] The Alaska Water Use Act of 1966 provides that " 'water' means all water of the state, surface and subsurfaces, occurring in a natural state, except mineral and medicinal water" and "wherever occurring in a natural state, the waters are reserved to the people for common use and are subject to appropriation and beneficial use as provided in this chapter."[26]

The Oregon ground water act stops short of purporting to make *all* ground water appropriable. It does make the statute applicable to all ground water to

---

[22] Kans. Stat. Ann. § 82a-707 (1969); Nev. Rev. Stat. § § 534.010 (Supp. 1969) and 534.020 (Supp. 1967).

[23] Idaho Code Ann. § 42-230 (Supp. 1969); S. Dak. Comp. Laws Ann. § § 46-1-6(7) and 46-6-3 (1967); Okla. Stat. Ann. tit. 82, § 1002 (1970); N. Dak. Cent. Code Ann. § 61-01-01 (1960).

[24] Wyo. Stat. Ann. § § 41-121 (1957) and 41-138 (Supp. 1969).

[25] Utah Code Ann. § § 73-1-1 and 73-3-1 (1968).

[26] Alaska Stat. § § 46.15.260 and 46.15.030 (Supp. 1966).

which it could have practical application. This appears to be consonant with principles of ground water hydrology. The definition reads: " 'Ground Water' means any water, except capillary moisture, beneath the land surface or beneath the bed of any stream, lake, reservoir or other body of surface water within the boundaries of this state, whatever may be the geological formation or structure in which such water stands, flows, percolates or otherwise moves."[27]

Ground water body with ascertainable bounderies.—Designations in the New Mexico and Washington ground water statutes fall within this category. The first group is "underground streams, channels, artesian basins, reservoirs, or lakes, having reasonably ascertainable boundaries."[28] The second is "All bodies of water that exist beneath the land surface and that there saturate the interstices of rocks or other materials—that is, the waters of underground streams or channels, artesian basins, underground reservoirs, lakes or basins, whose existence or whose boundaries may be reasonably established or ascertained. . . ."[29]

Definite underground stream and underflow of surface stream.—Statutes of Arizona, California, and Texas include subterranean streamflows in lists of appropriable waters. In Arizona, it is water flowing "in definite underground channels." In California, "subterranean streams flowing through known and definite channels." And in Texas, waters of the ordinary flow "and underflow" of every flowing river or natural stream.[30]

Miscellaneous

(1) The New Mexico statute includes a provision to the effect that artificial surface waters that pass from the domain of the owner or developer and enter a natural watercourse, and are not reclaimed by him for a period of 4 years, are subject to appropriation; but that continuance of their availability for such appropriation cannot be compelled.[31]

(2) Statutes passed in Colorado, Oregon, and Washington late in the 19th century provided that ditches for utilization of waste, seepage, or spring waters should be governed by the same laws relating to priority of right as those diverting from streams, provided that the owner of the lands upon which such water arose should have the prior right thereto. The Colorado and Oregon acts

---

[27] Oreg. Rev. Stat. § § 537.515 and 537.525 (Supp. 1969).

[28] N. Mex. Stat. Ann. § 75-11-1 (1968).

[29] Wash. Rev. Code § 90.44.035 (Supp. 1961).

[30] Ariz. Rev. Stat. Ann. § 45-101 (1956); Cal. Water Code § 1200 (West 1956); Tex. Rev. Civ. Stat. Ann. art. 7467 (Supp. 1970).

[31] N. Mex. Stat. Ann. § 75-5-25 (1968). For the purpose of this act, artificial surface waters are defined as waters whose appearance or accumulation is due to escape, seepage, loss, waste, drainage, or percolation from constructed works, either directly or indirectly, and which depend for their continuance upon acts of man. They are primarily private and subject to use by the owner or developer thereof.

are still in existence. The Washington act was repealed in the course of enactment of the water appropriation statute of 1917.[32]

The Colorado Supreme Court held that the foregoing statute was not applicable to waters that reached a natural stream by natural flow, by percolation, or by being artificially turned into the same.[33] In an Oregon decision, it was stated that the statutory preference in favor of the landowner did not apply under the circumstances of the case.[34] An early Idaho law containing the same authorization—but without the provision favoring the landowner—is still a part of the water appropriation statute.[35]

Previous Court Declarations

Stream Water Appropriative Rights

For a long period appropriative rights in the West related chiefly to diversions of water from surface streams. In the large majority of States and Territories, the legislatures spoke first, and the courts sooner or later extended their recognition to the appropriation doctrine and construed the already existing statutes. Thus, in most cases the designation of appropriable waters was originally a legislative function. It pertained specifically in certain instances to surface stream waters only; in others, to both streams and one or more other surface sources. In the other jurisdictions, judicial recognition of this doctrine necessarily related under the facts of each case to rights to the use of streamflow acquired pursuant to local customs, if any prevailed in the particular community. Or if not, it was extended simply to informal diversions of water and application thereof to beneficial use.

Alaska.—The situation in this jurisdiction differed from those elsewhere. The "Compiled Laws of the Territory of Alaska, 1913" contained reproductions of section 9 of the Act of Congress of 1866 and the amendment of 1870,[36] providing protection of rights to water vested by local laws, customs, and court decisions in the public domain jurisdictions.[37]

In the first volume of Alaska case reports, however, there is a decision, rendered in 1890, in which the Federal District Court recognized the appropriation doctrine. The court held that prior appropriators of water were

---

[32] Colo. Rev. Stat. Ann. § 148-2-2 (1963); Oreg. Rev. Stat. § 537.800 (Supp. 1969); Wash. Laws 1889-90, ch. 21, § 15; Laws 1917, ch. 117, § 47.

[33] *La Jara Creamery & Live Stock Assn.* v. *Hansen,* 35 Colo. 105, 108-109, 83 Pac. 644 (1905); *Nevius* v. *Smith,* 86 Colo. 178, 182-183, 279 Pac. 44 (1928); *De Haas* v. *Benesch,* 116 Colo. 344, 351, 181 Pac. (2d) 453 (1947).

[34] *Borman* v. *Blackmon,* 60 Oreg. 304, 310-311, 188 Pac. 848 (1911).

[35] Idaho Code Ann. § 42-107 (1948).

[36] 14 Stat. 253, § 9 (1866); 16 Stat. 218 (1870).

[37] Alaska Comp. Laws Ann. § § 47-3-7 and 47-3-8 (1949), deleted, Alaska Stat. Tables (Supp. 1966).

entitled to protection, under the Act of Congress of 1866, in their prior rights to divert stream water acquired pursuant to local customs before regulations relating to water rights had been adopted in the local mining district.[38] It is true a later decision in the first division, while not repudiating the appropriation doctrine but on the contrary specifically applying it to the facts of the case, held that the Act of Congress of July 26, 1866, was not in force in Alaska.[39] But several years later, the court for the same division disagreed emphatically with the holding of the latter case on this point. For many years, the court declared, Congress, the Alaska miners, and the courts had acted on the premise that this statute had been extended to Alaska.[40] In the meantime, the court for the third division held that section 9 of the Act of 1866 and the appropriation doctrine had been extended to Alaska by the Acts of 1884 and 1900.[41]

Judicial recognition of the appropriation doctrine in Alaska, then, preceded any Territory-wide water rights legislation. But this recognition in its turn was based on extension to Alaska of early Congressional statutes, the applicability of which was predicated on existence of local laws and customs in the mining areas of this jurisdiction. That such local customs were in effect, as well as rules and regulations of mining districts dating back at least to the 1880's, is noted in court opinions.[42]

Other jurisdictions. —In four other western jurisdictions, the doctrine of prior appropriation was recognized by the courts before the respective State or Territorial legislatures explicitly declared this basic water law policy. These are California, Nevada, Utah, and Oregon.

(1) California. In the California practice act of 1851, the legislature took note of the "customs, usages, or regulations established and in force at the bar, or diggings" in actions respecting mining claims and thereby indirectly or

---

[38] *Noland* v. *Coon,* 1 Alaska 36, 37 (1890).

[39] *Ketchikan Co.* v. *Citizens' Co.,* 2 Alaska 120, 123-126 (1903).

[40] *McFarland* v. *Alaska Perseverance Min. Co.,* 3 Alaska 308, 322-323 (1907), affirmed sub nom. *Thorndyke* v. *Alaska Perseverance Min. Co.,* 164 Fed. 657 (9th Cir. 1908).

[41] *Revenue Min. Co.* v. *Balderston,* 2 Alaska 363, 367-368 (1905). 23 Stat. 26, § 8 (1884), replaced by 31 Stat. 330, § 26 (1900), 48 U.S.C. § 356 (1964). In 1966, the State of Alaska provided specifically for the appropriation and use of water. Alaska Stat. § 46.15.010 *et seq.* (Supp. 1966).

[42] Rules and regulations governing appropriation and diversion of water from streams in the Harris mining district, adopted February 18, 1882, and mostly copied from the California Civil Code § § 1410-1422 (1872), are set out in the opinions in *McFarland* v. *Alaska Perseverance Min. Co.,* 3 Alaska 308 (1907), affirmed sub. nom. *Thorndyke* v. *Alaska Perseverance Min. Co.,* 164 Fed. 657 (9th Cir. 1908). See also, regarding mining district water rules, *Noland* v. *Coon,* 1 Alaska 36, 37 (1890); *Madigan* v. *Kougarok Min. Co.,* 3 Alaska 63, 67 (1906); *Miocene Ditch Co.* v. *Campion Min. & Trading Co.,* 3 Alaska 572, 585 (1908); *Anderson* v. *Campbell,* 4 Alaska 660, 665 (1913); *Alaska Juneau Gold Min. Co.* v. *Ebner Gold Min. Co.,* 239 Fed. 638, 640-641 (9th Cir. 1917).

impliedly recognized the appropriation doctrine.[43] However, there was no direct legislation pertaining to water rights until enactment of the Civil Code of 1872, which became effective January 1, 1873.[44] In the meantime—from 1853 to the end of 1872—52 decisions in controversies over the use of water were rendered by the California Supreme Court, the largest part of which involved diversions from watercourses for mining, milling, and irrigation purposes. In several cases decided in 1853 and 1855, actions involving mining water rights were decided pursuant to the principle of prior appropriation of water.[45] The Civil Code enactment in 1872 was essentially a codification of appropriative principles and practices that had developed in the various mining camps of the State.

(2) Nevada. A large part of the interstate boundary between California and Nevada lies along or close to the Sierra Nevada,—an area in which so many of the California mining camps were located. The influence of mining water customs which grew up on the California side was felt in Nevada as well as in other western mining jurisdictions. The appropriation doctrine "well settled in California," to the effect that as between appropriative claimants to the use of streamflow the first in time has the best right, was followed by the Nevada Supreme Court as early as 1866.[46] Legislative recognition of the appropriation doctrine, however, was not accorded until 1889.[47]

(3) Utah. In early Territorial days, rights to the use of Utah streamflows for irrigation and domestic purposes were acquired either by actual diversion and application of water to beneficial use, or by legislative grant.[48] For 50 years, diversions were so made without existence of specific statutory procedure for acquiring appropriative rights.

In the earliest Territorial supreme court decision that was rendered with respect to use of water, the principle of prior appropriation of water was recognized.[49] The first statutory recognition of accrued rights to water acquired by appropriation came 2 years later. The first statutory procedure for *future* appropriation of water was provided in 1897, shortly after the attainment of statehood.[50] Irrigation with water diverted from Utah streams, particularly close to the points of their emergence from the mouths of canyons

---

[43] Cal. Stat. 1851, ch. 5, § 621.

[44] Cal. Civ. Code § § 1410-1422 (1872).

[45] *Eddy* v. *Simpson*, 3 Cal. 249, 252 (1853); *Stiles* v. *Laird*, 5 Cal. 120, 122-123 (1855); *Irwin* v. *Phillips*, 5 Cal. 140, 145-147 (1855).

[46] *Lobdell* v. *Simpson*, 2 Nev. 274, 277-279 (1866).

[47] Nev. Laws 1889 ch. 113, repealed by Laws 1893, ch. 127. In 1875, the Nevada Supreme Court expressed its opinion that there was then no statute of the State that recognized the right of prior appropriation of water for purposes of irrigation: *Barnes* v. *Sabron*, 10 Nev. 217, 232 (1875).

[48] *Wrathall* v. *Johnson*, 86 Utah 50, 80, 40 Pac. (2d) 755 (1935).

[49] *Crane* v. *Winsor*, 2 Utah 248, 253 (1878).

[50] Utah Laws 1880, ch. 20; Laws 1897, ch. 52.

along the Wasatch Mountains, had reached a considerable stage of development before the judicial and legislative branches of government had occasion to declare appropriative principles pertaining to stream water rights.

(4) Oregon. In 1880, the Supreme Court of Oregon recognized the doctrine of prior appropriation of stream waters as between possessors of unsurveyed government lands, in accordance with the Act of Congress of 1866,[51] provided a local custom to this effect were alleged and proved.[52] Legislative recognition of the appropriation doctrine, of existing appropriative rights, and of the right to make further appropriations, was finally accorded in 1891.[53] Prior thereto, local customs were in effect under which an intending appropriator posted a notice of his claim and filed it in the county records.[54]

Ground Water Appropriative Rights

Definite underground stream.—It is noted earlier that application of the appropriative principle to definite underground streams is contained not only in statutes pertaining expressly to subterranean water of this class, but also in those acts that subject to appropriation all waters, or all ground waters, or water constituting underflow of a stream. Independently of these statutes, however, and before the enactment of statutes pertaining expressly to definite underground streams, courts had drawn their historic distinction between such streams and percolating waters. This distinction was made chiefly with respect to the riparian question—whether the owner of land in which ground water occurred had the rights of a riparian proprietor therein, or owned the water outright.

Independently, then, of statutes subjecting waters of definite underground streams to appropriation, courts of a large majority of Western States decided cases in which legal distinctions between such waters and diffused percolating waters were involved.

With marked unanimity the courts that considered these questions accepted the principle that the rules of law that govern uses of water of such streams are not the same as those that apply to other ground waters. In general, they took the view that definite underground streams are legally comparable to surface watercourses. This means that the subterranean water should be definitely found to be moving, either continuously or intermittently, in a definite channel with bed and banks, and that such water is subject to the law of watercourses, not to any theory of absolute ownership by the owner of overlying lands. From this, it followed that in a particular jurisdiction the

---

[51] 14 Stat. 253 (1866).
[52] *Lewis* v. *McClure,* 8 Oreg. 273, 274-275 (1880). The requirement of proof was later relaxed: *Speake* v. *Hamilton,* 21 Oreg. 3, 8, 26 Pac. 855 (1890).
[53] Oreg. Laws 1891, p. 52.
[54] *Cole* v. *Logan,* 24 Oreg. 304, 309, 33 Pac. 568 (1893).

doctrines of water law recognized therein with respect to streams on the surface would be applied to subterranean streams—the appropriation doctrine or the riparian doctrine, or both doctrines, as the case might be.

Underflow of surface stream.—By definition, this aspect of ground water is part of a watercourse—the subsurface portion which exists in the ground underlying and in immediate contact with the flow on the surface of the ground; and with subterranean sideflows extending in many situations, on one or both sides, for varying distances beyond the surface streambanks.

In a number of Western States, the high courts have had occasion to take cognizance of the existence of stream underflow. They agree that this water is as much a part of the stream as is the surface flow and that it is governed by the same rules—appropriation, riparian, or both.

An Arizona decision defined the "underflow, subflow or undercurrent" of a surface stream; and it laid down a judicial test to determine whether or not water is subflow and subject to the same rules of appropriation law as water of the surface stream itself.[55]

Percolating water.—The courts tenaciously clung to their longstanding distinction between definite underground streams and percolating waters, opinions of hydrologists to the contrary notwithstanding, and with it the application of the law of watercourses to streams in the ground. As a result of this distinction, wherever the appropriation doctrine was applied it was customarily applied to underground streams only, not to percolating water. It is therefore not surprising that in extending the appropriation doctrine to percolating water, the judiciary should lag behind the legislatures. As a matter of fact, in many States in which appropriative rights in percolating water are recognized, the legislatures spoke before there had been any indication of the official judicial attitude. (The laws concerning such water will be discussed in chapters 19 and 20.) Court action in some States was as follows.

(1) New Mexico. In 1927, the legislature enacted a law relating to appropriation of water in underground streams, channels, artesian basins, reservoirs, or lakes having reasonably ascertainable boundaries.[56] This act was held void by the New Mexico Supreme Court as being in contravention of a constitutional provision inhibiting extension of provisions of any existing law by reference only to its title. Despite this, the principles that it declared were unqualifiedly approved by the court.[57] The defective legislation was replaced in 1931 by an act which eliminated the objectionable features.[58]

By its terms, the New Mexico ground water enactment applied to ground waters of designated classes with ascertainable boundaries, not to percolating

---

[55] *Maricopa County M. W. C. Dist.* v. *Southwest Cotton Co.,* 39 Ariz. 65, 96, 4 Pac. (2d) 369 (1931).

[56] N. Mex. Laws 1927, ch. 182.

[57] *Yeo* v. *Tweedy,* 34 N. Mex. 611, 286 Pac. 970 (1929).

[58] N. Mex. Laws 1931 ch. 131.

waters in general. But it went beyond the underground streams and channels designation to a described class of artesian basins—probably far enough to arouse as much legal opposition and questioning as though it had extended to all percolating waters. In declaring that the 1927 law was declaratory of existing law and was fundamentally sound, although technically void, and that the waters of an artesian basin, the boundaries of which had been ascertained, were subject to appropriation even without the aid of the statute, the supreme court took the following broad view. This view was that the right of prior appropriation obtained in the jurisdiction under Mexican sovereignty and continued after the American acquisition of the region and that adoption of the common law did not change the rules already prevailing. In developing its thesis, the supreme court appeared to consider artesian basins with defined boundaries and percolating waters to be in the same logical category.

(2) Idaho. In 1899, "subterranean waters" were included in the still existing list of waters subject to appropriation in Idaho.[59] Comprehensive legislation governing appropriation of ground waters was enacted in 1951 and 1953.[60] In the interim, the Idaho Supreme Court rendered decisions respecting rights to the use of percolating waters which, while not uniform in the development of principles, nevertheless with one exception favored the doctrine of appropriation. The earlier decisions tended toward this doctrine. The latest ones embraced it completely.[61]

(3) Utah. Judicial fiat in Utah definitely preceded and led directly to legislative action. In 1935, after passing through successive stages of recognizing rules of absolute ownership and of correlative rights in percolating waters, the Utah Supreme Court rendered two decisions recognizing appropriative rights in waters of an artesian basin.[62] These cases were decided about a week apart. In the earlier one, the minority opinion included a recommendation that the legislature take action without delay in extending public control over percolating waters by means of State administrative authority. Within a few months, the legislature cooperated by enacting a statute removing the limitation of streams flowing "in known or defined natural channels" from the designation of appropriable waters. This left the designation as "All waters in this state, whether above or under the ground * * *."[63]

(4) California. In this State, the Water Code subjects no other ground water to appropriation except "subterranean streams flowing through known and

---

[59] Idaho Laws 1899, p. 380, § 2, Code Ann. 42-103 (1948).

[60] Idaho Code Ann. § § 42-226 to 42-239 (Supp. 1969).

[61] Controlling decisions: *Hinton* v. *Little*, 50 Idaho 371, 374-380, 296 Pac. 582 (1931); *Silkey* v. *Tiegs*, 51 Idaho 344, 351-353, 5 Pac. (2d) 1049 (1931).

[62] *Wrathall* v. *Johnson*, 86 Utah 50, 40 Pac. (2d) 755 (1935); *Justesen* v. *Olsen*, 86 Utah 158, 40 Pac. (2d) 802 (1935).

[63] Utah Laws 1935, ch. 105, Code Ann. § 73-1-1 (1968).

definite channels."[64] However, the California Supreme Court has held that surplus or excess percolating waters above the quantities to which the paramount rights of overlying landowners attach are subject to appropriation for nonoverlying uses, such as devotion to a public use or exportation beyond the basin or watershed.[65] Nevertheless, as this ground water is excluded from the Water Code declaration just noted, the appropriation procedure provided in the Water Code does not apply to it. The only way in which percolating water can be appropriated in California is by taking the water from the ground and applying it to beneficial use.[66]

(5) Colorado. Ground waters physically tributary to a stream system, whether originating from seepage and waste from irrigation or coming from natural sources, are held by the courts to be a part of the stream and subject to appropriation to the same extent as waters of surface tributaries.[67] This has been the consistent holding of the Colorado courts notwithstanding the proviso in a statute enacted in 1889—and still in effect—declaring that ditches constructed for the purpose of utilizing the waste, seepage, or spring waters of the State shall be governed by the same priority laws as those relating to stream waters, provided that the owner of the lands of origin has the prior right to the water if capable of being used on his lands.[68] This point has been noted earlier under "Statutory Declarations—Miscellaneous."

WHO MAY APPROPRIATE WATER

The legislatures of all Western States which recognize the doctrine of appropriation have something to say about the qualifications of those who are permitted to appropriate water. Some of the statutory provisions are brief, others detailed. Generally, appropriations of water may be made by various persons, public or private group organizations, or governmental agencies and entities.

Nongovernmental Applicants

Person

In providing for appropriation of water within their jurisdictions, the uniform purpose of State legislatures is to subject waters of the State to acquisition of rights of diversion and use by the public generally—pursuant of

---

[64] Cal. Water Code § 1200 (West 1956).

[65] *Pasadena* v. *Alhambra*, 33 Cal. (2d) 908, 925-926, 207 Pac. (2d) 17 (1949).

[66] *Katz* v. *Walkinshaw*, 141 Cal. 116, 134-135, 70 Pac. 663 (1902), 74 Pac. 766 (1903).

[67] *McClellan* v. *Hurdle*, 3 Colo. App. 430, 434-435, 33 Pac. 280 (1893); *Nevius* v. *Smith*, 86 Colo. 178, 181-183, 279 Pac. 44 (1928); *Black* v. *Taylor*, 128 Colo. 449, 459, 264 Pac. (2d) 502 (1953); *Genoa* v. *Westfall*, 141 Colo. 533, 349 Pac. (2d) 370, 378 (1960).

[68] Colo. Rev. Stat. Ann. § 148-2-2 (1963).

course to authorizations, safeguards, and limitations of the enabling statutes. If a particular supply of unappropriated water is available, any member of the public may appropriate it. The original thinking on this is exemplified by the Utah Supreme Court's statements in its second reported decision on rights to the use of water, rendered long before statutory procedure for making appropriations of water in the Territory had been enacted. The court said that if appellants failed to appropaiate the water in litigation, "any stranger could appropriate it," whether or not a member of the local irrigation company; that "This is a free country, * * * and the appropriation of water is open to all."[69] In more recent years, as noted later,[70] the legislative tendency throughout the West has been to authorize qualified applicants to appropriate unappropriated water only if certain prerequisites relating to the public welfare are met.

Natural person, organization, public entity.—Nearly all the statutes refer unqualifiedly either to "any person" or to "every person" as a potential appropriator. Utah requires that such person be a citizen of the United States or one who has filed his declaration of intention to become a citizen.[71] Nevada's specification in this particular is any person, or any citizen of the United States, or any person who has legally declared his intention to become such, "over the age of 21 years."[72] In an early case, the Montana Supreme Court held that an alien could acquire title to a ditch and water right, "and hold the same until office found, against collateral attacks by third persons other than the sovereign," and "in the absence of forfeiture by office found, may convey title to his grantee."[73] In a still earlier case, the Nevada Supreme Court recognized the right of an Indian to appropriate water on the public lands of the United States and to maintain an action for the diversion of such water against his interests.[74]

These western statutory references to qualifications of appropriators are in the form of specific authorizations to persons and other named groups or organizations or entities to appropriate water pursuant to the instant legislation. They are not in the form of a specific mandate that the privileges in question may not be equally enjoyed by others not literally named.

The authorization to "persons" to appropriate water is not confined to natural persons. The term is broader than this. Either expressly or by necessary implication, other classes of potential appropriators with certain rights and responsibilities are recognized. For example, in the Arizona statute the word

---

[69] *Munroe* v. *Ivie,* 2 Utah 535, 537-538 (1880).

[70] See "Methods of Appropriating Water of Watercourses—Restrictions and Preferences in Appropriation of Water—Restrictions on the Right to Appropriate Water."

[71] Utah Code Ann. § 73-3-2 (Supp. 1969).

[72] Nev. Rev. Stat. § § 533.010 (Supp. 1969) and 533.325 (Supp. 1967).

[73] *Quigley* v. *Birdseye,* 11 Mont. 439, 445-446, 28 Pac. 741 (1892).

[74] *Lobdell* v. *Hall* 3 Nev. 507 (1868).

"person" includes the United States, the State, or a municipality.[75] Nevada also includes these classes, with the exception of a municipality, as well as a corporation and association.[76] And in Kansas and South Dakota, all the foregoing, with the addition of a partnership, are included in the definition of "person".[77]

In various other States, the term "person" is impliedly a natural person and other classes are specifically added, such as "any person" and "the United States, the State, and any entity or organization capable of holding an interest in real property in this State."[78] A simple grouping such as "Every person, association or corporation"[79] is used in many statutes.

In other words, a broad statement in a water rights statute as to who may appropriate water propounds qualifications of an appropriator, but not always necessarily all essential qualifications.

Landownership in relation to appropriator qualifications.—This matter is discussed later under "The Land Factor in Appropriating Water," in connection with private lands. It is there brought out that in Arizona there is a judicial rule to the effect that an appropriator of water for irrigation must be either an owner or a possessor of land susceptible of being irrigated. The general subject has been involved in litigation in some other States as well.

Group Organizations

Early statutory and nonstatutory appropriations.—The history of water appropriation law in the Western States begins with appropriations of water made not only by individuals but by group organizations of various kinds.

Before New Mexico became a part of the United States, diversions of water from the Rio Grande and tributary streams had been made for many decades by many community acequias.[80] The Kearny Code, promulgated during the war with Mexico, undertook to protect the laws governing watercourses then in effect and to continue their enforecment.[81] The first Territorial legislature of New Mexico declared that all inhabitants should have the right to construct either private or common acequias and to divert water through such acequias.[82]

Earliest diversions of water by the Mormon settlers in Utah were made as the result of grants or appropriations of water. Originally, the diversions were made through the media of groups of settlers then unorganized, but which

---

[75] Ariz. Rev. Stat. Ann. § § 45-141(A) and 45-142(A) (Supp. 1970).
[76] Nev. Rev. Stat. § § 533.010 (Supp. 1969) and 533.325 (Supp. 1967).
[77] Kans. Stat. Ann. § § 82a-701(a) (1969); S. Dak. Comp. Laws Ann. § 46-1-6(1) (1967).
[78] Cal. Water Code § § 1252 (West Supp. 1970) and 1252.5 (West 1956).
[79] Colo. Rev. Stat. Ann. § 148-1-1 (1963).
[80] Hutchins, Wells A., "The Community Acequia: Its Origin and Development," 31 Southwestern Historical Quarterly 261 (1928).
[81] Kearny Code, § 1.
[82] N. Mex. Laws, July 20, 1851.

grew into towns and districts and eventually in most cases into incorporated or unincorporated mutual irrigation companies. (See the State summary for Utah in the appendix.)

Gold miners and their adversaries, whose controversies gave rise to the California system of appropriative water rights, comprised not only many individuals but also a considerable number of water and mining companies. In fact, in 15 of the 41 earliest reported water rights cases decided by the California Supreme Court (from 1853 to 1863, inclusive) companies were named as principal parties. Thus, the California Supreme Court in many decisions had recognized organizations as adversary appropriators long before the California legislature enacted the first western statute providing a procedure for appropriating water, and designating therein only "persons" as appropriators.[83]

On the other hand, early procedural statutes of several jurisdictions, inspired by the California Civil Code, related specifically to both persons and organizations.[84] In Oregon, the first detailed procedure applied to corporations only, although other sections of the act recognized the existence of appropriations by individuals and provided for their adjudication.[85]

Typical of litigation over water rights in relation to irrigation organizations are two early Colorado decisions—the earlier one pertaining to a company that carried water for hire, the later to a mutual irrigation company.[86]

These early procedures were not exclusive. One could appropriate water validly without complying with their requirements. But compliance with the statutory provisions was important in affording the benefit of the doctrine of relation, which was not accorded to those who failed to comply.

The author is not aware of any high court decision in the West to the effect that an early statutory procedure was not applicable to an intended appropriation by a natural person or an organization for the sole reason that the status of the claimant was not expressly listed in the act. And in the absence of statutes, appropriations of water were widely recognized by the courts regardless of the individual or group characteristics of intending appropriators. Questions over formal title to appropriations of water that arose in connection with diversions for the use of other parties did not necessarily concern the diverter's qualifications to appropriate water for his or its own use.

Appropriations under current statutes.—(1) Corporation. A majority of existing water rights statutes list corporations as potential appropriators.

---

[83] Cal Civ. Code § § 1410-1422 (1872).

[84] For example, person or corporation: Idaho Laws 1881, p. 267. Person, company, or corporation: Nebr. Laws 1889, ch. 68. Person, persons, or association: Wash. Laws 1891, ch. 142.

[85] Oreg. Laws 1891, p. 52.

[86] *Wheeler* v. *Northern Colorado Irr. Co.,* 10 Colo. 582, 17 Pac. 487 (1888); *Combs* v. *Agricultural Ditch Co.,* 17 Colo. 146, 28 Pac. 966 (1892).

Several statutes refer to a "public or private" corporation.[87] Nevada requires the corporation to be authorized to do business in the State.[88] Sections of the Oregon statutes relate variously to appropriations made by public utility water companies and by railway corporations.[89] The Nevada appropriation statute recognizes appropriations of water by commercial companies for transmission to lands of persons for compensation.[90] Many decisions have been rendered by the California Supreme Court relating to State regulation of the rates and services of public utility water corporations.[91]

In most Western States, statutes relating to the organizational affairs of corporations are separate from those relating to appropriation of water. In Texas, however, all statutes authorizing appropriation of water, from the first enactment to the present, likewise authorized and still authorize the formation of corporations for the purpose of supplying water to lands along their canals. The later statutes provide for public regulation of rates charged to consumers. Many of these essentially public-service corporations have been succeeded by irrigation, water improvement, water control and improvement, and other public water districts.[92]

The Oregon Supreme Court had occasion to observe that appropriation of water by a corporation follows the same general rule respecting priority of the right as though made by an individual.[93] The first case decided by the Oklahoma Supreme Court with respect to appropriative water rights involved a controversy between an individual claimant and a corporation of the type commonly known in the West as a mutual irrigation corporation, or cooperative irrigation company. In its corporate capacity, this organization made and defended an appropriation of water for the use of its farmer-shareholders.[94]

(2) Other private group organizations. The majority of western statutes include "association" in their statements of appropriative qualifications. This of course may comprise any number of associates from two or more. The Washington statute includes a water users' association, which was the type of

---

[87] N. Mex. Stat. Ann. § 75-5-1 (1968); S. Dak. Comp. Laws Ann. § 46-5-10 (1967); Tex. Rev. Civ. Stat. Ann. art. 7492 (1954).

[88] Nev. Rev. Stat. § 533.325 (Supp. 1967).

[89] Oreg. Rev. Stat. § § 541.010 and 537.310 (Supp. 1969).

[90] Nev. Rev. Stat. § 533.040 (Supp. 1967). This is in the form of one of the provisos inserted in this section providing for appurtenance of all water to the place of beneficial use. See *Prosole* v. *Steamboat Canal Co.,* 37 Nev. 154, 158-162, 140 Pac. 720, 144 Pac. 744 (1914); *Reno Power, Light & Water Co.* v. *Public Service Commission,* 300 Fed. 645, 648-650 (D. Nev. 1921).

[91] Cal. Railroad Comm., "Public Utility Regulation by the California Railroad Commission" (1927), brings together all supreme court decisions dealing with the jurisdiction and work of the Railroad Commission, now the Public Utilities Commission, to 1927. Of a total of 109 decisions thus reported, 39 were water cases.

[92] Hutchins, Wells A., "The Texas Law of Water Rights," pp. 266-283 (1961).

[93] *In re Hood River,* 114 Oreg. 112, 131, 181, 227 Pac. 1065 (1924).

[94] *Gates* v. *Settlers' Mill., Canal & Res. Co.,* 19 Okla. 83, 85-87, 91 Pac. 856 (1907).

cooperative organization originally preferred by the United States Reclamation Service (now Bureau of Reclamation) in its dealings with water uses on the Federal Reclamation projects. It was one form of the mutual irrigation company. The mutual company organization in its incorporated character is of significant importance in various parts of the West, notably Utah, southern California, and eastern Colorado. It is also found unincorporated in many places. A few statutes list "partnership" and "firm."

(3) Public districts. The only current water appropriation statutes that expressly refer to "irrigation district" are Oregon and Washington.[95] However, this important organization is covered in the all-inclusive language of other statutes. Examples may be cited of two States in which the district form of organization is widely used for distributing water to great aggregate acreages of irrigated land. Thus in California, the irrigation district and the many other kinds of public water districts are included in the statute under the phrase "any entity or organization capable of holding an interest in real property in this State."[96] Texas includes its water improvement district and water control and improvement district—successors of the irrigation district—and other districts and extensive water authorities in the category "political subdivision of the State."[97]

Riparian Proprietor

In the few Western States in which supreme courts have expressed opinions as to whether an owner of riparian land may successfully claim water rights both as a riparian owner and as an appropriator for the service of such land, a majority hold in the affirmative. That is to say, the landowner may be possessed of both riparian and appropriative rights for use on the same tract of land. In Oregon, on the contrary, it is held that for the purpose of the instant proceeding, election of either claim constitutes abandonment of the other.

Views on this question have been expressed in the several high courts as follows.

California. —"It is established in California that a person may be possessed of rights to the use of the waters of a stream both because of the riparian character of the land owned by him and also as an appropriator."[98] Under some circumstances it might be advantageous for such a riparian proprietor to exercise his riparian rather than his appropriative right—for example, if the appropriative right had been acquired after most of the riparian lands on the stream had passed into private ownership, and if the irrigation demands of other riparian owners were considerable. Or an appropriation of winter floodflow for storage might provide the riparian owner with water late in the

---

[95] Oreg. Rev. Stat. § 537.410 (Supp. 1969); Wash. Rev. Code § 90.03.250 (Supp. 1961).

[96] Cal. Water Code § § 1252 (West Supp. 1970) and 1252.5 (West 1956).

[97] Tex. Rev. Civ. Stat. Ann. art. 7942 (1954).

[98] *Rindge* v. *Crags Land Co.,* 56 Cal. App. 247, 252, 205 Pac. 36 (1922).

season after the normal flow becomes too low to be of material use under his riparian right.

However, the privilege of thus claiming dual water rights for the same piece of land does not necessarily result in giving the riparian owner the sum of the quantities of water claimed under each of his rights. It cannot be made a vehicle for acquiring the right to more water than can be put to reasonable beneficial use, which under the California constitution is the limit of all rights to the use of water in the State.[99] The privilege is "qualified only with the condition that the total water claimed under the combined rights does not amount to more than is reasonably necessary to satisfy the necessary uses to which it is designed to be put."[100]

Such an appropriation of water by a riparian owner takes its place in the order of priorities with respect to other appropriators on the same stream. But it has no effect upon an already existing upstream riparian right.[101]

Texas.—The Texas Supreme Court likewise recognizes that a landowner may be a riparian owner and also an appropriator of water for use on his riparian land, and may claim either right without prejudice to his assertion of the other.

Where a plaintiff had complied with the appropriation acts and, in addition as shown by his pleading, his land was clearly riparian, he was held to be entitled to equitable relief.[102] In the landmark case of *Motl* v. *Boyd,* the supreme court held also that the riparian right extends only to the ordinary flow and underflow of the stream, and that storm and floodwaters are open to appropriation. Hence, defendants were not required to obtain a permit to divert and use water under such rights as they had as riparian owners. And as riparians they were not concluded because they had made application for a permit to appropriate storm waters for use on their riparian land.[103]

The riparian landowner in Texas is limited to a reasonable share of the ordinary flow and underflow of the stream, so far as rights of other riparians are concerned. The appropriative right is specifically limited by statute to the quantity of water necessarily required and beneficially used for authorized purposes. Hence, it follows that the quantity of water that a riparian owner in this State might lawfully apply to his land by reason of an appropriation of high flow could not exceed the difference between the amount of his applications of riparian water and his total requirements for beneficial use.

Washington.—In this State also, one may claim rights to the use of water on the same tract of land both as an appropriator and as a riparian proprietor. It is true that in Washington the riparian doctrine has been considerably modified as

---

[99] Cal. Const., art. XIV, § 3.

[100] *Rindge* v. *Crags Land Co.,* 56 Cal. App. 247, 253, 205 Pac. 36 (1922). See *Senior* v. *Anderson,* 130 Cal. 290, 296-297, 62 Pac. 563 (1900).

[101] *McKissick Cattle Co.* v. *Anderson,* 62 Cal. App. 558, 567, 217 Pac. 779 (1923).

[102] *Hoefs* v. *Short,* 114 Tex. 501 510, 273 S.W. 785 (1925).

[103] *Motl* v. *Boyd,* 116 Tex. 82, 124, 286 S.W. 458 (1926).

the result of repeated decisions of the supreme court. (See the prior discussion in chapter 6. See also chapter 10.) However, this court specifically held that a mere assertion of rights by appropriation is not antagonistic to and a waiver of rights arising out of riparian ownership.[104]

In a case in which plaintiffs based their rights to the use of water on three grounds—(1) riparian, (2) appropriation, and (3) contract—the supreme court held that the plaintiffs could not be forced to elect to rely on one cause only.[105]

Oregon.—A riparian owner in Oregon is as competent as anyone else to make an appropriation of water for use on his land, even though it is riparian land. In such case, he may claim a right to the use of the water either as a riparian owner or as an appropriator—but he cannot be both at once.[106]

A reason for the foregoing principle is that one cannot at the same time hold title to the same thing both as a tenant in common and in severalty.[107] To segregate a fixed quantity of water from the whole flow of a stream as it passes one's land and to appropriate such quantity to his exclusive use, said the Oregon Supreme Court, is to destroy one of the essential characteristics of riparian use considered as a tenancy in common. Hence, one who does this abandons the role of a riparian owner and assumes that of a tenant in severalty. Assumption of one of these claims is abandonment of the other.[108] The profound effect of his principle on the development of Oregon water law has been considered elsewhere by this author.[109]

Governmental Agencies and Entities Other than Districts[110]

Municipality

The general situation in the West.—Municipalities occupy a unique place in the water appropriation philosophy of the West. Their identity with early development of water resources in various regions was close. For example, special studies in two of them show: (1) The community acequias in the Southwest, notably in what is now New Mexico, provided not only irrigation water for the lands of the members, but domestic water for their closely grouped homes as well. (2) After towns were incorporated in the settlement of Utah, many of their local councils took control of the water supply ditches and operated and maintained them for long periods of time, until they finally

---

[104] *Nesalhous* v. *Walker*, 45 Wash. 621, 626, 88 Pac. 1032 (1907).

[105] *Hutchinson* v. *Mt. Vernon Water & Power Co.*, 49 Wash. 469, 472, 95 Pac. 1023 (1908).

[106] *State ex rel. Pacific Livestock Co.* v. *Davis*, 116 Oreg. 232, 236, 240 Pac. 882 (1925).

[107] *Caviness* v. *La Grande Irr. Co.*, 60 Oreg. 410, 421-424, 119 Pac. 731 (1911).

[108] *Bowen* v. *Spalding*, 63 Oreg. 392, 395, 128 Pac. 37 (1912).

[109] Hutchins, Wells A., "The Common-Law Riparian Doctrine in Oregon: Legislative and Judicial Modification," 36 Oreg. Law Rev. 193, 200-201, 212-220 (1957).

[110] Districts are considered above under "Nongovernmental Applicants—Person" and "Group Organizations."

graduated into other forms of organization. In fact, the close association existing between the pioneer town, the farming community, and the irrigation system was similar in many respects in the early days in these two Territories.[111] As western municipalities grew apace both in number and in population, and as they naturally required more and more water, it became the accepted practice to give them special treatment in appropriating water for the service of their inhabitants. This of course is entirely aside from their rights of eminent domain in acquiring existing water rights.

The water appropriation statutes of a number of States specifically authorize municipalities to appropriate water. Whether or not the State statute refers in specific terms to municipal appropriations, a municipality in any western jurisdiction unquestionably is as fully qualified to appropriate water for its own beneficial purposes as is any other potential appropriator. On the other hand, as stated, they tend to have special consideration.

The high regard in which the right of a municipality to provide water by appropriation for the requirements of its citizens is held in the West, where demand for water has steadily encroached upon supply, is evidenced by statutes and court decisions in various jurisdictions. Some situations in point are as follows:

Policy declarations.—California: "It is hereby declared to be the established policy of this State that the right of a municipality to acquire and hold rights to the use of water should be protected to the fullest extent necessary for existing and future uses," but not with the right to waste water. "The application for a permit by a municipality for the use of water for the municipality or the inhabitants thereof for domestic purposes shall be considered first in right, irrespective of whether it is first in time."[112]

Texas: "The right to take waters necessary for domestic and municipal supply purposes is primary and fundamental, and the right to recover from other uses, waters essential to such purposes shall be paramount and unquestioned in the policy of the State," pursuant to constitutional and statutory law.[113]

---

[111] See, Hutchins, Wells A.: "The Community Acequia: Its Origin and Development," 31 Southwestern Historical Quarterly 261 (1928); "Mutual Irrigation Companies in Utah," Utah Agr. Expt. Sta. Bull. 199, pp. 16-20 (1927). See also Thomas, George, "The Development of Institutions under Irrigation," pp. 92-116 (1920).

[112] Cal. Water Code § § 106.5 and 1460 (West 1956).

[113] Tex. Rev. Civ. Stat. Ann. art. 7472b (1954).

The Texas Supreme Court has said "In our opinion, Article 7472b, supra, relates solely to the exercise of the power of eminent domain for acquisition of water for domestic, municipal and irrigation purposes and was not intended by the Legislature to be a directive to the Water Rights Commission in passing on competing applications for permits." *City of San Antonio* v. *Texas Water Comm'n,* 407 S. W. (2d) 752, 764 (Tex. 1966). See the discussion at notes 978-979 *infra* regarding articles 7471 and 7472c with respect to municipal and other preferences in appropriating water. See also the

Wyoming: "Municipal corporations shall have the same right as individuals to acquire rights by prior appropriation and otherwise to the use of water for domestic and municipal purposes,* * *."[114]

Preferences in obtaining water supplies.—Wherever preferences in appropriating water are provided for, domestic use stands highest and municipal use is closely associated with it. This results naturally from the indispensability of water to human life, and from the overriding need for water in other activities carried on in human communities.[115]

Appropriation of water by municipality for future use.—(1) Legislation. Statutes of several States provide for appropriation of water to meet the growing needs of municipalities. Thus, in Arizona and Oregon, applications for municipal uses may be approved to the exclusion of all subsequent appropriations if the estimated needs of the municipality so indicate.[116]

A California municipality may appropriate water in excess of its existing needs, the excess being subject to temporary appropriation by others pending the growth of the municipal requirements. When the municipality is ready to use the additional water to which it has claim, the holders of temporary permits are entitled to compensation for the loss of use of their facilities thus rendered valueless. Or in lieu of temporary permits, the municipality may be authorized to become as to the surplus a public utility, subject to the jurisdiction of the State Public Utilities Commission.[117]

In South Dakota, a municipality may appropriate water for contemplated future resonable needs under the procedure applicable to existing needs. Others may make temporary appropriations of the surplus above existing needs pending the time the municipality is ready to use it.[118]

The section of the Utah statute relating to forfeiture of a water right for nonuse for a period of 5 years authorizes extensions of time upon a showing of reasonable cause for such nonuse, one of the reasonable causes thus recognized being "the holding of a water right without use by any municipality * * * to meet the reasonable future requirements of the public."[119]

(2) Court decisions. The water appropriation act of Texas does not, in specific terms, authorize a municipality to make a present appropriation of water for future use. But a court of civil appeals indicated its approval of the

---

discussion at notes 1011-1012 regarding articles 7472 and 7472a which provide that certain appropriations shall be granted subject to the right of municipalities to make later appropriations for domestic and municipal purposes, without condemnation.

[114] Wyo. Const., art. XIII, § 5.

[115] Attention to this aspect of water rights law is given below under the subtopic "Restrictions and Preferences in Appropriation of Water—Preferences in Water Appropriation."

[116] Ariz. Rev. Stat. Ann. § 45-143(B) (1956); Oreg. Rev. Stat. § 537.190(2) (Supp. 1969).

[117] Cal. Water Code § § 1203, 1460, 1461, 1463 (West 1956), 1462 and 1464 (West Supp. 1970).

[118] S. Dak. Comp. Laws Ann. § 46-5-38 (1967).

[119] Utah Code Ann. § 73-1-4 (1968).

validity of such an appropriation.[120] With respect to Corpus Christi, the court observed that: "A city may be reasonably expected to grow and develop over a period of years, and if it does so, its demands for water, as well as other necessaries, would necessarily increase." Hence, the city's failure to make immediate use of all water specified in a 1927 permit did not support a hypothesis of "wilful abandonment."

Courts of several other States also have given sympathetic consideration to reasonable future needs of growing cities. Thus, in 1914, the Wyoming Supreme Court held that the City of Cheyenne was not limited in the amount of its appropriation to the needs of its citizens at the time its early rights were adjudicated. Furthermore, the city had the right to dispose of and apply its surplus water to a beneficial use even outside the city up to the amount of its appropriation, even though by so doing it left no water in the stream for subsequent appropriators.[121]

The Colorado Supreme Court recognized the right of Denver to appropriate water not only for immediate use but for the needs resulting from a normal increase in population within a reasonable time in the future, and to lease the use of water pending its need by the city.[122]

The Idaho Supreme Court has held to the same general effect. Furthermore, a municipality may purchase lands, if necessary, to acquire water for its municipal needs; but after purchase, it is not required to irrigate the lands to which water rights had attached, nor to cause them to be irrigated, in order to avoid loss of the water rights on a charge of abandonment. The power granted to a municipality to acquire and hold water for future needs is "an absolute necessity to the life and existence of a municipality."[123]

Salt Lake City, so the Supreme Court of Utah held, may acquire, develop, and manage such surplus water above its present requirements as is incident to needs reasonably anticipated in the future; it may construct and operate facilities necessary therefor; and it may sell and distribute the surplus outside its corporate limits pending the time the water is needed in the city, without regulation by the State Public Service Commission.[124]

[120] *Lower Nueces River Water Supply Dist.* v. *Cartwright,* 274 S. W. (2d) 199, 208 (Tex. Civ. App. 1954, error refused n.r.e.).

[121] *Holt* v. *Cheyenne,* 22 Wyo. 212, 232, 137 Pac. 876 (1914). See *Van Tassel Real Estate & Live Stock Co.* v. *Cheyenne,* 49 Wyo. 333, 357-359, 54 Pac. (2d) 906 (1936).

[122] *Denver* v. *Sheriff,* 105 Colo. 193, 203-208, 96 Pac. (2d) 836 (1939). The city is protected by statute against the vesting of rights under such leasings that would defeat the city's right to make eventual use of the water: Colo. Laws 1931, ch. 172, Rev. Stat. § 139-79-1 (1963).

[123] *Beus* v. *Soda Springs,* 62 Idaho 1, 6-7, 107 Pac.(2d) 151 (1940). It is not against public policy for a city to appropriate more water than necessary to supply its immediate needs: *Pocatello* v. *Murray,* 206 Fed. 72, 80 (D. Idaho 1913), affirmed, 214 Fed. 214 (9th Cir. 1914).

[124] *County Water System* v. *Salt Lake City,* 3 Utah (2d) 46, 53-54, 278 Pac. (2d) 285 (1954).

The New Mexico Supreme Court has held that a city's appropriative right may extend to its future use to satisfy its needs resulting from normal increase in population within a reasonable period of time. If not so applied, such right may be lost.[125]

Other means of reserving water for future needs of municipality.—A statute enacted by the Texas legislature in 1931, and incorporated into the water appropriation act, accords to "any city, town or municipality of this State" the right to make appropriations of water from streams—other than an international boundary stream, which of course is the Rio Grande—for domestic and municipal purposes, which will supersede appropriations already made after passage of the act for other purposes without the necessity of compensating the holders of the latter, "any law to the contrary notwithstanding."[126] The "appropriations or allotments of water hereafter made" that are subject to this burden are for "hydro-electric power, irrigation, manufacturing, mining, navigation, or any other purposes than domestic or municipal purposes."

In a Federal court suit, it was strongly contended that in granting this right of appropriation from certain streams "without the necessity of condemnation or paying therefor," the Texas act was unconstitutional as applying different rules of priority to the waters of the Rio Grande from those of the Colorado, Trinity, Brazos, and other Texas rivers. However, in holding the act to be not objectionable as reflecting any arbitrary discrimination or repugnant classification, the court observed that a number of things about this international stream tended to bring the statute within the permissible discretion of the legislature. "In short," said the court, "Texas does not and cannot have a free hand with this particular river.* * * The article in question [art. 7472a] is held constitutional."[127]

The legislature of Oregon grants to Portland and certain other cities in the State exclusive rights to appropriate waters of certain named streams for their municipal purposes.[128]

Some other special considerations.—The Oregon legislature's attention to municipal water supply matters is further evidenced by the following: Municipalities are exempted from certain general requirements concerning the time of beginning work under permits to appropriate water, and from cancellation of permits on certain grounds. Municipalities are granted the same rights as those accorded to the State with respect to public recapture of

---

[125] *State* v. *Crider,* 78 N. Mex. 312, 431 Pac. (2d) 45 (1967). The court indicated that such treatment was comparable to that accorded appropriations for anticipated expansion in irrigated acreage. See discussion below under "Methods of Appropriating Water of Watercourses—Completion of Appropriation—Gradual or Progressive Development."

[126] Tex. Rev. Civ. Stat. Ann. arts. 7472 and 7472a (1954).

[127] *El Paso County W. I. Dist. No. 1* v. *El Paso,* 133 Fed. Supp. 894, 906-907 (W. D. Tex. 1955), affirmed in part, reversed in part but not on the matter considered here, 243 Fed. (2d) 927 (5th Cir. 1957), certiorari denied, 355 U.S. 820 (1957).

[128] Oreg. Rev. Stat. § § 538.420-.450 (Supp. 1970).

waterpower rights and properties. Municipal water rights acquired before February 24, 1909—the effective date of the water code of 1909—are confirmed. The State Engineer is directed to reject, or to grant subject to municipal use, all appropriations where, in his judgment, appropriation of the waters applied for impairs a municipal water supply. Municipal corporations are to advise him on request as to the amount and source of the municipal water supply, and any probable increase or extension of the same.[129]

Some of the western water appropriation statutes provide for preferences in appropriating water and for preferred uses of appropriated water, in which domestic and municipal uses are favored.[130]

The State

General observations.—It is within the province of the legislature to declare generally that the State or its agencies may appropriate water. It is likewise the legislature's prerogative to provide special procedure for such appropriation, or even to ignore the subject completely.

If nothing is said in the statute about State appropriations of water, the State executive branch could not be viewed as being thereby precluded from appropriating water for its proper functions. For example, if a water supply were needed for a State administrative or medical or penal institution, and unappropriated water is found available therefor, the State agency in charge of the institution's affairs would be no less competent to appropriate the water for its official functions than would be any other intending appropriator of water for his private needs. Some western State statutes expressly recognize the State or agencies thereof as possible appropriators.

Some individual State situations.—(1) Oregon and Utah. Waters may be withdrawn from general appropriation for specific purposes, including State use, if the legislature chooses to do this or to permit it to be done. The Oregon legislature has so withdrawn waters of a number of streams for purposes, among others, of "maintaining and perpetuating the recreational and scenic resources of Oregon," for public park purposes, and for protection and propagation of game fish.[131] And the State Water Resources Board of Oregon is authorized to make withdrawals of water from appropriation when necessary to comply with requirements of the State water resources policy.[132] In Utah, water may be withdrawn from appropriation by the Governor, on recommendation of the State Engineer, for the purpose of preserving it for use by

---

[129] Oreg. Rev. Stat. § § 537.230, .290, .410 (Supp. 1969), and 538.410 (Supp. 1967).

[130] These matters are discussed later under "Methods of Appropriating Water of Watercourses—Restrictions and Preferences in Appropriation of Water."

[131] Oreg. Rev. Stat. § § 538.110-.300 (Supp. 1967). For a different approach (appropriation of the unappropriated water of a lake by the governor, in trust for the people), see Idaho Code Ann. § 67-4301 (1949), discussed in chapter 8 under "Elements of the Appropriative Right—Purpose of Use of Water—Other Purposes of Use of Water—Recreation".

[132] Oreg. Rev. Stat. § 536.410 (Supp. 1969).

irrigation districts and organized agricultural water users, or "for any use whatsoever," when the welfare of the State demands it. It may be restored to appropriation under the same procedure.[133]

(2) Montana and North Dakota. The Montana Water Resources Board has constructed irrigation projects and acquired and exercised water rights therefor.[134] Neither this Board nor any other public agency has jurisdiction over the acquisition of appropriative water rights. But the Board does have authority to bring action to adjudicate the waters of any stream.[135]

In North Dakota, the State Water Conservation Commission, which likewise has been engaged in water development, is given by the legislature full control over all unappropriated public water of the State to the extent necessary to fulfill the purposes of the statute. The North Dakota State Engineer is the secretary and chief engineer of the Commission and, subject to its approval, may grant water rights under the procedure provided by the statute. For its own purposes, the Commission may initiate a water right by executing a written declaration of intention and filing it in the office of the State Engineer. On completion of construction and application of water to beneficial use, a declaration of completion of the appropriation is filed.[136]

(3) California. The California Water Code specifically confers upon the State the privilege of appropriating water,[137] and contains a part entitled "Appropriation of Water by Department of Water Resources" which is applicable in connection with the State Water Plan.[138]

Restrictions imposed by the California legislature on taking water away from counties and watershed areas in which it originates, in such quantities as to interfere with the proper development of such counties and areas, are mentioned later in connection with preferences in appropriating water resulting from location of land.[139]

---

[133] Utah Code Ann. § § 73-6-1 and 73-6-2 (1968). Such matters are noted later in discussing "Methods of Appropriating Water of Watercourses—Restrictions and Preferences in Appropriation of Water."

[134] See, regarding one aspect of this, *Allendale Irr. Co.* v. *State Water Conservation Board,* 113 Mont. 436, 127 Pac. (2d) 227 (1942).

[135] Mont. Rev. Codes Ann. § § 89-848, -849, -851 (Supp. 1969), -850, and -852 to -855 (1964).

[136] N. Dak. Cent. Code Ann. § § 61-02-32 to 61-02-34, 61-03-01 (1960), 61-02-31, and 61-02-32 (Supp. 1969).

[137] Cal. Water Code § 1252.5 (West 1956).

[138] *Id.,* Div. 6, Pt. 2. The 1959 California Water Resources Development Bond Act (Stats. 1959, ch. 1762) which provided for a 1.75 billion dollar bond issue, was approved by the electorate in 1960. See "Implementation of the California Water Plan," Cal. Dept. of Water Resources Bul. 160-66, p. 18 (March 1966). See also, regarding the California Water Plan, "Water For California, The California Water Plan, Outlook in 1970" (Dec. 1970); *Id.,* Summary Report (Dec. 1970).

[139] See "Methods of Appropriating Water of Watercourses—Restrictions and Preferences in Appropriation of Water—Preferences in Water Appropriation—Acquisition of rights to appropriate water."

The United States

Specific authorization in most statutes.—Most of the western water appropriation statutes specifically include the United States among those who may appropriate water pursuant to the statutes. Kansas and South Dakota include in the definition of "person" any agency of the Federal Government.[140] The North Dakota State Water Conservation Commission, which has supervisory control over the acquisition of all water rights in the State, is fully empowered to contract with the United States, or any of its departments, agencies, or officers, with respect to planning, developing, and handling of any or all waters of the State, whether considered as intrastate or interstate.[141]

Appropriation without specific statutory authorization.—Appropriations of water by the United States pursuant to State laws are recognized in all Western States, regardless of specific enabling mention in the State statute. For example, the Wyoming water rights statute, from the time of its first enactment, has applied in specific terms only to persons, associations, or corporations. Yet in its decision in a leading interstate suit, in which the United States was granted leave to intervene, the United States Supreme Court pointed out that pursuant to the Reclamation Act[142] the Secretary of the Interior made filings for lands in both Wyoming and Nebraska in compliance with the Wyoming water appropriation law, and that these filings were accepted by the State officials as adequate under State law and established the priority dates for the projects.[143]

Special statutory provisions relating to the United States.—Several of the western water appropriation statutes contain special provisions concerning appropriation of water by the United States. These are directed chiefly, but not entirely, at facilitating construction of Federal projects under the Reclamation Act of 1902 as amended.[144]

Thus in Montana, New Mexico, and Oklahoma, prospective appropriations of water are held valid for 3 years in order to afford opportunity for investigation by the Federal Government before actually initiating the appropriative right.[145] The Washington statute authorizes a 1 year period for preliminary investigation of a proposed Federal project, a further period of 3 years, and even more time for detailed investigation if the undertaking appears feasible.[146] In South Dakota, unappropriated waters—except "for uses under

---

[140] Kans. Stat. Ann. § 82a-701(a) (1969); S. Dak. Comp. Laws Ann. § 46-1-6(1) (1967).
[141] N. Dak. Cent. Code Ann. § § 61-02-24, 61-02-24.1, 61-02-28 (Supp. 1969), and 61-02-25 to 61-02-27 (1960).
[142] 32 Stat. 388, § 8, 43 U.S.C. § § 372, 383 (1964).
[143] *Nebraska* v. *Wyoming,* 325 U. S. 589, 611-615 (1945).
[144] 32 Stat. 388, 43 U.S.C. § 371 *et seq.* (1964).
[145] Department of Interior: Mont. Rev. Codes Ann. § 89-808 (1964); Reclamation Act: N. Mex. Stat. Ann. § 75-5-31 (1968); United States: Okla. Stat. Ann. tit. 82, § 91 (1970).
[146] Wash. Rev. Code § 90.40.030 (Supp. 1961).

vested rights and dry draw uses"—may be withdrawn from appropriation for periods not specified in the statute pending the making of investigations by the United States.[147]

Nebraska specifically authorizes the United States to appropriate, develop, and store unappropriated flood or unused waters in compliance with Nebraska law in connection with any project constructed under the Reclamation Act. Detailed provisions, including conducting of water along natural streams, are contained in the enactment.[148]

Under the Idaho statute, the Division of Grazing, United States Department of the Interior, may appropriate water for the purpose of watering livestock on the public domain, subject to certain restrictions on use of the water and duration of the appropriation so required. The statute provides that this authorization shall not be construed to prevent the Bureau of Reclamation from filing application for or completing appropriation of water under the general water appropriation laws of the State.[149]

Oregon provides, among other things, that on any stream system where construction is contemplated by the United States under the Reclamation Act, the State Engineer shall make a hydrographic survey of the stream system and shall furnish to the Attorney General all data necessary for a determination of water rights. On request of the Secretary of the Interior, the State Attorney General and district attorneys in the areas affected are required to bring suit on behalf of the State for such determination of all water rights concerned.[150]

Without reliance upon any statute relating specifically to projects under the Reclamation Act, the Colorado Supreme Court held in 1967 that under the facts in that case there was no intent to take water and no physical demonstration from which such an intent could be inferred so as to constitute the initial step in an appropriation where the Bureau of Reclamation had made only a preliminary study "for information" along with several other studies throughout virtually all of the river basin without any determination as to which particular project might be undertaken.[151] In another case also decided in 1967, the court noted that similar studies had been made by the Bureau of Reclamation except that, since the projects involved in the latter case had been specifically identified in Congressional legislation, they were studied in more

---

[147] S. Dak. Comp. Laws Ann. § 46-5-42 (1967).

[148] Nebr. Rev. Stat. § 46-273 (1968).

[149] Idaho Code Ann. § § 42-501 to -505 (1948).

[150] Oreg. Rev. Stat. § 541.220 (Supp. 1969). Other provisions also relate to Federal reclamation. Section 537.290 exempts the United States from provisions relating to public recapture of water used for power purposes.

[151] *Four Counties Water Users Assn.* v. *Colorado River Water Conservation Dist.*, 161 Colo. 416, 425 Pac. (2d) 259 (1967), cert. denied, 389 U.S. 1049 (1967), reh. denied, 390 U.S. 976 (1968).

detail. But the court concluded that this did not constitute a determination to pursue the particular projects with a definite intention to actually go ahead with them and thereby appropriate water for such purposes.[152]

THE LAND FACTOR IN APPROPRIATING WATER

The general rule in the West is that one at least rightfully in possession of land, even though not the owner, may appropriate water for use in connection with such land. Suggestions have been made that under some circumstances a trespasser on land may appropriate water in connection with that land. Assertions pro and con on these matters of landownership qualification in appropriating water are discussed under succeeding topics. The matter of appurtenance of the appropriative right to land is dealt with in chapter 8.

Historical Development of the Relationship

Public Domain

Prior to Congressional legislation.—In California water law, the appropriation doctrine originated and developed on the public domain without specific guidance from either the California legislature or Congress, but as a result of local customs formulated and applied in the mining camps of the Sierra Nevada foothills, and of interpretations by the State courts of pertinent common law principles. The early California courts held that locations on public land for mining purposes and diversions of water from their natural channels stood on the same footing. Each was the exercise of an implied license from the State with the acquiescence of the Federal Government. As between conflicting claims of location of land and appropriation of water, priority in time would govern.[153] Thus, as between possessors of land or water, where the true owner was not intervening, principles of equity were applied. The presumed license to work the mines and to appropriate water was dependent upon a proviso that the prior rights of others be not thereby infringed.

The principle was thus established that the first appropriator of water of a stream passing over Federal public lands—who had no title to the soil because it was still in the Government—had the right to insist that the water be subject to

---

[152] *Four Counties Water Users Assn.* v. *Middle Park Water Conservation Dist.*, 161 Colo. 429, 425 Pac. (2d) 262 (1967), cert. denied, 389 U.S. 1049 (1967), reh. denied, 390 U.S. 976 (1968).

[153] See *Jennison* v. *Kirk*, 98 U. S. 453, 457-458 (1879); *Irwin* v. *Phillips*, 5 Cal. 140, 146-147 (1855); *Hill* v. *Newman*, 5 Cal. 445, 446 (1855); *Conger* v. *Weaver*, 6 Cal. 548, 555-556 (1856); *Hoffman* v. *Stone*, 7 Cal. 46, 48 (1857); *Crandall* v. *Woods*, 8 Cal. 136, 141, 144 (1857); *Bear River & Auburn Water & Min. Co.* v. *New York Min. Co.*, 8 Cal. 327, 332-333 (1857); *Palmer* v. *Railroad Commission*, 167 Cal. 163, 170-171, 138 Pac. 997 (1914).

his use and enjoyment,[154] to the extent that he thus appropriated it before the rights of others attached,[155] whether such others were locators of mining claims or appropriators of water.[156]

So far as public lands of the United States are concerned, the law of appropriation thus arose through the acts of persons who originally were technically trespassers on the public domain. Rights to water initiated in this way were later recognized by Congress, as against claims of subsequent entrymen, in statutes that contained no provision concerning the qualifications of appropriators. Hence the principle that one might appropriate water for use on public lands without regard to the question of title to the place of use.[157]

Congressional legislation and its effect. (1) Confirmation of right to appropriate water on the public domain. During the years immediately following the Civil War, Congress enacted three measures relating to appropriations of water on the public domain which profoundly influenced and stimulated the spread of the doctrine of prior appropriation throughout the Western States.[158] This topic has been treated heretofore in some detail in connection with establishment of the appropriation doctrine in the West (see chapter 6). Briefly, for the present purpose, the Act of 1866 provided that the owners and possessors of vested and accrued appropriative rights on the public domain as recognized by local customs, laws, and court decisions should be protected in the same. And it acknowledged and confirmed rights of way therefor. The 1870 amendment of section 9 of the 1866 law provided that all patents, preemptions, and homesteads should be subject to water and ditch rights recognized by the Act of 1866. And the Desert Land Act of 1877 provided that water rights on desert lands should depend upon prior appropriation, all surplus water above such rights to be subject to appropriation by others. The Desert Land Act was construed by the United States Supreme Court as applying not only to desert entries in the States and Territories named, but to entries under other land laws as well.[159]

Thus, the right to appropriate water on the public lands—customary in the West from times of earliest settlements—was confirmed by Congress. And the

---

[154] *Butte Canal & Ditch Co.* v. *Vaughn,* 11 Cal. 143, 153-154 (1858).

[155] *Union Water Co.* v. *Crary,* 25 Cal. 504, 509 (1864); *Smith* v. *O'Hara,* 43 Cal. 371, 375 (1872).

[156] *Irwin* v. *Phillips,* 5 Cal. 140, 146-147 (1855); *Crandall* v. *Woods,* 8 Cal. 136, 143-144 (1857).

[157] See discussions by Long, J. R., "A Treatise on the Law of Irrigation," 2d ed., § 102 (1916); Wiel, S. C., "Water Rights in the Western States," 3d ed., vol. I, § 319 (1911); Kinney, C. S., "A Treatise on the Law of Irrigation and Water Rights," 2d ed., vol. II, § § 687, 766, 767 (1912).

[158] 14 Stat. 253, § 9 (1866); 16 Stat. 218 (1870); 19 Stat. 377 (1877), 43 U.S.C. § 321 *et seq.* (1964).

[159] *California Oregon Power Co.* v. *Beaver Portland Cement Co.,* 295 U.S. 142. 160-163 (1935).

retroactive effect of the legislation upon appropriations already made on the public lands was declared and established by the United States Supreme Court. What Congress did, in the Court's opinion, was to recognize an existing right of possession—which by reason of the Government's silent acquiesence it was in duty bound to do—rather than to establish a new right.[160] But it did even more than that. The effect of the Acts of 1866 and 1870 was not limited to rights acquired before 1866 but reached into the future as well. It approved the policy of appropriation as recognized by local laws, customs, legislation, and judicial decisions, as the test and measure of private rights in and to the nonnavigable waters on the public domain.[161] Appropriators on unsurveyed public lands were no longer to be regarded as even technical trespassers. They were rightful occupants.[162]

(2) Relation to local customs and laws. The Act of 1866 applies specifically to appropriative rights that "have vested and accrued" and that "are recognized and acknowledged by the local customs, laws, and decisions of courts." The consistent policy of the United States Government, according to a Federal court in 1931, "has been * * * to allow the citizens of the various states to work out their own system of law with relation to water rights without intervention or adverse legislation by the federal government."[163]

A few years later the Supreme Court held that the effect of the Desert Land Act was not to curtail the power of the States affected to legislate as they might deem wise with respect to water rights. It left each of them free "to determine for itself to what extent the rule of appropriation or the common law rule in respect of riparian rights should obtain."[164] It follows that claims of right that are not recognized and acknowledged by these local laws are not protected by the Congressional legislation.[165]

(3) Early State court views regarding land-water relationship. For many years, high courts of California, Oregon, and Washington took the position that the right to appropriate water was confined to waters flowing over public lands of the United States or of the State. This came about because of the historical origin of the western appropriation doctrine on public lands, and of the measures taken by Congress to protect water rights acquired on the public

---

[160] *Jennison* v. *Kirk*, 98 U. S. 453, 459 (1879); *Broder* v. *Water Co.*, 101 U. S. 274, 276 (1879).

[161] *California Oregon Power Co.* v. *Beaver Portland Cement Co.* 295 U. S. 142, 154-155 (1935).

[162] *Ely* v. *Ferguson*, 91 Cal. 187, 190, 27 Pac. 587 (1891).

[163] *United States* v. *Central Stockholders' Corporation of Vallejo*, 52 Fed. (2d) 322, 329 (9th Cir. 1931).

[164] *California Oregon Power Co.* v. *Beaver Portland Cement Co.*, 295 U.S. 142, 163-164 (1935).

[165] *McKenzie* v. *Moore*, 20 Ariz. 1, 4-5, 176 Pac. 568 (1918); *San Joaquin & Kings River Canal & Irr. Co.* v. *Worswick*, 187 Cal. 674, 682-684, 685, 203 Pac. 999 (1922); *Taylor* v. *Abbott*, 103 Cal. 421, 423-424, 37 Pac. 408 (1894).

domain pursuant to local customs, laws, and court decisions. Most western lands were then in public ownership. Necessarily, the early relationship of appropriative rights to public lands was close and, at first, of vital importance.

Thus, in California, the claimant of an appropriative right had the burden of showing that it pertained to public lands of the United States.[166] As late as 1921, the California Supreme Court commented that an appropriation of waters flowing through private lands, made under the Civil Code, was but another form of prescription.[167] In Oregon, it was held that the doctrine of appropriation applied only to rights acquired under the Act of Congress of 1866.[168] And the Washington Supreme Court said that "the doctrine of appropriation applies only to public lands, and when such lands cease to be public and become private property, it is no longer applicable."[169] These views were expressed and reiterated in one form or another in many court decisions in these States.

This judicial association of appropriation of water with public land exclusively—except where prescriptive rights vested through adverse possession and use of water as against private lands—developed in jurisdictions in which the riparian doctrine was also accepted. It was based on the view that by these Acts of Congress, the United States waived its riparian streamflow rights with respect to its own riparian lands in these jurisdictions in favor of intending appropriators of water of the same stream; but that when any parcel of land contiguous to a stream passed to private ownership, it immediately became vested with a riparian water right in such stream. When this occurred, the now privately owned parcel contiguous to the stream, and use of the water flowing by or across the land and necessary for its enjoyment, were immune from attack by any subsequent appropriator. From this, there was deduced the narrow and artificial relationship of water appropriation to public land only.

The high courts of these jurisdictions clung tenaciously to this concept for a long time. They were sometimes disposed to revert to it even after the general tide had turned.[170] Eventually, however, in line with the trend toward restricting application of the riparian doctrine as against appropriations of water, the narrow concept was altered. Riparian rights, where recognized at all, were limited to the actual water needs of riparian landowners. Whether the stream flowed across public or private lands, or both, riparian owners had no claim on excess water.

Now the law in these jurisdictions is that surplus waters in a source of supply above the quantities to which prior appropriative rights and riparian

---

[166] *Santa Cruz* v. *Enright,* 95 Cal. 105, 113, 30 Pac. 197 (1892).

[167] *San Bernardino* v. *Riverside,* 186 Cal. 7, 13, 198 Pac. 784 (1921).

[168] *Simmons* v. *Winters,* 21 Oreg. 35, 42, 27 Pac. 7 (1891).

[169] *Benton* v. *Johncox,* 17 Wash. 277, 289, 49 Pac. 495 (1897).

[170] See *Wallace* v. *Weitman,* 52 Wash. (2d) 585, 586-587, 328 Pac. (2d) 157 (1958).

rights attach are public waters of the State, subject to appropriation.[171] The appropriable character of the stream flow does not change as it passes from public to private land and vice versa.

(4) Places of diversion and use. The cases dealing with appropriations of water on the public domain have been concerned chiefly with the location of the point of diversion of the water. Of course, this is an essential factor in orienting the diversions of conflicting claimants on the same stream and in establishing relative priorities. However, diversions of water from streams on the public lands for the purpose of making beneficial use of the water on other public lands were customarily made in the early mining period in the Sierra foothills of California, in the Mormon colonies in Utah under the Latter-day Saint Church leadership, and in many places elsewhere in the West both before and after the public land laws became locally operative. That this might be lawfully done was asserted in decisions in various cases.[172]

Relative possessory rights in the tract on which the diversion was made, and that to which the water was taken for mining or irrigation or other use, were matters of land law, not water law.

(5) Additional case references. Some additional decisions in courts of the United States and of Territories and States on the effect of the Congressional legislation discussed herein are cited in the accompanying footnote.[173]

---

[171] *Meridian* v. *San Francisco*, 13 Cal. (2d) 424, 445-447, 90 Pac. (2d) 537 (1939). An appropriation validly made on private land has fully as much force as one made on public land: *Caviness* v. *La Grande Irr. Co.*, 60 Oreg. 410, 423-424, 119 Pac. 731 (1911). "Defendants' contention that the doctrine of appropriation of water applies only to public lands has been rejected by this court." *Drake* v. *Smith*, 54 Wash. (2d) 57, 61, 337 Pac. (2d) 1059 (1959).

[172] For Some California cases, see *Ely* v. *Ferguson*, 91 Cal. 187, 190, 27 Pac. 587 (1891); *Williams* v. *Harter*, 121 Cal. 47, 50, 53 Pac. 405 (1898); *Sherwood* v. *Wood*, 38 Cal. App. 745, 749, 177 Pac. 491 (1918).

[173] Territorial and State courts: *Gila Water Co.* v. *Green*, 27 Ariz. 318, 324-327, 232 Pac. 1016 (1925); *Parker* v. *McIntyre*, 47 Ariz. 484, 491, 56 Pac. (2d) 1337 (1936).

Silver Lake Power & Irr. Co. v. *Los Angeles*, 176 Cal. 96, 101-102, 167 Pac. 697 (1917).

Coffin v. *Left Hand Ditch Co.*, 6 Colo. 443 (1882); *Beaver Brook Res. & Canal Co.* v. *St. Vrain Res. & Fish Co.*, 6 Colo. App. 130, 40 Pac. 1066 (1895); *Edwards* v. *Roberts*, 26 Colo. App. 538, 144 Pac. 856 (1914); *Bowers* v. *McFadzean*, 82 Colo. 138, 257 Pac. 361 (1927).

Youngs v. *Regan*, 20 Idaho 275, 278-280, 118 Pac. 499 (1911).

Gallagher v. *Basey*, 1 Mont. 457, 460-462 (1872), affirmed, 87 U. S. 670, 681-684 (1875); *Atchison* v. *Peterson*, 1 Mont. 561, 569 (1872), affirmed, 87 U. S. 507, 510-514 (1874); *Ryan* v. *Quinlan*, 45 Mont. 521, 531, 124 Pac. 512 (1912).

Jones v. *Adams*, 19 Nev. 78, 86, 6 Pac. 442 (1885); *Twaddle* v. *Winters*, 29 Nev. 88, 105-106, 85 Pac. 280 (1906), 89 Pac. 289 (1907).

State ex rel. State Game Commission v. *Red River Valley Co.*, 51 N. Mex. 207, 269-270, 182 Pac. (2d) 421 (1945); *State ex rel. Bliss* v. *Dority*, 55 N. Mex. 12, 21-22, 225 Pac. (2d) 1007 (1950), appeal dismissed, 341 U. S. 924 (1951).

Hough v. *Porter*, 51 Oreg. 318, 383-386, 95 Pac. 732 (1908), 98 Pac. 1083 (1909),

State Lands

Appropriation of water by State for use of State lands.—The power of the legislature of a State to authorize, either expressly or by implication, the State government or any of its agencies to appropriate water for proper purposes is no more debatable than its power to authorize individuals to do so. This is mentioned earlier under "Who May Appropriate Water." The instrumentality used in making water available for specific State lands, or for such lands in general—whether grant or appropriation, or as to permissible method of appropriation—is within the discretion of the law-making body.

Appropriation by others in relation to State lands.—In addition to what the State chooses to do in making unappropriated water available for use of its own lands, there is some legislation concerning appropriations by others in relation to State lands. Thus the State of California, by enactment of the Civil Code,[174] is held by its supreme court to have consented to the taking, by an appropriator pursuant to the code procedure, of the water of any stream in which the State held riparian rights, by virtue of its ownership of land contiguous to such streams, at the time of such appropriation. Appropriators under the Civil Code thereby acquired rights superior to the riparian rights of lands owned by the State on the same stream when the appropriations were made before the riparian lands passed into private ownership. But the riparian rights of lands acquired from the State are superior to appropriative rights of lands on the same stream which were *acquired after* the riparian lands passed into private ownership because, although the State might have reserved from its grants of land the waters flowing through them for the benefit of subsequent appropriators, it had not done so. Section 1422, which provided that the rights of riparian owners should not be affected by the provisions of the statute, saved and protected the rights of grantees who acquired land from the State before proceedings to appropriate water under the code provisions were initiated.[175]

---

102 Pac. 728 (1909); *Caviness* v. *La Grande Irr. Co.,* 60 Oreg. 410, 424, 119 Pac. 731 (1911); *Davis* v. *Chamberlain,* 51 Oreg. 304, 315, 98 Pac. 154 (1908); *Laurance* v. *Brown,* 94 Oreg. 387, 395, 185 Pac. 761 (1919).

Some Federal court decisions: *Krall* v. *United States,* 79 Fed. 241, 242-243 (9th Cir. 1897), appeal dismissed, 174 U. S. 385, 389-391 (1899); *Almo Water Co.* v. *Jones,* 39 Fed. (2d) 37, 38-39 (9th Cir. 1930); *United States* v. *Walker River Irr. Dist.,* 104 Fed. (2d) 334, 336-337, 339-340 (9th Cir. 1939).

Some United States Supreme Court decisions: *Atchison* v. *Peterson,* 87 U. S. 507 (1874); *Basey* v. *Gallagher,* 87 U. S. 670 (1875); *Sturr* v. *Beck,* 133 U. S. 541, 550-551 (1890); *United States* v. *Rio Grande Dam & Irr. Co.,* 174 U. S. 690, 703-710 (1899); *Gutierres* v. *Albuquerque Land & Irr. Co.,* 188 U. S. 545, 552-556 (1903); *San José Land & Water Co.* v. *San José Ranch Co.,* 189 U. S. 177, 183-184 (1903). See *Forbes* v. *Gracey,* 94 U. S. 762, 766-767 (1877).

174 Cal. Civ. Code § § 1410-1422 (1872).

175 *Lux* v. *Haggin,* 69 Cal. 255, 368-376, 4 Pac. 919 (1884), 10 Pac. 674 (1886). See also *Antioch* v. *Williams Irr. Dist.,* 188 Cal. 451, 463, 205 Pac. 688 (1922); *Palmer* v.

The declaration in the California Civil Code, while binding the State as to its proprietary lands bordering on nonnavigable streams, does not affect lands of other persons or water rights pertaining thereto.[176]

The Idaho Supreme Court held that a water right may be perfected by a lessee of State land for use in connection with such land. If a water right is initiated by a lessee of private land, according to the court, the water right is the lessee's property unless he was acting as agent of the owner. There is no reason why a lessee of State land should be excepted from this privilege.[177]

Montana, according to its supreme court, by necessary implication assumed to itself the ownership, *sub modo,* of the rivers and streams of the jurisdiction. By legislation authorizing appropriation of the water—first adopted by the Territory[178] and continued by the State[179]—Montana expressly granted the right to appropriate waters of such streams, and conferred upon anyone the right to make a valid appropriation of water on unsold State lands.[180] An appropriation of water for use on State school land, leased by the irrigator from the State, was held to be not invalid because title to the land was not in the appropriator.[181]

Under the facts and circumstances of an Oregon case, the supreme court held that a squatter on State land who initiated a water right thereon had a right to sell his improvements and water rights to one who later acquired title to the land.[182]

The first Texas statute authorizing appropriation of water and providing procedure for acquiring rights of use, enacted in 1889, was applicable only to the arid regions of the State.[183] This statute, the supreme court held, could not operate and probably was not intended to operate on the rights of existing owners of private riparian lands. It was intended to operate only on such interests as were in the State by reason of its ownership of riparian lands. The court concluded that the State, in authorizing appropriation of unappropriated waters of every river or natural stream in the arid areas, thereby consented to the making of such appropriations insofar as the rights of its own lands were concerned.[184]

Railroad Commission, 167 Cal. 163, 172, 138 Pac. 997 (1914); *Hand* v. *Carlson,* 138 Cal. App. 202, 209-210, 31 Pac. (2d) 1084 (1934).

[176] *Duckworth* v. *Watsonville Water & Light Co.,* 170 Cal. 425, 432, 150 Pac. 58 (1915).

[177] *First Security Bank of Blackfoot* v. *State,* 49 Idaho 740, 745-746, 291 Pac. 1064 (1930).

[178] Mont. Laws 1885, p. 130.

[179] Mont. Rev. Codes Ann. § 89-801 *et seq.* (1964).

[180] *Smith* v. *Denniff,* 24 Mont. 20, 22, 60 Pac. 398 (1900).

[181] *Sayre* v. *Johnson,* 33 Mont. 15, 20, 81 Pac. 389 (1905).

[182] *Campbell* v. *Walker,* 137 Oreg. 375, 385, 2 Pac. (2d) 912 (1931).

[183] Tex. Laws 1889, ch. 88.

[184] *McGhee Irr. Ditch Co.* v. *Hudson,* 85 Tex. 587, 591-592, 22 S.W. 398, 967 (1893).

Questions of rights-of-way granted by a State over its own lands are discussed later under "Rights-of-Way for Water Control and Related Purposes."

Private Lands

Appropriator's Ownership of Land Used

General rule: At least rightful possession.—According to the weight of authority, one at least rightfully in possession of land, even though not the owner, may make a valid appropriation in connection with such land, which water right remains his own property. Some variations that occur from State to State are refinements of this general rule.

On the public domain the original appropriators of water were technically trespassers—they were "squatters," with no formal right of possession or even of entry. But the Federal Government silently acquiesced in the occupancy of its lands by miners and appropriators of water, and Congress finally acknowledged and confirmed the right of these people to take these steps.[185] This legislation the United States Supreme Court held was both retroactive and prospective in its operation.[186]

When the Federal land laws became operative in these far western regions, lawful occupancy with intent to appropriate the land and the water, and accompanying acts that evidenced the intent, were sufficient to put in motion the process of acquiring patent to the land and completion of the appropriative right. The patent evidenced private title to the land. The priority of the appropriative right related back to the first act in the process of appropriation, whatever that may have been under the laws of the particular jurisdiction.

From the time of enactment of the Act of 1866, it was the clearly expressed intent of Congress that appropriations of water could be made on the public lands of the United States in accordance with local laws and customs, and that necessary rights of way across the public land could be obtained therefor. Questions of title to the land and title to the water right lay in different fields of jurisprudence. The former related to Federal land law, the latter to local water law. To allow individuals to appropriate water on the public domain during the long period in which the appropriation doctrine was developing in the West, it was necessary to authorize appropriations by possessors of the land for the simple reason that the United States was the only owner.

A glance at the western appropriation laws enacted during the last half of the 19th century shows that questions of relationships between appropriation of water and possession of the land on which the water might be applied and the appropriation completed, were in the minds of many early legislators. The first Territorial legislature of Colorado declared that persons claiming, owning, or possessing rights or title to land on the bank or margin or in the neighborhood of any stream should be entitled to use of the water thereof for purposes of irrigation and making the land available to the full extent of the

---

[185] 14 Stat. 253, § 9 (1866); 16 Stat. 218 (1870); 19 Stat. 377 (1877), 43 U.S.C. § 321 *et seq.* (1964).

[186] This is discussed above under "The Land Factor in Appropriating Water—Historical Development of the Relationship—Public Domain."

soil for agricultural purposes.[187] Montana followed suit in 1865,[188] and Wyoming in 1875.[189] The Territory of Dakota enacted a similar declaration in 1881.[190] These four Territorial statutes were not identical in wording—such as items including both grantees and holders of possessory title and recognition of pre-existing rights. But they were alike in relating the water right to land holdings or claims contiguous to or in the neighborhood of streams. The Washington State statute of 1890 provided that a person holding a possessory right to land in the vicinity of a natural stream or lake, but not abutting thereon, might take unappropriated water therefrom.[191]

As against a claim of riparian right under the Wyoming statute, the State supreme court held that the statute did not refer to riparian owners only, but extended to all those who claimed land in the neighborhood of a stream.[192] In commenting on this statute, Wyoming's first State Engineer, Elwood Mead, emphasized that it made the ownership of land rather than the construction of ditches the foundation of the water right.[193]

The early California cases were decided before the Congressional statutes were enacted. They emphasized that the right to running water existed "without private ownership of the soil—upon the ground of prior location upon the land, or prior appropriation and use of the water."[194] The California courts continued to hold to this principle.[195]

The Colorado Supreme Court held it unnecessary to determine whether predecessors of plaintiffs, who claimed water rights, held title to the land in fee simple. "It is sufficient, in order to perfect an appropriation to the right to use of water, if they had only an uncompleted or unfinished title. This right they could have acquired separate and apart from the land."[196]

Elsewhere in the West, the high courts hold to the view that a fee simple title to the land used is not necessary to the validity of an appropriation of water, but many of them require at least a possessory claim. The chief differences are as to what constitutes a possessor for such purpose. The overall situation can be best illustrated by some State examples, as follows.

[187] Colo. Laws 1861, p. 67.
[188] Bannack Stat., p. 367 (1865).
[189] Wyo. Comp. Laws, ch. 65 (1876).
[190] Terr. Dak. Laws 1881, ch. 142.
[191] Wash. Laws 1889-90, ch. 21, § § 7 and 8.
[192] *Moyer* v. *Preston*, 6 Wyo. 308, 318-320, 44 Pac. 845 (1896).
[193] Mead, Elwood, "Irrigation Institutions," p. 248 (1903).
[194] *Hill* v. *Newman*, 5 Cal. 445, 446 (1855). See also *Crandall* v. *Woods*, 8 Cal. 136, 142 (1857); *Hill* v. *King*, 8 Cal. 336, 338 (1857).
[195] Forty years later, in *Santa Paula Water Works* v. *Peralta*, 113 Cal. 38, 43, 45 Pac. 168 (1896), the court held that title or the right to acquire title in the place of intended use has never been a necessary element of the right to appropriate water in California. See *Joerger* v. *Pacific Gas & Electric Co.*, 207 Cal. 8, 34, 276 Pac. 1017 (1929).
[196] *Kountz* v. *Olson*, 94 Colo. 186, 191, 29 Pac. (2d) 627 (1934).

In Idaho, water may be appropriated for beneficial use on land not owned by the appropriator, who nevertheless becomes the owner of the water right.[197] The test of a valid appropriation of water is its diversion from the natural source and its application to a beneficial use, not title to the land as between water claimants.[198]

The right to appropriate water in Oregon exists without private ownership in the soil or without perfect title thereto, as against all persons except the Government or its grantees. "Such right acquired by an appropriation and beneficial use upon land in the quiet possession of the appropriator and upon which he had made valuable improvements and reclaimed in part, is not dependent upon the title to the soil upon which the water is used."[199]

The courts of Texas have not held that the validity of an appropriative right depends on the appropriator's holding title to the land in connection with which the right is exercised. However, in administering the current water appropriation act, the Texas Water Rights Commission refuses to accept an application from any individual who does not own the land to be irrigated.[200]

The Utah Supreme Court holds that one may appropriate water for use on a specific tract of land without having title to the land.[201] In general, says the court, a right to the use of water is independent of the right to land.[202] However, in refusing to sustain an attempted appropriation of water to irrigate unenclosed and unoccupied public land for the sole purpose of producing food for wild waterfowl, the Utah court held that there must be some type of possessory right in the appropriator good as against all but the Government.[203]

The Montana rule does not require fee simple title in the appropriator to land to be irrigated under his right.[204] It does apparently contemplate that if the appropriator does not own the land he intends to irrigate, at least rightful possession—that is, a possessory interest— is necessary to his acquisition of a valid water right.[205] This requirement is satisfied by lawful entry and settlement on public lands or a *bona fide* intent to acquire title to both land

---

[197] *First Security of Blackfoot* v. *State*, 49 Idaho 740, 746, 291 Pac. 1064 (1930); *Sanderson* v. *Salmon River Canal Co.*, 34 Idaho 145, 160, 199 Pac. 999 (1921).

[198] *Sarret* v. *Hunter*, 32 Idaho 536, 541-542, 185 Pac. 1072 (1919).

[199] *Laurance* v. *Brown*, 94 Oreg. 387, 396, 185 Pac. 761 (1919).

[200] Tex. Water Rights Comm'n, "Rules, Regulations and Modes of Procedure," rule 225.1 under "225. Additional Requirements for Irrigation" (1970 Rev., Jan. 1970).

[201] *Jensen* v. *Birch Creek Ranch Co.*, 76 Utah 356, 362, 289 Pac. 1097 (1930).

[202] *Witmore* v. *Salt Lake City*, 89 Utah 387, 397-400, 57 Pac. (2d) 726 (1936).

[203] *Lake Shore Duck Club* v. *Lake View Duck Club*, 50 Utah 76, 80-82, 166 Pac. 309 (1917).

[204] *St. Onge* v. *Blakely*, 76 Mont. 1, 18, 245 Pac. 532 (1926); *Thomas* v. *Ball*, 66 Mont. 161, 166, 213 Pac. 597 (1923).

[205] *Tucker* v. *Jones*, 8 Mont. 225, 229, 19 Pac. 571 (1888).

and water, or by one holding lands under contract for its purchase.[206] Also acceptable is rightful possession of land under a contract with the owner the nature of which does not appear in the record.[207]

The Washington Supreme Court rendered conflicting decisions on the question of landownership as a qualification of an appropriator of water. Apparently, it came to favor the principle that the appropriator need not own the land in order to initiate the appropriation, but that if the proposed appropriation is to be perfected, he must necessarily make some arrangements to operate the land on which he expects to complete the appropriation by application of the water to beneficial use.[208]

In 1924, without mentioning the earlier Washington cases, the supreme court stated that it was not necessary that an appropriator be the owner of any lands, riparian or otherwise.[209] Two years later, without referring to the 1924 decision and without citation of any authorities, the supreme court said that while it had held, as was done generally, that an appropriator of water need not own any land in order to make a valid appropriation, it is equally true that an appropriation of water is only valid to the extent of lands which may be acquired and to which the water is applied beneficially and with reasonable diligence.[210] The point at issue in this case was not landownership as a qualification of an appropriator. The question was whether an appropriative right could be "tacked" onto an original appropriation for a much larger tract than was ever irrigated or eventually acquired. This, it was held, could not be done.

The Arizona rule. – The Arizona rule with respect to the landownership qualification question, as declared by the courts of the State, is specific. For many decades this has been so. This is true despite the legislative recognition of "any person" as an appropriator under the statute.

In 1901, the Territorial supreme court stated that under the Spanish and Mexican laws enforced in the State of Sonora, of which Arizona had formed a part, landholding was the basis for any valid appropriation of water from a public stream, and that this became a part of the Territorial laws.[211] Long after

---

[206] *St. Onge* v. *Blakely,* 76 Mont. 1, 18, 23, 245 Pac. 532 (1926).

[207] *Smith* v. *Denniff,* 24 Mont. 20, 28-29, 60 Pac. 398 (1900).

[208] *Thorpe* v. *Tenem Ditch Co.,* 1 Wash. 566, 570, 20 Pac. 588 (1889), negated the requirement of landownership, referring to Wash. Laws 1873, p. 520, which authorizea holders of title or possessory right to agricultural lands in Yakima County to appropriate water for irrigation. In *Avery* v. *Johnson,* 59 Wash. 332, 334, 109 Pac. 1028 (1910), the court announced that one who seeks to claim water for irrigating agricultural land by appropriation must own the land or be an actual *bona fide* settler having a possessory interest, with evidence of an intent to acquire title, and that a mere squatter can claim no water right. This was followed in *Sander* v. *Bull,* 76 Wash. 1, 6, 135 Pac. 489 (1913).

[209] *In re Alpowa Creek,* 129 Wash. 9, 17, 224 Pac. 29 (1924).

[210] *In re Ahtanum Creek,* 139 Wash. 84, 98-99, 245 Pac. 758 (1926).

[211] *Slosser* v. *Salt River Valley Canal Co.,* 7 Ariz. 376, 385-386, 393 65 Pac. 332 (1901), appeal dismissed, 195 U.S. 639 (1904); *Biggs* v. *Utah Irrigating Ditch Co.,* 7 Ariz. 331, 350-351, 64 Pac. 494 (1901).

enactment of the water rights appropriation statute, the State supreme court agreed that this principle had been the law of the Territory since its foundation, and held that it still was the law.[212]

In Arizona, therefore, the appropriator of water for irrigation must be either the *owner* or the *possessor* of land susceptible of being irrigated. "Possessor" implies the following qualifications:[213]

(1) To make a valid appropriation of water for use on the land possessed, he must have a present intent and apparent future ability to acquire ownership of the land. A temporary possessor cannot make an appropriation.

(2) As a necessary corollary, a lessee of land cannot initiate an appropriative right that inures to the benefit of his lessor. The lessor must make the appropriation.

Initiation of Appropriative Right in Trespass

The first appropriations of water in Utah and California were made by trespassers on the public domain, which initially belonged to Mexico and in 1848 was ceded to the United States. As discussed previously in this chapter, the Federal Government silently acquiesced in the practice; and Congress eventually enacted legislation acknowledging and confirming the water rights and rights of way of these previously technical trespassers and authorized further appropriation of water on the public lands—if made in conformity with local laws, customs, and judicial decisions.

The situation with respect to private land, however, is different. The general rule is that an appropriative right initiated in trespass on private land is voidable as against the owner of the land.

Some early differences.—It is true that a few decisions—none rendered in recent years—favored recognition of appropriations initiated in trespass on private land. For example, in the early case of *Smith* v. *Logan,* the Nevada Supreme Court held that one who irrigated a tract of land in connection with which he was a trespasser had validly initiated an appropriative right therefor, which he could have changed to other land when he lost possession of the original tract. According to the court, the water had not become appurtenant to the disputed tract, and the successful possessor had not connected himself with the trespasser's right to the use of the water.[214] But the Nevada court later held that acts of trespass that threatened to become the foundation of a prescriptive right might be enjoined, because an intending appropriator has no right to go upon the land of another without either permission or condemnation for the purpose of appropriating water.[215]

A few years after rendition of the Nevada decision in *Smith* v. *Logan,* the California Supreme Court fully conceded that under that decision the use of

---

[212] *Tattersfield* v. *Putnam,* 45 Ariz. 156, 168-174, 41 Pac. (2d) 228 (1935).

[213] *Id.* at 171-172, 174.

[214] *Smith* v. *Logan,* 18 Nev. 149, 154, 1 Pac. 678 (1883).

[215] *Bidleman* v. *Short,* 38 Nev. 467, 471, 150 Pac. 834 (1915).

the water by a trespasser on private land does not make such water appurtenant to such land. But, the court stated, "it does not follow from this that the use of water upon land to which it is already appurtenant, by one who is a trespasser thereon, will give him such a right in the water as that he may thereafter divert it from the land, or upon being ejected therefrom, convey to a stranger a legal title in the water or in the use thereof."[216]

In 1910, the Utah Supreme Court rejected the concept of a necessary relationship between the right to use spring water on the public domain and "some right or title in and to" the lands around the spring or on which the water was applied. The court observed that the authorities sanction a rule that even a trespasser on land may acquire the exclusive right to the use of water used thereon; that when once acquired, such a right is paramount to the rights of the true owner or claimant of the land; and that when the water claimant is dispossessed of the land, he may divert and use the water elsewhere.[217] Some 40 years later, this court noted that the question had not been settled in Utah. The court stated that had one of the parties deliberately gone on another's land to make an appropriation of water, knowing that he was committing a trespass, "it might well be that such trespass would nullify his right to appropriate this water." However, the parties here had stipulated that defendant believed the area to be Government land.[218]

While making no decision on the point in the latter case, because under the circumstances none was called for, the more mature view of the Utah court is therefore opposed to giving an appropriator who deliberately trespasses on private land this advantage. Supreme courts of other Western States that have expressed themselves on this matter agree with Utah. However, there are differences in the extent of the penalty thus imposed.

Voidability as against the owner of land trespassed upon.—In some court opinions, it is stated broadly that a valid water right cannot be initiated by trespass on private land;[219] or that a permit to appropriate water cannot be acquired through such trespass;[220] or that one who appropriated water under the statutory procedure but who made the diversion on another's land by trespass thereon had no interest in or to such water by virtue of certificates of water right issued by the State Engineer.[221] There are, however, situations in

---

[216] *Alta Land & Water Co.* v. *Hancock,* 85 Cal. 219, 228-229, 24 Pac. 645 (1890). This case had to do with trespass on private riparian land. The court held that nothing was acquired by conveyances from the trespassers during pendency of the ejectment suit, for they had nothing to convey. Nothing was taken from the rights of the riparian owners by the trespassers' acts.

[217] *Patterson* v. *Ryan,* 37 Utah 410, 415, 108 Pac. 1118 (1910).

[218] *Riordan* v. *Westwood,* 115 Utah 215, 232-233, 203 Pac. (2d) 922 (1949).

[219] *Geary* v. *Harper,* 92 Mont. 242, 251, 12 Pac. (2d) 276 (1932).

[220] *Idaho Power Co.* v. *Buhl,* 62 Idaho 351, 357, 111 Pac. (2d) 1088 (1941).

[221] *Minton* v. *Coast Property Corp.,* 151 Oreg. 208-209, 217-218, 46 Pac. (2d) 1029 (1935).

which the gravamen of the complaint is injury to the owner of the land that is trespassed upon. Hence arises a different rule that such an appropriation is *void as against the landowner.*

The term "void" when used in this connection means no more than "voidable" when the landowner has the right to grant an easement.[222] Or even where a water right *initiated* in trespass is held invalid, a vested appropriative right *exercised* by committing a trespass is not necessarily void, even though it may not be asserted as against the owner of the land trespassed upon.[223]

The Washington Supreme Court acknowledged what might be a general rule that a valid appropriation cannot be so initiated, and that no rights can be obtained against the landowner. But the court could find no authority indicating that a *technical* trespass by posting notices of appropriation would render them unavailing to the appropriator where the water sought to be appropriated was neither flowing upon nor riparian to the land in question.[224]

The Idaho Supreme Court held that a permit issued by the State was of no force or effect where the applicant had trespassed on private land in obtaining data needed in making his appropriation.[225] In a case decided in 1931, however, the necessary data were obtained by means of a triangulation survey of the site of the contemplated diversion and right-of-way, made from a highway without entering upon the private property. Under these circumstances, the court held that this intending appropriator had a lawful right to apply for a permit, and that the permit issued on his application was lawful.[226] This decision was approved in a later case in which the supreme court said that trespass, in order to invalidate the appropriation, must be physical, not merely mental.[227]

Purposes of trespassing upon the land.—In the foregoing cases, the trespass upon private land was made for one or both of two purposes—one to obtain data required for an application to appropriate water; the other to construct a stream diversion and a ditch leading from the stream over the abutting and intervening land to the place of intended use.

Where the State law authorized an intending appropriator to condemn a right-of-way across private land for the purpose of obtaining data, as was

---

[222] *Scherck* v. *Nichols,* 55 Wyo. 4, 13-14 95 Pac. (2d) 74 (1939). In this case the landowner had not complained, but on the contrary the present owner stipulated that the water was being diverted with her consent. Hence a third party was not the one to object.

[223] *Osnes Livestock Co.* v. *Warren,* 103 Mont. 284, 295, 62 Pac. (2d) 206 (1936).

[224] *State ex rel. Ham, Yearsley & Ryrie* v. *Superior Court,* 70 Wash. 442, 464-466, 126 Pac. 945 (1912).

[225] *Marshall* v. *Niagara Springs Orchard Co.,* 22 Idaho 144, 153-158, 125 Pac. 208 (1912).

[226] *Bassett* v. *Swenson,* 51 Idaho 256, 259-262, 5 Pac. (2d) 722 (1931). In this action, the plaintiff was seeking the right to enter the property of the defendants in order to effectuate the diversion authorized by his permit. The right of condemnation therefor was upheld.

[227] *Idaho Power Co.* v. *Buhl,* 62 Idaho 351, 357-358, 111 Pac. (2d) 1088 (1941).

suggested in one of the Idaho cases,[228] as well as for the purpose of acquiring an easement in the land and constructing physical works for handling the water, the intending appropriator's legal course is clear enough. In many western jurisdictions, natural persons may condemn rights-of-way over other lands in order to effectuate appropriations of water (see "Rights-of-way for Water Control and Related Purposes," below). Barring agreement with the landowner, this appears to be the only practicable way of initiating an appropriation of public unappropriated water on privately owned land in a State in which the validity of a permit depends upon its having been obtained without committing trespass.

If the intending appropriator should go upon another's land, make surveys, build a diversion headgate, and dig a ditch across the land without the owner's permission and without any other formality, but with no interruption for the period of the statute of limitations—and if all the necessary elements of prescription are proved—the trespasser may then have legal title to the right-of-way and to the physical works. Under the Idaho Law he could then initiate his appropriation of the water, there being no further trespass—but not before then. But if the State rule were that the appropriation even though initiated in trespass is voidable only as against the landowner and only at his instigation, the appropriative process presumably could begin during the statutory prescriptive period, subject to interruption only if the landowner objects before the period expires. This, however, is subject to the willingness of the State administrative agency to accept an application for a permit from a person who does not have access to the source of supply of water. There are State administrators who are not willing to do so.

For example, the rules and regulations of the California Water Resources Control Board contain several sections relating to the intending appropriator's right of access, among which are: If it is necessary for an applicant to occupy private property or to use existing works which he does not own, he must secure the necessary right of access. If the proposed project will require a permit, license, or approval of a Federal agency or officer, such consent is necessary to approval of the application. And if the applicant does not own the land at the point of diversion, he must give the name and address of the owner and state what steps have been taken to secure right of access thereto.[229] The Texas Water Rights Commission requires, where the applicant does not have the power of condemnation and proposes to place any installation on the land

---

[228] *Marshall* v. *Niagara Springs Orchard Co.*, 22 Idaho 144, 153, 125 Pac. 208 (1912). The court stated that the right to enter the land in question for the purpose of investigating, inspecting, and making surveys, plans, and specifications for the purpose of making application for a permit to appropriate the water, should have been obtained from the landowner "either by an agreement of the parties, or by condemnation proceedings, and without such remedy being pursued, the respondent in making such entry would be a trespasser."

[229] Cal. Admin. Code, tit. 23, § § 670(s), and 747 to 749 (1969).

of another or to inundate other than his own land, a verified copy of written conveyance of easement or option therefor.[230] After all, the granting of a permit to one who does not have access to the source of supply would scarcely be a business-like proceeding. It could easily lead to trouble.

Late in the 19th century, long before the California Water Commission Act was passed, the supreme court of that State held that one might make an appropriation of water by taking peaceable possession of a constructed ditch, which would be good as against all the world except the true owner and those holding under or through him. Such appropriator, said the court, must account to the true owner until his possession ripens into a title by prescription. When this transpires, his right as against other appropriators would have priority from the date of his own possession and appropriation.[231]

RIGHTS-OF-WAY FOR WATER CONTROL AND RELATED PURPOSES

Public Lands

Public Lands of the United States

Early Acts of Congress.—Under "The Land Factor in Appropriating Water," above, attention is called to the effect of the Congressional legislation of 1866 and 1870[232] on the development of the appropriation doctrine in the West. These statutes related not only to water rights on the public lands, but also to rights-of-way necessary for their effectuation and enjoyment. Section 9 of the Act of 1866 provided that the right-of-way for construction of ditches and canals, for the purpose of effectuating appropriative rights on the public domain that had vested and accrued under local customs, laws, and court decisions, should be acknowledged and confirmed. The amendatory Act of 1870 was passed to clarify the Congressional intent that grantees of the United States would take their lands charged with the existing servitude.[233] This statute provided that all patents, preemptions, and homesteads should be subject, not only to vested and accrued water rights, but also to ditch and reservoir rights connected therewith, acquired or recognized by section 9 of the 1866 statute. In 1879, the United States Supreme Court construed the legislation in two decisions of major importance, both of which went to the United States Supreme Court from the Supreme Court of California.[234]

---

[230]Tex. Water Rights Comm'n, "Rules, Regulations and Modes of Procedure," rule 215.9 (1970 Rev., Jan. 1970).

[231]*Utt* v. *Frey,* 106 Cal. 392, 396, 39 Pac. 807 (1895).

[232]14 Stat. 253, § 9 (1866); 16 Stat. 218 (1870).

[233]*California Oregon Power Co.* v. *Beaver Portland Cement Co.,* 295 U.S. 142, 154-155 (1935).

[234]*Jennison* v. *Kirk,* 98 U.S. 453, 456-457, 459 (1879); *Broder* v. *Water Co.,* 101 U.S. 274, 275-277 (1879).

(1) *Jennison* v. *Kirk*. Counsel contended that only the right to the use of water on public lands acquired by priority of possession is dependent on local customs, laws, and decisions of courts, and that the rights-of-way over such lands for construction of ditches and canals is conferred absolutely on those who have acquired the water right. In rejecting this contention, the Supreme Court said that the object of the section was to give the sanction of the proprietor, the United States, to possessory rights and to prevent them from being lost on a sale of the lands. The section proposed no new system; it sanctioned, regulated, and confirmed a system already established. As so expounded, the section foreclosed further proprietary objection by the United States to applications that rested on local custom.[235]

(2) *Broder* v. *Water Company*. In this case private rights of ownership of lands of two groups were involved—those in one group acquired *after* the date of passage of the Act of 1866, and those of the other acquired *before* the enactment. As to a canal of one of the parties, so far as it ran on the date of enactment through land of the United States—in which private rights were subsequently acquired—"this act [of Congress] was an unequivocal grant of the right of way, if it was no more."[236] As to the other lands granted under an earlier act containing a reservation in favor of pre-existing rights, an appropriator who had constructed a canal across the lands before they were granted in 1862 and 1864 need not rely on the Act of 1866. The Court considered that legislation "rather a voluntary *recognition of a pre-existing right of possession,* constituting a valid claim to its continued use, than the establishment of a new one."[237]

That the Supreme Court in *Broder* v. *Water Company* regarded the Act of 1866 as "an unequivocal grant" for existing diversions on the public lands was reiterated by that Court in 1950.[238] "Thus Congress made good appropriations in being as against a later patent to riparian parcels of the public domain, and removed the cloud cast by adverse federal claims." And in 1935, the Court held that the effect of the Acts of 1866 and 1870 was not limited to rights acquired before 1866 but reach into the future as well.[239]

(3) Other cases. Although these Congressional statutes speak only of ditches, canals, and reservoirs, it was the view of a United States Court of Appeals that such terms are broad enough to include rights-of-way for "dams, flumes, pipes, and tunnels as analogous or incidental to, and discharging the functions of, such reservoirs, ditches and canals."[240]

---

[235] *United States* v. *Gerlach Live Stock Co.,* 339 U.S. 725, 748 (1950).

[236] *Broder* v. *Water Co.,* 101 U.S. 274, 275 (1879).

[237] *Id.* at 276.

[238] *United States* v. *Gerlach Live Stock Co.,* 339 U.S. 725, 748 (1950).

[239] *California Oregon Power Co.* v. *Beaver Portland Cement Co.,* 295 U.S. 142, 154-155 (1935).

[240] *Utah Light & Traction Co.* v. *United States,* 230 Fed. 343, 345 (8th Cir. 1915).
   For a recent case discussing these statutes, see *Hunter* v. *United States,* 388 Fed. (2d) 148, 154-155 (9th Cir. 1967).

No right vests as against the Government under these statutes until the work is completed. The United States Supreme Court held that the statutes create no title, legal or equitable, in the one who simply takes possession of the land. Under the statutes "no right or title to the land, or to a right of way over or through it, or to the use of water from a well thereafter to be dug, vests, as against the government, in the party entering upon possession from the mere fact of such possession unaccompanied by performance of any labor thereon."[241]

As the pueblo rights of the City of San Diego accrued prior to the passage of the Congressional acts granting rights-of-way over the public domain, rights-of-way acquired under such legislation were held by the California Supreme Court to be subordinate to the already vested rights of the city derived from its succession to the Mexican pueblo.[242] (See "The Pueblo Water Right," chapter 11.)

Later Acts of Congress. —An act passed in 1890 provided that all patents taken up after its date for lands west of the 100th meridian should contain reservations of rights-of-way thereon for ditches or canals constructed by authority of the United States.[243] A number of enactments regarding water and hydroelectric power followed.[244]

Legislation enacted in 1941 relates to grants of rights-of-way to States or political subdivisions thereof.[245]

Some other United States Supreme Court interpretations. —According to the United States Supreme Court, the Congressional Acts of 1866 and 1870 were primitive and works for generating and distributing electric power were unknown; hence, they were not in the mind of Congress. These pioneer statutes were limited to ditches, canals, and reservoirs; they did not cover power houses, transmission lines, or necessary subsidiary structures. So, when such modern works came into use, the early statutes were found inadequate. To meet this situation, Congress passed the Act of 1896, which related exclusively to rights-of-way for electric power purposes. The Court considered it plain that the Act of 1896 superseded those of 1866 and 1870 so far as they were applicable to such rights-of-way.[246]

The Supreme Court held in another decision that the difference of most significance between the acts of 1891 and 1896 related to the nature of

---

[241] *Bear Lake & River Waterworks & Irr. Co.* v. *Garland,* 164 U.S. 1, 18 (1896). See *United States* v. *Rickey Land & Cattle Co., 164 Fed. 496, 499 (N.D. Cal. 1908).

[242] *San Diego* v. *Cuyamaca Water Co., 209 Cal. 105, 131-132, 287 Pac. 475 (1930).

[243] 26 Stat. 391 (1890), 43 U.S.C. § 945 (1964).

[244] Of these, see 26 Stat. 1101 (1891), 43 U.S.C. §§ 946-949 (1964); 29 Stat. 120 (1896), 43 U.S.C. § 957 (1964); 30 Stat. 404 (1898); 43 U.S.C. § 951 (1964); 31 Stat. 790 (1901), 43 U.S.C. § 959 (1964). The Federal Power Act of 1920 provided that rights-of-way acquired prior to June 10, 1920, were not affected by this act. 41 Stat. 1063, 16 U.S.C. § 816 (1964).

[245] 55 Stat. 183, 43 U.S.C. § 931a (1964).

[246] *Utah Power & Light Co.* v. *United States,* 243 U.S. 389, 405-406 (1917), affirming in part and reversing in part, 209 Fed. 554 (8th Cir. 1913), reversing 208 Fed. 821 (D. Utah 1913).

the respective rights-of-way. The right-of-way intended by the 1891 act was neither a mere easement nor a fee simple absolute, but a limited fee on an implied condition of reverter in the event that the grantee ceased to use it or retain the land for the purpose indicated in the act. Under the Act of 1896, however, the beneficiary was intended to receive a revocable permit or license, not a limited fee.[247]

State Lands

Laws of some Western States grant the right-of-way across lands of the State for diversion and distribution works required in effectuating an appropriation. Some require the payment of compensation, others not. Some examples follow:

Nebraska.—Nebraska accords the right to occupy State lands and to obtain rights-of-way over highways, without compensation, to those who wish to construct the necessary water control works.[248]

South Dakota.—South Dakota grants to any person holding a valid statutory water right, over all school and public lands belonging to the State, a right of way for the construction of necessary waterworks when constructed by authority of the commissioner of School and Public Lands. The statute makes no mention of compensation.[249]

Idaho.—The Idaho statute grants the right-of-way over State lands to any person for construction and maintenance of works for conveyance of water. Just compensation, to be ascertained as provided for taking of private property for public use, must first be paid.[250]

Texas.—In Texas, the grant of right-of-way, not to exceed 100 feet in width, and the necessary area for any dam and reservoir site, for any of the purposes authorized by the water rights law, includes rock, gravel, and timber and the right-of-way for construction purposes. The beneficiary pays such compensation as the Texas Water Commission may determine.[251]

Oregon.—Oregon has several laws relating to grants of rights-of-way over State lands for ditches and other water facilities.[252] The earliest Oregon statute granting rights-of-way over State lands to individuals and corporations for the construction of water ditches was approved February 24, 1885.[253] This law provided that all patents issued by the State for any of its tide, swamp, overflowed, and school lands should be subject to any vested rights of the owners of such water ditches acquired under the law. This statute, said the

---

[247] *Kern River Co.* v. *United States,* 257 U.S. 147, 152 (1921).

[248] Nebr. Rev. Stat. § § 46-244 to -251 (1968).

[249] S. Dak. Comp. Laws Ann. § § 5-4-2 and 46-8-18 (1967).

[250] Idaho Code Ann. § 42-1104 (1948).

[251] Tex. Rev. Civ. Stat. Ann. art. 7582 (1954).

[252] Oreg. Rev. Stat. § § 541.030, .130, and .240 (Supp. 1969).

[253] Oreg. Laws 1885, p. 73, Rev. Stat. § 273.761 (Supp. 1969).

Oregon Supreme Court in 1898, was a legislative sanction, confirmatory of the customs of miners and, like the Act of Congress of July 26, 1866, "was the recognition of a pre-existing right, rather than a granting of a new easement in real property."[254]

Oregon also accords to the United States, the State, or any person, firm, cooperative association, or corporation the right to acquire the right-of-way across public, private, and corporate lands, or other rights-of-way across public, private, and corporate lands, or other rights-of-way, for necessary construction, maintenance, and use of all necessary works for securing, storing, and conveying water for irrigation, drainage, or other beneficial purposes, on payment of just compensation under the laws of eminent domain. Similar provision is made for acquiring the right to enlarge an already constructed conduit to convey the required quantity of water, upon payment of compensation for the damage, if any, caused thereby.[255]

Utah.—The Utah statute likewise grants to any person a right-of-way "across and upon public, private, and corporate lands" for construction and use of all necessary water control facilities "upon payment of just compensation therefor."[256] The authorization in another section,[257] to enlarge an existing ditch owned by someone else on payment of compensation, has been construed by the Utah Supreme Court as invoking the principle involved in eminent domain in the event that the parties cannot agree.[258]

California.—California municipal corporations are granted the right-of-way over public lands of the State for waterworks and powerplants, and the right to take materials for construction and also State waters under certain circumstances.[259]

Federal projects.—In some State statutes, special provision is made for grants of rights-of-way across State lands for project development works constructed by authority of the United States.[260]

California legislation granting rights-of-way to the United States over public lands of the State for certain purposes, including ditches and canals constructed under the provisions of the Reclamation Act, and providing that subsequent patents or conveyances of such lands located or filed on should be issued subject thereto, was repealed.[261]

---

[254] *Carson* v. *Gentner,* 33 Oreg. 512, 523, 52 Pac. 506 (1898).

[255] Oreg. Rev. Stat. § § 772.305 and .310 (Supp. 1963).

[256] Utah Code Ann. § 73-1-6 (1968).

[257] *Id.* § 73-1-7.

[258] *Nielson* v. *Sandburg,* 105 Utah 93, 96-102, 141 Pac. (2d) 696 (1943), citing *Salt Lake City* v. *East Jordan Irr. Co.,* 40 Utah 126, 121 Pac. 592 (1911); *Peterson* v. *Sevier Valley Canal Co.,* 107 Utah 45, 50-51, 151 Pac. (2d) 477 (1944).

[259] Cal. Pub. Utilities Code § § 10151-10155 (West 1956).

[260] See Oreg. Rev. Stat. § 541.240 (Supp. 1969); S. Dak. Comp. Laws Ann. § § 5-4-2 and 46-8-18 (1967).

[261] Cal. Pub. Resources Code § § 8351 and 8352, repealed, respectively, Stats. 1943, ch. 1124, and Stats. 1953, ch. 501.

Private Lands

"The United States and the state of Montana have recognized the right of an individual to acquire the use of water by appropriation * * *; but neither has authorized, nor, indeed, could authorize, one person to go upon the private property of another for the purpose of making an appropriation, except by condemnation proceedings."[262]

Use of Water for Beneficial Purposes a Public Use

That the use of water for beneficial purposes is a public use is recognized throughout the West. In most jurisdictions it applies even though the use is made by one individual for his own private purposes. Some State constitutions declare only that the use of water appropriated "for sale, rental, or distribution" is a public use.[263] Some other constitutional or statutory declarations of public use are broad enough to apply to the use of water generally, without restriction to its application to the delivery to others than the appropriator himself or itself.[264]

Whether declared in the fundamental law of the State, or in the legislative branch, or by the judiciary, this is a long recognized principle throughout the West. In 1901, the Kansas Supreme Court stated in *Lake Koen Navigation, Reservoir & Irrigation Company* v. *Klein* that: "We are met at the threshold of the inquiry in hand with the question as to whether, under the conditions existing in this state, irrigation is such a public purpose as to warrant the permission of the exercise of the power of eminent domain for its accomplishment. After careful consideration, we answer this question in the affirmative." The court found no difficulty in reaching the conclusion "that the promotion of irrigation in this state is a public use, and that the legislature is authorized in its discretion to commit the power of eminent domain to private persons or corporations for its promotion."[265] At this approximate time—in 1899—the irrigated area in Kansas was reported as only 0.3 percent of

---

[262] *Prentice* v. *McKay*, 38 Mont. 114, 117, 98 Pac. 1081 (1909).

[263] Cal. Const., art. XIV, § 1; Idaho Const., art. XV, § 1.

[264] Uses of water for mining and municipal and certain other purposes, by whomever utilized, are beneficial to the public and are public uses: Alaska Stat. § 09.55.240(b) (Supp. 1962). Sale, rental, distribution, "or other beneficial use" a public use: Mont. Const., art. III, § 15. Necessity of water for irrigation a natural want: Nebr. Const., art. XV, § 4. Use of ways and waterways for transporting water for beneficial use a public use: Oreg. Const., art. 1, § 18. Irrigation of arid lands a public purpose: S. Dak. Const., art. XXI, § 7. Conservation and development of water resources for all useful purposes are public rights and duties: Tex. Const., art. XVI, § 59a. Use of water for beneficial purposes as provided in the statute a public use: Utah Code Ann. § 73-1-5 (1968). Use of water for irrigation, mining, and manufacturing purposes a public use: Wash. Const., art. XXI, § 1.

[265] *Lake Koen Navigation, Res. & Irr. Co.* v. *Klein*, 63 Kans. 484, 488-489, 65 Pac. 684 (1901).

the total for the West, as contrasted with 2 percent for Nebraska, 13 percent for Montana, 19 percent for California, and 21 percent for Colorado.[266]

Before this time, considerable attention to commercialized irrigation development had been paid elsewhere in the West. The California and Montana constitutional declarations were made in 1879 and 1889, respectively. In 1888, the Colorado Supreme Court stated that: "The constitution unquestionably contemplates and sanctions the business of transporting water for hire from natural streams to distant consumers."[267] During the latter part of the 19th century, there was much financing of western land and water development projects on a commercial scale. This type of irrigation financing eventually proved to be infeasible and practically ceased during the first half of the present century.[268] However, in its conclusion in the *Lake Koen* case as to the value of irrigation in the State's economy, the Kansas Supreme Court took a forward looking view.

In 1935, in the course of holding that the State may appropriate private property under its inherent power of eminent domain, the New Mexico Supreme Court observed that "the question of the necessity and expediency of the taking is a legislative question," but that "Whether the use to which the property is to be put is a public use is a judicial question." The character of the use involved as public had been determined by the Territorial supreme court long previously.[269] Three decades earlier, the Utah Supreme Court said that "while it is for the legislature to determine, in the first instance, whether the use is a public use, and to provide the means of condemnation, yet the great weight of authority holds that the declaration of the Legislature is not final, and that it is ultimately for the courts to determine whether a particular use is public or not."[270]

Condemnation by Organization for Public Service

Once the principle that the use of water for irrigation is a public use was established by constitutional or legislative mandate or court decree, the way was paved for according to public and public-service organizations, that had been vested with the power of eminent domain, the right to condemn necessary rights-of-way for canals as well as sites for reservoirs, buildings, and structures needed for effectuating the storage, diversion, control, and delivery

---

[266] U.S. Bur. Census, Thirteenth Census of the United States: 1910, Irrigation of Agricultural Lands, Table 14, p. 845.

[267] *Wheeler* v. *Northern Colorado Irr. Co.,* 10 Colo. 582, 588, 17 Pac. 487 (1888).

[268] See Teele, R. P., "The Economics of Land Reclamation in the United States," pp. 148-152 (1927); Hutchins, Wells A., "Commercial Irrigation Companies," U. S. Dept. Agr. Tech. Bull. 177 pp. 6-14 (1930); Hutchins, Wells A., Selby, H. E., Voelker, Stanley W., "Irrigation-Enterprise Organizations," pp. 34-38, 78-79, 81-82, 84, 89-91 (1953).

[269] *State ex rel. Red River Valley Co.* v. *District Court,* 39 N. Mex. 523, 527-528, 51 Pac. (2d) 239 (1935).

[270] *Highland Boy Gold Min. Co.* v. *Strickley,* 28 Utah 215, 230-231, 78 Pac. 296 (1904).

of water to consumers. The commercial irrigation company—either public utility or private contract type of water enterprise—fitted into this concept. Indeed, these declarations relating to "sale, rental, or distribution" were made to facilitate the distribution of water for hire. That the State had the power to authorize privately owned organizations, created and operated for public service, to condemn land easements to effectuate this public use of water for irrigation purposes was recognized and established in the early decades of modern irrigation in the West.[271]

Condemnation by Individual for His Own Use

Although, as the Montana Supreme Court pointed out in 1909,[272] the State has no power to authorize an intending appropriator to enter private land without formality for the purpose of appropriating water there, it does have power to authorize him to do this by acquiring an easement under the law of eminent domain. And it may make such authorization to an individual whether for the purpose of supplying water to others for hire, or to acquire a water supply for his own private use. The basis for this admittedly long step forward is the recognition that, under typical western conditions, the irrigation of one's own land is so important to the welfare of the community and eventually to that of the State as to justify the declaration that it is a public use.

Constitutional foundation for the principle.—This was established by the United States Supreme Court in *Clark* v. *Nash,* decided in 1905, affirming a decision of the Utah Supreme Court.[273] At issue was the validity of a statute of the State authorizing any person, corporation, or association to enlarge an already constructed canal belonging to another party by compensating the owner for the damage so caused.[274] The constitutional issue involved was whether the land in question was being condemned for a public or for a private use.

The State court pointed out that the most vital of all industrial questions with which the people within the arid region had been confronted since the advent of the early pioneers was the method of appropriation and use of water. "The natural physical conditions of this State are such that in the great majority of cases the only possible way the farmer can supply his land with

---

[271] See discussions of these public water services by Wiel, S. C., "Water Rights in the Western States," 3d ed., vol. 2, §§ 1245 to 1328 (1911); Kinney, C. S., "A Treatise on the Law of Irrigation and Water Rights," 2d ed., vol. 3, §§ 1490 to 1529 (1912). A study of the practical usefulness of the commercial type of irrigation organization was made by the author in 1929: Hutchins, Wells A., "Commercial Irrigation Companies," U.S. Dept. Agr. Tech. Bull. 177 (1930).

[272] *Prentice* v. *McKay,* 38 Mont. 114, 117, 98 Pac. 1081 (1909).

[273] *Clark* v. *Nash,* 198 U. S. 361 (1905), affirming 27 Utah 158, 163-168, 75 Pac. 371 (1904).

[274] Utah Rev. Stat. § 1278 (1898), now Code Ann. § 73-1-7 (1968).

water is by conveying it by means of ditches across his neighbor's lands which intervene between his own and the source from which he obtains his supply." The court held that the condemnation was for a public use, as these words mean a use that will promote the public interest and develop the State's natural resources.

The United States Supreme Court agreed with the State court as to validity of the statute in question. But the Court cautioned that it was not to be understood as approving the broad proposition that private property may be taken *in all cases* where the taking may promote the public interest and tend to develop the State's natural resources.[275] What the Court held was that differences of climate and soil, which required different laws in the arid States from those in the humid ones, must be recognized.[276] Having reference to the physical conditions obtaining in Utah, the use sought to be condemned under the circumstances of this case was believed to be a public one, even though it was simply for the purpose of obtaining water for an individual. This was because it was absolutely necessary to enable this individual to make any use whatever of his land.[277] So the Supreme Court held that on the facts appearing in the record, the statute permitting enlargement of the neighbors' ditch, with compensation to them, was within the legislative power of the State.[278]

Thus, in *Clark* v. *Nash,* the United States Supreme Court sustained the constitutional soundness of a statute of a Western State, in the economy of which irrigation was a vital factor, authorizing an individual to condemn the right to enlarge his neighbor's ditch, as a facet of the whole concept of individual condemnation of rights-of-way over private lands. The same line of reasoning with respect to public use was applied to construction and operation of roads and tramways in the mining industry.[279]

Right-of-way for new ditch.—In nearly all Western States, an individual may condemn an easement across lands intervening between his own and the source of his water supply for the purpose of conveying to his own property the water to which his appropriation entitles him.

---

[275] *Clark* v. *Nash,* 198 U.S. 361, 369 (1905).

[276] *Id.* at 367-368.

[277] *Id.* at 369-370.

[278] *Id.* at 370

[279] *Highland Boy Gold Min. Co.* v. *Strickley,* 28 Utah 215, 230-236, 78 Pac. 296 (1904), affirmed, 200 U. S. 527 (1906). The Utah court said, 28 Utah at 232, that: "The mining industry in this State is second in importance only to that of irrigation, and this court held in the case of *Nash* v. *Clark,* supra, that the construction and operation of irrigation ditches is a public use." In affirming the judgment of the State court, the United States Supreme Court said, 200 U.S. at 531 that: "In the opinion of the legislature and the Supreme Court of Utah the public welfare of that State demands that the aërial lines between the mines upon its mountain sides and the railways in the valleys below should not be made impossible by the refusal of a private owner to sell the right to cross his land. The Constitution of the United States does not require us to say that they are wrong."

(1) Statutory authorizations. The earliest statutory authorization to this effect that has come to the author's attention was the Colorado Territorial right-of-way law enacted by the first legislative assembly. This provided that persons owning claims on the bank, margin, or in the neighborhood of any stream should have the right-of-way over adjacent lands for purposes of irrigation.[280] In construing this law in its first reported water rights decision, the Territorial supreme court observed that all lands were held in subordination to the dominant rights of others, who must necessarily pass over them to obtain a supply of water to irrigate their own lands. This right, said the court, arose not only by virtue of the statute, but sprang from the necessity arising from local pecularities of climate.[281] The Colorado State constitution accorded to all persons and corporations rights-of-way across both public and private lands for conveyance of water for domestic, irrigation, mining, and manufacturing purposes, and for drainage, upon payment of just compensation.[282]

Another early authorization was contained in the Arizona Territorial Howell Code of 1864. This provided for acquisition of rights-of-way for public or private acequias across private lands not benefited by the acequia, upon assessment and payment of damages.[283]

In granting such rights-of-way to an individual for his own benefit, the statutes either directly or impliedly relate the authorization to an exercise of the power of eminent domain. For example, the Oklahoma authorization is to "exercise the right of eminent domain to acquire" the necessary rights-of-way, such rights to be "acquired in the manner provided by law for the taking of private property for public use."[284] Or the right-of-way may be granted "upon payment of just compensation therefor."[285] With respect to the Utah statute granting the right of enlargement of an already constructed ditch upon payment of proper compensation,[286] the State supreme court held that proceedings under this section are controlled by the principle involved in the law of eminent domain.[287]

The California procedure differs markedly from the usual western pattern. Private ways for an irrigation, drainage, or seepage canal may be opened, laid out, or altered by order of the board of county supervisors for the convenience

---

[280] Colo. Laws 1861, p. 67.

[281] *Yunker* v. *Nichols,* 1 Colo. 551, 555, 570 (1872).

[282] Colo. Const., art. XVI, § 7. The current statutory provisions are in Colo. Rev. Stat. Ann. §§ 148-3-1 to 148-3-5 (Supp. 1969) and § 148-3-6 (1963).

[283] Terr. Ariz. Howell Code, ch. LV, § 4. The current authorization to landowners is Ariz. Rev. Stat. Ann. § 45-201 (1956).

[284] Okla. Stat. Ann. tit. 82, § 2 (1970). See Alaska Stat. § 09.55.240(b) (Supp. 1962); Nev. Rev. Stat. § 533.050 (Supp. 1967).

[285] Utah Code Ann. § 73-1-6 (1968).

[286] *Id.* § 73-1-7.

[287] *Nielson* v. *Sandberg,* 105 Utah 93, 96-102, 141 Pac. (2d) 696 (1943); *Peterson* v. *Sevier Valley Canal Co.,* 107 Utah 45, 50-51, 151 Pac. (2d) 477 (1944).

of one or more residents or freeholders of any road district under the procedure applying to public roads, except that only one petitioner is necessary. The person for whose benefit the private way is required must pay the damages awarded to landowners and must keep the canal in repair.[288]

North Dakota grants the right-of-way to appropriators of water, including the right to enlarge existing structures and use them in common with the former owner.[289] In Idaho, the right to cross another ditch as well as other land is granted.[290] Invocation of the doctrine of relation under the Washington statute is not impaired by the amount of time taken to condemn necessary sites for water control structures, inasmuch as such condemnation proceedings are as essential to the enterprise as is the actual construction of the physical works.[291]

Certain conditions are imposed in some statutes. Thus in Arizona, only "An owner of arable and irrigable lands" may exercise this right of condemnation.[292] Under the Texas procedure, persons or associations who seek to exercise this power must first make application to the Texas Water Rights Commission which, if it deems the proposal advisable, may institute condemnation proceedings in the name of the State for use of the individual concerned.[293]

Measures to protect the servient estates are declared. Thus: No landowner need grant a right-of-way across his land for irrigation works if there are already in operation across such property works sufficient for furnishing enough water for the dominant estate.[294] The shortest and most direct route must be followed, and no tract of improved or occupied land may be burdened unnecessarily by more than one ditch without the owner's consent.[295] There must be the least damage to private or public property, consistent with proper and economical engineering construction.[296] The practical use of any right-of-way or public or private road is not to be impaired, nor must public or private property be injured.[297]

---

[288] Cal. Water Code § § 7020-7026 (West 1956). Apparently these sections have not been directly construed by the appellate courts of California. Comparable legislation providing for acquisition of rights-of-way for private roads was upheld by the California Supreme Court in the early case of *Los Angeles County* v. *Reyes,* 3 Cal. U. 775, 777-778, 32 Pac. 233 (1893).

[289] N. Dak. Cent. Code Ann. § 61-01-04 (1960).

[290] Idaho Code Ann. § § 42-1102 to -1108 (1948).

[291] Wash. Rev. Code § 90.03.040 (Supp. 1961). *Grant Realty Co.* v. *Ham, Yearsley & Ryrie,* 96 Wash. 616, 624-626, 165 Pac. 495 (1917).

[292] Ariz. Rev. Stat. Ann. § 45-201 (1956).

[293] Tex. Rev. Civ. Stat. Ann. art. 7583 (1954).

[294] Kans. Stat. Ann. § 42-316 (1964).

[295] Colo. Rev. Stat. Ann. § § 148-3-4 and 148-3-5 (Supp. 1969).

[296] N. Mex. Stat. Ann. § 75-1-3 (1968); N. Dak. Cent. Code Ann. § 61-01-04 (1960); Okla. Stat. Ann. tit. 82, § 2 (1970); S. Dak. Comp. Laws Ann. § 46-8-1 (1967).

[297] Utah Code Ann. § 73-1-6 (1968).

(2) Judicial constructions of statutes. In many decisions the courts have dealt with constructions of the ditch right-of-way laws, a few of which may be cited.

In 1899, the Montana Supreme Court declared that the taking of private property from its owner can be done only pursuant to the procedure provided by the legislature therefor and with always "a rigorous compliance with the provisions of the statute, which points out when, in what manner, and under what conditions" the property can be taken.[298]

The Oregon Supreme Court holds that authority to condemn a right-of-way over the land of another for the purpose of obtaining a particular supply of water depends upon the applicant's right to make a lawful appropriation of such water.[299]

In a New Mexico case, it was held that the owners of a community acequia, whether private parties or a community acequia corporation, had the right to condemn a right-of-way for a ditch. And as irrigation was a public purpose, a city had no express or implied right to condemn the acequia for another public purpose.[300] This case was distinguished a few years later in a case in which it was held that a city had the power to condemn property already devoted to a public use, provided the first public use was not obliterated or destroyed, the property to be used jointly.[301]

In a recent case,[302] the New Mexico Supreme Court held that under the State's constitution and legislation a right of way to lay a pipeline to a watercourse to make beneficial use thereof under an appropriative right could be acquired by eminent domain by a private corporation for coal mining purposes. The court indicated that the same principles would be applied to irrigation and other beneficial uses of water.[303]

The Nebraska statute declares that "All persons" have authority to condemn rights-of-way over and through the lands of others for ditches, dams, and other necessary works for the storage and conveyance of water.[304] However, the State supreme court has held that the right of eminent domain cannot be exercised for purely private purposes, such as by an individual for

---

[298] *Glass* v. *Basin Min. & Concentrating Co.,* 22 Mont. 151, 155-156, 55 Pac. 1047 (1899). In view of the declaration in Mont. Const., art. III, § 15, that the right-of-way over land of others for necessary water conduits and structures is a public use, the supreme court held that the right to appropriate water on the land of another may be acquired by condemnation proceedings: *Prentice* v. *McKay,* 38 Mont. 114, 118, 98 Pac. 1081 (1909). See *Cocanougher* v. *Zeigler,* 112 Mont. 76, 79, 112 Pac. (2d) 1058 (1941).

[299] *Henrici* v. *Paulson,* 134 Oreg. 222, 224, 226, 293 Pac. 424 (1930). Oreg. Rev. Stat. § 772.305 (Supp. 1963).

[300] *Albuquerque* v. *Garcia,* 17 N. Mex. 445, 449-454, 130 Pac. 118 (1913). N. Mex. Stat. Ann. § 75-1-3 (1968).

[301] *Raton* v. *Raton Ice Co.,* 26 N. Mex. 300, 307, 191 Pac. 516 (1920).

[302] *Kaiser Steel Corp.* v. *W.S. Ranch Co.,* 81 N. Mex. 414, 467 Pac. (2d) 986 (1970).

[303] *Id.* at 467 Pac. (2d) 990-991.

[304] Nebr. Rev. Stat. § § 46-246 to -248 (1968).

irrigation of his own land.[305] In its holding, the Nebraska Supreme Court distinguished the decision of the United States Supreme Court in *Clark* v. *Nash*,[306] as limited by the highest Court itself to the circumstances of that case, wherein reference was had to the natural conditions of an arid State such as Utah. The Nebraska court pointed out the vast difference between the physical configuration and climatic conditions of Utah and of Nebraska. Under local conditions, it was held, the right of eminent domain rests upon the right to the control of rates by the public. Application of the statutory sections to irrigation districts and public service companies was conceded. What the court held was that the statutes could not, with due regard to the right of private property, be applied to circumstances in which a mere private interest is subserved.

The right of an individual to condemn a right-of-way across the land of another is declared by the legislature and sustained by the courts of Idaho.[307] However, the supreme court denied the right to condemn what it termed "a novel use of a canal system belonging to others."[308] The applicants in this case proposed to discharge water appropriated by them into the Low Line canal of Twin Falls Canal Company, and to pump a like quantity of water out of the main canal of that company at a point on the main system far above the point of discharge into the lowland canal. One cannot condemn the right to use a small part of a canal of another at a lower point, the court held, to discharge water into it and another small part at the higher point to pump the water out. "No legal fiction can support the theory that the water to be taken out of respondent's main canal is the same water as that proposed to be appropriated by appellants and placed in the Low Line Canal."

Right to enlarge another's existing ditch.—In addition to authorizing an individual to condemn a right-of-way across his neighbor's land for a new ditch from the source of supply to the place of use, a number of State statutes provide that in the same way he may acquire the right to enlarge or to use an existing ditch on the intervening land, in common with the former owners, upon payment of proper compensation.[309]

---

[305] *Vetter* v. *Broadhurst,* 100 Nebr. 356, 360-363, 160 N. W. 109 (1916), cited with approval in *Onstott* v. *Airdale Ranch & Cattle Co.,* 129 Nebr. 54, 58-59, 260 N. W. 556 (1935).

[306] *Clark* v. *Nash,* 198 U. S. 361, 367-370 (1905), affirming 27 Utah 158, 75 Pac. 371 (1904).

[307] Idaho Code Ann. § § 42-1101 to -1108 (1948). *Bassett* v. *Swenson,* 51 Idaho 256, 259-263, 5 Pac. (2d) 722 (1931).

[308] *Berg* v. *Twin Falls Canal Co.,* 36 Idaho 62, 64-66, 213 Pac. 694 (1922).

[309] Cal. Water Code § 1800 (West Supp. 1970); Colo. Rev. Stat. Ann. § 148-3-6 (1963); N. Mex. Stat. Ann. § § 75-1-3 and 75-5-14 (1968); N. Dak. Cent. Code Ann. § 61-01-04 (1960); Okla. Stat. Ann. tit. 82, § 2 (1970); Oreg. Rev. Stat. § 772.310 (Supp. 1963); S. Dak. Comp. Laws Ann. § 46-8-1 (1967); Utah Code Ann. § 73-1-7 (1968); Wash. Rev. Code § 90.03.040 (Supp. 1961); Wyo. Stat. Ann. § 1-794 (Supp. 1969).

An appropriator under the California Water Commission Act or Water Code may jointly occupy and use the works of another if the State Water Resources Control Board finds that the undeveloped capacity of the source of supply requires it, on payment of a pro rata share of the cost of the old and new work and of maintenance.[310] Under the same conditions and procedure, he may repair, improve, or enlarge at his own expense any works built or in process of being built, and may use the works jointly with the owners.[311]

With respect to compensation, Colorado provides for payment of a reasonable proportion of the cost of construction of the ditch;[312] Oregon for the damages, if any, caused by the enlargement.[313] New Mexico specifies that the person enlarging the ditch shall have the right to use of the quantity of water added to the capacity of the structure or other work caused by enlargement. Its statute makes further provision for recourse against a joint user who fails to pay his proper share of the cost of maintenance and operation.[314] Utah provides that: The person who makes the enlargement must compensate the original owner for the damage caused thereby, and he must pay an equitable proportion of the canal maintenance. The enlargement must be made during a certain period of the year if not otherwise agreed upon. The additional water turned into the enlarged ditch shall bear its proportion of loss by evaporation and seepage.[315] As noted above, it was the Utah statute authorizing enlargement of a neighbor's ditch that received the specific approval of the Utah Supreme Court and of the Supreme Court of the United States.[316]

Right of entry upon other land to obtain data.—In addition to and aside from grants of rights-of-way easements, statutes of several States authorize entrance upon private lands for the purpose of obtaining data—a temporary privilege rather than a permanent right of occupancy and use. Thus, the New Mexico statute provides that technicians of the United States, the State, and of any person, firm, or corporation may enter upon both public and private lands and waters for the purpose of making hydrographic surveys and examinations necessary for selecting sites for water works, subject to responsibility for any damage done.[317] That of Oregon authorizes any person to enter upon any land for the purpose of locating a point of diversion of water intended to be appropriated and for locating and surveying ditch lines and reservoir sites.[318] In

---

[310] Cal. Water Code § § 1775 (West Supp. 1970) and 1777 (West 1956).

[311] Cal. Water Code § 1800 (West Supp. 1970).

[312] Colo. Rev. Stat. Ann. § 148-3-6 (1963).

[313] Oreg. Rev. Stat. § 772.310 (Supp. 1963).

[314] N. Mex. Stat. Ann. § 75-5-14 (1968).

[315] Utah Code Ann. § 73-1-7 (1968).

[316] *Nash* v. *Clark.* 27 Utah 158, 162-168, 75 Pac. 371 (1904), affirmed, 198 U. S. 361, 367-370 (1905).

[317] N. Mex. Stat. Ann. § 75-1-3 (1968).

[318] Oreg. Rev. Stat. § 537.320 (Supp. 1969).

Texas, persons, associations, corporations, and districts may enter upon lands or waters of any person for examination and survey necessary to the selection of reservoir sites and rights-of-way.[319]

The author's attention has not been called to any high court decision in which the validity of this statutory right of entry upon private land for the sole purpose of obtaining data was called in question. As discussed above under "The Land Factor in Appropriating Water–Private Lands," the Idaho Supreme Court has held that such an entry for the purpose of obtaining data needed in applying for a permit to appropriate water, without the owner's permission, is a trespass. As such, it cannot be the foundation of a valid appropriative right.[320] Idaho has no statutory authorization to enter lands for this sole purpose comparable to these just noted. Query: What would be the attitude of the Idaho Supreme Court to such a statutory provision ignoring, as it does, questions of landowner permission and condemnation?

METHODS OF APPROPRIATING WATER OF WATERCOURSES

Procedures for acquiring stream water appropriative rights in the West developed from informal steps of taking water from a stream and turning it onto the ground, to administrative methods provided by State statutes under which all successive steps in the appropriative process are prescribed. In most jurisdictions, these requirements must be followed scrupulously if an intending appropriator is to perfect his right. Before public controls were imposed upon the appropriative process, one could appropriate water as a matter of right, so long as the water was available in the stream in excess of then existing rights and provided the would-be appropriator could get access to the source and to the place of intended use. But with the advent of the so-called "water codes"–State statutes providing for the acquisition of appropriative rights and generally for their adjudication and for distribution of the water under State administrative agencies–acquisition of the right thereunder became less and less a matter of positive right, and more and more a privilege accorded to an applicant whose proposed project does not, in the judgment of the State administrator, conflict with the public interest or impair the public welfare. In the determination of these factors the administrator is accorded a wide discretion, subject to judicial review. Restrictions on the right to appropriate water and preferences in acquiring and exercising the right, which constitute an important phase of the appropriative process, are discussed immediately following the present topic of "methods."

The current method of appropriating water generally under State administrative procedure is in effect in a large majority of Western States. It has operated so long as to be a well-established feature of the complex whole of western water control. Its major importance is commonly taken for granted.

---

[319] Tex. Rev. Civ. Stat. Ann. art 7580 (1954).
[320] *Marshall* v. *Niagara Springs Orchard Co.*, 22 Idaho 144, 153-158, 125 Pac. 208 (1912).

Nevertheless, this facet of administrative control over the handling of public water supplies can be understood more clearly by taking note of the two phases of appropriative procedure that preceded it—(a) the period of nonstatutory methods of appropriation, extending roughly from the 1840's to the 1870's; and (b) the ensuing period of early statutory methods which persisted—although they eventually were largely discarded—into the present century.

Let it be again emphasized that the instant discussion relates to *water of watercourses.* Ground water appropriative rights are considered later, in chapters 19 and 20.

Nonstatutory

Originally, all means of appropriating western stream waters were non-statutory—no Federal or State or Territorial statute declared the steps that must be taken in acquiring the right. At present, most Western States have statutes that provide for taking certain steps; and a majority of these statutory procedures are either held or generally considered to be the exclusive means of making valid appropriations. Idaho is an outstanding exception. There the law is settled to the effect that one who wishes to appropriate water may follow the statutory procedure or may disregard it completely, as he chooses. This feature is noted below in discussing current statutory methods.

Earliest Western Locations

The earliest appropriations of water in the West were made in Spanish settlements in certain areas in the Southwest, in the Mormon colonies of Utah, and during the California Gold Rush.

Spanish settlements in the Southwest.—As noted in chapter 6, questions concerning the existence of the appropriation doctrine in the American Southwest under Spanish rule have been debated and the answers are still subject to some disagreement. The New Mexico Supreme Court declared that the law of prior appropriation existed under the Republic of Mexico at the time New Mexico was acquired by the United States, but gave no details.[321] The Arizona Supreme Court said that in the Mexican State of Sonora, of which Arizona formed a part, prior rights arose under Mexican law only as the result of grants from the government, but that appropriations were permitted to some extent by local custom—again no details.[322] Many small community acequias were constructed by Spanish-Americans in San Luis Valley, Colorado, as well as by such settlers and Indians up and down the length of the Rio Grande in New Mexico and into Texas, the water rights of which came into existence with their first use of the water.

---

[321] *United States* v. *Rio Grande Dam & Irr. Co.,* 9 N. Mex. 292, 306-307, 51 Pac. 674 (1898). See also *State ex rel. State Game Commission* v. *Red River Valley Co.,* 51 N. Mex. 207, 217, 182 Pac. (2d) 421 (1945).

[322] *Maricopa County M.W.C. Dist.* v. *Southwest Cotton Co.,* 39 Ariz. 65, 74-75, 4 Pac. (2d) 369 (1931).

It is reasonable to conclude that in addition to the making of grants by the government, the taking of water for community and even for individual use was permitted, or perhaps tolerated, in various areas as a matter of local custom which did not rise to the dignity of a general statute. But as to whether the principle of *priority* of appropriation, in the form in which it spread throughout the West, and methods of enforcement, were a part of this customary law, there appears to be little or no available authoritative documentary evidence. The author is not aware of any published account of public enforcement of priorities of private appropriative water rights in the Spanish-American Southwest.

The Arizona court's conclusions that "the right to appropriate and use water for irrigation has been recognized longer than history, and since earlier than tradition"[323] need not be questioned. Regardless of those declarations, it can be stated with equal assurance that there is nothing in the present water laws of either Texas or California, in which States the Spaniards also made settlements, to suggest that a principle of *prior* appropriation of water prevailed in the jurisdiction under Spanish or Mexican sovereignty.[324] Spanish-Mexican water law made little if any impression on the water law of the State of California other than with respect to water rights of American cities that succeeded Spanish or Mexican pueblos. In Texas, after years of controversy, the high courts finally held that lands in Spanish and Mexican grants riparian to the Lower Rio Grande *do not* have appurtenant rights to irrigate with the river waters.[325] No question of Spanish or Mexican law relating to *appropriation* of water was involved in this suit.

Utah Mormon colonies.—Originally, rights to the use of public streams of water in Utah were acquired, either by actual diversion and application of water to beneficial use, or by legislative grant.[326] For 50 years after the beginning of irrigation in this region, appropriations of water were made by diverting the water from stream channels and applying it to beneficial use, without any specific statutory procedure for acquiring appropriative rights. In these cases, the intention of the appropriator and usefulness of the purpose were tests in determining validity of the right.[327]

In 1852, the Utah legislature authorized the county courts to make grants of water privileges.[328] As administered by the county courts, an appropriator was required to petition the court for a water privilege, which the court

---

[323] *Clough* v. *Wing*, 2 Ariz. 371, 380, 17 Pac. 453 (1888). "Evidences of it are to be found all over Arizona and New Mexico in the ancient canals of a pre-historic people, who once composed a dense and highly civilized population."

[324] Compare Hutchins, Wells A.: "The California Law of Water Rights," pp. 41-51 (1956), and "The Texas Law of Water Rights," pp. 102-106 (1961).

[325] *Valmont Plantations* v. *State of Texas*, 163 Tex. 381, 355 S. W. (2d) 502 (1962), affirming 346 S. W. (2d) 853 (Tex. Civ. App. 1961).

[326] *Wrathall* v. *Johnson*, 86 Utah 50, 80, 40 Pac. (2d) 755 (1935).

[327] *Hague* v. *Nephi Irr. Co.*, 16 Utah 421, 429-430, 52 Pac. 765 (1898).

[328] Terr. Utah Laws 1852, p. 38, § 39, "An Act in Relation to the Judiciary."

claimed the right either to grant or to reject; and he could make his appropriation only pursuant to the grant if he received one. This act was in effect until 1880.

The 1852 law was replaced in 1880 by a statute which made the county selectmen *ex officio* water commissioners of the county and which recognized accrued rights to water acquired by appropriation and provided for their determination and orderly recordation. But it contained no procedure for making new appropriations.[329] An intending appropriator diverted and applied water to beneficial use and thereby appropriated it, as before, but without the terms and conditions which the county court had previously been authorized to impose and which, in many instances, it apparently did. During this period, "rights to the use of unappropriated waters were not acquired without a taking and diverting and using them."[330] The 1880 law remained in effect until a procedural law was enacted in 1897.[331]

California Gold Rush.—Water laws that evolved during this vital period in California history were generated on public lands of the United States, which Mexico had ceded by virtue of the Treaty of Guadalupe Hidalgo.[332] This treaty was proclaimed July 4, 1848, less than 6 months after the discovery of gold in the Sierra foothills.

There was little or no organized government in the mining areas in these early years, and little or no law other than that made and enforced by the miners themselves.[333] The miners took possession of the land and the gold and the water needed to work the placer mining claims. They established and enforced rules and regulations governing acquisition and holding of mining claims, based on priority of discovery and diligence in working them; and they applied the same principles to the acquisition and exercise of rights to the water that they needed. These regulations and customs were strikingly characteristic of earlier mining enterprises in the Old World (see "Establishment of the Appropriation Doctrine in the West" in chapter 6).

Each mining camp made its own rules regarding location and working of mines and governing appropriation of water. The rules differed in detail from one locality to another, but the fundamental principles were substantially uniform. The right to appropriate water was customarily initiated by posting a notice at the place of intended diversion, and it was established by diverting water and applying it with due diligence to beneficial use. One who followed the rules acquired a right superior to those of later appropriators. The principle of "first in time, first in right" was fundamental. It was strictly enforced.

---

[329] Utah Laws 1880, ch. 20.

[330] *Coray* v. *Holbrook,* 40 Utah 325, 338, 121 Pac. 572 (1912).

[331] Utah Laws 1897, ch. 52.

[332] 9 Stat. 928.

[333] A very early statute provided that in actions respecting mining claims, proof should be admitted of the customs, usages, or regulations established at the bar or diggings embracing the claim: Cal. Stat. 1851, ch. 5, § 621.

The first act in appropriating water in a mining camp was the posting of a notice at the proposed point of diversion. This stated the appropriator's intention to divert a specified quantity of water through a ditch heading at that place. The notice was considered evidence of possession.[334] Although this was the customary way of initiating an appropriative right, it could be done by some other act that manifested the appropriator's intention in such manner as to put a prudent man upon inquiry—such as surveys, stakes, blazing of trees, and actual construction of works as well as notices.[335] In any event, the appropriation was initiated by the first act manifesting the intention; but title to the right did not vest until the appropriation was completed.[336] A valid appropriation of water could be made by constructing a conduit and actually diverting water from the source of supply in fulfillment of some useful purpose.[337]

The first appropriation procedural statute in California was enacted in 1872 in the Civil Code.[338]

Other western situations.—(1) The appropriative principles developed in the mining camps during the Gold Rush, which became an essential part of California water law, profoundly influenced the development of water appropriation law in the West. The reason for predominance of this influence over that of the Utah and Spanish-American customs was that the mining fever spread rapidly over the entire Northwest, as far east as Montana and Wyoming, and carried with it the pattern established in California with respect to acquisition, holding, and exercise of mining claims and mining water rights. From mining water right customs, the purposes of the procedure logically expanded to include irrigation, domestic, and manufacturing uses.

(2) Thus in Montana, according to its supreme court, originally "all appropriations were made pursuant to the rules and customs of the early settlers of California, which had been adopted in Montana territory and given the force of law, by recognition of the legislature * * * and the courts."[339]

(3) In not only California and Montana, but in most other Western States as well, appropriations of water were made before the State or Territorial legislatures provided procedure for making appropriations. In many of them, this was done before the legislatures had enacted any law at all respecting appropriative water rights. For example, in various parts of Oregon, before any legislation relating to methods of appropriating water had been enacted, there were in effect local customs under which an intending appropriator posted a notice of his claim and filed it in the county records. "Such a rule may be said to have become

---

[334] *Thompson* v. *Lee*, 8 Cal. 275, 280 (1857).

[335] *Kimball* v. *Gearhart*, 12 Cal. 27, 29-31 (1859).

[336] *Nevada County & Sacramento Canal Co.* v. *Kidd*, 37 Cal. 282, 310-311 (1869).

[337] *Utt* v. *Frey*, 106 Cal. 392, 395, 39 Pac. 807 (1895). See *Haight* v. *Costanich*, 184 Cal. 426, 431, 194 Pac. 26 (1920).

[338] Cal. Civ. Code § § 1410-1422 (1872).

[339] *Maynard* v. *Watkins*, 55 Mont. 54, 55, 173 Pac. 551 (1918).

established, under varying circumstances and conditions, in this state."[340] In fact, the first Oregon enactment on the subject declared that all existing appropriations made for beneficial purposes in accordance with laws, court decisions, or established local customs and regulations should be respected.[341]

Local customs prevailed in many western areas. They were often followed because the value of recording water claims in the event of later controversy became appreciated. But although valuable, posting and recording a customary notice was not indispensable to the validity of an appropriation.[342] A valid prestatutory appropriation could be made by actually diverting the water from the stream, with intent to apply the water to a beneficial use, followed by an application to such use within a reasonable time.[343]

In early decisions, the Washington Supreme Court referred to the matter of appropriating water pursuant to community customs, identified the right so acquired with the declarations of Congress in the Act of 1866, and held that lack of Territorial procedural legislation did not impair the validity of the right.[344] And in its first water rights decision, this court discussed the early establishment of local customs at miners' meetings, or by common agreement of all the people in the locality. Such agreement of all neighbors in a community that water can be and is appropriated by the first settlers in a certain way, said the court, was such a custom as the Congressional Act of 1866 designates as a vested right.[345]

In the statute of 1900 concerning a civil government for Alaska, Congress provided for recording notices and declarations of water rights, and authorized miners in any organized mining district to make rules and regulations governing such recording.[346] This legislation sanctioned a practice that had begun long before when, pursuant to local customs, rules and regulations were established in mining districts not only governing the recording of all claims of water rights, but providing also an orderly procedure for the appropriation of water.

---

[340] *In re silvies River,* 115 Oreg. 27, 39, 237 Pac. 322 (1925).

[341] Oreg. Laws 1891, p. 52.

[342] *Cook* v. *Evans,* 45 S. Dak. 31, 39, 45-46, 185 N.W. 262 (1921), 186 N. W. 571 (1922).

[343] *Application of Filippini,* 66 Nev. 17, 22, 202 Pac. (2d) 535 (1949). In 1875, the Nevada Supreme Court expressed its opinion that there was then no statute of the State that recognized the right of prior appropriation of water for irrigation purposes: *Barnes* v. *Sabron,* 10 Nev. 217, 232 (1875). Much later, after the water rights administrative statute had been in effect for several years, the Nevada court observed that the greater portion of water rights pertaining to the streams of this State had been acquired before enactment of any statute prescribing a method of appropriation, and that such rights had been recognized uniformly by the courts as vested under the common law of the State: *Ormsby County* v. *Kearney,* 37 Nev. 314, 352, 142 Pac. 803 (1914).

[344] *Ellis* v. *Pomeroy Improvement Co.,* 1 Wash. 572, 577-578, 21 Pac. 27 (1889); *Isaacs* v. *Barber,* 10 Wash. 124, 128, 38 Pac. 871 (1894); *Longmire* v. *Smith,* 26 Wash. 439, 448, 67 Pac. 246 (1901).

[345] *Thorpe* v. *Tenem Ditch Co.,* 1 Wash. 566, 570, 20 Pac. 588 (1889).

[346] 31 Stat. 321, ch. 786, tit. 1, ch. 1, § § 15 and 16, pp. 327-328 (1900), 48 U.S.C.A. § § 119 and 383 (1952).

(See "Statutory—Original Statutory Appropriation Procedures—Other Western States", below).

(4) On the other hand, early in the present century, the Nebraska Supreme Court stated that according to the weight of evidence in the case before it, there were very few settlers in northwestern Nebraska in 1880 and 1881. All took what water there was and without regulation or customs of any sort. No one respected any other's rights in water.[347] But appropriations of water were made in Nebraska prior to enactment of the first procedural statute in 1889;[348] and construction of one's works and diversion and application of the water constituted sufficient assertion of his rights until the rights were challenged.[349]

In neighboring Kansas, the supreme court said that prior to the first State legislation authorizing appropriation of water, enacted in 1886, rights to use water by priority of possession had not been recognized in the State. Irrigation had not been necessary for the needs of the early home builders, and local customs of appropriating water were invalid. Hence, there were no vested and accrued water rights to be protected by the Congressional Act of 1866.[350]

(5) In Colorado, there is no State administrative supervision over the acquisition of appropriative rights in water. Until 1969, there were statutory requirements for filing which had value, but which were not essential to the validity of the appropriation.[351]

Idaho has had successive statutes purportedly governing the appropriation of water but which, as noted both above and below, have never been the exclusive means of appropriating water. There is also a so-called "constitutional" or nonstatutory method which is completely informal and involves mere diversion of water and application to beneficial use.[352] It is advantageous to follow the statute, but not necessary.

(6) During the war with Mexico, New Mexico promulgated the Kearney Code, which provided for continued enforcement of existing laws concerning watercourses.[353] Declarations by the first Territorial Legislature of New Mexico, which then included what is now Arizona, impliedly recognized existence of the doctrine of appropriation by authorizing all inhabitants to construct either private or common acequias for their water supplies. But it established no procedure for obtaining water rights.[354] The first Legislature of the separate Territory of Arizona specifically affirmed the right to appropriate streams of

---

[347] *Meng* v. *Coffee,* 67 Nebr. 500, 518-520, 93 N. W. 713 (1903).

[348] Nebr. Laws 1889, ch. 68.

[349] *Kearney Water & Electric Powers Co.* v. *Alfalfa Irr. Dist.,* 97 Nebr. 139, 143-144, 149 N. W. 363 (1914).

[350] *Clark* v. *Allaman,* 71 Kans. 206, 240-241, 80 Pac. 571 (1905).

[351] Colo. Rev. Stat. § 148-4-1 to 148-4-7 (1963), repealed, Laws 1969, ch. 373, § 20. *Black* v. *Taylor,* 128 Colo. 449, 457-458, 264 Pac. (2d) 502 (1953).

[352] *Nielson* v. *Parker,* 19 Idaho 727, 730-731, 733, 115 Pac. 488 (1911).

[353] Kearney Code, § 1.

[354] N. Mex. Laws, July 20, 1851.

running water, but without indicating any formalities that must be or should be observed in so doing.[355] In both Territories, for decades, water was appropriated by constructing acequias or ditches, diverting it from streams, and applying it to beneficial use.

Statutory

Original Statutory Appropriation Procedures

The California procedure.—Enactment of the California Civil Code procedure[356]—which went into effect January 1, 1873, nearly a quarter century after the discovery of gold—was an important historical event. It not only remained California's only formal appropriation procedure for some 40 years, until about a quarter-century after Wyoming's adoption of the administrative procedure, but it also exerted considerable influence on the adoption of elementary statutory procedures in other Western States until the era of administrative procedures was well on its way.

The Civil Code made several declarations of substantive water law. These related to: appropriability of water flowing in a river or stream or down a canyon or ravine; cessation of right on cessation of use; changes in exercise of right; commingling of diverted water with other stream waters; priority as between appropriators; noninterference with riparian rights.

Procedural sections included: posting of notice at point of intended diversion, stating quantity of water claimed, purpose and place of use, means of diversion; recording notice with county recorder within 10 days; commencement of construction work within 60 days after posting of notice; continuance of work diligently and uninterruptedly to completion—which meant conducting the water to the place of use—unless temporarily interrupted by snow or rain. By compliance with these rules, the right related back to the time of posting notice. Failure to comply deprived the claimant of the prior right of use as against a subsequent claimant who complied therewith.

The California Civil Code procedure was not the exclusive method by which one could appropriate water. While it was in effect, an equally valid nonstatutory appropriation could still be made.[357] An advantage of conforming to the procedure, declared in the statute itself, was that it conferred on the claimant the benefit of the doctrine of relation.

Other Western States.—The importance of the California Civil Code procedure extended beyond the confines of that State. It became the prototype of the first statutory appropriation procedures adopted in several other western jurisdictions; and it influenced other legislatures as well. Although some

---

[355] Terr. Ariz. Bill of Rights, art. 22 (1864); Howell Code, ch. LV, "Of Acequias, or Irrigating Canals" (1864).

[356] Cal. Civ. Code § § 1410 to 1422 (1872).

[357] *Lower Tule River Ditch Co.* v. *Angiola Water Co.,* 149 Cal. 496, 499, 86 Pac. 1081 (1906).

features differed from one area to another, the overall situation may be summarized in general terms as follows:

(1) A substantial percentage of western legislatures followed the California pattern by enacting statutes providing for giving notice of intent to appropriate water by posting and recording in county records the details of their claims, for exercising diligence in completing the work, and for application of the principle of "relation back" to claimants who complied with the stated requirements.[358] In the above discussion of nonstatutory appropriation methods, the Congressional statute has been noted which provided for recording notices and declarations of water rights in organized mining districts in Alaska. Organization of the Harris mining district, and adoption in 1882 of rules and regulations governing water appropriations, are related in court decisions which show that they are a close copy of the first 10 sections of the California Civil Code legislation of 10 years earlier.[359]

(2) The influence of the California Civil Code is also evident in the Wyoming acts of 1886 and 1888.[360] The 1886 act required the intending appropriator to file a statement in the county records, to begin construction within 60 days after the filing, and to prosecute the work diligently to completion. The beginning of all surveys was to be construed as the beginning of construction. The Territorial law of 1888, enacted only 2 years prior to the new State legislation of 1890 which sparked the revolutionary trend toward administrative procedure in the West, required the county filing to be made within 90 days *after commencement* of construction. The priority, if construction was pursued diligently to completion, was to relate back to commencement of all necessary surveys. The Arizona legislation of 1893 also shows the influence,[361] but with these important exceptions: After posting notice, a copy had to be filed in the office of the county recorder, not only of the county in which the dam or canal was to be constructed, but of each county through which the canal was to pass, as well as with the Secretary of the Territory. Failure to construct the facilities within a reasonable time, or to use reasonable diligence in maintaining them, would be held to work a forfeiture of the water right.

---

[358] Cal. Civ. Code, § § 1410-1422 (1872); Idaho Laws 1881, p. 267; Mont. Laws 1885, p. 130; Kans. Laws 1886, ch. 115; Nebr. Laws 1889, ch. 68; Wash. Laws 1891, ch. 142 (in Wash. Laws 1889-90, ch. 21, constructor of ditch was required to file in county records, within 90 days after completion, map and verified statement; priority related back to commencement of work if filing made within time limit, otherwise only to date of filing; all rights forfeited unless due diligence exercised); Oreg. Laws 1891, p. 52; Utah Laws 1897, ch. 52, § § 8-11.

[359] *McFarland* v. *Alaska Perseverance Min. Co.*, 3 Alaska 308, 310-311 (1907), affirmed sub nom. *Thorndyke* v. *Alaska Perseverance Min Co.*. 164 Fed. 657 (9th Cir. 1908). See also *Alaska Juneau Gold Min. Co.* v. *Ebner Gold Min. Co.*, 239 Fed. 638 (9th Cir. 1917). Recording of claims of water rights in the Harris, Kougarok, Nome, and Mastodon Creek mining districts is noted in other decisions as well. (See the State summary for Alaska in the appendix.)

[360] Wyo. Laws 1886, ch. 61; Laws 1888, ch. 55.

[361] Ariz. Laws 1893, No. 86.

(3) A variation from the California plan of prescribing posting of notice as the initial statutory step in making an appropriation was to require the formalities to begin within a specified time *after* commencement of the construction work. This was done in the 1888 Wyoming act noted above. Before that, it was declared by the legislatures of Colorado and of Dakota Territory in 1881, and subsequently by Texas in 1889 and New Mexico in 1891.[362]

The 1881 Colorado statute provided that no priority of right should attach until the statement was recorded. The amendment of 1887 required filing not only with the county clerk, but also in the office of the State Hydraulic Engineer. If filed within the time limit, the priority of the right dated from commencement of the work, otherwise from the date of filing. The Dakota statute required first a filing of the location certificate in the county, followed by posting a copy thereof at or near the canal heading. Failure to commence work within 60 days and to prosecute the project to completion without unnecessary delay constituted abandonment of the right. In the Texas act of 1889, the claimant was required to record a sworn statement within 90 days after commencing work, by compliance with which his right related back to such commencement. New Mexico similarly required a recording within 90 days, required completion of the work within 5 years, and provided that no priority of right for any purpose should attach until the record was made.

(4) The last of these early procedural laws were enacted at the close of the 19th century—Oklahoma in 1897 and Nevada in 1899.[363] The Oklahoma statute provided for filing claims with the county recorders of deeds. Nevada provided for appropriating water solely upon application to county boards of water commissioners, consisting of the county commissioners and county surveyor. Whether the county should avail itself of the provisions of the act was left to the discretion of each county board. Apparently, this law was not generally put into effect.

Inadequacies of the Preadministrative Procedures

In the early days of water uses in the several Western States and Territories, local customs in making appropriations predominated, and legislation was either absent or was ineffectual in guiding the intending appropriator in acquiring his right. The California gold miners either invented a system of

---

[362] Colo. Laws 1881, p. 161; Laws 1887, p. 314. The 1881 act was declared unconstitutional on the ground that the subject matter was not adequately stated in the title of the act: *Lamar Canal Co.* v. *Amity Land & Irr. Co.,* 26 Colo. 370, 376-377, 58 Pac. 600 (1899). Terr. Dak. Laws 1881, ch. 142; Tex. Gen. Laws 1889, ch. 88; N. Mex. Laws 1891, p. 130.

[363] Okla. Laws 1897, ch. 19; Nev. Laws 1899, ch. 97. Although Nev. Laws 1866, ch. 100, provided for county records of certificates of intention to construct or maintain ditches or flumes, the State supreme court expressed its opinion that this act was not a recognition of the right of prior appropriation of water for irrigation purposes: *Barnes* v. *Sabron,* 10 Nev. 217, 232 (1875).

making appropriations, or they adopted methods developed in much older mining regions. (See "Origins of the Appropriation Doctrine" in chapter 6.) In any event, their overall system was followed in the extension of the mining industry to other western regions, particularly in the Northwest, and it was adopted by the California Legislature in enacting the first procedural water appropriation statute in the West.

Need for formal procedure.—In the absence of a statutory procedure for appropriating water, there is no record of the appropriation or, if a custom of filing and recording is followed, it is of local value only. And it is unofficial. Establishment of an appropriative right in such an environment depends largely upon testimony of other parties, which becomes increasingly unavailable as the "old-timer" witnesses grow old and die. Among conflicting claims upon a water source, many of which may have been made within a short period of time, relative priorities are understandably difficult to determine. As water uses, particularly for irrigation, developed in the West, something official became needed—some inducement to give specific notice of intent and to record it. Thus, there came a widespread practical need for formalizing appropriation procedures—for attaining at least an approach to order and legality in the initiation of an appropriation.

Purpose of early statutory procedures.—During the 1850's and 1860's, demands upon California water supplies grew enough to move the legislature to take action. This resulted in enacting a procedure as a part of the Civil Code of 1872.[364] By this time, the methods of appropriating water that were established by custom in the mining camps had become well-known, and they were appreciated as practical means of giving notice of and recording the appropriator's intention. So in effect the California Legislature codified, for statewide application, the substance of the mining camp rules and regulations, as construed by the courts. Various other western legislatures followed this lead. These other legislative bodies reached the stage of statutory declarations of appropriative methods at varying times as determined demands for improvement accumulated among their constituents. By far the greatest activity in this particular was in the 1880's.

The California Supreme Court viewed the whole purpose of the 1872 Civil Code procedure as a means of providing evidence whereby parties claiming under hostile diversions could establish their respective priorities in use of the water, and could avoid former difficulties in establishing the precise dates of inception of their respective enterprises.[365] In an earlier decision, this court stated that the legislative purpose "was merely to define with precision the conditions upon which the appropriator of water could have the advantage of the familiar doctrine of relation" which had been expounded and applied by the courts prior to the enactment.[366]

---

[364] Cal. Civ. Code § § 1410-1422 (1872).

[365] *Palmer v. Railroad Commission,* 167 Cal. 163, 172, 138 Pac. 997 (1914).

[366] *De Necochea v. Curtis,* 80 Cal. 397, 401, 20 Pac. 563, 22 Pac. 198 (1889).

Limited value of posting and filing.—In this aspect of providing evidence for the handling of conflicting priorities of right, the provisions of the several statutes had value in providing at least a *prima facie* record of initiation of the appropriation. That, however, was their chief practical contribution to a solution of western water problems. Objection to the requirement for posting notice at the point of intended diversion was that this place might be so isolated as to be seldom seen by human beings. Or it might be so far from ditches of other appropriators as not to come to their attention. Many important streams ran through more than one county. In States that required recordation only in the county in which the diversion was located, an interested party might have to visit several county seats in order to keep informed.[367]

The statutory procedures were optional with the intending appropriator. By using the prevailing statute, he obtained the advantage not only of having his claim on file in the official county records, but also of having his priority relate back to the first procedural step as against other claimants who chose to ignore the statute. But under most of the statutes, the *validity* of an appropriative right obtained by diversion and use without complying with the statute was equal to that of a right completed under the statutory provisions. For example, the Utah posting and filing statute was not enacted until irrigation development in the jurisdiction had been in progress for a half-century.[368] A report says that very few parties took advantage of this law and that it was therefore practically useless.[369]

Testimony of other parties was still necessary in establishing an appropriative right. The notice of intention posted and filed as required by the law, whatever value it may have had in resolving conflicting priorities, proved to be of little or no use in establishing the extent of an appropriative right.

In appraising the posting and filing method, it is necessary to consider how little the settlers who came from the East into a new western community knew about water measurement methods, or even estimates of water flow. Harding emphasizes the facts that although the posting and recording of the notice was a required item in the enactment of an appropriative right under the Civil Code and other statutes, no limitation was placed on the quantity of water that might be claimed, and that no fees proportional to the quantity stated in the notice were imposed. He points out further that many early appropriators had little definite knowledge of their actual needs, and that many plans were indefinite at the time the notice was posted; that many of these people had little knowledge of water measurement and claimed quantities entirely out of

---

[367] The Arizona statute provided for recording the notice in each county through which the canal passed, but not in each county through which the stream flowed. Ariz. Laws 1893, No. 86.

[368] Utah Laws 1897, p. 219 *et seq.*

[369] Teele, R. P., "Report of Irrigation Investigations in Utah," U. S. Dept. Agr. Bull. 124, p. 25 (1903).

proportion to the capacity of the conduit described in the notice; and that only a small fraction of all the notices posted were followed by actual completion of construction. As a natural result of these conditions, statements of claims in the notices were frequently indefinite and liberal.[370]

The California experience.—The California experience with posting and filing methods of appropriating water was publicized in 1901, with frank and sometimes sarcastic comments by the field agents about the absurdities that they encountered. This was done in reporting a study made by the United States Department of Agriculture in important areas of the State under the direction of Elwood Mead, who during much of the preceding decade had been the first State Engineer of Wyoming and had led that State in embarking upon its unprecedented pattern of water appropriation law.[371] It is indeed true that some of the aggregate recorded claims of appropriative water rights in the California areas that were studied border on the fantastic. For example, in the Cache Creek area, a portion of only one group of 64 recorded claims aggregated 147,600 second-feet (cubic feet per second). The claims were stated variously in miner's inches, cubic feet per second, inches per second, and cubic inches under a 4-inch pressure.[372] In the San Joaquin Valley, there were six different notices, each one of which claimed all the water of San Joaquin River. The total claims on the main San Joaquin River alone amounted to more than 700,000 second-feet, which is many times greater than the maximum floodflow of this stream.[373] In the Honey Lake Basin, notices of appropriation aggregated over 700,000 second-feet; yet at the rate which the field agent who wrote this report considered a permissible duty of water for this area—1 inch to 8 acres—62 second-feet would have been enough to supply the 20,000 acres then under irrigation.[374] In writing about the "absurd" claims recorded in two counties respecting Cache Creek and tributaries, and the total absence of record of many appropriations that were then actually being exercised, the investigator stated that such a situation was not exceptional. "In every county in California which I have had occasion to investigate and in every other State where this system of posting and filing prevails, the same conditions hold."[375]

In his introduction to the California study, Dr. Mead wrote that "the aggregate of all claims in California represents enough moisture to submerge the continent. * * * The evil comes in the failure of the law to afford any adequate protection to those who comply with its provisions."[376]

---

[370] Harding, S. T., "Water Rights for Irrigation," pp. 36-37 (1936).

[371] U. S. Dept. Agr. Bull. 100, "Report of Irrigation Investigations in California" (1901).

[372] *Id.* at 170.

[373] *Id.* at 232-233.

[374] *Id.* at 88-89.

[375] *Id.* at 170.

[376] *Id.* at 36.

One of the investigators in the study, a professor of civil engineering in the University of California, wrote that as a result of investigation and study of irrigation

The special agents who made the California study under the direction of Dr. Mead met at Berkeley on completion of the work and held a conference regarding the more important measures necessary to fully develop California's agricultural possibilities. There was "a practical unanimity of opinion among them" as to what should be done. In place of the then existing posting and filing method and complete absence of public supervision over the public waters, these men held it to be the duty of the State to take certain prescribed measures for supervising and controlling water appropriations under "an efficient administrative system."[377]

A decade later, while proposed legislation for water rights administration under a water commission was being considered at a public meeting in San Francisco, this author heard the proposal both warmly supported and bitterly assailed. One objection was that there was "no crying need" for it. Dr. Mead's group of engineers and technicians did not use the phrase "crying need" in their written reports. But one cannot read their accounts and recommendations, and sometimes sarcastic comments, without concluding that that was the way they felt about it.

It is remarkable that senseless claims of appropriated water, such as those stated in the foregoing examples, should be found in county records in so many parts of California. From this authentic study alone, the conclusion is inescapable that a recorded claim of quantity of water, without verification of quantitites actually diverted and used, could have had little or no evidential value.

The Utah experience.—The Utah experience with the posting and filing method came so late in the 19th century and lasted for such a short time as to be negligible. However, pro rata divisions of streamflow expressed either by fractional parts or by percentages of the flow were commonly made in Utah under an earlier law.[378]

Many examples of controlling agreements and decrees are disclosed in a report published in 1903 of a study of irrigation in Utah, comparable to the

---

problems in California, particularly as he found them in San Joaquin Valley, he had drawn among other conclusions the following: "The present method of posting notices and recording appropriations of water, under the existing State law previously referred to, is unsatisfactory to the last degree; in practice it results in great indefiniteness as to the amount of water claimed and uncertainty as to the locality mentioned. It countenances ignorance of water laws and water engineering, leads to obscurity of title, and, in many instances, renders the establishment of the validity and priority of claims almost impossible." *Id.* at 255.

[377] *Id.* at 397-400.

[378] Thomas, George, "The Development of Institutions under Irrigation," pp. 143-144 (1920).

Utah Laws 1880, ch. 20, § 8, provided that a right to the use of water might be measured by fractional parts of the whole supply, or by fractional parts with a limitation as to periods of time and use.

California report noted above, also made under the direction of Elwood Mead.[379] An extreme example—but in fairness not typical—was a stipulated decree awarding to a millowner 1265/4084 of water flowing in a small creek during a prescribed part of the year.[380]

As Dr. George Thomas has said, measurements and records of streamflow over a period of years would have been of inestimable value; "But the counties were poor, engineers were not available, * * *."[381] Agreement upon (a) a scheduled pro rata division of the flow of a fluctuating stream among parties owning varying acreages of land, and (b) upon actual division of the flow pursuant thereto at a particular time, without the benefit of technical assistance, must have been fraught with difficulty and frustration, to say the least.[382]

Abandonment of most posting and filing methods.—It is not strange that as water development and demands for further expansion increased throughout the West, and as the inadequacies of prestatutory and early statutory methods of appropriating water became widely appreciated, movements to obtain better legislative foundation for projected enterprises should appear in one State after another. Furthermore, a national reclamation program was getting under way in Congress.

Mead's experience in Wyoming convinced him that successful administrative control over public waters was no longer an illusory concept. It had become demonstrably a practicable reality. In the introductory article of the California report Dr. Mead made a strong case for public control, in which his group of expert assistants specifically concurred.[383] His letter of submittal of the Utah report repeated the recommendation.[384]

At the turn of the century, heavy pressures were developing in Utah for public supervision over adequate definitions of existing water rights and acquisition of new rights. This resulted in enactment of the first Utah

---

[379] U. S. Dept. Agr. Bull. 124, *supra* note 369. See also Mead, Elwood, "Irrigation Institutions," pp. 229-232 (1910).

[380] U. S. Dept. Agr. Bull. 124, *supra* note 369, at 283. Two typical examples: three-tenths of the flow to plaintiffs, the remainder in definite proportion to 13 of the 16 defendants; nine-elevenths of one-half the flow to plaintiffs, remainder to defendants. *Id.* at 284, 270.

[381] Thomas, G., *supra* note 378, at 140-141.

[382] Wayne D. Criddle, formerly State Engineer of Utah, advised the author in a letter dated April 5, 1962, that the determinations and stipulated decrees dividing streams of the State into fractions and awarding the divisions to various users (as well as those providing for multiple classes of water) "have caused us no end of trouble in water administration," but fortunately most of them were superseded by modern determinations under the special statutory procedure or in private litigation.

   Related old Utah statutory provisions and court decrees with respect to "primary" and "secondary" water rights are discussed below under "Restrictions and Preferences in Appropriation of Water—Preferences in Water Appropriation—Use of appropriated water: In time of water shortage."

[383] U.S. Dept. Agr. Bull. 100, *supra* note 371, at 51-65.

[384] U.S. Dept. Agr. Bull. 124, *supra* note 369, at 7-8.

administrative law in 1903,[385] almost coincidentally with publication of the Department of Agriculture's report. In the same year, neighboring Idaho also enacted an administrative statute.[386] In California, however, it was more than a decade after issuance of the Government report before the Water Commission Act was passed. Even after enactment of the strongly contested California bill in 1913, so much opposition continued as to cause the legislation to be withheld by referendum. It was finally approved by vote of the people in 1914.[387] Nebraska had followed Wyoming more closely in 1895.[388] Arizona enacted a centralized administrative procedure in 1919.[389] The last of the remaining western statutes providing procedure for appropriation of water under centralized administrative procedure was enacted by Alaska in 1966.[390]

Water Rights Administration

Administrative Control of Surface Water Rights

The changeover to administrative control of new appropriations.—(1) Beginning of public control. In the last decades of the 19th century and early in the present one, the growth of water development enterprises, particularly irrigation, in various parts of the West called for both protection of existing claims of appropriative rights and efficient means of acquiring new rights. This was not possible under the inadequate procedures for posting and filing claims, with no public supervision whatsoever.

Echoes of this were heard in various Western jurisdictions. The disfavor in which these procedures were held was emphasized with candor, clarity, and vigor in the 1901 California report of the Department of Agriculture.[391] It became increasingly evident that if the potential of the West's water resources was to be realized in the developing economy, something had to be done about public control of these resources and of their utilization. Necessarily, efficient public control went beyond legislative declarations as construed by the courts in individual controversies and as enforced by their decrees. It invoked continuing action by the executive arm of the State government, through the agency of administrative organizations equipped to find facts and to act upon them. It called for such action by applying clearly worded directives in exercising the police power of the State for the protection and utilization of public property.

The first experiments in State water rights administration were made in Colorado and Wyoming. What they were, and how they differed from each other, are stated immediately below.

---

[385] Utah Laws 1903, ch. 100.
[386] Idaho Laws 1903, p. 223.
[387] Cal. Stat. 1913, ch. 586.
[388] Nebr. Laws 1895, ch. 69.
[389] Ariz. Laws 1919, ch. 164.
[390] Alaska Laws 1966, ch. 50.
[391] U.S. Dept. Agr. Bull. 100, *supra* note 371.

(2) Colorado's efforts in pioneering a combined water rights adjudication and water distribution system will be discussed more fully in chapter 15. Undoubtedly, it was the first important attempt made by any State legislature to provide (a) a special proceeding for the determination of controversies over water rights,[392] which was strictly a judicial proceeding, and (b) a statewide administrative organization for controlling the distribution of water to those whose rights were thus adjudicated. The earliest statutory legislation was enacted in 1879 and 1881.[393]

Colorado did not then provide for administrative control over the *acquisition* of appropriative rights; and it never has done so. The 1881 legislature passed an act requiring the filing of a sworn statement in the county records within a certain period of time after commencement of work.[394] This act continued in effect, with various amendments, until repealed in 1969.[395] But the Colorado Supreme Court made it clear that the filing requirements were restricted to matters of evidence and that the lack thereof did not invalidate the appropriation.[396]

Colorado has no administrative procedure for control over the acquisition of appropriative rights, exclusive in operation, by which a State agency may choose among various applicants for permits and reject those which fail to meet statutory requirements.

Despite the fact that Colorado has not elected to join the great majority of her western sister States in imposing public control upon the acquisition of appropriative rights in the water of watercourses, this does not mean that the confusion and proliferation of exaggerated claims of appropriative rights that were characteristic of the posting and filing era now prevail in this State. Quite the contrary. Colorado's method of solving these difficulties consists of (a) special proceedings for determination and adjudication of water rights,[397] (b) tabulations of all decreed water rights, in order of seniority, and abandonments,[398] and (c) State control over the distribution of stream waters to all those parties whose rights have been adjudicated, pursuant to the applicable court decrees.[399]

(3) Wyoming's pioneering in the field of administrative control over public waters was two-fold. It extended first to providing procedure for initiating new appropriative rights by application to the State officials for permits to

---

[392] Long, Joseph R., "A Treatise on the Law of Irrigation," § 105 (1902).

[393] Colo. Laws 1879, p. 94; Laws 1881, pp. 119 and 142.

[394] Colo. Laws 1881, p. 161.

[395] Colo. Rev. Stat. Ann. § § 148-4-1 to 148-4-7 (1963), repealed, Laws 1969, ch. 373, § 20.

[396] *De Haas* v. *Benesch,* 116 Colo. 344, 351-352, 181 Pac. (2d) 453 (1947); *Archuleta* v. *Boulder & Weld County Ditch Co.,* 118 Colo. 43, 53, 192 Pac. (2d) 891 (1948); *Black* v. *Taylor,* 128 Colo. 449, 457-458, 264 Pac. (2d) 502 (1953).

[397] Colo. Rev. Stat. Ann. § § 148-21-18 to 148-21-23 (Supp. 1969).

[398] Id. § § 148-21-27 and 148-21-28.

[399] Id. § 148-21-34.

appropriate water, in place of the widespread "do-it-yourself" method of diverting water and putting it to use with or without the form of posting and filing a notice of intention. Second, it established a coordinated system of acquiring water rights, adjudicating them, and distributing water to the appropriators in accordance with their relative rights. This comprised the three broad functions of public water rights control, of which all administrative features were exercised by an organization headed by a single constitutional board.

The basis for this Wyoming system was laid in the State constitution, and it was promptly implemented by legislative action.[400] It was the forerunner of the varying administrative systems that were installed in most of the other Western States during the ensuing 30 years. For some of them, it served as a model.

Elwood Mead's part in creating this complete and unprecedented Wyoming water rights system was of major proportions. He was Assistant State Engineer of Colorado, among other occupations, before being appointed first Territorial Engineer of Wyoming in 1888. Then 30 years of age, Mead brought to Wyoming firsthand knowledge of the workings of the Colorado system and developing ideas of changes and additions needed to cope with the growing water problems of the West.

Events in Wyoming in 1888 were rapidly moving toward statehood, which was attained 2 years later. The Act of Congress admitting Wyoming to the Union provided "that the constitution which the people of Wyoming have formed for themselves be, and the same is hereby, accepted, ratified, and confirmed."[401] Within this 2-year period: (a) Mead clarified and organized his ideas of the place of water in the growing economy of the West, the inadequacy of current water laws in solving the growing problems, and the need for establishing certainty as to the nature, acquisition, and protection of water rights by recourse to public supervision. (b) He also made his ideas well-known in the Territory, and he took a leading part in the proceedings dealing with water problems in the constitutional convention.

The Wyoming convention produced a constitution that contains, in contrast to those of other Western States, an exceptionally large number of provisions relating to water. It created the first complete water rights administrative organization in the West. In Dr. Mead's own words, "accumulated water rights complications made irrigation one of the most important questions to be considered in the constitutional convention." Fortunately, he said, the membership of the convention included "a number of men who were unusually well informed on the subject, and who sought not simply to correct the mistakes of the past, but to create a system suited to the needs of the future."[402]

Mead also outlined the legislation necessary to implement the constitutional provisions. He became Wyoming's first State Engineer, and he held this office

---

[400] Wyo. Const. art. I, § § 31-33, art. VIII § § 1-5, art. XIII, § 5; Laws 1890-91, ch. 8.
[401] 26 Stat. 222 (1890).
[402] Mead, Elwood, "Irrigation Institutions," p. 252 (1903).

for 8 years during which the newly created Board of Control faced enormous problems in administering the statute. One such problem was an effort "to discredit the board before its labors began, by an appeal to the prejudice and selfishness of the older appropriators" in an area "where irrigators were already at war with each other."[403]

From the position of Wyoming State Engineer, Mead went to the United States Department of Agriculture, where he was in charge of irrigation investigations in the Office of Experiment Stations. In this capacity, he directed the California and Utah studies and preparation of the reports which are referred to repeatedly under the preceding topic "Inadequacies of the Preadministration Procedures."

(4) Other States. Neighboring Nebraska, into which the vitally important North Platte River flows from Wyoming, followed the Wyoming system closely in 1895. Variations were adopted by Idaho and Utah in 1903; Nevada, New Mexico, North Dakota, South Dakota, and Oklahoma in 1905; Oregon in 1909; Texas in 1913; California in 1914; Kansas and Washington in 1917; Arizona in 1919; and Alaska in 1966.[404]

The threefold State administrative systems pertaining to watercourses. — Hand in hand with the changeover from nonsupervision to State control of new appropriations of water went the installation of statutory procedures for adjudication of water rights and for control over distribution of water to those holding rights to its use. The Wyoming plan comprised this threefold arrangement. Not only did it borrow the ideas of special adjudication and administrative distribution of water from Colorado—although infusing into the adjudication process a strong administration component. It also produced for the first time an effective administrative control over making new appropriations, and coordinated it with adjudication and distribution under an administrative hierachy with a constitutional Board of Control at its summit. Dr. Mead's proposal, the essence of which was put into successful operation, was predominantly administrative. It was initiated at a time when the fields of administrative law and practice in the United States were in their early stages. This was a bold venture, of major significance in the water economy of the West.

The adjudication and water distribution facets of the complex whole of water administration are discussed in chapters 8 and 9, whereas the instant topic concerns appropriation procedures. However, before going into detail on matters of acquiring water rights, it is desirable at this point to emphasize the extent to which the legislatures of the several States have embraced

---

[403] *Id.* at pp. 252-259.

[404] Nebr. Law 1895, ch. 69; Idaho Laws 1903, p. 223; Utah Laws 1903, ch. 100; Nev. Laws 1905, ch. 46; N. Mex. Laws 1905, chs. 102 and 104; N. Dak. Laws 1905, ch. 34; S. Dak. Laws 1905, ch. 132; Terr. Okla. Laws 1905, ch. 21; Oreg. Laws 1909, ch. 216; Tex. Laws 1913, ch. 171; Cal. Stat. 1913, ch. 586; Kans. Laws 1917, ch. 172; Wash. Laws 1917, ch. 117; Ariz. Laws 1919, ch. 164; Alaska Stat. 1966, ch. 50.

administration principles in declaring control over rights to the use of public waters. To this end, a summary of the extent of western administrative policy follows:

(1) Appropriation of water. In all but 3 of the 19 Western States, an intending appropriator of water of a surface watercourse is required by statute to make application to a State official for a permit to make the appropriation. In most but not all of these 16 States, the statutory procedure is declared or commonly considered to be the exclusive method of initiating such an appropriation. Idaho is a definite exception, as noted later under "Current Administrative Procedures—Administrative—Exclusiveness of the statutory procedure."

In Nebraska and Texas, although the appropriation is not complete until water has been diverted and applied to beneficial use, there are no statutory formalities that must be followed after issuance of the permit. The other States in this group provide for supervision over matters connected with completion of the appropriation and final issuance of a certificate or license evidencing the perfected right.

The excepted three States are: Hawaii, in which the doctrine of prior appropriation is not recognized. Colorado, in which diversion and application to beneficial use completes the appropriation, which may then be judicially recognized. Montana, which provides by statute for nonadministrative methods of appropriating: (a) unadjudicated water, by posting notice and filing a copy in the county records;[405] and (b) adjudicated water, the process including an engineering survey, petition to court, and decree of the court.[406]

(2) Adjudication of water rights. All 19 Western States have some kind of special statutory procedure relating to the determination and adjudication of water rights. Necessarily, inasmuch as these procedures involve questions of ownership and exercise or private property rights, the processes are primarily judicial and the final pronouncements are made in court judgments and decrees. However, in most of them, there are provisions for active participation of State administrative agencies in some capacity. This may be by way of making preliminary determinations of the water rights, or assisting the courts by obtaining and providing hydrologic information for use in reaching the judicial decisions.

The Wyoming system provided the earliest integrated administrative-judicial procedures under which the administrative body makes a determination or adjudication of all relative rights on a stream or stream system, which is final unless appealed to the courts.[407] This was followed in Nebraska, where it is still in operation.[408] It was also copied by the Texas Legislature,[409] held to violate

---

[405] Mont. Rev. Codes Ann. § § 89-810 to -814 (1964).
[406] Id. § § 89-829 to -844.
[407] Wyo. Laws 1890-91, ch. 8, Stat. Ann. § § 41-165 to -200 (1957).
[408] Nebr. Laws 1895, ch. 69, Rev. Stat. § § 41-165 to -231 (Supp. 1968).
[409] Tex. Gen. Laws. 1917, ch. 88.

the State constitutional requirements for separation of governmental powers,[410] and was reenacted in modified form in 1967.[411] The original Nevada procedure likewise followed this plan, but was changed to conform to the Oregon variation noted below.[412]

A variation of the Wyoming plan originated in Oregon and was adopted in California, Arizona, and Nevada.[413] This provides for an initial administrative determination of conflicting water rights, which on completion is filed in court as the basis of a civil action. As approved or modified by the court, in whole or in part, it results in a court decree of adjudication. Here the administrative procedure is concluded before the judicial procedure begins. The adjudication is complete when the court judgment is rendered and the decree issued.

In Utah and Washington, the procedure begins with a filing in the appropriate court.[414] Thereafter, in Utah, the State administrator makes the necessary studies and formulates a report and proposed determination.[415] In Washington, the proceeding is referred to the administrator for the purpose of taking testimony as referee.[416] In each of these States, the administrative functions are performed after the judicial proceeding begins and are followed by final judical proceedings and determination of the rights involved.

In New Mexico, North Dakota, and Oklahoma the State administrator's participation is confined to preparation of basic hydrographic data to be offered in evidence in a statutory judicial proceeding. He makes the technical study, and the Attorney General enters suit on behalf of the State for a determination of all rights on the stream system.[417] The data thus obtained by the administrative study are introduced as evidence in the court proceeding. The Montana State administrative agency is authorized to bring action to adjudicate water rights, and may make hydrographic studies and introduce them in evidence.[418] The South Dakota administrative agency shall be requested to make or furnish a hydrographic survey in adjudications of water rights instituted by the State Attorney General or other parties.[419] In Kansas, in any suit brought to adjudicate water rights in which the state is not a

---

[410] *Board of Water Engineers* v. *McKnight,* 111 Tex. 82, 229 S. W. 301 (1921).

[411] Tex. Rev. Civ. Stat. Ann. art. 7542a (Supp. 1970). This requires a court review.

[412] Nev. Laws 1907, ch. 18; Laws 1915, ch. 253, Rev. Stat. § § 533.090-.320 (Supp. 1967-1969).

[413] Oreg. Laws 1909, ch. 216, Rev. Stat., ch. 539 (Supp. 1955); Cal. Stat. 1913, ch. 586, Water Code, Div. 2, pt. 3, ch. 3 (West 1956); Ariz. Laws 1919, ch. 164, Rev. Stat. Ann. § § 45-231 to -245 (1956).

[414] Utah Code Ann. § 73-4-1 (1968); Wash. Rev. Code § 90.03.110 (Supp. 1961).

[415] Utah Code Ann. § 73-4-11 (1968).

[416] Wash. Rev. Code § 90.03.160 (Supp. 1961).

[417] N. Mex. Stat. Ann. § 75-4-4 (1968); N. Dak. Cent. Code Ann. § § 61-03-15 and 61-03-16 (1960); Okla. Stat. Ann. tit. 82, § § 11 and 12 (1970).

[418] Mont. Rev. Codes Ann. § § 89-848 and -851 (Supp. 1969).

[419] S. Dak. Comp. Laws Ann. § 46-10-4 (1967).

"proper party," the court may request the administrative agency to act as referee to investigate and report on any or all physical facts involved.[420]

The Colorado system was said in 1900 to have been "noteworthy as the first important attempt made by any state legislature to provide a special proceeding for the determination of controversies over water rights."[421] These special proceedings are strictly judicial. This system has been augmented by a statutory procedure in which the State Engineer (and a division engineer) provides the water clerk with a tabulated list, in order of seniority, of all decreed water rights.[422]

Hawaii was not a State, or even a part of the United States, when the Colorado legislature enacted its first adjudication statute in 1879. However, the legislature of the Hawaiian Kingdom in 1860 authorized the commissioners of rights-of-way to hear and determine all controversies respecting rights in water.[423] The commissioners' functions are now performed by judges of the circuit courts. Their jurisdiction in this respect is differentiated from the concurrent jurisdiction of the circuit judges sitting as courts of equity.[424]

In several States, provision is made for the technical assistance of the State administrator in water rights actions—a matter of only furnishing evidence.

In addition, there is the court reference procedure. This is utilized considerably in California and, in varying regard and extent, it appears also in the water administrative statutes of some other States.[425] Under this plan, a court in which a water rights controversy is being tried may, at its discretion, call upon the State administrator for assistance on such matters of fact or questions of law as it deems necessary.[426] On a number of occasions, the California trial courts have been encouraged by the State supreme court to take advantage of this opportunity to obtain the skilled and unbiased services of the State agency for help in solving their baffling technical questions.[427]

(3) Distribution of water. All Western States except Hawaii have some kind of statutory procedure respecting the distribution of water to those entitled to receive it. Montana has provisions respecting the appointment, under certain conditions, of water commissioners by courts, to act under their orders, but no administrative function is involved.[428] In Nevada, the State administrative

---

[420] Kans. Stat. Ann. § 82a-725 (1969).

[421] Long, Joseph R., "A Treatise on the Law of Irrigation," p. 193 (1902).

[422] Colo. Rev. Stat. Ann. § 148-21-27(4) (Supp. 1969).

[423] Haw. Laws 1860, p. 12.

[424] Haw. Rev. Stat. § § 664-31 to -37 (1968).

[425] See, e.g., Nev. Rev. Stat. § 533.240 (Supp. 1967); Oreg. Rev. Stat. § 539.020 (Supp. 1955).

[426] Cal. Water Code § 2000 (West Supp. 1970).

[427] *Rancho Santa Margarita* v. *Vail,* 11 Cal. (2d) 501, 81 Pac. (2d) 533 (1938); *Tulare Irr. Dist.* v. *Lindsay-Strathmore Irr. Dist.,* 3 Cal. (2d) 489, 45 Pac. (2d) 972 (1935).

[428] Mont. Rev. Codes Ann. § § 89-1001 to -1024 (1964).

officials, in distributing water pursuant to a court adjudication, are deemed to be officers of the court, under its supervision and control.[429]

The other 16 States have statutory administration procedures of varying character. The Colorado system unquestionably set the pattern for the numerous procedures, beginning with Wyoming, which followed. This is a purely administrative proceeding. Its original and still basic purpose is to execute and enforce the water rights decrees of the courts. After adjudicating the water rights in such an action, the courts do not again become involved unless and until called upon to settle some particular controversy connected with the administrative program.

The extent of the water administrative organizations of these 16 States, the degree to which they are being utilized in the several jurisdictions, and their relative importance in the water rights control programs of these States, all vary considerably.

The oldest systems of the three neighboring States of Colorado, Wyoming, and Nebraska, have effectively operated throughout these jurisdictions. Each State is divided into many areas based on hydrological considerations—a few major divisions that take account of main drainage lines, and a considerable number of subdivisions pertaining to the lesser streams or sections of main ones. Active control emanates from the State administrative agency to the main division officials and thence to those in charge of the subdivisions.[430] These State representatives are charged with the responsibility of delivering water pursuant to the rights of each water user. They open, adjust, and close headgates in order to control outflow from the streams.[431] And they frequently have power to make arrests.[432]

As a practical matter, the wide divergence from one State to another in the importance and utilization of this arm of the water administrative program results from the volume of demands for its functioning. In general, water distribution areas are required by the statutes to be established and put into operation as the need therefor develops. This need may vary with the rate of water development in the State, but not necessarily so. Some examples follow:

California, with its vast and widespread water uses, has one of the simpler distribution plans. An outstanding use of this plan in California is on Kings River, in San Joaquin Valley, where for many decades the water rights situation has been extremely complicated.[433]

---

[429] Nev. Rev. Stat. § 533.220 (Supp. 1967).

[430] Wyo. Const., art. VIII, § § 4 and 5; Wyo. Stat. Ann. § § 41-54 and -61 (1967); Colo. Rev. Stat. Ann. § § 148-21-8, 148-11-3, and 148-11-5 (Supp. 1969); Nebr. Rev. Stat. § § 46-215 to -217, -222, and -223 (Supp. 1968).

[431] Wyo. Stat. Ann. § § 41-57, -58, -63 (1957), and -64 (Supp. 1969); Colo. Rev. Stat. Ann. § § 148-11-3, 148-21-17, and 148-21-34 (Supp. 1969); Nebr. Rev. Stat. § § 46-218, -219, and -224 (Supp. 1968).

[432] Wyo. Rev. Stat. § 41-65 (1957).

[433] For an interesting and authoritative account of that era on this important stream system, see Kaupke, Charles L., "Forty Years on Kings River, 1917-1957" (1957).

North Dakota and South Dakota started out with ambitious water distribution schemes inspired by those of Colorado and Wyoming, yet with very small aggregate areas under irrigation. Not only this, but the watered areas were concentrated mostly in the extreme western regions. Both States eventually discarded these plans as obsolete. Instead, North Dakota simply places all water distribution functions under the Water Conservation Commission.[434] Her sister State of South Dakota authorizes organization of water use control areas and appointment of watermasters when necessary.[435]

Idaho also started out with a statewide plan which was never put into operation. Instead, there is an operating plan of districts for adjudicated streams and elected watermasters under central State supervision.[436] The Kansas water rights law contains provisions for appointment of water commissioners to serve under central control in field offices.[437]

(4) Completeness of the State administrative system authorizations. In the overall view, then, the water rights laws of 16 Western States prescribe procedures governing exercise of all three basic administrative functions of State control over water rights: (a) supervision by an administrative agency over acquisition of appropriative water rights, (b) participation of the administrative agency in water rights adjudications in proceedings initiated by the State, either on its own motion or on petition of water users, and (c) administrative supervision over the distribution of water to those entitled to receive it. These States are Alaska, Arizona, California, Idaho, Kansas, Nebraska, Nevada, New Mexico, North Dakota, Oklahoma, Oregon, South Dakota, Texas, Utah, Washington, and Wyoming. It should be emphasized that this classification takes account only of outstanding statutes—not of the degree to which the statutory authorizations are put into effect, or whether they are used at all.

Two States authorize one administrative function only: Montana, adjudication of water rights; Colorado, distribution of water. Only in Hawaii is there no administrative procedure pertaining to the control of surface water rights.

Administrative Agencies

In most water administration States, exercise of the several administrative functions is delegated to a single agency or official. California is an exception. In 1956, the office of California State Engineer was abolished and its functions pertaining to water and dams were transferred to two newly created agencies: to a State Water Resources Control Board, having functions (a) control of acquisition of appropriative water rights, and (b) participation in adjudication procedures; and to a Department of Water Resources, having function (c) distribution of water in watermaster service areas.

---

[434] N. Dak. Cent. Code Ann. ch. 61-02 (1960).
[435] S. Dak. Comp. Laws Ann. § § 46-10-9 and 46-10-14 (1967).
[436] Idaho Code Ann. § 46-602 (1948).
[437] Kans. Stat. Ann. § 82a-706e (1969).

The Wyoming administrative organization is unique. Acquisition of appropriative rights (a) is supervised by the State Engineer. Adjudication of rights (b) is a function of the Board of Control, which consists of the State Engineer as president and the four water division superintendents. Distribution of water (c) is under the general supervision of the State Engineer, under whom are the four water division superintendents and the water district commissioners. The commissioners are under the immediate direction of the respective superintendents.

Preeminence of office of State Engineer.—The title of "State Engineer" has been prominent in the area of water administration. In the public eye it has tended to symbolize the chief water administrator of the State. Boards and commissions likewise have been prominent. In several instances, the State Engineer has been a board member—usually but not invariably the president. In most of the States there has been, at some time, an individual water official designated variously as State Engineer, State Water Commissioner, State Reclamation Engineer, Chief Engineer, or State Hydraulic Engineer. Usually his office was independent, at least with respect to some of its functions. In other cases, this official headed an organization which was part of an overall agency vested with other functions as well—such as the present Chief Engineer, Division of Water Resources of the Kansas State Board of Agriculture.

The State Engineer office or an equivalent arrangement currently operates in a majority of the western jurisdictions, although in several of them the exercise of at least some of its water rights functions is subject to a certain amount of supervision by an overriding State agency. In some, such as Colorado and Utah, the State Engineer office has always been an individual agency with respect to discharge of its water rights duties. During part of California's water administration experience, this official performed these duties as head of a division in a State department. The North Dakota State Engineer office was absorbed by the State Water Conservation Commission, of which he became secretary and chief engineer. The Commission's approval is required for the exercise of some of his delegated functions, but not for others. In South Dakota, the duties of the State Engineer pertaining to water rights control were transferred to a newly established State Water Resources Commission.

For many years, the officials who administer State water rights control policies—whether designated "State Engineer" or members of a comparable State agency—have maintained an organization known as the Association of Western State Engineers. This organization holds annual meetings in the Western States. Its programs attract Federal, State, and other speakers on current and prospective water problems. The presidency of the association is rotated annually among the States.

Changes over the years.—Very few of the agencies and offices that have been vested with supervision over surface water rights laws of 18 Western States (excluding Hawaii, in which there is no such State agency) have escaped reorganization and hence have remained unchanged throughout the water administration histories of their respective States.

Wyoming's original water administration organization has persisted to the present time—a Board of Control, comprising the State Engineer as president and the four water commissisioners. Utah likewise has had but one water administrative agency—the State Engineer. In Colorado, the only change in designation was an early one in name only—from State Hydraulic Engineer to State Engineer.

In most of the other States, however, several changes have taken place. This is exemplified in Nebraska—adjacent to both Colorado and Wyoming, both of which are noteworthy in that they have continued their organizations unchanged over more than seven decades. In Nebraska, the water administrative agency was first concerned solely with irrigation, later with other State functions as well, and finally with water resources only. Another contrasting State is California, which entered the water administration field comparatively late with a State Water Commission. The commission was subsequently included as a division in a department of public works, the water resource functions of which were later, by specific direction of the legislature, administered and exercised through the State Engineer. Currently, these California functions are divided between two independent State agencies—a five-member Water Resources Control Board, and a major department in the State Government vested with large powers in the field of water resource protection and development.

Changes in water administration organizations have resulted from various causes. Some are changes in name only. Of course, some changes stem from the frequently evidenced impulse to reorganize State agencies in order to meet changing and developing public needs. This is not a difficult legislative process where the demands are strong enough. In Wyoming, where legislation creating the water agencies is imbedded in the State constitution, it would be considerably more difficult, but not impossible if the need were to arise. Cutbacks in several jurisdictions resulted from lack of necessity for large organizations.

Thus in both Dakotas, the originally elaborate water distribution organizations proved unnecessary and were abolished. Experience with the Oregon Board of Control led to successive elimination of the two superintendent members and transfer of their duties to the remaining member, the State Engineer. Yet the development of Oregon's water economy has since resulted in requiring approval of the State Water Resources Board in case of issuance of certain permits of certain types prior to action thereon by the State Engineer, at the same time vesting the duties of the Hydroelectric Commission in the State Engineer. New Mexico for a time had a Board of Water Commissioners, the function of which was to hear and decide appeals from the State Engineer's acts and decisions, subject to appeal therefrom to the courts. This was finally abolished as an unnecessary link in the chain of appeal from the State Engineer—the highest administrative official—to the courts.

In other States, to cope with growing water needs, increases in personnel have been made to discharge properly the statutory functions of water rights control. And additional duties pertaining to conservation and development of water supplies either have been added to those of the existing organization, or have been vested in new agencies with which the State Engineer may or may not be associated.

Along with water agency reorganizations have gone some reassignments of the three water rights control functions—appropriation of water, determination of conflicting water rights, and distribution of public waters to the users. Trends in the several States with respect to policies of concentrating all three water rights functions in one agency, or of dividing them among more than one, may be charted as follows—with the caution that vesting certain functions in the State Engineer, and others in a board of which the State Engineer is a member, is listed as dividing the functions between *two* agencies:

(1) No change in policy: (a) Concentration of all functions in a single agency: Alaska, Arizona, Colorado, Montana, Nebraska, Oklahoma, Utah, Washington. (b) Dividing functions between two agencies: Wyoming.

(2) Functions originally consolidated in one agency, later divided between two: California.

(3) Functions originally divided between agencies, later consolidated in one: Idaho, Nevada, New Mexico, South Dakota.

(4) Functions originally divided between agencies, later consolidated in one, still later divided between two: North Dakota, Oregon.

In addition to the foregoing policy changes with respect to 16 States, all functions concentrated in a single agency were: (a) increased in number: Kansas. (b) Reduced and later increased in number: Texas.

Declarations of unconstitutionality of statutory provisions by the Texas Supreme Court resulted in elimination of the adjudication and distribution functions from the water rights statute for several years until the reenactment of such provisions in modified form in 1967. Comparable decisions in Idaho and South Dakota led to modifications of statutory adjudication provisions but without completely eliminating this function from the State programs.

Changes in the several States.—Under the ensuing paragraph headings by States, the successive changes in each of these 18 Western States are indicated with respect to both agencies and functions. Numerals in parentheses are used to designate original, intermediate, and current periods. Letters in parentheses refer to the three basic functions of (a) appropriating water, (b) participation in water rights adjudication, (c) distribution of water, (d) all three functions.

Alaska.—(1) Original and current. Department of Natural Resources: (d) All functions.

Arizona.—(1) Original. State Water Commissioner: (d) all functions.

(2) Intermediate. State Land Commissioner: (d) all functions.

(3) Current. State Land Department: (d) all functions.

California.—(1) Original. State Water Commission: (a) appropriation; (b) adjudication.

(2) Intermediate. Department of Public Works, Division of Water Rights: (d) all functions.

(3) Intermediate. Department of Public Works, Division of Water Resources, State Engineer: (d) all functions.

(4) Intermediate. State Water Rights Board: (a) appropriation; (b) adjudication. Department of Water Resources: (c) distribution.

(5) Current. State Water Resources Control Board: (a) appropriation; (b) adjudication. Department of Water Resources: (c) distribution.

Colorado.—(1) Original. State Hydraulic Engineer: (c) distribution.

(2) Current. State Engineer: (c) distribution.

Idaho.—(1) Original. State Engineer: (a) appropriation. Water commissioners and State Engineer: (b) adjudication. State Board of Irrigation (State Engineer and commissioners): (c) distribution.

(2) Intermediate. State Engineer: (d) all functions.

(3) Intermediate. Department of Reclamation, State Reclamation Engineer: (d) all functions.

(4) Current. Department of Reclamation, State Reclamation Engineer: (d) all functions. State Water Resources Board: (a) appropriation for impoundments of more than 10,000 acre-feet; (b) adjudication.

Kansas.—(1) Original. Kansas Water Commission: (a) appropriation.

(2) Intermediate. Division of Water Resources, State Board of Agriculture: (a) appropriation.

(3) Current. Chief Engineer, Division of Water Resources, State Board of Agriculture: (d) all functions.

Montana.—(1) Original. State Engineer, at direction of State Water Conservation Board: (b) adjudication.

(2) Current. State Water Resources Board: (b) adjudication.

Nebraska.—(1) Original. State Board of Irrigation: (d) all functions.

(2) Intermediate. State Board of Irrigation, Highways, and Drainage: (d) all functions.

(3) Intermediate. Department of Public Works, Bureau of Irrigation, Water Power, and Drainage: (d) all functions.

(4) Intermediate. Department of Roads and Irrigation, Bureau of Irrigation, Water Power, and Drainage: (d) all functions.

(5) Current. Department of Water Resources: (d) all functions.

Nevada.—(1) Original. Water commissioners: (c) distribution.

(2) Intermediate. State Engineer: (b) adjudication. State Board of Irrigation: (c) distribution.

(3) Intermediate. State Engineer: (a) appropriation; (b) adjudication. State Board of Irrigation: (c) distribution.

(4) Intermediate. State Engineer: (a) appropriation; (b) adjudication. State Board of Irrigation (State Engineer a member): (c) distribution.

(5) Intermediate. State Engineer: (d) all functions.

(6) Current. State Engineer, executive head Division of Water Resources, Department of Conservation and Natural Resources: (d) all functions.

New Mexico.—(1) Original. Territorial Irrigation Engineer: (a) appropriation. Board of Control (Territorial Irrigation Engineer and water commissioners): (b) adjudication; (c) distribution.

(2) Intermediate. Territorial Engineer, subject to appeal to Board of Water Commissioners: (d) all functions.

(3) Intermediate. State Engineer, subject to appeal to Board of Water Commissioners: (d) all functions.

(4) Current. State Engineer: (d) all functions.

North Dakota.—(1) Original. State Engineer: (a) appropriation; (b) adjudication. Board of Water Commissioners (State Engineer and water commissioners): (c) distribution.

(2) Intermediate. State Engineer: (d) all functions.

(3) Current. State Engineer, subject to State Water Conservation Commission: (a) appropriation. State Engineer, State Water Conservation Commission: (b) adjudication. State Water Conservation Commission: (c) distribution.

Oklahoma.—(1) Original. Statutory office of State Engineer, but duties performed by State Board of Agriculture: (d) all functions.

(2) Intermediate. Oklahoma Planning and Resources Board: (d) all functions.

(3) Current. Oklahoma Water Resources Board: (d) all functions.

Oregon.—(1) Original. State Engineer: (a) appropriation. State Board of Control (State Engineer and division superintendents): (b) adjudication; (c) distribution.

(2) Intermediate. State Engineer: (a) appropriation. State Water Board (State Engineer and division superintendents): (b) adjudication; (c) distribution.

(3) Intermediate. State Engineer: (d) all functions.

(4) Current. State Engineer, State Water Resources Board: (a) appropriation. State Engineer: (b) adjudication; (c) distribution.

South Dakota.—(1) Original. State Engineer: (a) appropriation; (b) adjudication. Board of Water Commissioners (State Engineer and water commissioners): (c) distribution.

(2) Intermediate. State Engineer: (a) appropriation; (b) adjudication.

(3) Intermediate. State Engineer: (d) all functions.

(4) Current. Water Resources Commission: (d) all functions.

Texas.—(1) Original. State Board of Water Engineers: (d) all functions.

(2) Intermediate. State Board of Water Engineers: (a) appropriation.

(3) Intermediate. Texas Water Commission: (a) appropriation.

(4) Current. Texas Water Rights Commission: (d) all functions.

Utah.—(1) Original and current. State Engineer: (d) all functions.

Washington.—(1) Original. State Hydraulic Engineer: (d) all functions.

(2) Intermediate. Department of Conservation and Development, Supervisor of Hydraulics: (d) all functions.

(3) Intermediate. Department of Conservation and Development, Supervisor of Water Resources: (d) all functions.

(4) Intermediate. Department of Conservation, Supervisor of Water Resources: (d) all functions.

(5) Intermediate. Department of Water Resources, Director of Water Resources: (d) all functions.

(6) Current. Department of Ecology, Director of Ecology: (d) all functions.

Wyoming.—(1) Original and current. State Engineer, Board of Control: (a) appropriation. Board of Control (State Engineer and superintendents): (b) adjudication; (c) distribution.

Current Appropriation Procedures

Administrative

States and agencies vested with supervision over appropriation of water.— To recapitulate:

(1) States. All Western States except Colorado, Hawaii, and Montana provide statutory procedure for the acquisition of appropriative water rights under the supervision of a central State administrative agency.

(2) State Engineer. In New Mexico, Utah, and Wyoming, the State Engineer is the supervising official, acting independently.

In Nevada, the State Engineer heads a division in a State department.

In North Dakota, with approval of the commission of which he is secretary and chief engineer, the State Engineer may accept and process applications to appropriate water.

In Oregon, the State Engineer must refer applications for permits that may involve the public welfare to a water resources board for consideration and action.

(3) In the remaining 10 Western States that have public supervision, the supervising State agency is a department, board, or commission. The concept of several statutes is that the agency vested with this function acts through a specified official thereof.

Purposes of the legislation.—Some of the influences and pressures that led one Western State after another to abandon its posting and filing method of appropriating water—or its lack of any statutory method—and to move over into the field of administrative control are discussed above under "Statutory— Inadequacies of the Preadministration Procedures." Broadly, so far as acquisition of rights was concerned, the chief purpose was to provide an orderly method for the appropriation of unappropriated waters.[438]

This new method consisted of (a) making applications to an informed and experienced State agency for specific quantities of water which bore some relation to the purposes and needs of the appropriator; (b) denying

---

[438] *Temescal Water Co.* v. *Department of Public Works*, 44 Cal. (2d) 90, 95, 280 Pac. (2d) 1 (1955).

applications for unavailable water or the approval of which would conflict with existing rights or would not be in the public interest; and (c) recording all details of the proposed appropriation from start to finish in a central State office where they would be readily available for use as evidence in a judicial determination of the rights involved.

There was nothing in the posting and filing method—as it operated in actual practice—to prevent an intending appropriator from initiating a right and beginning construction of work, so long as he was not stopped by litigation. This was the case even though claims on file often reached absurd totals. The administrative procedure, on the other hand, aimed at discouraging the making of applications for water in streams with respect to which the administrator had determined, for his own official purposes, that appropriative rights in being already laid claim to more water than the stream carried in ordinary seasons. It tended to warn the would-be appropriator of the risk, in quantitative measure, that he would run of having his right attach to only high floodflows, if he insisted on carrying it through to completion. Of course, he might obtain a storage right of considerable value. But the only available direct flow right might be such as to give him access to water only in occasional years, or at least only in the early seasons. Of inestimable value were the accumulating of available records incident to operation of the administrative programs, and results of the hydrographic surveys and hydrologic studies that were encouraged or commanded by the new laws.

An important purpose of the legislation in some States, also discussed in chapter 6 (in connection with interrelationships between appropriative and riparian principles), was to make it possible, by reason of adequate legislation, to strengthen the standing of appropriative rights in the jurisdiction as against claims of superior riparian rights. Oregon took the first orderly and well-prepared step in this direction in its water code of 1909. In this act, an efficient system of acquiring appropriative rights and of adjudicating them was worked out. Provisions were made for affirming and protecting riparian rights put to actual beneficial use prior to the enactment or within a short time thereafter, and for adjudicating all rights under the procedure provided in the statute.[439]

In 1945 the Kansas legislature, faced with decisions of the State supreme court that resulted in leaving the appropriation doctrine almost unworkable, enacted a new appropriation statute in which the Oregon precedent was invoked. Important amendments were made in 1957 for the purpose of strengthening the appropriation position in regard to riparian claims.[440] South Dakota followed the lead of Oregon and Kansas.[441]

---

[439] Oreg. Laws 1909, ch. 216.

[440] Kans. Laws 1945, ch. 390; Laws 1957, ch. 539.

[441] S. Dak. Laws 1955, ch. 430.

Constitutionality of the legislation.—(1) Exercise of the State's police power. Provisions for the appropriation of water under administrative control have been before the courts of many States on various points. The fundamental principle that the State has the right to provide for the appropriation of unappropriated public waters and to control the issuance of appropriative water rights has not been denied by any high court in the West. In many cases, the validity of the statutory provisions for acquisition of appropriative rights appears to have been taken for granted. In others, the court expressed its general approval, although some particular item may have been considered objectionable. As discussed later, some features of the adjudication statutes were held unconstitutional.

Aside from the protection of any proprietary interest that the State might have in the waters of its public streams, the State and Federal courts in Nevada agreed that regulation of such waters, including their appropriation, is clearly within the lawful exercise of the State's police power.[442] The Idaho Supreme Court held it to be settled law that the legislature might regulate the appropriation and use of public waters.[443] This is not to be confused with the Idaho rule that the statutory procedure in appropriating water is not exclusive; nor with the unconstitutionality of certain features of the statutory adjudication procedure, noted below.

Constitutionality of the Wyoming water administration law was considered at length and was sustained by the supreme court of that State.[444] "That the state may supervise and control the appropriation, diversion and distribution of the public waters, and impose that duty upon administrative officers, is settled by our former decisions, and is equally well settled in other states, where the doctrine of prior appropriation of water prevails."[445] By such supervision, no rights of private property are invaded. Under the police power, in the interest of the public welfare, and for the protection of private as well as public rights, said the court, property intended to be used for no other purpose than that of diverting public waters is regulated. The same result was reached in Nebraska with respect to the water rights law of that jurisdiction, which was based upon that of Wyoming.[446]

The California Supreme Court held that the conclusions arrived at by the administrative agency in determining due diligence and other matters involved

---

[442] *Ormsby County* v. *Kearney,* 37 Nev. 314, 336-338, 142 Pac. 803 (1914); *Humboldt Land & Cattle Co.* v. *Allen,* 14 Fed. (2d) 650, 653 (D. Nev. 1926); *Humboldt Lovelock Irr. Light & Power Co.* v. *Smith,* 25 Fed. Supp. 571, 573, 575 (D. Nev. 1938).

[443] *Big Wood Canal Co.* v. *Chapman,* 45 Idaho 380, 401-402, 263 Pac. 45 (1927).

[444] *Farm Investment Co.* v. *Carpenter,* 9 Wyo. 110, 132-139, 61 Pac. 258 (1900); *Wyoming Hereford Ranch* v. *Hammond Packing Co.,* 33 Wyo. 14, 31-36, 236 Pac. 764 (1925).

[445] *Hamp* v. *State,* 19 Wyo. 377, 391-392, 118 Pac. 653 (1911).

[446] *Farmers' Irr. Dist.* v. *Frank,* 72 Nebr. 136, 138-140, 100 N. W. 286 (1904).

in completing an appropriation are not judicial findings but are merely for their own guidance in performing their statutory duties. Hence, they are not such as to render the provision unconstitutionl.[447] On the other hand, provisions in the California statute for judicial review of administrative action were held unconstitutional. They were replaced by a procedure which the supreme court declared would constitute the proper remedy.[448]

(2) Effect on riparian rights. Validity of some of the State appropriation statutes with respect to their effect upon riparian rights has been called in question. For example, the Texas Supreme Court declared that the several water appropriation statutes down to and including that of 1917 were valid in so far as they authorized appropriation of stream waters without violation of existing riparian rights.[449]

Under "Purposes of the legislation," mention has been made of the Oregon, Kansas, and South Dakota statutes which contained provisions restricting operation of the riparian doctrine when it conflicted with the appropriative principles that were being propounded by the legislation. The Oregon provisions were approved by the State supreme court and by a United States Court of Appeals.[450] The Kansas provisions likewise were held by State and Federal courts to be not invalid on the issues involved.[451] Constitutionality of the South Dakota legislation of 1955 has been upheld by the State supreme court in 1964.[452]

Exclusiveness of the statutory procedure.—(1) Generally held to be exclusive. In most States in which administrative procedure for appropriating

---

[447] *Department of Public Works* v. *Superior Court,* 197 Cal. 215, 221-222, 239 Pac. 1076 (1925).

[448] *Mojave River Irr. Dist.* v. *Superior Court,* 202 Cal. 717, 725-726, 262 Pac. 724 (1927); *Temescal Water Co.* v. *Department of Public Works,* 44 Cal. (2d) 90, 99-100, 106, 280 Pac. (2d) 1 (1955); Cal. Water Code § 1360 (West Supp. 1970).

[449] *Motl* v. *Boyd,* 116 Tex. 82, 124, 286 S.W. 458 (1926).

[450] *In re Hood River,* 114 Oreg. 112, 173-182, 227 Pac. 1065 (1924); *California-Oregon Power Co.* v. *Beaver Portland Cement Co.,* 73 Fed. (2d) 555, 562-569 (9th Cir. 1934). Compare *California Oregon Power Co.* v. *Beaver Portland Cement Co.,* 295 U. S. 142, 155-165 (1935). See *Fitzstephens* v. *Watson,* 218 Oreg. 185, 344 Pac. (2d) 221 (1959).

[451] *State ex rel. Emery* v. *Knapp,* 167 Kans. 546, 555-556, 207 Pac. (2d) 440 (1949); *Baumann* v. *Smrha,* 145 Fed. Supp. 617 (D. Kans. 1956), affirmed per curiam, 352 U. S. 863 (1956); *Williams* v. *Wichita,* 190 Kans. 317, 374 Pac. (2d) 578 (1962), appeal dismissed, 375 U.S. 7 (1963), rehearing denied, 375 U.S. 936 (1963).

[452] *Belle Fourche Irr. Dist.* v. *Smiley,* 176 N. W. (2d) 239 (S. Dak. 1970); *Knight* v. *Grimes,* 80 S. Dak. 517, 127, N. W. (2d) 708 (1964). In the *Belle Fourche* case the court said that the "Decision in the Knight case concerned with underground waters is equally applicable to surface waters." 176 N. W. (2d) at 245.

Regarding the validity of North Dakota legislation, see *Baeth* v. *Hoisveen,* 157 N. W. (2d) 728, 733-734 (N. Dak. 1968), discussed in chapter 6 under "Establishment of the Riparian Doctrine in the West—Interrelationships of the Dual Water Rights Systems—The Status in Summary: By States—North Dakota."

water is in effect, the procedure provided by the current statute is either held or assumed to be the only way in which an intending appropriator may acquire an appropriative right. Idaho is a definite exception, as discussed later in this subtopic.

The intent of the legislatures that this specific, detailed procedure shall be exclusive is generally apparent from the wording of their declarations. Some, such as that of North Dakota, state that any intending appropriator, before commencing construction of works or taking water from any constructed works "shall make an application to the State Engineer for a water permit unless such construction or taking from such constructed works is for domestic or livestock purposes or for fish, wildlife and other recreational uses."[453] Others go further. For example, after such an introductory statement, Oregon adds emphasis by declaring that no person shall use, store, or divert any water until after issuance of such a permit.[454] Several statutes provide that no water right may be acquired solely by adverse use or adverse possession.[455] The Texas legislature adds a provision that anyone who willfully takes water for any purpose without first complying with all provisions of the act is guilty of a misdemeanor.[456] And the California Water Code declares that the diversion or use of water contemplated by the statute other than as authorized therein is a trespass, which the Board may bring action to have enjoined.[457]

Except in Idaho, high courts that have been called upon to pass on these legislative declarations have usually interpreted them literally. For example, the requirements of the pioneer statute—Wyoming—were so construed as to make a permit mandatory. This was held to be in the public interest, reasonable, and constitutional.[458] And in Arizona—the latest of the 17 contiguous Western States to adopt an administrative statute—the supreme court pointed out that prior to the 1919 water rights enactment an intending appropriator had the choice of following the then current statute or of disregarding it and relying solely on mere application of water to beneficial use. Thereafter, it was stated,

---

[453] N. Dak. Cent. Code Ann. § 61-04-02 (Supp. 1969).

[454] Oreg. Rev. Stat. § 537.130 (Supp. 1969).

[455] Kans. Stat. Ann. § 82a-705 (1969); Nev. Rev. Stat. § 533.060(3) (Supp. 1967); Utah Code Ann. § 73-3-1 (1968).

[456] Tex. Rev. Civ. Stat. Ann. art. 7520 (1954). See the declaration of an emergency respecting this matter in Laws 1953, ch. 358, § 3.

[457] Cal. Water Code § 1052 (West Supp. 1970). Citing this provision, the California Supreme Court observed that therefore there need be no apprehension lest rights become vested, by prescription or otherwise, in an excessive use of water or in a use for unauthorized purposes: *Meridian* v. *San Francisco*, 13 Cal. (2d) 424, 450, 90 Pac. (2d) 537 (1939).

[458] Wyo. Stat. Ann. § 41-201 (1957); *Laramie Rivers Co.* v. *Le Vasseur*, 65 Wyo. 414, 431, 202 Pac. (2d) 680 (1949); *Wyoming Hereford Ranch* v. *Hammond Packing Co.*, 33 Wyo. 14, 29-36, 236 Pac. 764 (1925).

he had no choice.[459] Judicial expressions were made in some other States.[460]

(2) The Utah experience. For a time there was a question in Utah as to whether the current method of appropriating water was exclusive, but the doubt was resolved in the affirmative. After holding in the *Hooppiania* and *Torsak* cases that the statutory requirements must be complied with,[461] the Utah Supreme Court 10 years later purported to overrule the *Hooppiania* case in this respect, although the statement appears to have been *dictum*.[462] However, the legislature, then in session, so amended the appropriation statute as to provide in explicit terms that no appropriation of water could be made and no right to the use thereof initiated otherwise than in the manner provided in the statute.

Four years later, the Utah legislature further declared its intent that the statutory provisions relating to abandonment and forfeiture of appropriative rights should be applicable whether the unused or abandoned water is permitted to run to waste or is used by others without right. It was further declared that no right to the use of water, either appropriated or unappropriated, can be acquired by adverse use or adverse possession.[463]

The Utah Supreme Court accepted the legislative position. The court declared that the 1939 amendment left no doubt that thereafter no right to the use of unappropriated water could be acquired without complying with the statutory requirements.[464]

(3) Definite exception in Idaho. As above stated, Idaho water law presents a definite exception to the general rule as to exclusiveness of the current statutory procedure.

There are in this jurisdiction two prevailing methods of appropriating water of watercourses, of equal validity—the "so-called constitutional" method and the "statutory" method.[465] The "constitutional" method stems from the fact that the

[459] *Parker* v. *McIntyre*, 47 Ariz. 484, 489, 56 Pac. (2d) 1337 (1936); *Tattersfield* v. *Putnam*, 45 Ariz. 156, 174, 41 Pac. (2d) 228 (1935); *England* v. *Ally Ong Hing*, 105 Ariz. 65, 459 Pac. (2d) 498, 504 (1969).

[460] *Crane* v. *Stevinson*, 5 Cal. (2d) 387, 398, 54 Pac. (2d) 1100 (1936); *Meridian* v. *San Francisco*, 13 cal. (2d) 424, 450, 90 Pac. (2d) 537 (1939); *Enterprise Irr. Dist.* v. *Tri-State Land Co.*, 92 Nebr. 121, 147-148, 138 N. W. 171 (1912); *Harkey* v. *Smith*, 31 N. Mex. 521, 526, 247 Pac. 550 (1926). The extant statutory method is the only way since the act became effective in which water rights may be acquired in Oregon: *Staub* v. *Jensen*, 180 Oreg. 682, 686-687, 178 Pac. (2d) 931 (1947).

[461] *Deseret Live Stock Co.* v. *Hooppiania*, 66 Utah 25, 34-37, 239 Pac. 479 (1925); *Torsak* v. *Rukavina*, 67 Utah 166, 170, 246 Pac. 367 (1926).

[462] *Wrathall* v. *Johnson*, 86 Utah 50, 120, 40 Pac. (2d) 755 (1935).

[463] Utah Laws 1935, ch. 105, Laws 1939, ch. 111, Code Ann. §§ 73-1-4 and 73-3-1 (1968).

[464] *Hanson* v. *Salt Lake City*, 115 Utah 404, 415, 205 Pac. (2d) 255 (1949).

[465] *Pioneer Irr. Dist.* v. *American Ditch Assn.*, 50 Idaho 732, 737, 1 Pac. (2d) 196 (1931). See *Vineyard Land & Stock Co.* v. *Twin Falls Salmon River Land & Water Co.*, 245

1889 constitution provided that the right to divert and appropriate the unappropriated waters of any natural stream for beneficial uses should never be denied.[466] This declaration has been construed as authorizing appropriation of stream water "by actually diverting the water and applying it to a beneficial use."[467]

It is true that when enacted, the statute provided that all rights to divert and use the waters of the State for beneficial purposes shall be acquired and confirmed under its provisions. It still so provides.[468] Despite this, the Idaho Supreme Court holds that in view of the constitutional declaration, legislation providing for a specific method of appropriating water *does not* thereby set up an exclusive method.[469]

There is no superiority of the right obtained under either method over that obtained under the other. There is an advantage in following the statutory procedure with respect to application of the doctrine of relation.

Nature of powers of administrators.—(1) Administrative and quasi-judicial. State officials vested with supervision and control over the unappropriated stream waters within their jurisdiction are part of the executive arm of the State Government. Primarily and essentially, they are just what they are commonly designated—administrative officers. In the performance of some of their delegated functions these officials exercise quasi-judicial powers. But this is no more than is done by many other regulatory boards and commissions throughout the United States. In no case is a water user or water claimant denied recourse to the truly judicial processes of the courts from an action, or from a failure to act, on the part of a water official which impairs a substantial right.

A few examples may be cited of instances in which the courts have commented or passed upon the nature of water administration powers, chiefly in the fields of determination or adjudication of water rights and distribution of water.

Objection was made to the Wyoming administrative law on the ground that it conferred judicial power on the Board of Control. The supreme court answered that this was a purely statutory proceeding which did not depend on the complaint of an injured party, and did not result in a judgment for damages nor issuance of any customary judicial process. The court concluded that the determination of relative water rights by the Board of Control was primarily administrative rather than judicial in character, inasmuch as in such proceeding no claimant obtained redress for injury but obtained evidence of title to a

Fed. 9, 20-21 (9th Cir. 1917). Also see *Village of Peck* v. *Denison,* 92 Idaho 747, 450 Pac. (2d) 310, 313 (1969).

[466] Idaho Const., art XV, § 3. In 1928, this section was amended to authorize the State to regulate and limit the use thereof for power purposes.

[467] *Sand Point Water & Light Co.* v. *Panhandle Development Co.,* 11 Idaho 405, 413-414, 83 Pac. 347 (1905).

[468] Idaho Code Ann. § 42-201 (1948).

[469] *Nielson* v. *Parker,* 19 Idaho 727, 730-731, 733, 115 Pac. 488 (1911); *Bachman* v. *Reynolds Irr. Dist.,* 56 Idaho 507, 514, 55 Pac. (2d) 1314 (1936).

valuable right. "The board, it is true, acts judicially, but the power exercised is quasi-judicial only, and such as under proper circumstances may appropriately be conferred upon executive officers or boards."[470] Considering the facts that the determination of the Wyoming Board of Control was made final unless appealed to the courts, and that the decision was rendered in the youth of administrative law and practice in the United States, this was indeed an advanced position for a State supreme court to take.

A few years after this Wyoming decision, the Supreme Court of Nebraska passed on the sections of the Nebraska statute of 1895 conferring upon the State administrative agency authority to ascertain and determine the amount of past appropriations and to allow further appropriations. This legislation, the court held, was not unconsitutional as conferring upon such agency the exercise of judicial functions. As a matter of fact, said the court, these powers were of a quasi-judicial character and were a valid exercise of the legislative power.[471]

By contrast with the Wyoming and Nebraska courts, the Texas Supreme Court, in *Board of Water Engineers* v. *McKnight,* held unconstitutional a legislative attempt to incorporate in the water law of that State a procedure for statutory determination of water rights based on those of Wyoming and Nebraska.[472] The Texas court's objection was that the legislature had attempted to confer on persons belonging to the executive branch of the State government powers that properly attach to another branch, without express permission of the constitution. Hence the statute was held void.[473] Years later, in an oil and gas case, the Texas Supreme Court decided a parallel question of public policy as to which the *McKnight* decision was held to be not controlling. This holding resulted from a State constitutional amendment[474] adopted after the effective date of the statutes found objectionable in the *McKnight* decision.[475]

The original water administration law of Nevada contained a provision based on those of Wyoming and Nebraska purporting to make the State Engineer's determination of water rights conclusive, subject to the right of appeal. This was believed by a majority of the Nevada Supreme Court to be unconstitutional.[476] The law was promptly changed by the legislature to conform to the Oregon system in which judicial as well as administrative process is requisite to

---

[470] *Farm Investment Co.* v. *Carpenter,* 9 Wyo. 110, 132-135, 61 Pac. 258 (1900).

[471] *Crawford Co.* v. *Hathaway,* 67 Nebr. 325, 365-368, 93 N. W. 781 (1903), overruled on different matters by *Wasserburger* v. *Coffee,* 180 Nebr. 147, 141 N. W. (2d) 738 (1966).

[472] Tex. Gen. Laws 1917, ch. 88. In 1967, Texas enacted integrated administrative-judicial procedures for the determination of water rights. Tex. Rev. Civ. Stat. Ann. art. 7542a (Supp. 1970).

[473] *Board of Water Engineers* v. *McKnight,* 111 Tex. 82, 299 S. W. 301 (1921).

[474] Tex. Const., art. XVI, § 59(a), adopted August 21, 1917.

[475] *Corzelius* v. *Harrell,* 143 Tex. 509, 186 S. W. (2d) 961 (1945).

[476] *Ormsby County* v. *Kearney,* 37 Nev. 314, 355-392, 142 Pac. 803 (1914).

the effectiveness of the determination.[477] The amended Nevada procedure was held valid.[478]

(2) No judicial powers. In issuing and refusing to issue permits to appropriate water, the administrator exercises no judicial powers; his powers are administrative only.[479] From the evidence, he must ascertain the conditions affecting certain matters as a guide in making his decision on the application for a permit. These are administrative determinations for his official use only. In no sense are they intended to be adjudications of private rights. And they are not binding on persons not party to an adjudication.[480]

(3) Exercise of discretion. In reaching various decisions on water matters by an administrator with quasi-judicial powers, exercise of a considerable measure of discretion is required, particularly in appraising the effect of granting or amending a permit upon the public interest.[481] These powers and duties are not in any sense judicial. Essential to their fulfillment is the exercise of a sound and reasonable discretion. "Fact finding," said the Texas court of civil appeals, "is not an exclusive judicial function. In respects in which discretion inheres or is vested in a governmental official or agency, fact finding is an element or ingredient essential to a proper exercise of such discretion, whether the function of such official or agency be executive, legislative or administrative."[482]

These discretionary powers of the administrator are necessary and important in the exercise of his duties. They are deserving of great respect. However, on review in water cases, the judiciary is not bound by the administrative findings but is the sole arbiter of law and fact.[483] Seldom if ever, said the Oregon Supreme Court, would there be interference by the court with the administrator's discretionary action on matters involving administration of water laws and substitution of its judgment for his. "Judges are not super engineers."[484] And in statutory adjudication proceedings, the Washington

---

[477] Nev. Laws 1915, ch. 253.

[478] *Vineyard Land & Stock Co. v. District Court*, 42 Nev. 1, 14-26, 171 Pac. 166 (1918); *Bergman* v. *Kearney*, 241 Fed. 884, 906, 908-910 (D. Nev. 1917).

[479] *East Bay Municipal Utility Dist. v. State Department of Public Works*, 1 Cal. (2d) 476, 479-481, 35 Pac. (2d) 1027 (1934); *Mojave River Irr. Dist. v. Superior Court*, 202 Cal. 717, 721-722, 262 Pac. 724 (1927); *Crawford Co. v. Hathaway*, 67 Nebr. 325, 365-368, 93 N. W. 781 (1903); *Farm Investment Co. v. Carpenter*, 9 Wyo. 110, 132-135, 61 Pac. 258 (1900).

[480] *Temescal Water Co. v. Department of Public Works*, 44 Cal. (2d) 90, 99-100, 280 Pac. (2d) 1 (1955); *Bullock* v. *Tracy*, 4 Utah (2d) 370, 373, 294 Pac. (2d) 707 (1956); *Funk* v. *Bartholet*, 157 Wash. 584, 593-595, 289 Pac. 1018 (1930); *Mack* v. *Eldorado Water Dist.*, 56 Wash. (2d) 584, 587, 354 Pac. (2d) 917 (1960).

[481] *Temescal Water Co. v. Department of Public Works*, 44 Cal. (2d) 90, 99-100, 280 Pac. (2d) 1 (1955); *State v. Oliver Bros.*, 119 Nebr. 302, 304, 228 N. W. 864 (1930); *Smyth* v. *Jenkins*, 208 Oreg. 92, 100, 299 Pac. (2d) 819 (1956).

[482] *Clark* v. *Briscoe Irr. Co.*, 200 S.W. (2d) 674, 683 (Tex. Civ. App., 1947).

[483] *American Fork Irr. Co. v. Linke*, 121 Utah 90, 93-94, 239 Pac. (2d) 188 (1951).

[484] *Smyth* v. *Jenkins*, 208 Oreg. 92, 100, 299 Pac. (2d) 819 (1956).

Supreme Court observed that the Court would be slow to make any changes in the findings of fact of the referee (the State administrator) unless it were as qualified as such official to dispose of such complicated matters.[485]

Judicial review of administrative action.—Statutes of all water administration States make provision for recourse to the courts from an action of the administrator that denies a substantial right. This might be denial of a permit to an applicant who considers that he has fully complied with all the statutory requirements. Or it might be the approval of an application in the face of protests that existing rights would be seriously impaired, or that the proposed appropriation would not be conducive to the public welfare. In many other situations, an administrative act, or a failure to act, would conflict with the aims of some interested party. For example: cancellation of a permit; refusal to issue a final license or certificate of appropriation; application for change in exercise of a water right; prolonged delay in taking some expected action; requirement that a headgate be repaired, or a measuring device installed, at the expense of the appropriator; or regulation of water distribution in claimed violation of decreed rights.

In some of the statutes, this recourse to the courts of one who deems himself aggrieved is referred to as an appeal, in others a review. The Nevada water law provides that the aggrieved party "may have the same review by a proceeding for that purpose, insofar as may be in the nature of an appeal * * *."[486]

In the view of the Oregon Supreme Court, the "appeal" granted by the Oregon statute[487] to the circuit court from any order or regulation of the State Engineer contemplated an original proceeding in the circuit court for a review of the administrative order, governed by the procedure in suits in equity.[488] The circuit court's function in reviewing such an order would be limited to determining whether the official acts were within the authority conferred upon him, and whether they were arbitrary or not justified by the facts. The Oregon Supreme Court has held further that the trial court may voluntarily limit its review by refusing to disturb administrative findings in those areas in which the administrative agency is expert.[489]

The original California provision for a review of action on an application to appropriate water, by bringing an action in the superior court, was held unconstitutional.[490] It has been replaced by authorization to file a petition for a writ of mandamus in the superior court to inquire into the validity of the action.[491] This procedure, provided by the Civil Code, the supreme court had

---

[485] *In re Ahtanum Creek,* 139 Wash. 84, 91, 245 Pac. 758 (1926); *In re Crab Creek & Moses Lake,* 134 Wash. 7, 17-18, 235 Pac. 37 (1925).

[486] Nev. Rev. Stat. § 533.450 (Supp. 1969).

[487] Oreg. Rev. Stat. § 536.060 (Supp. 1969).

[488] *Broughton's Estate* v. *Central Oregon Irr. Dist.,* 165 Oreg. 435, 462, 101 Pac. (2d) 425, 108 Pac. (2d) 276 (1940).

[489] *Warner Valley Stock Co.* v. *Lynch,* 215 Oreg. 523, 557-558, 336 Pac. (2d) 884 (1959).

[490] *Mojave River Irr. Dist.* v. *Superior Court,* 202 Cal. 717, 725-726, 262 Pac. 724 (1927).

[491] Cal. Water Code § 1360 (West Supp. 1970).

held to be the proper remedy for reviewing issuance of a permit despite protests on the ground of unavailability of unappropriated water.[492]

In most cases, the court to which such an appeal is taken is the trial court of the appropriate county. From this court's decision, appeal lies to the State supreme court. Nebraska allows an interested party who is dissatisfied with any decision or order of the Department of Water Resources to institute proceedings in the State supreme court to reverse, vacate, or modify the order. The procedure in such action is governed by that pertaining to appeals and error proceedings from the district court to the supreme court.[493] In Wyoming, an applicant for a permit may appeal from the action of the State Engineer to the Board of Control. From the board's decision, appeals may be taken to the district court of the county in which the greatest use of water is proposed to be made.[494]

A few water statutes specify that the trial on review of an administrative action shall be *de novo* (anew). Although in New Mexico the proceeding on appeal is *de novo,* evidence taken in hearings before the State Engineer may be considered as original evidence subject to legal objection.[495]

A Texas statute providing for *de novo* trial in suits for review was declared unconstitutional by the State supreme court. This, however, did not render invalid other sections of the act in which there remained a complete and workable law under which review of the reasonableness of the administrative order might be had under the substantial evidence rule.[496]

The Utah legislation providing for a plenary review in the district court in which the hearing proceeds as a trial *de novo* has been considered by the supreme court in several cases. Use of the terms "review" and "trial de novo" indicate that the trial court shall review only the issues of law and fact that were determinable by decision of the State Engineer.[497] The court does not

---

[492] *Temescal Water Co.* v. *Department of Public Works,* 44 Cal. (2d) 90, 99-100, 106, 280 Pac. (2d) 1 (1955).

[493] Nebr. Rev. Stat. § 46-210 (1968).

[494] Wyo. Stat. Ann. § 41-216 (1957).

[495] N. Mex. Stat. Ann. § 75-6-1 (1968). One of the conclusions reached by Clark, R.E., "New Mexico Water Law Since 1955," 2 Natural Resources J. 484, 560 (1962), is: "The precise nature of the *de novo* appeal to the district court should be clarified by the legislature. At the present time the proceeding seems to be somewhere between an original proceeding and an appeal on the record with evidence admissible and merited weight given to the State Engineer's decision. This is not what the statute specifies and is not what good administrative and judicial practice recommends." A 1967 constitutional amendment, which does not necessarily clarify the point raised by Clark, provides, "In any appeal to the district court from the decision, act or refusal to act of any state executive officer or body in matters relating to water rights, the proceeding upon appeal shall be de novo as cases originally docketed in the district court unless otherwise provided by law." N. Mex. Const., art. XVI, § 2.

[496] *Southern Canal Co.* v. *State Board of Water Engineers,* 159 Tex. 227, 318 S. W. (2d) 619 (1958), affirming 311 S. W. (2d) 938 (Tex. Civ. App. 1958).

[497] *United States* v. *District Court,* 121 Utah 1, 7, 11, 238 Pac. (2d) 1132 (1951).

adjudicate any rights except those on which the State Engineer's decision is final unless it is set aside.[498] The Utah Supreme Court recently declared it to be well-settled that in these judicial review proceedings, the trial *de novo* specified in the statute comprehends a trial of all pertinent issues to determine whether the applicant has made his burden of showing that the necessary conditions exist to warrant approval of his application.[499]

Procedural steps in appropriating water.—(1) In general. The procedure for acquiring an appropriative right in the 16 States that have water administrative systems for control of such function conform to a generally similar pattern. In some phases of the process, as would be expected, there are important differences from State to State. The typical procedure originated in the water administration act passed by the first State Legislature of Wyoming.

Except for a few States in which there are certain preapplication provisions (see "(2) Exceptional preapplication provisions," below), the first step in the appropriative process in all 16 appropriation-permit States is the making of a written *application* for permission to appropriate water. The application is filed in the office of the State Engineer or other comparable official or agency. The statutes provide for giving notice of the application, and for hearing and acting upon protests from persons concerned with the possible effect of the proposed provision on their own water enterprises, or who may advance other objections. The administrator is directed by the legislature to consider the implications of the proposal, if consummated, on the public welfare and on the rights of interested parties. The Oregon State Engineer is authorized to hold a hearing to determine whether the proposed use may prejudicially affect the public interest.[500] If in his judgment this will be the result, he must refer the application to the State Water Resources Board for consideration before acting upon it pursuant to the board's order.[501] In Arizona, approval of an application to appropriate water for generation of electrical energy in excess of 25,000 horsepower, or to build a dam therefor, requires an act of the legislature.[502]

As a result of investigations required by the statute, the administrator reaches a determination either that the application be refused, or that it be approved with or without modification of the proposed plan. If the proposal

---

[498] *United States* v. *District Court,* 121 Utah 18, 24, 242 Pac. (2d) 774 (1952). See further, *Bullock* v. *Tracy,* 4 Utah (2d) 370, 373, 294 Pac. (2d) 707 (1956); *East Bench Irr. Co.* v. *Utah,* 5 Utah (2d) 235, 238-240, 300 Pac. (2d) 603 (1956).

[499] *Shields* v. *Dry Creek Irr. Co.,* 12 Utah (2d) 98, 101-102, 363 Pac. (2d) 82 (1961). In another recent case, it is said that the trial court's approval of certain applications to appropriate water should be affirmed if the supreme court finds probable cause to believe that unappropriated waters are available and that the application can be made without interfering with prior rights to the use of the water by others: *Reimann* v. *Richards,* 12 Utah (2d) 109, 111, 363 Pac. (2d) 499 (1961).

[500] Oreg. Rev. Stat. § 537.180 (Supp. 1969).

[501] *Id.* § 537.170(1).

[502] Ariz. Rev. Stat. Ann. § 45-146 (1956).

and the application therefor conform to all requirements of the statute and of the rules and regulations of the State administrator issued pursuant thereto—including correctness and completeness of form, availability of unappropriated water, freedom from taint of impairment of the public welfare or infringement of existing water rights—and if in the administrator's judgment there are no other compelling reasons for dismissing the application (see discussion of Restrictions and Preferences in Appropriation of Water, below), the application is approved. Otherwise, it must be denied.

The next step in the statutory process is issuance of a *permit* to one whose application is approved. This is the intended appropriator's authorization to proceed with his proposed project, or with some modification of it insisted upon by the administrator acting within his delegated discretion. In some States, the permit is a separate document. In most of them, however, the application, with the State's approval endorsed thereon, is returned to the applicant and becomes thereby his permit to make the appropriation.

The permit contains certain directions which, together with specific requirements of the statute, must be followed by the permittee in constructing his water control works, diverting water, and applying it to beneficial use. In the majority of the States under consideration, the permittee makes proof to the administrative agency of completion of construction and of diversion and application of water to beneficial use. This proof, if accepted as full compliance with the statutory requirements, entitles the permittee to the issuance by the State of a document which evidences the State's acknowledgment that the applicant has completed his appropriation. In several States, this final administrative document is called a *license.* In the others, it is a *certificate,* or a *certificate of appropriation,* or a *water rights certificate.*

Procedures in three States require the permittee to make proof of completion of construction of works when that stage has been accomplished. On doing this, he receives a *certificate of construction* before being required to go through the final formality of obtaining his license.[503] This may precede the making of proof of application of water to beneficial use and issuance of an ensuing license by a short period of time or perhaps by a very long one, depending upon the circumstances. However, in most of these cases, the official inspection to determine the quantity of water applied to beneficial use may be made at the same time as that of the constructed work if requested by the permittee and approved by the administrator.

After issuing the permit in Nebraska and Texas, the permittee receives no further documents. A previous requirement in the Nebraska statute (that the State agency, when satisfied that the appropriation had been perfected in accordance with law, should send a certificate to the county clerk for

---

[503] N. Mex. Stat. Ann. § 75-5-9 (1968); Okla. Stat. Ann. tit. 82, § § 52 and 53 (1970); S. Dak. Comp. Laws Ann. § § 46-5-27 to 46-5-29 (1967).

recordation) was repealed in 1955.[504] Statutes of both Nebraska and Texas require reports to the administrative agency for the purpose, among other things, of revealing indications of uncompleted appropriations. And in Nebraska, there is a procedure provided by the original 1895 statute, and well established by judicial construction, under which "any appropriator might have his claim adjudicated by the state board."[505] The administrative decision is appealable to the supreme court but it is final unless so appealed.[506]

Appropriations of water in Oregon for generation of electricity by individuals and private corporations are governed by provisions of the "hydroelectric act."[507] Administration of this act was originally vested in the Hydroelectric Commission of Oregon. In 1961, the Commission was abolished and all its functions were transferred to the State Engineer, who had been an ex-officio member of the commission.[508]

A Nevada statute supplements the general water rights law with respect to acquisition of rights for watering livestock, particularly range livestock. Subject to the protection of subsisting rights to water range livestock at particular places and in sufficient numbers to utilize substantially all the public range readily available to livestock watering at such places, livestock watering rights may be acquired under the general water appropriation procedure. However, a sufficient measure of the quantity of water required for such a livestock water appropriation is specification of the number and kind of animals to be watered or which have been watered there.[509]

South Dakota has a special procedure known as the "Dry Draw" law for acquiring rights to use waters of small streams flowing in minor channels. Water rights evidenced by location certificates are processed through the Water Resources Commission. A somewhat comparable procedure in North Dakota was repealed in 1963.[510]

---

[504] Nebr. Rev. Stat. § 46-239 (1943), repealed, Laws 1955, ch. 183, § 6. A letter to the author from Dan S. Jones, Jr., Director of Water Recourses, Nebraska, dated August 18, 1961, advised that the value of the water rights certificates filed in county records had long been questioned, inasmuch as approved applications and other records in the State administrative office are sufficient evidence of a water right.

[505] *Kearney Water & Elec. Powers Co.* v. *Alfalfa Irr. Dist.,* 97 Nebr. 139, 145-146, 149 N. W. 363 (1914).

[506] Nebr. Rev. Stat. § § 46-226 to -231 (1968). See *Farmers' Irr. Dist.* v. *Frank,* 72 Nebr. 136, 145-154, 100 N. W. 286 (1904); *Enterprise Irr. Dist.* v. *Tri-State Land Co.,* 92 Nebr. 121, 139-151, 138 N. W. 171 (1912); *Kearney Water & Elec. Powers Co.* v. *Alfalfa Irr. Dist.,* 97 Nebr. 139, 145-146, 149 N. W. 363 (1914); *North Loup River Public Power & Irr. Dist.* v. *Loup River Public Power Dist.,* 162 Nebr. 22, 26, 74 N. W. (2d) 863 (1956).

[507] Oreg. Rev. Stat. ch. 543, "Hydroelectric Power Projects" (Supp. 1965), originally enacted, Laws 1931, ch. 67.

[508] Oreg. Laws 1961, ch. 224.

[509] Nev. Rev. Stat. § § 533.485-.510 (Supp. 1967).

[510] S. Dak. Comp. Laws Ann. § § 46-1-6(3), 46-6-1 to 46-4-8 (1967); N. Dak. Cent. Code Ann. § § 61-04-18 to 61-04-21 (1960), repealed, Laws 1963, ch. 419, § 7.

The Oklahoma courts had impressed upon the appropriative process in that State a statutory construction not found elsewhere in the West. This was that a hydrographic survey and a determination of existing rights were prerequisite to the issuance by the State of a permit to appropriate water for irrigation purposes, although not for the development of waterpower. Since 1963, however, this is no longer required for appropriating water for irrigation or other purposes.[511]

Procedures for the acquisition of storage water rights are noted later (see "Storage Water Appropriation").

(2) Exceptional preapplication provisions. (a) An intending appropriator in New Mexico may file with the State Engineer a *notice of intention* to make formal application for a permit to appropriate certain public water. The State Engineer may allow a reasonable time for making the surveys and obtaining the data required for a formal application. If the applicant files his application with all necessary data within the time specified, priority dates from the time of filing notice of intention.[512]

(b) Prior to its repeal in 1967, a Texas statute provided that a prospective Texas appropriator who wished, before making application, to investigate the feasibility of a project involving use of a large quantity of water, could tender a *presentation* to the Texas Water Rights Commission. To qualify, prospective projects had to involve more than 20,000 acre-feet of storage or 50 second feet of diversion, or generation of 2,000 hydroelectric horsepower, with engineering forces adequate for making an expeditious investigation. Before filing a tendered presentation the Commission had to approve it as to extent, purpose, and good faith. The total time a presentation could remain in effect was 3 years. Priority of an application to appropriate water based on a presentation, and of a permit based on such application, dated from the time the Commission filed the approved presentation.[513]

(c) The Washington statutes contain a provision for issuance of a preliminary permit to an applicant requiring him to obtain and furnish more information than he shows in his application, in order that proper action may

---

[511] *Gay* v. *Hicks,* 33 Okla. 675, 686, 124 Pac. 1077 (1912); *Owens* v. *Snider,* 52 Okla. 772, 153 Pac. 833 (1915); *Grand-Hydro* v. *Grand River Dam Authority,* 192 Okla. 693, 695-696, 139 Pac. (2d) 798 (1943); Okla. Stat. Ann. tit. 82, § § 11 and 12 (1970).

[512] N. Mex. Stat. Ann. § 75-5-1 (1968).

[513] Tex. Rev. Civ. Stat. Ann. arts 7496-7499a (1954), repealed, Laws 1967, ch. 111, § 1. "Presentations filed by the Texas Water Rights Commission before the effective date of this Act are not affected by this Act." Laws 1967, ch. 111, § 2. Regarding the repealed statute, see *Board of Water Engineers* v. *Briscoe,* 35 S. W. (2d) 804, 806-807 (Tex. Civ. App. 1930, error dismissed); *Board of Water Engineers* v. *San Antonio,* 273 S. W. (2d) 913, 914-915 (Tex. Civ. App. 1954), affirmed, 155 Tex. 111, 283 S. W. (2d) 722 (1955). See also *City of San Antonio* v. *Texas Water Comm'n,* 392 S. W. (2d) 200, 205-210 (Tex. Civ. App. 1962). For a discussion of temporary permits, see "(5) Permit: Types," below.

be taken upon it (see "(5) Permit: Types," below).[514] Its purpose is similar to that of the Texas presentation which, however, is applied for voluntarily.

(3) Application to State administrator. (a) Necessity of filing application. With a few exceptions, the western water rights laws provide that an application for permission to appropriate water must be filed—not necessarily before anything is done in anticipation of an application, inasmuch as necessary studies, surveys, and estimates may require a long period of time—but before any actual construction of storage, diversion, or distribution facilities is performed, or before water is diverted from constructed works.[515] The Kansas statute is exceptional in stating specifically that the application to the Chief Engineer may be filed either before or after commencement of any work in connection with construction, enlargement, or extension of any works for the diversion, storage, or use of water.[516]

The Washington law does not undertake to forbid the construction of works prior to making an application to the Director. It does prohibit an intending appropriator from using or diverting the water in question until he has received a permit. And it declares that construction of any waterworks, or performance of any work in connection with construction or use of water, "shall not be an appropriation of such water nor an act for the purpose of appropriating water unless a permit," other than a temporary permit, has first been granted.[517] This "spells out" the apparent intention of the legislature—expressed explicitly in another section[518]—that priority of an appropriative right acquired under the administrative procedure is not to be determined by the time of beginning construction of works or diverting water, or of performing any act in connection with the proposed appropriation other than filing the application.[519]

Most of the other western legislatures depend upon providing for relation back to the time of filing the application, and on prohibiting the beginning of an appropriation before obeying the statutory admonition.

(b) Required contents of application. The water rights statutes prescribe certain items which the application to the administrator must contain. They leave to the State agency's promulgated rules and regulations announcement of additional requirements that the agency may deem necessary. The purpose of the required contents, supported by maps, drawings, and documents, is to provide the administrator with a proper description and limitation of the right applied for.

---

[514] Wash. Rev. Code § 90.03.290 (Supp. 1961).

[515] In some States, no permit is required for certain uses of water such as domestic use. See the discussion in chapter 8 under "Elements of the Appropriative Right—Purposes of the Use of Water."

[516] Kans. Stat. Ann. § 82a-709 (1969).

[517] Wash. Rev. Code § 90.03.250 (Supp. 1961).

[518] "The right acquired by appropriation shall relate back to the date of filing of the original application in the office of the supervisor of water resources." *Id.* § 90.03.340.

[519] Application of the doctrine of relation requires, of course, that all subsequent steps be properly taken and that there be no hiatus in continuity of the proceeding.

Customary items include:
- Name and address of applicant.
- Source of proposed water supply.
- Nature and amount of proposed use of water
    direct flow diversions in cubic feet per second
    storage in acre-feet
    periods of annual use of the water
    total quantity of annual use.
- Location and description of works for diversion, storage, and distribution of water, and of places of return of unconsumed water to the stream.
- Place of use of water.
- Times of beginning construction of facilities and estimated times of completing construction and application of the water to beneficial use.

Data pertaining to specific purposes of use are required in some of the States:
- For agriculture,
    legal subdivisions of the land and acreage to be irrigated.
- For power,
    nature of the works
    pressure head
    places of diversion, release, and return of water to the stream.
- For storage of water,
    details of reservoir construction
    dimensions
    capacity
    area inundated
    uses of water
    feeder canal
    distribution facilities.
- For municipal use,
    current population
    estimates of future growth.
- For mining,
    location and character of the mines
    methods of supplying and utilizing water.

Some further provisions in a few statutes include:
- For corporate applicants,
    place of incorporation
    capital stock paid in
    directors.
- For large projects,
    practicability and estimated cost of works

  financial resources of applicant
  means of providing construction funds.

Several statutes authorize the administrator to call for information not stated in the rules and regulations in a case of contemplated diversions of 500 second feet or more, or proposed dams exceeding specified heights.

An incomplete, ambiguous or otherwise defective application is returned to the applicant for correction. Priority is not impaired if the corrected application is refiled within the prescribed time.

(c) Administrative advice to the applicant. In its rules and regulations issued in 1960, the California State Water Rights Board offered some pertinent advice to the permit applicant about the legal effect of his application and of the permit if one is issued thereon, and respecting the relation of the permit to unappropriated water in the source of supply and to the possible impairment of preexisting water rights:[520]

> *It should be understood that neither the filing of an application nor its approval by the board will give one a water right.* Issuance of permit merely signifies consent of the State that unappropriated water may be appropriated and right acquired in accordance with law and the terms of the permit. The right is created by beneficial use in accordance with law and the terms and conditions of the permit. Diligence is required from the filing of an application and undue delay in final disposition of the application will not be allowed.* * *
>
> The purpose of an application is to initiate a right to use unappropriated water, i.e., water which is not already in use under prior and existing rights, and to establish a record of such right so that its status in relation to other rights may be more readily determined. * * * *The approval of an application and issuance of a permit is, however, no assurance of a water supply,* or that the full amount of water for which the application is approved may be diverted without impairment of existing rights. On these points an applicant must assure himself. Likewise he must himself defend the right if it is attacked by others. A water right is a property right and the owner has the same obligation to defend it against encroachment as in the case of any other kind of property.

In 1964, the State Water Rights Board issued, in place of the 1960 edition, a pamphlet entitled "Regulations and Information Pertaining to Appropriation of Water in California," which has no Foreword and does not repeat in any one place the two paragraphs above quoted. (A similar pamphlet was issued in 1969 by its successor, the State Water Resources Control Board.) However, the correctness of this information has not diminished with the passage of time.

---

[520] "Rules, Regulations and Information Pertaining to Appropriation of Water in California." Cal. Admin. Code, tit. 23, ch. 2.1, subchs. 1 and 2, Foreword (1960).

(d) Force and effect of an application to appropriate water. An application to the State administrator for a permit to make an appropriation of water is not an appropriation. And the applicant is not an appropriator.

Practical effects of filing an application that conforms to all the statutory requirements are: The applicant gives formal notice of his intention to acquire the water right in question. He places his proposal in line for consideration by the State authorities. If the water right is eventually acquired by performance of all acts made necessary by the statute and the rules and regulations, its priority is determined by the time of filing the application.

The applicant has the right to have his application considered and acted upon by the properly constituted authorities.[521] But unless and until the statutory requirements and conditions are met, the applicant obtains no property right or any other right against the State.[522]

The Utah Supreme Court holds that when an application to appropriate water lapses without having occurred as a result of fraud or mistake on the part of the State Engineer, he is without authority to reinstate the original priority date.[523]

The discussion under "Restrictions and Preferences in Appropriations of Water," emphasizes that in most of the States that have administrative procedures governing appropriation of water, no one has the unqualified right to make an appropriation. If an intending appropriator possesses the requisite qualifications therefor, he may ask the State for the privilege of acquiring such a right. It is true that an application that conforms to all statutory requirements is entitled to approval by the State administrator. But one of these prerequisites is that the administrator shall consider questions, not only of availability of unappropriated water, but also the possibility of conflict with the public interest should the appropriation be consummated, including the possibility that use of the water for some other purpose than that proposed by the applicant may better serve the public welfare.

The foregoing question may arise in the event that two or more conflicting applications are pending in the State office at the same time.[524] It may also

---

[521] "The board shall consider and act upon all applications for permits to appropriate water and shall do all things required or proper relating to such applications." Cal. Water Code § 1250 (West Supp. 1970).

[522] East Bay Municipal Utility Dist. v. State Department of Public Works, 1 Cal. (2d) 476, 480-481, 35 Pac. (2d) 1027 (1934).

[523] Mosby Irr. Co. v. Criddle, 11 Utah (2d) 41, 46, 354 Pac. (2d) 848 (1960).

[524] In Baeth v. Hoisveen, 157 N.W. (2d) 728, 733-734 (N. Dak. 1968), the court stated that it did not approve of the State Water Commission's granting to one of two owners of adjacent lands overlying an underground stream who had applied "at approximately the same time . . . so much water that the other was in effect denied use of any water." This case is discussed in more detail in chapter 6 under

arise, and be determined, even should there be only one application under consideration, where a long range view of prospective water development fails to support the applicant's proposal. In the development of this principle, the California Supreme Court concluded in 1921 that the legislature did not intend to vest in the administrative agency more than a supervisory discretion in issuing permits to appropriate unappropriated water.[525] But in 1955, the same court acknowledged that the cumulative effects of subsequent statutory changes were to vest in the State agency a broad discretion in determining whether the issuance of a permit will best serve the public interest.[526]

(4) Permit to appropriate water. (a) What it constitutes and evidences. A permit, whether in the form of an endorsement on an application or a separate document, evidences the State's approval of a proposal to appropriate water contained in the application.

On this matter, the California Water Code declares as follows: As prerequisites to the issuance of a permit to appropriate water, (a) there must be an applicant; (b) the application must contain all matters prescribed by the statute and in the form required by the State Water Rights Board; (c) the intended use must be beneficial; (d) there must be available unappropriated water; and (e) all fees must be paid. On the approval of an application, the Board shall issue a permit. This gives the right to take and use water only to the extent and for the purpose allowed in the permit. All permits shall be issued under the terms and conditions prescribed in the statute.[527]

Another typical declaration is in the Oregon statute. This is to the effect that on receipt of an approved application, the applicant may proceed with construction of the necessary works and take all steps required to apply the water to beneficial use and to perfect the proposed appropriation. But if the application is refused, "the applicant shall take no steps toward construction of the proposed work or the diversion and use of water so long as the refusal continues in force."[528]

Receipt of a permit, then, does not constitute an appropriation of water. It is (a) the State's notification to the applicant that his proposal has been found adequate in satisfying all pertinent legal requirements; and (b) its authorization to him to proceed with his plan to completion. What he holds is a contingent right which may ripen into a complete appropriation. Or on the contrary, it

---

"Interrelationships of the Dual Water Rights Sytems–The Status in Summary: By States–North Dakota."

[525] *Tulare Water Co.* v. *State Water Commission,* 187 Cal. 533, 536-537, 202 Pac. 874 (1921).

[526] *Temescal Water Co.* v. *Department of Public Works,* 44 Cal. (2d) 90, 99-100, 280 Pac. (2d) 1 (1955).

[527] Cal Water Code § § 1375, 1380 (West Supp. 1970), 1381, and 1382 (West 1956).

[528] Oreg. Rev. Stat. § 537.210 (Supp. 1969).

may be defeated by failure of the permittee to comply with the necessary requirements.[529]

According to the California statute, "A permit shall be effective for such time as the water actually appropriated under it is used for a useful and beneficial purpose in conformity with this division, but no longer."[530] The California Supreme Court says that a permit under the Water Code is merely evidence of initiation of an appropriation.[531]

Similarly, the Texas Legislature declares that a permit, when filed as required with the county clerk, shall be constructive notice of the filing of the application, issuance of the permit, and of all the rights arising thereunder.[532] And it is the view of the Texas courts that "permit," being synonymous with "leave or license," means only that the permittee has the license of the State to become an appropriator of water under statutory conditions;[533] that the mere granting of a permit by the administrator does not constitute a preexisting preferential right to the use of water, but is only evidence of it.[534]

(b) Permit terms and conditions. (i) Contents of permit. The permit's importance lies in the fact that it fully describes the appropriative water right which the applicant is specifically authorized by the State to acquire, and which he will acquire if he completes the designated process successfully.

Whether in a particular State the permit is in the form of an application to appropriate water with official approval endorsed thereon, or is an entirely separate document, it contains the terms of the intended appropriative right. These include, for example, date of filing the application, quantity of water, point of diversion, place of use, and purpose of use. Also set forth are the terms and conditions under which the right shall be acquired, such as periods of time for performing essential requirements and anything else provided for in the statute. In addition, the permit sets out restrictions, such as periods of annual use of water and maximum rate of diversion; general requirements, including making of reports; and possibly matters pertaining especially to the desired right in question. See "Restrictions and Preferences in Appropriation of Water," below.

---

[529] *Speer* v. *Stephenson,* 16 Idaho 707, 716, 102 Pac. 365 (1909). Therefore, the permit is not an appropriation and is not real property under the statute. It is the consent given by the State to construct and acquire real property. Until all requirements have been complied with, the permit holder has nothing but an inchoate right: *Basinger* v. *Taylor,* 30 Idaho 289, 297-298, 164 Pac. 522 (1917). See also *Morse* v. *Gold Beach Water, Light & Power Co.,* 160 Oreg. 301, 305, 84 Pac. (2d) 113 (1938).

[530] Cal. Water Code § 1390 (West 1956).

[531] *Yuba River Power Co.* v. *Nevada Irr. Dist.,* 207 Cal. 521, 525, 279 Pac. 128 (1929).

[532] Tex. Rev. Civ. Stat. Ann. art. 7518 (1954).

[533] *Motl* v. *Boyd,* 116 Tex. 82, 124-126, 286 S. W. 458 (1926). The permittee obtains no property right in the water while flowing in the stream, and his appropriative right does not actually mature until he has taken the steps prescribed in the statute.

[534] *Board of Water Engineers* v. *Briscoe,* 35 S. W. (2d) 804, 806 (Tex. Civ. App. 1930, error dismissed).

(ii) Time periods. Times for beginning construction of works, completing construction, and applying the water to beneficial use are prescribed in the permit. In a few States, the fixing of these time periods is left by statute to the administrator. In Kansas, for example, the only statutory instruction to the Chief Engineer in this respect is to limit the time for perfecting an appropriation "to a reasonable period within which the proposed works can be completed by expeditious procedure * * *."[535] In most administration States, however, the legislature designates one or more of the maximum time periods, which the administrator may shorten if he deems it desirable, and leaves the others to administrative discretion.

California provides an example of liberal delegation of authority. Construction must begin within the time specified in the permit, not less than 60 days from its date. All other time limits are fixed in the permit.[536]

In Nevada, construction work must begin within 1 year from the date of the permit and must be completed within 5 years; application of water to beneficial use must be completed within 10 years.[537] The statute of South Dakota provides that if one-fifth of the construction work is not completed within one-half of the time allowed for completion, and if there has been no extension of time, the water in question shall be open to general appropriation.[538]

(iii) Extensions of time periods. All 16 administration appropriation statutes authorize the State administrator to extend the periods of time prescribed in the permit "for good cause." The aim of the statutes is to require prosecution of the work diligently and uninterruptedly to completion unless delayed by circumstances over which the permittee has no control. Circumstances that would qualify for an extension of time include, variously, magnitude of the undertaking, physical and engineering difficulties, and high cost of the work not reasonably anticipated; litigation over title to use of the water in question; and unfavorable action of the elements. The Nebraska legislature requires vigorous, diligent, and uninterrupted prosecution of the work to completion "unless temporarily interrupted by some unavoidable and natural cause," with a construction force adequate to complete the work within the time stipulated in the permit "notwithstanding the ordinary delays and casualties that must be expected and provided against."[539]

In a majority of these States, both the granting of extensions and the lengths of time involved are left to the discretion of the administrative agency. Several statutes authorize extensions of 3 years for completion of construction and 2 years more for application of the water to beneficial use. Idaho makes special provision for extensions in case of projects involving more than 200,000 acre-feet of storage capacity or a diversion of more than 25,000 acre-feet in

[535] Kans. Stat. Ann. § 82a-713 (1969).
[536] Cal. Water Code § 1395 (West 1956).
[537] Nev. Rev. Stat. § 533.380 (Supp. 1967).
[538] S. Dak. Comp. Laws Ann. § 46-5-25 (1967).
[539] Nebr. Rev. Stat. § 46-238 (1968).

one irrigation season for a project of no less than 5,000 acres.[540] The Utah law limits extensions to 50 years from the date of the permit. It provides further that extensions not exceeding 14 years may be granted by the State Engineer upon a sufficient showing by affidavit, and that those exceeding 14 years require application, publication of notice, and hearing at which any interested person may protest. If, however, works are constructed with which to make beneficial use of the water, additional time beyond the 50-year period may be granted in which to make proof.[541]

Factors involved in the determination of good cause for extending the prescribed limits for taking of steps in appropriating water are discussed in connection with "Completion of Appropriation—Diligence," below.

(iv) Some other permit conditions. The Nebraska water appropriation statute requires the holder of an approved application for water power to enter into a contract with the State for the leasing from the State of all water so appropriated. The lease runs for a period not to exceed 50 years. The value of improvements made by a lessee is paid to him by a subsequent lessee.[542]

Every person who accepts a permit from the State of California does so under the conditions precedent that no value therefor in excess of the actual amount paid to the State shall ever be claimed with respect to either (a) public regulation of services to be rendered by him; or (b) valuation for purposes of sale to or purchase by, whether through condemnation proceedings or otherwise, the State or any of its political subdivisions, municipalities, or districts of designated types.[543] The Arizona and Oregon water rights laws contain provisions to the same effect.[544]

An express condition of each appropriation of ground water in Nevada is that the appropriator's right relates to a specific quantity of water. It must allow for a reasonable lowering of the static water level at the appropriator's point of diversion. In Kansas, the condition applies to either surface or ground water; and to a reasonable raising or lowering of the static water level and reasonable increase or decrease of streamflow at the appropriator's point of diversion. Also, in Kansas, impairment of an existing use includes unreasonable deterioration of the water quality at the water user's point of diversion beyond a reasonable economic limit. In the determination of these matters the economics of diversion of pumping and the economy of the area are considered.[545]

The objective of these statutes is that so long as the rights of holders of existing appropriations of water from the same source of supply can be satisfied under such express conditions, permits to applicants later in time are

---

[540] Idaho Code Ann. § 42-204 (Supp. 1969).

[541] Utah Code Ann. § 73-3-12 (1969).

[542] Nebr. Rev. Stat. § 46-236 (1968).

[543] Cal. Water Code § 1392 (1956).

[544] Ariz. Rev. Stat. Ann. § 45-149(B) (1956); Oreg. Rev. Stat. § 537.280 (Supp. 1969).

[545] Nev. Rev. Stat. § 534.110(4) (Supp. 1967); Kans. Stat. Ann. § 82a-711 and 711a (1969).

not denied on the ground that diversions under such later appropriations may cause a change in the static water level at the prior appropriator's point of diversion, or impairment of quantity or quality of surface water.

The Idaho ground water law recognizes the prior right of the first appropriator, but declares that a reasonable exercise of this right shall not block full economic development of ground water resources. It is further declared that early appropriations of ground water shall be protected in the maintenance of reasonable ground water pumping levels established by the State administrator.[546] The general topic of protection and means of diversion of water supplies is discussed later in chapter 13.

(c) Action by the permittee. Within the time limits specified in the permit, or within an extension thereof for reasonable cause, the holder of the permit or approved application is expected (a) to construct his diversion, storage, and distribution works; (b) to divert or impound water, or both, from the source of supply to which his permit relates; and (c) to apply the water to the beneficial use to which he is authorized to put it.

The permittee will make such progress reports to the administrative agency as the rules and regulations of the latter provide for. In some instances, he may expect inspection visits from officers or technical employees of the agency.

The permittee will report to the administrator completion of construction of his water service facilities. In several States, he is required to make proof of such completion and thereby to become entitled to a certificate of completion, as stated below. When he is ready to make proof of application of the water to beneficial use, which completes the steps he is required to take, the State issues to him a certificate or license evidencing the acquisition of his appropriative right, provided his proof is satisfactory. As stated before, in Nebraska and Texas no documents are issued after issuance of a permit. The permittee's appropriation is not complete, however, until he has applied the water to beneficial use. He may be required to furnish reports to the administrator, and he is subject to inquiry as to the status of his work. In the event that his work is not kept up, there is a prospect of his losing his permit. This is noted immediately below.

(d) Revocation or cancellation of permit. A permit is valid and effective only so long as the holder takes his progressive steps with reasonable expedition, considering all the circumstances, and within the times allowed therefor in the permit or in any extensions thereof.

Most of the States, through legislative declarations relating to forfeiture and abandonment and procedures leading thereto, take cognizance of inactive appropriative rights. These declarations of status and procedure contemplate *matured* water rights. But statutes of some States are silent as to the status of a permit—which of course is not an appropriative right—the requirements of which are not being met by the holder, and as to what should be done about it.

---

[546] Idaho Code Ann. § 42-226 (Supp. 1969).

The Idaho water rights law deals with the situation by declaring that such a permittee "shall be deemed to have abandoned all right under his permit."[547] In Nebraska, failure of a permittee to comply with the statutory requirements "shall work a forfeiture of the appropriation and all rights thereunder."[548] One State has legislation to the effect that if one-fifth of the construction work is not completed within one-half of the time allowed, and if there is no extension of the time, the administrator may accept an application to appropriate the waters involved. The right under the former permit is thereupon forfeited.[549]

The water rights laws of seven other States call for direct action by the administrator. In most cases, this is mandatory when the situation comes to his attention. In one State, his intervention is invoked by protest of an interested party that the work is not being diligently prosecuted. The procedural details differ from State to State. All statutes provide for giving notice to the permittee, in some instances requiring him to furnish lacking proof, in others to show cause. Several laws contemplate hearings. In all cases, establishment of default on the part of the permittee is ground for revoking or cancelling the permit and declaring the water available for further appropriation, subject to judicial review.[550]

(5) Permit: Types. (a) In addition to regular permits, storage permits are issued in some States (see "Storage Water Appropriation," below).

(b) The Texas appropriation procedure includes both seasonal and temporary permits as well as those of the regular type.

Operation of the seasonal permit is limited to the part or parts of the calendar year expressly stated in the permit, whereas the regular permit is effective throughout the year.[551] A seasonal permit is usually granted where irrigation is desired for seasonal crops or where the applicant proposes to appropriate water to fill an off-channel reservoir during the wet season for use during the dry season.[552] A temporary permit may be issued for not to exceed 3 years' duration.[553] It is usually sought where water is required for a job of

---

[547] Id. § 42-204.

[548] Nebr. Rev. Stat. § 46-238 (1968).

[549] S. Dak. Comp. Laws Ann. § 46-5-25 (1967).

[550] The controlling statutes are: Cal. Water Code §§ 1410-1415 (West Supp. 1970); Nev. Rev. Stat. §§ 533.390, .395, and .410 (Supp. 1967); Oreg. Rev. Stat §§ 537.260, .410-.450 (Supp. 1969); Tex. Rev. Civ. Stat. Ann. arts. 7474, 7519 (1954), 7519a, and 7519b (Supp. 1970); Utah Code Ann. § 73-3-13 (1968); Wash. Rev. Code § 90.03.320 (Supp. 1961); Wyo. Stat. Ann. § 41-206 (1957).

[551] Tex. Water Rights Comm'n, "Rules, Regulations and Modes of Procedure," rules 205.1 and 205.2 (1970 Rev., Jan. 1970.)

[552] Id. rule 205.2. The Commission shall set forth in each seasonal permit "such conditions as may be necessary to fully protect prior appropriations or vested rights on the stream." Tex. Rev. Civ. Stat. Ann. art. 7467c. (Supp. 1970).

[553] ". . . where the same will not interfere with or adversely affect prior appropriations of vested rights on the stream. Such temporary permits shall be subject to all the

short duration in a particular locality, such as drilling an oil well or highway construction. It does not vest in the holder any permanent right to use water and expires in accordance with its terms.[554]

(c) In Washington, a temporary permit may be granted upon a proper showing to the administrator. It is valid only during the pendency of an application for a regular permit.

A preliminary permit may be issued by the Washington administrator to an applicant who does not furnish sufficient information upon which the administrator may make his findings necessary for action upon the application. The preliminary permit is issued for not to exceed 3 years. Within this time the applicant is required to make the necessary investigations and progress reports.[555] The Washington preliminary permit corresponds in a measure to the former Texas presentation, except that the latter was applied for by the intending appropriator before making his application for a permit (see "(2) Exceptional preapplication provisions." above).

(d) The Utah State Engineer may issue a temporary permit to drill a water well at any time after the filing of an application to appropriate water therefrom.[556]

(6) Permit: Effect on preexisting rights. A permit is the permission granted by the State to appropriate unappropriated public water. It is not permission to appropriate water already appropriated by someone else. The authorized appropriation, when perfected, takes its place in the line of priorities that attach to the particular source of supply, and it is junior to all those already established. This is a fundamental principle of the doctrine of prior appropriation. Under the administrative system of appropriating water, determining water rights, and distributing water, the new permit appropriation is served with water after all adjudicated or determined prior rights have received the quantities of water to which they are entitled. But this may be subject to certain restrictions and preference provisions. See "Restrictions and Preferences in Appropriation of Water," below.

That the granting and exercise of a permit shall not interfere with existing rights is the intent of the legislature. The Nevada water rights statute devotes a two-paragraph section to the declarations that every permit and every certificate of appropriation relating to water of an adjudicated system shall be subject to: existing rights, the decree of adjudication, and regulation and control by the administrative agency. On unadjudicated streams, they are

---

requirements of this chapter relating to the use of water and shall have priorities as against each other as of the time of making application therefor." Tex. Rev. Civ. Stat. Ann. art. 7467c (Supp. 1970).

[554] Tex. Water Rights Comm'n, *supra* note 551, rule 205.3. Rule 205.4 provides that a "term" permit may be issued for a specific number of years (which apparently may exceed 3 years) that expires automatically under its terms.

[555] Wash. Rev. Code § § 90.03.250 and 90.03.290 (Supp. 1961).

[556] Utah Code Ann. § 73-3-5 (1968).

subject to the same administrative control as is provided for adjudicated waters.[557]

The legislative intent is likewise expressed in all State statutes that vest the administrator with authority, or that direct him, to reject applications which in his judgment will impair existing water rights. (See "Restrictions and Preferences in Appropriation of Water–Restrictions on the Right to Appropriate Water," below.) The California statute lists as one of the prerequisites to the issuance of a permit that "There must be unappropriated water available to supply the applicant."[558] Even if the intent is not stated in direct language, the whole purpose of the administrative statute with its system of priorities embraces this requirement. Validity of the statute would be compromised if this were not true.

The conclusion of the administrator that the permit applied for will or will not impair existing water rights is not conclusive or binding on any party.[559] It is made for the administrative use of the State agency in passing on the application pending before it. This decision is subject to review in the courts, in which the matter of impairment of existing rights may be judicially determined as between the conflicting claimants.

The State Engineer is an administrative, not a judicial officer. In deciding whether an application to appropriate water should be approved or rejected, he exercises an executive function—to ascertain for his own guidance whether there is reason to believe from the evidence that there are unappropriated waters in the proposed source of supply which can be appropriated without impairing existing rights.[560] This determination merits consideration by the judiciary, but it has no binding force on the final determination of the latter.[561] But even if a permit should be issued, and the administrative act be not overturned by the reviewing court, the permit still would be junior to all preexisting rights of appropriation that attach to the same source of supply. An attempt to exercise it in contravention of these preexisting rights would be subject to injunction.

We speak here of preexisting *rights of appropriation.* This refers to appropriative rights already in being, whether so declared by existing court decrees or by outstanding final permits and licenses or certificates not yet adjudicated. It refers also to rights about to be established in current proceedings involving issuance of the proposed new permit.

The question of impairment of existing riparian rights is discussed later under "Restrictions and Preferences in Appropriation of Water–Restrictions on the Right to Appropriate Water–Nonimpairment of existing rights." It is a factor for consideration in only some Western States.

---

[557] Nev. Rev. Stat. § 533.430 (Supp. 1967).

[558] Cal. Water Code § 1375(d) (West Supp. 1970).

[559] *Motl* v. *Boyd,* 116 Tex. 82, 126-127, 286 S. W. 458 (1926).

[560] *Bullock* v. *Tracy,* 4 Utah (2d) 370, 373, 294 Pac. (2d) 707 (1956).

[561] *American Fork Irr. Co.* v. *Linke,* 121 Utah 90, 93-94, 239 Pac. (2d) 188 (1951).

The underlying reason, of course, for denying the exercise of a permit right that impairs preexisting rights is invocation of the constitutional prohibition against taking private property without due process of law. The State can go far toward reducing unnecessary waste of water through regulation of diversions so long as its acts are fairly an exercise of its police power, because no appropriator has a vested right to waste any of his appropriated water supply.[562] One may generalize with a reasonable degree of assurance as to these distinctions. When, however, the principles are applied to actual controversies, the line at which the police power stops and confiscation begins is not always so sharply drawn. A highly controversial decision of the New Mexico Supreme Court in a controversy involving pueblo rights versus rights of prior appropriation is evidence of this.[563]

(7) Certificate of completion of construction. The water rights laws of three States provide for the issuance of a certificate of completion of construction. This takes place after issuance of the permit, and before that of the final license evidencing the perfected appropriative right.[564]

On or before the date set in the permit for completion of construction of facilities, the permittee is required to notify the administrator that he is ready to submit proof that construction of the works he has built under the permit is complete and the works ready for inspection. The administrator makes or causes to be made an inspection, at least in case of larger projects. If not found properly and safely constructed, the administrator may require the necessary changes to be made. A finding that the works are in satisfactory condition results in issuance to the permittee of a certificate showing that the completed construction meets with the State's approval. This report may be in some detail. In any event, it sets forth the actual capacity of the works and such limitations upon the water right as may be warranted by their condition, but not such as to extend the rights described in the permit.

(8) Certificate of appropriation or license. (a) What it is. In all except two of the 16 administration appropriation States, this is the final document issued by the State administrative agency in the process of making an appropriation of water. The two exceptions are Nebraska and Texas, in which no certificates follow the permit.

This document is called a license in the three States that issue certificates of completion of construction work. Thus, this avoids the possible confusion of

---

[562] *Eden Irr. Co.* v. *District Court,* 61 Utah 103, 113, 211 Pac. 957 (1922); *Finney County Water Users' Assn.* v. *Grahm Ditch Co.,* 1 Fed. (2d) 650, 652 (D. Colo. 1924); Cal. Const., art. XIV, § 3.

[563] *Cartwright* v. *Public Serv. Co. of New Mexico,* 66 N. Mex. 64, 85-87, 343 Pac. (2d) 654 (1959). An attempt by the parties to litigate the same issues again, under a claim of continuation of the first suit, was blocked on *res adjudicata* grounds, 68 N. Mex. 418, 362 Pac. (2d) 796 (1961).

[564] N. Mex. Stat. Ann. § 75-5-9 (1968); Okla. Stat. Ann. tit. 82, § § 52 and 53 (1970); S. Dak. Comp. Laws Ann. § 46-5-27 to 46-5-29 (1967).

two successive certificates in the same proceeding. In California, also, which does not have certificates of construction, it is called a license. In the other States, it is a certificate, or certificate of appropriation, or certificate of water right.

(b) Procedures. The immediate steps leading to issuance of this document vary. In some States, with the approach of the time set in the permit for making proof of application of water to beneficial use, the administrator notifies the permittee of his impending obligation. In others, the permittee takes the initiative by reporting to the State the completion of his requirements. The administrator makes an inspection of the situation or causes it to be made. Most of the statutes that provide for certificates of completion of construction state that the inspection to determine the amount of water applied to beneficial use shall be made at the same time as that of the constructed work if requested by the permittee and deemed proper by the administrator.

Issuance of the certificate may be made or denied, depending upon the results of the inspection. As no certificate may be issued for more water than has been applied to beneficial use, an intending appropriator who has not been able to accomplish it all within the time limit may possibly be granted an extension of time, or a certificate for a lesser quantity of water than was intended. For example, the Oregon water rights statute declares that the State Engineer "shall limit the certificate * * * to a description of such appropriation as has been actually perfected to the extent that the water applied for has been actually applied to the beneficial use contemplated in the permit."[565]

In some of the laws, specific provision is made for hearing protests against issuance of certificates or licenses. A permittee who deems himself aggrieved at the action of the administrator in connection with issuance or refusal to issue a certificate or license may have the same reviewed in court.

Issuance of certificates and licenses is recorded in the administrator's office and in the appropriate county records.

The Wyoming procedure differs from those of other States. When an appropriation of water has been perfected, the appropriator may submit final proof before one of the members of the water administration organization. The water division superintendent advertises notice of when and where proofs will be open to public inspection. An interested party may contest any proof. Thereafter, the materials are transmitted to the Board of Control which, if satisfied that the appropriation has been perfected in accordance with the permit, issues a certificate of appropriation of the water and sends it for recording to the county in which the use of water has been made.[566]

(c) Contents of certificate or license. Some statutes list the main items to be included in a certificate or license, while others leave the required contents to

---

[565] Oreg. Rev. Stat. § 537.260(2) (Supp. 1969).
[566] Wyo. Stat. Ann. § 41-211 (Supp. 1969).

the decision of the administrator. The purpose of this document is to define completely the water right which has been acquired, particularly the extent and conditions of actual diversion and application of the water to beneficial use.

Important items to be included will be the name and address of the appropriator; date of priority; source of water supply; extent and purpose of the water right; quantity of water found by inspection to have been applied to beneficial use; place of diversion and place of use, including land descriptions in case of irrigation. In various instances, description of irrigated land by legal subdivisions is required, except for large projects. Reference is made in the certificate to the permit under which the water was appropriated. As this final document evidences the water right which the State thus certifies has been acquired, the quantity of water to which it relates cannot exceed the quantity found to have been actually put to beneficial use. Likewise, it is sometimes declared that the certificate cannot extend the rights described in the application for a permit.

(d) Conditions. Under "(4) Permit to appropriate water," above, some conditions that the statutes impose upon those who receive permits to appropriate water are noted. The conditions respecting leases of power (in Nebraska[567]), limitation on valuations to be claimed in rate fixing and condemnation proceedings, and effect of junior rights on means of diversion of prior appropriators, are all permanent features of the perfected water rights, in addition to being imbedded in the permit. In California, Arizona, and Oregon, holders of licenses and certificates of appropriation are bound by the conditions imposed in permits, noted above, with respect to claims of value therefor.[568]

In Arizona, certificates for rights to the use of water for power development must limit the right or franchise to a period of 40 years from date of application, subject to a preferred right of renewal under laws existing at the date of expiration. Priority of the appropriation dates from the time of filing the application with the State officer.[569]

(e) Effect of certificate or license. Typical legislative declarations are:

— The license "confirms the right to the appropriation of such an amount of water as has been determined to have been applied to beneficial use." A license shall be effective for such time as the water actually appropriated under it is used for a useful and beneficial purpose in conformity with the statute but no longer.[570]

---

[567] Nebr. Rev. Stat. § 46-236 (Supp. 1968).

[568] Cal. Water Code § 1629 (West 1956). The Arizona statute apparently reaches the same result by referring to "the permittee, his successors or assigns": Ariz. Rev. Stat. Ann. § 45-149(B) (1956). In Oregon, the prohibition relates to "the actual cost to the owner of perfecting" the rights in accordance with the provisions of the statute: Oreg. Rev. Stat. § 537.280 (Supp. 1969).

[569] Ariz. Rev. Stat. Ann. § 45-152(B) (1956).

[570] Cal. Water Code § § 1610 (West Supp. 1970) and 1627 (West 1956).

— The license "shall be binding upon the state as to the right of such licensee to use the amount of water mentioned therein, and shall be *prima facie* evidence as to such right."[571] The Idaho Supreme Court held that a license is invalid if issued with respect to use of water on land not mentioned in the original application for a permit.[572]

— Rights set forth in a certificate shall continue in the owner so long as the water shall be applied to a beneficial use in accordance with its terms, subject only to loss by nonuse as provided in the statute. A certificate that has passed the time allowed for contesting and cancellation "shall be conclusive evidence of the priority and extent of the appropriation therein described in any proceeding in any court or tribunal of the state," except where the rights have been subsequently abandoned.[573]

— "The certificate * * * shall be prima facie evidence of the owner's right to the use of the water in the quantity, for the purpose, at the place, and during the time specified therein, subject to prior rights."[574]

(f) Revocation and cancellation. The California statute gives the Water Resources Control Board authority to revoke a license, subject to judicial review, "at any time" after its issuance if the water is not being put to beneficial use or if any of its terms and conditions are not being observed.[575] The Oregon State Engineer, subject to appeal to the circuit court, may cancel a certificate (and the permit on which it is based) as a result of a contest brought within 3 months after its issuance.[576] Most of the States, however, make no provision for revocation or cancellation of a certificate or license as such. The appropriative water right which this document evidences is of course subject to loss under the forfeiture statutes by reason of failure to make use of the water as provided therein (see chapter 14).

Additional appropriation.—It is legally possible for a water user to make more than one appropriation for use on his land so long as he does not exceed, with respect to a particular tract, the statutory limitation (if there is one) or the quantity reasonably necessary for beneficial use thereon. Any additional appropriations, unless provided otherwise by statute, take their places in the line of priorities attaching to the particular water supply. For example, an irrigator may hold the first, third, and fifth priorities and only those. In this case, his third priority is junior to the second and senior to the fourth priorities held by other parties.

Wyoming and Nebraska are among the few States in which there are quantitative statutory limitations upon the water that may be appropriated

---

[571] Idaho Code Ann. § 42-220 (1948).

[572] *Basinger* v. *Taylor*, 36 Idaho 591, 597-598, 211 Pac. 1085 (1922).

[573] Oreg. Rev. Stat. § § 537.250(2) and .270 (Supp. 1969).

[574] Utah Code Ann. § 73-3-17 (1968).

[575] Cal. Water Code § § 1675-1677 (West Supp. 1970).

[576] Oreg. Rev. Stat. § 537.260(1) (Supp. 1969).

(see "Specific Quantity of Water" under "Elements of the Appropriative Right," in chapter 8). The Wyoming limitation proved to be less than enough for many appropriators. As a result, the legislature provided in 1945 that rights to the use of surplus water—water in excess of the total quantity of all appropriations from a stream—might be acquired by all holders of adjudicated appropriations or permits relating to the direct flow of such stream, with priority as of March 1, 1945. In this way, the statutory limit was raised for the benefit of existing appropriators in the cases in which surplus water was available therefor.[577]

In 1953, the Nebraska legislature likewise acted, but without raising the statutory limit. Existing appropriators of water for agricultural purposes within a drainage basin who had less than the statutory limit of direct flow were authorized to make supplemental appropriations of direct flow therein, with this proviso: that their total appropriations for particular lands would not thereby be raised above the limits provided by law, as well as by the requirements of good husbandry. Priorities should date from the time of filing applications therefor.[578]

Not Administratively Controlled

In Colorado and Montana, although the doctrine of prior appropriation of water is recognized, there is no administrative procedure for supervising the acquisition of appropriative rights.[579]

Colorado.—In this State, the intending appropriator does not apply to the State Engineer or to any other State official or agency for a permit to make an appropriation, subject as in the appropriation administration States to refusal if statutory conditions so require or if they authorize denial of the application. The constitution of Colorado provides that: "The right to divert the unappropriated waters of any natural stream to beneficial uses shall never be denied."[580] The method of acquiring appropriative rights to the use of natural stream waters of this State adheres strictly and literally to this prohibition in the fundamental law.

For two decades following establishment of the Territory of Colorado in 1861, no formalities for making appropriations were prescribed by the legislature. An appropriative right to the use of stream water was initiated by taking the first essential step—diverting the water with intent to apply it to a

---

[577] Wyo. Stat. Ann. § § 41-181 to 41-188 (1957).

[578] Nebr. Rev. Stat. § 46-240.01 (1968).

[579] Prior to 1966, Alaska, like Colorado and Montana, had no centralized State administrative procedure for appropriating water. However, in 1966 the Alaska Legislature enacted a comprehensive "Water Use Act." Alaska Stat. § 46.15.010 *et seq.* (Supp. 1966).

[580] Colo. Const., art. XVI, § 6.

beneficial use. This has always been the first essential step.[581] The appropriation was completed by applying the water to the intended use.[582] This is still
the method of acquiring a right to the use of such unappropriated water.
However, until 1969, there was a statutory requirement for filing which had
value but which the claimant need not have complied with to insure the
soundness of his appropriation.

The statute provided that within 60 days after commencement of work,
everyone who constructed or enlarged any works for the diversion or storage of
water of a natural stream for any beneficial use had to file a sworn statement
of his claim, with maps, in the office of the State Engineer. If the facts were
adequately presented, the State Engineer accepted the claim for filing in his
office. Reproductions were made and filed in the appropriate county records.
A certified copy of such a filing was *prima facie* evidence, in any court having
jurisdiction, of the claimant's intent to complete the construction and to
utilize the rights described therein.[583]

The Colorado Supreme Court so construed the statutory requirements for
filing maps and statements as to restrict their purpose and effect to matters of
evidence. It cautioned that the purpose and effect of filing "must not be
extended beyond the statute."[584] Further, said the court, compliance with the
statutory requirements is not strictly part of the act of appropriation, which is
completed when the works are constructed and the water diverted and put to a
beneficial use. "The filing of maps and statements under our irrigation
statutes is a means of fixing and holding the rights which a party already
has acquired by appropriation and are only prima facie evidence of the
appropriation."[585]

In 1969, the Colorado Legislature repealed this filing requirement[586] and
enacted legislation providing that any appropriator who desires a determination
of his water right and the amount and priority thereof, shall file an application
for such determination with the water clerk.[587] Jurisdiction to hear and

---

[581] The rule is elementary that the first essential of an appropriation is the actual diversion
of the water with intent to apply to a beneficial use: *Denver v. Northern Colorado
Water Conservancy Dist.*, 130 Colo. 375, 386, 276 Pac. (2d) 992 (1954).

[582] Application of water to a beneficial use is essential to a completed appropriation:
Denver v. Sheriff, 105 Colo. 193, 199, 96 Pac. (2d) 836 (1939); *Sterling v. Pawnee
Ditch Extension Co.*, 42 Colo. 421, 428, 94 Pac. 339 (1908).

[583] Colo. Rev. Stat. Ann. § § 148-4-1 to 148-4-7 (1963), repealed, Laws 1969, ch. 373, § 20.

[584] *De Hass v. Benesch,* 116 Colo. 344, 351-352, 181 Pac. (2d) 453 (1947). The lack of
filing maps or statements does not invalidate the appropriation: *Black v. Taylor*, 128
Colo. 449, 457-458, 264 Pac. (2d) 502 (1953).

[585] *Archuleta v. Boulder & Weld County Ditch Co.*, 118 Colo. 43, 53, 192 Pac. (2d) 891
(1948).

[586] Colo. Laws 1969, ch 373, § 20.

[587] Colo. Rev. Stat. Ann. § 148-21-18(1) (Supp. 1969). Regarding "Conditional Decrees in
Colorado," see in chapter 8, "Inchoate Appropriative Right."

adjudicate such questions is vested exclusively in the water judges and their designated referees.[588]

Montana.—There is no centralized State administrative procedure for acquisition of appropriative rights in Montana. A procedure provided by statute now governs the appropriation of water from *adjudicated* streams or other sources of supply which must be followed in appropriating such waters. A separate statutory procedure, which apparently is optional with the intending appropriator, applies to *unadjudicated* sources. The State Water Resources Board has no control in any case.

(1) Nonstatutory procedure for appropriating *unadjudicated* water. With respect to *unadjudicated* water only, a valid appropriation may still be made by actually diverting water and applying it to beneficial use, even without compliance with the statute which purports to govern such appropriations (see the immediately following subtopic).[589]

(2) Statutory procedure for appropriating *unadjudicated* water. The intending appropriator is required to post a notice at the point of intended diversion, to file a notice in the county records and begin construction within prescribed periods of time, and to prosecute the work diligently to completion. Only by compliance with the statute does the right of use relate back to the date of posting notice.[590]

According to the Montana Supreme Court, the statutory method is not the exclusive procedure by which one may appropriate unappropriated water. It is, however, the only way in which an intending appropriator may obtain the advantage of the doctrine of relation.[591]

(3) Procedure for appropriating *adjudicated* water. The statutory procedure now in force was provided in 1921.[592] An intending appropriator of water of an *adjudicated* stream or other source of supply must provide an engineering survey and an aerial photograph.[593] This is followed by a court action in which the petitioner accepts the priority of any outstanding court decree and in

---

[588] *Id.* § 148-21-10 (1) and (2). This is subject to certain rights of appeal to higher courts. *Id.* § 148-21-20(9). The 1969 legislation provided for these special water clerks, water judges, and their designated referees. Such matters were previously handled by regular courts and judicial officers. For further discussions of these and other provisions of the 1969 Colorado "Water Right Determination and Adjudication Act," see chapter 15 and the State summary for Colorado in the appendix.

[589] *Vidal* v. *Kensler,* 100 Mont. 592, 594-595, 51 Pac. (2d) 235 (1935); *Clausen* v. *Armington,* 123 Mont. 1, 14, 212 Pac. (2d) 440 (1949).

[590] Mont. Rev. Codes Ann. § § 89-810 to 89-814 (1964).

[591] *Musselshell Valley Farming and Livestock Co.* v. *Cooley,* 86 Mont. 276, 288, 283 Pac. 213 (1929); *Bailey* v. *Tintinger,* 45 Mont. 154, 171-172, 122 Pac. 575 (1912). See *Morris* v. *Bean,* 146 Fed. 423, 427 (D. Mont. 1906).

[592] Mont. Laws 1921, ch. 228, Rev. Codes Ann. § § 89-829 to -844 (1964). Sec. 89-829 defines an adjudicated stream or other source as one "concerning which there has been an adjudication of rights between appropriators or claimants, as contemplated in section 89-839."

[593] Mont. Rev. Codes Ann. § 89-829 (1964).

which parties who may be affected are made defendants.[594] At the conclusion of the trial, the court may enter either an interlocutory or a permanent decree allowing the appropriation subject to all prior decrees.[595] By interlocutory decree, the court may prescribe the conditions under which both the work necessary to a completion of the right and the time of completion may be prescribed. On full compliance the court enters its decree establishing the appropriation.[596] Failure to comply with the statutory provisions deprives the appropriator of the right to use water as against a subsequent appropriator mentioned in or bound by a decree of the court.[597]

The Montana Supreme Court holds that the statute is applicable equally to appropriations of so-called normal flow and to those of flood or excess waters in the stream.[598] Water stored in a reservoir pursuant to an appropriation of water of an adjudicated stream is protected by the statute, when released into the stream from storage, from being identified as part of the normal flow.[599]

It was the legislature's intention that there shall be a substantial compliance with the requirements of this statute. Hence, it provides the exclusive method for appropriating water from an adjudicated stream or other source. One who thus appropriates adjudicated water is simply a junior appropriator, with the rights and disabilities incident to one whose water right thus decreed is subject to the superior rights adjudicated in the original decree.[600]

Not Exclusively Administratively Controlled

Idaho.—In this State, there are two methods of equal validity of appropriating water. One of these is the statutory method. This is comparable to the procedures contained in the water rights statutes of the other 15 States in which administrative supervision over water appropriations is the established procedure and, in probably most cases, the exclusive one. These matters have been discussed previously in this chapter.

The other Idaho method of making an appropriation of water, established by the judiciary is the "so-called constitutional, as distinguished from the statutory method of appropriating water."[601] The constitutional aspect relates to a declaration in the original constitution of 1889 that "The right to divert and appropriate the unappropriated waters of any natural stream to beneficial uses shall never be denied."[602] In 1928, long after this method was established, this sentence was amended by adding thereto a clause "except that the state may regulate and limit the use thereof for power purposes." The

---

[594] *Id.* § 89-832.
[595] *Id.* § 89-831.
[596] *Id.* § 89-834.
[597] *Id.* § 89-837.
[598] *Quigley* v. *McIntosh,* 88 Mont. 103, 107-108, 290 Pac. 266 (1930).
[599] Mont. Rev. Codes Ann. § 89-829(3) (1964).
[600] *Quigley* v. *McIntosh,* 88 Mont. 103,109, 290 Pac. 266 (1930).
[601] *Pioneer Irr. Dist.* v. *American Ditch Assn.,* 50 Idaho 732, 737, 1 Pac. (2d) 196 (1931).
[602] Idaho Const., art. XV, § 3.

effect of the constitutional provision on the acquisition of water rights for irrigation and purposes other than power was not altered by the amendment.

The Idaho Supreme Court construed this constitutional declaration as authorizing a person to appropriate the water of a stream simply "by actually diverting the water and applying it to a beneficial use."[603] In view of this provision in the fundamental law, said the court, legislation providing for a specific procedure for appropriating water does not thereby set up an exclusive method. A right may still be acquired by diversion and use of the water without conforming to statutory requirements.[604]

In *Nielson* v. *Parker,* the supreme court stated that so far as it had been advised, it never was the intention of the legislature to cut off the right an appropriator and user of water might acquire by actually diverting and applying the water to beneficial use. This, said the court, constituted actual notice to every intending appropriator of water of such stream.[605]

The 1903 legislature, in enacting the administrative statute, may indeed have had no intention of impairing the validity of an appropriation initiated under the previous law and carried to completion with reasonable diligence under the present one. As a general principle of statutory water law, the legislature certainly would not be suspected of intending any such thing. So far as rights already initiated are concerned, it is commonly the intent of the framers of a new statute to recognize inchoate rights and to allow them to be perfected. But as to *future* rights, the literal language of the 1903 statute is that all rights to divert and use water "shall hereafter" be acquired under the provisions of the new law. No succeeding legislature repealed this provision.[606]

In the first report of the Idaho State Engineer, it is stated that the irrigation law enacted in 1903 "completely changed the manner of obtaining rights to divert and use the waters of the streams of the State."[607] It was after this, in 1905, that the Idaho Supreme Court first declared that the administrative provision in the new statute was not exclusive.[608] The actual decision in this case had to do with relative priorities of (a) a right initiated before the new enactment took place and completed thereafter and (b) an appropriation initiated under the new law. However, it was cited by the same court a few years later as upholding appropriation by mere diversion and application to beneficial use despite statutory laws that established a formal procedure.[609]

---

[603] *Sand Point Water & Light Co.* v. *Panhandle Development Co.,* 11 Idaho 405, 413-414, 83 Pac. 347 (1905).

[604] *Nielson* v. *Parker,* 19 Idaho 727, 730-731, 733, 115 Pac. 488 (1911). See also *Bachman* v. *Reynolds Irr. Dist.,* 56 Idaho 507, 514, 55 Pac. (2d) 1314 (1936).

[605] *Nielson* v. *Parker,* 19 Idaho 727, 733, 115 Pac. 488 (1911).

[606] Idaho Laws 1903, § 41, Code Ann. § 42-201 (1948).

[607] Biennial Report, State Engineer to Governor of Idaho, p. 7 (1903-1904).

[608] *Sand Point Water & Light Co.* v. *Panhandle Development Co.,* 11 Idaho 405, 412-414, 83 Pac. 347 (1905).

[609] *Nielson* v. *Parker,* 19 Idaho 727, 730-731, 115 Pac. 488 (1911).

Other than with respect to the date of priority of the right, there is no superiority of right obtained under either of these methods over that obtained under the other method. Under the statutory procedure, priority of the completed right relates back to the time of filing the application for a permit with the State administrator and so dates its inception therefrom. Under the "constitutional" method, the priority dates from the time of completion of the appropriation–the time of applying the water to beneficial use.[610] The act of 1903, according to the Idaho Supreme Court, was intended to provide an exclusive method by which an appropriator should be entitled to the benefit of the doctrine of relation.[611] In order to obtain the benefit of the doctrine of relation, it is necessary that in all respects the statutory procedure be followed strictly.[612]

This valuable legal device that is accorded to the statutory appropriator who conforms strictly to the procedural requirements thus results in preserving the priority intact pending completion of the project. This is true, even though years elapse before making final proof and obtaining a license. A "constitutional" appropriator, on the contrary, has no priority to protect prior to completion of his project. Thus, he may find his right subordinate to those of others who both make proper filings with the administrator before the constitutional right is perfected and also complete their appropriations in proper time thereafter. The practical advantages of the statutory method in a competitive area, particularly in the case of a large project, become evident.

The "constitutional" appropriator has no fees to pay to the State in acquiring his right. Nevertheless, he is under a disadvantage with respect to necessary records when the times come for him to assert or to defend his right against other claimants. Unless forewarned as to the value of keeping records, he may fail to do so until, with passage of time, competent evidence becomes increasingly difficult to obtain. For the statutory appropriator, on the other hand, a continuing record is kept in the State administrator's office with respect to all matters of initiation, process of acquisition, and perfection of the appropriation.

Storage Water Appropriation

Public Policy

Recognition of reservoir storage as one of the chief features of water utilization appears in the water rights jurisprudence throughout the West. Storage is a means of conserving water, by capturing it when plentiful and holding it back for future use, as well as an implement in flood protection programs. Thus, with use of upstream reservoirs, spring floodflows may not only be prevented from inundating downstream lands, but may be stored and

---

[610] *Crane Falls Power & Irr. Co.* v. *Snake River Irr. Co.,* 24 Idaho 63, 81-82, 133 Pac. 655 (1913).

[611] *Reno* v. *Richards,* 32 Idaho 1, 11, 178 Pac. 81 (1918).

[612] *Big Wood Canal Co.* v. *Chapman,* 45 Idaho 380, 405-406, 263 Pac. 45 (1927).

made available for late-season use when unregulated flows are low. And they may even be carried over from so-called "wet" years to mitigate the deficiencies of "dry" seasons.

Encouragement of reservoir construction in the West is a matter of public policy. In Montana, the constitution declares that sites necessary for collecting and storing water shall be held to be a public use.[613] Its legislation provides that "an appropriator may impound flood, seepage, and waste waters in a reservoir and thereby appropriate the same."[614] And the supreme court rejected a contention of counsel that as a broad principle reservoirs should not be permitted in the course of or at the headwaters of adjudicated streams. The court acknowledged that the public is interested in having water conserved, and that construction and maintenance of reservoirs for conservation of flood waters and prevention of waste is of very high public importance.[615]

The constitution of Texas includes in its declaration of public rights and duties the "control, storing, preservation and distribution" of storm and flood waters.[616] And the supreme court agreed that reservoir storage is one of the established methods of complying with the constitutional mandate.[617]

From early times in California, the right to store water for later use under an appropriative right has been implicit in the water law.[618]

In a decision rendered in 1918, the California Supreme Court stated that storage of water in a reservoir is not in itself a beneficial use, but is a mere means to the end of applying the water to public use.[619] Later, the electorate adopted a constitutional amendment which commands that conservation of the State's water resources be exercised in the interest of the people and for the public welfare.[620] In construing this amendment, the same court declared, as inherent in the fundamental plan, that storage of water for flood control, equalization, and stabilization of the flow and future use is within the beneficial uses to which the public waters may be put. This right of storage, said the court, is to be exercised only pursuant to lawful appropriations.[621]

---

[613] Mont. Const., art. III, § 15.

[614] Mont. Rev. Codes Ann. § 89-801(1) (Supp. 1969).

[615] *Donich* v. *Johnson,* 77 Mont. 229, 239-241, 250 Pac. 963 (1926).

[616] Tex. Const. art. XVI, § 59(a).

[617] *Motl* v. *Boyd,* 116 Tex. 82, 115-116, 286 S. W. 458 (1926).

[618] In *Rupley* v. *Welch,* 23 Cal. 452, 454-457 (1863), the priority of an appropriation exercised by means of a reservoir in the bed of a ravine was sustained as against the claim of a later appropriator.

[619] *Lindblom* v. *Round Valley Water Co.,* 178 Cal. 450, 456, 173 Pac. 994 (1918).

[620] Cal. Const., art. XIV, § 3.

[621] *Meridian* v. *San Francisco,* 13 Cal. (2d) 424, 449-450, 90 Pac. (2d) 537 (1939).

California legislation enacted in 1969 provides that, subject to pertinent provisions regarding beneficial use of water and if considered to be in the public interest, the State Water Resources Control Board may approve appropriations by storage of water to be released for the purposes of protecting or enhancing the quality of other waters

In California, detention of surplus water above the immediate needs of a riparian owner from a wet season to a dry season is not a proper riparian use. It constitutes an appropriation of the water.[622]

Along with recognition of the value and encouragement of the principle of reservoir storage have gone admonitions of the necessity of proceeding with full regard for established water rights. Thus, in the *Meridian* case, the California Supreme Court cautioned that the right of storage must necessarily be subordinate to beneficial uses of the stream water made in the exercise of riparian and prior appropriative rights therein.[623] And the Montana Supreme Court placed upon subsequent reservoir users the burden of showing that the construction, maintenance, and use of their reservoirs does not interfere with the rights of prior appropriators.[624]

Nearly all western water appropriation statutes take specific note of storage as a means of effectuating and exercising an appropriation of water. In some cases, this is done in requiring that an application to appropriate water in which storage is included shall state certain particulars of the storage plan. In other States, storage appropriations require more than one permit. And still other statutes contain special features pertaining to the storage water right.

Method of Appropriation

One appropriation method followed in the West makes no distinction between direct flow and storage rights. It treats them as steps in the acquisition of a single appropriative right. Another method deals with these as separate segments of the overall plan of water utilization and provides separate complementary procedures therefor. Under a third plan, entirely separate appropriations are involved.

Storage and direct flow procedures integrated.—This plan is followed in the larger number of Western States. In acquiring an appropriative right that includes storage, the procedures of diverting, impounding, distributing, and applying the water to beneficial use are simply phases of one complete administrative procedure. Included in the application for a permit are statements of proposed storage facilities, capacity of reservoir, quantity of water to be collected in an on-channel reservoir and rediverted after release for direct use downstream, quantity to be diverted for storage away from the stream, and periods of impounding and release from storage.

---

which are put to beneficial uses. Cal. Laws 1969, ch. 482, § 9, Water Code § 1242.5 (West Supp. 1970).

[622] *Lodi* v. *East Bay Municipal Utility Dist.,* 7 Cal. (2d) 316, 335, 60 Pac. (2d) 439 (1936).

[623] *Meridian* v. *San Francisco,* 13 Cal. (2d) 424, 449-450, 90 Pac. (2d) 537 (1939).

[624] *Donich* v. *Johnson,* 77 Mont. 229, 239-241, 250 Pac. 963 (1926). See *Kelly* v. *Granite Bi-Metallic Consolidated Min. Co.,* 41 Mont. 1, 10-12, 108 Pac. 785 (1910); *Knutson* v. *Huggins,* 62 Idaho 662, 668, 115 Pac. (2d) 421 (1941).

Such a project may involve: (a) an on-channel reservoir in which streamflow is captured and from which stored water is released into the stream and diverted therefrom for use, with no direct flow diversion; or (b) on-channel storage and direct flow diversion; or (c) diversion from the stream of not only water to be impounded in a distant reservoir, but also of direct flow for immediate use. Whatever the combination, the permit authorizes construction of the whole project with storage as one of its features. The certificate or license confirms completion of the project and the water right therefor. The storage water right, right of diversion, and the right of use of water are complementary parts of one complete appropriative right.

The completeness of integration of these processes is exemplified by an authorization in the water rights law of Kansas. This section declares that subject to vested rights and prior appropriation rights, any person entitled to use water for beneficial purposes may collect and store the same for use thereafter—with a proviso that such collection, storage, use, and times of use are consistent with reasonable storage and cultivation practices.[625]

The Montana statute provides that an appropriator may impound flood, seepage, and waste waters in a reservoir and thereby appropriate the same.[626] The procedure for appropriating water of an adjudicated stream in this State includes presentation of information concerning proposed diversion, conveyance, storage, and distribution works. If a storage reservoir is proposed, details respecting it and the means of conveying the stored water to the place of contemplated use must be stated. Included in this statute is a proviso that water released from storage in a reservoir constructed on an already adjudicated stream shall not be considered a part of the natural flow of such stream.[627]

The Utah statute provides that in an application for a permit to appropriate water to be stored in an on-channel reservoir, the storage shall be regarded as a diversion. The point of diversion is the point where the longitudinal axis of the dam crosses the center of the streambed. The place at which released water is taken from the stream is designated as a point of rediversion.[628]

With respect to water impounded in a reservoir constructed on a public watercourse in New Mexico—some of the water to be used for irrigation downstream and some held in storage for flood control—the supreme court held that the mere act of impounding the water did not clothe it with appropriative status. Since to constitute an appropriation there must be a diversion and an application to beneficial use, it was held that the impounded water was all public water until applied to beneficial use. Necessarily, therefore, such water was not appropriated until this requirement had been effected.[629]

---

[625] Kans. Stat. Ann. § 42-313 (1964).
[626] Mont. Rev. Codes Ann. § 89-801(1) (Supp. 1969), noted under "Public Policy," above.
[627] Mont. Rev. Codes Ann. § 89-829 (1964).
[628] Utah Code Ann. § 73-3-2 (1968).
[629] *State ex rel. State Game Commission* v. *Red River Valley Co.,* 51 N. Mex. 207, 223-224, 182 Pac. (2d) 421 (1945).

Separate permits for storage and for application of stored water to beneficial use.—In a somewhat smaller group are statutes that provide, where storage of water is involved, for separate but nonetheless complementary procedures.

Several of these statutes contain almost identical provisions. An application for a reservoir permit is subject to the general requirements of the appropriation statute, except that it is exempted from the provision in the general procedure—if there is one—requiring enumeration of lands proposed to be irrigated. This is generally known as the *primary* permit. One who wishes to apply to beneficial use water so stored under the primary permit files an application for a *secondary* permit. This application refers to the reservoir for a supply of water. It also presents evidence that an agreement has been entered into with the reservoir owner for a permanent interest in the reservoir for impounding therein an adequate quantity of water. On completion of beneficial use of the water, proof is taken under the secondary permit. The final certificate of appropriation refers to both the works for conveyance of water from the reservoir described in the secondary permit, and the reservoir described in the primary permit.[630]

With several exceptions, the foregoing procedure is also followed in Nebraska. Certain exceptions are: If the purpose to which the stored water is to be applied is irrigation, the application for a permit to make beneficial use must describe the land to be irrigated. For 6 months from the time limited for completion of the reservoir, the reservoir owner has a preferred right to file application for a permit to apply the water to beneficial use. No final certificate of appropriation of water is issued by the administrator on completion of the appropriation of water, whether with or without storage.[631]

The Texas Water Rights Commission likewise issues to the appropriator no documents after the permit. Before commencing construction or enlargement of any storage work, an application must be made to the Texas Water Rights Commission for a permit.[632] Separate permits are required: (a) to build either an on-channel or an off-channel reservoir; (b) to appropriate water to fill the reservoir; and (c) to divert and use water from storage.[633] However, if requested, permission for all of these proposals has usually been contained in one permit.[634]

---

[630] Ariz. Rev. Stat. Ann. § 45-151 (1956); Nev. Rev. Stat. § 533.440 (Supp. 1967); Oreg. Rev. Stat. § 537.300 (Supp. 1969); Wash. Rev. Code § 90.03.370 (Supp. 1961); Wyo. Stat. Ann. §§ 41-26 and -27 (1957).

[631] Nebr. Rev. Stat. §§ 46-241 and -242 (1968).

[632] Tex. Rev. Civ. Stat. Ann. arts. 7492-7494 (1954).

[633] Tex. Water Rights Comm'n, "Rules, Regulations and Modes of Procedure," rules 210.1-.3 (1970 Rev., Jan. 1970).

[634] Letter to the author dated November 28, 1958, from Joe D. Carter, formerly Examiner and later Chairman of the Board of Water Engineers and of its successor the Texas Water Commission.

If completion of a reservoir project in Arizona within a reasonable time does not appear probable, the administrative agency may, on application of the secondary permittee, permit him joint occupancy and use under the primary permit to the extent deemed advisable. The applicant must pay to the primary permittee a pro rata portion of the total cost of the works.[635]

In a Nevada permit to appropriate water that is to be stored for subsequent irrigation use, reservoir evaporation losses are taken into consideration in determining the acre-footage of storage to be allowed. This is in addition to the factors which the State Engineer must take into account in issuing permits for direct-irrigation rights.[636]

An Oregon enactment in 1961 provides for a single application for stock ponds or other small reservoirs in which diversion from the reservoir is not contemplated and there is no requirement for continuous flow through the pond.[637]

An article in the Wyoming water rights statute is devoted to reservoirs, storage of water, and storage water rights. A large part of this legislation was enacted in 1903.[638] One of the many provisions declares that by contrast with direct flow rights, reservoir water and rights acquired under reservoir permits and adjudications do not attach to particular lands except by deed or other sufficient instrument of conveyance executed by reservoir owners. Except when so attached, reservoir water and water rights may be sold, leased, transferred, and used for beneficial purposes in such manner and on such lands as the owners desire. Water may be withdrawn for beneficial use by those entitled to it at such times as they may elect.[639] This provision, which was enacted in 1921, changed the previous rule established in 1909. That rule provided that no water rights (whether direct flow or storage rights) could be detached from the land for which the water was acquired without loss of priority.[640]

Questions relating to primary and secondary permits in Wyoming were involved in litigation in the supreme court late in the 1950's.[641] This was an action for adjudication of ownership of a reservoir and water rights therein. Controlling questions related to appurtenance of the reservoir and rights to certain lands at the time they were mortgaged, and passing of title when the mortgage was foreclosed. So far as the present discussion is concerned, two points may be noted:

(1) From a careful reading of the statutes in the light of the rather involved facts, the supreme court was convinced that the primary permit contemplates

---

[635] Ariz. Rev. Stat. Ann. § 45-151(C) (1956).

[636] Nev. Rev. Stat. § 533.070(2) (Supp. 1967).

[637] Oreg. Laws 1961, ch. 187, Rev. Stat. § 537.300(2) (Supp. 1969).

[638] Wyo. Laws 1903, ch. 69, Stat. Ann. § 41-26 et seq. (1957).

[639] Wyo. Stat. Ann. § 41-37 (1957).

[640] Wyo. Laws 1909, ch. 68; Laws 1921, ch. 141. See Condict v. Ryan, 79 Wyo. 231, 233, 335 Pac. (2d) 792 (1959); Sturgeon v. Brooks, 73 Wyo. 436, 453-457, 281 Pac. (2d) 675 (1955).

[641] Condict v. Ryan, 79 Wyo. 211, 225-230, 333 Pac. (2d) 684 (1958), rehearing denied, 79 Wyo. 231, 234-235, 335 Pac. (2d) 792 (1959).

the authority from the State to construct a reservoir. A secondary permit is the State's authority to appropriate to beneficial use the waters impounded in a reservoir.

(2) Under the circumstances of this case, in which the reservoir owners and persons intending to use its impounded waters were the same, the statute was not mandatory, but was permissive only. As a result, its procedures need not be followed. However, the question as to whether a secondary permit had or had not been granted in this case was not debatable.

Separate appropriations. —Colorado water law has recognized appropriations of two classes—(a) one for diversion of water for immediate application to a particular beneficial use; (b) the other for storage of water to be used subsequently.[642] An appropriation of water for one of these functions has not been an appropriation for the other.[643] In the *Handy Ditch Company* case, the supreme court held that an appropriator could not claim storage rights for even temporary periods under an appropriation for direct irrigation. Other cases have indicated that a reservoir appropriation is limited to one filling in each year.[644]

The Colorado Adjudication Act of 1943 included in its definitions of terms as used therein the following:[645]

(6) "Direct water right" shall mean the right to divert water for immediate use.

(7) "Storage water right" shall mean the right of impounding water for future beneficial use.

However, this was repealed in 1969.[646]

More on the distinction between appropriation of these classes in Colorado appears in the following subtopic.

Relative priorities of direct flow and storage water rights. —In most western jurisdictions, it is the rule that all appropriative rights on a stream system are integrated on a basis of relative priorities attaching to the several rights, regardless of whether they pertain to direct flow or to storage, or to both. No preference attaches to either group. There is nothing in the statutes of most States nor in most high court decisions that suggests preferential treatment other than that accorded on the basis of relative priorities.

There is an exception to the general rule in Nebraska where the water rights law provides that: "The owners or possessors of reservoirs shall not have the

---

[642] *Handy Ditch Co.* v. *Greeley & Loveland Irr. Co.*, 86 Colo. 197, 198-200, 280 Pac. 481 (1929).

[643] *Holbrook Irr. Dist.* v. *Fort Lyon Canal Co.*, 84 Colo. 174, 191, 269 Pac. 574 (1928); *City and County of Denver* v. *Northern Colorado Water Cons. Dist.*, 130 Colo. 375, 276 Pac.(2d) 992, 999 (1954).

[644] *Windsor Res. & Canal Co.* v. *Lake Supply Ditch Co.*, 44 Colo. 214, 223-225, 98 Pac. 729 (1908); *Holbrook Irr. Dist.* v. *Fort Lyon Canal Co.*, 84 Colo. 174, 192, 269 Pac. 547 (1928).

[645] Colo. Rev. Stat. Ann. § 148-9-1 (1963).

[646] Colo. Laws 1969, ch. 373, § 20.

right to impound any water whatever in such reservoirs during the time that such water is required in ditches for direct irrigation or for the reservoirs holding senior rights."[647] This principle in one form or another has been declared repeatedly by the legislature since the early enactments of administrative appropriation law.

In Colorado prior to 1935, there was a serious question—and considerable contention—as to the relative preferences of direct flow and storage rights on the same stream. In *People ex rel. Park Reservoir Company* v. *Hinderlider,* a case finally decided in 1936, this question came to a head.[648] An opinion of the supreme court originally handed down April 15, 1935, sustained a judgment of the trial court, the result of which would have been to deny a reservoir with *senior* priority the right to store water at a time when ditches with direct-flow priorities *junior* in time to the reservoir priority needed the water for direct irrigation.

Three days later, the legislature amended the statute providing that persons might store "any of the unappropriated waters of the State not thereafter needed for immediate use for domestic or irrigating purposes * * *." This was done by adding a proviso which, as codified, reads: " * * * that after April 18, 1935, the appropriation of water for any reservoirs hereafter constructed, when decreed, shall be superior to an appropriation of water for direct application claiming a date of priority subsequent in time to that of such reservoirs."[649]

The entire cause in the *Park Reservoir* case was represented to the supreme court in September 1935. In February 1936, the supreme court withdrew its earlier opinion and reversed the trial court decision without referring to this statute, which in any event was not controlling in this litigation. The effect of the reversal was to deny preference to either appropriation group other than on a basis of priority. Whether direct flow or storage, therefore, the individual priority now governs.

In a recent case, the Montana Supreme Court said, "The primary right to the use of water in a stream is that of the appropriator of the natural flow, not the storage claimant."[650] But in an earlier case, the court said "the laws of Montana that apply to the acquisition of running water equally apply to the

---

[647] Nebr. Rev. Stat. § 46-241(2) (1968).

[648] *People ex rel. Park Res. Co.* v. *Hinderlider,* 98 Colo. 505, 507-511, 57 Pac. (2d) 894 (1936). Plaintiff had a decree for storage with priority as of October 1, 1888. When spring floods had subsided, the stream did not furnish sufficient water for direct irrigation from ditches diverting from it. Priorities of some direct-use ditches were senior to that of plaintiff and some were junior.

[649] Colo. Laws 1935, ch. 147, Rev. Stat. Ann. § 148-5-1 (1963).

The Colorado Adjudication Act of 1943 distinguished "direct water rights" and "storage water rights," § § 148-9-1(6) and (7), but was repealed, Laws 1969, ch. 373, § 20. This is discussed in the preceding subtopic.

[650] *Gwynn* v. *City of Philipsburg,* __ Mont. __, 478 Pac. (2d) 855, 859 (1970), citing *Whitcomb* v. *Helena Water Works Co.,* 151 Mont. 443, 444 Pac. (2d) 301 (1968).

storage and use of flood or waste water, and the doctrine of 'first in time, first in right' applies to both."[651]

As a related matter, it may be noted that in a 1969 decision, the Texas Court of Civil Appeals applied a system of "weighted priorities" to distribute water from the lower Rio Grande River for irrigation purposes among the several claimants in what the court called "unprecedented" circumstances in that case.[652] The court stressed, among other things, that the Texas water appropriation acts were primarily intended to apply to free-flowing streams and any constructed storage facilities of the appropriators whereas the Rio Grande River had been changed from a free-flowing stream by the construction of government dams. The court concluded that the legislature had failed to "specifically treat of rights in stored waters when such storage made greater quantities of water available for irrigation purposes by the construction of dams by agencies of the national or state governments. The statutes of 1895 and 1913 sound as an uncertain trumpet in the complicated situation which now confronts us, involving as it does the mixing and impounding of two classes of water,—flood and ordinary flow. There is room for some equitable adjustment."[653] The court also said that "although the Legislature in 1895 and 1913 never envisioned or contemplated the present existing situation, we would not be justified in saying that the statutes have no application to the case. However, the equity arm of a court is not inoperative in the presence of an unprecedented situation."[654] This was preceded by the statement that:

> While it may be impossible to state with accuracy the proportions of the two classes of water that may be impounded in Falcon reservoir at any particular time or within any particular year, it is reasonably safe to assume that the greater portion of said waters is and will be storm or flood waters, and it could be argued with force that those certified filings and permits calling for storm waters should be allowed a preference over those calling only for the ordinary flow and underflow of the river. In our opinion, there is no practical value to be realized in recognizing a distinction between certified filings and permits, nor between permits of different dates. All of such filings and permits were issued under laws which were adopted in contemplation of free flowing as contrasted with controlled rivers or streams.[655]

---

[651] *Federal Land Bank* v. *Morris*, 112 Mont. 445, 116 Pac. (2d) 1007, 1012 (1941). This case was not mentioned in either of the 1968 or 1970 opinions.

[652] *State* v. *Hidalgo County Water Control & Improvement Dist. No. 18*, 443 S. W. (2d) 728, 739, 760 (Tex. Civ. App. 1969). The case dealt with water rights on the segment of the river system lying below the Falcon dam. *Id.* at 730.

Among additional complicating factors, the court referred to the past uncertainty regarding water rights along the lower Rio Grande, discussed below.

[653] *Id.* at 745.

[654] *Id.* at 744-745.

[655] *Id.* at 744. Regarding difficulties in distinguishing flood waters and normal flows,

The court applied a weighted priorities system in which it divided those with water rights into two classes: A (legal) and B (equitable). Class A (legal) included those who had acquired a right to use waters of the Rio Grande River by virtue of having complied with the appropriation statutes of the State or those whose rights had been recognized by the State. Class B (equitable) included those who had been "making good faith use of the waters of the Rio Grande for irrigation purposes prior to the institution of this suit but do not qualify as Class A users."[656] The latter included those who had been held not to have riparian rights in *Valmont Plantations* v. *State of Texas,* decided in 1962,[657] and others who had been receiving water from certain water districts by various means.[658] The court stressed that there had been uncertainty as to the nature and origin of water rights along the lower Rio Grande River prior to the *Valmont Plantations* decision and that, although certain water users did not have legal rights, the State had never taken action to cancel or limit the scope or operations under any certified filing or permit relating to waters of the Rio Grande.[659] The court also said:

... there is in this state a strong public policy against waste. It hardly seems appropriate to say that in times of abundant water, we must nevertheless adopt a strict literal construction of statutes that were not designed for and hence in part are not suited to the regulation of rights in and to waters stored by governmental action when such course would deprive good faith users of water and allow the same to flow unused to the Gulf. These good faith users are before the court for the purpose of having their rights adjudicated. If it rests within the power and authority of the court to adjudicate such claims, relief should not be denied. In our opinion, equitable rights may be recognized because of the considerations above mentioned. We think classifications based roughly upon legal and equitable bases can be made effectively operative and that a 1.7 to 1 weighted priority plan will be substantially in accord with the trial court's theory of the division of available waters.[660]

... Considering the water as may be available to meet the irrigation needs of

see 739-740.

Incidentally, Tex. Rev. Civ. Stat. Ann. art. 7545 (1954), repealed, Laws 1967, ch. 159, § 1, provided that an application by one who constructs a dam across any watercourse for the purpose of storing the water thereof "shall have priority over all other applicants." The court did not mention this provision.

[656] *State* v. *Hidalgo County Water Control & Improvement Dist. No. 18,* 443 S. W. (2d) 728, 748-749 (Tex. Civ. App. 1969).

[657] 163 Tex. 381, 355 S. W. (2d) 502 (1962), discussed in chapter 6 under "Interrelationships of the Dual Water Rights Systems—The Status in Summary: By States—Texas."

[658] *State* v. *Hidalgo County Water Control & Improvement Dist. No. 18,* 443 S. W. (2d) 728, 749-750 (Tex. Civ. App. 1969).

[659] *Id.* at 745-746, 760.

[660] The trial court had further provided that "The unallocated water periodically will be

the area, we are in agreement with the trial court that a plan of weighted priorities will operate with less hardship than a system based upon a strict time priority basis. As stated by that court:

> "Under a strict priority allocation, the first priority acreage will receive all water flowing into the reservoir until its full quota would be received.* * * This procedure would result in some land receiving no water for an entire year; in fact records show that since construction of Falcon dam, there would be four years that no water would be received by any acreage other than that of the first priority.* * * Under the weighted allocation procedure, first priority acreage would receive less water than under a strict priority basis. The water not allocated to (the first priority acreage) would go to lower priority acreage. Under this procedure all land would receive water every year."

The trial court also found as a fact that the economy of the lower Rio Grande Valley would be served by the adoption of a weighted priority system. While there are imaginable circumstances under which strict priority would operate more benefically than a "weighted priority" plan, we are in agreement with the court below, despite the recognized danger inherent in attempting to predict climatic, meteorological and weather conditions along the Rio Grande in future years. In times of severe drought, public policy calling for efficient and effective use of water as opposed to waste and enforceable under the police power of the state, is available to ameliorate extreme conditions.

Although, so far as we have been able to find, a system of weighted priorities has never been adopted by a court decree, the concept is not entirely new.[661]

Storage Location

Natural lake.—Sources of water supply specifically named in the water appropriation statutes may include natural lakes.[662] Or by necessary implication, they may be included in an overall designation. In any event, the

---

divided into equal parts per acre for each Priority class" after a certain deduction for water reserved for domestic and urban uses. *Id.* at 732. The Court of Appeals apparently approved this general approach, although it made modifications in the trial court's priority classes and the deduction for urban uses (*Id.* at 731 *et seq.*) and also said "it could be argued with force that those certified filings and permits calling for storm waters should be allowed a preference over those calling only for the ordinary flow" as quoted above at note 655.

[661] *Id.* at 747-748.

[662] For example, the Nebraska statute authorizes appropriation of unappropriated waters of any "natural lake or reservoir" to supplement existing rights inadequate in time of water scarcity: Nebr. Rev. Stat. § 46-240 (1968).

unappropriated water of a natural lake would undoubtedly be recognized as a legitimate source of water supply in any western jurisdiction, subject to the ever present restriction that existing property rights shall not be impaired. In discussing the relation of a watercourse to connected sources of water supply, chapter 3 stresses the reciprocal importance of lake level and outflow to the use of littoral lands, as well as to persons who depend upon the outflow. It cites two area examples of major importance.

In addition to the question of appropriation of water of a natural lake is that of using such a body of water for storage purposes. The Texas statute authorizes both appropriation of water of lakes and storage of appropriated water in lakes.[663]

Maintenance of the water level of a lake in its natural surroundings, with a reasonable alteration of lake level to permit artificial storage and withdrawal of water, is important. Rights of lake level maintenance for purposes of preserving attractive surroundings, recreational opportunities, and land values were sustained in several western decisions.[664]

A Washington decision authorized parties (a) to store water in a navigable lake and to divert therefrom what they put in, after proper allowance for evaporation and seepage, and (b) to take from the lake such portion of any surplus as they might need. This was made subject to the requirement that rights of a prior appropriator in the use of his appliances be protected.[665]

Relation of storage site to watercourse. —Whether a proposed reservoir is to be located on the channel of a watercourse or away from it involves geographical and topographical considerations of available reservoir sites and other controlling features of the project. Great impounding dams in the West are characteristically built across stream channels. They hold back waters that collect for considerable distances upstream in the channel and on each side of it. On the other hand, many reservoirs of widely varying sizes are located away from watercourses and are filled through feeder canals which bring water from the natural source of supply.

The character of water rights that attach to storage waters does not depend upon the location of the reservoir with respect to the stream. However, the storage and diversion features differ, and procedures for acquiring the water rights vary in some particulars.

The water rights statutes that provide for primary and secondary permits differentiate between the functions of storing water and applying it to

---

[663] Tex. Rev. Civ. Stat. Ann. arts. 7467 and 7468 (Supp. 1970).

[664] *Los Angeles* v. *Aitken,* 10 Cal. App. (2d) 460, 473-475, 52 Pac. (2d) 585 (1935); *Elsinore* v. *Temescal Water Co.,* 36 Cal. App. (2d) 116, 129-130, 97 Pac. (2d) 274 (1939); *Litka* v. *Anacortes,* 167 Wash. 259, 262-263, 9 Pac. (2d) 88 (1932); *In re Martha Lake Water Co. No. 1,* 152 Wash. 53, 55-57, 277 Pac. 382 (1929). See *Petition of Clinton Water Dist. of Island County,* 36 Wash. (2d) 284, 286-291, 218 Pac. (2d) 309 (1950).

[665] *Ortel* v. *Stone,* 119 Wash. 500, 503-504, 205 Pac. 1055 (1922).

beneficial use, but not between on-channel and off-channel storage. Whether in these particular States it is the practice to require separate permits for feeder canals and for reservoirs, or one permit for both operations, apparently is optional with the administrator.

In the Cache la Poudre Valley of Colorado is the *locus* of a system of exchanging water that will be touched upon in chapter 9. This, however, is pertinent to the present discussion, in that much of the water stored in this area is impounded at sites lower than the lands for the irrigation of which the rights were acquired. The Colorado water rights statute specifically authorizes, with prescribed safeguards, the exchange of water stored downstream for direct-flow diversions upstream.[666] As carried out in the Cache la Poudre Valley, this system makes it possible for an irrigation company to store water in a reservoir located below its canals and its irrigated lands. The water so stored is to be delivered eventually to downstream canals in return for late season use by the reservoir owner of river water to which the downstream projects are entitled under their early direct-flow rights.[667]

The Montana Supreme Court rejected an argument of counsel that reservoirs should not be permitted in the course of or at the headwaters of adjudicated streams—provided that there be no interference by the reservoir with other rights to the use of the natural flow.[668] In 1948, this court stated that it is of course elementary that a natural depression may be utilized as a reservoir if no one is injured thereby.[669]

Storage of water in the ground.—Water rights statutes of several States take notice of the practice of storing surface water in the ground for later withdrawal, and make provision for it.

Thus in California, in parts of which this operation is extensively carried out,[670] the storing of water in the ground, including diversion of stream water therefor, constitutes a beneficial use thereof if the stored water is thereafter applied to the beneficial purposes for which the storage appropriation was made.[671] The Water Resources Control Board specifies for such appropriations

---

[666] Colo. Rev. Stat. Ann. § 148-6-4 (1963).

[667] Hemphill, R. G., "Irrigation in Northern Colorado," U. S. Department of Agriculture Bulletin 1026 (1922).

[668] *Donich* v. *Johnson,* 77 Mont. 229, 240, 250 Pac. 963 (1926); *Kelly* v. *Granite Bi-Metallic Consolidated Min. Co.,* 41 Mont. 1, 10-12, 108 Pac. 785 (1910).

[669] *Perkins* v. *Kramer,* 121 Mont. 595, 599, 198 Pac. (2d) 475 (1948).

[670] Richter, Raymond C. and Chun, Robert Y. D., "Artificial Recharge of Ground Water Reservoirs in California," Trans. Am. Soc. Civ. Eng. vol. 126, part III, No. 3274, pp. 742-761 (1961); Smith, Stephen C. and Bittinger, Morton W., "Managing Artificial Recharge through Public Districts," Am. Soc. Agr. Eng., Paper No. 62-709 (1962); Muckel, Dean C., "Replenishment of Ground Water Supplies by Artificial Means," USDA Tech. Bull. 1195 (1959); Mitchelson, A. T. and Muckel, Dean C., "Spreading Water for Storage Underground," USDA Tech. Bull. 578 (1937).

[671] Cal. Water Code § 1242 (West 1956). Water replenishment districts: Cal. Water Code § § 60000-60449 (West 1966).

location of points of diversion or rediversion from a natural channel, or of taking water under control for direct percolation; description and capacities of all physical works and surface and subterranean areas; and methods of water measurement.[672]

The Texas statute was amended in 1957 to authorize appropriation of "Those unappropriated public waters consisting of only storm and flood waters" for the purpose of recharging fresh water-bearing aquifers in a specified portion of the Edwards underground reservoir, to be withdrawn subsequently for application to a beneficial use. However, the legislature was careful not to disturb the prevailing Texas judicial and legislative concept of ownership by the landowner of percolating water in his land. It stopped the appropriative relationship of this recharging function when the water once entered the ground. Any water so appropriated, "upon being put or allowed to sink into the ground, shall thereupon lose its character and classification and be considered percolating ground water."[673] One of the purposes for which a ground water district may be created is recharging the water supply of ground water reservoirs or subdivisions thereof.[674]

Recognition of the practice by the Utah Legislature is expressed in a declaration that "If water is to be stored in an underground area or basin" the application to appropriate the water shall follow certain requirements as to the point of the area of intake, location of the basin, and points of collection therefrom.[675]

The Washington ground water statute defines "artificially stored ground water" as water made available in ground storage artificially, either intentionally or incidentally to irrigation and that otherwise would have been dissipated by natural waste. Artificially stored ground waters that have been abandoned or forfeited are declared to be public and subject to appropriation.[676]

Reservoir Functions

On-channel versus off-channel storage. — An on-channel reservoir is physically a part of the watercourse. Hence, one of its functions—in many instances the only one—is (a) to withhold from the natural flow of the stream the rightful supply of water to be stored, while (b) allowing the excess to flow down the stream channel to rightful claimants below, and (c) to release its stored waters into the stream for pickup at the project's downstream diversion headgates. If this is a multiple-purpose project, other obligations may be added, such as flood control and hydroelectric development.

The engineering features of an off-channel storage reservoir differ from those of one constructed across the watercourse. The irrigated lands (a) may be

---

[672] Cal. Admin. Code, tit. 23, § § 688 and 689 (1969).

[673] Tex. Rev. Civ. Stat. Ann. art. 7470 (Supp. 1970).

[674] Tex. Rev. Civ. Stat. Ann. art. 7880-3c-B (1954).

[675] Utah Code Ann. § 73-3-2 (1968).

[676] Wash. Rev. Code § § 90.44.035 and 90.44.040 (Supp. 1961).

served entirely with water released from the reservoir directly into distribution ditches, or (b) partly in that way and partly with natural flow diverted directly from the stream. In the latter case, the stream diversion may be made either through the same headgate that supplies the feeder canal or through a separate one.

From the standpoint of rights to store water and to apply stored water to the land, there is no difference between on-channel and off-channel storage.

Storage versus regulation.—The *storage* function consists of impounding water for later use, usually in a later season or later year. A *regulating* reservoir holds water for brief periods. It is a valuable operational aid in delivering water to meet the fluctuating demands of project irrigators.[677]

The distinction between these functions is thus set forth in the rules and regulations of the California State Water Resources Control Board pertaining to appropriation of water:[678]

— The use of a tank or reservoir is considered *storage* when water is collected during a time of high streamflow and held over for use in a time of deficient streamflow. The quantity of water is expressed as a definite volume.

— It is considered *regulation* if water is collected in order that a supply may be available for use at a rate other than that at which it may be conveniently diverted from the source. The quantity is expressed as a definite rate of flow.

— If a tank or reservoir is wholly or partially filled more than once during a single water-year, water held less than 30 days shall be considered *regulation* and water held for 30 days or more shall be considered *storage*.

— An applicant for a permit to store water must specify the volume and the dates between which storage will be collected. If he proposes to store more than one year's supply in order to secure cyclic or hold-over storage, he must state (a) the maximum quantity to be put into storage in any one year and (b) the maximum annual amount to be drawn from storage.

The Colorado Supreme Court recognizes a legal distinction between diversions of water for immediate application to beneficial use and for storage of water for subsequent use. An appropriation for either function is not an appropriation for the other.[679] This court holds also that an appropriator cannot claim storage rights for even temporary periods under an appropriation for direct irrigation.[680] Nevertheless, the Colorado court agrees realistically that in the practical operation of an irrigation project, water passing through

---

[677] Hutchins, Wells A., "Delivery of Irrigation Water," USDA Tech. Bull. 47 (1928).

[678] Cal. Admin. Code, tit. 23, § § 685 and 670(b) (1969).

[679] *Holbrook Irr. Dist.* v. *Fort Lyon Canal Co.,* 84 Colo. 174, 191, 269 Pac. 574 (1928).

[680] *Handy Ditch Co.* v. *Greeley & Loveland Irr. Co.,* 86 Colo. 197, 198-200, 280 Pac. 481 (1929).

reservoirs should not and cannot, by reason of that fact alone, become storage water.[681]

A type of reservoir formed by a high diversion dam impounds water only in "dead" storage. It serves the purpose of raising the stream water level to a height at which the flow can be diverted into ditch headgates. Water so withheld below the level of the diversion gate of course remains there after the irrigation season unless an outlet in the dam or a pumping plant is provided.[682]

Storage carry-over.—To store water in one year for use in a later year is common practice. Conservation and better utilization of water are furthered by impounding water when it is available in a wet season in order to meet demands in a later season or later year of short water supply.

The Montana Supreme Court expressed its approval of the principle of utilizing a reservoir to store water in any year for use in that or in succeeding years.[683] But in two recent cases it appears to have taken a more restrictive approach regarding the refilling of a reservoir or other storage of water during the irrigating season at the expense of irrigation appropriators of the natural streamflow.[684]

The Colorado Supreme Court has construed the Colorado water rights statute[685] as not allowing more than one filling of a reservoir on one priority in any one year.[686] However, this court concluded that nothing in the statute limited the beneficial use of water for adjudication purposes to the year of diversion and storage. Hence, water need not be withdrawn from the reservoir in the season of storage in order to receive proper credit for adjudication purposes.[687] All requirements of the law are fulfilled, said the court, when the water is applied to a beneficial use within a reasonable time after storage.

---

[681] *Nepesta Ditch & Res. Co.* v. *Espinosa,* 73 Colo. 302, 303, 215 Pac. 141 (1923). "It is a matter of common knowledge, of which we must take notice, that a vast amount of water applied to direct irrigation comes through reservoirs and we can see no objection. The fact that water diverted for direct irrigation passes through reservoirs on its way to the land on which it will be used does not make it storage water."

[682] The Nebraska water rights statute provides that a reservoir constructed for the purpose of withholding water and raising it to permit its being applied to lands of a higher level or given a greater head for power shall not be considered a storage reservoir. But to perfect an appropriation of such flowing water, the reservoir and the dam must be described in the application: Nebr. Rev. Stat. § 46-243 (1968).

[683] *Federal Land Bank* v. *Morris,* 112 Mont. 445, 454-456, 116 Pac. (2d) 1007 (1941).

[684] *Whitcomb* v. *Helena Water Works Co.,* 151 Mont. 443, 444 Pac. (2d) 301 (1968); *Gwynn* v. *City of Philipsburg,* __ Mont. __, 478 Pac. (2d) 855, 859 (1970), in which the court said, "The primary right to the use of water in a stream is that of the appropriator of the natural flow, not the storage claimant." This is mentioned above under "Method of Appropriation—Relative priorities of direct flow and storage water rights."

[685] Colo. Rev. Stat. Ann. § 148-5-1 *et seq.* (1963).

[686] *Windsor Res. & Canal Co.* v. *Lake Supply Ditch Co.,* 44 Colo. 214, 223-225, 98 Pac. 729 (1908); *Holbrook Irr. Dist.* v. *Fort Lyon Canal Co.,* 84 Colo. 174, 192, 269 Pac. 574 (1928).

[687] *North Sterling Irr. Dist.* v. *Riverside Res. & Land Co.,* 119 Colo. 50, 200 Pac. (2d) 933 (1948).

The section of the Wyoming statute that provides for furnishing excess stored water to applicants contains a provision reading that: "Nothing contained in this section shall be construed to deny the right to store water for use for more than one year."[688]

The rules and regulations of the California State Water Resources Control Board recognize the right of storage carryover in a requirement that a proposal in an application "to store more than one year's supply in a reservoir in order to secure cyclic or holdover storage" must state the maximum quantity of water to be stored in any one year and the maximum to be withdrawn annually.[689]

Some small storages.—In several States, special provision is made for small reservoir storages, chiefly for domestic and livestock purposes. Some examples follow.

Provisions relating to appropriation of water in the New Mexico law do not apply to stockmen or stockowners who construct water tanks or ponds for storing water with capacity of 10 acre-feet or less.[690] And the declaration that water sources are free for all travelers to take water for the use of themselves and their animals does not apply to wells, nor to ponds or reservoirs constructed by persons for their own use.[691] People living in the upper valleys of stream systems have the right to impound and utilize a reasonable share of the waters originating there. Exercise of the right is subject to the appropriation laws.[692]

An Oregon statute enacted in 1961 authorizes a single application for stock ponds or other small reservoirs where there is no contemplated diversion of water from the reservoir nor any requirement for continued flow through the ponds.[693]

The South Dakota "dry draw" law contemplates storage of floodwaters for irrigation or livestock purposes on ravines "not having an average daily flow of at least 0.4 cubic feet per second" from May 1 to September 30, inclusive. One who takes advantage of this authorization adhers to certain formalities in filing a location certificate in the county records. If he desires a certificate from the State, he may obtain one by taking prescribed steps.[694]

In Texas, a permit is not required for construction on one's own property of a dam or reservoir to contain not more than 200 acre-feet of water for domestic and livestock purposes.[695]

---

[688] Wyo. Stat. Ann. § 41-39 (1957).
[689] Cal. Admin. Code, tit. 23, § 670(b)(5) (1969).
[690] N. Mex. Stat. Ann. § 75-8-3 (1968).
[691] *Id.* § 75-1-4.
[692] *Id.* § 75-5-27.
[693] Oreg. Laws 1961, ch. 187, Rev. Stat. § 537.300(2) (Supp. 1969).
[694] S. Dak. Comp. Laws Ann. § § 46-1-6, 46-4-1 to 46-4-8 (1967).
[695] Tex. Rev. Civ. Stat. Ann. art. 7500a (Supp. 1970).

Disposal of Impounded Water

Water rights statutes of several States make provision for the disposal of water stored in excess of the needs of the reservoir owners. The owners of the storage (or diversion or distribution) works are required to deliver the excess at reasonable rates to parties entitled to put it to beneficial use.[696] In several of these States, a reservoir owner who refuses to deliver such excess water at reasonable rates as determined by the State administrator may be compelled to do so by the appropriate court.

The Wyoming statute contains many provisions relating to reservoirs and storage of water. With respect to the instant subtopic, an early enactment—still in the statute—prohibits the owner of a ditch, canal, or reservoir from receiving a royalty for the use thereof. It further declares that those furnishing surplus waters to others shall be considered common carriers, subject to the same governing laws as such carriers.[697]

A later Wyoming enactment provides that those who impound more water than they necessarily use on or in connection with their own lands shall deliver the excess to owners of lands capable of using such water and who apply therefor. On refusal to comply, the owners may be compelled by court proceedings to do so. A user of such water in any particular year has preference to the same for the next following year. On application of any interested party, a board of special commissioners is constituted consisting of the State Engineer, water commissioner, and water superintendent having jurisdiction of the area in question. Its purpose is to establish reasonable maximum rates after notice and hearing.[698]

Proceedings followed by one such Wyoming board of special commissioners were litigated in a 1956 case.[699] A general observation made by the court was that the basic right to store reservoir water for irrigation proposed under the statute depends upon provisions for use of the water by the holders of primary permits, by the holders of secondary permits, and by the owners of other lands lying under and capable of being irrigated from the reservoir, in the order named. These provisions for furnishing excess stored water to applicants on a public utility basis are aside from those sections providing for the sale and lease of portions of the overall right to the use of waters impounded in a reservoir.[700]

---

[696] N. Mex. Stat. Ann. § 75-5-16 (1968); N. Dak. Cent. Code Ann. § § 61-04-03 and 61-04-17 (1960); Okla. Stat. Ann. tit. 82, § 101 (1970); S. Dak. Comp. Laws Ann. § 46-7-1 (1967).

[697] Wyo. Stat. Ann. § 41-47 (1957).

[698] *Id.* § 41-39.

[699] *Lake De Smet Reservoir Co.* v. *Kaufmann,* 75 Wyo. 87, 93-103, 292 Pac. (2d) 482 (1956).

[700] Wyo. Stat. Ann. § § 41-28, -33, -34, -37, and -38 (1957).

Completion of Appropriation

Elements of a Valid Appropriation

The elements of a valid appropriation of water were thus stated by a California court in 1920:[701]

> To constitute a valid appropriation of water, three elements must always exist: (1) An intent to apply it to some existing or contemplated beneficial use; (2) an actual diversion from the natural channel by some mode sufficient for the purpose; and (3) an application of the water within a reasonable time to some beneficial use. * * *

This undoubtedly expresses the consensus of the western judiciary, not only when the opinion was written but currently. However, conflicting views were expressed in earlier cases. Contrasts appear between administration water statutes and some of those that preceded them.

The doctrine of relation was an important factor. In essence, the doctrine of relation contemplates the performance of two acts by the intending appropriator at different times in the process of appropriating the water. If the doctrine is applicable to a given set of circumstances, its effect is that the priority of appropriation relates back from the time of performing one act—completion of appropriation—to that of a previous act—initiation of the right. It is obvious, therefore, that in order to determine the question of applicability of this doctrine to the facts of a particular appropriation, both "initiation" and "completion" must be clearly defined. The later discussion of the doctrine of relation herein lays stress on questions pertaining to initiation of the right. Here we emphasize questions of completion.

What Constitutes Completion of an Appropriation

Development of the rules.—(1) Wiel, writing in 1911, stated that:[702]

> Throughout the law of appropriation there is now occurring a transition regarding the attributes of a right of appropriation within itself, irrespective of any question of riparian rights or of Federal rights. The transition is from a possessory system, based upon possession of the stream, to a 'particular purpose system' based upon the requirements of a specific use, such as the

---

[701] *Simons* v. *Inyo Cerro Gordo Min. & Power Co.*, 48 Cal. App. 524, 537, 192 Pac. 144 (1920). See also the discussion at notes 707 and 708, *infra*.

Some comparable expressions: *Hoogendorn* v. *Nelson Gulch Min. Co.*, 4 Alaska 216, 220 (1910); *Clough* v. *Wing*, 2 Ariz. 371, 382-383, 17 Pac. 453 (1888); *Larimer County Res. Co.* v. *People ex rel. Luthe*, 8 Colo. 614, 616-617, 9 Pac. 794 (1886); *Walsh* v. *Wallace*, 26 Nev. 299, 327, 67 Pac. 914 (1902); *Snow* v. *Abalos*, 18 N. Mex. 681, 694, 140 Pac. 1044 (1914); *Gates* v. *Settlers' Mill., Canal & Res. Co.*, 19 Okla. 83, 89, 91 Pac. 856 (1907); *Hutchinson* v. *Stricklin*, 146 Oreg. 285, 297, 28 Pac. (2d) 225 (1933); *Tanner* v. *Provo Res. Co.*, 99 Utah 139, 149, 98 Pac. (2d) 695 (1940); *Moyer* v. *Preston*, 6 Wyo. 308, 321, 44 Pac. 845 (1896).

[702] Wiel, S.C., "Water Rights in the Western States, 3d ed., vol. 1, § § 139 and 362 (1911).

irrigation of a specific tract of land or the running of specific machinery. With this change of attitude the law of appropriation is being modified throughout, old decisions are becoming obsolete, and old rules are giving place to new.

* * * *

[Under the possessory system,] the right to the water is not complete until the water is actually taken into one's possession, or rather, until all work preparatory to the actual use of the water is completed, since that is the equivalent of taking possession; it is the nearest to possession that the nature of the right makes possible. The appropriator acquires no right until he actually takes possession.

(2) The theory of this "possessory system," which arose under the practices of appropriating water on the public domain, is reflected in preadministration water statutes as well as decisions of courts. Several of the early western posting and filing statutes provided that construction of the works should be prosecuted diligently and continuously to completion. "Completion" was defined as conducting the water to the place of intended use.[703]

Some other early statutes did not attempt to define "completion" of the appropriative right, but left the matter open to court interpretation. Thus, the Montana Supreme Court held that under the statute of 1885 actual use of the water could not be exacted as prerequisite to a completed appropriation. On the contrary, compliance with the statute was "the equivalent of actual possession." Hence, a claimant who complied with the statute had a completed appropriation on completion of construction work even before actually applying the water to beneficial use.[704] And the South Dakota Supreme Court took a similar view of operations under the 1881 statute of Dakota Territory. In the court's view, this law did not contemplate an actual use prior to a completed appropriation. An appropriation thereunder was complete when the water was diverted into the ditch and the location certificate was filed and posted. The rights were acquired "under the so-called 'possessory basis' of the right of appropriation."[705]

(3) California. Conflicting statements appear in opinions of the California courts as to just when a nonstatutory appropriation—in the absence of an intervening Civil Code appropriation with its principle of relation back—was deemed complete. Expressions made from time to time differed as to whether the final act was completion of the ditch, or diversion of water, or application of the water to beneficial use.

---

[703] Cal. Civ. Code § § 1416 and 1417 (1872); Nebr. Laws 1889, ch. 68, § § 9 and 10; Tex. Laws 1889, ch. 88, § § 6 and 7; Laws 1895, ch. 21, § § 8 and 9.
[704] *Bailey* v. *Tintinger,* 45 Mont. 154, 174, 122 Pac. 575 (1912).
[705] *Butte County* v. *Lovinger,* 64 S. Dak. 200, 209, 266 N. W. 127 (1936).

In a very early case, it was said that title to the water right is not perfected until the ditch has been so far completed as to convey the water.[706] Six decades later a district court of appeal, after making the unqualified statement quoted above at the beginning of this subtopic, tended to hedge with the following:[707]

> The third, and perhaps the most essential, element to the legal appropriation of water is its application within a reasonable time to some useful purpose of industry. It is, perhaps, not strictly true that this application is essential to the appropriation; for if diversion is actually made with *intent* to use the water for such purposes, the appropriation is then complete in the sense that the rights of the appropriator cannot be defeated by acts done or appropriations attempted to be made by others after such diversion and while he is proceeding with reasonable diligence to apply the water appropriated by him to the purpose contemplated.* * *

As against an intervening appropriation under the California Civil Code, the final act in an appropriation made without conforming to the code requirements appears to have been application to a beneficial use of the maximum quantity of water so diverted and applied prior to posting of notice by the Civil Code appropriator. In the latter case, the court held that the water right of a party who had not posted notice (as against one who had followed the code) "could not exceed the greatest amount of water ever actually taken by him and applied to a beneficial use or uses prior to the time when others appropriated waters from the springs. * * * Actual diversion (the taking of possession) creates the right; actual use (the amount in possession) measures the right. * * * "[708]

Another point of view was that a diversion of water ripened into a valid appropriation only where the water so diverted was utilized by the appropriator for a beneficial purpose.[709]

(4) Idaho. Under the preadministration acts of 1881 and 1899, the appropriation was complete on completion of construction and conducting of the water to the point of intended use, subject to loss of the right by failure to apply the water to a beneficial use within a reasonable time.[710]

(5) Water permit statutes. Under these statutes, the final act performed by the permittee in completing his appropriation is application of the water to the

---

[706] *Kimball* v. *Gearhart*, 12 Cal. 27, 29-30 (1859).

[707] *Simons* v. *Inyo Cerro Gordo Min. & Power Co.*, 48 Cal. App. 524, 537, 192 Pac. 144 (1920).

[708] *Id.* at 537-538.

[709] *Hewitt* v. *Story*, 64 Fed. 510, 514-515 (9th Cir. 1894); *Miller & Lux* v. *Rickey*, 127 Fed. 573, 585 (C.C.D. Nev. 1904); *Nevada County & Sacramento Canal Co.* v. *Kidd*, 37 Cal. 282, 310 (1869), ("The right to the water, or water right, as it is commonly called, is only acquired by an actual appropriation and use of the water"); *De Necochea* v. *Curtis*, 80 Cal. 397, 402, 20 Pac. 563, 22 Pac. 198 (1889).

[710] *Basinger* v. *Taylor*, 30 Idaho 289, 299, 164 Pac. 522 (1917).

beneficial use or uses authorized in the permit. In a majority of the States, this act is evidenced by a license or certificate of appropriation.

Thus in Idaho, under the statutory administration statute, "no appropriation is complete until the water has been applied to a beneficial use." Thereupon the permittee is entitled to the issuance of a license which is *prima facie* evidence of his water right. But the statutory procedure is not the exclusive method of appropriating water in this State. An intending appropriator may follow the "constitutional" method in disregard of the statute. In this event, he "must depend upon actual appropriation, that is to say, actual diversion and application to beneficial use."[711]

The same necessity of completing an appropriation by application of the water to the intended beneficial use prevails under the current statutes of Nebraska and Texas which, however, do not provide for issuance of evidentiary documents such as a license or certificate. The fact that the permit is the last document to be issued does not affect in any way the requirement of beneficial use.

(6) Nonpermit statutes. In Colorado, the appropriation "is completed when the ditch or conduit is constructed and the water is diverted therethrough and applied to a beneficial use."[712]

In Montana, there are two water appropriation statutes. One applies to adjudicated waters, the other to waters of streams that have not been adjudicated. The Montana statute pertaining to *unadjudicated* waters is permissive in operation; but to obtain the benefit of the doctrine of relation, it must be followed. It provides for posting a notice, filing notice in the county records, beginning construction within a prescribed time, and prosecuting "the same with reasonable diligence to completion."[713] Said the Montana Supreme Court: "These are all the requirements of the Code, and by what authority shall any additional exaction be made? * * * from one who proceeds under the statute, actual use of the water cannot be exacted as a prerequisite to a completed appropriation."[714]

A considerable number of decisions of the Montana Supreme Court involved appropriations made after enactment of the first statute of 1885, but not in compliance therewith. In stating, in a number of these cases, the circumstances

---

[711] *Basinger* v. *Taylor,* 30 Idaho 289, 299, 164 Pac. 522 (1917), 36 Idaho 591, 598, 211 Pac. 1085 (1922).

[712] *Archuleta* v. *Boulder & Weld County Ditch Co.,* 118 Colo. 43, 53, 192 Pac. (2d) 891 (1948). See also *Rocky Mountain Power Co.* v. *White River Electric Assn.,* 151 Colo. 45, 48-49, 376 Pac. (2d) 158, 161 (1962); *Denver* v. *Northern Colorado Water Conservancy Dist.,* 130 Colo. 375, 388, 276 Pac. 992 (1954). See *Jefferson County* v. *Rocky Mountain Water Co.,* 102 Colo. 351, 361, 79 Pac. (2d) 373 (1938).

[713] Mont. Rev. Codes Ann. § § 89.870 and .811 (1964).

[714] *Anderson* v. *Spear-Morgan Livestock Co.,* 107 Mont. 18, 27-28, 79 Pac. (2d) 667 (1938), quoting from *Bailey* v. *Tintinger,* 45 Mont. 154, 173-174, 122 Pac. 575 (1912).

connected with completed appropriative rights, the court included words denoting actual application of the water to beneficial use.[715] The implication of these repeated statements is that actual use of the water is either important, or is essential, in arriving at a determination of completion of an appropriation made without complying with statutory requirements. In no case examined in connection with this study has the Montana Supreme Court specifically held a nonstatutory appropriation to have been complete on completion of the ditch, or other means of diversion and conveyance, prior to *any* actual use of the water.

The current Montana statute pertaining to *adjudicated* waters provides the exclusive method of appropriating waters from an adjudicated stream or other source.[716] This involves a petition to the court and decree thereof. The statutory provision as to completion of such an appropriation is as follows:[717]

> The court may provide by interlocutory decree awarding the appropriation, the condition under which the ditch, aqueduct, dam, or other work, necessary to the complete appropriation, shall be done and the time within which the same shall be completed until the conditions imposed are complied with. Upon a full compliance with the terms prescribed by the court, it shall enter its order and decree establishing the appropriation and fixing the date thereof, which, if the appropriator shall have been diligent in complying with the court order, shall be the date of the filing of the petition. The court may fix a later date if the facts warrant.

Intent.—The intention of the appropriator to divert and apply the water to beneficial use—his object and purpose in making the appropriation, his acts and conduct in regard thereto—is stressed in various decisions, particularly the earlier ones.[718]

It must be a *bona fide* intention.[719] One who locates a water right with intent to hold it for speculation and not for beneficial use gains no rights by simply going through the forms.[720]

---

[715] See *Murray* v. *Tingley,* 20 Mont. 260, 261-262, 269, 50 Pac. 723 (1897); *Allen* v. *Petrick,* 69 Mont. 373, 384, 222 Pac. 451 (1924); *Anaconda National Bank* v. *Johnson,* 75 Mont. 401, 410, 244 Pac. 141 (1926); *Musselshell Valley Farming & Livestock Co.* v. *Cooley,* 86 Mont. 276, 290, 291, 283 Pac. 213 (1929); *Vidal* v. *Kensler,* 100 Mont. 592, 594-595, 51 Pac. (2d) 235 (1935); *Clausen* v. *Armington,* 123 Mont. 1, 14, 212 Pac. 440 (1949). See also *Cruse* v. *McCauley,* 96 Fed. 369, 371 (C.C.D. Mont. 1899); *Oscarson* v. *Norton,* 39 Fed. (2d) 610, 613 (9th Cir. 1930).

[716] *Anaconda National Bank* v. *Johnson,* 75 Mont. 401, 411, 244 Pac. 141 (1926).

[717] Mont. Rev. Codes Ann. § 89-834 (1964).

[718] *Hewitt* v. *Story,* 64 Fed. 510, 514-515 (9th Cir. 1894); *Harkey* v. *Smith,* 31 N. Mex. 521, 525, 247 Pac. 550 (1926).

[719] *Simons* v. *Inyo Cerro Gordo Min. & Power Co.,* 48 Cal. App. 524, 536-537, 192 Pac. 144 (1920).

[720] *Miocene Ditch Co.* v. *Campion Min. & Trading Co.,* 3 Alaska 572, 586 (1908).

Under the administrative method of appropriating water, the intent is expressed in the application for a permit in whatever particulars the State agency requires.

Diversion of water.—Actual diversion of water from the stream is also stressed in various decisions,[721] including such language as " * * * a completed ditch, actually diverting water,* * * "[722] and " * * * an actual diversion from the stream,* * *."[723] Parties who offered no proof of their diversion of water from a stream were held to have failed to establish an appropriation of the water.[724]

However, there are cases in which the diversion requirement was satisfied by natural overflow from the stream, as well as those in which it was denied. The necessity and materiality of diversion are discussed in chapter 9 under "Diversion, Distribution, and Storage Works."

In an application for a permit to appropriate water, the means of diversion is specified. If approved by the administrator, it is authorized in the permit.

Completion of construction.—Under "Development of the rules," above, it has been brought out that the early "possessory system" of appropriative rights contemplated prosecution of construction work diligently and continuously to completion, whereupon the would-be appropriator acquired a completed water right (subject to abandonment for nonuse) without the necessity of promptly putting the water to actual use. This theory was developed in various court decisions. It was reflected in some of the preadministration statutes, either specifically or by necessary implication as judicially construed.

However, some other courts held that appropriations made before pre-administration statutes went into effect were not complete until the water had been applied to beneficial use. Here the statutes changed the rule with respect to appropriations made in compliance with their provisions, but not as to those persons who, deliberately or otherwise, ignored the legislative requirements.

Under the water administrative-permit statutes now in force, an appropriation is not deemed complete at the time construction work is finished. In three of these States a certificate of completion of construction is given to the

---

[721] In a New Mexico case, water impounded in a reservoir on a public watercourse, part being intended for later use and part held in storage for flood control, was held, for lack of diversion and application to beneficial use, to be not appropriated: *State ex rel. State Game Commission* v. *Red River Valley Co.,* 51 N. Mex. 207, 223-224, 182 Pac. (2d) 421 (1945).

[722] *Murray* v. *Tingley,* 20 Mont. 260, 269, 50 Pac. 723 (1897).

[723] *Rodgers* v. *Pitt,* 129 Fed. 932, 939-940 (C.C.D. Nev. 1904).

[724] *Sherlock* v. *Greaves,* 106 Mont. 206, 216, 76 Pac. (2d) 87 (1938). "* * * repeatedly decided in this jurisdiction" that an actual diversion is necessary to an appropriation: *Windsor Res. & Canal Co.* v. *Lake Supply Ditch Co.,* 44 Colo. 214, 217, 98 Pac. 729 (1908). To preserve a water right, it is necessary to provide means for continual diversion of the water from its natural channel: *McPhail* v. *Forney,* 4 Wyo. 556, 561, 35 Pac. 773 (1894).

permittee when he demonstrates to the satisfaction of the administrative agency that the works are done and are ready for inspection.[725] This, however, does not represent perfection of the water right. That ultimate goal is not reached until the water is applied to the beneficial use or uses covered in the permit. The certificate of completion of construction is a document that follows the permit and precedes the final document, the license evidencing the perfected right. As is true with respect to the other permit system statutes, actual application of the water to beneficial use is essential to a valid appropriative right.

Application of water to beneficial use.—"The sine qua non of making a valid appropriation is and was to apply the water attempted to be appropriated to some beneficial use."[726] As against a subsequent appropriator, the right extends to, and only to, the quantity of water actually diverted and applied to a beneficial use.[727] This of course is the aim of appropriating water—to make use of it for some definite valuable purpose. The purpose must be a beneficial one. That accomplishment of this purpose is necessary to the completion of the appropriation is now generally true, although as above stated this was not always the case.

Thus, an appropriation made in Idaho under the "constitutional" method is complete on application of the water to the beneficial use for which the water is appropriated.[728] Under the current administrative statute, likewise, no appropriation is complete until this has taken place. However, previous statutory appropriations were completed when the works were constructed and water was conducted through the same to the place of intended use, subject to being lost by failure to apply the water to beneficial use within a reasonable time.[729]

What developed into the later western view is expressed by the Utah Supreme Court in an opinion rendered several years after enactment of the first complete water appropriation statute of that State. After stating the three principal elements necessary to constitute a valid appropriation, the court said that:[730]

> But we think the filing of a written application with the state engineer, as required by the statute, is but declaring, or the giving of a notice of, an intention to appropriate unappropriated public water. The final step, and the most essential element, to constitute a completed valid appropriation of water, is the application of it to a beneficial purpose. Whatever else is required to be or is done, until the actual application of the water is made

---

[725] N. Mex. Stat. Ann. § 75-5-9 (1968); Okla. Stat. Ann. tit. 82, § § 52 and 53 (1970); S. Dak. Comp. Laws Ann. § § 46-5-27 to 46-5-29 (1967).

[726] *Robinson* v. *Schoenfeld,* 62 Utah 233, 238, 218 Pac. 1041 (1923).

[727] *Kernan* v. *Andrus,* 6 Alaska 54, 59-60 (1918).

[728] *Reno* v. *Richards,* 32 Idaho 1, 10, 178 Pac. 81 (1918).

[729] *Basinger* v. *Taylor,* 30 Idaho 289, 299, 164 Pac. 522 (1917).

[730] *Sowards* v. *Meagher,* 37 Utah 212, 223, 108 Pac. 1112 (1910).

for a beneficial purpose, no valid appropriation has been effected. This was so before the statute, and it is still so under the statute.* * *

Application of the water to a beneficial use is necessary to the validity of an appropriation made under any of the other western administration statutes, as well as that of Utah. Statutes of these States, other than those of Nebraska and Texas, require further action (a) in the form of an inspection by the administrative agency of the completed work and determination that the permittee has completed appropriation of the water, followed (b) by issuance to him of a certificate of appropriation or equivalent license declaring that he has appropriated a specific quantity of water not exceeding that stated in the permit.

As stated above in discussing the nature and effect of a certificate or license, this final document is evidence of the completed appropriative right. It is acknowledgment by the State that the right has been perfected in accordance with law.[731] And it is binding on the State in the absence of subsequent failure of the holder to keep the right in good standing. The document confirms only the right that has been perfected. Regardless of the maximum quantity of water authorized by the permit to be appropriated, the certificate or license confirms the right to only the quantity which the permittee has actually put to beneficial use. In Nebraska and Texas, the State administrative agencies by reports and investigations keep in touch with the status of work done under permits and may cancel the rights thereunder for failure to proceed diligently. The administrators of these States do not issue certificates or licenses confirming completion.

Diligence

Basic requirement of diligence.—It is a general principle, that the validity of an appropriation of water as against intervening rights depends upon its being completed within a reasonable time with the exercise of due diligence. This principle has been applicable throughout the entire history of the appropriation doctrine in the West.

In a decision rendered in 1869, the California Supreme Court referred to its previous holdings concerning the necessity of diligence and good faith in relation to the doctrine of relation (discussed below) and declared the principles to be founded in reason. Their meaning and intent is that no man shall follow "dog in the manger" tactics, by claiming water because of certain preliminary acts and preventing others from enjoying what he lets alone, thereby preventing development of natural resources by others.[732] In early

---

[731] The Oregon Supreme Court has said that by the legislation of that State "the legislative assembly intended the water right certificate, not the permit, even when followed by a beneficial use, to mark the point at which a water right becomes vested." *Green* v. *Wheeler*, 254 Ore. 424, 458 Pac. (2d) 938, 940-941 (1969), certiorari denied, 397 U. S. 990 (1969).

[732] *Nevada County & Sacramento Canal Co.* v. *Kidd*, 37 Cal. 282, 314 (1869).

decisions of other courts, it was emphasized that following up the initial act of appropriation with reasonable diligence extended to consummation of the purpose without unnecessary delay.[733]

Principles respecting diligence.—The principles respecting diligence in relation to acquisition of appropriative rights were established in decisions of many courts prior to the era of statutory control and such principles have continued to be applied. These principles are important both in fixing times in permits for performance of certain acts, and in allowing extensions of such time periods.

What the law requires is reasonable diligence, with a fixed purpose on the part of the intending appropriator to carry through his project.[734] The diligence required does not involve unusual or extraordinary effort.[735] What is required is that the attempt to appropriate water be pursued with all the expedition and constant effort to accomplish the undertaking that is usual with men engaged in like enterprises who desire a speedy accomplishment of their designs.[736] There must be such assiduity in prosecution of the enterprise as will manifest to the world a *bona fide* intention to complete it within a reasonable time.[737]

Question of fact.—The question of reasonable diligence is one of fact for the court or the jury to decide.[738] It depends on the facts and circumstances of each particular case.[739] And it necessarily varies with each individual case.[740] Thus a lapse of 25 years, unexplained, in reconstructing a destroyed dam would be considered in determining, as a question of fact, whether due diligence had been used under all the circumstances of the case.[741]

---

[733] *Larimer County Res. Co.* v. *People ex rel. Luthe,* 8 Colo. 614, 616-617, 9 Pac. 794 (1886); *Clough* v. *Wing,* 2 Ariz. 371, 382-383, 17 Pac. 453 (1888).

[734] *Denver* v. *Northern Colorado Water Conservancy Dist.,* 130 Colo. 375, 388, 276 Pac. (2d) 992 (1954); *Four Counties Water Users Assn.* v. *Colorado River Water Cons. Dist.,* 159 Colo. 499, 514-516, 414 Pac. (2d) 469 (1966).

[735] *In re Deschutes River & Tributaries,* 134 Oreg. 623, 647-648, 286 Pac. 563, 294 Pac. 1049 (1930).

[736] *Carbon Canal Co.* v. *Sanpete Water Users Assn.,* 10 Utah (2d) 376, 380, 353 Pac. (2d) 916 (1960).

[737] *Ophir Silver Min. Co.* v. *Carpenter,* 4 Nev. 534, 542-543, 546 (1869); *In re Hood River,* 114 Oreg. 112, 130-131, 227 Pac. 1065 (1924).

[738] *Weaver* v. *Eureka Lake Co.,* 15 Cal. 271, 273-274 (1860); *Gates* v. *Settlers' Mill., Canal & Res. Co.,* 19 Okla. 83, 91, 91 Pac. 856 (1907).

[739] *Parker* v. *McIntyre,* 47 Ariz. 484, 492-495, 56 Pac. (2d) 1337 (1936); *Klug* v. *Ireland,* 99 Colo. 542, 543, 64 Pac. (2d) 131 (1936); *Conant* v. *Jones,* 3 Idaho 606, 612-613, 32 Pac. 250 (1893); *Rodgers* v. *Pitt,* 129 Fed. 932, 941-942 (C.C.D. Nev. 1904); *In re Silvies River,* 115 Oreg. 27, 61, 237 Pac. 322 (1925).

[740] *Gates* v. *Settlers' Mill., Canal & Res. Co.,* 19 Okla. 83, 89-90, 91 Pac. 856 (1907). "The time within which the appropriation must be completed varies according to circumstances, as what may be reasonable diligence in one case may be a great lack of diligence in another,* * * " *Maricopa County M. W. C. Dist.* v. *Southwest Cotton Co.,* 39 Ariz. 65, 103, 4 Pac. (2d) 369 (1931).

[741] *Gilia Water Co.* v. *Green,* 29 Ariz. 304, 306, 241 Pac. 307 (1925).

Determination of what constituted reasonable diligence in connection with the nonstatutory appropriations was within the sound discretion of the courts.[742] In determining the question in an early case, the California Supreme Court said that consideration might be given to such surrounding circumstances as nature of the country, climate, and difficulty of procuring labor and materials.[743]

Some circumstances excusing delays.—Some of the early posting and filing statutes declared that work must be prosecuted diligently and uninterruptedly to completion, but carried a proviso excusing temporary interruptions caused by snow or rain.[744]

Magnitude of the undertaking has been mentioned as an item for consideration in determining whether construction work was completed within a reasonable time.[745] A Texas court of appeals felt that the failure of an irrigation project, which was watering thousands of acres under its appropriation, to build distribution works to furnish water to a particular or small tract of land should not constitute a failure within the meaning of the statutes to prosecute its project "diligently and continuously to completion."[746] Drainage necessities and water shortage were considered an excuse in Nevada.[747]

The Montana Supreme Court indicated its belief that a farmer struggling for a livelihood, who cultivates his land and irrigates it as fast as he is able to provide the means, may not be guilty of unreasonable delay in applying his water to beneficial use.[748] Yet 2 years later, in a case arising in Montana, a Federal court cautioned that in determining the question of reasonableness the effect on later appropriators must be taken into account. In view of the rights of newcomers, said the court, there should be no unnecessary delay on the part of the earlier settlers.[749] All this simply supports the concept that circumstances affecting diligence vary with each particular case, and that the judgment varies accordingly.

Some inexcusable circumstances.—(1) In general. Obstructive weather conditions and matters incidental to the enterprise itself that could not reasonably be avoided, therefore, have been accepted in certain cases as excusing delay. But matters personal to the appropriator—such as sickness,

---

[742] *Morris* v. *Bean,* 146 Fed. 423, 427 (C. C. D. Mont. 1906).

[743] *Kimball* v. *Gearhart,* 12 Cal. 27, 30 (1859).

[744] Cal. Civ. Code § 1416 (1872); Nebr. Laws 1889, ch. 68, § 9.

[745] *Bailey* v. *Tintinger,* 45 Mont. 154, 178-179, 122 Pac. 575 (1912); *Oviatt* v. *Big Four Min. Co.,* 39 Oreg. 118, 126-127, 65 Pac. 811 (1901); *Water Supply & Storage Co.* v. *Larimer & Weld Irr. Co.,* 24 Colo. 322, 325, 51 Pac. 496 (1897). Compare *Antero & Lost Park Res. Co.* v. *Ohler,* 65 Colo. 161, 162-163, 176 Pac. 286 (1918), and dissenting opinion by Justice Garrigues.

[746] *Fairbanks* v. *Hidalgo W. I. Dist. No. 2,* 261 S. W. 542, 546 (Tex. Civ. App. 1923, error dismissed).

[747] *Rodgers* v. *Pitt,* 129 Fed. 932, 941-942 (C.C.D. Nev. 1904).

[748] *Arnold* v. *Passavant,* 19 Mont. 575, 580-581, 49 Pac. 400 (1897).

[749] *Cruse* v. *McCauley,* 96 Fed. 369, 372 (C. C. D. Mont. 1899).

pecuniary inability, occupation with other work, and other conditions incident to the person—are not generally recognized as excusing great delay in the construction of works necessary to actual diversion and use of water.[750]

(2) Lack of pecuniary means. The distaste for impecuniosity as an excuse for not prosecuting and completing the work of appropriation with reasonable diligence within a reasonable time has appeared in the court decisions from early times.[751] "Financial inability is not under the statute, as it was not without the statute, such a cause as will excuse lack of diligence in the prosecution of the work."[752] However, some of the statutes list cost of the work as a factor for consideration by the administrator.[753]

(3) Lack of pecuniary means: Leniency under exceptional or uncontrollable circumstances. The Oregon Supreme Court recognized the general rule before the water code of 1909 was enacted.[754] However, even prior to the national financial depression that reached its intensity in the early 1930's, leniency was shown where great difficulties were encountered and exceptionally high expenditures were found necessary.[755] And in a decision rendered in 1932, the supreme court gave controlling weight to the impact of the depression in ordering an extension of time within which an appropriation under the water code could be completed.[756]

---

[750] Grant Realty Co. v. Ham, Yearsley & Ryrie, 96 Wash. 616, 624, 165 Pac. 495 (1917). Cal. Admin. Code tit. 23, § 779 (1969).

[751] Kimball v. Gearhart, 12 Cal. 27, 31 (1859); Mitchell v. Amador Canal & Min. Co., 75 Cal. 464, 482-483, 17 Pac. 246 (1888).

[752] Rio Puerco Irr. Co. v. Jastro, 19 N. Mex. 149, 155, 141 Pac. 874 (1914).
   See also Carbon Canal Co. v. Sampete Water Users Assn., 19 Utah (2d) 6, 425 Pac. (2d) 405, 409 (1967).

[753] For example, in fixing permit times for completion, the Director "shall take into consideration the cost and magnitude of the project and the engineering and physical features to be encountered." Wash. Rev. Code § 90.03.320 (Supp. 1961). For good cause shown, the Department may extend the period for completion "if the magnitude, physical difficulties and cost of the work justify extension." Ariz. Rev. Stat. Ann. § 45-150 (1956).

[754] "The authorities clearly show that the claimant's pecuniary condition is not an excuse, and, though the doctrine may seem harsh, it is nevertheless right." Cole v. Logan, 24 Oreg. 304, 310-311, 33 Pac. 568 (1893); Oviatt v. Big Four Min. Co., 39 Oreg. 118, 126-127, 65 Pac. 811 (1901).

[755] In re Owyhee River, 124 Oreg. 44, 48-49, 259 Pac. 292 (1927); State ex rel. Van Winkle v. People's West Coast Hydro-Electric Corp., 129 Oreg. 475, 483-484, 278 Pac. 583 (1929). Under such circumstances, where the claimants pursued their work to the best of their ability, such showing was given considerable weight in determining the question of diligence.

[756] In re White River and Its Tributaries, 141 Oreg. 504, 515-519, 16 Pac. (2d) 1109 (1932). "The law does not require of an appropriator extraordinary efforts or impossible things. At a time when moratoriums are considered and banks take long holidays and many of them close, the question of finances, it seems to us, must of necessity be taken into account in determining as to the diligence and good faith of the company in completing its appropriation."

(4) Lack of diligence. In a considerable number of decisions in which no extraordinary difficulties were apparent, lack of diligence was measured by the excessive length of time taken to accomplish an act or series of acts in making an appropriation of water.

Some holdings that under the circumstances of the particular case the length of time actually taken was immoderate and unreasonable, and therefore to be considered as imputing lack of diligence, follow:

— Submission for 18 years or more to a temporary injunction without making any effort to have it removed.[757]

— Periods of 14 years between initiation of the project and completion of a part of the work.[758]

— Period of 20 years from initiation to application to beneficial use.[759]

— In an interstate case, the United States Supreme Court considered that a failure for a period of nearly 40 years to put waters to beneficial use precluded the claimants from now asserting their rights.[760]

— On the premise that an appropriator is allowed a reasonable time—and only such—within which to complete application of water to the contemplated beneficial use, the Oregon Supreme Court held that the installation of an elaborate system of irrigation after 67 years of flooding native vegetation was an attempted new appropriation and hence inferior to an intervening right.[761]

Gradual or Progressive Development

General principles.—From early times, courts have recognized the principle that the right to the use of water for irrigation is not necessarily confined to

---

Compare *Antero & Lost Park Res. Co.* v. *Ohler,* 65 Colo. 161, 162-163, 176 Pac. 286 (1918). From 1891 to June 1894 some actual construction work was carried on. Then for several years the only work was on maintenance of fences and buildings. From 1898 to 1907 no construction work was done. The supreme court supported the trial court's finding that diligence had not been exercised from 1894 to 1907 and that there was no right to a priority antedating 1907. Justice Garrigues dissented on the grounds that the delays were excusable by reason of the magnitude and difficulties of the work, death of one of the active parties, and the financial stringency attending the panic of 1893.

[757] *Sierra Land & Water Co.* v. *Cain Irr. Co.,* 219 Cal. 82, 83-84, 25 Pac. (2d) 223 (1933).
[758] *Hindman* v. *Rizor,* 21 Oreg. 112, 120, 27 Pac. 13 (1891); *Stickney* v. *Hanrahan,* 7 Idaho 424, 431, 63 Pac. 189 (1900); *Vineyard Land & Stock Co.* v. *Twin Falls Salmon River Land & Water Co.,* 245 Fed. 9, 21-22 (9th Cir. 1917).
[759] *Oscarson* v. *Norton,* 39 Fed. (2d) 610, 613 (9th Cir. 1930). An unexplained lapse of 25 years in reconstructing a destroyed dam would be considered in determining *as a question of fact* whether due diligence had been exercised *under all the circumstances of the case: Gila Water Co.* v. *Green,* 29 Ariz. 304, 306, 241 Pac. 307 (1925).
See also *Carbon Canal Co.* v. *Sampete Water Users Assn.,* 19 Utah (2d) 6, 425 Pac. (2d) 405, 409 (1967).
[760] *Washington* v. *Oregon,* 297 U. S. 517, 528-529 (1936).
[761] *Oliver* v. *Skinner & Lodge,* 190 Oreg. 423, 437-438, 226 Pac. (2d) 507 (1951).

the quantity actually applied at the time the appropriation is made.[762] "He would be entitled, not only to his needs and necessities at that time, but to such other and further amount of water, within the capacity of his ditch, as would be required for the future improvement and extended cultivation of his lands, if the right is otherwise kept up."[763] And the actual quantity must be such as the appropriator could put to a useful purpose on his land within a reasonable time by the use of reasonable diligence.[764]

This principle—that an appropriation is not necessarily to be measured by the application of the water during the first one or two, or even a series of years—"was not intended * * * to give an appropriator a quarter of a century in which to apply water to a beneficial use."[765] The court had reference to an individual appropriator, not to a great project the magnitude and complicated conditions of which present a very different problem. In the instant case, within a period of 24 years, the appropriator had reclaimed not quite one-half of his 160-acre tract. So he was accorded a right for only the quantity of water necessary to irrigate the land so reclaimed.

Development of the rule.—The rule of gradual development carried two invariable conditions which the appropriative claimant must meet: (a) the enlarged use of water over that accomplished in the early stages must have been within the original intent of the appropriator, and claimed at the time of initiating the appropriation; and (b) the intending appropriator proceeded with reasonable diligence to apply the water to the use intended.[766]

---

[762] The claim of an appropriator must be for a useful and beneficial purpose or in contemplation of a future use of the water for such purpose: *Weaver* v. *Eureka Lake Co.,* 15 Cal. 271, 275 (1860).

[763] *Hewitt* v. *Story,* 64 Fed. 510, 514 (9th Cir. 1894).

[764] *Senior* v. *Anderson,* 115 Cal. 496, 503-504, 47 Pac. 454 (1896).

[765] *Bennett* v. *Nourse,* 22 Idaho 249, 256, 125 Pac. 1038 (1912).

[766] "It is not requisite that the use of water appropriated be made immediately to the full extent of the needs of the appropriator. It may be prospective and contemplated, provided there is a present ownership or possessory right to the lands upon which it is to be applied, coupled with a *bona fide* intention to use the water, and provided that the appropriator proceeds with due diligence to apply the water to his needs." *St. Onge* v. *Blakely,* 76 Mont. 1, 23, 245 Pac. 532 (1926). "But where such appropriator, for illustration, only originally intended to irrigate forty acres of land, and he applied water on such land, this forty acres would be the limit of his right as such appropriator under his original appropriation." *State ex rel. Community Ditches* v. *Tularosa Community Ditch,* 19 N. Mex. 352, 371, 143 Pac. 207 (1914). See also generally regarding the rule of gradual development, *State* v. *Crider,* 78 N. Mex. 312, 431 Pac. (2d) 45, 48-49 (1967).

Some other court opinions in which both conditions were stated are: *Barnes* v. *Sabron,* 10 Nev. 217, 239-240, 244 (1875); *Union Mill & Min. Co.* v. *Dangberg,* 81 Fed. 73, 113 (C.C.D. Nev. 1897); *Elliot* v. *Whitmore,* 23 Utah 342, 352-353, 65 Pac. 70 (1901); *Smith* v. *Duff,* 39 Mont. 382, 387-388, 102 Pac. 984 (1909); *Ison* v. *Sturgill,* 57 Oreg. 109, 116, 109 Pac. 579, 110 Pac. 535 (1910); *Haight* v. *Costanich,* 184 Cal. 426, 431-432, 194 Pac. 26 (1920); *In re Doan Creek,* 125 Wash. 14, 25, 215 Pac. 343 (1923).

Granted that the two conditions are met in such an enterprise involving gradual development, any subsequent appropriator diverts water subject to such prior claim.[767] The priority of the entire right, if progressively developed properly, relates back to the date on which it was initiated.[768] But if the diligence required in developing the right is not exercised, rights of other appropriators that are initiated after the expiration of an allowable time for reasonable use become fixed as against the original appropriator, with priorities attaching to their own initiation dates. Hence, they take precedence over any enlargement—which is viewed as an attempted new appropriation—that the original appropriator may attempt after these other rights intervene.[769]

Early in the 20th century, the Oklahoma Supreme Court recognized the right to make gradual or progressive development without loss of priority where one continuous project is carried on with no lack of diligence. But the court imposed a qualification which, to this author's knowledge, is unique in western jurisprudence. This qualification is (a) that the original priority of the senior appropriator would extend to the quantity of water actually applied by him to beneficial use at the time a junior appropriator made his appropriation; (b) but that after this quantity is taken by the senior, the junior's right would become effective with respect to the quantity of water he applied to beneficial use; after which (c) the senior's right would again attach to any excess.[770] This of course disregards the doctrine of relation. It is squarely in conflict with the authorities cited in the immediately preceding paragraph, which adhere to the general western rule.

In *Cole* v. *Logan*, the Oregon Supreme Court cautioned that the privilege of gradual development without loss of priority does not mean that the appropriator can suspend his improvements for an unreasonable time and then, by adding to the area of his cultivated land, be restored to his original individual diversion as against subsequent appropriators who have acquired rights in the stream.[771] And the Montana Supreme Court declared that the

---

[767] *Kleinschmidt* v. *Greiser*, 14 Mont. 484, 497, 37 Pac. 5 (1894). Otherwise, said the Montana Supreme Court, in overruling the trial court, "The priority under such rule would depend largely upon the time appropriators brought their lands under cultivation, and not upon the priority of appropriation and diversion of the water necessary to irrigate the land owned by the appropriator, as the law provides." To the same effect: *Cole* v. *Logan*, 24 Oreg. 304, 311, 33 Pac. 568 (1893).

[768] *Ison* v. *Sturgill*, 57 Oreg. 109, 116, 109 Pac. 579, 110 Pac. 535 (1910). Applied to the circumstances of a large project: *In re Deschutes River and Tributaries*, 134 Oreg. 623, 649, 286 Pac. 563, 294 Pac. 1049 (1930).

[769] *Oliver* v. *Skinner & Lodge*, 190 Oreg. 423, 437-438, 226 Pac. (2d) 507 (1951). See *Washington* v. *Oregon*, 297 U. S. 517, 528-529 (1936).

[770] *Gates* v. *Settlers' Mill., Canal & Res. Co.*, 19 Okla. 83, 89-91, 91 Pac. 856 (1907).

[771] *Cole* v. *Logan*, 24 Oreg. 304, 312, 33 Pac. 568 (1893). In such event, his appropriation would be confined to his necessary use as applied to the lands he brought under cultivation within a reasonable time before any subsequent rights accrued.

privilege is not accorded "for mere future speculative profit or advantage, without regard to existing or contemplated beneficial uses."[772]

The Washington Supreme Court declined to apply the rule of gradual development in cases in which the projected uses were too remote and speculative,[773] or where the growth was extremely slow.[774] In determining what should be considered reasonable diligence under the circumstances of the particular case, said the court, "The doctrine of common sense applies."[775]

Application of the rule under the administration statutes.—The considerations which govern solutions of questions relating to gradual or progressive development are found chiefly in controversies over appropriative rights that were initiated before the administrative statutes were enacted. Thus, they had to do primarily with acts that already had taken place. Now the administrative statutes which are in effect in most Western States grant authority to administrators to fix time periods for constructing works and applying water to beneficial use. Thus, these statutes contemplate acts to be performed in the future.

Under this administration statute arrangement, the intent of the prospective appropriator is expressed in his application for a permit as clearly as the State administrative officer requires. In fixing the time periods, this officer takes into consideration all the circumstances to the extent that they can be ascertained at the time. If for one reason or another the permittee finds the going difficult and fears that he cannot fulfill his obligations within the prescribed time, he may ask for an extension. In acting upon such request, the administrator has access to the extant judicial principles as to reasonableness and diligence. If an extension is granted and the permittee completes his appropriation within the extended time and pursuant to his recorded intention, his priority relates back to the time his application was filed. In other words, the same basic principles are involved now as before the administrative era, but they are applied under publicity regulated methods of appropriation.

In a 1956 case involving administrative fixing of rates for reservoir water, the Wyoming Supreme Court took occasion to quote with approval one of its own previous statements which in turn was quoted from the opinion in a Utah case decided in 1910. This was: " ' " * * * an application [for a permit to appropriate water] may properly be made when it is made in good faith and with an actual bona fide intention and a present design to appropriate the

---

[772] *Toohey* v. *Campbell,* 24 Mont. 13, 17, 60 Pac. 396 (1900). In this case, the intent of an appropriator of water in 1868, as to the then present and contemplated use of water diverted in that year, was held to have never reached beyond the purpose of irrigating a tract of 25 acres then enclosed. It did not extend to an additional area within a larger tract, taken up in 1876, embracing the former enclosure and possessory claim.

[773] *Thorp* v. *McBride,* 75 Wash. 466, 469-470, 135 Pac. 228 (1913).

[774] *In re Doan Creek,* 125 Wash. 14, 215 Pac. 343 (1923).

[775] *In re Alpowa Creek,* 129 Wash. 9, 14-15, 224 Pac. 29 (1924).

water for a beneficial use, though contemplated in the future, and when it is not made for the purposes of mere speculation or monopoly." ' "[776]

The Wyoming water rights statute is typical of those that authorize the administrative agency to grant extensions of time for beginning and completing construction and making application of water to beneficial use "for good cause shown," without particularizing the causes.[777] Policies of some other States are:

In Nebraska, the applicant must "vigorously, diligently, and uninterruptedly prosecute such work to completion unless temporarily interrupted by some unavoidable and natural cause" and "with such a force as shall assure the average rate of constructional progress necessary to complete such work or works within the time stipulated in the approval of such application, notwithstanding the ordinary delays and casualties that must be expected and provided against."[778]

In South Dakota, an extension may equal the time during which work was prevented "by the operation of law beyond the power of such applicant to avoid."[779] In North Dakota, times may be extended "for good cause shown."[780]

The New Mexico legislature authorizes the State Engineer to allow extensions of the times specified in the permit for completion of works "equal to the time during which work was prevented by acts of God, operation of law, or other causes beyond the control of the applicant."[781]

Extensions of time are allowed in Idaho when an applicant is prevented from proceeding because of some matter under the jurisdiction of the United States, or by litigation over his title. Extensions in case of large reservoirs (involving more than 200,000 acre-feet capacity) or diversions (involving more than 25,000 acre-feet in one irrigation season for a project of no less than 5,000 acres) because of the time required for organizing, financing, and construction may be granted, provided that at least $100,000 has already been expended toward purchases of property and construction of works.[782]

---

[776] *Lake De Smet Res. Co.* v. *Kaufmann,* 75 Wyo. 87, 99, 292 Pac. (2d) 482 (1956), quoting from *Scherck* v. *Nichols,* 55 Wyo. 4, 18, 95 Pac. (2d) 74 (1939), quoting from *Sowards* v. *Meagher,* 37 Utah 212, 221-222, 108 Pac. 1112 (1910). In this last cited case, the Utah Supreme Court confessed that the question was open to debate and not free from doubt, but that the conclusion indicated had been reached under circumstances of good faith and freedom from mere speculation or monopoly.

[777] Wyo. Stat. Ann. § 41-206 (1957).

[778] Nebr. Rev. Stat. § 46-238 (1968).

[779] S. Dak. Comp. Laws Ann. § 46-5-25 (1967).

[780] N. Dak. Cent. Code Ann. § 61-04-14 (Supp. 1969); Okla. Stat. Ann. tit. 82, § 56 (1970).

[781] N. Mex. Stat. Ann. § 75-5-7 (1968).

[782] Idaho Code Ann. § 42-204 (Supp. 1969), discussed and applied in *Keller* v. *Magic Water Co.,* 92 Idaho 276, 441 Pac. (2d) 725, 732 (1968).

The rules and regulations of the California Water Resources Control Board state that extensions of time stated in a permit may be granted only upon a showing of good cause, in that failure to fulfill the terms has been occasioned by causes which could not reasonably be avoided. Causes not generally acceptable are lack of finances, occupation with other work, physical disability, and other conditions incident to the person and not to the enterprise.[783]

Progressive development versus future use.—There is a sharp distinction between (a) the principle of gradual or progressive development of a projected appropriation of water, which is generally accepted in the West with the essential qualifications of original intent and due diligence, and (b) the concept of appropriating water for future use and reserving the right indefinitely without doing much if anything in the way of developing the project.

The right of appropriation for use in the indefinite future is commonly granted to municipalties, with temporary rights of use by others pending the time the city needs the water. (This is noted above under "Who May Appropriate Water.") This concession, however, is owing to the peculiar circumstances surrounding municipalities. Towns and cities are commonly expected to grow, and to need more water for additional citizens but at uncertain times in the future. By contrast, an attempted reservation of water by an individual, the project to lie dormant until he chooses to revive it while remaining immune from attack by other intending appropriators, conforms to the idea of a "dog in the manger" attitude. Never, to this author's knowledge, has this been sanctioned by any high court in the West.[784]

Gradual or progressive development, then, implies (a) the setting aside of quantities of water to be applied to beneficial use from time to time over a specified period of years, (b) within the scope of the appropriator's announced plan, and (c) predicated upon his exercise of reasonable diligence all the way along. This principle was accepted by the courts in the early history of the appropriation doctrine, and it is applied in operation of the current State administrative control statutes. Obviously, the holding out of water from general appropriation for the future use of an individual who has no intention of commencing development immediately, or for a protracted time, would violate the diligence requirement of the progressive development concept. It is alien to that generally accepted principle. The requisite conditions that are imposed are sound.

Doctrine of Relation

Nature and importance.—The doctrine of relation, or relation back, is important in the appropriation water rights jurisprudence of the West. Its

---

[783] Cal. Admin. Code, tit. 23, § § 778 and 779 (1969).

[784] On the contrary, said a Federal court in Nevada, "In the appropriation of water, there cannot be any "dog in the manger" business by either party, to interfere with the rights of others, when no beneficial use of the water is or can be made by the party causing such interference." *Union Mill & Min. Co.* v. *Dangberg,* 81 Fed. 73, 119 (C. C. D. Nev. 1897).

importance lies in its bearing on the priority of an appropriation—its function of holding the claimant's priority intact pending his completion of the appropriative process with due diligence, at which time his priority relates back to the time at which acquisition of the right was initiated.

The doctrine was recognized by the Supreme Court of California in one of its very early cases, decided within a few years after gold was discovered. The first water rights case in which the doctrine was expounded appears to have been *Kelly* v. *Natoma Water Company,* decided in 1856.[785] Reference was made to *Stark* v. *Barnes,* an 1853 decision (not a water case) wherein a correct statement of the doctrine was said to be that " 'where a number of acts are to be performed, in virtue of which a right accrues, the time of performance of the last act, when all have been performed in good faith, relates back to the commencement of the series of acts which create the right, so as to make it perfect when the first act was being commenced.' "[786]

In the *Kelly* case the supreme court stated that in the *Stark* case "the doctrine of relation, as between the acts of the plaintiff, first and last, was simply applied to the thing possessed, and not to the intention of possessing." The actual holding in the *Kelly* case is that the right does not relate back to the intention to appropriate water. The *dictum* in the case is that it does relate back to the first act of possession in the series of acts constituting the appropriation.

In absence of statute.—The doctrine of relation as applied to acquisition of appropriative rights was recognized throughout the West. It was the subject of many court pronouncements.[787]

(1) Statement of the doctrine. In many court opinions, the doctrine of relation back has been expressed in various ways. The doctrine embodies the features that (a) if a party embarks in good faith upon a project to appropriate water, (b) if he consummates his purpose without unnecessary delay by exercising reasonable diligence in every step required in constructing facilities, diverting water, and completing the appropriation, (c) then although his power of enjoyment will not commence until completion is accomplished, yet his right as against those who initiate their appropriations after he does will have relation back to the time of commencement.[788] As discussed

---

[785] *Kelly* v. *Natoma Water Co.,* 6 Cal. 105, 108 (1856).

[786] *Stark* v. *Barnes,* 4 Cal. 412, 413-414 (1853).

[787] Early adoptions in other jurisdictions following *Kelly* v. *Natoma Water Co.* were *Ophir Silver Min. Co.* v. *Carpenter,* 4 Nev. 534, 543-544 (1869); *Woolman* v. *Garringer,* 1 Mont. 535, 544 (1872); *Keeney* v. *Carillo,* 2 N. Mex. 480, 493 (1883); *Sieber* v. *Frink,* 7 Colo. 148, 153, 2 Pac. 901 (1884).

[788] *Maricopa County M. W. C. Dist.* v. *Southwest Cotton Co.,* 39 Ariz. 65, 102-103, 4 Pac. (2d) 369 (1931); *Maeris* v. *Bicknell,* 7 Cal. 261, 263 (1857); *Ophir Silver Min. Co.* v. *Carpenter,* 4 Nev. 534, 543-544 (1869); *Keeney* v. *Carillo,* 2 N. Mex. 480, 483 (1883); *Gay* v. *Hicks,* 33 Okla. 675, 682, 124 Pac. 1077 (1912); *Morgan* v. *Shaw,* 47 Oreg. 333, 336, 83 Pac. 534 (1906); *Salt Lake City* v. *Salt Lake City Water & Electrical Power Co.,* 24 Utah 249, 264, 67 Pac. 672 (1902); *Grant Realty Co.* v. *Ham, Yearsley & Ryrie,* 96 Wash. 616, 623, 165 Pac. 495 (1917); *Moyer* v. *Preston,* 6 Wyo. 308, 321, 44

earlier,[789] the act of completion from which the priority of the right relates back to the beginning may be (a) completion of construction of works, or (b) application of water to beneficial use, depending upon the era and the statutes and court decisions in point. Under the current statutes regulating appropriations of water under permit from the State Engineer, completion of appropriation invariably refers to actual application of the water to beneficial use.

Therefore, as between two persons digging ditches at the same time, and prosecuting work thereon, with reasonable diligence, to completion, the one who first began work had the prior right, even though the other had completed his first. This was the doctrine of "relation back."[790]

While, then, in the absence of a statute requiring notice, or other action, the right relates back to the time when the first step was taken, "it does not apply, or protect the intending appropriator however, unless he prosecutes his work of diversion with reasonable diligence."[791] In such case, the priority "generally dates from the time when the work is completed or the appropriation is fully perfected."[792] This would usually be "the time of actual application of the water" to the intended beneficial use.[793] Until this is done, the claimant's rights are inchoate.[794]

Relation back is not to be confused with the perfecting of title to the water right. The title is perfected when the appropriation is complete, whether or not diligence was exercised. When completion of the appropriation occurs, then the priority dates back, by operation of the doctrine of relation to the beginning of the work, *provided* that the invariable prerequisites have been fulfilled.[795]

(2) Reason for the doctrine. In a very early case, the California Supreme Court observed that the right of relation back was necessary for the protection

---

Pac. 845 (1896); *Union Mill & Min. Co.* v. *Dangberg,* 81 Fed. 73, 109 (C. C. D. Nev. 1897); N. Mex. Stat. Ann. § 75-1-2 (1968); N. Dak. Cent. Code Ann. § 61-01-03 (1960).

[789] Under "What Constitutes Completion of Appropriation—Completion of construction" and "Application of water to beneficial use."

[790] *Murray* v. *Tingley,* 20 Mont. 260, 268, 50 Pac. 723 (1897).

[791] *Rio Puerco Irr. Co.* v. *Jastro,* 19 N. Mex. 149, 153, 141 Pac. 874 (1914); *Still* v. *Palouse Irr. & Power Co.,* 64 Wash. 606, 612-614, 117 Pac. 466 (1911).

[792] *Ophir Silver Min. Co.* v. *Carpenter,* 4 Nev. 534, 543, 544 (1869).

[793] *Maricopa County M. W. C. Dist.* v. *Southwest Cotton Co.,* 39 Ariz. 65, 102-103, 4 Pac. (2d) 369 (1931).

[794] An 1889 decree had both absolute and interlocutory features. "At the time of the entry of the decree, the court established in each ditch an absolute right to the full amount of water per second of time that had been applied to a beneficial use, and gave such appropriation a number, and, to that extent, it was absolute. It tentatively recognized an inchoate right to additional water, which inchoate right, if of any validity, might become an absolute right, under the doctrine of relation, if the water was applied to a beneficial use with due diligence." *Crawford Clipper Ditch Co.* v. *Needle Rock Ditch Co.,* 50 Colo. 176, 181, 114 Pac. 655 (1911).

[795] *Kimball* v. *Gearhart,* 12 Cal. 27, 29-30 (1859); *Nevada County & Sacramento Canal Co.* v. *Kidd,* 37 Cal. 282, 311 (1869).

of prior appropriators. If the right were not to commence until completion of the canal, the value of a large water right could be destroyed by a small appropriation made after nearly the entire work on the prior appropriation had been completed.[796]

In a stream adjudication decision rendered nearly three-quarters of a century later, the Oregon Supreme Court expressed much the same thought. Diligence and relation back must be considered together, said the court, because the rule with its basis on diligence grew out of necessity through conflicting claims of settlers in the arid districts. "Except for its application the doctrine of appropriation would have resolved itself into a scrambling rush for the possession of the water right, and the question would always be decided in favor of the one who either had the most money or the one who had the least to do to effect a diversion of water."[797]

(3) Initiation of the claim. The date to which the completed right related back was variously referred to as initiation of the claim, commencement of the appropriation, or first step in appropriating water.

In the absence of a well-recognized custom (as well as absence of statute), the first act must have been such as to indicate the intention of appropriating the water in such manner as to put a prudent man upon inquiry.[798] This may have been the giving of notice of intention to appropriate water;[799] or the beginning of construction of a diversion dam or ditch or other appliance by means of which the appropriation is effected;[800] or the commencement of surveys for the canal route.[801]

Trivial labor and small expenditures will not carry the appropriation back by relation to the "first substantial act of the appropriator for its acquisition."[802] There must be an open, notorious, physical demonstration, conclusively indicating a fixed purpose of pursuing and, within a reasonable time, acquiring a water right.[803]

In an interstate case, the United States Supreme Court expressed its view that under the doctrine of appropriation as applied in the States that were parties to the controversy, in the absence of statute, the right when perfected by use is deemed effective from the time the purpose to make the appropriation is definitely formed and actual work on the project is

---

[796] *Conger* v. *Weaver*, 6 Cal. 548, 558 (1856).

[797] *In re Hood River*, 114 Oreg. 112, 142, 227 Pac. 1065 (1924).

[798] *Kimball* v. *Gearhard*, 12 Cal. 27, 31 (1859).

[799] *De Necochea* v. *Curtis*, 80 Cal. 397, 401, 20 Pac. 563, 22 Pac. 198 (1889).

[800] *Kelly* v. *Natoma Water Co.*, 6 Cal. 105, 108 (1856); *Union Mill & Min. Co.* v. *Dangberg*, 81 Fed. 73, 109 (C. C. D. Nev. 1897).

[801] *Conger* v. *Weaver*, 6 Cal. 548, 558 (1856). Early Wyoming Territorial statutes directed that the beginning of all necessary surveys should be considered as commencement of the work of construction: Wyo. Laws 1886, ch. 61, § 13; Laws 1888, ch. 55, § 12.

[802] *Klug* v. *Ireland*, 99 Colo. 542, 543, 64 Pac. (2d) 131 (1936).

[803] *Holbrook Irr. Dist.* v. *Fort Lyon Canal Co.*, 84 Colo. 174, 190, 269 Pac. 574 (1928).

begun—provided the work is carried to completion and the water is applied to beneficial use with reasonable diligence.[804]

(4) Local custom. Before enactment of the legislative acts authorizing acquisition of appropriative rights which were initiated by posting and filing notice of appropriation, local customs to that effect had developed in many areas of the West. In California, this custom was adopted in the gold mining regions from similar mining practices.[805]

> [In Oregon, before the legislative enactment of 1891,] it was a recognized rule that the appropriation of water of a stream, initiated by the posting and recording of a notice of appropriation, in accordance with a custom, and perfected by diversion and application of the water to a beneficial use within a reasonable time, dates back under the doctrine of relation to the first step taken.* * * Such a rule may be said to have become established, under varying circumstances and conditions, in this state.[806]

In one of its earliest water rights decisions, the Montana Supreme Court held that notices of appropriation posted on a stream, and immediate entering on the work of constructing dam and ditch, were sufficient to put other parties on their guard and to apprise them of the initiated appropriation.[807]

Nonadministration statutes.—The early statutes of a number of Western States and Territories embodied the posting and filing procedure in their provisions for acquiring water rights. Some of them provided specifically for application of the doctrine of relation. (See "Statutory—Original Statutory Appropriation Procedures," above.) For example, the California Civil Code—which was the earliest of these statutes, and which became the prototype for several of them—provided with respect to this feature that:[808]

> Sec. 1418. By a compliance with the above rules the claimant's right to the use of the water relates back to the time the notice was posted.
> Sec. 1419. A failure to comply with such rules deprives the claimants of the first right to the use of the water as against a subsequent claimant who complies therewith.

Although these early statutory procedures were not regarded as exclusive methods of appropriating water, it was necessary that they should be followed by one who wished to obtain the advantage of the doctrine of relation.[809] But

---

[804] *Arizona* v. *California,* 298 U. S. 558, 565-566 (1936).

[805] Harding, S. T., "Water Rights for Irrigation," p. 24 (1936).

[806] *In re Silvies River,* 115 Oreg. 27, 39, 237 Pac. 322 (1925). By compliance with the rules and regulations of the Harris mining district, Alaska, adopted in 1882, a claimant's right to the use of water related back to the time the notice was posted: *McFarland* v. *Alaska Perserverance Min. Co.,* 3 Alaska 308, 336 (1907). The rule, said the court, stated the law, even in the absence of a miners' rule or custom.

[807] *Woolman* v. *Garringer,* 1 Mont. 535, 544-545 (1872).

[808] Cal. Civ. Code §§ 1418 and 1419 (1872).

[809] *Duckworth* v. *Watsonville Water & Light Co.,* 158 Cal. 206, 211, 110 Pac. 927 (1910), 170 Cal. 425, 431, 150 Pac. 58 (1915); *Sand Point Water & Light Co.* v. *Panhandle Development Co.,* 11 Idaho 405, 412-414, 83 Pac. 347 (1905); *Murray* v. *Tingley,* 20

where a notice was not filed or posted as required by the statute,[810] or where reasonable diligence in prosecuting the work was lacking,[811] there could be no relation back to the time of beginning.

The Texas and Wyoming preadministration statutes provided that an intending appropriator should file a notice in the county records within a prescribed time after commencement of construction, which in Wyoming went back to the beginning of necessary surveys.[812]

Until 1969, the Colorado statute provided that an intending appropriator had to file a statement of his claim in the office of the State Engineer within 60 days after construction of his ditch or reservoir.[813] Nothing was said about relation back. However, the Colorado Supreme Court has recognized the doctrine of relation, and has held that to obtain its benefit, construction must have been prosecuted with reasonable diligence, with a fixed purpose to carry through the project, and completed within a reasonable time.[814] "Once the decision has been made to proceed with the project, continuing investigations and changes are simply evidence of diligence and endeavor to accomplish the greatest good at a minimum of cost to the public, not abandonment of the project."[815] In 1969, the Colorado Legislature repealed the above-mentioned filing requirement,[816] and enacted provisions for the voluntary determination of water rights and conditional water rights, amounts and priorities thereof, approval of plans for augmentation, and bienniel findings of reasonable diligence.[817] In establishing standards for such determinations the legislature recognized the doctrine of relation back by providing:[818]

> In the determination of a water right the priority date awarded shall be that date on which the appropriation was initiated if the appropriation was

---

Mont. 260, 269, 50 Pac. 723 (1897); *State ex rel. Van Winkle* v. *People's West Coast Hydro-Electric Corp.,* 129 Oreg. 475, 481-482, 278 Pac. 583 (1929); *Robinson* v. *Schoenfeld,* 62 Utah 233, 238-239, 218 Pac. 1041 (1923); *State ex rel. Ham, Yearsley & Ryrie* v. *Superior Court,* 70 Wash. 442, 462, 126 Pac. 945 (1912).

[810] *Pyke* v. *Burnside,* 8 Idaho 487, 490, 69 Pac. 477 (1902).

[811] *Still* v. *Palouse Irr. & Power Co.,* 64 Wash. 606, 612-614, 117 Pac. 466 (1911).

[812] Tex. Gen. Laws 1889, § 8; Wyo. Laws 1888, ch. 55, §§ 11 and 12. "And many appropriations now existing, made before the adoption of the present statutes, have been established, and others will be established, in respect to priorities, upon evidence as to time of commencing work or making surveys." *Whalon* v. *North Platte Canal & Colonization Co.,* 11 Wyo. 313, 344, 71 Pac. 995 (1903).

[813] Colo. Rev. Stat. Ann. §§ 148-4-1 to 148-4-7 (1963). The Colorado Supreme Court held that compliance with the filing requirements was not necessary to the validity of the appropriation. *Black* v. *Taylor,* 128 Colo. 449, 457-458, 264 Pac. (2d) 502 (1953).

[814] *Denver* v. *Northern Colorado Water Conservancy Dist.,* 130 Colo. 375, 384, 388, 276 Pac. (2d) 992 (1954).

[815] *Four Counties Water Users Assn.* v. *Colorado River Water Conservation Dist.,* 159 Colo. 499, 514-516, 414 Pac. (2d) 469 (1966).

[816] Colo. Laws 1969, ch. 373, § 20.

[817] Colo. Rev. Stat. Ann. §§ 148-21-1 to 148-21-45 (Supp. 1969).

[818] *Id.* § 148-21-21 (1).

completed with reasonable diligence. If the appropriation was not completed with reasonable diligence following the initiation thereof, then the priority date thereof shall be that date from which the appropriation was completed with reasonable diligence.

Montana has two nonadministration water statutes. (a) With respect to *unadjudicated* waters, compliance with the statutory requirements is necessary to invocation of the doctrine of relation back to the time of taking the first step, posting of notice.[819] (b) In awarding an appropriation from a source that has been *adjudicated,* the court by interlocutory decree may prescribe the conditions to be fulfilled. On full compliance, the court enters a decree establishing the appropriation and fixing the date of priority which, if the appropriator has complied diligently, is the date of filing the petition. If the facts warrant, the court may fix a later date.[820]

In a case decided in 1906 involving rights to the use of water of a stream rising in Montana and flowing into Wyoming, a Federal court cautioned that the early appropriation statutes were not enacted for the purpose of enabling an appropriator to claim by relation to the date when the work was begun, because that was the rule prior to any legislation on the subject with respect to causes in which the work was prosecuted with reasonable diligence. Nor were they ever intended to destroy the right of appropriation by methods other than those defined by them. Their only effect, said the court, was to deny the power of an appropriator who failed to file the notice to claim as of the date of his beginning work. The penalty for such failure in this instance was to limit the right to the time when the water was actually applied and used.[821] (See "Completion of Appropriation," above, for circumstances under which completion meant completion of construction of works, and those under which it referred to application of water to use.)

Administration statutes.—(1) Relation back to first step. A feature of the modern statutes providing administrative control over the appropriation of water is that the priority of a right that is acquired by full compliance with the law relates back to the date of filing, in the office of the State administrator, the application for a permit to appropriate the water.

A majority of the statutes include a concise statement similar to that of Oregon: "The right acquired by an appropriation shall date from the filing of the application in the office of the State Engineer."[822] Several add a proviso such as that of New Mexico:" * * * subject to compliance with the provisions of this article, and the rules and regulations established thereunder."[823]

---

[819] *Murray* v. *Tingley,* 20 Mont. 260, 269, 50 Pac. 723 (1897).

[820] Mont. Rev. Codes Ann. § 89-834 (1964).

[821] *Morris* v. *Bean,* 146 Fed. 423, 427 (C. C. D. Mont. 1906).

[822] Oreg. Rev. Stat. § 537.250(3) (Supp. 1969).

[823] N. Mex. Stat. Ann. § 75-1-2 (1968).

In Kansas, the priority of appropriation right to use water for any purpose *except* domestic dates from the time of filing the application. For domestic purposes, it dates from the time of filing the application or from the time of first making actual use of the water therefor, whichever is earlier.[824]

The general appropriation statute of Nevada does not state explicity that the date of filing the application shall constitute the date of priority of an appropriation made in strict compliance with the statutory procedure. This, however, is clearly implied. And it is followed by the State Engineer's office in processing applications and permits. For example, if, according to the statute, an application is returned for correction and is refiled in proper form within the time allowed, the application does not lose its "priority of filing" on account of such defects. And the ground water statute declares explicitly that the date of priority of an appropriation of ground water is the date of filing the application in proper form in the office of the State Engineer pursuant to the provisions of the general water law.[825]

(2) Postponement of priority. Several statutes provide for postponement of priority for failure to take necessary acts with reasonable diligence, or within the times allowed or extensions thereof.

In New Mexico, North Dakota, Oklahoma, and South Dakota, postponement takes place as a result of inadequate work toward completion of construction. The administrator examines the works and requires those improperly constructed to be put in good condition within a specified time. Failure to put them in proper condition within such time is cause for postponing the priority. Postponement is measured by the time elasping between the date set for completing such changes and the date they are made to the satisfaction of the administrator.[826]

In Idaho, the postponement relates to failure to make beneficial use of water within the time allowed. It extends for a period of time equal to that elapsing between the date allowed for making proofs of beneficial use and the date of actually making such proof.[827]

If an application approved by the Utah State Engineer lapses for failure of the applicant to comply with the statutory law or with an order of the State Engineer, and if it is reinstated on a showing of reasonable cause, the date of priority is changed to the date of reinstatement.[828]

Appropriation of Water for Use in Another State

The question of appropriating water within one State for the purpose of diverting it across the stateline for use in a sister State merges into the much

---

[824] Kans. Stat. Ann. § 82a-707 (1969).

[825] Nev. Rev. Stat. § § 533.355 and 534.080 (Supp. 1967).

[826] N. Mex. Stat. Ann. § 75-5-8 (1968); N. Dak. Cent. Code Ann. § 61-04-09 (Supp. 1969); Okla. Stat. Ann. tit. 82, § 52 (1970); S. Dak. Comp. Laws Ann. § 46-5-28 (1967).

[827] Idaho Code Ann. § 42-219 (Supp. 1969).

[828] Utah Code Ann. § 73-3-18 (1968).

larger and vastly more important question of rights to the use of waters of interstate streams. This is because most—but not all—[829] of such cases arise with respect to streams which themselves cross statelines. The topographic features of river valleys are conducive to this result. At this point, however, attention is concentrated on the immediate question of transstateline diversions of water, regardless of whether the streams from which the water is diverted flow entirely within the upper State or cross the interstate boundary—leaving the larger questions to be considered later in chapter 22.

Questions respecting diversions across statelines arose early in the 20th century and became the subject of litigation before there was any legislation to guide the administrators and the courts. A majority of the Western States now have statutes which grant, restrict, or forbid the initiation of an appropriation of water within their borders for use in another jurisdiction.

Court Decisions

Some fundamental points recognized by the judiciary and problems involved.—These are:

(1) "A water right may be acquired under the doctrine of prior appropriation by the diversion of water at a point on a stream in one state and its application to beneficial use on lands in another state where the stream flows in both states."[830] But that:

(2) The water statutes of the States involved have no extraterritorial effect.[831] And that:

(3) The State in its sovereign capacity may exercise its authority over the waters flowing in the streams within its borders. And it has the right to prohibit their diversion within the State boundaries for use outside of them.[832] However,

(4) Whatever power a State may have to prevent the acquisition of an appropriative right within its territory for use of water in another State cannot be exercised to the impairment of a preexisting validly established appropriative

---

[829] "First of all, it should be remembered that Bear Creek is not an interstate stream. It is located wholly within the state of Idaho and does not reach into the state of Montana, and so no question of the appropriation and diversion of the waters of an interstate stream for use within this state or in a neighboring state arises in this case." *Walbridge* v. *Robinson,* 22 Idaho 236, 240-241, 125 Pac. 812 (1912).

[830] *Lindsy* v. *McClure,* 136 Fed. (2d) 65, 69 (10th Clr. 1943).

[831] *Id.* at 70; *West End Irr. Co.* v. *Garvey,* 117 Colo. 109, 114-115, 184 Pac. (2d) 476 (1947).

[832] *Walbridge* v. *Robinson,* 22 Idaho 236, 240-247, 125 Pac. 812 (1912). The supreme court sustained an act of the State Engineer in refusing to issue, in the absence of legislative authority therefor, a certificate of completion of construction in connection with a proposed appropriation of water within Idaho for purposes of irrigation in Montana.

right of a project that overlaps the stateline. Protection of such a right is secured to its holder by the constitution of the United States.[833]

In absence of State statutes.—In the absence of State statutes pertaining specifically to exports or imports of water across statelines:

(1) In 1903, the Wyoming Supreme Court observed that: "Upon the general principles governing such appropriation, we perceive no reason, if the same be not prohibited by statute, why the owner of lands in another state may not at a point in this State lawfully divert the water of a stream flowing in both states and conduct such water upon his lands for their irrigation, and thereupon secure a valid water right."[834] Subsequently, as noted below, the Wyoming Legislature *did* place restrictions on such diversions of water.

(2) In 1947, the Colorado Supreme Court held that statements that it had made in an opinion delivered nearly a half-century earlier, while spoken concerning a ditch diverting water within the State for irrigation of lands outside of it, apply equally to ditches that divert water outside the State for use within it. These statements were to the effect that it cannot be presumed that the legislature intended to enact a law (for the adjudication of priorities) that would operate beyond the territorial limits of the State, or that it was legislating for the reclamation or irrigation of lands beyond its boundaries, or was making provision by way of police regulations over a territory beyond its jurisdiction.[835] These two Colorado decisions, then, did not pass on the legality of diversions of water across the stateline. They held that under the State statutory procedure there was no provision for adjudicating claimed rights to make diversions of water for transportation either into or out of the State. Without determination of the claimed rights, there could of course be no enforcement under the statutory procedure.

---

[833] *Weiland* v. *Pioneer Irr. Co.,* 259 U. S. 498, 501-502 (1922). The appropriation in this case, with a priority as of 1890, was made for the diversion of water from an interstate stream (North Fork of the Republican River) within Colorado. About one-third of the water was used within Colorado, and the remainder was transported into Nebraska for beneficial use therein. Suit to enjoin the Colorado water administration officials from interfering with the right of the irrigation company to divert water into Nebraska under its 1890 priority was brought in 1913 in the Federal court for the District of Colorado. Decree of injunction was affirmed in *Weiland* v. *Pioneer Irr. Co.,* 258 Fed. 519 (8th Cir. 1916). In 1917, the Colorado legislature passed a statute forbidding diversion of water into another State for use therein: Colo. Laws 1917, p. 539, Rev. Stat. Ann. § 148-1-1 (1963).

[834] *Willey* v. *Decker,* 11 Wyo. 496, 534, 73 Pac. 210 (1903).

[835] Adjudication of out-of-State diversions would not be within the purview of the statutory proceedings, the purpose of which is to furnish the basis for division of the stream waters among the ditches diverting water therefrom through control of their headgates by public water officials: *West End Irr. Co.* v. *Garvey,* 117 Colo. 109, 113-114, 184 Pac. (2d) 476 (1947). Under the adjudication statute of Colorado, the district court of La Plata County did not have jurisdiction to award priority to a ditch which, though having its headgate in Colorado, was intended to and did carry water into New Mexico for irrigation there: *Lamson* v. *Vailes,* 27 Colo. 201, 203-204, 61 Pac. 231 (1900).

In a somewhat analogous decision, the New Mexico Supreme Court held that in the water appropriation act of that State the legislature did not intend to give the Territorial Engineer authority to grant permits to be exercised beyond the boundaries of New Mexico—permits, that is, to divert water within Colorado, from a stream flowing into New Mexico, for conveyance into the latter jurisdiction for use there.[836]

The problems in these cases, then, were matters of statutory construction.

(3) Late in the 19th century, Mitchell Irrigation District, with lands situated wholly in Nebraska, located its diversion headgate on the south bank of North Platte River within Wyoming, about one-half mile west of the Wyoming-Nebraska stateline. This was indeed a strategic location of the headworks from the standpoint of Mitchell District. But it led to considerable controversy with neighboring Nebraska irrigation projects, contention with water administrative officials of both States, and litigation in both State and Federal courts.

As a result of a decision by the Wyoming Supreme Court, the Mitchell District water right was adjudicated with a priority as of 1890 by the Wyoming State Board of Control.[837] Previously, the Wyoming Board had refused to accept proofs because of advice from the Attorney General that it had no jurisdiction over an appropriation solely for the irrigation of lands in another State. However, the supreme court held that the Board had jurisdiction and should act upon the proofs of appropriation. Thus, the priority of the Mitchell appropriation was determined and established under the Wyoming procedure and as a part of the Wyoming schedule of priorities, whereas the rights of Mitchell's neighboring projects east of the stateline—in its own State—were on the Nebraska schedule.

Complications ensued. For a long time, Mitchell district was in contention with the water administrative officials of Nebraska over its refusal to comply with headgate closing orders of the State in favor of Nebraska appropriators with earlier priorities. This culminated in a judgment of the Nebraska Supreme Court in the *Sorensen* case that despite the district's diversion within Wyoming, this appropriator and its appropriation were subject to control of the State of Nebraska as soon as the water was brought into the State. Hence, the Wyoming priority of the Mitchell district was held junior to earlier priorities of appropriators on the North Platte within Nebraska, and its exercise was restricted accordingly.[838]

Several years later, Mitchell went into the Federal court in Wyoming in an action to require the Wyoming State officials to administer water rights along the North Platte according to the strict order of priorities on the stream section within Wyoming. On appeal, the United States Court of Appeals for the 10th

---

[836] *Turley* v. *Furman*, 16 N. Mex. 253, 255-257, 114 Pac. 278 (1911).

[837] *State ex rel. Mitchell Irr. Dist.* v. *Parshall*, 22 Wyo. 318, 329-330, 140 Pac. 830 (1914).

[838] *State ex rel. Sorensen* v. *Mitchell Irr. Dist.*, 129 Nebr. 586, 594, 262 N. W. 543 (1935), certiorari denied, 297 U. S. 723 (1936).

Circuit held that the district's appropriation had been lawfully made and had vested long prior to enactment of the Wyoming statute of 1939, which provided that no water of Wyoming should ever be appropriated for use outside the State without specific authorization of the legislature. In any event, this statute failed to indicate a legislative intent to disturb vested rights. A judgment of dismissal was reversed.[839]

Still later, Mitchell district brought an action in a Wyoming State court for a mandatory injunction requiring the State water commissioner to prevent the diversion of water from the North Platte in Wyoming by five canals having priorities junior to the Mitchell appropriation. This found no favor with the Wyoming Supreme Court. The supreme court considered it far from established that if the water commissioner during particular seasons had closed the headgates of junior appropriators in Wyoming, Mitchell would have received the water thus released. That is to say, Farmers Irrigation District of Nebraska, located just below Mitchell on the river, held priority earlier than Mitchell's which must be satisfied before Mitchell could take any water. The Nebraska State administration officials, after the decision in the *Sorensen* case, did not permit Mitchell to take water ahead of earlier Nebraska priorities. Wyoming officials obviously had no jurisdiction over the river waters after they crossed the stateline. Hence, the Wyoming watermaster was not to blame when the district obeyed the Nebraska officials and kept its headgate closed at certain times. It was concluded that no purpose would be served by closing the junior Wyoming headgates at times when Mitchell would receive no benefit therefrom.[840]

(4) One aspect of the general question of appropriation of water within one State for use in another was touched upon in the decision in a Federal suit which was primarily a contest over rights to the waters of the Rio Grande in the vicinity of El Paso, Texas. However, "along with that are a cluster of satellite controversies."[841]

A water district that was formed on the Texas portion of the Federal Rio Grande reclamation project contended that its New Mexico appropriation in effect had extraterritorial force, and that it supplanted the law of Texas in control of water brought down the river from New Mexico for use in the Texas part of the project. This contention the court dismissed. Also dismissed was plaintiffs' other view that water rights under the New Mexico appropriation became appurtenant to the project lands in Texas. This proposition, as handled

---

[839] *Mitchell Irr. Dist.* v. *Sharp,* 121 Fed. (2d) 964, 967-968 (10th Cir. 1941), certiorari denied, 314 U. S. 667 (1941).

[840] *Mitchell Irr. Dist.* v. *Whiting,* 59 Wyo. 52, 70-79, 136 Pac. (2d) 502 (1943), certiorari denied, 322 U. S. 727 (1944).

[841] *El Paso County W.I. Dist. No. 1* v. *El Paso,* 133 Fed. Supp. 894, 904-905, 923-924 (W.D. Tex. 1955), affirmed in part, reversed in part but not on the matters considered here, 243 Fed. (2d) 927 (5th Cir. 1957), certiorari denied, 355 U. S. 820 (1957).

by the court, merged into the question of State rights to the waters of an interstate stream, which is outside the scope of the instant topic.

State Statutes: Salient Points Summarized

(1) Arizona. Water may be appropriated for projects that overlap the statelines. However, at its discretion, the State department may decline to issue a permit if the proposed point of diversion is within Arizona and the place of use is within another State.[842]

(2) California. With respect to any stream flowing across the State boundary—but not including interstate lakes, or streams flowing into or out of them—provided the sister State reciprocates: (a) An appropriation of water may be made in California for use in the other State. (b) A right of appropriation with diversion and use in the other State, and recognized by its laws, has the same force and effect as if located in California, except that this does not apply to Walker River and its tributaries in Nevada.[843]

(3) Colorado. It is unlawful to divert or transport, by any artificial or natural means, the waters of streams or other sources of the State into any other State for use therein. It is the duty of the State officials to carry out this mandate.[844]

(4) Idaho. (a) Issuance of permits to appropriate water within Idaho for diversion into another State for use therein is prohibited unless the sister State has reciprocal legislation. (b) Special provisions relate to appropriation of public waters of Idaho for use in Oregon, Wyoming, and Nevada.[845]

(5) Montana. (a) Appropriation of water in the State for use outside the State boundaries requires approval of the legislature. (b) A later act authorizes appropriations by the State of Wyoming, for use therein, on issuance of certificates of appropriation therefor by the Montana State Water Resources Board, provided Wyoming enacts reciprocal legislation.[846]

(6) Nebraska. (a) On specific legislative authorization, water may be appropriated for diversion or storage in Nebraska and use in an adjoining State which grants reciprocal rights. Application therefor and rights thereunder are governed by the laws of Nebraska. (b) Operators of interstate ditches are required to construct and maintain suitable measuring devices in Nebraska at or near the stateline.[847]

(7) Nevada. (a) Projects having works or lands located partly in Nevada and partly in another State may appropriate water, provided the sister State authorizes diversions of water therefrom into Nevada. (b) On any stream

---

[842] Ariz. Rev. Stat. Ann. § 45-153 (1956).

[843] Cal. Water Code § § 1230, 1232 (West 1956), and 1231 (Supp. 1970).

[844] Colo. Rev. Code § § 148-1-1 and 148-1-2 (1963).

[845] Idaho Code Ann. § § 42-408, -402, -405 to -407, -409 (1948), -401, -403, -404, and -410 (Supp. 1969).

[846] Mont. Rev. Codes Ann. § § 89-846 and 89-809 (1964).

[847] Nebr. Rev. Stat. § § 46-233.01, 46-233.02, 46-213 (1968).

flowing across the stateline—provided there is reciprocal legislation—water may be appropriated in Nevada for use in the adjoining State, and an appropriation having diversion and place of use in the other State and recognized by the laws thereof has the same force and effect as if the diversion and use were in Nevada. (c) The place of use of water may not be changed for use outside the State, except with respect to waters so diverted before March 23, 1951, and still used for domestic or industrial purposes outside the State.[848]

(8) Oregon. Express consent of the legislature is required for the diversion, impounding, or appropriation, for diversion or use outside the State, of (a) any water within Oregon, or (b) waters inside the State boundary which form part of any stream or other body of water serving as part of the common boundary of Oregon and any other State and over which Oregon has concurrent jurisdiction, except for development of hydroelectric energy, flood control, irrigation, or other uses without diversion from the drainage basin wherein located. On receiving legislative permission, coupled with any conditions that the legislature may choose to impose in the interest of the State, the permittee may proceed under the regular statutory procedure.[849]

(9) Utah. (a) Water may be appropriated from interstate streams, in Utah, to be conveyed into any border State for use therein, provided the sister State has reciprocal legislation. (b) The State Engineer is directed to cooperate with administrative officials of adjoining States and, with consent of the Governor, to enter into agreements with them, in the determination and regulation of all water and water rights in interstate streams.[850]

(10) Washington. Provided reciprocity in legislation exists: (a) If the diversion point or any of the works or place of use or part of the irrigable lands of a project are within Washington, water may be appropriated. (b) At the Director's discretion, issuance of permit may be refused where the point of diversion is within Washington but the place of beneficial use is in some other State or nation.[851]

(11) Wyoming. (a) Reservoir water may not be used outside the State boundaries without special permit from the State Engineer. (b) Water may be diverted or stored in Wyoming for use in any adjoining State if specifically authorized by the legislature and if the sister State reciprocates. (c) The Board of Control may adjudicate such water rights. (d) Special provisions apply to interstate appropriations for use in Utah and Montana. (e) Other provisions apply to purchasers of water originating outside the State and flowing into Wyoming, but not legally available for either State or

---

[848] Nev. Rev. Stat. § § 533.515, .522, .524, and .520 (Supp. 1969).
[849] Oreg. Rev. Stat. § § 537.810 to 537.870 (Supp. 1967).
[850] Utah Code Ann. § 73-2-8 (1968).
[851] Wash. Rev. Code § 90.03.300 (Supp. 1961).

private use in Wyoming as against another State or appropriators therein. (f) Procedure is provided for transferring, from an adjoining State to a location within Wyoming, the point of diversion of an appropriation of water of an interstate stream entering Wyoming that was acquired from the sister State.[852]

Priority of Appropriation

Importance and Value of Fixed Priority

Essential element of the doctrine.—As the term implies, priority is an essential ingredient of the law of prior appropriation. "One of the essential elements of a valid appropriation is that of priority over others."[853]

This principle was established in California by the customs of the miners and by the supreme court in its earliest decisions over rights to the use of water.[854] As the appropriation doctrine became established in the western jurisdictions by customs, statutes, and court decisions, it included the essential principle of "First in time, first in right"—that priority in time of making an appropriation confers superiority of right over those who follow.[855]

This principle still prevails in the water rights jurisprudence of the West except as noted below under "Restrictions and Preferences in Appropriation of Water."

The date of priority.—The priority of a particular appropriation is represented by a date. With respect to such water right, all appropriations of water of the same source of supply having earlier dates of priority are senior in right, and all having later dates of priority are junior in right.

---

[852] Wyo. Stat. Ann. § § 41-34, -150 to -153, and -11 to -25 (1957).

[853] *Joerger* v. *Pacific Gas & Electric Co.,* 207 Cal. 8, 26, 276 Pac. 1017 (1929). The appropriator first in time is prior in right over others on the same stream: *Arizona* v. *California,* 298 U. S. 558, 565-566 (1936). This is the fundamental principle of appropriation of water: *Caviness* v. *La Grande Irr. Co.,* 60 Oreg. 410, 424, 119 Pac. 731 (1911). It is the cardinal rule of the doctrine: *Lindsey* v. *McClure,* 136 Fed. (2d) 65, 69 (10th Cir. 1943).

[854] *Eddy* v. *Simpson,* 3 Cal. 249, 252 (1853); *Stiles* v. *Laird,* 5 Cal. 120, 122-123 (1855). Conflicting rights to the working of mines and to the diversion of streams from their natural channels were held to stand on an equal footing, and "when they conflict, they must be decided by the fact of priority upon the maxim of equity, *qui prior est in tempore potior est in jure.*" *Irwin* v. *Phillips,* 5 Cal. 140, 146-147 (1855). *Jennison* v. *Kirk,* 98 U. S. 453, 457-458, 461 (1879).

[855] See *Bower* v. *Moorman,* 27 Idaho 162, 180-181, 147 Pac. 496 (1915); *Mettler* v. *Ames Realty Co.,* 61 Mont. 152, 159-160, 169, 201 Pac. 702 (1921); *Proctor* v. *Jennings,* 6 Nev. 83, 87 (1870); *Biggs* v. *Miller,* 147 S. W. 632, 636 (Tex. Civ. App. 1912); *Lehi Irr. Co.* v. *Moyle,* 4 Utah 327, 340, 9 Pac. 867 (1886); *Willey* v. *Decker,* 11 Wyo. 496, 510, 73 Pac. 210 (1903); *Vineyard Land & Stock Co.* v. *Twin Falls Oakley Land & Water Co.,* 245 Fed. 30, 34 (9th Cir. 1917); *Basey* v. *Gallagher,* 87 U. S. 670, 682 (1875). Compare *Sturr* v. *Beck,* 6 Dak. 71, 50 N. W. 486 (1888), affirmed, 133 U. S, 541, 552 (1890).

It is the duty of a watermaster in charge of distribution of water of an adjudicated stream—whether appointed by court or by the State—to distribute the water according to the rights of those entitled to receive it. Thus, in the watermaster's routine of opening, closing, and adjusting diversion headgates, his guide is a schedule of all appropriative rights in good standing that attach to the stream system, arranged in the chronological order of their respective dates of priority. Each right relates to a specific flow of water, usually in cubic feet per second. As the natural streamflow diminishes with the advancing season, headgates are lowered or closed in the reverse order of priorities, beginning with the latest in time and working backward in time, always reserving sufficient water to fill completely the requirements of the earlier rights. Should there be an increase in the natural flow, the gates are opened or raised to give the junior appropriators the benefit of the available supply.

The Utah legislature expressed its understanding of this relationship of priorities, and of what is incumbent upon the watermaster to effectuate it, thus: "Appropriators shall have priority among themselves according to the dates of their respective appropriations, so that each appropriator shall be entitled to receive his whole supply before any subsequent appropriator shall have any right; * * *."[856]

The date of priority of an appropriation, then, is of outstanding and often of vital importance. In 1891, the Colorado Supreme Court observed that: "The authorities seem to concur in the conclusion that the priority to the use of water is a property right."[857] Two years later this court made a statement concerning the value of a priority, which has been quoted on several occasions.[858]

Property rights in water consist not alone in the amount of the appropriation, but, also, in the *priority* of the appropriation. It often happens that the chief value of an appropriation consists in its *priority* over other appropriations from the same natural stream. Hence, to deprive a person of his priority is to deprive him of a most valuable property right. * * *

The Priority Principle in Operation

Priorities of successive appropriations on one stream.—It is possible for an intending appropriator to obtain a valid right to all the water that flows in a stream if he has need for it. Such an appropriation of the entire streamflow was

---

[856] Utah Code Ann. § 73-3-21 (1968). Following the semicolon is a proviso regarding preferences in time of scarcity, noted later.

[857] *Strickler* v. *Colorado Springs,* 16 Colo. 61, 70, 26 Pac. 313 (1891).

[858] *Nichols* v. *McIntosh,* 19 Colo. 22, 27, 34 Pac. 278 (1893); *Whitmore* v. *Murray City,* 107 Utah 445, 452-453, 154 Pac. (2d) 748 (1944). "It necessarily follows that the owner of a priority right to the use of water is the owner of property and he cannot be deprived thereof without due process of law." *Vonberg* v. *Farmers Irr. Dist.,* 132 Nebr. 12, 20, 270 N. W. 835 (1937).

sustained by the California Supreme Court in an early decision.[859] In several later decisions, the validity of such rights was recognized.[860] Of course, these situations are exceptional.

If, as is usual, the first appropriator does not make a valid appropriation of the entire water supply, the surplus waters of such source are subject to successive appropriations. As a result, the total number of rights so attaching to a stream system may be small, or it may be very large, running into the hundreds or even thousands.[861]

Succeeding appropriations by first user. —The first appropriator himself may also be one of the succeeding appropriators, for use of water on either the same land or on other land, without losing his first priority provided others are not injured.[862] If a prior appropriator wishes to acquire a succeeding appropriation, he must make a new appropriation therefor on each occasion. Each such new appropriation on his part will be inferior in priority to all rights of others that have intervened since his first appropriation was made.[863] The difference between this situation and a deliberately acquired right of gradual development has been discussed earlier.

Relation of priority to diversion works. —It has been long established that a single headgate and diversion ditch may be used for the service of several different priorities. These may be successive and several appropriations under rights owned by the same water user.[864] Or they may be several rights owned by different appropriators.

It was doubtless a matter of mutual convenience for Nichols and his associates to convey the water for the use of their respective farms for a certain distance through the same irrigating ditch; and in so doing they were entitled to have their respective rights protected the same as if the water had been conveyed through separate ditches, or through ditches having separate and independent head gates.[865]

---

[859] *Brown* v. *Mullin,* 65 Cal. 89, 90, 3 Pac. 99 (1884).

[860] *Larsen* v. *Appollonio,* 5 Cal. (2d) 440, 444, 55 Pac. (2d) 196 (1936); *Huffner* v. *Sawday,* 153 Cal. 86, 94, 94 Pac. 424 (1908); *Baxter* v. *Gilbert,* 125 Cal. 580, 581-582, 58 Pac. 129 (1899).

[861] "Any person or number of persons may have an interest in, or become the exclusive owner or owners of, different water rights, each of which rights may have had their inception at different times, and in such cases the order of their respective priorities must necessarily depend upon the dates of the initiation of each particular right." *Whited* v. *Cavin,* 55 Oreg. 98, 106, 105 Pac. 396 (1909).

[862] *Caviness* v. *La Grande Irr. Co.,* 60 Oreg. 410, 428, 119 Pac. 731 (1911).

[863] *Tudor* v. *Jaca,* 178 Oreg. 126, 158, 164 Pac. (2d) 680 (1945), 165 Pac. (2d) 770 (1946); *Union Grain & Elevator Co.* v. *McCammon Ditch Co.,* 41 Idaho 216, 221-223, 240 Pac. 443 (1925); *Union Mill & Min. Co.* v. *Dangberg,* 81 Fed. 73, 106 (C.C.D. Nev. 1897).

[864] *Simpson* v. *Bankofier,* 141 Oreg. 426, 432, 16 Pac. (2d) 632 (1932), 18 Pac. (2d) 814 (1933).

[865] *Nichols* v. *McIntosh,* 19 Colo. 22, 24, 34 Pac. 278 (1893).

Location of diversion works on watercourse.—From a strict legal standpoint, the point of location of the diversion works on the source of supply has nothing to do with priority of the right. The first appropriator who locates his point of diversion on a stream has the prior right to the use of the waters thereof, regardless of whether subsequent appropriators locate above him or below him on the same stream. And the same rule applies to all subsequent appropriators with respect to all others on the same stream.[866] Without having any bearing on relative dates of acquisition of the right, priority number one may be located near the headwaters of the stream, or near its mouth, or at any point between these extremes.

A physical advantage in being situated high up the stream is that late in the season the natural flow may be large enough to be diverted there, yet not enough to reach downstream appropriators in sufficient quantity to be useful to them if left alone. In that event, the law does not require the upstream junior appropriator to do such a vain thing as to release water that would simply be lost in the stream channel and hence be of no benefit to those downstream. On unpoliced streams in the pioneer days, junior appropriators upstream sometimes enforced their advantage of location by means of gunplay, which accounted for the saying that under such circumstances "a high-ority is better than a priority."[867] With increasing water development and use, and administration of streams by officials empowered to make arrests, this type of open disregard of prior rights became impracticable.

Current legislative declarations.—The constitutions and water administration statutes of several Western States variously express the theme—but usually with important exceptions discussed later in connection with restrictions and preferences—that "As between appropriators, the first in time is the first in right."[868]

---

[866] *McCall* v. *Porter*, 42 Oreg. 49, 57, 70 Pac. 820 (1902), 71 Pac. 976 (1903); *Beecher* v. *Cassia Creek Irr. Co.*, 66 Idaho 1, 9-10, 154 Pac. (2d) 507 (1944). Where appropriations are made at different points of diversion on a stream and by means of different ditches, the diversion made by each ditch is of necessity an independent appropriation: *Spring Creek Irr. Co.* v. *Zollinger,* 58 Utah 90, 98, 197 Pac. 737 (1921). Compare *Keller* v. *Magic Water Co.,* 92 Idaho 226, 441 Pac. (2d) 725, 732-734 (1968) where collective diversion works constituted one diversion. See chapter 8, note 394.

[867] In one of the upper Rocky Mountain valleys, it was said, the custom was to choose the ugliest man in the community and to arm him with the longest available rifle for protection of the upstream headgates against attacks by justly indignant irrigators downstream.

[868] S. Dak. Code Comp. Laws Ann. § 46-5-7 (1967). See Ariz. Rev. Stat. Ann. § 45-141(A) (Supp. 1970); Colo. Const., art. XVI, § 6; Idaho Const., art. XV, § 3; Idaho Code Ann. § 42-106 (1948); Kans. Stat. Ann. § 82a-707(c) (1969); Mont. Rev. Codes Ann. § 89-807 (1964); Nebr. Const., art. XV, § 6; Nebr. Rev. Stat. § 46-204 (1968); N. Mex. Const., art. XVI, § 2; N. Mex. Stat. Ann. § 75-1-2 (1968); N. Dak. Cent. Code Ann. § 61-01-02 (Supp. 1969); Tex. Rev. Civ. Stat. Ann. art. 7472 (1954); Utah Code Ann. § 73-3-1 (1968); Wash. Rev. Code § 90.30.010 (Supp. 1961); Wyo. Const., art. VIII, § 3.

Apparently, the first legislative pronouncement in which this appears was in the California Civil Code of 1872, in the first western statutory procedure for appropriating water.[869] It was not repealed or replaced by the present California Water Code.

Effect of statutory administration restrictions.—The flat declarations of "First in time, first in right," which the water administration statutes picked up from early customs and judicial declarations, are now modified in nearly all Western States with respect to the essential time factor by administrative restrictions and preferences directed or authorized by the legislatures.

This facet of the law of prior appropriation is becoming increasingly important in the field of legislative and administrative control over the conservation and utilization of public water supplies. It is the subject of the next ensuing topics. Some further discussion of the priority principle appears in chapter 8, under "Elements of the Appropriative Right."

Restrictions and Preferences in Appropriation of Water

The administrative systems for control of water appropriations, which in most States are the exclusive means of acquiring such rights, accord to no one the unqualified right to appropriate water. These statutory systems contain restrictions on the approval of applications for permits. A result of the restrictions may be refusal on the part of the administrator to approve the application, in whole or in part. Also, many of the statutes designate preferences, either in the process of making appropriations or in the use of water already appropriated, or both. In addition, there are some provisions for taking possession of existing senior rights to the use of water for low preference purposes, in order that they may be exercised by junior appropriators for high preference purposes.

It is true that several State constitutions or statutes prohibit the denial of rights to appropriate stream waters. But in the States that have water appropriation-permit statutes, this inhibition is coupled with certain exceptions.

A general rule in the appropriation-permit States is (1) that to be approved, an application for a permit to appropriate water must conform to the specific requirements of the statute; but (2) that the application must be denied (a) if there is no unappropriated water available in the proposed source, or (b) if the granting would threaten the stability or value of preexisting water rights, or (c) if the proposed project appears inimical to the public welfare. It is also a general rule that the administrator may grant a qualified or limited right consonant with the statutory restrictions.

The statutory preferences in appropriation of water place domestic water use highest on the lists. This results from the indispensability of water in preserving human life. Municipal use is generally coupled with domestic, either

---

[869] Cal. Civ. Code § 1414 (West 1954).

in the literal wording of the law or in practice. This is because the primary use of water within a municipality serves the life, health, welfare, and safety of human beings in the aggregate—a composite domestic purpose. Next on the list in most States is agriculture, particularly irrigation. Industrial uses of various kinds—manufacturing, waterpower, mining—usually follow. Purposes such as recreation, wildlife protection, and navigation, if they are mentioned, usually come afterward.

The policy of curbing the indiscriminate acquisition and exercise of rights to the use of water is an important phase of State administrative control over this vital natural resource. Available water supplies, despite their periodical replenishment from the inexhaustible ocean, are not unlimited. Great as is their potential in the West, demands upon them tend to increase with development of communities, farm lands, and industries. The purpose of restrictions on the right to make appropriations of available water supplies, and the purpose of preferences relating to uses of water in the order of their value to the public welfare, are to secure the greatest possible benefit to the public from administrative control and regulation of the State's water resources.

Problems in the fields of restrictions and preferences in water appropriation are considered separately below.

Restrictions on the Right to Appropriate Water

Constitutional prohibitions against denial of the right to appropriate water.—Wiel, writing in 1911, stated that "most States put the 'free development' theory into their constitutions or statutes by providing, 'The right to appropriate unappropriated water shall never be denied,' or words to the same effect."[870]

To say "most States" is incorrect. In only two constitutions (Colorado and Idaho) and one statute (Nebraska) did this flat, unqualified declaration appear in 1911.[871] After the publication of Mr. Wiel's text, one of these two constitutions (Idaho) was so amended as to add an exception; and the one statute of Nebraska, although not amended, was overshadowed by a subsequent qualified constitutional declaration.

Constitutional provisions on this subject follow:

(1) Colorado. "The right to divert the unappropriated waters of any natural stream to beneficial uses shall never be denied."[872]

---

[870] Wiel, S.C., "Water Rights in the Western States," 3d ed., vol. 1, § 108 (1911).

[871] It is true that this declaration appeared in the New Mexico law of 1905, but it was deleted 2 years later. New Mexico Laws 1905, ch. 102: "Section 1. All natural waters within the limits of New Mexico are hereby declared to belong to the public, and no person shall be denied the right to appropriate said waters for beneficial use." Laws 1907, ch. 49: "Section 1. All natural waters flowing in streams and water courses, whether such be perennial, or torrential, within the limits of the Territory of New Mexico, belong to the public and are subject to appropriation for beneficial use."

[872] Colo. Const., art. XVI, § 6.

(2) Idaho. "The right to divert and appropriate the unappropriated waters of any natural stream to beneficial uses, shall never be denied, except that the state may regulate and limit the use thereof for power purposes."[873] The last clause, respecting power purposes, was added by amendment in 1928.

(3) Nebraska. "The right to divert unappropriated waters of every natural stream for beneficial use shall never be denied except when such denial is demanded by the public interest."[874] This section was adopted in 1920.

(4) Wyoming. "No appropriation shall be denied except when such denial is demanded by the public interests."[875]

What are the results of these mandates in the fundamental laws?

Colorado has no administrative procedure for control over the acquisition of appropriative rights, exclusive in its operation, under which a State agency may choose among applications for permits and reject those which fail to meet the statutory requirements, thus preventing an applicant from making his desired appropriation.

Idaho has an administrative procedure which, however, is not exclusive in its operation. An application for a permit which fails to measure up to the standards may be rejected. This prevents the applicant from obtaining a permit to make his appropriation under the statutory procedure. But unless the proposed appropriation is for power development, which the State may control and regulate, the applicant is not precluded from appropriating water by diversion and application to beneficial use without regard to the statutory requirements.

The constitutional inhibitions in Nebraska and Wyoming against denial of the right to appropriate water contain only one exception—conflict with the public interest. However, if certain other unfavorable conditions exist—such as insufficient water supply, or conflict with preexisting rights—issuance of permits is not conducive to the public welfare. The Wyoming water rights statute includes both of these conditions, together with threat of detriment to the public interest, as grounds for rejection of applications. And in Nebraska—the water rights law of which as originally enacted and in its present form states that "The right to divert unappropriated waters of every natural stream for beneficial use shall never be denied," but without the constitutional exception added in 1920 concerning public interest demands—the statute specifically recognizes that approval of an application if there is no unappropriated water in the source of supply is not conducive to the public welfare.[876] In both States, rights obtained by applicants may be specifically qualified and limited by the administrators.

---

[873] Idaho Const., art. XV, § 3.

[874] Nebr. Const. art. XV, § 6.

[875] Wyo. Const. art. VIII, § 3.

[876] Wyo. Stat. Ann. §§ 41-203 and 41-206 (1957); Nebr. Rev. Stat. §§ 46-204, 46-234, and 46-235 (1968). "If there is unappropriated water in the source of supply named in the application, and if such application and appropriation when perfected is not

In practical operation, it is doubtful that the administrative agencies of these two States are more hampered by reason of this constitutional feature than are those of other Western States the constitutions of which are silent on this matter.

But no unqualified right of appropriation under water permit statutes.—In the 16 Western States in which control over appropriation of water is imposed by statute, no person has an unqualified right to appropriate water.[877] It is his privilege to apply to the State authorities for a permit to make the appropriation. But this will be granted to him only if certain conditions and prerequisites prevail. And as stated later in discussing preferences in acquiring the right, his application may be prior in time to applications of other parties who, however, may have a preferential status which entitles them to priorities senior to that of the first applicant.

The statutory listings of these restrictions on the privilege of obtaining permits to appropriate water are grouped into several categories below. Generally, the legislative directions are mandatory. If a prescribed condition exists, such for example as unavailability of unappropriated water in the proposed source, the evident intent usually is that the application shall be denied. However, in some instances it is provided that the State agency "may" refuse to issue the permit, or may issue one with respect to less water or land than is applied for.

Conformance to specific requirements of the statute.—The State administrative agency is not required to approve an application that is not in proper form. Such an application is returned for correction to the applicant, who has a prescribed period of time within which to refile it in the State office in order to hold the original priority of filing.

Likewise the application must comply with all governing provisions of the law and with the rules and regulations of the State administrative agency. It must also be accompanied by the required filing fees.[878] Whether or not specifically declared in the statute, this is common administrative practice.

Availability of unappropriated water.—(1) A practically uniform requirement. In order to obtain a permit to appropriate water in the 16 appropriation control States, a *sine qua non* is the availability of unappropriated water in the proposed source of supply.

In most of these statutes, this condition is expressly stated in the directions to the administrative agency to approve permits. In the others, it appears

---

otherwise deterimental to the public welfare, the Department of Water Resources shall approve the same, * * *." *Id.* § 46-235.

[877] In *Tanner* v. *Bacon,* 103 Utah 494, 504-505, 136 Pac. (2d) 957 (1943), the Utah Supreme Court rejected a contention of counsel that under the doctrine of priorities, every person who makes an application to appropriate unappropriated water of Utah has an unqualified right to have his application approved.

[878] See S. Dak. Comp. Laws Ann. § § 46-5-18 and 46-5-20 (1967); Tex. Rev. Civ. Stat. Ann. art. 7507 (1954).

elsewhere in the statute.[879] Or if not, it is certainly by necessary implication an administrative requirement. In view of the widespread importance of and attention to this factor in western water administration, any supposed legislative intent that, in passing on an application for a permit, the administrator be excused from investigating and weighing the question of available water is not credible.[880]

(2) Difficulties in determining the question. Occasionally, in practice, there have been what amount to contentions that the question of unavailability of unappropriated water in the proposed source may be adequately answered by the application of simple arithmetic to available office records. Despite this, the problem is administrative not clerical; and it involves consideration of many factors. Any question as to this that arises in the course of processing an application for a permit to appropriate water must be answered. In the last analysis, such an answer becomes a careful administrative estimate, subject to review in a judicial proceeding. Some situations that have reached the courts may be noted:

(a) New Mexico. The State Engineer of New Mexico, according to the statute, "shall determine from the evidence presented by the parties interested, from such surveys of the water supply as may be available, and from the records, whether there is unappropriated water available for the benefit of the applicant" and, if so, he shall approve the application.[881]

In 1914, the New Mexico Supreme Court held that: "Where an application for a permit to appropriate water for a beneficial use is approved by the district court, on appeal the appellate court will presume, in the absence of anything in the record to the contrary, that there is unappropriated water available to supply the requirements under the permit."[882]

---

[879] For example, in determining whether the proposed use will prejudicially affect the public interest, the administrative agency must take into consideration, among other things, the condition of the proposed water supply: Kans. Stat. Ann. § 82a-711 (1969); Oreg. Rev. Stat. § 537.170 (Supp. 1969). California legislation enacted in 1969 provides that in determining the amount of water available for appropriation, the State Water Resources Control Board shall take into account, whenever it is in the public interest, the amounts of water needed for protection of beneficial uses including any uses specified to be protected in any relevant water quality control plan established pursuant to applicable legislation. Cal. Laws 1969, ch. 482, § 10, Water Code § 1243.5 (West Supp. 1970).

[880] In *Cantin* v. *Carter,* 88 Idaho 179, 397 Pac. (2d) 761, 765-766 (1964), the court said:
"A subsequent appropriator attempting to justify his diversion has the burden of proving that it will not injure prior appropriations . . . .
"It is a fundamental concept that under our constitution, water which has already been appropriated is not subject to appropriation by another, unless it has been abandoned . . . . Idaho Const. Art. 15, § § 3, 4, 5. Before any permit to appropriate water to a beneficial use can ripen into a right to use the water, it is basic that the permit holder must show a supply of unappropriated water. Idaho Const. Art. 15, § 3."

[881] N. Mex. Stat. Ann. § 75-5-5 (1968).

[882] *Rio Puerco Irr. Co.* v. *Jastro,* 19 N. Mex. 149, 155, 141 Pac. 874 (1914).

(b) Texas. In noting that under the statute the administrator's duty is to reject applications when there is no unappropriated water in the source of supply, the Texas Supreme Court stated that: "The facts as to that question can be determined by the board by the mere matter of adding up the amount of water previously appropriated and shown on their records, and subtracting it from the amount of state water which they had previously determined the stream furnished. That is clearly administrative."[883]

This comment makes an unsuccessful attempt to oversimplify a situation that in actual practice is well known by administrators to be far from simple. This is owing to complications of available streamflows, status of unappropriated rights of record, effects of return flow from diversion and use of water, riparian rights where recognized by the courts, and other factors.

(c) California. Much the same contention was made in a California case to the effect that an independent judicial determination of the issue of availability of unappropriated water could be made simply by comparing the aggregate of existing rights with estimated supplies, with the result that the expense of numerous hearings on applications for permits before the State agency could be avoided.[884] The supreme court, however, was not impressed.

In this case, the court referred to one of its previous decisions[885] in which the opinion stated that it was manifestly impracticable for the State agency to authoritatively determine that there is not water in a given stream subject to appropriation, that "What is unappropriated water is a constantly fluctuating question, depending upon the seasonal flow of the stream, the annual rainfall, the forteiture of prior appropriations, and default in the use of riparian rights." Following this quotation from an earlier decision, the supreme court went on to say that a future determination as to existing appropriative and riparian rights rests upon then present uses which may be quite different at a later time. Hence, a determination as to the future availability of water can be only an estimate. If, said the court, the administrator erroneously concludes that unappropriated water is available to supply an applicant, when there actually is no reasonable expectation of such a supply, the error may be corrected upon a review of the determination. "But a holding that such a danger is so imminent as to justify an independent judicial proceeding to determine the availability of unappropriated water before the department considers an application, would deprive the administrative proceeding of all of its proper functions in the issuance of a permit. No such danger will be presumed."

(d) Washington. In the view of the Washington Supreme Court, the Director of Ecology is vested with a considerable degree of discretion in making investigations and findings and otherwise exercising his delegated functions. He

---

[883] *Motl v. Boyd,* 116 Tex. 82, 126, 286 S.W. 458 (1926).
[884] *Temescal Water Co.* v. *Department of Public Works,* 44 Cal. (2d) 90, 105-106, 280 Pac. (2d) 1 (1955).
[885] *Tulare Water Co.* v. *State Water Comm'n,* 187 Cal. 533, 537, 202 Pac. 874 (1921).

must determine, preliminarily and tentatively, certain questions of public interest including availability of unappropriated water. But he is an administrator, not a judicial officer. Hence, his decisions in granting permits—and the refusal of the superior court to set his decisions aside—do not constitute adjudications of existing private water rights.[886]

(e) Utah. On the whole, in its consideration of the statutory powers of the Utah State Engineer in a number of decisions, the supreme court of that State has taken a liberal view of the legislative intent that the public waters of the State be made available for beneficial use—that in view of the State policy in this respect, "new appropriations should be favored and not hindered."[887]

The Utah statute requires rejection of applications under specified conditions in the interest of the public welfare. This is the case even though all waters of the stream have not been appropriated.[888] But when the question of unappropriated water is in doubt, the State Engineer should have power to approve the application and afford an orderly recourse to the courts.[889] He determines whether under the evidence there is reason to believe that there are unappropriated waters in the proposed source available for appropriation under the statutory restrictions.[890] The State Engineer's decision, in short, is that there is probable cause to believe that the applicant either may or may not be able to establish rights under his application without impairing the rights of others.[891]

(f) The West as a whole. The requirement that a permit shall not be granted if there is no unappropriated water in the proposed source of supply involves difficult questions of administrative policy.

It is often stated that the usual flow of many western streams is overappropriated. On occasions, when an application to appropriate water of a given stream is filed, the State administrator's records may disclose no reasonably anticipated supply above the requirements of existing claimants. However, unless complete water supply studies have been made on that stream system, there may be a question as to whether the absence of unappropriated flood flows and return water supplies is so clearly established as to justify denial of the application. The permit, if granted, attaches to only whatever

---

[886] *Funk* v. *Bartholet*, 157 Wash. 584, 593-595, 289 Pac. 1018 (1930); *Madison* v. *McNeal*, 171 Wash. 669, 680, 19 Pac. (2d) 97 (1933); *Mack* v. *Eldorado Water Dist.*, 56 Wash. (2d) 584, 587, 354 Pac. (2d) 917 (1960).

[887] *Little Cottonwood Water Co.* v. *Kimball*, 76 Utah 243, 248-249, 289 Pac. 116 (1930). See *Whitmore* v. *Welch*, 114 Utah 578, 586-587, 201 Pac. (2d) 954 (1949); *Brady* v. *McGonagle*, 57 Utah 424, 432-433, 195 Pac. 188 (1921).

[888] *Tanner* v. *Bacon*, 103 Utah 494, 504, 136 Pac. (2d) 957 (1943).

[889] *Rocky Ford Irr. Co.* v. *Kents Lake Res. Co.*, 104 Utah 202, 212, 135 Pac. (2d) 108 (1943). See *Lehi Irr. Co.* v. *Jones*, 115 Utah 136, 142-146, 202 Pac. (2d) 892 (1949).

[890] *Bullock* v. *Tracy*, 4 Utah (2d) 370, 373, 294 Pac. (2d) 707 (1956).

[891] *United States* v. *District Court*, 121 Utah 1, 11-12, 238 Pac. (2d) 1132 (1951); *Eardley* v. *Terry*, 94 Utah 367, 376, 77 Pac. (2d) 362 (1938).

supply may be found above the requirements of holders of existing rights. Hence, the question of better public policy—to deny the application, with the possibility that the conclusions of the administrative officer may be in error and a proposed beneficial use of water be thereby foreclosed, or to grant the application and allow the intending appropriator to take the risk of failure of his project if no water supply proves to be available.

In 1922, in the interstate case of *Wyoming* v. *Colorado,* the United States Supreme Court referred to an assertion by counsel that permits issued by the Wyoming State Engineer constituted "solemn adjudications" by that official that the supply was adequate to cover them. The Court stated:[892]

> But in this the nature of the permits is misapprehended. In fact and in law they are not adjudications, but mere licenses to appropriate, if the requisite amount of water be there. As to many nothing ever is done under them by the intending appropriators. In such cases there is no appropriation, and even in others the amount of the appropriation turns on what is actually done under the permit. In late years the permits relating to these streams have contained a provision, saying:
>
> "The records of the state engineer's office show the waters of [the particular stream] to be largely appropriated. The appropriator under the permit is hereby notified of this fact, and the issuance of this permit grants only the right to divert and use the surplus or waste water of the stream and confers no rights which will interfere with or impair the use of water by prior appropriators."
>
> It therefore is plain that these permits have no such probative force as Colorado seeks to have attributed to them.

From the statutes and decisions, there is no doubt that the determination of the State water control agency in any appropriation-permit State in the West: (a) is an administrative function; (b) is not an adjudication of outstanding private rights; and (c) is to be made from a consideration of all pertinent factors solely for the guidance of the administrative agency in passing upon the intending appropriator's application for a permit. All this is true in the course of administrative processing of the application. It is equally valid during and after review of the administrative decision in a court of competent jurisdiction, where the procedure for obtaining the requested permit merges into and ends in a judicial adjudication.

Nonimpairment of existing water rights.—(1) Nearly all the water appropriation statutes of the West that provide administrative control over acquisition of water rights contain language forbidding the issuance of permits the effect of which will be to impair the value of existing water rights. In jurisdictions in which riparian rights are recognized, this applies to impairment of riparian as well as appropriative water rights. The Texas statute directs that this protection

---

[892] *Wyoming* v. *Colorado,* 259 U. S. 419, 488-489 (1922). See *Ide* v. *United States,* 263 U. S. 497, 507-508 (1924).

be provided for "existing water rights" and "vested riparian rights."[893] The extent to which riparian rights have become vested and are protected against appropriative rights in such States are discussed in chapter 6 under "Interrelationships of the Dual Water Rights Systems—The Status in Summary: By States."

Even without a specific statutory command to the administrator to refuse approval of an application, the granting of which would appear to threaten the value of existing water rights in good standing, the legislative intent—as in case of lack of unappropriated water—is clearly implied by the whole context of the water control provisions. In this connection, the very few administrative statutes that do not specifically include possible infringement of existing water rights as ground for refusal of a permit *do* include detriment to the public interest. Among matters detrimental to the public welfare, as noted later, is impairment of the value of vested water rights.

(2) The Kansas statute directs the Chief Engineer to reject an application if the proposed use will impair a use under an existing water right, or to require its modification to conform to the public interest. Further, with regard to whether a proposed use will have this effect, "impairment shall include the unreasonable raising or lowering of the static water level or the unreasonable increase or decrease of the streamflow or the unreasonable deterioration of the water quality at the water user's point of diversion beyond a reasonable economic limit."[894]

(3) The Nebraska statute contains an unusual provision that "if a prior appropriation has been perfected to water the same land to be watered by the applicant, the Department * * * may refuse such application * * *."[895]

(4) The discussion under "Availability of unappropriated water" regarding the nature of the administrator's findings as strictly administrative, and not a determination of existing water rights, applies equally here. In fact the Kansas reenactment of 1957, in directing the Chief Engineer to make a determination of the rights of all users of water (other than for domestic purposes) as of June 28, 1945, at which time the current administrative procedure went into effect, added this: "*Provided*, That no such determination shall be deemed an adjudication of the relation between any vested right holders with respect to the operation or exercise of their vested rights."[896] The purpose of this authorization is to provide the Chief Engineer with data on uses of water under preexisting "vested rights." Such data, together with records of subsequent

---

[893] Tex. Rev. Civ. Stat. Ann. arts. 7506 and 7507 (1954). Other provisions respecting protection of private property rights include arts. 7469 and 7620. Noninterference with rights of riparian proprietors: Tex. Rev. Civ. Stat. Ann. arts. 7612 and 7612B (Supp. 1970).

[894] Kans. Stat. Ann. §82a-711 (1969).

[895] Nebr. Rev. Stat. §46-234 (1968).

[896] Kans. Stat. Ann. §82a-704 (1969).

applications and permits and water supply statistics, will be expected to furnish a rational basis for reaching conclusions as to the availability of unappropriated water in a particular stream system.

Some States have statutory provisions regarding the filing of claims regarding preexisting rights.[897]

(5) In approving applications and issuing and processing permits to appropriate water, the State assumes no responsibility for the availability of unappropriated water, nor for noninterference with existing water rights. The State directs the administrative agency to inquire into these factors and, on the basis of all accessible information, to reach reasonable conclusions respecting them before issuing or refusing to issue permits. But once a permit is accepted, it is the holder's responsibility to exercise it in a lawful manner—not to use it as a means of depreciating preexisting water rights values. Assuming it to be incumbent upon the water administrator to call the applicant's attention to official conclusions as to water supply and prior commitments, then if the latter desires to proceed despite apparent hazards, it is his duty to stay within the law. And, as the California agency in its rules and regulations, above noted, makes very clear, it is the permittee's own obligation—not that of the State—to protect his permit right against encroachment.

The question of detriment to the public welfare.—(1) Some general observations. The terms "public interest" and "public welfare" as used in this phase of water law have the same connotations. In this discussion they are used interchangeably.

Nearly all the 16 appropriation-permit statutes contain specific provisions relating to the handling of prospective appropriations that threaten to prove detrimental to the public interest or public welfare. All of these statutes include restrictions against prescribed conditions unquestionably inimical to the commonweal.

"Public policy," said a learned California jurist in 1907, "is at best a vague and uncertain guide."[898] This criticism was directed at a concept that public policy might justify so reducing a riparian owner's right to the use of water as to limit him to reasonableness and economy as against an appropriator. This action, in the view that the California Supreme Court then took of the scope of the riparian right, would amount to the taking of private property without compensation. (No longer is this the California judicial policy. Pursuant to a constitutional mandate, the supreme court has since progressed. See chapter 10).

---

[897] See Wash. Rev. Code §§ 90.14.010 to .121 (Supp. 1970); Alaska Stat. §46.15.135 (Supp. 1966); Tex. Rev. Civ. Stat. Ann. art. 7542a, §4 (Supp. 1970). These are mentioned in chapter 6 under "Interrelationships of the Dual Water Rights Systems—The Status in Summary: By States."

[898] Justice M. C. Sloss in *Miller & Lux v. Madera Canal & Irr. Co.,* 155 Cal. 59, 65, 99 Pac. 502 (1907).

Regardless of the context in which the above observation was made, "public interest" and "public welfare" most assuredly are often illusive terms. One may assert, with reason, that the public welfare is not being served by the continued issuance of permits to appropriate water from a supply that, according to all the evidence, already is grossly over-appropriated. Nor is it advanced by the exercise of permit rights certain to cause injury to existing water rights in good standing. On the other hand, there are considerations of State water policy as to which public spirited citizens sincerely disagree. Disagreements inevitably occur whenever new water control questions arise. This has been the case throughout the history of water development in this country. However, in reaching a decision as to whether an appropriation should be rejected as potentially dangerous to the public welfare, legislative direction to the administrator to consider certain clearly specified matters tends to narrow the issues and to bring the perplexing problem more clearly into focus.

In the West, then, there prevails the basic principle that an application to appropriate water, the consummation of which would threaten the public welfare, should be rejected by the administrator, subject to judicial review. This concept appears in the constitutions of both Wyoming and Nebraska in the mandate, above noted, that the right to appropriate water shall never be denied *except* when the public interest so demands. In one form or another, the principle is expressed in all the western administrative appropriation statutes.

In the following paragraphs some particular State situations are noted. In a few instances, brief mention is made of court decisions respecting the nature of the powers of administrators that are pertinent to the present topic, but which are discussed more fully under "Current Appropriation Procedures: Administrative," above.

(2) California. The State Water Resources Control Board is directed by the statute to allow appropriations of water "under such terms and conditions as in its judgment will best develop, conserve, and utilize in the public interest the water sought to be appropriated." Otherwise the proposal must be rejected.[899] The beneficial uses which the Board shall consider include, but are not limited to, "domestic, irrigation, municipal, industrial, preservation and enhancement of fish and wildlife,[900] recreational, mining and power purposes, and any uses specified to be protected in any relevant water quality control plan," as well as

---

[899] Cal. Water Code § § 1253 and 1255-1257 (West Supp. 1970).

[900] It also may be noted that, with respect to public fishing rights, in a 1966 Montana case the court said "under the proper circumstances we feel that such a public interest should be recognized." *Paradise Rainbows* v. *Fish and Game Comm'n,* 148 Mont. 412, 421 Pac. (2d) 717, 721 (1966). In so stating, the court referred to *People* v. *Glenn - Colusa Irr. Dist.,* 127 Cal. App. 30, 15 Pac. (2d) 549 (1932). Regarding such public rights in navigable waters, see in chapter 4 "Water Rights in Navigable Waterways—Appropriative Rights—State Law."

"the reuse or reclamation of the water."[901] Consideration also shall be given to general coordinated water resource plans.[902]

Note the quoted language of the legislature as to what the Board shall do *in its judgment*. "In carrying out its present duty," said the California Supreme Court,[903] "the department [now the Board] *exercises a broad discretion* in determining whether the issuance of a permit will best serve the public interest." (Emphasis supplied.) This determination requires an administrative adjudication which, in any case in which the issuance of a permit is protested, may be made only after a hearing. The administrative decision is subject to judicial review by way of writ of mandate.[904]

(3) Kansas. As noted above, the water rights statute requires the Chief Engineer to reject an application if the proposed use will prejudicially and unreasonably affect the public interest, or to require its modification to conform to the public interest to the end that the highest public benefit and maximum economical development may result from the use of such water. In ascertaining such question, the Chief Engineer is directed to take into consideration the area, safe yield, and recharge rate of the appropriate water supply; the priority of existing claims of all persons to use water thereof; the amount of each such claim; and all other matters pertaining to such question.[905]

(4) Texas. The Texas Water Rights Commission is directed by the legislature to reject an application if the proposed use is detrimental to the public welfare. It is also charged with the duty of conserving natural water resources "in the greatest practicable measure for the public welfare." The Commission must not only follow the statutory rule relating to preferential uses of water, but must also give preference to those applications the purposes of which contemplate and will effectuate the maximum utilization of waters and are designed to prevent waste of water.[906] The subject of preferences in Texas water law is discussed later under "Preferences in Water Appropriation".

(5) New Mexico. The question of public interest was considered by the Supreme Court of New Mexico shortly before the attainment of statehood. The court expressed its belief that matters of public interest went beyond questions of danger to public health and safety—that the purpose of the statute

[901] Cal. Water Code § 1257 (West Supp. 1970).

[902] *Id.* §1256.

[903] Citing § § 1253 and 1255.

[904] *Temescal Water Co.* v. *Department of Public Works*, 44 Cal. (2d) 90, 99-101, 280 Pac. (2d) 1 (1955). For the development of this principle, see *Tulare Water Co.* v. *State Water Commission*, 187 Cal. 533, 536-537, 202 Pac. 874 (1921); *Yuba River Power Co.* v. *Nevada Irr. Dist.*, 207 Cal. 521, 522-523, 279 Pac. 128 (1929); *East Bay Municipal Utility Dist.* v. *State Department of Public Works*, 1 Cal. (2d) 476, 477-481, 35 Pac. (2d) 1027 (1934).

[905] Kans. Stat. Ann. §82a-711 (1969).

[906] Tex. Rev. Civ. Stat. Ann. arts. 7506, 7507, 7472c (1955), and 7471 (Supp. 1970).

was to obtain the greatest possible benefit to the public. By way of illustration, the public interest would be served by protecting investors against making worthless investments in the Territory, especially if made after official approval of unsound enterprises. Further, said the court, while the question of relative costs of two competing water supply projects was not conclusive on the issue of public interest, it was believed that it should be taken into account.[907]

Until 1923, there was a New Mexico Board of Water Commissioners, whose duty was to hear and determine appeals from the acts and decisions of the State Engineer. Its decisions were final, subject to appeal to the district court.[908] The supreme court held that the board was not called upon to review the discretion of the State Engineer, but that on appeal the board would determine for itself the question as to whether an application should be approved or rejected. The hearing in the district court likewise was *de novo*, without review of the discretion of the State Engineer or of the board.[909]

This case was expressly overruled in 1963 to the extent that former case law allowed the district court to hear new or additional evidence, and based thereon to form its own conclusions.[910] The scope of review is limited to evidence adduced at the hearing before the state engineer or the board or both and the issue is whether or not the state engineer acted fraudulently, capriciously or arbitrarily. The determination of the state engineer must be based upon substantial evidence.[911]

(6) The Washington Director of Ecology is directed to reject an application to appropriate water if, among other things, the proposed use "threatens to prove detrimental to the public interest, having due regard to the highest feasible development of the use of the waters belonging to the public." In making his determination, it is the duty of the Director to investigate "all facts relevant and material to the application."[912]

The statute vests the Director with a considerable degree of discretion in making investigations and findings and otherwise performing his delegated functions.[913] He must determine, for the purpose of deciding for or against the issuance of a permit, matters of public interest.[914] But as stated above in discussing questions of availability of unappropriated water, the Director is an administrator and his findings are in no sense intended to be adjudications of private rights.

---

[907] *Young & Norton* v. *Hinderlider*, 15 N. Mex. 666, 667-668, 110 Pac. 1045 (1910).

[908] N. Mex. Stat. Ann. §75-2-11 (1968).

[909] *Farmers' Development Co.* v. *Rayado Land & Irr. Co.*, 18 N. Mex. 1, 9, 133 Pac. 104 (1913).

[910] *Kelley* v. *Carlsbad Irr. Co.*, 71 N. Mex. 464, 466-467, 379 Pac. (2d) 763 (1963).

[911] See *Ingram* v. *Malone Farm*, 382 Pac. (2d) 981, 982 (N. Mex. 1963).

[912] Wash. Rev. Code §90.03.290 (Supp. 1961).

[913] *Id.* §§90.03.250-90.03.330.

[914] *Funk* v. *Bartholet*, 157 Wash. 584, 593-595, 289 Pac. 1018 (1930).

(7) Utah. The statutory restrictions on approval of applications include a finding that the "proposed plan is physically and economically feasible unless the application is filed by the United States Bureau of Reclamation and would not prove detrimental to the public welfare."[915]

The Utah Supreme Court recognized that even though all waters of a stream had not been appropriated, the statute required rejection of applications under specified conditions in the interest of the public welfare.[916] Noting that the Utah statute concerning preferences (see below) indicates that the legislature considered domestic and agricultural uses as the most beneficial uses to which water may be applied, the court took the view that anything which is not for the best interest of the public would be "detrimental to the public welfare." Therefore it was in the interest of the public welfare for the State Engineer—provided he did not act arbitrarily or capriciously—to reject or limit an application for power purposes in favor of a later application for agriculture and domestic uses.

Necessarily, in reaching various conclusions on these matters, an exercise of discretion by the Utah State Engineer is required, and to this end he is vested by the legislature with broad discretionary powers. The question of abuse of discretion is subject to a judicial review.[917] The important—but not conclusive—discretionary powers and duties of the State Engineer are deserving of great respect. As a safeguard against possible injustices, however, and by plenary review on trial *de novo,* the court is invested with the final word as to conflicting contentions of applicants and contestants.[918]

(8) Oregon. The current water rights statute provides that certain applications for permits to appropriate water must be referred by the State Engineer to the State Water Resources Board for consideration. Included is an application to appropriate water for purposes other than generation of electricity if, in the State Engineer's judgment, the proposed use may prejudicially affect the public interest. In the hydroelectric act is a provision that under prescribed circumstances an application for a preliminary permit or a license to generate electricity must be referred by the State Engineer to the Board for consideration. If in any such case the Board determines that the proposed use would impair or be detrimental to the public interest so far as the coordinated, integrated State water resources policy is concerned, it enters an order rejecting the application or requiring its modification to conform to the public interest. The application is then referred back to the State Engineer for further proceedings not inconsistent with the Board's order.

---

[915] Utah Code Ann. § 73-3-8 (1968).

[916] *Tanner* v. *Bacon,* 103 Utah 494, 505-510, 136 Pac. (2d) 957 (1943).

[917] *United States* v. *District Court,* 121 Utah 1, 5-8, 238 Pac. (2d) 1132 (1951); *In re Application 7600 to Appropriate Water,* 73 Utah 50, 55-56, 272 Pac. 225 (1928).

[918] *American Fork Irr. Co.* v. *Linke,* 121 Utah 90, 93-94 239 Pac. (2d) 188 (1951).

In determining the question of detriment to the public, the Oregon Board is directed to have due regard for conserving the highest use of water for all purposes, many purposes being specifically named. It must take into consideration maximum economic development of water; control for all beneficial purposes, including drainage, sanitation, flood control; amount of water available for appropriation; prevention of wasteful and other undesirable uses of water; protection of all vested and inchoate water rights; and the State water resources policy.[919]

In the early history of the Oregon water rights statute, the Board of Control (subsequently abolished) performed the function of deciding questions of public interest referred to it by the State Engineer. In one case decided during that period, the Oregon Supreme Court observed that the Board had the duty of refusing an application if, after full hearing, the public interest demanded it.[920] In another case, the court cautioned that it was only when the contemplated use was a menace to the safety and welfare of the public that the application should be referred to the Board for consideration.[921] The current directive of the legislature to the State Water Resources Board, briefed above is in its statutory language so detailed and all-embracing that the Board necessarily must exercise a broad discretion in applying the declared policy to its deliberations and conclusions respecting approval or rejection of applications.

Important observations of the Oregon Supreme Court in this field include the following:

Under the water rights act, the State Engineer is vested with a wide discretion in exercising his primary responsibility for proper distribution of State waters for beneficial uses. Judges are not super engineers. Hence seldom if ever will the court interfere with his discretionary action on matters involving administration of the water laws and substitute its judgment for his.[922]

Statutes providing for review of the State Engineer's action would be unconstitutional if so construed as to vest in the courts the power to substitute their judgment for his on matters of legislative policy. This does not mean that all such administrative orders must be affirmed if supported by substantial evidence, for the court may have power to reassess all the evidence. The court may voluntarily limit its review by refusing to disturb administrative findings in those areas in which the administrative agency is expert.[923]

(9) Alaska. The 1966 Alaska Water Use Act provides that in determining the

---

[919] Oreg. Rev. Stat. § § 537.170(3) (Supp. 1969) and 543.225(3) (Supp. 1965).

[920] *Cockinham* v. *Lewis*, 58 Oreg. 484, 487-497, 114 Pac. 88, 115 Pac. 342 (1911).

[921] *In re Schollmeyer*, 69 Oreg. 210, 215, 138 Pac. 211 (1914).

[922] *Smyth* v. *Jenkins*, 208 Oreg. 92, 100, 299 Pac. (2d) 819 (1956).

[923] *Warner Valley Stock Co.* v. *Lynch*, 215 Oreg. 523, 547-561, 336 Pac. (2d) 884 (1959)

public interest for the purpose of acting on applications for permits, the Commissioner of Natural Resources shall consider:

(1) the benefit to the applicant resulting from the proposed appropriation;

(2) the effect of the economic activity resulting from the proposed appropriation;

(3) the effect on fish and game resources and on public recreational opportunities;

(4) the effect on public health;

(5) the effect of loss of alternate uses of water that might be made within a reasonable time if not precluded or hindered by the proposed appropriation;

(6) harm to other persons resulting from the proposed appropriation;

(7) the intent and ability of the applicant to complete the appropriation; and

(8) the effect upon access to navigable or public waters.[924]

The Commissioner may issue a permit subject to terms, conditions, restrictions, and limitations he considers necessary to protect the public interest and the rights of others, although permits shall be subject to termination only as provided in the act.[925]

(10) In summary. An application to appropriate water for any project the fulfilment of which threatens to be detrimental to the safety, health, and general welfare of the public should be rejected. Conversely, an application that meets all formal requirements and that appears to be conducive to the public interest or public welfare should be approved.

Matters stated in the foregoing legislative and judicial declarations governing approval and rejection of permits, as conducive to the public welfare, fall generally into the following categories:

Effective conservation of the State's natural water resources, including prevention of wasteful and other undesirable uses of water. Control of water resources for all beneficial purposes, including consumptive uses, drainage, sanitation, flood prevention. Maximum economic development of water resources. Utilization of water by projects that are feasible, economic, and financially sound. Effectuation of the State water policy, and of specific general and coordinated water resources plans. Availability of water for appropriation. And protection of all rights to the use of water, both perfected and inchoate.

Qualified and limited right.—If a proposed project appears to the State administrator to be somewhat less than wholly desirable, but to have potential

---

[924] Alaska Stat. §46.15.080(b) (Supp. 1966).
[925] *Id.* §46.15.100.

merit if substantially revised, it need not be rejected altogether. Instead, if a qualified and limited right of appropriation appears justified, the State agency may approve a proposal modified to an extent consonant with conditions that actually exist.[926]

The statutory duty of water which prevails in some States is discussed in chapter 8, under "Elements of the Appropriative Right—Measure of the Appropriative Right—Duty of Water." In these jurisdictions an applicant may apply for the maximum allowed by law. However, if in his particular situation such quantity is patently more than he can apply to beneficial use, the administrator would not be justified in authorizing such quantity and it is doubtful if he would do so. Several statutes specifically authorize the State agency to approve an application for a lesser quantity of water than is applied for if there exist substantial reasons therefor.[927] The California Water Code provides that "The issuance of a permit gives the right to take and use water only to the extent and for the purpose allowed in the permit."[928] In view of this, a district court of appeal held that an application to appropriate water may be granted in part and denied in part.[929]

Even without such specific authorization, the statutory power to grant or to completely deny an application, according to the conditions that exist respecting it, would include by necessary implication the power to approve less water than asked for. A contrary construction of the legislation would be unreasonable. The cumulative effect of the administrative discretionary powers in issuing and refusing permits, granted by western legislatures and authorized by the courts, and of the prevailing policies of limiting water uses to beneficial requirements and forbidding unnecessary waste of water, negatives any likelihood that any western administrative statute would be so construed as to require the State to grant to an applicant a permit for a quantity of water substantially in excess of his needs, simply because he applies for it.

The same comments apply to the imposition of other qualifications and limitations in the issuance of permits. For example, certain statutes provide specifically for the approval of applications under terms and on conditions necessary to protect the public interest.[930] Others authorize the administrator

---

[926] *Kirk* v. *State Board of Irr.*, 90 Nebr. 627, 631-632, 134 N.W. 167 (1912); *East Bay Municipal Utility Dist.* v. *State Department of Public Works,* 1 Cal. (2d) 476, 481, 35 Pac. (2d) 1027 (1934).

[927] Ariz. Rev. Stat. Ann. § 45-143 (1956); Idaho Code Ann. § 42-203 (Supp. 1969); Nebr. Rev. Stat. § 46-235 (1968); Nev. Rev. Stat. § 533.380 (Supp. 1967); N. Mex. Stat. Ann. § 75-5-5 (1968); Oreg. Rev. Stat. § 537.190(1) (Supp. 1969); S. Dak. Comp. Laws Ann. § 46-5-21 (1967); Wash. Rev. Code § 90.03.290 (Supp. 1961).

[928] Cal. Water Code § 1381 (West 1956).

[929] *Rich* v. *McClure,* 78 Cal. App. 209, 213, 248 Pac. 275 (1926).

[930] Cal. Water Code § 1253 (West Supp. 1970); Oreg. Rev. Stat. § 537.190(1) (Supp. 1969).

to limit the applicant to less periods of time for taking steps than requested;[931] or to a smaller area of land;[932] or to vary the periods of annual use.[933]

Development of hydroelectric power.—Several statutes contain special provisions governing appropriation of water for development of electric energy. This is in addition to the usual requirements for specifying particulars in applications to appropriate water for specific purposes, as well as matters of procedure in connection with proposals for large water supply projects.

(1) Arizona. The statute provides that no application to appropriate water for generating electric energy in excess of 25,000 horsepower, or for a permit to build a dam on a stream for such purpose and quantity, shall be approved without authorization by the legislature. The same authorization is required for changes in use of water appropriated for domestic, municipal, or irrigation uses if the change contemplates generation of that quantity of power.[934]

It is also provided that a certificate for power development appropriation of water shall limit the right to a period of 40 years from date of application, subject to a preferred right of renewal under laws existing at the date of expiration of the right. Priority of the appropriation dates from the time of filing the application with the Department.[935]

(2) Idaho. The State constitution provides that the right to divert and appropriate the unappropriated waters of any natural stream to beneficial uses shall never be denied, except that the State may regulate and limit the use thereof for power purposes.[936]

This matter appears above in connection with discussion of the alternative methods of appropriating water in Idaho.

(3) Nebraska. There is a provision in the State constitution that the use of water for power purposes shall be deemed a public use and shall never be alienated, but may be leased or otherwise developed as prescribed by law.[937]

An applicant for a waterpower appropriation in Nebraska must enter into a contract with the State, through the Department, for leasing the water from the State for not longer than 50 years. On expiration of such lease, the Department appraises the value of improvements made thereunder by any lessee, subject to appeal to the district court. The value of the improvements as finally determined must be paid by any subsequent lessee to the lessee who owns the improvements.[938]

---

[931] Nebr. Rev. Stat. §46-235 (1968); Nev. Rev. Stat. §533.380 (Supp. 1967); Wyo. Stat. Ann § 41-206 (1957).

[932] Nebr. Rev. Stat. §46-235 (1968).

[933] N. Mex. Stat. Ann. §75-5-5 (1968); S. Dak. Comp. Laws Ann. §46-5-21 (1967).

[934] Ariz. Rev. Stat. Ann. §45-146 (1956).

[935] *Id.* §45-152.

[936] Idaho Const., art. XV, §3.

[937] Nebr. Const., art. XV, §7.

[938] Nebr. Rev. Stat. § 46-236 (1968).

Early in the 20th century, the Nebraska Supreme Court held that the State has such a proprietary interest in the waters of its streams and in their beneficial use that (a) it may transfer a qualified ownership or right of use thereof; that (b) in doing so it may impose such limitations and conditions as its public policy demands; that (c) in reserving such ownership and control, it may even prohibit the transmission or use of waterpower beyond the confines of the State; and that (d) undoubtedly it had granted to the State administrative agency the power and duty to determine such questions and impose such conditions.[939]

(4) Oregon. The State constitution contains no provisions regarding water other than the control and development of waterpower.[940] This article in the fundamental law provides that the rights to all water for the development of waterpower and to waterpower sites then owned or thereafter acquired by the State shall be held in perpetuity. The State is empowered to control and/or develop waterpower within the State; to lease water and waterpower sites therefor; to control and distribute electrical energy; to develop, separately or in cooperation with the United States or with political subdivisions of the State, waterpower, and to acquire, build, and operate projects therefor; to cooperate to this effect with such agencies and with other States and subdivisions thereof; to fix necessary rates and charges for the use of water therefor; and to loan the credit of the State in carrying out such programs. Nothing in the article is to be construed to affect in any way the Oregon water rights laws "other than for the development of water power."

Appropriations of water in Oregon for generation of electricity are governed by provisions of the "hydroelectric act."[941] But this act does not apply to any waterpower project constructed by the United States, nor to cities, towns, or other municipal corporations of the State including public utility districts but saving thereto certain rights and preferences.

Administration of the hydroelectric act is now vested in the State Engineer. Certain applications, however, must be referred to the State Water Resources Board for consideration before he acts upon them. Preliminary permits may be granted to enable the applicant to do preliminary work. An application may be denied if it appears (a) that the applicant has failed to comply substantially with the terms and conditions of the preliminary permit, or (b) that notwithstanding issuance of a preliminary permit, the project now is unfeasible or the public interest requires denial of the license. Licenses are limited to 50 years, subject to renewals under certain conditions. The State or any of its municipalities may take over any project constructed under a license on payment of fair value, the right of eminent domain being expressly reserved.

---

[939] *Kirk* v. *State Board of Irr.*, 90 Nebr. 627, 631-632, 134 N. W. 167 (1912).
[940] Oreg. Const., art. XI-D.
[941] Oreg. Rev. Stat. § § 543.010-.620 and .990 (Supp. 1965).

When the whole net investment is amortized and repaid, the project becomes the property of the State.

Other factors.—(1) Other matters stressed in some of the statutes as essential to the approval of an application to appropriate water include:[942]

— The applicant should demonstrate his intention to construct his proposed works in good faith and with due diligence. Purposes of speculation or monopoly are not acceptable.

— Particularly in case of large undertakings, the applicant must show to the satisfaction of the State administrative agency that the plans are physically and economically feasible.

— Also particularly with respect to large projects, the applicant's financial ability to carry the construction satisfactorily to completion must be shown.

The Idaho Department is prohibited from issuing a permit to appropriate waters of any lake 5 acres or less in surface area, pond, pool, or spring located wholly on lands of another except to such other owner or with his written permission, formally verified.[943]

In Nebraska, no application is exclusive of any of the lands included therein until the owners formally consent thereto. No application made or canal constructed prior to perfection of the appropriation, or filing of such consent, prevents other applications from being allowed and canals constructed to irrigate the same lands.[944]

(2) Restrictions against allowing diversions of water from one watershed into another, to the injury of persons living in the areas of origin, appear in some western statutes. This matter is considered in chapter 8 under "Elements of the Appropriative Right—Diversion of Water from Watershed".

(3) Also see the earlier discussion under "Storage Water Appropriation—Method of Appropriation—Relative priorities of direct flow and storage water rights." This includes a discussion of a 1969 Texas case applying a system of "weighted priorities" in what the court called an "unprecedented" situation.[945]

(4) For additional considerations regarding navigable watercourses and their tributaries, see chapter 4.

Preferences in Water Appropriation

Order of preferences in purpose of use.—Certain preferences in the field of water appropriation exist with respect to: (a) the acquisition of rights to appropriate water under the statutory procedure; (b) the use of water already

---

[942] See Idaho Code Ann. §§42-203 and 204 (1948); Oreg. Rev. Stat. §537 .150 and .160 (Supp. 1969); Utah Code Ann. §73-3-8 (1968); Wyo. Stat. Ann. §41-205 (1957).

[943] Idaho Code Ann. §§42-212 and -213 (1948).

[944] Nebr. Rev. Stat. §46-234 (1968).

[945] *State* v. *Hidalgo County Water Control Improvement Dist. No. 18,* 443 S. W. (2d) 728, 739, 745 (Tex. Civ. App. 1969).

appropriated; and (c) the taking for a superior use of a right to water already appropriated for an inferior use.

Statutes or constitutions in a majority of the Western States provide orders of preference for one or more of these categories. Some of the statements are brief, others somewhat elaborate. These are summarized under the next ensuing subtopic; but first, some comments about the several purposes of use that are included therein. Bear in mind that each State list of preferences does not necessarily include all of the following purposes.

(1) Domestic and municipal. In declarations in which a specific order of preference is stated, domestic use generally has first place. Municipal use is closely associated with domestic. In two States, the first preference goes to domestic and municipal, without distinction. In two others, municipal use takes second place. In the other States, a specific category is not assigned to municipal use.[946]

The tenor of the statutory preferences is to ignore any distinction between (a) the strictly domestic use of water by the inhabitants of a municipality for drinking, laundering, and culinary purposes and for the watering of residential lawns and gardens, and (b) the strictly municipal uses of water by the city for firefighting, sanitation, street-cleaning, public parks, public buildings, and the like. An individual may appropriate stream water for his own domestic use in a rural area. A city may make such an appropriation for the combined domestic uses of its inhabitants, in addition to water required for its public functions. The domestic use of water within the city is not deprived of its perferential status by being served along with municipal use.

Each of the California and South Dakota statutes declares that the established policy of the State embraces two fundamental aims: (a) recognition of the use of water for domestic purposes as the highest use, and (b) protection of the water rights of municipalities for existing and future uses without waste.[947]

The Kansas and South Dakota laws grant special privileges to users of water for domestic purposes—"domestic use" pertaining to small quantities of water by individuals or family units for household purposes including watering of small gardens and lawns. They appear to be applicable particularly to rural areas, for nothing in either statute contemplates a breakdown of a city's water supply into individual citizen use and public municipal use. On the contrary, in

---

[946] One Oregon statute accords "human consumption" the first preference although an earlier statute places domestic use first. For a discussion of a 1970 Oregon Court of Appeals decision which appears to have construed these statutes as having a limited effect, see "Use of appropriated water: In time of shortage," below. In view of this decision, the Oregon provisions dealing with other types of uses, as listed in the next subtopic, are not noted in this subtopic.

[947] Cal. Water Code § §106 and 106.5 (West 1956); S. Dak. Comp. Laws Ann. §46-1-5 (1967).

the South Dakota statute there is a definition of "municipal use" as the use of water by a municipality and its inhabitants to promote the life, safety, health, comfort, and business pursuits of the inhabitants.[948]

The rules and regulations of the California State Water Resources Control Board pertaining to appropriation of water define domestic uses as those "common to homes, resorts, motels, organization camps, camp grounds, etc.;" including the incidental watering of domestic stock for family sustenance and the irrigation of not to exceed one-half acre in lawn, ornamental shrubbery, gardens and truck at any single establishment," and municipal use as including "all those uses common to the municipal water supply of a city, town, or other similar population group, and use incidental thereto for any beneficial purpose."[949] Those of the Texas Water Rights Commission define domestic use of water by an individual, or by a family unit or household, for usual household purposes, including watering of domestic animals, and municipal use as:

> the use of water within or without a municipality and its environs, whether supplied by a person, a political subdivision, a privately-owned public utility, or other agency or party, primarily to promote the safety, life, health, comfort and business pursuits of the users. It specifically includes the use of water for fighting fires, flushing sewers, sprinkling streets, watering parks and parkways, and small quantities of water for recreational purposes such as swimming pools; the use of water in public and private buildings, industrial enterprises supplied by a municipal distribution system without special construction to meet its demands, and homes, and the irrigation of lawns and family gardens.[950]

Neither the South Dakota statute, nor the California or Texas administrative rules, draw—or suggest—any distinction between the use of water supplied by a municipality to its population for drinking and other household purposes, and of water supplied by the city for the varied living and business needs of the segment of civilization—the aggregate human organism—comprising its individual inhabitants.

Preferences in the use of water as among domestic, municipal, manufacturing, or other purposes—however well adapted they may be to competing uses of water as among diversions from a stream system—may be difficult to apply to the many facets of use of a municipal water supply system within a complicated metropolitan area.[951] Cities may serve water from comprehensive

---

[948] Kans. Stat. Ann. § § 82a-701, -705, -705a, and -709 (1969); S. Dak. Comp. Laws Ann. § § 46-1-5, 46-1-6(4) and (5), and 46-5-8 (1967).

[949] Cal. Admin. Code, tit. 23, § § 661 and 664 (1969).

[950] Tex. Water Rights Comm'n, "Rules, Regulations and Modes of Procedure," rule 115.1(s) (1970 Rev., Jan. 1970) and (u) (June 4, 1970 addendum to 1970 Rev.).

[951] Compare the discussion of "Purpose of Use of Water," under the riparian doctrine, in chapter 10. The City of Brownwood, Texas, had acquired contractual rights from riparian owners to use water for "general municipal purposes." This was held to give it

artificial systems—often comprising storage, diversion, and distribution for long distances—to their inhabitants who may number tens of thousands or even hundreds of thousands. Water may be supplied for domestic, trade, local transportation, and professional consumption, production of commodities, and airconditioning, as well as sanitation, firefighting, and other public safety measures.

(2) Agriculture, stock watering, manufacturing. In a number of the lists of preferences, agriculture—in practice, particularly irrigation—stands second to domestic use.[952] In Kansas, North Dakota, and Texas, it is third. It is preceded in Kansas and Texas by both domestic and municipal, and in Texas also by industrial, including development of electric power by other than hydroelectric means. Irrigation is far down the list in Wyoming. After declaring the first four preferred groups, in which irrigation is not mentioned, the legislature makes irrigation "superior and preferred to any use where water turbines or impulse water wheels are installed for power purposes."

In four of the States in which manufacturing or industrial use is listed, it is in third place, preceded by domestic and agricultural uses. In Texas, it is in the second group, the first group comprising both domestic and municipal uses; hence it precedes irrigation which is next in order. In Kansas and Wyoming, manufacturing takes fourth place. In North Dakota, irrigation and industry together occupy third place, preceded by domestic and livestock use.

Stock watering, which of course is an important phase of agricultural enterprise, is named as a preference in Arizona (where it occupies second place with irrigation, preceded by the combined domestic and municipal preference) and North Dakota (where it occupies second place, preceded by domestic use). In a number of other states, the watering of livestock, or of certain livestock is considered a domestic use. For example: (a) In South Dakota, stock watering is a domestic use. (b) In Kansas, watering of domestic livestock used in operating a farm is included in the term "domestic use." (c) In Idaho, a sufficient amount of water for use of domestic animals kept for the use of the household is a domestic use. (d) In Texas, water for sustaining the life of domestic animals is a domestic use.[953]

---

a preference right to the use of water for domestic purposes within its city limits; but it did not thereby acquire a right to sell water to railroads and others for nondomestic purposes and to persons outside the city limits because, in doing this, the city was not disposing of the water "for any municipal purpose." *Grogan* v. *Brownwood,* 214 S. W. 532, 536-539 (Tex. Civ. App. 1919). This early decision for such purposes contrasts with the administrative definition employed for the municipal use preference provision in Texas discussed above.

[952] References to the various statutory provisions for this and the following uses appear in the next subtopic, "Order of preferences in individual States."

[953] S. Dak. Comp. Laws Ann. § 46-1-6(4) (1967); Kans. Stat. Ann. § 82a-701(c) (1969); Idaho Code Ann. § 42-111 (1948); Tex. Rev. Civ. Stat. Ann. art. 7471 (Supp. 1970). See also Tex. Water Rights Comm'n, "Rules, Regulations and Modes of Procedure," rule 115.1(s) (1970 Rev., Jan. 1970), regarding domestic use. These rules also include

(3) Hydroelectric power. The preferential status of the use of water for developing hydroelectric energy is third in Arizona, along with mining. It is fifth in Texas; sixth and last in Kansas, where it follows even recreational uses.

(4) Mining. This, the use of water which gave birth to the California appropriation doctrine law, is mentioned as a preferred use in Arizona (where it occupies third place, along with power), Idaho (where it has a preference over manufacturing and agriculture *only* in an organized mining district), and in Texas (where it occupies fourth place).

(5) Recreation. This is becoming an increasingly important use of water of large storage projects. It is as yet listed in only four statutes—fifth place in Kansas, seventh place in Texas, and fourth and last in Arizona and North Dakota.

(6) Other uses of water. Texas lists navigation in sixth place, just ahead of recreation and pleasure, and in last place, "other beneficial use." Alaska also expressly recognizes other beneficial uses.

In Arizona and North Dakota, wildlife uses, including fishing, occupy last place, along with recreation.

Wyoming's third place, following drinking by humans and livestock and municipal uses, and preceding industrial and irrigation, is given to an assortment of uses including steam engines and general railway use, culinary, laundry, bathing, refrigeration, heating, and steam power plants.

Order of preferences in individual States. —These are summarized as follows:

(1) Alaska. First to public water supply and then to the most beneficial uses.[954]

(2) Arizona. First, domestic (including gardens not exceeding one-half acre) and municipal; second, irrigation and stock watering; third, power and mining; last, recreation and wildlife uses including fish.[955]

(3) California. Established policy of the State: Use of water for domestic purposes is highest use and irrigation next highest;[956] protection of water rights of municipalities for existing and future uses without waste.[957]

(4) Colorado. First, domestic. Agriculture has preference over manufacturing.[958]

---

separate definitions of livestock use (watering livestock in connection with farming, ranching or dairy enterprises, rule 115.1(t)) and stockraising use (watering livestock connected with the operation of commercial feedlots, rule 115.1(ff)).

The Cal. Admin. Code, tit. 23, § 668 (1969), provides that water for domestic stock is considered a domestic use, but watering of commercial livestock is a stock watering use. See also § 661.

[954] Alaska Const., art VIII, § 13; Stat. § § 46.15.090 and 46.15.150 (Supp. 1966).
[955] Ariz. Rev. Stat. Ann. § 45-147 (Supp. 1970). See also § § 45-141(A) and (B) (Supp. 1970) and (C) (1956).
[956] Cal. Water Code § § 106 (West 1956) and 1254 (West Supp. 1970).
[957] Cal. Water Code § 106.5 (West 1956).
[958] Colo. Const., art. XVI, § 6.

(5) Idaho. First, domestic. Agriculture has preference over manufacturing; but in an organized mining district, mining and milling connected with mining have preference over manufacturing and agriculture.[959]

(6) Kansas. In the following order: (a) domestic, (b) municipal, (c) irrigation, (d) industrial, (e) recreational, (f) waterpower.[960]

(7) Nebraska. First, domestic. Agriculture has preference over manufacturing.[961]

(8) North Dakota. (a) Domestic, (b) livestock, (c) irrigation and industry, (d) fish, wildlife, and other outdoor recreational uses.[962]

(9) Oregon. (a) Under an early enactment still in the statute: First, domestic. Agriculture has preference over manufacturing.[963]

(b) Under a statute enacted in 1955: First, human consumption. Second, livestock consumption. Thereafter, other beneficial uses in an order consistent with the public interest under existing circumstances.[964]

Subject to the foregoing, the State Water Resources Board may prescribe preferences for the future for the particular uses of any source of water supply in aid of the highest and best beneficial use of the water, considering physical characteristics and economy of the area, water requirements, and proposed uses of water as between consumptive and nonconsumptive.[965]

(10) South Dakota. Established policy of the State: Use of water for domestic purposes is highest use; protection of water rights of municipalities for existing and future requirements without waste.[966]

(11) Texas. In following order: (a) domestic and municipal—human life and life of domestic animals; (b) industrial, including development of electric power by means other than hydroelectric; (c) irrigation; (d) mining and recovery of minerals; (e) hydroelectric power; (f) navigation; (g) recreation and pleasure; (h) other beneficial uses.[967] "The right to take waters necessary for domestic and municipal supply purposes is primary and fundamental * * *."[968]

---

[959] Idaho Const., art. XV, § 3.

[960] Kans. Stat. Ann. § 82a-707(b) (1969).

[961] Nebr. Const., art. XV, § 6; Rev. Stat. § 46-204 (1968).

[962] N. Dak. Cent. Code Ann. § 61-01-01.1 (Supp. 1969).

[963] Oreg. Laws 1893, p. 150, § 3, Rev. Stat. § 540.140 (Supp. 1969).

[964] Oreg. Rev. Stat. § 536.310(12) (Supp. 1969). For a discussion of a 1970 Oregon Court of Appeals decision which appears to have construed this and the earlier statute as having a limited effect see "Use of appropriated water: In time of shortage," below.

[965] Id. § 536.340(3).

[966] S. Dak. Comp. Laws Ann. § 46-1-5 (1967).

[967] Tex. Rev. Civ. Stat. Ann. art. 7471 (Supp. 1970).

[968] Tex. Rev. Civ. Stat. Ann. art. 7472b (1954).

(12) Utah. First, domestic; second, agriculture.[969]

(13) Washington. To be determined by court. Protection as among irrigators in condemnation proceedings accorded to the most economical method of artificial irrigation.[970]

(14) Wyoming. (a) Drinking for both man and beast; (b) municipal; (c) steam engines and general railway use, culinary, laundry, bathing, refrigeration (including manufacture of ice), steam and hot water heating plants, steam power plants; (d) industrial. Irrigation superior to any use by water turbines or impulse water wheels for power.[971]

Acquisition of rights to appropriate water.—(1) Preferences regarding application for permit.

(a) Arizona. When pending applications conflict, first preference goes to domestic (including small gardens) and municipal uses; second to irrigation and stockwatering; third to power and mining; last to recreation and wildlife including fish.[972]

(b) California. In acting upon applications to appropriate water the board shall be guided by the policy that domestic use is the highest use and irrigation is the next highest use of water.[973]

An express and candidly stated deviation from the originally strict principle of "First in time, first in right" in the doctrine of prior appropriation is the declaration of the California Legislature that "The application for a permit by a municipality for the use of water for the municipality or the inhabitants thereof for domestic purposes shall be considered first in right, irrespective of whether it is first in time."[974]

The Water Resources Control Board is directed to take a broad view of the benefit to the public from a proposed project in relation to other beneficial uses of the water applied for. The beneficial uses which the Board must consider include, but are not limited to, "domestic, irrigation, municipal, industrial, preservation and enhancement of fish and wildlife, recreational, mining and power purposes, and any uses specified to be protected in any relevant water control plan." (There is no suggestion of preferences in this listing.) In its decision, the Board may subject the proposed appropriation "to such terms and conditions as in its judgment will best develop, conserve, and utilize in the public interest, the water sought to be appropriated."[975]

---

[969] Utah Code Ann. §73-3-21 (1968).

[970] Wash. Rev. Code §90.03.040 (Supp. 1961).

[971] Wyo. Stat. Ann. §41-3 (1957).

[972] Ariz. Rev. Stat. Ann. §45-147 (Supp. 1970). See also §45-141(C) (1956).

[973] Cal. Water Code §§106 (West 1956) and 1254 (West Supp. 1970).

[974] Cal. Water Code §1460 (West 1956).

[975] Cal. Water Code § 1257 (West Supp. 1970). See also §§ 1253, 1255, 1256, and 1258; *Johnson Rancho County Water Dist.* v. *State Water Rights Bd.*, 235 Cal. App. (2d) 863, 45 Cal. Rptr. 589 (1965).

(c) Oregon. In 1955, the Oregon legislature created the State Water Resources Board, with powers and duties of major significance in the field of water law. Among several declarations of policy that the Board is directed to take into consideration is the following: "When proposed uses of water are in mutually exclusive conflict," preference is given first to human consumption purposes and next to livestock consumption. Thereafter it goes to other beneficial purposes in an order consistent with the public interest under the existing circumstances.[976]

The State Water Resources Board may, subject to existing rights and existing statutory preferential uses, prescribe preferences for the future for particular uses of any source of water supply in aid of highest and beneficial use thereof. Consideration must be given to natural characteristics and economy of the area, water requirements, type of proposed use as between consumptive and nonconsumptive uses, and other pertinent data.[977]

(d) Texas. In the allotment and appropriation of water, the public policy of the State is that preference and priority be given in the order listed above under "Order of preferences in individual States." This declaration, the Federal court at El Paso believed, simply regulates priorities prospectively in the subsequent issuance of permits, and does not affect outstanding permits duly issued.[978] The statute further directs the Texas Water Rights Commission to observe the rule that as between applicants for water rights, preference be given not only in the order of preferential uses so declared, but that preference also be given those applications the purposes for which contemplate and will effectuate the maximum utilization of water and are designed to prevent waste of water.[979]

---

[976] Oreg. Rev. Stat. § 536.310(12) (Supp. 1969). The question of the applicability of this act with respect to competing applications appears to have been left unresolved in *Phillips* v. *Gardner,* 469 Pac. (2d) 42 (Oreg. App. 1970), discussed later under "Use of appropriated water: In times of shortage."

[977] *Id.* § 536.340 (3).

[978] *El Paso County W. I. Dist. No. 1* v. *El Paso,* 133 Fed. Supp. 894, 907-908 (W. D. Tex. 1955), affirmed in part, reversed in part but not on the matter considered here, 243 Fed. (2d) 927 (5th Cir. 1957), certiorari denied, 355 U. S. 820 (1957).

[979] Tex. Rev. Civ. Stat. Ann. art. 7472c (1954). In *City of San Antonio* v. *Texas Water Comm'n,* 407 S. W. (2d) 752, 764 (Tex. Sup. Ct. 1966), the court said that art. 7472c "specifically admonishes the Water Rights Commission 'that as between applicants for rights to use the waters of the State, preference be given not only in the order of preferential uses declared [by Article 7471], but that preference also be given those applications the purposes for which contemplate and will effectuate the maximum utilization of waters and are designated and calculated to prevent the escape of waters without contribution to a beneficial public service.' San Antonio answers this by arguing that if Article 7472c gives the Commission discretion to ignore the priorities established in Article 7471, then Article 7472c is unconstitutional because such purpose is not contained in the caption of the Act. The question of violating the order of priority of uses is not presented in this case."

(2) Preferences regarding location of land. Restrictions against allowing diversions of water from one watershed into another or to the injury of persons living in the areas of origin appear in some western statutes. This matter is considered in chapter 8 under "Elements of the Appropriative Right—Diversion of Water from Watershed or Area of Origin."

(3) Withdrawal of unappropriated water from appropriation.

(a) Oregon. In a series of enactments, certain waters of the State have been withdrawn from appropriation by the legislature. The purposes are, variously, maintenance and perpetuation of the recreational and scenic resources of Oregon; establishment of State parks, maintenance and perpetuation of game fish and game fish propagation; service of domestic, stock, municipal, and irrigation purposes.[980]

The State Water Resources Board of Oregon may order unappropriated waters withdrawn from appropriation when deemed necessary to insure compliance with the State water resources policy or to otherwise serve the public interest. The order of withdrawal, issued after notice and hearing, particularly specifies the waters withdrawn, the uses for which withdrawn, duration of withdrawal, and reasons therefor. The order may be modified or revoked at any time. While the order is in effect, no application to appropriate the waters for the specified uses will be received.[981]

(b) Utah. When, in the judgment of the Governor and the State Engineer, the welfare of the State demands it, the Governor of Utah by proclamation may suspend the right of the public to appropriate surplus waters of any stream or other source of water supply. This is for the purpose of preserving such unappropriated waters for use by irrigation districts and organized water users, "or for any use whatsoever." Waters withdrawn from appropriation may be restored by the proclamation of the Governor upon recommendation of the State Engineer. Applications to appropriate such water may not be filed during the period of withdrawal.[982]

(c) To permit investigations by the United States. As stated earlier under "Who May Appropriate Water—Governmental Agencies Other than Districts—The United States," statutes of several States authorize the withdrawal of waters from general appropriation for certain periods of years in order to

---

[980] Oreg. Rev. Stat. § § 538.110-.300 (Supp. 1967).

For a different approach (appropriation of the unappropriated water of a lake by the governor in trust for the people), see Idaho Code Ann. § 67-4301 (1949), discussed in chapter 8 under "Elements of the Appropriative Right—Purpose of Use of Water—Other Purposes of Use of Water—Recreation."

Regarding possibilities of denying or restricting individual water appropriations so as to protect recreational and other uses or interests, see the above discussion under "Restrictions on the Right to Appropriate Water—The question of detriment to the public welfare."

[981] Oreg. Rev. Stat. § 536.410 (Supp. 1969).

[982] Utah Code Ann. § § 73-6-1 and 73-6-2 (1968).

afford investigation by the United States before actually initiating rights to appropriate such waters for proposed Federal projects.[983]

(d) By establishing minimum streamflows or lake levels. This, in effect, may constitute a partial withdrawal of stream or lake waters from appropriation.

Under a 1969 statute, the Washington Department of Ecology may establish minimum water flows or levels for streams, lakes or other public waters for the purposes of protecting fish, game, birds or other wildlife resources, or recreational or aesthetic values, whenever this appears to be in the public interest. The statute provides that the Department shall establish such minimum flows or levels as are needed to protect the resource when requested to do so by the Department of Fisheries or the Game Commission, or by the Water Pollution Control Commission to preserve water quality. (However, the Water Pollution Control Commission was abolished in 1970 and its powers transferred to the Department of Ecology.[984]) In establishing such minimum flows, the Department also shall be guided by the State's policy to retain sufficient minimum flows or levels to provide adequate waters for stock on riparian grazing lands to drink from such streams or lakes if this does not result in an unconscionable waste. Regulations establishing minimum flows or levels shall be preceded by required public notices and hearings and shall be filed in a "Minimum Water Level and Flow Register." No right to direct or store public waters shall be granted by the Department which shall conflict with the regulations establishing flows or levels, but such regulations establishing flows or levels shall not affect water and storage rights in existence prior to the enactment of this legislation in 1969.[985]

Use of appropriated water: Priority of right.—Preference in use of appropriated water in order of priority of right was the original rule in the West as a fundamental facet of the law of prior appropriation. Unless altered by statute, as described above, it still prevails.

Use of appropriated water: In time of water shortage.—(1) The Arizona water rights statute repeats what is said in the laws of some other Western States to the effect that "The person or the state of Arizona or a political subdivision thereof first appropriating the water shall have the better right."[986]

Another section of the Arizona statute, however, provides that in years of scarce water supply, landowners shall have preference to the water for irrigation "according to the dates of their appropriation or their occupation of the lands, either by themselves or their grantors. The oldest titles shall have

---

[983] Mont. Rev. Codes Ann. § 89-808 (1964); N. Mex. Stat. Ann. § 75-5-31 (1968); Okla. Stat. Ann. tit. 82, § 91 (1970); S. Dak. Comp. Laws Ann. § 46-5-42 (1967); Wash. Rev. Code § § 90.40.030 and 90.40.040 (Supp. 1961).

[984] Wash. Laws 1970, ch. 62, § § 6 and 30 (15).

[985] Wash. Rev. Code § § 90.22.010 to 90.22.040 (Supp. 1970), modified by Laws 1970, ch. 62, § § 4, 6, and 30(15).

[986] Ariz. Rev. Stat. Ann. § 45-141(A) (Supp. 1970).

preference."[987] This was based on a provision in the Howell Code, adopted early in the Territorial regime.[988] With respect to this the State supreme court stated in 1901 that: "As applied to private ditches, the statute must be construed as a declaration that not mere priority of diversion, but priority of use and application of water upon particular lands, shall govern in determining conflicting rights."[989]

(2) Constitutions or statutes of several States recognize the general rule that priority in appropriation gives the better right as between water appropriators, but that in time of water shortage users for domestic purposes have preference over all others, and agriculture has preference over manufacturing.[990]

(a) The Colorado constitution makes no mention of compensation in the event that a junior appropriator of domestic water should assert the constitutional preference over a senior appropriator for irrigation at a time when there is not enough water for both. However, while recognizing the preference, the Colorado Supreme Court held that it does not entitle one to exercise it without payment of just compensation.[991]

(b) In the Idaho constitution there is an additional provision that in an organized mining district, mining purposes and milling connected with mining are preferred over manufacturing and agriculture. But, it goes on to say, the exercise of such preferences is subject to the laws regulating exercise of the power of eminent domain. And the Idaho Supreme Court agreed that water could not be taken from prior appropriators without compensation in order to supply the domestic needs of others.[992]

It is held further that the constitutional preference in favor of mining does not authorize or excuse the filling up of natural stream channels or the discharge of poisonous minerals into their waters.[993]

(c) The Nebraska constitutional provision, adopted in 1920, also declares that no inferior right may be acquired by a superior right without compensation.

---

[987] Ariz. Rev. Stat. Ann. § 45-175 (1956).

[988] Terr. Ariz. Howell Code, ch. LV, § 17 (1864).

[989] *Biggs* v. *Utah Irrigating Ditch Co.,* 7 Ariz. 331, 349, 64 Pac. 494 (1901). This construction, when considered in connection with the section giving owners of irrigable lands the right to construct acequias and to obtain the necessary water, was regarded by the court as the underlying principle in its broad application to all appropriations of water for irrigation.

[990] Colo. Const., art. XVI, § 6; Idaho Const., art. XV, § 3; Nebr. Const. art. XV, § 6; Nebr. Rev. Stat. § 46-204 (1968).

[991] *Sterling* v. *Pawnee Ditch Extension Co.,* 42 Colo. 421, 426-428, 94 Pac. 339 (1908), cited and quoted with approval in *Black* v. *Taylor,* 128 Colo. 449, 457, 264 Pac. (2d) 502 (1953). See *Montrose Canal Co.* v. *Loutsenhizer Ditch Co.,* 23 Colo. 233, 236-238, 48 Pac. 532 (1896). *Strickler* v. *Colorado Springs,* 16 Colo. 61, 72-75, 26 Pac. 313 (1891).

[992] *Basinger* v. *Taylor,* 30 Idaho 289, 294-295, 164 Pac. 522 (1917); *Montpelier Mill. Co.* v. *Montpelier,* 19 Idaho 212, 219-220, 113 Pac. 741 (1911).

[993] *Ravndal* v. *Northfork Placers,* 60 Idaho 305, 311, 91 Pac. (2d) 368 (1939); *Bunker Hill & Sullivan Min. & Concentrating Co.* v. *Polak,* 7 Fed. (2d) 583, 585 (9th Cir. 1925).

As originally enacted in 1895, and as still in the statute, the water rights law declares these preferences in times when the available water is not enough for all, but it does not include the final proviso forbidding acquisition of an inferior right without payment of just compensation.[994] In other words, the legislature did not amend this preexisting statute to conform to the constitutional inhibition.

Before the Nebraska constitution added this limiting proviso, the supreme court held that vested rights of completed appropriations cannot be destroyed without compensation.[995] And more recently, the supreme court observed that the framers of the constitution clearly intended to provide that water previously appropriated for power purposes may be taken and appropriated for irrigation use upon payment of just compensation, and not otherwise.[996]

(d) The Oregon statutory provision cited above was first enacted in 1893.[997] It declares the domestic preference to be "subject to such limitations as may be presecribed by law."

In 1955, the Oregon Legislature created the State Water Resources Board, with powers and duties of major significance in the field of water law. Among several declarations of policy that the Board is directed to take into consideration in formulating a coordinated program for use and control of the State water resources is the following: When "available supplies of water are insufficient for all who desire to use them," preference must go first to human consumption, second to livestock consumption, and thereafter other beneficial uses in an order consonant with the public interest under the existing circumstances.[998] No reference was made to the earlier enactment.

So far as has been ascertained, neither of the foregoing sections has been construed by the Oregon Supreme Court.[999] But in a recent case, the Oregon Court of Appeals appears to have concluded that they have only a limited effect. With respect to the earlier 1893 statutory provision (section 540.140), it stated that the 1909 Oregon Water Act had substituted "priority based on time of appropriation for the pre-1909 statutory preference (ORS 540.140)

---

[994] Nebr. Laws 1895, ch. 69, § 43, Rev. Stat. § 46-204 (1968).

[995] *Kearney Water & Electric Power Co.* v. *Alfalfa Irr. Dist.,* 97 Nebr. 139, 146, 149 N. W. 363 (1914). In *Crawford Co.* v. *Hathaway,* 67 Nebr. 325, 371-372, 93 N. W. 781 (1903), the supreme court construed the statutory preference as intending to protect the riparian owner in the use of water for drinking, cooking, and stock watering; that it did not extend to general municipal purposes nor to flushing sewers. This case was overruled on other matters by *Wasserburger* v. *Coffee,* 180 Nebr. 147, 141 N. W. (2d) 738 (1966).

[996] *Loup River Public Power Dist.* v. *North Loup River Public Power & Irr. Dist.,* 142 Nebr. 141, 152-153, 5 N. W. (2d) 240 (1942).

[997] Oreg. Laws 1893, p. 150, § 3, Rev. Stat. § 540.140 (Supp. 1969).

[998] Oreg. Rev. Stat. § 536.310(12) (Supp. 1969).

[999] However, from a proper construction of another provision authorizing approval of applications for municipal water supplies "to the exclusion of all subsequent appropriations" (*id.* § 537.190), the supreme court in 1914 thought it apparent that

based on the nature of the uses."[1000] However, the court said, "It may be that ORS 540.140 still has viability as to rights which were perfected prior to 1909 or as to rights bearing the same effective date. Since neither is involved in the case at bar, we need not consider those possibilities here."[1001] The court also said:

> ORS 536.210, et seq., enacted in 1955, establish a water resources board, direct it to develop comprehensive programs for conserving and augmenting water resources for all purposes, and outline factors to be considered by the board in formulating a water resources program. It is clear from a reading of these sections that it was not intended that they supersede the previously prescribed laws governing the issuance and priority of water rights certificates. In fact, ORS 536.320 specifically provides:
> "The board shall not have power:
> " * * *.
> "(2) To modify, set aside or alter any existing right to use water or the priority of such use established under existing laws * * *.
> " * * *."

The appropriative rights involved in the case were domestic use rights with 1947 priority dates and an irrigation right with a 1919 priority date. From its language quoted above, the court appears to have concluded that the 1955 preference provision did not apply to such previously existing appropriative rights. But the question of its possible application to later acquired rights appears to have been left unresolved.

(3) A Utah statute contains a provision very similar to the above. It accords preferences in times of scarcity first to domestic purposes without unnecessary waste and second to agricultural purposes. The original version as enacted in 1880 contained a proviso that such preference should not be exercised to the injury of any vested right without just compensation. This was included in the 1903 water administration law, but without the requirement of compensation.[1002]

"priorities of appropriation constitute a species of property in the proprietor which cannot be taken from him except by the right of eminent domain upon suitable compensation first assessed and tendered." *In re Schollmeyer,* 69 Oreg. 210, 215, 138 Pac. 211 (1914).

[1000] *Phillips* v. *Gardner,* 469 Pac. (2d) 42, 44 (Oreg. App. 1970). The court added that "Although the 1909 Act did not directly state that priorities should be based on priority in time and not on nature of use, the whole thrust of the Act clearly indicates such a purpose." *Id.* The Court also said "The Act, § 73, provides 'All laws and parts of laws so far as in conflict or inconsistent with the provisions of this Act are hereby repealed.' " *Id.* at 43.

[1001] *Id.* at 44.

[1002] Utah Laws 1880, ch. 20, § 14, Laws 1903, ch. 100, § 54, Code Ann. § 73-3-21 (1968).

So far as ascertained, the Utah provision for preference without compensation has not been construed by the supreme court.[1003] In one case the court observed that the Utah statute did not include this rule of preferences for the express guidance of the State Engineer in rejecting or approving applications, as the California statute had done. But, said the court, it did indicate clearly that the legislature considered these two purposes as the most beneficial uses to which water may be applied.[1004]

An important feature of the development of the Utah law of appropriative water rights was the classification of "primary" and "secondary" water rights. This prevailed for nearly 40 years. It was finally eliminated in the 1919 statutory revision.[1005]

An effect of this primary-secondary classification was to group earlier appropriators into one class and later ones into another class. In two of the laws, the average flow at low-water mark was a controlling factor. The 1897 law provided that all appropriators of water from streams, springs, and lakes up to "their average flow at low water mark" should be "deemed equal in rights to, the said waters, according to their vested rights;" secondary rights, as described in the 1880 legislation, were to be recognized, subject to "prior rights."[1006]

Related old Utah statutory provisions, court decrees, and agreements regarding prorata divisions of streamflow measured by fractional parts or percentages of flow, are discussed above under "Statutory—Inadequacies of the Preadministrative Procedure—The Utah experience." Statutory recognition of

---

[1003] The current version of the statute had the attention of the court in a decision concerning the water rights implications of allowing livestock to drink directly from a stream. But this had no bearing on relative rights of use, because the livestock owner had made no appropriation of the water: *Bountiful City* v. *DeLuca*, 77 Utah 107, 118-119, 292 Pac. 194 (1930).

[1004] *Tanner* v. *Bacon*, 103 Utah 494, 507-508, 136 Pac. (2d) 957 (1943).

[1005] Utah Laws 1880, ch. 20, § § 6 and 7; Laws 1897, ch. 52, § § 5 and 6; Laws 1903, ch. 100, § 72; Laws 1919, ch. 67, § 10.

[1006] Utah Laws 1897, ch. 52, § § 5 and 6.

Mead, Elwood, "Irrigation Institutions" p. 228 (1910), stated that: "The law of 1880 defined two classes, primary and secondary rights. Primary rights include all rights acquired up to the time when the sum of the rights equals the average flow of the stream at low-water stage. Secondary rights are rights acquired to any supply in excess of the average low-water flow, and are subject to the complete enjoyment of primary rights. Whenever there is not water enough for all primary rights, the flow of the stream is divided among them pro rata. When there is more than enough for the primary rights, but not enough for all secondary rights, the excess over the primary rights is divided among the secondary rights pro rata. The law carries the classification no farther, but numerous court decrees have divided the rights into more than two classes. In adjudicating the rights on the upper section of the Provo River in 1899 the court divided the rights into ten classes, on the same basis as the primary and secondary rights defined in the law."

primary and secondary water rights is reflected in several opinions of the Utah Supreme Court respecting early water rights.[1007]

(4) The Kansas declaration of principles governing appropriations of water was first enacted in 1945. It was extensively revised in 1957.[1008]

The 1945 Kansas version declared that where appropriations of water for different purposes conflict they must take precedence in a stated order (repeated in 1957 and given verbatim below); and that as between appropriators the first in time is the first in right. The 1957 legislature undertook to reconcile these apparently unreconcilable declarations by enacting the following:

(b) Where uses of water for different purposes conflict such uses shall conform to the following order of preference: Domestic, municipal, irrigation, industrial, recreational and water power uses. However, the date of priority of an appropriation right, and not the purpose of use, determines the right to divert and use water at any time when the supply is not sufficient to satisfy all water rights that attach to it. The holder of a water right for an inferior beneficial use of water shall not be deprived of his use of the water either temporarily or permanently as long as he is making proper use of it under the terms and conditions of his water right and the laws of this state, other than through condemnation.

(c) As between persons with appropriation rights, the first in time is the first in right.* * *

The Kansas legislature did not in terms authorize the condemnation of early priority rights for inferior uses of water for the purpose of putting the water to superior use. However, the above language in section 82a-707(b) is probably to be construed as an implied authorization to this effect. If not, the purpose of declaring an order of preference and then stating explicitly that in time of water shortage it is the date of priority, not the purpose of use, that controls the exercise of the appropriative right, is not evident.

Taking for a superior use a right to water already appropriated for an inferior use.—(1) The matter of compensation. The constitutional and statutory provisions of Colorado, Idaho, Nebraska, Oregon, and Kansas with respect to the taking of a senior right for an inferior use of water, in order that a junior right may be exercised with the use of water of a higher preference, are discussed immediately above.

The importance of this question lay in the fact that early appropriations of water were usually made for irrigation and, in many areas, for mining, whereas

---

[1007] See *Manning* v. *Fife*, 17 Utah 232, 236-237, 54 Pac. 111 (1898); *Salt Lake City* v. *Salt Lake City Water & Electrical Power Co.*, 24 Utah 249, 266, 67 Pac. 672 (1902), 25 Utah 456, 71 Pac. 1069 (1903); *Bishop* v. *Duck Creek Irr. Co.*, 121 Utah 290, 295-296, 241 Pac. (2d) 162 (1952).

[1008] Kans. Laws 1945, ch. 390, § 7, Stat. Ann. § 82a-707 (1969).

large quantity rights for domestic purposes in municipalities were often sought after much of the streamflows were already appropriated. Yet irrigation, although having a high preference rating, is superseded by higher preference domestic and municipal uses. As shown in the above discussion, some constitutional and statutory declarations of preferences in time of water shortage include a proviso inhibiting the taking of earlier rights without compensation, and some do not. In cases in which courts of record passed on the question, however, compensation was required.

(2) Subjection of future appropriations to taking without compensation. In most cases, these declarations have not been construed as subjecting rights acquired after their enactment to the hazard of uncompensated loss to preferred rights.

In Texas there is an exception. A statute enacted in 1931—the "Wagstaff Act"[1009]—declared, among other things, that: "The right to take waters necessary for domestic and municipal supply purposes is primary and fundamental, and the right to recover from other uses, waters essential to such purposes shall be paramount and unquestioned in the policy of the State, and in the manner Constitutional and Statutory authority provide."[1010] The section then goes on to recognize, in all political subdivisions of the State and constitutional government agencies exercising general legislative powers, the right of eminent domain, to be exercised as permitted by law for water purposes. This authorization to take waters necessary for the preferred uses, then, includes payment of compensation.

However, another provision initiated in the Wagstaff Act provides that as between appropriators the first in time is the first in right; *provided* that all appropriations *thereafter* made with respect to streams other than an international boundary stream—in other words, the Rio Grande—for any purposes other than domestic or municipal, "shall be granted subject to the right of any city, town or municipality of this State to make further appropriations of said water thereafter without the necessity of condemnation or paying therefor, for domestic and municipal purposes" as defined in the act as "including water for sustaining human life and the life of domestic animals," "any law to the contrary notwithstanding."[1011]

The validity of this Texas legislation negating compensation, but eliminating from its applicability the Rio Grande, has been questioned on many occasions. In a controversy pertaining to the waters of this particular river, it was brought

---

[1009] Tex. Laws 1931, ch. 128.

[1010] Tex. Rev. Civ. Stat. Ann. art. 7472b (1954).

[1011] Tex. Rev. Civ. Stat. Ann. arts. 7472, 7472a (1954), and 7471 (Supp. 1970). Regarding this provision and some possible limitations on its exercise, see McCall, J. D., "Rights of Impounded Water," in Proceedings, Water Law Conferences, Univ. of Tex., pp. 251, 257-262 (1952, 1954).

to the attention of the Federal court at El Paso. This court, in answer to a contention that article 7472a is unconstitutional in making the legislation inapplicable to any stream constituting the international boundary between the United States and Mexico, sustained the validity of the section. This elimination of the Rio Grande, the court considered, did not reflect any arbitrary discrimination or repugnant classification, and was not irrational.[1012]

(3) Procedures for condemning prior low preference water rights.

(a) Washington. The State constitution provides that the use of water for irrigation, mining, and manufacturing purposes shall be deemed a public use.[1013]

The water rights statute of Washington declares the beneficial use of water to be a public use. It extends to any person (meaning individuals, associations, corporations, districts, and municipalities) the right to exercise the power of eminent domain for acquiring property and rights needed for water control and use, including the right to condemn an inferior use of water for a superior use. The court is vested with the function of determining what use will be for the greatest public benefit and therefore to be deemed a superior use. A limitation is

That no property right in water or the use of water shall be acquired hereunder by condemnation for irrigation purposes, which shall deprive any person of such quantity of water as may be reasonably necessary for the irrigation of his land then under irrigation to the full extent of the soil, by the most economical method of artificial irrigation applicable to such land according to the usual methods of artificial irrigation employed in the vicinity where such land is situated. In any case, the court shall determine what is the most economical method.[1014]

In construing the statute, the Washington Supreme Court held that although incidental benefits to be derived by the public from the establishment of a private enterprise could not be considered sufficient to make the intended use a public one, this nevertheless does not apply to the portions of the State in which water supplies are limited and generally cannot be duplicated—where water is life itself. Hence under such circumstances the use of water for irrigation, or for domestic purposes when the desired domestic purpose is the foundation of an agricultural enterprise, becomes a public use.[1015]

(b) Wyoming. Preferred uses include rights for domestic and transportation purposes, steam powerplants, and industrial purposes. Existing rights not

---

[012] *El Paso County W. I. Dist. No. 1* v. *El Paso,* 133 Fed. Supp. 894, 906-907 (W. D. Tex. 1955), affirmed in part, reversed in part but not on the matter considered here, 243 Fed. (2d) 927 (5th Cir. 1957), certiorari denied, 355 U. S. 820 (1957).

[1013] Wash. Const., art. XXI, § 1.

[1014] Wash. Rev. Code § § 90.03.040 and 90.03.480 (Supp. 1961).

[1015] *State ex rel. Andersen* v. *Superior Court,* 119 Wash. 406, 410-411, 205 Pac. 1051 (1922).

preferred may be condemned to supply water for preferred uses other than steam powerplants and industrial purposes. Preferred water uses have preferences in the order stated above under "Order of preferences in individual States."

This order of preferences contains four groups, none of which includes agriculture or irrigation. The only reference to agriculture or irrigation is in the sentence immediately following the last group. This is to the effect that the use of water for irrigation shall be superior to any use where water turbines or impulse water wheels are installed for power purposes.

A change to a preferred use may be made with the approval of the State Board of Control, after notice and hearing, if necessary, before the division superintendent. Payment of just compensation must be made.[1016]

The Wyoming Supreme Court held that a change to a preferred use under this statute carries only the rights and priorities pertaining to the use that is the subject of the condemnation. It does not operate to subordinate the rights of other users in the source of supply unless their rights are likewise acquired or condemned.[1017] In other words, simply changing a use of water to a preferred use does not alter the priority of its right.

(c) Alaska. The 1966 Alaska Water Use Act provides that an applicant for a permit shall be granted a permit and is entitled to a preference over other appropriators if the use is for a public water supply. However, to be entitled to a preference the applicant must show that the preferred use will be prevented or substantially interfered with by a *prior* appropriator and agree to compensate the prior appropriator for any damages sustained by the preferred use.[1018]

[1016] Wyo. Stat. Ann. § § 41-3 and -4 (1957).

[1017] *Newcastle* v. *Smith,* 28 Wyo. 371, 376-378, 205 Pac. 302 (1922).

[1018] Alaska Stat. § 46.15.150 (Supp. 1966).

Chapter 8

THE APPROPRIATIVE RIGHT

In 1894, a United States Court of Appeals stated what is believed to be the western judicial consensus as to general principles of the appropriative right. At this time, Wyoming's pioneer program of administrative control over acquisition of water rights was just getting under way. Administrative principles were being put into practice, but had not yet been subjected to judicial review. Many western court decisions involving appropriative rights had been rendered. The Federal court's summation was then, and still is, a valid statement of fundamentals in this area of substantive law. The statement follows:[1]

> We consider the law to be well settled that the right to water flowing in the public streams may be acquired by an actual appropriation of the water for a beneficial use; that, if it is used for irrigation, the appropriator is only entitled to the amount of water that is necessary to irrigate his land by making a reasonable use of the water; that the object had in view at the time of the appropriation and diversion of the water is to be considered in connection with the extent and right of appropriation; that if the capacity of the flume, ditch, canal, or other aqueduct, by means of which the water is conducted, is greater than is necessary to irrigate the lands of the appropriator, he will be restricted to the quantity of water needed for the purposes of irrigation, for watering his stock, and for domestic use; that the same rule applies to an appropriation made for any other use or purpose; that no person can, by virtue of his appropriation, acquire a right to any more water than is necessary for the purpose of his appropriation; that, if the water is used for the purpose of irrigating lands owned by the appropriator, the right is not confined to the amount of water used at the time the appropriation is made. He would be entitled, not only to his needs and necessities at that time, but to such other and further amount of water, within the capacity of his ditch, as would be required for the future improvement and extended cultivation of his lands, if the right is otherwise kept up; that the intention of the appropriator, his object and purpose in making the appropriation, his acts and conduct in regard thereto, the quantity and character of land owned by him, his necessities, ability, and surroundings, must be considered by the courts, in connection with the extent of his actual appropriation and use, in determining and defining his rights; that the mere act of commencing the construction of a ditch with the

---

[1] *Hewitt* v. *Story,* 64 Fed. 510, 514-515 (9th Cir. 1894). Cited were decisions of the supreme courts of California, Nevada, Colorado, and Idaho, and of the Supreme Court of the United States. The instant case arose in California.

avowed intention of appropriating a given quantity of water from a stream gives no right to the water unless this purpose and intention are carried out by the reasonable, diligent, and effectual prosecution of the work to the final completion of the ditch, and diversion of the water to some beneficial use; that the rights acquired by the appropriator must be exercised with reference to the general condition of the country and the necessities of the community, and measured in its extent by the actual needs of the particular purpose for which the appropriation is made, and not for the purpose of obtaining a monopoly of the water, so as to prevent its use for a beneficial purpose by other persons; that the diversion of the water ripens into a valid appropriation only where it is utilized by the appropriator for a beneficial use; that the surplus or waste water of a stream may be appropriated, subject to the rights of prior appropriators, and such an appropriator is entitled to use all such waters; that, in controversies between prior and subsequent appropriators of water, the question generally is whether the use and enjoyment of the water for the purposes to which the water is applied by the prior appropriator have been in any manner impaired by the acts of the subsequent appropriator. These general principles are of universal application throughout the states and territories of the Pacific coast. * * *

PROPERTY CHARACTERISTICS

Right of Beneficial Use

The concept that use of public water must be made for beneficial purposes is fundamental in western water jurisprudence. In chapter 1 there is some discusssion of constitutional, statutory, and judicial declarations of the relation between the appropriative water right and the beneficial use of water.

State Constitutions and Statutes

The conceptual relationship of beneficial use of water to the right of its appropriation runs through much of fundamental as well as statutory water law of the West.

Constitutions.—Briefly, in the constitutions of Arizona, New Mexico, and Utah, water rights for beneficial purposes are recognized and confirmed.[2] Since riparian rights to the use of water of watercourses are generally not recognized in these States, the declarations relate to rights of appropriation therein. Other manifestations of the concept appear elsewhere.[3]

---

[2] Ariz. Const., art. XVII, § 2; N. Mex. Const., art. XVI, § 1; Utah Const., art. XVII, § 1.
[3] Cal. Const., art. XIV, § 3; Colo. Const., art. XVI, § 6; Idaho Const., art. XV, § § 1 and 3; Mont. Const. art. III, § 15; Nebr. Const., art. XV, § § 5 and 6; N. Mex. Const., art. XVI, § § 2 and 3; Tex. Const., art. XVI, § 59a; Wyo. Const., art. VIII, § 3.

Statutes.—The statutes show the correlation to be not only significant, but vital. It appeared first in the California Civil Code of 1872—the first statute to provide procedures for appropriating water. "The appropriation must be for some useful or beneficial purpose, and when the appropriator or his successor in interest ceases to use it for such a purpose, the right ceases."[4] The California Water Code reenacts the constitutional declaration of 1928 that the general welfare requires that the State water resources "be put to beneficial use to the fullest extent of which they are capable," and that the right to use water of any natural stream "is and shall be limited to such water as shall be reasonably required for the beneficial use to be served."[5]

Several statutes declare the historical principle, thus expressed in the Nevada statute: "Beneficial use shall be the basis, the measure and the limit of the right to the use of water."[6]

Wyoming defines "water right" as "a right to use the water of the state, when such use has been acquired by the beneficial application of water under laws of the state relating thereto, and in conformity with the rules and regulations dependent thereon."[7] Texas defines "beneficial use," for the purposes of the statute, as "the use of such a quantity of water, when reasonable intelligence and reasonable diligence are exercised in its application for a lawful purpose, as is economically necessary for that purpose," and restricts appropriative rights thereto.[8] South Dakota brings in the element of public welfare by defining "beneficial use" as "any use of water that is reasonable and useful and beneficial to the appropriator, and at the same time is consistent with the interests of the public in the best utilization of water supplies," and declaring that appropriations shall remain subject to this principle.[9]

Still other legislative declarations expressly tie the principle of beneficial use to the right of appropriation.[10]

---

[4] Cal. Civ. Code § 1411 (1872). Several current statutes contain this declaration: Idaho Code Ann. § 42-104 (1948); Mont. Rev. Codes Ann. § 89-802 (1964); Nebr. Rev. Stat. § 46-229 (1968).

[5] Cal. Water Code § 100 (West 1956); Cal. Const., art. XIV, § 3.

[6] Nev. Rev. Stat. § 533.035 (Supp. 1969); Ariz. Rev. Stat. Ann. § 45-101(B) (1956); N. Mex. Stat. Ann. § 75-1-2 (1968); N. Dak. Cent. Code Ann. § 61-01-02 (Supp. 1969); Okla. Stat. Ann. tit. 82, § 1-A (1970); Oreg. Rev. Stat. § 540.610 (Supp. 1969); S. Dak. Comp. Laws Ann. § 46-1-8 (1967); Tex. Rev. Civ. Stat. Ann. art. 7542 (1954); Utah Code Ann. § 73-1-3 (1968); Wyo. Stat. Ann. § 41-2 (1957). This also appears in N. Mex. Const., art. XVI, § 3.

[7] Wyo. Stat. Ann. § 41-2 (1957).

[8] Tex. Civ. Stat. Ann. arts. 7476 and 7543 (1954).

[9] S. Dak. Comp. Laws Ann. §§ 46-1-6(6) and 46-5-5 (1967).

[10] Appropriation rights shall remain subject to the principle of beneficial use: Kans. Stat. Ann. §§ 82a-707(a) and -718 (1969). Water may be appropriated for beneficial use: Oreg. Rev. Stat. § 537.120 (Supp. 1969); Wash. Rev. Code § 90.03.250 (Supp. 1961). "Beneficial use means a use of water for the benefit of the appropriator, other persons or the public, that is reasonable and consistent with the public interest, including, but

Under the current administrative control procedures for appropriating water, which prevail in 16 of the Western States,[11] this correlation is an essential element in completing and perfecting the water right. In 14 of these States, the appropriator's final step in perfecting the right is making proof of beneficial use of the water, in consequence of which he receives a license or certificate of appropriation from the State.[12] In Nebraska and Texas in which the permit is the last document issued by the administrator, the right nevertheless is not completed until the water has been applied to the intended beneficial use.

In the 14 States which issue licenses or certificates of appropriation, the administrator puts his stamp of approval on the projected appropriation only when convinced that application of tl.e water to beneficial use in accordance with the terms of the permit has been made. In Nebraska and Texas, it is this official's function to ascertain, by reports and investigations, what progress has been made by the permittee and, if the circumstances so justify, to bring proceedings for cancelling the permit.

In none of these 16 States does the statute contemplate the acquisition of an appropriative right by any conduct, or any amount of work, short of application of the water to beneficial use. The right of appropriation and the principle of beneficial use are correlated, in both law and practice, in the administrative procedures.

The Concurring Judicial Rule

The appropriative right does not extend to ownership of the *corpus* of water while it remains in the natural source of supply. It is a right to the *use* of the water—a usufruct. Inherent in the right of appropriation are the requirements that the use made of the appropriated water shall be a beneficial one, and that the right to divert and use the water extends only to the quantity actually applied to such beneficial use. The appropriative right, therefore, is not merely a right to the use of the water; it is a right of *beneficial use*. This is the view that the courts have taken through the years, probably without significant dissent.

Various facets of the general rule were involved in many judicial controversies and were discussed in a considerable number of court opinions. Major points follow:

Intent to apply water to beneficial use.—An appropriation of water begins with crystallization of the intent of the appropriator to divert and apply water

---

not limited to, domestic, agricultural, irrigation, industrial, manufacturing, mining, power, public, sanitary, fish and wildlife, and recreational uses." Alaska Stat. § 46.15.260(3) (Supp. 1966).

[11] The excepted States are Colorado, Hawaii, and Montana.

[12] This is discussed in chapter 7 under "Methods of Appropriating Water of Water-courses—Current Appropriation Procedures—Administrative—Procedural steps in appropriating water—(8) Certificate of appropriation or license."

to specific beneficial use or uses.[13] The early decisions emphasized that there must be "some open, physical demonstration of the intent, and for some valuable use."[14] In the early controversies, such demonstrations might take the form of beginning construction of works, or even of making surveys. Later it might be done by posting a notice at the point of intended diversion of the water and filing a copy of the claim in the county courthouse. Currently, under the administrative control laws, the intent is crystallized by filing in the State office a formal application for a permit to make the appropriation.

Usufruct.—The appropriator acquires no specific property in the particles of water—the *corpus* of the water—while flowing in the stream. What he acquires is a right of diversion and use of some specific quantity of water that at that time may be flowing in the stream.[15] This is a usufructuary right[16] —sometimes termed a usufruct[17]—a right of possession and use only.[18] The basis of acquisition of this right is beneficial use of the water.[19]

The right of usufruct of the appropriator is subject to a reasonable use and consumption of the water for beneficial purposes.[20] Hence, the appropriative right is a right of beneficial use.[21]

Consummation of the intended use.—The true test of an appropriation of water is successful application thereof to the beneficial use designed.[22] This consummation of beneficial use is a *sine qua non* of a valid appropriation under most State statutory laws.[23]

---

[13] *Tattersfield* v. *Putnam,* 45 Ariz. 156, 172, 41 Pac. (2d) 228 (1935); *Genoa* v. *Westfall,* 141 Colo. 533, 349 Pac. (2d) 370, 378 (1960); *Crawford* v. *Lehi Irr. Co.,* 10 Utah (2d) 165, 168-169, 350 Pac. (2d) 147 (1960).

[14] *McDonald* v. *Bear River & Auburn Water & Min. Co.,* 13 Cal. 220, 232-233 (1859); *Larimer County Res. Co.* v. *People ex rel. Luthe,* 8 Colo. 614, 616-617, 9 Pac. 794 (1886).

[15] *Rickey Land & Cattle Co.* v. *Miller & Lux,* 152 Fed. 11, 18 (9th Cir. 1907); *Bergman* v. *Kearney,* 241 Fed. 884, 893 (D. Nev. 1917); *In re Hood River,* 114 Oreg. 112, 181, 227 Pac. 1065 (1924); *Garner* v. *Anderson,* 67 Utah 553, 565, 248 Pac. 496 (1926).

[16] *Murphy* v. *Kerr,* 296 Fed. 536, 541 (D. N. Mex. 1923).

[17] *Salt Lake City* v. *Salt Lake City Water & Elec. Power Co.,* 24 Utah 249, 266, 67 Pac. 672 (1902).

[18] *Brennan* v. *Jones,* 101 Mont. 550, 567, 55 Pac. (2d) 697 (1936).

[19] *In re Manse Spring and Its Tributaries,* 60 Nev. 280, 286, 108 Pac. (2d) 311 (1940); *Application of Filippini,* 66 Nev. 17, 21-22, 202 Pac. (2d) 535, 537 (1949).

[20] *Big Rock Mutual Water Co.* v. *Valyermo Ranch Co.,* 78 Cal. App. 266, 274, 248 Pac. 264 (1926).

[21] *Hufford* v. *Dye,* 162 Cal. 147, 153, 121 Pac. 400 (1912); *Dalton* v. *Kelsey,* 58 Oreg. 244, 253-254, 114 Pac. 464 (1911).

[22] *Genoa* v. *Westfall,* 141 Colo. 533, 349 Pac. (2d) 370, 378 (1960).

[23] See *Fourzan* v. *Curtis,* 43 Ariz. 140, 146, 29 Pac. (2d) 722 (1934); *Albrethsen* v. *Wood River Land Co.,* 40 Idaho 49, 60, 231 Pac. 418 (1924); *Gates* v. *Settlers' Mill., Canal & Res. Co.,* 19 Okla. 83, 89-91, 91 Pac. 856 (1907); *Cundy* v. *Weber,* 68 S. Dak. 214, 222-223, 300 N. W. 17 (1941); *Crawford* v. *Lehi Irr. Co.,* 10 Utah (2d) 165, 168-169, 350 Pac. (2d) 147 (1960); *State* v. *Laramie Rivers Co.,* 59 Wyo. 9, 39, 136 Pac. (2d) 487 (1943).

As discussed earlier in chapter 7 under "Methods of Appropriating Water of Watercourses—Completion of Appropriation," the so-called "possessory basis" of a right of appropriation, which arose under practices of appropriating water on the public domain and was reflected in preadministrative water statutes as well as some court decisions, contemplated "completion" of the appropriation as conducting the water to the place of intended use. A right thus "completed," however, was subject to loss by abandonment if the water was not applied to beneficial use with reasonable diligence within a reasonable time.

Under the current statutes providing administrative control over appropriation of water, as above noted, proof of application of the water to the intended beneficial use is the final step taken by the appropriator in acquiring an appropriative right. Application of the water to such use is absolutely essential to acquisition of the right.

Measure of the right of beneficial use.—"The courts recognize that beneficial use is the basis, the measure, and the limit of the right to use of water, Section 2, Article 16, Constitution of New Mexico,* * *."[24] (See "State Constitutions and Statutes," above.) Thus, as against a subsequent appropriator, the appropriative water right extends to, and only to, the quantity of water actually diverted and applied to a beneficial use.[25]

Under the administrative statutes, water may not be appropriated in excess of the reasonable quantity that may be used for the beneficial purpose designated in the application for a permit.[26] The allowable quantity of water is first measured by the original appropriation and, if that proves to be more than can be beneficially used, then by the factual measure of beneficial use.[27]

This facet of the right of beneficial use is developed further under "Elements of the Appropriative Right—Measure of the Appropriative Right," below.

Right of Property[28]

Briefly, as stated immediately above, the appropriative right is a right of beneficial use, a usufruct only, and hence it does not include an ownership of the *corpus* of water while still in the natural source of supply. A necessary result is that (a) ownership of a private appropriative right and (b) ownership of the public water to which the right relates are entirely different things.

---

[24] *Holloway* v. *Evans,* 55 N. Mex. 601, 607, 238 Pac. (2d) 457 (1951).

[25] *Kernan* v. *Andrus,* 6 Alaska 54, 59-60 (1918); *Ortel* v. *Stone,* 119 Wash. 500, 503, 205 Pac. 1055 (1922).

[26] *Crawford* v. *Lehi Irr. Co.,* 10 Utah (2d) 165, 168-169, 350 Pac. (2d) 147 (1960).

[27] *Silver King Consolidated Min. Co.* v. *Sutton,* 85 Utah 297, 331, 39 Pac. (2d) 682 (1934).

[28] See chapter 5 which comprises discussions of the property nature of (1) water (a) flowing in a natural stream and (b) reduced to physical possession by means of artificial structures, and (2) water rights.

Whatever ownership concept of water flowing in a natural stream—(a) public ownership, or (b) State ownership, or (c) ownership in the "negative community" or by no one—is favored in a particular western jurisdiction, State administrative control over the handling of water and rights to the use thereof is not affected by doctrinaire differences between the concepts. Pragmatically, the important principle is that private ownership of stream water while in its natural environment does not exist; but private rights to abstract and use such waters—under State supervision and control in the exercise of its police powers—do exist, and they are property rights.

Right of Private Property

Other matters important to the present context are brought out in chapter 5. These include:

— The appropriative right is a right of private property. It is subject to ownership, disposition, and litigation as in the case of other forms of private property.

— The appropriative right is valuable property.

— The general rule in the West is that the appropriative right is real property. Although the general rule is followed with respect to certain points in Montana, there is an important exception with respect to taxation.[29] As a corollary to the general rule, an action to quiet title to an appropriative right is in the nature of an action to quiet title to real estate.

Ownership of the Appropriative Right

In general.—The appropriative right is an interest in real estate.[30] As a general practical matter, a person who is legally competent to own title to land in a particular jurisdiction has equal competence to hold title to an appropriative water right therein, subject to any special qualifications that the State law may impose upon those who exercise appropriative water rights. (See, in chapter 7, "Who May Appropriate Water".)

Multiple ownerships of appropriative right.—The possibility of ownership by more than one person of a single appropriative right was acknowledged in the early mining days. In one case, the California Supreme Court remarked that, with reference to the right to water, "we do not see why this right may not be acquired by two or more acting together, or why, when they do acquire it, they do not hold it as other property, and may not sue as such for any unlawful interference with it."[31]

Water companies appeared as litigants in many early California water rights controversies. From the first, throughout the West, recognition of group ownership of water privileges, whether informal or organized, was either

---

[29] This is discussed in chapter 5 under "Water Rights—Appropriative Right—Real Property: The Montana Rule."

[30] Although an interest in realty, the appropriative right is a right of use and is subject to loss as a result of nonuse. It thus differs from title to land.

[31] *Kimball* v. *Gearhart,* 12 Cal. 27, 47 (1859).

explicit or implicit in both statutory and case law. Thus, appropriators of water include natural persons, private associations, corporations, water districts and other public entities, municipalities, States, and the United States. (See, in chapter 7, "Who May Appropriate Water," and see "Elements of the Appropriative Right—Sale, Rental, or Distribution of Water," below.)

Separable ownerships of ditch and water right.—The water right—an incorporeal hereditament in the flow and use of the stream as a natural resource—is entirely distinct from the property right in the works by which the water is diverted, stored, and carried to the land for beneficial use thereon, or in connection therewith, and each may exist without the other.[32] "We have held repeatedly that water rights and ditch rights are separate and distinct property rights. One may own a water right without a ditch right, or a ditch right without a water right."[33]

The Montana Supreme Court observed that "so far distinct are the water rights and ditch rights that the abandonment of one does not necessarily imply an abandonment of the other."[34]

It has been long established that a single diversion may be used for the service of several different priorities owned by different appropriators for use in connection with their respective farms.[35] An example in some jurisdictions is a public service company which, as a common carrier, may serve many individual farmers in whom title to the water rights is vested but who have no ownership interest in the water system. (See "Elements of the Appropriative Right—Sale, Rental or Distribution of Water," below. See also, in chapter 9, "Diversion, Distribution, and Storage Works.")

Separable ownerships of land and water right.—According to the weight of authority in the West, one at least rightfully in possession of land, even though not the owner, may make a valid appropriation of water in connection with such tract. Variations and refinements of the general rule occur from State to State. This matter is discussed under "The Land Factor in Appropriating Water" in chapter 7.

This, however, is a facet of the question of qualifications of an appropriator. Titles to the land and to the appropriative right acquired for and exercised in connection with the land are not merged by reason of their being held by the same party. They remain separate and distinct items of ownership. As recently as 1962, the Utah Supreme Court declared that: "The right to make use of one's land and the right to use water are two severable things."[36]

---

[32] *Murphy* v. *Kerr,* 296 Fed. 536, 541 (D. N. Mex. 1923); *First State Bank of Alamogordo* v. *McNew,* 33 N. Mex. 414, 437, 269 Pac. 56 (1928).

[33] *Connolly* v. *Harrel,* 102 Mont. 295, 300-301, 57 Pac. (2d) 781 (1936).

[34] *McDonnell* v. *Huffine,* 44 Mont. 411, 423, 120 Pac. 792 (1912).

[35] *Simpson* v. *Bankofier,* 141 Oreg. 426, 432, 16 Pac. (2d) 632 (1932), 18 Pac. (2d) 814 (1933); *Nichols* v. *McIntosh,* 19 Colo. 22, 24, 34 Pac. 278 (1893).

[36] *Stubbs* v. *Ercanbrack,* 13 Utah (2d) 45, 368 Pac. (2d) 461, 463 (1962). See *Whitmore* v. *Salt Lake City,* 89 Utah 387, 397-400, 57 Pac. (2d) 726 (1936).

Right to the Flow of Water

The general rule.—The appropriator owns an easement in the stream from which he diverts water and in its tributaries above his point of diversion. This consists of the right to have the water flow from the head of the stream and from the head of each tributary above his point of diversion, in sufficient quantity to the head of his ditch or place of diversion, and to have it of such quality as will meet his needs as protected by his water right.[37] See chapter 13.)

If diverted from the natural channel by other appropriators for their convenience, the prior appropriator is entitled to have the water delivered to him at available points by subsequent appropriators and at their expense.[38]

At this point, it is well to emphasize the elemental proposition that this right of the appropriator applies to the flow of water *to* his point of diversion—that it does not remain attached to the streamflow after it has passed down the channel from his premises. The principle was established in early California cases that after the water leaves his premises the appropriator no longer has any right or interest in it, and that he cannot complain of any uses made by others downstream.[39] This distinction between the relative locations of the water has an important place in the law of adverse possession of water (see chapter 14).

Incorporeal hereditament.—The right of the prior appropriator to have the water flow in the stream to the head of his ditch is generally held to be an incorporeal hereditament.[40] This does not prejudice the conclusion that although the appropriative right is an incorporeal hereditament, "It savors of, and is a part of, the realty itself."[41]

Wiel submits the proposition that although a water right by appropriation is often called an easement, this is not the better view. Being not subordinate to any land, but independent thereof and of equal dignity, it is not an easement therein. "Being but a usufruct, or privilege of flow and use, it is incorporeal."[42]

---

[37] *Helena* v. *Rogan,* 26 Mont. 452, 469-470, 68 Pac. 798 (1902).

[38] *Pima Farms Co.* v. *Proctor,* 30 Ariz. 96, 106-107, 245 Pac. 369 (1926). See *Salt Lake City* v. *Gardner,* 39 Utah 30, 45-47, 114 Pac. 147 (1911); *Joseph W. Bowles Res. Co.* v. *Bennett,* 92 Colo. 16, 22-24, 18 Pac. (2d) 313 (1932); *State ex rel. Crowley* v. *District Court,* 108 Mont. 89, 97-98, 88 Pac. (2d) 23 (1939).

[39] *Eddy* v. *Simpson,* 3 Cal. 249, 252 (1853); *Hanson* v. *McCue,* 42 Cal. 303, 310 (1871); *Lakeside Ditch Co.* v. *Crane,* 80 Cal. 181, 182-183, 187, 22 Pac. 76 (1889).

[40] *Rickey Land & Cattle Co.* v. *Miller & Lux,* 152 Fed. 11, 14 (9th Cir. 1907); *Madison* v. *McNeal,* 171 Wash. 669, 675, 19 Pac. (2d) 97 (1933); *Wyatt* v. *Larimer & Weld Irr. Co.,* 18 Colo. 298, 315, 33 Pac. 144 (1893).

[41] *Rickey Land & Cattle Co.* v. *Miller & Lux,* 152 Fed. 11, 14 (9th Cir. 1907).

[42] Wiel, S. C., "Water Rights in the Western States," 3d ed., vol. 1, § § 53 and 287, vol. 2, § 1340 (1911).

The appropriative right is generally appurtenant to the land the water is used on, but in most States it may be severed therefrom, transferred, and made appurtenant to

Quantity of water in stream.—The right to the requisite flow of water extends to the headgate of the ditch (or other place of diversion, such, for example, if possession is legally taken of natural overflow).[43] The flow must then be allowed to continue out from the stream into the diversion ditch,[44] and thence through the ditch to the place of use.[45]

The first appropriator has the right to insist that the water continue to flow to his headgate or point of diversion substantially as it did when he first made the appropriation.[46] An early Utah court says that the right of the prior appropriators is to have the water flow to them "in its natural state."[47]

That to be actionable, the interference with or injury to the prior appropriator's use of his appropriated water supply must be material or substantial, appears to be the general rule.[48]

A mere temporary or trivial irregularity, which does not cause him any actual injury, would, of course, not be a cause of suit; but, if the interruption is of such a character as to interfere with his use of the water, and cause sensible or positive injury to him, a suit may be maintained to enjoin the further commission of the wrong.[49]

Materiality of injury caused by a junior appropriator is illustrated by the facts in a Utah case.[50]

Quantity of water in tributaries.—The right of continued flow extends to the tributaries; that is, the rights of a prior appropriator are entitled to protection against material infringement by subsequent appropriations of water from its tributaries. This rule has been recognized since early times in the

---

other land under certain conditions as discussed below. See "Appurtenance of Water Right to Land—Generally Appurtenant, but Severable."

[43] *Rickey Land & Cattle Co.* v. *Miller & Lux,* 152 Fed. 11, 18 (9th Cir. 1907); *McDonald* v. *Askew,* 29 Cal. 200, 206 (1865); *Tulare Irr. Dist.* v. *Lindsay-Strathmore Irr. Dist.,* 3 Cal. (2d) 489, 546-547, 45 Pac. (2d) 972 (1935); *Willey* v. *Decker,* 11 Wyo. 496, 73 Pac. 210 (1903); *Moe* v. *Harger,* 10 Idaho 302, 307, 77 Pac. 645 (1904); *Naches & Cowiche Ditch Co.* v. *Weikel,* 87 Wash. 224, 227-228, 151 Pac. 494 (1915).

[44] *Lower Kings River Water Ditch Co.* v. *Kings River & Fresno Canal Co.,* 60 Cal. 408, 410 (1882).

[45] *Lakeside Irr. Co.* v. *Markham Irr. Co.,* 116 Tex. 65, 74-77, 285 S. W. 593 (1926).

[46] *Carson* v. *Hayes,* 39 Oreg. 97, 102, 65 Pac. 814 (1901).

[47] *Crane* v. *Winsor,* 2 Utah 248, 253 (1878).

[48] *Noh* v. *Stoner,* 53 Idaho 651, 655-657, 26 Pac. (2d) 1112 (1933); *Rocky Ford Irr. Co.* v. *Kents Lake Res. Co.,* 104 Utah 202, 213-214, 135 Pac. (2d) 108 (1943).

[49] *Carson* v. *Hayes,* 39 Oreg. 97, 102, 65 Pac. 814 (1901).

[50] *Logan, Hyde Park & Smithfield Canal Co.* v. *Logan,* 72 Utah 221, 223-226, 269 Pac. 776 (1928). The junior appropriator's upstream power plant caused frequent fluctuations in the streamflow, varying in a 24-hour period from 1 to 15 cubic feet per second, which seriously interfered with the prior appropriators downstream in the proper exercise of their rights. The court held that the junior appropriator had no right to cause this interference.

West.[51] "All streams are dependent upon tributaries for a supply of water," said the Colorado Supreme Court late in the 19th century. If the prior appropriator had no claim on the water of tributaries, his water supply might be cut off by settlers above at any time—"a conclusion so manifestly unjust that it must be discarded."[52]

The logic of the foregoing comment, which was applied to the relationship between an appropriation made on a main stream and a subsequent appropriation on an upstream tributary, is readily apparent. Less simple, but equally equitable, is its application to a situation in which the first appropriation is made on a stream below the junction of a tributary, a second appropriation is made on the main stream above this tributary junction, and a third appropriation is made on the tributary. The principle involved is well stated in the syllabus of a Colorado case. It was also adopted several years later in Montana.[53]

If the result of the appropriation from the tributary is to require the prior appropriator to surrender the use of water for the benefit of senior appropriations below the point where such tributary joins the main stream, then such prior appropriator may require the junior appropriator from the tributary to first surrender the use of water, before such prior appropriator is required to surrender his use, and may maintain an action for that purpose.

The Utah Supreme Court made the sweeping statement that an appropriator of water from the central channel of a stream is entitled to rely upon "all the sources which feed the main stream above his own diversion point, clear back to the farthest limits of the watershed."[54] But coincident with this right, on his part, to insist as against the public that his water come to him, is the right of the public to insist that no more than his quantity come to him.[55]

---

[51] *Weaver* v. *Eureka Lake Co.*, 15 Cal. 271, 274 (1860); *Baxter* v. *Gilbert*, 125 Cal. 580, 582, 58 Pac. 129 (1899); *Malad Valley Irr. Co.* v. *Campbell*, 2 Idaho 411, 415, 18 Pac. 52 (1888); *Josslyn* v. *Daly*, 15 Idaho 137, 149, 96 Pac. 568 (1908); *Beaverhead Canal Co.* v. *Dillon Elec. Light & Power Co.*, 34 Mont. 135, 141, 85 Pac. 880 (1906); *Strait* v. *Brown*, 16 Nev. 317, 323-324 (1881); *Tonkin* v. *Winzell*, 27 Nev. 88, 96-97, 73 Pac. 593 (1903); *Low* v. *Schaffer*, 24 Oreg. 239, 244, 33 Pac. 678 (1893); *Moyer* v. *Preston*, 6 Wyo. 308, 317-318, 44 Pac. 845 (1896); *Ryan* v. *Tutty*, 13 Wyo. 122, 126-127, 78 Pac. 661 (1904).

[52] *Strickler* v. *Colorado Springs*, 16 Colo. 61, 67, 26 Pac. 313 (1891).

[53] *Platte Valley Irr. Co.* v. *Buckers Irr., Mill & Improvement Co.*, 25 Colo. 77, 53 Pac. 334 (1898); *Helena* v. *Rogan*, 26 Mont. 452, 469-470, 68 Pac. 798 (1902). See also *Water Supply & Storage Co.* v. *Larimer & Weld Res. Co.*, 25 Colo. 87, 91-92, 53 Pac. 386 (1898).

[54] *Richlands Irr. Co.* v. *Westview Irr. Co.*, 96 Utah 403, 418, 80 Pac. (2d) 458 (1938).

[55] *Adams* v. *Portage Irr., Res. & Power Co.*, 95 Utah 1, 13, 72 Pac. (2d) 648 (1937).

The commonly recognized right of protection to the appropriator on the main stream extends only to waters of a tributary that reach his point of diversion at the time he has need of the water.[56] As stated by a Federal court: "An appropriator from a main channel can complain of a diversion from a 'tributary' only if and when such tributary would, if not interferred with, make a valuable contribution to the main stream."[57] Thus, the question as to whether one stream or other source of water supply is a tributary of another becomes, for this purpose, a question of fact.[58]

The burden of proof in controversies between prior appropriators on a main stream and junior appropriators of water of an upstream tributary is discussed in the last part of this chapter under "Relative Rights of Senior and Junior Appropriators—Reciprocal Rights and Obligations of Appropriators."

Quality of the water.—(1) As a general principle, the appropriator is entitled to the flow of water in the stream to his diversion works in such state of natural purity as to substantially fulfill the purposes for which his appropriation was made. If not protected in this particular, the usefulness of his water right may be depreciated or even destroyed. The necessity for the rule is self-evident.

In its first reported water rights decision, the Utah Supreme Court held that an appropriator was entitled to protection by the court against a subsequent material deterioration in quality of the stream water by an ore crusher.[59] Three-fourths of a century later, the same court said that: "The owner of a water right has a vested right to the quality as well as the quantity which he has beneficially used."[60]

(2) Development of the rule in California. As might be anticipated, the question of stream pollution arose early in California as a result of the predominant emphasis at that time on use of water for mining purposes. The courts came to recognize that if these mountain stream waters were to be put to maximum beneficial use, preservation of their original pristine quality was neither practical nor necessary for many useful purposes. That is, some deterioration in quality of the water might not impair the usefulness of a particular downstream appropriation, that question to be determined as one of fact in consideration of the purpose to which the water was being or was to be applied.[61]

---

[56] *Leonard* v. *Shatzer*, 11 Mont. 422, 426-427, 28 Pac. 457 (1892).

[57] *United States* v. *Haga*, 276 Fed. 41, 43 (D. Idaho 1921).

[58] *Loyning* v. *Rankin*, 118 Mont. 235, 246, 165 Pac. (2d) 1006 (1946). In *Anderson* v. *Spear-Morgan Livestock Co.*, 107 Mont. 18, 29-30, 79 Pac. (2d) 667 (1938), it was held that where the testimony of all witnesses showed that only in time of flood did water from a certain creek flow into another creek, such evidence did not justify the court in finding that the first creek was a tributary of the second one.

[59] *Crane* v. *Winsor*, 2 Utah 248, 253 (1878).

[60] *Salt Lake City* v. *Boundary Springs Water Users Assn.*, 2 Utah (2d) 141, 144, 270 Pac. (2d) 453 (1954).

[61] *Hill* v. *Smith*, 27 Cal. 476, 483 (1865).

Some divergences in judicial views were expressed in the earliest decisions.[62] The California Supreme Court, however, settled upon the principle that the appropriator is entitled to protection against acts that materially deteriorate the quality of the water for the uses to which he wishes to apply it.[63]

(3) Relation to purposes of use of the injured appropriator. In the formulation of the general rule in California, it was recognized that in the use of waters of a stream by appropriators up and down the channel, the carrying of some impurity from one water use location to another is inevitable—that preservation of the water in its original state of purity is of course a desirable attainment but, in a developing economy, quite impracticable.[64] In a case decided in 1919 by a district court of appeal, this pragmatic conclusion was expressed as follows:[65]

> A prior locator cannot insist that the stream above him shall not be used by subsequent locators or appropriators for mining purposes, and that the water shall flow to his claim in a state of absolute purity. While the subsequent locator will not be permitted so to conduct his operations as to unreasonably interfere with the fair enjoyment of the stream by the prior locator, or to destroy or substantially injure the latter's superior rights as a prior locator, nevertheless, the law recognizes the necessity for some deterioration, which, within reasonable limits, is *damnum absque injuria*. Any other rule might involve an absolute prohibition of the use of all the water of a stream above a prior locator in order to preserve the quality of a small portion taken therefrom.* * *

The right of the prior appropriator to have the water at his headgate "of such quality as will meet his needs as protected by his water right" was

---

[62] See *Bear River & Auburn Water & Min. Co.* v. *New York Min. Co.*, 8 Cal. 327, 333-336 (1857); *Mokelumne Hill Canal & Min. Co.* v. *Woodbury*, 10 Cal. 185, 186-187 (1858); *Butte Canal & Ditch Co.* v. *Vaughn*, 11 Cal. 143, 153-154 (1858); *Pilot Rock Creek Canal Co.* v. *Chapman*, 11 Cal. 161, 162 (1858). See also *Esmond* v. *Chew*, 15 Cal. 137, 143 (1860).

[63] *Phoenix Water Co.* v. *Fletcher*, 23 Cal. 481, 487 (1863). See *Dripps* v. *Allison's Mines Co.*, 45 Cal. App. 95, 99, 187 Pac. 448 (1919); *Wright* v. *Best*, 19 Cal. (2d) 368, 378, 121 Pac. (2d) 702 (1942); *Joerger* v. *Pacific Gas & Elec. Co.*, 207 Cal. 8, 25-26, 276 Pac. 1017 (1929). Compare the facts in *Antioch* v. *Williams Irr. Dist.*, 188 Cal. 451, 457-458, 465, 205 Pac. 688 (1922).

[64] In 1942, the California Supreme Court mistakenly said it to be an established rule that an appropriator of stream water, as against upper owners with inferior rights of user, "is entitled to have the water at his point of diversion preserved in its natural state of purity." *Wright* v. *Best*, 19 Cal. (2d) 368, 378, 121 Pac. (2d) 702 (1942). However, the court then went on to qualify this flat statement by adding that "any use which corrupts the water so as to *essentially impair its usefulness for the purposes* to which he originally devoted it, is an invasion of his rights." [Emphasis supplied.]

[65] *Dripps* v. *Allison's Mines Co.*, 45 Cal. App. 95, 99, 187 Pac. 448 (1919).

acknowledged by other western courts as well.[66] In a 1959 Washington case, a finding that logging operations had permanently polluted the domestic water supply of a community, destroyed the usefulness of its prior appropriative rights, and depreciated the value of the members' real estate was sustained by the Washington Supreme Court.[67] In a 1967 Colorado case, the court concluded that although all the water used in a State fish hatchery was returned to the stream, the water was returned to the stream in a contaminated and damaged condition as a direct result of which financial loss was suffered by the plaintiffs who held appropriative rights. Judgments for damages and the issuance of an injunction were sustained.[68]

Much earlier, the Washington Supreme Court had acknowledged the correctness of the general rule that a prior appropriator is entitled to injunctive protection against pollution of his water supply by the discharge therein of such deleterious matter as to render it unfit for purposes of irrigation.[69] In the instant case, however, domestic use had ceased long before the action was brought, and there was no eivdence that the water had been rendered unfit for irrigation. The damage to plaintiff's irrigation system from waste waters discharged upstream consisted of silt deposits in the canal and, in some cases, clogging of outlet pipes. The court took the view that plaintiff had appropriated water knowing that, in time, the country above might be settled and cultivated and that the settlers would be entitled to use the stream reasonably for both drainage and irrigation. "The plaintiff must accomodate its appliances for irrigation to the conditions which a reasonable use may require. * * * Until the plaintiff can show an unreasonable use by the defendants in conveying waste waters into this creek, there is clearly, we think, no cause for an injunction."

(4) The question of substantial injury. As noted above, California early adhered to the qualification that in order to afford an appropriator a ground of action, deterioration of water quality must be material in its injurious effect upon his use of the water.[70] A Colorado court has said that the appropriator has the right to have the streamflow unimpaired in any *permanent* and *unreasonable way.*[71]

Courts of equity are not warranted in interfering with upstream mining industries solely because they cause slight inconveniences or occasional annoyance or even some degree of interference, so long as they do no *substantial* damage. But to permit a subsequent appropriator to so pollute the

---

[66] *Helena* v. *Rogan*, 26 Mont. 452, 469-470, 68 Pac. 798 (1902).

[67] *Drake* v. *Smith*, 54 Wash. (2d) 57, 60-63, 337 Pac. (2d) 1059 (1959).

[68] *Game and Fish Comm'n* v. *Farmers Irr. Co.,* ____Colo.____ , 462 Pac. (2d) 562 (1967).

[69] *Naches & Cowiche Ditch Co.* v. *Weikel*, 87 Wash. 224, 227-233, 151 Pac. 494 (1915).

[70] *Phoenix Water Co.* v. *Fletcher*, 23 Cal. 481, 487 (1863).

[71] *Cushman* v. *Highland Ditch Co.,* 3 Colo. App. 437, 439, 33 Pac. 344 (1893). Regarding reasonable use criteria, see also *Suffolk Min. & Mill Co.* v. *San Miguel Consol. Min. & Mill Co.,* 9 Colo. App. 407, 48 Pac. 828, 832 (1897); and dicta, citing cases, in *State* v. *California Packing Corp.,* 105 Utah 182, 141 Pac. (2d) 386, 388 (1943).

stream as to render it less available to the downstream senior is as injurious as depriving the latter of a part of his appropriated water.[72]

This rule works both ways as between prior and subsequent appropriators.

Numerous authorities announce the doctrine that while a prior use of the water of a stream for mining purposes necessarily contaminates it to some extent, such contamination or deterioration of the quality of the water cannot be carried to such a degree as to inflict substantial injury upon another user of the waters of said stream.[73]

To the extent that contamination of the water by the senior appropriator begins or is increased *after* the junior appropriation is made, this proposition is a logical derivative of the well-recognized general rule that a junior appropriator has a vested right as against his senior to insist upon a continuance of the conditions that existed at the time the later appropriation was made, provided that a change would injure him.[74] Some points concerning mining vis-à-vis agricultural water rights are discussed below in this subtopic.

(5) Material deterioration of quality a question of fact. In the opinion in its early landmark western water rights case of *Atchison* v. *Peterson,* the United States Supreme Court stated that:[75]

What diminution of quantity, or deterioration in quality, will constitute an invasion of the rights of the first appropriator will depend upon the special circumstances of each case, considered with reference to the uses to which the water is applied. A slight deterioration in quality might render the water unfit for drink or domestic purposes, whilst it would not sensibly impair its value for mining or irrigation. In all controversies, therefore, between him and parties subsequently claiming the water, the question for determination is necessarily whether his use and enjoyment of the water to the extent of his original appropriation have been impaired by the acts of the defendant.* * *

(6) Remedies for substantial injury. "Any material deterioration of the quality of the stream by subsequent appropriators or others without superior

---

[72] *Arizona Copper Co.* v. *Gillespie,* 12 Ariz. 190, 202-203, 100 Pac. 465 (1909), affirmed, 230 U. S. 46 (1913).

[73] *Ravndal* v. *Northfork Placers,* 60 Idaho 305, 311-312, 91 Pac. (2d) 368 (1939).

[74] *Bennett* v. *Nourse,* 22 Idaho 249, 253, 125 Pac. 1038 (1912); *Hill* v. *Standard Min. Co.,* 12 Idaho 223, 234, 85 Pac. 907 (1906).

[75] *Atchison* v. *Peterson,* 87 U. S. 507, 514-515 (1874). See *Arizona Copper Co.* v. *Gillespie,* 230 U. S. 46, 56-57 (1913); *Montana Co.* v. *Gehring,* 75 Fed. 384, 388 (9th Cir. 1896); *Ravndal* v. *Northfork Placers,* 60 Idaho 305, 312, 91 Pac. (2d) 368 (1939); "The reasonableness of the use is a question for the jury, to be determined by them upon the facts and circumstances of each particular case," *Dripps* v. *Allison's Mines Co.,* 45 Cal. App. 95, 99, 187 Pac. 448 (1919). As to reasonable use criteria applied by court or jury, see also cases in note 71 *supra.*

rights entitles him [the downstream appropriator] to both injunctive and legal relief." So said the California Supreme Court in 1942.[76]

Decades earlier, the United States Supreme Court expressed its views as to the factors that distinguish equitable from legal relief.[77] The following quotation follows that given immediately above in connection with material deterioration of quality:

> But whether, upon a petition or bill asserting that his prior rights have been thus invaded, a court of equity will interfere to restrain the acts of the party complained of, will depend upon the character and extent of the injury alleged whether it be irremediable in its nature, whether an action at law would afford adequate remedy, whether the parties are able to respond for the damages resulting from the injury, and other considerations which ordinarily govern a court of equity in the exercise of its preventive process of injunction.

The Court reviewed the circumstances relating to the alleged pollution of water diverted downstream and concluded that the injury—which was only slightly if at all attributable to defendants' operations—was scarcely appreciable by contrast with the damage that would result to defendants from indefinite suspension of their work. The defendants were capable of answering for damages that they might cause. Under these circumstances, the lower court was upheld in refusing to interfere by injunction and in leaving plaintiffs to their remedy, if any, by an action of law.

(7) Mining versus agriculture. Much of the western law of appropriative water rights was first propounded, expounded, and established in early decisions of the California Supreme Court. In the earliest of these decisions, there is an ever-recurring consciousness of the importance of mining in the State and of hydraulic mining water rights. In 1857, the court observed that the judiciary of California had had thrown upon it responsibilities not incurred by the courts of any other State in the Union with respect to a large class of cases—unknown in the jurisprudence of other States—involving the great mining interest dependent upon the use of water.[78]

The principle of priority of appropriation was applied in the first California cases as between appropriators of water for mining purposes.[79] Inevitably

---

[76] *Wright* v. *Best,* 19 Cal. (2d) 368, 378, 121 Pac. (2d) 702 (1942). (See also *Game and Fish Comm'n* v. *Farmers Irr. Co.,*___Colo.___, 462 Pac. (2d) 562 (1967), discussed above at note 68.) But see *Heil* v. *Sawada,* 187 Cal. App. (2d) 633, 637-638, 10 Cal. Rptr. 61 (1960), indicating that an injunction will not be granted if no advantage would result to the plaintiff, but harm would accrue to the defendant.

[77] *Atchison* v. *Peterson,* 87 U. S. 507, 515-516 (1874).

[78] *Bear River & Auburn Water & Min. Co.* v. *New York Min. Co.,* 8 Cal. 327, 332 (1857). See *Crandall* v. *Woods,* 8 Cal. 136, 141 (1857); *Hoffman* v. *Stone,* 7 Cal. 46, 49 (1857); *Conger* v. *Weaver,* 6 Cal. 548, 555-556 (1856).

[79] *Eddy* v. *Simpson,* 3 Cal. 249, 252 (1853).

conflicts arose between claimants of water for mining, who contended that only appropriations for this purpose were valid, and claimants for other purposes. The California Supreme Court first held that the State policy toward settlers extended to all pursuits with no partiality except in the single case in which the rights of the agriculturalist, when gold was discovered on the land he occupied, were made as the result of a statute to yield to those of the miner.[80] Several years later, the court held that a threatened diversion of water, for mining purposes, from an irrigation reservoir was a violation of a property right acquired by virtue of a prior appropriation.[81]

The Arizona Supreme Court held that although the Territorial laws recognized the right to appropriate public stream water for mining as well as for agriculture, no superior right is accorded the miner. The only superiority of right arises by prior appropriation. This does not mean that an agriculturist may captiously complain of the reasonable use of water by the miner upstream so long as no substantial damage is done. It does mean that such stream pollution or burdening the stream channel with debris as to render the stream substantially unavailable to the agriculturist is actionable.[82]

The United States Supreme Court agreed. The Court stated that "The Arizona statute places a water user for mining purposes upon no higher plane than a user for irrigation." And without force, it was declared, was the suggestion that the right to use water for mining and reduction purposes cannot be exercised without polluting the streams with waste material, and that the lower user therefore cannot complain of the necessary consequences of the legal right conferred by the statute. Sufficiency of water for necessary uses of the first appropriator includes quality as well as quantity. Extent of the effect of diminution of quality is a factual question.[83]

The Idaho constitution states several preferences in use of appropriated water,[84] one of which is that "in any organized mining district those using the water for mining purposes or milling purposes connected with mining, shall have preference over those using the same for manufacturing or agricultural purposes," such preferred usage to be subject to the laws governing exercise of the power of eminent domain.[85] There is nothing in this or any other provision of the constitution that authorizes miners or others "to fill up the natural

---

[80] *Tartar* v. *Spring Creek Water & Min. Co.*, 5 Cal. 395, 397-399 (1855).

[81] *Rupley* v. *Welch*, 23 Cal. 452, 455-457 (1863). It was held, however, that the question of injury to growing crops involved a right vested in the miner by the State Possessory Act of 1852 and subject to regulation under the Indemnity Act of 1855.

[82] *Arizona Copper Co.* v. *Gillespie*, 12 Ariz. 190, 202-203, 100 Pac. 465 (1909), affirmed, 230 U. S. 46 (1913).

[83] *Arizona Copper Co.* v. *Gillespie*, 230 U. S. 46, 56-57 (1913).

[84] In chapter 7, see "Methods of Appropriating Water of Watercourses—Restrictions and Preferences in Appropriation of Water—Preferences in Water Appropriation."

[85] Idaho Const., art. XV, § 3.

channel of any of the public streams of the state to the injury of any other user of the waters of the stream."[86] A Federal court likewise took a dim view of such a contention, saying that it "asserts for the miner in Idaho constitutional rights unknown to American constitutional law—the right not only to a preference in the use of a stream, but the right to inflict unlimited injury upon property of those who have acquired vested rights as manufacturers or agriculturists."[87]

(8) Grant by appropriator of easement to pollute a stream. A nonriparian appropriator of water of a California stream granted to a mining company, for a consideration, a perpetual right to pollute the stream by using it as a conduit to carry off the debris deposited from mining claims. There was no showing in the case that pollution from the mining operations was so extensive as to amount to a public nuisance. The California Supreme Court held that although no authority had been cited for or against the proposition that an easement may be attached to a water right, there was no legal or practical objection to it. An appropriative right constitutes an interest in realty, and it therefore can appropriately serve as a servient estate to which an easement may be annexed.[88]

Appurtenance of Water Right to Land

Early and Widespread Recognition in the West

The concept of appurtenance of an appropriative right to the land on or in connection with which the water is used received early acceptance in California. The Civil Code included the following enactment:[89]

A thing is deemed to be incidental or appurtenant to land when it is by right used with the land for its benefit, as in the case of a way, or watercourse, or of a passage for light, air, or heat from or across the land of another.

Prior to this enactment the California Supreme Court held, with respect to public lands, that the water privilege used in connection with a sawmill on the public domain passed with a conveyance of the mill. The reason was that the mill would have been wholly valueless without the water.[90]

---

[86] *Hill* v. *Standard Mining Co.*, 12 Idaho 223, 233, 85 Pac. 907 (1906), quoted with approval in *Ravndal* v. *Northfork Placers*, 60 Idaho 305, 311, 91 Pac. (2d) 368 (1939).

[87] *Bunker Hill & Sullivan Min. & Concentrating Co.* v. *Polak*, 7 Fed. (2d) 583, 585 (9th Cir. 1925).

[88] *Wright* v. *Best*, 19 Cal. (2d) 368, 382-383, 121 Pac. (2d) 702 (1942). The court stated that the novelty of the incident was no bar to its recognition as an easement if its creation violated no principle of public policy.

[89] Cal. Civ. Code § 662 (1872).

[90] *McDonald* v. *Bear River & Auburn Water & Min. Co.*, 13 Cal. 220, 233, 235-236 (1859).

It was later held that the fact that land to which water appropriated on the public domain was taken was then unsurveyed public land did not prevent the water right from becoming appurtenant thereto.[91] With respect to private lands: The appropriative right becomes appurtenant to the land on or in connection with which the use of water is made under the right.[92] The water right necessary for the reasonable enjoyment of the land is an easement;[93] hence, where the land cannot be used advantageously without it, the water right is an appurtenance.[94]

Among various declarations of the relationship of appurtenance to appropriative rights is that of the Utah Supreme Court to the effect that: "A right to divert and use the waters of a stream, acquired by appropriation, is a hereditament appurtenant to the land for the benefit of which the appropriation is made."[95] And another pertinent declaration in a water case is by a Texas court that:[96]

> An appurtenance is that which belongs to another thing, but which has not belonged to it immemorially. The thing appurtenant need not be one of necessity. It may be one of convenience only; but it must be connected in use with the principal thing; in other words, "a thing is appurtenant to something else only when it stands in the relation of an incident to a principal, and is necessarily connected with the use and enjoyment of the latter." *Humphreys* v. *McKissock,* 140 U.S. 304.* * *

The widespread legislative and judicial acceptance of the concept throughout the West is revealed in the ensuing discussion. (Other aspects of the general topic of appurtenance of water rights to land are discussed later in this chapter under "Elements of the Appropriative Right—Sale, Rental, or Distribution of Water.")

Generally Appurtenant, but Severable

Of general application in the West is the rule that an appropriative right becomes appurtenant to the land for the benefit of which the water is applied. As will appear later, in most jurisdictions the right may be severed from the land to which it became initially appurtenant and, subject to certain conditions, it may be transferred to and become simultaneously appurtenant to other land.

---

[91] *Ely* v. *Ferguson,* 91 Cal. 187, 190, 27 Pac. 587 (1891).

[92] *Senior* v. *Anderson,* 138 Cal. 716, 723, 72 Pac. 349 (1903).

[93] *Cave* v. *Crafts,* 53 Cal. 135, 140 (1878). See *Farmer* v. *Ukiah Water Co.,* 56 Cal. 11, 15 (1880).

[94] *Crooker* v. *Benton,* 93 Cal. 365, 369, 28 Pac. 953 (1892).

[95] *Conant* v. *Deep Creek & Curlew Valley Irr. Co.,* 23 Utah 627, 629-630, 66 Pac. 188 (1901).

[96] *Hunstock* v. *Limburger,* 115 S. W. 327, 329 (Tex. Civ. App. 1909, error refused).

Statutes.—Declarations that the appropriative right shall be appurtenant to the land in connection with which it is acquired are contained in many of the water rights statutes.[97]

Some of the declarations are that the "water" remains appurtenant to the place of use—disregarding the legal distinction between the *corpus* of the water itself and the incorporeal right to its use. Others refer to both the water and the right of use. However, the legislative intent is clear enough.

The Alaska statute[98] provides that:

> The right to use water under an appropriation or permit shall be appurtenant to the land or place where it has been or is to be beneficially used, provided, that water supplied by one person to another person's property shall not be appurtenant to the property unless the parties so intend. An appurtenant water right shall pass with a conveyance of the land, or transfer, or by operation of law unless specifically exempted from the conveyance.

However, with the permission of the Commissioner of the Department of Natural Resources, "all or any part of an appropriation may be severed from the land to which it is appurtenant, may be sold, leased or transferred for other purposes or to other lands and be made appurtenant to other lands."

It is currently provided by the Arizona statute[99] that:

> A water right may be severed from the land to which it is appurtenant or from the site of its use if for other than irrigation purposes and with the consent and approval of the owner of such right may be transferred for use for irrigation of agricultural lands or for municipal, stock watering, power and mining purposes and to the State or its political subdivisions for use for recreation and wildlife purposes (including fish) without losing priority theretofore established, subject to [a number of] limitations and conditions.

The Washington statute makes a general declaration that the right to the use of water that has been applied to a beneficial use shall remain appurtenant to the land or place of use; but it also provides that where water applied for in the application for a permit is to be used for irrigation purposes, it shall become appurtenant only to such land as may be reclaimed thereby to the full extent of the soil for agricultural purposes.[100]

---

[97] Idaho Code Ann. § § 42-101, -220 (1948), -1402 (Supp. 1969); Kans. Stat. Ann. § § 42-121 (1964) and 82a-701(g) (1969); Nev. Rev. Stat. § 533.040 (Supp. 1969); Oreg. Rev. Stat. § 540.510 (Supp. 1969); Wash. Rev. Code § 90.03.380 (Supp. 1961).

[98] Alaska Stat. § 46.15.160 (Supp. 1966).

[99] Ariz. Rev. Stat. Ann. 45-172 (Supp. 1970).

[100] Wash. Rev. Code § § 90.03.380 and 90.03.290 (Supp. 1961).

In Wyoming, it is provided by statute (a) that (except as stated under (b), below) rights to the use of water shall attach to the land for irrigation, or to other beneficial purposes; but (b) that reservoir water rights acquired under reservoir permits and adjudications shall not attach to any particular lands except by formal conveyance executed by the reservoir owner.[101] The provision with respect to optional attachment of reservoir rights was added in 1921.[102]

Some court decisions in harmony with the statutes.—These are cited in the accompanying footnote.[103]

Some individual State situations.—(1) Arizona. Appurtenance of shares of capital stock of Salt River Valley Water Users' Association to the lands of shareholders, as provided in the articles of incorporation, was sustained by the Arizona Supreme Court.[104]

(2) California. By contrast with the riparian right, the appropriative right is not inseparably annexed to the land as part and parcel of it, but is separable and alienable from the land to which it became initially appurtenant.[105]

Whether the shares of stock of a mutual irrigation company are appurtenant to the land on which the water served by the company is used is a question of fact, to be determined from the circumstances of the case.[106] Severance of the appropriative right from the land to which initially appurtenant does not take place when the landowner and his neighbors convey their several water rights to a mutual irrigation company for the mere purpose of convenience in the

---

[101] Wyo. Stat. Ann. § § 41-2 and -37 (1957).

[102] Wyo. Laws 1921, ch. 141.

[103] *Tattersfield* v. *Putnam,* 45 Ariz. 156, 170, 171, 41 Pac. (2d) 228 (1935); *Anderson* v. *Cummings,* 81 Idaho 327, 331-332, 340 Pac. (2d) 1111 (1959); a water right acquired in Idaho by the "constitutional" method—diversion and use without needing to conform to the statute—becomes an appurtenance of the land to which it is applied, as well as one acquired under the statute: *Furey* v. *Taylor,* 22 Idaho 605, 611, 127 Pac. 676 (1912); it took no legislation to establish the principle of appurtenance in arid Nevada: *Zolezzi* v. *Jackson,* 72 Nev. 150, 153-154, 297 Pac. (2d) 1081 (1956); *Middle Rio Grande Water Users Assn.* v. *Middle Rio Grande Conservancy Dist.,* 57 N. Mex. 287, 299, 258 Pac. (2d) 391 (1953); the provision "is a valid exercise of the legislative power to regulate and control the use and distribution of the waters of the state," *Broughton* v. *Stricklin,* 146 Oreg. 259, 272, 28 Pac. (2d) 219 (1933), 30 Pac. (2d) 332 (1934); appurtenant to the land, and therefore realty: *Madison* v. *McNeal,* 171 Wash. 669, 675, 19 Pac. (2d) 97 (1933); in 1909, the Wyoming legislature adopted the policy that a water right by direct flow from a stream shall be attached to the land: *Hunziker* v. *Knowlton,* 78 Wyo. 241, 249-251, 322 Pac. (2d) 141 (1958).

[104] *Greene & Griffin Real Estate & Inv. Co.* v. *Salt River Valley Water Users' Assn.,* 25 Ariz. 354, 359, 360-362, 217 Pac. 945 (1923).

[105] *Wright* v. *Best,* 19 Cal. (2d) 368, 382, 121 Pac. (2d) 702 (1942).

[106] *Bank of Visalia* v. *Smith,* 146 Cal. 398, 400-401, 81 Pac. 542 (1905); *Smith* v. *Hallwood Irr. Co.,* 67 Cal. App. 777, 782, 228 Pac. 373 (1924).

management and distribution of the water back to them according to their respective rights.[107] In such case, a right that was held and exercised under one title before the conveyance is held and exercised under a (formally) different title afterward. The water right remains appurtenant to the land.

The "mere use of water with land for its benefit" does not make the water right appurtenant to such land. A thing is deemed to be appurtenant to land when it is by *right* used with the land for its benefit.[108] The use of water by a trespasser on the land of another does not make the water appurtenant to the land on which it is wrongfully used.[109]

(3) Colorado. "It is recognized in this state that water may or may not be appurtenant to land."[110] Irrigation water rights, even though appurtenant to the lands in connection with which the rights were acquired, cannot be held to be inseparably annexed thereto.[111] On the contrary, the principle is established that the right to use water is a property right which may be sold and transferred separately from the land in connection with which the right was acquired, so long as the rights of others are not injuriously affected thereby.[112]

"The ownership of a prior right to the use of water is essentially different from the ownership of stock in an irrigation company." A stockholder in such a company who makes actual application of water from the company's ditch to a beneficial use may, by means of such use, acquire a prior right thereto. But his title to the stock without such use gives him no title to the water priority. If he has a priority and wishes to transfer it, he can grant it only to someone who will continue to use the water.[113]

(4) Kansas. The water right "is a real property right appurtenant to and severable from the land on or in connection with which the water is used * * *."[114]

(5) Montana. The general rule is that a water right acquired by appropriation and used for a beneficial and necessary purpose in connection with a given tract of land, is an appurtenance thereto.[115] But this is not invariably so. Under some circumstances, the water right may not be appurtenant to the land on which the water is being used.[116] Claims that water rights had become appurtenant to certain lands or other properties were denied by the Montana Supreme Court in several cases.[117]

---

[107] *In re Thomas' Estate,* 147 Cal. 236, 242, 81 Pac. 539 (1905).

[108] *Gause* v. *Pacific Gas & Elec. Co.,* 60 Cal. App. 360, 374, 212 Pac. 922 (1923).

[109] *Alta Land & Water Co.* v. *Hancock,* 85 Cal. 219, 228, 24 Pac. 645 (1890).

[110] *Hastings & Heyden Realty Co.* v. *Gest,* 70 Colo. 278, 283, 201 Pac. 37 (1921).

[111] *Oppenlander* v. *Left Hand Ditch Co.,* 18 Colo. 142, 151, 31 Pac. 854 (1892).

[112] *Strickler* v. *Colorado Springs,* 16 Colo. 61, 70, 72, 26 Pac. 313 (1891).

[113] *Combs* v. *Agricultural Ditch Co.,* 17 Colo. 146, 151-152, 28 Pac. 966 (1892).

[114] Kans. Stat. Ann. § 82a-701(g) (1969).

[115] *Leggat* v. *Carroll,* 30 Mont. 384, 387, 76 Pac. 805 (1904).

[116] *Maclay* v. *Missoula Irr. Dist.,* 90 Mont. 344, 353, 3 Pac. (2d) 286 (1931).

[117] *Smith* v. *Denniff,* 24 Mont. 20, 28-29, 60 Pac. 398 (1900); *Leggat* v. *Carroll,* 30 Mont. 384, 387, 76 Pac. 805 (1904); *Bullerdick* v. *Hermsmeyer,* 32 Mont. 541, 553, 81 Pac.

It appears that in Montana the question as to whether a water right is appurtenant to the land on which the water is used is a question of fact.[118] One who asserts that a water right and ditch are appurtenant to certain lands has the burden of proving that they are appurtenances.[119]

(6) Nevada. The fact that the appropriative right is an appurtenance to the realty in connection with which the use of water is made is recognized by the courts.[120] However, the use of water by a trespasser did not make the water appurtenant to the land. Hence, the trespasser's use of the water thereon did not inure to the benefit of one who subsequently acquired valid title to the land.[121]

In a case arising in Nevada, a Federal court said it to be a generally accepted principle in the arid States that shares of capital stock in a mutual irrigation company—a nonprofit enterprise—are appurtenant to the land of the shareholder irrigated through the system of the company.[122]

The section of the Nevada water rights statute providing that all water used in the State for beneficial purposes shall remain appurtenant to the place of use contains a proviso reading: "That the provisions of this section shall not apply in cases of ditch or canal companies which have appropriated water for diversion and transmission to the lands of private persons at an annual charge."[123] This proviso had the attention of both the Nevada Supreme Court and the United States District Court for Nevada. Although the situation is discussed in more detail later (under "Elements of the Appropriative Right—Sale, Rental, or Distribution of Water—Public Regulation of Rates and Services" and "The Real Appropriator—Commercial Enterprise"), brief references on the matter of appurtenance of water right to land are in order at this point.

In the State case, the supreme court held that any rights that the consumer had acquired by application of the water to beneficial use prior to enactment of the statute were not affected by it. But as to the statute, the court expressed its

---

334 (1905); *Pew* v. *Johnson*, 35 Mont. 173, 180, 88 Pac. 770 (1907); *Hays* v. *Buzard*, 31 Mont. 74, 82, 77 Pac. 423 (1904).

[118] *Yellowstone Valley Co.* v. *Associated Mortgage Investors, Inc.*, 88 Mont. 73, 84, 290 Pac. 255 (1930).

[119] *Smith* v. *Denniff*, 24 Mont. 20, 29, 60 Pac. 398 (1900).

[120] *Rickey Land & Cattle Co.* v. *Miller & Lux*, 152 Fed. 11, 15 (9th Cir. 1907). To be available and effective, a water right for agricultural purposes must be attached to the land and become in a sense appurtenant thereto by actual application of the water: *Prosole* v. *Steamboat Canal Co.*, 37 Nev. 154, 161, 164, 140 Pac. 720, 144 Pac. 744 (1914).

[121] *Smith* v. *Logan*, 18 Nev. 149, 154, 1 Pac. 678 (1883).

[122] *Pacific States Savings & Loan Corp.* v. *Schmitt*, 103 Fed. (2d) 1002, 1004 (9th Cir. 1939).

[123] Nev. Rev. Stat. § 533.040 (Supp. 1969).

view that an agricultural consumer is the appropriator and that the water right attaches to his land.[124] The Federal court suit was brought by the water company to restrain the State Public Service Commission from fixing a certain schedule of rates and charges for water to be supplied by the company. The court viewed the statutory language as recognition of the right to appropriate water for the purpose of distribution and sale, and stated that "The theory that the right vests exclusively in the customer is illogical under a statute which declares that the use of the water is not appurtenant to the land on which he uses it."[125]

(7) New Mexico. The general rule of appurtenance of an appropriative right to the particular land on which the water is applied to beneficial use is recognized in New Mexico.[126] However, the supreme court held that a right to the use of water for raising stock on the public domain, although appurtenant to the possessory right in the range land on which the water is being beneficially used, it is not necessarily appurtenant to any particular part of the range; and it is not transferred to a homestead entryman of a part of such range land, as an appurtenance to the land, by virtue of his entry alone.[127]

An exception to the general rule in New Mexico is provided by statute. It is declared that "all waters appropriated for irrigation purposes, except as otherwise provided by written contract between the owner of the land and the owner of any ditch, reservoir or other works for the storage or conveyance of water, shall be appurtenant to specified lands" owned by the holder of the right to use the water.[128]

(8) South Dakota. The shares of capital stock of a reorganized irrigation company were held, under the circumstances of a case, to be not appurtenant to land of shareholders. The water rights held by the company were located in the pioneer days, long before enactment of the water code, and were not affected by its enactment. These water rights, the court reasoned, became vested in those who actually located them as distinguished from

---

[124] *Prosole* v. *Steamboat Canal Co.*, 37 Nev. 154, 158-166, 140 Pac. 720, 144 Pac. 744 (1914). The issue was whether the company should be enjoined from failing to deliver to a customer the full quantity of water it had been customarily delivering him, so long as he complied with reasonable regulations and paid a reasonable charge.

[125] *Reno Power, Light & Water Co.* v. *Public Serv. Comm'n,* 300 Fed. 645, 647-652 (D. Nev. 1921). The actual holding of the court was that the reasonable value of the water right, so far as it was used and useful in supplying the company's customers, was a part of the total value on which the company was entitled to a fair return.

[126] *Murphy* v. *Kerr,* 296 Fed. 536, 541 (D. N. Mex. 1923); *Carlsbad Irr. Dist.* v. *Ford,* 46 N. Mex. 335, 341, 128 Pac. (2d) 1047 (1942).

[127] *First State Bank of Alamogordo* v. *McNew,* 33 N. Mex. 414, 423-429, 269 Pac. 56 (1928).

[128] N. Mex. Stat. Ann. § 75-1-2 (1968).

users of the water; they never became appurtenant to the lands of the shareholders.[129]

(9) Texas. The appropriative right is an incorporeal hereditament appurtenant to the land for the benefit of which the appropriation was made, and it is therefore a part of the freehold.[130]

(10) Utah. Essential to attachment of the appropriative right as an appurtenance to the land for the use of which the appropriation was made are the facts that (a) the use of the water is beneficial to the land, and (b) it is necessary to the use and enjoyment of such land.[131] It is not the water itself that becomes an appurtenance; it is the right to take and use the water that sustains this relation.[132]

In Utah, the general question of appurtenance of mutual irrigation company stock to land and of the water rights represented by such shares of corporate stock has long been of major importance, owing to the outstanding place of such organizations in the agricultural development and irrigation economy of this State.[133] Whether a water right evidenced by such corporate shares is appurtenant to the land on which the water is used is a question of fact.

The Utah water rights statute contains a provision which, in its present form, provides that water rights shall be transferred by deed in substantially the same manner as real estate, except when they are represented by shares of stock in a corporation, "in which case water shall not be deemed to be appurtenant to the land."[134] The effect of the 1943 enactment,[135] which added the quoted phrase, as construed by the Utah Supreme Court, was to establish a rebuttable presumption that a water right represented by corporate shares did not pass to the grantee as an appurtenance to the land on which used, but that the grantee could overcome such presumption by clear and convincing evidence that the water right in fact was appurtenant and that the grantor intended to transfer it with the land, even though not expressly mentioned in the deed. In other words, the amendment made water rights represented by such stock "presumably not appurtenant."[136]

The foregoing construction was approved in a subsequent Utah case. In this decision, the majority of the court held that a purchaser of land failed to establish by clear and convincing evidence that the water right in controversy (owned by the grantee at the time of the sale but not mentioned in the deed)

---

[129] *Butte County* v. *Lovinger*, 64 S. Dak. 200, 209-213, 266 N. W. 127 (1936).
[130] *Lakeside Irr. Co.* v. *Markham Irr. Co.*, 116 Tex. 65, 74-77, 285 S. W. 593 (1926).
[131] *Thompson* v. *McKinney*, 91 Utah 89, 93-98, 63 Pac. (2d) 1056 (1937).
[132] *Cortella* v. *Salt Lake City*, 93 Utah 236, 247, 72 Pac. (2d) 630 (1937).
[133] Hutchins, Wells A., "Mutual Irrigation Companies in California and Utah," U. S. Farm Credit Admin., Coop. Div. Bull. 8 (1936).
[134] Utah Code Ann. § 73-1-10 (1968).
[135] Utah Laws 1943, ch. 105, § 1.
[136] *Brimm* v. *Cache Valley Banking Co.*, 2 Utah (2d) 93, 99-100, 269 Pac. (2d) 859 (1954).

was appurtenant to the land. It was the majority opinion that proof that water represented by water stock was used on certain land by the owner during the entire period of his ownership is not alone sufficient to rebut the presumption of nonappurtenance.[137]

(11) Washington. A right to the flow of water, considered as appurtenant to the land on which it is used and as real property, is subject to adjudication under the water code.[138]

In a mutual irrigation company the stock certificate represents the water right. A transfer or sale of the certificate may be made separate from the land and will transfer the water right. But where not thus sold or transferred, the question whether the water right is appurtenant to the stockholder's land is generally a question of fact.[139]

Appurtenant and not Generally Severable Without Loss of the Right

Wyoming.—The Wyoming statute provides that rights to the direct use of water shall attach to the land for irrigation, or to other beneficial purposes. In the same section is the declaration that "Water rights for the direct use of the natural unstored flow of any stream cannot be detached from the lands, place or purpose for which they are acquired," except for changes to a preferred use, correction of errors in permits and certificates of appropriation, and various other exceptions.[140]

Prior to enactment of this provision in 1909,[141] it was well established in this State that appurtenant streamflow water rights might be sold separate and apart from the lands.[142] The only limitation was that the change should not injuriously affect the rights of other appropriators.[143]

---

[137] *Hatch* v. *Adams,* 7 Utah (2d) 73, 75-76, 318 Pac. (2d) 633 (1957). Evidence as to whether the grantees had used the water on this land continuously after they acquired it was conflicting. Evidence established that other water was used on the land in question.

[138] *Thompson* v. *Short,* 6 Wash. (2d) 71, 87-88, 106 Pac. (2d) 720 (1940).

[139] *Berg* v. *Yakima Valley Canal Co.,* 83 Wash. 451, 455-456, 145 Pac. 619 (1915). Appurtenant to mill property: *Murray* v. *Briggs,* 29 Wash. 245, 260-261, 69 Pac. 765 (1902).

[140] Wyo. Stat. Ann. § § 41-2 to -8 (1957), 41-9 to -10.2:1 (Supp. 1969).

The exceptions are summarized in chapter 9, note 206. Regarding these and perhaps certain other exceptions, see Trelease, Frank J., and Lee, Dellas W., "Priority and Progress—Case Studies in the Transfer of Water Rights," 1 Land and Water Law Rev. 1 (1966); Trelease, Frank J., "Transfer of Water Rights—Errata and Addenda—Sales For Recreational Purposes And To Districts," 2 Land and Water Law Rev. 321 (1967).

[141] Wyo. Laws 1909, ch. 68.

[142] *Hunziker* v. *Knowlton,* 78 Wyo. 241, 249-251, 322 Pac. (2d) 141 (1958).

[143] *Johnston* v. *Little Horse Creek Irrigating Co.,* 13 Wyo. 208, 226, 228, 79 Pac. 22 (1904).

In addition, the attachment of reservoir rights to land in Wyoming is optional with the reservoir owners and those to whom they grant storage water rights. This provision was added to the statute in 1921.[144] The previous rule, established in 1909,[145] was that no water rights, whether direct flow or storage, could be detached from the land for which acquired, without loss of priority. The primary purpose of making the change, according to the Wyoming Supreme Court, was to permit reservoir rights to be diverted from any particular land, which "was doubtless to enable the waters of the state to be utilized more extensively than would otherwise have been possible."[146] Some discussion of this Wyoming situation with respect to reservoir waters appears in chapter 7 under "Methods of Appropriating Water of Watercourses—Storage Water Appropriation."

Nebraska. An 1895 statute included a provision the extant version of which requires an application for a permit to appropriate water, if for irrigation purposes, to include "a description of the land to be irrigated thereby and the amount thereof . . . ."[147] In 1904 the Nebraska Supreme Court declared that by enacting this statute the State adopted a policy "by which the right to use the water shall not be granted separate from the land to which it is to be applied, and that the right to use the water should attach to the land, and, when the land is sold, be sold with it; for this reason, the statute is explicit in requiring a description of the land to be irrigated, and the amount thereof, to be set forth in the application."[148]

A statute enacted in 1889 provided that one entitled to the use of water "may change the place of diversion if others are not injured by such change and may extend the ditch, flume or aqueduct by which the diversion is made to places beyond that where the first use was made." As amended in 1911, the statute provided that an owner of a ditch, storage reservoir, or other water appropriation device "may change the point of diversion, or the line of any flume, ditch or aqueduct if others are not injured thereby," with approval of the State administrative agency. The extant version is similar

---

[144] Wyo. Laws 1921, ch. 141, Stat. Ann. § 41-37 (1957).

[145] Wyo. Laws 1909, ch. 68.

[146] *Sturgeon* v. *Brooks,* 73 Wyo. 436, 454, 281 Pac. (2d) 675 (1955). See also *Condict* v. *Ryan,* 79 Wyo. 211, 225-230, 333 Pac. (2d) 684 (1958), 335 Pac. (2d) 792 (1959).

[147] Nebr. Laws 1895, ch. 69, Rev. Stat. § 46-233 (1968).

[148] *Farmers' Irr. Dist.* v. *Frank,* 72 Nebr. 136, 138-139, 100 N. W. 286 (1904). The court at the outset mentioned as a feature of such a doctrine "that the right to the use of water should never be separated from the land to which it is to be applied. . . ." 72 Nebr. at 138.

Orders of the Nebraska Department of Water Resources approving petitions to change points of diversion have specifically stated that the right to make such change does not carry with it any right to irrigate lands not entitled to water under the appropriation at the original point of diversion, as was stated in a letter to the author from Dan S. Jones, Jr., Director of the Department, dated September 5, 1963.

in wording although the words "if others are not injured thereby" have been omitted.[149]

A decision of the Nebraska Supreme Court was rendered in 1905 while the 1889 legislative authorization to extend the ditch beyond the first place of use was still in effect. The supreme court held that the statute was merely declaratory of the law governing changes in place of use as it had previously existed, but that the declaration must be construed together with the act of 1895 with the result that such changes were now under State administrative control.[150] Six years later, in 1911, the legislature in amending the 1889 statute expressly added such a requirement regarding State administrative permission. However, in the same amendment it withdrew its express authorization to extend the conduit to new places of use. Conceivably, so far as the matter of changes in locational use is concerned, the present authority to change the *point of diversion* and the *line of a ditch* could be so interpreted as to "take in a lot of territory"—with complete change in places of use, if the State administrator approved. However, why should the legislature adopt what would be a needlessly roundabout and cryptic way of authorizing changes in place of use? The legislature's explicit action in 1911 in withdrawing express authorization to extend the conduit to new places of use is significant. It is reasonable to assume that in consonance therewith, the legislative intent was to authorize desirable changes in conduit line that would *not* involve changes in locational use.

Another statute was enacted in 1895 that pertained to irrigation districts. It included a provision the extant version of which reads: "It is hereby expressly provided that all water distributed for irrigation purposes shall attach to and follow the tract of land to which it is applied . . . ."[151] In a case decided in 1951, the Nebraska Supreme Court observed that "While it is true that prior to the Irrigation Act of 1895 a freedom to change the location of the use apparently existed, no such right now exists except by permission" of the State administrative agency. Such requirement, said the court, does not divest the right; it is a valid exercise of the police power of the State in the regulation of its public waters.[152] The literal language of the quoted opinion may indicate

---

[149] Nebr. Laws 1889, ch. 68, § 5; Laws 1911, S.F. 263. The extant version, Nebr. Rev. Stat. § 46-250 (1968), reads: "The owner of any ditch, storage reservoir, storage capacity, or other device for appropriating water may, upon petition to the Department of Water Resources, and upon its approval, change the point at which the water under any water appropriation of record is diverted from a natural stream or reservoir, *change the line of any flume, ditch, or aqueduct,* or change a storage site; Provided, that no reclamation district or power appropriator may change the established return flow point without the approval of the Department of Water Resources." [Emphasis added.]

[150] *Farmers' & Merchants' Irr. Co.* v. *Gothenburg Water Power & Irr. Co.,* 73 Nebr. 223, 227-228, 102 N.W. 487 (1905).

[151] Nebr. Laws 1895, ch. 70, § 9, p. 275, Rev. Stat. § 46-122 (1968).

[152] *State* v. *Birdwood Irr. Dist.,* 154 Nebr. 52, 62-63, 46 N.W. (2d) 884 (1951). The court apparently was referring to this 1895 act regarding irrigation districts.

acceptance of the rule that the right to change the place of use with the State agency's permission still exists. However, the court went on to say that any such right in the case of canal company service was always qualified by lack of power in the company to deprive landowners of their dedicated use of water without their express consent. The statutory procedure for bringing lands within an irrigation district for the purpose of sharing its appropriation of water—which is the exclusive procedure for so doing—was not followed in this case. Thus, it was held, the outside landowners had acquired no right to the use of the district water, despite any use that they had in fact been making of the water for many years.[153] Moreover, in this opinion the court cited a 1941 opinion by the Federal Circuit Court of Appeals, Eighth Circuit. In that opinion, the court said:

> By act of the Nebraska legislature, all appropriations for irrigation purposes made since 1895 are inseparably appurtenant to specific land, and so follow the land to which the water was intended to be and has been applied.[154] Appropriative rights acquired prior to 1895, however, were not necessarily required to be attached to specific land, and so could, generally speaking, be transferred or assigned for use on other property . . . . But any change in the locational use of previously appropriated waters could, after 1895, only be made "under the permission and subject to the administrative control of the state irrigation authorities."[155]

Unlike the quoted statement from this 1941 Federal case, the Nebraska Supreme Court in its 1951 decision did not expressly limit its quoted language regarding permissible changes in locational use to appropriative rights acquired prior to 1895. But the appropriative right in dispute had in fact been acquired (in 1893) prior to 1895.[156] Moreover, although the statement in the 1951

---

[153] *Id.* at 63.

[154] Citing Nebr. Comp. St. 1929, § 46-109, forerunner of Nebr. Rev. Stat. § 46-122 (1968) which is the extant version of the provision of the act of 1895 regarding irrigation districts described above (Laws 1895, ch. 70, § 9, p. 276).

[155] *United States* v. *Tilley,* 124 Fed. (2d) 850, 856-857 (8th Cir. 1941), certiorari denied, 316 U. S. 691 (1942), citing in the latter regard the 1905 decision of the Nebraska Supreme Court discussed at note 150, *supra.*

[156] *State* v. *Birdwood Irr. Dist.,* 154 Nebr. 52, 54, 46 N. W. (2d) 884 (1951).

In an earlier case, *Farmers' & Merchants' Irr. Co.* v. *Gothenburg Water Power & Irr. Co.,* 73 Nebr. 223, 227-228, 102 N. W. 487 (1905), discussed above at note 150, the court spoke of the "irrigation law of 1895." It appears to have been referring entirely or largely to the 1895 statute mentioned above at note 147 (which was similarly so described in *Farmers' Irr. Dist.* v. *Frank,* 72 Nebr. 136, 138-139, 100 N. W. 286 (1904), *supra* note 148). It perhaps also had in mind this provision of the 1895 act pertaining to irrigation districts. But at any rate, as in the 1951 Nebraska case, the water appropriations in dispute were made prior to 1895. As mentioned above in note 155, this case was cited in the 1941 Federal case which expressly distinguished appropriative rights acquired before 1895. It also was cited, in addition to the 1941 Federal case, in the 1951 Nebraska case.

opinion regarding permissible changes in locational use of appropriated water was woven into the judicial argument, it was not necessary to the actual decision. In the last analysis, the decision rested on the points that the purpose of an irrigation district is to furnish water to lands within its boundaries; that no one can gain a right to use of district waters merely by using them for irrigation purposes for a period of time; that the statutory procedure for bringing outside lands within an irrigation district and its water rights is exclusive; and that in the instant case such procedure had not been followed.

Severability and Conditions of Severance

Absolutely inseparable appurtenance of an appropriative right to a specific tract of land does not appear to be legally practicable. Even should the State law be adamant in providing that such a right shall not be detached from the tract to which it is appurtenant without loss of priority—without which priority the right would be unenforceable as against other appropriators—it is nevertheless subject to loss in several ways. These are chiefly voluntary abandonment, involuntary statutory forfeiture for nonuse, and adverse possession that ripens into prescription. Even though abandonment is voluntary, there is no such thing as abandonment to a particular person or for a consideration. In short, an appropriative right requires constant attention and substantially continuous beneficial use to keep it in good standing and to avoid loss to the owner in some way sanctioned by law.

The right to change the place of use of water under an appropriative right is granted by statute or court decision, or both, in a large majority of the Western States. (See "Exercise of the Appropriative Right," below.) Qualifications and conditions are provided for the exercise of this right; but an appropriator who qualifies may make the change. Hence, although in most instances the appropriative right becomes attached or appurtenant to the initial place of use, the appurtenance is not inseparable when conditions prevail under which a change in the place of use is authorized. As stated earlier in this topic, if all conditions are met, the appropriative right may be detached from one tract of land and transferred to other land, in which event the right becomes appurtenant to the tract to which it is transferred, and without loss of priority.

Most of the western water rights statutes provide procedures under which such a change of place of use, with detachment from the one tract and simultaneous attachment to another designated tract, may be effectuated. All the administrative control statutes require petition to and approval of the State administrative agency before such a change may be made. In reaching his decision, the administrator must take into consideration the reasons advanced by the petitioner, the possible effect of the proposed change on stream water conditions, and any matters of public welfare that may be involved.

An invariable condition of the right to make such a change in place of use, whether or not under the jurisdiction of a State administrative agency, is that no injury shall be inflicted upon holders of other water rights. Those who fear that injury may result may be heard by the administrator—whose decision is subject to judicial review—when the proposed change is under official consideration.

The administration statutes make noninfringement of other rights an express condition of the administrator's decision. In Colorado, where there is no administrative control over this function, the supreme court observed that the right to change the place of use and point of diversion relating to an appropriation of water is an inherent property right, not conferred by the remedial statute. It was said to be preexisting as an incident of ownership, and always enforceable so long as the vested rights of others are not injuriously affected.[157]

Likewise in Montana, with a statute authorizing changes in place of use of water[158] but without procedure for effectuating them, the supreme court has held that "A water right is not an inseparable appurtenance to land in Montana;"[159] and that an appropriator has the right to change the place of use of the water so long as the change does not injuriously affect other appropriators.[160]

Several statutes authorize changes of place of use under a condition comparable to that of Nevada. This includes, as a proviso to a declaration that all water used for beneficial purposes shall remain appurtenant to the place of use, the following:[161]

> That if for any reason it should at any time become impracticable to use water beneficially or economically at the place to which it is appurtenant, the right may be severed from such place of use and simultaneously transferred and become appurtenant to other place or places of use, in the manner provided in this chapter, and not otherwise, without losing priority of right heretofore established; * * *.

In declaring that all water used in New Mexico for irrigation purposes, except as otherwise provided by the statute, shall be considered appurtenant to the land on which it is used, the statute of the State adds that the right to use the same on such land shall never be severed therefrom without the owner's consent. By consent of the owner, however, all or part of the right may be so severed and simultaneously transferred and become appurtenant to other land or for other purposes, without losing priority. The usual

---

[157] *Brighton Ditch Co.* v. *Englewood,* 124 Colo. 366, 372-373, 237 Pac. (2d) 116 (1951).
[158] Mont. Rev. Codes Ann. § 89-803 (1964).
[159] *Kofoed* v. *Bray,* 69 Mont. 78, 84, 220 Pac. 532 (1923).
[160] *Whitcomb* v. *Murphy,* 94 Mont. 562, 565, 23 Pac. (2d) 980 (1933).
[161] Nev. Rev. Stat. § 533.040 (Supp. 1969); Okla. Stat. Ann. tit. 82, § 34 (1970); S. Dak. Comp. Laws Ann. § 46-5-34 (1967).

conditions relating to detriment to existing rights and approval of the State Engineer are included.[162]

The Wyoming statute declaring that water rights for the natural unstored flow of a stream cannot be detached from the lands, place, or purpose for which they are acquired, with various exceptions, is noted above.[163]

Conveyance of Title to Appropriative Right

Sale and Assignment of Water Right

An appropriative water right is "a distinct subject of grant."[164] Early in the development of California water law, it was established that the right to use water by priority of appropriation, "as a substantive and valuable property, * * * may be transferred like other property."[165]

Various limitations upon the exercise of this right of sale and assignment have been disclosed above in connection with the general topic of appurtenance and will be further discussed below. But the basic right of ownership and divestiture of ownership was so well established in the early development of the appropriation doctrine in the West, and so consistently confirmed, as to be axiomatic. In fact, in a case in which certain parties who owned water rights and placer-mining lands covenanted among themselves that none of them should sell his interest in the water rights or make any compromise or settlement with anyone attempting to take possession of them, except with written consent of all the others, the Montana Supreme Court held that such a contract was against public policy.[166]

It is well to emphasize here that the *assignability* of a water right and the *transfer of place of use* are altogether different things. This is true, even though they may be involved in the same transaction. Appurtenance of the right has no bearing upon its assignability if the place of use is not changed; but in a transfer of place of use, appurtenance may be involved.

For example, the owner of an appropriative water right and of the land on or in connection with which the water is being used may sell both land and water right, whether appurtenant or nonappurtenant, to someone else. If the purchaser possesses the qualifications imposed in the particular jurisdiction

---

[162] N. Mex. Stat. Ann. § 75-5-22 (1968).

[163] At note 140.

[164] *Arnett* v. *Linhart,* 21 Colo. 188, 190, 40 Pac. 355 (1895); *Nielson* v. *Newmyer,* 123 Colo. 189, 192-193, 228 Pac. (2d) 456 (1951).

[165] *McDonald* v. *Bear River & Auburn Water & Min. Co.,* 13 Cal. 220, 232-233 (1859). "Under the law of this state as established at the beginning, the water-right which a person gains by diversion from a stream for a beneficial use is a private right, a right subject to ownership and disposition by him, as in the case of other private property. All the decisions recognize it as such," *Thayer* v. *California Development Co.,* 164 Cal. 117, 125, 128 Pac. 21 (1912).

[166] *Ford* v. *Gregson,* 7 Mont. 89, 93-94, 98, 14 Pac. 659 (1887).

upon intending appropriators, he simply replaces the former owner, and there is no change in place of use. And in States that sanction changes in place of use—as most of them do (see, in chapter 9, "Change in Exercise of Water Right")—the original owner, whether or not he sells the original land may, if properly authorized, transfer the use of the water right to other land that he possesses.

On the other hand, the original owner may retain the original land, while selling the water right to someone else who, if properly authorized, changes the place of use to other land of his own possession. One who thus buys an appropriative right separate from the land on or in connection with which it is being exercised, with the intention of moving the water right elsewhere, must comply with whatever formalities are prescribed by the enabling State law for both (1) assignment of the water right and (2) transfer of the place of use. The problem of appurtenance in connection with such a properly authorized and executed transaction is solved by application of a legal device—simultaneous detachment of the water right from one tract of land and transferance of its appurtenance to another tract.

Some Aspects of Conveyance of Appropriative Titles

Conveyance of possessory rights on the public domain.—The earliest transfers of appropriative rights that appeared in western decisions related to possessory rights on the public domain.[167] Such appropriative water rights could be "held, granted, abandoned or lost by the same means as a right of the same character issuing out of lands to which a private title exists."[168] Except as against the Government, a settler in good faith might convey his possessory interest in the land and in the water right thereto, by voluntary surrender to one who takes possession from him; and the transferee would become vested with all the right his predecessor had in the premises.[169]

Conveyance of land on or in connection with which water rights are exercised.—(1) This situation was thus summed up by Weil in 1911:[170]

It is well settled that a water-right *may* pass with land as an appurtenance thereto, or as a parcel thereof, but not *necessarily* so; and whether a water-right passes as an appurtenance involves two questions,

---

[167] See *Stephens* v. *Mansfield,* 11 Cal. 363, 365-366 (1858); *McDonald* v. *Bear River & Auburn Water & Min. Co.,* 13 Cal. 220, 233 (1859).

[168] *Union Water Co.* v. *Crary,* 25 Cal. 504, 509 (1864).

[169] *Hindman* v. *Rizor,* 21 Oreg. 112, 116-118, 27 Pac. 13 (1891); *Low* v. *Rizor,* 25 Oreg. 551, 555-556, 37 Pac. 82 (1894). See also *Brown* v. *Newell,* 12 Idaho 166, 170-173, 85 Pac. 385 (1906); *Osnes Livestock Co.* v. *Warren,* 103 Mont. 284, 303-304, 62 Pac. (2d) 206 (1936); *First State Bank of Alamogordo* v. *McNew,* 33 N. Mex. 414, 423-424, 427-429, 269 Pac. 56 (1928).

[170] Wiel, S.C., "Water Rights in the Western States," 3d ed., vol. 1, § 550 (1911). Mr. Wiel commented extensively on various ramifications of this subject.

viz: (*a*) Whether the water-right is an appurtenance; and (*b*) whether, being such, it was intended to pass. Both of these are questions of fact in each case.

Although, as shown earlier under "Appurtenance of Water Right to Land," the appropriative right is generally—but not invariably—considered to be appurtenant or attached to the place of use, either by statutory declaration or rule of the courts, or both, yet it is not such an inseparable appurtenance that it cannot be alienated from the place of use either voluntarily by the holder of the right or, under certain circumstances, against his will.

Some details of the situation in the West as disclosed by statutes and court decisions follow.

(2) The water right statutes of several States contain provisions concerning the passing of appurtenant water rights with conveyances of the land.[171]

Thus, in Kansas, under one statute, a water right is appurtenant to the place on which established by use of water thereon and it passes with every conveyance of the land whether mentioned in the deed or not, unless expressly excepted therefrom. Under the other law more recently enacted, the water right passes as an appurtenance to the land of use with a conveyance of such land by deed, lease, will, or other voluntary disposal, or by inheritance.

In Idaho: (a) Every water right confirmed under the statute, or by any court decree, shall become appurtenant to and pass with a conveyance of the land for which the right was granted. (b) Irrigation water rights allotted in a statutory adjudication become a part of the land and pass with conveyance thereof.

In North Dakota, any conditional or perfected water appropriation permit for irrigation purposes shall be transferred only with the approval of the State engineer. Any conditional or perfected water appropriation permit may also be assigned, with the approval of the State engineer, to other land owned by the water permit holder. The transfer of title to land in whatever manner shall carry with it all rights to use the appurtenant water for irrigation purposes unless such rights to use water have been severed according to the statute.

Oklahoma and South Dakota provide that: (a) No right to appropriate water for irrigation purposes shall be assigned or the ownership in any way transferred apart from the land to which it is appurtenant except in the manner expressly provided by law. (b) Transfer of title to land "in any manner" shall carry with it all rights to the use of water appurtenant thereto for irrigation purposes. New Mexico conforms to the same pattern as Oklahoma and South

---

[171] Idaho Code Ann. § § 42-220 (1948) and -1402 (Supp. 1969); Kans. Stat. Ann. § § 42-121 (1964) and 82a-701(g) (1969); N. Mex. Stat. Ann. § 75-5-21 (1968); N. Dak. Cent. Code Ann. § 61-04-15 (Supp. 1969); Okla. Stat. Ann. tit. 82, § 27 (1970); S. Dak. Comp. Laws Ann. § 46-5-33 (1967); Utah Code Ann. § 73-1-11 (1968).

Dakota but with two variations, thus: in (a) "water for storage reservoirs" is excepted; and at the end of (b) there is added "unless previously alienated in the manner provided by law."

The Utah statute declares that a right to the use of water appurtenant to land shall pass to the grantee of such land, unless (a) the right or a part of it is reserved by the grantor in express terms in the conveyance, or (b) the water right is separately conveyed.

It is true that these specific statutory sections, other than as stated, contain no exceptions to the flat declaration that an appurtenant water right shall pass with the land in a conveyance thereof. However, all these statutes contain other sections authorizing an appropriator to change the place of use of water under his appropriative right, subject to prescribed conditions, in which case the right ceases to be an appurtenance to the land from which conveyed and becomes simultaneously appurtenant to the new tract. (See, in chapter 9, "Change in Exercise of Water Right.") In other words, the statutory directive that the appurtenant right *shall* pass with conveyance of the land does not propound an inflexible rule. It states a principle of general application, subject to equally authoritative exceptions provided elsewhere in the statute. Thus construed, the provisions are not in hopeless conflict.

(3) Numerous controversies over conveyances of lands on which water rights were exercised have been decided in the western courts. The general principle stated in these statutes has also been acknowledged judicially. "Whoever grants a thing grants by implication that which is necessary to the beneficial use and enjoyment of the thing granted," including water rights.[172] Early in the century, the Nebraska Supreme Court construed the water appropriation statute as having adopted such a policy.[173]

It was said to be the rule that appurtenances to land, including water rights, pass by a deed for the land without being especially mentioned.[174] In a 1959 case, the Washington Supreme Court rejected a contention that water rights

---

[172] *Frank* v. *Hicks,* 4 Wyo. 502, 526, 35 Pac. 475 (1894). Where water has been appropriated for use on certain land, and the land could not be used advantageously without it, the water right was an adjunct to the land and passed in a conveyance as appurtenant to the land: *Crooker* v. *Benton,* 93 Cal. 365, 369, 28 Pac. 953 (1892). "In the first place, it is well established that a water right is an appurtenance to the land on which it has been used and will pass by conveyance of the land." *Russell* v. *Irish,* 20 Idaho 194, 198, 118 Pac. 501 (1911).

[173] By such policy, "the right to use the water shall not be granted separate from the land to which it is to be applied, and that the right to use the water should attach to the land, and, when the land is sold, be sold with it." *Farmers' Irr. Dist.* v. *Frank,* 72 Nebr. 136, 138-139, 100 N. W. 286 (1904).

[174] *Hogan* v. *Thrasher,* 72 Mont. 318, 332, 233 Pac. 607 (1925); "Without even a mention thereof," *Day* v. *Buckeye Water Conservation & Drainage Dist.,* 28 Ariz. 466, 478, 237 Pac. 636 (1925); *Coventon* v. *Seufert,* 23 Oreg. 548, 553-554, 32 Pac. 508 (1893).

were not acquired with a purchase of property "because water rights were not specifically mentioned in certain deeds."[175]

The Utah Supreme Court approved the statutory rule of that State that a deed in statutory form, *without reservation of water,* conveys whatever appurtenant rights the grantor has to the water used on the land.[176] Other courts that approve the general rule also adopt the proviso that the conveyance will carry the rights appurtenant to the land unless expressly reserved from the grant.[177] Another recognized exception is separate conveyance of the appurtenant water right away from the land on which the water is used.[178]

Likewise, where questions as to the intent of the parties have arisen, courts have held that the intent of the parties, at least where lawfully expressed, must control the question of passing title to an appurtenant water right in a conveyance of the land.[179] The above quotation from Wiel makes this point.[180]

Where a water right intended to be conveyed with land is so stated in the deed in express terms, the grantee takes that only which is expressly conveyed, and does not take any additional rights by implication.[181] But in absence of language indicating a different intention on the part of the grantor, everything essential to the beneficial use and enjoyment of the property conveyed is to be considered as passing by the conveyance.[182]

When the deed conveying title to land does not specify the particular appurtenant water right alleged to have been conveyed with the land, or to what extent the use of water was appurtenant to it, extrinsic evidence must be resorted to in order to establish the fact.[183]

---

[175] *Drake* v. *Smith,* 54 Wash. (2d) 57, 61, 337 Pac. (2d) 1059 (1959). "A water right is an interest in real property appurtenant to the land and passes to the grantee when the land is conveyed."

[176] *Thompson* v. *McKinney,* 91 Utah 89, 92-93, 63 Pac. (2d) 1056 (1937); *Anderson* v. *Hamson,* 50 Utah 151, 153, 167 Pac. 254 (1917). Utah Code Ann. § 73-1-11 (1968) provides that a right to the use of water appurtenant to land shall pass to the grantee of the land; but any such right or a part thereof may be reserved by the grantor in express terms in the conveyance, or it may be separately conveyed.

[177] *Hogan* v. *Thrasher,* 72 Mont. 318, 332, 233 Pac. 607 (1925); *Russell* v. *Irish,* 20 Idaho 194, 198-199, 118 Pac. 501 (1911).

[178] *Frank* v. *Hicks,* 4 Wyo. 502, 528-529, 35 Pac. 475 (1894). This case was decided before the Wyoming Legislature changed the rule with respect to detachment of direct-flow rights from the land to which appurtenant. However, the rule as stated is applicable in most States. See, for example, Utah Code Ann. § 73-1-11 (1968).

[179] *Lensing* v. *Day & Hansen Security Co.,* 67 Mont. 382, 384, 215 Pac. 999 (1923); *Stinson* v. *Murray,* 8 Alaska 167, 174 (1930).

[180] Applied in *Dill* v. *Killip,* 174 Oreg. 94, 98, 147 Pac. (2d) 896 (1944).

[181] *Kofoed* v. *Bray,* 69 Mont. 78, 84, 220 Pac. 532 (1923).

[182] *Yellowstone Valley Co.* v. *Associated Mortgage Investors, Inc.,* 88 Mont. 73, 84, 290 Pac. 255 (1930).

[183] *Bullerdick* v. *Hermsmeyer,* 32 Mont. 541, 550, 81 Pac. 334 (1905).

In early Wyoming cases, it was held with respect to direct-flow rights that a conveyance of the realty, by the owner of the land and water right, carried with it the ditch and water right without specifically mentioning the latter.[184] This rule was referred to with approval and was applied in recent cases in which *storage* water rights were in litigation. As noted earlier under "Appurtenance of Water Rights to Land—Appurtenant and not Generally Severable Without Loss of the Right," reservoir rights in Wyoming, as distinguished from direct-flow rights, do not attach to land except by conveyance executed by the reservoir owner. When reservoir rights are so established, as contemplated by the statute,[185] they pass as appurtenances with conveyance of the land, under the general rule governing such appurtenances.[186]

The Idaho Supreme Court rendered several decisions involving conveyance of parts of tracts to which water rights were appurtenant. In our opinion, in which a deed to 20 acres out of a 160-acre tract also conveyed a right to 6.5 inches out of a decreed right of 50 inches for the entire quarter-section, and in which the evidence showed irrigation of the 20-acre parcel, this water-right conveyance was approved, the court stating that: "It is certainly neither unlawful, nor unusual, for the owner of a parcel of land, with an appurtenant water right, to convey a part of the land together with a portion of the appurtenant water right."[187] Elsewhere, a landowner might convey part of his land together with part of an appurtenant water right, and likewise might include in or omit from the lien of the mortgage all or any part of the water rights appurtenant to the land mortgaged.[188] And "A division of a tract of land to which water is appurtenant, without segregating or reserving the water right, works a division of such water right in proportion as the land is divided."[189]

It has been held in California that unless a water right becomes inseparably appurtenant to the whole of a parcel, the owner can convey a part of the land with a reservation of the right for use on the land retained. Here, a conveyance of 62 acres of a 118-acre parcel, with an express reservation in the deed of the entire water right, operated to reserve validly the entire right for use on the retained 56 acres.[190]

---

[184] *Frank* v. *Hicks*, 4 Wyo. 502, 526, 531, 35 Pac. 475 (1894); *McPhail* v. *Forney*, 4 Wyo. 556, 560, 35 Pac. 773 (1894).

[185] Wyo. Stat. Ann. § 41-37 (1957).

[186] *Sturgeon* v. *Brooks*, 73 Wyo. 436, 455-456, 281 Pac. (2d) 675 (1955); *Condict* v. *Ryan*, 79 Wyo. 211, 227-230, 333 Pac. (2d) 684 (1958).

[187] *Harvey* v. *Deseret Sheep Co.*, 40 Idaho 450, 453, 234 Pac. 146 (1925).

[188] *Harris* v. *Chapman*, 51 Idaho 283, 294-295, 5 Pac. (2d) 733 (1931).

[189] *Hunt* v. *Bremer*, 47 Idaho 490, 493, 276 Pac. 964 (1929).

[190] *Locke* v. *Yorba Irr. Co.*, 35 Cal. (2d) 205, 209-211, 217 Pac. (2d) 425 (1950). The court stated that if the grantor had conveyed the land without mention of the water rights, those rights would have passed with the conveyance.

Questions of conveyance of land on which water had been used by trespassers were involved in a few cases. The Nevada Supreme Court held that the use of water on land by a trespasser did not make the water appurtenant to the land, hence such use did not inure to the benefit of one who subsequently acquired valid title to the land.[191] Later, the California Supreme Court conceded the proposition, based on the Nevada decision, that the use of water by a trespasser does not make the water appurtenant to the land on which it is wrongfully used. "But," said the California court, "it does not follow from this that the use of water upon land to which it is already appurtenant, by one who is a trespasser thereon, will give him such a right in the water as that he may thereafter divert it from the land, or, upon being ejected therefrom, convey to a stranger a legal title in the water or in the use thereof."[192]

Under the circumstances of two cases, on the other hand, the Oregon Supreme Court took a different view. In the first decision, the court sustained the validity of an appropriation of water initiated by a trespasser on private land, the trespasser having conveyed his interest subsequently to the lawful lessee thereof. Later the court upheld a sale of improvements and water rights initiated by squatters on State land, the sale being made to one who later acquired legal title to the land.[193]

.A discussion of initiation of appropriative rights in trespass appears in chapter 7 "The Land Factor in Appropriating Water."

Conveyance of land together with appurtenances.—It is a general rule, as expressed in a fairly early California water case, that a thing used by right with land for its benefit, such as a water right, is an appurtenance thereto and passes with the land in a conveyance of the land together with its appurtenances.[194] Such a conveyance of land "with appurtenances" operates without any further express grant of a water right to convey to the grantee a water right appropriated, owned, and used by the grantor and necessary for the proper irrigation of the land granted.[195] A Texas court of civil appeals, in holding to the same effect, cautioned that: "The word 'appurtenances' in a deed covers only what is legally appurtenant to the land described. It does not, without particular mention, convey any rights which do not naturally and necessarily belong to the thing granted in the hands of the grantor."[196]

---

[191] *Smith* v. *Logan*, 18 Nev. 149, 154, 1 Pac. 678 (1883).

[192] *Alta Land & Water Co.* v. *Hancock*, 85 Cal. 219, 228-229, 24 Pac. 645 (1890).

[193] *Seaweard* v. *Pacific Livestock Co.*, 49 Oreg. 157, 161-163, 88 Pac. 963 (1907); *Campbell* v. *Walker*, 137 Oreg. 375, 385, 2 Pac. (2d) 912 (1931).

[194] *Farmer* v. *Ukiah Water Co.*, 56 Cal. 11, 14-15 (1880).

[195] *Tucker* v. *Jones*, 8 Mont. 225, 231-232, 19 Pac. 571 (1888); *Beisell* v. *Wood*, 182 Oreg. 66, 72-73, 185 Pac. (2d) 570 (1947).

[196] *Hunstock* v. *Limburger*, 115 S. W. 327, 329 (Tex. Civ. App. 1909, error refused.).

But use of the word "appurtenances" is not in all cases necessary. An easement that is necessary for the reasonable enjoyment of the land may pass in a conveyance of the land without mention of the water right and without any reference thereto.[197] In several cases, the rule has been stated that where the right to the use of water exists in favor of land conveyed by deed, and without which the land would be valueless or of much less value, and which constituted perhaps the principal inducement for the purchase, the water right will pass by deed without use of the word "appurtenances." This is based on the maxim of the law that "whoever grants a thing is supposed also tacitly to grant that without which the grant would be of no avail."[198] This includes water rights.

On the other hand, as stated under the immediately preceding subtopic, the intent of the parties if clearly expressed, or determined, is held in various cases to control the question of passing of title to an appurtenant water right. So far as a positive intention in use of the term "appurtenances" is concerned, "A water right which is used in irrigating lands may pass as a grant of the lands themselves, under the word 'appurtenances', if such was the intention of the grantor, and of this intention there is not the shadow of a doubt in this case."[199] And as to a negative intent, a deed of land *together with the appurtenances* would carry with it the water right appurtenant to the land at the time of conveyance, unless specifically reserved in the deed "or it could be clearly shown that it was known to both parties that the water right was not intended to be conveyed."[200]

When a deed to land with its appurtenances describes the water rights that are conveyed in connection with the land, there can be no implication that other water rights not so described were intended by the parties to be included by reason of the appurtenances clause.[201]

Reservation of water right in conveyance of land. —In various jurisdictions there is express recognition of the rule that a grantor of land to which a water right is appurtenant—unless the right has become inseparably attached to the

---

[197] *Stanislaus Water Co.* v. *Bachman*, 152 Cal. 716, 724, 93 Pac. 858 (1908).

[198] *Simmons* v. *Winters*, 21 Oreg. 35, 44, 27 Pac. 7 (1891). "Whoever grants a thing grants by implication that which is necessary to the beneficial use and enjoyment of the thing granted." *Frank* v. *Hicks*, 4 Wyo. 502, 526, 35 Pac. 475 (1894).

[199] *King* v. *Ackroyd*, 28 Colo. 488, 494, 66 Pac. 906 (1901).

[200] *Russell* v. *Irish*, 20 Idaho 194, 198-199, 118 Pac. 501 (1911).

[201] *Paddock* v. *Clark*, 22 Idaho 498, 510, 126 Pac. 1053 (1912). It was held subsequently, by reference to *Paddock* v. *Clark,* that the general appurtenances clause in each of the deeds in litigation did not enlarge the specific water right described therein: *Harris* v. *Chapman*, 51 Idaho 283, 295, 5 Pac. (2d) 733 (1931). Where, in conveyance of land, a part only of the appurtenant water right is described and specified as being conveyed therewith, such specific designation destroys any presumption of intention to convey the remainder: *Nielson* v. *Newmyer*, 123 Colo. 189, 228 Pac. (2d) 456, 458-459 (1951).

whole of a parcel—may convey the land with an express reservation of the water right from the conveyance.[202]

Reservation of the appurtenant water right in express terms in conveyances of the land involved is recognized in the water rights statutes of Kansas and Utah.[203] The New Mexico statute provides that transfer of title to land in any manner whatsoever shall carry with it all rights to the use of water appurtenant thereto for irrigation purposes, "unless previously alienated in the manner provided by law."[204]

Conveyance of water right separate and apart from the land.—"The owner of land with an appurtenant water right may, by appropriate conveyance, convey the land to one person and the water right to another."[205] In such case, the right becomes appurtenant to the land to which transferred.[206] "It is settled beyond dispute that a water right may be sold and transferred and its place of use changed, when such change does not injure the rights of others."[207] And more recently, as above noted, the Colorado Supreme Court reaffirmed the principles that (a) a water right is a property right, separate and apart from the land on which it is used; (b) the land for which the water was appropriated or on which it has been used may be conveyed or held without the water; and (c) the water may be conveyed or held without the land.[208]

Of course, in the States that prescribe statutory procedures for transferring the place of use of water, as most of them do, conveyances apart from the land would be ineffective without conformance to the water transfer statute. These statutes usually require State administrative approval, which is conditioned, on avoidance of injury to other water rights. And even if statutory formalities are not prescribed, no change will be sanctioned by the courts if material injury to others results or is threatened.

In Utah, where the water rights statute provides that an appurtenant right to the use of water, or any part thereof, may be separately conveyed from the

---

[202] *Locke* v. *Yorba Irr. Co.*, 35 Cal. (2d) 205, 209-211, 217 Pac. (2d) 425 (1950); *Harris* v. *Chapman*, 51 Idaho 283, 294-295, 5 Pac. (2d) 733 (1931); *Kofoed* v. *Bray*, 69 Mont. 78, 84, 220 Pac. 532 (1923). The Colorado Supreme Court observed in 1951 that land for which water was appropriated or on which it has been used may be conveyed or held without the water, and the water may be conveyed or held without the land; or any part of the land may be conveyed together with any part of the water right and the remainder be retained: *Nielson* v. *Newmyer*, 123 Colo. 189, 228 Pac. (2d) 456, 458 (1951).

[203] Kans. Stat. Ann. § 42-121 (1964); Utah Code Ann. § 73-1-11 (1968).

[204] N. Mex. Stat. Ann. § 75-5-21 (1968).

[205] *Yellowstone Valley Co.* v. *Associated Mortgage Investors, Inc.*, 88 Mont. 73, 84, 290 Pac. 255 (1930).

[206] *In re Robinson*, 61 Idaho 462, 469, 103 Pac. (2d) 693 (1940).

[207] *Haney* v. *Neace-Stark Co.*, 109 Oreg. 93, 116, 216 Pac. 757 (1923).

[208] *Nielson* v. *Newmyer*, 123 Colo. 189, 228 Pac. (2d) 456, 458 (1951).

land,[209] the supreme court says that this has long been the law in this jurisdiction.[210] Statutes of several States provide that no right to appropriate water for irrigation purposes shall be transferred apart from the land to which appurtenant "except in the manner specially provided by law."[211] Statutes of these States—and of most others in the West—provide procedure for making changes in place of use, with transfers of appropriative rights from one tract to another, subject to prescribed conditions. (See, in chapter 9, "Change in Exercise of Water Right.")

There are exceptions to the general situation. A number of relevant Wyoming and Nebraska statutes and cases in this regard have been discussed earlier under "Appurtenance of Water Rights to Land."[212] In Wyoming, originally, appurtenant streamflow water rights might be sold separate and apart from the lands, provided the change did not injuriously affect others.[213] Later Wyoming statutes provide, with certain exceptions, that such rights for "the direct use of the natural unstored flow of any stream cannot be detached from the lands, place or purpose for which they are acquired," but that reservoir water rights may be sold or leased unless attached to particular lands by conveyances from the reservoir owners to the water users.[214]

Conveyance of water right represented by shares in mutual irrigation corporation.—(1) Nature of the mutual company. Mutual or cooperative irrigation companies are private associations of irrigation farmers, voluntarily organized for the purpose of providing irrigation water at cost, primarily for use on the farms of their members, and usually for domestic purposes also. The larger ones are incorporated. Each State has a general corporation law, which is adapted to the functioning of irrigation enterprises and, in the West, is widely used for their incorporation. (See the discussions of water-supply enterprises under "Elements of the Appropriative Right—Sale, Rental, or Distribution of Water.")

The capital stock of a mutual irrigation corporation, as is the case with private corporations generally, represents ownership of the corporate assets. Hence, an irrigation water user who owns shares of stock in the mutual company that serves his land has an undivided ownership interest in the

---

[209] Utah Code Ann. § 73-1-11 (1968).

[210] *Salt Lake City* v. *McFarland*, 1 Utah (2d) 257, 260-261, 265 Pac. (2d) 626 (1954).

[211] Okla. Stat. Ann. tit. 82, § 27 (1970); S. Dak. Comp. Laws Ann. § 46-5-33 (1967); water for storage reservoirs excepted, N. Mex. Stat. Ann. § 75-5-21 (1968); in the manner provided in this chapter and not otherwise, Nev. Rev. Stat. § 533.040 (Supp. 1969); as provided in this section, N. Dak. Cent. Code Ann. § 61-04-15 (Supp. 1969).

[212] See thereunder "Appurtenant and not Generally Severable Without Loss of the Right."

[213] *Hunziker* v. *Knowlton*, 78 Wyo. 241, 249-251, 322 Pac. (2d) 141 (1958); *Johnston* v. *Little Horse Creek Irrigating Co.*, 13 Wyo. 208, 226, 228, 79 Pac. 22 (1904).

[214] Wyo. Stat. Ann. § § 41-2 and -37 (1957).

irrigation system from which his supply of water is obtained.[215] But this share of the capital stock also represents the right to service of water from the company's system. A shareholder pays for this service in the form of stock assessments or toll charges, or both. Dividends on the capital stock are paid to the shareholders in water service, rather than in money.[216]

Some discussion of appurtenance of water rights to land appears under the immediately preceding title. Questions in the area of mutual company water rights vis-à-vis shares of capital stock have been litigated in a considerable number of cases in the Western States, many of which involve organizational and operation matters. Some points related to the instant subtopic may be briefly noted.

(2) General observations. Title to water rights exercised by a mutual company may be vested in the irrigation organization or in individual shareholders, depending upon State law or upon the action taken in acquiring the rights. If the mutual company makes the appropriation in its own name, it of course holds the formal title. If farmers who hold individual rights organize a company and transfer their rights to it, again the company holds formal title. Or the farmers may organize the company without making any transfer of their rights. As a rule, mutual company shareholders are considered holders of the water rights, or at least as the beneficial owners.

Shares of stock of a mutual company may or may not be attached to specific tracts of land. Attachment to land may result either by way of "location" on specific tracts—resulting from contract between company and shareholders evidenced by articles of incorporation, bylaws, and stock certificates—or by representing the right to receive water considered appurtenant to such tracts. If not attached to specific tracts, they are known as "floating" shares. These floating shares may pass freely from one holder to another and may be used for irrigation of any tract that can be served from the irrigation system as normally operated. Restrictions are sometimes imposed by the management upon transfer of water from one lateral to another, based upon capacities and operation requirements. This is a matter of expedience in

---

[215] The stock certificate in a mutual irrigation company "is really a certificate showing an undivided part ownership in a certain water supply." *Genola* v. *Santaquin,* 96 Utah 88, 101-102, 80 Pac. (2d) 930 (1938).

[216] For detailed studies of the organization, financing, and operation of these enterprises including specifically matters relating to shares of capital stock, see Hutchins, Wells A., Selby, H.E., and Voelker, Stanley W., "Irrigation-Enterprise Organizations," U. S. Dept. Agr. Cir. 934 (1953); Hutchins, Wells A.: "Mutual Irrigation Companies in California and Utah," U. S. Farm Credit Admin., Coop. Div. Bul. 8 (1936), and "Mutual Irrigation Companies," U. S. Dept. Agr. Tech. Bul. 82 (1929). For comment relating particularly to legal features, see Bennett, J. S., "Mutual Water Companies in California," 2 Southwestern Law Rev. 12 (1917); Wiel, S. C., "Water Rights in the Western States," 3d ed., vol. 2, §§ 1266-1271 (1911); Kinney, C. S., "A Treatise on the Law of Irrigation and Water Rights," 2d ed., vol. 3, §§ 1449-1489 (1912).

operation and maintenance, and within such limitations the shares are freely transferable.

Appurtenance of water right, which is a legal matter, then, is to be distinguished from appurtenance of mutual-company stock to land, which is a contractual matter between the company and its stockholders. In practice, the two terms often amount to the same thing. The water rights under which a mutual company operates may be appurtenant to the individual parcels of land served by the company. This might result, for example, from operation of State water law, as in Arizona (see below); or from original appurtenance of water rights to lands of individual neighboring farmers who later organized a company for better service of their pooled water supplies; or from action of the company in attaching its shares to specifically designated tracts of land. In any of these cases, the water right becomes an appurtenance to the individual tract of land in connection with which it is exercised, and both water right and stock shares pass with conveyance of the land. If changes of place of use of water are permitted by law or by company policy, the water right and the stock which represents it may be transferred to other land.

On the other hand, the water rights may be appurtenant to the general service area of the company by reason of its appropriating water for the area as a whole, and the company may not take action in "locating" its shares on specific parcels. In such case, within the limits of transferability set by operational needs, any farmer may transfer his floating stock and the right to water service to any other part of the service area. The only attachment to land that is involved is a temporary one, necessarily recorded on the water delivery schedules of the company superintendent for operational purposes only. And the only appurtenance of water right is to the general service area.

(3) Some litigated examples. Water rights in Arizona belong to the landowner. The Salt River Valley Water Users' Association—one of the largest mutual irrigation companies in the nation—performed the function of furnishing water to lands to which the shares "and the rights and interests represented thereby are appurtenant," not as owner of the irrigation water, "because it cannot and does not *own* the water," but as a carrier for its shareholders.[217] In another case, this water users' association was adjudged to

---

[217] *Adams* v. *Salt River Valley Water Users' Assn.*, 53 Ariz. 374, 382-383, 89 Pac. (2d) 1060 (1939). There is a clear distinction between the water works properties of an unincorporated association held in common by the members, and the right of appropriation possessed by each member by virtue of landownership: *Biggs* v. *Utah Irrigating Ditch Co.*, 7 Ariz. 331, 345, 64 Pac. 494 (1901). A water user who owned less than the average number of shares per acre was entitled to have served to him his adjudicated water supply on payment of the same reasonable rate charged all other appropriators served by the company canal, "regardless of whether or not he did or did not own a single share of stock of the company," *Olsen* v. *Union Canal & Irr. Co.*, 58 Ariz. 306, 317-318, 119 Pac. (2d) 569 (1941); *Whiting* v. *Lyman Water Co.*, 59 Ariz. 121, 123-124, 458, 459-460, 124 Pac. (2d) 316, 129 Pac. (2d) 995 (1942).

have the right to provide in its articles of incorporation that shares of capital stock, which merely evidence the right to a certain quantity of water, should be inseparably appurtenant to the lands of the shareholders. The lien for a stock assessment is superior to a mortgage lien given and recorded prior to the levy of assessment.[218]

The Colorado Supreme Court has viewed neither the canal company alone nor the water users alone as appropriators in the strict sense of the term. The result of their combined acts of diverting the water and applying it to a beneficial use is to constitute a completed appropriation.[219] The cited case involved the question of inclusion of value of water rights in the rate base of a commercial company; but in cases dealing with mutual companies the courts likewise insist that both diversion and application of the water to beneficial use within a reasonable time are necessary to a valid appropriation, so that completion requires performance on the part of the water users.

In pointing out, in an early Colorado case, the essential differences between prior right to the use of water and ownership of stock in an irrigation company, the supreme court stated that "A stockholder in an irrigating company who makes an actual application of water from the company's ditch to beneficial use may, by means of such use, acquire a prior right thereto; but his title to the stock without such use gives him no title to the priority. He may transfer his stock to whom he will; but he can only transfer his priority to some one who will continue to use the water."[220]

Another view—and a logical one—is that a mutual corporation is simply the agent of the stockholder-appropriators to carry their water to where they may make the beneficial use.[221] "It would seem to be immaterial at what stage of the proceedings the water users, or real appropriators, employed or organized a corporation as an instrumentality in constructing a ditch as a means of conveying to their lands the water which they were in this manner attempting to appropriate, and to which they afterwards secured a complete right."[222] If the group begin as independent appropriators and subsequently exercise their water rights through a mutual company ditch, their water rights remain even though a community ditch is substituted for their original means of diversion.[223] "Water rights are pooled in a mutual company for convenience of operation and more efficient distribution, and perhaps far more convenient

---

[218] *Green & Griffin Real Estate & Investment Co.* v. *Salt River Valley Water Users' Assn.*, 25 Ariz. 354, 359-362, 217 Pac. 945 (1923).

[219] *Jefferson County* v. *Rocky Mountain Water Co.*, 102 Colo. 351, 356, 361, 79 Pac. (2d) 373 (1938).

[220] *Combs* v. *Agricultural Ditch Co.*, 17 Colo. 146, 150-152, 28 Pac. 966 (1892).

[221] *In re Walla Walla River*, 141 Oreg. 492, 498, 16 Pac. (2d) 939 (1932); *Eldredge* v. *Mill Ditch Co.*, 90 Oreg. 590, 596, 177 Pac. 939 (1919).

[222] *In re Silvies River*, 115 Oreg. 27, 100-103, 237 Pac. 322 (1925).

[223] Compare *Oppenlander* v. *Left Hand Ditch Co.*, 18 Colo. 142, 147-148, 31 Pac. 854 (1892).

transfer." The stock certificate embraces the right to call for the holder's undivided part of the water supply according to the method of distribution.[224]

The California Supreme Court thus expressed its conclusions as to the relationship of capital stock to water rights of mutual companies holding rights of appropriation of water of the Kaweah River system:[225]

> The capital stock of the foregoing corporations is transferable in the ordinary manner provided by law, and the owners thereof are the equitable owners of that proportion of the properties of each of such corporations which their respective number of the shares of stock thereof bear to the entire subscribed capital stock of the corporation, and as such equitable owners of the properties of the corporation are also equitably entitled to the proportionate distribution of such waters as such corporation acquires by appropriation or otherwise for the various uses for which such waters are acquired. Such stockholders are in that sense and to that extent, but to none other, owners of the water and water rights which the corporation possesses, and over the distribution of which it exercises under general laws and under its particular by-laws full and exclusive control.* * *

The stockholders in irrigation corporations of this character, said the court, have a definite right to their proportion of the distribution of such water when so acquired. But no stockholder possesses a legal right to take the quantity of water to which he is entitled by any means other than those supplied by the corporation itself in the exercise of its control over the distribution of such water as is covered by its appropriation, and as is receivable in the quantities and at the points of intake designated in the acquisition of its appropriative rights. It was held that a district that acquired stock in these corporations had no authority to go higher up the river above the companies' regular points of intake and divert its proportion of the aggregate water supply up there.

In the majority of western jurisdictions, as heretofore noted, appurtenance of a water right to land is a question of fact, and whether it passes with a conveyance of the land involves questions of both fact and intent of the parties. This appears to be the general rule as well with respect to water rights represented by shares of capital stock in a mutual irrigation company.[226] Under certain circumstances, a sale and transfer of the certificate may be made apart from the land for use on other land and will operate to transfer the water right thereto. But if not thus sold or transferred, the water rights and the shares pass as appurtenances with conveyance of the land.[227]

---

[224] *Genola* v. *Santaquin*, 96 Utah 88, 101-102, 80 Pac. (2d) 930 (1938).

[225] *Consolidated People's Ditch Co.* v. *Foothill Ditch Co.*, 205 Cal. 54, 62-64, 269 Pac. 915 (1928).

[226] *Berg* v. *Yakima Valley Canal Co.*, 83 Wash. 451, 455-456, 145 Pac. 619 (1915).

[227] *Pacific States Savings & Loan Corp.* v. *Schmitt*, 103 Fed. (2d) 1002, 1004-1005 (9th Cir. 1939); *Berg* v. *Yakima Valley Canal Co.*, 83 Wash. 451, 455-456, 145 Pac. 619 (1915). The "mere exchange of one muniment of title to the water right for another [deed for stock] cannot be deemed a severance thereof from the land to which it was

Under the then prevailing water laws and the circumstances of the case cited below, it was held in South Dakota that: the water rights to which a mutual company succeeded vested in the original locators of the water rights and not in those who used the water; the shares of stock and water rights never became appurtenant to the irrigated land; and the shares and water rights were not included in a mortgage of the land.[228]

The Utah water rights statute provides that water rights shall be transferred by deed "in substantially the same manner as real estate, except when they are represented by shares of stock in a corporation, in which case water shall not be deemed to be appurtenant to the land * * *."[229] The effect of this statute, the supreme court held, was to establish a *rebuttable* presumption that a water right represented by corporate shares did not pass to the grantee as an appurtenance to the land on which the water was used.[230]

Mortgage of water right.—It is recognized in various decisions that a water right, being an interest in realty subject to alienation by the holder of the title, may be mortgaged to the same extent as other interests in real property.[231] The practice of including the water rights in mortgages of irrigated lands and irrigation company systems is common. Such lands would be reduced in value and in many cases would have none, if deprived of the right to the use of water. An irrigation system without water rights would have little or no value for any purpose.[232]

A water right that is appurtenant to land, then, is subject to any mortgage of such land.[233] But, just as a landowner may convey part of his land together with part of an appurtenant water right, he may include in or omit from the lien of a mortgage all or any part of the water rights appurtenant to the land

---

concededly appurtenant." *Woodstoone Marble & Tile Co.* v. *Dunsmore Canyon Water Co.*, 47 Cal. App. 72, 76-77, 190 Pac. 213 (1920).

[228] *Butte County* v. *Lovinger*, 64 S. Dak. 200, 209-212, 266 N. W. 127 (1936).

[229] Utah Code Ann. § 73-1-10 (1968).

[230] *Hatch* v. *Adams,* 7 Utah (2d) 73, 75, 318 Pac. (2d) 633 (1957); *Brimm* v. *Cache Valley Banking Co.,* 2 Utah (2d) 93, 99-100, 269 Pac. (2d) 859 (1954).

[231] The Kansas water rights statute provides that a water right passes as an appurtenance with a conveyance of the land by voluntary disposal, including "mortgage." Kans. Stat. Ann. § 82a-701(g) (1969).

[232] In a study published in 1936, this author discussed the course which the creditor of a mutual irrigation company might pursue in realizing on the value of water rights on foreclosure of a mortgage of the company's physical assets and water rights, and the uncertainty as to whether in at least some jurisdictions the water may be diverted away from the service area by a foreclosing creditor in view of the beneficial interest which the former stockholders have in the water rights. Hutchins, Wells A., "Mutual Irrigation Companies in California and Utah," Farm Credit Admin. Coop. Bull. 8 at pp. 87-91 and 136-138 (1936). See the view of the Idaho Supreme Court on this as expressed in *Hobbs* v. *Twin Falls Canal Co.,* 24 Idaho 380, 393, 133 Pac. 899 (1913).

[233] *Reconstruction Finance Corp.* v. *Schmitt,* 20 Fed. Supp. 816, 820 (D. Nev. 1937).

mortgaged.[234] A mortgage of the land with the appurtenances covers the incorporeal hereditaments annexed to the realty, and also such physical property, or rights to or in connection with them, as are used with and for the benefit of the land and are reasonably necessary for its proper enjoyment. Unless expressly reserved, the appurtenant water rights pass with the mortgage conveyance.[235]

The California Supreme Court went a step farther in holding that as an appropriative right is an incident of the land and will pass as such by a conveyance thereof, without express mention and without any reference thereto such as use of the word "appurtenances," therefore: "A conveyance of land upon a foreclosure sale must, of necessity, at least as between the parties to the mortgage, carry with it a water-right appurtenant to the land acquired and used by the mortgagor for the benefit of the land, *although obtained after the execution of the mortgage and before the sale on foreclosure.*" [Emphasis supplied.][236]

Formalities of conveyance.—(1) The general rule. As a water right is real estate, and as any interest in it therefore is perforce an interest in real estate, the water right cannot generally be transferred to another except by a written conveyance such as would convey the title to real property.[237] A conveyance or an agreement to convey such an interest is within the statute of frauds and hence must be in writing.[238]

A Kansas statute provides that water rights (or shares in irrigation companies) may be the subject of separate transfers by deeds executed and recorded as conveyances of real estate, subject to the laws relating to the registration and recording of conveyances affecting title to real estate.[239]

The Texas water appropriation statute provides that every conveyance of a "ditch, canal, or reservoir, or other irrigation work, or any interest therein," shall be executed, acknowledged, and recorded in the same manner as conveyances of real estate.[240] "Water right" is not specifically mentioned in

---

[234] *Harris* v. *Chapman*, 51 Idaho 283, 294-295, 5 Pac. (2d) 733 (1931).

[235] *Yellowstone Valley Co.* v. *Associated Mortgage Investors, Inc.,* 88 Mont. 73, 82, 290 Pac. 255 (1930). Regardless of whether the right to certain spring waters was deemed part of the land on which they arose, or an appurtenance thereto, the right to such water passed by virtue of mortgage of the land, foreclosure decree, sale, and sheriff's deeds: *Skinner* v. *Silver*, 158 Oreg. 81, 97-100, 75 Pac. (2d) 21 (1938).

[236] *Stanislaus Water Co.* v. *Bachman*, 152 Cal. 716, 724, 93 Pac. 858 (1908).

[237] *Hale* v. *McCammon Ditch Co.,* 72 Idaho 478, 488, 244 Pac. (2d) 151 (1951); *Gard* v. *Thompson*, 21 Idaho 485, 496, 123 Pac. 497 (1912).

[238] *Stepp* v. *Williams*, 52 Cal. App. 237, 253, 198 Pac. 661 (1921).

[239] Kans. Stat. Ann. § 42-121 (1964). In 1900, the Kansas Supreme Court held that the accumulation of water above a dam built in a navigable stream by a riparian landowner was, in a sense, a reducing of personal property to possession, so that a grant of a right to use power thereby created need not be made by deed, but could be validly made by parol: *Johnston* v. *Bowersock*, 62 Kans. 148, 161-162, 61 Pac. 740 (1900).

[240] Tex. Rev. Civ. Stat. Ann. art. 7571 (1954).

this statute, but the water right is real estate and the formalities of conveyances would be expected to be applicable. A provision in the Wyoming water rights statute is comparable to that of Texas.[241]

The Utah statute provides that water rights shall be transferred by deed in substantially the same manner as real estate, except when they are represented by shares of stock in a corporation, "in which case water shall not be deemed to be appurtenant to the land."[242] As construed by the Utah Supreme Court, the effect of this statute was to establish a rebuttable presumption that a water right represented by corporate shares did not pass to the grantee as an appurtenance to the land on which used. The grantee could overcome such presumption by clear and convincing evidence that the water right was appurtenant and that the grantor intended to transfer it with the land, even though not expressly mentioned in the deed.[243]

Wyoming reservoir rights do not attach to any particular lands except by conveyance executed by the reservoir owners. Except as so attached, they may be sold or leased for beneficial use on such lands as the parties may desire. Deeds and leases for periods of 3 years or more must be executed, acknowledged, and recorded in the same way as deeds, and also filed with the State Engineer; and leases for shorter periods must be in writing and filed with the State Engineer.[244]

(2) Assignment of permit. Water rights statutes of several States provide that a permit to appropriate water may be assigned.[245] The assignment is not binding, except on the parties, unless filed for record in the office of the State administrator. Nevada and Washington extend the provision to applications as well as to permits, but the latter requires prior approval of assignment of the application as well as filing for record. Utah has a more elaborate procedure for assigning rights claimed under applications prior to issuance of certificate of appropriation.[246] California provides for assignment of applications in connection with State water plans.[247]

The Idaho Supreme Court held that the right given in a permit is merely a contingent right, which may or may not ripen into a complete appropriation.

---

[241] Wyo. Stat. Ann. § 41-254 (1957).

[242] Utah Code Ann. § 73-1-10 (1968).

[243] *Hatch* v. *Adams*, 7 Utah (2d) 73, 75, 318 Pac. (2d) 633 (1957); *Brimm* v. *Cache Valley Banking Co.*, 2 Utah (2d) 93, 99-100, 269 Pac. (2d) 859 (1954).

[244] Wyo. Stat. Ann. § § 41-37 and -38 (1957). Ineffective acknowledgment under § 41-38: *Condict* v. *Ryan*, 79 Wyo. 231, 233-236, 335 Pac. (2d) 792 (1959).

[245] Ariz. Rev. Stat. Ann. § 45-149 (1956); Nev. Rev. Stat. § 533.385 (Supp. 1967); N. Mex. Stat. Ann. § 75-5-21 (1968); N. Dak. Cent. Code Ann. § 61-04-15 (Supp. 1969); Okla. Stat. Ann. tit. 82, § 27 (1970); Oreg. Rev. Stat. § 537.220 (Supp. 1969); S. Dak. Comp. Laws Ann. § 46-5-33 (1967); Wash. Rev. Code § 90.03.310 (Supp. 1961).

[246] Transfer must be by written instrument in the manner provided for conveyance of real estate. It may be filed with the State Engineer; if not so recorded, it is void vis-à-vis a subsequent recorded assignment accepted in good faith. Utah Code Ann. § 73-3-18 (1968).

[247] Cal. Water Code § § 10504, 10505, and 12640 (West 1956).

Hence it is not an appropriation of water, and is not real property, but it is a consent given by the State to construct works and acquire real property.[248] Despite this, the supreme court held that the holder of a permit must make a formal assignment or conveyance.[249] The syllabus by the court in this case states that: "A water right is real estate and must be conveyed as real estate, and where one has a valid water permit issued to him by the state engineer, he cannot convey the water right secured thereby by simply handing the permit to a would-be purchaser."

A Texas court of civil appeals adopted a rule of construction of the Texas water statutes "to the effect that water appropriations, permits, and irrigation systems may be sold and assigned without invalidating the appropriation."[250]

(3) Possessory rights on the public domain. It was the rule of the courts that a settler in good faith on the public domain acquired a possessory right with respect to the land on which he settled, and that he might convey the possessory interest in the land and in the water right appurtenant thereto, by parol or otherwise, to one who took possession from him.[251]

(4) Effect of informal transfer upon priority of right. One early result of the general rule that a written deed of conveyance is necessary to transfer an appropriative right was the concept that a transfer lacking all formalities operated as an abandonment of the water right, thus forfeiting the original priority and relegating the priority of the transferee to the date of his own beginning actual use of the water. Although this found favor in a few decisions, it tended to operate on the parties to the transaction with unnecessary severity. And it was clearly irrational in disregarding the fundamental rule that abandonment is an *intentional* process. The importance of the fallacious concept in the few jurisdictions in which it was accepted diminished or ended long ago.[252]

---

[248] *Big Wood Canal Co.* v. *Chapman,* 45 Idaho 380, 401-402, 263 Pac. 45 (1927); *Speer* v. *Stephenson,* 16 Idaho 707, 716, 102 Pac. 365 (1909).

[249] *Gard* v. *Thompson,* 21 Idaho 485, 496, 123 Pac. 497 (1912).

[250] *Fiarbanks* v. *Hidalgo County W. I. Dist. No. 2,* 261 S. W. 542, 545 (Tex. Civ. App. 1923, error dismissed.)

[251] *Hindman* v. *Rizor,* 21 Oreg. 112, 116-118, 27 Pac. 13 (1891); *McDonald* v. *Lannen,* 19 Mont. 78, 83-86, 47 Pac. 648 (1897); *Featherman* v. *Hennessy,* 42 Mont. 535, 539-540, 113 Pac. 751 (1911); *Lobdell* v. *Hall,* 3 Nev. 507, 517 (1868); *First State Bank of Alamogordo* v. *McNew,* 33 N. Mex. 414, 423-424, 427-429, 269 Pac. 56 (1928).

[252] Wiel, writing in 1911, concluded that it might properly be held that a parol sale is evidence of an abandonment, but not conclusive; and that the rule "properly has no ground for existence to-day." Wiel, S.C., "Water Rights in the Western States," 3d ed. vol. 1, § 555 (1911). For a sequence of pertinent California and Montana decisions, see *Smith* v. *O'Hara,* 43 Cal. 371, 376-377 (1872), but compare, *McLeran* v. *Benton,* 43 Cal. 467, 476 (1872); *Barkeley* v. *Tieleke,* 2 Mont. 59, 62-65 (1874); *Middle Creek Ditch Co.* v. *Henry,* 15 Mont. 558, 572-581, 39 Pac. 1054 (1895); *McDonald* v. *Lannen,* 19 Mont. 78, 83-86, 47 Pac. 648 (1897); *Wood* v. *Lowney,* 20 Mont. 273, 277-278, 50 Pac. 794 (1897); *Griseza* v. *Terwilliger,* 144 Cal. 456, 461-462, 77 Pac. 1034 (1904); *Featherman* v. *Hennessy,* 42 Mont. 535, 539-540, 113 Pac. 751 (1911).

(5) Executed parol license. As above stated, it was the rule that a settler in good faith on the public domain might convey his possessory right by parol license or otherwise. A different question is involved with respect to parol sales of water rights under circumstances of equity, where the transferee entered into possession and made use of the water as well as making investments on the strength of the parol title. The validity of such conveyances was sustained in a considerable number of cases. That is to say, an oral grant, made for a valuable consideration, and carried into execution, may be held to constitute an executed parol grant, an equitable title to use of the water.[253] These parol transfers in equity have been enforced not only as between the parties to the transactions, but also with respect to successors in interest of the original parties.[254]

The reasoning of the Texas Supreme Court with respect to a contract for the use of water rights, works, and easements was, first, that it affected real estate to such an extent as to come within the statute of frauds. However, the contract was taken out of the statute by full compliance on the part of the landowner, part performance on the part of the other contractor, and inducement of the landowner to alter his position on the strength of an oral extension of the contract to such an extent that it would be fraud on him to permit the other party to set up its invalidity.[255]

The basis of the holding of irrevocability of an oral license in many of these cases is, either expressly or impliedly, that under such circumstances and with full consideration of equity the grantor ought to be, and is, estopped to deny his grantee's title. This is exemplified in a fairly recent Oregon decision.[256] Even more recently, the Oregon Supreme Court, speaking through Justice O'Connell, advanced a thesis which may be summarized as follows:[257]

> Previous cases accept the theory that the oral grant may be taken out of the statute of frauds by part performance; but they do not always clearly indicate the principle involved. However, if the promisee has acted in reasonable reliance on the promisor's promise, the court will enforce it. A better statement of the doctrine of part performance—better than merely resting on the theory of equitable estoppel—would be that it recognizes that the terms of an oral grant will be enforced (a) if there is enough conduct

---

[253] *Fogarty* v. *Fogarty*, 129 Cal. 46, 47-49, 61 Pac. 570 (1900); *Stepp* v. *Williams*, 52 Cal. App. 237, 253, 198 Pac. 661 (1921); *Campbell* v. *Shivers*, 1 Ariz. 161, 174, 25 Pac. 540 (1874). Oral license accepted, fully executed, and used to advantage by the parties is valid and enforceable: *Keim* v. *Downing*, 157 Nebr. 481, 490, 59 N. W. (2d) 602 (1953), "A parol grant of an easement or license like any other contract may rest in implication."

[254] *Churchill* v. *Russell*, 148 Cal. 1, 4-5, 82 Pac. 440 (1905); *Reynolds Irr. Dist.* v. *Sproat*, 70 Idaho, 217, 221-222, 214 Pac. (2d) 880 (1950).

[255] *Texas Co.* v. *Burkett*, 117 Tex. 16, 29-30, 296 S. W. 273 (1927).

[256] *Shepard* v. *Purvine*, 196 Oreg. 348, 374, 248 Pac. (2d) 352 (1952).

[257] *Luckey* v. *Deatsman*, 217 Oreg. 628, 343 Pac. (2d) 723, 725 (1959).

based. on the oral grant to satisfy the statute for minimizing perjured claims and opportunities for fraud, and (b) if there are equitable grounds for enforcing the contract, whether found in facts supporting an equitable estoppel or facts justifying avoidance of unjust enrichment or relief from fraud.

Privity between claimant and original appropriator.—The doctrine of prior appropriation as recognized and applied throughout most of the West had its initiation and early development on the public domain. As a result, the judicial rules with respect to conveyance of appropriative rights were developed largely in connection with public lands. A settler in good faith on the public domain had in the first instance, of course, only possessory rights in the land and water, which he could validly transfer to another settler by verbal sale as well as by way of written instrument. In this case the purchaser entered upon possession, and he eventually obtained from the United States formal title to the parcel of land with its appurtenant water right.

But settlers did not always sell their rights to newcomers. In various instances they simply abandoned their possessions and moved elsewhere. In some such situations, another settler would come upon the previously occupied tract, with perhaps some buildings, planted crops, and an irrigation ditch, of which he would take possession and would begin operations. In others, there may have been three or more successive occupants, each of whom took over a partly developed but clearly abandoned settlement and operated it for a time, the last one remaining and eventually obtaining his patent. The question then was, to what date did the completed water right relate?

Although, as noted above, there was for a time some disagreement among the courts as to whether a verbal sale of a water right exercised in connection with privately owned land operated *ipso facto* as an abandonment of the water right, there was general agreement on the principle that where there was *in fact* an abandonment and cessation of use by the original appropriator, another person with whom there was no privity of estate, who resumed the discontinued use of the water through the same ditch and on the same land, could not thereby relate his priority back to the date of the original appropriation.[258] The right of the latest claimant in such case, as against other appropriators, will have priority from the date of his own possession and appropriation, and not from the date of the original construction of the ditch and appropriation by some other person under whom he does not hold, and

---

[258] *Union Mill & Min. Co.* v. *Dangberg,* 81 Fed. 73, 103 (C.C.D. Nev., 1897). "The right of a person claiming an appropriation of water cannot be tacked on to that of a mere squatter who, while he may have irrigated the land, has abandoned it and has not transferred his interest in the land or irrigation works to the claimant or his predecessors," *In re Silvies River,* 115 Oreg. 27, 105, 237 Pac. 322 (1925).

between whom and himself there is no privity of estate. "His appropriation in such a case is a new and independent one, and must stand or fall upon its own merits."[259]

Summarizing the principle, then: The mere possession by one person of a water right originated by another does not show the requisite privity of estate. In order to make good his claim to the right as of the date at which it was in fact initiated, the possessor must show some contractual relation between himself and the original appropriator, or privity with him under the laws of succession. Otherwise, initiation of the presently claimed right will be fixed as of the date at which possession was taken.[260]

ELEMENTS OF THE APPROPRIATIVE RIGHT

Priority of the Right

The Basic Rule

The California Supreme Court observed that:[261]

One of the essential elements of a valid appropriation is that of priority over others. Under this doctrine he who is first in time is first in right, and so long as he continues to apply the water to a beneficial use, subsequent appropriators may not deprive him of the rights his appropriation gives him, by diminishing the quantity or deteriorating the quality of the water.* * *

Current Application of the Rule

This principle—that priority in time conferred superiority of right—was a *sine qua non* in appropriation of water from the earliest years of water rights laws in the West. And so it continued without significant exception until, in the latter part of the 19th century, there appeared some constitutional and statutory provisions stating the basic principle of time priority but containing some exceptions in the form of preferences in use of appropriated water in periods of shortage. In addition, under the permit appropriation statutes, there

---

[259] *Utt* v. *Frey,* 106 Cal. 392, 396, 39 Pac. 807 (1895); *Chiatovich* v. *Davis,* 17 Nev. 133, 136, 28 Pac. 239 (1882); *Head* v. *Hale,* 38 Mont. 302, 308, 100 Pac. 222 (1909).

[260] *Kenck* v. *Deegan,* 45 Mont. 245, 249, 122 Pac. 746 (1912). See *Osnes Livestock Co.* v. *Warren,* 103 Mont. 284, 290, 62 Pac. (2d) 206 (1936). See also *Oklahoma Water Resources Bd.* v. *Central Oklahoma Master Conservancy Dist.,* 464 Pac. (2d) 748, 752 (Okla. 1968).

[261] *Joerger* v. *Pacific Gas & Electric Co.,* 207 Cal. 8, 26, 276 Pac. 1017 (1929). The "fundamental principle of appropriation of water, as distinguished from riparian use, is that he who is prior in time is superior in right to the extent of his appropriation," *Caviness* v. *La Grande Irr. Co.,* 60 Oreg. 410, 424, 119 Pac. 731 (1911). A basic principle applicable to all appropriations of water is that "He who is first in time is first in right," *Reagle* v. *Square S. Land & Cattle Co.,* 133 Colo. 392, 394, 296 Pac. (2d) 235 (1956).

emerged the concept that no unqualified right of appropriation was accorded. This was further implemented by express grants to administrators of broad powers (1) to deny permits in the interest of the public welfare, and (2) to choose between conflicting applications to appropriate water pursuant (a) to a legislatively declared list of purposes of use and (b) to further considerations of public interest.

In view of these developments of expressed legislative intent, and of sympathetic consideration by the courts so long as existing property rights are adequately protected, the basic principle of time priority in applying for a permit to appropriate water, while it still exists, is no longer—and it has not been for many years—the sole criterion in approval of an application. Development of many large-scale storage projects throughout the West inevitably left less and less streamflow available for individual appropriation. The trend is still in this direction and will continue into the foreseeable future. Administrative attention is necessarily called more and more to overall problems of conservation and best use of water for multiple purposes in which public welfare has prime consideration, and—except with respect to ground water—less and less to formal applications by individuals for appropriation of small quantities of irrigation water for their small tracts of land.

The foregoing comments apply to *acquisition* of appropriative rights. Exercise of an acquired right is a different matter. Once priorities are established, whether in favor of specified individuals or of large projects, priority of the right governs the schedules according to which diversions and reservoir fillings are regulated by State administrative agencies.

Some Facets of the Subject of Priority of Right

Chapter 7 ends with a considerable treatment of related topics concerning priority of appropriation and restrictions and preferences in appropriation. They include the importance and value of a fixed priority, successive appropriations on one stream by the first user and by other parties, and relation of the priority to diversion works and to the stream as a whole. They also pertain to constitutional and statutory restrictions on the right to make appropriations, consideration of other obligations pertaining to the stream, and granting of qualified permit rights. And they relate to various orders of preferences in acquiring appropriative rights and in use of appropriated water. Further discussion of these matters here is unnecessary.

Specific Quantity of Water

The General Rule

The appropriative right refers in most instances to a definite quantity of water. From the early mining days, this has been the case.[262] Indeed, this has

---

[262] "* * * the right to appropriate a specific amount, in preference to others, must be determined by a suit brought for that purpose,* * *." *Owens* v. *Snider,* 52 Okla. 772, 781, 153 Pac. 833 (1915).

been one of the most distinctive features of the appropriative right a contrasted with the riparian right.[263] "Another important distinction between riparian rights and appropriation rights is that the riparian's use measure o water is elusive and shrouded in the word 'reasonable', more unknown than foreknown, while the appropriator's use measure of water is predetermined, a least the maximum."[264]

In a series of decisions which, in conjunction with legislative declarations resulted in progressive modification of the common-law riparian doctrine, the Oregon Supreme Court pointed out that the right of prior appropriation was incompatible with the rule of riparian ownership. One of the distinctions between the two doctrines is that appropriation contemplates a tenancy in severalty and riparian a tenancy in common. Thus, the appropriative right excludes the idea of equality among appropriators, and contemplates the use of a definite, certain, and fixed quantity of water. On the other hand, the riparian right is correlated with a similar right of every other owner of land riparian to the same stream, and in the nature of things contemplates the right to use a variable quantity of water.[265]

Some Exceptions

There have been cases in western courts in which appropriative rights have related to specific fractions of the total available flow of streams.[266] In Utah, in the early days, prorata divisions of streamflow measured either by fractional parts or by percentages of the flow were commonly made.[267] The old determinations and stipulated decrees based on proportion of available flow caused considerable trouble in water administration, but fortunately most of them were superseded by modern determinations under the special statutory procedure or in private litigation.[268] In other parts of the West they do not appear to have reached any such proportions.

---

[263] A right of appropriation is a right to a definite quantity of water, but a riparian right is not: *Wallace* v. *Weitman,* 52 Wash. (2d) 585, 588, 328 Pac. (2d) 157 (1958).

[264] *El Paso County W. I. Dist. No. 1* v. *El Paso,* 133 Fed. Supp. 894, 910 (W.D. Tex. 1955).

[265] *In re Deschutes River & Tributaries,* 134 Oreg. 623, 704-705, 286 Pac. 563, 294 Pac. 1049 (1930). For futher discussion and citations of authorities, see Hutchins, Wells A., "The Common-Law Riparian Doctrine in Oregon: Legislative and Judicial Modification." 36 Oreg. Law Rev. 193 (1957).

[266] See *Trimble* v. *Hellar,* 23 Cal. App. 436, 446-447, 138 Pac. 376 (1913).

[267] Thomas, George, "The Development of Institutions under Irrigation," pp. 143-144 (1920). Preadministration statutes provided that a right to the use of water might be measured by fractional parts of the whole supply, or by fractional parts with a limitation as to periods of time and use: Utah Laws 1880, ch. 20, § 8; Laws 1897, ch. 52, § 34.

[268] Letter to the author from Wayne D. Criddle, formerly State Engineer of Utah, April 5, 1962.

Examples of such decrees and agreements are discussed in chapter 7 under "Methods of Appropriating Water of Watercourses—Statutory—Inadequacies of the Preadministrative Procedures—The Utah experience." Related old Utah statutory provisions and court decrees with respect to "primary" and "secondary" water rights

In other cases, rights to make valid appropriations of the entire flows of streams have been recognized by the courts when the claimant could establish his need for the entire flow.[269]

Appropriations Made Under Water Administrative Procedures

One who seeks to appropriate streamflow in a permit-system State must state in his application the quantity of water that he wishes to appropriate for a specific purpose or purposes. This is usually expressed in cubic feet per second (or second-feet) for direct diversion, and in acre-feet for reservoir storage. Approval of his application, which is usually the permit, may not apply to the entire quantity of water that he requests, but it does declare the specific quantity that he is authorized to appropriate under the permit. His final license or certificate of appropriation, likewise, confirms the exact quantity of water that he has put to beneficial use in accordance with the prescribed requirements, which is the amount that the State recognizes as the quantitative limit of his appropriative right. And in the States in which no license or certificate is issued, the right recognized by the State refers to the quantity which the intending appropriator demonstrates that he has put to beneficial use. Likewise, in the special proceedings for determination of completed appropriative rights, the specific quantity of water adjudged to each claimant, and listed in the court decree, is that which he proves to have put to beneficial use. See chapter 15.

Measure of the Appropriative Right

The measure of an appropriative right was thus summarized by a California district court of appeal:[270]

The extent of an appropriator's or adverse user's right is limited, not by the quantity of water actually diverted, nor by the capacity of his ditch, but by the quantity which is, or may be, applied by him to his beneficial uses. * * * An appropriator's right is limited to such quantity, not exceeding the capacity of his ditch, as he may put to a useful purpose upon his land within a reasonable time, by use of reasonable diligence. * * * A diversion over and above what is reasonably necessary for the uses to which he devotes the water cannot be regarded as a diversion for a beneficial use. He cannot waste. * * *

---

also are discussed in chapter 7 under "Methods of Appropriating Water of Watercourses—Restrictions and Preferences in Appropriation of Water—Preferences in Water Appropriation—Use of appropriated water: In time of water shortage."

[269] See for example, *Brown* v. *Mullin,* 65 Cal. 89, 90, 3 Pac. 99 (1884); *Drake* v. *Earhart,* 2 Idaho 750, 757, 23 Pac. 541 (1890); *Larsen* v. *Apollonio,* 5 Cal. (2d) 440, 444, 55 Pac. (2d) 196 (1936); *Keller* v. *Magic Water Co.,* 92 Idaho 276, 441 Pac. (2d) 725, 733 (1968).

[270] *Felsenthal* v. *Warring,* 40 Cal. App. 119, 133, 180 Pac. 67 (1919).

Capacity of Ditch as a Factor

"The early cases measured the appropriator's right by the capacity of his ditch."[271] However, by the end of the 19th century, ditch capacity was being generally rejected as a measure of an appropriator's right, at least without full consideration of his necessary beneficial uses.[272] Such rejection, that is, was not always sharp and complete. Rather, in some instances, it was a matter of reducing emphasis of ditch capacity as a factor and shifting the emphasis to the growing realization that it was not the sole factor. For example, there was the statement that "The amount of water to which an appropriator is entitled may *occasionally* be determined by the capacity of his ditch at its smallest part." [Emphasis supplied][273] Again, "The size of the ditch is a factor in aid of the intention of the party making the appropriation of the water. It is not, however, conclusive. The true test is the amount actually used for beneficial purpose."[274]

In 1912, the Montana Supreme Court made some loose statements concerning appropriators' "needs" and capacities of diversion and conveyance facilities as measuring the extent of their appropriations.[275] After all, one's needs might substantially exceed his present intention to make both immediate use of a certain quantity of water and a reasonably prospective increase in use. If carried out diligently, the total beneficial use—not his needs—would measure the appropriation, which obviously could not be completed without adequate diversion and conveyance capacity. In other words, capacity of physical works must necessarily be adequate to serve the contemplated beneficial use—a necessary means to that end. But extent of use of water, not ditch capacity nor possible needs, must be looked to in determining the limit and extent of the

---

[271] *Tulare Irr. Dist.* v. *Lindsay-Strathmore Irr. Dist.*, 3 Cal. (2d) 489, 547, 45 Pac. (2d) 972 (1935). In a statutory adjudication proceeding, "the capacity of the various ditches outweighed all other considerations," *Fort Morgan Land & Canal Co.* v. *South Platte Ditch Co.*, 18 Colo. 1, 3, 30 Pac. 1032 (1892); *Hillman* v. *Hardwick*, 3 Idaho 255, 262, 28 Pac. 438 (1891); *Caruthers* v. *Pemberton*, 1 Mont. 111, 117 (1869); *Ophir Silver Min. Co.* v. *Carpenter*, 6 Nev. 393, 394 (1871); *Coventon* v. *Seufert*, 23 Oreg. 548, 554, 32 Pac. 508 (1893). In *White* v. *Todd's Valley Water Co.*, 8 Cal. 443, 444-445 (1857), it was stated that the appropriator would be allowed a reasonable time to make corrections in the plan and grade of his ditch in order to give it the intended capacity. Compare *Hufford* v. *Dye*, 162 Cal. 147, 159, 121 Pac. 400 (1912).

[272] *Smith* v. *Hawkins*, 120 Cal. 86, 88, 52 Pac. 139 (1898); *Woods* v. *Sargent*, 43 Colo. 268, 271-272, 95 Pac. 932 (1908); *Gotelli* v. *Cardelli*, 26 Nev. 382, 386-387, 69 Pac. 8 (1902); *Millheiser* v. *Long*, 10 N. Mex. 99, 104, 117, 61 Pac. 111 (1900); *Donnelly* v. *Cuhna*, 61 Oreg. 72, 76, 119 Pac. 331 (1911); *Biggs* v. *Miller*, 147 S. W. 632, 636 (Tex. Civ. App. 1912).

[273] *Glaze* v. *Frost*, 44 Oreg. 29, 32-33, 74 Pac. 336 (1903).

[274] *Trimble* v. *Hellar*, 23 Cal. App. 436, 443-444, 138 Pac. 376 (1913), rehearing denied by supreme court, 1914. See *Union Mill & Min. Co.* v. *Dangberg*, 81 Fed. 73, 110 (C. C. D. Nev. 1897); *Smith* v. *Duff*, 39 Mont. 382, 388-390, 102 Pac. 984 (1909).

[275] *Bailey* v. *Tintinger*, 45 Mont. 154, 178, 122 Pac. 575 (1912).

completed appropriation. Two years after deciding the cited case, the Montana court took a more rational approach in stating that: "The tendency of recent decisions of the courts in the arid states is to disregard entirely the capacity of the ditch and regard the actual beneficial use, installed within a reasonable time after the appropriation has been made, as the test of the extent of the right."[276] Statutes of both Nevada and Texas specifically reject carrying capacity of one's ditch as a measure of his appropriative water right.[277]

In the permit appropriation States, an application to appropriate water sets out details of physical works. If the applicant is to perfect an appropriation of water for his intended project, his ditch necessarily must be adequate to convey the water to his land. But after making his final proof of appropriation, it is the quantity of water shown therein to have been put to beneficial use on the acreage involved, not exceeding the quantity authorized in the permit, that goes into his license or certificate of appropriation. In this formal and controlled appropriative process, ditch capacity was a necessary element in getting the permittee's authorized quantity of water to his land. It did not become an element of his State-certified appropriative right.

Beneficial Use of Water[278]

Earlier, under "Property Characteristics," there is a discussion of the appropriative right as a *right of beneficial use* of water. In the instant discussion of elements of the appropriative right the subject is approached, with as little duplication as practicable, from the standpoint of beneficial use as a *measure of the extent* of an appropriative right.[279]

Questions of beneficial use of water are also involved in some of the discussions of restrictions and preferences in appropriation of water in the last part of chapter 7.

---

[276] *Conrow* v. *Huffine,* 48 Mont. 437, 444, 138 Pac. 1094 (1914). See *Haight* v. *Costanich,* 184 Cal. 426, 431, 194 Pac. 26 (1920).

[277] Nev. Rev. Stat. § 533.060 (Supp. 1967); Tex. Rev. Civ. Stat. Ann. art. 7543 (1954).

[278] See Trelease, Frank J., "The Concept of Reasonable Beneficial Use in the Law of Surface Streams," 12 Wyo. Law Journal 1 (1957). The subject of this article is a speech given by Professor Trelease to the Committee on the Economics of Water Resources Development of the Western Agricultural Economics Research Council and Western Regional Research Committee W-42, Rept. No. 5, at 7, Berkeley, California, December 20-21, 1956.

[279] For some other statements, see *Kernan* v. *Andrus,* 6 Alaska 54, 59-60 (1918); *Santa Cruz Res. Co.* v. *Rameriz,* 16 Ariz. 64, 68, 70, 141 Pac. 120 (1914); *Wheldon Valley Ditch Co.* v. *Farmers Pawnee Canal Co.,* 51 Colo. 545, 549-550, 119 Pac. 1056 (1911); *Lee* v. *Hanford,* 21 Idaho 327, 331, 332, 121 Pac. 558 (1912); *Ortel* v. *Stone,* 119 Wash. 500, 503, 205 Pac. 1055 (1922); *State* v. *Laramie Rivers Co.,* 59 Wyo. 9, 39, 136 Pac. (2d) 487 (1943); *Miller & Lux* v. *Rickey,* 127 Fed. 573, 584 (C. C. D. Nev. 1904).

Beneficial use defined.—According to the Texas Legislature:[280]

> For the purpose of this chapter, beneficial use shall be held to mean the use of such a quantity of water, when reasonable intelligence and reasonable diligence are exercised in its application for a lawful purpose, as is economically necessary for that purpose.

And in the South Dakota water rights statute, the section on "Definitions" of terms used in the statute, "unless the context otherwise plainly requires," includes:[281]

> "Beneficial Use" [is] any use of water that is reasonable and useful and beneficial to the appropriator, and at the same time is consistent with the interests of the public in the best utilization of water supplies.

The rule and its reasons.—In 1935, after mentioning the ditch-capacity rule, long since repudiated in the State, the California Supreme Court observed that:[282]

> As the pressure of population has led to the attempt to bring under cultivation more and more lands, and as the demands for water to irrigate these lands have become more and more pressing, the decisions have become increasingly emphatic in limiting the appropriator to the quantity reasonably necessary for beneficial uses. * * * If the appropriator uses more than the amount so required, he gains no right thereto. An excessive diversion of water for any purpose cannot be regarded as a diversion for a beneficial use. In so far as the diversion exceeds the amount reasonably necessary for beneficial purposes, it is contrary to the policy of the law and is a taking without right and confers no title, no matter for how long continued.* * *

Substantially the same observations, in one form or another, were made by many courts.[283] More picturesquely phrased was the earlier observation of Federal District Judge Thomas P. Hawley, who 45 years before, in 1852, crossed the plains to the Carson River area of Nevada: "In the appropriation of water, there cannot be any 'dog in the manger' business by either party, to

---

[280] Tex. Rev. Civ. Stat. Ann. art. 7476 (1954).

[281] S. Dak. Comp. Laws Ann. § 46-1-6(6) (1967).

[282] *Tulare Irr. Dist.* v. *Lindsay-Strathmore Irr. Dist.*, 3 Cal. (2d) 489, 546-547, 45 Pac. (2d) 972 (1935). See *Thorne* v. *McKinley Bros.*, 5 Cal. (2d) 704, 710, 56 Pac. (2d) 204 (1936).

[283] Some examples: *Allen* v. *Petrick*, 69 Mont. 373, 377, 222 Pac. 451 (1924); *Steptoe Live Stock Co.* v. *Gulley*, 53 Nev. 163, 172, 295 Pac. 772 (1931); *State ex rel. Community Ditches* v. *Tularosa Community Ditch*, 19 N. Mex. 352, 371, 143 Pac. 207 (1914); *Whited* v. *Cavin*, 55 Oreg. 98, 107, 105 Pac. 396 (1909); *Crawford* v. *Lehi Irr. Co.*, 10 Utah (2d) 165, 168-169, 350 Pac. (2d) 147 (1960); *Quinn* v. *John Whitaker Ranch Co.*, 54 Wyo. 367, 378, 92 Pac. (2d) 568 (1939).

nterfere with the rights of others, when no beneficial use of the water is or can
be made by the party causing such interference."[284]

Constitutional and statutory declarations.—Provisions in the constitutions of
10 Western States relate the right to the use of water to beneficial use. These
are Arizona, California, Colorado, Idaho, Montana, Nebraska, New Mexico,
Texas, Utah, and Wyoming. The water rights statutes of 10 States contain the
historical pronouncement that beneficial use shall be the basis, the measure, and the limit of the right to the use of water.[285] Statutes of nearly all Western States contain either positive declarations of the essential relationship between appropriative rights and beneficial use of water,
or incidental references to beneficial use in the procedures for appropriating
water, or both.

Some incidents of the rule of beneficial use.—(1) The *intention* of one who
seeks to appropriate water in any of the permit States is disclosed in his
application for a permit. In seeking the State's permission to appropriate a
specific quantity of water for the purpose of applying it to a stated beneficial
use, the applicant expressly declares his intent to do these things. But prior to
the era of administrative control over appropriation of water, the courts had
come to consider appropriator's intent as a necessary element in their
determination of both the validity of his appropriation and the extent of it.
This is briefly noted above under "Property Characteristics—Right of Beneficial
Use—The Concurring Judicial Rule."

Thus, the courts looked into the appropriator's intention, his object, and his
purpose before going on to consider his acts, reasonableness, and diligence in
consummating the intent.[286] And essential to the *initiation* of the appropriation were the *bona fides* of the claimant's intent to appropriate the water and
apply it to a beneficial use.[287] "The law will not encourage anyone to play the
part of the dog in the manger, and therefore the intention must be *bona fide*
and not a mere afterthought."[288]

The *bona fide* intent may be to apply the water not only to an existing
beneficial use, but to prospective or contemplated beneficial use. As noted
earlier in chapter 7 under "Methods of Appropriating Water of Watercourses—

---

[284] *Union Mill & Min. Co.* v. *Dangberg,* 81 Fed. 73, 119 (C. C. D. Nev. 1897). The phrase
was used in *Bailey* v. *Tintinger,* 45 Mont. 154, 178, 122 Pac. 575 (1912); *Vineyard
Land & Stock Co.* v. *Twin Falls Salmon River Land & Water Co.,* 245 Fed. 9, 21 (9th
Cir. 1917); *Harkey* v. *Smith,* 31 N. Mex. 521, 531, 247 Pac. 550 (1926).

[285] Citations of the applicable constitutional and statutory provisions are given above
under "Property Characteristics—Right of Beneficial Use."

[286] *Hewitt* v. *Story,* 64 Fed. 510, 514 (9th Cir. 1894); *Power* v. *Switzer,* 21 Mont. 523,
530, 55 Pac. 32 (1898); *Crawford* v. *Lehi Irr. Co.,* 10 Utah (2d) 165, 168-169, 350
Pac. (2d) 147 (1960); *In re Alpowa Creek,* 129 Wash. 9, 13-14, 224 Pac. 29 (1924).

[287] *Millheiser* v. *Long,* 10 N. Mex. 99, 106, 61 Pac. 111 (1900); *Nevada Ditch Co.* v.
Bennett, 30 Oreg. 59, 97, 45 Pac. 472 (1896).

[288] *Bailey* v. *Tintinger,* 45 Mont. 154, 178, 122 Pac. 575 (1912).

Completion of Appropriation", this must be consummated with reasonable diligence pursuant to the initial intent.[289]

The *future,* therefore, must have been within the appropriator's *original* intent in undertaking such appropriations.[290] Indeed, when the beneficial use of water covered by an appropriation is not immediate, but is prospective or contemplated, the intention of the party becomes of prime importance.

(2) Streamflow not appropriated by others. A number of courts have held that one can make an appropriation of the entire flow of a stream if he can and does apply the entire quantity to beneficial use.[291] The California Supreme Court held that as a result of the constitutional amendment of 1928,[292] excess waters over the requirements of riparian owners and prior appropriators constitute public waters of the State "to be used, regulated and controlled by the state on or under its direction."[293] Hence, if an intending appropriator can make reasonable beneficial use of all such excess waters in a stream, he can lawfully appropriate the entire quantity.[294]

(3) The privilege granted by the State to divert water only for uses truly beneficial rules out speculation.[295]

(4) If, after an appropriation is made, conditions change and the necessity for the original beneficial use diminishes, then to the extent of the lessened necessity the appropriator no longer has use for that additional quantity of water and the change inures to the benefit of subsequent appropriators who have need for it.[296] Cognizance of this facet of the rule of beneficial use of water was taken by the California Supreme Court in stating that:[297]

> What is a beneficial use, of course, depends upon the facts and circum-
> stances of each case. What may be a reasonable beneficial use, where water

---

[289] *Hutchinson* v. *Stricklin,* 146 Oreg. 285, 297, 28 Pac. (2d) 225 (1933). In 1900, the Montana Supreme Court declared that as every appropriation must be for a beneficial or useful purpose as commanded by the statute, "it becomes the duty of the courts to try the question of claimant's intent by his acts and the circumstances surrounding his possession of the water, its actual or contemplated use and the purposes thereof." *Toohey* v. *Campbell,* 24 Mont. 13, 17-18, 60 Pac. 396 (1900).

[290] *Haight* v. *Costanich,* 184 Cal. 426, 431-432, 194 Pac. 26 (1920).

[291] *Brown* v. *Mullin,* 65 Cal. 89, 90, 3 Pac. 99 (1884); *Larsen* v. *Apollonio,* 5 Cal. (2d) 440, 444, 55 Pac. (2d) 196 (1936); *Lockwood* v. *Freeman,* 15 Idaho 395, 398, 98 Pac. 295 (1908); *Mettler* v. *Ames Realty Co.,* 61 Mont. 152, 159-160, 201 Pac. 702 (1921); *Marks* v. *Hilger,* 262 Fed. 302, 304 (9th Cir. 1920). See also *Keller* v. *Magic Water Co.,* 92 Idaho 276, 441 Pac. (2d) 725, 733 (1968); *Village of Peck* v. *Denison,* 92 Idaho 747, 450 Pac. (2d) 310, 313-314 (1969).

[292] Cal. Const., art. XIV, § 3.

[293] *Meridian* v. *San Francisco,* 13 Cal. (2d) 424, 445, 459, 90 Pac. (2d) 537 (1939).

[294] *Albaugh* v. *Mt. Shasta Power Corp.,* 9 Cal. (2d) 751, 762, 73 Pac. (2d) 217 (1937).

[295] *Combs* v. *Agricultural Ditch Co.,* 17 Colo. 146, 152, 28 Pac. 966 (1892).

[296] *Conrow* v. *Huffine,* 48 Mont. 437, 444-445, 138 Pac. 1094 (1914); *Huffine* v. *Miller,* 74 Mont. 50, 52, 237 Pac. 1103 (1925).

[297] *Tulare Irr. Dist.* v. *Lindsay-Strathmore Irr. Dist.,* 3 Cal. (2d) 489, 567, 45 Pac. (2d) 972 (1935).

is present in excess of all needs, would not be a reasonable beneficial use in an area of great scarcity and great need. What is a beneficial use at one time may, because of changed conditions, become a waste of water at a later time.

(5) Because a *sine qua non* of a valid appropriation of water is that it should be applied to some beneficial use, a quantity of water too small to be used beneficially is not subject to appropriation.[298] Furthermore, the mere watering of land with intent to promote plant growth cannot be classed as beneficial if the conditions are such as to produce only meager, insubstantial results.[299]

However, beneficial use of water upon lands, and the possibility of the landowner's making a profit from the crops raised by means of irrigation upon his lands, are not one and the same thing. In other words, in the instant case, the question of profitableness of rice culture by a landowner had no bearing upon his right to receive and use water for that purpose.[300]

(6) Irrigation is a beneficial use of water in an arid land. "It is true that the diversion of the water only ripens into a valid appropriation when it is utilized by the appropriator for a beneficial use. But it need not be alleged in the complaint that the irrigation of lands is a beneficial use. If irrigation in a dry and arid climate like Nevada is not a beneficial use of the water, it would be difficult to determine what is."[301]

Other Terms Associated with Beneficial Use

Exclusion of unnecessary waste. —Unnecessary or unreasonable waste of water is incompatible with its beneficial use. Water in arid areas of the West "is too scarce, needful, and precious" to admit of waste.[302] Hence, "An excessive diversion of water for any purpose cannot be regarded as a diversion to a beneficial use." In an interstate case, the United States Supreme Court warned that "There must be no waste in arid lands of the 'treasure' of a river. * * * The essence of the doctrine of prior appropriation is beneficial use, not a stale or barren claim."[303]

As a result, an appropriation of water does not include the right to waste it when waste can be avoided.[304] It was said by the United States Supreme Court

---

[298] *Fourzan* v. *Curtis,* 43 Ariz. 140, 146, 29 Pac. (2d) 722 (1934).

[299] *Vineyard Land & Stock Co.* v. *Twin Falls Salmon River Land & Water Co.,* 245 Fed. 9, 21-22 (9th Cir. 1917).

[300] *Nelson* v. *Anderson-Cottonwood Irr. Dist.,* 51 Cal. App. 92, 96, 196 Pac. 292 (1921).

[301] *Miller & Lux* v. *Rickey,* 127 Fed. 573, 585, (C. C. D. Nev. 1904). This statement was made in the opinion of the court in a suit concerning rights to use of waters of Walker River, which rises in California and flows into Nevada.

[302] *Union Mill & Min. Co.* v. *Dangberg,* 81 Fed. 73, 97 (C. C. D. Nev. 1897); *Combs* v. *Agricultural Ditch Co.,* 17 Colo. 146, 153-154, 28 Pac. 966 (1892).

[303] *Washington* v. *Oregon,* 297 U. S. 517, 527-528 (1936).

[304] *Twin Falls Land & Water Co.* v. *Twin Falls Canal Co.,* 7 Fed. Supp. 238, 251-252 (D. Idaho 1933).

in an early case, and repeated by other courts, that an appropriation does not confer such an absolute right to the body of the water diverted that the owner can allow it, after diversion, to run to waste and thus prevent others from using it for legitimate purposes.[305] Custom in a community cannot authorize unreasonable waste of water.[306] Nor does a decreed right to the use of a specified quantity of water authorize a wasteful or excessive use at such times as the maximum is not needed for the decreed purposes.[307] Such practices that result in injury to junior appropriators may be restricted by a proper action.[308]

It must be emphasized that the waste of water that is frowned upon is *unreasonable* waste.[309] Mathematical exactness in determining unreasonable excesses is seldom practicable, but a reasonable approximation to substantial accuracy should be aimed at.[310]

The prohibition against unnecessary waste does not mean that an appropriator is required to take extraordinary precautions to prevent waste of water if he is making a reasonable use of the water according to the general custom of the locality,[311] "so long as the custom does not involve unnecessary waste."[312] It is recognized, furthermore, that in operating an irrigation system—particularly a large one—there is practically always some unpreventable waste which is to be deemed a part of the appropriation.[313]

Claimants on a stream have the right to demand that water in excess of the reasonable requirements of those upstream be left in the channel to supply their own proper demands.[314] And an appropriator who does not divert more

---

[305] *Atchison* v. *Peterson,* 87 U. S. 507, 514 (1874); *Mann* v. *Parker,* 48 Oreg. 321, 323, 86 Pac. 598 (1906); *Custer* v. *Missoula Public Service Co.,* 91 Mont. 136, 145, 6 Pac. (2d) 131 (1931).

[306] *Shafford* v. *White Bluffs Land & Irr. Co.,* 63 Wash. 10, 14-15, 114 Pac. 883 (1911).

[307] *Fort Collins Mill. & Elevator Co.* v. *Larimer & Weld Irr. Co.,* 61 Colo. 45, 53, 156 Pac. 140 (1916); *Tucker* v. *Missoula Light & Ry. Co.,* 77 Mont. 91, 101-102, 250 Pac. 11 (1926).

[308] *Wall* v. *Superior Court of Yavapai County,* 53 Ariz. 344, 356, 89 Pac. (2d) 624 (1939); *Burley Irr. Dist.* v. *Ickes,* 116 Fed. (2d) 529 (D. C. Cir. 1940); *Clausen* v. *Armington,* 123 Mont. 1, 17-18, 212 Pac. (2d) 440 (1949).

[309] *Bennett* v. *Salem,* 192 Oreg. 531, 544, 545, 235 Pac. (2d) 772 (1951). "This court has held that all unreasonable wasting of water should be suppressed by the court in adjudicating water rights."

[310] *Combs* v. *Agricultural Ditch Co.,* 17 Colo. 146, 153-154, 28 Pac. 966 (1892).

[311] *Joerger* v. *Pacific Gas & Electric Co.,* 207 Cal. 8, 23, 276 Pac. 1017 (1929).

[312] *Tulare Irr. Dist.* v. *Lindsay-Strathmore Irr. Dist.,* 3 Cal. (2d) 489, 547, 45 Pac. (2d) 972 (1935). He "cannot be compelled to divert according to the most scientific method known." See *Worden* v. *Alexander,* 108 Mont. 208, 215, 90 Pac. (2d) 160 (1939).

[313] *Thayer* v. *California Development Co.,* 164 Cal. 117, 137, 128 Pac. 21 (1912); *Bidleman* v. *Short,* 38 Nev. 467, 470-471, 150 Pac. 834 (1915).

[314] *Barrows* v. *Fox,* 98 Cal. 63, 66, 32 Pac. 811 (1893); *Fort Lyon Canal Co.* v. *Chew,* 33 Colo. 392, 404-405, 81 Pac. 37 (1905); *In re Hood River,* 114 Oreg. 112, 188, 227 Pac. 1065 (1924).

than the quantity of water to which he is lawfully entitled must return the surplus to the stream without unnecessary waste.[315] The taking of more than the quantity of water actually put to reasonable beneficial use is a taking without right,[316] for the excess water is subject to appropriation by any other person who may put it to beneficial use.[317]

Actual needs of water user.—An appropriative right is limited by the actual reasonable needs of the appropriator, and he can acquire no right to the use of more water than is necessary for the purposes of his appropriation. As said by the Idaho Supreme Court, "it is against the public policy of the state, as well as against express enactments, for a water user to take from an irrigation canal more water, of that to which he is entitled, than is necessary for the irrigation of his land and for domestic purposes."[318] This principle has been declared in many cases decided by many western courts.[319]

It follows that both beneficial use of water and actual need for the water are measures of the extent of one's appropriative water right. As noted above in discussing ditch capacity as a measurement factor, these terms do not necessarily mean the same thing, for the quantity of water reasonably required for the water user's needs may not be the quantity he has put to beneficial use. To say that a particular appropriator is making beneficial use of more water than he needs would be contradictory. But it would not be irrational to find that he is making beneficial use of *less* water than he needs. He might be utilizing only a small part of his farming potential. In any event, if beneficial use is less than needs, the water right will be measured by beneficial use unless, of course, the original intent includes additional use and is being pursued diligently.

---

[315] *Natoma Water & Min. Co.* v. *Hancock,* 101 Cal. 42, 51-52, 31 Pac. 112 (1892), 35 Pac. 334 (1894); *Burkart* v. *Meiberg,* 37 Colo. 187, 190, 86 Pac. 98 (1906); *Clausen* v. *Armington,* 123 Mont. 1, 17-18, 212 Pac. (2d) 440 (1949).

[316] *Thayer* v. *California Development Co.,* 164 Cal. 117, 137, 128 Pac. 21 (1912).

[317] *Hufford* v. *Dye,* 162 Cal. 147, 153-154, 121 Pac. 400 (1912).

[318] *Coulson* v. *Aberdeen Springfield Canal Co.,* 39 Idaho 320, 323-324, 227 Pac. 29 (1924). And earlier in Oregon: "If more water is diverted by a settler than is needed for the purpose intended, or is actually used for such need, he acquires a right only to the amount so needed and used." *Porter* v. *Pettengill,* 57 Oreg. 247, 249, 110 Pac. 393 (1910).

[319] For example: *Clough* v. *Wing,* 2 Ariz. 371, 378, 17 Pac. 453 (1888); *Senior* v. *Anderson,* 130 Cal. 290, 296-297, 62 Pac. 563 (1900); *Fort Lyon Canal Co.* v. *Chew,* 33 Colo. 392, 398-400, 81 Pac. 37 (1905); *Cook* v. *Hudson,* 110 Mont. 263, 282-283, 103 Pac. (2d) 137 (1940); *Barnes* v. *Sabron,* 10 Nev. 217, 243-244 (1875); *Simmons* v. *Winters,* 21 Oreg. 35, 51, 27 Pac. 7 (1891); *Quinn* v. *John Whitaker Ranch Co.,* 54 Wyo. 367, 378, 92 Pac. (2d) 568 (1939); *Hewitt* v. *Story,* 64 Fed. 510, 514 (9th Cir. 1894); *Vineyard Land & Stock Co.* v. *Twin Falls Oakley Land & Water Co.,* 245 Fed. 30, 34 (9th Cir. 1917); *Dern* v. *Tanner,* 60 Fed. (2d) 626, 628 (D. Mont. 1932).

Reasonable use. – The term "reasonable" came to be adopted by the courts as a qualification of the appropriator's use of water for a beneficial purpose.[320] As aptly stated by the Oregon Supreme Court, "The use must not only be beneficial to the lands of the appropriator, but it must also be reasonable in relation to the reasonable requirements of subsequent appropriators."[321] The California Supreme Court elaborated a little on the term by saying that:[322]

> It is further substantially declared wherever the question has been considered that beneficial use is not what is actually consumed, but what is reasonably necessary for the purpose to which the water is devoted, and that an excessive diversion of water for any purpose cannot be regarded as a diversion for a beneficial use, in so far as it is in excess of any reasonable requirement for that purpose.* * *
>
> The effect of the decisions clearly appears to be that one actually diverting water under a claim of appropriation for a useful or beneficial purpose, cannot by such diversion acquire any right to divert more water than is reasonably necessary for such use or purpose, no matter how long a diversion in excess thereof has continued,* * *.[323]

But an interpretation of reasonableness is not to be pushed to the point of imposing unreasonableness upon the prior appropriator. Thus, a Federal district court has said "a reasonable method of farming must prevail and a farmer is not required to use methods which are costly in labor and money simply because some waste can be saved thereby."[324] In an earlier case in the same court, it was agreed that conservation of water is a wise public policy, but that so also is conservation of the energy and well-being of the water user; that economy of use is not synonymous with minimum use, and so an appropriator

---

[320] *Hewitt* v. *Story,* 64 Fed. 510, 514 (9th Cir. 1894); *Anderson* v. *Bassman,* 140 Fed. 14, 28 (N.D. Cal. 1905); *Barnes* v. *Sabron,* 10 Nev. 217, 233, 243-244 (1875); "An appropriator of water for irrigation is entitled to so much water only as is necessary to irrigate his land, and is bound to make a reasonable use of it," Syllabus, *Clough* v. *Wing,* 2 Ariz. 371, 17 Pac. 453 (1888). Under the appropriation doctrine, "diversion and application of water to a beneficial use constitute an appropriation, and entitle the appropriator to a continuing right to use the water, to the extent of the appropriation, but not beyond that reasonably required and actually used." *Arizona* v. *California,* 298 U. S. 558, 565-566 (1936).

[321] *Tudor* v. *Jaca,* 178 Oreg. 126, 143, 164 Pac. (2d) 680 (1945), 165 Pac. (2d) 770 (1946).

[322] *California Pastoral & Agricultural Co.* v. *Madera Canal & Irr. Co.,* 167 Cal. 78, 84, 85, 86, 138 Pac. 718 (1914).

[323] See also *Natoma Water & Min. Co.* v. *Hancock,* 101 Cal. 42, 51-52, 31 Pac. 112 (1892), 35 Pac. 334 (1894); *Hufford* v. *Dye,* 162 Cal. 147, 153-154, 159-160, 121 Pac. 400 (1912).

[324] *Twin Falls Land & Water Co.* v. *Twin Falls Canal Co.,* 7 Fed. Supp. 238, 252 (D. Idaho 1933).

of water should not reasonably be limited in his water right to his minimum needs.[325]

Reasonableness of use of water is a question of fact to be determined by the jury (or the court) according to the facts and circumstances of each particular case.[326]

Under current administrative procedures for appropriating water pursuant to permits to do so: "Water may be appropriated in excess of the reasonable amount that may be used for the beneficial use designated in the application.[327]

Reasonable beneficial use.—An amendment to the constitution of California in 1928 provided that "The right to water or to the use or flow of water in or from any natural stream or water course in this State is and shall be limited to such water as shall be reasonably required for the beneficial use to be served, * * *." Riparian as well as appropriative rights are governed by the limitation.[328]

In construing the amendment and its impact upon the State law of water rights, the California Supreme Court employed the term "reasonable beneficial use" (considering in connection therewith reasonable methods of use and reasonable methods of diversion) as denoting the measure of the water right, appropriative and riparian alike, as now commended by the fundamental law of the State.[329] The term has been applied to the measure of water rights in subsequent cases as well.[330]

Economical use.—To the requirements of beneficial and reasonable use the courts added the concept of economy in the use of water—that the appropriator's use must be economical, in accordance with his needs.[331] The

---

[325] *Caldwell* v. *Twin Falls Salmon River Land & Water Co.,* 225 Fed. 584, 596 (D. Idaho 1915).

The prior appropriator cannot prevent others from using the surplus above his own economical and reasonable needs: *Roeder* v. *Stein,* 23 Nev. 92, 97, 42 Pac. 867 (1895); *Doherty* v. *Pratt,* 34 Nev. 343, 349-350, 124 Pac. 574 (1912); *Vineyard Land & Stock Co.* v. *Twin Falls Salmon River Land & Water Co.,* 245 Fed. 9, 22 (9th Cir. 1917).

[326] *Dripps* v. *Allison's Mines Co.,* 45 Cal. App. 95, 99-100, 187 Pac. 448 (1919); *Barnes* v. *Sabron,* 10 Nev. 217, 243-244 (1875). And the method commonly used in the community has a bearing in determining the quantity of water to which a user is entitled: *Beasley* v. *Engstrom,* 31 Idaho 14, 18, 168 Pac. 1145 (1917).

[327] *Crawford* v. *Lehi Irr. Co.,* 10 Utah (2d) 165, 168, 350 Pac. (2d) 147 (1960).

[328] Cal. Const., art. XIV, § 3.

[329] *Peabody* v. *Vallejo,* 2 Cal. (2d) 351, 368-369, 381, 40 Pac. (2d) 486 (1935).

[330] *Tulare Irr. Dist.* v. *Lindsay-Strathmore Irr. Dist.,* 3 Cal. (2d) 489, 547, 567, 568, 45 Pac. (2d) 972 (1935); *Lodi* v. *East Bay Municipal Utility Dist.,* 7 Cal. (2d) 316, 339, 60 Pac. (2d) 439 (1936); *Pasadena* v. *Alhambra,* 33 Cal. (2d) 908, 925, 207 Pac. (2d) 17 (1949). See also *Joslin* v. *Marin Municipal Water Dist.,* 67 Cal. (2d) 132, 429 Pac. (2d) 889, 60 Cal. Rptr. 377 (1967), discussed in chapter 6 under "Interrelationships of the Dual Water Rights Systems—The Status in Summary: By States—California."

[331] *Dalton* v. *Kelsey,* 58 Oreg. 244, 253-254, 114 Pac. 464 (1911); he "should be required to make an economic as well as a reasonable use of the water," *Union Mill & Min. Co.*

Idaho Supreme Court observed in 1952 that a determination of the duty of water, which involved many factors, is based upon "two primary considerations: beneficial and economical use," and is a determination of a fact.[332]

The Montana Supreme Court cautioned that the limitation of economy of use is to be applied within reasonable limits; that is, the objective of a determination of the duty of water is the quantity necessary to irrigate land not only economically, but successfully. Emphasis should of course be placed upon economy of use, but not "to such an extent as to imperil success."[333] And the system of irrigation in common use in the locality, if reasonable and proper under existing conditions, may be taken as a standard, even though a more economical method might be adopted.[334]

As considered and applied in the decisions, economical use is an antonym of waste. If an appropriator wastes water, he necessarily is not using it economically. As he has no right to waste water unreasonably or unnecessarily, then of necessity he must make economical as well as reasonable and beneficial use.

The limitation of the appropriative right to economical and reasonable use thus precludes any waste of water that can be reasonably avoided.[335] The use of water is so necessary as to preclude its being allowed to run to waste. Its "full beneficial and economical use requires" that when the wants of one appropriator are supplied, another may be permitted to use the flow.[336] The Colorado Supreme Court "recognizes the urgent and ever increasing necessity" for enforcing economical use of water for irrigation. "Whenever there is a wasteful, or other unnecessary or unlawful use of water, it should be promptly and efficiently dealt with under the law."[337]

---

v. *Dangberg,* 81 Fed. 73, 113 (C. C. D. Nev. 1897); *Anderson* v. *Bassman,* 140 Fed. 14, 28 (N. D. Cal. 1905); "A prior appropriator is only entitled to the water to the extent that he has use for it when economically and reasonably used," *Washington State Sugar Co.* v. *Goodrich,* 27 Idaho 26, 44, 147 Pac. 1073 (1915); "Under the law and the specific terms of the decree as it has been directed to be modified, the allowance of a prior right to plaintiffs for one hundred and eighty-four inches is limited to such times as that quantity, by reasonable and economical use, is necessary for the irrigation of their lands," *Twaddle* v. *Winters,* 29 Nev. 88, 109-110, 85 Pac. 280 (1906), 89 Pac. 289 (1907).

[332] *Uhrig* v. *Coffin,* 72 Idaho 271, 274, 240 Pac. (2d) 480 (1952).

[333] *Allen* v. *Petrick,* 69 Mont. 373, 376, 380, 222 Pac. 451 (1924).

[334] *Worden* v. *Alexander,* 108 Mont. 208, 215, 90 Pac. (2d) 160 (1939). See *Rodgers* v. *Pitt,* 129 Fed. 932, 943-944 (C.C.D. Nev. 1904).

[335] *Vineyard Land & Stock Co.* v. *Twin Falls Oakley Land & Water Co.,* 245 Fed. 30, 33-34, 35 (9th Cir. 1917).

[336] *Hufford* v. *Dye,* 162 Cal. 147, 159, 121 Pac. 400 (1912).

[337] *Comstock* v. *Larimer & Weld Res. Co.,* 58 Colo. 186, 205-206, 145 Pac. 700 (1914).

The overall association.—These several terms associated with beneficial use of water lend themselves to classification because, while they are all associated with beneficial use, they do have recognizable connotations from that term. Yet they all must have consideration in arriving at the quantity of water to which an appropriative claimant is entitled.

In summary, the water to which an appropriator is found to be entitled (1) is limited by the statement in his permit or claim, depending on the enabling statute, and by its availability for his use above the quantities required to satisfy preexisting rights, and within such limitations (2) it will be measured by his reasonable, economical, beneficial use, without unreasonable or unnecessary waste, not to exceed the quantity necessary to meet his actual needs. This is discussed further in chapter 9 under "Efficiency of Practices."

Period of Use of Water

The established rule.—In the last quarter of the 19th century, courts of several States adopted the rule that the right to the use of a specific supply of water might be acquired by one person for certain months, days, or parts of days, and by someone else for other specified periods of time not in conflict with those of the first appropriator. This was based on the premise that there is no difference in principle between appropriations of water measured by time and those measured by volume.[338] The rule is elementary said the Utah Supreme Court in 1924.[339] And in 1960, this court observed that:[340]

> We have held one of the basic elements of a water right is the time, period or season when the right to the use exists. This must be unequivocally determined and set out. We now add to supplement such element that a water right is based upon annual use during the water use period of each year, or the entire year.* * *

It is the policy of the law that no water shall be permitted to go to waste when it can be appropriated for a beneficial use elsewhere.[341] Stated differently, the value of water is too great to allow a landowner to gain a right

---

[338] *Smith* v. *O'Hara,* 43 Cal. 371, 376 (1872); *Barnes* v. *Sabron,* 10 Nev. 217, 245 (1875); *Turner* v. *Cole,* 31 Oreg. 154, 159, 49 Pac. 971 (1897); *Cache la Poudre Res. Co.* v. *Water Supply & Storage Co.,* 25 Colo. 161, 167, 53 Pac. 331 (1898).

[339] *Hardy* v. *Beaver County Irr. Co.,* 65 Utah 28, 40, 234 Pac. 524 ((1924).

[340] *In re Water Rights of Escalante Valley Drainage Area,* 10 Utah (2d) 77, 82-83, 348 Pac. (2d) 679 (1960). See also *Mountain Meadow Ditch & Irr. Co.* v. *Park Ditch & Res. Co.,* 130 Colo. 537, 539, 277 Pac. (2d) 527 (1954); *Galiger* v. *McNulty,* 80 Mont. 339, 354, 260 Pac. 401 (1927); *Wilson* v. *Angelo,* 176 Wash. 157, 160-161, 28 Pac. (2d) 276 (1934).

[341] *Turner* v. *Cole,* 31 Oreg. 154, 159, 49 Pac. 971 (1897).

thereto for the entire 24 hours of each day by using the same for only a half or any other portion of the time less than the whole.[342]

Some questioning or nonapplication of the rule. — Thus, measurement of an appropriative right not only by quantity but also by time, or by period of use of water, became well established in western jurisprudence. In some cases, however, questions were raised, or the rule was not applied to the factual situation.

Near the close of the 19th century, in *McGinness* v. *Stanfield,* the Idaho Supreme Court expressed itself as of the opinion that so long as an appropriator applied the water to a beneficial purpose, he was the judge within the limits of his appropriation of the times and place of use; and that a trial court was exceeding its province in dictating time of use.[343] This decision was distinguished 30 years later by the same court, which declared its agreement with the general western rule.[344] Despite this disapproval of *McGinness* v. *Stanfield* by the Idaho Supreme Court, Judge Bourquin of the United States District Court for the District of Idaho a few years later expressed his approval of that decision, saying "and why, when, and where departed from, prior to the suits herein, has not been made known to the court."[345] The judge was skeptical of the practicability of measuring an appropriation by time. He took the position that as quantity of water and requirements therefor vary so greatly from time to time, its application must be left to the judgment of the irrigator, subject to control by the court's water master.

Shortly after the start of the 20th century, a Federal court in Nevada approved the general rule followed by the courts of the State, but held that under the facts of the instant case the appropriation had been made without

---

[342] *Northern California Power Co., Consolidated* v. *Flood,* 186 Cal. 301, 306, 199 Pac. 315 (1921). This case dealt with acquisition of rights by prescription, but the principle is equally applicable to appropriation without the element of adverse use.

For some examples of division of water supply based on period of use, see *Smith* v. *O'Hara,* 43 Cal. 371, 372 (1872); *Santa Paula Water Works* v. *Peralta,* 113 Cal. 38, 44, 45 Pac. 168 (1896); *Suisun* v. *De Freitas,* 142 Cal. 350, 351-353, 75 Pac. 1092 (1904); *Thorne* v. *McKinley Bros.,* 5 Cal. (2d) 704, 710-712, 56 Pac. (2d) 204 (1936); *Cache la Poudre Res. Co.* v. *Water Supply & Storage Co.,* 25 Colo. 161, 162-167, 53 Pac. 331 (1898); *In re North Powder River,* 75 Oreg. 83, 94-95, 144 Pac. 485 (1914), 146 Pac. 475 (1915); *Smyth* v. *Jenkins,* 148 Oreg. 165, 168-169, 33 Pac. (2d) 1007 (1934); *Oliver* v. *Skinner & Lodge,* 190 Oreg. 423, 436, 442-443, 226 Pac. (2d) 507 (1951); *Cleary* v. *Daniels,* 50 Utah 494, 500, 167 Pac. 820 (1917). In South Dakota, an injunction was issued against the injurious practice of a junior appropriator in withholding by a dam three-fourths of the streamflow during the daytime for the purpose of discharging in large quantities at night for power purposes: *Lone Tree Ditch Co.* v. *Rapid City Elec. & Gas Light Co.,* 16 S. Dak. 451, 455, 462, 93 S. W. 650 (1903).

[343] *McGinness* v. *Stanfield,* 6 Idaho 372, 374-375, 55 Pac. 1020 (1898).

[344] *Dunn* v. *Boyd,* 46 Idaho 717, 721-723, 271 Pac. 2 (1928).

[345] *United States* v. *American Ditch Assn.,* 2 Fed. Supp. 867, 869 (D. Idaho 1933).

reference to any particular period and hence was not limited as to time.[346] And the Colorado Supreme Court held that an appropriation of water for operation of mill machinery had been made for a specific quantity of the water for use whenever it was available in the stream, and that the fact that the volume of streamflow, by reason of climatic conditions, was sufficient for use during only certain parts of the year did not, of itself, limit the appropriation to such periods. The appropriation was operative whenever the flow was sufficient.[347]

Appropriation under permit pursuant to administrative statute.—As stated in chapter 7, under "Methods of Appropriating Water of Watercourses—Current Appropriation Procedures—Administrative," a permit granted by the State to appropriate water sets out—or may set out—restrictions including periods of annual use. This is the administrative application of the general rule as to measurement of an appropriation by time periods. The restrictions so imposed in the permit become essential features of the particular appropriation.[348]

In 1926, the New Mexico Supreme Court decided a case in which plaintiff had obtained a permit for the year-round use of 5 second-feet, and defendant later obtained a permit for 4½ second-feet out of plaintiff's supply for winter use only, that is, from October 15 to March 15.[349] The court noted the rule of measurement by time as well as by quantity which prevailed under the arid region doctrine of appropriation, but did not consider it well adapted to general agriculture. Despite this, the court took the position that the water appropriation statute of the State had departed from the arid region doctrine in this particular, inasmuch as the statute regulated the acquisition, means, and manner of enjoyment of water rights, which controlled the whole matter. Attention was called to the fact that the statute required an applicant to state in his application the quantity of water and period or periods of annual use of the water,[350] so that now the right of the water user is measured by the State Engineer's permit or by decree of the court.

---

[346] *Rodgers* v. *Pitt,* 129 Fed. 932, 938-939 (C. C. D. Nev. 1904).

[347] *Telluride* v. *Blair,* 33 Colo. 353, 355, 80 Pac. 1053 (1905).

[348] Note that the South Dakota statute provides that the allowance of water for irrigation shall not exceed 1 second-foot per 70 acres, or the equivalent thereof, and the volume of diverted water is limited to 3 acre-feet per acre, delivered on the land "for a specified time each year," S. Dak. Comp. Laws Ann. § 46-5-6 (1967). In Oklahoma, the amount of water to be diverted for irrigation shall be no more than 4 acre-feet at the point of diversion for each acre of irrigated land "each calendar year." Okla. Stat. Ann. tit. 82, § 33 (1970).

[349] *Harkey* v. *Smith,* 31 N. Mex. 521, 523-529, 247 Pac. 550 (1926). Defendant's claim was based on plaintiff's nonuse during the winter months, resulting in forfeiture, which the supreme court rejected as inapplicable to the facts herein. Plaintiff had the right to use the 5 second-feet at any time of the year in accordance with his necessities. Defendant could acquire no primary right to use his claimed 4½ second-feet in the year, for his claim was subservient to that of plaintiff and could be exercised only after plaintiff's needs had been supplied.

[350] N. Mex. Stat. Ann. § 75-5-1 (1968).

Relevant to this topic is the specific authorization in the water rights statute of Texas for the granting of "seasonal" permits.[351] The right to which a seasonal permit relates is limited to the portion of the calendar year expressly stated in the permit. The rules and regulations of the Texas Water Rights Commission describe the seasonal permit as limiting the taking of water to certain months or dates during the year. "This type of permit is usually granted where irrigation is desired for seasonal crops or where the applicant proposes to appropriate water to fill an off-channel reservoir during the wet season for use during the dry season."[352]

Duty of Water

Significance of the term.—"In determining what is a reasonable quantity for beneficial uses," said the California Supreme Court in 1935, "it is the policy of the state to require within reasonable limits the highest and greatest duty from the waters of the state."[353] In the absence of a statute definitely regulating the duty of water, the question becomes one of fact for the court in each case to determine on the evidence presented to it; and "it is apparent there can be no exact uniform rule for computing the duty or reasonable quantity of water for irrigation to be applied in all cases alike."[354]

"Although," said the Colorado Supreme Court in 1954, "the expression 'Duty of Water', in the opinions of some present-day scholarly hydrologists and technical engineers, may be outmoded, provincial, unscientific and otherwise objectionable, nevertheless it is a term well understood and accepted by every rancher and farmer who has had practical experience in the artificial irrigation of land for the production of crops. It is that measure of water, which by careful management and use, without wastage, is reasonably required to be applied to any given tract of land for such period of time as may be adequate to produce therefrom a maximum amount of such crops as ordinarily are grown thereon. It is not a hard and fast unit of measurement, but is variable according to conditions."[355]

The term "duty of water"—so generally used some decades ago—has not been eliminated from western water law parlance. It is nevertheless true that other terms have come into prominence, and are being increasingly used, not only in technical literature but also in litigation over rights to the use of water.

---

[351] Tex. Rev. Civ. Stat. Ann. art. 7467c(1) (Supp. 1970).

[352] Tex. Water Rights Comm'n, "Rules, Regulations and Modes of Procedure," rule 205.2 (1970 Rev., Jan. 1970).

[353] *Tulare Irr. Dist.* v. *Lindsay-Strathmore Irr. Dist.,* 3 Cal. (2d) 489, 547, 45 Pac. (2d) 972 (1935).

[354] *Joerger* v. *Pacific Gas & Electric Co.,* 207 Cal. 8, 21-22, 276 Pac. 1017 (1929).

[355] *Farmers Highline Canal & Res. Co.* v. *Golden,* 129 Colo. 575, 584-585, 272 Pac. (2d) 629 (1954).

A 1945 publication on irrigation requirements of California crops, published by the California Department of Public Works, Division of Water Resources, in cooperation with United States Department of Agriculture, Soil Conservation Service, Division of Irrigation,[356] contains a section entitled "Definition of Terms." Terms defined there, in the following order, are: Irrigation requirement, water requirement, consumptive use (evapotranspiration), transpiration, duty of water, irrigation efficiency, field capacity, permanent wilting percentage, moisture equivalent, available moisture, moisture percentage, apparent specific gravity (volume weight), soil moisture, and subirrigation. Comparisons of two commonly used newer terms with duty of water may be made from the following definitions:

Irrigation Requirement: The quantity of water, exclusive of precipitation, that is required for crop production. It includes surface evaporation and other economically unavoidable wastes. Usually expressed in depth for given time (volume per unit area for given time). (See also water requirement.)

Water Requirement: The quantity of water, regardless of its source, required by a crop in a given period of time, for its normal growth under field conditions. It includes surface evaporation and other economically unavoidable wastes. Usually expressed as depth (volume per unit area) for a given time. (See also irrigation requirement.)

Duty of Water: The quantity of irrigation water applied to a given area for the purpose of maturing its crop, expressed as acre-feet or acre-inches per acre or as depth in feet or inches.

For large areas, the term "consumptive use," including loss by evaporation and transpiration, may be employed.

How the quantity is determined. – In the settlement of early controversies between claimants of rights to the use of water, scientific assistance was not available. Quantities of flowing water were measured in miner's inches flowing over a wier or through the orifice in a structure installed for the purpose; and observations were made and evidence was given as to the relation of measured quantities to cultivated tracts of land for given periods of time. Thus, in areas of irrigation farming, local standards were developed.

The introduction of questions of quantitative irrigation requirements into western water jurisprudence appears to have been accepted with some diffidence by some high courts. Late in the 19th century, it was observed that "It is always *proper* to inquire into the question of the necessity and ability to

---

[356] Young, Arthur A., "Irrigation Requirements of California Crops," Cal. Dept. Pub. Works, Div. Water Resources, Bul. 51, pp. 10-11 (1945).

use the quantity of water appropriated and diverted." [Emphasis supplied.] [357] By contrast, there is the forthright statement a half-century later that: "Many factors enter into a determination of the duty of water, which is based upon two primary considerations: beneficial and economical use. The determination of this question is a determination of a fact." [358] In 1924, the Montana Supreme Court observed that: "A fundamental error into which the early day courts fell was the result of their failure to appreciate what has been termed the duty of water; that is, the extent to which and the manner in which the water should be used by the appropriator." [359]

The courts came to agree in principle that in fixing the extent of an appropriative right, "The quantity of water acquired by appropriation must be determined by the amount of land irrigated and the quantity of water needed therefor." [360] This principle recognized not only, as a limiting factor, the *need* for water for a particular area, but also the necessity for determining the *specific quantity* of water needed.

Specific quantities are mentioned in various State supreme court opinions, none of which evince any illusion as to the difficulties of arriving at figures that would do justice to all parties according to their respective rights. Federal District Judge Bourquin was frankly skeptical of the practicability of such an undertaking. "But how any court can predetermine the duty of water, passeth understanding. So variable are the essential factors of soil, cultivation, skill, crop, weather, time, that omnipotence, but not human wisdom, might solve the problem." [361] Nevertheless, many courts essayed solution of the problem. In some areas, for example, the judicial general rule became 1 inch per acre unless the evidence disclosed that a greater or lesser quantity was required—a fact for the court or jury, and never to be considered a question of law for the courts. [362] In one region in which the general rule for certain situations was ½ inch per acre, an allowance of 2 inches was made where the smaller stream

---

[357] *Kleinschmidt* v. *Greiser*, 14 Mont. 484, 496, 37 Pac. 5 (1894). In determining the amount so appropriated, it is "proper" for the courts to take into consideration the number of acres of land susceptible of irrigation and the amount of water necessary to irrigate the same: *Kirk* v. *Bartholomew*, 3 Idaho 367, 372, 29 Pac. 40 (1892).

[358] *Uhrig* v. *Coffin*, 72 Idaho 271, 274, 240 Pac. (2d) 480 (1952).

[359] *Allen* v. *Petrick*, 69 Mont. 373, 379-380, 222 Pac. 451 (1924). Continuing, the court said that: "In determining the duty of water the court should ascertain the quantity which is essential to irrigate economically but successfully the tract of land to be irrigated. Emphasis should be placed upon economy of use. But economy should not be insisted upon such an extent as to imperil success."

[360] *Porter* v. *Pettengill*, 57 Oreg. 247, 250, 110 Pac. 393 (1910).

[361] *United States* v. *American Ditch Assn.*, 2 Fed. Supp. 867, 869 (D. Idaho 1933).

[362] *Stearns* v. *Benedick*, 126 Mont. 272, 276-277, 247 Pac. (2d) 656 (1952); *Conrow* v. *Huffine*, 48 Mont. 437, 445-446, 138 Pac. 1094 (1914).

would require an unduly expensive conduit.[363] In other cases, extremely porous soil was cause for allowances of water higher than the norm.[364]

Factors for consideration in arriving at the quantity of water to be allowed an appropriator were announced by courts from time to time.[365] In 1954, the Colorado Supreme Court listed "suggestions of matters properly to be considered in determining the duty of water." These were:[366]

> Land characteristics at the place of use are important; location; slope; depth of soil; whether it is loose or close; if underlain with gravel or impervious material; its composition and general adaptability for the growing of irrigated crops; all are taken into consideration. Climate is a feature not to be overlooked, as also are the kinds of crops ordinarily grown thereon and the proportion of the area devoted to each type of crop and the rotation thereof. In fact, every element that concerns or affects the consumption of water in the particular case before the court is to be considered. * * *

Although evidence as to duty of water has long been widely presented by trained technicians, some courts accorded a warmer welcome to testimony by local farmers with long experience in practices of farming under irrigation. Thus, in a Montana case: "Again, as to the evidence, while that of the experts is very valuable on location and measurements, still the testimony of the men on the land, who know the soil, the kind of crops that can be raised on it, and who have spread the water and dug into that soil, and watched the effect during the entire growing season, brings in evidence of considerable weight."[367]

---

[363] *Hedges* v. *Riddle,* 75 Oreg. 197, 198, 146 Pac. 99 (1915).

[364] *In re Rogue River,* 117 Oreg. 477, 481, 244 Pac. 662 (1926); *Worden* v. *Alexander,* 108 Mont. 208, 212-213, 90 Pac. (2d) 160 (1939).

[365] Some of the earlier declarations included: Character of area, climatic conditions, location and altitude of lands, kind of crops, period of irrigation time, necessary method of irrigation, and head of water at the intake: *Hough* v. *Porter,* 51 Oreg. 318, 417-420, 95 Pac. 732 (1908), 98 Pac. 1083 (1909), 102 Pac. 728 (1909). Acreage of irrigable land, degree of sterility of premises, most profitable crops to be raised under irrigation, quantity of water required by careful husbandry: *Donnelly* v. *Cuhna,* 61 Oreg. 72, 76, 119 Pac. 331 (1911). Character of soil, climate, and other conditions, as well as manner of application of water: *Little Walla Walla Irr. Union* v. *Finis Irr. Co.,* 62 Oreg. 348, 351, 124 Pac. 666, 125 Pac. 270 (1912). Character of soil: intended irrigated area; climatic conditions; location, quality, and altitude of lands; kinds of intended crops; length of irrigation season; other conditions peculiar to each particular case: *Joerger* v. *Pacific Gas & Electric Co.,* 207 Cal. 8, 21-22, 276 Pac. 1017 (1929).

[366] *Farmers' Highline Canal & Res. Co.* v. *Golden,* 129 Colo. 575, 584-585, 272 Pac. (2d) 629 (1954).

[367] *Federal Land Bank* v. *Morris,* 112 Montana 445, 452-453, 116 Pac. (2d) 1007 (1941). Two years earlier, the same court declined to give controlling weight to the testimony of qualified irrigation engineers that all lands involved required only 1 inch per acre for

Statutory provisions.— (1) Beneficial use as limit of right. Beneficial use of water as an essential measure of the appropriative right runs throughout the water rights legislation of the West, either expressly or by necessary implication, or both. As brought out earlier under "Beneficial Use of Water," water rights statutes of 10 States repeat the historic declaration that beneficial use shall be the basis, the measure, and the limit of the right to the use of water.[368] Additional provision for implementing the declaration is made in some of these acts; and various specific references to beneficial use or reasonable requirements of appropriators appear in the statutes of the remaining eight mainland States.[369]

(2) Quantitative limitations. In the water rights statutes of several States are limitations upon the quantity of water that may be used per acre of land devoted to agriculture under irrigation.

(a) California. As used in the division of the Water Code pertaining to water rights, the term "useful or beneficial purposes" is not to be construed to mean the use in any 1 year of more than 2½ acre-feet of water per acre in the irrigation of land not devoted to cultivated crops.[370]

The rules and regulations of the State Water Resources Control Board state the amounts of water considered reasonably necessary for certain uses in typical parts of the State.[371]

(b) Idaho. No permit shall authorize the diversion for irrigation purposes of more than 1 second-foot for each 50 acres of land, or more than 5 acre-feet

---

successful and economical irrigation, whereas qualified farmers with wide and long experience in local irrigation testified that two to three inches were necessary. The engineers had no personal experience in the local area and, according to the court, based their testimony "upon a mere casual examination thereof." The supreme court fortified its decision in the premises by the skeptical observation that: "While, in determining the weight of the evidence in this case, we should consider the interest of the parties, we should also consider the fact that the engineers were employed by the appellants herein, and in their testimony would likely favor the parties by whom they were employed." *Worden* v. *Alexander,* 108 Mont. 208, 214-215, 90 Pac. (2d) 160 (1939). Compare *Joerger* v. *Pacific Gas & Electric Co.,* 207 Cal. 8, 21-22, 35-36, 276 Pac. 1017 (1929).

[368] Ariz. Rev. Stat. Ann. § 45-101(B) (1956); Nev. Rev. Stat. §533.035 (Supp. 1969); N. Mex. Const., art. XVI, § 3; N. Mex. Stat. Ann. § 75-1-2 (1968); N. Dak. Cent. Code Ann. § 61-01-02 (Supp. 1969); Okla. Stat. Ann. tit. 82, § 1-A (1970); Oreg. Rev. Stat. § 540.610 (Supp. 1969); S. Dak. Comp. Laws Ann. § 46-1-8 (1967); Tex. Rev. Civ. Stat. Ann. art. 7542 (1954); Utah Code Ann. § 73-1-3 (1968); Wyo. Stat. Ann. § 41-2 (1957).

[369] Alaska Stat. § § 46.15.030 and 46.15.260 (Supp. 1966); Cal. Water Code § 1240 (West 1956); Colo. Rev. Stat. Ann. § 148-21-3(7) (Supp. 1969); Idaho Code Ann. § 42-220 (1948); Kans. Stat. Ann. § 82a-707(d) (1969); Mont. Rev. Codes Ann. § 89-802 (1964); Nebr. Rev. Stat. § 46-231 (1968); Wash. Rev. Code § 90.03.010 (Supp. 1961).

[370] Cal. Water Code § 1004 (West 1956).

[371] Cal. Admin. Code, tit. 23, § 657 (1969).

of stored water per acre per annum, unless the administrator finds a greater quantity to be necessary. No licence or court decree shall confirm the right to use more than 1 second-foot per 50 acres unless the administrator or the court so decides.[372]

(c) Nebraska. For irrigation purposes, the limit is 1 second-foot for 70 acres, or 3 acre-feet per acre in the aggregate each year. However, for irrigation of 40 acres or less, where the statutory limit is too small for proper distribution and application of water, additional heads of water may be allotted for limited times. Stored water appropriations for irrigation are limited to 3 acre-feet per acre in a calendar year.[373]

(d) Oklahoma. For irrigation purposes, the limit is 4 acre-feet at the point of diversion for each acre of land irrigated each calendar year.[374]

(e) South Dakota. For irrigation, the allowance does not exceed 1 second-foot per 70 acres, or the equivalent thereof, not to exceed 3 acre-feet per acre, delivered on the land for a specified time in each year. However, this limitation does not apply at times when the floodflow of a stream much exceeds the quantity required for approved rights thereon.[375]

(f) Wyoming. For direct use of the natural unstored flow of any stream, no allotment may exceed 1 second-foot for each 70 acres for which the appropriation is made. However, a statute enacted in 1945 provided for allocation to holders of adjudicated or permit rights, with priority as of March 1, 1945, rights in the surplus waters (over and above existing appropriations) of the stream in question, not to exceed (1) 1 second-foot per 70 acres of irrigated land and (2) his proportionate share of previously appropriated water.[376] The limitation does not apply to reservoir storage waters.

(3) Criteria in directives to administrators. (a) Nevada. In determining the quantity of water to be granted for irrigation in a permit, the State Engineer is directed to consider the local irrigation requirements; the duty of water as established by court decree or by experimental work; the growing season, type of culture, and reasonable ditch conveyance losses; and any other pertinent data necessary to arrive at a reasonable duty of water. In case of storage of water, reasonable evaporation losses are to be taken into consideration.[377]

(b) New Mexico. In the issuance of permits to appropriate water for irrigation, the State Engineer "shall permit the amount allowed to be diverted at a rate consistent with good agricultural practices and which will result in the most effective use of available water in order to prevent waste."[378]

---

[372] Idaho Code Ann. § § 42-202 (Supp. 1969) and -220 (1948).
[373] Nebr. Rev. Stat. § § 46-231, -240.01, and -242 (1968).
[374] Okla. Stat. Ann. tit. 82, § 33 (1970).
[375] S. Dak. Comp. Laws Ann. § 46-5-6 (1967).
[376] Wyo. Stat. Ann. § § 41-181 to -188 (1957).
[377] Nev. Rev. Stat. § 533.070 (Supp. 1967).
[378] N. Mex. Stat. Ann. § 75-5-17 (Supp. 1969).

(c) In both Nevada and New Mexico, prior to amendment in 1945 and 1955, respectively,[379] the statutes prescribed quantitative limitations upon irrigation water rights.

Conveyance losses.—(1) Place of measurement of appropriated water. Water is measured to appropriators at the point at which it is diverted from the stream. This was the practice of the early water users, and the courts recognized it as practicable.[380] The measurement at the point of diversion not only includes the quantity of water intended to be delivered at the place of beneficial use, but it is also so regulated as to compensate for necessary transmission losses.[381]

(2) Reasonable conveyance loss allowable. Always and inevitably there is a difference between the quantity of water diverted from a stream and the quantity that reaches the place of use through an open ditch or flume.[382] Particularly is this true in the case of a large and long irrigation system.[383] Hence, an appropriator "is entitled to hold and divert, as incident to his appropriative rights, such amount of water as may be reasonably necessary to take care of normal storage and transportation losses."[384]

(3) Obligation imposed on water user. Granted, then, that some conveyance loss in an open ditch is generally unavoidable, a water user who expects

---

[379] Nev. Stats. 1945, ch. 56; N. Mex. Laws 1955, ch. 91.

[380] *Caruthers* v. *Pemberton,* 1 Mont. 111, 117, (1869); *Kleinschmidt* v. *Greiser,* 14 Mont. 484, 498, 37 Pac. 5 (1894); *Bennett* v. *Nourse,* 22 Idaho 249, 254, 125 Pac. 1038 (1912); *Basinger* v. *Taylor,* 30 Idaho 289, 300, 164 Pac. 522 (1917); *Ramelli* v. *Sorgi,* 38 Nev. 552, 559, 149 Pac. 71 (1915).

[381] *In re Althouse Creek,* 85 Oreg. 224, 226-227, 162 Pac. 1072 (1917); *Wheat* v. *Cameron,* 64 Mont. 494, 501-502, 210 Pac. 761 (1922).

[382] *Barrows* v. *Fox,* 98 Cal. 63, 66, 32 Pac. 811 (1893).

[383] *Thayer* v. *California Development Co.,* 164 Cal. 117, 137, 128 Pac. 21 (1912).

[384] *Oliver* v. *Skinner and Lodge,* 190 Oreg. 423, 440-441, 226 Pac. (2d) 507 (1951); *Bennett* v. *Salem,* 192 Oreg. 531, 544, 235 Pac. (2d) 772 (1951); *Tulare Irr. Dist.* v. *Lindsay-Strathmore Irr. Dist.,* 3 Cal. (2d) 489, 546-547, 45 Pac. (2d) 972 (1935). "In offering evidence as to the duty of water, the inquiry is properly directed to the amount of water necessary to be diverted from the stream in order to properly irrigate the land, and the question of reasonableness or unreasonableness of the loss from the ditch through seepage and evaporation is a proper subject for inquiry." *Clark* v. *Hansen,* 35 Idaho 449, 455, 206 Pac. 808 (1922). In holding that a party, whose right of appropriation for 0.96 second-foot dated back to 1858, was entitled to have enough additional water diverted at the headgate to compensate for seepage, evaporation, and loss necessarily resulting from proper conveyance of the water in order to produce 0.96 second-foot at the irrigated land, the Oregon Supreme Court explained by saying that: "Under existing conditions to measure out at the place of diversion the exact amount which the claimant is entitled actually to put on the land is for all practical purposes equivalent to admitting a right and at the same time denying part of it." *In re Althouse Creek,* 85 Oreg. 224, 226-227, 162 Pac. 1072 (1917).

to have his full water supply delivered at his land is required to use reasonable care and diligence in holding the transmission losses to a practical minimum.[385] And he may be compelled to do so.[386]

As said by the Oregon Supreme Court in 1923, "We have not arrived at the state of irrigation when farmers can practically lay iron water pipes, or construct concrete ditches; yet the question that water for irrigation must be used economically and without needless waste is no longer debatable."[387] A Federal court observed that although the water user is not bound to extraordinary diligence in means and methods of use, and may proceed according to local custom, he is bound to reasonable care in construction and maintenance of appliances to the end that others be not unnecessarily deprived of the water.[388]

(4) In granting permits under the water administration statutes, reasonable conveyance losses are taken into account.[389]

---

[385] *Joseph Mill. Co.* v. *Joseph,* 74 Oreg. 296, 302, 304, 144 Pac. 465 (1914).

[386] *Roeder* v. *Stein,* 23 Nev. 92, 96-97, 42 Pac. 867 (1895). In the adjudication of rights to the use of Hood River waters, the various water users were required to put their conveyance works "in good serviceable condition * * * in a good and husband-like manner" by taking certain prescribed steps prior to a specified date: *In re Hood River,* 114 Oreg. 112, 188, 227 Pac. 1065 (1924).

[387] *Foster* v. *Foster,* 107 Oreg. 355, 363, 366, 213 Pac. 895 (1923). The parties were required, by a certain date, to repair their ditches and flumes and keep them in condition, which could be done "without building concrete or new ditches and at a reasonable expense." An appropriator has no right to run water into a swamp and cause the loss of two-thirds of a stream simply because he is following lines of least resistance. *Doherty* v. *Pratt,* 34 Nev. 343, 348, 124 Pac. 574 (1912). A loss of 50 percent of the water between the point of diversion and place of use was held by the Idaho Supreme Court to be not reasonable. "The farmers could not reasonably have been expected to build a cement ditch at the cost of $100,000, as suggested by one of the witnesses. But they could have been reasonably expected to prevent the water spreading out at several places as shown by the evidence." *Basinger* v. *Taylor,* 36 Idaho 591, 597, 211 Pac. 1085 (1922).

[388] *Dern* v. *Tanner,* 60 Fed. (2d) 626, 628 (D. Mont. 1932). "To secure the amount to which the appropriator is entitled admeasured at his land, no excess can be diverted from the source to cover unreasonable loss in transit." Losses from the ditch in litigation were held to be excessive.

[389] An appropriation is effectual only as to so much water as is actually applied to beneficial use, together with a reasonable allowance for waste, seepage, and evaporation: Kans. Stat. Ann. § 42-302 (1964); "reasonable transportation losses" and "reservoir evaporation losses" are taken into consideration in Nev. Rev. Stat. § 533.070 (Supp. 1967); "reasonable conveyance losses" are included in Cal. Admin. Code, tit. 23, § 655 (1969); Okla. Stat. Ann. tit. 82, § 33 (1970), and S. Dak. Comp. Laws Ann. § 46-5-6 (1967), in limiting the permitted amount of water to be taken, do not mention conveyance losses, but in view of the declarations in the statutes respecting beneficial use, a limitation to reasonable conveyance loss is clearly to be implied.

Excessive Allowance of Water

Previously in this topic "Measure of the Appropriative Right," attention has been called to a wealth of authoritative expressions of legislatures and courts pointing up the need for conserving and making beneficial use of water and avoiding unnecessary waste, for better service of the public welfare. The policy statements that appear in so many court opinions do not deviate from the principle that reasonable beneficial use is the goal and that, as a necessary corollary, unnecessary waste of water is abhorrent. They show no trace of compromise.

Despite all this, wasteful practices were tolerated by the courts in many areas, chiefly in the earlier decades. At first, when water was plentiful, the accepted practice in various communities was to use it lavishly. Thus were precedents set for careless handling of what was to become an increasingly scarce natural resource. Appropriative rights to the use of unnecessarily large quantities of water were litigated and decreed. The farmer's right to more water than he needed became of record. Added to this were the burden of increasing costs of making substantial improvements. Further complications grew out of the widespread efforts of water users to hold title to maximum quantities of water to which their rights related. Unfortunately, a result was much excessive and therefore wasteful use of water which contributed to shortages in quantities available to newcomers.

Comments on these early extravagances in authorized uses of water were made in an opinion of the Montana Supreme Court in a case decided in 1924. Although the court's discourse pertains especially to practices in that State, comparable conditions obtained in various other western regions as well. With this reminder, several pertinent paragraphs of the court's thesis are reproduced here:[390]

In Montana, as elsewhere, when the early settlers made their original appropriations they had little knowledge of the quantity of water necessary to irrigate their lands to good advantage. Ample quantities of water being available in the streams the settlers claimed extravagant amounts. * * * Almost every irrigator used an excessive amount of water, some all they could get. * * * When the country became more thickly settled and the people began to farm more thoroughly and according to more approved methods, it began to be understood by practical as well as scientific experience that the use of excessive quantities of water was detrimental rather than beneficial to the land. * * * Yet here, as well as elsewhere, many still adhere to extravagant use of water, although it is apparent to the enlightened that these users are raising smaller and poorer crops than they would raise if they used water more sparingly and intelligently. * * *

---

[390] *Allen v. Petrick,* 69 Mont. 373, 377-380, 222 Pac. 451 (1924).

It is a matter of common knowledge in the several judicial districts of this state where irrigation has been practiced since the early days that extravagant quantities of water were awarded the litigants by the courts. In instances more water was awarded than some of the ditches of the litigants ever would carry; in others much greater quantities of water than the litigants ever did or could use beneficially. In some cases the courts were not to blame. The litigants tried to get all they could. They even stipulated to the use of quantities of water ridiculously large for the amount of land indicated. * * *

A fundamental error into which the early day courts fell was the result of their failure to appreciate what has been termed the duty of water; that is, the extent to which and the manner in which the water should be used by the appropriator. In determining the duty of water the court should ascertain the quantity which is essential to irrigate economically but successfully the tract of land to be irrigated. * * *

With respect to material and expensive changes in practice, "Decrees fixing the extent of rights follow rather than lead in such improvements in practice."[391] Although this comment was made with respect to conditions that existed in the first one-third of the present century as well as earlier, it undoubtedly reflects also the situation that existed in the very early years of irrigation development when so little unbiased information as to water requirements for crops was available. Furthermore, appropriators were generally protected, not only in quantities of water appropriated, but in means of diversion if reasonable.

At an address in Reno, Nevada, in 1953, an official of the Bureau of Reclamation elaborated on what he termed the practice of "padding and pyramiding" State water rights and its adverse effect on planning water use projects in the mountain States. By "padding" he meant creating records of rights to the use of water in excess of that actually beneficially used. By "pyramiding" he referred to filing and maintaining in good standing more applications to appropriate water than are required for a given purpose. "It is my opinion," he said, "based upon more than 30 years of reclamation work, that this practice is one of the most serious problems we are encountering in developing western water resources. The seriousness increases as the water available for appropriation diminishes."[392]

Point of Diversion of Water

The necessity of a diversion of water under an appropriative right is discussed in chapter 9. The place of diversion of the water is an element of the

---

[391] Harding, S.T., "Water Rights for Irrigation," p. 38 (1936).
[392] Larson, E.O., "Planning of Water Use Projects under Federal and State Law." 22 Proc. National Reclamation Assn. 100 (1953).

appropriative right—a focal point in the establishment and exercise of the right. It is there that the water right attaches to the flow of the stream—the place at which the appropriator takes control of the quantity of water that he is entitled to divert. And it is to that point that he is entitled to have the stream flow without substantial interference or impairment of quality by those junior in right or without right.

The place of diversion of an appropriator is also important from the standpoint of other appropriators of the flow of the same stream (see, in chapter 7, "Methods of Appropriating Water of Watercourses—Priority of Appropriation").[393] It is so important in this respect that a change in point of diversion of an appropriative right may be made only if the rights of others are not thereby adversely affected and, in most jurisdictions, only by following a prescribed statutory procedure. (See, in chapter 9, "Change in Exercise of Water Right—Point of Diversion.")

Under the administrative procedures for appropriating water, the proposed point of diversion is stated by the intending appropriator in his application. As approved or altered by the administrator in the permit, and as fixed by construction of the diversion works, this place becomes an essential part of the completed appropriative right.[394]

---

[393] The decision in an early Nevada case was based on most unusual facts. An appropriator used alternative points of diversion, taking out all the water at one point at one time and all the water at another point at another time, as his convenience dictated. Inasmuch as the practice had been begun before an objecting party purchased lands lying on the stream between the two points of diversion, the supreme court saw no reason to deny the prior appropriator's right to continue the alternative uses. *Hobart* v. *Wicks,* 15 Nev. 418, 420-421 (1880). See S. Dak. Comp. Laws Ann. § 46-5-13 (1967), regarding overhead sprinkling diversions.

[394] In *Keller* v. *Magic Water Co.,* 92 Idaho 226, 441 Pac. (2d) 725, 732-734 (1968), the facts in the case were said to constitute merely an amendment of a permit to show the correct point of diversion rather than an authorized change in the point of diversion. The court also concluded that there was only one diversion even though the diversion works consisted of a dam and two pumping units separated by location and time of construction, with the natural channel constituting part of the transportation system. When the second pumping unit was completed, the appropriator's date of priority dated back to the initial date of application for all waters beneficially used. (The court refuted the contention that two separate and different points of diversion were being utilized, the second point being subsequent in time and thus subsequent in priority to others' rights.)

The South Dakota water rights statute provides that each application and permit for irrigation by the overhead sprinkler method, or by the use of portable diversion pumping equipment, may authorize diversions from one or more points at a time from a reach of the stream or other water sources between two fixed points on the stream as described in the application and permit; provided, that the total quantity diverted from two or more permissible points at one time under the provisions of a water right shall not exceed the total withdrawal rate allowed by said water right per unit of time. S. Dak. Comp. Laws Ann. § 46-5-13 (1967).

Place of Use of Water

The place of use of water under an appropriative right may or may not be located on land contiguous to the stream from which the water is diverted. In this respect the doctrine of appropriation differs from the riparian doctrine, with the requirement of the latter that use of water be made in general only on riparian land. On many large irrigation projects in the West, the area of land which would conform to the accepted definition of "riparian" land is a very small fraction of the total area irrigated. Even in the States in which the riparian doctrine is recognized, the water rights of most of the large irrigation enterprises consist chiefly or entirely of appropriative rights.

Earlier in this chapter, the topic "Appurtenance of Water Right to Land" reveals the intimate association of appurtenance with place of use of water under the appropriative right.

The western administrative procedures for appropriating water invariably require the applicant for a permit to designate his proposed place of use of the water which he desires to appropriate. Some of the statutes require an applicant for an irrigation water supply to describe the lands proposed to be irrigated, with legal subdivisions and total acreages stated as nearly as practicable. Others leave this to the rules and regulations of the State administrator. Some statutes specifically except large projects; if not expressly excepted, the required information can of course be presented on maps without detailed listings of subdivisions. A few statutes provide that final certificates of appropriation shall designate legal subdivisions of irrigated land on which the rights were acquired and for which they are confirmed. A majority, however, describe the certificate in general terms as confirmatory of the completed right. The purpose of the license or certificate of appropriation is to define completely the water right that it evidences, particularly the extent and conditions of actual diversion of water and its application to beneficial use. Whether specifically "spelled out" in the statute or not, inclusion of an adequate description of the irrigated area would seem to be an implicit requirement.

The matter of effecting changes in place of use of appropriated water is discussed in chapter 9 under "Change in Exercise of Water Right—Place and Purpose of Use."

Diversion of Water from Watershed or Area of Origin

Long Recognition of the Qualified Right

Under the appropriation doctrine, a right of use acquired in the flow of a stream is not limited to lands contiguous thereto nor to any other lands solely because of their location. From this it follows that the use is not generally restricted to the watershed, subject of course to the rule that applies to other features of exercise of the appropriative right, that the prior rights of others be not adversely affected by diverting the water outside the original drainage area.

The practice of taking water out of the watershed in which it originates has been followed from the earliest years of hydraulic mining in the Sierra foothills of California, wherein numerous streams rising in the mountains tend to parallel each other in their descent into the vast central valley. This right of the appropriator to divert, from one watershed to another, water in excess of the quantity necessary to satisfy the requirements of prior rights, riparian and appropriative, was specifically recognized by the California courts.[395] The acknowledged right to take water out of the watershed, however, was always qualified by the limitation that no injury be thereby inflicted upon prior or superior rights.[396] See also the discussion below regarding "Some Statutory Authorizations and Restrictions—California."

In an early decision, the Colorado Supreme Court concluded that it was lawful to carry appropriated water out of the watershed in which it originates, across an intervening divide, into another watershed for irrigation of lands in the latter valley, provided it could be done without detriment to holders of existing priorities in the original watershed.[397] Other courts held to the same effect.[398]

In some instances, the Montana Supreme Court used caution in discussing the right to take waters out of the watershed. For example, in one case in

---

[395] *Miller* v. *Bay Cities Water Co.,* 157 Cal. 256, 280-281, 107 Pac. 115 (1910); *San Joaquin & Kings River Canal & Irr. Co.* v. *Fresno Flume & Irr. Co.,* 158 Cal. 626, 627-630, 112 Pac. 182 (1910); *Gallatin* v. *Corning Irr. Co.,* 163 Cal. 405, 413, 126 Pac. 864 (1912).

[396] *Southern California Investment Co.* v. *Wilshire,* 144 Cal. 68, 72-74, 77 Pac. 767 (1904); *Huffner* v. *Sawday,* 153 Cal. 86, 90, 94, 94 Pac. 424 (1908); *Scott* v. *Fruit Growers' Supply Co.,* 202 Cal. 47, 51-55, 258 Pac. 1095 (1927).

[397] "In the absence of legislation to the contrary, we think that the right to water acquired by priority of appropriation is not in any way dependent upon the *locus* of its application to the beneficial use designed." *Coffin* v. *Left Hand Ditch Co.,* 6 Colo. 443, 449-451 (1882). See also *Oppenlander* v. *Left Hand Ditch Co.,* 18 Colo. 142, 144, 31 Pac. 854 (1892).

[398] *Saunders* v. *Robison,* 14 Idaho 770, 95 Pac. 1057 (1908), syllabus by the court. Commencing in 1864, miners conveyed waters of Gold Creek across a divide into the watershed of Pioneer Creek: *Mannix & Wilson* v. *Thrasher,* 95 Mont. 267, 268, 26 Pac. (2d) 373 (1933). Immaterial whether the lands to which the waters are applied are within or without the watershed of the stream from which the waters are taken: *Mettler* v. *Ames Realty Co.,* 61 Mont. 152, 159, 201 Pac. 702 (1921). In various decrees of water rights, appropriators were authorized to take the water out of the watershed for use on outside lands: *Thrasher* v. *Mannix & Wilson,* 95 Mont. 273, 277-278, 26 Pac. (2d) 370 (1933).

which the right had been acquired many years previously, it was said that:[399]

> Waters primarily belong in the watershed of their origin, if there is land therein which requires irrigation. * * * Courts have many times sustained such foreign appropriation, and perhaps each case would be determined upon its own individual merit. It is sufficient here to say that the right to the use of this water for placer mining purposes by the appellants has been sustained, but it may be appropriate to remark that the burden placed upon the water should not be added to, to the detriment of appropriations made for irrigating lands within the area of the stream from which the water is diverted. * * *

An objection to taking water away from its watershed is that the benefit from return flow from lands irrigated with such water will accrue to the new watershed, and thus be lost to the lands lying within the original watershed. This merges into the subject of changes in place of use of appropriated water, which is discussed in chapter 9 under "Change in Exercise of Water Right—Place and Purpose of Use."

Under many circumstances, preexisting rights are not injured by a diversion out of the watershed of an appropriation specifically made for that purpose, which usually attaches only to the surplus in the streamflow above the requirements of these senior rights.

Some Statutory Authorizations and Restrictions

California. —The Water Code imposes certain restrictions upon the taking of water, pursuant to State and Federal plans, away from the localities in which it originates, aimed at protection of these localities from deprivation of water reasonably required for their beneficial needs and development. Statewide restrictions relate to counties of origin.[400] Central Valley Project restrictions relate to watersheds or areas of origin.[401] These restrictions have not yet been construed by the State supreme court. The California Attorney General has rendered opinions with respect to their scope and applicability.[402] Federal

---

[399] *Galliger* v. *McNulty,* 80 Mont. 339, 356, 260 Pac. 401 (1927); *Spokane Ranch & Water Co.* v. *Beatty,* 37 Mont. 342, 351-352, 96 Pac. 727, 97 Pac. 838 (1908). In a case decided in 1942, an appropriator unsuccessfully claimed title to the return flow from water brought into the watershed by another party: *Allendale Irr. Co.* v. *State Water Conservation Board,* 113 Mont. 436, 439, 449, 127 Pac. (2d) 227 (1942).

[400] Cal. Water Code § § 10500 to 10507 (West Supp. 1970).

[401] Cal. Water Code § § 11128 (West 1956) and 11460-11463 (West Supp. 1970).

[402] 25 Cal. Op. Atty. Gen. 8 (1955); 29 Cal. Op. Atty. Gen. 136 (1957).

courts discussed them in several related actions pertaining to waters of the San Joaquin River.[403]

New Mexico.—A section of the water appropriation statute provides that water may be transferred from one stream or drainage into another and diverted therefrom, less transmission losses determined by the State Engineer. Another section makes it unlawful to divert the waters of any public stream for use in a valley other than that of such stream, to the impairment of subsisting prior appropriations.[404]

North Dakota.—The State Water Conservation Commission has authority to conserve and develop waters within the natural watershed areas of the State and, subject to vested and riparian rights, to divert waters from one watershed area to another watershed area, and the waters of any river, lake, or stream into another river, lake, or stream.[405]

Texas.—The legislature had undertaken to protect holders of rights to the use of water originating in a given watershed from such exportation of the water therefrom as will adversely affect their rights. The water rights statute makes it unlawful to divert any of the flow, underflow, or stormflow of any watercourse or watershed into any other to the prejudice of any person or property within the original watershed. Before any water may be so taken application must be made to the Texas Water Rights Commission for a permit therefor, which is not to be issued until after notice and hearing by the Commission as to the rights that may be affected thereby. Appeal may be taken from the Commission's decision to the courts under the usual procedure for judicial review. Penalties are provided for violations of these provisions.[406] Procedure for obtaining a permit to divert water from a watershed for use in another is noted and particularized in the rules and regulations of the Commission.[407]

The Texas Supreme Court has refused to construe this statute's language so as to "have the intolerable consequence of defeating a project promising

---

[403] *Rank* v. *(Krug) United States,* 142 Fed. Supp. 1, 149-154 (S. D. Cal. 1956); *Rank* v. *(Krug) United States,* 155 Fed. Supp. 872, 874 (S. D. Cal. 1957); *State of California* v. *Rank,* 293 Fed. (2d) 340, 352-353, 360 (9th Cir. 1961); *State of California* v. *Rank,* 307 Fed. (2d) 96 (9th Cir. 1962); *City of Fresno* v. *State of California,* 372 U. S. 627, 630 (1963); *Dugan* v. *Rank,* 372 U. S. 609, 617 (1963).

[404] N. Mex. Stat. Ann. § § 75-5-24 and 75-7-5 (1968).

Another section (75-5-27), in order, *inter alia,* to distribute water "as equitably as possible without interfering with vested rights, recognizes the natural right of the people living in the upper valleys of the several stream systems to impound and utilize a reasonable share of the waters which are precipitated upon and have their source in such valleys and superadjacent mountains," provided, however, that the exercise of this right is subject to the laws governing the appropriation of water.

[405] N. Dak. Cent. Code Ann. § 61-02-14(1)(d) (Supp. 1969).

[406] Tex. Rev. Civ. Stat. Ann. arts. 7589, 7591 (1954), 7477, § 12, 7590 (Supp. 1970).

[407] Tex. Water Rights Comm'n, "Rules, Regulations and Modes of Procedure," rule 620.1 (1970 Rev., Jan. 1970).

immense benefits to the receiving region or the State as a whole upon a mere showing of a slight harm to present or future interests." It noted that another statute (the Wagstaff Act) charges the Commission, in passing on all applications for appropriative rights, to give preference to those which will maximize utilization of waters and prevent their escape without contribution to a beneficial public service.[408] The court said "it is apparent that the Legislature intended to prohibit diversion out of the basin of origin only to the extent such diversion would impair water rights in existence at the time of the proposed diversion" and "we have also concluded that as to any water in the originating basin found to be in excess of that amount required to protect existing rights, the Legislature intended that the Commission should, in a balancing process, take into consideration future benefits and detriments expected to result from a proposed transbasin diversion and that there would be 'prejudice' only if the benefits from the diversion were outweighed by detriments to the originating basin. See Johnson and Knippa, Transbasin Diversion of Water, 43 Tex. L. R. 1035, 1044 (1965)."[409] In another case, a specific statutory prohibition against withdrawal of water from a particular watershed[410] was held unconstitutional.[411]

---

[408] Tex. Rev. Civ. Stat. Ann. art. 7472c (1954).

[409] City of San Antonio v. Texas Water Comm'n, 407 S. W. (2d) 752, 758-759 (Tex. Sup. Ct. 1966).

The court further held that Tex. Rev. Civ. Stat. Ann. art. 7589 (1954) was not modified or repealed by provisions of the Wagstaff Act (arts. 7471-7472d) giving priority to municipal use. Id. at 762-763.

The court also concluded that a restriction on transbasin diversions of surface water included in the Water Resources Administration & Development Act of 1965 "is directed solely at the 'State Water Plan' to be formulated by the Texas Water Development Board and not the Water Rights Commission. This is reinforced by the further provision that after the Plan is adopted it shall be a 'flexible guide' by which the Commission need not be bound but rather shall take 'into consideration in matters coming before the Commission.' " Id. at 757, citing Acts 1965, ch. 297, Tex. Rev. Civ. Stat. Ann. art. 8280-9, § 3(b) (Supp. 1970) which, among other things, provides that "the Board shall not prepare or formulate any plan which contemplates or results in the removal from the basin of origin of any surface water to some other river basin or area outside of such basin of origin if the water supply involved in such plan or project will be required to supply the reasonably foreseeable future water supply requirements for the next ensuing fifty-year period within the river basin of origin, except on a temporary, interim basis."

Concerning the amount of water available for appropriation, the court said "There is evidence in the record that water retained within the watershed is susceptible to multiple use because all water uses are not consumptive uses. It is apparent that water unappropriated and available for use within the originating watershed is not necessarily the equivalent of water unappropriated within the originating watershed but to be used outside the watershed." Id. at 762.

[410] Tex. Rev. Civ. Stat. Ann. art. 1434a, § 1-a (1962).

[411] Board of Water Engineers v. San Antonio, 273 S. W. (2d) 913, 914-915 (Tex. Civ. App. 1954), affirmed, 155 Tex. 111, 283 S. W. (2d) 722 (1955).

Nebraska.—Two sections in the water rights statute of Nebraska relating to the return of unused water to the stream bear directly upon the question of diverting water out of the watershed in which it originates.

(1) One section, originally a part of the 1889 law, provides that appropriated water shall not be turned into any stream other than that from which diverted unless such stream exceeds in width 100 feet, in which event not more than 75 percent of the regular flow shall be taken.[412]

(2) Another section, enacted in 1919, directs that unused water from an irrigation ditch be returned with as little waste as possible to the stream from which taken or to the Missouri River.[413]

The Nebraska Supreme Court construed these two sections together as necessarily limiting location of canals "to within the watershed of the stream that furnishes the source of supply." It was held that under the established policy of the State, water for irrigation and power purposes taken from the Platte River or its tributaries may not be lawfully diverted over and beyond the southern watershed of that stream and applied to lands situated without the basin of this river.[414]

The Nebraska Department of Water Resources approved an application to appropriate water from the Snake River, a tributary of Niobrara River, and to transport it out of the Snake watershed and into that of the Niobrara for irrigation purposes. In affirming this order, the supreme court distinguished the facts in the *earlier* case, where there was an admitted attempt to transport water to lands wholly outside the Platte River valley basin, and here where to all intents and purposes the Snake and Niobrara comprised one watershed and basin. All unused waters would be returned to the Niobrara, where they would have naturally flowed, and thence to the Missouri River, never out of the overall watershed. Under the circumstances of this case, the statutes were not in conflict.[415]

Purpose of Use of Water

The Use Must be Beneficial

So long as the use of water made under an appropriative right is a beneficial one, no distinction is made between appropriations for different useful purposes, and no appropriator for any one useful purpose has any preference

---

[412] Nebr. Rev. Stat. § 46-206 (1968).

[413] *Id.* § 46-265.

[414] *Osterman* v. *Central Nebraska Public Power & Irr. Dist.,* 131 Nebr. 356, 369-370, 268 N. W. 334 (1936).

[415] *Ainsworth Irr. Dist.* v. *Bejot,* 170 Nebr. 257, 102 N. W. (2d) 416 (1960). In addition, the evidence showed that in various stretches the Snake River exceeded 100 feet in width and that less than 50 percent of the flow would be taken.

or superior right over an appropriator for any other useful purpose, other than with respect (a) to priority of appropriation, and (b) to cases in which statutory preferences apply.

In 1875, the United States Supreme Court referred to a California case decided 20 years before and stated that:[416]

> Ever since that decision it has been held generally throughout the Pacific States and Territories that the right to water by prior appropriation for any beneficial purpose is entitled to protection. Water is diverted to propel machinery in flour-mills and saw-mills, and to irrigate land for cultivation, as well as to enable miners to work their mining claims; and in all such cases the right of the first appropriator, exercised within reasonable limits, is respected and enforced. * * *

Referring to its own recent decision in *Atchison* v. *Peterson*,[417] in which there were considered the respective rights of miners to running waters on the mineral lands of the public domain, the Court said that:[418]

> The views there expressed and the rulings made are equally applicable to the use of water on the public lands for the purposes of irrigation. No distinction is made in those States and Territories by the custom of miners or settlers, or by the courts, in the rights of the first appropriator from the use made of the water, if the use be a beneficial one.

Some Statutory Listings

The chief purpose of the earliest water appropriation statutes of various Western States was to authorize diversions from stream channels for the irrigation of agricultural land, and some of them mentioned irrigation only. In fact, the first State water official in South Dakota was designated "State Engineer of Irrigation,"[419] and the first North Dakota water rights administration statute was entitled "Irrigation Code."[420]

Some of the present administrative control statutes list several purposes for which water may be appropriated. Some others state generally that the purpose must be beneficial, and later they single out purposes of use in providing for the type of information with respect to specific purposes that must be contained in the application to make an appropriation, or in directing attention to some other matter. A few of the more comprehensive current listings are:

---

[416] *Basey* v. *Gallagher,* 87 U. S. 670, 681-683 (1875), referring to *Tartar* v. *Spring Creek Water & Min. Co.,* 5 Cal. 395 (1855).

[417] *Atchison* v. *Peterson,* 87 U. S. 507, 510-513 (1874).

[418] *Basey* v. *Gallagher,* 87 U. S. 670, 682 (1875).

[419] S. Dak. Laws 1890, ch. 104. His duties were concerned with developing irrigation within the State, not supervision over water rights.

[420] N. Dak. Laws 1905, ch. 34.

— Domestic, municipal, irrigation, stockwatering, water power, recreation, wildlife, including fish, and mining.[421]

— Domestic, irrigation, municipal, industrial, preservation of fish and wildlife, recreation, mining, power, any uses specified to be protected in any relevant water quality control plan, reuse of reclamation of water, and storing of water underground.[422]

— Irrigation, domestic, municipal, power, public recreation, commercial and game fishing and wildlife, fire protection, mining, industrial, navigation, scenic attraction, or any other beneficial use having special public value.[423]

— Irrigation, mining, milling, manufacturing, power, waterworks for cities and towns, stockraising, public parks, game preserves, recreation and pleasure, industrial purposes and plants, domestic, navigation, recharging a specified ground water reservoir and other beneficial uses.[424]

— Drinking for man and beast, municipal, steam engines and general railway use, culinary, laundry, bathing, refrigeration (including manufacture of ice), steam and hot water heating, steam power plants, industrial, irrigation, and water power.[425]

Purposes of use of water named in the current statutes are discussed at some length in connection with restrictions and preferences in appropriation of water in the last part of chapter 7.

Constitutional Mandates

Constitutions of several States contain declarations relating to specific purposes of use of water.

In North Dakota, it is provided that all flowing streams and natural watercourses shall forever remain the property of the State for mining, irrigation, and manufacturing purposes.[426]

Preferences among domestic, agriculture, and manufacturing are declared in Colorado, and among those uses are mining or milling connected with mining in Idaho.[427] (In chapter 7, see "Methods of Appropriating Water of Watercourses—Restrictions and Preferences in Appropriation of Water—Preferences in Water Appropriation.")

In Nebraska, the necessity of water for domestic and irrigation purposes is declared to be a natural want.[428] In South Dakota, irrigation of arid lands is a

---

[421] Ariz. Rev. Stat. Ann. § 45-141(A) (Supp. 1970).

[422] Cal. Water Code § § 1242 (West 1956), 1243, and 1257 (West Supp. 1970).

[423] Oreg. Rev. Stat. § § 537.170 (3) (a) (Supp. 1969) and 543.225(3)(a) (Supp. 1965). These are included in "the highest use of the water" which must be conserved in determining whether a proposed use of water would impair or be detrimental to the public interest.

[424] Tex. Rev. Civ. Stat. Ann. arts. 7470 and 7471 (Supp. 1970).

[425] Wyo. Stat. Ann. § 41-3 (1957). These are the uses of water that are named in the section providing for condemnation of existing rights not preferred to supply water for preferred uses.

[426] N. Dak. Const., art. XVII, § 210.

[427] Colo. Const., art. XVI, § 6; Idaho Const., art. XV, § 3.

[428] Nebr. Const., art. XV, § 4.

public purpose.[429] Texas declares that the conservation and development of natural resources including water for irrigation, power, and other useful purposes are public rights and duties.[430] Use of water in Washington for irrigation, mining, and manufacturing purposes is a public use.[431]

The Oregon constitution declares that the right to all water for development of water power and to water power sites owned by the State shall be held in perpetuity, and it clothes the State with broad powers to control and develop water and to distribute electric energy.[432]

Early Uses of Water in the West

(1) The Indians of the Southwest carried on agricultural operations with the aid of irrigation for centuries before the Spanish explorers came. The Spaniards brought to this continent a knowledge of irrigation institutions and practice acquired chiefly from the Moors and proceeded to adapt their irrigation experience to the new country. As a result, Indian customs were modified but not extinguished, and out of the merging of the Spanish and Indian methods of public or community handling of irrigation affairs there developed the Spanish-American community acequia. Thus, the community acequia provided the southwestern settlements with water both for domestic purposes and for irrigation.[433]

(2) The same result was achieved by use of ditches built by the Mormons in Utah and surrounding regions from the time in July 1847 when the first pioneer company, led by Brigham Young, entered Great Salt Lake Valley and established there the nucleus of a great colonization enterprise.[434] In addition to domestic and irrigation purposes, water of Utah settlements was put to use in providing power for operating milling machinery.[435] An act passed at the first session of the Territorial Legislative Assembly gave the county courts control of all water privileges and authority "to grant mill sites."[436]

---

[429] S. Dak. Const., art. XXI, § 7.

[430] Tex. Const., art. XVI, § 59(a).

[431] Wash. Const., art. XXI, § 1.

[432] Oreg. Const., art. XI-D.

[433] Hutchins, Wells A., "The Community Acequia: Its Origin and Development," 31 Southwestern Historical Quarterly 261 (1928). The first Spanish settlement in what is now the Southwestern United States was at San Juan, New Mexico, near the junction of the Rio Chama and the Rio Grande. There Juan de Oñate established his colony in 1598. "On August 11 of that year work was begun on an irrigation ditch, the Spaniards being assisted in their labor by some 1500 Indians." *Id.* at 275, citing Bancroft, H. H., "Arizona and New Mexico," p. 132 (1889).

[434] Hutchins, Wells A., "Mutual Irrigation Companies in Utah," Utah Agricultural Experiment Station Bull. 199 pp. 9-16 (1927).

[435] Thomas, George, "The Development of Institutions under Irrigation," pp. 46-48 (1920).

[436] Terr. Utah Laws 1852, p. 38 § 39, "An Act in Relation to the Judiciary," approved February 4, 1852.

(3) Use of water in the West for mining purposes sprang into prominence with the California Gold Rush, which followed the discovery of gold in the Sierra foothills in January 1848. The association of gold and water came about because much of the gold was extracted from the ground by means of hydraulic or placer mining processes in which the use of water was essential.[437] From California the hydraulic mining practices spread to other States in the Northwest and to Alaska.

(4) With the growth of western settlements into villages, towns, and cities, community water requirements rose from domestic to municipal status. Industrial purposes that required the use of water came to include not only grist and saw mills and milling connected with mining, but manufacturing of other kinds and development of hydraulic power.

Mining and Irrigation

During the feverish activity that prevailed during the gold-mining activity in California—where the western appropriation doctrine in its present form received its greatest impetus—uses of water for mining purposes predominated in the water cases that reached the supreme court. The principle of priority of appropriation was applied in the first cases as between appropriations of water for mining purposes,[438] and soon afterward to other purposes,[439] including domestic and irrigation.[440] In 1857, the California Supreme Court commented that the judiciary of that State had had thrown upon it responsibilities not incurred by the courts of any other State in the Union with respect to a large class of cases—unknown in the jurisprudence of other States—involving the great mining interest dependent upon the use of water.[441]

With the eventual decline in the far-flung mining industry and increase in irrigation of lands, controversies over irrigation water rights that reached the high courts of California and other Western States became relatively more numerous.[442]

---

[437] Harding, S.T., "Water Rights for Irrigation," p. 3-4 (1936).

[438] *Eddy* v. *Simpson,* 3 Cal. 249, 252 (1853).

[439] Saw milling: *Tartar* v. *Spring Creek Water & Min. Co.,* 5 Cal. 395 (1855). Mining versus milling: *Conger* v. *Weaver,* 6 Cal. 548 (1856).

[440] *Crandall* v. *Woods,* 8 Cal. 136 (1857).

[441] *Bear River & Auburn Water & Min. Co.* v. *New York Min. Co.,* 8 Cal. 327, 332 (1857).

[442] Of 52 water rights decisions rendered by the California Supreme Court to the end of 1872—in which year the Civil Code appropriation procedure was enacted—45 involved claims of appropriative rights for mining purposes, ten for milling, nine for irrigation, four for domestic or municipal, and one for stockwatering. In 16 of these cases, more than one purpose of use of water was involved. Eight cases included both mining and milling, four both mining and irrigation. Of 19 cases in the 10-year period 1873-1882, 16 involved irrigation, four each involved domestic, municipal, and mining, and two stockwatering.

Of 42 decisions of the Montana Supreme Court relating to water rights rendered to 1900 inclusive, 13 were in the approximate Territorial period 1869 to 1889, inclusive,

Eventually, the placer mining claims became largely exhausted. As this occurred on an increasingly widespread scale, the less affluent gold seekers had the choice of giving up their livelihood or moving on to virgin territory.[443] With respect to those who elected to remain in the area, questions arose as to the status of their appropriative rights for mining claims now rendered useless. In one such case in California, certain parties undertook to take water away from claims that had been "worked out" to other mining localities. The supreme court indicated that it saw no plausible reason why one who appropriates water for mining in a given locality could not extend his ditch to another mining area, or erect a mill and use the water for motive power without forfeiting his prior right.[444] Ten years earlier, the same court approved a rule that a change in *place* of use of water from one mining locality to another would not affect the priority of the right; but properly refused to express an opinion as to whether a change in *purpose* of use would affect the priority "as the point does not arise in this case."[445] The right to make such changes in place and purpose of use under appropriative rights, with certain limitations, has become an established principle of western water law (see chapter 9).

In the rules and regulations of the California Water Resources Control Board relating to appropriation of water under the Water Code there appears the following definition: "Mining Use. Mining use includes any use wherein the water is applied to mining processes as for hydraulicking, for drilling and on concentrator tables, but not in connection with air blasts, compressors, etc."[446] In those of the Texas Water Rights Commission: "Mining Use is the application of water to mining processes, as for hydraulic use, drilling, washing sand and gravel, and oil field repressuring."[447]

Before approval of an application to appropriate navigable water in Utah for the purpose of recovering therefrom salts and other minerals by precipitation or otherwise, the applicant must file with the State Engineer a copy of a contract for payment of royalties to the State. Approval will be revoked if the applicant fails to comply with the contract terms.[448] The Utah Supreme Court

---

and 29 in the State period 1891 to 1900, inclusive. Of the 13 Territorial cases, eight concerned mining and milling connected with mining, three irrigation, and two conflicts between mining and irrigation interests. Of the 29 ensuing State court cases, 21 concerned irrigation water rights and only three mining and milling purposes solely.

[443] See Shinn, Charles H., "Mining Camps, A Study in American Frontier Government," pp. 276-280 (1948, originally published in 1885).

[444] *Davis* v. *Gale*, 32 Cal. 26, 32-35 (1867).

[445] *Maeris* v. *Bicknell,* 7 Cal. 261, 263 (1857). Compare *Louden* v. *Frey,* 67 Cal. 474, 477, 8 Pac. 31 (1885).

[446] Cal. Admin. Code, tit. 23, § 665 (1969).

[447] Tex. Water Rights Comm'n, "Rules, Regulations and Modes of Procedure," rule 115.1(x) (1970 Rev., Jan. 1970).

[448] Utah Code Ann. § 73-3-8 (1968).

sustained the validity of this statute with its requirement for filing a copy of a royalty contract prior to approval of an application to appropriate water. It was apparent, said the court, that the salt found in the waters of the Great Salt Lake was a valuable "mineral." Being navigable, the lake bed belongs to the State subject to Congressional control over navigation in commerce. As such owner, the State is entitled to all valuable minerals in or on such beds; and it is within its authority in providing procedure by which rights to the salt may be acquired from the State government.[449]

Irrigation

Irrigation of cultivated land.—(1) By far the greatest number of controversies over water rights that reached the high courts of the West had to do with rights for the irrigation of cultivated land.

(2) Emergence of irrigation. In California, the right to appropriate water for the purpose of irrigating land and to establish the priority of such an appropriation as against a later appropriation for another purpose—in this case mining—was sustained by the supreme court in 1863.[450] In a few other early cases, irrigation was involved along with other purposes.[451]

Before this occurred in California, irrigation water rights were being acquired in various parts of Utah; and they were recognized in Arizona and New Mexico long before. (See, in chapter 7, "Methods of Appropriating Water of Watercourses—Nonstatutory.") The Act of Congress of July 26, 1866, provided for the protection of prior rights to the use of water on the public domain "for mining, agricultural, manufacturing, or other purposes."[452] In a decision construing this statute, the United States Supreme Court recognized the development of such rights "for purposes of agricultural irrigation" as well as for mining on the public domain.[453]

(3) Crops. An appropriator's water right for irrigation purposes is not limited by the character of crops he raises, unless the soil should be adapted to only one kind of crop or to limited kinds. Ordinarily, he may change the character of crops grown at will.[454]

---

[449] *Deseret Livestock Co.* v. *State,* 110 Utah 239, 242-245, 171 Pac. (2d) 401 (1946).

[450] *Rupley* v. *Welch,* 23 Cal. 452, 455-457 (1863).

[451] Domestic and irrigation: *Crandall* v. *Woods,* 8 Cal. 136, 144 (1857); *Hanson* v. *McCue,* 42 Cal. 303, 306-307 (1871); domestic, milling, and irrigation: *Higgins* v. *Barker,* 42 Cal. 233, 235 (1871).

[452] 14 Stat. 253, § 9 (1866), amended, 16 Stat. 218 (1870).

[453] *Broder* v. *Water Co.,* 101 U. S. 274, 276-277 (1879). See the statement of general principles of appropriative rights in *Hewitt* v. *Story,* 64 Fed. 510, 514-515 (9th Cir. 1894), in which irrigation is specially mentioned.

[454] *Muir* v. *Allison,* 33 Idaho 146, 159-160, 191 Pac. 206 (1920). The principle that one may use no more water than is necessary according to the standards and practices of good husbandry for the particular crops sought to be grown, all essential factors being taken into consideration, does not place any restraint on the kinds of crops one may desire to raise: *In re Robinson,* 61 Idaho 462, 469, 103 Pac. (2d) 693 (1940).

The California Supreme Court concluded that a policy of eliminating the irrigation of low-duty crops from a classification of purposes sufficiently beneficial to be the foundation of an appropriative right would be a legislative question, not one for the judiciary. It was contended in the instant case that rice growing requires such an excessive quantity of water, as compared with any other crop, that it practically amounts to a waste; that rice cultivation should not be tolerated in California, where water for other crops and uses is so indispensable and so scarce. "It may be," said the court, "that under these circumstances rice culture in this state should not be encouraged, or that, in the exercise of the police power, the use of waters of the state in that business might be lawfully forbidden. But that is a legislative question which the court cannot consider. The making of such a rule is beyond our power."[455]

In another California case involving rice culture under irrigation, it was held that "beneficial use of water upon lands, and the possibility of the land owner making a profit upon the crops raised by means of irrigation upon his lands, are not one and the same thing."[456]

(4) Minor streams in South Dakota. Special procedure is provided for acquiring rights to the use of minor streams known as "dry draws" for purposes of irrigation and stockwatering. Somewhat comparable procedure in North Dakota was repealed in 1963.[457]

(5) Oklahoma was unique among the Western States in providing, as construed by the supreme court, that hydrographic surveys and adjudications of existing rights were conditions precedent to issuance of permits for irrigation purposes. This, however, was not required with respect to development of water power,[458] and, since 1963, is no longer required for appropriating water for irrigation or other purposes.[459]

(6) The period of use of water is important in connection with an appropriative right for irrigation purposes. The irrigation season in the Southwest is long, lasting in some sections throughout most or all of the year. However, in most western regions the season ordinarily lasts 5 to 7 months. The same crop is not necessarily irrigated on a single farm throughout the irrigation season. For example, in some areas alfalfa may be irrigated at intervals from spring into the fall, whereas grain might be irrigated only into June and sugar beets only from then on. And in parts of the Southwest, citrus groves may be watered throughout the year—even in December and January. It

---

[455] *Antioch* v. *Williams Irr. Dist.*, 188 Cal. 451, 467-468, 205 Pac. 688 (1922).

[456] *Nelson* v. *Anderson-Cottonwood Irr. Dist.*, 51 Cal. App. 92, 96, 196 Pac. 292 (1921).

[457] S. Dak Comp. Laws Ann. § § 46-1-6 (3) and 46-4-1 to 46-4-8 (1967); N. Dak. Cent. Code Ann. § 61-04-18 to 61-04-21 (1960), repealed, Laws 1963, ch. 419, § 7.

[458] *Gay* v. *Hicks*, 33 Okla. 675, 124 Pac. 1077 (1912); *Owens* v. *Snider*, 52 Okla. 772, 153 Pac. 833 (1915); *Grand-Hydro* v. *Grand River Dam Authority*, 192 Okla. 693, 139 Pac. (2d) 798 (1943).

[459] Okla. Stat. Ann. tit. 82, § § 11 and 12 (1970).

is to the appropriator's advantage to have the period of use under his water right coincide with the period customarily followed in the region. If this is arranged, he gains flexibility in adapting his water supply to choice of crops and general farming requirements.

Some legal questions involved in the subject of period of use of water have been discussed earlier under "Measure of the Appropriative Right."[460]

(7) "Irrigation use includes any application of water to the production of irrigated crops or the maintenance of large areas of lawns, shrubbery, or gardens."[461]

Irrigation of uncultivated land.—(1) The general rule. Irrigation of lands used variously for "wild hay," "wild meadow," "native grasses," "pasture," "grazing" was recognized in a number of cases in various States as a valid purpose for which water might be appropriated.[462] "The use of water for the irrigation of pasture land, as counsel agree, constitutes a beneficial use of water."[463] When there is evidence that wild hay and pasture lands are materially increased in productiveness by reason of application of water, a valid appropriation of such water may be made.[464]

Early in the present century, in pointing out that the evidence showed positively that by irrigation the amount of grass for pasture was greatly increased, the Montana Supreme Court stated logically that:[465]

> If the respondent should cut the grass for hay, it would hardly be contended that the use of the water was not then beneficial, within the meaning of the statute; and if so, it can hardly be that the question whether the use is a beneficial one can be made to depend upon the particular manner in which respondent feeds the grass produced by the irrigation.

As used in the division of the California Water Code relating to water rights, "useful or beneficial purposes" is not to be construed to mean "the use in any one year of more than 2½ acre-feet of water per acre in the irrigation of uncultivated areas of land not devoted to cultivated crops."[466]

[460] Compare *Harkey* v. *Smith,* 31 N. Mex. 521, 525-530, 247 Pac. 550 (1926).
[461] Cal. Admin. Code, tit. 23, § 662 (1969).
[462] *Campbell* v. *Ingram,* 37 Cal. App. 728, 730-731, 174 Pac. 366 (1918); *Oliver* v. *Skinner and Lodge,* 190 Oreg. 423, 437-438, 226 Pac. (2d) 507 (1951); *In re Silvies River,* 115 Oreg. 27, 41, 237 Pac. 322 (1925); *Jensen* v. *Birch Creek Ranch Co.,* 76 Utah 356, 361-362, 289 Pac. 1097 (1930); *Rodgers* v. *Pitt,* 129 Fed. 932, 942 (C. C. D Nev. 1904); *Anderson Land & Stock Co.* v. *McConnell,* 188 Fed. 818, 822 (C. C. D. Nev. 1910). Decrees sustained in *Vineyard Land & Stock Co.* v. *Twin Falls Oakley Land & Water Co.,* 245 Fed. 30, 33, 35 (9th Cir. 1917); *Pacific Live Stock Co.* v. *Read,* 5 Fed. (2d) 466, 468 (9th Cir. 1925).
[463] *In re Escalante Valley Drainage Area,* 11 Utah (2d) 77, 80, 355 Pac. (2d) 64 (1960).
[464] *Rudge* v. *Simmons,* 39 Idaho 22, 27-28, 226 Pac. 170 (1924).
[465] *Sayre* v. *Johnson,* 33 Mont. 15, 19, 81 Pac. 389 (1905).
[466] Cal. Water Code § 1004 (West 1956).

(2) Some exceptions regarding particular circumstances. A Federal court, in determining conflicting rights on an interstate stream flowing from Nevada into Idaho, refused to approve any prior right for a practice under which water was simply cast out over high lying sagebrush land for the purpose of increasing the growth of the native grasses found among the sagebrush. The grasses were scant and sparse and their growth was not largely promoted by the irrigation.[467]

The Utah Supreme Court refused to approve an appropriation of water for irrigation of unenclosed and unoccupied public domain of the United States for the sole purpose of propagating wild water fowl.[468] "To our minds," said the court, "it is utterly inconceivable that a valid appropriation of water can be made under the laws of this state, when the beneficial use of which, after the appropriation is made, will belong equally to every human being who seeks to enjoy it." This general opinion, it will be noted, was expressed before provision for recreational facilities became an important part of large water project development in the West.

It was held in Nevada that cutting of wild grass produced by the natural overflow of a stream would found no right of appropriation.[469] In Colorado, on the other hand, an early statute, still extant, authorizes persons who have received the benefits of natural overflow from streams in irrigation of meadowland, in event of diminution of the streamflow, to construct ditches for such purpose with priorities as of the time of first use of the meadow.[470] This statute, with pertinent judicial citations, is discussed in chapter 9 under "Diversion, Distribution, and Storage Works—Some Features of Waterworks."

Domestic and Municipal Relationships

Domestic.—"The fact that the water was used for culinary and domestic purposes by plaintiff, its agents and employees, was of itself sufficient to establish a beneficial use of the water."[471]

The question as to what constitutes domestic use of water in farming communities appears to have been considered more generally in decisions involving riparian rights than in questions concerning appropriations of water

---

[467] *Vineyard Land & Stock Co.* v. *Twin Falls Salmon River Land & Water Co.*, 245 Fed. 9, 12-13, 21, 22 (9th Cir. 1917). Although the court made a substantial allowance for uncultivated pasture land that produced good results, it stated with respect to the scant-return areas that: "The employment of water for this purpose can scarcely, in this day of agricultural progress in the arid states, be classed as a beneficial use."

[468] *Lake Shore Duck Club* v. *Lake View Duck Club*, 50 Utah 76, 80-81, 166 Pac. 309 (1917).

[469] *Walsh* v. *Wallace*, 26 Nev. 299, 327-328, 67 Pac. 914 (1902); *Anderson Land & Stock Co.* v. *McConnell*, 188 Fed. 818, 822 (C. C. D. Nev. 1910).

[470] Colo. Rev. Stat. Ann. § 148-3-14 (1963), first enacted, Laws 1879, p. 106.

[471] *Silver Peak Mines* v. *Valcalda*, 79 Fed. 886, 890 (C. C. D. Nev. 1897).

for domestic purposes. The right to the use of the streamflow for the sustenance of the riparian owner and family is inherent in the riparian doctrine in those jurisdictions which recognize such right. Water likewise may be appropriated for domestic purposes in all of the mainland western jurisdictions. But the riparian cases seem to constitute most of the judicial authority as to what this use actually contemplates.

Domestic and municipal.—(1) The terms are closely related but are not truly synonymous. Domestic use by individuals or small groups in farming communities has both physical and legal connotations quite different from large uses of water by municipalities and their inhabitants. As distinguished from use in municipalities, domestic use in rural areas means primarily the use of water for drinking and other household purposes. Incidentally, in various jurisdictions, it includes water for small gardens and for the family domestic animals, to the specific exclusion of both industrial use in irrigation and watering of commercial herds of stock. On the other hand, appropriation of water for municipal use by public water districts, cities, and public utility corporations contemplates such public uses for the benefit of the citizenry as fire protection, sprinkling of streets, watering of parks, and use in public buildings, as well as personal use of individual citizens in connection with their business establishments as well as their homes and lawns.

It follows that although the terms "domestic use" and "municipal use" are sometimes used interchangeably, they are not in every sense synonymous. Use of water for drinking and household use in rural areas conforms to the elemental classification of domestic use. On the other hand, such use within a municipality, while still domestic, is within the overall concept of municipal. This household use is made with water acquired by the city and supplied to its inhabitants without differentiation from other uses for which the city acquires and provides water within its political limits.

(2) Some definitions. To clarify well-considered distinctions between domestic and municipal uses of water, attention is called to three sets of definitions of the two uses summarized below. In each group the definitions were prepared for administrative use in control of appropriative water rights; and in each instance the contrasts between domestic and municipal are purposely highlighted for guidance of the administrator.[472]

---

[472] Compare the meaning of the term "domestic use" as used in an ordinance of the City of Albuquerque fixing rates for the supplying of water, as defined by the New Mexico Supreme Court: "Domestic use, as the term is used in the ordinance fixing the schedule of rates to be charged, means the use to which water is applied by the family, or for family use, and includes all uses to which water is applied around the home, and includes the watering of animals, but it does not include the use of water in public parks or public pleasure resorts maintained by the city, or the temporary quenching of the thirst of animals while engaged in labor upon the streets." *Water Supply Co. of Albuquerque* v. *Albuquerque,* 17 N. Mex. 326, 334, 128 Pac. 77 (1912).

(a) California.[473] *Domestic*: Uses common to homes, resorts, motels, organization camps, and campgrounds (for human consumption, cooking, and sanitary purposes). Included are incidental watering of domestic stock for family sustenance, and irrigation of one-half acre in lawn, ornamental shrubbery, gardens and truck.

Municipal: All uses common to the municipal water supply of a city, town, or other similar population group, and use incidental thereto for any beneficial purpose.

(b) South Dakota.[474] *Domestic:* Use by an individual or family unit or household for drinking, washing, sanitary, culinary, and other ordinary household purposes. Included are one-half acre in family garden, trees, shrubbery, or orchard, and stockwatering.

Municipal: Use by the State through its institutions, facilities and properties or a municipality and its inhabitants whether supplied by the government or by a privately-owned public utility or other agency, primarily to promote the life, safety, health, comfort, and business pursuits of the inhabitants. Does *not* include crop irrigation on a commercial scale, even within the limits of the State institution, facility, property or municipality, nor large recreational uses such as lakes.

(c) Texas.[475] *Domestic:* Use by an individual or family unit or household for drinking, washing, culinary purposes. Includes irrigation of family garden or orchard for family food, and watering of domestic animals.

Municipal: Use within or without a municipality and its environs, whether supplied by a person, a political subdivision, a privately-owned public utility, or other agency or party, primarily to promote the safety, life, health, comfort, and business pursuits of the users. Specifically includes use for fighting fires, flushing sewers, sprinkling streets, watering parks and parkways, small recreational uses such as swimming pools; use in public and private buildings, industrial enterprises supplied by a municipal distribution system without special construction, and homes, and irrigation of lawns and family gardens.

(3) Highly favored uses of water. (a) Domestic use of water in rural areas, and municipal use with which domestic use is integrated in organized urban communities, are highly favored in the law. Consumption of water for drinking—without which life ceases—and its use for culinary and sanitation purposes, are obviously necessary to serve human life, health, and comfort whether on the farm or in town. Use of water for business pursuits of the

---

[473] Cal. Admin. Code, tit. 23, § § 661 and 664 (1969).

[474] S. Dak. Comp. Laws Ann. § § 46-1-6(4) and (5) (1967).

[475] Tex. Water Rights Comm'n, "Rules, Regulations and Modes of Procedure," rule 115.1(s) (1970 Rev., Jan. 1970) and (u) (June 1970 addendum to 1970 Rev.).

inhabitants of a city, as well as for domestic use, is integrated with the general municipal needs of the municipality and is thus in the favored class; use of water for business pursuits of farmers in the form of irrigation and commercial stockraising is not.

In much of the early western development, the distinction between irrigation and domestic purposes was not of practical importance in the acquisition and exercise of appropriative water rights. In the Southwest, before the dawn of written history, the two uses were served in various Indian communities; and from the beginning of modern history water was supplied for these purposes by Spanish-American community acequias. This experience was repeated in Utah's Mormon settlements, and in non-Mormon developments elsewhere in the West. Individual farmers who diverted water for irrigation often used part of the supply for their domestic needs. As group organizations came into general use, they often appropriated water for both irrigation and domestic purposes. Controversies over a claim of favored classification were more likely to arise when a community endeavored to obtain a municipal water supply with a higher preference standing, at the expense of irrigationists.[476] And as western cities grew in numbers of inhabitants and in area, arbitrary preferences in use of water in the complex whole of a metropolitan area, as among domestic, municipal, industrial, or other purposes, became more and more outdated and impracticable.[477]

(b) In any event, as stated at length in the final parts of chapter 7 in discussing restrictions and preferences in the appropriation doctrine, there is considerable legislation in the western water appropriation statutes, and indeed there are some constitutional provisions, relating to restrictions and preferences in the appropriation and use of water. As there noted, in all declarations in which a specific order of preference is stated, domestic use has first place; closely associated with domestic use in the statutes and court decisions is municipal use, and the tenor of the statutory preferences is to ignore any distinction between the strictly domestic use of water by the city's inhabitants and the strictly municipal uses of water by the city. This simply means that in rural areas, domestic use is most highly favored; in urban areas, domestic and municipal share this position without prejudice to either use.

(c) Aside from the question of statutory and constitutional preferences, special attention is given in some of the appropriation statutes and high court decisions to domestic and municipal uses of water. Some details follow

---

[476] *Sterling* v. *Pawnee Ditch Extension Co.,* 42 Colo. 421, 426-427, 94 Pac. 339 (1908); *Montrose Canal Co.* v. *Loutsenhizer Ditch Co.,* 23 Colo. 233, 236-237, 48 Pac. 532 (1896).

[477] In chapter 7, see "Methods of Appropriating Water of Watercourses—Restrictions and Preferences in Appropriation of Water—Preferences in Water Appropriation—Order of preferences in purpose of use."

(d) Domestic. The New Mexico water appropriation statute authorizes travelers to take water for their own use, and for animals under their charge, from water currents flowing from natural sources.[478]

An early Kansas statute, still extant, provides that any person may take water from a natural stream "for filling barrels or other vessels for his domestic uses."[479]

The Utah Supreme Court held that while flowing naturally in a stream channel, water is common property to which all have equal rights, subject at all times not only to the same rights in others, but also to the special rights to divert and use water of the stream recognized by the law of appropriation. Thus, subject to vested rights of appropriation by others, anyone may drink or dip water from the stream or water his animals therein. This is sharply distinguished from the special right of appropriation, which is a limitation on these rights of public use, and which requires a diversion from the stream or other interference with the natural free flow.[480]

In Kansas, use of water for domestic purposes instituted after the 1945 water appropriation law went into effect, to the extent that it is beneficial, constitutes an appropriation right without the necessity of first obtaining approval of the administrator. However, any person using water for domestic purposes after that date, or intending to make such use after the 1957 amendment, *may* apply for a permit pursuant to the formal statutory procedure.[481]

(e) Municipal. The California statute provides that "The application for a permit by a municipality for the use of water for the municipality or the inhabitants thereof for domestic purposes shall be considered first in right, irrespective of whether it is first in time."[482]

In Oregon, the State Engineer is directed to reject, or to grant subject to municipal use, all applications leading to appropriations which in his judgment would impair municipal water supplies.[483] In addition, elsewhere in the water rights statute, many privileges and exemptions are accorded to municipalities.

---

[478] N. Mex. Stat. Ann. § § 75-1-4 and 75-1-5 (1968).

[479] Kans. Stat. Ann. § 42-311 (1964), first enacted, Laws 1891, ch. 133.

[480] *Adams* v. *Portage Irr. Res. & Power Co.*, 95 Utah 1, 11-16, 72 Pac (2d) 648 (1937).

[481] Kans. Stat. Ann. § § 82a-705, -705a, -709 (1969).

South Dakota is another of the States that sets domestic use apart. The water appropriation statute declares, among other things, that it is the established policy of the State that the use of water for domestic purposes is the highest use of water "and takes precedence over all appropriative rights." The term "Vested Rights" includes "Use for domestic purposes as that term is herein defined* * *." Any person or persons desiring to make reasonable use of water from any source for domestic purposes may do so without obtaining a permit from the commission for such use." S. Dak. Comp. Laws Ann. § § 46-1-5(1), 46-1-9, and 46-5-8 (1967).

[482] Cal. Water Code § 1460 (West 1956).

[483] Oreg. Rev. Stat. § § 537.190(2) (Supp. 1969) and 538.410 (Supp. 1967).

In almost identical language, the statutes of California and South Dakota declare the established policy of the State to be that the right of a municipality to acquire and hold rights to the use of water should be protected to the fullest extent necessary for existing and future uses. However, no municipality may waste water or use it for other than municipal purposes. Nor may waters in excess of reasonable existing needs of the municipality be prevented from being temporarily appropriated by others, subject to the municipality's right of recovery when needed.[484]

A section of the Texas water rights statute as enacted in 1931 provided that all appropriations of water thereafter made—from the waters of any stream other than the Rio Grande—for any purpose other than domestic or municipal, should be granted subject to the right of any municipality of the State to make further appropriation thereof for domestic and municipal purposes without the necessity of compensating the existing appropriators.[485] The validity of this provision was sustained by a Federal court as against a contention that the exclusion of the waters of the Rio Grande was unconstitutional.[486]

The Wyoming Supreme Court pointed out one of the differences between an appropriation for irrigation and one for municipal purposes. This was to the effect that although water stored for agricultural purposes is not put to a beneficial use until actually used therefor, nevertheless part of a city's stored water supply is a continuing benefit to the community from the time it is first impounded, in that it "stands as a partial protection against the spread of fire in the city every minute of the day, and therefore, at all times subserves a most beneficial purpose."[487]

The right of a municipality to appropriate water to meet its reasonably anticipated future needs is declared and approved in legislation and court decisions of several States. This facet of the topic of municipal water rights is discussed in chapter 7 under "Who May Appropriate Water—Governmental Agencies and Entities Other than Districts—Municipality."

Domestic and stockwatering.—At common law, the right to water cattle in a stream flowing through one's land appears to have been as much a part of the landowner's prerogative as his right to use the stream for drinking and culinary purposes.[488] As developed in various American and English cases, and as specifically recognized in California, uses of water for domestic purposes and for the watering of domestic animals at the farmstead are classed as "natural" uses of water, and uses for business purposes including watering of large herds

---

[484] Cal. Water Code § 106.5 (West 1956); S. Dak. Comp. Laws Ann. § 46-1-5(2) (1967).
[485] Tex. Rev. Civ. Stat. Ann. arts. 7472 and 7472a (1954).
[486] *El Paso County W. I. Dist. No. 1* v. *El Paso,* 133 Fed. Supp. 894, 906-907 (W. D. Tex. 1955). The court held that the statute does not reflect any arbitrary discrimination or repugnant classification and is not irrational.
[487] *Van Tassel Real Estate & Live Stock Co.* v. *Cheyenne,* 49 Wyo. 333, 362, 54 Pac. (2d) 906 (1936).
[488] *Bathgate* v. *Irvine,* 126 Cal. 135, 142, 58 Pac. 442 (1899).

of livestock are "artificial" or less preferential purposes.[489] This association of domestic use with watering of farmstead domestic animals, but not with commercial herds of stock, was carried over into the appropriation doctrine.

The rules and regulations of the California Water Resources Control Board define "domestic uses" as including "the incidental watering of domestic stock for family sustenance." "Stockwatering" use is use of water for commercial livestock, while repeating that "Water for domestic stock shall be considered a domestic use."[490]

The rules and regulations of the Texas Water Rights Commission define "domestic use" as including "the watering of domestic animals." "Livestock use" is the watering of "livestock connected with farming, ranching or dairy enterprises." "Stockraising use" is the watering of "livestock connected with the operation of a commercial feedlot."[491]

The Idaho water rights statute defines "domestic purposes" as including water for household, "and a sufficient amount for the use of domestic animals kept with and for the use of the household."[492] The Texas statute gives highest preference to "domestic and municipal uses, including water for sustaining human life and the life of domestic animals."[493] And the current South Dakota water appropriation statute, in defining "domestic use," ends with the flat statement that "Stockwatering shall be considered a domestic use."[494]

An application to appropriate water in Oregon included a specific quantity for "domestic and farm power purposes and domestic supplies." The applicant had a dairy farm on which he kept milk cows, horses, and hogs. The Oregon Supreme Court held that the application for domestic purposes properly included the average number of these domestic animals.[495]

Although, therefore, some conflict unquestionably exists, the weight of authority appears to be that in the appropriation doctrine, as well as the riparian, domestic use includes watering of domestic farm animals immediately concerned with the family life, but not the watering of large numbers of livestock utilized as a farm business.

Stockwatering

Watering of livestock was a daily task at the early settlements in the far West performed by immigrants who came from the East and Middle West and

---

[489] Hutchins, Wells A., "The California Law of Water Rights," pp. 235-237 (1956).

[490] Cal. Admin. Code, tit. 23, § § 661 and 668 (1969).

[491] Tex. Water Rights Comm'n, "Rules, Regulations and Modes of Procedure," rules 115.1(s), (t), and (ff) (1970 Rev., Jan. 1970).

[492] Idaho Code Ann. § 42-111 (1948).

[493] Tex. Rev. Civ. Stat. Ann. art. 7471 (Supp. 1970).

[494] S. Dak. Comp. Laws Ann. § 46-1-6(4) (1967).

[495] In re Schollmeyer, 69 Oreg. 210, 212, 216, 138 Pac. 211 (1914).

brought livestock with them. Conditions surrounding the early uses of wa
for agricultural purposes in Carson Valley, Nevada, in the early 1850's we
described graphically in an opinion by a Federal judge who himself crossed t
plains to this area in 1852.[496] Carson Valley attained a place in western histo
in the middle of the 19th century, for a large proportion of the mai
thousands of people who crossed the country from the Missouri River to tl
far West from 1841 to 1859 used the Carson Route.[497]

Stockwatering is expressly listed in some of the water rights statutes as
purpose for which water may be appropriated.[498] Courts have specifical
recognized it as a beneficial use.[499]

Special attention is paid to stockwatering in some of the water righ
statutes. A Nevada statute enacted in 1925 supplements the general wate
rights statute by prescribing certain conditions with respect to the acquisitio
of rights for watering livestock, particularly range livestock (see the end of th:
subtopic).[500] New Mexico extends to travelers the right to take water for thei
own use, and for their animals, from waters flowing from natural sources an
also exempts from the statutory requirements for appropriating water thos
who may construct tanks or ponds having capacity of 10 acre-feet or less fo
the purpose of watering stock.[501] Oregon accords special treatment in case o
an application to appropriate water for stock ponds or other small reservoir:
from which water is not to be diverted or required to flow through the
ponds.[502] South Dakota makes special provision for appropriations from minoi
streams for irrigation or stock purposes.[503] A Texas statute authorizes any
landowner to construct on his own property a reservoir to impound not more
than 200 acre-feet of water for domestic and livestock purposes "without the

---

[496] Judge Thomas P. Hawley, *Union Mill & Min. Co.* v. *Dangberg,* 81 Fed. 73, 100-103
(C. C. D. Nev. 1897). The account is based not only on the record in the case, but also
on the judge's own experiences. The earliest settlers were squatters on the public
domain, raising cattle which roamed at large and taking advantage of stream water for
agricultural purposes chiefly by means of its overflow. The water flowed in sloughs and
spread over the lowlands at high stage; cuts were made through the banks to let the
water out when the stream was not flowing bank-full. In general, there were no specific
appropriations of the water and but few genuine ditches and substantial diversions.

[497] Stewart, George R., "The California Trail" (1962).

[498] For example: Ariz. Rev. Stat. Ann. § 45-141(A) (Supp. 1970); Nev. Rev. Stat. § 533.340
(Supp. 1967); Tex. Rev. Civ. Stat. Ann. art. 7470 (Supp. 1970).

[499] For example: *First State Bank of Alamogordo* v. *McNew,* 33 N. Mex. 414, 422, 269
Pac. 56 (1928); *Farmers' Development Co.* v. *Rayado Land & Irr. Co.,* 28 N. Mex. 357,
371, 213 Pac. 202 (1923). See also *Stevenson* v. *Steele,* 93 Idaho 4, 453 Pac. (2d) 819,
826 (1969).

[500] Nev. Rev. Stat. § § 533.485 to .510 (Supp. 1967). Constitutionality upheld, under
attack: *In re Calvo,* 50 Nev. 125, 131-141, 253 Pac. 671 (1927). See *Adams-McGill Co.*
v. *Hendrix,* 22 Fed. Supp. 789, 791 (D. Nev. 1938).

[501] N. Mex. Stat. Ann. § § 75-1-4, 75-1-5, and 75-8-3 (1968).

[502] Oreg. Rev. Stat. § 537.300(2) (Supp. 1969).

[503] S. Dak. Comp. Laws Ann. § § 46-1-6(3) and 46-4-1 to 46-4-8 (1967).

necessity of securing a permit therefor," but apparently requires him to obtain a permit if he desires to withdraw water from such impoundment for purposes other than domestic or livestock use.[504]

Methods of watering the stock have come into the cases. The Utah Supreme Court held that acts of merely permitting animals *to drink directly from a stream* gave no right to or possession of use of the water;[505] but that any member of the public might water his stock in a stream without making a diversion of water therefrom, subject to all vested rights of appropriation of the streamflow, from which special rights of appropriation the public right was explicitly distinguished.[506]

The Nevada Supreme Court held that the general rule that to constitute a valid appropriation of streamflow there must be an actual diversion, does not apply to an appropriation for watering livestock in natural watering places formed by natural depressions.[507] The Nevada stockwatering act, noted earlier in this subtopic, relates to particular watering places, to which the quantity of water appropriated is measured by the number and kind of animals watered. It obviously contemplates use of the water in place, with no question about diverting it from a stream. (See the discussion in chapter 9 under "Diversion, Distribution, and Storage Works—Some Features of Waterworks—Use of Streamflow Without Conduit—Dipping or drinking from stream.")

Other Purposes of Use of Water

In general.—Other purposes specifically designated as beneficial from the standpoint of appropriating water, in addition to those noted immediately below, include protection and propagation of wildlife including fish culture, game preserves, scenic attraction, public parks, transportation.[508] Attention is called particularly to the following:

Power.—One of the earliest water rights exercised under the riparian doctrine was the utilization of streamflow as power for propelling mill wheels.[509] The decision in one of the earliest California water rights cases

---

[504] Tex. Rev. Civ. Stat. Ann. art. 7500a (Supp. 1970). Although the statute does not say that the landowner may *use* the water for the stated purpose without a permit, such a legislative intent was necessarily implied: *Anson* v. *Arnett,* 250 S. W. (2d) 450, 452-453 (Tex. Civ. App. 1952, error refused n.r.e.). But it does not authorize *irrigation* from a *watercourse* without a permit: Tex. Atty. Gen., Opinion No. WW-97, May 17, 1957.

[505] *Bountiful City* v. *De Luca,* 77 Utah 107, 118-119, 292 Pac. 194 (1930).

[506] *Adams* v. *Portage Irr., Res. & Power Co.,* 95 Utah 1, 11-16, 72 Pac. (2d) 648 (1937).

[507] *Steptoe Live Stock Co.* v. *Gulley,* 53 Nev. 163, 171-173, 295 Pac. 772 (1931).

[508] Regarding the consideration of water quality, see Cal. Water Code § § 1242.5 and 1257 (West Supp. 1970) discussed in chapter 7 in note 621 and at note 975, respectively.

[509] "The use of the water in its passage through his [the riparian owner's] land to operate a power plant thereon is as clearly within his rights as is his right to operate a mill thereon with which to grind grain or to operate any other machinery, than which there is no more ancient or well-established feature of riparian rights." *Mentone Irr. Co.* v. *Redlands Elec. Light & Power Co.,* 155 Cal. 323, 327, 100 Pac. 1082 (1909). Use of

involved, and established, the priority of right of an appropriation for a use other than mining—in this case water-power for operating a sawmill—over that of a later appropriation for mining purposes.[510]

The use of waterpower for production of hydroelectric energy has become of major importance in the industrial economy of the West, in addition to its growing use in providing electrical power for pumping water from the ground. In chapter 7, under "Methods of Appropriating Water of Watercourses— Restrictions and Preferences in Appropriation of Water—Restrictions on the Right to Appropriate Water—Development of hydroelectric power," data are given respecting important authorizations and restrictions in Arizona, Idaho, Nebraska, and Oregon. In addition, in chapter 7, under the subtopic "Preferences in Water Appropriation—Order of preferences in individual States," the Texas list is shown to include in *second* place industrial including "development of electric power by means other than hydro-electric," and in *fifth* place hydroelectric power.[511]

Also to be mentioned is the unique Oklahoma judicial distinction between procedures for issuance of permits for (a) irrigation and (b) power development purposes. Hydrographic surveys and adjudications of existing rights were conditions precedent to issuance of permits for irrigation purposes—but not for development of waterpower.[512] However, in 1963 the Oklahoma Legislature expressly declared that such hydrographic surveys and adjudications are not conditions precedent to the issuance of permits for irrigation or other purposes.[513]

Administrative rules and regulations relating to appropriation of water in California and Texas include almost identical definitions of "power use" as including "use for hydroelectric and hydromechanical power and for air blasts and other mechanical devices of like nature."[514]

The Federal Power Act[515] is one in a series of acts of Congress which deals with rights-of-way on public lands of the United States for control of water and hydroelectric power. Enacted June 10, 1920, as the Federal Water Power Act, it provides for administration of rights-of-way on public lands for power purposes, and of all power developments which affect navigable waters of the United States and waters over which Congress has jurisdiction in regulation of

---

the streamflow for propelling mill machinery was recognized as a riparian right at common law: *Bathgate* v. *Irvine*, 126 Cal. 135, 142, 58 Pac. 442 (1899).

[510] *Tartar* v. *Spring Creek Water & Min. Co.,* 5 Cal. 395, 397-399 (1855).

[511] Tex. Rev. Civ. Stat. Ann. art. 7471 (Supp. 1970).

[512] *Gay* v. *Hicks,* 33 Okla. 675, 124 Pac. 1077 (1912); *Owens* v. *Snider,* 52 Okla. 772, 153 Pac. 833 (1915); *Grand-Hydro* v. *Grand River Dam Authority,* 192 Okla. 693, 139 Pac. (2d) 798 (1943).

[513] Okla. Stat. Ann. tit. 82, § § 11 and 12 (1970).

[514] Cal. Admin. Code, tit. 23, § 663 (1969); Tex. Water Rights Comm'n, "Rules, Regulations and Modes of Procedure," rule 115.1(y) (1970 Rev., Jan. 1970).

[515] 41 Stat. 1063, 16 U.S.C. § 791a *et seq.* (1964). These acts are noted in chapter 7 under

commerce. Administration is exercised through the issuance of preliminary permits for not to exceed 3 years for purposes of investigation, and licenses for definite periods of time not exceeding 50 years.

An applicant for a water power license is required to submit "Satisfactory evidence that the applicant has complied with the requirements of the laws of the State or States within which the proposed project is to be located with respect to bed and banks and to the appropriation, diversion, and use of water for power purposes * * * ."[516] According to the United States Supreme Court, section 9(b) of the Federal Power Act

> does not itself require compliance with any state laws. Its reference to state laws is by way of suggestion to the Federal Power Commission of subjects as to which the Commission may wish some proof submitted to it of the applicant's progress. The evidence required is described merely as that which shall be 'satisfactory' to the Commission. The need for compliance with applicable state laws, if any, arises not from the federal statute but from the effectiveness of the state statutes themselves.[517]

Industrial use.—In the early history of the arid region doctrine of prior appropriation, industrial use was not clearly defined. Appropriations of water were made for milling purposes connected with mining, and for power to operate sawmills and grist mills. In the latter case, the purpose of use of the water could with reason be classed either as power or as industrial; under the appropriation doctrine, it mattered not which. That manufacturing, an industrial use, was a beneficial purpose of water was specifically recognized by Congress in authorizing appropriation of water on the public domain.[518]

Rules and regulations governing appropriation of water in California classify industrial use broadly as including "those many uses wherein the water serves the purposes of commerce, trade, or industry."[519]

The comparable Texas rule is "the use of water in processes designed to convert materials of a lower order of value into forms having greater usability and commercial value, and includes water necessary for the development of electric power by means other than hydro-electric."[520] This definition follows literally the language of the statute providing preferences in the allotment and appropriation of water.[521]

"Rights-of-Way for Water Control and Related Purposes—Public Lands—Public Lands of the United States."

[516] 41 Stat. 1068, § 9(b), 16 U.S.C. § 802(b) (1964).

[517] *First Iowa Hydro-Elec. Coop.* v. *Federal Power Comm'n,* 328 U. S. 152, 177-178 (1946).

[518] 14 Stat. 253, § 9 (1866); 16 Stat. 218 (1870); 19 Stat. 377 (1877), 43 U. S. C. § 321 *et seq.* (1964).

[519] Cal. Admin. Code, tit. 23, § 666 (1969).

[520] Tex. Water Rights Comm'n, "Rules, Regulations and Modes of Procedure," rule 115.1(v) (1970 Rev., Jan 1970).

[521] Tex. Rev. Civ. Stat. Ann. art. 7471 (Supp. 1970).

By this Texas statutory classification of development of electric power by means other than hydroelectric as an industrial use, it is placed in the second class of preferred uses, whereas hydroelectric power is relegated to fifth place. It is true that in the same enactment the Texas Water Rights Commission is directed to observe the rule that as between applicants for permits, "preference be given not only in the order of preferential uses declared," but that preference also be given those applications the purposes of which contemplate and will effectuate the maximum utilization of water and are designed to prevent waste of water.[522] Construing these sections together, it is clear that the Texas legislature did not intend the declaration of preferences to be either the sole guide to the administrator or to be meaningless. Its intent was to vest the State agency with a broad discretion in choosing between conflicting applications to appropriate water, with full consideration of all the guidelines specified in the statute. As a result, the deliberate distinction made by the legislature in power classifications must be considered by the administrator in deciding between pending conflicting applications; hence it is of practical importance.[523]

Recreation.—(1) The California Water Code provides that the use of water for recreation and for the preservation and enhancement of fish and wildlife resources is a beneficial use of water. The quantities of water required therefor must be taken into account by the Water Resources Control Board, in determining quantities of water available for appropriation for other beneficial purposes, whenever it is in the public interest to do so.[524] Within certain limitations, the California Department of Water Resources is authorized to plan recreation development associated with State-constructed water projects, in consultation with affected local, State, and Federal agencies. With the approval of the Department of General Services, real property necessary therefor may be acquired.[525]

California's definition of recreational use for administrative purposes respecting appropriation of water "includes those uses, except the irrigation of golf courses, which are common to a resort or other recreational establishment such as boating, swimming, fishing, etc.." Not included is use of water at a campground or resort for human consumption, cooking, or sanitary purposes, this being considered a domestic use.[526]

---

[522] Tex. Rev. Civ. Stat. Ann. art. 7472c (1954).

[523] In *City of San Antonio* v. *Texas Water Comm'n,* 407 S. W. (2d) 752, 764 (Tex. Sup. Ct. 1966), the city had argued that "if Article 7472c gives the Commission discretion to ignore the priorities established in Article 7471, then Article 7472c is unconstitutional because such purpose is not contained in the caption of the Act." But the court refused to decide this question because "The question of violating the order of priority of uses is not presented in this case."

[524] Cal. Water Code § 1243 (West 1956).

[525] *Id.* § § 345 and 346.

[526] Cal. Admin. Code, tit. 23, § 667 (1969).

(2) In its list of preferences, the Kansas water rights statute places recreation next to last, ahead of waterpower.[527] That of Texas relegates recreation and pleasure to seventh place, followed only by other unspecified beneficial uses.[528]

(3) The Nevada statutes provide that the use of water "for any recreational purpose, is hereby declared a beneficial use."[529]

(4) The supreme courts of Montana and New Mexico rejected claims that beneficial uses of public waters did not include "swimming pool or fish pond" and "recreation and fishing," respectively.[530]

(5) In the list of beneficial uses which must be considered by the administrative agency of Oregon in determining whether a proposed use of water would be detrimental to the public interest, the water rights statute includes "public recreation" and "scenic attraction."[531] In a series of legislative enactments, certain Oregon waters have been specifically withdrawn from appropriation for purposes including "maintaining and perpetuating the recreational and scenic resources of Oregon."[532] Utah legislation authorizes the Governor to withdraw particular waters from appropriation.[533] Idaho legislation employs a different approach. It authorizes and directs the Governor to appropriate, in trust for the people, all or so much of the unappropriated water of certain lakes as may be necessary for their preservation for scenic beauty, health, recreation or other specified purposes. The legislation provides, among other things, that no proof of completion of any works of diversion shall be required.[534] Colorado legislation authorizes river conservancy districts to "file upon and hold for the use of the public" sufficient water to maintain a constant streamflow to preserve fish and for use in retaining ponds for fish

[527] Kans. Stat. Ann. § 82a-707 (1969).

[528] Tex. Rev. Civ. Stat. Ann. art. 7471 (Supp. 1970).

[529] Nev. Rev. Stat. § 533.030 (Supp. 1969).

[530] *Osnes Livestock Co.* v. *Warren,* 103 Mont. 284, 300-302, 62 Pac. (2d) 206 (1936); *State ex rel. State Game Comm'n* v. *Red River Valley Co.,* 51 N. Mex. 207, 218, 182 Pac. (2d) 421 (1945).

Regarding public fishing rights in Montana, see the discussion of *Paradise Rainbows* v. *Fish and Game Comm'n,* 148 Mont. 412, 421 Pac. (2d) 717 (1966), cited in chapter 7, note 900.

[531] Oreg. Rev. Stat. § § 537.170(3)(a) (Supp. 1969) and 543.225(3)(a) (Supp. 1965).

[532] Oreg. Rev. Stat. § § 538.110–.300 (Supp. 1967).

[533] Utah Code Ann. § § 73-6-1 and 73-6-2 (1968). The Oregon and Utah legislation, and Washington legislation regarding the establishment of minimum streamflows or lake levels, Wash. Rev. Code § § 90.40.030 and 90.40.040 (Supp. 1961), are discussed in chapter 7 under "Methods of Appropriating Water of Watercourses–Restrictions and Preferences in Appropriation of Water–Preferences in Water Appropriation–Acquisition of rights to appropriate water–(3) Withdrawal of unappropriated water from appropriation."

[534] Idaho Code Ann. § § 67-4301 to -4306 (1949).

propagation.[535] But the Colorado Supreme Court held that water may not be so appropriated without a diversion of water from the stream.[536]

(6) Public versus private fishing rights were involved in litigation in New Mexico and Texas.

The New Mexico case involved waters impounded behind a dam in a public stream, part intended for irrigation downstream, part classified as dead storage, and part held back for flood control to be released from time to time as waste water. All the water was held to be public water until beneficially applied to the purposes of its potential use. The organization that impounded these waters had no exclusive privilege in their use while they remained public, and no right of recreation or fishing distinct from the right of the general public therein when properly authorized by the State Game Commission. Access to these waters could be had without trespassing upon private property.[537]

One of the chief issues in the Texas controversy was the force and effect of a permit granted by the Board of Water Engineers to a recreation club to appropriate and use water impounded in an artificial lake on a statutory navigable stream "for the purpose of game preserve, recreation and pleasure resort." The permittee had no title to the bed of the stream, nor to a public road that crossed the lake near its upper end; but it did own land contiguous to the streambed and submerged by the lake. Although the permittee fenced the land and stocked the lake with fish, it did not have the exclusive right to fish in the lake and it could not prevent the public from fishing therein. And although the public had no right to trespass on the club's privately owned land, fishing from a boat over the club's submerged land was not trespass. This was because the water remained public water even though it spread away from the river channel and overlay private land.[538]

Recharge of ground water supply.—(1) In California, according to the water rights statute, the storing of water in the ground, including the diversion of streams and the flowing of water on lands necessary to the accomplishment thereof, constitutes a beneficial use of water if the water so stored is thereafter applied to the beneficial purposes for which the appropriation for storage was

---

[535] Colo. Rev. Stat. Ann. § 150-7-5(10) (1963).

[536] *Colorado River Water Conservation Dist.* v. *Rocky Mountain Power Co.,* 158 Colo. 331, 406 Pac. (2d) 798 (1965), citing earlier Colorado cases, an Idaho case, and a United States Supreme Court case arising from Idaho. This and other cases concerning the question of the necessity of a diversion in making an appropriation of water are discussed in chapter 9 under "Diversion, Distribution, and Storage Works—Some Features of Waterworks."

[537] *State ex rel State Game Comm'n* v. *Red River Valley Co.,* 51 N. Mex. 207, 223-229, 182 Pac. (2d) 421 (1945). See chapter 4, note 98, regarding related aspects of this case, a Wyoming case, *Day* v. *Armstrong,* 362 Pac. (2d) 137, 143 (Wyo. 1961), and a contrary Colorado case, *Hartman* v. *Tresise,* 36 Colo. 146, 84 Pac. 685, 686-687 (1905).

[538] *Diversion Lake Club* v. *Heath,* 126 Tex. 129, 138-140, 143-146, 86 S. W. (2d) 441 (1935).

made.[539] So-called "water spreading" is an important feature of water development in parts of southern and central California.

(2) The Texas water rights statute authorizes the appropriation of storm and flood waters for the purpose of recharging fresh water-bearing aquifers in a specified portion of a named underground reservoir, when expert testimony shows that an unreasonable loss of water will not occur and that the water can be later withdrawn for application to a beneficial use. It is specifically provided that on being discharged into the ground, such water "shall thereupon lose its character and classification and be considered percolating ground water." The appropriations for such purpose are subject to the priority of appropriations set forth in the statute.[540] One of the purposes for which "underground water conservation districts" may be created is recharging the ground water supply of ground water reservoirs or subdivisions.[541]

Navigation.—(1) The Oregon water rights statute provides that in determining whether a proposed use of water would be detrimental to the public interest, due regard must be given by the administrative agency to conserving the highest use of water for all purposes including navigation.[542]

(2) In the list of preferences in the allotment and appropriation of water in Texas, navigation is in sixth place, ahead of recreation and pleasure and other unspecified beneficial uses.[543]

Uses of Water Held to be not Beneficial

California.—Certain uses of water were held in early cases, as well as subsequently, to be not beneficial when considered as bases of claimed appropriative rights. For example, diverting water for the purpose of drainage only was held in one of the earliest cases to be not appropriating it to a beneficial purpose; that is, one who so diverts water gains no priority over others who in good faith appropriate the water for mining or other useful purposes.[544] A bare claim for no object other than speculation is invalid as the foundation of an appropriative right.[545] And in 1935, a use of water for the sole purpose of exterminating gophers and squirrels during the winter period in an area of great need of water was held to be not such a beneficial use as will support an appropriative right for that purpose.[546]

---

[539] Cal. Water Code § 1242 (West 1956).

[540] Tex. Rev. Civ. Stat. Ann. art. 7470 (Supp. 1970).

[541] Tex. Rev. Civ. Stat. Ann. art. 7880-3c(B) (1954).

[542] Oreg. Rev. Stat. § § 537.110(3)(a) (Supp. 1969) and 543.225(3)(a) (Supp. 1965).

[543] Tex. Rev. Civ. Stat. Ann. art. 7471 (Supp. 1970).

[544] *Maeris* v. *Bicknell,* 7 Cal. 261, 262-263 (1857). But use of a ditch for drainage as well as conveyance of water for a recognized beneficial use under an appropriative right does not invalidate the right: *Marius* v. *Bicknell,* 10 Cal. 217, 221-222 (1858).

[545] *Weaver* v. *Eureka Lake Co.,* 15 Cal. 271, 275 (1860).

[546] *Tulare Irr. Dist.* v. *Lindsay-Strathmore Irr. Dist.,* 3 Cal. (2d) 489, 567-568, 45 Pac. (2d) 972 (1935).
    See also *Joslin* v. *Marin Municipal Water Dist.,* 67 Cal. (2d) 132, 140-141, 429 Pac. (2d) 889, 60 Cal. Rptr. 377 (1967), discussed in chapter 6, note 239.

Idaho.—Use of water during the winter for the purpose of overflowing lands so that the water might freeze and form an icecap and thus be conserved for later use was held to be not a beneficial use. It had been claimed that the formation of the icecap, sometimes to a depth of several feet, was very beneficial in that the moisture was retained by the soil into the summer, thereby considerably aiding plant growth. Both the referee and the trial court found that this was not a beneficial use. The Idaho Supreme Court sustained this finding because the evidence, while conflicting, was sufficient to support it.[547]

Nevada-Idaho.—In the adjudication of rights to the use of waters of a stream system originating in Nevada and flowing into Idaho, the allowance of water for irrigating pasture land was one-half the quantity awarded to cultivated hay and grain land. However, there were high-lying areas of pasture land on which water was turned loose over sagebrush land for the purpose of increasing growth of the native grasses among the sagebrush. It was found that these grasses were sparse and that their growth was not greatly promoted. For these reasons, the Federal court found that the use of water was not beneficial, and hence refused to allow a water right therefor.[548]

Oregon.—In a stream system adjudication in Oregon, it was held that an allowance of 30 second-feet for the purpose of carrying off debris during the irrigation season would not be a beneficial use of the water, because it would be equivalent to depriving about 1,600 acres of water for irrigation. The court believed, however, that such use during the nonirrigating season, when the river waters were not desired for storage purposes, would be a beneficial use of the water.[549]

Sale, Rental, or Distribution of Water

A Public use

The constitutions of several States contain declarations to the effect that the use of water appropriated for sale, rental, or distribution is a public use.[550] Oregon has a statutory declaration to this effect.[551] "It is undoubtedly true that the diversion and distribution of water for irrigation and other domestic purposes in New Mexico, and other Western States where irrigation is necessary, is a public purpose."[552]

---

[547] *Blaine County Investment Co.* v. *Mays,* 49 Idaho 766, 773, 291 Pac. 1055 (1930).

[548] *Vineyard Land & Stock Co.* v. *Twin Falls Salmon River Land & Water Co.,* 245 Fed. 9, 21-22 (9th Cir. 1917).

[549] *In re Deschutes River & Tributaries,* 134 Oreg. 623, 665-668, 286 Pac. 563, 294 Pac. 1049 (1930).

[550] Cal. Const., art. XIV, § 1; Idaho Const., art. XV, § 1, Mont. Const., art. III, § 15.

[551] Oreg. Rev. Stat. § 541.010(1) (Supp. 1969).

[552] *Albuquerque Land & Irr. Co.* v. *Gutierrez,* 10 N. Mex. 177, 231, 61 Pac. 357 (1900), affirmed, 188 U. S. 545 (1903).

These declarations have several meanings. They support the principle that the Western States, which contain large areas in which available water supplies are not adequate for full requirements of good lands, the utilization of streamflow in meeting as far as practicable the requirements of private users is a public purpose in that it contributes to the public welfare. Again, as stated in chapter 7 under "Rights-of-Way for Water Control and Related Purposes— Private lands," their characterization as public uses of water provides a basis for clothing the controlling organizations with the power of eminent domain in acquiring rights-of-way for diversion, storage, and delivery of the water. And they also provide the basis for subjecting the sale or rental of the water to State control under the laws regulating public utilities. In fact, the California and Idaho constitutional declarations specifically include phrases subjecting such sales or rentals to regulation and control of the State under procedure prescribed by law. And the Oregon statute provides that the right to collect rates for such use of water is a franchise, and that the rights shall be fixed by public authority.

What is meant in these provisions by "sale" and "rental" of water is readily understandable, but the meaning of the word "distribution" is less obvious. It may have been intended originally as a catchall phrase to include all water deliveries made by appropriators to persons other than themselves, whether or not technically pursuant to sale or rental. However, State regulation of rates and charges for delivery of water has not been imposed upon irrigation districts, which serve users of water on or in connection with lands within their boundaries, nor upon mutual irrigation companies, which serve their own stockholders at cost, both of which are self-operated and controlled and are not in the business of serving the public for profit. Nor is such regulation imposed upon commercial irrigation companies of the type which deal, not with the public generally, but only under private contracts with water users of their own choosing.

A more reasonable interpretation of the term "distribution," whether or not so intended, is to apply it to the diversion and delivery to consumers of water which the irrigation company does not sell or rent because, under the circumstances in the particular jurisdiction, it has no title to the water. It is simply charging the consumers, not a price for the sale of a commodity that it does not own, but for the cost of services performed in obtaining physical possession of the water and transporting it to the consumers' places of use. This view is supported by a holding of the Arizona Supreme Court in 1904 to the effect that water diverted from a public stream by a public service irrigation company remains public water until it is actually used by the appropriator-consumers.[553]

An anomalous situation developed when the California Code of Civil Procedure was amended in 1917 for the purpose of extending the power of

---

[553] *Gould* v. *Maricopa Canal Co.*, 8 Ariz. 429, 446-447, 76 Pac. 598 (1904).

eminent domain to incorporated mutual irrigation companies.[554] This section included in "public uses," on behalf of which the right of eminent domain might be exercised, the works for irrigating lands "furnished with water by corporations supplying water to the lands of the stockholders thereof only." However, the previous concept that use of water by shareholders of a corporation which, pursuant to the purpose of its organization, supplies water only to its own shareholders at cost, is a private use, still prevails.[555] The California Public Utilities Code reenacts a former section declaring that such a company is not a public utility, and is not subject to the jurisdiction, control, or regulation of the Public Utilities Commission.[556]

Construing together these two California statutes, both of which are still in effect, the apparent conclusion is: (a) for the purpose of exercising the power of eminent domain, the use of water by a mutual company is deemed a public use; (b) with respect to public regulation of rights and services, it is a private use. Inasmuch as the functions of condemning rights-of-way and of delivering water to users are strictly separate, the two contrasting concepts for practical purposes are not incompatible.[557]

Appropriation Initiated by One Party and Completed by Another

The general rule that an appropriation of water may be initiated by one party and completed by another has been recognized throughout practically the entire history of the appropriation doctrine in the West. The purpose of completion by another may have been part of the appropriator's original plan, or it may have resulted from circumstances that developed after the project was under way. These differences will appear in the ensuing discussion. (For various aspects of the subject of completing an appropriation, see, in chapter 7, "Methods of Appropriating Water of Watercourses—Completion of Appropriation.")

Thus, in a stream system adjudication, the Oregon Supreme Court declared that it was the plan of the 1891 law, "and runs through all the cases," that an appropriation of water may be made for the future use of another. This includes future use on lands which the appropriator does not then own, or which he does not contemplate owning and which he never does own.[558] The

---

[554] Cal. Civ. Pro. Code § 1238(4) (West Supp. 1970).

[555] "* * * a mutual water company, devoting the water which it diverts exclusively to the use of its own stockholders, and not to the general public* * *is not engaged in public service and is not a public utility." *J. M. Howell Co.* v. *Corning Irr. Co.,* 177 Cal. 513, 519, 171 Pac. 100 (1918).

[556] Cal. Pub. Util. Code § 2507 (Supp. 1970).

[557] See discussion of distinctions between mutual and commercial service of water, and between private-contract and public-utility service, in Hutchins, Wells A., Selby, H. E., and Voelker, Stanley W., "Irrigation-Enterprise Organizations," U. S. Dept. Agr. Cir. 934, pp. 19-20 and 68-71 (1953).

[558] *In re Deschutes River and Tributaries,* 134 Oreg. 623, 655, 286 Pac. 563, 294 Pac. 1049 (1930).

Oregon court previously inclined to the view that the appropriator whose *bona fide* intent contemplates a use by another person or on other lands than his is the principal and the other person the agent, but concluded that "in whatever capacity the parties to the appropriation may be considered, the result is the same."[559] Subsequently, this court realized that the result is not the same when ownership of the water right is involved.[560] This important question is discussed later under "The Real Appropriator—Principal and agent."

In an action to declare certain water rights null and void, the Wyoming Supreme Court expressed its belief that if the law is complied with in other respects, one person may act as volunteer for another in connection with the steps leading up to a perfected appropriation.[561]

The rule applies to transfer of an inchoate right; that is, the purchaser may complete the appropriation.[562]

The possessor of an appropriative right initiated by another must show some contractual relation or privity with him in order to be entitled to succeed to the original date of priority. Otherwise he cannot "tack" his own title onto that of his predecessor, but takes only by recapture. The effect is that of a new appropriation, with priority as of the time of such taking.[563] (See "Property Characteristics—Conveyance of Title to Appropriative Right," above.)

The water appropriation statute of Kansas provides that any person may apply for a permit to appropriate water to a beneficial use, "notwithstanding that the application pertains to the use of water by another, or upon or in connection with the lands of another." There is a proviso that rights perfected under such an application "shall attach to the lands on or in connection with which the water is used and shall remain subject to the control of the owners of the lands as in other cases provided by law."[564]

The provisions in the Texas statute relating to contracts to supply water pertain specifically to persons as well as to associations, corporations, and public districts.[565]

Appropriation of Water by Individuals and Organizations for Delivery to Consumers

"Any person or the State of Arizona or a political subdivision thereof may appropriate unappropriated water * * * for his personal use or for delivery to consumers."[566]

---

[559] *Nevada Ditch Co.* v. *Bennett,* 30 Oreg. 59, 97-98, 45 Pac. 472 (1896); *Nevada Ditch Co.* v. *Canyon & Sand Hollow Ditch Co.,* 58 Oreg. 517, 521, 114 Pac. 86 (1911).

[560] *In re Walla Walla River,* 141 Oreg. 492, 498, 16 Pac. (2d) 939 (1932).

[561] *Scherck* v. *Nichols,* 55 Wyo. 4, 21, 95 Pac. (2d) 74 (1939).

[562] *Nevada Ditch Co.* v. *Bennett,* 30 Oreg. 59, 93, 45 Pac. 472 (1896).

[563] *Kenck* v. *Deegan,* 45 Mont. 245, 249, 122 Pac. 746 (1912). See *Osnes Livestock Co.* v. *Warren,* 103 Mont. 284, 290, 62 Pac. (2d) 206 (1936).

[564] Kans. Stat. Ann. § 82a-708a (1969).

[565] Tex. Rev. Civ. Stat. Ann. arts. 7547, 7554, *et seq.* (1954).

[566] Ariz. Rev. Stat. Ann. § 45-141(A) (Supp. 1970).

In 1900, the New Mexico Supreme Court declared that to constitute a valid appropriation of water a rightful diversion and an application to some beneficial use must be established, neither being sufficient without the other, and that:

It is not essential that the water shall be used by the person or corporation diverting the water from the stream, for the law is well settled that the water may be diverted from the streams by canals and ditches owned by individuals or corporations, and conducted long distances and beneficially used by others. This is fully established by the large canal and ditch systems existing in California, Colorado, Arizona and many other States."[567]

Whether explicitly or implicitly, all western water appropriation statutes authorize individuals, groups, formal organizations, and public agencies and entities to make such appropriations either for their own uses, or for disposition to consumers, that is, those who put the water to beneficial use. And long prior to enactment of the general water statutes in the several Western States and Territories, such practices were followed pursuant to local custom and judicial recognition. In chapter 6, references are made to these practices in the Mormon settlements in Utah, gold mining regions of California and other northwestern States and Territories, and in Indian, Spanish, and Mexican communities in the Southwest.

Water Supply Enterprises[568]

Organizations may be formed to supply water for any of the purposes for which water may be appropriated. The great majority of such enterprises in the West were formed initially for the supplying of water for irrigation of land.

The purpose of an irrigation organization is to provide water for the use of agricultural lands that cannot be irrigated by individual means as conveniently

---

[567] *Albuquerque Land & Irr. Co.* v. *Gutierrez,* 10 N. Mex. 177, 240-241, 61 Pac. 357 (1900), affirmed, 188 U. S. 545 (1903). Even earlier, the Colorado Supreme Court held that the State constitution "unquestionably contemplates and sanctions the business of transporting water for hire from natural streams to distant consumers." *Wheeler* v. *Northern Colorado Irr. Co.,* 10 Colo. 582, 588, 17 Pac. 487 (1888). In 1912, in a suit to determine relative appropriative rights of two irrigation systems in the waters of Pecos River, a Texas court of civil appeals observed that "statutory appropriations, when filed in compliance with law, give to such appropriators the right to take the water to nonriparian lands, there to use it for themselves or to dispose of it to water consumers." *Biggs* v. *Miller,* 147 S. W. 632, 637 (Tex. Civ. App. 1912). And in Montana in 1938: "An appropriation of water may be made for purposes of sale or rental." *Sherlock* v. *Greaves,* 106 Mont. 206, 218, 76 Pac. (2d) 87 (1938).

[568] For further discussions of water supply enterprises in this chapter, see "Property Characteristics—Conveyance of Title to Appropriative Right—Some Aspects of Conveyance of Appropriative Right—Conveyance of water right represented by shares in mutual corporation" and "Elements of the Appropriative Right—Purpose of Use of Water." In chapter 7, see "Who May Appropriate Water" and "Methods of Appropriating Water of Watercourses—Restrictions and Preferences in Appropriation of Water—Preferences in Water Appropriation."

or economically as by group enterprise, if at all. The purpose is the same whether the organization is an informal group of a few neighboring farmers or is a multiple-purpose project covering a great area of land.

Irrigation organizations of various types may acquire, hold, and exercise appropriative rights for the purpose of providing water for land which they were organized to serve. Such water rights as they acquire by appropriation, purchase, or otherwise are held—whether only formally or in substance—in trust for the performance of their several functions. Questions regarding actual ownership of water rights pertaining to water served by organizations will be revealed as the discussion progresses.

In the accompanying footnote is a list of published reports pertaining to water supply organizations in the West written by the author over a 30-year period.[569] Comments under this subtopic are based largely on these studies as well as on supplementary sources.

By classification according to the organizational complexity of the undertaking, these water appropriating enterprises are:

(1) Individual, for the service of a single farm, or a group of farms operated by the appropriator and served through a common diversion and ditch.

(2) Unincorporated group of appropriators. Such associations result from the physical and financial advantages to be gained by a common water diversion and distribution system for the service of a group of neighboring farms. They may be operated under either verbal or written agreements. Some of the larger ones are united under articles of association which in content, though not in legal effect, resemble formal articles of incorporation. Although sometimes referred to as "partnership" enterprises, this designation is misleading, for in legal contemplation these associations are coownerships, not partnerships. In appropriating water and making it physically available to their lands, and generally in doing things respecting their water system in which an individual may lawfully engage, members of an unincorporated association may take action jointly.

---

[569] Hutchins, Wells A.: "Irrigation District Operation and Finance," U. S. Dept. Agr. Bul. 1177 (1923); "Mutual Irrigation Companies in Utah," Utah Agr. Expt. Sta. Bul. 199 (1927); "The Community Acequia: Its Origin and Development," 31 Southwestern Historical Quarterly 261 (1928); "Community Acequias or Ditches in New Mexico," State Eng. N. Mex. 8th Bien. Rep., 1926-1928, 227 (1928); "Mutual Irrigation Companies," U. S. Dept. Agr. Tech. Bul. 82 (1929); "Financial Settlements of Defaulting Irrigation Enterprises," U. S. Dept. Agr. Cir. 72 (1929); "Commercial Irrigation Companies," U. S. Dept. Agr. Tech. Bul. 177 (1930); "Summary of Irrigation-District Statutes of Western States," U. S. Dept. Agr. Misc. Pub. 103 (1931); "Irrigation Districts, Their Organization, Operation and Financing," U. S. Dept. Agr. Tech. Bul. 254 (1931); "Organization and Operation of Cooperative Irrigation Companies," U. S. Farm Credit Admin., Coop. Div. Cir. C-102 (1936); "Mutual Irrigation Companies in California and Utah," U. S. Farm Credit Admin., Coop. Div. Bul. 8 (1936); with Selby, H. E., and Voelker, Stanley W., "Irrigation-Enterprise Organizations," U. S. Dept. Agr. Cir. 934 (1953).

(3) Incorporated water company. Included in this classification are (a) mutual irrigation companies and (b) commercial irrigation companies. These companies are organized and they operate under the general corporation laws of the State. The capital stock of mutual irrigation companies—which are nonprofit enterprises—is held by the owners of lands served with water by the company. Except in isolated instances, that of commercial companies is held by outsiders whose investments were made for the purpose of gain, as in case of other businesses. Other profit and nonprofit distinctions are noted below. Appropriation of water is initiated and carried through the administrative process by the corporation, which thus holds formal title to the appropriative right; questions as to actual ownership of the right are noted under the ensuing discussion of relations between organization and consumers.

(4) Public agency. Included are irrigation districts and water districts of various types, water authorities, municipalities, other political subdivisions, and agencies of the State and of the United States.

Profit and Nonprofit Enterprises

Private nonprofit irrigation enterprises.—These comprise mutual or cooperative irrigation companies organized for the purpose of providing irrigation water at cost, primarily for the use of their members. The larger mutual companies are incorporated. Unincorporated mutual irrigation enterprises are divided into (1) those that were never incorporated, and (2) those that were once incorporated but lost their corporate status and continued to function with the form but without the powers of a corporation.

In California, where public rate regulation of water utilities attained importance, the supreme court held that a mutual irrigation or water company, devoting the water which it diverts exclusively to the use of its own shareholders, and not to the general public, "is not engaged in public service and is not a public utility."[570] The Public Utilities Code declares that a company that supplies water to its own shareholders at cost is not a public utility and is not subject to the jurisdiction of the Public Utilities Commission.[571]

In early cases, it was held that persons who hold water rights individually and who form a corporation and delegate thereto the function of handling the diversion and distribution facilities, reserving to themselves their water rights, do not thereby dedicate or appropriate to public use the water thus reserved and used by themselves.[572] Furthermore, even if the holders do convey their water rights to the company for the mere purpose of convenient management and distribution of the water to the users according to their respective rights, there is no severance of the right from the land to which it was appurtenant.[573]

---

[570] *J. M. Howell Co.* v. *Corning Irr. Co.*, 177 Cal. 513, 519, 171 Pac. 100 (1918).
[571] Cal. Pub. Util. Code § 2705 (Supp. 1970).
[572] *Hildreth* v. *Montecito Creek Water Co.*, 139 Cal. 22, 29, 72 Pac. 395 (1903).
[573] *In re Thomas' Estate*, 147 Cal. 236, 242, 81 Pac. 539 (1905).

Mutual irrigation companies reached their major importance in Utah, southern California, and eastern Colorado.

Public nonprofit enterprises.—These consist of districts, municipalities,[574] and other public agencies and entities.

All of the contiguous Western States have general statutes governing the organization and operation of irrigation districts, which are public, quasi-municipal corporations, political subdivisions of a State. Some such districts are created by special act of the legislature.

Despite its vicissitudes, including heavy losses of invested capital in many areas and during various periods, the irrigation district was a major factor in attracting private capital to the irrigation development of the West. As against the financial failures, there were and are many outstanding successes. In addition, there are other types of water districts (water control and improvement districts, water conservancy districts, metropolitan water districts, etc.), water authorities comprising entire watersheds, and other political subdivisions concerned primarily with water supply. The West is dotted with such public agencies and entities. A political entity authorized by the legislature to embrace a vast area, for multiple purposes, empowered to issue bonds, and with broad powers of taxation, can have a potent influence on the water economy of the region.

Private profit enterprises.—These are the commercial irrigation companies. In the last part of the 19th century, they were organized on a considerable scale in various parts of the West for the purpose of building and operating irrigation works for the profit of persons who provided the capital and undertook to retain temporary or permanent ownership of the irrigation system. Thus, with respect to ownership of irrigation facilities, commercial companies differed from both public districts and private mutual companies, in that the latter two groups comprise nonprofit, cooperative enterprises under local ownership and control.[575]

The two types of commercial irrigation companies formed solely for operational purposes (as distinguished from the construction or development companies) consisted of (a) private contract companies for the service of selected consumers, and (b) public utility companies intended to serve all applicants within the service area to the extent of the water supply—that is, the public. These enterprises in the (b) group, then, are privately owned but are engaged in service to the public.

---

[574] For discussions of municipalities in their various relationships to water rights problems, see, in chapter 7, "Who May Appropriate Water" and "Methods of Appropriating Water of Watercourses—Restrictions and Preferences in Appropriation of Water—Preferences in Water Appropriations," and in this chapter, "Elements of the Appropriative Right—Purpose of Use of Water."

[575] Ownership of properties of an irrigation district may be held to be in the public or in the State, depending upon the legal questions involved, but control is vested in representatives selected by the local community.

The distinction between classes of water service rendered by private contract companies and public utility companies, long established in ratemaking cases, is of fundamental importance when the question of public regulation of the commercial company rates is raised. Public utility rates and services are subject to public regulation, whether or not consumers have permanent water contracts with the companies, whereas rates fixed by contracts which in the technical legal sense are private contracts cannot be disturbed by public authority. The practical application of this principle involves some fine distinctions and legal technicalities.

Investments in these private "profit" (so-called) water enterprises, while contributing substantially to the agricultural development of the West, were so generally unprofitable to the investors that new capital practically ceased to be available many years ago. Most of the going commercial enterprises were succeeded by public and private nonprofit organizations. Except in a few areas, not many are left.

Public Supervision and Regulation of Water Supply Enterprises

Statutes of various States provide for public supervision over organization and bond issues of irrigation districts. Other statutes govern the incorporation of water companies, both mutual and commercial. The so-called "blue-sky laws," or corporate security acts, of the Western States apply to mutual irrigation companies and to private contract commercial companies that seek to issue securities.

In a few States, long-term securities may not be issued by public utility irrigation companies without approval of the State commission that has jurisdiction over the rates of such companies. This is of practical importance chiefly in California, in which State the provisions of the blue sky law do not apply to any security (other than an interest in a real estate development) the issuance of which has been authorized by the State Public Utilities Commission.[576]

Public Regulation of Rates and Services

What enterprises are subject to public regulation.—An individual, as well as an association or formal organization or entity, may appropriate water for delivery to consumers.[577] It follows logically that the venture of an individual who appropriates water for delivery to the general consumer public is engaged in public utility service of water and that it may thereby be classed as a public utility, subject to whatever regulation the State may provide for the service of water to the public.[578] In most irrigation cases in which regulatory bodies have taken jurisdiction, however, organizations have been involved.

---

[576] Cal. Corp. Code § 25100(e) (Supp. 1970).
[577] See "Appropriation of Water by Individuals and Organizations for Delivery to Consumers," *supra.*
[578] The Cal. Pub. Util. Code § § 2701 (West 1956) and 2704 (West Supp. 1970) provides that

In contrasting the two types of commercial irrigation companies formed solely for operational purposes, it is stated earlier under "A Public Use" that public regulation of rates and services applies only to companies engaged in public service—the supplying of water to the public generally. It does not apply to sales or rentals of water to consumers pursuant to strictly private contracts which they hold with the company. If a commercial company is engaged in both kinds of service—public service to some of the consumers and private contract service to others— only the public utility part of its service is subject to regulation.

Likewise, in contrasting profit and nonprofit enterprises in general, it has been shown that a mutual irrigation company that provides water for its own shareholders only, at cost, is not of the nature of a public utility and is not subject to rate regulation by public utilities commissions.

Here again is a possible exception in situations in which both private and public service are rendered. A California company originally organized as a purely mutual irrigation company began the practice of delivering, in addition to irrigation water to only its own stockholders, domestic water to both shareholders and nonshareholders. So it became technically in part a public utility. At the suggestion of the then State Railroad Commission a subordinate public utility company was formed to take over the domestic service. This subsidiary acquired shares of stock in the parent company sufficient to cover its domestic water requirements; and the mutual company held all the stock of the domestic company. Under this arrangement, the Commission regulated the rates of the domestic company, but it did not inquire into the cost of water to the domestic company so long as the latter received the same treatment as all other mutual shareholders.

Regulatory agencies.—In the earlier discussion of "A Public Use," there are noted constitutional and statutory provisions subjecting sales and rentals of water to such regulation and control of the State as is provided by law. Rate regulation at first was generally imposed on the water selling or renting enterprises through the medium of ordinances passed by the county governing bodies. Later, as the use of regulatory procedures administered by State commissions increased, the function in most Western States in which it was important was vested in the State commission that had jurisdiction over other public utilities.

There are deviations from this generalization. Texas vests regulation of water company rates in the State Water Rights Commission which administers

---

"any person" who sells water under contract or otherwise shall be a public utility. However, it exempts from public regulation the owner of a water supply who uses it primarily for his own domestic or irrigation purposes, who either (a) sells the surplus for such purposes, or (b) in an emergency water shortage sells water from his supply for not more than one irrigation season, or who (c) sells part of the water as an accomodation to neighbors who have no other water supply.

the water rights act.[579] Colorado still delegates this authority to the boards of county commissioners, which was formerly general practice in the West.[580]

As stated in chapter 7 under "Methods of Appropriating Water of Watercourses–Storage Water Appropriation," water rights statutes of New Mexico, North Dakota, Oklahoma, and South Dakota provide that surplus waters over the needs of appropriators in "storage, diversion, or carriage" works must be delivered, at reasonable rates, to any person entitled to its use.[581] In the last three named States, determination of the reasonableness of rates is vested in the water rights administrator and enforcement in the courts. New Mexico leaves both determination and enforcement to the judicial process.

The Montana water rights statute authorizes the sale of surplus water, and requires it to be sold at "the usual and customary rates per inch" to the person entitled thereto who tenders payment. Enforcement may be effectuated by the latter in an action at law or in equity.[582]

Two Wyoming statutes respecting the disposal of surplus stored waters are also noted at this point in chapter 7. One statute prohibits receipt of a royalty for the use of water facilities, and classes those who furnish surplus water to others as common carriers. The other provides for (a) delivery of excess impounded waters to applicants, enforcement to be compelled by court proceedings; and (b) on application of any interested party, creation of a temporary board of special commissioners consisting of the State Engineer, water commissioner, and local water superintendent, for the purpose of establishing maximum reasonable rates for the waters in dispute.[583]

Value of water right as element of rate base.—Field studies of irrigation enterprises published in 1930 and 1953 revealed instances in which valuations of water rights were included in rate bases of companies in which ownership of water rights was vested, but none in those of enterprises the water rights of which were held by the water users. It was found that on the whole, State commissions were averse to placing substantial values on water rights beyond

---

[579] Tex. Rev. Civ. Stat. Ann. art. 7563 (1954). Historically, all Texas statutes authorizing appropriation of water likewise authorized formation of corporations for the purpose of supplying water to lands along their canals. The first water administration statute, enacted in 1913, created a Board of Water Engineers to supervise acquisition of water rights, and also vested the Board with regulation of rates for water supplies to users. This is discussed at some length in Hutchins, Wells A., "The Texas Law of Water Rights," pp. 266-283 (1961). In 1962, the Board of Water Engineers was succeeded by the Texas Water Commission, since renamed the Texas Water Rights Commission.

[580] Colo. Rev. Stat. Ann. § 148-8-1 *et seq.* (1963).

[581] N. Mex. Stat. Ann. § 75-5-16 (1968); N. Dak. Cent. Code Ann. §§ 61-04-03 and 61-04-17 (1960); Okla. Stat. Ann. tit. 82, § 101 (1970); S. Dak. Comp. Laws Ann. § 46-7-1 (1967).

[582] Mont. Rev. Codes Ann. §§ 89-823 to -826 (1964).

[583] Wyo. Stat. Ann. §§ 41-47 and -39 (1957).

the actual cost of their acquisition even if, as a matter of law, they belonged to the companies.[584]

Acceptance of a permit or license to appropriate water in California carries an express statutory condition that no value therefor, in excess of the actual amount paid to the State, shall ever be claimed with respect to, among other things, public regulation of services to be rendered by the appropriator.[585] The Arizona and Oregon water rights statutes contain provisions to the same effect.[586]

The Colorado Supreme Court from early times emphasized the collaborative relationship of commercial companies and their water consumers, the company being the trustee and representative for protection of their rights. In 1938, in the review of a ratemaking proceeding, this court concluded that neither the whole nor any part of the value of project water rights should be included in the rate base. Particular emphasis was laid on the fact that the company's decreed appropriations were of necessity dependent upon the joint acts of company and water users, neither of which could be considered the appropriator in the strict sense of that term.[587]

In a case arising in California shortly before the State commission procedure was established, the United States Supreme Court held that a public service company was entitled to have the value of its water rights taken into account by boards of county supervisors in fixing the rates to be charged by the company. But the Court did not decide the principle on which the valuation should be measured.[588]

The Idaho Supreme Court, which has adhered to the view that an appropriation of water for sale, rental, or distribution belongs to the water company, stated that such an appropriator has a valuable property right entitled to protection. The court held that the State Public Utilities Commission was in error in refusing to include in the rate base of a public-service enterprise the value of its water right other than the actual cost of acquiring this right.[589]

---

[584] Hutchins, Wells A., "Commercial Irrigation Companies," U. S. Dept. Agr. Tech. Bul. 177, pp. 30-31 (1930); Hutchins, Wells A., Selby, H. E., and Voelker, Stanley W., "Irrigation-Enterprise Organizations," U. S. Dept. Agr. Cir. 934, pp. 72-73 (1953).

[585] Cal. Water Code § § 1392 and 1629 (West 1956).

[586] Ariz. Rev. Stat. Ann. § 45-149(B) (1956); Oreg. Rev. Stat. § 537.280 (Supp. 1969).

[587] *Jefferson County* v. *Rocky Mountain Water Co.,* 102 Colo. 351, 355-361, 363, 79 Pac. (2d) 373 (1938).

[588] *San Joaquin & Kings River Canal & Irr. Co.* v. *County of Stanislaus,* 233 U. S. 454, 459-461 (1914), reversing, 191 Fed. 875 (N. D. Cal. 1911). The lower court had held that the water right was the property of the consumer and attached to his land, and not to that of the company attached to its canal system; hence, the company was not entitled to have it valued as its property right in this case.

[589] *Murray* v. *Public Utilities Commission,* 27 Idaho 603, 619-620, 150 Pac. 47 (1915); *Capital Water Co.* v. *Public Utilities Commission,* 44 Idaho 1, 16-20, 262 Pac. 863 (1926).

In a case concerning the relative status of commercial company and consumer, the Nevada Supreme Court concluded that the water user was in fact the actual appropriator, even though the water was supplied through the agency of the company. The question as to whether the company had a property interest in the right to furnish the water was not an issue.[590] Seven years later, the Federal court for the District of Nevada expressed its disbelief that the water right of a commercial water company in Nevada rested exclusively in the customer, and held squarely that the reasonable value of the water right, insofar as it was used and useful in supplying the company's customers, was a part of the total value on which the company was entitled to a fair return.[591] These cases are noted elsewhere in this chapter in connection with appurtenance of water right to land under "Property Characteristics," and in more detail later under "The Real Appropriator—Commercial enterprise."

Formal Title to the Appropriative Right

It has been long settled that a public service corporation may make an appropriation of water for distribution to the public generally, and may hold formal title to the appropriative right.[592] This is the case regardless of the question of actual legal ownership of the appropriative right, discussed below. Whether this real ownership is held to be vested in the consumers, or in the organization company, the company may serve the users through its facilities and represent them in protecting their water rights.[593]

Mutual water companies and public agencies, likewise, to the extent of their fundamental authority, may appropriate water or acquire existing appropriative rights and hold formal title thereto.

---

[590] *Prosole* v. *Steamboat Canal Co.*, 37 Nev. 154, 158-162, 166-167, 140 Pac. 720, 144 Pac. 744 (1914).

[591] *Reno Power, Light & Water Co.* v. *Public Serv. Comm'n*, 300 Fed. 645, 647-652 (D. Nev. 1921). The court emphasized that no valuation should be allowed for the right to water that was being wasted.

[592] *Pima Farms Co.* v. *Proctor*, 30 Ariz. 96, 112-113, 245 Pac. 369 (1926); *Happy Valley Land & Water Co.* v. *Nelson*, 169 Cal. 694, 695-696, 147 Pac. 966 (1915); *Combs* v. *Farmers' High Line Canal & Res. Co.*, 38 Colo. 420, 429-432, 88 Pac. 396 (1907); *Farmers' Co-op Ditch Co.* v. *Riverside Irr. Dist.*, 14 Idaho 450, 457-459, 94 Pac. 761 (1908); *Bailey* v. *Tintinger*, 45 Mont. 154, 177-178, 122 Pac. 575 (1912); *Prosole* v. *Steamboat Canal Co.*, 37 Nev. 154, 158-162, 140 Pac. 720, 144 Pac. 744 (1914); *Reno Power, Light & Water Co.* v. *Public Serv. Comm'n*, 300 Fed. 645, 648-650 (D. Nev. 1921); *Albuquerque Land & Irr. Co.* v. *Gutierrez*, 10 N. Mex. 177, 240-241, 61 Pac. 357 (1900), affirmed, 188 U. S. 545, 555-556 (1903); *Biggs* v. *Miller*, 147 S. W. 632, 637-638 (Tex. Civ. App. 1912); *State* v. *Laramie Rivers Co.*, 59 Wyo. 9, 41-46, 136 Pac. (2d) 487 (1943).

[593] *Montezuma Canal Co.* v. *Smithville Canal Co.*, 218 U. S. 371, 382 (1910); *Salt River Valley Water Users' Assn.* v. *Norviel*, 29 Ariz. 360, 374, 375, 241 Pac. 503 (1925); *Combs* v. *Farmers' High Line Canal & Res. Co.*, 38 Colo. 420, 429-432, 88 Pac. 396 (1907); *Nampa & Meridian Irr. Dist.* v. *Barclay*, 56 Idaho 13, 18-19, 47 Pac. (2d) 916 (1935); *Biggs* v. *Miller*, 147 S. W. 632, 637-638 (Tex. Civ. App. 1912).

The Real Appropriator

Commercial enterprise. —The western decisions on this matter conflict. This topic is associated with that entitled "Methods of Appropriating Water of Watercourses—Completion of Appropriation—What Constitutes Completion of an Appropriation" in chapter 7.

(1) Ownership of water right by company. (a) In California, where public regulation of water utilities became increasingly prominent early in this century, an important case was decided by the United States Supreme Court with respect to water rates fixed by boards of county supervisors, shortly before the changeover to State regulatory control became effective. The chief issue was inclusion in the rate base of valuation of the company's water rights. In holding that this valuation should be taken into account, the Court was obviously convinced that the water rights had been acquired, paid for, and confirmed by prescription against riparian owners and that they belonged to the company.[594]

(b) A number of other courts have held or declared that the appropriative water rights exercised by commercial irrigation companies belong to the company, not to the consumers.[595]

(c) In a statutory adjudication suit, the Oregon Supreme Court held squarely that a corporation organized for profit for the purpose of supplying water to all persons whose lands are within reach of its ditch for general rental, by contrast with a mutual corporation organized for the purpose of carrying the water appropriated by its mutual stockholders, became the owner of the use of water appropriated.[596] In so doing, the court took occasion to remove

---

[594] *San Joaquin & Kings River Canal & Irr. Co.* v. *County of Stanislaus,* 233 U. S. 454, 459-461 (1914).

[595] The appropriation of water carried in a ditch operated for sale, rental, or distribution of water belongs to the water company, not to the water user. The right of the latter is only that of a *user and consumer: Nampa & Meridian Irr. Dist.* v. *Barclay,* 56 Idaho 13, 18-19, 47 Pac. (2d) 916 (1935); *Farmers Co-operative Ditch Co.* v. *Riverside Irr. Dist.,* 14 Idaho 450, 457-459, 94 Pac. 761 (1908). The appropriation of "a public service corporation * * * is complete when it has fully complied with the statute and has its distributing system completed and is ready and willing to deliver water to users upon demand, and offers to do so." *Bailey* v. *Tintinger,* 45 Mont. 154, 177-178, 122 Pac. 575 (1912). To the same effect with respect to the statutes of 1881 and 1899, subject to loss of the right by failure to apply the water to a beneficial use within a reasonable time: *Basinger* v. *Taylor,* 30 Idaho 289, 299, 164 Pac. 522 (1917). Also to the same effect, with respect to the 1881 South Dakota water appropriation law, the water rights being held to have vested in the original locators at the time that they were acquired, and not in those who used the water: *Butte County* v. *Lovinger,* 64 S. Dak. 200, 209, 266 N. W. 127 (1936). Irrigation company held to be the appropriator, and parties with whom it had contracted for water service were customers of an appropriator: *Willis* v. *Neches Canal Co.,* 16 S. W. (2d) 266, 268-269 (Tex. Com. App. 1929). See *Biggs* v. *Miller,* 147 S. W. 632, 637-638 (Tex. Civ. App. 1912).

[596] *In re Walla Walla River,* 141 Oreg. 492, 496-499, 16 Pac. (2d) 939 (1932). Some dissatisfied customers of the public service corporation who discontinued their

any misapprehension that had resulted from its statement in the opinion in an earlier case in which it had observed gratuitously that the water and ditch rights exercised by a public service water corporation "really belong to the individual appropriator" and are appurtenant to the place of use, and then proceeded to its actual holding that *a fortiori* "must this be true in the case of a mutual water company."[597]

(d) The Nevada Supreme Court and the Federal court for the District of Nevada rendered opinions as to the purport of a statute enacted in 1913, which is still in effect. This law provides that water used for beneficial purposes shall remain appurtenant to the place of use, subject to two exceptions, one being that the provisions in question shall not apply in cases of companies that have appropriated water for diversion and transmission to lands of private persons at an annual charge.[598]

In the year following enactment, this Nevada statute was referred to by the State supreme court, but was held inapplicable to water rights in the case at bar on the ground that they were acquired prior to the enactment. The court held that the consumer in the case was entitled to receive the quantity of water he had been customarily served so long as he complied with reasonable regulations and paid a reasonable charge; that the consumer, not the company, was the actual appropriator.[599] After this decision was rendered, the United States Supreme Court case with respect to a California company, noted above, was decided.[600] Referring to observations in the opinion of Justice Holmes therein, the Nevada court held, on petition for rehearing (petition denied) that "whether or not the appellant [consumer] had a property interest in the right to furnish the water is not an issue in the case at bar, and our observations made in the opinion are not to be considered as decisive of this matter."

Several years later, the Federal court for Nevada, referring to the statute and its exception noted above, expressed its belief that "The theory that the right vests explicitly in the customer is illogical under a statute which declares that his use of the water is not appurtenant to the land on which he uses it," and

---

patronage and formed for themselves a mutual company were not entitled to carve any water rights out of their previous public utility patronage, inasmuch as the water right belonged to the company. The date of priority of their rights under their own mutual company was relegated to the date on which the mutual company operations began.

[597] *Eldredge* v. *Mill Ditch Co.,* 90 Oreg. 590, 596-597, 177 Pac. 939 (1919).

[598] Nev. Rev. Stat. § 533.040 (Supp. 1967). This statute and the State and Federal cases have been noted more briefly under "Property Characteristics—Appurtenance of Water Right to Land," and in the instant topic under "Public Regulation of Rates and Services."

[599] *Prosole* v. *Steamboat Canal Co.,* 37 Nev. 154, 162-167, 140 Pac. 720, 144 Pac. 744 (1914).

[600] *San Joaquin & Kings River Canal & Irr. Co.* v. *County of Stanislaus,* 233 U. S. 454, 459-461 (1914).

held that the reasonable value of the water right was a part of the total value on which the company was entitled to a fair return.[601]

(2) Ownership of water right by consumer. (a) Other decisions have been rendered to the effect that the consumer owns the water right, even though the company holds formal title for purposes of exercise of the right and for protection of the interests of all concerned.

(b) In early years, the Colorado Supreme Court took the view that the carrier of water, while having a special status in some respects different from that of the ordinary common carrier, does not become "a proprietor of the water diverted."[602] Rather, it must be regarded as an intermediate agency existing for the purpose of aiding consumers in the exercise of their constitutional rights, as well as a private enterprise prosecuted for the benefit of its owners.[603] Such a company, by means of which consumers enjoy their appropriation, is their trustee and representative for protection of their rights.[604]

Years later, in an action to enjoin the enforcement of a rate established by a board of county commissioners, the Colorado Supreme Court concluded that neither the whole nor any part of the value of the water rights should be included in the rate base. But, the court pointed out, the decreed appropriations of the company were of necessity dependent upon the joint and practically concurrent acts of the company and the water users. "The cases in Colorado dealing with situations analogous to the one before us all hold that neither the ditch company alone nor the users alone are appropriators in the strict sense of that term." Both diversion of the water and its beneficial application are necessary not only to constitute an appropriation, but also to its continued existence, whether performed by the same person or by different ones.[605]

In a 1962 case, the Colorado court said, among other things, that:

The carrier creates the means of diverting water from the natural stream, carrying it to the place where the consumer can economically accept delivery from the carrier ditch (along with other consumers) and apply it to irrigation. Until the water has been actually applied to beneficial use there is no water right.

The legal title to the decreed appropriation from the natural stream, however, belongs to the carrier which has a duty to protect it for the benefit of the consumers under the ditch. The carrier also has sufficient interest in

---

[601] *Reno Power, Light & Water Co.* v. *Public Serv. Comm'n,* 300 Fed. 645, 648-650 (D. Nev. 1921).

[602] *Wheeler* v. *Northern Colorado Irr. Co.,* 10 Colo. 582, 587-588, 17 Pac. 487 (1888).

[603] *Wyatt* v. *Larimer & Weld Irr. Co.,* 18 Colo. 298, 308, 33 Pac. 144 (1893).

[604] *Combs* v. *Farmers' High Line Canal & Res. Co.,* 38 Colo. 420, 429-432, 88 Pac. 396 (1907).

[605] *Jefferson County* v. *Rocky Mountain Water Co.,* 102 Colo. 351, 355-361, 79 Pac. (2d) 373 (1938).

the water right that unused rights of the consumer do not cease to exist but may be held by the carrier for sale to other consumers and thus no part of the full decreed appropriation to the carrier ditch need be abandoned to the source stream.

. . . .

A carrier ditch that also applies water to beneficial use has the right to legal ownership of the stream appropriation for all the water allocated to the ditch, and also the complete ownership of the ripened water right effectuated by application of a portion of that water to beneficial use by the carrier itself.[606]

(c) In 1900, the New Mexico Supreme Court held the law to be well settled that water might be diverted from a stream by an individual or a corporation and served to others for their beneficial use, the beneficial user having constituted the company his agent to divert and transport the water for his use.[607] In affirming this decision, the United States Supreme Court held that Congress did not intend, in enacting the Desert Land Act,[608] that surplus water on the public domain must be *directly* appropriated by the owners of the land on which beneficial use of water was to be made. That is, a corporation could be lawfully empowered to become an intermediary for furnishing water to irrigate the lands of third parties, for the rights conferred upon irrigation companies by Congressional legislation were not limited to such corporations as were "mere combinations of owners of irrigable land"[609]—in other words, not limited to individuals and mutual irrigation companies.

The Federal court for the District of New Mexico, in reviewing principles of water law developed in the West, stated that a development company that contracts with land purchasers to supply them with water owns the irrigation works, but "the water right is appurtenant to the land and belongs to the owner thereof."[610]

(d) Likewise in Arizona, in 1901, it was held that a corporation organized for the purpose of furnishing water for agricultural purposes, but which itself owns no arable and irrigable land, becomes the mere agency of the water users in making the appropriation therefor.[611] All persons who own lands under a canal

---

[606] *City and County of Denver* v. *Miller,* 149 Colo. 96, 368 Pac. (2d) 982, 984 (1962). In the latter regard, the court cited *City and County of Denver* v. *Brown,* 56 Colo. 216, 138 Pac. 44 (1914). The court concluded that since the City of Denver was both the owner of the carrier ditch and the beneficial user of the water in dispute, "the city did not hold, like the ordinary carrier, as a trustee for the next consumer. The city was itself the consumer of and held every element of legal and equitable ownership possible, with respect to the 62 inches of water at issue here." 368 Pac. (2d) at 985.

[607] *Albuquerque Land & Irr. Co.* v. *Gutierrez,* 10 N. Mex. 177, 240-241, 61 Pac. 357 (1900).

[608] 19 Stat. 377 (1877), 43 U. S. C. § 321 *et seq.* (1964).

[609] *Gutierres* v. *Albuquerque Land & Irr. Co.,* 188 U. S. 545, 555-556 (1903).

[610] *Murphy* v. *Kerr,* 296 Fed. 536, 545 (D. N. Mex. 1923), affirmed, 5 Fed. (2d) 908 (8th Cir. 1925).

[611] *Slosser* v. *Salt River Valley Canal Co.,* 7 Ariz. 376, 390, 65 Pac. 332 (1901).

in this State, irrigated by means of water furnished by and through such canal, become appropriators and possessed of appropriative rights in the order of their several priorities.[612]

(e) The Wyoming Supreme Court has held that "The carrier of water is but the agent or trustee for others. The actual appropriator of the water is the party who puts it to beneficial use." A common carrier has the duty to distribute the water to applicants as they come, and to distribute only the quantity of water over which it has control. And reciprocally, no landowner can have any right to the water unless he appropriates it and uses it for a beneficial purpose. The court emphasized that regardless of whether, in the instant case, the organization should be regarded as a common carrier or a strictly private corporation, owners of land under the canal could acquire no right to any part of the water without taking certain essential steps, including making an application to or purchase from the company respecting a right of use, and thereafter applying the water to a beneficial purpose.[613]

(f) A section of the Kansas water rights statute provides in part that:[614]

Any person may apply for a permit to appropriate water to a beneficial use, notwithstanding that the application pertains to the use of water by another, or upon or in connection with the lands of another: *Provided,* Any rights to the beneficial use of water perfected under such applications shall attach to the lands on or in connection with which the water is used and shall remain subject to the control of the owners of the lands as in other cases provided by law.

This section, vesting ownership of the appropriative right in the landowner-consumer, would be applicable whether the initial appropriation is made by a commercial irrigation company or by a mutual company.

Mutual enterprise.—(1) Formal title to water rights exercised by a mutual company may be held either by the irrigation organization or by individual shareholders, depending upon State law and upon the action taken in acquiring the rights. However, it is the general rule in the West that regardless of holding of formal title, actual ownership of appropriative rights is vested in the water users and is represented by shares of stock in the corporation. Some questions of appurtenance of mutual company stock to land have been discussed earlier in this chapter under "Property Characteristics—Appurtenance of Water Right to Land."

---

[612] *Gould* v. *Maricopa Canal Co.,* 8 Ariz. 429, 447, 76 Pac. 598 (1904). In *Pima Farms Co.* v. *Proctor,* 30 Ariz. 96, 112-113, 245 Pac. 369 (1926), the supreme court referred to the defendant public service corporation as doing the appropriating, but this obviously was simply a convenient way of referring to the defendant as doing the construction and operation work for, and as representing the interests of, its many consumers. The contest was between prior and subsequent appropriators; there was no issue of ownership of the appropriative right. The attitude of the supreme court on the question of water right ownership was not changed thereby. See *Olsen* v. *Union Canal & Irr. Co.,* 58 Ariz. 306, 317-318, 119 Pac. (2d) 569 (1941); *Whiting* v. *Lyman Water Co.,* 59 Ariz. 121, 123-124, 458, 459-460, 124 Pac. (2d) 316, 129 Pac. (2d) 995 (1942).

[613] *State* v. *Laramie Rivers Co.,* 59 Wyo. 9, 41-46, 136 Pac. (2d) 487 (1943).

[614] Kans. Stat. Ann. § 82a-708a (1969).

(2) The Utah mutual company was devised and came into being merely as a convenient means of distributing water among members of a group who were the real owners of the water rights and users of the water represented by the stock issued by the corporation.[615]

In Utah, the purpose of organizing these corporations was commonly, though not exclusively, for taking over existing unincorporated systems which the benefitted landowners held in common ownership. Many of them were originally built under the supervision of the community leaders and subsequently were operated by the towns which the irrigated lands surrounded. According to the Utah Supreme Court, "Water rights are pooled in a mutual company for convenience of operation and more efficient distribution, and perhaps for more convenient transfer." And the stock certificate in such a company "is really a certificate showing an undivided part ownership in a certain water supply."[616]

(3) The Oregon Supreme Court observed that the relation of a mutual water corporation "seems to be clearly that of a holding company, trustee, or agent for the real owners of the water who are putting it to beneficial use upon their lands."[617]

(4) The mutual water company was used extensively in agricultural development in California, particularly in the southern part of the State, as a vehicle for taking over and operating irrigation systems built in connection with the subdivision and sale of farmlands. Purchasers of irrigable lands received, as part of their purchase, shares of stock in the mutual company while it was still only a paper organization. When 50 percent, or some other prearranged segment of the irrigation company stock, passed to the landowners, management and operation of the irrigation system was turned over to the mutual company by the construction and development company and thereafter was under the control of the mutual shareholders.

According to the rather numerous California decisions relating to the affairs of these organizations, the stockholders of a mutual water company are at least the beneficial holders of the water rights, if not the formal holders, particularly—but not necessarily—if either the water rights or the shares of stock are specifically appurtenant to the land. For example, a mutual company formed in connection with a typical land development enterprise of the character mentioned above succeeded the development company in formal title to the appropriative rights; but the water user-stockholders became the beneficial owners.

In a case involving some nine mutual companies, capital stock of which had not been made appurtenant to land but was purchased by an irrigation district for use of district lands, the California Supreme Court held that water rights

---

[615] *Nash* v. *Alpine Irr. Co.,* 58 Utah 84, 197 Pac. 603 (1921).

[616] *Genola* v. *Santaquin,* 96 Utah 88, 101-102, 80 Pac. (2d) 930 (1938).

[617] *Eldredge* v. *Mill Ditch Co.,* 90 Oreg. 590, 596-597, 177 Pac. 939 (1919). See *In re Walla Walla River,* 141 Oreg. 492, 498, 16 Pac. (2d) 939 (1932).

acquired by appropriation or otherwise by a mutual company for the service of its shareholders' lands, though held formally by the company, belong equitably to the stockholders.[618]

Incorporators who transfer their several water rights to the company in exchange for shares of capital stock surrender to the corporation their right of control or regulation in use of the water; but no impairment of the original water right results therefrom, and no severance from the land to which it was appurtenant.[619] Nor is there any change in substance in the ownership of the right. It remains the subject of individual ownership after the transaction as well as before, the only distinction being that it is held and exercised by the corporation under a formally different title. The corporation becomes merely the agent of its shareholders for the purpose of serving their several interests.[620]

(5) A contract between the corporation that constructed the Twin Falls Carey Act project in Idaho and the mutual company that was eventually to operate the project provided, among other things, that each share of stock in the mutual company would represent a water right for a specified quantity of water per acre, plus a proportionate interest in the property which the construction company would hold in trust for the mutual company until the project should be transferred to the latter. But, said a Federal court:

a water right can only exist when appropriated for and appurtenant to land upon which a beneficial use of the flow can be made. They [the shares] were, when issued, only indicia of a water right dedicated to a definite parcel of land. If sold and appurtenant to land, each share constitutes a proportionate interest in the works and water. Unsold, a share is of potential value only under peculiar conditions.[621]

(6) The Salt River Valley project, Arizona, is operated by the same mutual water users' association to which the project was transferred by the construction agency, the United States Bureau of Reclamation. One of the objects for which the association was organized is to furnish water for the irrigation of lands of holders of shares appurtenant to such lands. According to the Arizona Supreme Court, "The Association performs this function not as the owner of the irrigation water, because it cannot and does not *own* the water. It is a carrier of the water for its shareholders, who have delegated to it, subject of course to review by the courts, the power to determine in the first instance the source or sources from which each shareholder is entitled to have his irrigation water."[622]

[618] *Consolidated People's Ditch Co.* v. *Foothill Ditch Co.,* 205 Cal. 54, 62-63, 269 Pac. 915 (1928).

[619] *Fuller* v. *Azusa Irrigating Co.,* 138 Cal. 204, 213-214, 71 Pac. 98 (1902); *Turner* v. *Lowell Avenue Mutual Water Co.,* 104 Cal. App. (2d) 204, 209, 231 Pac. (2d) 115 (1951); *In re Thomas' Estate,* 147 Cal. 236, 242, 81 Pac. 539 (1905).

[620] *Locke* v. *Yorba Irr. Co.,* 35 Cal. (2d) 205, 209, 217 Pac. (2d) 425 (1950); *Hildreth* v. *Montecito Creek Water Co.,* 139 Cal. 22, 29, 72 Pac. 395 (1903).

[621] *Twin Falls Land & Water Co.* v. *Twin Falls Canal Co.,* 7 Fed. Supp. 238, 246 (D. Idaho 1933).

[622] *Adams* v. *Salt River Valley Water Users' Assn.,* 53 Ariz. 374, 382-383, 89 Pac. (2d) 1060 (1939).

This is in line with the long established water policy of Arizona that ownership and possession of land is essential to a valid appropriation of streamflow, and that therefore the appropriative water rights of a canal company, whether public utility or mutual, vest in the landholding water users and not in the company.[623]

Principal and agent.—In explaining the interrelationship of parties who perform different parts of the appropriative process—one performing the service of diversion and distribution of water and the other applying the water to a beneficial use—courts have sometimes designated them as principal and agent.

(1) Thus, if the consumer who actually applies to beneficial use the water delivered by a commercial irrigation company is held to be the real appropriator, the company is said to be his agent in making the water available for his use.[624] And a mutual corporation formed by water users for the purpose of convenience in management and water distribution "becomes merely their agent for the purpose of serving their several interests."[625]

(2) It has been said that whether the irrigation company is commercial or mutual, it "becomes an intermediary agent of the owner of the land and water right and diverts and carries the water" from the stream to the land—a carrier of the water.[626] The Arizona Supreme Court has taken this view, regardless of whether the water rights are acquired before or after formation of the company organization.[627]

(3) On the other hand, in pointing out the distinction between (a) a corporation organized for profit in supplying water to all potential consumers in its service area, and (b) a mutual irrigation company organized to carry water appropriated by its stockholders, the Oregon Supreme Court stated that: "The former corporation [commercial] becomes the owner of the use of the water appropriated and the irrigator becomes its agent to apply the water supplied to a beneficial

---

[623] *Slosser* v. *Salt River Valley Canal Co.,* 7 Ariz. 376, 390, 393, 65 Pac. 332 (1901); *Gould* v. *Maricopa Canal Co.,* 8 Ariz. 429, 447, 76 Pac. 598 (1904); *Olsen* v. *Union Canal & Irr. Co.,* 58 Ariz. 306, 317-318, 119 Pac. (2d) 569 (1941). The right to delivery of water by owners of a canal and reservoir system "depends entirely upon the right of appropriation held by the water user, and is not in any manner dependent upon his owning stock in such a corporation." *Whiting* v. *Lyman Water Co.,* 59 Ariz. 121, 123-124, 458, 124 Pac. (2d) 316, 129 Pac. (2d) 995 (1942). The last sentence quoted from this opinion in the *Whiting* case is not applicable to situations such as in the Salt River Valley Water Users' Association, as pointed out later under "Right of Consumer to Receive Water From the Distributing Agency—Mutual irrigation company."

[624] *Prosole* v. *Steamboat Canal Co.,* 37 Nev. 154, 158-162, 140 Pac. 720, 144 Pac. 744 (1914); *State* v. *Laramie Rivers Co.,* 59 Wyo. 9, 42, 45-46, 136 Pac. (2d) 487 (1943).

[625] *Hildreth* v. *Montecito Creek Water Co.,* 139 Cal. 22, 29, 72 Pac. 395 (1903). Water rights acquired by a mutual company for the service of its stockholders belong equitably to the latter: *Consolidated People's Ditch Co.* v. *Foothill Ditch Co.,* 205 Cal. 54, 62-63, 269 Pac. 915 (1928).

[626] *Murphy* v. *Kerr,* 296 Fed. 536, 545 (D. N. Mex. 1923).

[627] The corporation is "a mere agency" by which the consumer appropriations are made effective: *Slosser* v. *Salt River Valley Canal Co.,* 7 Ariz. 376, 390, 65 Pac. 332 (1901). Mutual corporations, in this respect, "have duties similar to that of common carriers." *Whiting* v. *Lyman Water Co.,* 59 Ariz. 121, 124, 458, 124 Pac. (2d) 316, 129 Pac. (2d) 995 (1942).

use. The latter corporation [mutual] is simply the agent of the appropriator to carry his water to where he makes the beneficial use."[628]

(4) In a rate-fixing case, the Colorado Supreme Court in effect took a middle position on the matter of principal and agency. The court held that neither the company alone nor the consumers alone were appropriators in the strict sense of the term, inasmuch as their combined acts were necessary to constitute the appropriation and to keep it alive.[629]

Public agency.—Appropriative water rights of irrigation districts are generally held by the organization and are appurtenant to the entire area included within the district boundaries. Some exceptions have occurred, for example, when the districts did not acquire title to all preexisting individual rights. These rights retained their priorities and their appurtenance to specific tracts of land.

Water rights of districts other than the standard irrigation district—of which there are many kinds in the West—may be appurtenant to individual tracts, or to entire areas within the district boundaries, depending upon applicable State laws and the particular circumstances under which the rights were acquired.

Municipalities are both formal and real appropriators of the water which they divert and supply to their inhabitants.

Right of Consumer to Receive Water from the Distributing Agency

Commercial company.—An owner of land under a commercial company canal can acquire no right to any part of the water carried by the canal without performing essential acts in acquiring the right—making application to the company for service, and applying the water to beneficial use.[630] It is the duty of a common carrier to distribute the water only to applicants as they come.[631] But the right to water once sold to an applicant "becomes a perpetual right subject to defeat only by failure to pay annual water rents and comply with the lawful requirements as to the conditions of the use."[632]

If the company is deemed to own the water right, a *bona fide* customer receives not only service, but an interest in the company's priority proportionate to the quantity of water beneficially used by him.[633] If the customer is the real appropriator, he acquires by his relation to the company an easement in its irrigation system.[634]

Again, where the company is the real appropriator, water must be supplied to all lands adjacent to or within reach of the canal system without discrimination on payment of charges.[635]

---

[628] *In re Walla Walla River*, 141 Oreg. 492, 498, 16 Pac. (2d) 939 (1932).

[629] *Jefferson County* v. *Rocky Mountain Water Co.*, 102 Colo. 351, 356, 361, 79 Pac. (2d) 373 (1938).

[630] *State* v. *Laramie Rivers Co.*, 59 Wyo. 9, 45-46, 136 Pac. (2d) 487 (1943).

[631] *Id.* at 44.

[632] *Farmers' Co-op. Ditch Co.* v. *Riverside Irr. Dist.*, 14 Idaho 450, 458-459, 94 Pac. 761 (1908).

[633] *Reno Power, Light & Water Co.* v. *Public Serv. Comm'n*, 300 Fed. 645, 648, 649 (D. Nev. 1921).

[634] *Bolles* v. *Pecos Irr. Co.*, 23 N. Mex. 32, 41, 167 Pac. 280 (1917); *Murphy* v. *Kerr*, 296 Fed. 536, 546-549 (D. N. Mex. 1923), affirmed, 5 Fed. (2d) 908 (8th Cir. 1925).

[635] *In re Walla Walla River*, 141 Oreg. 492, 496-497, 16 Pac. (2d) 939 (1932).

But if the right vests in the consumer by reason of his application of the water to beneficial use, then it may be necessary to discriminate between the consumer-appropriators by giving preference to those whose priorities are earliest in time.[636]

In Arizona, a canal company has the duty to distribute the water to which its consumers are entitled in the order of priorities and upon equal terms.[637] These individual water user priorities control whether the organization is a public service irrigation company[638] or a mutual irrigation company.[639]

Mutual irrigation company.—(1) In most Western States, the privilege of obtaining water from a standard incorporated mutual company is derived from the holding of shares of its capital stock. Exceptional circumstances in Arizona are mentioned below.

A mutual company that has an appropriative right covering its entire service area may limit itself by its own articles of incorporation and policies to an inflexible basis of apportionment of water, such as only one share of stock to the acre. Or it may authorize the holding of any number of shares per acre. Consumers pay for the service through the media of capital stock assessments, or toll charges for quantities of water delivered, or both.

(2) The rule in Arizona is that one who has a valid right by virtue of appropriation to the use of water served through a canal system owned and operated by a company does not need to own shares of stock in the company in order to be entitled to the delivery of water therefrom[640]—unless, of course, in a situation comparable to that on the Salt River Valley Project, as stated immediately below. "Such companies have duties similar to that of common carriers, and must carry the water which they do not, and can never, own, to the person who has the right to use it by virtue of an appropriation under the laws of the state, upon the payment of proper carriage charges, regardless of the ownership of stock in the corporation."[641]

As stated earlier under "The Real Appropriator—Mutual enterprise," the Salt River Valley Water Users' Association is held to be "a carrier of water for its shareholders," such shares being made appurtenant to the land of each member. Thus, all landowners who did not hold preexisting appropriative rights acquired, by virtue of purchase of stock in the association, the right to

---

[636] *Prosole* v. *Steamboat Canal Co.,* 37 Nev. 154, 166, 140 Pac. 720, 144 Pac. 744 (1914).

[637] *Olsen* v. *Union Canal & Irr. Co.,* 58 Ariz. 306, 317, 119 Pac. (2d) 569 (1941).

[638] *Gould* v. *Maricopa Canal Co.,* 8 Ariz. 429, 447, 76 Pac. 598 (1904).

[639] *Hargrave* v. *Hall,* 3 Ariz. 252, 253-255, 73 Pac. 400 (1891).

[640] *Olsen* v. *Union Canal & Irr. Co.,* 58 Ariz. 306, 317-318, 119 Pac. (2d) 569 (1941). In this case, the company attempted to compel those who held less shares of stock than acres of land to pay sums in addition to their proportionate share of the operating expenses, or get no water. The court held that all water users were entitled to the delivery of water in order of priority of appropriation, and upon equal terms.

[641] *Whiting* v. *Lyman Water Co.,* 59 Ariz. 121, 123-124, 458, 459, 124 Pac. (2d) 316, 129 Pac. (2d) 995 (1942).

have the association's irrigation system bring water to their land in order that they thereby could, in the first instance, appropriate such water by use on such lands and, in the second place, continue thereafter to exercise such right so long as they paid the necessary operation and maintenance charges comprising, or including, assessments on their shares of stock. Under such circumstances, necessarily, the qualifying phrase in the opinion in the *Whiting* case, "regardless of the ownership of stock in the corporation,"[642] is not applicable.

District.—As distinguished from the water right to which an irrigation district holds formal title, the right of a holder of irrigable land within the district to receive water from the irrigation system is usually appurtenant to the specific tract of irrigable land as it is listed on the assessment roll. The landowners pay for the service of water in the form of assessments levied upon the land, or through toll charges for water actually delivered, or both assessments and tolls.

The right of an individual to receive water from districts of some other types vests in the landowner solely by reason of inclusion of the land therein because of the anticipated benefit. In still others, the right is derived from execution of a voluntary water-service contract between the individual landowner and the district.

Municipality.—The right of an inhabitant of a municipality to receive water from its facilities is incident to his residence within the city limits.

RELATIVE RIGHTS OF SENIOR AND JUNIOR APPROPRIATORS

Rights of Senior Appropriator

Exclusive to Extent of Prior Appropriation

(1) A fundamental facet of the Western States doctrine of prior appropriation, as developed in the early mining days, was that the one who first appropriates water has the sole right to use the same for the purpose for which it was appropriated,[643] to the exclusion of any subsequent appropriation for the same purpose or for any other use of the water,[644] and to the full extent of his appropriation if necessary for his beneficial uses.[645] According to the California Supreme Court about a century later, "As between appropriators * * * the one first in time is the first in right, and a prior appropriator is entitled to all the water he needs, up to the amount that he has taken in the past, before a subsequent appropriator may take any."[646] In this case, the

---

[642] *Id.*

[643] *Hoffman* v. *Stone,* 7 Cal. 46, 49 (1857).

[644] *Ortman* v. *Dixon,* 13 Cal. 33, 38 (1859).

[645] *Butte Canal & Ditch Co.* v. *Vaughn,* 11 Cal. 143, 153-154 (1858); *Senior* v. *Anderson,* 130 Cal. 290, 297, 62 Pac. 563 (1900).

[646] *Pasadena* v. *Alhambra,* 33 Cal. (2d) 908, 926, 207 Pac. (2d) 17 (1949).

rights in litigation were ground water rights, not subject to the administrative procedure in the Water Code.

(2) As a result of statutory preferences and restrictions that now prevail generally in the West with respect to permits for the appropriation of streamflow, the first applicant is not necessarily the one who acquires the first priority (see the discussions of restrictions and preferences at the end of chapter 7). With respect to such appropriations, it is more nearly correct to say that the one who holds the highest priority—who may or may not have been the *earliest applicant*—is first in right.

(3) However, the rule as it was emphasized in the early decisions was recognized throughout the West. "The senior appropriator may lawfully demand that he have at his headgate sufficient water to supply his present needs,"[647] so that "Each junior appropriator is entitled to divert water only at such times as all prior appropriators are being supplied under their appropriations under conditions as they existed at the time the appropriation was made."[648] Many other decisions from many States stated or applied this historic fundamental facet of the appropriation doctrine.[649]

Except where statutory exceptions intervene, the principle is still valid. In fact, the Utah water appropriation statute provides that, subject to a proviso concerning statutory preferences in time of scarcity of water, "Appropriators shall have priority among themselves according to the dates of their respective appropriations, so that each appropriator shall be entitled to receive his whole supply before any subsequent appropriator shall have any right; * * * ."[650]

Maintenance of Stream Conditions

(1) One of the most important of the junior appropriator's safeguards, discussed later,[651] is his right to have the stream conditions maintained

---

[647] *Vogel* v. *Minnesota Canal & Res. Co.,* 47 Colo. 534, 540, 107 Pac. 1108 (1910).

[648] *Beecher* v. *Cassia Creek Irr. Co.,* 66 Idaho 1, 9-10, 154 Pac. (2d) 507 (1944). "The right of a prior appropriator of water is paramount." *In re Rogue River,* 102 Oreg. 60, 65, 201 Pac. 724 (1921). The right of defendants (junior appropriators) "is at all times subservient to the primary right of plaintiffs, and can be exercised only after plaintiffs' needs have been supplied." *Harkey* v. *Smith,* 31 N. Mex. 521, 530, 247 Pac. 550 (1926). Subsequent appropriators are bound to take notice of the accrued rights of prior appropriators: *Kearney Water & Electric Powers Co.* v. *Alfalfa Irr. Dist.,* 97 Nebr. 139, 145, 149 N. W. 363 (1914).

[649] Some typical cases are *Mettler* v. *Ames Realty Co.,* 61 Mont. 152, 159, 169, 201 Pac. 702 (1921); *Jerrett* v. *Mahan,* 20 Nev. 89, 98, 17 Pac. 12 (1888); *Gay* v. *Hicks,* 33 Okla. 675, 682, 124 Pac. 1077 (1912); *Scoggins* v. *Cameron County W. I. Dist. No. 15,* 264 S. W. (2d) 169, 173-174, (Tex. Civ. App. 1954, error refused n.r.e.); *McNaughton* v. *Eaton,* 4 Utah (2d) 223, 225-226, 291 Pac. (2d) 886 (1955); *Avery* v. *Johnson,* 59 Wash. 332, 335, 109 Pac. 1028 (1910).

[650] Utah Code Ann. § 73-3-21 (1968).

[651] Under "Rights of Junior Appropriator—Maintenance of Stream Conditions."

substantially as they were when he made his appropriation. This principle applies equally to the senior appropriator.[652]

The junior's grievance in most situations would be that changes in the exercise of the senior rights after the junior appropriates water interfere with the proper exercise of the latter's subsequently acquired rights. The senior, on the other hand, is concerned with the effect that new junior projects may have on the continued operation of his own.

(2) In 1953, the Colorado Supreme Court, while acknowledging the principle that an appropriator of waters of a stream "has a vested right to the continued maintenance of conditions on the stream as they existed at the time he made his appropriation," pointed out that "This doctrine, of course, applies only to interference by man with natural conditions upon the stream in existence at the time of the appropriation."[653]

(3) In 1939, the Oregon Supreme Court held that the rights of a downstream appropriator are not infringed by upstream construction of structures for the purpose of controlling soil erosion in the stream channel—provided water is not diverted, the streambed is restored as nearly as possible to its original condition, and the work can be done without material interference with the rights of the downstream appropriator. This question, it was held, depends largely upon the facts, "and we do not presume to determine it as a matter of law." As to the policy invoked, the court held that:[654]

> To deny our water users the right to control such streams and prevent the erosion that would soon take place would mean the utter destruction of much of our most valuable irrigated lands throughout the state. It is the duty of the landowner to prevent the construction of dams to a point where diversion from the channel will occur, but the landowner has a right to use or permit such dams for the purpose of erosion control, where they do not divert water from the channel or from the diversion works of another appropriator. It is shown that if the erosion is permitted to continue the water would be drained from the lands bordering on the creek and they would become dry and worthless.

A section added to the California Water Code in 1953 provides that:[655]

> An appropriation of water of any stream or other source of water under this part does not confer authority upon the appropriator to prevent or interfere with soil conservation practices above the point of diversion in the watershed in which such stream or other source originates, which practices

---

[652] *Vogel* v. *Minnesota Canal & Res. Co.,* 47 Colo. 534, 540, 107 Pac. 1108 (1910); *East Bench Irr. Co.* v. *Deseret Irr. Co.,* 2 Utah (2d) 170, 177-178, 271 Pac. (2d) 449 (1954).

[653] *Mendenhall* v. *Lake Meredith Res. Co.,* 127 Colo. 444, 446-447, 257 Pac. (2d) 414 (1953).

[654] *State ex rel. Johnson* v. *Stewart,* 163 Oreg. 585, 605, 96 Pac. (2d) 220 (1939).

[655] Cal. Water Code § 1252.1 (West 1956).

do not themselves constitute an appropriation for which a permit is required by this part.

Quantity and Quality of the Water, and Right to the Flow of Tributaries

The prior appropriator's right of protection against material or substantial diminution of quantity or deterioration in quality of water for the purposes for which he appropriated it, and extension of such protection to the flow of tributaries as well as that of the stream on which he has his diversion, have been discussed at some length earlier in this chapter under "Property Characteristics— Right of Property."

Increase in Amount of Appropriation, When Lawful

As will be brought out below in discussing rights of junior appropriators, no senior appropriation can be actually enlarged above its original content at the expense of junior appropriators. However, enlargements of the senior right may be lawfully made *before* any junior rights attach,[656] provided there is excess water in the source of supply available for further appropriation.

Furthermore, as discussed in chapter 7 (see "Methods of Appropriating Water of Watercourses—Completion of Appropriation—Gradual or Progressive Development"), the right to the use of water for irrigation is not necessarily confined to the quantity actually applied during the first year or two—or even within a series of years—subject to two invariable conditions: (1) the enlarged use of the water over that accomplished in the early stages must have been within the original intent of the appropriator, and claimed at the time of initiating the appropriation and (2) the intending appropriator proceeded with reasonable diligence to apply the water to the use intended. Provided these conditions are met, the priority of the right on completion relates back to the date on which it was initiated; hence, any subsequent appropriator diverts water subject to such prior claim. Under the western administrative statutes governing appropriation of water, these pragmatic principles are applied in the making of applications to appropriate water and the subsequent granting to the applicant of permits and licenses or certificates of appropriation.

Noninjurious Changes in Exercise of the Senior Right

As noted below,[657] the senior appropriator is not entitled to make any changes in the conditions of his appropriation of the streamflow to the material injury of junior appropriators. But this restriction on the senior applies only to activities that infringe the junior right. Subsequent appropriators cannot successfully complain of changes that do not substantially injure them.[658]

---

[656] *Healy* v. *Woodruff,* 97 Cal. 464, 466-467, 32 Pac. 528 (1893).

[657] Under "Rights of Junior Appropriator—Maintenance of Stream Conditions."

[658] *Farmers Res. & Irr. Co.* v. *Lafayette,* 93 Colo. 173, 177, 24 Pac. (2d) 756 (1933); *Thrasher* v. *Mannix & Wilson,* 95 Mont. 273, 277-278, 26 Pac. (2d) 370 (1933).

Reasonable Means of Diversion

The matter of protection of a prior appropriator in a reasonable means of diversion of water is discussed in chapter 13.

Rights of Junior Appropriator

Appropriation of Unappropriated Water

The rule that subsequent appropriators may acquire rights in the surplus water over that to which prior rights attach was recognized in the pioneer mining days.[659] Thus, if the person who first appropriates water from a stream appropriates only a part of the supply, "another person may appropriate a part or the whole of the residue; and when appropriated by him his right thereto is as perfect, and entitled to the same protection, as that of the first appropriator to the portion appropriated by him."[660] Although, to appropriate surplus water, one does not need the consent of earlier appropriators, he must respect all prior rights.[661] This rule, obviously essential in agricultural development in the West, became well settled in the law of appropriative water rights.[662]

Protection Against Enlargement of Senior Right

Those who acquire prior rights on a stream "can in no way change or extend their use of the water" to the prejudice of subsequent appropriators.[663] As pointed out earlier in discussing "Increase in Amount of Appropriation, When Lawful" under "Rights of Senior Appropriator," this inhibition applies to actual enlargements above the specific terms of the prior appropriation, not to gradual development within the original intent of the appropriator and pursued with due diligence. Such an actual enlargement above the specific terms of prior appropriation constitutes a new appropriation.

---

[659] *Ortman* v. *Dixon,* 13 Cal. 33, 38-40 (1859).

[660] *Smith* v. *O'Hara,* 43 Cal. 371, 375 (1872).

[661] *Custer* v. *Missoula Public Service Co.,* 91 Mont. 136, 143-145, 6 Pac. (2d) 131 (1931).
Certain types of water use may leave possibilities of multiple-use of water to take into account. See, for example, the discussion of waste, seepage, and return waters in chapter 18 and *City of San Antonio* v. *Texas Water Comm'n,* 407 S. W. (2d) 752, 762 (Tex. Sup. Ct. 1966), discussed in note 409 *supra.*

[662] *Hewitt* v. *Story,* 64 Fed. 510, 515 (9th Cir. 1894); "The residue, after a prior appropriation, may be appropriated by others out of the water of the same stream, if there is no interference with a prior appropriator," *Fairbury* v. *Fairbury Mill & Elevator Co.,* 123 Nebr. 588, 592, 243 N. W. 774 (1932); *Barnes* v. *Sabron,* 10 Nev. 217, 233, 245 (1875); *State ex rel. Community Ditches* v. *Tularosa Community Ditch,* 19 N. Mex. 352, 371, 143 Pac. 207 (1914); *Gates* v. *Settlers' Mill., Canal & Res. Co.,* 19 Okla. 83, 91, 91 Pac. 856 (1907); *In re Willow Creek,* 74 Oreg. 592, 647, 144 Pac. 505 (1914), 146 Pac. 475 (1915); *Biggs* v. *Miller,* 147 S. W. 632, 636 (Tex. Civ. App. 1912); *Adams* v. *Portage Irr., Res. & Power Co.,* 95 Utah 1, 13-14, 72 Pac. (2d) 648 (1937). When a prior appropriator has diverted the quantity of water to which he is entitled, he may not so impede the remaining streamflow as to prevent it from reaching the junior appropriator's headgate: *Van Camp.* v. *Emery,* 13 Idaho 202, 208, 89 Pac. 752 (1907).

[663] *Union Mill & Min. Co.* v. *Dangberg,* 81 Fed. 73, 106 (C.C.D. Nev. 1897).

It follows, then, that rights acquired by juniors after senior rights attach are themselves senior, not only to subsequent appropriations by third parties, but also to further appropriations by the first one on the stream. Thus, if A should hold the first, third, and fifth priorities on a stream, B the second, and C the fourth, A cannot merge his later priorities with his first to the prejudice of the intervening rights acquired by B and C.[664]

Use of Water When not Needed by Senior

(1) Not only may a junior claimant appropriate water in excess of the quantities to which prior appropriations attach, but he may also use water to which a prior appropriation attaches at such times as the water is not needed by the prior appropriator.[665]

Despite the fact that in many areas the waters of streams are overappropriated, "there are always times when prior appropriators do not need the water."[666] At such times, "such prior right is temporarily suspended and the next right or rights in the order of priority may use the water until such time as the prior appropriator's needs justify his demanding that the junior appropriator or appropriators give way to his superior claim."[667]

No diversion or use of any surplus beyond the quantity which the prior appropriator has the ability to use for his needs is actionable by him.[668] On the contrary, by court action, subsequent appropriators may compel a prior appropriator to release, for their use, water which he does not need for a beneficial purpose.[669]

---

[664] *Union Grain & Elevator Co.* v. *McCammon Ditch Co.*, 41 Idaho 216, 221-223, 240 Pac. 443 (1925); *Quigley* v. *McIntosh*, 110 Mont. 495, 505, 103 Pac. (2d) 1067 (1940); *Ophir Silver Min. Co.* v. *Carpenter*, 4 Nev. 534, 542-544, 548 (1869); *Gates* v. *Settlers' Mill., Canal & Res. Co.*, 19 Okla. 83, 91, 91 Pac. 856 (1907); *Oliver* v. *Skinner & Lodge*, 190 Oreg. 423, 438, 226 Pac. (2d) 507 (1951); *Jensen* v. *Birch Creek Ranch Co.*, 76 Utah 356, 362, 289 Pac. 1097 (1930).

[665] *Hufford* v. *Dye*, 162 Cal. 147, 153-154, 159-160, 121 Pac. 400 (1912); *Knutson* v. *Huggins*, 62 Idaho 662, 668-669, 115 Pac. (2d) 421 (1941); *Tudor* v. *Jaca*, 178 Oreg. 126, 141, 164 Pac. (2d) 680 (1945), 165 Pac. (2d) 770 (1946); *Biggs* v. *Miller*, 147 S. W. 632, 636 (Tex. Civ. App. 1912); *Johnston* v. *Little Horse Creek Irrigating Co.*, 13 Wyo. 208, 227-228, 79 Pac. 22 (1904).

[666] *Clay Spring Cattle Co.* v. *Bassett*, 76 Colo. 510, 512-513, 233 Pac. 156 (1925).

[667] *Cook* v. *Hudson*, 110 Mont. 263, 282-283, 103 Pac. (2d) 137 (1940).

[668] *Nevada County & Sacramento Canal Co.* v. *Kidd*, 37 Cal. 282, 313 (1869); *Clough* v. *Wing*, 2 Ariz. 371, 377-378, 17 Pac. 453 (1888); *Vineyard Land & Stock Co.* v. *Twin Falls Salmon River Land & Water Co.*, 245 Fed. 9, 22 (9th Cir. 1917). The upstream prior appropriator cannot complain of any use made of the water while permitted to flow downstream past his closed headgate: *Lakeside Ditch Co.* v. *Crane*, 80 Cal. 181, 187, 22 Pac. 76 (1889).

[669] *Clausen* v. *Armington*, 123 Mont. 1, 17-18, 212 Pac. (2d) 440 (1949). Compare *Wall* v. *Superior Court of Yavapai County*, 53 Ariz. 344, 356, 89 Pac. (2d) 624 (1939), at note 672 *infra*.

The policy reason for the rule is thus explained by the Nebraska Supreme Court:[670]

> The use of water for irrigation in this state is a natural want. The inadequacy of supply to meet the demands of the public requires strict administration to prevent waste. It is therefore the policy of the law that junior appropriators may use available water within the limits of their own appropriations so long as the rights of senior appropriators are not injured or damaged.

(2) In view of this long recognized right of junior appropriators, it is obviously to their advantage—as well as in the interest of water conservation generally—that the practices of their seniors be carried out without unnecessary waste. As then the senior appropriator's right does not include the reasonably avoidable waste of water,[671] by a proper action a junior appropriator may so limit the use by his senior as to avoid unnecessary waste.[672] The New Mexico Supreme Court held, however, that a downstream senior appropriator must have demanded the water in order to have a cause of action.[673] Otherwise, said the court, water may be wasted.[674]

(3) An appropriator of water, therefore, has no surplus which he can either sell or give to another party as against subsequent appropriators.[675] It follows

---

[670] *State ex rel. Cary* v. *Cochran,* 138 Nebr. 163, 172-173, 292 N. W. 239 (1940).

[671] *Santa Cruz Res. Dist.* v. *Rameriz,* 16 Ariz. 64, 70, 141 Pac. 120 (1914). The right of a prior appropriator with respect to a later one does not extend to use of a wasteful method of diversion, nor of ditches and structures that are not in good serviceable condition: *Warner Valley Stock Co.* v. *Lynch,* 215 Oreg. 523, 536-542, 336 Pac. (2d) 884 (1959). "When his requirements have been satisfied, he no longer has a right to the use of water, but must permit others to use it." *Snow* v. *Abalos,* 18 N. Mex. 681, 695, 140 Pac. 1044 (1914). In the arid State of Utah, to waste water is to injure the public welfare; hence, it is "the duty of the user of water to return surplus or waste water into the stream from which it was taken so that further use can be made by others." *Brian* v. *Fremont Irr. Co.,* 112 Utah 220, 224-225, 186 Pac. (2d) 588 (1947).

[672] *Wall* v. *Superior Court of Yavapai County,* 53 Ariz. 344, 356, 89 Pac. (2d) 624 (1939). Compare *Clausen* v. *Armington,* 123 Mont. 1, 17-18, 212 Pac. (2d) 440 (1949), at note 669 *supra.*

[673] *Worley* v. *U. S. Borax & Chemical Corp.,* 78 N. Mex. 112, 428 Pac. (2d) 651, 653-655 (1967), citing, at 654, *Vogel* v. *Minnesota Canal & Reservoir Co.,* 47 Colo. 534, 107 Pac. 1108 (1910), and *Cook* v. *Hudson,* 110 Mont. 263, 103 Pac. (2d) 137 (1940). The court said, at 654, "We are not required to decide whether the demand must be made upon the State Engineer (see § § 75-2-1 and 75-2-9, N.M.S.A. 1953), the water master (see § § 75-3-1 and 75-3-2, N.M.S.A. 1953), the upstream junior appropriators or one or more of them. Here, it is undisputed that no demand of any kind was made."

[674] "Once the water passes the diversion point of the upstream appropriator, his opportunity to use the water is lost. If the downstream appropriator does not use the water, the opportunity to use this water is wasted." 428 Pac. (2d) at 654, citing N. Mex. Const., art. XVI, § 3 which provides "Beneficial use shall be the basis, the measure and the limit of the right to use water."

[675] *Johnston* v. *Little Horse Creek Irrigating Co.,* 13 Wyo. 208, 227-228, 79 Pac. 22 (1904); *Manning* v. *Fife,* 17 Utah 232, 238, 54 Pac. 111 (1898).

that when his needs have been supplied, he should leave the water in the stream to flow down to those next in priority[676] or, if he does divert an excessive quantity, the excess must be returned to the stream.[677] The Nebraska situation with respect to the return of unused water to the stream has been discussed earlier under "Elements of the Appropriative Right—Diversion of Water from Watershed."

(4) It is held by the Utah Supreme Court that between the time of inception of an appropriative right and its full consummation, intermediate or intervening appropriators may acquire rights to use the water by appropriating it. This is but a temporary right and must give way to the rights of the prior appropriator when he has completed his appropriation and is ready to use the water.[678]

Reasonable Limitation of Senior Right

From what has been said it is clear that the prior appropriator does not have an unlimited right to the use of water, but is subject to a reasonable limitation of his right for the benefit of junior appropriators. He may thus be limited to the quantity of water reasonably required to raise crops under reasonably efficient methods of applying water to the land—a result which a court of equity has inherent power to bring about. This judicial power of limitation is itself a limited power; it cannot be used to eliminate or modify established water rights.[679] (See "Efficiency of Practices" in chapter 9.)

The Utah Supreme Court held that at the discretion of the trial court, reasonable regulations may be imposed in a decree of adjudication upon the use of water by the parties.[680] But, the supreme court cautioned in another case, the trial court should avoid making a regulation which has the potentiality of depriving prior appropriators of a substantial part of the quantity of water which it found that they are entitled to use.[681]

Maintenance of Stream Conditions

(1) The junior appropriator initiates his right with notice of existing stream conditions and rights of diversion and use, and in the belief that the water previously appropriated by others will continue to be used as it is then being

---

[676] *Fort Lyon Canal Co.* v. *Chew,* 33 Colo. 392, 404-405, 81 Pac. 37 (1905); *In re Hood River,* 114 Oreg. 112, 188, 227 Pac. 1065 (1924). See Nev. Rev. Stat. § 533.060(1) (Supp. 1967).

[677] *Natoma Water & Min. Co.* v. *Hancock,* 101 Cal. 42, 51-52, 31 Pac. 112 (1892), 35 Pac. 334 (1894); *Gunnison Irr. Co.* v. *Gunnison Highland Canal Co.,* 52 Utah 347, 357, 174 Pac. 852 (1918). See Mont. Rev. Codes Ann. § 89-805 (1964).

[678] *Whitmore* v. *Murray City,* 107 Utah 445, 451-452, 154 Pac. (2d) 748 (1944); *Salt Lake City* v. *Salt Lake City Water & Elec. Power Co.,* 24 Utah 249, 266-267, 67 Pac. 672 (1902).

[679] *In re Water Rights of Escalante Valley Drainage Area,* 10 Utah (2d) 77, 82, 348 Pac. (2d) 679 (1960).

[680] *McKean* v. *Lasson,* 5 Utah (2d) 168, 173, 298 Pac. (2d) 827 (1956).

[681] *McNaughton* v. *Eaton,* 4 Utah (2d) 223, 225-226, 291 Pac. (2d) 886 (1955).

used. Therefore, he has a vested right, as against his senior, to insist that such conditions be not changed to the detriment of his own right.[682]

The foregoing rule—that a junior appropriator is entitled to maintenance of the stream conditions as of the time he makes his appropriation—is followed generally in the West. However, after recognizing this general rule, the Idaho Supreme Court felt concerned that in some situations this might not afford adequate protection to the junior. So "we now declare and determine the rule, generally applicable, to be that junior appropriators have a vested right to a continuance of the conditions existing on the stream at *and subsequent to* the time they made their appropriations, and that no proposed change in place of use or diversion will be permitted when it will injuriously affect such established rights." [Emphasis supplied.][683] And as noted above in discussing rights of the senior appropriator, the Colorado Supreme Court, likewise acknowledging the general principle, took occasion to point out that it applies only to interference by man with natural conditions on the stream in existence at the time of the appropriation.[684]

(2) In order to establish this well-recognized rule, an actual impairment or irreparable injury to the legal rights of the junior appropriator must be demonstrated by evidential facts and not by potentialities.[685]

(3) The general rule is frequently invoked, and applied, with respect to proposed changes in point of diversion, place of use, and manner of use that threaten material injury to junior rights.[686] Safeguards against injurious changes are accorded to senior appropriators as well. (See "Change in Exercise of Water Right" in chapter 9.)

(4) Some references respecting the right of an appropriator vis-à-vis upstream erosion-control practices appear earlier under "Rights of Senior Appropriator—Maintenance of Stream Conditions." The relationship would apply regardless of the appropriator's priority.

Substitution of Water

The right of a junior appropriator to substitute water of equivalent quantity and quality has been recognized. Specifically, he has been allowed to divert

---

[682] *East Bench Irr. Co.* v. *Deseret Irr. Co.,* 2 Utah (2d) 170, 177-178, 271 Pac. (2d) 449 (1954); *Oliver* v. *Skinner & Lodge,* 190 Oreg. 423, 441, 226 Pac. (2d) 507 (1951); *Dannenbrink* v. *Burger,* 23 Cal. App. 587, 595, 138 Pac. 751 (1913); *Faden* v. *Hubbell,* 93 Colo. 358, 369, 28 Pac. (2d) 247 (1933); *Union Mill & Min. Co.* v. *Dangberg,* 81 Fed. 73, 106 (C. C. D. Nev. 1897); *Smith* v. *Duff,* 39 Mont. 382, 389-390, 102 Pac. 984 (1909).

[683] *Crockett* v. *Jones,* 47 Idaho 497, 503-504, 277 Pac. 550 (1929).

[684] *Mendenhall* v. *Lake Meredith Res. Co.,* 127 Colo. 444, 446-447, 257 Pac. (2d) 414 (1953).

[685] *Del Norte Irr. Dist.* v. *Santa Maria Res. Co.,* 108 Colo. 1, 7, 113 Pac. (2d) 676 (1941). Compare *Ireland* v. *Henrylyn Irr. Dist.,* 113 Colo. 555, 558-559, 160 Pac. (2d) 364 (1945), in which on the facts the general rule was held not applicable.

[686] *Farmers Highline Canal & Res. Co.* v. *Golden,* 129 Colo. 575, 579, 272 Pac. (2d) 629 (1954).

water from a stream at a point above a prior appropriator's place of diversion
and to turn water from the same stream, or from a different stream, if equal in
quantity and quality, into the ditch of the prior appropriator if done at a point
where the latter can make full use of the water and without injury to him, and
at the expense of the junior appropriator.[687] This aspect of the junior
appropriator's right merges into the topic "Exchange or Substitution of Water,"
which is developed in chapter 9 under "Natural Channels and Reservoirs—Use
of Natural Channel."

Reciprocal Rights and Obligations of Appropriators

No Encroachment by Either Party

Early in the development of the appropriation doctrine in California,
the supreme court said that: "When the right has once vested in the
defendants, the plaintiff is no more justified, by extending its own claim,
or changing the means of appropriation, in interfering with the full enjoyment
of the right vested in the defendants, than the defendants would be, in
encroaching upon the prior rights of the plaintiff."[688]

A half-century later, a California district court of appeal summarized these
reciprocal rights thus: Of two or more appropriators on the same stream, each
must so use his right as not to interfere materially with the others, the matter
of superiority by reason of priority being of course considered. The excessive
use of any right to the injury of others is against public policy. "The mere
inconvenience, or even the matter of extra expense, within limits which are not
unreasonable, to which a prior user may be subjected, will not avail to prevent
a subsequent appropriator from utilizing his right. There must be a substantial
as distinguished from a mere technical or abstract damage to the right of the
prior appropriator by the exercise by the subsequent appropriator of his right
to entitle the former to relief against any attempt of the latter to utilize his
right."[689]

Relative Locations on Stream

In an early decision, the California Supreme Court had occasion to redeclare
the principle that as against subsequent locators below the diversion point of
the first appropriator, the latter had a superior right enforceable at law, and to
state that the principle should be equally applicable whether subsequent

---

[687] *United States* v. *Caldwell,* 64 Utah 490, 497-498, 231 Pac. 434 (1924); *Maricopa
County M. W. C. Dist.* v. *Southwest Cotton Co.,* 39 Ariz. 367, 370, 7 Pac. (2d) 254
(1932); *Reno* v. *Richards,* 32 Idaho 1, 5, 178 Pac. 81 (1918).

[688] *Nevada Water Co.* v. *Powell,* 34 Cal. 109, 119 (1867). To the same effect: *Proctor* v.
Jennings, 6 Nev. 83, 87-88 (1870).

[689] *Waterford Irr. Dist.* v. *Turlock Irr. Dist.,* 50 Cal. App. 213, 221, 194 Pac. 757 (1920).
In *Peabody* v. *Vallejo,* 2 Cal. (2d) 351, 376, 40 Pac. (2d) 486 (1935), the California
Supreme Court quoted the first sentence of the above quotation, with the words
"within limits which are not unreasonable" italicized, and said that the rule with its
appropriate limitations in the italicized words was correct as so stated.

appropriators located above or below him on the stream.[690] This, of course, is a cardinal principle of the doctrine of prior appropriation.[691]

Likewise, the rule that each junior appropriator is entitled to divert water only at such times as all prior appropriators are being supplied under their appropriations, under conditions as they existed when the appropriation was made, applies regardless of the relative locations of the parties on the stream.[692] Reciprocally, each prior appropriator is limited to the receipt at his point of diversion of water in the quantity and of the quality concerning which he made his appropriation; and regardless of diversions made upstream by junior appropriators, the prior appropriator has no grounds for complaint if he receives the quantity to which he is entitled whenever he has occasion to use it.[693]

Effect of Losses of Water in Stream Channel

Appropriator not penalized because of natural upstream losses.—Natural losses of water, owing to "seepage, evaporation, and channel absorption or other physical conditions beyond the control of the appropriators,"[694] that may occur in large quantities on long stream channels raise questions as to their effect on the right of the appropriator whose diversion is located below a heavily losing section of the stream channel.

The general rule is that notwithstanding heavy natural losses above him, a prior appropriator is entitled to have the streamflow reach his headgate in quantity necessary to satisfy his appropriative right. In the abstract, said a Federal court, more people might be benefitted by allowing the entire flow to be diverted by junior appropriators upstream, inasmuch as the flow through a sandy and gravelly stretch of 10 miles or more may result in substantial waste, "but equity does not consist in taking the property of a few for the benefit of the many, even though the general average of benefits would be greater."[695]

Upstream appropriator entitled to flow that would be lost.—Under ordinary circumstances it is elementary that "where there are two water rights upon a stream, one above the other, and where the water becomes diminished during a certain period of the year, so that it will not flow down and reach the lower user, the upper user may use all of it for the time it will not reach the lower one."[696]

Such a factual situation was featured in an interstate case involving a stream flowing from Oregon into Washington. It was found that if certain dams in

[690] *Hill* v. *King,* 8 Cal. 336, 337-338 (1857).

[691] *Proctor* v. *Jennings,* 6 Nev. 83, 87 (1870); *Kaler* v. *Campbell,* 13 Oreg. 596, 597-598, 11 Pac. 301 (1886); *Union Mill & Min. Co.* v. *Dangberg,* 81 Fed. 73, 106 (C. C. D. Nev. 1897).

[692] *Beecher* v. *Cassia Creek Irr. Co.,* 66 Idaho 1, 9-10, 154 Pac. (2d) 507 (1944).

[693] *Kelly* v. *Granite Bi-Metallic Consolidated Min. Co.,* 41 Mont. 1, 10-12, 108 Pac. 785 (1910); *Featherman* v. *Hennessy,* 42 Mont. 535, 542, 113 Pac. 751 (1911).

[694] *Albion-Idaho Land Co.* v. *Naf Irr. Co.,* 97 Fed. (2d) 439, 444 (10th Cir. 1938).

[695] *Morris* v. *Bean,* 146 Fed. 423, 435-436 (D. Mont. 1906).

[696] *Fenstermaker* v. *Jorgensen,* 53 Utah 325, 333, 178 Pac. 760 (1919).

Oregon were removed during the period of water shortage, the streamflow would be quickly absorbed and lost in the gravel underlying the channel leading across the stateline into Washington.[697] "To restrain the diversion at the bridge," said the United States Supreme Court, "would bring distress and even ruin to a long-established settlement of tillers of the soil for no other or better purpose than to vindicate a barren right. This is not the high equity that moves the conscience of the court in giving judgment between states." The Court expressed its conclusion thus:[698]

> The case comes down to this: The court is asked upon uncertain evidence of prior right and still more uncertain evidence of damage to destroy possessory interests enjoyed without challenge for over half a century. In such circumstances, an injunction would not issue, if the contest were between private parties, at odds about a boundary. Still less will it issue here in a contest between states, a contest to be dealt with in the large and ample way that alone becomes the dignity of the litigants concerned.

Accordingly, as the Montana Supreme Court observed in 1892, it is not the law that when none of the water in controversy could, if left in the stream, reach the prior appropriator's point of diversion at a distant point below, the junior upstream appropriator should be restrained from using the water on the sole ground that the downstream appropriation is prior in right. But, cautioned the court, these observations should not be so misconstrued or misapplied as to allow wrongful diversion or diminution of a stream on the pretense that the water would be lost, unless that possible result can be clearly substantiated.[699]

But downstream appropriator entitled to a usable quantity.—However, the prior appropriator is not to be penalized by junior diversions upstream if a *useful* or *usable* quantity could reach his headgate in its natural course.[700] Quantitatively, if 45 inches of water were flowing at the upstream diversion and only 1 inch would reach the downstream diversion, 15 miles below, if the 45 inches were left in the stream, that residue of 1 inch would be of little or no use to the downstream irrigator.[701] Furthermore, when a large quantity of water will be rendered useless and a large water surface area laid open to evaporation upstream in the complicated process of getting water from one

---

[697] *Washington* v. *Oregon,* 297 U. S. 517, 522-523 (1936). In *Mitchell Irr. Dist.* v. *Whiting,* 59 Wyo. 52, 77-79, 136 Pac. (2d) 502 (1943), certiorari denied, 322 U. S. 727 (1944), the Wyoming Supreme Court quoted from this language of the United States Supreme Court and applied the Court's ruling to an analogous situation in the case at bar.

[698] *Washington* v. *Oregon,* 297 U. S. 512, 529 (1936).

[699] *Raymond* v. *Wimsette,* 12 Mont. 551, 560-561, 31 Pac. 537 (1892).

[700] *Union Mill & Min. Co.* v. *Dangberg,* 81 Fed. 73, 119 (C. C. D. Nev. 1897); *Tonkin* v. *Winzell,* 27 Nev. 88, 96-97, 73 Pac. 593 (1903); *Dameron Valley Res. & Canal Co.* v. *Bleak,* 61 Utah 230, 234-235, 211 Pac. 974 (1922).

[701] *Raymond* v. *Wimsette,* 12 Mont. 551, 560-561, 31 Pac. 537 (1892).

area to another, the resulting use made by downstream appropriators could not justly be deemed beneficial.[702]

Whether a definite quantity of water passing a given point on a river would, if not diverted or interrupted in its course, reach the headgate of a prior appropriator's canal "in a usable quantity creates a very complicated question of fact." Under a State administrative system governing the distribution of water according to priorities, such as that of Nebraska, it is therefore the duty of the State administrators to determine from all available means whether or not a usable quantity can be delivered at the downstream headgate. This finding of fact must be determined in the first instance by the officers charged with administration of the particular stream. The finding of fact thus made, which is an administrative function, is final unless unreasonable or arbitrarily made.[703]

In *State ex rel. Cary* v. *Cochran,* the Nebraska Supreme Court held that after determining that a given quantity of water passing a certain point on the river would not, even if uninterrupted, reach the prior appropriator's headgate in usable quantities, the administrative officers of the State may lawfully permit upstream junior appropriators to divert it for irrigation purposes. The court pointed out that this often results in the receipt by junior appropriators of a head of water when a prior appropriator downstream is getting none. "Such situations are not therefore conclusive evidence of unlawful diversions."

Difficulties of enforcement of prior rights on a long, losing stream channel.—These were stated graphically in the opinion of the Colorado Supreme Court in a case involving transfer of early priorities from downstream ditches to the canal of the latest priority some 25 to 30 miles upstream. In times of scarcity of water, the loss in the river was so great that 60 to 70 second-feet must be released at this junior upstream canal in order to deliver 18 second-feet to the early rights downstream, even when augmented by natural accretions en route. An excerpt from the opinion follows:[704]

> The evidence shows the owners exhausted every legitimate means within their power to get this water down the river, past protestants' headgates for use in their own ditches, and most of them became impoverished by the loss of their crops, and expenses of litigation in these attempts. At their request the county officials placed numerous patrolmen on the river, but they were unable to keep the gates above, closed down. In some instances the deputies were thrown into the river, in others they were fired upon, the gates were raised, and the water taken by ditches that were not entitled to it. Finally

---

[702] *Warner Valley Stock Co.* v. *Lynch,* 215 Oreg. 523, 543-545, 336 Pac. (2d) 884 (1959). The factual situation in this case was most complicated.

[703] *State ex rel. Cary* v. *Cochran,* 138 Nebr. 163, 173-174, 292 N.W. 239 (1940); *Robinson* v. *Dawson County Irr. Co.,* 142 Nebr. 811, 816-817, 8 N.W. (2d) 179 (1943).

[704] *Ironstone Ditch Co.* v. *Ashenfelter,* 57 Colo. 31, 36-45, 140 Pac. 177 (1914).

the state engineer, the division engineer, and the water commissioner of district 41 gave up trying to force this early priority water down to 2 and 3 headgates in times of scarcity, when the decrees had to be enforced. After personally investigating the conditions on the river they saw the impracticability of trying to bring so small a stream over so large a river bed with so great a loss, for the purpose of delivering 18 feet of early priority water at the headgates of 2 and 3. They were convinced that it would be a benefit to everyone on the river, and an injury to none, to have this early water transferred into the Montrose canal.* * *

Burden of Proof

(1) The New Mexico Supreme Court adopted the rule that in contests over water rights, prior appropriators who complain of injury must prove that their use of the water is reasonable and beneficial, and the junior appropriator then must show that there is a surplus in the source of water supply from which water may be taken without injuring prior rights.[705] Previously, this rule had been applied by the California Supreme Court as between riparian claimants and prior appropriators on the one hand and junior appropriators on the other.[706]

(2) In 1908, the Colorado Supreme Court took the view that:[707]

Where a senior seeks to enjoin a junior appropriator of water from diverting the same to the injury of the former, and the junior appropriator seeks to avoid the same upon the ground that if the use which he threatens to make of it is restrained, the owner of the senior right will derive no benefit, such a defense ought to be established by clear and satisfactory evidence. The infringement of a prior by the owner of a junior right constitutes a legal injury, and, before the junior can justify his acts of interference with the prior right upon the ground stated, a strong showing should be made.* * *

(3) A facet of the question of upstream interference by junior appropriators pertains to the flow of upstream tributaries. In a later 1908 opinion, the Colorado Supreme Court held that: "The presumption is that the water of a tributary of a stream, less the evaporation, if not interfered with, will naturally reach the main stream either by surface or subterranean flow."[708] Hence, the burden of establishing a contention that water proposed to be diverted from an upstream tributary would not in its natural course reach the headgate of a prior

---

[705] *Pecos Valley Artesian Conservancy Dist.* v. *Peters,* 52 N. Mex. 148, 152-154, 193 Pac. (2d) 418 (1948).

[706] *Tulare Irr. Dist.* v. *Lindsay-Strathmore Irr. Dist.,* 3 Cal. (2d) 489, 535, 45 Pac. (2d) 972 (1935).

[707] *Alamosa Creek Canal Co.* v. *Nelson,* 42 Colo. 140, 149-150, 93 Pac. 1112 (1908). The evidence on this point was conflicting, and the defense was not established to the satisfaction of the trial court. The supreme court held that the evidence was legally sufficient to uphold the finding of the trial court in favor of the downstream seniors.

[708] *Petterson* v. *Payne,* 43 Colo. 184, 186-187, 95 Pac. 301 (1908).

appropriator on the main stream below, rests upon the junior claimant. Several decades later, this court reaffirmed the principle, stating that on the issue of whether water is or is not tributary to a stream ·the burden is upon the party who asserts that it is *not* tributary—not on the one who asserts that it is. "The natural presumption is, that all flowing water finds its way to a stream."[709]

(4) Whether the alleged upstream interference occurs on the main stream or on a tributary, the affirmative defense of the junior diversion must show that under all the surrounding conditions it does not adversely affect the senior's receipt of the full appropriation to which he is entitled. This might include a showing that the full quantity of water was received despite the upstream taking; or that the runoff was slight and the streambed sufficiently dry to absorb the entire flow enroute.[710] Under some circumstances, the burden rests upon the upstream junior appropriator to show that neither the surface flow nor underflow, if uninterrupted, would reach the senior's point of diversion.[711]

(5) In *Irion* v. *Hyde,* the Montana Supreme Court held it to be "well settled that a subsequent appropriator attempting to justify his diversion has the burden of proving that it does not injure prior appropriators."[712] The result of the junior appropriator's actually making the required strong affirmative showing appears in two other cases decided by this court, as follows:

When the evidence given by the upstream junior appropriator tends to show that the waters of Stream A would not, even if uninterrupted, reach Stream B on which senior headgates are located, this junior appropriator whose diversion is located on Stream A is *prima facie* entitled to make use of the water if such use does not interfere with the use by senior appropriators of the natural flow in Stream B. The burden then is upon the latter to show that, if uninterrupted, the waters of Stream A *would* reach Stream B by a defined channel either on the surface or in the ground, and that the junior's appropriation of it diminishes the volume of water flowing in Stream B.[713]

INCHOATE APPROPRIATIVE RIGHT

Nature and Extent of the Right

In chapter 7, under "Definitions," appears the following:

Inchoate appropriative right is an incomplete appropriative right in good standing. It comes into being at the taking of the first step provided by law for acquisition of an appropriative right. It remains in good standing so long as the requirements of law are being fulfilled. And it matures into an appropriative right on completion of the last step provided by law.

---

[709] *De Haas* v. *Benesch,* 116 Colo. 344, 350-351, 181 Pac. (2d) 453 (1947).

[710] *Irion* v. *Hyde,* 110 Mont. 570, 584, 105 Pac. (2d) 666 (1940).

[711] *Neil* v. *Hyde,* 32 Idaho 576, 586, 186 Pac. 710 (1919); *Jackson* v. *Cowan,* 33 Idaho 525, 528, 196 Pac. 216 (1921).

[712] *Irion* v. *Hyde,* 110 Mont. 570, 581, 105 Pac. (2d) 666 (1940).

[713] *Ryan* v. *Quinlan,* 45 Mont. 521, 531-532, 124 Pac. 512 (1912); *Loyning* v. *Rankin,* 118 Mont. 235, 249, 165 Pac. (2d) 1006 (1946).

Thus, one who has undertaken to appropriate water but who has not completed his appropriation does not have a water right in the full sense of the term, but he nevertheless has a substantial right.

This phase of the appropriative right to the use of water came to judicial attention in the early development of the appropriation doctrine in California. The supreme court held that one who initiates an appropriation has a "preliminary, inchoate right to acquire in the future a right to water," but that before an appropriation is completed, "The right to the water does not *yet exist, and it may never vest. The most that is in esse*, is, a *right to acquire, by reasonable diligence, a future right to the water.* * * * "[714]

Sixty years later, in a case arising in Montana, a Federal court stated: "True, this inchoate right may not be defeated by an intervening appropriation so long as the holder thereof, after the construction of his diversion works, exercises due diligence in making such application of the water; but it still remains true that to perfect the right, actual use is indispensable."[715]

Inchoate rights on the public domain were subjected to an important qualification. Referring to decisions rendered by the United States Supreme Court, the Supreme Court of California stated that "until the completion of the work no title, legal or equitable, vests in the appropriator, no right vests which the government of the United States is compelled to recognize." Therefore, one who initiates such an appropriation of water on the public domain acquires a possessory right to continue with diligence the prosecution of the work to completion as against "all the world but the United States."[716]

Property Nature of the Inchoate Right

The courts of California and Idaho differ in their views as to the property nature of an inchoate right. The California Supreme Court held that upon completion of an appropriation prior to enactment of the Civil Code in 1872, by diligent construction, diversion, and application of the water to a useful purpose, the appropriator's title would become complete and perfect, but that in the meantime he had "an existing conditional right, manifested by actual visible possession of the works. It would be clearly a property right, and it being incidental and appurtenant to land, it was real property." It was also held that an incomplete appropriative right initiated pursuant to the Civil Code by

---

[714] *Nevada County & Sacramento Canal Co.* v. *Kidd*, 37 Cal. 282, 311, 313, 316 (1869), quoted with approval in *Mitchell* v. *Amador Canal & Min. Co.*, 75 Cal. 464, 482-483, 17 Pac. 246 (1888), in which it was also said that: "The mere act of commencing a ditch, with the intention of appropriating the water, of itself gives no right to the water of a stream. The right depends upon the effectual prosecution of the work."

[715] *Oscarson* v. *Norton*, 39 Fed. (2d) 610, 613 (9th Cir. 1930).

[716] *Silver Lake Power & Irr. Co.* v. *Los Angeles*, 176 Cal. 96, 101-102, 167 Pac. 697 (1917). See also *United States* v. *Rickey Land & Cattle Co.*, 164 Fed. 496, 499 (N. D. Cal. 1908).

posting notice, and in good standing, was likewise an interest in the realty, even though not yet a title.[717]

The Idaho Supreme Court holds that a permit to appropriate water is not real property under the statute, but is a consent given by the State to construct and acquire real property.[718] Notwithstanding statements in the Idaho decisions to the effect that a permit is not real property, the supreme court has held that the holder of a permit cannot convey the water right represented thereby by handing the permit to a would-be purchaser, but must make a formal assignment or conveyance.[719]

Permit to Appropriate Water

In California, the statutory administrative procedure is the sole means by which water of watercourses may be appropriated. In Idaho, there are two methods by which such an appropriation may be made: (1) the statutory procedure, and (2) what is called the "constitutional" method, by which one may validly appropriate water by diverting it and applying it to a beneficial use without recourse to the State administrator. Insofar as validity of the completed right is concerned, neither method is superior to the other. With respect to application of the doctrine of relation, the statutory method is more advantageous. These matters are discussed in chapter 7 under "Methods of Appropriating Water of Watercourses—Current Appropriation Procedures—Administrative—Exclusiveness of the statutory procedure."

The first step in the administrative appropriation procedure in each of these States is the filing of an application with the State administrative agency for a permit to make the appropriation of water. If all requisites are fulfilled, the applicant receives from the State a permit which authorizes him to proceed with construction of works, diversion of water, and application of the water to beneficial use. When all conditions have been complied with and proof of completion of the appropriation has been made, the permittee receives from the State a license. In California, the license "confirms the right to the appropriation of such an amount of water as has been determined to have been applied to beneficial use."[720] In Idaho, the license "shall be binding upon the state as to the right of such licensee to use the amount of water mentioned therein, and shall be prima facie evidence as to such right."[721]

---

[717] *Inyo Consolidated Water Co.* v. *Jess,* 161 Cal. 516, 519-521, 119 Pac. 934 (1912). See *Merritt* v. *Los Angeles,* 162 Cal. 47, 50-51, 120 Pac. 1064 (1912); *Haight* v. *Costanich,* 184 Cal. 426, 431-432, 194 Pac. 26 (1920).

[718] *Big Wood Canal Co.* v. *Chapman,* 45 Idaho 380, 401-402, 263 Pac. 45 (1927); *Speer* v. *Stephenson,* 16 Idaho 707, 716, 102 Pac. 365 (1909). See also *Griffiths* v. *Cole,* 264 Fed. 369, 372-373 (D. Idaho 1919); *Sauve* v. *Abbott,* 19 Fed. (2d) 619, 620 (D. Idaho 1927).

[719] *Gard* v. *Thompson,* 21 Idaho 485, 496, 123 Pac. 497 (1912).

[720] Cal. Water Code § 1610 (West Supp. 1970).

[721] Idaho Code Ann. § 42-220 (1948).

It is evident, then, that a permit to appropriate water represents an inchoate right. Formerly, in California, an inchoate right could be obtained by an applicant prior to issuance of the permit, because it was then the judicial view that the State administrative agency had no discretion to issue or deny a permit; that depending upon the availability of unappropriated water and the sufficiency of an application, its duty to grant or deny was mandatory.[722] However, as a result of statutory changes the administrative agency now exercises a broad discretion in determining whether the issuance of a permit will best serve the public interest. This determination requires an administrative adjudication which, in any case in which an application is protested, may be made only after a hearing.[723] In the Foreword to the "Rules, Regulations and Information Pertaining to Appropriation of Water in California," issued by the State Water Rights Board in 1960, it was stated that:[724]

> *It should be understood that neither the filing of an application nor its approval by the board will give one a water right.* Issuance of permit merely signifies consent of the State that unappropriated water may be appropriated and right acquired in accordance with law and the terms of the permit.* * *

In 1964, the State Water Rights Board issued, in place of the 1960 edition, a pamphlet entitled "Regulations and Information Pertaining to Appropriation of Water in California," which has no Foreword and does not repeat this statement. (A similar pamphlet was issued in 1969 by its successor, the State Water Resources Control Board.) However, the correctness of this information has not diminished with the passage of time.

The Idaho Supreme Court has thus expressed its views as to the nature of a permit issued by the State: The right given therein is merely a contingent right, which may ripen into a complete appropriation, or on the other hand may be defeated by the failure of the holder to comply with the requirements of the statute. Hence, it is not an appropriation of water.[725] The permit simply evidences the consent of the State that the applicant may proceed under the law and make an appropriation of public water.[726] The applicant obtains from a permit no right to the use of water unless he complies substantially with every provision of the statute affecting the issuance of the permit and fulfills all the conditions and limitations therein; but such compliance initiates a right to the use of water in the applicant.[727] Until all the requirements have been complied with, the holder of the permit has nothing but an inchoate right; but

---

[722] *Tulare Water Co.* v. *State Water Commission,* 187 Cal. 533, 536, 202 Pac. 874 (1921).

[723] *Temescal Water Co.* v. *Department of Public Works,* 44 Cal. (2d) 90, 99-100, 280 Pac. (2d) 1 (1955).

[724] Cal. Admin. Code, tit. 23, ch. 2.1, subchs. 1 and 2 (1960).

[725] *Big Wood Canal Co.* v. *Chapman,* 45 Idaho 380, 401-402, 263 Pac. 45 (1927); *Speer* v. *Stephenson,* 16 Idaho 707, 716, 102 Pac. 365 (1909).

[726] *Marshall* v. *Niagara Springs Orchard Co.,* 22 Idaho 144, 153, 125 Pac. 208 (1912).

[727] *Washington State Sugar Co.* v. *Goodrich,* 27 Idaho 26, 38, 147 Pac. 1073 (1915).

after fulfilling all requirements, he is entitled to a license confirming his right of use of the water.[728]

Conditional Decrees and Water Rights in Colorado

Prior to 1969, the comprehensive Colorado statutory system for the adjudication of water rights made specific provision for conditional decrees of rights to the use of water under appropriations only partially completed or not perfected. If proof of partial completion by the claimant was satisfactory to the court, a conditional decree was issued, conditioned upon application of the water to beneficial use within a reasonable time thereafter, the final decree in a subsequent proceeding to fix a quantity of water not in excess of the maximum fixed in the conditional decree. In this way, rights of partially completed appropriations were safeguarded pending completion and final adjudication, or forfeiture and cancellation, as the case might have been.[729]

With the enactment of the "Water Right Determination and Adjudication Act of 1969," the legislature provided for determinations of, among other things, a conditional water right and the amount and priority thereof, including a determination that a conditional water right has become a water right by virtue of a completed appropriation. A person desiring such a determination shall file an application with the water clerk, setting forth facts in support of the ruling sought.[730] Jurisdiction to hear and adjudicate such questions is vested exclusively in the water judges and their designated referees[731] who determine the place of diversion or storage, means of diversion, type of use, amount and priority of use, "and other pertinent information."[732] In every second calendar year following the year in which a conditional water right has been determined, the owner or user of the right, if he wishes to maintain the right, must obtain a finding by the referee of reasonable diligence in the development of the appropriation; failure to do so shall be considered an abandonment of the conditional water right.[733]

---

[728] *Basinger* v. *Taylor*, 30 Idaho 289, 297-298, 164 Pac. 522 (1917).

[729] Colo. Rev. Stat. Ann. § § 148-10-6 to 148-10-9 (1963), repealed, Laws 1969, ch. 373, § 20. In the case of *Denver* v. *Northern Colorado Water Conservancy Dist.,* 130 Colo. 375, 276 Pac. (2d) 992 (1954), headnote no. 20 in the Pacific Reporter reads: "Requirement of statute authorizing conditional water right decrees is not that claimant shall not have abandoned but rather that he has prosecuted his claims of appropriation and the financing and construction of his enterprise with reasonable diligence."

[730] Colo. Rev. Stat. Ann. § 148-21-18(1) (Supp. 1969).

[731] *Id.* § § 148-21-10(1) and (2). This 1969 legislation provided for these special water clerks, referees, and judges. Such matters were previously handled by regular courts and judicial officers. For further discussions of these and other provisions of this 1969 Colorado legislation, see chapter 15 and the State summary for Colorado in the appendix.

[732] *Id.* § § 148-21-19(1) and 148-21-20(7).

[733] *Id.* § 148-21-17(4).

Some supreme court decisions refer to decrees of adjudication entered in 1888 and 1889, both of which had both absolute and interlocutory or conditional features. The practical reasons for including conditional decrees in the 1888 general adjudication were stated.[734] Inclusion of both absolute and interlocutory features in the decree of 1889 were thus explained:[735]

> At the time of the entry of the decree, the court established in each ditch an absolute right to the full amount of water per second of time that had been applied to a beneficial use, and gave such appropriation a number, and, to that extent, it was absolute. It tentatively recognized an inchoate right to additional water, which inchoate right, if of any validity, might become an absolute right, under the doctrine of relation, if the water was applied to a beneficial use with due diligence.* * *

The question of abandonment of an inchoate or conditional appropriation was the subject of some debate. In the two decisions just noted, the Colorado Supreme Court held that the principles of abandonment are not to be applied to these contingent interests, inasmuch as in the absence of diligence no appropriation would exist and so the inchoate interest, tentatively recognized, would terminate.[736] Kinney criticized this, stating that the better rule is to treat such an inchoate right as abandoned where there has been an unreasonable time in the final consummation of the right, after the rights of others have intervened, unless there should be a failure to comply with some specific statute in which case the right should be treated as forfeited.[737] This statement by Kinney is inconsistent with a statement several sections later in which he points out correctly the decided distinction in legal significance between "abandonment" and "forfeiture" which "should be observed," abandonment being the "relinquishment of the right by the owner with the intention to forsake and desert it." Several years later, the supreme court referred to the decisions and to Kinney's criticism of them, but did not find it necessary to decide the question in this case. The court said: "However that may be, the party may not, in the same defense, plead that his adversary never had any rights, and that such rights, as once existed, had been abandoned.* * * "[738]

---

[734] *Conley* v. *Dyer,* 43 Colo. 22, 23-25, 95 Pac. 304 (1908).

[735] *Crawford Clipper Ditch Co.* v. *Needle Rock Ditch Co.,* 50 Colo. 176, 181, 114 Pac. 655 (1911).

[736] *Conley* v. *Dyer,* 43 Colo. 22, 28-29, 95 Pac. 304 (1908); *Crawford Clipper Ditch Co.* v. *Needle Rock Ditch Co.,* 50 Colo. 176, 182, 114 Pac. 655 (1911).

[737] Kinney, C. S., "A Treatise on the Law of Irrigation and Water Rights," 2d ed., vol. 2, §§ 1102 and 1118 (1912).

[738] *Bieser* v. *Stoddard,* 73 Colo. 554, 560, 216 Pac. 707 (1923). The court apparently believed that abandonment of a conditionally decreed right could be shown, but decided that it had not been established herein.

In a 1939 decision, the Colorado Supreme Court reiterated the fundamental proposition that application of water to a beneficial use is essential to a completed appropriation, and that all acts preceding this—even diversion from the natural stream—constitute but an inchoate right or interest which terminates if beneficial use does not follow. In such event, the water goes to junior claimants who have complied with all requirements of the law. And to obtain a priority dating from the commencement of work, beneficial use must take place within a reasonable time, which depends upon the facts and circumstances of each particular case.[739]

As noted above, the 1969 legislation provides that in every second calendar year following the year in which a conditional right has been determined, the owner or user of the right must obtain a finding from the referee of reasonable diligence in the development of the appropriative right; failure to do so shall constitute an abandonment of the right.[740] Abandonment of a conditional water right is defined as the "termination of a conditional water right as a result of the failure to develop with reasonable diligence the proposed appropriation upon which such water right is to be based."[741] This definition differs from the act's definition of the "abandonment of a water right," apparently meaning a completed appropriation, as "the termination of a water right in whole or in part as a result of the intent of the owner thereof to discontinue permanently the use of all or part of the water available thereunder."[742]

---

[739] *Denver* v. *Sheriff,* 105 Colo. 193, 199, 96 Pac. (2d) 836 (1939).

    Other cases dealing with conditional decrees regarding water appropriations include *Four Counties Water Users Ass'n* v. *Colorado River Water Conservation Dist.,* 159 Colo. 499, 414 Pac. (2d) 469 (1966); *Id.,* 161 Colo. 416, 425 Pac. (2d) 259 (1967); *Id.,* 161 Colo. 424, 425 Pac. (2d) 266 (1967); *Four Counties Water Users Ass'n* v. *Middle Park Water Conservation Dist.,* 161 Colo. 429, 425 Pac. (2d) 262 (1967).

[740] Colo. Rev. Stat. Ann. § 148-21-17(4) (Supp. 1969).

[741] *Id.* § 148-21-3(14).

[742] *Id.* § 148-21-3(13).

Chapter 9

EXERCISE OF THE APPROPRIATIVE RIGHT

DIVERSION, DISTRIBUTION, AND STORAGE WORKS

Some Features of Waterworks

Diversion and Distribution Works

A common phenomenon in the West.—The familiar system of artificial works for diverting water from a stream and conveying it to the place of use is a common phenomenon in the irrigation-conscious West. In parts of the southwestern region, this has been so from time immemorial.

In a typical case, a dam built across a stream diverts water into and through a headgate, from which it flows in a canal or ditch to the area to be served. In common parlance, "canal" and "ditch" are often interchangeable, "canal" being more usually applied to the larger and longer artificial waterways. The next subdivision includes "laterals," which branch off from the main ditch into smaller and smaller arteries. In 1951, the Colorado Supreme Court, having occasion to decide whether a particular ditch was or was not a "lateral," stated that: "A ditch normally has its headgate in a stream or other primary source of water supply. A lateral is a branch ditch which has its headgate in the main ditch and not in a natural watercourse."[1] Many main ditches, particularly the large and long canals, are lined to reduce transmission losses and to facilitate maintenance. The system may include flumes and pipes for conveying the water; and there may be pumping plants for lifting water over the streambank or out of a sump at the place of diversion, or for boosting diverted water from a lowline to a highline canal.

Statutory mention of works.—Some of the water appropriation statutes specifically mention kinds of physical works by which water may be taken from streams and conveyed to places of use. For example: "To effect the beneficial use, the person or the state of Arizona or a political subdivision thereof appropriating the water may construct and maintain reservoirs, dams, canals, ditches, flumes and other necessary waterways."[2] Appropriable waters "may be held or stored by dams, in lakes or reservoirs, or diverted by means of canals, ditches, intakes, pumping plants, or other works."[3] Wheels or other machinery may be placed on banks of streams for the purpose of raising water to the level required for its use in irrigating land.[4] In the process of

---

[1] *New Multa Trina Ditch Co.* v. *Patch,* 123 Colo. 444, 447, 230 Pac. (2d) 597 (1951).
[2] Ariz. Rev. Stat. Ann. § 45-141(B) (Supp. 1969).
[3] Tex. Rev. Civ. Stat. Ann. art. 7468 (Supp. 1970).
[4] Oreg. Rev. Stat. § 541.410 (Supp. 1969).

(590)

appropriating water in South Dakota, the statute takes cognizance of the overhead sprinkler system of irrigation by providing that:[5]

Each application and permit for irrigation by the overhead sprinkler method, or by the use of portable diversion pumping equipment, may divert from one or more points at a time from a reach of the stream or other watercourse between two fixed points on the stream described in the application and permit provided that the total amount diverted from two or more permissible points under the provisions of a water right at one time shall not exceed the total withdrawal rate allowed by said water right per unit of time.

Artificial diversion works usually necessary.—As noted below, use of water of natural sources without the aid of artificial devices has been held sufficient under certain circumstances to support the acquisition of appropriative rights. However, in the water use economy of the West, control of the water by taking it from the source of supply and conveying it to the place of intended use in artificial works is necessary in most cases in exercising an appropriative right. Generally, from early times in the West, it was recognized that there must be some adequate means of diverting the water from the natural supply.[6] Said the Utah Supreme Court in 1960: "In appropriating water it is necessary * * * [among other requirements] to have a diversion from the natural channel by means of a ditch, canal or other structure, * * *."[7]

Mode of diversion not material.—But it is the fact of diversion, not the mode, that is material. Only such acts are necessary as are practicable to accomplish the purpose of making beneficial use of the water.[8] As stated by a Federal court in 1904, "It is immaterial, in acquiring the right, whether the water was taken from the river by means of a canal, ditch, flume, or pipe, or by

---

[5] S. Dak. Comp. Laws Ann. § 46-5-13 (1967).

[6] *Simons* v. *Inyo Cerro Gordo Min. & Power Co.*, 48 Cal. App. 524, 537, 192 Pac. 144 (1920). "It seems the settled law" in the irrigation States that in the acquisition of a vested right to the use of water from public streams, there must be construction of ditches or conduits, through which to divert water and conduct it to the place of use, followed by actual application of the water to beneficial use: *Gates* v. *Settlers' Mill., Canal & Res. Co.*, 19 Okla. 83, 89, 91 Pac. 856 (1907). To perfect an appropriation "there must be the physical works by which the water is diverted and carried directly to the land for beneficial use thereon, or carried to storage reservoirs where it is stored temporarily, and then carried to land for beneficial use thereon." *Murphy* v. *Kerr*, 296 Fed. 536, 542 (D. N. Mex. 1923). "It appears from the record that, in the irrigation of arid lands, waste ditches for the disposition of the surplus water are as necessary as the irrigation itself." *Brand* v. *Lienkaemper*, 72 Wash. 547, 549, 130 Pac. 1147 (1913).

[7] *Crawford* v. *Lehi Irr. Co.*, 10 Utah (2d) 165, 168, 350 Pac. (2d) 147 (1960).

[8] *Simons* v. *Inyo Cerro Gordo Min. & Power Co.*, 48 Cal. App. 524, 537, 192 Pac. 144 (1920). "It is well settled that in the appropriation of water any means adopted to convey it to the place of use is legitimate for the purpose of the appropriation." *Turvey* v. *Kincaid*, 111 Oreg. 237, 241, 226 Pac. 219 (1924).

any other method."[9] And in 1960, the Colorado Supreme Court quoted with approval a statement that it had made in the opinion in a case decided in 1883 that: " 'The true test of appropriation of water is the successful application thereof to the beneficial use designed; and the method of diverting or carrying the same, or making such appropriation, is immaterial.' "[10]

The right to continuance of one's reasonable means of diversion is discussed in chapter 13.

Use of Streamflow Without Conduit

Dipping or drinking from stream. – In Nevada and Colorado, it has been held that under some circumstances appropriative rights may be founded on practices of dipping or drinking from streams. The Utah Supreme Court recognizes this as a public privilege, subject to rights of prior appropriation to the use of the streamflow, but rejects it as the basis of an appropriative right.

Thus, the Nevada Supreme Court observed that the method of taking water from streams by the use of dams, ditches, or other artificial structures was the natural thing to do. However, it would not necessarily follow that a diversion by artificial means was necessary to constitute an appropriation where the water could be put to a beneficial use without such diversion, where there was a practice of doing so, at less cost so far as the use of water was a factor, that had developed into a well-established custom. Hence, the controlling reason for requiring an artificial diversion to establish an appropriative right did not apply to an appropriation for watering livestock in natural watering places formed by natural depressions, such appropriation having been made prior to enactment of any statute specifying the manner of appropriating water.[11]

As stated in chapter 8 under "Elements of the Appropriative Right—Purpose of Use of Water—Stockwatering," a Nevada statute, enacted in 1925, supplements the general water rights statute by prescribing certain conditions with respect to the acquisition of rights for the watering of livestock, particularly range livestock. It states the circumstances under which new appropriations may be made in conformity with the stated policy of protecting the grazing use of the portion of the public range already fully utilized by holders of stockwatering rights. A sufficient measure of the quantity of water for this kind of an appropriation is to specify the number and kind of animals to be watered. The legislation relates to the "right to water range livestock at a particular place" and to "the watering place"—obviously contemplating use of

---

[9]*Miller & Lux* v. *Rickey,* 127 Fed. 573, 584 (C.C.D. Nev. 1904). "The right to use the water is the essence of appropriation; the means by which it is done are incidental." *Offield* v. *Ish,* 21 Wash. 277, 281, 57 Pac. 809 (1899).

[10]*Genoa* v. *Westfall,* 141 Colo. 533, 349 Pac. (2d) 370, 378 (1960), quoting from *Thomas* v. *Guiraud,* 6 Colo. 530, 533 (1883).

[11]*Steptoe Live Stock Co.* v. *Gulley,* 53 Nev. 163, 171-173, 295 Pac. 772 (1931). Note that the circumstances of this case related peculiarly to the livestock industry.

the water in place, with no question about diverting it from the spring or stream channel.[12] The constitutionality of this stockwatering act was sustained, under attack, by the Nevada Supreme Court, and it was referred to, with approval, by the Federal District Court for Nevada.[13]

A Colorado case decided in 1960 involved a claim of right to a long exercised use of small quantities of water in potholes or ponds in a streambed, augmented by installation of an artificial sump, some water being collected in troughs for watering stock and some dipped or drawn in buckets—and at times pumped—for "household and other domestic uses." In affirming the judgment of the trial court, the supreme court held that "an appropriation of water to beneficial uses," as that phrase is understood in the water law of Colorado, had been made, and that the prior appropriator was entitled to continued maintenance of conditions as they existed at the time the appropriation was made. The general principle was declared that:[14]

> It is not necessary in every case for an appropriator of water to construct ditches or artificial ways through which the water might be taken from the stream in order that a valid appropriation be made. The only indispensable requirements are that the appropriator intends to use the waters for a beneficial purpose and actually applies them to that use.

The Utah Supreme Court stated one aspect of the principal question in a case before it as "the right of users on grazing range to water their livestock at springs or streams flowing in natural channels, without interference, without making a statutory appropriation." Rights of two kinds to the use of such waters were recognized: (a) The right of a prior appropriator of water, in the exercise of which "there must be a diversion from the natural channel or an interference with the natural free flow, for storage, effected by the work, labor, or art of man." (b) While water is flowing naturally in a stream channel or other source of supply, and its ownership therefor of necessity in the public, "everyone may drink or dip therefrom or water his animals therein, subject to the limitations above noted as to the rights of the appropriator as fixed by law to his quantity and quality."[15]

---

[12]Nev. Rev. Stat. § § 533.485-.510 (Supp. 1967).

[13]*In re Calvo,* 50 Nev. 125, 131-141, 253 Pac. 671 (1927). "Because of natural conditions particularly, an arid mountainous region covering the major portion of the state's areas of more than 100,000 square miles, the state has recognized and provided for the protection of stockmen who have been first to make use of springs and small water channels to enable them to graze their live stock in adjacent regions which, with the possible exception of mining, is not adaptable to any other use." *Adams-McGill Co.* v. *Hendrix,* 22 Fed. Supp. 789, 791 (D. Nev. 1938).

[14]*Genoa* v. *Westfall,* 141 Colo. 533, 349 Pac. (2d) 370, 378 (1960).

[15]*Adams* v. *Portage Irr., Res. & Power Co.,* 95 Utah 1, 12-14, 72 Pac. (2d) 648 (1937). The right of plaintiffs to take water from streams for camp purposes and to water their sheep in the creek was held to be a lawful right, recognized by the constitution and the

Natural overflow.—With respect to irrigation—a beneficial use of water which is usually served away from the stream channel rather than within it—the Nevada Supreme Court in *Walsh* v. *Wallace* held that to constitute a valid appropriation of water there must be an actual diversion of the same. The cutting of wild grass produced by the overflow of a stream, said the court, or "by the water of Reese river coming down and spreading over the land," was not an appropriation of water within the meaning of that term.[16] According to a description of early Nevada conditions in the opinion in a Federal case decided in 1897, based not only on the record in the case but also on the judge's own experiences as one who came to Carson Valley in 1852, it was then common practice to take advantage of the irrigation water chiefly through its overflow.[17] However, standards apparently had risen in the half-century that passed before *Walsh* v. *Wallace* was decided in 1902; and the 1897 Federal opinion itself contains an excellent summary of the principles by which the extent of one's appropriation is determined, as developed by the courts prior to the era of administrative practice and procedure.[18] In 1910, a Federal court stated that the watering of meadowland by use of natural overflow would found no right of appropriation, citing *Walsh* v. *Wallace.*[19]

In an early case, the Colorado Supreme Court took a broad view of the question of appliances in getting irrigation water from a stream to the land to be moistened. In the court's opinion "a dam or contrivance of any kind," with or without ditches, would be legally sufficient if physically effective. Or even if production could be attained "by the natural overflow of water thereon, without the aid of any applicances whatever," such natural moistening would be a sufficient appropriation of the reasonably necessary quantity of water.[20]

A few years earlier than the supreme court's rendering of this decision, the Colorado Legislature enacted a statute, still extant, which provides that persons who shall have enjoyed the use of water from a natural stream for irrigation of meadowland by the natural overflow or operation of the stream may, in case of diminution of flow, construct ditches for that purpose with priorities as of the

---

statute, unless in so doing they appreciably decreased the quantity or deteriorated the quality of the waters to the use of which defendants had a priority.

See also *Hunter* v. *United States,* 388 Fed. (2d) 148, 153 (9th Cir. 1967), arising from California, regarding appropriation for livestock use as well as by placing water wheels in a stream to operate mills, citing *Ortman* v. *Dixon,* 13 Cal. 33 (1859; *Tartar* v. *Spring Creek Water & Mining Co.,* 5 Cal. 395 (1855).

[16]*Walsh* v. *Wallace,* 26 Nev. 299, 327-328, 67 Pac. 914 (1902).

[17]*Union Mill & Min. Co.* v. *Dangberg,* 81 Fed. 73, 100-103 (C.C.D. Nev. 1897), opinion by Judge Thomas P. Hawley. See, in chapter 8, "Elements of the Appropriative Right—Purpose of Use of Water—Stockwatering."

[18]*Id.* at 94-95.

[19]*Anderson Land & Stock Co.* v. *McConnell,* 188 Fed. 818, 822 (C.C.D. Nev. 1910).

[20]*Thomas* v. *Guiraud,* 6 Colo. 530, 533 (1883). Successful application of water to beneficial use is the true test, the method of getting the water there being immaterial.

time of first use of the meadows.[21] The supreme court held that this statute gives the meadowland owner an appropriation of the water "without any affirmative act of his own in withdrawing water from the stream."[22] However, it was held in the following year that such an appropriator is not exempt from the necessity of proving his claim in the event of an adjudication. If he fails to do this, and later builds a ditch on account of diminution of the streamflow, he is not entitled to have his priority date back by relation to his meadow appropriation ahead of priorities fixed by a previous statutory decree the making and limitations of which he completely ignored.[23]

Development of the very considerable water law of Oregon progressed with a liberal recognition that, at least in pioneer communities, valid appropriative rights could originate in use of natural stream overflow in times of flood, priorities therefor dating from the time shown by the evidence at which honest efforts were made to use both land and water for beneficial purposes.[24] In 1933, the supreme court stated that "It is now well settled that where practically no artificial works for irrigation are necessary, the requirement of a valid appropriation that there be a diversion from the natural channel is satisfied, when the appropriator accepts the gift of nature, and indicates his intention to reap the benefits of natural irrigation."[25]

Despite this broad statement in 1933, there was previously for years a growing consciousness of the anachronism of recognizing and protecting prior appropriative rights to the use of uncontrolled natural stream overflow while controlled methods of diversion and use were being subjected to requirements of reasonable efficiency. The continued practice of utilizing uncontrolled

---

[21]Colo. Rev. Stat. Ann. § 148-3-14 (1963), first enacted, Laws 1879, p. 106.

[22]*Humphreys Tunnel & Min. Co. v. Frank*, 46 Colo. 524, 528-529, 105 Pac. 1093 (1909). In a proceeding begun for the purpose of procuring an adjudication of priorities, a claim was that ditches were constructed for the purpose of taking the place of irrigation by overflow which had become depreciated by reason of natural causes: *Means v. Stow*, 31 Colo. 282, 283-284, 73 Pac. 48 (1903). The appeal was dismissed on procedural grounds without discussing the validity of the statute or of the appropriation.

[23]*Broad Run Investment Co. v. Deuel & Snyder Improvement Co.*, 47 Colo. 573, 577-583, 108 Pac. 755 (1910). The claimant stood by during the adjudication, while other meadow owners who had constructed ditches to replace their meadow overflow irrigation appeared and had their priorities adjudicated and decreed. He did nothing toward utilizing the meadow appropriation through a ditch until after expiration of the applicable statutory period of limitations. His claim was therefore barred by the statute. See also *San Luis Valley Land & Cattle Co. v. Hazard*, 114 Colo. 233, 234-235, 157 Pac. (2d) 144 (1945).

[24]*McCall v. Porter*, 42 Oreg. 49, 55-56, 70 Pac. 820 (1902), 71 Pac. 976 (1903; *In re Silvies River*, 115 Oreg. 27, 66, 237 Pac. 322 (1925); *Campbell v. Walker*, 137 Oreg. 375, 379, 382, 2 Pac. (2d) 912 (1931); *Smyth v. Jenkins*, 148 Oreg. 165, 166, 168-169, 33 Pac. (2d) 1007 (1934).

[25]*Masterson v. Pacific Live Stock Co.*, 144 Oreg. 396, 408, 24 Pac. (2d) 1046 (1933).

natural overflow in crop irrigation came to be recognized as wasteful. It was no longer to be regarded as a right, but as a privilege to be tolerated only while no injury resulted to others, no deprivation of the use by junior appropriators of water that simply served the purpose of lifting the flood flow over the banks for the benefit of prior appropriative overflow rights, and to be changed to a control system within a reasonable time.[26] After reaffirming the previously recognized rule that "the law does not vainly require" artificial works if the overflow system is adequate, the supreme court insisted that "in most cases the building of some kind of an irrigation system" is eventually requisite "to effect an economical beneficial use of such water and prevent waste" and that this "should be accomplished within a reasonable time as circumstances permit and necessities require."[27] And in 1959, the Oregon Supreme Court held squarely that the time had come when the method of diversion of water by way of natural overflow in Warner Valley was a privilege only, and that it could not be insisted upon if it interfered with appropriation by others of the waters for a beneficial use.[28]

Scenic beauty and other purposes.—A controversy in the Federal courts early in the present century involved relative appropriative rights to the use of a stream which flowed through a canyon several miles from Colorado Springs, Colorado. The canyon was about three-fourths of a mile long and very deep. Its floor and sides were covered with an exceptionally luxuriant growth of trees, shrubbery, and flowers produced by streamflow through the canyon and the mist and spray from its falls, which were almost continuous throughout the canyon. At this locality, complainant and its predecessors had owned and operated a summer resort for more than 20 years. Defendant proposed to divert water away from the stream above the canyon for the generation of electricity.

The trial court held that maintenance of vegetation in the canyon by the flow and seepage of the stream and the mist and spray of its falls constituted a beneficial use of such waters, and had been appropriated for the purposes of serving complainant's properties in the manner indicated. The court relied on the Colorado rule that an appropriator was not required to construct artificial waterways through which water might be taken from the stream.[29]

---

[26]*In re Willow Creek,* 74 Oreg. 592, 621, 622, 144 Pac. 505 (1914), 146 Pac. 475 (1915).

[27]*In re Silvies River,* 115 Oreg. 27, 66, 237 Pac. 322 (1925).

[28]*Warner Valley Stock Co.* v. *Lynch,* 215 Oreg. 523, 536-541, 336 Pac. (2d) 884 (1959). This does not mean, in the cited case, that these appropriators had no vested right to use the quantity of water they had appropriated from Hart Lake. They no longer had the *privilege* of a natural overflow *method* of diversion; but they were entitled to pump their appropriated quantity of water provided it would overflow if no water (other than the water appropriated under a prior right) were withdrawn from the lake or prevented from reaching it.

[29]*Cascade Town Co.* v. *Empire Water & Power Co.,* 181 Fed. 1011, 1016-1019 (C.C.D. Colo. 1910), reversed, 205 Fed. 123 (8th Cir. 1913).

The court of appeals recognized the beneficial effect of resorts, such as the one owned by complainant, in promoting health by affording rest and relaxation, but questioned the basing of an appropriation of water on the continued natural falls and flow of a stream. Complainant was not entitled to continuance of the falls "solely for their scenic beauty. The state laws proceed upon more material lines." All the water could not be held for the scant vegetation lining the banks, but must be used more efficiently by applying it to the land. If water is appropriated without diverting it from the stream, as is permissible under some circumstances in Colorado, such use must not be unnecessarily or wastefully excessive. The trial court was criticized for basing its decision on this branch of the case largely on the artistic value of the falls, and for making no inquiry into effectiveness of such use of the water as compared with the customary methods of irrigation. Accordingly, the decree was reversed and remanded.[30]

Idaho legislation authorizes and directs the Governor to appropriate, in trust for the people, all or so much of the unappropriated water of certain lakes as may be necessary for their preservation for scenic beauty, health, recreation or other specified purposes.[31] The legislation provides, among other things, that no proof of completion of any works of diversion shall be required.[32]

Colorado legislation authorizes river conservancy districts to "file upon and hold for the use of the public" sufficient water to maintain a constant streamflow to preserve fish and for use in retaining ponds for fish propagation.[33] However, the Colorado Supreme Court held that water may not be so appropriated without a diversion of water from the stream. Among other things, the court said:

> There is no support in the law of this state for the proposition that a minimum flow of water may be "appropriated" in a natural stream for piscatorial purposes without diversion of any portion of the water "appropriated" from the natural course of the stream. By the enactment of C.R.S. 1963, 150-7-5(10) the legislature did not intend to bring about such an extreme departure from well established doctrine, and we hold that no such departure was brought about by said statute.[34]

---

[30]*Empire Water & Power Co.* v. *Cascade Town Co.,* 205 Fed. 123, 128-129 (8th Cir. 1913).

[31]Including (for three named lakes) transportation and commercial purposes.

[32]Idaho Code Ann. § § 67-4301 to 67-4306 (1949).

Regarding Oregon and Utah legislation concerning the withdrawal of water from appropriation, and Washington legislation concerning the establishment of minimum streamflows or lake levels for similar purposes, see the discussion in chapter 7 under "Methods of Appropriating Water of Watercourses—Restrictions and Preferences in Appropriation of Water—Preferences in Water Appropriation—Acquisition of rights to appropriate water—(3) Withdrawal of unappropriated water from appropriation."

[33]Colo. Rev. Stat. Ann. § 150-7-5(10) (1963).

[34]*Colorado River Water Conservation Dist.* v. *Rocky Mountain Power Co.,* 158 Colo. 331, 406 Pac. (2d) 798, 800 (1965), citing earlier Colorado cases, an Idaho case, and a

Storage Works

In chapter 7, under "Methods of Appropriating Water of Water-courses—Storage Water Appropriation," storage reservoir characteristics and functions are discussed at some length. Further discussion at this point is not needed.

Relation of Physical Works to Water Right

Control of Waterworks

Ownership and control of the system of works through which water is diverted from a source of supply and carried to a particular unit of land, or to any combination of land units, may be vested either in a single individual or in an association, corporation, or governmental entity.

Types of private and public organizations and governmental entities having to do with the service of water are discussed in chapter 8 under "Elements of the Appropriative Right—Sale, Rental, or Distribution of Water." The consumers served by a diversion and distribution agency may be members of an unincorporated association, holders of shares of stock in a corporation, customers of or contract-holders with a commercial water company, landowners within an irrigation district, and persons resident within a municipality or public district or water authority who are entitled to water service therefrom by reason of their residence within the service area or their holding of contracts for water service. In some States, local improvement districts are formed within irrigation districts for purposes of lining or otherwise improving laterals, operating and maintaining them, or providing for drainage, costs being allocated locally.

The control of a consumer over the waterworks through which he is supplied varies, then, from (a) sole ownership and management of an individual ditch, (b) up through common ownership and management exercised through officers whom he helps to elect, (c) to participation in very diffuse public ownership and very indirect control over public management exercised through his franchise as a citizen.

United States Supreme Court case arising from Idaho. The court did not mention its 1960 opinion regarding stock watering, discussed above under "Dipping or drinking from the stream," in which it had said "It is not necessary in every case for an appropriator of water to construct ditches or artificial ways through which the water might be taken from the stream in order that a valid appropriation be made. The only indispensable requirements are that the appropriator intends to use the waters for a beneficial purpose and actually applies them to that use." *Genoa* v. *Westfall,* 141 Colo. 533, 349 Pac. (2d) 370, 378 (1960). Nor did the court mention the earlier Colorado cases discussed above under "Natural overflow" or the Federal appellate case regarding scenic beauty discussed above at note 30. In these and other regards, see Ellis, Willis H., "Watercourses—Recreational Uses for Water Under Prior Appropriation Law," 6 Natural Resources J. 181 (1966); Comment, "Water Appropriation for Recreation," 1 Land and Water Law Rev. 209, 214 *et seq.* (1966).

Many changes in the form of organization of water supply enterprises have taken place in the West. Control passed in some cases from pioneer towns to mutual companies. Elsewhere commercial companies were replaced by mutual companies or by irrigation districts. The mutual-type water users organizations formed on the early Federal reclamation projects were mostly converted to irrigation districts, a notable exception being the Salt River Valley Project, Arizona. One of the largest western irrigation projects, in Imperial Valley, California, was originally planned for a diversion of water from Colorado River by a commercial company and distribution to more than 500,000 acres of land through the systems of 14 mutual companies. The works of the development company were later acquired by Imperial Irrigation District, which eventually also acquired the systems of all mutual companies and has since operated the project as a single district unit. In recent years, large-scale district, water authority, and State water plans have come into prominence. Even interstate projects are now in various stages of planning and execution.

The overall trend is toward larger and more integrated plans, with the probability of more comprehensive areawide and even regional projects for management of both surface streams and ground waters.

Separable Ownerships of Waterworks and Water Right

It was early recognized, as shown by the growing diversity in type of water supply organizations over the years, that the means of diversion might be owned by a single appropriator, or owned in common by a number of appropriators or water users, or such means might be owned by one person and the water appropriated by another—in short, that ownership of the means of diversion of water is not essential to perfect the right of appropriation.[35]

In chapter 8, under "Property Characteristics—Right of Property—Ownership of the Appropriative Right," it is shown that water rights and ditch rights are separate and distinct property rights; that one may own a water right without a ditch right, or vice versa; and that abandonment of one does not necessarily imply an abandonment of the other.[36] And so the water right and the ditch right for conveyance of the water may each "be owned, held and conveyed independently of the other."[37] Each of several water appropriators using a ditch in common may separately abandon his right thereto.[38]

The waterworks and water right are so separated in their property nature that they "are capable of several and distinct injuries, giving rise to separate

[35] *Slosser* v. *Salt River Valley Canal Co.,* 7 Ariz. 376, 389, 65 Pac. 332 (1901); *Gould* v. *Maricopa Canal Co.,* 8 Ariz. 429, 447, 76 Pac. 598 (1904).

[36] *Connolly* v. *Harrell,* 102 Mont. 295, 300-301, 57 Pac. (2d) 781 (1936); *McDonnell* v. *Huffine,* 44 Mont. 411, 423, 120 Pac. 792 (1912).

[37] *Simonson* v. *Moon,* 72 Idaho 39, 47, 237 Pac. (2d) 93 (1951); *Marks* v. *Twohy Bros. Co.,* 98 Oreg. 514, 533, 534, 194 Pac. 675 (1921).

[38] *Brighton Ditch Co.* v. *Englewood,* 124 Colo. 366, 373, 237 Pac. (2d) 116 (1951).

and distinct causes of action, for which there are separate and distinct remedies."[39] Despite this separation in property nature, it is true that the water right and ditch right are closely related in their functioning, for under most circumstances the exercise of the water right depends upon the use of some method of diverting and conveying the water.

Joint Occupancy and Use of Works

From the rule respecting separable ownerships of water rights and waterworks, it results that a single diversion and distribution system may be used for the service of any number of different priorities owned by different appropriators for use in connection with their respective farms. (See in chapter 7 "Methods of Appropriating Water of Watercourses—Priority of Appropriation.") "The joint use of the common conduit does not vary the legal consequences which flow from the possession of these several water rights. These remain exactly the same as though the fourteen users had constructed fourteen separate ditches in which to carry their water from Mann Creek to their respective lands."[40] Several parties may appropriate water simultaneously by means of a common ditch for lands even though held in severalty, and may hold ownership of the water right jointly or in common. Distribution of the water after diversion into their ditch is their own affair.[41] In a Colorado case, two parties acted together in appropriating water and construcing a ditch, and there was a unity of possession while the water was being diverted and carried in the ditch; but such unity of possession ceased when the water reached the separate places of use, so that the water right was not jointly owned.[42]

It is a fundamental rule of irrigation law in Colorado that a decree entered in a statutory adjudication proceeding does not and cannot determine ownership of the various water priorities awarded to any given ditch; it merely awards the ditch its proper number, and adjudicates the quantity of water to which it is entitled from water priorities of various dates which will use it.[43]

In several decisions rendered over the years, the Colorado Supreme Court has held that any one of several appropriators of water diverted and carried through the same ditch may—as against the other appropriators through the

---

[39]*Nevada County & Sacramento Canal Co.* v. *Kidd,* 37 Cal. 282, 309 (1869).

[40]*Cronwall* v. *Talboy,* 45 Idaho 459, 463, 262 Pac. 871 (1928).

[41]*Miller* v. *Lake Irr. Co.,* 27 Wash. 447, 451-452, 67 Pac. 996 (1902).

[42]*Telluride* v. *Davis,* 33 Colo. 355, 356-358, 80 Pac. 1051 (1905).

[43]*Saunders* v. *Spina,* 140 Colo. 317, 344 Pac. (2d) 469, 473 (1959). It does not and cannot adjudge the respective rights and claims of water users under any ditch: *Loshbaugh* v. *Benzel,* 133 Colo. 49, 54, 291 Pac. (2d) 1064 (1956). Nor does it purport to determine what persons own the ditch, or their respective interests in the ditch or in the water which it carries: *Putnam* v. *Curtis,* 7 Colo. App. 437, 440-441, 43 Pac. 1056 (1896).

same ditch—remove his water from the ditch and divert it at another point, for use at another place, or by other means, or for some other purpose of use.[44]

A Colorado statute first enacted in 1879, and still in effect, provides that in time of shortage, when there is not enough water for all appropriators supplied from any ditch or reservoir, all owners and consumers shall receive a share of the available supply in proportion to the quantity which each would have received had there been no deficiency.[45] However, the Colorado Supreme Court held that the several priorities served by a single ditch are protected by the constitution and cannot be interfered with by legislative action. "The most favorable view that can be taken of the statute is that in times of scarcity of water it may be resorted to to compel the prorating of water among consumers having priorities of the same, or nearly the same, date."[46]

There is no vested right by one ditch cotenant to rotation in use of water with another, in the absence of contract therefor or of long-continued custom.[47]

NATURAL CHANNELS AND RESERVOIRS

Use of Natural Channel

Three Interrelated Functions

This topic embraces three related, but to a greater or lesser extent distinguishable, uses. These are: (1) Conveyance of water in the natural channel, which is substituted for a major or minor fraction of a ditch length, and which is usually dry and therefore without complications of conflicting appropriative rights of others. (2) Discharging one's appropriated water into a natural watercourse and commingling it there with flowing water to which existing rights attach. The purpose is to use the watercourse as a conduit for conveying the water to a downstream point at which an adjusted comparable quantity is diverted for distribution and use. (3) Exchange or substitution of water, which involves either (a) discharge of water into a stream and diversion of an adjusted comparable quantity from the stream either above or below the

---

[44]*Telluride* v. *Davis,* 33 Colo. 355, 359-360, 80 Pac. 1051 (1905); *Hallett* v. *Carpenter,* 37 Colo. 30, 32, 86 Pac. 317 (1906); *Ironstone Ditch Co.* v. *Ashenfelter,* 57 Colo. 31, 40, 140 Pac. 177 (1914); *Compton* v. *Knuth,* 117 Colo. 523, 526, 190 Pac. (2d) 117 (1948).

[45]Colo. Laws 1879, p. 79, Rev. Stat. Ann. § 148-3-13 (1963).

[46]*Larimer & Weld Irr. Co.* v. *Wyatt,* 23 Colo. 480, 491, 48 Pac. 528 (1897). "It may therefore be considered as *stare decisis* in this jurisdiction that there may be circumstances in which water consumers from the same ditch may not be compelled to pro-rate with each other." *Farmers' High Line Canal & Res. Co.* v. *White,* 32 Colo. 114, 118-119, 75 Pac. 415 (1904).

[47]*Brighton Ditch Co.* v. *Englewood,* 124 Colo. 366, 374, 237 Pac. (2d) 116 (1951).

point of discharge, or (b) diversion of water from a stream and substitution therefor of water taken from storage or another source.

The first two functions, then, relate to uses of natural channels for conveying water from one place to another and thus avoiding costs of building artificial ditches over such distances. In the first case, the channel carries little or no natural streamflow; in the second case, the flow already there is substantial. The third function emphasizes substitution of water supplies, in the course of which conveyance from one point to another in the natural channel is either incidental or nonexistent.

The three functions are discussed separately below. Inasmuch as to some extent they overlap, with a particular transaction involving more than one function, another section summarizing the separate State statutory provisions includes them all.

Conveyance of Water

The well settled rule. –The California Supreme Court stated in 1906 that:[48]

A person who is making an appropriation of water from a natural source or stream, is not bound to carry it to the place of use through a ditch or artificial conduit, nor through a ditch or canal cut especially for that purpose. He may make use of any natural or artificial channel, or natural depression, which he may find available and convenient for that purpose, so long as other persons interested in such conduit do not object, and his appropriation so made will, so far as such means of conducting the water is concerned, be as effectual as if he had carried it through a ditch or pipe-line made for that purpose and no other. * * *

Responsibility for injury. –The person who takes advantage of this privilege is responsible for any injury resulting from the negligent or unlawful use of the channel.[49] Such limited use of natural channels to the extent that nature has

---

[48]*Lower Tule River Ditch Co.* v. *Angiola Water Co.,* 149 Cal. 496, 498, 86 Pac. 1081 (1906). Much earlier the court had said, "It would be a harsh rule * * * to require those engaged in these enterprises to construct an actual ditch along the whole route through which the waters were carried, and to refuse them the economy that nature occasionally afforded in the shape of a dry ravine, gulch, or canyon." *Hoffman* v. *Stone,* 7 Cal. 46, 49 (1857). *Miller* v. *Wheeler,* 54 Wash. 429, 436, 103 Pac. 641 (1909). One may adopt as a part of his ditch a depression or slough and thus save construction cost: *Bennett* v. *Nourse,* 22 Idaho 249, 255, 125 Pac. 1038 (1912); *Barker* v. *Sonner,* 135 Oreg. 75, 79, 80, 294 Pac. 1053 (1931); *Clark* v. *North Cottonwood Irr. & Water Co.,* 79 Utah 425, 432, 11 Pac. (2d) 300 (1932).

[49]*Blaine County Investment Co.* v. *Mays,* 49 Idaho 766, 775-776, 291 Pac. 1055 (1930). Such use of the channel as to wash excessive quantities of soil into it and to cause winter overflow was enjoinable. One whose use causes overflow is liable in damages under the statute: *Hagadone* v. *Dawson County Irr. Co.,* 136 Nebr. 258, 265, 285 N. W. 600 (1939).

made them such is not inconsistent with ownership of the bed of the stream by the owner of adjoining farm lands.[50]

Privilege impermanent.—The requirement that means of diversion and distribution must be reasonably efficient (see "Efficiency of Practices," later) applies to natural channels used for the conveyance of water as well as to artificial conduits. The courts took the view long ago that an old natural depression in such condition as to result in considerable waste of water should be replaced by a good ditch.[51] Readily avoidable waste of water finds less and less favor with courts and administrators.

Statutes.—It will be noted later, under "Summary of State Statutory Provisions," that authorization to use natural channels for conveying water, with appropriate limitations and safeguards, is contemplated by various statutes, but chiefly with respect to commingling in flowing streams and to exchanges of water.

Commingling

The general rule.—Most Western State statutes very specifically authorize the practice of commingling—that water appropriated out of one stream may be turned into the channel of another stream, mingled with the water already flowing there, and then reclaimed, provided that the quantity of water to which prior appropriators are entitled shall not be diminished or its quality impaired, and that due allowance is made for losses by evaporation and seepage. In the water administration States, these acts are necessarily carried out under the supervision of the local administrative agents. The high courts that have had occasion to consider this widespread statutory and judicial rule generally have approved it.[52]

---

[50]*Pleasant Valley Irr. & Power Co.* v. *Barker,* 98 Wash. 459, 462-463, 167 Pac. 1092 (1917).

[51]*Stickney* v. *Hanrahan,* 7 Idaho 424, 433, 63 Pac. 189 (1900). In a statutory adjudication, the Oregon Supreme Court criticized as obviously wasteful the long established custom of utilizing sloughs and natural depressions for carrying water, and declared that such means should be sanctioned only until a fair opportunity arises to replace them with artificial works: *In re Silvies River,* 115 Oreg. 27, 44, 237 Pac. 322 (1925).

[52]*Sorenson* v. *Norell,* 24 Colo. App. 470, 471-472, 135 Pac. 119 (1913); *Pleasant Valley Irr. & Power Co.* v. *Barker,* 98 Wash. 459, 462-463, 167 Pac. 1092 (1917); *MacKinnon* v. *Black Pine Min. Co.,* 32 Idaho 228, 230, 179 Pac. 951 (1919); *United States* v. *Caldwell,* 64 Utah 490, 496-497, 231 Pac. 434 (1924). Waters conveyed in the Rio Grande from place of storage to places of use did not become part of the streamflow to which a riparian owner was entitled: *Parker* v. *El Paso County W. I. Dist. No. 1,* 116 Tex. 631, 643-644, 297 S. W. 737 (1927). Citing this *Parker* case, the City of El Paso was held by a Federal court to have the right to use the riverbed as a conduit to convey

No abandonment.—In mingling one's waters with those flowing in a stream for the purpose of diverting an equivalent quantity below, there is obviously no intention of abandoning the water; certainly abandonment does not result from such temporary release of the waters from the appropriator's control with the avowed intent to recapture.[53] While approving this rule for situations in which there is no intent to abandon, but on the contrary a specific purpose to effectuate a planned recapture, the Nevada Supreme Court in an early decision correctly pointed out that it did not apply to the circumstances of the case at bar, where "the water was discharged into the stream as a matter of convenience, and without intention of recapturing it."[54]

Limitations on exercise.—Exercise of the practice of commingling is subject to important limitations declared from time to time in the statutes or in decisions of the courts. (The statutory limitations are stated later under "Summary of State Statutory Provisions.") In the first place, the appropriator has no claim to any part of the natural flow by virtue of exercising the practice; hence, he is not entitled to take from the stream any larger quantity of water than he turned into it.[55]

There must be no deprivation of the quantities of water to which prior appropriators are entitled.[56] Nor must there be an injurious impairment of the quality of the water for the purposes for which the prior user appropriated it, such as for domestic uses.[57] The quality requirement is most important in that

---

water that it had pumped from wells: *El Paso County W. I. Dist. No. 1* v. *El Paso,* 133 Fed. Supp. 894, 926-927 (W. D. Tex. 1955).

In *State ex rel. Reynolds* v. *Luna Irr. Co.,* 80 N. Mex. 515, 458 Pac. (2d) 590, 591 (1969), the New Mexico Supreme Court held that waters released from a dam in Arizona, conveyed over a largely dry river bed, and intercepted by diversion dams for irrigation use in New Mexico, became public waters of New Mexico within the meaning of New Mex. Stat. Ann. § 75-1-1 (1968) and hence were subject to adjudication in New Mexico. The court added that "When surface waters are released from storage into a 'dry' river bed they necessarily merge and interchange with the ground waters of the stream system." However, the court apparently did not conclude anything regarding the nature of the rights in such waters other than to merely refute Luna Irrigation Company's contention that, since such waters were its own private waters, it should be excluded from an action begun by the State Engineer to adjudicate water rights in the stream in New Mexico.

[53] *Butte Canal & Ditch Co.* v. *Vaughn,* 11 Cal. 143, 151-152, 154 (1858); *Los Angeles* v. *Glendale,* 23 Cal. (2d) 68, 76, 142 Pac. (2d) 289 (1943); *Herriman Irr. Co.* v. *Keel,* 25 Utah 96, 115, 69 Pac. 719 (1902).

[54] *Schulz* v. *Sweeny,* 19 Nev. 359, 361-362, 11 Pac. 253 (1886).

[55] *Paige* v. *Rocky Ford Canal & Irr. Co.,* 83 Cal. 84, 94-96, 21 Pac. 1102 (1889); *Meine* v. *Ferris,* 126 Mont. 210, 217, 247 Pac. (2d) 195 (1952); *Miller* v. *Wheeler,* 54 Wash. 429, 438, 103 Pac. 641 (1909).

[56] *Miller* v. *Wheeler,* 54 Wash. 429, 438, 103 Pac. 641 (1909).

[57] *Missoula Pub. Serv. Co.* v. *Bitter Root Irr. Dist.,* 80 Mont. 64, 68-69, 257 Pac. 1038 (1927). The fact that the water deposited in the stream never caused the flow to reach the high-water mark did not excuse the junior appropriator from the consequences of infringing the prior appropriator's right by impairing the quality of the water.

it concerns the public as well as private interests, and it must be strictly complied with.[58]

The Utah statute authorizing commingling and recovery or substitution of water requires prior written application to and approval of the State Engineer.[59] The supreme court holds that one who seeks to take advantage of the statute by allowing surplus or waste water to enter a slough, but without complying with the statutory provisions, loses dominion over such water.[60]

A water appropriator who makes use of a natural channel for conveyance of water is responsible for any injury resulting from negligent or unlawful use, such as causing overflow above the accustomed high-water level.[61]

Burden of proof.—Early in the history of the appropriation doctrine in the West, it was established that the burden of proof is on the party who exercises the privilege of commingling, to show that he is not taking out more water than the quantity that belongs to him.[62] In one of its earliest mining decisions, the California Supreme Court recognized the difficulty of determining with accuracy the quantity of water the parties are entitled to divert after commingling, and stated that:[63]

If exact justice cannot be obtained, an approximation to it must be sought, care being taken that no injury is done to the innocent party. The burden of proof rests with the party causing the mixture. He must show clearly to what portion he is entitled. He can claim only such portion as is established by decisive proof. The enforcement of his right must leave the opposite party in the use of the full quantity to which he was originally entitled.

When commingling practices are carried out under supervision of a watermaster, and gains and losses in transit are determined by the administrative authority as a result of reliable measurements, the determination of what the opposing parties are entitled to is reduced to an impartial, scientific basis.

---

[58]*Little Cottonwood Water Co.* v. *Kimball,* 76 Utah 243, 252-253, 289 Pac. 116 (1930). The supreme court affirmed a trial court order directing rejection by the State Engineer of an application to commingle water, on the ground that the inferior quality of the water proposed to be turned into a creek would render the entire stream below the place of entry unfit for domestic and culinary purposes. The scheme for supplying potable water for domestic use through a pipeline to all persons entitled thereto from the stream "does not meet the requirements of the statute" that the original water in the stream "must not be deteriorated in quality * * * for the purpose used."

[59]Utah Code Ann. § 73-3-20 (1968). *United States* v. *Caldwell,* 64 Utah 490, 496-497, 231 Pac. 434 (1924).

[60]*Lasson* v. *Seely,* 120 Utah 679, 687, 238 Pac. (2d) 418 (1951).

[61]*Blaine County Investment Co.* v. *Mays,* 49 Idaho 766, 775-776, 291 Pac. 1055 (1930); *Hagadone* v. *Dawson County Irr. Co.,* 136 Nebr. 258, 265, 285 N. W. 600 (1939).

[62]*Herriman Irr. Co.* v. *Keel,* 25 Utah 96, 115, 69 Pac. 719 (1902). " * * * it is an elementary principle, firmly established, that one who, without consent, intentionally confounds his property with the property of a stranger, though they be of the same kind, will lose the whole unless he can prove the true quantity belonging to himself." *Herriman Irr. Co.* v. *Butterfield Min. Co.,* 19 Utah 453, 464, 57 Pac. 537 (1899).

[63]*Butte Canal & Ditch Co.* v. *Vaughn,* 11 Cal. 143, 152-153 (1858).

Exchange or Substitution of Water

Interrelationships.—This topic is closely related to (a) use of a natural channel for conveyance of water and (b) commingling and recapture of water. Acts of exchange or substitution may involve one or both of these previous topics, or neither of them. For example:

(a) Acts of discharging impounded water or direct flow into a stream, and rediverting an equivalent quantity of water at a distant point below, involves them both. Although there is no pretense—or even a legal fiction—that the same particles of water are recaptured, the processes of using the channel for transportation, for commingling and recapture, and for exchange of stored or direct flow waters for waters already in the stream are all carried out. This is the case, regardless of whether the downstream diversion is made at the same time as the upstream discharge into the channel, or at an earlier or a later date.

(b) On the other hand, the acts of discharging into a stream either stored water or direct flow from another source, and of diverting comparable quantities at a higher point or from an upstream tributary, involve neither channel transportation nor commingling and rediversion of this artificial increment.

The principle.—A good abridgment of this long recognized principle appears in a decision of the Oregon Supreme Court in 1943:[64]

A subsequent appropriator may assert the right to take the waters of the stream from which the prior appropriation has been made and give the prior appropriator in return therefor other water from a different source, but of like quantity and quality delivered at such a place that the prior appropriator can make full use thereof without being injured in any way.* * *

* * * the substitution of impounded water in the same quantity and of the same quality for water normally flowing in the natural stream does not constitute a trespass or infringement upon or a restriction of the rights of lower appropriators.

Nor does such an exchange or substitution of water constitute an abandonment of the water rights involved. "Abandonment is a matter of intention."[65]

---

[64]*Dry Gulch Ditch Co.* v. *Hutton,* 170 Oreg. 656, 675, 681, 133 Pac. (2d) 601 (1943). Exchange of water in artificial ditch for right-of-way: *Methow Cattle Co.* v. *Williams,* 64 Wash. 457, 460, 117 Pac. 239 (1911). Water exchange agreements between Salt Lake City and mutual irrigation companies: *Baird* v. *Upper Canal Irr. Co.,* 70 Utah 57, 257 Pac. 1060 (1927); *Salt Lake City* v. *McFarland,* 1 Utah (2d) 257, 265 Pac. (2d) 626 (1954).

[65]*Middle Creek Ditch Co.* v. *Henry,* 15 Mont. 558, 560-565, 572-581, 39 Pac. 1054 (1895). In this case, the exchange contract was in writing, but was not acknowledged or recorded. The court held that by conveying, by an instrument in writing sufficient for the purpose, the use of water for a valuable consideration, the acts of the parties indicated an intention precisely opposite to that of abandonment. For some one-time

Where a clear case of benefit and noninjury is made, the power to execute such an exchange may be exercised.[66] It has been held in Utah that an application to make such an exchange cannot be rejected by the State Engineer without a showing that vested rights will thereby be substantially impaired.[67]

Limitations on exercise.—In Oregon, the supreme court cautioned that: "While an exchange of waters is permitted, such exchange cannot be given the effect of changing priority rights to the extent that one holding an older priority before such exchange thereafter should be deemed no longer the owner of a senior priority but only that of a priority junior to the other party to such exchange."[68]

The foregoing statement accords with the rule that under no circumstances can an exchange of water be lawfully brought about where it would be to the detriment of prior users, or would result in depriving them of a property right.[69] Thus, an attempt to acquire the right to turn appropriated water into the lowline canal of an irrigation company, and to pump an equivalent quantity out of its highline canal far higher than the point of entry, was rejected by the Idaho Supreme Court.[70] Another proposed exchange was disapproved because of excessive deterioration of the quality of streamflow that would result.[71]

In a fairly early Colorado case, it was held that the question of exchanges of water between the same or different owners of ditches or reservoirs is a matter wholly foreign to the object of a statutory adjudication proceeding, and should be determined in some other appropriate proceeding brought for that specific purpose. But, said the court, no such system of exchange that necessarily converts a junior into a senior right can be sanctioned by a court of equity.[72] In Utah, one who proposes to exercise this privilege must first have the formal approval of the State Engineer.[73]

---

conflicting views as to the effect of informal transfer upon priority of water right. see in chapter 8 "Property Characteristics—Conveyance of Title to Appropriative Right—Some Aspects of Conveyance of Appropriative Titles—Formalities of Conveyance."

[66]*Board of Directors of Wilder Irr. Dist.* v. *Jorgensen,* 64 Idaho 538, 546-550, 136 Pac. (2d) 461 (1943); *King* v. *Ackroyd,* 28 Colo. 488, 495, 66 Pac. 906 (1901).

[67]*Salt Lake City* v. *Boundary Springs Water Users Assn.,* 2 Utah (2d) 141, 143-144, 270 Pac. (2d) 453 (1954).

[68]*Dry Gulch Ditch Co.* v. *Hutton,* 170 Oreg. 656, 684, 133 Pac. (2d) 601 (1943).

[69]*Daniels* v. *Adair,* 38 Idaho 130, 135, 220 Pac. 107 (1923). In this case, an unsuccessful attempt was made to enforce an acceptance of undecreed waters in exchange for decreed waters.

[70]*Berg* v. *Twin Falls Canal Co.,* 36 Idaho 62, 64-66, 213 Pac. 694 (1922). Further mention is made of this case in discussing statutory constructions, below.

[71]*Little Cottonwood Water Co.* v. *Kimball,* 76 Utah 243, 252-253, 289 Pac. 116 (1930).

[72]*Windsor Res. & Canal Co.* v. *Lake Supply Ditch Co.,* 44 Colo. 214, 226, 98 Pac. 729 (1908).

[73]Utah Code Ann. § 73-3-20 (1968). *United States* v. *Caldwell,* 64 Utah 490, 496-497, 231 Pac. 434 (1924).

Burden of proof.—The person who seeks to exercise the privilege of exchanging water has the general burden of showing that no impairment of vested rights will result from the change.[74] The earlier comments on burden of proof under "Commingling," would be either directly or impliedly applicable here.

Substitution of prior appropriator's diversion.—This feature is stated as follows:[75]

An appropriator of water from a running stream is entitled to have it flow down the natural channel to his point of diversion undiminished in quantity and quality or, if diverted from the natural channel by other appropriators for their conveneince, to have it delivered to him at available points by other means provided by subsequent appropriators and at their expense. This seems to be a rule of general accommodation and utility and has been universally followed by the courts when applied to surface streams. * * *

In adhering to this rule in several cases, the Utah Supreme Court emphasized that changes in established means of diversion of prior appropriators by junior claimants must be at the expense of the latter,[76] and that the substitute water "be returned into the stream or into the ditch or canal of the prior appropriator, if that is done at a point where the prior appropriator can make full use of the water, and without injury or damage to him."[77]

Some statutory constructions.—Herein are judicial comments and constructions of several of the State statutes relating to uses of natural channels that are summarized and cited later under "Summary of State Statutory Provisions".

(1) Colorado. The plan of exchange of water authorized by statute was operated extensively in Cache la Poudre Valley. This plan, which embraced a

---

[74]*Salt Lake City* v. *Boundary Springs Water Users Assn.,* 2 Utah (2d) 141, 143-144, 270 Pac. (2d) 453 (1954).

[75]*Pima Farms Co.* v. *Proctor,* 30 Ariz. 96, 106-107, 245 Pac. 369 (1926). For administrative complications foreseen by the court, see *Maricopa County M.W.C. Dist.* v. *Southwest Cotton Co.,* 39 Ariz. 367, 370, 7 Pac. (2d) 254 (1932). Substitution of pipeline for headgates on a heavily losing channel by agreement of the parties: *Basinger* v. *Taylor,* 30 Idaho 289, 293, 164 Pac. 522 (1917), 36 Idaho 591, 596, 211 Pac. 1085 (1922).

[76]*Salt Lake City* v. *Gardner,* 39 Utah 30, 45-47, 114 Pac. 147 (1911); *Big Cottonwood Tanner Ditch Co.* v. *Shurtliff,* 56 Utah 196, 204-205, 189 Pac. 587 (1919).

[77]*United States* v. *Caldwell,* 64 Utah 490, 497-498, 231 Pac. 434 (1924). A decree authorizing a power company entitled, for the purpose of operating its power plant to a secondary use of the water of a river, to take the water from the river above a prior appropriator's point of diversion and to convey it down to its powerhouse, and then to flume it into the canal of the former appropriator, does not destroy that part of the canal above the point where such water is thus discharged into it, nor take from such prior appropriator the right to control the flow of its own water; the prior appropriator having the right to convey the water which such power company does not use, and it also having the right to control its canal: *Salt Lake City* v. *Salt City Water & Elec. Power Co.,* 24 Utah 249, 266, 67 Pac. 672 (1902), 25 Utah 456, 71 Pac. 1069 (1903).

most intricate system of exchanging water among mutual irrigation companies under local administrative supervision, made possible the storage of waters in reservoirs located below the canals of companies that owned them, for eventual delivery to downstream canals in return for late-season use by the upper canals of direct streamflow to which the lower canals were entitled by virtue of their direct-flow rights. It was studied and reported upon in a Bulletin of the United States Department of Agriculture published in 1922.[78] According to this account, 12 reservoirs in Cache la Poudre Valley, with an aggregate capacity of about 50,000 acre-feet, were built by the several companies below their distributing canals, and "in 1916, an average year, the operation of the exchange system made available for use on higher land about 55,000 acre-feet of water stored in low reservoirs, or 14 percent of the total supply used by all the canals of the valley."

In a case decided in 1918, the Colorado Supreme Court observed, with respect to the Cache la Poudre Valley, that: "It appears * * * that by reason of the exchange of water for irrigation among various appropriators, the rights of water users are unusually complicated and interrelated."[79] Ten years earlier it was held that the question of exchanges of water between the same or different owners of ditches or reservoirs was a matter wholly foreign to the object of a statutory adjudication proceeding, and should be determined in some other appropriate proceeding brought for that specific purpose; but that no such system of exchange that necessarily converts a junior into a senior right can be sanctioned by a court of equity.[80] Insofar as Cache la Poudre Valley is concerned, the major direct-flow rights were fixed by court decree in 1882 and storage rights in 1909.[81]

Another Colorado statute, originally enacted in 1899 and still in effect,[82] provides that for the purpose of saving crops, and under the supervision of the water commissioner, appropriators of water from the same stream may exchange with and loan to each other, for a limited time, the water to which they are entitled. The supreme court promptly took a rather critical view of this statute by holding, in *Fort Lyon Canal Company* v. *Chew,* that if it is operative at all, it must be with due regard to the rights of other appropriators who may be affected; that such exchanges or loans should not be permitted, "if at all," without a clear showing that the vested rights of others are not injured.[83] Two years later, the court appeared to relent a little. In answer to a

---

[78]Hemphill, Robert G., "Irrigation in Northern Colorado," U.S. Dept. Agr. Bull. 1026, at pp. 12-13 and 80-81 (1922).
[79] *Water Supply & Storage Co.* v. *Larimer & Weld Res. Co.,* 65 Colo. 504, 505, 179 Pac. 870 (1918).
[80] *Windsor Res. & Canal Co.* v. *Lake Supply Ditch Co.,* 44 Colo. 214, 226, 98 Pac. 729 (1908).
[81]Hemphill, *supra* note 78, at 81.
[82]Colo. Laws 1899, p. 236, Rev. Stat. Ann. § 148-6-5 (1963).
[83] *Fort Lyon Canal Co.* v. *Chew,* 33 Colo. 392, 400-405, 81 Pac. 37 (1905).

contention that the act was unconstitutional, it was held that the *Fort Lyon* decision had disposed of the difficulty "by placing a construction upon the statute in question, which permits an exchange or loan of water under circumstances and conditions which do not injuriously affect the vested rights of other appropriators."[84]

(2) Idaho. The water rights statute authorizes the substitution of direct flow from a stream or tributary for stored or other waters discharged into it, provided rights of prior appropriators are properly protected and approval of the State administrative agency has been obtained. Where a clear case of benefit and noninjury is made, such an exchange may be and has been approved.[85] But it is not sanctioned if the exchange would be detrimental to prior appropriators or would result in depriving them of a property right.[86]

The statute provides that "water may be turned into any *ditch,* natural channel or waterway from reservoirs or other sources of water supply, and such water may be substituted or exchanged for an equal amount of water diverted from the *stream, creek or river* into which such water flows, or any tributary thereof, * * *."[87] [Emphasis supplied.] A novel attempt to invoke the rule, but without reference to any natural channel or stream, was frowned upon by the Idaho Supreme Court. The attempt was to acquire the right to turn appropriated water into the lowline canal of a mutual irrigation company, and to pump an equivalent quantity out of the company's main canal at a point on the system far higher than the point of discharge into the lowline. It was held that there was no statutory authorization for such utilization of the company's property without compensation, and that the right could not be acquired by condemning the use of a small part of the lowline for the purpose of turning creek water into it and a small part of the main canal for the purpose of taking out a like amount.[88]

(3) Montana. Long before the statute authorizing exchange of stored water for direct flow was enacted,[89] the Montana Supreme Court approved an exchange of appropriative rights for natural flow diverted from one stream into another stream—involving a conveyance of water rights by an unrecorded deed.[90]

---

[84]*Bowman* v. *Virdin,* 40 Colo. 247, 249-251, 90 Pac. 506 (1907).

[85]*Reno* v. *Richards,* 32 Idaho 1, 5, 178 Pac. 81 (1918); *Board of Directors of Wilder Irr. Dist.* v. *Jorgensen,* 64 Idaho 538, 546-550, 136 Pac. (2d) 461 (1943). See also *Keller* v. *Magic Water Co.,* 92 Idaho 276, 441 Pac. (2d) 725, 732-734 (1968).

[86]*Daniels* v. *Adair,* 38 Idaho 130, 135-136, 220 Pac. 107 (1923).

[87]Idaho Code Ann. § 42-105 (Supp. 1969).

[88]*Berg* v. *Twin Falls Canal Co.,* 36 Idaho 62, 64-66, 213 Pac. 694 (1922). "Whether appellants could condemn a right to use the whole system for the purpose contemplated is not before us, and need not be decided."

[89]Mont. Rev. Codes Ann. § 89-806 (1964).

[90]*Middle Creek Ditch Co.* v. *Henry,* 15 Mont. 558, 560-565, 572, 39 Pac. 1054 (1895). There was no abandonment of water rights, despite the lack of formality in making the conveyance. See the discussion of this case at note *65 supra.*

(4) New Mexico. The statutory provision not only authorizes delivery of water into a stream or watercourse in exchange for water diverted therefrom above or below the point of delivery, but also includes "any ditch" in the authorization.[91] To the extent that this authorizes the taking of a property right without compensation, in failing to provide for compensation to the owner of a ditch in a case in which a nonowner attempts to take advantage of the statute, this was held unconstitutional.[92] The court specifically confined its disapproval to cases in which the question concerns the use of senior ditches, constructed and maintained at cost to the owners, without compensation. It has no application to cases in which the use of natural watercourses is involved, concerning which the court saw no objection.

(5) Wyoming. Referring to the statute that authorizes appropriators to arrange among themselves for the delivery of either storage or direct flow water from another source,[93] the Wyoming Supreme Court quoted the first section and stressed that: "It will be observed that this exchange must be made 'by agreement.' "[94]

Other waters at the surface.—Decisions have been rendered from time to time with respect to rights to exchange salvaged, developed, and return waters for natural streamflow. These matters are discussed later in chapter 18.

Summary of State Statutory Provisions

The several State statutory provisions relating to use of natural channels for conveyance of water, commingling, and exchange or substitution of water are summarized in the following paragraphs:

Arizona.—Natural channels may be used to convey water, but without diminishing the flow already appropriated. If necessary, the water superintendent divides the water (§ 45-173). Procedure is provided for the use of a streambed to convey stored water from a reservoir to the consumer under supervision of the water division superintendent (§ 45-174).[95]

California.—Nothing in the chapter relating to maintenance of flow in streams is to prevent the use or enlargement of any natural channel for (1) municipal purposes, or for use in connection with any artificial irrigation, drainage, or flood control system that does not lower the quantity of appropriated water (§ 7043), or (2) for conveyance of appropriated water where the channel is designated as part or all of the means of conveyance (§ 7044). Appropriated water may be turned into another stream channel,

---

[91]N. Mex. Stat. Ann. § 75-5-24 (1968).

[92]*Miller* v. *Hagerman Irr. Co.*, 20 N. Mex. 604, 612-614, 151 Pac. 763 (1915). The State can compel such portage of water in a private ditch only when just compensation is made.

[93]Wyo. Stat. Ann. § § 41-5 to -8 (1957).

[94]*In re Owl Creek Irr. Dist.*, 71 Wyo. 70, 258 Pac. (2d) 220 (1953).

[95]Ariz. Rev. Stat. Ann. § § 45-173 and -174 (1956).

mingled with its water, and reclaimed, but without diminishing the quantity already appropriated by another (§ 7075).[96]

Colorado.—Natural streams may be used to transport reservoir waters to specific points under the supervision of State water officials, losses to be determined by the State Engineer (§§ 148-5-2 and 148-5-3). Water may be diverted from one stream and turned into and mingled with the water of another, from which the same quantity may be taken minus losses determined by the State Engineer (§§ 148-6-1 to 148-6-3). If other rights are not injured, stored water may be delivered into a ditch or stream to supply appropriations therefrom, and an equal quantity less deductions for loss (to be determined by the State Engineer) may be taken from the stream higher up, under the supervision of the water commissioner (§ 148-6-4). Under the supervision of the water commissioner, appropriators from the same stream may exchange with and loan to each other, for a limited time, the water to which they are entitled for the purpose of saving crops (§ 148-6-5).[97]

Idaho.—(1) Appropriated water may be turned into another stream channel, mingled with its water, and reclaimed. (2) Stored or other waters may be turned into any ditch, natural channel, or waterway from reservoirs or other sources, and substituted for an equal quantity (minus transmission losses) diverted from the watercourse into which such water flows or from any tributary, the rights of prior appropriators not to be impaired, State administrative approval required, and written agreement among parties to be filed with State in form approved by the attorney general (42-105 and -240). Procedure is provided for the conveyance of stored water through natural channels under the supervision of the Department of Reclamation (§§ 42-801 and -802).[98]

Kansas.—Natural streams or channels may be used to convey water, due allowance to be made for evaporation and seepage losses.[99]

Montana.—Stream channels may be used to convey appropriated waters but without injury to other rights (§ 89-804). Stored water may be discharged into a stream in exchange for equal quantities of natural flow if prior appropriators are not injured (§ 89-806). With respect to unadjudicated streams only, procedure is provided for regulating conveyances of stored water through natural stream channels on petition of reservoir controllers (§ 89-857 to -864).[100]

Nebraska.—Appropriated water may be returned to the stream and the same quantity diverted less transit losses to be determined by the

[96]Cal. Water Code §§ 7043, 7044, and 7075 (West 1956).
[97]Colo. Rev. Stat. Ann. §§ 148-5-2, 148-5-3, 148-6-1, to 148-6-5 (1963).
[98]Idaho Code Ann. § 42-105, -240 (Supp. 1969), -801, and -802 (1948).
[99]Kans. Stat. Ann. § 42-303 (1964).
[100]Mont. Rev. Codes Ann. §§ 89-804, -806, and -857 to -864 (1964).

Department of Water Resources, not to the prejudice of a prior appropriator (§ 46-241(2)). Such commingling and withdrawal may be made "without regard to any prior appropriation" with prior written consent of a majority of the contiguous residents and landowners, liability for damages from overflow to be imposed (§ 46-252).[101]

Nevada.—Water stored either in Nevada or in an adjoining State may be turned into any natural channel or watercourse and claimed for beneficial use below, allowance for losses to be made by the State Engineer (§ 533.055). Other sections authorize commingling and reclamation of stored water (§ 533.525); procedure for State regulation therefor (§ 533.445); installation of measuring devices (§ 536.010).[102]

New Mexico.—Water may be turned into any ditch, stream, or watercourse to supply appropriations therefrom in exchange for water taken above or below the point of delivery, less transmission losses determined by the State Engineer, if other appropriators are not injured.[103]

North Dakota.—Water turned into a natural or artificial watercourse by any party entitled to its use may be reclaimed below, subject to existing rights, allowance for losses to be determined by the State Engineer (§ 61-01-05). The Water Conservation Commission, in using streams for conveying water to the place of use, is directed to adopt proper means of determining the natural flow when insufficient to satisfy prior rights (§ 61-02-36).[104]

Oklahoma.—Water turned into a natural or artificial watercourse by any party entitled to its use may be reclaimed and diverted below, subject to existing rights, conveyance losses to be determined by the Water Resources Board.[105]

Oregon.—The bed of a stream or other watercourse may be used to transport water from a reservoir, constructed under the provisions of the Water Rights Act, to the consumers. The district watermaster adjusts stream headgates. One-half of the watermaster expense is charged to the reservoir.[106]

South Dakota.—Water turned into a natural or artificial watercourse by any person entitled to its use may be reclaimed and diverted below, subject to existing rights, due allowance for losses to be determined by the State Water Resources Commission.[107]

Texas.—For conveyance of stored water to the place of use or point of diversion, natural stream channels may be used under rules and regulations

[101] Nebr. Rev. Stat. § § 46-241(2) and -252 (1968).
[102] Nev. Rev. Stat. § § 533.055, .525 (Supp. 1967), .445, and 536.010 (Supp. 1969).
[103] N. Mex. Stat. Ann. § 75-5-24 (1968).
[104] N. Dak. Cent. Code Ann. § § 61-01-05 and 61-02-36 (1960).
[105] Okla. Stat. Ann. tit. 82, § 3 (1970).
[106] Oreg. Rev. Stat. § 540.410 (Supp. 1969).
[107] S. Dak. Comp. Laws Ann. § 45-5-14 (1967).

prescribed by the Texas Water Rights Commission (art. 7548). As directed by the statute, the Commission has promulgated rules and regulations governing such use of natural stream channels (rules 520.1 to 520.6). When stored storm and flood waters are released from storage on an international stream and are designated for capture downstream by a specified user entitled thereto, interference with the passage of such waters is declared unlawful and the Commission is empowered to effectuate the statutory provisions (art. 7550a).[108]

Utah.—With approval of the State Engineer, appropriated water may be turned into a natural stream channel or body of water, or into an on-channel reservoir, commingled with its waters, and rediverted, minus transmission losses, either above or below the point of discharge into the stream, but without injuriously affecting the quantity or quality of water already there. Incoming water bears its equitable share of reservoir costs. Withdrawals are not to interfere with rights of others.[109]

Washington.—Water may be conveyed along a natural stream or lake, allowance for transmission losses to be determined by the Director of Ecology. Compensation is payable for injuries caused by raising the water level above high water mark.[110]

Wyoming.—A streambed may be used to carry impounded water to the consumer, or a ditch may be used to carry such water to a person having the right to have the water carried therethrough, under regulations by the water commissioner. Part of the expense of supervision is charged against the reservoir operator (§ 41-29). If prior appropriators are not injured, junior appropriators may divert from a stream, for irrigation, industrial, or municipal purposes, direct flow to which downstream seniors are entitled, in lieu of an equal quantity of water stored by the upstream juniors in reservoirs located below their lands and discharged into the stream above the lands of the downstream seniors. The exchange is authorized by secondary permit from the State Engineer and is administered by the water commissioner (§§ 41-42 to -44). Appropriators of waters of streams or springs or collections of still water may arrange among themselves such agreements for delivery and use of either storage or direct flow water from another source to fill out their appropriations or accomplish fuller use of public water, but with no adverse effect upon other rights. Such use is without prejudice to the original appropriator (§§ 41-5 to -8).[111]

---

[108]Tex. Rev. Civ. Stat. Ann. arts. 7548 (1954) and 7550a (Supp. 1970). Tex. Water Rights Comm'n, "Rules, Regulations and Modes of Procedure," rules 520.1 to 520.6 (1970 Rev., Jan 1970).

[109]Utah Code Ann. § 73-3-20 (1968).

[110]Wash. Rev. Code § 90.03.030 (Supp. 1961).

[111]Wyo. Stat. Ann. §§ 41-5 to -8, -29, -44 (1957), -42, and -43 (Supp. 1969).

Use of Natural Reservoir

"It is of course elementary that a natural depression may be utilized as a reservoir if no one is injured thereby."[112]

In one of its very early decisions, the Colorado Supreme Court held that in the absence of any written law on the subject, a person would have the legal right to construct a dam on a nonnavigable stream on the public domain for the purpose of creating a storage reservoir, so long as he did not encroach on the superior rights of others. "The act of utilizing as a reservoir a natural depression, which included the bed of the stream, or which was found at the source thereof, was not in and of itself unlawful."[113]

In 1943, the long established rule authorizing the use of natural channels in the handling of water was extended by the California Supreme Court to natural reservoirs. The City of Los Angeles was engaged in spreading waters for underground storage as the most practical method of storage under the local conditions. The court referred to the fact that in the early history of the State it had recognized the advantage of permitting the use of natural surface facilities, streambeds, dry canyons, and the like for transportation of water. This rule so established by the judiciary was incorporated in the Civil Code in 1872;[114] and the court now believed that in codifying this rule in the Water Code in 1943[115] the legislature could hardly have intended to abrogate the right to use other natural facilities for similar purposes. "It would be as harsh to compel plaintiff to build reservoirs when natural ones were available as to compel the construction of an artificial ditch beside a stream bed."[116]

Although the use of natural lakes and reservoirs for storage of water has apparently not been involved in controversies that have gone to the high courts of Texas, there seems to be ample reason to conclude that under the statutes of that State water may be stored in natural reservoirs, as well as in those created artificially, provided of course that the littoral rights of surrounding landowners are not infringed.[117]

ROTATION IN USE OF WATER

The Problem and the Plan

Rotation in the use of a considerable stream of water is regularly practiced within many irrigation projects for the purpose of avoiding the losses and

---

[112] *Perkins* v. *Kramer,* 121 Mont. 595, 599, 198 Pac. (2d) 475 (1948).

[113] *Larimer County Res. Co.* v. *People ex rel. Luthe,* 8 Colo. 614, 615, 617, 9 Pac. 794 (1886).

[114] Cal. Civ. Code § 1413 (1872).

[115] Cal. Water Code § 7075 (West 1956).

[116] *Los Angeles* v. *Glendale,* 23 Cal. (2d) 68, 76-77, 142 Pac. (2d) 289 (1943).

[117] Appropriable waters may be held or stored by dams, in *lakes or reservoirs.* Tex. Rev. Civ. Stat. Ann. art. 7468 (Supp. 1970). Storm and floodwaters may be appropriated for storage in a part of the Edwards underground reservoir for later use. *Id.* art. 7470.

inefficiency which so often are found to attend the continuous delivery to farms of a multiplicity of small "heads" or "streams," as they are variously called.[118]

Likewise, rotation is sometimes practiced as among independent diversions of water from watercourses as a result of court decrees or agreement of the water users. The practice requires a schedule under which each water user is entitled to divert the entire flow of the stream (or that fraction of the flow to which those involved in the plan are entitled to divert in the aggregate) for, say, one, two, or three consecutive days during each 15-day period. The length of each particular water user's time of use—or turn—during each period is computed according to the ratio which his appropriative right bears to all rights involved in the schedule. Like all other variations from the strict plan of diversion of streamflow according to priorities of right, a rotation plan imposed by court decree upon a group of water users must be equitable to them all with full regard for their rights as against each other; and such a plan, whether imposed by the court or entered into by common agreement of the parties, must not infringe the rights of others on the stream who are not parties to the plan.

Under many sets of circumstances, and particularly during periods of water shortage, rotation in the complete diversion of a streamflow to the use of which a number of users are collectively entitled gives better results than does the continuous diversion by each water-right holder of his small fraction of the total flow. It is true that in certain areas the prevailing topographic and soil conditions, landownerships, character of crops grown, and cultural habits of the farmers are such as to encourage the use of small streams for long periods of time. Under other circumstances, large heads for shorter periods are preferable.[119]

Where conditions are such as to favor the use of large streams for short periods, and appropriators therefore have only intermittent need for the quantities of water they have appropriated, a plan of rotation may improve the exercise of the junior rights without materially impairing those of their seniors.

Statutory Authorization to Rotate Water Uses

Statutes of several Western States specifically authorize appropriations of water from a common supply to rotate in the use of water to which they are collectively entitled.[120]

---

[118]Hutchins, Wells A., "Delivery of Irrigation Water," U. S. Dept. Agr., Tech. Bull. 47, pp. 7-24 (1928).

[119]Hutchins, supra note 118, at pp. 22-24.

[120]Ariz. Rev. Stat. Ann. § 45-245(B) (1956); Kans. Stat. Ann. § § 42-340 to -347 (1964); Nebr. Rev. Stat. § 46-231 (1968); Nev. Rev. Stat. § 533.075 (Supp. 1967); Oreg. Rev. Stat. § 540.150 (Supp. 1969); Wash. Rev. Code § 90.03.390 (Supp. 1961); Wyo. Stat. Ann. § 41-70 (1957).

The purpose of such legislation, whether expressed or implied, is to enable irrigators to exercise their water rights more efficiently, and thus to bring about more economical use of available water supplies. Nevada's authorization is made "to the end that each user may have an irrigation head of at least 2 cubic feet per second."

Most of these statutes confer this right upon users of water who own lands to which water rights are attached or appurtenant. Kansas extends it to proprietors of two or more irrigation works who, with the written consent of their water users, agree to rotate all or part of their combined supply. Arizona and Oregon provide for written agreements in accordance with which the local State administrative official makes the agreed distribution. Washington requires approval of the local watermaster or the State Director of Ecology. In Wyoming, prior written notice of intention to rotate must be given to the district water commissioner. The Kansas statute requires that the agreement be delivered to the superintendent of the ditch, conduit, reservoir or lateral and, in the event the agreement covers more than one season, that the agreement be recorded with the county register of deeds.

In Nevada, Washington, and Wyoming, like authorization is also granted to an individual user who holds water rights of more than one priority to rotate in their use.

Kansas extends the privilege also to users of water from irrigation works who agree in writing among themselves to rotate their water supplies.

Nebraska authorizes rotation in cases in which the statutory allotment of continuous flow for irrigation of an area of 40 acres or less is too small for proper distribution and application of water.

Necessarily, whether or not written into the enabling legislation, rotation practices are lawful only when their exercise inflicts no injury upon nonparticipants. None of the statutes purports to divest any appropriator of any part of a quantity of water to which he is entitled by virtue of his priority, or of the time at which he is entitled to divert it. On the contrary, there is included in a majority of them a specific condition that the rotation be practiced without injury to other appropriators or infringement of their water rights.

A section of the Oklahoma law relating to the organization and operation of irrigation districts provides for rotation of streamflow among different localities in time of water shortage, the apportionment to be made with due regard to existing rights by water commissioners consisting of chairmen of the boards of directors of the districts affected.[121] This section was identical with provisions in other early irrigation district laws of several Western States. It is doubtful, however, that the provision was ever put into effect on any substantial scale in any State, for it conflicts with procedures for distribution

---

[121]Okla. Stat. Ann. tit. 82, § 201 (1970).

of stream waters under the State administrative laws. It is generally omitted from current codifications.[122]

Rotation Agreements

Appropriators on Watercourse

In 1904, the Wyoming Supreme Court observed that an agreement between several persons who had appropriated water, as tenants in common, to use the entire quantity on alternate weeks, respectively, where the evidence disclosed no injury to any of them, "does not seem objectionable in itself."[123] Other agreements elsewhere have been similarly approved in cases in which no injury to outsiders was shown.[124]

Users on Enterprise Ditch System

The Washington Supreme Court refused to hold that an irrigation company regulation providing for rotation through intermittent flow was unreasonable as a matter of law, and refused to disapprove such a regulation so long as the consumers received the quantities of water to which they were entitled.[125]

The Idaho Supreme Court recognized the right of consumers under an irrigation company ditch to enter into an agreement providing for the use of water in rotation as among themselves, and observed that: "Rotation in irrigation undoubtedly tends to conserve the waters of the state and to increase and encourage their duty and service, and is, consequently, a practice that deserves encouragement in so far as it may be done within legal bounds."[126] As this practice is recognized by leading authorities as most efficient and desirable, contracts providing it will be enforced by the courts.[127] But in the absence of contract, there is no vested right in one ditch cotenant to rotation in use of water by and with another.[128]

The Idaho Supreme Court has reaffirmed its earlier policy by holding that where the method of distribution of water by a mutual irrigation company

---

[122]For example, after having been a part of the California Irrigation District Act since its original enactment March 7, 1887 (Cal. Stat. 1887, p. 29, § 43), but never having been construed by the appellate courts of that State and apparently never having been put to use, the section was omitted from the enactment of the California Water Code in 1943. The reason for omission was that the section was obsolete and unworkable, in view of provisions of the Water Code and preceding legislation relating to the utilization of water rights in California.

[123]*Johnston* v. *Little Horse Creek Irrigating Co.,* 13 Wyo. 208, 237, 79 Pac. 22 (1904).

[124]*Peake* v. *Harris,* 48 Cal. App. 363, 378, 192 Pac. 310 (1920), hearing denied by California Supreme Court, August 27, 1920; *In re Crab Creek,* 194 Wash. 634, 642-644, 79 Pac. (2d) 323 (1938).

[125]*Shafford* v. *White Bluffs Land & Irr. Co.,* 63 Wash. 10, 13-15, 114 Pac. 883 (1911).

[126]*Helphery* v. *Perrault,* 12 Idaho 451, 454, 86 Pac. 417 (1906).

[127]*State* v. *Twin Falls Canal Co.,* 21 Idaho 410, 441-443, 121 Pac. 1039 (1911).

[128]*Brighton Ditch Co.* v. *Englewood,* 124 Colo. 366, 374, 237 Pac. (2d) 116 (1951).

provides the user with a larger flow of water when available than his shares of stock represent, thus enabling him to complete his irrigation in a comparatively short time after the water is shut off—which results in better irrigation and less waste of water than can be accomplished with a smaller stream of continuous flow over a longer period—the court should not limit the user to the quantity of water represented by his shares in the company.[129]

Appellate court cases in a few other jurisdictions involving rotation of water within canal enterprises have come to attention.[130]

Imposition of Rotation Plan by Court Decree

After having recognized the judicial remedy of rotation as among riparian owners to permit the beneficial use of water by all landowners concerned, the California Supreme Court early in this century applied it to appropriators also, in view of the fact that the appropriative right extends only to beneficial use of water. As a guide to trial courts faced by the problem of imposing rotation systems as between appropriators, the supreme court said that:[131]

If there is not water enough (and this appears to be the fact) to permit a diversion of the stream and a simultaneous use of part by both parties without injury, the court may by its decree fix the times when, by rotation, the whole may be used by each at different times in proportion to their respective rights. In doing so, the court should recognize the paramount and primary right of the respondent to the first flow in a full ditch and the use of all of it, or a lesser quantity, for given periods during the irrigating season, as it may be required. If this can be done so that by giving respondent the first flow for a week or every other week, or on certain days in the week, and the appellant the right thereto in the intervals, the wants of respondent are fully supplied, he obtains all he is entitled to and has no ground of complaint. While this remedy of rotation and use of waters for irrigation purposes has been more generally \applied as between riparian proprietors * * * , in principle there is no reason why it should not be made applicable as between claimants by appropriation. * * *

At about the same time, the Oregon Supreme Court stated that "The trend of the later decisions is to apply this method where practicable."[132]

---

[129]*Ramseyer* v. *Jamerson,* 78 Idaho 504, 514-515, 305 Pac. (2d) 1088 (1957);*Simonson* v. *Moon,* 72 Idaho 39, 47, 237 Pac. (2d) 93 (1951).

[130]*Anderson* v. *Cook,* 25 Mont. 330, 331-339, 64 Pac. 873, 65 Pac. 113 (1901);*Honaker* v. *Reeves County W. I. Dist. No. 1,* 152 S. W. (2d) 454, 456 (Tex. Civ. App. 1941, error refused).

[131]*Hufford* v. *Dye,* 162 Cal. 147, 160-161, 121 Pac. 400 (1912).

[132]*McCoy* v. *Huntley,* 60 Oreg. 372, 376, 119 Pac. 481 (1911). See also *Cantrall* v. *Sterling Min. Co.,* 61 Oreg. 516, 526, 122 Pac. 42 (1912).

The theme is reiterated in both earlier and later decisions in cases in which the plan could be equitably applied.[133]

A South Dakota decision was to the effect that if the head of water to which the holder of a small tract of land is entitled is not sufficient for practicable irrigation, the court should award him a stream of adequate size and should limit the time of use.[134] The Nebraska statute to the same effect with respect to tracts of 40 acres or less[135] is noted earlier under "Statutory Authorization to Rotate Water Uses." Also noted there is Nevada's legislative purpose to enable each water user to have an irrigation head of at least 2 second-feet.[136]

Courts of review have had occasion to pass on compulsory rotation systems provided by Oregon administrators in statutory stream system adjudications.[137]

Qualification, Questioning, or Disapproval of Compulsion

Despite the considerable number of high court decisions approving not only the principle of rotation in water uses, but also its imposition by court decree where this was considered justified by the surrounding circumstances, the approach to rotation issues has been taken in other cases with some reservation or even actual dissent. A few examples follow.

---

[133]*Cundy* v. *Weber*, 68 S. Dak. 214, 226-227, 300 N. W. 17 (1941); *Ward County W. I. Dist. No. 3* v. *Ward County Irr. Dist. No. 1*, 117 Tex. 10, 14-16, 295 S. W. 917 (1927), reforming and affirming 237 S. W. 584 (Tex. Civ. App. 1921); *Crawford* v. *Lehi Irr. Co.*, 10 Utah (2d) 165, 169, 350 Pac. (2d) 147 (1960); having the power to make such a judgment or decree, the court also has the power to enforce it by injunction: *Hidalgo County W. I. Dist. No. 2* v. *Cameron County W. C. & I. Dist. No. 5*, 253 S. W. (2d) 294, 296 (Tex. Civ. App. 1952, error refused n.r.e.); *Becker* v. *Marble Creek Irr. Co.*, 15 Utah 225, 229, 49 Pac. 892 (1897); *Dameron Valley Res. & Canal Co.* v. *Bleak*, 61 Utah 230, 237, 211 Pac. 974 (1922); *Rocky Ford Canal Co.* v. *Cox*, 92 Utah 148, 158, 59 Pac. (2d) 935 (1936); *Union Mill & Min. Co.* v. *Dangberg*, 81 Fed. 73, 121 (C.C.D. Nev. 1897); *Anderson* v. *Bassman*, 140 Fed. 14, 29 (C.C.N.D. Cal. 1905).

[134]*Cook* v. *Evans*, 45 S. Dak. 31, 42, 185 N. W. 262 (1921).

[135]Nebr. Rev. Stat. § 46-231 (1968).

[136]Nev. Rev. Stat. § 533.075 (Supp. 1967).

[137]*In re Willow Creek*, 74 Oreg. 592, 629, 144 Pac. 505 (1914), 146 Pac. 475 (1915); *In re North Powder River*, 75 Oreg. 83, 96, 144 Pac. 485 (1914), 146 Pac. 475 (1915). In a controversy over rights decreed in the *North Powder River* adjudication, the supreme court saw no reason why, if a postadjudication appropriation was not interfered with, a projected rotation plan could not be carried out if the earliest appropriator did not need all the water for a short period of time, as this would be purely a matter of administration: *Hutchinson* v. *Stricklin*, 146 Oreg. 285, 302-303, 28 Pac. (2d) 225 (1933). In one case, the supreme court approved establishment of a plan of rotation provided by decree without objection at the time, inasmuch as no appeal had been taken from that part of the decree; objection now made by some of the parties came too late: *Krebs* v. *Perry*, 134 Oreg. 290, 303-304, 292 Pac. 319, 293 Pac. 432 (1930).

A New Mexico case involved the relative rights of a prior appropriator who had a permit for the all-year use of 5 second-feet of water, and a junior appropriator who applied for and obtained a permit for 4½ second-feet out of the same supply for winter use only, basing his application upon a claim that the earlier appropriator's right to such water, as a result of nonuse during the winter, had been lost by forfeiture for such season. The supreme court rejected the later appropriator's claim of forfeiture and held that he was a junior appropriator only, at any time of the year. In doing so, the court held that no case of rotation was involved here; and observed that even if it were, whether a rule of rotation could be worked out under the circumstances was doubtful. "This case differs from those arising on community ditches, where all of the rights are usually of the same dignity, and rotation is frequently awarded as a means of dividing the water on an equitable basis."[138]

The Utah Supreme Court said that as rotation of irrigation waters aids materially in saving of water and enlarging its duty, "the courts favor, whenever possible, that system." It was admitted that the power to compel rotation as against a nonconsenting water user might not then (in 1917) be thoroughly settled.[139] But subsequent decisions of this court appear to have settled this matter in the affirmative, particularly one rendered in 1960 in which the court said:

> It appears that the objective of achieving the most economical use of the water will be served by the order made directing that it be used under a rotation system, and that it will result neither in hardship nor injustice to the plaintiff. Accordingly we see no basis to justify interference with the conclusion reached by the trial court in refusing to issue an injunction.[140]

In a Washington case, the rights of the parties to the action were defined on a percentage basis by court decree. After certain of these parties petitioned the State administrator to adopt a plan of rotation, the administrator entered an order suggesting such a plan. The supreme court held that unless the parties could agree upon some plan of rotation, all that the administrator could do was to give each party the percentage awarded him by the decree.[141] In a subsequent decision rendered in the course of a statutory adjudication, this court declared that inclusion of a plan of rotation should first be considered and adjusted by the State administrator, which had not been "adopted entirely" by him here. "We think that neither the trial court nor ourselves

---

[138]*Harkey* v. *Smith*, 31 N. Mex. 521, 530-531, 247 Pac. 550 (1926).
[139]*Big Cottonwood Tanner Ditch Co.* v. *Shurtliff*, 49 Utah 569, 589, 164 Pac. 856 (1917).
[140]*Crawford* v. *Lehi Irr. Co.*, 10 Utah (2d) 165, 169, 350 Pac. (2d) 147 (1960). See also *Rocky Ford Canal Co.* v. *Cox*, 92 Utah 148, 158, 59 Pac. (2d) 935 (1936), "When necessary, periods of rotation may be imposed;" *Dameron Valley Res. & Canal Co.* v. *Bleak*, 61 Utah 230, 237, 211 Pac. 974 (1922).
[141]*Osborn* v. *Chase*, 119 Wash. 476, 479, 205 Pac. 844 (1922).

should, in the first instance, decree such method of distribution, without much more conclusive and compelling evidence than is in this case."[142]

It has been noted earlier under "Rotation Agreements" that the Idaho Supreme Court gave its blessing to voluntary rotation agreements and their enforcement. However, in 1920, this court refused to adopt a rule *compelling* the use of water by rotation. The court was not convinced that the time had arrived for the adoption of such a rule in Idaho. This stand was taken because of the long-standing practice of many irrigation communities of giving each user a continuous flow of water, and of the preponderance of water rights in the State that had passed by decree which were based upon the rule of continuous flow. The practice of rotation was not condemned, but on the contrary would be enforced where the parties had contracted for it. However, until the practice had become established by custom, it would not be imposed upon water users accustomed to the continuous-delivery plan, without their consent.[143] In a subsequent proceeding to change the point of diversion and place of use of certain waters, the Idaho Supreme Court interpreted a trial court decree providing for rotation, *provided* only that there was sufficient water in the stream system to supply other appropriators as authorized by their decreed water rights and priority dates thereof.[144]

Interstate Compact

In 1922, the States of Colorado and New Mexico entered into a compact with respect to the equitable distribution of the waters of La Plata River, which rises in Colorado and flows into New Mexico. The compact was ratified by both States in 1923,[145] and it received Congressional consent in 1925.[146]

Litigation ensued over a provision in article II, section 3, of the La Plata River Compact to the effect that whenever the river flow is so low that in the judgment of the two State Engineers it would be advantageous to distribute the entire streamflow to each State in alternating periods, rather than according to criteria elsewhere provided in the compact, such use may be rotated between the States "in such manner, for such periods, and to continue for such time as the State engineers may jointly determine." The Colorado Supreme Court held that such compact, which interfered with a Colorado appropriator's use of his decreed water by requiring the water to be delivered to New Mexico appropriators part of the time, could not be pleaded by the State water officials as excusing their failure to enforce such priority.[147]

---

[142]*In re Ahtanum Creek,* 139 Wash. 84, 95-96, 245 Pac. 758 (1926).

[143]*Muir v. Allison,* 33 Idaho 146, 162-163, 191 Pac. 206 (1920).

[144]*Beecher v. Cassia Creek Irr. Co.,* 66 Idaho 1, 8-10, 154 Pac. (2d) 507 (1944).

[145]N. Mex. Laws 1923, p. 13; Colo. Sess. Laws 1923, p. 696.

[146]43 Stat. 796.

[147]*La Plata River & Cherry Creek Ditch Co.* v. *Hinderlider,* 93 Colo. 128, 130-134, 25 Pac. (2d) 187 (1933). Later, in the same cause, the court said that the compact attempted

On appeal—for which certiorari was substituted—the United States Supreme Court reversed the State court's decision. It was held that under the principle of an equitable apportionment of benefits between the States, the Colorado State decree could not confer upon the appropriator any rights in excess of Colorado's share of the streamflow, which was only an equitable portion thereof. The fact that the apportionment by means of rotation in periods of low streamflow was made by compact between the States with the consent of Congress made it binding to the same extent as would have been an apportionment by the Court itself.

That such alternate rotating flow was then a more efficient use of the stream than if the flow had been steadily divided equally between the Colorado and New Mexico appropriators was conclusively established by the evidence. * * * The delegation to the State Engineers of the authority to determine when the waters should be so rotated was a matter of detail clearly within the constitutional power.[148]

CHANGE IN EXERCISE OF WATER RIGHT [149]

Major Changes

Questions of making substantial alterations in the exercise of one's appropriative right arose in the very early years of mining in the Sierra Nevada of California. This resulted from the "playing out" of mining claims and the necessity of either changing the point of diversion or place of use or purpose of use of the water—or of all three—to another mining location or to an agricultural use elsewhere or, if none of these possibilities were available, of abandoning the entire undertaking. Later changes came to embrace means of diversion, or use or time of use of the water such as from direct flow to storage. However, most of the activity in this field, and of legislation and case determination respecting it, centered in the three segments of point of diversion, place of use, and purpose of use of the appropriated water. State statutory provisions now in effect are summarized at the end of this topic.

The exercise of the privilege is generally permitted by legislation and court decisions—but with important exceptions noted below—without loss of priority of the appropriative right, so long as the rights of others are not thereby impaired. It has been stated many times that the appropriator is entitled to have the stream conditions maintained substantially as they existed at the time he made his appropriation. (See, in chapter 8, "Elements of the Appropriative

---

to provide for the equitable apportionment of waters in defiance of ownership and that it did not finally settle anything: *Hinderlider* v. *La Plata River & Cherry Creek Ditch Co.*, 101 Colo. 73, 75, 70 Pac. (2d) 849 (1937).

[148] *Hinderlider* v. *La Plata River & Cherry Creek Ditch Co.*, 304 U. S. 92, 108-109 (1938).

[149] A related but different subject, "Conveyance of Title to Appropriative Right," is discussed in chapter 8 under "Property Characteristics."

Right" and "Relative Rights of Senior and Junior Appropriators".) This applies equally to senior and junior appropriators. Not only is the *senior* appropriator entitled to protection against any impairment of his right by those who come later; the *junior* appropriator initiates his right in the belief that the water previously appropriated by others will continue to be used as it is then being used. Therefore, the junior has a vested right, as against the senior, to insist that such conditions be not changed to the detriment of his own right. Some examples of injury against which protection is afforded are noted below.

Generally, changes in the point of diversion, place of use, or character of use of water, if made in conformity with any statutory requirements that may exist, and which do not impair the rights of others, do not affect the validity of the appropriation in question, nor do they forfeit or work an abandonment of the water right or alter the priority of the appropriation. The use simply continues with all its rights and obligations under the changed conditions.

The changes in exercise of appropriative rights do not contemplate or countenance any increase in the quantity of water diverted under the original exercise of the right.[150]

In no event would an increase in the appropriated water supply be authorized solely by virtue of a change in point of diversion, place of use, or purpose of use of water. This is for the elemental reason that an enlargement in the quantity of water appropriated can be made only by acquiring a new appropriative right to the additional quantity, which new right is junior in priority to all other rights—by whomsoever initiated—intervening between the dates of the original appropriation and of this additional one. (See, in chapter 7, "Methods of Appropriating Water of Watercourses—Priority of Appropriation—Succeeding Appropriations by First User." Gradual development, if within the appropriator's original intent and carried out diligently, is not an enlargement.)[151]

---

[150] On the contrary, the New Mexico statute placing restrictions on the right to change the point of diversion do not apply to community acequias established and in operation before the water rights statute of 1907 went into effect, "Provided that by such change no increase in the amount of water appropriated shall be made beyond the amount to which the acequia was formerly entitled." N. Mex. Stat. Ann. § 75-14-60 (1968).

[151] Rigidities of the appropriation doctrine respecting appurtenance of water rights, difficulties in effectuating transfers of the place or purpose of use or of diversion points, and effects upon the water economy, have been dealt with in a number of articles, papers, or reports. Contrasting views are expressed in Gaffney, M. M., "Diseconomies Inherent in Western Water Laws: A California Case Study," in "Water and Range Resources and Economic Development of the West," Conf. Proc., Comm. on Econ. of Water Resources Devel. and Comm. on Econ. of Range Use and Devel., of the Western Agric. Econ. Research Council, Report No. 9, p. 55 (Tucson 1961); Trelease, F. J., "Water Law and Economic Transfers of Water," 43 Jour. of Farm Econ. 1147 (1961); Gaffney, M. M., "Water Law and Economic Transfers of Water: A Reply," 44 Jour. of Farm Econ. 427 (1962); Trelease, F. J., "Water Law and Economic Transfers of Water: A Rejoinder," *Id.* at 435. Some other publications

Point of Diversion

Legislation

With the exception of Alaska, Arizona, and Texas, the water rights statutes of the appropriation doctrine States specifically authorize appropriators to change their points of diversion of the water. In these three excepted States, the right is expressly or impliedly recognized by the judiciary.

In the majority of the States, such change requires prior approval of the State water administrative agency. In most of these, some kind of procedure is prescribed, often including findings and hearings of objections. California specifies a detailed compulsory procedure for changes in rights acquired under the Water Commission Act and of the Water Code which succeeded it, such rights being administered under the State Water Resources Control Board. With respect to California appropriations otherwise made, there is simply a statutory authorization carrying a requirement that no injury be inflicted upon others.[152] In Colorado, a person desiring a determination with respect to a change in point of diversion may obtain a decree from the water judge or his designated referee.[153]

Many statutes impose a specific condition that the right of change may be exercised only if there is no impairment of other existing water rights. In some, a finding to this effect by the State administrator is required. Nevada requires a finding that the proposed change will not tend to impair the value of existing rights or to be otherwise detrimental to the public welfare.[154] Colorado authorizes a decree permitting the requested change if it appears that the rights of others will not be injuriously affected or that the imposition of terms and conditions will prevent such injury.[155] In Idaho, a requested change may be approved in whole or in part, or upon conditions, provided no other water rights are injured thereby and the change does not constitute an enlargement in

---

dealing with such matters include "Water Resources and Economic Development of the West," Report No. 10, "Water Transfer Problems," and "International River Basin Development," Conf. Proc., Comm. on Econ. of Water Resources Devel. of the Western Agr. Econ. Research Council (Las Vegas 1966); Trelease, F. J., and Lee, D. W., "Priority and Progress—Case Studies in the Transfer of Water Rights," 1 Land and Water Law Rev. 1 (1966); Trelease, F. J., "Transfers of Water Rights—Errata and Addenda—Sales for Recreational Purposes and to Districts," 2 Land and Water Law Rev. 321 (1967); Ellis, W. H. "Water Transfer Problems: Law," in Kneese, A. V., and Smith, S. V., eds., "Water Research", p. 233 (1966); Comment, "Water Law—Legal Impediments to Transfers of Water Rights," 7 Natural Resources Jour. 433 (1967); Trelease, F. J., "Changes and Transfers of Water Rights," 13 Rocky Mt. Mineral Law Inst. 507 (1967); Hartman, L. M., and Seastone, D., "Water Transfers: Economic Efficiency and Alternative Institutions" (1970).

[152]Cal. Water Code § § 1700, 1706 (West 1956), and 1701-1705 (West Supp., 1970).
[153]Colo. Rev. Stat. Ann. § § 148-21-3(11) and 148-21-18 to 148-21-21 (Supp. 1969).
[154]Nev. Rev. Stat. § 533.370 (Supp. 1967).
[155]Colo. Rev. Stat. Ann. § 148-21-21 (Supp. 1969).

use of the original right.[156] In New Mexico, no such change shall be allowed to the detriment of the rights of others having valid and existing rights in the stream system and it shall be subject to the rules and regulations of the State Engineer.[157] The condition in the Utah statute centers in uncompensated injury; that is, changes are not to be rejected for the sole reason that they would impair vested rights of others, for if otherwise proper they may be approved as to part of the water involved, or on condition that the conflicting rights be acquired.[158]

Not many of the statutes specifically mention the item that a change in point of diversion, properly made, carries with it the priority of the right in question. However, it is a widely recognized judicial rule, as noted in the next subtopic.

Judicial Decisions

Independent of statutes.—As previously noted, in Alaska, Arizona, and Texas there is no express statutory authority for changes in point of diversion of appropriative rights.

In Alaska, the supreme court has recognized that the prior appropriator may change the point of diversion or place of use of the water to which he has a right, without affecting the priority of his right, so long as such change does not prejudice the rights of later appropriators.[159]

The Arizona Supreme Court has sanctioned such changes by holding that if occasioned by abandonment of the original ditch and substitution of another, they were not evidence of intent to abandon the water rights and did not affect their validity.[160] This court also stated that the means of appropriation may be

---

[156]Idaho Code Ann. § 42-108 and -222 (Supp. 1969).

[157]N. Mex. Stat. Ann. §§ 75-5-3 and 75-5-23 (1968). Section 75-5-23.1 (Supp. 1971) includes a procedure for granting temporary approval of changes in points of diversion or storage or in use of water in emergency situations.

In *W. S. Ranch Co.* v. *Kaiser Steel Corp.,* 79 N. Mex. 65, 439 Pac. (2d) 714, 718 (1968), the court noted that the State Engineer, having determined that a change could be made without detriment to existing rights, in granting the change nevertheless took the precautionary measure of imposing conditions that limited the amount of water to be diverted, required measurement and recording of water diversions and return flow, protected certain junior appropriators, and generally prohibited any detriment to existing rights. The court also noted that the appropriator making the change could take no more water than would have been available at the old point of diversion as provided in an adjudication decree.

[158]Utah Rev. Code Ann. § 73-3-3 (1968). Either permanent or temporary changes are defined as changes for definite periods of no more than one year. Somewhat different procedures, including requirements regarding notice to others, are specified for temporary changes.

[159]*Eglar* v. *Baker,* 4 Alaska 142, 144-145 (1910); *Miocene Ditch Co.* v. *Campion Min. & Trading Co.,* 3 Alaska 572, 584 (1908).

[160]*Slosser* v. *Salt River Valley Canal Co.,* 7 Ariz. 376, 394-395, 65 Pac. 332 (1901); *Gould* v. *Maricopa Canal Co.,* 8 Ariz. 429, 448, 76 Pac. 598 (1904). See *Miller* v.

changed by the appropriator from time to time if no injury results to others, or may be changed by direction of the courts in proper cases in order to enlarge the use of the waters of the stream.[161]

In a Texas case, it was urged that an alleged prior right had been forfeited because the holder had changed the headgate without authority of the State administrative agency. A court of civil appeals held that: "The statute fixes a penalty, but does not forfeit water rights in such instances."[162] Rules and regulations of the State water agency require its permission for changes in point of diversion of appropriated water.[163]

The Wyoming Legislature has provided administrative procedure for making changes in point of diversion on an interstate stream that enters Wyoming, from a point outside the State to one within it, if the irrigated land is in Wyoming.[164] Until 1965, it had not expressly authorized such changes within the State; but the supreme court approved the general western rule allowing changes of point of diversion if no other appropriators would be injured, and it noted that this has been said to be a property right.[165] Legislation enacted in 1965 expressly provides that anyone having heretofore acquired an adjudicated or unadjudicated right to the beneficial use of "any stream in the State" may change the point of diversion upon applying for and obtaining the permission of the appropriate State agency.[166] No such permission shall be granted unless the right of other appropriators shall not be injuriously affected.[167]

Purpose of statutory procedure.—With respect to the statutes of New Mexico and Colorado authorizing changes in exercise of appropriative rights, a Federal court expressed the view that:[168]

Douglas, 7 Ariz. 41, 44, 60 Pac. 722 (1900); *Salt River Valley Water Users' Assn.* v. *Norviel,* 29 Ariz. 360, 370, 374, 499, 502, 241 Pac. 503 (1925), 242 Pac. 1013 (1926).

[161]*Pima Farms Co.* v. *Proctor,* 30 Ariz. 96, 105, 245 Pac. 369 (1926).

[162]*Ward County W. I. Dist. No. 3* v. *Ward County Irr. Dist. No. 1,* 237 S. W. 584, 588 (Tex. Civ. App. 1921), reformed and affirmed, 117 Tex. 10, 295 S. W. 917 (1927).

[163]Tex. Water Rights Comm'n, "Rules, Regulations and Modes of Procedure," rules 605.1 to 610.2 (1970 Rev., Jan. 1970).

[164]Wyo. Stat. Ann. § § 41-19 to -25 (1957).

[165]*Ramsay* v. *Gottsche,* 51 Wyo. 516, 530, 69 Pac. (2d) 535 (1937); *Van Tassel Real Estate & Live Stock Co.* v. *Cheyenne,* 49 Wyo. 333, 350-351, 54 Pac. (2d) 906 (1936); *Holt* v. *Cheyenne,* 22 Wyo. 212, 232, 137 Pac. 876 (1914).

[166]If an adjudicated right, the State Board of Control; if an unadjudicated right, the State Engineer.

[167]Wyo. Laws 1965, ch. 138, § 1, Stat. Ann. § 41-10.4 (Supp. 1969).

In *White* v. *Wheatland Irr. Dist.,* 413 Pac. (2d) 252, 258-259 (Wyo. 1966), the court noted that although prior to this legislation State agency approval for a change of diversion point was not required, if an appropriator chose to submit to the jurisdiction of the State agency for purposes of having a change already made confirmed and his certificate amended accordingly "we perceive no reason why that could not have been done."

[168]*Lindsey* v. *McClure,* 136 Fed. (2d) 65, 69-70 (10th Cir. 1943).

* * * a water right is a property right and inherent therein is the right to change the place of diversion, storage, or use of the water if the rights of other water users will not be injured thereby. Hence, the statutes above referred to are a recognition rather than a grant of the right to make such changes and they merely lay down a procedure whereby it may be determined whether such changes can be effected without injuriously affecting the rights of other users."

Exclusiveness of statutory procedure.—In most Western States in which there are statutory procedures for making changes in points of diversion, these procedures generally are exclusive. For example, the Utah Supreme Court has held that no change in place of diversion, place of use, or purpose of use "can be initiated or accomplished under our law" without approval of the State administrator or of the district court on review.[169]

The Idaho Supreme Court held that any change in point of diversion of water appropriated under the water administration act requires an application to the State administrator.[170] In a later case, in which all water rights of which the origin is given in the opinion were initiated long before the 1903 enactment of the Idaho water administration statute and in which such a change had been made without authority of the State agency, the supreme court observed that such change without such approval "does not forfeit the water right."[171] Although the supreme court failed to note in this case the significant difference between statutory and nonstatutory appropriations in Idaho, the statutory procedure for appropriating water in this State is *not* the exclusive procedure.[172] The current Idaho statutes, however, apparently provide that an application be made to the State administrator for changes in diversion points of water rights acquired under either the statutory or constitutional methods.[173]

In Colorado, the current statutory procedure apparently is not exclusive. A person desiring a determination with respect to a change in point of diversion may obtain a decree from the water judge or his designated referee.[174]

The Rule Respecting Change of Diversion as Announced by the Courts

The general rule.—In a very early decision, the California Supreme Court approved an instruction by the trial court to the jury to the effect that a

---

[169]*United States* v. *District Court,* 121 Utah 1, 5-6, 238 Pac. (2d) 1132 (1951). Procedural questions both before the State administrator and before the district court on appeal: *East Bench Irr. Co.* v. *Utah,* 5 Utah (2d) 235, 300 Pac. (2d) 603 (1956).

[170]*Washington State Sugar Co.* v. *Goodrich,* 27 Idaho 26, 40-41, 147 Pac. 1073 (1915). The State agency was correct in denying an application for a change in point of diversion that would interfere with the rights of others.

[171]*Harris* v. *Chapman,* 51 Idaho 283, 297, 5 Pac. (2d) 733 (1931).

[172]See, in chapter 7, "Methods of Appropriating Water of Watercourses—Current Appropriation Procedures—Exclusiveness of the Statutory Procedure."

[173]Idaho Code Ann. § § 42-108 and -222 (Supp. 1969).

[174]Colo. Rev. Stat. Ann. § § 148-21-3(11) and 148-21-18 to 148-21-21 (Supp. 1969).

person entitled to divert a given quantity of water from a stream may take the same at any point on the stream, and may change the point of diversion at pleasure, if the rights of others are not thereby injuriously affected.[175] Other courts announced the rule from time to time.[176] "There is nothing in the law of prior appropriation that prevents" operation of the qualified rule.[177] And by the same token, "Under the statute and decisions, a prior appropriator has no right to change the point of diversion when it will in any manner injure a subsequent appropriator."[178]

Some other aspects of the rule.—"The right to change the place of diversion and use of water depends upon and must be controlled by the facts of each particular case, and no inflexible rulé applicable to all conditions can be laid down."[179]

An appropriator may change the point of diversion of a portion of his appropriative right, as well as the entire quantity.[180]

---

[175]*Kidd* v. *Laird,* 15 Cal. 161, 179,181 (1860). Two years later, this court pointed out that the right to make such changes was not "absolute and unqualified," but included the condition that no injury be inflicted upon the rights of others: *Butte T. M. Co.* v. *Morgan,* 19 Cal. 609, 616 (1862).

[176]*Hague* v. *Nephi Irr. Co.,* 16 Utah 421, 434, 52 Pac. 765 (1898); *Spring Creek Irr. Co.* v. *Zollinger,* 58 Utah 90, 95, 197 Pac. 737 (1921); *Twaddle* v. *Winters,* 29 Nev. 88, 103, 85 Pac. 280 (1906); 89 Pac. 289 (1907); "The law seems to be well settled" to this effect: *Mally* v. *Weidensteiner,* 88 Wash. 398, 403-404, 153 Pac. 342 (1915); "It must be conceded that generally" this is true: *In re Johnson, Appeal from Department of Reclamation,* 50 Idaho 573, 578, 300 Pac. 492 (1931).

[177]*Johnston* v. *Little Horse Creek Irrigating Co.,* 13 Wyo. 208, 237, 79 Pac. 22 (1904).

[178]*Bennett* v. *Nourse,* 22 Idaho 249, 254, 125 Pac. 1038 (1912). A well established proposition: *Loyning* v. *Rankin,* 118 Mont. 235, 247, 165 Pac. (2d) 1006 (1946).

In *Farmers Highline Canal & Reservoir Co.* v. *Golden,* 129 Colo. 575, 272 Pac. (2d) 629, 634 (1954), involving a proceeding to change the diversion point by a city that had acquired decreed water rights formerly used for irrigation, the court said, "Petitioner contends . . . that it is entirely within the right of an appropriator of water to enlarge upon his use, and now that the City of Golden is the owner, it may enlarge upon the use to the extent of the entire decree. Counsel for petitioner here confuse two altogether different principles. This doctrine even on behalf of an original appropriator, may be applied only to the extent of use contemplated at the time of appropriation. It has no application whatever to a situation where a decree is sought for change of point of diversion or use. There the right is strictly limited to the extent of former actual usage." This case was quoted and discussed in *City of Westminster* v. *Church,* 167 Colo. 1, 445 Pac. (2d) 52, 58 (1968), involving a change of use, discussed at note 234 *infra.*

[179]*Crockett* v. *Jones,* 47 Idaho 497, 503-504, 277 Pac. 550 (1929). An earlier, lengthier statement to the same effect appears in *Vogel* v. *Minnesota Canal & Res. Co.,* 47 Colo. 534, 537-538, 107 Pac. 1108 (1910).

In *Keller* v. *Magic Water Co.,* 92 Idaho 226, 441 Pac. (2d) 725, 732-734 (1968), there was merely an amendment of a permit to show the correct point of diversion rather than an authorized change in the point of diversion. See chapter 8, note 394.

[180]*Perry* v. *Calkins,* 159 Cal. 175, 179, 113 Pac. 136 (1911). Citing this case, an appellate court said later that: "We fail to discover any sound reason why an appropriator of

"It is immaterial, in acquiring the right, whether the water was taken from the river by means of a canal, ditch, flume, or pipe, or by any other method." And at any time after the right is acquired, the means of diversion as well as the point at which contact is made with the stream may be changed if no injury results to others.[181]

Effect of Change on Validity of Appropriation

No abandonment or forfeiture.—In the course of development of the rule authorizing and restricting the right to make a change in point of diversion, attempts were made to obtain rulings that the making of such a change effected either an abandonment or a statutory forfeiture of the appropriation in question. So far as abandonment is concerned, such advocated concept overlooks the essential requirement of this way of losing an appropriative right—an *intention* to abandon it, that is, to forsake it completely. Here, of course, on the contrary, intent is to continue full exercise of the right after taking the water from the stream at a different place. Nor does statutory forfeiture apply, provided there is no failure to use the water for the prescribed period of years, and the statute does not say that the water must continue to be diverted at the original place. On the contrary, most Western water rights statutes specifically authorize changes in point of diversion. Hence, there is no merit in the concept with respect to either abandonment or forfeiture.[182]

No effect on priority of right.—In an early Colorado case, it was held that a change of point of diversion which effected no change in quantity of water diverted, and injured no one, did not affect the right of priority of the

---

water from a stream may not divide the appropriation provided it does not appear that by such division injury will result to others who have vested rights in such water." *People's Ditch Co.* v. *Foothill Irr. Dist.,* 112 Cal. App. 273, 276-277, 297 Pac. 71 (1931, hearing denied by supreme court).

[181]*Miller & Lux* v. *Rickey,* 127 Fed. 573, 584 (C.C.D. Nev. 1904). "Plaintiffs had the right to change this means of diversion of the waters to which they were entitled, since said change injured no one." *Hand* v. *Clease,* 202 Cal. 36, 45, 258 Pac. 1090 (1927). *Anderson* v. *Baumgartner,* 4 Cal. (2d) 195, 196, 47 Pac. (2d) 724 (1935). "The right to use the water is the essence of appropriation; the means by which it is done are incidental." *Offield* v. *Ish,* 21 Wash. 277, 281, 57 Pac. 809 (1899).

Regarding the right of an evicted squatter on the public domain to change the point of diversion, see *Hunter* v. *United States,* 388 Fed. (2d) 148, 154-155 (9th Cir. 1967).

[182]Not abandonment: *Anderson* v. *Baumgartner,* 4 Cal. (2d) 195, 196, 47 Pac. (2d) 724 (1935); *In re Deschutes River and Tributaries,* 134 Oreg. 623, 639-640, 286 Pac. 563, 294 Pac. 1049 (1930); not statutory forfeiture: *Van Tassel Real Estate & Live Stock Co.* v. *Cheyenne,* 49 Wyo. 333, 350-351, 54 Pac. (2d) 906 (1936). See *Ward County W. I. Dist. No. 3* v. *Ward County Irr. Dist. No. 1,* 237 S. W. 584, 588 (Tex. Civ. App. 1921), reformed and affirmed, 117 Tex. 10, 295 S. W. 917 (1927). Neither forfeiture nor abandonment: *Graham* v. *Leek,* 65 Idaho 279, 292, 144 Pac. (2d) 475 (1943).

appropriation.[183] This is recognized as an essential component of the general rule.[184]

The Question of Resulting Injury

Resulting injury bars a change of diversion.—That this is an essential condition of the right to make such a change in exercising one's water right is stated repeatedly in the decisions, as reflected in the foregoing discussion. Specifically, this right of change is not an absolute or vested right, but is only a conditional or qualified one. "No such change can be made if thereby the public, or any other appropriator, prior or subsequent, is adversely affected." Nor can a prior appropriator prevent a junior from appropriating any unappropriated water merely because the former in the future may wish to change his place of diversion. But when no material injury is in sight, a mere exchange of water violates no property rights.[185]

Hence, where a change caused or threatened to cause injury to others, the right to make the change was not sustained. This occurred in a very early Montana case in which a senior appropriator wished to transfer his point of diversion above the headgate of a junior appropriator,[186] and likewise in a case decided decades later in Washington.[187] In the Montana case, the junior appropriator had located his mill at a point where he could validly use the water previously appropriated but without consuming it, which conditions he was entitled to have continued. The change upstream in Washington was denied because it would result in depriving the lands through which the stream flowed of the benefits of subirrigation and of domestic use from springs fed by the stream. A Wyoming situation differed from the foregoing in that between the junior diversion and the downstream senior headgate the volume of water in the stream was substantially increased by springs—a benefit to the upstream junior. If the senior carried out his proposed change, the spring accretion would no longer be available so that the difference would have to be deducted from the junior's water supply—a material alteration of the conditions under which the latter made his appropriation, with a resulting substantial injury.[188]

The question of injury to lands dependent upon the continuance of return flow conditions which would result from changes in exercise of upstream rights has arisen in situations in which changes in either point of return or place of use—or both—were sought. A Colorado case involved both loss of return flow, in that the lands proposed to be irrigated were outside the drainage of the main stream and hence would contribute no return above the diversions of the

---

[183]*Sieber* v. *Frink,* 7 Colo. 148, 154, 2 Pac. 901 (1884).

[184]*In re Ahtanum Creek,* 139 Wash. 84, 100, 245 Pac. 758 (1926). The quantity of water covered by the original right is not affected.

[185]*United States* v. *Caldwell,* 64 Utah 490, 499-503, 231 Pac. 434 (1924).

[186]*Columbia Min. Co.* v. *Holter,* 1 Mont. 296, 299-300 (1871).

[187]*Haberman* v. *Sander,* 166 Wash. 453, 460-463, 7 Pac. (2d) 563 (1932).

[188]*Groo* v. *Sights,* 22 Wyo. 19, 31, 134 Pac. 269 (1913).

downstream irrigator, and harmful diminution in the flow of the main stream. The supreme court applied the oft-repeated rule that a junior appropriator of water has a vested right, as against his senior, to a continuation of the conditions on the stream as they existed at the time he made his appropriation.[189] On the other hand, under the complicated circumstances of another Colorado case, the evidence showed that the change in point of diversion was a benefit to everyone concerned.[190]

To bar a proposed change of point of diversion of water, the injury that threatens to accrue must be to a water right[191] and must be a readily determinable injury, not merely a *possible* injury that *might* result.[192] Proof is indeed required that vested rights will not be impaired; but this is not carried to the point "where every remote but presently indeterminable vested right must be pinpointed" and a beneficial change denied because it *could* interfere with vested rights.[193] In other words, it must be "not merely a fanciful injury but a real and actual injury."[194]

The action in a Nevada case centered solely in a construction of a decree of adjudication. An order authorizing a change in point of diversion and place of use was made long after the decree was issued and bore no relation to it. The supreme court felt that such suit was not a proper action in which to try the question of injury from the change. That matter, said the court, should be determined in a proper proceeding involving that specific issue, in which all parties whose rights might be affected could be given a change to be heard.[195]

In an Idaho case, a change of point of diversion and use, "whether regular and legal or not, was actually accomplished and thereafter used and enjoyed adversely."[196]

Burden of proof of injury.—The applicant for permission to change the point of diversion of water has the burden of establishing the necessary facts to make out a *prima facie* case that vested rights will not be thereby adversely affected.[197] On the other hand, the party who affirmatively alleges injury as a result of the change of place of diversion thereby assumes the burden of proving such injury.[198] The rule was thus restated in a 1954 case: "While the

---

[189]*Vogel* v. *Minnesota Canal & Res. Co.*, 47 Colo. 534, 537-542, 107 Pac. 1108 (1910).

[190]*Ironstone Ditch Co.* v. *Ashenfelter*, 57 Colo. 31, 45-46, 140 Pac. 177 (1914).

[191]*Colthorp* v. *Mountain Home Irr. Dist.*, 66 Idaho 173, 180-182, 157 Pac. (2d) 1005 (1945). Plaintiff did not plead that the change would in any way injure the water or the decreed right to use the water on his land. For this and other reasons, it was held that the complaint failed to state a cause of action.

[192]*Application of Boyer*, 73 Idaho 152, 160-161, 248 Pac. (2d) 540 (1952).

[193]*American Fork Irr. Co.* v. *Linke*, 121 Utah 90, 94-95, 239 Pac. (2d) 188 (1951).

[194]*Beecher* v. *Cassia Creek Irr. Co.*, 66 Idaho 1, 7, 8, 154 Pac. (2d) 507 (1944).

[195]*Kent* v. *Smith*, 62 Nev. 30, 39-40, 140 Pac. (2d) 357 (1943).

[196]*Hillcrest Irr. Dist.* v. *Nampa & Meridian Irr. Dist.*, 57 Idaho 403, 412, 66 Pac. (2d) 115 (1937).

[197]*Tanner* v. *Humphreys*, 87 Utah 164, 171, 48 Pac. (2d) 484 (1935).

[198]*Thrasher* v. *Mannix & Wilson*, 95 Mont. 273, 276, 26 Pac. (2d) 370 (1933); *Lokowich* v. *Helena*, 46 Mont. 575, 577, 129 Pac. 1063 (1913).

applicant has the general burden of showing that no impairment of vested rights will result from the change, the person opposing such application must fail if the evidence does not disclose that his rights will be impaired."[199]

Uninjured party may not complain.—The holder of a water right who cannot show injury thereto as a result of a proposed change in another's point of diversion has no cause for complaint.[200] Nor can one who can assert no legal right to the water complain of such a change.[201]

Place and Purpose of Use

Place of Use

Some statutory situations.—In a majority of Western States, the water rights statutes provide for making changes in both place and purpose of use of appropriated water. Generally, the authorizations, procedures, and restrictions upon exercise of the right of change apply to each of the three major functions—diversion, place of use, and purpose. In most instances, approval of the State administrative agency is required.[202] However, there are some exceptions.

A Nevada statute provides that all appropriated water shall remain appurtenant to the place of use except that it may be transferred to another place of use whenever it becomes impracticable to use the water beneficially or economically at the place to which it is appurtenant. Such a transfer will not result in loss of priority.[203] Permission of the State administrative agency is

---

[199]*Salt Lake City* v. *Boundary Springs Water Users Assn.*, 2 Utah (2d) 141, 143-144, 270 Pac. (2d) 453 (1954).

[200]*Gallagher* v. *Montecito Valley Water Co.*, 101 Cal. 242, 246, 35 Pac. 770 (1894); *In re Deschutes River and Tributaries*, 134 Oreg. 623, 639-640, 286 Pac. 563, 294 Pac. 1049 (1930); *Tanner* v. *Provo Res. Co.*, 99 Utah 139, 152-153, 98 Pac. (2d) 695 (1940); *Sain* v. *Montana Power Co.*, 20 Fed. Supp. 843, 848 (D. Mont. 1937).

[201]*Vineland Irr. Dist.* v. *Azusa Irrigating Co.*, 126 Cal. 486, 495-497, 58 Pac. 1057 (1899); *Mettler* v. *Ames Realty Co.*, 61 Mont. 152, 158, 201 Pac. 702 (1921).

[202]Prior to 1969, Colorado, which is one State requiring no permit to appropriate water, had legislation which applied specifically only to changes in points of diversion. Colo. Rev. Stat. Ann. § § 148-9-22 to 148-9-25 (1963). But in many cases, the supreme court has sanctioned changes in place of use if no injury results to vested rights of other appropriators. "We take it that no citations are necessary in this connection." *Hassler* v. *Fountain Mutual Irr. Co.*, 93 Colo. 246, 249, 26 Pac. (2d) 102 (1933). This is an inherent property right, long existing as an incident of ownership and always enforceable so long as the vested rights of others are not infringed. *Brighton Ditch Co.* v. *Englewood*, 124 Colo. 366, 372-373, 237 Pac. (2d) 116 (1951). In 1969, § § 148-9-22 to 148-9-25 were repealed and new provisions enacted permitting "change of water rights," which is defined as a change in type, place, or time of use or place of diversion. Colo. Laws 1969, ch. 373, § § 1 and 20(1), pp. 1202, 1207-1212, and 1223, Rev. Stat. Ann. § § 148-21-18 to 148-21-21 and 148-21-3(11) (Supp. 1969).

[203]Nev. Rev. Stat. § 533.040 (Supp. 1969). This provision does not apply to ditch or canal companies which have appropriated water for transmission to lands of private persons at an annual charge.

required.[204] There are similar statutory provisions in Oklahoma and South Dakota which, however, pertain only to water used for irrigation purposes.[205]

The Wyoming statute, with various exceptions,[206] does not authorize an appropriator to change the place of use of appropriated direct-flow water and declares that water rights for the direct use of natural unstored streamflow can not be detached from the lands or place of use for which acquired.[207] This, however, does not apply to reservoir water rights. Unless attached to particular lands by deed or other instruments of conveyance, reservoir rights may be transferred for use elsewhere.[208]

The Nebraska legislation may constitute another exception to the usual provisions regarding changes in place of use although its effect, as construed by the courts, is rather unsettled. This is discussed in chapter 8 under "Property Characteristics—Appurtenance of Water Right to Land—Appurtenant and not Generally Severable Without Loss of the Right."

The limitations on taking water out of the watershed or area of origin, noted in chapter 8 ("Elements of the Appropriative Right—Diversion of Water From Watershed or Area of Origin"), necessarily apply to changes in place of use as well as to location of the original place of use.

Some judicial points.—In a very early decision, the California Supreme Court saw no reason why a miner's appropriative right should be impaired or forfeited by a mere change in the place of use of the water from one mining

---

[204]*Id.,* § 533.325 (Supp. 1967).

[205]Okla. Stat. Ann. tit. 82, § 34 (1970); S. Dak. Comp. Laws Ann. § § 46-5-34 and 46-5-35 (1967). These expressly provide that no such change may be made if it will be detrimental to existing rights.

[206]These include acquisition of water for preferred uses or for highway and certain other temporary purposes, correction of errors in permits and certificates of appropriation, certain voluntary exchange agreements, and replacement of irrigated lands submerged by certain reservoirs. Wyo. Stat. Ann. § § 41-2 to -8 (1957), -9 to -10.2:1 (Supp. 1969). Pre-1909 water rights perhaps are also excepted. This was discussed but left undecided in *State* v. *Laramie Rivers Co.,* 59 Wyo. 9, 136 Pac. (2d) 487, 496 (1943), referring *inter alia* to *Hughes* v. *Lincoln Land Co.,* 27 Fed. Supp. 972 (D. Wyo. 1939), and *United States* v. *Tilley,* 124 Fed. (2d) 850, 857 (8th Cir. 1942). *Hunziker* v. *Knowlton,* 78 Wyo. 241, 322 Pac. (2d) 141 (1958), rehearing denied, 324 Pac. (2d) 266 (1958), apparently indicates that pre-1909 water rights ordinarily could have been transferred before 1909 but it found it unnecessary to decide the question of attempted transfers of such rights after the 1909 legislation restricting transfers. Other possible exceptions may include authorized rotation agreements and the acquisition of water for fish hatcheries and public fishing areas and by irrigation districts, water conservancy districts, water and sewer districts, and watershed improvement districts. In this regard, see Trelease, Frank J., and Lee, Dellas W., "Priority and Progress—Case Studies in the Transfer of Water Rights," 1 Land and Water Law Rev. 1 (1966); Trelease, Frank J., "Transfer of Water Rights—Errata and Addenda—Sales for Recreational Purposes and to Districts," 2 Land and Water Law Rev. 321 (1967).

[207]Wyo. Stat. Ann. § § 41-2 to -4 (1957) and -213 (Supp. 1969).

[208]Wyo. Stat. Ann. § 41-37 (1957).

locality to another.[209] In the earliest California decisions, the rule with respect to change of place of use was stated without the limitation of no injury to the rights of others.[210] That essential limitation, which was recognized promptly by the California courts in connection with rights to change one's point of diversion and which is general in the West, came later.

It was declared in an Oregon decision that the rule allowing a change in place of use may be properly applied only if the new place of use is equivalent in area and water requirements to the original place of use—that there be a continuing intention to irrigate a well defined acreage. "If the intention to irrigate Whiteacre is abandoned before the intention to irrigate Blackacre becomes fixed, the water right is lost." If such a lapse in intent occurs, the formation of a new intention to irrigate other lands marks the beginning of a new appropriation.[211] In another stream adjudication, this court held that the extension of a ditch to additional land did not appear under the evidence to be an enlargement or a new appropriation, but rather completion of application of the water to beneficial use with due diligence and within a reasonable time—in other words, gradual development as contemplated when the appropriation was made.[212]

A change in place of use, lawfully made, does not work a forfeiture and is not an abandonment of the water right.[213] Even an injurious change, though subject to challenge by the injured party, does not affect the validity of the appropriative right—at least in the absence of a statute declaring a forfeiture under such conditions.[214]

Under the statute,[215] said the Oregon Supreme Court, it is a condition precedent to exercise of the right to change the place of use of water specified in an adjudication proceeding that the holder of the right make application to the State Engineer and obtain his approval of the change.[216] Respecting the Idaho statute,[217] the supreme court of that State held that the procedure therein must be followed where the statute applies, and that if it is not applicable the owner of the water right may proceed in a court of equity.[218]

---

[209]*Maeris* v. *Bicknell*, 7 Cal. 261, 263 (1857).

[210]*Davis* v. *Gale*, 32 Cal. 26, 33-34 (1867), criticized in *Fuller* v. *Swan River Placer Mining Co.*, 12 Colo. 12, 16-19, 19 Pac. 836 (1888).

[211]*In re Umatilla River*, 88 Oreg. 376, 396-397, 168 Pac. 922 (1917), 172 Pac. 97 (1918).

[212]*In re Silvies River*, 115 Oreg. 27, 49, 237 Pac. 322 (1925).

[213]*In re Johnson, Appeal from Department of Reclamation*, 50 Idaho 573, 579, 300 Pac. 492 (1931).

[214]*Hansen* v. *Larsen*, 44 Mont. 350, 353, 120 Pac. 229 (1911).

[215]Oreg. Rev. Stat. § § 540.510-.530 (Supp. 1969).

[216]*Broughton* v. *Stricklin*, 146 Oreg. 259, 271, 28 Pac. (2d) 219 (1933), 30 Pac. (2d) 332 (1934).

[217]Idaho Code Ann. § § 42-108 and -222 (Supp. 1969).

[218]*First Security Bank of Blackfoot* v. *State*, 49 Idaho 740, 744, 745, 291 Pac. 1064 (1930). "The statute empowering the commissioner of reclamation to authorize a

The physical interrelationship of upstream and downstream appropriative diversions is such that injury in change of place of use is voiced in most ordinary situations by downstream appropriators against those above. Thus, a change in point of return to the stream of upstream nonconsumptive uses—or the excess from consumptive uses—may deprive the lower diversion of water on which it has been depending, and in that case it is an actionable injury.[219] In a number of cases, the downstream user complains of the loss of return flow on which he has been depending when an upstream use is changed to a new locality. This violates the "continuance of conditions" philosophy and, if the original use was not excessive, the change may be enjoined.[220]

It appears, however, that not in all situations does the downstream appropriator have an unqualified right to the continuance of return flow conditions upstream upon which he claims dependence. Under the circumstances of two cases, the Idaho Supreme Court denied the claim because the return flow from upper lands was so excessive as to impute wastefulness rather than beneficial use to the exercise of the original appropriative right. Thus, in one case, it was held that the upstream owner could not be required to continue to irrigate the original land nor to waste 75 percent of the decreed water for the benefit of the lower appropriator. And in the other case, "It is axiomatic that no appropriator can compel any other appropriator to continue the waste of water whereby the former may benefit." In other words, the rule that a junior appropriator has the right to a continuation of stream conditions as they were when he made his appropriation will not be so construed as to compel the senior to waste his water by use on the original land.[221]

Statutory authorization to a State administrator to approve applications to change place of use of water appropriated from streams does not clothe him

---

change in the place of use was designed to provide a method for making such changes which would eliminate friction and a multiplicity of lawsuits among water users. But it neither added to nor detracted from a property right which already existed."

[219]*Mannix & Wilson* v. *Thrasher*, 95 Mont. 267, 271, 26 Pac. (2d) 373 (1933); *Gassert* v. *Noyes*, 18 Mont. 216, 223, 44 Pac. 959 (1896); *Last Chance Min. Co.* v. *Bunker Hill & S. Min. & Concentrating Co.*, 49 Fed. 430 (C.C.D. Idaho 1892).

[220]*Hall* v. *Blackman*, 22 Idaho 556, 558, 126 Pac. 1047 (1912). A Federal court approved a decree restricting the use of certain water to certain lands, by reason of the fact that approximately two-thirds of the water found its way back to the stream by percolation, so that junior appropriators downstream were afforded the opportunity of making use of that quantity: *Vineyard Land & Stock Co.* v. *Twin Falls Salmon River Land & Water Co.*, 245 Fed. 9, 28 (9th Cir. 1917). But a change in place of use from one tributary valley to another is not injurious to a junior appropriator on the main stream below the junction of the two forks because he obtains the benefit of all return flow from water used in the valley of either tributary: *Saunders* v. *Robison*, 14 Idaho 770, 774, 95 Pac. 1057 (1908).

[221]*Colthorp* v. *Mountain Home Irr. Dist.*, 66 Idaho 173, 179-182, 157 Pac. (2d) 1005 (1945); *Application of Boyer*, 73 Idaho 152, 162-163, 248 Pac. (2d) 540 (1952). See also *Jones* v. *Big Lost River Irrig. Dist.*, 93 Idaho 227, 459 Pac. (2d) 1009, 1012 (1969).

with authority to interfere in the affairs and self-government of an irrigation district by granting an application to make such change from one area to another within the district. This is a judicial, not administrative, function.[222]

Purpose of Use

Some statutory situations.—Most of the water rights statutes authorize changes in purpose or character of use of appropriated water along with changes in point of diversion and place of use, and generally subject to the same qualifications and restrictions.

There are several exceptions. The legislatures of Idaho, Nebraska, and Texas do not expressly authorize changes of use. However, in answer to an objector who had not initiated his own appropriation until after a change in kind of use had been made, the Idaho Supreme Court stated that a change from one kind of mining, or from one use in mining to another use, did not invalidate an appropriation for mining purposes.[223] In 1905, the Nebraska Supreme Court held that the purpose of use of water under an appropriation made before the water rights statute was enacted could be changed from power to irrigation, so long as the water continued to be put to beneficial use.[224] No further litigation on this matter in the Nebraska Supreme Court has come to attention. In Texas, the right to make changes in purpose of use under administrative control would seem to be implied by the abundant authority conferred by the legislature upon the Texas Water Rights Commission with respect to the issuance of and control over water permits.[225]

The statutory provisions in Arizona respecting changes in purpose of use are that administrative approval is required for any change from domestic, municipal, or irrigation purposes, and legislative authorization is required for a change that contemplates generating hydroelectrical energy of more than

---

[222]*Wenatchee Reclamation Dist.* v. *Titchenal,* 175 Wash. 398, 402-404, 27 Pac. (2d) 734 (1933).

[223]*Zezi* v. *Lightfoot,* 57 Idaho 707, 711-712, 68 Pac. (2d) 50 (1937).

[224]*Farmers' & Merchants' Irr. Co.* v. *Gothenburg Water Power & Irr. Co.,* 73 Nebr. 223, 226-227, 102 N. W. 487 (1905). The change to irrigation was made both before and after the downstream appropriation was made, but the statement of facts is not clear as to the extent of actual injury from the change of use and extension of the ditches *after* the junior claimant initiated its right. Nor is the question of injury to junior appropriators mentioned in the opinion, aside from the point that the evidence disclosed diversion of no more water than was originally appropriated.

[225]Hutchins, Wells A., "The Texas Law of Water Rights," pp. 287-290 (1961). *Clark* v. *Briscoe Irr. Co.,* 200 S. W. (2d) 674, 682-685 (Tex. Civ. App. 1947). The court held squarely that there was implicit in the constitutional and statutory laws a vesting in the State agency of the continuing duty of supervision over the distribution and use of water, carrying with it the requirement that any substantial change in use or place of use not authorized in the original permit must have the administrative approval. Tex. Water Rights Comm'n, "Rules, Regulations and Modes of Procedure," rules 605.2(1)(e) and 610.1(c) (1970 Rev., Jan. 1970).

25,000 horsepower.[226] In Wyoming, with various exceptions, water rights for the direct use of the natural unstored flow of any stream *cannot* be detached from the purpose for which acquired.[227]

Some judicial points.—"The owner may change the use of the water to any other beneficial use, so long as the change does not interfere with the vested rights of others."[228] From early times, this has been a well-recognized judicial rule.[229] Where the water rights statute provides a procedure for making such change, it must be followed by the appropriator.[230]

Many changes in purpose of use were made in the early years of water uses in the mining States, such as California and Montana, as a consequence of the "playing-out" of placer-mining claims and contemporaneous development of agriculture under irrigation and of other industries as well. In California, severe restrictions on hydraulic mining in areas tributary to the Sacramento River were eventually imposed because of widespread damage from debris. A succinct and informative account of use of water in mining in California from the earliest uses to 1960 is given in a 1960 work by S. T. Harding.[231] With respect to changes in use of the early mining appropriations, he stated that extensive revival of hydraulic mining does not appear probable under existing conditions and that: "The water supplies formerly used for hydraulic mining are not largely in use for power and irrigation at locations below the elevations of the main gravel areas."[232]

---

[226] Ariz. Rev. Stat. Ann. § 45-146(B) (1956). See § 45-172 (Supp. 1970) relating to changes in place of water use which also contains references to certain purposes of use.

[227] Wyo. Stat. Ann. § 41-2 to -4 (1957) and -213 (Supp. 1969). The various exceptions are summarized in note 206, *supra*.

[228] Kinney, S. C., "A Treatise on the Law of Irrigation and Water Rights," 2d ed., vol. 4, § 768 (1912), quoted in *Blanchard* v. *Hartley*, 111 Oreg. 308, 312, 226 Pac. 436 (1924), and *In re Willow Creek*, 74 Oreg. 592, 144 Pac. 505 (1914), 146 Pac. 475 (1915). Although he can change the purpose of his appropriation, he cannot increase the quantity to the injury of existing subsequent appropriators, and he will be subject to the same rule after the change as before: *Manning* v. *Fife*, 17 Utah 232, 238, 54 Pac. 111 (1898). See also *W. S. Ranch Co.* v. *Kaiser Steel Corp.*, 79 N. Mex. 65, 439 Pac. (2d) 714, 715 (1968).

[229] *Atchison* v. *Peterson*, 87 U. S. 507, 514 (1874); *Gallagher* v. *Montecito Valley Water Co.*, 101 Cal. 242, 246, 35 Pac. 770 (1894); *In re Alpowa Creek*, 129 Wash. 9, 16-17, 224 Pac. 29 (1924).

[230] *Oliver* v. *Skinner and Lodge*, 190 Oreg. 423, 448-449, 226 Pac. (2d) 507 (1951).

[231] Harding, S. T., "Water in California," ch. 4, pp. 61-70 (1960).

[232] In several early California cases in which the right to change purpose of use was mentioned but was not in issue, the supreme court either withheld expression of opinion, *Maeris* v. *Bicknell*, 7 Cal. 261, 263 (1857), or did express opinion that the change was not an abandonment of the right, *McDonald* v. *Bear River & Auburn Water & Min. Co.*, 13 Cal. 220, 236-237 (1859); *Davis* v. *Gale*, 32 Cal. 26, 33-34 (1867). Positive expressions of approval came later. Change from mining to irrigation and domestic, *Happy Valley Land & Water Co.* v. *Nelson*, 169 Cal. 694, 696, 147 Pac. 966 (1915). For some Montana changes: Mining to irrigation, *Meagher* v. *Hardenbrook*, 11 Mont. 385, 28 Pac. 451 (1891); mining and agricultural to municipal, *Spokane Ranch*

A change of irrigated crops would be simply a substitution of one phase of irrigation agriculture to another and not a change in purpose of use. If it were, a farmer who practiced rotation of crops—which is widely done in irrigated areas—would be penalized to no purpose. Of course, a change that required more water—such as from alfalfa to rice—would call for an additional water supply not within the terms of the original appropriation. In an Oregon stream adjudication in which major changes were made from pasturing to raising hay, involving some reduction in use of water, a reverse effect was urged—that the testimony indicated abandonment of the right. The supreme court did not think it did.[233]

In a 1968 case, *City of Westminster* v. *Church,* the Colorado Supreme Court said:

> Plaintiffs' action against the City of Westminster is but one of several cases in this jurisdiction involving a municipality's purchase of agricultural water rights with the intention of devoting such rights to municipal and domestic purposes. The municipality, of course, has the legal right to devote its acquired water rights to municipal uses, provided that no injury accrues to the vested rights of other appropriators . . . . The principal dangers attending the municipality's altered use are that the city will attempt to use a continuous flow, where the city's grantor only used the water for intermittent irrigation . . . and that the municipality will enlarge its use of the water to the full extent of the decreed rights, regardless of historical usage. . . . To protect against the possibility of such extended use of the water rights, the courts will impose conditions upon the change of use and point of diversion sufficient to protect the rights of other appropriators. We have reviewed and upheld such restrictive conditions in numerous cases.[234]

The court also said:

> We hold that the trial court erred in ruling that the storage rights were limited to historical use. A reservoir right permits one filling of the reservoir per year.[235] Change of use does not create a greater burden as to storage water. We believe the City of Westminster is entitled under its storage right decree to whatever water is available each year to fill that storage decree.
>
> . . . .
>
> Defendant City of Westminster could not enlarge upon its predecessors' use of the water rights by changing periodic direct flow for irrigation to a

& *Water Co.* v. *Beatty,* 37 Mont. 342, 96 Pac. 727, 97 Pac. 838 (1908); milling to irrigation, *Featherman* v. *Hennessy,* 43 Mont. 310, 115 Pac. 983 (1911).

[233]*In re Silvies River,* 115 Oreg. 27, 41, 237 Pac. 322 (1925). "It does not appear to have been the intention of the company to relinquish its rights to the use of these waters but rather to delay or partly suspend the application of the waters to a beneficial use."

[234]*City of Westminster* v. *Church,* 167 Colo. 1, 445 Pac. (2d) 52, 58 (1968), citing earlier Colorado cases and Hutchins, W. A., "Selected Problems in the Law of Water Rights in the West," USDA Misc. Pub. 418 (1942), p. 384.

[235]See chapter 7 at note 644.

continuous flow for storage. Such a change would necessarily increase the ultimate consumption from the stream to the detriment of other appropriators.

. . . .

The district court ascertained the extent of historical usage of defendant's water rights during the period 1938 to 1959 on the basis of the state engineer's certified records. This data established that in this twenty-year period, average annual diversions were 306 acre-feet under the direct flow decrees and 123 acre-feet under the storage decrees. To eliminate fluctuations in availability from year to year, the court devised a ten-year moving average of 3060 acre-feet and 1230 acre-feet for the defendant's direct flow and storage rights respectively. Defendant maintained adequate storage facilities for these diversions, so that the direct flow rights could be transformed into storage rights, with no greater quantity being diverted in any ten-year period for storage purposes than had been historically diverted for direct flow irrigation. Except as to the storage rights previously discussed, in light of the circumstances of the case, this method of ascertaining due restraints on defendant's altered use of the water rights is eminently reasonable.[236]

An obvious injury to downstream appropriators from upstream change of purpose of use may result from change of a nonconsumptive to a consumptive use. Thus, a change from a use in which none of the water is consumed, as for power purposes, to one in which nearly all is consumed, as in case of irrigation, is apt to affect others injuriously.[237] Hence, a milling company, which had no appropriation for any purpose except operating the mill, could not change the use to irrigation of lands controlled by itself or of upstream lands of others to the detriment of a downstream appropriator who depended upon the stream after it passed the mill.[238] The same result may flow from a change from mining to irrigation.[239] In one instance, the holder of a prior appropriation for

---

[236] The court added that: "We also note that at the times free water is available in the river, the restrictions would not apply since all appropriators may then divert beyond the measure of their decree without infringing the rights of other persons." 445 Pac. (2d) at 58-59.

   In regard to effects of changing the water use upon direct flow rights, the court quoted and discussed an earlier case that involved a proceeding to change a diversion point by a city that had acquired decreed water rights formerly used for irrigation. *Farmers Highline Canal & Reservoir Co.* v. *Golden*, 129 Colo. 575, 584, 272 Pac. (2d) 629, 634 (1954), discussed in note 178 *supra*.

[237] *Broughton* v. *Stricklin*, 146 Oreg. 259, 270, 28 Pac. (2d) 219 (1933), 30 Pac. (2d) 332 (1934).

[238] *Cache la Poudre Res. Co.* v. *Water Supply & Storage Co.*, 25 Colo. 161, 169-171, 53 Pac. 331 (1898); *Hutchinson* v. *Stricklin*, 146 Oreg. 285, 296-297, 300, 28 Pac. (2d) 225 (1933).

[239] *Head* v. *Hale*, 38 Mont. 302, 307-308, 100 Pac. 222 (1909). An equitable adjustment was made in *Featherman* v. *Hennessy*, 43 Mont. 310, 316-317, 115 Pac. 983 (1911).

operation of a sawmill attempted to transfer his appropriation to others upstream for irrigation purposes. Here, the proposed change was injurious to downstream junior appropriators on two counts: (a) purpose of use, from nonconsumptive to consumptive; and (b) place of use, *upstream* above the diversions of holders of junior rights who had appropriated water for irrigation purposes, which if accomplished would have defeated their rights.[240]

A logical interpretation of the Montana nonadministration statute, the State supreme court believed, was to hold that the burden is on the party who insists that such change affected him adversely, to allege and to prove the facts; the restrictive words "If others are not thereby injured" being matters of defense. This is consonant with rules disclosed earlier under "Point of Diversion—The Question of Resulting Injury—Burden of proof of injury" that (a) under a nonadministration statute the party who affirmatively alleges injury has the burden of proving it; and (b) one who applies for permission to make a change under an administration statute has the burden of establishing the facts necessary to make out a *prima facie* case of noninjury. In the instant case, the court explained that the statute does not apply or by implication declare that a change, even if it affects others adversely, shall impair the appropriative right in any respect; what it might do if injurious is to give rise to an action for damages or for an injunction.[241]

A person who is not injured by a change in purpose of use is in no position to complain. Thus, a change from mining to agriculture does not impair the rights of others for use of the water on *upstream* lands.[242] Nor may one be heard to complain of a change in use of a water right in which he had no legal interest.[243]

Summary of Statutory Authorizations and Restrictions

Following is a summary of the salient features of statutory authorizations to make changes in point of diversion, place of use, and purpose of use of appropriated water, and of restrictions thereon:

Alaska.—Place and purpose of use. State administration approval required. Instrument of change must be filed with State administrative agency and recorded in the county of the appropriation.[244]

Arizona.—(1) Place of use. For prescribed uses only, without loss of priority, with State administration approval, no injury to other rights, and,

---

[240]*Washington State Sugar Co.* v. *Goodrich*, 27 Idaho 26, 44, 147 Pac. 1073 (1915).

[241]*Hansen* v. *Larsen*, 44 Mont. 350, 353, 120 Pac. 229 (1911).

[242]*Hand* v. *Carlson*, 138 Cal. App. 202, 208, 31 Pac. (2d) 1084 (1934).

[243]*Campbell* v. *Goldfield Consolidated Water Co.*, 36 Nev. 458, 462, 136 Pac. 976 (1913). The contested water supply was a spring, the source of a natural watercourse, the spring being located allegedly within the boundaries of a mining claim owned by the contestor. Under Nevada law, he could have no right in such a spring otherwise than through appropriation; and he had made no claim of appropriation.

[244]Alaska Stat. § 46.15.160(b) (Supp. 1966).

in the case of irrigation districts, agricultural improvement districts, or water users associations, with the approval of the governing body of such organizations. (2) Purpose of use. For domestic, municipal, or irrigation, State administration approval required. For generation of 25,000 horsepower hydroelectric energy, legislative authorization required.[245]

California.—Point of diversion, place of use, or purpose of use. (1) Appropriation made under Water Commission Act or Water Code. State administration permission required; agency must find no resulting injury to any legal water user, and hold hearing on protest. (2) Appropriation otherwise made. (a) No injury to others. (b) Extension of conduit to places beyond first use.[246]

Colorado.—Permissive determination of change in type, place, or time of use, or points of diversion; ruling by water judge or designated referee in accord with no injury to other vested rights, or prevention of injury by imposing terms.[247]

Idaho.—Point of diversion or place of use. State administration approval required; hearing of protest; finding of no injury to others. Any person aggrieved by administrator's decision may appeal to court. If right represented by shares of corporate stock, or if system controlled by irrigation district, organization consent required for change to outside lands.[248]

Kansas.—(1) Point of diversion, place of use, or purpose of use. State administration approval required; finding of reasonableness and no impairment of any existing right, and that change relates to the same local source of supply as that to which water right relates. No loss of priority. (2) Extension of ditch to new place of diversion. Caused by unfavorable change in natural stream channel. No injury to others. No loss of priority.[249]

Montana.—Point of diversion, extension of conduit beyond place of first use, purpose of use. No injury to others.[250]

Nebraska.—(1) Point of diversion, line of conduit, or storage site. State administration approval required. (2) Established return flow point of reclamation district or power appropriator. State administration approval required.[251]

---

[245] Ariz. Rev. Stat. Ann. § § 45-146(B) (1956) and 45-172 (Supp. 1970). The latter section, relating to changes in place of water use, also contains references to certain purposes of use.

[246] Cal. Water Code § § 1700, 1706 (West 1956), and 1701-1705 (West Supp. 1970).

[247] Colo. Rev. Stat. Ann. § § 148-21-3(11) and 148-21-18 to 148-21-21 (Supp. 1969).

[248] Idaho Code Ann. § § 42-108 and -222 (Supp. 1969).

[249] Kans. Stat. Ann. § § 42-304 (1964) and 82a-708b (1969).

[250] Mont. Rev. Codes Ann. § 89-803 (1964).

[251] Nebr. Rev. Stat. § 46-250 (1968). The composite effect of this and § § 46-122 and -233 (1968) in regard to changes in place of use, as construed by the courts, is rather unsettled. This is discussed in chapter 8 under "Property Characteristics—Appurtenance of Water Right to Land—Appurtenant and not Generally Severable Without Loss of the Right."

Nevada.—(1) Point of diversion, place of use, or manner of use. State administration approval required; hearing on protest if deemed necessary; finding of no tendency to impair value of existing rights or be otherwise detrimental to public welfare. (2) Place of use, additional requirement. For prescribed cause only, without loss of priority.[252]

New Mexico.—(1) Point of diversion, place of storage, place of use, or purpose of use. Requires State administration approval, after published notice. No detriment to existing rights. (2) Place of use, additional requirement. Severance of water right from land to which appurtenant only with consent of landowner, without loss of priority. (3) Point of diversion, community acequia. Restrictions do not apply to community acequias in operation before March 19, 1907, provided no accompanying increase thereby in quantity of water appropriated.[253]

North Dakota.—(1) Point of diversion, place of storage, place of use, or purposes of use. (2) Change in means or place of diversion or control shall not affect priority if others not injured.[254]

Oklahoma.—(1) Point of diversion, place of storage, place of use, or purpose of use. Requires State administration approval, after published notice. A party interested in same source of water supply may bring action to review decision. No detriment to existing rights. (2) Place of use, additional requirement. For prescribed causes only, without loss of priority.[255]

Oregon.—Point of diversion, place of use, or purpose of use. Requires State administration approval, after published notice and hearing if objections filed, subject to appeal. No loss of priority. No injury to existing rights.[256]

South Dakota.—(1) Point of diversion, place of storage, place of use, or purpose of use. Requires State administration approval, after published notice. A party interested in same source of water supply may bring action

---

[252]Nev. Rev. Stat. § § 533.040 (Supp. 1969) and .325-.435 (Supp. 1967).

[253]N. Mex. Stat. Ann. § § 75-5-3, 75-5-22, 75-5-23, and 75-14-60 (1968).

[254]N. Dak. Cent. Code Ann. § § 61-02-31 (Supp. 1969) and 61-14-05 (1960). The latter section provides that "Any appropriator of water may use the same for a purpose other than that for which it was appropriated, or may change the place of diversion, storage, or use, *in the manner, and under the conditions prescribed in section 61-14-04.*" [Emphasis added.] Prior to 1963 § 61-14-04 had provided, among other things, for administrative approval of such changes. However, in 1963 § 61-14-04 was repealed. N. Dak. Laws 1963, ch. 417, §26. The 1963 laws, in ch.417, §1, amended §61-01-02 of the statutes so as to provide that appropriations for irrigation purposes shall be appurtenant to specified owned lands "unless such rights to use water have been severed for other beneficial uses as provided by section 61-04-15." As amended in 1963, 1965, and 1969, §61-04-15, among other things, provides that irrigation appropriations may be assigned or may be transferred to other lands owned by the holder, with administrative approval.

[255]Okla. Stat. Ann. tit. 82, § § 34 and 35 (1970).

[256]Oreg. Rev. Stat. § § 540.510-.530 (Supp. 1969).

to review decision. No detriment to existing rights. (2) Place of use, additional requirement. For prescribed causes only, without loss of priority.[257]

Texas.—None.

Utah.—Point of diversion, place of use, or purpose of use. Requires State Engineer approval, subject to judicial review. No vested right to be impaired without just compensation. (1) Permanent change. Procedure same as for appropriating water. (2) Temporary change, fixed period not exceeding one year. Investigation and order by State Engineer. If possibility of impairing vested rights, applications may be approved as to part of the water involved or upon condition that such conflicting rights be acquired.[258]

Washington.—(1) Permanent change. (a) Place of use. Without loss of priority if no detriment to existing rights. (b) Point of diversion or purpose of use. No detriment to existing rights. (c) In every case, requries State administrative approval, application to be published as in case of appropriating water. (2) Temporary or seasonal change of point of diversion of place of use. Requires administrative approval. No detriment to existing rights.[259]

Wyoming.—(1) Point of diversion from another State, on an interstate stream that enters Wyoming, to a location within Wyoming. Requires administration approval, after public hearing, subject to appeal to court. By virtue of 1965 legislation, similar requirements expressly apply to changing the diversion point by anyone having heretofore acquired a right to beneficially use any stream in the State. (2) Place of use or purpose of use. With various exceptions,[260] water rights for direct use of natural unstored streamflow cannot be detached from the lands, place, or purpose for which acquired. Reservoir water rights, unless attached by deed or other instrument of conveyance to particular lands, may be transferred and used on other lands and for other purposes.[261]

EFFICIENCY OF PRACTICES

In diverting, conveying, distributing, and using water, the appropriator is held to reasonable efficiency—not absolute efficiency.[262] The reasonableness of efficiency of his practices is measured largely in the more careful decisions by the higher standards prevalent in the community, with some evidence of a tendency to encourage improvements in standards when it can be done without excessive financial burden on the water users. "These features with relation to

---

[257]S. Dak. Comp. Laws Ann. § § 46-5-24 and 46-5-31 to 46-5-36 (1967).

[258]Utah Code Ann. § 73-3-3 (1968).

[259]Wash. Rev. Code § § 90.03.380 and 90.03.390 (Supp. 1961).

[260]Which are summarized in note 206, *supra.*

[261]Wyo. Stat. Ann. § § 41-2 to -10, -19 to -25, -37 (1957), -10.1 to -10.4, and -213 (Supp. 1969).

[262]See in chapter 8 "Elements of the Appropriative Right—Measure of the Appropriative Right—Other Terms Associated With Beneficial Use."

water litigation are deemed to be questions of fact for the reasonable determination of the trial court."[263]

Diversion, Conveyance, and Distribution of Water

The prior appropriator must use reasonable diligence, reasonable care, and reasonably efficient appliances in making his diversion and transporting the water to the place of intended use in order that the surplus water may not be rendered unavailable to those who are entitled to it.[264] One whose means of diversion becomes insufficient, because of its inherent defects, when the surplus is diverted upstream must take the usual and reasonable measures to perfect such means. There is no requirement of absolute efficiency with respect to artificial appliances.[265] Nor is it necessary that one should divert and distribute water according to the most scientific method known.[266] But the appropriator is bound to the exercise of reasonable care in the construction and maintenance of his appliances to the end that others be not unnecessarily deprived of the use of the water.[267]

In a 1922 Idaho case, the Idaho Supreme Court said that an appropriator who had effected a saving of a 10 percent loss of water by changing the point of diversion

has materially augmented the amount of water available from the stream for beneficial use and should have a prior right to its use. This is not the case with the saving of 50 per cent. which is brought about by eliminating the loss from the old Farmers' ditch. . . . The loss of 50 per cent. in the Farmers' ditch between the old point of diversion of the individual appellants and the place where they applied the water on their land was not a reasonable loss. The farmers could not reasonably have been expected to build a cement lined ditch at the cost of $100,000, as suggested by one of the witnesses. But they could have been reasonably expected to prevent the water spreading out at several places. . . .[268]

---

[263]*Mt. Shasta Power Corp.* v. *McArthur,* 109 Cal. App. 171, 183, 292 Pac. 549 (1930, hearing denied by supreme court).

[264]*Natoma Water & Min. Co.* v. *Hancock,* 101 Cal. 42, 51-52, 31 Pac. 112 (1892), 35 Pac. 334 (1894); *Kent* v. *Smith,* 62 Nev. 30, 39, 140 Pac. (2d) 357 (1943); *Tudor* v. *Jaca,* 178 Oreg. 126, 141-143, 164 Pac. (2d) 680 (1945), 165 Pac. (2d) 770 (1946); *Hardy* v. *Beaver County Irr. Co.,* 65 Utah 28, 41, 234 Pac. 524 (1924).

[265]*State ex rel. Crowley* v. *District Court,* 108 Mont. 89, 97-98, 88 Pac. (2d) 23 (1939).

[266]*Tulare Irr. Dist.* v. *Lindsay-Strathmore Irr. Dist.,* 3 Cal. (2d) 489, 547, 45 Pac. (2d) 972 (1935); *Worden* v. *Alexander,* 108 Mont. 208, 215, 90 Pac. (2d) 160 (1939).

[267]*Dern* v. *Tanner,* 60 Fed. (2d) 626, 628 (D. Mont. 1932). Hence, if a less wasteful method can be devised, even at additional expense, "an appropriator has no right to run water into a swamp and cause the loss of two-thirds of a stream simply because he is following lines of least resistance." *Doherty* v. *Pratt,* 34 Nev. 343, 348, 124 Pac. 574 (1912).

[268]*Basinger* v. *Taylor,* 36 Idaho 591, 597, 211 Pac. 1085 (1922).

The Arizona court of appeals held in 1966 that appropriators who had conserved water by improvement and concrete lining of their irrigation ditches did not have the right to use the saved water on adjacent lands for which they held no appropriative rights without applying for the right to do so from the State Land Department. The court said:

> Certainly any effort by users of water in Arizona tending toward conservation and more economical use of water is to be highly commended. However, commendable practices do not in themselves create legal rights.
>   . . . .
>
> The appellees may only appropriate the amount of water from the Verde River as may be beneficially used in any given year upon the land to which the water is appurtenant even though this amount may be less than the maximum amount of their appropriation. . . . [I]n those years when water in excess of that which appellees may beneficially use upon the appurtenant land to which their water right attaches, all water which may flow to lower and subordinate owners of water rights is no longer of concern to appellees. Any practice, whether through water-saving procedures or otherwise, whereby appellees may in fact reduce the quantity of water actually taken inures to the benefit of other water users and neither creates a right to use the waters saved as a marketable commodity nor the right to apply same to adjacent property having no appurtenant water rights.[269]

The court noted that Arizona legislation had placed matters pertaining to application of waters to new lands or changes in use of waters under the jurisdiction of the State Land Department with certain prescribed standards to be followed.

With Particular Reference to Diversions of Water

The Utah Supreme Court held that it was the settled law of the jurisdiction that a junior appropriator could divert water from a stream at a point above the prior appropriator's diversion and return it into the latter's ditch if undiminished in quantity and unaffected in quality,[270] at his own expense.[271] But he has no right to cause frequent and substantial fluctuations in the streamflow to suit his own purposes, the result of which is to seriously impair the usefulness of the flow to prior appropriators downstream.[272]

---

[269] *Salt River Valley Water Users' Ass'n* v. *Kovacovich,* 3 Ariz. App. 28, 411 Pac. (2d) 201, 202-204 (1966), discussed in Dickenson, R. W., "Installation of Water Saving Devices as a Means of Enlarging an Appropriative Right to Use of Water," 2 Natural Resource Lawyer 272, 274 (1969); Case Note, 46 Oreg. Law Rev. 243 (1967).

See chapter 18 regarding rights to use salvaged and other kinds of waters, which deals with related although different matters.

[270] *United States* v. *Caldwell,* 64 Utah 490, 497-498, 231 Pac. 434 (1924).

[271] *Big Cottonwood Tanner Ditch Co.* v. *Shurtliff,* 56 Utah 196, 204-205, 189 Pac. 587 (1919).

[272] *Logan, Hyde Park & Smithfield Canal Co.* v. *Logan,* 72 Utah 221, 224-226, 269 Pac. 776 (1928).

In a 1952 Colorado case in which the right of certain appropriators to construct a channel in the streambed for the purpose of conducting the water to their headgate was in issue, the supreme court held that their right to divert and use water from the stream at that headgate "included the right to make and change the necessary dams, channels or other diversion works within the stream bed which might be necessary to enable them to continue the diversion of water at their headgate, provided no additional burden were made upon defendants' lands thereby."[273] Also, appropriators have the right to repair and improve their physical works in order to divert their full decreed supply of water. As against junior appropriators, this is not an enlarged use of the water appropriated.[274]

With Particular Respect to Conveyance and Distribution of Water

A long established rule is that in conveying water to the place of use, the appropriator is required to keep his flumes and ditches in good repair in order to prevent *unnecessary* waste.[275]

It is recognized that always and inevitably there is a difference between the quantity of water diverted from the stream and the quantity that reaches the place of use through open ditches and flumes. Hence, some loss by absorption and evaporation takes place even in conduits well constructed and maintained. "So much of the water as may be unavoidably wasted is to be deemed a part of that which is appropriated" to beneficial use.[276] So a reasonable conveyance loss is allowable, the "reasonableness" in a particular case depending upon the circumstances thereof.[277]

But when the inevitable loss "becomes extreme by reason of the porous character of the soil, and water is scarce, it becomes necessary for an irrigator to take reasonable means to lessen the amount of loss."[278] In a California case,

---

[273] *Downing* v. *Copeland,* 126 Colo. 373, 375-376, 249 Pac. (2d) 539 (1952).

[274] *Flasche* v. *Westcolo Co.,* 112 Colo. 387, 393, 149 Pac. (2d) 817 (1944). "The rule of law that gives junior appropriators a vested right to a continuance of conditions on the stream does not include the right to a continuance of the senior appropriators' misfortunes with their ditch."

[275] *Barrows* v. *Fox,* 98 Cal. 63, 66-67, 32 Pac. 811 (1893).

[276] *Thayer* v. *California Development Co.,* 164 Cal. 117, 137, 128 Pac. 21 (1912).

[277] *Clark* v. *Hansen,* 35 Idaho 449, 456, 206 Pac. 808 (1922); *Almo Water Co.* v. *Jones,* 39 Fed. (2d) 37, 38 (9th Cir. 1930); although farmers could not reasonably have been expected to build a cement ditch at a cost of $100,000, they have been reasonably expected to prevent the water from spreading out at several places and thus causing considerable waste: *Basinger* v. *Taylor,* 36 Idaho 591, 597, 211 Pac. 1085 (1922); *In re Willow Creek,* 74 Oreg. 592, 622, 144 Pac. 505 (1914), 146 Pac. 475 (1915); the law contemplates an economical use of water and will not countenance a loss many times the deliverable quantity resulting from the condition of the conveyance appliances: *Sterling* v. *Pawnee Ditch Extension Co.,* 42 Colo. 421, 429-430, 94 Pac. 339 (1908).

[278] *Shotwell* v. *Dodge,* 8 Wash. 337, 341, 36 Pac. 254 (1894).

prior appropriators found themselves penalized when they finally attempted to correct a long-time wastage of water.[279]

The ditch owner has the duty of exercising ordinary care in keeping the conduit clean and free from debris.[280] He has the right, as against the owner of the servient estate, to recondition the ditch by making reasonable improvements for the purpose of increasing its efficiency.[281]

A long drawn-out lawsuit in San Joaquin Valley, California, culminated after many years in a decision rendered by the California Supreme Court, in which a long opinion was written and many important matters were covered.[282] Appropriators had been conveying water in earth ditches for long periods of time—some of them for more than 50 years—and it appeared that in many instances conveyance losses amounted to 40 to 45 percent. Insofar as the instant topic is concerned, the supreme court held that these appropriators as a matter of law had the right to divert and distribute the water by means of earth ditches and could not be compelled to construct impervious conduits in order that seepage water might be made available to a junior appropriator. The supreme court appeared to be sympathetic toward any feasible plan of affecting a substantial saving of water at a reasonable cost, to be apportioned as justice might require, but refused to hold that the prior appropriators' methods were wasteful. It was stated that: "if appellant sincerely desires to save some of the conveyance loss, on the retrial, it can offer to defray the expenses of straightening some of the major ditches, or of building, in some cases, impervious ditches." The court summarized the California rule as to efficiency of appliances and practices in diverting and distributing water by declaring that in determining what is a reasonable quantity for beneficial uses the State policy requires "within reasonable limits" the highest duty from the public waters, but that on the contrary the appropriator is not restricted to the most scientific method known.[283] "He is entitled to make a reasonable use of the water according to the general custom of the locality, so long as the custom does not involve unnecessary waste."[284]

---

[279] Dannenbrink v. Burger, 23 Cal. App. 587, 593-595, 138 Pac. 751 (1913, hearing denied by supreme court). For a long time, these parties diverted water by means of an imperfect dam and flume through which substantial quantities of water were wasted into the stream. When they eventually repaired and replaced the structures, they were held to be not thereby entitled to withhold from downstream appropriators who, for a period of about 25 years had been making use of the wastage, the quantities of water claimed thereby to be saved.

[280] Big Cottonwood Tanner Ditch Co. v. Hyland Realty, Inc., 8 Utah (2d) 341, 344, 334 Pac. (2d) 755 (1959).

[281] Big Cottonwood Tanner Ditch Co. v. Moyle, 109 Utah 213, 231-238, 174 Pac. (2d) 148 (1946). Compare Harvey v. Haights Bench Irr. Co., 7 Utah (2d) 58, 68-69, 318 Pac. (2d) 343 (1957).

[282] Tulare Irr. Dist. v. Lindsay-Strathmore Irr. Dist., 3 Cal. (2d) 489, 45 Pac. (2d) 972 (1935).

[283] Id. at 572-574.

[284] Id. at 574.

Use of Water

The standards governing the use of water made by an appropriator are essentially the same or comparable to those that apply to diversion and conveyance practices and appliances.[285]

Fundamentally, it is the policy of the law to encourage efficiency and to avoid unnecessary waste in applying water to the soil.[286]

A pragmatic application of the rule to situations that appear so frequently in litigation recognizes that an appropriator should be allowed to exercise his right to its full extent, but that such exercise must be a reasonable one. Thus, "it is necessary and proper to limit prior appropriators to the volume of water reasonably required to raise crops under reasonably efficient methods of applying water to the land."[287] As with diversion and conveyance of water, the appropriator is not compelled to irrigate his land in the most scientific manner known.[288] The system of irrigation in common use in the locality, if reasonable and proper under existing conditions, is to be taken as a standard, even though a more economical method might be installed at a higher cost to the irrigator.[289] In the attainment of this aim, it is *unnecessary* waste that is not countenanced.[290]

In an early case, the California Supreme Court held that in watering his land the irrigator is subject to the maxim *sic utere tuo ut alienum non laedas.* "An action cannot be maintained against him for the reasonable exercise of his right, although an annoyance or injury may thereby be occasioned to the plaintiffs."[291]

---

[285] *Tudor* v. *Jaca*, 178 Oreg. 126, 141-143, 164 Pac. (2d) 680 (1945), 165 Pac. (2d) 770 (1946); *Doherty* v. *Pratt*, 34 Nev. 343, 348, 124 Pac. 574 (1912).

[286] *Tulare Irr. Dist.* v. *Lindsay-Strathmore Irr. Dist.*, 3 Cal. (2d) 489, 547, 45 Pac. (2d) 972 (1935); *Ramseyer* v. *Jamerson*, 78 Idaho 504, 515, 305 Pac. (2d) 1088 (1957); *Court House Rock Irr. Co.* v. *Willard*, 75 Nebr. 408, 411-412, 106 N. W. 463 (1906); *United States* v. *Caldwell*, 64 Utah 490, 499-500, 231 Pac. 434 (1924). See *Mammoth Canal & Irr. Co.* v. *Burton, Judge*, 70 Utah 239, 256, 259 Pac. 408 (1927).

[287] *In re Water Rights of Escalante Valley Drainage Area*, 10 Utah (2d) 77, 82, 348 Pac. (2d) 679 (1960); *Hardy* v. *Beaver County Irr. Co.*, 65 Utah 28, 41, 234 Pac. 524 (1924).

[288] *Tulare Irr. Dist.* v. *Lindsay-Strathmore Irr. Dist.*, 3 Cal. (2d) 489, 573, 45 Pac. (2d) 972 (1935).

[289] *Worden* v. *Alexander*, 108 Mont. 208, 215-216, 90 Pac. (2d) 160 (1939); *Joerger* v. *Pacific Gas & Electric Co.*, 207 Cal. 8, 23, 276 Pac. 1017 (1929).

[290] *Comstock* v. *Larimer & Weld Res. Co.*, 58 Colo. 186, 205-206, 145 Pac. 700 (1914); the appropriative right includes no surplus water: *Johnston* v. *Little Horse Creek Irrigating Co.*, 13 Wyo. 208, 227, 79 Pac. 22 (1904); an excessive diversion of water cannot be regarded as a diversion to beneficial use: *Combs* v. *Agricultural Ditch Co.*, 17 Colo. 146, 153-154, 28 Pac. 966 (1892).

[291] *Gibson* v. *Puchta*, 33 Cal. 310, 316 (1867), quoted in *Stroup* v. *Frank A. Hubbell Co.* 27 N. Mex. 35, 37-39, 192 Pac. 519 (1920).

The Utah Supreme Court has held that whether regulations on the use of water by the parties shall be imposed in the adjudication of water rights is within the discretion of the trial court, but that detailed regulations should be imposed "with great caution." The reason is that usually the parties can agree upon necessary regulations to meet occasions as they arise and it is better to allow this than to impose hard and fast regulations which cannot be changed to meet emergencies.[292]

---

[292]*Mckean* v. *Lasson,* 5 Utah (2d) 168, 173, 298 Pac. (2d) 827 (1956); *McNaughton* v. *Eaton.* 4 Utah (2d) 223, 224, 291 Pac. (2d) 886 (1955).

333.3

Hutchins, R.

AUTHOR

Water rights laws   vol.1

TITLE

DATE LOANED	BORROWER'S NAME	DATE RETURNED
9/21/77	Rod Thompson	9/21/77

333.3

Water rights laws.   vol. 1